T0142127

Lecture Notes in Computer Science 13666

Founding Editors

Gerhard Goos
Karlsruhe Institute of Technology, Karlsruhe, Germany

Juris Hartmanis
Cornell University, Ithaca, NY, USA

Editorial Board Members

Elisa Bertino
Purdue University, West Lafayette, IN, USA

Wen Gao
Peking University, Beijing, China

Bernhard Steffen
TU Dortmund University, Dortmund, Germany

Moti Yung
Columbia University, New York, NY, USA

More information about this series at https://link.springer.com/bookseries/558

Shai Avidan · Gabriel Brostow ·
Moustapha Cissé · Giovanni Maria Farinella ·
Tal Hassner (Eds.)

Computer Vision – ECCV 2022

17th European Conference
Tel Aviv, Israel, October 23–27, 2022
Proceedings, Part VI

Springer

Editors
Shai Avidan
Tel Aviv University
Tel Aviv, Israel

Gabriel Brostow 🄬
University College London
London, UK

Moustapha Cissé
Google AI
Accra, Ghana

Giovanni Maria Farinella 🄬
University of Catania
Catania, Italy

Tal Hassner 🄬
Facebook (United States)
Menlo Park, CA, USA

ISSN 0302-9743   ISSN 1611-3349 (electronic)
Lecture Notes in Computer Science
ISBN 978-3-031-20067-0   ISBN 978-3-031-20068-7 (eBook)
https://doi.org/10.1007/978-3-031-20068-7

© The Editor(s) (if applicable) and The Author(s), under exclusive license
to Springer Nature Switzerland AG 2022
This work is subject to copyright. All rights are reserved by the Publisher, whether the whole or part of the material is concerned, specifically the rights of translation, reprinting, reuse of illustrations, recitation, broadcasting, reproduction on microfilms or in any other physical way, and transmission or information storage and retrieval, electronic adaptation, computer software, or by similar or dissimilar methodology now known or hereafter developed.
The use of general descriptive names, registered names, trademarks, service marks, etc. in this publication does not imply, even in the absence of a specific statement, that such names are exempt from the relevant protective laws and regulations and therefore free for general use.
The publisher, the authors, and the editors are safe to assume that the advice and information in this book are believed to be true and accurate at the date of publication. Neither the publisher nor the authors or the editors give a warranty, expressed or implied, with respect to the material contained herein or for any errors or omissions that may have been made. The publisher remains neutral with regard to jurisdictional claims in published maps and institutional affiliations.

This Springer imprint is published by the registered company Springer Nature Switzerland AG
The registered company address is: Gewerbestrasse 11, 6330 Cham, Switzerland

Foreword

Organizing the European Conference on Computer Vision (ECCV 2022) in Tel-Aviv during a global pandemic was no easy feat. The uncertainty level was extremely high, and decisions had to be postponed to the last minute. Still, we managed to plan things just in time for ECCV 2022 to be held in person. Participation in physical events is crucial to stimulating collaborations and nurturing the culture of the Computer Vision community.

There were many people who worked hard to ensure attendees enjoyed the best science at the 16th edition of ECCV. We are grateful to the Program Chairs Gabriel Brostow and Tal Hassner, who went above and beyond to ensure the ECCV reviewing process ran smoothly. The scientific program includes dozens of workshops and tutorials in addition to the main conference and we would like to thank Leonid Karlinsky and Tomer Michaeli for their hard work. Finally, special thanks to the web chairs Lorenzo Baraldi and Kosta Derpanis, who put in extra hours to transfer information fast and efficiently to the ECCV community.

We would like to express gratitude to our generous sponsors and the Industry Chairs, Dimosthenis Karatzas and Chen Sagiv, who oversaw industry relations and proposed new ways for academia-industry collaboration and technology transfer. It's great to see so much industrial interest in what we're doing!

Authors' draft versions of the papers appeared online with open access on both the Computer Vision Foundation (CVF) and the European Computer Vision Association (ECVA) websites as with previous ECCVs. Springer, the publisher of the proceedings, has arranged for archival publication. The final version of the papers is hosted by SpringerLink, with active references and supplementary materials. It benefits all potential readers that we offer both a free and citeable version for all researchers, as well as an authoritative, citeable version for SpringerLink readers. Our thanks go to Ronan Nugent from Springer, who helped us negotiate this agreement. Last but not least, we wish to thank Eric Mortensen, our publication chair, whose expertise made the process smooth.

October 2022

Rita Cucchiara
Jiří Matas
Amnon Shashua
Lihi Zelnik-Manor

Preface

Welcome to the proceedings of the European Conference on Computer Vision (ECCV 2022). This was a hybrid edition of ECCV as we made our way out of the COVID-19 pandemic. The conference received 5804 valid paper submissions, compared to 5150 submissions to ECCV 2020 (a 12.7% increase) and 2439 in ECCV 2018. 1645 submissions were accepted for publication (28%) and, of those, 157 (2.7% overall) as orals.

846 of the submissions were desk-rejected for various reasons. Many of them because they revealed author identity, thus violating the double-blind policy. This violation came in many forms: some had author names with the title, others added acknowledgments to specific grants, yet others had links to their github account where their name was visible. Tampering with the LaTeX template was another reason for automatic desk rejection.

ECCV 2022 used the traditional CMT system to manage the entire double-blind reviewing process. Authors did not know the names of the reviewers and vice versa. Each paper received at least 3 reviews (except 6 papers that received only 2 reviews), totalling more than 15,000 reviews.

Handling the review process at this scale was a significant challenge. To ensure that each submission received as fair and high-quality reviews as possible, we recruited more than 4719 reviewers (in the end, 4719 reviewers did at least one review). Similarly we recruited more than 276 area chairs (eventually, only 276 area chairs handled a batch of papers). The area chairs were selected based on their technical expertise and reputation, largely among people who served as area chairs in previous top computer vision and machine learning conferences (ECCV, ICCV, CVPR, NeurIPS, etc.).

Reviewers were similarly invited from previous conferences, and also from the pool of authors. We also encouraged experienced area chairs to suggest additional chairs and reviewers in the initial phase of recruiting. The median reviewer load was five papers per reviewer, while the average load was about four papers, because of the emergency reviewers. The area chair load was 35 papers, on average.

Conflicts of interest between authors, area chairs, and reviewers were handled largely automatically by the CMT platform, with some manual help from the Program Chairs. Reviewers were allowed to describe themselves as senior reviewer (load of 8 papers to review) or junior reviewers (load of 4 papers). Papers were matched to area chairs based on a subject-area affinity score computed in CMT and an affinity score computed by the Toronto Paper Matching System (TPMS). TPMS is based on the paper's full text. An area chair handling each submission would bid for preferred expert reviewers, and we balanced load and prevented conflicts.

The assignment of submissions to area chairs was relatively smooth, as was the assignment of submissions to reviewers. A small percentage of reviewers were not happy with their assignments in terms of subjects and self-reported expertise. This is an area for improvement, although it's interesting that many of these cases were reviewers hand-picked by AC's. We made a later round of reviewer recruiting, targeted at the list of authors of papers submitted to the conference, and had an excellent response which helped provide enough emergency reviewers. In the end, all but six papers received at least 3 reviews.

The challenges of the reviewing process are in line with past experiences at ECCV 2020. As the community grows, and the number of submissions increases, it becomes ever more challenging to recruit enough reviewers and ensure a high enough quality of reviews. Enlisting authors by default as reviewers might be one step to address this challenge.

Authors were given a week to rebut the initial reviews, and address reviewers' concerns. Each rebuttal was limited to a single pdf page with a fixed template.

The Area Chairs then led discussions with the reviewers on the merits of each submission. The goal was to reach consensus, but, ultimately, it was up to the Area Chair to make a decision. The decision was then discussed with a buddy Area Chair to make sure decisions were fair and informative. The entire process was conducted virtually with no in-person meetings taking place.

The Program Chairs were informed in cases where the Area Chairs overturned a decisive consensus reached by the reviewers, and pushed for the meta-reviews to contain details that explained the reasoning for such decisions. Obviously these were the most contentious cases, where reviewer inexperience was the most common reported factor.

Once the list of accepted papers was finalized and released, we went through the laborious process of plagiarism (including self-plagiarism) detection. A total of 4 accepted papers were rejected because of that.

Finally, we would like to thank our Technical Program Chair, Pavel Lifshits, who did tremendous work behind the scenes, and we thank the tireless CMT team.

October 2022

Gabriel Brostow
Giovanni Maria Farinella
Moustapha Cissé
Shai Avidan
Tal Hassner

Organization

General Chairs

Rita Cucchiara   University of Modena and Reggio Emilia, Italy
Jiří Matas   Czech Technical University in Prague, Czech Republic
Amnon Shashua   Hebrew University of Jerusalem, Israel
Lihi Zelnik-Manor   Technion – Israel Institute of Technology, Israel

Program Chairs

Shai Avidan   Tel-Aviv University, Israel
Gabriel Brostow   University College London, UK
Moustapha Cissé   Google AI, Ghana
Giovanni Maria Farinella   University of Catania, Italy
Tal Hassner   Facebook AI, USA

Program Technical Chair

Pavel Lifshits   Technion – Israel Institute of Technology, Israel

Workshops Chairs

Leonid Karlinsky   IBM Research, Israel
Tomer Michaeli   Technion – Israel Institute of Technology, Israel
Ko Nishino   Kyoto University, Japan

Tutorial Chairs

Thomas Pock   Graz University of Technology, Austria
Natalia Neverova   Facebook AI Research, UK

Demo Chair

Bohyung Han   Seoul National University, Korea

Social and Student Activities Chairs

Tatiana Tommasi   Italian Institute of Technology, Italy
Sagie Benaim   University of Copenhagen, Denmark

Diversity and Inclusion Chairs

Xi Yin   Facebook AI Research, USA
Bryan Russell   Adobe, USA

Communications Chairs

Lorenzo Baraldi   University of Modena and Reggio Emilia, Italy
Kosta Derpanis   York University & Samsung AI Centre Toronto,
                             Canada

Industrial Liaison Chairs

Dimosthenis Karatzas   Universitat Autònoma de Barcelona, Spain
Chen Sagiv   SagivTech, Israel

Finance Chair

Gerard Medioni   University of Southern California & Amazon,
                             USA

Publication Chair

Eric Mortensen   MiCROTEC, USA

Area Chairs

Lourdes Agapito   University College London, UK
Zeynep Akata   University of Tübingen, Germany
Naveed Akhtar   University of Western Australia, Australia
Karteek Alahari   Inria Grenoble Rhône-Alpes, France
Alexandre Alahi   École polytechnique fédérale de Lausanne,
                             Switzerland
Pablo Arbelaez   Universidad de Los Andes, Columbia
Antonis A. Argyros   University of Crete & Foundation for Research
                             and Technology-Hellas, Crete
Yuki M. Asano   University of Amsterdam, The Netherlands
Kalle Åström   Lund University, Sweden
Hadar Averbuch-Elor   Cornell University, USA

Hossein Azizpour	KTH Royal Institute of Technology, Sweden
Vineeth N. Balasubramanian	Indian Institute of Technology, Hyderabad, India
Lamberto Ballan	University of Padova, Italy
Adrien Bartoli	Université Clermont Auvergne, France
Horst Bischof	Graz University of Technology, Austria
Matthew B. Blaschko	KU Leuven, Belgium
Federica Bogo	Meta Reality Labs Research, Switzerland
Katherine Bouman	California Institute of Technology, USA
Edmond Boyer	Inria Grenoble Rhône-Alpes, France
Michael S. Brown	York University, Canada
Vittorio Caggiano	Meta AI Research, USA
Neill Campbell	University of Bath, UK
Octavia Camps	Northeastern University, USA
Duygu Ceylan	Adobe Research, USA
Ayan Chakrabarti	Google Research, USA
Tat-Jen Cham	Nanyang Technological University, Singapore
Antoni Chan	City University of Hong Kong, Hong Kong, China
Manmohan Chandraker	NEC Labs America, USA
Xinlei Chen	Facebook AI Research, USA
Xilin Chen	Institute of Computing Technology, Chinese Academy of Sciences, China
Dongdong Chen	Microsoft Cloud AI, USA
Chen Chen	University of Central Florida, USA
Ondrej Chum	Vision Recognition Group, Czech Technical University in Prague, Czech Republic
John Collomosse	Adobe Research & University of Surrey, UK
Camille Couprie	Facebook, France
David Crandall	Indiana University, USA
Daniel Cremers	Technical University of Munich, Germany
Marco Cristani	University of Verona, Italy
Canton Cristian	Facebook AI Research, USA
Dengxin Dai	ETH Zurich, Switzerland
Dima Damen	University of Bristol, UK
Kostas Daniilidis	University of Pennsylvania, USA
Trevor Darrell	University of California, Berkeley, USA
Andrew Davison	Imperial College London, UK
Tali Dekel	Weizmann Institute of Science, Israel
Alessio Del Bue	Istituto Italiano di Tecnologia, Italy
Weihong Deng	Beijing University of Posts and Telecommunications, China
Konstantinos Derpanis	Ryerson University, Canada
Carl Doersch	DeepMind, UK

Matthijs Douze	Facebook AI Research, USA
Mohamed Elhoseiny	King Abdullah University of Science and Technology, Saudi Arabia
Sergio Escalera	University of Barcelona, Spain
Yi Fang	New York University, USA
Ryan Farrell	Brigham Young University, USA
Alireza Fathi	Google, USA
Christoph Feichtenhofer	Facebook AI Research, USA
Basura Fernando	Agency for Science, Technology and Research (A*STAR), Singapore
Vittorio Ferrari	Google Research, Switzerland
Andrew W. Fitzgibbon	Graphcore, UK
David J. Fleet	University of Toronto, Canada
David Forsyth	University of Illinois at Urbana-Champaign, USA
David Fouhey	University of Michigan, USA
Katerina Fragkiadaki	Carnegie Mellon University, USA
Friedrich Fraundorfer	Graz University of Technology, Austria
Oren Freifeld	Ben-Gurion University, Israel
Thomas Funkhouser	Google Research & Princeton University, USA
Yasutaka Furukawa	Simon Fraser University, Canada
Fabio Galasso	Sapienza University of Rome, Italy
Jürgen Gall	University of Bonn, Germany
Chuang Gan	Massachusetts Institute of Technology, USA
Zhe Gan	Microsoft, USA
Animesh Garg	University of Toronto, Vector Institute, Nvidia, Canada
Efstratios Gavves	University of Amsterdam, The Netherlands
Peter Gehler	Amazon, Germany
Theo Gevers	University of Amsterdam, The Netherlands
Bernard Ghanem	King Abdullah University of Science and Technology, Saudi Arabia
Ross B. Girshick	Facebook AI Research, USA
Georgia Gkioxari	Facebook AI Research, USA
Albert Gordo	Facebook, USA
Stephen Gould	Australian National University, Australia
Venu Madhav Govindu	Indian Institute of Science, India
Kristen Grauman	Facebook AI Research & UT Austin, USA
Abhinav Gupta	Carnegie Mellon University & Facebook AI Research, USA
Mohit Gupta	University of Wisconsin-Madison, USA
Hu Han	Institute of Computing Technology, Chinese Academy of Sciences, China

Bohyung Han	Seoul National University, Korea
Tian Han	Stevens Institute of Technology, USA
Emily Hand	University of Nevada, Reno, USA
Bharath Hariharan	Cornell University, USA
Ran He	Institute of Automation, Chinese Academy of Sciences, China
Otmar Hilliges	ETH Zurich, Switzerland
Adrian Hilton	University of Surrey, UK
Minh Hoai	Stony Brook University, USA
Yedid Hoshen	Hebrew University of Jerusalem, Israel
Timothy Hospedales	University of Edinburgh, UK
Gang Hua	Wormpex AI Research, USA
Di Huang	Beihang University, China
Jing Huang	Facebook, USA
Jia-Bin Huang	Facebook, USA
Nathan Jacobs	Washington University in St. Louis, USA
C. V. Jawahar	International Institute of Information Technology, Hyderabad, India
Herve Jegou	Facebook AI Research, France
Neel Joshi	Microsoft Research, USA
Armand Joulin	Facebook AI Research, France
Frederic Jurie	University of Caen Normandie, France
Fredrik Kahl	Chalmers University of Technology, Sweden
Yannis Kalantidis	NAVER LABS Europe, France
Evangelos Kalogerakis	University of Massachusetts, Amherst, USA
Sing Bing Kang	Zillow Group, USA
Yosi Keller	Bar Ilan University, Israel
Margret Keuper	University of Mannheim, Germany
Tae-Kyun Kim	Imperial College London, UK
Benjamin Kimia	Brown University, USA
Alexander Kirillov	Facebook AI Research, USA
Kris Kitani	Carnegie Mellon University, USA
Iasonas Kokkinos	Snap Inc. & University College London, UK
Vladlen Koltun	Apple, USA
Nikos Komodakis	University of Crete, Crete
Piotr Koniusz	Australian National University, Australia
Philipp Kraehenbuehl	University of Texas at Austin, USA
Dilip Krishnan	Google, USA
Ajay Kumar	Hong Kong Polytechnic University, Hong Kong, China
Junseok Kwon	Chung-Ang University, Korea
Jean-Francois Lalonde	Université Laval, Canada

Ivan Laptev	Inria Paris, France
Laura Leal-Taixé	Technical University of Munich, Germany
Erik Learned-Miller	University of Massachusetts, Amherst, USA
Gim Hee Lee	National University of Singapore, Singapore
Seungyong Lee	Pohang University of Science and Technology, Korea
Zhen Lei	Institute of Automation, Chinese Academy of Sciences, China
Bastian Leibe	RWTH Aachen University, Germany
Hongdong Li	Australian National University, Australia
Fuxin Li	Oregon State University, USA
Bo Li	University of Illinois at Urbana-Champaign, USA
Yin Li	University of Wisconsin-Madison, USA
Ser-Nam Lim	Meta AI Research, USA
Joseph Lim	University of Southern California, USA
Stephen Lin	Microsoft Research Asia, China
Dahua Lin	The Chinese University of Hong Kong, Hong Kong, China
Si Liu	Beihang University, China
Xiaoming Liu	Michigan State University, USA
Ce Liu	Microsoft, USA
Zicheng Liu	Microsoft, USA
Yanxi Liu	Pennsylvania State University, USA
Feng Liu	Portland State University, USA
Yebin Liu	Tsinghua University, China
Chen Change Loy	Nanyang Technological University, Singapore
Huchuan Lu	Dalian University of Technology, China
Cewu Lu	Shanghai Jiao Tong University, China
Oisin Mac Aodha	University of Edinburgh, UK
Dhruv Mahajan	Facebook, USA
Subhransu Maji	University of Massachusetts, Amherst, USA
Atsuto Maki	KTH Royal Institute of Technology, Sweden
Arun Mallya	NVIDIA, USA
R. Manmatha	Amazon, USA
Iacopo Masi	Sapienza University of Rome, Italy
Dimitris N. Metaxas	Rutgers University, USA
Ajmal Mian	University of Western Australia, Australia
Christian Micheloni	University of Udine, Italy
Krystian Mikolajczyk	Imperial College London, UK
Anurag Mittal	Indian Institute of Technology, Madras, India
Philippos Mordohai	Stevens Institute of Technology, USA
Greg Mori	Simon Fraser University & Borealis AI, Canada

Vittorio Murino	Istituto Italiano di Tecnologia, Italy
P. J. Narayanan	International Institute of Information Technology, Hyderabad, India
Ram Nevatia	University of Southern California, USA
Natalia Neverova	Facebook AI Research, UK
Richard Newcombe	Facebook, USA
Cuong V. Nguyen	Florida International University, USA
Bingbing Ni	Shanghai Jiao Tong University, China
Juan Carlos Niebles	Salesforce & Stanford University, USA
Ko Nishino	Kyoto University, Japan
Jean-Marc Odobez	Idiap Research Institute, École polytechnique fédérale de Lausanne, Switzerland
Francesca Odone	University of Genova, Italy
Takayuki Okatani	Tohoku University & RIKEN Center for Advanced Intelligence Project, Japan
Manohar Paluri	Facebook, USA
Guan Pang	Facebook, USA
Maja Pantic	Imperial College London, UK
Sylvain Paris	Adobe Research, USA
Jaesik Park	Pohang University of Science and Technology, Korea
Hyun Soo Park	The University of Minnesota, USA
Omkar M. Parkhi	Facebook, USA
Deepak Pathak	Carnegie Mellon University, USA
Georgios Pavlakos	University of California, Berkeley, USA
Marcello Pelillo	University of Venice, Italy
Marc Pollefeys	ETH Zurich & Microsoft, Switzerland
Jean Ponce	Inria, France
Gerard Pons-Moll	University of Tübingen, Germany
Fatih Porikli	Qualcomm, USA
Victor Adrian Prisacariu	University of Oxford, UK
Petia Radeva	University of Barcelona, Spain
Ravi Ramamoorthi	University of California, San Diego, USA
Deva Ramanan	Carnegie Mellon University, USA
Vignesh Ramanathan	Facebook, USA
Nalini Ratha	State University of New York at Buffalo, USA
Tammy Riklin Raviv	Ben-Gurion University, Israel
Tobias Ritschel	University College London, UK
Emanuele Rodola	Sapienza University of Rome, Italy
Amit K. Roy-Chowdhury	University of California, Riverside, USA
Michael Rubinstein	Google, USA
Olga Russakovsky	Princeton University, USA

Mathieu Salzmann	École polytechnique fédérale de Lausanne, Switzerland
Dimitris Samaras	Stony Brook University, USA
Aswin Sankaranarayanan	Carnegie Mellon University, USA
Imari Sato	National Institute of Informatics, Japan
Yoichi Sato	University of Tokyo, Japan
Shin'ichi Satoh	National Institute of Informatics, Japan
Walter Scheirer	University of Notre Dame, USA
Bernt Schiele	Max Planck Institute for Informatics, Germany
Konrad Schindler	ETH Zurich, Switzerland
Cordelia Schmid	Inria & Google, France
Alexander Schwing	University of Illinois at Urbana-Champaign, USA
Nicu Sebe	University of Trento, Italy
Greg Shakhnarovich	Toyota Technological Institute at Chicago, USA
Eli Shechtman	Adobe Research, USA
Humphrey Shi	University of Oregon & University of Illinois at Urbana-Champaign & Picsart AI Research, USA
Jianbo Shi	University of Pennsylvania, USA
Roy Shilkrot	Massachusetts Institute of Technology, USA
Mike Zheng Shou	National University of Singapore, Singapore
Kaleem Siddiqi	McGill University, Canada
Richa Singh	Indian Institute of Technology Jodhpur, India
Greg Slabaugh	Queen Mary University of London, UK
Cees Snoek	University of Amsterdam, The Netherlands
Yale Song	Facebook AI Research, USA
Yi-Zhe Song	University of Surrey, UK
Bjorn Stenger	Rakuten Institute of Technology
Abby Stylianou	Saint Louis University, USA
Akihiro Sugimoto	National Institute of Informatics, Japan
Chen Sun	Brown University, USA
Deqing Sun	Google, USA
Kalyan Sunkavalli	Adobe Research, USA
Ying Tai	Tencent YouTu Lab, China
Ayellet Tal	Technion – Israel Institute of Technology, Israel
Ping Tan	Simon Fraser University, Canada
Siyu Tang	ETH Zurich, Switzerland
Chi-Keung Tang	Hong Kong University of Science and Technology, Hong Kong, China
Radu Timofte	University of Würzburg, Germany & ETH Zurich, Switzerland
Federico Tombari	Google, Switzerland & Technical University of Munich, Germany

James Tompkin	Brown University, USA
Lorenzo Torresani	Dartmouth College, USA
Alexander Toshev	Apple, USA
Du Tran	Facebook AI Research, USA
Anh T. Tran	VinAI, Vietnam
Zhuowen Tu	University of California, San Diego, USA
Georgios Tzimiropoulos	Queen Mary University of London, UK
Jasper Uijlings	Google Research, Switzerland
Jan C. van Gemert	Delft University of Technology, The Netherlands
Gul Varol	Ecole des Ponts ParisTech, France
Nuno Vasconcelos	University of California, San Diego, USA
Mayank Vatsa	Indian Institute of Technology Jodhpur, India
Ashok Veeraraghavan	Rice University, USA
Jakob Verbeek	Facebook AI Research, France
Carl Vondrick	Columbia University, USA
Ruiping Wang	Institute of Computing Technology, Chinese Academy of Sciences, China
Xinchao Wang	National University of Singapore, Singapore
Liwei Wang	The Chinese University of Hong Kong, Hong Kong, China
Chaohui Wang	Université Paris-Est, France
Xiaolong Wang	University of California, San Diego, USA
Christian Wolf	NAVER LABS Europe, France
Tao Xiang	University of Surrey, UK
Saining Xie	Facebook AI Research, USA
Cihang Xie	University of California, Santa Cruz, USA
Zeki Yalniz	Facebook, USA
Ming-Hsuan Yang	University of California, Merced, USA
Angela Yao	National University of Singapore, Singapore
Shaodi You	University of Amsterdam, The Netherlands
Stella X. Yu	University of California, Berkeley, USA
Junsong Yuan	State University of New York at Buffalo, USA
Stefanos Zafeiriou	Imperial College London, UK
Amir Zamir	École polytechnique fédérale de Lausanne, Switzerland
Lei Zhang	Alibaba & Hong Kong Polytechnic University, Hong Kong, China
Lei Zhang	International Digital Economy Academy (IDEA), China
Pengchuan Zhang	Meta AI, USA
Bolei Zhou	University of California, Los Angeles, USA
Yuke Zhu	University of Texas at Austin, USA

Todd Zickler   Harvard University, USA
Wangmeng Zuo   Harbin Institute of Technology, China

Technical Program Committee

Davide Abati
Soroush Abbasi
    Koohpayegani
Amos L. Abbott
Rameen Abdal
Rabab Abdelfattah
Sahar Abdelnabi
Hassan Abu Alhaija
Abulikemu Abuduweili
Ron Abutbul
Hanno Ackermann
Aikaterini Adam
Kamil Adamczewski
Ehsan Adeli
Vida Adeli
Donald Adjeroh
Arman Afrasiyabi
Akshay Agarwal
Sameer Agarwal
Abhinav Agarwalla
Vaibhav Aggarwal
Sara Aghajanzadeh
Susmit Agrawal
Antonio Agudo
Touqeer Ahmad
Sk Miraj Ahmed
Chaitanya Ahuja
Nilesh A. Ahuja
Abhishek Aich
Shubhra Aich
Noam Aigerman
Arash Akbarinia
Peri Akiva
Derya Akkaynak
Emre Aksan
Arjun R. Akula
Yuval Alaluf
Stephan Alaniz
Paul Albert
Cenek Albl

Filippo Aleotti
Konstantinos P.
    Alexandridis
Motasem Alfarra
Mohsen Ali
Thiemo Alldieck
Hadi Alzayer
Liang An
Shan An
Yi An
Zhulin An
Dongsheng An
Jie An
Xiang An
Saket Anand
Cosmin Ancuti
Juan Andrade-Cetto
Alexander Andreopoulos
Bjoern Andres
Jerone T. A. Andrews
Shivangi Aneja
Anelia Angelova
Dragomir Anguelov
Rushil Anirudh
Oron Anschel
Rao Muhammad Anwer
Djamila Aouada
Evlampios Apostolidis
Srikar Appalaraju
Nikita Araslanov
Andre Araujo
Eric Arazo
Dawit Mureja Argaw
Anurag Arnab
Aditya Arora
Chetan Arora
Sunpreet S. Arora
Alexey Artemov
Muhammad Asad
Kumar Ashutosh

Sinem Aslan
Vishal Asnani
Mahmoud Assran
Amir Atapour-Abarghouei
Nikos Athanasiou
Ali Athar
ShahRukh Athar
Sara Atito
Souhaib Attaiki
Matan Atzmon
Mathieu Aubry
Nicolas Audebert
Tristan T.
    Aumentado-Armstrong
Melinos Averkiou
Yannis Avrithis
Stephane Ayache
Mehmet Aygün
Seyed Mehdi
    Ayyoubzadeh
Hossein Azizpour
George Azzopardi
Mallikarjun B. R.
Yunhao Ba
Abhishek Badki
Seung-Hwan Bae
Seung-Hwan Baek
Seungryul Baek
Piyush Nitin Bagad
Shai Bagon
Gaetan Bahl
Shikhar Bahl
Sherwin Bahmani
Haoran Bai
Lei Bai
Jiawang Bai
Haoyue Bai
Jinbin Bai
Xiang Bai
Xuyang Bai

Yang Bai
Yuanchao Bai
Ziqian Bai
Sungyong Baik
Kevin Bailly
Max Bain
Federico Baldassarre
Wele Gedara Chaminda
    Bandara
Biplab Banerjee
Pratyay Banerjee
Sandipan Banerjee
Jihwan Bang
Antyanta Bangunharcana
Aayush Bansal
Ankan Bansal
Siddhant Bansal
Wentao Bao
Zhipeng Bao
Amir Bar
Manel Baradad Jurjo
Lorenzo Baraldi
Danny Barash
Daniel Barath
Connelly Barnes
Ioan Andrei Bârsan
Steven Basart
Dina Bashkirova
Chaim Baskin
Peyman Bateni
Anil Batra
Sebastiano Battiato
Ardhendu Behera
Harkirat Behl
Jens Behley
Vasileios Belagiannis
Boulbaba Ben Amor
Emanuel Ben Baruch
Abdessamad Ben Hamza
Gil Ben-Artzi
Assia Benbihi
Fabian Benitez-Quiroz
Guy Ben-Yosef
Philipp Benz
Alexander W. Bergman

Urs Bergmann
Jesus Bermudez-Cameo
Stefano Berretti
Gedas Bertasius
Zachary Bessinger
Petra Bevandić
Matthew Beveridge
Lucas Beyer
Yash Bhalgat
Suvaansh Bhambri
Samarth Bharadwaj
Gaurav Bharaj
Aparna Bharati
Bharat Lal Bhatnagar
Uttaran Bhattacharya
Apratim Bhattacharyya
Brojeshwar Bhowmick
Ankan Kumar Bhunia
Ayan Kumar Bhunia
Qi Bi
Sai Bi
Michael Bi Mi
Gui-Bin Bian
Jia-Wang Bian
Shaojun Bian
Pia Bideau
Mario Bijelic
Hakan Bilen
Guillaume-Alexandre
    Bilodeau
Alexander Binder
Tolga Birdal
Vighnesh N. Birodkar
Sandika Biswas
Andreas Blattmann
Janusz Bobulski
Giuseppe Boccignone
Vishnu Boddeti
Navaneeth Bodla
Moritz Böhle
Aleksei Bokhovkin
Sam Bond-Taylor
Vivek Boominathan
Shubhankar Borse
Mark Boss

Andrea Bottino
Adnane Boukhayma
Fadi Boutros
Nicolas C. Boutry
Richard S. Bowen
Ivaylo Boyadzhiev
Aidan Boyd
Yuri Boykov
Aljaz Bozic
Behzad Bozorgtabar
Eric Brachmann
Samarth Brahmbhatt
Gustav Bredell
Francois Bremond
Joel Brogan
Andrew Brown
Thomas Brox
Marcus A. Brubaker
Robert-Jan Bruintjes
Yuqi Bu
Anders G. Buch
Himanshu Buckchash
Mateusz Buda
Ignas Budvytis
José M. Buenaposada
Marcel C. Bühler
Tu Bui
Adrian Bulat
Hannah Bull
Evgeny Burnaev
Andrei Bursuc
Benjamin Busam
Sergey N. Buzykanov
Wonmin Byeon
Fabian Caba
Martin Cadik
Guanyu Cai
Minjie Cai
Qing Cai
Zhongang Cai
Qi Cai
Yancheng Cai
Shen Cai
Han Cai
Jiarui Cai

Bowen Cai
Mu Cai
Qin Cai
Ruojin Cai
Weidong Cai
Weiwei Cai
Yi Cai
Yujun Cai
Zhiping Cai
Akin Caliskan
Lilian Calvet
Baris Can Cam
Necati Cihan Camgoz
Tommaso Campari
Dylan Campbell
Ziang Cao
Ang Cao
Xu Cao
Zhiwen Cao
Shengcao Cao
Song Cao
Weipeng Cao
Xiangyong Cao
Xiaochun Cao
Yue Cao
Yunhao Cao
Zhangjie Cao
Jiale Cao
Yang Cao
Jiajiong Cao
Jie Cao
Jinkun Cao
Lele Cao
Yulong Cao
Zhiguo Cao
Chen Cao
Razvan Caramalau
Marlène Careil
Gustavo Carneiro
Joao Carreira
Dan Casas
Paola Cascante-Bonilla
Angela Castillo
Francisco M. Castro
Pedro Castro

Luca Cavalli
George J. Cazenavette
Oya Celiktutan
Hakan Cevikalp
Sri Harsha C. H.
Sungmin Cha
Geonho Cha
Menglei Chai
Lucy Chai
Yuning Chai
Zenghao Chai
Anirban Chakraborty
Deep Chakraborty
Rudrasis Chakraborty
Souradeep Chakraborty
Kelvin C. K. Chan
Chee Seng Chan
Paramanand Chandramouli
Arjun Chandrasekaran
Kenneth Chaney
Dongliang Chang
Huiwen Chang
Peng Chang
Xiaojun Chang
Jia-Ren Chang
Hyung Jin Chang
Hyun Sung Chang
Ju Yong Chang
Li-Jen Chang
Qi Chang
Wei-Yi Chang
Yi Chang
Nadine Chang
Hanqing Chao
Pradyumna Chari
Dibyadip Chatterjee
Chiranjoy Chattopadhyay
Siddhartha Chaudhuri
Zhengping Che
Gal Chechik
Lianggangxu Chen
Qi Alfred Chen
Brian Chen
Bor-Chun Chen
Bo-Hao Chen

Bohong Chen
Bin Chen
Ziliang Chen
Cheng Chen
Chen Chen
Chaofeng Chen
Xi Chen
Haoyu Chen
Xuanhong Chen
Wei Chen
Qiang Chen
Shi Chen
Xianyu Chen
Chang Chen
Changhuai Chen
Hao Chen
Jie Chen
Jianbo Chen
Jingjing Chen
Jun Chen
Kejiang Chen
Mingcai Chen
Nenglun Chen
Qifeng Chen
Ruoyu Chen
Shu-Yu Chen
Weidong Chen
Weijie Chen
Weikai Chen
Xiang Chen
Xiuyi Chen
Xingyu Chen
Yaofo Chen
Yueting Chen
Yu Chen
Yunjin Chen
Yuntao Chen
Yun Chen
Zhenfang Chen
Zhuangzhuang Chen
Chu-Song Chen
Xiangyu Chen
Zhuo Chen
Chaoqi Chen
Shizhe Chen

Xiaotong Chen
Xiaozhi Chen
Dian Chen
Defang Chen
Dingfan Chen
Ding-Jie Chen
Ee Heng Chen
Tao Chen
Yixin Chen
Wei-Ting Chen
Lin Chen
Guang Chen
Guangyi Chen
Guanying Chen
Guangyao Chen
Hwann-Tzong Chen
Junwen Chen
Jiacheng Chen
Jianxu Chen
Hui Chen
Kai Chen
Kan Chen
Kevin Chen
Kuan-Wen Chen
Weihua Chen
Zhang Chen
Liang-Chieh Chen
Lele Chen
Liang Chen
Fanglin Chen
Zehui Chen
Minghui Chen
Minghao Chen
Xiaokang Chen
Qian Chen
Jun-Cheng Chen
Qi Chen
Qingcai Chen
Richard J. Chen
Runnan Chen
Rui Chen
Shuo Chen
Sentao Chen
Shaoyu Chen
Shixing Chen

Shuai Chen
Shuya Chen
Sizhe Chen
Simin Chen
Shaoxiang Chen
Zitian Chen
Tianlong Chen
Tianshui Chen
Min-Hung Chen
Xiangning Chen
Xin Chen
Xinghao Chen
Xuejin Chen
Xu Chen
Xuxi Chen
Yunlu Chen
Yanbei Chen
Yuxiao Chen
Yun-Chun Chen
Yi-Ting Chen
Yi-Wen Chen
Yinbo Chen
Yiran Chen
Yuanhong Chen
Yubei Chen
Yuefeng Chen
Yuhua Chen
Yukang Chen
Zerui Chen
Zhaoyu Chen
Zhen Chen
Zhenyu Chen
Zhi Chen
Zhiwei Chen
Zhixiang Chen
Long Chen
Bowen Cheng
Jun Cheng
Yi Cheng
Jingchun Cheng
Lechao Cheng
Xi Cheng
Yuan Cheng
Ho Kei Cheng
Kevin Ho Man Cheng

Jiacheng Cheng
Kelvin B. Cheng
Li Cheng
Mengjun Cheng
Zhen Cheng
Qingrong Cheng
Tianheng Cheng
Harry Cheng
Yihua Cheng
Yu Cheng
Ziheng Cheng
Soon Yau Cheong
Anoop Cherian
Manuela Chessa
Zhixiang Chi
Naoki Chiba
Julian Chibane
Kashyap Chitta
Tai-Yin Chiu
Hsu-kuang Chiu
Wei-Chen Chiu
Sungmin Cho
Donghyeon Cho
Hyeon Cho
Yooshin Cho
Gyusang Cho
Jang Hyun Cho
Seungju Cho
Nam Ik Cho
Sunghyun Cho
Hanbyel Cho
Jaesung Choe
Jooyoung Choi
Chiho Choi
Changwoon Choi
Jongwon Choi
Myungsub Choi
Dooseop Choi
Jonghyun Choi
Jinwoo Choi
Jun Won Choi
Min-Kook Choi
Hongsuk Choi
Janghoon Choi
Yoon-Ho Choi

Yukyung Choi
Jaegul Choo
Ayush Chopra
Siddharth Choudhary
Subhabrata Choudhury
Vasileios Choutas
Ka-Ho Chow
Pinaki Nath Chowdhury
Sammy Christen
Anders Christensen
Grigorios Chrysos
Hang Chu
Wen-Hsuan Chu
Peng Chu
Qi Chu
Ruihang Chu
Wei-Ta Chu
Yung-Yu Chuang
Sanghyuk Chun
Se Young Chun
Antonio Cinà
Ramazan Gokberk Cinbis
Javier Civera
Albert Clapés
Ronald Clark
Brian S. Clipp
Felipe Codevilla
Daniel Coelho de Castro
Niv Cohen
Forrester Cole
Maxwell D. Collins
Robert T. Collins
Marc Comino Trinidad
Runmin Cong
Wenyan Cong
Maxime Cordy
Marcella Cornia
Enric Corona
Huseyin Coskun
Luca Cosmo
Dragos Costea
Davide Cozzolino
Arun C. S. Kumar
Aiyu Cui
Qiongjie Cui

Quan Cui
Shuhao Cui
Yiming Cui
Ying Cui
Zijun Cui
Jiali Cui
Jiequan Cui
Yawen Cui
Zhen Cui
Zhaopeng Cui
Jack Culpepper
Xiaodong Cun
Ross Cutler
Adam Czajka
Ali Dabouei
Konstantinos M. Dafnis
Manuel Dahnert
Tao Dai
Yuchao Dai
Bo Dai
Mengyu Dai
Hang Dai
Haixing Dai
Peng Dai
Pingyang Dai
Qi Dai
Qiyu Dai
Yutong Dai
Naser Damer
Zhiyuan Dang
Mohamed Daoudi
Ayan Das
Abir Das
Debasmit Das
Deepayan Das
Partha Das
Sagnik Das
Soumi Das
Srijan Das
Swagatam Das
Avijit Dasgupta
Jim Davis
Adrian K. Davison
Homa Davoudi
Laura Daza

Matthias De Lange
Shalini De Mello
Marco De Nadai
Christophe De
    Vleeschouwer
Alp Dener
Boyang Deng
Congyue Deng
Bailin Deng
Yong Deng
Ye Deng
Zhuo Deng
Zhijie Deng
Xiaoming Deng
Jiankang Deng
Jinhong Deng
Jingjing Deng
Liang-Jian Deng
Siqi Deng
Xiang Deng
Xueqing Deng
Zhongying Deng
Karan Desai
Jean-Emmanuel Deschaud
Aniket Anand Deshmukh
Neel Dey
Helisa Dhamo
Prithviraj Dhar
Amaya Dharmasiri
Yan Di
Xing Di
Ousmane A. Dia
Haiwen Diao
Xiaolei Diao
Gonçalo José Dias Pais
Abdallah Dib
Anastasios Dimou
Changxing Ding
Henghui Ding
Guodong Ding
Yaqing Ding
Shuangrui Ding
Yuhang Ding
Yikang Ding
Shouhong Ding

Haisong Ding
Hui Ding
Jiahao Ding
Jian Ding
Jian-Jiun Ding
Shuxiao Ding
Tianyu Ding
Wenhao Ding
Yuqi Ding
Yi Ding
Yuzhen Ding
Zhengming Ding
Tan Minh Dinh
Vu Dinh
Christos Diou
Mandar Dixit
Bao Gia Doan
Khoa D. Doan
Dzung Anh Doan
Debi Prosad Dogra
Nehal Doiphode
Chengdong Dong
Bowen Dong
Zhenxing Dong
Hang Dong
Xiaoyi Dong
Haoye Dong
Jiangxin Dong
Shichao Dong
Xuan Dong
Zhen Dong
Shuting Dong
Jing Dong
Li Dong
Ming Dong
Nanqing Dong
Qiulei Dong
Runpei Dong
Siyan Dong
Tian Dong
Wei Dong
Xiaomeng Dong
Xin Dong
Xingbo Dong
Yuan Dong

Samuel Dooley
Gianfranco Doretto
Michael Dorkenwald
Keval Doshi
Zhaopeng Dou
Xiaotian Dou
Hazel Doughty
Ahmad Droby
Iddo Drori
Jie Du
Yong Du
Dawei Du
Dong Du
Ruoyi Du
Yuntao Du
Xuefeng Du
Yilun Du
Yuming Du
Radhika Dua
Haodong Duan
Jiafei Duan
Kaiwen Duan
Peiqi Duan
Ye Duan
Haoran Duan
Jiali Duan
Amanda Duarte
Abhimanyu Dubey
Shiv Ram Dubey
Florian Dubost
Lukasz Dudziak
Shivam Duggal
Justin M. Dulay
Matteo Dunnhofer
Chi Nhan Duong
Thibaut Durand
Mihai Dusmanu
Ujjal Kr Dutta
Debidatta Dwibedi
Isht Dwivedi
Sai Kumar Dwivedi
Takeharu Eda
Mark Edmonds
Alexei A. Efros
Thibaud Ehret

Max Ehrlich
Mahsa Ehsanpour
Iván Eichhardt
Farshad Einabadi
Marvin Eisenberger
Hazim Kemal Ekenel
Mohamed El Banani
Ismail Elezi
Moshe Eliasof
Alaa El-Nouby
Ian Endres
Francis Engelmann
Deniz Engin
Chanho Eom
Dave Epstein
Maria C. Escobar
Victor A. Escorcia
Carlos Esteves
Sungmin Eum
Bernard J. E. Evans
Ivan Evtimov
Fevziye Irem Eyiokur
  Yaman
Matteo Fabbri
Sébastien Fabbro
Gabriele Facciolo
Masud Fahim
Bin Fan
Hehe Fan
Deng-Ping Fan
Aoxiang Fan
Chen-Chen Fan
Qi Fan
Zhaoxin Fan
Haoqi Fan
Heng Fan
Hongyi Fan
Linxi Fan
Baojie Fan
Jiayuan Fan
Lei Fan
Quanfu Fan
Yonghui Fan
Yingruo Fan
Zhiwen Fan

Zicong Fan
Sean Fanello
Jiansheng Fang
Chaowei Fang
Yuming Fang
Jianwu Fang
Jin Fang
Qi Fang
Shancheng Fang
Tian Fang
Xianyong Fang
Gongfan Fang
Zhen Fang
Hui Fang
Jiemin Fang
Le Fang
Pengfei Fang
Xiaolin Fang
Yuxin Fang
Zhaoyuan Fang
Ammarah Farooq
Azade Farshad
Zhengcong Fei
Michael Felsberg
Wei Feng
Chen Feng
Fan Feng
Andrew Feng
Xin Feng
Zheyun Feng
Ruicheng Feng
Mingtao Feng
Qianyu Feng
Shangbin Feng
Chun-Mei Feng
Zunlei Feng
Zhiyong Feng
Martin Fergie
Mustansar Fiaz
Marco Fiorucci
Michael Firman
Hamed Firooz
Volker Fischer
Corneliu O. Florea
Georgios Floros

Wolfgang Foerstner
Gianni Franchi
Jean-Sebastien Franco
Simone Frintrop
Anna Fruehstueck
Changhong Fu
Chaoyou Fu
Cheng-Yang Fu
Chi-Wing Fu
Deqing Fu
Huan Fu
Jun Fu
Kexue Fu
Ying Fu
Jianlong Fu
Jingjing Fu
Qichen Fu
Tsu-Jui Fu
Xueyang Fu
Yang Fu
Yanwei Fu
Yonggan Fu
Wolfgang Fuhl
Yasuhisa Fujii
Kent Fujiwara
Marco Fumero
Takuya Funatomi
Isabel Funke
Dario Fuoli
Antonino Furnari
Matheus A. Gadelha
Akshay Gadi Patil
Adrian Galdran
Guillermo Gallego
Silvano Galliani
Orazio Gallo
Leonardo Galteri
Matteo Gamba
Yiming Gan
Sujoy Ganguly
Harald Ganster
Boyan Gao
Changxin Gao
Daiheng Gao
Difei Gao

Chen Gao
Fei Gao
Lin Gao
Wei Gao
Yiming Gao
Junyu Gao
Guangyu Ryan Gao
Haichang Gao
Hongchang Gao
Jialin Gao
Jin Gao
Jun Gao
Katelyn Gao
Mingchen Gao
Mingfei Gao
Pan Gao
Shangqian Gao
Shanghua Gao
Xitong Gao
Yunhe Gao
Zhanning Gao
Elena Garces
Nuno Cruz Garcia
Noa Garcia
Guillermo
    Garcia-Hernando
Isha Garg
Rahul Garg
Sourav Garg
Quentin Garrido
Stefano Gasperini
Kent Gauen
Chandan Gautam
Shivam Gautam
Paul Gay
Chunjiang Ge
Shiming Ge
Wenhang Ge
Yanhao Ge
Zheng Ge
Songwei Ge
Weifeng Ge
Yixiao Ge
Yuying Ge
Shijie Geng

Zhengyang Geng
Kyle A. Genova
Georgios Georgakis
Markos Georgopoulos
Marcel Geppert
Shabnam Ghadar
Mina Ghadimi Atigh
Deepti Ghadiyaram
Maani Ghaffari Jadidi
Sedigh Ghamari
Zahra Gharaee
Michaël Gharbi
Golnaz Ghiasi
Reza Ghoddoosian
Soumya Suvra Ghosal
Adhiraj Ghosh
Arthita Ghosh
Pallabi Ghosh
Soumyadeep Ghosh
Andrew Gilbert
Igor Gilitschenski
Jhony H. Giraldo
Andreu Girbau Xalabarder
Rohit Girdhar
Sharath Girish
Xavier Giro-i-Nieto
Raja Giryes
Thomas Gittings
Nikolaos Gkanatsios
Ioannis Gkioulekas
Abhiram
    Gnanasambandam
Aurele T. Gnanha
Clement L. J. C. Godard
Arushi Goel
Vidit Goel
Shubham Goel
Zan Gojcic
Aaron K. Gokaslan
Tejas Gokhale
S. Alireza Golestaneh
Thiago L. Gomes
Nuno Goncalves
Boqing Gong
Chen Gong

Yuanhao Gong
Guoqiang Gong
Jingyu Gong
Rui Gong
Yu Gong
Mingming Gong
Neil Zhenqiang Gong
Xun Gong
Yunye Gong
Yihong Gong
Cristina I. González
Nithin Gopalakrishnan
    Nair
Gaurav Goswami
Jianping Gou
Shreyank N. Gowda
Ankit Goyal
Helmut Grabner
Patrick L. Grady
Ben Graham
Eric Granger
Douglas R. Gray
Matej Grcić
David Griffiths
Jinjin Gu
Yun Gu
Shuyang Gu
Jianyang Gu
Fuqiang Gu
Jiatao Gu
Jindong Gu
Jiaqi Gu
Jinwei Gu
Jiaxin Gu
Geonmo Gu
Xiao Gu
Xinqian Gu
Xiuye Gu
Yuming Gu
Zhangxuan Gu
Dayan Guan
Junfeng Guan
Qingji Guan
Tianrui Guan
Shanyan Guan

Denis A. Gudovskiy
Ricardo Guerrero
Pierre-Louis Guhur
Jie Gui
Liangyan Gui
Liangke Gui
Benoit Guillard
Erhan Gundogdu
Manuel Günther
Jingcai Guo
Yuanfang Guo
Junfeng Guo
Chenqi Guo
Dan Guo
Hongji Guo
Jia Guo
Jie Guo
Minghao Guo
Shi Guo
Yanhui Guo
Yangyang Guo
Yuan-Chen Guo
Yilu Guo
Yiluan Guo
Yong Guo
Guangyu Guo
Haiyun Guo
Jinyang Guo
Jianyuan Guo
Pengsheng Guo
Pengfei Guo
Shuxuan Guo
Song Guo
Tianyu Guo
Qing Guo
Qiushan Guo
Wen Guo
Xiefan Guo
Xiaohu Guo
Xiaoqing Guo
Yufei Guo
Yuhui Guo
Yuliang Guo
Yunhui Guo
Yanwen Guo

Akshita Gupta
Ankush Gupta
Kamal Gupta
Kartik Gupta
Ritwik Gupta
Rohit Gupta
Siddharth Gururani
Fredrik K. Gustafsson
Abner Guzman Rivera
Vladimir Guzov
Matthew A. Gwilliam
Jung-Woo Ha
Marc Habermann
Isma Hadji
Christian Haene
Martin Hahner
Levente Hajder
Alexandros Haliassos
Emanuela Haller
Bumsub Ham
Abdullah J. Hamdi
Shreyas Hampali
Dongyoon Han
Chunrui Han
Dong-Jun Han
Dong-Sig Han
Guangxing Han
Zhizhong Han
Ruize Han
Jiaming Han
Jin Han
Ligong Han
Xian-Hua Han
Xiaoguang Han
Yizeng Han
Zhi Han
Zhenjun Han
Zhongyi Han
Jungong Han
Junlin Han
Kai Han
Kun Han
Sungwon Han
Songfang Han
Wei Han

Xiao Han
Xintong Han
Xinzhe Han
Yahong Han
Yan Han
Zongbo Han
Nicolai Hani
Rana Hanocka
Niklas Hanselmann
Nicklas A. Hansen
Hong Hanyu
Fusheng Hao
Yanbin Hao
Shijie Hao
Udith Haputhanthri
Mehrtash Harandi
Josh Harguess
Adam Harley
David M. Hart
Atsushi Hashimoto
Ali Hassani
Mohammed Hassanin
Yana Hasson
Joakim Bruslund Haurum
Bo He
Kun He
Chen He
Xin He
Fazhi He
Gaoqi He
Hao He
Haoyu He
Jiangpeng He
Hongliang He
Qian He
Xiangteng He
Xuming He
Yannan He
Yuhang He
Yang He
Xiangyu He
Nanjun He
Pan He
Sen He
Shengfeng He

Songtao He
Tao He
Tong He
Wei He
Xuehai He
Xiaoxiao He
Ying He
Yisheng He
Ziwen He
Peter Hedman
Felix Heide
Yacov Hel-Or
Paul Henderson
Philipp Henzler
Byeongho Heo
Jae-Pil Heo
Miran Heo
Sachini A. Herath
Stephane Herbin
Pedro Hermosilla Casajus
Monica Hernandez
Charles Herrmann
Roei Herzig
Mauricio Hess-Flores
Carlos Hinojosa
Tobias Hinz
Tsubasa Hirakawa
Chih-Hui Ho
Lam Si Tung Ho
Jennifer Hobbs
Derek Hoiem
Yannick Hold-Geoffroy
Aleksander Holynski
Cheeun Hong
Fa-Ting Hong
Hanbin Hong
Guan Zhe Hong
Danfeng Hong
Lanqing Hong
Xiaopeng Hong
Xin Hong
Jie Hong
Seungbum Hong
Cheng-Yao Hong
Seunghoon Hong

Yi Hong
Yuan Hong
Yuchen Hong
Anthony Hoogs
Maxwell C. Horton
Kazuhiro Hotta
Qibin Hou
Tingbo Hou
Junhui Hou
Ji Hou
Qiqi Hou
Rui Hou
Ruibing Hou
Zhi Hou
Henry Howard-Jenkins
Lukas Hoyer
Wei-Lin Hsiao
Chiou-Ting Hsu
Anthony Hu
Brian Hu
Yusong Hu
Hexiang Hu
Haoji Hu
Di Hu
Hengtong Hu
Haigen Hu
Lianyu Hu
Hanzhe Hu
Jie Hu
Junlin Hu
Shizhe Hu
Jian Hu
Zhiming Hu
Juhua Hu
Peng Hu
Ping Hu
Ronghang Hu
MengShun Hu
Tao Hu
Vincent Tao Hu
Xiaoling Hu
Xinting Hu
Xiaolin Hu
Xuefeng Hu
Xiaowei Hu

Yang Hu
Yueyu Hu
Zeyu Hu
Zhongyun Hu
Binh-Son Hua
Guoliang Hua
Yi Hua
Linzhi Huang
Qiusheng Huang
Bo Huang
Chen Huang
Hsin-Ping Huang
Ye Huang
Shuangping Huang
Zeng Huang
Buzhen Huang
Cong Huang
Heng Huang
Hao Huang
Qidong Huang
Huaibo Huang
Chaoqin Huang
Feihu Huang
Jiahui Huang
Jingjia Huang
Kun Huang
Lei Huang
Sheng Huang
Shuaiyi Huang
Siyu Huang
Xiaoshui Huang
Xiaoyang Huang
Yan Huang
Yihao Huang
Ying Huang
Ziling Huang
Xiaoke Huang
Yifei Huang
Haiyang Huang
Zhewei Huang
Jin Huang
Haibin Huang
Jiaxing Huang
Junjie Huang
Keli Huang

Lang Huang
Lin Huang
Luojie Huang
Mingzhen Huang
Shijia Huang
Shengyu Huang
Siyuan Huang
He Huang
Xiuyu Huang
Lianghua Huang
Yue Huang
Yaping Huang
Yuge Huang
Zehao Huang
Zeyi Huang
Zhiqi Huang
Zhongzhan Huang
Zilong Huang
Ziyuan Huang
Tianrui Hui
Zhuo Hui
Le Hui
Jing Huo
Junhwa Hur
Shehzeen S. Hussain
Chuong Minh Huynh
Seunghyun Hwang
Jaehui Hwang
Jyh-Jing Hwang
Sukjun Hwang
Soonmin Hwang
Wonjun Hwang
Rakib Hyder
Sangeek Hyun
Sarah Ibrahimi
Tomoki Ichikawa
Yerlan Idelbayev
A. S. M. Iftekhar
Masaaki Iiyama
Satoshi Ikehata
Sunghoon Im
Atul N. Ingle
Eldar Insafutdinov
Yani A. Ioannou
Radu Tudor Ionescu

Umar Iqbal
Go Irie
Muhammad Zubair Irshad
Ahmet Iscen
Berivan Isik
Ashraful Islam
Md Amirul Islam
Syed Islam
Mariko Isogawa
Vamsi Krishna K. Ithapu
Boris Ivanovic
Darshan Iyer
Sarah Jabbour
Ayush Jain
Nishant Jain
Samyak Jain
Vidit Jain
Vineet Jain
Priyank Jaini
Tomas Jakab
Mohammad A. A. K.
    Jalwana
Muhammad Abdullah
    Jamal
Hadi Jamali-Rad
Stuart James
Varun Jampani
Young Kyun Jang
YeongJun Jang
Yunseok Jang
Ronnachai Jaroensri
Bhavan Jasani
Krishna Murthy
    Jatavallabhula
Mojan Javaheripi
Syed A. Javed
Guillaume Jeanneret
Pranav Jeevan
Herve Jegou
Rohit Jena
Tomas Jenicek
Porter Jenkins
Simon Jenni
Hae-Gon Jeon
Sangryul Jeon

Boseung Jeong
Yoonwoo Jeong
Seong-Gyun Jeong
Jisoo Jeong
Allan D. Jepson
Ankit Jha
Sumit K. Jha
I-Hong Jhuo
Ge-Peng Ji
Chaonan Ji
Deyi Ji
Jingwei Ji
Wei Ji
Zhong Ji
Jiayi Ji
Pengliang Ji
Hui Ji
Mingi Ji
Xiaopeng Ji
Yuzhu Ji
Baoxiong Jia
Songhao Jia
Dan Jia
Shan Jia
Xiaojun Jia
Xiuyi Jia
Xu Jia
Menglin Jia
Wenqi Jia
Boyuan Jiang
Wenhao Jiang
Huaizu Jiang
Hanwen Jiang
Haiyong Jiang
Hao Jiang
Huajie Jiang
Huiqin Jiang
Haojun Jiang
Haobo Jiang
Junjun Jiang
Xingyu Jiang
Yangbangyan Jiang
Yu Jiang
Jianmin Jiang
Jiaxi Jiang

Jing Jiang
Kui Jiang
Li Jiang
Liming Jiang
Chiyu Jiang
Meirui Jiang
Chen Jiang
Peng Jiang
Tai-Xiang Jiang
Wen Jiang
Xinyang Jiang
Yifan Jiang
Yuming Jiang
Yingying Jiang
Zeren Jiang
ZhengKai Jiang
Zhenyu Jiang
Shuming Jiao
Jianbo Jiao
Licheng Jiao
Dongkwon Jin
Yeying Jin
Cheng Jin
Linyi Jin
Qing Jin
Taisong Jin
Xiao Jin
Xin Jin
Sheng Jin
Kyong Hwan Jin
Ruibing Jin
SouYoung Jin
Yueming Jin
Chenchen Jing
Longlong Jing
Taotao Jing
Yongcheng Jing
Younghyun Jo
Joakim Johnander
Jeff Johnson
Michael J. Jones
R. Kenny Jones
Rico Jonschkowski
Ameya Joshi
Sunghun Joung

Felix Juefei-Xu
Claudio R. Jung
Steffen Jung
Hari Chandana K.
Rahul Vigneswaran K.
Prajwal K. R.
Abhishek Kadian
Jhony Kaesemodel Pontes
Kumara Kahatapitiya
Anmol Kalia
Sinan Kalkan
Tarun Kalluri
Jaewon Kam
Sandesh Kamath
Meina Kan
Menelaos Kanakis
Takuhiro Kaneko
Di Kang
Guoliang Kang
Hao Kang
Jaeyeon Kang
Kyoungkook Kang
Li-Wei Kang
MinGuk Kang
Suk-Ju Kang
Zhao Kang
Yash Mukund Kant
Yueying Kao
Aupendu Kar
Konstantinos Karantzalos
Sezer Karaoglu
Navid Kardan
Sanjay Kariyappa
Leonid Karlinsky
Animesh Karnewar
Shyamgopal Karthik
Hirak J. Kashyap
Marc A. Kastner
Hirokatsu Kataoka
Angelos Katharopoulos
Hiroharu Kato
Kai Katsumata
Manuel Kaufmann
Chaitanya Kaul
Prakhar Kaushik

Yuki Kawana
Lei Ke
Lipeng Ke
Tsung-Wei Ke
Wei Ke
Petr Kellnhofer
Aniruddha Kembhavi
John Kender
Corentin Kervadec
Leonid Keselman
Daniel Keysers
Nima Khademi Kalantari
Taras Khakhulin
Samir Khaki
Muhammad Haris Khan
Qadeer Khan
Salman Khan
Subash Khanal
Vaishnavi M. Khindkar
Rawal Khirodkar
Saeed Khorram
Pirazh Khorramshahi
Kourosh Khoshelham
Ansh Khurana
Benjamin Kiefer
Jae Myung Kim
Junho Kim
Boah Kim
Hyeonseong Kim
Dong-Jin Kim
Dongwan Kim
Donghyun Kim
Doyeon Kim
Yonghyun Kim
Hyung-Il Kim
Hyunwoo Kim
Hyeongwoo Kim
Hyo Jin Kim
Hyunwoo J. Kim
Taehoon Kim
Jaeha Kim
Jiwon Kim
Jung Uk Kim
Kangyeol Kim
Eunji Kim

Daeha Kim
Dongwon Kim
Kunhee Kim
Kyungmin Kim
Junsik Kim
Min H. Kim
Namil Kim
Kookhoi Kim
Sanghyun Kim
Seongyeop Kim
Seungryong Kim
Saehoon Kim
Euyoung Kim
Guisik Kim
Sungyeon Kim
Sunnie S. Y. Kim
Taehun Kim
Tae Oh Kim
Won Hwa Kim
Seungwook Kim
YoungBin Kim
Youngeun Kim
Akisato Kimura
Furkan Osman Kınlı
Zsolt Kira
Hedvig Kjellström
Florian Kleber
Jan P. Klopp
Florian Kluger
Laurent Kneip
Byungsoo Ko
Muhammed Kocabas
A. Sophia Koepke
Kevin Koeser
Nick Kolkin
Nikos Kolotouros
Wai-Kin Adams Kong
Deying Kong
Caihua Kong
Youyong Kong
Shuyu Kong
Shu Kong
Tao Kong
Yajing Kong
Yu Kong

Zishang Kong
Theodora Kontogianni
Anton S. Konushin
Julian F. P. Kooij
Bruno Korbar
Giorgos Kordopatis-Zilos
Jari Korhonen
Adam Kortylewski
Denis Korzhenkov
Divya Kothandaraman
Suraj Kothawade
Iuliia Kotseruba
Satwik Kottur
Shashank Kotyan
Alexandros Kouris
Petros Koutras
Anna Kreshuk
Ranjay Krishna
Dilip Krishnan
Andrey Kuehlkamp
Hilde Kuehne
Jason Kuen
David Kügler
Arjan Kuijper
Anna Kukleva
Sumith Kulal
Viveka Kulharia
Akshay R. Kulkarni
Nilesh Kulkarni
Dominik Kulon
Abhinav Kumar
Akash Kumar
Suryansh Kumar
B. V. K. Vijaya Kumar
Pulkit Kumar
Ratnesh Kumar
Sateesh Kumar
Satish Kumar
Vijay Kumar B. G.
Nupur Kumari
Sudhakar Kumawat
Jogendra Nath Kundu
Hsien-Kai Kuo
Meng-Yu Jennifer Kuo
Vinod Kumar Kurmi

Yusuke Kurose
Keerthy Kusumam
Alina Kuznetsova
Henry Kvinge
Ho Man Kwan
Hyeokjun Kweon
Heeseung Kwon
Gihyun Kwon
Myung-Joon Kwon
Taesung Kwon
YoungJoong Kwon
Christos Kyrkou
Jorma Laaksonen
Yann Labbe
Zorah Laehner
Florent Lafarge
Hamid Laga
Manuel Lagunas
Shenqi Lai
Jian-Huang Lai
Zihang Lai
Mohamed I. Lakhal
Mohit Lamba
Meng Lan
Loic Landrieu
Zhiqiang Lang
Natalie Lang
Dong Lao
Yizhen Lao
Yingjie Lao
Issam Hadj Laradji
Gustav Larsson
Viktor Larsson
Zakaria Laskar
Stéphane Lathuilière
Chun Pong Lau
Rynson W. H. Lau
Hei Law
Justin Lazarow
Verica Lazova
Eric-Tuan Le
Hieu Le
Trung-Nghia Le
Mathias Lechner
Byeong-Uk Lee

Chen-Yu Lee
Che-Rung Lee
Chul Lee
Hong Joo Lee
Dongsoo Lee
Jiyoung Lee
Eugene Eu Tzuan Lee
Daeun Lee
Saehyung Lee
Jewook Lee
Hyungtae Lee
Hyunmin Lee
Jungbeom Lee
Joon-Young Lee
Jong-Seok Lee
Joonseok Lee
Junha Lee
Kibok Lee
Byung-Kwan Lee
Jangwon Lee
Jinho Lee
Jongmin Lee
Seunghyun Lee
Sohyun Lee
Minsik Lee
Dogyoon Lee
Seungmin Lee
Min Jun Lee
Sangho Lee
Sangmin Lee
Seungeun Lee
Seon-Ho Lee
Sungmin Lee
Sungho Lee
Sangyoun Lee
Vincent C. S. S. Lee
Jaeseong Lee
Yong Jae Lee
Chenyang Lei
Chenyi Lei
Jiahui Lei
Xinyu Lei
Yinjie Lei
Jiaxu Leng
Luziwei Leng

Jan E. Lenssen
Vincent Lepetit
Thomas Leung
María Leyva-Vallina
Xin Li
Yikang Li
Baoxin Li
Bin Li
Bing Li
Bowen Li
Changlin Li
Chao Li
Chongyi Li
Guanyue Li
Shuai Li
Jin Li
Dingquan Li
Dongxu Li
Yiting Li
Gang Li
Dian Li
Guohao Li
Haoang Li
Haoliang Li
Haoran Li
Hengduo Li
Huafeng Li
Xiaoming Li
Hanao Li
Hongwei Li
Ziqiang Li
Jisheng Li
Jiacheng Li
Jia Li
Jiachen Li
Jiahao Li
Jianwei Li
Jiazhi Li
Jie Li
Jing Li
Jingjing Li
Jingtao Li
Jun Li
Junxuan Li
Kai Li

Kailin Li
Kenneth Li
Kun Li
Kunpeng Li
Aoxue Li
Chenglong Li
Chenglin Li
Changsheng Li
Zhichao Li
Qiang Li
Yanyu Li
Zuoyue Li
Xiang Li
Xuelong Li
Fangda Li
Ailin Li
Liang Li
Chun-Guang Li
Daiqing Li
Dong Li
Guanbin Li
Guorong Li
Haifeng Li
Jianan Li
Jianing Li
Jiaxin Li
Ke Li
Lei Li
Lincheng Li
Liulei Li
Lujun Li
Linjie Li
Lin Li
Pengyu Li
Ping Li
Qiufu Li
Qingyong Li
Rui Li
Siyuan Li
Wei Li
Wenbin Li
Xiangyang Li
Xinyu Li
Xiujun Li
Xiu Li

Xu Li
Ya-Li Li
Yao Li
Yongjie Li
Yijun Li
Yiming Li
Yuezun Li
Yu Li
Yunheng Li
Yuqi Li
Zhe Li
Zeming Li
Zhen Li
Zhengqin Li
Zhimin Li
Jiefeng Li
Jinpeng Li
Chengze Li
Jianwu Li
Lerenhan Li
Shan Li
Suichan Li
Xiangtai Li
Yanjie Li
Yandong Li
Zhuoling Li
Zhenqiang Li
Manyi Li
Maosen Li
Ji Li
Minjun Li
Mingrui Li
Mengtian Li
Junyi Li
Nianyi Li
Bo Li
Xiao Li
Peihua Li
Peike Li
Peizhao Li
Peiliang Li
Qi Li
Ren Li
Runze Li
Shile Li

Sheng Li
Shigang Li
Shiyu Li
Shuang Li
Shasha Li
Shichao Li
Tianye Li
Yuexiang Li
Wei-Hong Li
Wanhua Li
Weihao Li
Weiming Li
Weixin Li
Wenbo Li
Wenshuo Li
Weijian Li
Yunan Li
Xirong Li
Xianhang Li
Xiaoyu Li
Xueqian Li
Xuanlin Li
Xianzhi Li
Yunqiang Li
Yanjing Li
Yansheng Li
Yawei Li
Yi Li
Yong Li
Yong-Lu Li
Yuhang Li
Yu-Jhe Li
Yuxi Li
Yunsheng Li
Yanwei Li
Zechao Li
Zejian Li
Zeju Li
Zekun Li
Zhaowen Li
Zheng Li
Zhenyu Li
Zhiheng Li
Zhi Li
Zhong Li

Zhuowei Li
Zhuowan Li
Zhuohang Li
Zizhang Li
Chen Li
Yuan-Fang Li
Dongze Lian
Xiaochen Lian
Zhouhui Lian
Long Lian
Qing Lian
Jin Lianbao
Jinxiu S. Liang
Dingkang Liang
Jiahao Liang
Jianming Liang
Jingyun Liang
Kevin J. Liang
Kaizhao Liang
Chen Liang
Jie Liang
Senwei Liang
Ding Liang
Jiajun Liang
Jian Liang
Kongming Liang
Siyuan Liang
Yuanzhi Liang
Zhengfa Liang
Mingfu Liang
Xiaodan Liang
Xuefeng Liang
Yuxuan Liang
Kang Liao
Liang Liao
Hong-Yuan Mark Liao
Wentong Liao
Haofu Liao
Yue Liao
Minghui Liao
Shengcai Liao
Ting-Hsuan Liao
Xin Liao
Yinghong Liao
Teck Yian Lim

Che-Tsung Lin
Chung-Ching Lin
Chen-Hsuan Lin
Cheng Lin
Chuming Lin
Chunyu Lin
Dahua Lin
Wei Lin
Zheng Lin
Huaijia Lin
Jason Lin
Jierui Lin
Jiaying Lin
Jie Lin
Kai-En Lin
Kevin Lin
Guangfeng Lin
Jiehong Lin
Feng Lin
Hang Lin
Kwan-Yee Lin
Ke Lin
Luojun Lin
Qinghong Lin
Xiangbo Lin
Yi Lin
Zudi Lin
Shijie Lin
Yiqun Lin
Tzu-Heng Lin
Ming Lin
Shaohui Lin
SongNan Lin
Ji Lin
Tsung-Yu Lin
Xudong Lin
Yancong Lin
Yen-Chen Lin
Yiming Lin
Yuewei Lin
Zhiqiu Lin
Zinan Lin
Zhe Lin
David B. Lindell
Zhixin Ling

Zhan Ling
Alexander Liniger
Venice Erin B. Liong
Joey Litalien
Or Litany
Roee Litman
Ron Litman
Jim Little
Dor Litvak
Shaoteng Liu
Shuaicheng Liu
Andrew Liu
Xian Liu
Shaohui Liu
Bei Liu
Bo Liu
Yong Liu
Ming Liu
Yanbin Liu
Chenxi Liu
Daqi Liu
Di Liu
Difan Liu
Dong Liu
Dongfang Liu
Daizong Liu
Xiao Liu
Fangyi Liu
Fengbei Liu
Fenglin Liu
Bin Liu
Yuang Liu
Ao Liu
Hong Liu
Hongfu Liu
Huidong Liu
Ziyi Liu
Feng Liu
Hao Liu
Jie Liu
Jialun Liu
Jiang Liu
Jing Liu
Jingya Liu
Jiaming Liu

Jun Liu
Juncheng Liu
Jiawei Liu
Hongyu Liu
Chuanbin Liu
Haotian Liu
Lingqiao Liu
Chang Liu
Han Liu
Liu Liu
Min Liu
Yingqi Liu
Aishan Liu
Bingyu Liu
Benlin Liu
Boxiao Liu
Chenchen Liu
Chuanjian Liu
Daqing Liu
Huan Liu
Haozhe Liu
Jiaheng Liu
Wei Liu
Jingzhou Liu
Jiyuan Liu
Lingbo Liu
Nian Liu
Peiye Liu
Qiankun Liu
Shenglan Liu
Shilong Liu
Wen Liu
Wenyu Liu
Weifeng Liu
Wu Liu
Xiaolong Liu
Yang Liu
Yanwei Liu
Yingcheng Liu
Yongfei Liu
Yihao Liu
Yu Liu
Yunze Liu
Ze Liu
Zhenhua Liu

Zhenguang Liu
Lin Liu
Lihao Liu
Pengju Liu
Xinhai Liu
Yunfei Liu
Meng Liu
Minghua Liu
Mingyuan Liu
Miao Liu
Peirong Liu
Ping Liu
Qingjie Liu
Ruoshi Liu
Risheng Liu
Songtao Liu
Xing Liu
Shikun Liu
Shuming Liu
Sheng Liu
Songhua Liu
Tongliang Liu
Weibo Liu
Weide Liu
Weizhe Liu
Wenxi Liu
Weiyang Liu
Xin Liu
Xiaobin Liu
Xudong Liu
Xiaoyi Liu
Xihui Liu
Xinchen Liu
Xingtong Liu
Xinpeng Liu
Xinyu Liu
Xianpeng Liu
Xu Liu
Xingyu Liu
Yongtuo Liu
Yahui Liu
Yangxin Liu
Yaoyao Liu
Yaojie Liu
Yuliang Liu

Yongcheng Liu
Yuan Liu
Yufan Liu
Yu-Lun Liu
Yun Liu
Yunfan Liu
Yuanzhong Liu
Zhuoran Liu
Zhen Liu
Zheng Liu
Zhijian Liu
Zhisong Liu
Ziquan Liu
Ziyu Liu
Zhihua Liu
Zechun Liu
Zhaoyang Liu
Zhengzhe Liu
Stephan Liwicki
Shao-Yuan Lo
Sylvain Lobry
Suhas Lohit
Vishnu Suresh Lokhande
Vincenzo Lomonaco
Chengjiang Long
Guodong Long
Fuchen Long
Shangbang Long
Yang Long
Zijun Long
Vasco Lopes
Antonio M. Lopez
Roberto Javier
    Lopez-Sastre
Tobias Lorenz
Javier Lorenzo-Navarro
Yujing Lou
Qian Lou
Xiankai Lu
Changsheng Lu
Huimin Lu
Yongxi Lu
Hao Lu
Hong Lu
Jiasen Lu

Juwei Lu
Fan Lu
Guangming Lu
Jiwen Lu
Shun Lu
Tao Lu
Xiaonan Lu
Yang Lu
Yao Lu
Yongchun Lu
Zhiwu Lu
Cheng Lu
Liying Lu
Guo Lu
Xuequan Lu
Yanye Lu
Yantao Lu
Yuhang Lu
Fujun Luan
Jonathon Luiten
Jovita Lukasik
Alan Lukezic
Jonathan Samuel Lumentut
Mayank Lunayach
Ao Luo
Canjie Luo
Chong Luo
Xu Luo
Grace Luo
Jun Luo
Katie Z. Luo
Tao Luo
Cheng Luo
Fangzhou Luo
Gen Luo
Lei Luo
Sihui Luo
Weixin Luo
Yan Luo
Xiaoyan Luo
Yong Luo
Yadan Luo
Hao Luo
Ruotian Luo
Mi Luo

Tiange Luo
Wenjie Luo
Wenhan Luo
Xiao Luo
Zhiming Luo
Zhipeng Luo
Zhengyi Luo
Diogo C. Luvizon
Zhaoyang Lv
Gengyu Lyu
Lingjuan Lyu
Jun Lyu
Yuanyuan Lyu
Youwei Lyu
Yueming Lyu
Bingpeng Ma
Chao Ma
Chongyang Ma
Congbo Ma
Chih-Yao Ma
Fan Ma
Lin Ma
Haoyu Ma
Hengbo Ma
Jianqi Ma
Jiawei Ma
Jiayi Ma
Kede Ma
Kai Ma
Lingni Ma
Lei Ma
Xu Ma
Ning Ma
Benteng Ma
Cheng Ma
Andy J. Ma
Long Ma
Zhanyu Ma
Zhiheng Ma
Qianli Ma
Shiqiang Ma
Sizhuo Ma
Shiqing Ma
Xiaolong Ma
Xinzhu Ma

Gautam B. Machiraju
Spandan Madan
Mathew Magimai-Doss
Luca Magri
Behrooz Mahasseni
Upal Mahbub
Siddharth Mahendran
Paridhi Maheshwari
Rishabh Maheshwary
Mohammed Mahmoud
Shishira R. R. Maiya
Sylwia Majchrowska
Arjun Majumdar
Puspita Majumdar
Orchid Majumder
Sagnik Majumder
Ilya Makarov
Farkhod F.
    Makhmudkhujaev
Yasushi Makihara
Ankur Mali
Mateusz Malinowski
Utkarsh Mall
Srikanth Malla
Clement Mallet
Dimitrios Mallis
Yunze Man
Dipu Manandhar
Massimiliano Mancini
Murari Mandal
Raunak Manekar
Karttikeya Mangalam
Puneet Mangla
Fabian Manhardt
Sivabalan Manivasagam
Fahim Mannan
Chengzhi Mao
Hanzi Mao
Jiayuan Mao
Junhua Mao
Zhiyuan Mao
Jiageng Mao
Yunyao Mao
Zhendong Mao
Alberto Marchisio

Diego Marcos
Riccardo Marin
Aram Markosyan
Renaud Marlet
Ricardo Marques
Miquel Martí i Rabadán
Diego Martin Arroyo
Niki Martinel
Brais Martinez
Julieta Martinez
Marc Masana
Tomohiro Mashita
Timothée Masquelier
Minesh Mathew
Tetsu Matsukawa
Marwan Mattar
Bruce A. Maxwell
Christoph Mayer
Mantas Mazeika
Pratik Mazumder
Scott McCloskey
Steven McDonagh
Ishit Mehta
Jie Mei
Kangfu Mei
Jieru Mei
Xiaoguang Mei
Givi Meishvili
Luke Melas-Kyriazi
Iaroslav Melekhov
Andres Mendez-Vazquez
Heydi Mendez-Vazquez
Matias Mendieta
Ricardo A. Mendoza-León
Chenlin Meng
Depu Meng
Rang Meng
Zibo Meng
Qingjie Meng
Qier Meng
Yanda Meng
Zihang Meng
Thomas Mensink
Fabian Mentzer
Christopher Metzler

Gregory P. Meyer
Vasileios Mezaris
Liang Mi
Lu Mi
Bo Miao
Changtao Miao
Zichen Miao
Qiguang Miao
Xin Miao
Zhongqi Miao
Frank Michel
Simone Milani
Ben Mildenhall
Roy V. Miles
Juhong Min
Kyle Min
Hyun-Seok Min
Weiqing Min
Yuecong Min
Zhixiang Min
Qi Ming
David Minnen
Aymen Mir
Deepak Mishra
Anand Mishra
Shlok K. Mishra
Niluthpol Mithun
Gaurav Mittal
Trisha Mittal
Daisuke Miyazaki
Kaichun Mo
Hong Mo
Zhipeng Mo
Davide Modolo
Abduallah A. Mohamed
Mohamed Afham
    Mohamed Aflal
Ron Mokady
Pavlo Molchanov
Davide Moltisanti
Liliane Momeni
Gianluca Monaci
Pascal Monasse
Ajoy Mondal
Tom Monnier

Aron Monszpart
Gyeongsik Moon
Suhong Moon
Taesup Moon
Sean Moran
Daniel Moreira
Pietro Morerio
Alexandre Morgand
Lia Morra
Ali Mosleh
Inbar Mosseri
Sayed Mohammad
    Mostafavi Isfahani
Saman Motamed
Ramy A. Mounir
Fangzhou Mu
Jiteng Mu
Norman Mu
Yasuhiro Mukaigawa
Ryan Mukherjee
Tanmoy Mukherjee
Yusuke Mukuta
Ravi Teja Mullapudi
Lea Müller
Matthias Müller
Martin Mundt
Nils Murrugarra-Llerena
Damien Muselet
Armin Mustafa
Muhammad Ferjad Naeem
Sauradip Nag
Hajime Nagahara
Pravin Nagar
Rajendra Nagar
Naveen Shankar Nagaraja
Varun Nagaraja
Tushar Nagarajan
Seungjun Nah
Gaku Nakano
Yuta Nakashima
Giljoo Nam
Seonghyeon Nam
Liangliang Nan
Yuesong Nan
Yeshwanth Napolean

Dinesh Reddy
    Narapureddy
Medhini Narasimhan
Supreeth
    Narasimhaswamy
Sriram Narayanan
Erickson R. Nascimento
Varun Nasery
K. L. Navaneet
Pablo Navarrete Michelini
Shant Navasardyan
Shah Nawaz
Nihal Nayak
Farhood Negin
Lukáš Neumann
Alejandro Newell
Evonne Ng
Kam Woh Ng
Tony Ng
Anh Nguyen
Tuan Anh Nguyen
Cuong Cao Nguyen
Ngoc Cuong Nguyen
Thanh Nguyen
Khoi Nguyen
Phi Le Nguyen
Phong Ha Nguyen
Tam Nguyen
Truong Nguyen
Anh Tuan Nguyen
Rang Nguyen
Thao Thi Phuong Nguyen
Van Nguyen Nguyen
Zhen-Liang Ni
Yao Ni
Shijie Nie
Xuecheng Nie
Yongwei Nie
Weizhi Nie
Ying Nie
Yinyu Nie
Kshitij N. Nikhal
Simon Niklaus
Xuefei Ning
Jifeng Ning

Yotam Nitzan
Di Niu
Shuaicheng Niu
Li Niu
Wei Niu
Yulei Niu
Zhenxing Niu
Albert No
Shohei Nobuhara
Nicoletta Noceti
Junhyug Noh
Sotiris Nousias
Slawomir Nowaczyk
Ewa M. Nowara
Valsamis Ntouskos
Gilberto Ochoa-Ruiz
Ferda Ofli
Jihyong Oh
Sangyun Oh
Youngtaek Oh
Hiroki Ohashi
Takahiro Okabe
Kemal Oksuz
Fumio Okura
Daniel Olmeda Reino
Matthew Olson
Carl Olsson
Roy Or-El
Alessandro Ortis
Guillermo Ortiz-Jimenez
Magnus Oskarsson
Ahmed A. A. Osman
Martin R. Oswald
Mayu Otani
Naima Otberdout
Cheng Ouyang
Jiahong Ouyang
Wanli Ouyang
Andrew Owens
Poojan B. Oza
Mete Ozay
A. Cengiz Oztireli
Gautam Pai
Tomas Pajdla
Umapada Pal

Simone Palazzo
Luca Palmieri
Bowen Pan
Hao Pan
Lili Pan
Tai-Yu Pan
Liang Pan
Chengwei Pan
Yingwei Pan
Xuran Pan
Jinshan Pan
Xinyu Pan
Liyuan Pan
Xingang Pan
Xingjia Pan
Zhihong Pan
Zizheng Pan
Priyadarshini Panda
Rameswar Panda
Rohit Pandey
Kaiyue Pang
Bo Pang
Guansong Pang
Jiangmiao Pang
Meng Pang
Tianyu Pang
Ziqi Pang
Omiros Pantazis
Andreas Panteli
Maja Pantic
Marina Paolanti
Joao P. Papa
Samuele Papa
Mike Papadakis
Dim P. Papadopoulos
George Papandreou
Constantin Pape
Toufiq Parag
Chethan Parameshwara
Shaifali Parashar
Alejandro Pardo
Rishubh Parihar
Sarah Parisot
JaeYoo Park
Gyeong-Moon Park

Hyojin Park
Hyoungseob Park
Jongchan Park
Jae Sung Park
Kiru Park
Chunghyun Park
Kwanyong Park
Sunghyun Park
Sungrae Park
Seongsik Park
Sanghyun Park
Sungjune Park
Taesung Park
Gaurav Parmar
Paritosh Parmar
Alvaro Parra
Despoina Paschalidou
Or Patashnik
Shivansh Patel
Pushpak Pati
Prashant W. Patil
Vaishakh Patil
Suvam Patra
Jay Patravali
Badri Narayana Patro
Angshuman Paul
Sudipta Paul
Rémi Pautrat
Nick E. Pears
Adithya Pediredla
Wenjie Pei
Shmuel Peleg
Latha Pemula
Bo Peng
Houwen Peng
Yue Peng
Liangzu Peng
Baoyun Peng
Jun Peng
Pai Peng
Sida Peng
Xi Peng
Yuxin Peng
Songyou Peng
Wei Peng

Weiqi Peng
Wen-Hsiao Peng
Pramuditha Perera
Juan C. Perez
Eduardo Pérez Pellitero
Juan-Manuel Perez-Rua
Federico Pernici
Marco Pesavento
Stavros Petridis
Ilya A. Petrov
Vladan Petrovic
Mathis Petrovich
Suzanne Petryk
Hieu Pham
Quang Pham
Khoi Pham
Tung Pham
Huy Phan
Stephen Phillips
Cheng Perng Phoo
David Picard
Marco Piccirilli
Georg Pichler
A. J. Piergiovanni
Vipin Pillai
Silvia L. Pintea
Giovanni Pintore
Robinson Piramuthu
Fiora Pirri
Theodoros Pissas
Fabio Pizzati
Benjamin Planche
Bryan Plummer
Matteo Poggi
Ashwini Pokle
Georgy E. Ponimatkin
Adrian Popescu
Stefan Popov
Nikola Popović
Ronald Poppe
Angelo Porrello
Michael Potter
Charalambos Poullis
Hadi Pouransari
Omid Poursaeed

Shraman Pramanick
Mantini Pranav
Dilip K. Prasad
Meghshyam Prasad
B. H. Pawan Prasad
Shitala Prasad
Prateek Prasanna
Ekta Prashnani
Derek S. Prijatelj
Luke Y. Prince
Véronique Prinet
Victor Adrian Prisacariu
James Pritts
Thomas Probst
Sergey Prokudin
Rita Pucci
Chi-Man Pun
Matthew Purri
Haozhi Qi
Lu Qi
Lei Qi
Xianbiao Qi
Yonggang Qi
Yuankai Qi
Siyuan Qi
Guocheng Qian
Hangwei Qian
Qi Qian
Deheng Qian
Shengsheng Qian
Wen Qian
Rui Qian
Yiming Qian
Shengju Qian
Shengyi Qian
Xuelin Qian
Zhenxing Qian
Nan Qiao
Xiaotian Qiao
Jing Qin
Can Qin
Siyang Qin
Hongwei Qin
Jie Qin
Minghai Qin

Yipeng Qin
Yongqiang Qin
Wenda Qin
Xuebin Qin
Yuzhe Qin
Yao Qin
Zhenyue Qin
Zhiwu Qing
Heqian Qiu
Jiayan Qiu
Jielin Qiu
Yue Qiu
Jiaxiong Qiu
Zhongxi Qiu
Shi Qiu
Zhaofan Qiu
Zhongnan Qu
Yanyun Qu
Kha Gia Quach
Yuhui Quan
Ruijie Quan
Mike Rabbat
Rahul Shekhar Rade
Filip Radenovic
Gorjan Radevski
Bogdan Raducanu
Francesco Ragusa
Shafin Rahman
Md Mahfuzur Rahman
    Siddiquee
Hossein Rahmani
Kiran Raja
Sivaramakrishnan
    Rajaraman
Jathushan Rajasegaran
Adnan Siraj Rakin
Michaël Ramamonjisoa
Chirag A. Raman
Shanmuganathan Raman
Vignesh Ramanathan
Vasili Ramanishka
Vikram V. Ramaswamy
Merey Ramazanova
Jason Rambach
Sai Saketh Rambhatla

Clément Rambour
Ashwin Ramesh Babu
Adín Ramírez Rivera
Arianna Rampini
Haoxi Ran
Aakanksha Rana
Aayush Jung Bahadur
    Rana
Kanchana N. Ranasinghe
Aneesh Rangnekar
Samrudhdhi B. Rangrej
Harsh Rangwani
Viresh Ranjan
Anyi Rao
Yongming Rao
Carolina Raposo
Michalis Raptis
Amir Rasouli
Vivek Rathod
Adepu Ravi Sankar
Avinash Ravichandran
Bharadwaj Ravichandran
Dripta S. Raychaudhuri
Adria Recasens
Simon Reiß
Davis Rempe
Daxuan Ren
Jiawei Ren
Jimmy Ren
Sucheng Ren
Dayong Ren
Zhile Ren
Dongwei Ren
Qibing Ren
Pengfei Ren
Zhenwen Ren
Xuqian Ren
Yixuan Ren
Zhongzheng Ren
Ambareesh Revanur
Hamed Rezazadegan
    Tavakoli
Rafael S. Rezende
Wonjong Rhee
Alexander Richard

Christian Richardt
Stephan R. Richter
Benjamin Riggan
Dominik Rivoir
Mamshad Nayeem Rizve
Joshua D. Robinson
Joseph Robinson
Chris Rockwell
Ranga Rodrigo
Andres C. Rodriguez
Carlos Rodriguez-Pardo
Marcus Rohrbach
Gemma Roig
Yu Rong
David A. Ross
Mohammad Rostami
Edward Rosten
Karsten Roth
Anirban Roy
Debaditya Roy
Shuvendu Roy
Ahana Roy Choudhury
Aruni Roy Chowdhury
Denys Rozumnyi
Shulan Ruan
Wenjie Ruan
Patrick Ruhkamp
Danila Rukhovich
Anian Ruoss
Chris Russell
Dan Ruta
Dawid Damian Rymarczyk
DongHun Ryu
Hyeonggon Ryu
Kwonyoung Ryu
Balasubramanian S.
Alexandre Sablayrolles
Mohammad Sabokrou
Arka Sadhu
Aniruddha Saha
Oindrila Saha
Pritish Sahu
Aneeshan Sain
Nirat Saini
Saurabh Saini

Takeshi Saitoh
Christos Sakaridis
Fumihiko Sakaue
Dimitrios Sakkos
Ken Sakurada
Parikshit V. Sakurikar
Rohit Saluja
Nermin Samet
Leo Sampaio Ferraz
    Ribeiro
Jorge Sanchez
Enrique Sanchez
Shengtian Sang
Anush Sankaran
Soubhik Sanyal
Nikolaos Sarafianos
Vishwanath Saragadam
István Sárándi
Saquib Sarfraz
Mert Bulent Sariyildiz
Anindya Sarkar
Pritam Sarkar
Paul-Edouard Sarlin
Hiroshi Sasaki
Takami Sato
Torsten Sattler
Ravi Kumar Satzoda
Axel Sauer
Stefano Savian
Artem Savkin
Manolis Savva
Gerald Schaefer
Simone Schaub-Meyer
Yoni Schirris
Samuel Schulter
Katja Schwarz
Jesse Scott
Sinisa Segvic
Constantin Marc Seibold
Lorenzo Seidenari
Matan Sela
Fadime Sener
Paul Hongsuck Seo
Kwanggyoon Seo
Hongje Seong

Dario Serez
Francesco Setti
Bryan Seybold
Mohamad Shahbazi
Shima Shahfar
Xinxin Shan
Caifeng Shan
Dandan Shan
Shawn Shan
Wei Shang
Jinghuan Shang
Jiaxiang Shang
Lei Shang
Sukrit Shankar
Ken Shao
Rui Shao
Jie Shao
Mingwen Shao
Aashish Sharma
Gaurav Sharma
Vivek Sharma
Abhishek Sharma
Yoli Shavit
Shashank Shekhar
Sumit Shekhar
Zhijie Shen
Fengyi Shen
Furao Shen
Jialie Shen
Jingjing Shen
Ziyi Shen
Linlin Shen
Guangyu Shen
Biluo Shen
Falong Shen
Jiajun Shen
Qiu Shen
Qiuhong Shen
Shuai Shen
Wang Shen
Yiqing Shen
Yunhang Shen
Siqi Shen
Bin Shen
Tianwei Shen

Xi Shen
Yilin Shen
Yuming Shen
Yucong Shen
Zhiqiang Shen
Lu Sheng
Yichen Sheng
Shivanand Venkanna
  Sheshappanavar
Shelly Sheynin
Baifeng Shi
Ruoxi Shi
Botian Shi
Hailin Shi
Jia Shi
Jing Shi
Shaoshuai Shi
Baoguang Shi
Boxin Shi
Hengcan Shi
Tianyang Shi
Xiaodan Shi
Yongjie Shi
Zhensheng Shi
Yinghuan Shi
Weiqi Shi
Wu Shi
Xuepeng Shi
Xiaoshuang Shi
Yujiao Shi
Zenglin Shi
Zhenmei Shi
Takashi Shibata
Meng-Li Shih
Yichang Shih
Hyunjung Shim
Dongseok Shim
Soshi Shimada
Inkyu Shin
Jinwoo Shin
Seungjoo Shin
Seungjae Shin
Koichi Shinoda
Suprosanna Shit

Palaiahnakote
  Shivakumara
Eli Shlizerman
Gaurav Shrivastava
Xiao Shu
Xiangbo Shu
Xiujun Shu
Yang Shu
Tianmin Shu
Jun Shu
Zhixin Shu
Bing Shuai
Maria Shugrina
Ivan Shugurov
Satya Narayan Shukla
Pranjay Shyam
Jianlou Si
Yawar Siddiqui
Alberto Signoroni
Pedro Silva
Jae-Young Sim
Oriane Siméoni
Martin Simon
Andrea Simonelli
Abhishek Singh
Ashish Singh
Dinesh Singh
Gurkirt Singh
Krishna Kumar Singh
Mannat Singh
Pravendra Singh
Rajat Vikram Singh
Utkarsh Singhal
Dipika Singhania
Vasu Singla
Harsh Sinha
Sudipta Sinha
Josef Sivic
Elena Sizikova
Geri Skenderi
Ivan Skorokhodov
Dmitriy Smirnov
Cameron Y. Smith
James S. Smith
Patrick Snape

Mattia Soldan
Hyeongseok Son
Sanghyun Son
Chuanbiao Song
Chen Song
Chunfeng Song
Dan Song
Dongjin Song
Hwanjun Song
Guoxian Song
Jiaming Song
Jie Song
Liangchen Song
Ran Song
Luchuan Song
Xibin Song
Li Song
Fenglong Song
Guoli Song
Guanglu Song
Zhenbo Song
Lin Song
Xinhang Song
Yang Song
Yibing Song
Rajiv Soundararajan
Hossein Souri
Cristovao Sousa
Riccardo Spezialetti
Leonidas Spinoulas
Michael W. Spratling
Deepak Sridhar
Srinath Sridhar
Gaurang Sriramanan
Vinkle Kumar Srivastav
Themos Stafylakis
Serban Stan
Anastasis Stathopoulos
Markus Steinberger
Jan Steinbrener
Sinisa Stekovic
Alexandros Stergiou
Gleb Sterkin
Rainer Stiefelhagen
Pierre Stock

Ombretta Strafforello
Julian Straub
Yannick Strümpler
Joerg Stueckler
Hang Su
Weijie Su
Jong-Chyi Su
Bing Su
Haisheng Su
Jinming Su
Yiyang Su
Yukun Su
Yuxin Su
Zhuo Su
Zhaoqi Su
Xiu Su
Yu-Chuan Su
Zhixun Su
Arulkumar Subramaniam
Akshayvarun Subramanya
A. Subramanyam
Swathikiran Sudhakaran
Yusuke Sugano
Masanori Suganuma
Yumin Suh
Yang Sui
Baochen Sun
Cheng Sun
Long Sun
Guolei Sun
Haoliang Sun
Haomiao Sun
He Sun
Hanqing Sun
Hao Sun
Lichao Sun
Jiachen Sun
Jiaming Sun
Jian Sun
Jin Sun
Jennifer J. Sun
Tiancheng Sun
Libo Sun
Peize Sun
Qianru Sun

Shanlin Sun
Yu Sun
Zhun Sun
Che Sun
Lin Sun
Tao Sun
Yiyou Sun
Chunyi Sun
Chong Sun
Weiwei Sun
Weixuan Sun
Xiuyu Sun
Yanan Sun
Zeren Sun
Zhaodong Sun
Zhiqing Sun
Minhyuk Sung
Jinli Suo
Simon Suo
Abhijit Suprem
Anshuman Suri
Saksham Suri
Joshua M. Susskind
Roman Suvorov
Gurumurthy Swaminathan
Robin Swanson
Paul Swoboda
Tabish A. Syed
Richard Szeliski
Fariborz Taherkhani
Yu-Wing Tai
Keita Takahashi
Walter Talbott
Gary Tam
Masato Tamura
Feitong Tan
Fuwen Tan
Shuhan Tan
Andong Tan
Bin Tan
Cheng Tan
Jianchao Tan
Lei Tan
Mingxing Tan
Xin Tan

Zichang Tan
Zhentao Tan
Kenichiro Tanaka
Masayuki Tanaka
Yushun Tang
Hao Tang
Jingqun Tang
Jinhui Tang
Kaihua Tang
Luming Tang
Lv Tang
Sheyang Tang
Shitao Tang
Siliang Tang
Shixiang Tang
Yansong Tang
Keke Tang
Chang Tang
Chenwei Tang
Jie Tang
Junshu Tang
Ming Tang
Peng Tang
Xu Tang
Yao Tang
Chen Tang
Fan Tang
Haoran Tang
Shengeng Tang
Yehui Tang
Zhipeng Tang
Ugo Tanielian
Chaofan Tao
Jiale Tao
Junli Tao
Renshuai Tao
An Tao
Guanhong Tao
Zhiqiang Tao
Makarand Tapaswi
Jean-Philippe G. Tarel
Juan J. Tarrio
Enzo Tartaglione
Keisuke Tateno
Zachary Teed

Ajinkya B. Tejankar
Bugra Tekin
Purva Tendulkar
Damien Teney
Minggui Teng
Chris Tensmeyer
Andrew Beng Jin Teoh
Philipp Terhörst
Kartik Thakral
Nupur Thakur
Kevin Thandiackal
Spyridon Thermos
Diego Thomas
William Thong
Yuesong Tian
Guanzhong Tian
Lin Tian
Shiqi Tian
Kai Tian
Meng Tian
Tai-Peng Tian
Zhuotao Tian
Shangxuan Tian
Tian Tian
Yapeng Tian
Yu Tian
Yuxin Tian
Leslie Ching Ow Tiong
Praveen Tirupattur
Garvita Tiwari
George Toderici
Antoine Toisoul
Aysim Toker
Tatiana Tommasi
Zhan Tong
Alessio Tonioni
Alessandro Torcinovich
Fabio Tosi
Matteo Toso
Hugo Touvron
Quan Hung Tran
Son Tran
Hung Tran
Ngoc-Trung Tran
Vinh Tran

Phong Tran
Giovanni Trappolini
Edith Tretschk
Subarna Tripathi
Shubhendu Trivedi
Eduard Trulls
Prune Truong
Thanh-Dat Truong
Tomasz Trzcinski
Sam Tsai
Yi-Hsuan Tsai
Ethan Tseng
Yu-Chee Tseng
Shahar Tsiper
Stavros Tsogkas
Shikui Tu
Zhigang Tu
Zhengzhong Tu
Richard Tucker
Sergey Tulyakov
Cigdem Turan
Daniyar Turmukhambetov
Victor G. Turrisi da Costa
Bartlomiej Twardowski
Christopher D. Twigg
Radim Tylecek
Mostofa Rafid Uddin
Md. Zasim Uddin
Kohei Uehara
Nicolas Ugrinovic
Youngjung Uh
Norimichi Ukita
Anwaar Ulhaq
Devesh Upadhyay
Paul Upchurch
Yoshitaka Ushiku
Yuzuko Utsumi
Mikaela Angelina Uy
Mohit Vaishnav
Pratik Vaishnavi
Jeya Maria Jose Valanarasu
Matias A. Valdenegro Toro
Diego Valsesia
Wouter Van Gansbeke
Nanne van Noord

Simon Vandenhende
Farshid Varno
Cristina Vasconcelos
Francisco Vasconcelos
Alex Vasilescu
Subeesh Vasu
Arun Balajee Vasudevan
Kanav Vats
Vaibhav S. Vavilala
Sagar Vaze
Javier Vazquez-Corral
Andrea Vedaldi
Olga Veksler
Andreas Velten
Sai H. Vemprala
Raviteja Vemulapalli
Shashanka
    Venkataramanan
Dor Verbin
Luisa Verdoliva
Manisha Verma
Yashaswi Verma
Constantin Vertan
Eli Verwimp
Deepak Vijaykeerthy
Pablo Villanueva
Ruben Villegas
Markus Vincze
Vibhav Vineet
Minh P. Vo
Huy V. Vo
Duc Minh Vo
Tomas Vojir
Igor Vozniak
Nicholas Vretos
Vibashan VS
Tuan-Anh Vu
Thang Vu
Mårten Wadenbäck
Neal Wadhwa
Aaron T. Walsman
Steven Walton
Jin Wan
Alvin Wan
Jia Wan

Jun Wan
Xiaoyue Wan
Fang Wan
Guowei Wan
Renjie Wan
Zhiqiang Wan
Ziyu Wan
Bastian Wandt
Dongdong Wang
Limin Wang
Haiyang Wang
Xiaobing Wang
Angtian Wang
Angelina Wang
Bing Wang
Bo Wang
Boyu Wang
Binghui Wang
Chen Wang
Chien-Yi Wang
Congli Wang
Qi Wang
Chengrui Wang
Rui Wang
Yiqun Wang
Cong Wang
Wenjing Wang
Dongkai Wang
Di Wang
Xiaogang Wang
Kai Wang
Zhizhong Wang
Fangjinhua Wang
Feng Wang
Hang Wang
Gaoang Wang
Guoqing Wang
Guangcong Wang
Guangzhi Wang
Hanqing Wang
Hao Wang
Haohan Wang
Haoran Wang
Hong Wang
Haotao Wang

Hu Wang
Huan Wang
Hua Wang
Hui-Po Wang
Hengli Wang
Hanyu Wang
Hongxing Wang
Jingwen Wang
Jialiang Wang
Jian Wang
Jianyi Wang
Jiashun Wang
Jiahao Wang
Tsun-Hsuan Wang
Xiaoqian Wang
Jinqiao Wang
Jun Wang
Jianzong Wang
Kaihong Wang
Ke Wang
Lei Wang
Lingjing Wang
Linnan Wang
Lin Wang
Liansheng Wang
Mengjiao Wang
Manning Wang
Nannan Wang
Peihao Wang
Jiayun Wang
Pu Wang
Qiang Wang
Qiufeng Wang
Qilong Wang
Qiangchang Wang
Qin Wang
Qing Wang
Ruocheng Wang
Ruibin Wang
Ruisheng Wang
Ruizhe Wang
Runqi Wang
Runzhong Wang
Wenxuan Wang
Sen Wang

Shangfei Wang
Shaofei Wang
Shijie Wang
Shiqi Wang
Zhibo Wang
Song Wang
Xinjiang Wang
Tai Wang
Tao Wang
Teng Wang
Xiang Wang
Tianren Wang
Tiantian Wang
Tianyi Wang
Fengjiao Wang
Wei Wang
Miaohui Wang
Suchen Wang
Siyue Wang
Yaoming Wang
Xiao Wang
Ze Wang
Biao Wang
Chaofei Wang
Dong Wang
Gu Wang
Guangrun Wang
Guangming Wang
Guo-Hua Wang
Haoqing Wang
Hesheng Wang
Huafeng Wang
Jinghua Wang
Jingdong Wang
Jingjing Wang
Jingya Wang
Jingkang Wang
Jiakai Wang
Junke Wang
Kuo Wang
Lichen Wang
Lizhi Wang
Longguang Wang
Mang Wang
Mei Wang

Min Wang
Peng-Shuai Wang
Run Wang
Shaoru Wang
Shuhui Wang
Tan Wang
Tiancai Wang
Tianqi Wang
Wenhai Wang
Wenzhe Wang
Xiaobo Wang
Xiudong Wang
Xu Wang
Yajie Wang
Yan Wang
Yuan-Gen Wang
Yingqian Wang
Yizhi Wang
Yulin Wang
Yu Wang
Yujie Wang
Yunhe Wang
Yuxi Wang
Yaowei Wang
Yiwei Wang
Zezheng Wang
Hongzhi Wang
Zhiqiang Wang
Ziteng Wang
Ziwei Wang
Zheng Wang
Zhenyu Wang
Binglu Wang
Zhongdao Wang
Ce Wang
Weining Wang
Weiyao Wang
Wenbin Wang
Wenguan Wang
Guangting Wang
Haolin Wang
Haiyan Wang
Huiyu Wang
Naiyan Wang
Jingbo Wang

Jinpeng Wang
Jiaqi Wang
Liyuan Wang
Lizhen Wang
Ning Wang
Wenqian Wang
Sheng-Yu Wang
Weimin Wang
Xiaohan Wang
Yifan Wang
Yi Wang
Yongtao Wang
Yizhou Wang
Zhuo Wang
Zhe Wang
Xudong Wang
Xiaofang Wang
Xinggang Wang
Xiaosen Wang
Xiaosong Wang
Xiaoyang Wang
Lijun Wang
Xinlong Wang
Xuan Wang
Xue Wang
Yangang Wang
Yaohui Wang
Yu-Chiang Frank Wang
Yida Wang
Yilin Wang
Yi Ru Wang
Yali Wang
Yinglong Wang
Yufu Wang
Yujiang Wang
Yuwang Wang
Yuting Wang
Yang Wang
Yu-Xiong Wang
Yixu Wang
Ziqi Wang
Zhicheng Wang
Zeyu Wang
Zhaowen Wang
Zhenyi Wang

Zhenzhi Wang
Zhijie Wang
Zhiyong Wang
Zhongling Wang
Zhuowei Wang
Zian Wang
Zifu Wang
Zihao Wang
Zirui Wang
Ziyan Wang
Wenxiao Wang
Zhen Wang
Zhepeng Wang
Zi Wang
Zihao W. Wang
Steven L. Waslander
Olivia Watkins
Daniel Watson
Silvan Weder
Dongyoon Wee
Dongming Wei
Tianyi Wei
Jia Wei
Dong Wei
Fangyun Wei
Longhui Wei
Mingqiang Wei
Xinyue Wei
Chen Wei
Donglai Wei
Pengxu Wei
Xing Wei
Xiu-Shen Wei
Wenqi Wei
Guoqiang Wei
Wei Wei
XingKui Wei
Xian Wei
Xingxing Wei
Yake Wei
Yuxiang Wei
Yi Wei
Luca Weihs
Michael Weinmann
Martin Weinmann

Congcong Wen
Chuan Wen
Jie Wen
Sijia Wen
Song Wen
Chao Wen
Xiang Wen
Zeyi Wen
Xin Wen
Yilin Wen
Yijia Weng
Shuchen Weng
Junwu Weng
Wenming Weng
Renliang Weng
Zhenyu Weng
Xinshuo Weng
Nicholas J. Westlake
Gordon Wetzstein
Lena M. Widin Klasén
Rick Wildes
Bryan M. Williams
Williem Williem
Ole Winther
Scott Wisdom
Alex Wong
Chau-Wai Wong
Kwan-Yee K. Wong
Yongkang Wong
Scott Workman
Marcel Worring
Michael Wray
Safwan Wshah
Xiang Wu
Aming Wu
Chongruo Wu
Cho-Ying Wu
Chunpeng Wu
Chenyan Wu
Ziyi Wu
Fuxiang Wu
Gang Wu
Haiping Wu
Huisi Wu
Jane Wu

Jialian Wu
Jing Wu
Jinjian Wu
Jianlong Wu
Xian Wu
Lifang Wu
Lifan Wu
Minye Wu
Qianyi Wu
Rongliang Wu
Rui Wu
Shiqian Wu
Shuzhe Wu
Shangzhe Wu
Tsung-Han Wu
Tz-Ying Wu
Ting-Wei Wu
Jiannan Wu
Zhiliang Wu
Yu Wu
Chenyun Wu
Dayan Wu
Dongxian Wu
Fei Wu
Hefeng Wu
Jianxin Wu
Weibin Wu
Wenxuan Wu
Wenhao Wu
Xiao Wu
Yicheng Wu
Yuanwei Wu
Yu-Huan Wu
Zhenxin Wu
Zhenyu Wu
Wei Wu
Peng Wu
Xiaohe Wu
Xindi Wu
Xinxing Wu
Xinyi Wu
Xingjiao Wu
Xiongwei Wu
Yangzheng Wu
Yanzhao Wu

Yawen Wu
Yong Wu
Yi Wu
Ying Nian Wu
Zhenyao Wu
Zhonghua Wu
Zongze Wu
Zuxuan Wu
Stefanie Wuhrer
Teng Xi
Jianing Xi
Fei Xia
Haifeng Xia
Menghan Xia
Yuanqing Xia
Zhihua Xia
Xiaobo Xia
Weihao Xia
Shihong Xia
Yan Xia
Yong Xia
Zhaoyang Xia
Zhihao Xia
Chuhua Xian
Yongqin Xian
Wangmeng Xiang
Fanbo Xiang
Tiange Xiang
Tao Xiang
Liuyu Xiang
Xiaoyu Xiang
Zhiyu Xiang
Aoran Xiao
Chunxia Xiao
Fanyi Xiao
Jimin Xiao
Jun Xiao
Taihong Xiao
Anqi Xiao
Junfei Xiao
Jing Xiao
Liang Xiao
Yang Xiao
Yuting Xiao
Yijun Xiao

Yao Xiao
Zeyu Xiao
Zhisheng Xiao
Zihao Xiao
Binhui Xie
Christopher Xie
Haozhe Xie
Jin Xie
Guo-Sen Xie
Hongtao Xie
Ming-Kun Xie
Tingting Xie
Chaohao Xie
Weicheng Xie
Xudong Xie
Jiyang Xie
Xiaohua Xie
Yuan Xie
Zhenyu Xie
Ning Xie
Xianghui Xie
Xiufeng Xie
You Xie
Yutong Xie
Fuyong Xing
Yifan Xing
Zhen Xing
Yuanjun Xiong
Jinhui Xiong
Weihua Xiong
Hongkai Xiong
Zhitong Xiong
Yuanhao Xiong
Yunyang Xiong
Yuwen Xiong
Zhiwei Xiong
Yuliang Xiu
An Xu
Chang Xu
Chenliang Xu
Chengming Xu
Chenshu Xu
Xiang Xu
Huijuan Xu
Zhe Xu

Jie Xu
Jingyi Xu
Jiarui Xu
Yinghao Xu
Kele Xu
Ke Xu
Li Xu
Linchuan Xu
Linning Xu
Mengde Xu
Mengmeng Frost Xu
Min Xu
Mingye Xu
Jun Xu
Ning Xu
Peng Xu
Runsheng Xu
Sheng Xu
Wenqiang Xu
Xiaogang Xu
Renzhe Xu
Kaidi Xu
Yi Xu
Chi Xu
Qiuling Xu
Baobei Xu
Feng Xu
Haohang Xu
Haofei Xu
Lan Xu
Mingze Xu
Songcen Xu
Weipeng Xu
Wenjia Xu
Wenju Xu
Xiangyu Xu
Xin Xu
Yinshuang Xu
Yixing Xu
Yuting Xu
Yanyu Xu
Zhenbo Xu
Zhiliang Xu
Zhiyuan Xu
Xiaohao Xu

Yanwu Xu
Yan Xu
Yiran Xu
Yifan Xu
Yufei Xu
Yong Xu
Zichuan Xu
Zenglin Xu
Zexiang Xu
Zhan Xu
Zheng Xu
Zhiwei Xu
Ziyue Xu
Shiyu Xuan
Hanyu Xuan
Fei Xue
Jianru Xue
Mingfu Xue
Qinghan Xue
Tianfan Xue
Chao Xue
Chuhui Xue
Nan Xue
Zhou Xue
Xiangyang Xue
Yuan Xue
Abhay Yadav
Ravindra Yadav
Kota Yamaguchi
Toshihiko Yamasaki
Kohei Yamashita
Chaochao Yan
Feng Yan
Kun Yan
Qingsen Yan
Qixin Yan
Rui Yan
Siming Yan
Xinchen Yan
Yaping Yan
Bin Yan
Qingan Yan
Shen Yan
Shipeng Yan
Xu Yan

Yan Yan
Yichao Yan
Zhaoyi Yan
Zike Yan
Zhiqiang Yan
Hongliang Yan
Zizheng Yan
Jiewen Yang
Anqi Joyce Yang
Shan Yang
Anqi Yang
Antoine Yang
Bo Yang
Baoyao Yang
Chenhongyi Yang
Dingkang Yang
De-Nian Yang
Dong Yang
David Yang
Fan Yang
Fengyu Yang
Fengting Yang
Fei Yang
Gengshan Yang
Heng Yang
Han Yang
Huan Yang
Yibo Yang
Jiancheng Yang
Jihan Yang
Jiawei Yang
Jiayu Yang
Jie Yang
Jinfa Yang
Jingkang Yang
Jinyu Yang
Cheng-Fu Yang
Ji Yang
Jianyu Yang
Kailun Yang
Tian Yang
Luyu Yang
Liang Yang
Li Yang
Michael Ying Yang

Yang Yang
Muli Yang
Le Yang
Qiushi Yang
Ren Yang
Ruihan Yang
Shuang Yang
Siyuan Yang
Su Yang
Shiqi Yang
Taojiannan Yang
Tianyu Yang
Lei Yang
Wanzhao Yang
Shuai Yang
William Yang
Wei Yang
Xiaofeng Yang
Xiaoshan Yang
Xin Yang
Xuan Yang
Xu Yang
Xingyi Yang
Xitong Yang
Jing Yang
Yanchao Yang
Wenming Yang
Yujiu Yang
Herb Yang
Jianfei Yang
Jinhui Yang
Chuanguang Yang
Guanglei Yang
Haitao Yang
Kewei Yang
Linlin Yang
Lijin Yang
Longrong Yang
Meng Yang
MingKun Yang
Sibei Yang
Shicai Yang
Tong Yang
Wen Yang
Xi Yang

Xiaolong Yang
Xue Yang
Yubin Yang
Ze Yang
Ziyi Yang
Yi Yang
Linjie Yang
Yuzhe Yang
Yiding Yang
Zhenpei Yang
Zhaohui Yang
Zhengyuan Yang
Zhibo Yang
Zongxin Yang
Hantao Yao
Mingde Yao
Rui Yao
Taiping Yao
Ting Yao
Cong Yao
Qingsong Yao
Quanming Yao
Xu Yao
Yuan Yao
Yao Yao
Yazhou Yao
Jiawen Yao
Shunyu Yao
Pew-Thian Yap
Sudhir Yarram
Rajeev Yasarla
Peng Ye
Botao Ye
Mao Ye
Fei Ye
Hanrong Ye
Jingwen Ye
Jinwei Ye
Jiarong Ye
Mang Ye
Meng Ye
Qi Ye
Qian Ye
Qixiang Ye
Junjie Ye

Sheng Ye
Nanyang Ye
Yufei Ye
Xiaoqing Ye
Ruolin Ye
Yousef Yeganeh
Chun-Hsiao Yeh
Raymond A. Yeh
Yu-Ying Yeh
Kai Yi
Chang Yi
Renjiao Yi
Xinping Yi
Peng Yi
Alper Yilmaz
Junho Yim
Hui Yin
Bangjie Yin
Jia-Li Yin
Miao Yin
Wenzhe Yin
Xuwang Yin
Ming Yin
Yu Yin
Aoxiong Yin
Kangxue Yin
Tianwei Yin
Wei Yin
Xianghua Ying
Rio Yokota
Tatsuya Yokota
Naoto Yokoya
Ryo Yonetani
Ki Yoon Yoo
Jinsu Yoo
Sunjae Yoon
Jae Shin Yoon
Jihun Yoon
Sung-Hoon Yoon
Ryota Yoshihashi
Yusuke Yoshiyasu
Chenyu You
Haoran You
Haoxuan You
Yang You

Quanzeng You
Tackgeun You
Kaichao You
Shan You
Xinge You
Yurong You
Baosheng Yu
Bei Yu
Haichao Yu
Hao Yu
Chaohui Yu
Fisher Yu
Jin-Gang Yu
Jiyang Yu
Jason J. Yu
Jiashuo Yu
Hong-Xing Yu
Lei Yu
Mulin Yu
Ning Yu
Peilin Yu
Qi Yu
Qian Yu
Rui Yu
Shuzhi Yu
Gang Yu
Tan Yu
Weijiang Yu
Xin Yu
Bingyao Yu
Ye Yu
Hanchao Yu
Yingchen Yu
Tao Yu
Xiaotian Yu
Qing Yu
Houjian Yu
Changqian Yu
Jing Yu
Jun Yu
Shujian Yu
Xiang Yu
Zhaofei Yu
Zhenbo Yu
Yinfeng Yu

Zhuoran Yu
Zitong Yu
Bo Yuan
Jiangbo Yuan
Liangzhe Yuan
Weihao Yuan
Jianbo Yuan
Xiaoyun Yuan
Ye Yuan
Li Yuan
Geng Yuan
Jialin Yuan
Maoxun Yuan
Peng Yuan
Xin Yuan
Yuan Yuan
Yuhui Yuan
Yixuan Yuan
Zheng Yuan
Mehmet Kerim Yücel
Kaiyu Yue
Haixiao Yue
Heeseung Yun
Sangdoo Yun
Tian Yun
Mahmut Yurt
Ekim Yurtsever
Ahmet Yüzügüler
Edouard Yvinec
Eloi Zablocki
Christopher Zach
Muhammad Zaigham
    Zaheer
Pierluigi Zama Ramirez
Yuhang Zang
Pietro Zanuttigh
Alexey Zaytsev
Bernhard Zeisl
Haitian Zeng
Pengpeng Zeng
Jiabei Zeng
Runhao Zeng
Wei Zeng
Yawen Zeng
Yi Zeng

Yiming Zeng
Tieyong Zeng
Huanqiang Zeng
Dan Zeng
Yu Zeng
Wei Zhai
Yuanhao Zhai
Fangneng Zhan
Kun Zhan
Xiong Zhang
Jingdong Zhang
Jiangning Zhang
Zhilu Zhang
Gengwei Zhang
Dongsu Zhang
Hui Zhang
Binjie Zhang
Bo Zhang
Tianhao Zhang
Cecilia Zhang
Jing Zhang
Chaoning Zhang
Chenxu Zhang
Chi Zhang
Chris Zhang
Yabin Zhang
Zhao Zhang
Rufeng Zhang
Chaoyi Zhang
Zheng Zhang
Da Zhang
Yi Zhang
Edward Zhang
Xin Zhang
Feifei Zhang
Feilong Zhang
Yuqi Zhang
GuiXuan Zhang
Hanlin Zhang
Hanwang Zhang
Hanzhen Zhang
Haotian Zhang
He Zhang
Haokui Zhang
Hongyuan Zhang

Hengrui Zhang
Hongming Zhang
Mingfang Zhang
Jianpeng Zhang
Jiaming Zhang
Jichao Zhang
Jie Zhang
Jingfeng Zhang
Jingyi Zhang
Jinnian Zhang
David Junhao Zhang
Junjie Zhang
Junzhe Zhang
Jiawan Zhang
Jingyang Zhang
Kai Zhang
Lei Zhang
Lihua Zhang
Lu Zhang
Miao Zhang
Minjia Zhang
Mingjin Zhang
Qi Zhang
Qian Zhang
Qilong Zhang
Qiming Zhang
Qiang Zhang
Richard Zhang
Ruimao Zhang
Ruisi Zhang
Ruixin Zhang
Runze Zhang
Qilin Zhang
Shan Zhang
Shanshan Zhang
Xi Sheryl Zhang
Song-Hai Zhang
Chongyang Zhang
Kaihao Zhang
Songyang Zhang
Shu Zhang
Siwei Zhang
Shujian Zhang
Tianyun Zhang
Tong Zhang

Tao Zhang
Wenwei Zhang
Wenqiang Zhang
Wen Zhang
Xiaolin Zhang
Xingchen Zhang
Xingxuan Zhang
Xiuming Zhang
Xiaoshuai Zhang
Xuanmeng Zhang
Xuanyang Zhang
Xucong Zhang
Xingxing Zhang
Xikun Zhang
Xiaohan Zhang
Yahui Zhang
Yunhua Zhang
Yan Zhang
Yanghao Zhang
Yifei Zhang
Yifan Zhang
Yi-Fan Zhang
Yihao Zhang
Yingliang Zhang
Youshan Zhang
Yulun Zhang
Yushu Zhang
Yixiao Zhang
Yide Zhang
Zhongwen Zhang
Bowen Zhang
Chen-Lin Zhang
Zehua Zhang
Zekun Zhang
Zeyu Zhang
Xiaowei Zhang
Yifeng Zhang
Cheng Zhang
Hongguang Zhang
Yuexi Zhang
Fa Zhang
Guofeng Zhang
Hao Zhang
Haofeng Zhang
Hongwen Zhang

Hua Zhang

Jiaxin Zhang

Zhenyu Zhang

Jian Zhang

Jianfeng Zhang

Jiao Zhang

Jiakai Zhang

Lefei Zhang

Le Zhang

Mi Zhang

Min Zhang

Ning Zhang

Pan Zhang

Pu Zhang

Qing Zhang

Renrui Zhang

Shifeng Zhang

Shuo Zhang

Shaoxiong Zhang

Weizhong Zhang

Xi Zhang

Xiaomei Zhang

Xinyu Zhang

Yin Zhang

Zicheng Zhang

Zihao Zhang

Ziqi Zhang

Zhaoxiang Zhang

Zhen Zhang

Zhipeng Zhang

Zhixing Zhang

Zhizheng Zhang

Jiawei Zhang

Zhong Zhang

Pingping Zhang

Yixin Zhang

Kui Zhang

Lingzhi Zhang

Huaiwen Zhang

Quanshi Zhang

Zhoutong Zhang

Yuhang Zhang

Yuting Zhang

Zhang Zhang

Ziming Zhang

Zhizhong Zhang

Qilong Zhangli

Bingyin Zhao

Bin Zhao

Chenglong Zhao

Lei Zhao

Feng Zhao

Gangming Zhao

Haiyan Zhao

Hao Zhao

Handong Zhao

Hengshuang Zhao

Yinan Zhao

Jiaojiao Zhao

Jiaqi Zhao

Jing Zhao

Kaili Zhao

Haojie Zhao

Yucheng Zhao

Longjiao Zhao

Long Zhao

Qingsong Zhao

Qingyu Zhao

Rui Zhao

Rui-Wei Zhao

Sicheng Zhao

Shuang Zhao

Siyan Zhao

Zelin Zhao

Shiyu Zhao

Wang Zhao

Tiesong Zhao

Qian Zhao

Wangbo Zhao

Xi-Le Zhao

Xu Zhao

Yajie Zhao

Yang Zhao

Ying Zhao

Yin Zhao

Yizhou Zhao

Yunhan Zhao

Yuyang Zhao

Yue Zhao

Yuzhi Zhao

Bowen Zhao

Pu Zhao

Bingchen Zhao

Borui Zhao

Fuqiang Zhao

Hanbin Zhao

Jian Zhao

Mingyang Zhao

Na Zhao

Rongchang Zhao

Ruiqi Zhao

Shuai Zhao

Wenda Zhao

Wenliang Zhao

Xiangyun Zhao

Yifan Zhao

Yaping Zhao

Zhou Zhao

He Zhao

Jie Zhao

Xibin Zhao

Xiaoqi Zhao

Zhengyu Zhao

Jin Zhe

Chuanxia Zheng

Huan Zheng

Hao Zheng

Jia Zheng

Jian-Qing Zheng

Shuai Zheng

Meng Zheng

Mingkai Zheng

Qian Zheng

Qi Zheng

Wu Zheng

Yinqiang Zheng

Yufeng Zheng

Yutong Zheng

Yalin Zheng

Yu Zheng

Feng Zheng

Zhaoheng Zheng

Haitian Zheng

Kang Zheng

Bolun Zheng

Haiyong Zheng
Mingwu Zheng
Sipeng Zheng
Tu Zheng
Wenzhao Zheng
Xiawu Zheng
Yinglin Zheng
Zhuo Zheng
Zilong Zheng
Kecheng Zheng
Zerong Zheng
Shuaifeng Zhi
Tiancheng Zhi
Jia-Xing Zhong
Yiwu Zhong
Fangwei Zhong
Zhihang Zhong
Yaoyao Zhong
Yiran Zhong
Zhun Zhong
Zichun Zhong
Bo Zhou
Boyao Zhou
Brady Zhou
Mo Zhou
Chunluan Zhou
Dingfu Zhou
Fan Zhou
Jingkai Zhou
Honglu Zhou
Jiaming Zhou
Jiahuan Zhou
Jun Zhou
Kaiyang Zhou
Keyang Zhou
Kuangqi Zhou
Lei Zhou
Lihua Zhou
Man Zhou
Mingyi Zhou
Mingyuan Zhou
Ning Zhou
Peng Zhou
Penghao Zhou
Qianyi Zhou

Shuigeng Zhou
Shangchen Zhou
Huayi Zhou
Zhize Zhou
Sanping Zhou
Qin Zhou
Tao Zhou
Wenbo Zhou
Xiangdong Zhou
Xiao-Yun Zhou
Xiao Zhou
Yang Zhou
Yipin Zhou
Zhenyu Zhou
Hao Zhou
Chu Zhou
Daquan Zhou
Da-Wei Zhou
Hang Zhou
Kang Zhou
Qianyu Zhou
Sheng Zhou
Wenhui Zhou
Xingyi Zhou
Yan-Jie Zhou
Yiyi Zhou
Yu Zhou
Yuan Zhou
Yuqian Zhou
Yuxuan Zhou
Zixiang Zhou
Wengang Zhou
Shuchang Zhou
Tianfei Zhou
Yichao Zhou
Alex Zhu
Chenchen Zhu
Deyao Zhu
Xiatian Zhu
Guibo Zhu
Haidong Zhu
Hao Zhu
Hongzi Zhu
Rui Zhu
Jing Zhu

Jianke Zhu
Junchen Zhu
Lei Zhu
Lingyu Zhu
Luyang Zhu
Menglong Zhu
Peihao Zhu
Hui Zhu
Xiaofeng Zhu
Tyler (Lixuan) Zhu
Wentao Zhu
Xiangyu Zhu
Xinqi Zhu
Xinxin Zhu
Xinliang Zhu
Yangguang Zhu
Yichen Zhu
Yixin Zhu
Yanjun Zhu
Yousong Zhu
Yuhao Zhu
Ye Zhu
Feng Zhu
Zhen Zhu
Fangrui Zhu
Jinjing Zhu
Linchao Zhu
Pengfei Zhu
Sijie Zhu
Xiaobin Zhu
Xiaoguang Zhu
Zezhou Zhu
Zhenyao Zhu
Kai Zhu
Pengkai Zhu
Bingbing Zhuang
Chengyuan Zhuang
Liansheng Zhuang
Peiye Zhuang
Yixin Zhuang
Yihong Zhuang
Junbao Zhuo
Andrea Ziani
Bartosz Zieliński
Primo Zingaretti

Nikolaos Zioulis
Andrew Zisserman
Yael Ziv
Liu Ziyin
Xingxing Zou
Danping Zou
Qi Zou

Shihao Zou
Xueyan Zou
Yang Zou
Yuliang Zou
Zihang Zou
Chuhang Zou
Dongqing Zou

Xu Zou
Zhiming Zou
Maria A. Zuluaga
Xinxin Zuo
Zhiwen Zuo
Reyer Zwiggelaar

Contents – Part VI

UnrealEgo: A New Dataset for Robust Egocentric 3D Human Motion Capture

Hiroyasu Akada[1,2(✉)] , Jian Wang[1] , Soshi Shimada[1], Masaki Takahashi[2], Christian Theobalt[1], and Vladislav Golyanik[1]

[1] Max Planck Institute for Informatics, SIC, Saarbrücken, Germany
hakada@mpi-inf.mpg.de
[2] Keio University, Tokyo, Japan

Abstract. We present *UnrealEgo, i.e.,* a new large-scale naturalistic dataset for egocentric 3D human pose estimation. UnrealEgo is based on an advanced concept of eyeglasses equipped with two fisheye cameras that can be used in unconstrained environments. We design their virtual prototype and attach them to 3D human models for stereo view capture. We next generate a large corpus of human motions. As a consequence, UnrealEgo is the first dataset to provide in-the-wild stereo images with the largest variety of motions among existing egocentric datasets. Furthermore, we propose a new benchmark method with a simple but effective idea of devising a 2D keypoint estimation module for stereo inputs to improve 3D human pose estimation. The extensive experiments show that our approach outperforms the previous state-of-the-art methods qualitatively and quantitatively. UnrealEgo and our source codes are available on our project web page (https://4dqv.mpi-inf.mpg.de/UnrealEgo/).

Keywords: Egocentric 3D human pose estimation · Naturalistic data

1 Introduction

Egocentric 3D human pose estimation has been actively researched recently [27,43,46,47,52,53,55,56]. Compared to cumbersome motion capture systems that require a fixed recording volume, the egocentric setup is more suitable to capture daily human activities in unconstrained environments. Example applications include XR technologies [19] and motion analysis for sport and health [39].

Several setup types were proposed for egocentric 3D human pose estimation. Some methods work on mobile devices such as a cap [53], a helmet [43] or a head-mounted display [46,47] equipped with a camera to capture egocentric views of a user's whole body. Although these methods show promising results, their setups

Supplementary Information The online version contains supplementary material available at https://doi.org/10.1007/978-3-031-20068-7_1.

© The Author(s), under exclusive license to Springer Nature Switzerland AG 2022
S. Avidan et al. (Eds.): ECCV 2022, LNCS 13666, pp. 1–17, 2022.
https://doi.org/10.1007/978-3-031-20068-7_1

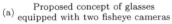

(a) Proposed concept of glasses equipped with two fisheye cameras   (b) Human model wearing the glasses   (c) Egocentric fisheye views

Fig. 1. Overview of the proposed UnrealEgo setup.

are still not satisfactory for daily use; the cameras are mounted far from the user's body, which is inconvenient and restrictive. The recently introduced EgoGlass approach [56] tackles this issue by an eyeglasses-based setup with two cameras attached to the glasses frame. Their setup imposes fewer restrictions on users' activities. We envision that with the recent development of smaller cameras [2] and smart glasses [4,6], the eyeglasses-based setup can be a de facto standard to capture daily human activities in various situations.

Along with that, there is a lack of datasets that would account for this new and advanced capture setting and that would allow developing algorithmic frameworks involving it. Furthermore, existing egocentric datasets are limited in several ways and cannot be easily re-purposed for 3D human pose estimation with the compact eyeglasses-based setup. First, the existing datasets do not contain complex human motions (such as breakdance and backflip) that are seen in daily human activities [43,47,53,56]. Second, the available egocentric datasets do not faithfully model the 3D environment [47,53]. Next, the existing stereo-based datasets [43,56] do not contain in-the-wild images. All in all, we note that there is no large-scale stereo-based dataset currently available. Consequently, a lack of a comprehensive and versatile egocentric dataset is a severely limiting factor in the development of methods for egocentric 3D perception.

To alleviate the issues mentioned above, we present *UnrealEgo, i.e.,* a new large-scale naturalistic and synthetic dataset for egocentric 3D human pose estimation. UnrealEgo is based on an advanced concept of an eyeglasses-based setup with two fisheye cameras symmetrically attached to the glasses frame. Fisheye cameras are getting more and more compact; they can capture a wider range of views than normal cameras which is beneficial for egocentric human pose estimation [43]. We use Unreal Engine [10] to synthetically design the eyeglasses as shown in Fig. 1(a). We then attach the eyeglasses to realistic 3D human models (*RenderPeople*) [7] and capture in-the-wild stereo views in various 3D environments as shown in Fig. 1(b) and (c). Note that we prioritize the motion diversity in UnrealEgo. Figure 2 shows examples of 3D human models in diverse poses

Fig. 2. Samples of characters and poses from UnrealEgo. We use 17 high-quality 3D RenderPeople models [7]. Also, we utilize Mixamo motions [5] and modify them to diversify our motion data. Please refer to our video for better visualizations and our supplementary asset list for characteristics of each human model.

from UnrealEgo. In total, UnrealEgo contains 450k in-the-wild stereo views (900k images in total) with the largest variety of motions among the existing egocentric datasets. UnrealEgo allows developing new methods that account for temporal changes of surrounding 3D environments (see Sect. 3) and evaluating the current state-of-the-art methods in highly challenging scenarios (see Sect. 5).

Furthermore, we propose a new benchmark approach that achieves state-of-the-art accuracy on UnrealEgo. At the core of our method is a heatmap-based 2D keypoint estimation module. It accepts stereo inputs and passes them to two weight-sharing encoders that produce feature maps in the latent space. The obtained feature maps are concatenated along with the channel dimensions and processed by a decoder that estimates 2D keypoint heatmaps (see Fig. 5). In extensive experiments, we observe that this simple but effective architecture brings significant improvements compared with existing methods [47,56] qualitatively and quantitatively by 13.5% on MPJPE and 14.65% on PA-MPJPE metrics.

In summary, the primary **contributions** of this work are as follows:

- *UnrealEgo, i.e.,* a new large-scale naturalistic dataset for egocentric 3D human motion capture.
- A new approach for 3D human pose estimation achieving state-of-the-art accuracy on the new benchmark dataset.

UnrealEgo is the first to provide (1) naturalistic in-the-wild stereo images with the largest variety of motions and (2) sequences with realistically and accurately-modeled changes of the surrounding 3D environments. This allows a more thorough evaluation of existing and upcoming methods for egocentric 3D vision, including the temporal component and global 3D poses.

2   Related Work

2.1   Datasets for Outside-in 3D Human Pose Estimation

Many datasets were proposed for 3D pose estimation with ground-truth annotations. Some of them are captured with optical markers [26,45,49], while the
others use marker-less mocap systems [28,36,37,54]. However, these datasets
are mostly captured in the studio and usually lack the diversity of clothing,
occlusions, and environments.

In the meantime, synthetic datasets have become popular because no costly
mocap setups are required for annotations. Many such datasets are created by
compositing people on background images [24,36,37,41,42,51]. Because of such
composition, however, their images do not match real-world scenes in terms of the
local pixel intensity statistics and distributions. Butler *et al.* [15] provide images
rendered using underlying detailed 3D geometry and corresponding optical flows
that can be used for tracking purposes. However, this dataset does not provide
3D joint annotations unlike ours.

The recent works by Zhu *et al.* [57] and Patel *et al.* [40] use 3D modeling tools
and game engines [1,9,10] to render realistic images of rigged 3D human models
in 3D environments. Unfortunately, these datasets are designed for outside-in
pose estimation from an external camera viewpoint; they are not suitable and
cannot be easily repurposed for egocentric 3D pose estimation.

2.2   Datasets for Egocentric 3D Human Pose Estimation

There exist several datasets specifically recorded for egocentric 3D human poses.
Mo^2Cap^2 [53] is the first cap-based setup with a single wide-view fisheye camera attached 8cm away from the user. With this setup, Xu *et al.* [53] create a
large-scale dataset by compositing SMPL models [33] on randomly-chosen backgrounds (real images), resulting in 530k images with 15 annotated keypoints per
image. xR-EgoPose [47] approach uses a head-mounted display with a single fisheye camera equipped 2 cm away from a user's nose. This work uses the Mixamo
motion dataset [5] to animate 3D human models and renders egocentric views
with HDR backgrounds with the help of the 3D rendering tool V-Ray [3]. Their
dataset contains 380k photorealistic synthetic images with 25 body and 40 hand
keypoints. However, both datasets contain only monocular images. They feature only simple (every-day) human motions (due to the restrictions imposed by
their setups) and do not accurately model 3D environments and complex human
trajectories in them. Hence, they do not cover most motions that can arise in
egocentric 3D human pose estimation using a compact eyeglass-based setup.
Ego4D [22] is a new large-scale dataset for egocentric vision. Unfortunately, it
does not contain 3D annotations of human poses.

On the other hand, existing stereo egocentric datasets have several limitations. Rhodin *et al.* [43] proposed EgoCap, *i.e.,* a headgear with a pair of
fisheye cameras equipped 25cm away from users to capture stereo views. Their
dataset contains only 30k stereo image pairs with a limited variety of motions

	Monocular Setting		Stereo Setting		
	Mo2Cap2[54]	xR-EgoPose[48]	EgoCap[44]	EgoGlass[57]	UnrealEgo
Device					
Example Data	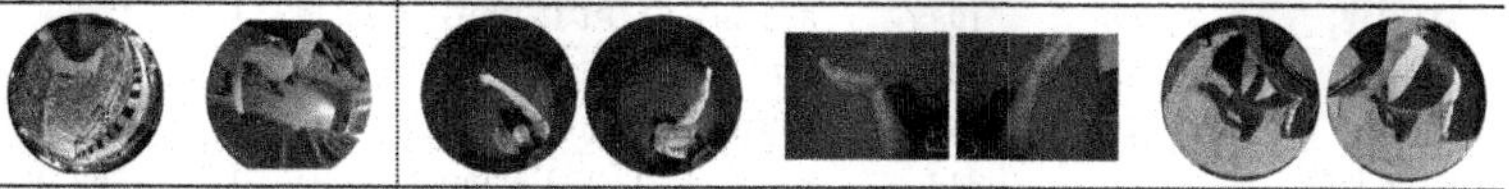				
Distance to user's face	~8cm from the head	~2cm from the nose	~25cm from the head	~1cm from the head	~1cm from the head
Number of egocentric views	530k	380k	30k × 2 views	170k × 2 views	450k × 2 views
Number of keypoints	body: 15	body: 25 hand: 40	body: 17	body: 13	body: 32 hand: 40
Image generation	composite	composite	lab environments	lab environments	3D environments
Image quality	low	realistic	real	real	realistic
Motion diversity	middle	middle	low	low	high

Fig. 3. Comparison of datasets for egocentric 3D human pose estimation.

in a lab environment. More recently, EgoGlass [56] simplified the stereo setup with eyeglasses and two cameras equipped on the glasses frames. Although Ego-Glass captured a relatively large-scale of images, *i.e.*, total 170k stereo pairs, *the dataset is captured only in a studio environment and is not publicly available.*

In contrast to existing datasets, UnrealEgo addresses the above shortcomings. Figure 3 illustrates the differences among existing datasets and UnrealEgo. Firstly, UnrealEgo provides stereo images in indoor and outdoor scenes. Secondly, it offers the largest number of images, *e.g.*, 15 times larger than EgoCap [43] and 2.5 times larger than EgoGlass [56]. Next, it contains naturalistic image sequences with accurately modeled geometry changes in the surrounding 3D environments. Also, it offers the largest number of body and hand keypoints. Furthermore, it is the most challenging egocentric dataset in terms of motion variety.

2.3 Methods for Egocentric 3D Human Pose Estimation

Existing methods for egocentric 3D human pose estimation can be divided into two groups in terms of egocentric settings. The first group aims at estimating 3D keypoints from monocular views. Mo2Cap2 [53] is the first CNN-based system to predict 3D poses. Tome *et al.* [46,47] follow a two-step approach using a multi-branch autoencoder to capture uncertainty in their predicted 2D heatmaps and to leverage rotation constraints [46]. Jiang *et al.* [27] predict 3D poses by utilizing the information of surrounding environments and extremities of the user's body. Zhang *et al.* [55] estimate 3D poses with fisheye distortions using an automatic

Table 1. Comparison of human motion capture datasets.

Dataset	Subjects	Motions	Minutes	Dataset	Subjects	Motions	Minutes
ACCAD [11]	20	252	26.74	KIT [35]	55	4232	661.84
BMLhandball [31]	10	649	101.98	MPI HDM05 [38]	4	215	144.54
BMLmovi [21]	89	1864	174.39	MPI Limits [12]	3	35	20.82
BMLrub [48]	111	3061	522.69	MPI MoSh [32]	19	77	16.53
CMU [16]	96	1983	543.49	MPI-INF-3DHP [36]	8	–	–
D-FAUST [14]	10	129	5.73	SFU [50]	7	44	15.23
DanceDB [13]	20	151	203.38	SSM [34]	3	30	1.87
EKUT [35]	4	349	30.74	TCD Hands [25]	1	62	8.05
Eyes Japan [20]	12	750	363.64	TotalCapture [49]	5	37	41.1
Human3D [26]	11	–	–	Transitions [34]	1	110	15.1
Human4D [18]	8	148	72.60	AMASS [34]	344	11265	2420.86
HumanEva [45]	3	28	8.48	Ours	17	45520	3174.63

calibration module. More recently, Wang *et al.* [52] proposed an optimization-based approach with a motion prior learned from an additional dataset for global 3D human motion capture. Even with their competitive results, these monocular methods often fail on complex motions (*e.g.,* due to the depth ambiguity).

The second group follows multi-view settings, including our work. Ego-Cap [43] is an optimization-based approach using a body-part detector and personalized 3D skeleton models. Cha *et al.* [17] developed a headset equipped with eight cameras; they introduced a CNN-based method to reconstruct a human body and an environment in 3D. EgoGlass [56] builds upon xR-EgoPose [47] and is one of the most accurate methods; its architecture contains two separate UNets for the stereo inputs in the 2D joint estimation module. In contrast to the reviewed works, this paper proposes a simple yet effective idea of devising a new 2D joint estimation module that accepts stereo inputs to significantly improve 3D pose estimation compared with the existing best-performing methods.

3   UnrealEgo Dataset

This section provides details of the UnrealEgo dataset, focusing on our setup, motions, and rendered egocentric data. Please also see our supplementary video for dynamic visualizations and our supplementary asset list.

3.1   Setup

We use Unreal Engine [10] to synthetically design the eyeglasses with two fisheye cameras equipped on the glasses frame as shown in Fig. 1(a). The distance between the cameras is 12 cm. The cameras' field of view amounts to 170°. We attach the glasses to 3D human models (RenderPeople) that perform different motions in various 3D environments. Figure 1(b) and (c) show an example of the human models in a Kyoto-inspired environment in Japan, and fisheye views.

Characters. We use 17 realistic RenderPeople 3D human models (commercially available) [7], nine female and eight male. These models are rigged and skinned based on the default 3D human skeleton of Unreal Engine [10]. Their skin color tones include pale white, white, light brown, moderate brown, dark brown, and black. Their clothing types include athletic pants, jeans, shorts, tights, dress pants, skirts, jackets, t-shirts, and long sleeves with diffident colors. Please see Fig. 2 for an overview of the 3D human models we use. Also, please see our supplement for detailed characteristics of each human model.

Table 2. Motion categories in our dataset.

Motion types	Motions	Minutes	Motion types	Motions	Minutes
1: jumping	1343	36.35	16: standing - whole body	3791	307.95
2: falling down	714	35.27	17: standing - upper body	5820	708.74
3: exercising	1225	82.07	18: standing - turning	1785	82.73
4: pulling	272	28.31	19: standing - to crouching	680	38.21
5: singing	1054	149.21	20: standing - forward	3417	93.68
6: rolling	136	4.69	21: standing - backward	1207	21.69
7: crawling	612	22.47	22: standing - sideways	1496	30.42
8: laying	612	30.92	23: dancing	5728	800.13
9: sitting on the ground	68	10.88	24: boxing	4012	160.53
10: crouching - normal	1802	127.90	25: wrestling	2958	119.63
11: crouching - turning	612	12.74	26: soccer	1892	69.63
12: crouching - to standing	850	29.46	27: baseball	476	27.31
13: crouching - forward	1020	29.50	28: basketball	272	7.54
14: crouching - backward	493	8.82	29: american football	85	6.07
15: crouching - sideways	646	11.69	30: golf	442	80.07

Motions. It is our top priority to include a wider variety of motions that can represent as many daily human activities as possible. Therefore, we first create a new large corpus of motions. Specifically, we utilize Mixamo motions [5] and modify them using Unreal Engine [10] to enhance their plausibility and diversify the motion data. We first manually fix some motions that involve self-penetration and then modify the motions in various ways, including the speed of motions, arm movements, foot stances, and head rotations. For further details, please refer to our supplement. In total, we created 45,520 natural motions for the 17 human models, *i.e.*, ≈2700 motions per model. We provide the details of our dataset in Tables 1 and 2. Table 1 compares existing mocap datasets and our motion data. Note that AMASS [34] is a collection of several existing motion capture datasets [11–14,16,18,20,21,25,31,32,35,35,38,45,48–50]. Our dataset contains the largest number of motions with the longest consecutive 3D human motions. Table 2 summarises the included motion categories.

3D Environments. We use 14 realistic 3D environments. They include a variety of indoor and outdoor scenes (*e.g.*, parks, roads, bridges, offices, gardens, playrooms, laboratories, cafeterias, trains, tennis courts, baseball fields, football fields, factories, European boulevards, North-American houses, Chinese rooms, Kyoto towns, and Japanese restaurants, at different times of day and night). Please see our supplementary asset list for further details.

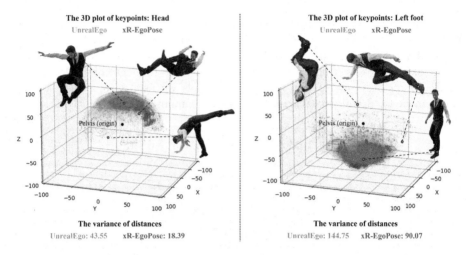

Fig. 4. Distributions of head and left foot locations in xR-EgoPose [47] (blue) and UnrealEgo (orange). The pelvis-relative 3D coordinates are on cm-scale. (Color figure online)

Spawning Human Characters. It is important to create populated scenes to simulate real-world situations. To this end, we develop an algorithm to randomly place human models in 3D environments in Unreal Engine. As a preliminary step, we manually place K rectangles $B=\{B_1,...,B_K\}$ where several human models can be spawned on even grounds. Here, let $S=\{S_1,...,S_K\}$ be the areas of rectangles and $C=\{C_1,...,C_K\}$ be their center positions in the world frame in Cartesian coordinate, respectively. As a first step, we choose i-th area $B_i \in B$ using area weighted probability $S_i/\sum_{i=1}^{K}S_i$. Secondly, we select T surrounding rectangles $B_t \in B$, $t = \{1,...,T\}$ with their center positions $C_t \in C$ being within 10m from C_i. Next, from all of the selected rectangles, we randomly sample world positions to place human models. The sampled positions are at least 1m far from each other. Lastly, we place human models by adjusting the heights of the lowest vertices of the human models to those of the sampled positions. About five models are spawned on average at once, and we render egocentric views from them. After that, we go back to the first step. This way, we randomly place the human models closer to each other in the 3D environment, and some rendered views can capture multiple models.

Rendering. We use a fisheye plugin [8] to render images until motions are completed, or a collision is detected. Here, we use the physics engine of Unreal Engine to detect collisions based on the pre-defined collision proxies (volumes) of the human models and the 3D environments. Around 100 stereo views per motion are rendered on average. The environments contain multiple light sources, including sky, points, and directional lights. Ray-tracing is enabled if the environments support it; rasterization rendering is used otherwise. Also, the rendering process of Unreal Engine includes deferred shading, global illumination, lit translucency,

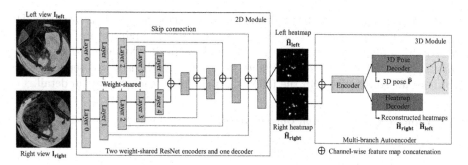

Fig. 5. Overview of the proposed method. Our network consists of a 2D module to predict 2D heatmaps of joint positions from stereo inputs (Sect. 4.1) and a 3D module to estimate 3D joint positions from the heatmaps (Sect. 4.2).

post-processing, and GPU particle simulation utilizing vector fields. Please refer to our supplement for more details on the asset rendering. All images are rendered on NVIDIA RTX 3090. The rendering speed is two frames per second.

3.2 Egocentric Dataset

We capture stereo fisheye images and depth maps with a resolution of 1024×1024 pixels each with 25 frames per second. Metadata is provided for each frame, including 3D joint positions, camera positions, and 2D coordinates of reprojected joint positions in the fisheye views. We randomly choose 10% of our motion data over all motion types, and capture 450k in-the-wild stereo views (900k images) in total. See Fig. 3 for the comparison with existing egocentric datasets.

As mentioned in Sect. 2.2, the motion variety is our top priority. UnrealEgo contains many complex motions in daily activities, some of which are difficult to capture with corresponding egocentric views in real-world settings. Example motions include breakdance and backflip in the dancing category shown in Table 2. To highlight the diversity of motions in UnrealEgo, we visualize the distributions of the keypoints in our UnrealEgo and xR-EgoPose [47] datasets in Fig. 4. Here, we use pelvis-relative 3D coordinates for head and left foot positions. Overall, the keypoints of UnrealEgo are more widespread with a larger variance of distances from the pelvis (origin) than those of xR-EgoPose. For example, in the left 3D plot of Fig. 4, the head is moving through a larger 3D space in UnrealEgo, even to areas below the pelvis, whereas head locations of xR-EgoPose are predominantly fixed above the pelvis. This shows that the UnrealEgo motions have a higher diversity of head positions.

4   Egocentric 3D Human Pose Estimation

In this section, we describe our egocentric 3D human pose estimation method. We firstly adopt a 2D module to predict 2D heatmaps of joint positions from stereo inputs and, next, a 3D module to generate 3D joint positions from the 2D heatmaps. Figure 5 shows the overview of our network architecture. The main contribution of our method lies in the 2D module specifically designed for stereo inputs. This differs from the previous work [56], which uses two separate 2D modules for stereo views. In the following, we explain each module in detail.

Table 3. Comparisons on UnrealEgo with and w/o ImageNet pre-training.

Methods	Settings	MPJPE (σ)	PA-MPJPE (σ)
xR-EgoPose	Monocular	112.86 (1.16) / 123.15 (2.05)	88.71 (0.98) / 96.56 (1.27)
EgoGlass	Stereo	91.44 (0.84) / 107.70 (1.88)	70.21 (0.90) / 84.22 (0.99)
Ours	Stereo	**79.06 (0.25) / 87.31 (0.57)**	**59.95 (0.74) / 64.65 (0.93)**

4.1 2D Module

Our 2D module consists of two weight-sharing encoders and one decoder with unified skip connections [44] for stereo features as shown in Fig. 5. Here, we follow Zhao *et al.* [56] to use ResNet18 [23] as our encoder backbone. The 2D module takes stereo RGB images $\{\mathbf{I}_{\text{Left}}, \mathbf{I}_{\text{Right}}\} \in \mathbb{R}^{256 \times 256 \times 3}$ as inputs, and infers 2D joint locations represented as a set of heatmaps $\{\mathbf{H}_{\text{Left}}, \mathbf{H}_{\text{Right}}\} \in \mathbb{R}^{64 \times 64 \times 15}$. Here, we predict 15 joints in the neck, upper arms, lower arms, hands, thighs, calves, feet and balls of the feet. From each layer of the two weight-sharing encoders, we extract the features and concatenate them along the channel dimension. These features are then forwarded to corresponding decoder layers via skip connections. Unlike the 2D module of the previous work [56], our 2D module utilizes stereo information for heatmap estimation and, thus, boosts the performance of the 3D pose estimation task. For the training of the 2D module, we apply the mean squared error (mse) between the ground-truth heatmaps $\mathbf{H}_{\text{Left}}$ and $\mathbf{H}_{\text{Right}}$ and the estimated 2D heatmaps $\widehat{\mathbf{H}}_{\text{Left}}$ and $\widehat{\mathbf{H}}_{\text{Right}}$:

$$L_{\text{2D}} = \text{mse}(\mathbf{H}_{\text{Left}}, \widehat{\mathbf{H}}_{\text{Left}}) + \text{mse}(\mathbf{H}_{\text{Right}}, \widehat{\mathbf{H}}_{\text{Right}}). \tag{1}$$

4.2 3D Module

Following previous work [56], we adopt the same multi-branch autoencoder for our 3D module. Given the heatmaps $\widehat{\mathbf{H}}_{\text{Left}}$ and $\widehat{\mathbf{H}}_{\text{Right}}$ predicted by the 2D module as inputs, the 3D module firstly encodes them to get embedding features. These features are used in two decoder branches. The first branch is a 3D pose branch, which outputs the final 3D pose $\hat{\mathbf{P}} \in \mathbb{R}^{16 \times 3}$. Here, the number of output 3D joints is 16 as the head position is included. The second branch is a heatmap branch, which tries to reconstruct the predicted 2D heatmaps $\widehat{\mathbf{H}}_{\text{Left}}$ and $\widetilde{\mathbf{H}}_{\text{Right}}$ so that the network can capture the uncertainty of the heatmaps.

Similar to [56], the overall loss function for the 3D module is as follows:

$$L_{\text{3D}} = \lambda_{\text{pose}}(\text{mpjpe}(\mathbf{P}, \hat{\mathbf{P}}) + \lambda_{\text{cos}}\cos(\mathbf{P}, \hat{\mathbf{P}})) +$$
$$\lambda_{\text{hm}}(\text{mse}(\widehat{\mathbf{H}}_{\text{Left}}, \widetilde{\mathbf{H}}_{\text{Left}}) + \text{mse}(\widehat{\mathbf{H}}_{\text{Right}}, \widetilde{\mathbf{H}}_{\text{Right}})), \tag{2}$$

Table 4. Quantitative evaluation on the general motions of UnrealEgo (MPJPE).

Methods	Jumping	Falling down	Exercising	Pulling,	Singing	Rolling	Crawling	Laying
xR-EgoPose	106.30	167.18	133.19	119.49	99.62	166.14	223.51	146.67
EgoGlass	88.55	135.25	105.11	89.96	75.54	143.64	199.27	114.85
Ours	**76.81**	**125.22**	**90.54**	**80.61**	**65.53**	**94.97**	**179.98**	**97.56**

Methods	Sitting on the ground	Crouching - normal	Crouching - turning	Crouching - to standing	Crouching - forward	Crouching - backward	Crouching - sideways	Standing - whole body
xR-EgoPose	274.99	172.25	173.77	108.96	119.95	136.52	145.81	94.34
EgoGlass	216.52	129.72	151.71	93.71	90.76	100.39	122.23	78.57
Ours	**195.28**	**120.65**	**131.82**	**81.28**	**76.04**	**81.31**	**88.54**	**67.67**

Methods	Standing - upper body	Standing - turning	Standing - to crouching	Standing - forward	Standing - backward	Standing - sideways	–	All
xR-EgoPose	93.36	103.28	101.60	99.72	105.86	114.28	–	112.61
EgoGlass	76.83	84.12	82.03	82.96	85.15	93.61	–	91.27
Ours	**65.92**	**74.55**	**73.21**	**70.86**	**70.40**	**79.06**	–	**79.57**

Table 5. Quantitative evaluation on the sports motions of UnrealEgo (MPJPE).

Methods	Dancing	Boxing	Wrestling	Soccer	Baseball	Basketball	American football	Golf	All
xR-EgoPose	116.75	97.33	116.65	104.65	103.75	98.65	149.76	117.50	113.28
EgoGlass	95.37	77.66	96.63	88.30	93.60	74.31	118.34	79.35	91.71
Ours	**79.86**	**69.34**	**84.02**	**76.54**	**74.27**	**62.09**	**103.79**	**72.06**	**78.19**

where $\mathbf{P}$ is a ground-truth 3D pose, mpjpe($\cdot$) is the mean per joint position error and cos($\cdot$) is a negative cosine similarity, $i.e.$,

$$\text{mpjpe}(\mathbf{P}, \hat{\mathbf{P}}) = \frac{1}{BJ} \sum_{i=1}^{B} \sum_{j=1}^{J} ||\mathbf{P}_i^j - \hat{\mathbf{P}}_i^j||_2, \tag{3}$$

$$\cos(\mathbf{P}, \hat{\mathbf{P}}) = -\frac{1}{B} \sum_{i=1}^{B} \sum_{l=1}^{L} \frac{\mathbf{P}_i^l \cdot \hat{\mathbf{P}}_i^l}{||\mathbf{P}_i^l|| \, ||\hat{\mathbf{P}}_i^l||}, \tag{4}$$

where B is the batch size, J is the number of joints, L is the number of limbs, and $\mathbf{P}_i^l \in \mathbb{R}^3$ is the l-th bone of the human skeleton.

5   Experiments

5.1   Implementation Details

We randomly split UnrealEgo into 3,821 motions (357,317 stereo views) for training, 494 motions (46,207 stereo views) for validation, and 526 motions (48,080 stereo views) for testing. The input images and ground-truth 2D heatmaps are resized to 256×256 and 64×64, respectively. The 2D module and the 3D module are trained separately on a Quadro RTX 8000 with a batch size of 16. We set the hyper-parameters as $\lambda_{\text{pose}} = 0.1$, $\lambda_{\text{cos}} = 0.01$, and $\lambda_{\text{hm}} = 0.001$. The modules are trained with Adam optimizer [30] for ten epochs, starting with a learning rate of 10^{-3} for the first half epochs and applying a linearly decaying rate for the next half. We perform the experiments three times and report average scores and standard deviations (denoted by σ).

Stereo inputs   EgoGlass [57]   Ours   Stereo inputs   EgoGlass [57]   Ours

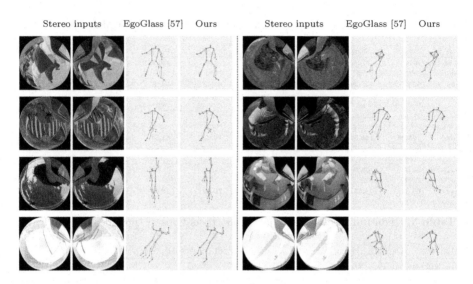

Fig. 6. Qualitative results on UnrealEgo (blue: ground truth; red: prediction). (Color figure online)

5.2   Comparisons

As our comparison methods, we adopt state-of-the-art methods for egocentric 3D human pose estimation, *i.e.*, EgoGlass [56] and xR-EgoPose [47]. Since their source codes are not available, we re-implement and tailor them for UnrealEgo. We train xR-EgoPose on the left views of UnrealEgo. For the sake of evaluation under the same conditions, we remove a body part branch with segmentation supervision in EgoGlass as xR-EgoPose does not use it. We follow the previous works and report the Mean Per Joint Position Error (MPJPE) and the Mean Per Joint Position Error with Procrustes alignment [29] (PA-MPJPE). Here, Procrustes alignment finds optimal rigid transformation and scale between the predicted and ground-truth 3D poses.

5.3   Results

We present results on the UnrealEgo test sequence. Table 3 quantitatively evaluates our approach and competing methods with and without ImageNet pretraining for the encoder. Overall, our method outperforms the previous best-performing method [56], across all metrics for both experiments with and without ImageNet. Specifically, our method with the pre-trained encoder shows significant improvement by 13.5% on MPJPE and 14.65% on PA-MPJPE compared to EgoGlass [56]. All methods, including ours, benefit from the ImageNet pretraining; the performance of our approach is boosted by 9.4% on MPJPE and 7.2% on PA-MPJPE.

We also break down the test sequence into 30 motion types as shown in Table 4 for general motions and Table 5 for sports motions. Both tables indicate

Stereo inputs   EgoGlass [57]   Ours   Right view End-to-end Separate   GT

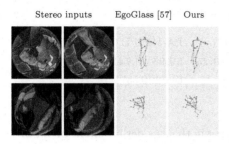   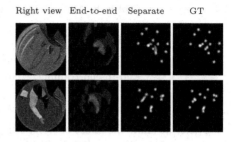

Fig. 7. Qualitative results for failure cases on UnrealEgo.

Fig. 8. Heatmap estimation results with two different training strategies.

Table 6. Ablation study for the backbone of the 2D heatmap module.

Backbones	MPJPE (σ)	PA-MPJPE (σ)
ResNet18	**79.06 (0.25)**	**59.95 (0.74)**
ResNet34	80.50 (0.78)	60.04 (0.60)
ResNet50	80.07 (0.45)	60.08 (0.63)
ResNet101	80.15 (0.06)	60.57 (0.79)

Table 7. Ablation study for the weight sharing in the 2D heatmap module.

Backbones	MPJPE (σ)	PA-MPJPE (σ)
Weight sharing	**79.06 (0.25)**	**59.95 (0.74)**
No weight sharing	83.54 (1.30)	62.29 (0.45)

that our method achieves significant superiority for all motion types. See Fig. 6 for the qualitative results. Even with the occlusions and complex poses in various environments, our method estimates the 3D poses much better than EgoGlass.

It is also worth analyzing failure cases. According to Table 4, bending motions (such as sitting on the ground or crouching) are reconstructed with comparably low accuracy. This is because the lower body parts are occluded by the upper body, especially when people crouch down as shown in Fig. 7. Even with the stereo inputs, these methods still can not perform well on some motions that are occasionally seen in daily human activities.

5.4 Ablation Study

We first ablate different encoder backbone architectures for our 2D module in Table 6. All variants generate the heatmap with the same resolution and the 3D module shares the same architecture. The experiment suggests that all of the models yield similar results but at a higher computational cost for a larger backbone. For example, the difference between ResNet18 and Resnet50 is only 0.2% on PA-MPJPE. This result is also observed in the previous work [46], showing that a larger backbone does not necessarily lead to performance improvements.

Table 8. Ablation study on the training strategy.

Backbones	MPJPE (σ)	PA-MPJPE (σ)
Separate training	**79.06 (0.25)**	**59.95 (0.74)**
End-to-end training	80.67 (0.58)	61.72 (0.55)

Next, we show the effect of weight sharing in the encoder backbone of our 2D keypoint estimation module in Table 7. The weight-sharing backbone performs better than the encoder without weight sharing by 5.4% on MPJPE and 3.8% on PA-MPJPE. One possible reason for this result is that the weight-sharing backbone can see more views during training, leading to a better feature extractor. Therefore, we use the weight-sharing strategy for all experiments.

Lastly, we conduct the experiment with different training strategies, *i.e.,* separate training and end-to-end training for our 2D keypoint estimation and 3D estimation module, as shown in Table 8. The result indicates that the separate training yields slightly better performance than the end-to-end training by 2.0% on MPJPE and 2.9% on PA-MPJPE. We also visualize the heatmaps predicted by our network with the different training strategies in Fig. 8. It is interesting to note that separate training leads to relatively accurate heatmap estimation while the network trained in an end-to-end manner tries to capture the whole body. Although this visual result can change depending on the hyper-parameters, we follow the same hyper-parameter setting in the previous work [56] and choose the separate training strategy for all experiments.

6   Conclusions

We presented *UnrealEgo*, *i.e.,* a new large-scale naturalistic dataset for egocentric 3D human pose estimation. It allows a comprehensive evaluation of existing and upcoming methods for egocentric 3D vision, including the temporal component and global 3D poses. Our simple yet effective architecture for egocentric 3D human pose estimation brings significant improvement compared to previous best-performing methods qualitatively and quantitatively. In addition, our extensive ablation studies validate our architectural design choices for the stereo inputs and the training strategy. Although our method achieved state-of-the-art results, there are still failure cases due to occlusions and complex motions. In future work, we are interested in incorporating explicit 3D geometry obtained from our stereo fisheye setup for further performance improvements.

Acknowledgements. We thank Silicon Studio Corp. for providing the fisheye plugin. Hiroyasu Akada and Masaki Takahashi were supported by the Core Research for Evolutional Science and Technology of the Japan Science and Technology Agency (JPMJCR19A1). Jian Wang, Soshi Shimada, Vladislav Golyanik and Christian Theobalt were supported by the ERC Consolidator Grant 4DReply (770784).

References

1. Blender (2022). https://www.blender.org
2. Calicam fisheye stereo camera (2022). https://astar.ai/products/stereo-camera
3. Chaos v-ray (2022). https://www.chaos.com/
4. glass (2022). https://www.google.com/glass/start/
5. Mixamo (2022). https://www.mixamo.com
6. Ray-ban stories smart glasses (2022). https://www.ray-ban.com/usa/ray-ban-stories
7. Renderpeople (2022). https://renderpeople.com
8. Siliconstudio (2022). https://www.siliconstudio.co.jp/en/
9. Unity (2022). https://unity.com
10. Unreal engine (2022). https://www.unrealengine.com
11. Advanced Computing Center for the Arts and Design: ACCAD MoCap Dataset. https://accad.osu.edu/research/motion-lab/mocap-system-and-data
12. Akhter, I., Black, M.J.: Pose-conditioned joint angle limits for 3D human pose reconstruction. In: IEEE Conference on Computer Vision and Pattern Recognition (CVPR) (2015)
13. Aristidou, A., Shamir, A., Chrysanthou, Y.: Digital dance ethnography: Organizing large dance collections. J. Comput. Cult. Herit. **12**(4), 1–27 (2019)
14. Bogo, F., Romero, J., Pons-Moll, G., Black, M.J.: Dynamic FAUST: Registering human bodies in motion. In: Computer Vision and Pattern Recognition (CVPR) (2017)
15. Butler, D.J., Wulff, J., Stanley, G.B., Black, M.J.: A naturalistic open source movie for optical flow evaluation. In: Fitzgibbon, A., Lazebnik, S., Perona, P., Sato, Y., Schmid, C. (eds.) ECCV 2012. LNCS, vol. 7577, pp. 611–625. Springer, Heidelberg (2012). https://doi.org/10.1007/978-3-642-33783-3_44
16. Carnegie Mellon University: CMU MoCap Dataset. http://mocap.cs.cmu.edu
17. Cha, Y.W., et al.: Towards fully mobile 3d face, body, and environment capture using only head-worn cameras. IEEE Trans. Vis. Comput. Graph. **24**(11), 2993–3004 (2018)
18. Chatzitofis, A., et al.: Human4d: A human-centric multimodal dataset for motions and immersive media. IEEE Access **8**, 176241–176262 (2020)
19. Elgharib, M., et al.: Egocentric videoconferencing. ACM Trans. Graph. **39**(6), 1–16 (2020)
20. Eyes JAPAN Co., Ltd.: Eyes Japan MoCap Dataset. http://mocapdata.com
21. Ghorbani, S., et al.: Movi: A large multi-purpose human motion and video dataset. PLOS ONE **16**(6), 1–15 (2021)
22. Grauman, K., Westbury, A., Byrne, E., Chavis, Z., Furnari, A., Girdhar, R., Hamburger, J., et al.: Ego4d: Around the world in 3,000 hours of egocentric video. In: Computer Vision and Pattern Recognition (CVPR) (2022)
23. He, K., Zhang, X., Ren, S., Sun, J.: Deep residual learning for image recognition. In: Proceedings of the IEEE conference on computer vision and pattern recognition (CVPR) (2016)
24. Hoffmann, D.T., Tzionas, D., Black, M.J., Tang, S.: Learning to train with synthetic humans. In: Fink, G.A., Frintrop, S., Jiang, X. (eds.) DAGM GCPR 2019. LNCS, vol. 11824, pp. 609–623. Springer, Cham (2019). https://doi.org/10.1007/978-3-030-33676-9_43
25. Hoyet, L., Ryall, K., McDonnell, R., O'Sullivan, C.: Sleight of hand: Perception of finger motion from reduced marker sets. In: Proceedings of the ACM SIGGRAPH Symposium on Interactive 3D Graphics and Games, I3D '12, pp. 79–86 (2012)

26. Ionescu, C., Papava, D., Olaru, V., Sminchisescu, C.: Human3.6m: Large scale datasets and predictive methods for 3d human sensing in natural environments. IEEE Trans. Pattern Anal. Mach. Intell. **36**(7), 1325–1339 (2014)
27. Jiang, H., Ithapu, V.K.: Egocentric pose estimation from human vision span. In: IEEE/CVF International Conference on Computer Vision (ICCV) (2021)
28. Joo, H.: Panoptic studio: A massively multiview system for social motion capture. In: International Conference on Computer Vision (ICCV) (2015)
29. Kendall, D.G.: A survey of the statistical theory of shape. Stat. Sci. **4**(2), 87–99 (1989)
30. Kingma, D., Ba, J.: Adam: A method for stochastic optimization. In: International Conference on Learning Representations (ICLR) (2015)
31. Lab, B.M.: BMLhandball Motion Capture Database. https://www.biomotionlab. ca//
32. Loper, M., Mahmood, N., Black, M.J.: MoSh: Motion and shape capture from sparse markers. ACM Trans. Graph. **33**(6), 1–13 (2014)
33. Loper, M., Mahmood, N., Romero, J., Pons-Moll, G., Black, M.J.: SMPL: A skinned multi-person linear model. ACM Trans. Graph. (Proc. SIGGRAPH Asia) **34**(6), 248:1-248:16 (2015)
34. Mahmood, N., Ghorbani, N., Troje, N.F., Pons-Moll, G., Black, M.J.: AMASS: Archive of motion capture as surface shapes. In: IEEE/CVF International Conference on Computer Vision (ICCV) (2019)
35. Mandery, C., Terlemez, O., Do, M., Vahrenkamp, N., Asfour, T.: The KIT whole-body human motion database. In: International Conference on Advanced Robotics (ICAR) (2015)
36. Mehta, D.: Monocular 3d human pose estimation in the wild using improved cnn supervision. In: International Conference on 3D Vision (3DV) (2017)
37. Mehta, D.: Single-shot multi-person 3d pose estimation from monocular rgb. In: International Conference on 3D Vision (3DV) (2018)
38. Müller, M., Röder, T., Clausen, M., Eberhardt, B., Krüger, B., Weber, A.: Documentation mocap database HDM05. Tech. Rep. CG-2007-2 (2007)
39. Núñez-Marcos, A., Azkune, G., Arganda-Carreras, I.: Egocentric vision-based action recognition: A survey. Neurocomputing **472**, 175–197 (2022)
40. Patel, P., Huang, C.H.P., Tesch, J., Hoffmann, D.T., Tripathi, S., Black, M.J.: AGORA: Avatars in geography optimized for regression analysis. In: Proceedings IEEE Conference on Computer Vision and Pattern Recognition (CVPR) (2021)
41. Pumarola, A., Sanchez, J., Choi, G., Sanfeliu, A., Moreno-Noguer, F.: 3DPeople: Modeling the geometry of dressed humans. In: International Conference in Computer Vision (ICCV) (2019)
42. Ranjan, A., Hoffmann, D.T., Tzionas, D., Tang, S., Romero, J., Black, M.J.: Learning multi-human optical flow. Int. J. Comput. Vis. (IJCV) **128**, 873–890 (2020)
43. Rhodin, H., et al.: Egocap: Egocentric marker-less motion capture with two fisheye cameras. ACM Trans. Graph. (TOG) **35**(6), 1–11 (2016)
44. Ronneberger, O., Fischer, P., Brox, T.: U-Net: Convolutional networks for biomedical image segmentation. In: Navab, N., Hornegger, J., Wells, W.M., Frangi, A.F. (eds.) MICCAI 2015. LNCS, vol. 9351, pp. 234–241. Springer, Cham (2015). https://doi.org/10.1007/978-3-319-24574-4_28
45. Sigal, L., Balan, A., Black, M.J.: HumanEva: Synchronized video and motion capture dataset and baseline algorithm for evaluation of articulated human motion. Int. J. Comput. Vis. (IJCV) **87**(4), 4–27 (2010)

46. Tomè, D., et al.: Selfpose: 3d egocentric pose estimation from a headset mounted camera. IEEE Trans. Pattern Anal. Mach. Intell. (2020). https://doi.org/10.1109/TPAMI.2020.3029700
47. Tome, D., Peluse, P., Agapito, L., Badino, H.: xr-egopose: Egocentric 3d human pose from an hmd camera. In: Proceedings of the IEEE/CVF International Conference on Computer Vision (ICCV) (2019)
48. Troje, N.F.: Decomposing biological motion: A framework for analysis and synthesis of human gait patterns. J. Vis. **2**(5), 371–387 (2002)
49. Trumble, M., Gilbert, A., Malleson, C., Hilton, A., Collomosse, J.: Total capture: 3d human pose estimation fusing video and inertial sensors. In: British Machine Vision Conference (BMVC) (2017)
50. University, S.F., of Singapore, N.U.: SFU Motion Capture Database. http://mocap.cs.sfu.ca/
51. Varol, G.: Learning from synthetic humans. In: Proceedings IEEE Conference on Computer Vision and Pattern Recognition (CVPR) (2017)
52. Wang, J., Liu, L., Xu, W., Sarkar, K., Theobalt, C.: Estimating egocentric 3d human pose in global space. In: Proceedings of the IEEE/CVF International Conference on Computer Vision (ICCV) (2021)
53. Xu, W., et al.: Mo^2Cap^2: Real-time mobile 3d motion capture with a cap-mounted fisheye camera. IEEE Trans. Vis. Comput. Graph. **25**, 2093 (2019)
54. Yu, Z., et al.: Humbi: A large multiview dataset of human body expressions. In: Proceedings of the IEEE/CVF Conference on Computer Vision and Pattern Recognition (CVPR) (2020)
55. Zhang, Y., You, S., Gevers, T.: Automatic calibration of the fisheye camera for egocentric 3d human pose estimation from a single image. In: Proceedings of the IEEE/CVF Winter Conference on Applications of Computer Vision (2021)
56. Zhao, D., Wei, Z., Mahmud, J., Frahm, J.M.: Egoglass: Egocentric-view human pose estimation from an eyeglass frame. In: International Conference on 3D Vision (3DV) (2021)
57. Zhu, T., Karlsson, P., Bregler, C.: SimPose: Effectively learning densepose and surface normals of people from simulated data. In: Vedaldi, A., Bischof, H., Brox, T., Frahm, J.-M. (eds.) ECCV 2020. LNCS, vol. 12374, pp. 225–242. Springer, Cham (2020). https://doi.org/10.1007/978-3-030-58526-6_14

Skeleton-Parted Graph Scattering Networks for 3D Human Motion Prediction

Maosen Li[1,2], Siheng Chen[1,2(✉)], Zijing Zhang[3], Lingxi Xie[4], Qi Tian[4], and Ya Zhang[1,2(✉)]

[1] Cooperative Medianet Innovation Center, Shanghai Jiao Tong University, Shanghai, China
{maosen_li,sihengc,ya_zhang}@sjtu.edu.cn
[2] Shanghai AI Laboratory, Shanghai, China
[3] Zhejiang University, Hangzhou, China
[4] Huawei Cloud & AI, Shenzhen, China
tian.qi1@huawei.com

Abstract. Graph convolutional network based methods that model the body-joints' relations, have recently shown great promise in 3D skeleton-based human motion prediction. However, these methods have two critical issues: first, deep graph convolutions filter features within only limited graph spectrums, losing sufficient information in the full band; second, using a single graph to model the whole body underestimates the diverse patterns on various body-parts. To address the first issue, we propose adaptive graph scattering, which leverages multiple trainable band-pass graph filters to decompose pose features into richer graph spectrum bands. To address the second issue, body-parts are modeled separately to learn diverse dynamics, which enables finer feature extraction along the spatial dimensions. Integrating the above two designs, we propose a novel skeleton-parted graph scattering network (SPGSN). The cores of the model are cascaded multi-part graph scattering blocks (MPGSBs), building adaptive graph scattering on diverse body-parts, as well as fusing the decomposed features based on the inferred spectrum importance and body-part interactions. Extensive experiments have shown that SPGSN outperforms state-of-the-art methods by remarkable margins of 13.8%, 9.3% and 2.7% in terms of 3D mean per joint position error (MPJPE) on Human3.6M, CMU Mocap and 3DPW datasets, respectively (The codes are available at https://github.com/MediaBrain-SJTU/SPGSN).

Keywords: Human motion prediction · Adaptive graph scattering · Spatial separation · Bipartite cross-part fusion

Supplementary Information The online version contains supplementary material available at https://doi.org/10.1007/978-3-031-20068-7_2.

© The Author(s), under exclusive license to Springer Nature Switzerland AG 2022
S. Avidan et al. (Eds.): ECCV 2022, LNCS 13666, pp. 18–36, 2022.
https://doi.org/10.1007/978-3-031-20068-7_2

1   Introduction

3D skeleton-based human motion prediction has attracted increasing attention and shown broad applications, such as human-computer interaction [17] and autonomous driving [6]. Human motion prediction aims to generate the future human poses, in form of the 3D coordinates of a few key body joints, given the historical motions. Early attempts develop state models [31,48,55,56] to capture the shallow dynamics. In the deep learning era, more implicit patterns are learned. For example, some recurrent-network-based methods [12,16,43,58] aggregate the states and predict poses frame-by-frame; some feed-forward models [18,32] directly output the predictions without state accumulation.

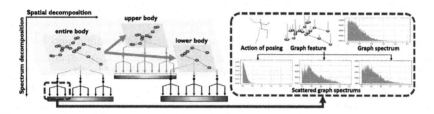

Fig. 1. Feature decomposition along the spatial and spectrum domains. For example, we separate the body into the upper and lower bodies, each of which uses a three-branch graph scattering tree with band-pass filtering to exploit rich graph spectrums.

Recently, numerous graph-convolution-based models [7,9,35,36,38,40,41,53] have achieved remarkable success in motion prediction by explicitly modeling the inherent body relations and extracting spatio-temporal features [27,49,59]. However, further development of graph-based methods encounters two critical issues. First, as long as the graph structure is given, standard graph convolution just filters the features within limited graph spectrum but cannot significantly preserve much richer bands (e.g., smoothness and difference on the graphs) at the same time. However, the pattern learning of human motions needs not only to capture the similarity or consistency of body-joints under the spatial constraints (low-frequency), but also to enhance the difference for diverse representation learning (high-frequency). For example, when the graph edge weights are purely positive or negative, deep graph convolution tends to average the distinct body-joints to be similar but ignores their specific characteristics. Second, existing methods usually use a single graph to model the whole body [40,41], which underestimates diverse movement patterns in different body-parts [18]. For example, the upper and lower bodies have distinct motions, calling for using different graphs to represent them separately.

To address the first issue, we propose the adaptive graph scattering technique, which leverages multiple trainable band-pass graph filters arranged in a tree structure to decompose input features into various graph bands. With the

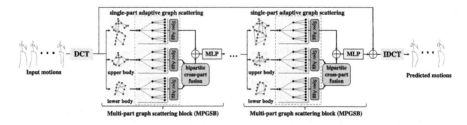

Fig. 2. Architecture of the SPGSN. The SPGSN first applies discrete cosine transform (DCT) to convert the body-joint positions along time to the frequency domain. Then, cascaded multi-part graph scattering blocks (MPGSBs) are built for deep feature extraction. Finally, we build a skip-connection between input and output features and use inverse DCT (IDCT) to recover the temporal information.

mathematically designed band-specific filters, adaptive filter coefficients and feature transform layers, it preserves information from large graph spectrum. To address the second issue, we decompose a body into multiple body-parts, where comprehensive dynamics could be extracted. Therefore, our method achieves finer feature extraction along both graph spectrum and spatial dimensions. Fig. 1 sketches both the spatial and spectrum decomposition. As an example, we show three body-parts: the upper body, the lower body and the entire body. To understand the graph scattering, we show the output graph spectrums on different bands after the corresponding filtering processes.

Integrating the above two designs, we propose a novel *skeleton-parted graph scattering network* (SPGSN). The core of SPGSN is the *multi-part graph scattering block* (MPGSB), consisting of two key modules: the single-part adaptive graph scattering, which uses multi-layer graph scatterings to extract spectrum features for each body-part, and bipartite cross-part fusion, which fuses body-part features based on part interactions. The SPGSN consists of multiple MPGSBs in a sequence; see Fig. 2. Taking the 3D motions as inputs, SPGSN first converts the feature along temporal dimension by discrete cosine transform (DCT) to obtain a more compact representation, which removes the complexity of temporal modeling [40,41]. Followed by the network pipeline, an inverse DCT recovers the responses to the temporal domain. A cross-model skip-connection is built to learn the residual DCT coefficients for stable prediction.

Extensive experiments are conducted for both short-term and long-term motion prediction on large-scale datasets, i.e., Human3.6M [24], CMU Mocap[1] and 3DPW [42]. Our SPGSN significantly outperforms state-of-the-art methods in terms of mean per joint position error (MPJPE). The main contributions of our work are summarized here:

- We propose the skeleton-parted graph scattering networks (SPGSN) to promote finer feature extraction along both graph spectrum and spatial dimen-

---

[1] http://mocap.cs.cmu.edu/.

sions, resulting in more comprehensive feature extraction in large graph spectrum and spatially diverse dynamics learning to improve prediction.

- In SPGSN, we develop the multi-part graph scattering block (MPGSB), which contains single-part adaptive graph scattering and cross-part bipartite fusion to learn rich spectral representation and aggregate diverse part-based features for effective dynamics learning.
- We conduct experiments to verify that our SPGSN significantly outperforms existing works by 13.8%, 9.3% and 2.7% in terms of MPJPE for motion prediction on Human3.6M, CMU Mocap and 3DPW datasets, respectively.

2   Related Works

2.1   Human Motion Prediction

For human motion prediction, early methods are developed based on state models [31,48,55,56]. Recently, some recurrent-network-based models consider the sequential motion states. ERD [12] and Pose-VAE [58] build encoder-decoder in recurrent forms. Structural-RNN [25] transfers information between body-parts recurrently. Res-sup [43], AGED [16] and TPRNN [35] model the pose displacements in RNN models. Besides, some feed-forward networks use spatial convolutions to directly predict the whole sequences without state accumulation [18,32]. Furthermore, considering an articulated pose, some methods exploit the correlations between body-components [4,7,40,41,53]. DMGNN [35] and MSR-GCN [9] build multiscale body graphs to capture local-global features. TrajCues [38] expands motion measurements to improve feature learning. Compared to previous models, our method leverages rich band-pass filters to preserve both smoothness and diversity of body joints and achieve more precise prediction.

2.2   Graph Representation Learning

Graphs explicitly depict the structural format [50,62] of numerous data, such as social networks [34,54], human poses and behaviors [5,11,20,30,39,49,51, 59,60,62–64], and dynamic systems [21,22,27,29,33,61]. As effective methods of graph learning, some studies of the graph neural networks (GNNs) are developed to perform signal filtering based on the graph Laplacian eigen-decomposition [3,10,28,65] or to aggregate vertex information [8,19,37,46,57]. Recently, graph scattering transform (GST) and related models are developed, promoting to capture rich graph spectrum with large bandwidth [15,23,44,47]. GSTs generalize the image-based scattering transforms [1,2,14,52], combining various graph signal filters with theoretically justified designs in terms of spectrum properties. [13,66] develop diffusion wavelets. [44,45] integrate designed scattering filters and parameterized feature learners. [47] expands GSTs on the spatio-temporal domain. In this work, we employ mathematical prior to initialize an adaptive graph scattering with trainable band-pass filters, filter coefficients and feature mapping.

3 Skeleton-Parted Graph Scattering Network

3.1 Problem Formulation

Skeleton-based motion prediction aims to generate the future poses given the historical ones. Mathematically, let $\mathbf{X}^{(t)} \in \mathbb{R}^{M \times 3}$ be a pose carrying the 3D coordinates of M body joints at time t, $\mathbb{X} = [\mathbf{X}^{(1)}, \ldots, \mathbf{X}^{(T)}] \in \mathbb{R}^{T \times M \times 3}$ be a three-mode tensor that concatenates moving poses within T timestamps. In motion prediction, let $\mathbb{X}^- = [\mathbf{X}^{(-T+1)}, \ldots, \mathbf{X}^{(0)}] \in \mathbb{R}^{T \times M \times 3}$ represent T historical poses, $\mathbb{X}^+ = [\mathbf{X}^{(1)}, \ldots, \mathbf{X}^{(\Delta T)}] \in \mathbb{R}^{\Delta T \times M \times 3}$ represent ΔT future poses. We aim to propose a predictor $\mathcal{F}_{\text{pred}}(\cdot)$ to predict the future motions $\widehat{\mathbb{X}}^+ = \mathcal{F}_{\text{pred}}(\mathbb{X}^-)$ to approximate the ground-truth $\mathbb{X}^+$.

3.2 Model Architecture

Here we propose the model architecture and the operation pipeline of the *Skeleton-Parted Graph Scattering Network* (SPGSN), which is sketched in Fig. 2.

Taking the historical motion tensor $\mathbb{X}^- = [\mathbf{X}^{(1)}, \ldots, \mathbf{X}^{(T)}]$ as the input, we first apply the discrete cosine transform (DCT) along the time axis to convert the temporal dynamics of motions into the frequency domain, leading to a compact representation that eliminates the complexity of extra temporal embedding to promote easy learning [40,41]. Mathematically, we reshape $\mathbb{X}^-$ into $\mathcal{X}^- \in \mathbb{R}^{T \times 3M}$ to consider all the joint coordinates at each timestamp independently as the basic units in the spatial domain; then we encode $\mathbf{X}^- = \text{DCT}(\mathcal{X}^-) \in \mathbb{R}^{M' \times C}$, where $M' = 3M$, and C denotes the number of DCT coefficients, also the feature dimension. In this way, although we triple the spatial scale, we compress the long sequence into a compact coefficient representation, resulting in a feature vector, and we do not need the additional sequential feature modeling. Compared to other frequency transformations, DCT fully preserves the temporal smoothness. The Fourier transform and wavelet transform usually introduce complex and multiscale responses, making the downstream modeling more complicated.

In the SPGSN, we develop a deep feed-forward architecture to learn the dynamics from the DCT-formed motion features $\mathbf{X}^-$. The network is constructed with cascaded *multi-part graph scattering blocks* (MPGSBs) as the core components. All MPGSBs do not share parameters, and the input of the following MPGSB is the output of the last one. In each MPGSB, the input motion is first decomposed into different body-parts. For example, Fig. 2 sketches the entire body, the upper and lower bodies, but different body separation strategies could be employed. There are trainable graphs on these body-parts. On each body-part, MPGSB takes a single-part adaptive graph scattering to preserve large-band spectrums of motion representation (see Sect. 4.1). On multiple body-parts, an bipartite cross-part fusion automatically performs body-part fusion based on the learned cross-part interaction for more coordinated motion estimation (see Sect. 4.2). Moreover, we build skip connections across all the MPGSBs, thus we force the SPGSN to capture the feature displacements for stable prediction. At the output end, we apply inverse DCT to recover the temporal information.

4   Multi-part Graph Scattering Block

Here we present the *Multi-Part Graph Scattering Blocks* (MPGSBs). Each MPGSB contains two key modules, **(1) single-part adaptive graph scattering** and **(2) bipartite cross-part fusion**, to extract large graph spectrum from distinct body-parts and fuse body-parts into hybrid representation, respectively.

4.1   Single-part Adaptive Graph Scattering

Given the determined graph topology, the information-aggregation-based graph filtering only captures features in limited spectrums, losing the rich frequency bands of the inputs. To address this problem, the single-part adaptive graph scattering learns sufficient large-band information on each body-part. The single-part adaptive graph scattering contains two main operations: (1) *adaptive graph scattering decomposition* and (2) *adaptive graph spectrum aggregation*, which parses graph spectrum and aggregates the important bands, respectively.

Adaptive Graph Scattering Decomposition. The adaptive graph scattering decomposition forms a tree-structure network with L layers and exponentially increasing tree nodes. These tree nodes perform graph filtering on the motion corresponding to various graph spectral bands.

We consider the first layer for example, and we could expand the design to any layers. Let the DCT-formed pose feature be $\mathbf{X} \in \mathbb{R}^{M' \times C}$, and the adaptive pose graph have adjacency matrix $\mathbf{A} \in \mathbb{R}^{M' \times M'}$. We utilize a series of band-pass graph filters: $\{h_{(k)}(\widetilde{\mathbf{A}}) | k = 0, 1, \ldots, K\}$, which are derived based the graph structure. Note that we have the normalized $\widetilde{\mathbf{A}} = 1/2(\mathbf{I} + \mathbf{A}/\|\mathbf{A}\|_F^2)$ to handles the amplitudes of the trainable elements. Given the filter bank, $\{h_{(k)}(\widetilde{\mathbf{A}})\}_{k=0}^K$, we obtain features $\{\mathbf{H}_{(k)} \in \mathbb{R}^{M' \times C'}\}_{k=0}^K$ through

$$\mathbf{H}_{(k)} = \sigma(h_{(k)}(\widetilde{\mathbf{A}})\mathbf{X}\mathbf{W}_{(k)}), \tag{1}$$

where $\mathbf{W}_{(k)}$ is the trainable weights corresponding to the kth filter, and the nonlinear $\sigma(\cdot)$ (e.g. Tanh) disperses the graph frequency representation [23]. Note that $\widetilde{\mathbf{A}}$ is also a parameterized matrix automatically tuned during training to adapt to the implicit interaction in motion data.

To ensure that various filters work on specific graph spectrums, we initialize $\{h_{(k)}(\widetilde{\mathbf{A}})\}_{k=0}^K$ by leveraging the mathematical priors to constrain their filtering bands. Furthermore, we apply trainable coefficients in $\{h_{(k)}(\widetilde{\mathbf{A}})\}_{k=0}^K$ to adaptively tune spectrum responses based on the predefined guidance; that is,

$$\begin{aligned}
h_{(k)}(\widetilde{\mathbf{A}}) &= \alpha_{(0,0)}\widetilde{\mathbf{A}}, & k &= 0; \\
h_{(k)}(\widetilde{\mathbf{A}}) &= \alpha_{(1,0)}\mathbf{I} + \alpha_{(1,1)}\widetilde{\mathbf{A}}, & k &= 1; \\
h_{(k)}(\widetilde{\mathbf{A}}) &= \sum\nolimits_{j=1}^k \alpha_{(k,j)}\widetilde{\mathbf{A}}^{2^{j-1}}, & k &= 2, \ldots, K,
\end{aligned} \tag{2}$$

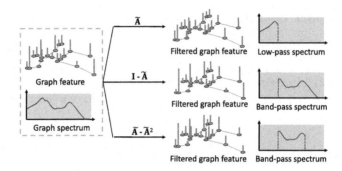

Fig. 3. Sketch of the graph filtering with graph filters. Note that we just show the initialized filters, and we apply trainable coefficients to achieve more flexible filtering.

where $\alpha_{(k,j)}$ is the trainable coefficient. For $k = 0$, we initialize $\alpha_{(0,0)} = 1$; for $k > 0$, we set $\alpha_{(k,k-1)} = 1$, $\alpha_{(k,k)} = -1$ and any other $\alpha_{(k,j)} = 0$. Notably, for $k > 0$, we could approximately obtain a series of graph wavelets to emphasize different frequencies. For example, we initialize $h_3(\widetilde{\mathbf{A}}) = 0\widetilde{\mathbf{A}} + \widetilde{\mathbf{A}}^2 - \widetilde{\mathbf{A}}^4$ to depict the joint difference under the 2-order relations at the beginning. The power 2^{j-1} are utilized based on diffusion wavelets, theoretically promoting optimal localization [13]. Besides, the intuition of this design is sketched in Fig. 3. Suppose all the edge weights are positive, $h_0(\widetilde{\mathbf{A}})$ only preserves the low-frequency to enhance smoothness; the other filters obtain the band-pass features and promote joints' varieties. The real feature responses of the graph scattering during model inference is visualized in Appendix to analyze this module.

Plugging Eqs. (2) to (1), we output the spectrum channels $\{\mathbf{H}_{(k)}\}$. At the next layer of the graph scattering, we repeat Eq. (1) on each $\mathbf{H}_{(k)}$. Thus, each non-leaf feature has $K + 1$ new branches; eventually, the output has $(K + 1)^L$ channels corresponding to different spectrums.

Adaptive Graph Spectrum Aggregation. To abstract the key information from the $(K + 1)^L$ graph scattering responses and provide information to the downstream MPGSB, we propose the adaptive graph spectrum aggregation to fuse the spectral channels based on the inferred spectrum scores, which measure the importance of each channel over the whole spectrum. Given the output channels $\{\mathbf{H}_{(k)}\}$, the spectrum aggregation is formulated as

$$\mathbf{H} = \sum_{k=0}^{(K+1)^L} \omega_k \mathbf{H}_{(k)} \in \mathbb{R}^{M' \times C'}, \qquad (3)$$

where ω_k is the inferred spectrum importance score of the kth feature $\mathbf{H}_{(k)}$, which is computed through

$$\omega_k = \frac{\exp\left(f_2\left(\tanh\left(f_1\left([\mathbf{H}_{\mathrm{sp}}, \mathbf{H}_{(k)}]\right)\right)\right)\right)}{\sum_{j=0}^{(K+1)^L} \exp\left(f_2\left(\tanh\left(f_1\left([\mathbf{H}_{\mathrm{sp}}, \mathbf{H}_{(j)}]\right)\right)\right)\right)}, \qquad (4)$$

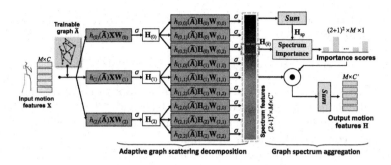

Fig. 4. A sketch of single-part adaptive graph scattering.

where $f_1(\cdot)$ and $f_2(\cdot)$ are MLPs, and $[\cdot, \cdot]$ is concatenation along feature dimensions. $\mathbf{H}_{\mathrm{sp}} \in \mathbb{R}^{M' \times C'}$ carries the whole graph spectrum, which is

$$\mathbf{H}_{\mathrm{sp}} = \mathrm{ReLU}\left(\frac{1}{(K+1)^L} \sum\nolimits_{k=0}^{(K+1)^L} \mathbf{H}_{(k)} \mathbf{W}_{\mathrm{sp}}\right), \tag{5}$$

where $\mathbf{W}_{\mathrm{sp}}$ denotes trainable weights and $\mathrm{ReLU}(\cdot)$ is the ReLU activation. $\mathbf{H}_{\mathrm{sp}}$ employs the embedded spectrum to benefit the representation understanding.

For clearer understanding, Fig. 4 sketches an examplar architecture of the single-part adaptive graph scattering ($L = 2$ and $K = 2$), where we briefly note various filtering with different subscripts. For multiple body-parts, we leverage shared parameters but different pose graphs on them to reduce the model complexity, since different body-parts carry the same feature modality but different graph views. In this way, we can capture the diverse features that reflects rich structural information.

4.2 Bipartite Cross-Part Fusion

To combine the diverse and hybrid features learned from different body-parts, we propose a bipartite cross-part fusion module based on body-part interactions, which allow the isolated single-part features to adapt to each other, leading to more coordinated and reasonable patterns on the whole body.

In this paper, we mainly consider to separate the body into two parts besides the entire body, because according to the experiences, the separation of the two parts (e.g. separating as upper and lower bodies or left and right bodies) can distinguish the different global movement patterns and explore their interactions to reflect the movement coordination. Meanwhile, the two-part separation needs only one interaction-based fusion, which reduces the model complexity. As an example, we consider the upper-lower-separation. We first model their cross-part influence, to reflect the implicit upper-lower interactions. Two directed bipartite graphs are adaptively constructed to propagate influence from the upper to the lower bodies and vice versa. Here we present the 'upper-to-lower' graph as an example. Let the joint features on the upper body and lower body be $\mathbf{H}_{\uparrow} \in$

$\mathbb{R}^{M_\uparrow \times C'}$ and $\mathbf{H}_\downarrow \in \mathbb{R}^{M_\downarrow \times C'}$, respectively, where $M_\uparrow$ and $M_\downarrow$ are the numbers of nodes in these two parts; we calculate the upper-to-lower affinity matrix through

$$\mathbf{A}_{\uparrow 2 \downarrow} = \mathrm{softmax}(f_\uparrow(\mathbf{H}_\uparrow) f_\downarrow(\mathbf{H}_\downarrow)^\top) \in [0,1]^{M_\uparrow \times M_\downarrow}, \tag{6}$$

where $\mathrm{softmax}(\cdot)$ is the softmax function across rows to normalize the affinity effects and enhance the strong correlations; $f_\uparrow(\cdot)$ and $f_\downarrow(\cdot)$ are two embedding networks. Each column of $\mathbf{A}_{\uparrow 2 \downarrow}$ reflects the influence levels of all the upper-body-joints to the corresponding lower-body-joint.

Given the $\mathbf{A}_{\uparrow 2 \downarrow}$, we update the lower body via

$$\mathbf{H}'_\downarrow = \mathbf{H}_\downarrow + \mathbf{A}_{\uparrow 2 \downarrow}^\top \mathbf{H}_\uparrow, \tag{7}$$

where the new lower body aggregates the information from the upper body by emphasizing the influence across body-parts. In the similar manner, we also update the upper body based on the bipartite lower-to-upper graph.

Finally, given the updated upper and lower body, $\mathbf{H}'_\uparrow$ and $\mathbf{H}'_\downarrow$, we fuse them on the whole body and obtain the hybrid feature $\mathbf{H}' \in \mathbb{R}^{M' \times C'}$ by

$$\mathbf{H}' = \mathrm{MLP}(\mathbf{H} + (\mathbf{H}'_\uparrow \oplus \mathbf{H}'_\downarrow)), \tag{8}$$

where $\oplus : \mathbb{R}^{M_\uparrow \times C'} \times \mathbb{R}^{M_\downarrow \times C'} \to \mathbb{R}^{M' \times C'}$ places joints from different body-parts to align with the original body. $\mathrm{MLP}(\cdot)$ further embeds the fused body. In this way, the output features carry the comprehensive graph spectrum and multi-part representation to promote motion prediction.

4.3   Loss Function

To train the proposed SPGSN, we define the loss function. Suppose that we take N samples in a mini-batch as inputs, and let the nth ground-truth and predicted motion sample be $\mathbb{X}_n^+$ and $\widehat{\mathbb{X}}_n^+$. The loss function $\mathcal{L}$ is defined as the average ℓ_2 distance between the targets and predictions:

$$\mathcal{L} = \frac{1}{N} \sum_{n=1}^{N} \|\mathbb{X}_n^+ - \widehat{\mathbb{X}}_n^+\|^2. \tag{9}$$

All the trainable parameters in our SPGSN are tuned end-to-end, including the body graph structures, adaptive filter coefficients and the network weights.

5   Experiments

5.1   Datasets

Dataset 1: Human 3.6M (H3.6M). There are 7 subjects performing 15 classes of actions in H3.6M [24], and each subject has 22 body joints. All sequences are downsampled by two along time. Following previous paradigms [9], the models are trained on the segmented clips in the 6 subjects and tested on the clips in the 5th subject.

Dataset 2: CMU Mocap. CMU Mocap consists of 5 general classes of actions. On each pose, we use 25 joints in the 3D space. Following [9,41], we use 8 actions: 'basketball', 'basketball signal', 'directing traffic', 'jumping', 'running', 'soccer', 'walking' and 'washing window'.

Dataset 3: 3D Pose in the Wild (3DPW). 3DPW [42] contains more than 51k frames with 3D poses for indoor and outdoor activities. We adopt the training, test and validation separation suggested by the official setting. Each subject has 23 joints. The frame rate of the motions is 30Hz.

5.2 Model and Experimental Settings

Implementation Details. We implement SPGSN with PyTorch 1.4 on one NVIDIA Tesla V100 GPU. We set 10 MPGSBs to form the entire model. In each MPGSB, the single-part adaptive graph scattering has $L = 2$ layers of graph scattering decomposition, and the filter order $K = 2$. The hidden dimension in a MPGSB is 256. We use Adam optimizer [26] to train the SPGSN with batch size 32. The learning rate is 0.001 with a 0.96 decay for every two epochs. To obtain more generalized evaluation with lower test bias, we utilize all the clips in

Table 1. Prediction MPJPEs of various models for short-term motion prediction on 5 representative actions in H3.6M. We also introduce an SPGSN variant called SPGSN (1body), which only considers the entire non-separated bodies. Since the original STS-GCN [53] uses a different protocol from all the other methods, we update its code for a fair comparison; see results in STSGCN*.

Motion	Walking				Eating				Smoking				Discussion				Directions			
Millisecond	80	160	320	400	80	160	320	400	80	160	320	400	80	160	320	400	80	160	320	400
Res-sup [43]	29.36	50.82	76.03	81.52	16.84	30.60	56.92	68.65	22.96	42.64	70.24	83.68	32.94	61.18	90.92	96.19	35.36	57.27	76.30	87.67
CSM [32]	21.70	43.56	66.29	75.48	14.50	26.13	47.47	55.63	19.42	37.70	62.49	68.55	26.35	53.41	79.12	83.01	27.07	44.72	63.94	75.37
SkelNet [18]	20.49	34.36	59.64	68.76	11.80	22.38	39.88	48.11	11.33	23.71	45.30	52.85	21.79	40.24	65.93	77.91	16.06	27.12	62.97	72.75
DMGNN [35]	17.32	30.67	54.56	65.20	10.96	21.39	36.18	43.88	8.97	17.62	32.05	40.30	17.33	34.78	61.03	69.80	13.14	24.62	64.68	81.86
Traj-GCN [41]	12.29	23.03	39.77	46.12	8.36	16.90	33.19	40.70	7.94	16.24	31.90	38.90	12.50	27.40	58.51	71.68	8.97	19.87	43.35	53.74
HisRep [40]	10.53	19.96	34.88	42.05	7.39	15.53	31.26	38.58	7.17	14.54	28.83	35.67	10.89	25.19	56.15	69.30	7.77	18.23	41.34	51.61
MSR-GCN [9]	12.16	22.65	38.64	45.24	8.39	17.05	33.03	40.43	8.02	16.27	31.32	38.15	11.98	26.76	57.08	69.74	8.61	19.65	43.28	53.82
STSGCN* [53]	16.26	24.63	40.06	45.94	14.32	22.14	37.91	45.03	13.10	20.20	37.71	44.65	14.33	24.28	52.62	68.53	14.24	24.27	44.24	53.21
SPGSN (1body)	**10.13**	19.51	35.52	44.67	7.13	15.02	31.87	41.18	6.83	13.94	28.77	36.78	10.42	23.90	54.13	69.99	7.38	17.48	40.54	53.09
SPGSN	10.14	**19.39**	**34.80**	**41.47**	**7.07**	**14.85**	**30.48**	**37.91**	**6.72**	**13.79**	**27.97**	**34.61**	**10.37**	**23.79**	53.61	**67.12**	**7.35**	**17.15**	**39.80**	**50.25**

Table 2. MPJPEs for short-term motion prediction on other 9 actions in H3.6M.

Motion	Greeting				Phoning				Posing				Purchases				Sitting			
Millisecond	80	160	320	400	80	160	320	400	80	160	320	400	80	160	320	400	80	160	320	400
Res-sup [43]	34.46	63.36	124.60	142.50	37.96	69.32	115.00	126.73	36.10	69.12	130.46	157.08	36.33	60.30	86.53	95.92	42.55	81.40	134.70	151.78
DMGNN [35]	23.30	50.32	107.30	132.10	12.47	25.77	48.08	58.29	15.27	29.27	71.54	96.65	21.35	38.71	75.67	92.74	11.92	25.11	44.59	50.20
Traj-GCN [41]	18.65	38.68	77.74	93.39	10.24	21.02	42.54	52.30	13.66	29.89	66.62	84.05	15.60	32.78	65.72	79.25	10.62	21.90	46.33	57.91
MSR-GCN [9]	16.48	36.95	77.32	93.38	10.10	20.74	41.51	51.26	12.79	29.38	66.95	85.01	14.75	32.39	66.13	79.64	10.53	21.99	46.26	57.80
STSGCN* [53]	15.02	**30.70**	**67.11**	87.63	14.88	21.40	46.55	52.03	15.01	25.69	**58.38**	**73.08**	15.26	**26.26**	63.45	**74.25**	15.19	22.95	46.82	58.34
SPGSN (1body)	15.16	33.61	71.89	88.74	8.78	18.50	39.85	51.53	10.92	25.46	61.38	78.87	12.78	28.86	62.59	77.01	**9.25**	19.58	43.47	56.32
SPGSN	**14.64**	32.59	70.64	**86.44**	**8.67**	**18.32**	**38.73**	**48.46**	**10.73**	**25.31**	59.91	76.46	**12.75**	28.58	**61.01**	74.38	9.28	**19.40**	**42.25**	53.56
Motion	Sitting down				Taking photo				Waiting				Walking together				Average			
Millisecond	80	160	320	400	80	160	320	400	80	160	320	400	80	160	320	400	80	160	320	400
Res-sup [43]	47.28	85.95	145.75	168.86	26.10	47.61	81.40	94.73	30.62	57.82	106.22	121.45	26.79	50.07	80.16	92.23	34.66	61.97	101.08	115.49
DMGNN [35]	14.95	32.88	77.06	93.00	13.61	28.95	45.99	58.76	12.20	24.17	59.62	77.54	14.34	26.67	50.08	63.22	16.95	33.62	65.90	79.65
Traj-GCN [41]	16.14	31.12	61.47	75.46	9.88	20.89	44.95	56.58	11.43	23.99	50.06	61.48	10.47	21.04	38.47	45.19	12.68	26.06	52.27	63.51
MSR-GCN [9]	16.10	31.63	62.45	76.84	9.89	21.01	44.56	56.30	10.68	23.06	48.25	59.23	10.56	20.92	37.40	43.85	12.11	25.56	51.64	62.93
STSGCN* [53]	16.70	28.05	**56.15**	72.03	14.61	24.84	45.98	61.79	16.30	24.33	48.12	59.79	11.38	22.39	39.90	47.48	15.34	25.52	50.64	60.61
SPGSN (1body)	14.34	28.10	58.23	74.44	**8.72**	18.95	42.62	55.22	9.24	20.02	43.80	56.80	**8.91**	18.46	34.88	42.98	10.55	22.63	48.21	60.96
SPGSN	**14.18**	**27.72**	56.75	**70.74**	8.79	**18.90**	**41.49**	**52.66**	**9.21**	**19.79**	**43.10**	**54.14**	8.94	**18.19**	**33.84**	**40.88**	**10.44**	**22.33**	**47.07**	**58.26**

the 5th subject of H3.6M and the test folder of CMU Mocap, instead of testing on a few samples picked from the test sequences like in [16, 32, 35, 41, 43].

Baselines. We compare our model to many state-of-the-art methods, including the RNN-based Res-sup [43], feed-fordward-based CSM [32], SkelNet [18], and graph-based Traj-GCN [41], DMGNN [35], HisRep [40], STSGCN [53] and MSR-GCN [9]. We test these methods under the same protocol.

Evaluation Metrics. We use the Mean Per Joint Position Error (MPJPE), where we record the average ℓ_2 distance between predicted joints and target ones in 3D Euclidean space at each prediction timestamp. Compared to previous mean angle error (MAE) [35, 43], the MPJPE relfects larger degrees of freedom of human poses and covers larger ranges of errors for clearer comparison.

5.3   Comparison to State-of-the-Art Methods

To validate SPGSN, we show the quantitative results for both short-term and long-term motion prediction on H3.6M, CMU Mocap and 3DPW. We also illustrate the predicted samples for qualitative evaluation.

Table 3. Prediction MPJPEs of methods for long-term prediction on 8 actions in H3.6M and the average MPJPEs across all the actions.

Motion	Walking		Eating		Smoking		Directions		Phoning		Sitting		TakingPhoto		Waiting		Average	
Millisecond	560	1k	560	1k	560	1k	560	1k	560	1k	560	1k	560	1k	560	1k	560	1k
Res-sup. [43]	81.73	100.68	79.87	100.20	94.83	137.44	110.05	152.48	143.92	186.79	166.20	185.16	107.03	162.38	126.70	153.14	129.19	164.96
Traj-GCN [41]	54.05	59.75	53.39	77.75	50.74	72.62	71.01	101.79	69.55	104.19	77.63	118.36	78.73	120.06	79.08	107.32	81.07	113.01
DMGNN [35]	71.36	95.82	58.11	86.66	50.85	72.15	102.06	135.75	71.33	108.37	75.51	115.44	78.38	123.65	85.54	113.68	93.57	127.62
MSR-GCN [9]	52.72	63.05	52.54	77.11	49.45	71.64	71.18	100.59	68.28	104.36	78.19	120.02	77.94	121.87	76.33	106.25	81.13	114.18
STSGCN* [53]	50.64	64.74	56.46	75.08	55.55	74.13	75.61	109.89	79.19	109.88	82.32	119.83	87.70	119.79	78.41	108.04	80.66	113.33
SPGSN	**46.89**	**53.59**	**49.76**	**73.39**	**46.68**	**68.62**	**70.05**	**100.52**	**66.70**	**102.52**	**75.00**	116.24	**75.58**	**118.22**	**73.50**	**103.62**	**77.40**	**109.64**

Table 4. Prediction MPJPEs of methods on CMU Mocap for both short-term and long-term prediction, as well as the average prediction results across all the actions.

Motion	Basketball					Basketball Signal					Directing Traffic					Jumping				
Millisecond	80	160	320	400	1000	80	160	320	400	1000	80	160	320	400	1000	80	160	320	400	1000
Res-sup. [43]	15.45	26.88	43.51	49.23	88.73	20.17	32.98	42.75	44.65	60.57	20.52	40.58	75.38	90.36	153.12	26.85	48.07	93.50	108.90	162.84
DMGNN [35]	15.57	28.72	59.01	73.05	138.62	5.03	9.28	20.21	26.23	52.04	10.21	20.90	41.55	52.28	111.23	31.97	54.32	96.66	119.92	224.63
Traj-GCN [41]	11.68	21.26	40.99	50.78	97.99	3.33	6.25	13.58	17.98	54.00	6.92	13.69	30.30	39.97	114.16	17.18	32.37	60.12	72.55	127.41
MST-GCN [9]	10.28	18.94	**37.68**	**47.03**	**86.96**	3.03	5.68	12.35	16.26	47.91	5.92	12.09	28.36	38.04	111.04	14.99	28.66	**55.86**	69.05	124.79
STSGCN [53]	12.56	23.04	41.92	50.33	94.17	4.72	6.69	14.53	17.88	49.52	6.41	12.38	29.05	38.86	109.42	17.52	31.48	58.74	72.06	127.40
SPGSN	**10.24**	**18.54**	38.22	48.68	89.58	**2.91**	**5.25**	**11.31**	**15.01**	**47.31**	**5.52**	**11.16**	**25.48**	**37.06**	**108.14**	**14.93**	**28.16**	56.72	**71.16**	125.20

Motion	Soccer					Walking					Washing Window					Average				
Millisecond	80	160	320	400	1000	80	160	320	400	1000	80	160	320	400	1000	80	160	320	400	1000
Res-sup. [43]	17.75	31.30	52.55	61.40	107.37	44.35	76.66	126.83	151.43	194.33	22.84	44.71	86.78	104.68	202.73	24.21	43.75	76.19	88.93	139.00
DMGNN [35]	14.86	25.29	52.21	65.42	111.90	9.57	15.53	26.03	30.37	67.01	7.93	14.68	33.34	44.24	82.84	14.07	24.44	45.90	55.45	104.33
Traj-GCN [41]	13.33	24.00	43.77	53.20	108.26	6.62	10.74	17.40	20.35	**34.41**	5.96	11.62	24.77	31.63	66.85	9.94	18.02	33.55	40.95	81.85
MSR-GCN [9]	10.92	19.50	37.05	46.38	**99.32**	**6.31**	10.30	17.64	21.12	39.70	5.49	11.07	25.05	32.51	71.30	8.72	15.83	30.57	38.10	79.01
STSGCN [53]	13.49	25.24	39.87	51.58	109.63	7.18	10.99	17.84	22.61	44.12	6.79	12.10	24.92	36.66	69.48	10.80	18.19	31.18	41.05	81.76
SPGSN	**10.86**	**18.99**	**35.05**	**45.16**	99.51	6.32	**10.21**	**16.34**	**20.19**	34.83	**4.86**	**9.44**	**21.50**	**28.37**	**65.08**	**8.30**	**14.80**	**28.64**	**36.96**	**77.82**

Short-Term Prediction. Short-term motion prediction aims to predict the poses within 400 ms. First, on H3.6M, Table 1 presents the MPJPEs of SPGSN and many previous methods on 5 representative actions at multiple prediction timestamps. We see that, SPGSN obtains superior performance at most timestamps; also, learning the diverse patterns from separated body-parts, SPGSN outperforms the variant SPGSN (1body) that only uses the entire human body. Besides, Table 2 presents the MPJPEs on other 9 actions in H3.6M and the average MPJPEs over the dataset. Compared to the baselines, SPGSN achieves much lower MPJPEs by 9.3% in average. Notably, the original STSGCN [53] uses a different protocol from all the other methods, we update its code for a fair comparison; see STSGCN* and more details are in Appendix.

Long-Term Prediction. Long-term motion prediction aims to predict the poses over 400 milliseconds, which is challenging due to the pose variation and elusive human intention. Table 3 presents the prediction MPJPEs of various methods at the 560 ms and 1000 ms on 8 actions in H3.6M. We see that, SPGSN achieves more effective prediction on most actions and has lower MPJPEs by 3.6% in average. The results on the other actions are shown in Appendix.

We also test the SPGSN for both short-term and long-term prediction on CMU Mocap. Table 4 shows the MPJPEs on 7 actions within the future 1000 ms. We see that, SPGSN outperforms the baselines on most actions, and the average prediction MPJPE is much lower by 9.3% than previous methods.

Furthermore, we test the SPGSN on 3DPW dataset for both short-term and long-term motion prediction. We present the average MPJPEs across all the test samples at different prediction steps in Table 5. Compared to the state-of-the-art methods, SPGSN reduces the MPJPE by 2.7% in average.

Table 5. The average prediction MPJPEs across the test set of 3DPW at various prediction time steps.

Millisecond	Average MAE							
	100	200	400	500	600	800	900	1000
Res-sup. [43]	102.28	113.24	173.94	185.35	191.47	201.39	205.12	210.58
CSM [32]	57.83	71.53	124.01	142.47	155.16	174.87	183.40	187.06
Traj-GCN [41]	16.28	35.62	67.46	80.19	**90.36**	106.79	113.93	117.84
DMGNN [35]	17.80	37.11	70.38	83.02	94.12	109.67	117.25	123.93
HisRep [40]	15.88	35.14	66.82	78.49	93.55	107.63	114.59	114.75
MSR-GCN [9]	15.70	33.48	65.02	77.59	93.81	108.15	114.88	116.31
STSGCN [53]	18.32	37.79	67.51	77.34	92.75	106.65	113.14	112.22
SPGSN	**15.39**	**32.91**	**64.54**	**76.23**	91.62	**103.98**	**109.41**	**111.05**

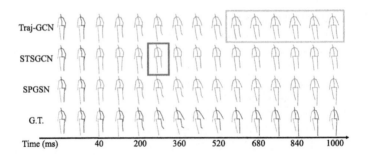

Fig. 5. Prediction samples of different methods on action 'Walking' of H3.6M for long-term prediction. The predictions of Traj-GCN collapse to static 'mean poses' after the 600th ms (orange box); STSGCN starts to suffer from large errors at the 280th ms (red box); SPGSN completes the action more accurately.

Prediction Visualization. To qualitatively evaluate the prediction, we compare the synthesized samples of SPGSN to those of Traj-GCN and STSGCN on H3.6M. Figure 5 illustrates the future poses of 'Walking' in 1000 ms with the frame interval of 80 ms. Compared to the baselines, SPGSN completes the action more accurately. The predictions of Traj-GCN collapse to static 'mean poses' after the 600th ms (orange box). STSGCN starts to suffer from large errors at the 280th ms (red box). See more results in Appendix.

5.4   Model Analysis

Numbers of MPGSBs and Graph Scattering Layers. We test the SPGSN frameworks with various numbers of MPGSBs (8-11) and layers of adaptive graph scattering (1-3) on H3.6M for both short-term and long-term prediction. Table 6 presents the average MPJPEs of different architectures. The SPGSN with 10 MPGSBs and 2 layers of adaptive graph scattering obtains the lowest MPJPEs. The models have stable prediction for 9-11 MSGCBs, and 2 or 3 graph scattering layers usually show better results than only using one layer.

Numbers of Spectral Channels. We investigate the numbers of graph scattering decomposition channels, K, in each MPGSB. We test the model that applies 1 to 5 channels on H3.6M; see the average MPJPEs in Table 7. We see that 3 channels lead to the lowest prediction errors. The model with only 1 channel cannot capture the sufficiently large spectrums and rich information. Five channels cause much heavy model and over-fitting.

Table 6. Performance analysis of SPGSNs with different numbers of graph scattering blocks and graph scattering layers.

	Scatter-layers			Average MPJPE					
MPGSB number	1	2	3	80	160	320	400	560	1000
8	✓			11.34	23.86	49.66	61.22	80.32	114.26
		✓		11.05	23.27	48.58	59.97	78.81	112.29
			✓	10.88	23.12	48.43	59.76	79.32	112.86
9	✓			10.91	23.22	48.39	59.63	79.31	113.09
		✓		10.58	22.56	47.49	58.73	78.49	112.06
			✓	**10.40**	22.33	47.29	58.58	77.79	110.55
10	✓			10.48	22.41	47.53	58.78	78.81	111.29
		✓		10.44	**22.33**	**47.07**	**58.26**	**77.40**	**109.64**
			✓	10.46	22.46	47.25	58.48	77.86	110.64
11	✓			10.51	22.39	47.24	58.42	77.91	110.35
		✓		10.57	22.53	47.15	58.49	79.06	112.05
			✓	10.66	22.69	47.43	58.66	79.18	112.83

Table 7. SPGSNs with different numbers of graph scattering channels on each non-leaf scattering feature.

	Average MAE					
Channel numbers ($K+1$)	80	160	320	400	560	1000
1	12.03	25.87	51.40	61.98	80.52	113.15
2	10.50	22.39	47.40	58.44	77.53	110.35
3	**10.44**	**22.33**	**47.07**	**58.26**	77.40	**109.64**
4	10.47	22.41	47.23	58.32	**77.37**	109.89
5	10.57	22.46	47.38	58.46	77.66	110.52

Bipartite Cross-Part Interaction. To investigate the proposed body-part separation and cross-part interaction, we compare the SPGSN with two model variants. First, SPGSN that directly aligns the independent part features on the entire body; second, SPGSN separates the body into left and right parts. We test these variants on H3.6M; see Table 8. The SPGSN with upper-lower interaction and fusion consistently outperforms the baselines. For SPGSN (no CrossPart), due to the lack of mutual influence, it is hard to ensure higher coordination and rationality. As for SPGSN (left-right), given the interaction of body-parts, the prediction error is reduced, while the upper-lower separation promotes more special dynamics than the left-right separation due to the movement diversity.

To verify the inferred interactions between the upper and lower bodies, we visualize the learned bipartite graphs on different actions. We show the upper-to-lower and lower-to-upper graphs on 'walking' and 'posing', where we plot the

Table 8. Comparison between SPGSN and its variants, including the model without cross-part fusion, i.e., SPGSN (no CrossPart), and the model separating the body into left and right parts, i.e., SPGSN (left-right).

Prediction time	80	160	320	400	560	1000
SPGSN (no CrossPart)	10.55	22.63	48.21	60.96	78.02	111.74
SPGSN (left-right)	10.47	22.51	47.48	58.85	77.79	110.16
SPGSN (ours, upper-lower)	**10.44**	**22.33**	**47.07**	**58.26**	**77.40**	**109.64**

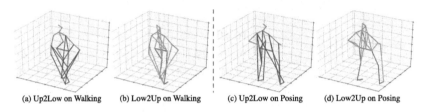

(a) Up2Low on Walking (b) Low2Up on Walking (c) Up2Low on Posing (d) Low2Up on Posing

Fig. 6. Inferred directed bipartite cross-part graphs on posing and walking. We denote the upper-to-lower and the lower-to-upper graphs as 'Up2Low' and 'Low2Up'.

Table 9. Comparison of running time, model sizes and MPJPE

	DMGNN [35]	Traj-GCN [41]	MSR-GCN [9]	STSGCN [53]	HisRep [40]	SPGSN (Ours)
RunTime (ms)	33.13	26.35	42.36	17.6	31.57	30.07
ParaSize (M)	4.82	2.56	6.30	0.04	3.18	5.66
FLOPs (M)	2.82	0.49	3.89	1.35	3.08	1.77
MPJPE	49.03	38.63	38.06	38.03	36.41	**34.53**

edges whose weights are larger than 0.25; see Fig. 6. Different actions reflect different bipartite graphs: walking connects the contralateral hands and feet on both upper-to-lower and lower-to-upper graphs; posing connects the ipsilateral joints on the two body-parts, which delivers near-torso features to the body.

Efficiency Analysis. To verify the applicability of SPGSN, we compare SPGSN to existing methods in terms of the running times, parameter numbers, FLOPs and prediction results in short-term prediction on H3.6M (Table 9). SPGSN has the lowest MPJPE and efficient running based on the parallel computation. SPGSN also has the acceptable model size.

6   Conclusion

We propose a novel skeleton graph scattering network for human motion prediction, which contains cascaded multi-part graph scattering blocks (MPGSBs) to capture fine representation along both spatial and spectrum dimensions. Each MPGSB builds adaptive graph scattering on separated body-parts. In this way, the model carries large graph spectrum and considers the distinct part-based dynamics for precise motion prediction. Experiments reveal the effectiveness of our model for motion prediction on Human3.6M, CMU Mocap and 3DPW datasets.

Acknowledgements. This work is supported by the National Key Research and Development Program of China (2020YFB1406801), the National Natural Science Foundation of China under Grant (62171276), 111 plan (BP0719010), STCSM (18DZ2270700, 21511100900), State Key Laboratory of UHD Video and Audio Production and Presentation.

References

1. Andén, J., Mallat, S.: Deep scattering spectrum. IEEE Trans. Signal Process. **62**(16), 4114–4128 (2014)
2. Bruna, J., Mallat, S.: Invariant scattering convolution networks. IEEE Trans. Pattern Anal. Mach. Intell. **35**(8), 1872–1886 (2013)
3. Bruna, J., Zaremba, W., Szlam, A., LeCun, Y.: Spectral networks and locally connected networks on graphs. In: ICLR (Apr 2014)
4. Cai, Y., Huang, L., Wang, Y., Cham, T.-J., Cai, J., Yuan, J., Liu, J., Yang, X., Zhu, Y., Shen, X., Liu, D., Liu, J., Thalmann, N.M.: Learning progressive joint propagation for human motion prediction. In: Vedaldi, A., Bischof, H., Brox, T., Frahm, J.-M. (eds.) ECCV 2020. LNCS, vol. 12352, pp. 226–242. Springer, Cham (2020). https://doi.org/10.1007/978-3-030-58571-6_14
5. Chen, G., Song, X., Zeng, H., Jiang, S.: Scene recognition with prototype-agnostic scene layout. IEEE Trans. Image Process. **29**, 5877–5888 (2020)
6. Chen, S., Liu, B., Feng, C., Vallespi-Gonzalez, C., Wellington, C.: 3d point cloud processing and learning for autonomous driving. IEEE Sig. Process. Mag. **38**, 68–86 (2020)
7. Cui, Q., Sun, H., Yang, F.: Learning dynamic relationships for 3d human motion prediction. In: CVPR (June 2020)
8. Dai, H., Dai, B., Song, L.: Discriminative embeddings of latent variable models for structured data. In: ICML (June 2016)
9. Dang, L., Nie, Y., Long, C., Zhang, Q., Li, G.: Msr-gcn: Multi-scale residual graph convolution networks for human motion prediction. In: Proceedings of the IEEE/CVF International Conference on Computer Vision (ICCV), pp. 11467–11476 (October 2021)
10. Defferrard, M., Bresson, X., Vandergheynst, P.: Convolutional neural networks on graphs with fast localized spectral filtering. In: NeurIPS (Dec 2016)
11. Fan, L., Wang, W., Huang, S., Tang, X., Zhu, S.C.: Understanding human gaze communication by spatio-temporal graph reasoning. In: ICCV (Oct 2019)
12. Fragkiadaki, K., Levine, S., Felsen, P., Malik, J.: Recurrent network models for human dynamics. In: ICCV, pp. 4346–4354 (December 2015)
13. Gama, F., Ribeiro, A., Bruna, J.: Diffusion scattering transforms on graphs. In: ICLR (May 2019)
14. Gama, F., Ribeiro, A., Bruna, J.: Stability of graph scattering transforms. In: NeurIPS, vol. 32 (December 2019)
15. Gao, F., Wolf, G., Hirn, M.: Geometric scattering for graph data analysis. In: ICML, pp. 2122–2131 (June 2019)

16. Gui, L.-Y., Wang, Y.-X., Liang, X., Moura, J.M.F.: Adversarial geometry-aware human motion prediction. In: Ferrari, V., Hebert, M., Sminchisescu, C., Weiss, Y. (eds.) ECCV 2018. LNCS, vol. 11208, pp. 823–842. Springer, Cham (2018). https://doi.org/10.1007/978-3-030-01225-0_48

17. Gui, L., Zhang, K., Wang, Y., Liang, X., Moura, J., Veloso, M.: Teaching robots to predict human motion. In: The IEEE/RSJ International Conference on Intelligent Robots and Systems (IROS) (Oct 2018)

18. Guo, X., Choi, J.: Human motion prediction via learning local structure representations and temporal dependencies. In: Proceedings of the AAAI Conference on Artificial Intelligence, vol. 33, pp. 2580–2587 (2019)

19. Hamilton, W., Ying, Z., Leskovec, J.: Inductive representation learning on large graphs. In: NeurIPS (Dec 2017)

20. Hu, G., Cui, B., Yu, S.: Skeleton-based action recognition with synchronous local and non-local spatio-temporal learning and frequency attention. In: ICME (July 2019)

21. Hu, Y., Chen, S., Zhang, Y., Gu, X.: Collaborative motion prediction via neural motion message passing. In: CVPR (June 2020)

22. Huang, Y., Bi, H., Li, Z., Mao, T., Wang, Z.: Stgat: Modeling spatial-temporal interactions for human trajectory prediction. In: ICCV, pp. 6272–6281 (2019)

23. Ioannidis, V.N., Chen, S., Giannakis, G.B.: Pruned graph scattering transforms. In: ICLR (Apr 2020)

24. Ionescu, C., Papava, D., Olaru, V., Sminchisescu, C.: Human3.6m: Large scale datasets and predictive methods for 3d human sensing in natural environments. IEEE Trans. Pattern Anal. Mach. Intell. **36**(7), 1325–1339 (2013)

25. Jain, A., Zamir, A., Savarese, S., Saxena, A.: Structural-rnn: Deep learning on spatio-temporal graphs. In: CVPR, pp. 5308–5317 (June 2016)

26. Kingma, D.P., Ba, J.: Adam: A method for stochastic optimization. arXiv:1412.6980 (2014)

27. Kipf, T., Fetaya, E., Wang, K.C., Welling, M., Zemel, R.: Neural relational inference for interacting systems. In: ICML. pp. 2688–2697 (2018)

28. Kipf, T., Welling, M.: Semi-supervised classification with graph convolutional networks. In: ICLR (Apr 2017)

29. Kosaraju, V., Sadeghian, A., Martín-Martín, R., Reid, I., Rezatofighi, S.H., Savarese, S.: Social-bigat: Multimodal trajectory forecasting using bicycle-gan and graph attention networks. arXiv preprint arXiv:1907.03395 (2019)

30. Lee, S., Lim, J., Suh, I.H.: Progressive feature matching: Incremental graph construction and optimization. IEEE Trans. Image Process. **29**, 6992–7005 (2020)

31. Lehrmann, A., Gehler, P., Nowozin, S.: Efficient nonlinear markov models for human motion. In: CVPR, pp. 1314–1321 (June 2014)

32. Li, C., Zhang, Z., Sun Lee, W., Hee Lee, G.: Convolutional sequence to sequence model for human dynamics. In: CVPR (June 2018)

33. Li, J., Yang, F., Tomizuka, M., Choi, C.: Evolvegraph: Multi-agent trajectory prediction with dynamic relational reasoning. NeurIPS (2020)

34. Li, M., Chen, S., Zhang, Y., Tsang, I.: Graph cross networks with vertex infomax pooling. In: NeurIPS, vol. 33, pp. 14093–14105 (2020)

35. Li, M., Chen, S., Zhao, Y., Zhang, Y., Wang, Y., Tian, Q.: Dynamic multiscale graph neural networks for 3d skeleton based human motion prediction. In: CVPR (June 2020)

36. Li, M., Chen, S., Zhao, Y., Zhang, Y., Wang, Y., Tian, Q.: Multiscale spatio-temporal graph neural networks for 3d skeleton-based motion prediction. IEEE Trans. Image Process. **30**, 7760–7775 (2021)

37. Li, Y., Tarlow, D., Brockschmidt, M., Zemel, R.: Gated graph sequence neural networks. In: ICLR (May 2016)
38. Liu, Z., Su, P., Wu, S., Shen, X., Chen, H., Hao, Y., Wang, M.: Motion prediction using trajectory cues. In: Proceedings of the IEEE/CVF International Conference on Computer Vision (ICCV), pp. 13299–13308 (October 2021)
39. Lu, X., Wang, W., Danelljan, M., Zhou, T., Shen, J., Van Gool, L.: Video object segmentation with episodic graph memory networks. In: Vedaldi, A., Bischof, H., Brox, T., Frahm, J.-M. (eds.) ECCV 2020. LNCS, vol. 12348, pp. 661–679. Springer, Cham (2020). https://doi.org/10.1007/978-3-030-58580-8_39
40. Mao, W., Liu, M., Salzmann, M.: History repeats itself: Human motion prediction via motion attention. In: Vedaldi, A., Bischof, H., Brox, T., Frahm, J.-M. (eds.) ECCV 2020. LNCS, vol. 12359, pp. 474–489. Springer, Cham (2020). https://doi.org/10.1007/978-3-030-58568-6_28
41. Mao, W., Liu, M., Salzmann, M., Li, H.: Learning trajectory dependencies for human motion prediction. In: ICCV (Oct 2019)
42. von Marcard, T., Henschel, R., Black, M.J., Rosenhahn, B., Pons-Moll, G.: Recovering accurate 3D human pose in the wild using IMUs and a moving camera. In: Ferrari, V., Hebert, M., Sminchisescu, C., Weiss, Y. (eds.) ECCV 2018. LNCS, vol. 11214, pp. 614–631. Springer, Cham (2018). https://doi.org/10.1007/978-3-030-01249-6_37
43. Martinez, J., Black, M., Romero, J.: On human motion prediction using recurrent neural networks. In: CVPR, pp. 4674–4683 (July 2017)
44. Min, Y., Wenkel, F., Wolf, G.: Scattering gcn: Overcoming oversmoothness in graph convolutional networks. In: Advances in Neural Information Processing Systems (NeurIPS), pp. 14498–14508 (Dec 2020)
45. Min, Y., Wenkel, F., Wolf, G.: Geometric scattering attention networks. In: ICASSP, pp. 8518–8522 (2021)
46. Niepert, M., Ahmed, M., Kutzkovl, K.: Learning convolutional neural networks for graphs. In: ICML (June 2016)
47. Pan, C., Chen, S., Ortega, A.: Spatio-temporal graph scattering transform. In: ICLR (May 2021)
48. Pavlovic, V., Rehg, J.M., MacCormick, J.: Learning switching linear models of human motion. In: NeurIPS (2001)
49. Qi, S., Wang, W., Jia, B., Shen, J., Zhu, S.C.: Learning human-object interactions by graph parsing neural networks. In: ECCV, pp. 401–417 (2018)
50. Rizkallah, M., Su, X., Maugey, T., Guillemot, C.: Geometry-aware graph transforms for light field compact representation. IEEE Trans. Image Process. **29**, 602–616 (2020)
51. Shi, L., Zhang, Y., Cheng, J., Lu, H.: Skeleton-based action recognition with directed graph neural networks. In: CVPR (June 2019)
52. Sifre, L., Mallat, S.: Rotation, scaling and deformation invariant scattering for texture discrimination. In: CVPR, pp. 1233–1240 (June 2013)
53. Sofianos, T., Sampieri, A., Franco, L., Galasso, F.: Space-time-separable graph convolutional network for pose forecasting. In: Proceedings of the IEEE/CVF International Conference on Computer Vision (ICCV), pp. 11209–11218 (October 2021)
54. Tabassum, S., Pereira, F.S., Fernandes, S., Gama, J.: Social network analysis: An overview. Wiley Interdiscip. Rev. Data Min. Knowl. Discov. **8**(5), e1256 (2018)
55. Taylor, G., Hinton, G.: Factored conditional restricted Boltzmann machines for modeling motion style. In: ICML (June 2009)
56. Taylor, G., Hinton, G., Roweis, S.: Modeling human motion using binary latent variables. In: NeurIPS (December 2007)

57. Velickovic, P., Cucurull, G., Casanova, A., Romero, A., Liò, P., Bengio, Y.: Graph attention networks. In: ICLR (Apr 2018)
58. Walker, J., Marino, K., Gupta, A., Hebert, M.: The pose knows: Video forecasting by generating pose futures. In: ICCV, pp. 3332–3341 (Oct 2017)
59. Wang, W., Zhu, H., Dai, J., Pang, Y., Shen, J., Shao, L.: Hierarchical human parsing with typed part-relation reasoning. In: CVPR (June 2020)
60. Xu, C., Chen, S., Li, M., Zhang, Y.: Invariant teacher and equivariant student for unsupervised 3d human pose estimation. In: Proceedings of the AAAI Conference on Artificial Intelligence, vol. 35, pp. 3013–3021 (2021)
61. Xu, C., Li, M., Ni, Z., Zhang, Y., Chen, S.: Groupnet: Multiscale hypergraph neural networks for trajectory prediction with relational reasoning. In: Proceedings of the IEEE/CVF Conference on Computer Vision and Pattern Recognition (CVPR), pp. 6498–6507 (2022)
62. Yan, S., Xiong, Y., Lin, D.: Spatial temporal graph convolutional networks for skeleton-based action recognition. In: AAAI (Feb 2018)
63. Zhang, J., Shen, F., Xu, X., Shen, H.T.: Temporal reasoning graph for activity recognition. IEEE Trans. Image Process. **29**, 5491–5506 (2020)
64. Zhang, X., Xu, C., Tian, X., Tao, D.: Graph edge convolutional neural networks for skeleton-based action recognition. IEEE Trans. Neural Netw. Learn. Syst. **31**(8), 3047–3060 (2019)
65. Zheng, C., Pan, L., Wu, P.: Multimodal deep network embedding with integrated structure and attribute information. IEEE Trans. Neural Netw. Learn. Syst. **31**(5), 1437–1449 (2020)
66. Zou, D., Lerman, G.: Graph convolutional neural networks via scattering. Appl. Comput. Harmon. Anal. **49**(3), 1046–1074 (2020)

Rethinking Keypoint Representations: Modeling Keypoints and Poses as Objects for Multi-person Human Pose Estimation

William McNally[1,2]([⊠]) [ID], Kanav Vats[1,2] [ID], Alexander Wong[1,2] [ID], and John McPhee[1,2] [ID]

[1] Systems Design Engineering, University of Waterloo, Waterloo, Canada
{wmcnally,k2vats,a28wong,mcphee}@uwaterloo.ca
[2] Waterloo Artificial Intelligence Institute, University of Waterloo, Waterloo, Canada

Abstract. In keypoint estimation tasks such as human pose estimation, heatmap-based regression is the dominant approach despite possessing notable drawbacks: heatmaps intrinsically suffer from quantization error and require excessive computation to generate and post-process. Motivated to find a more efficient solution, we propose to model individual keypoints and sets of spatially related keypoints (*i.e.*, poses) as objects within a dense single-stage anchor-based detection framework. Hence, we call our method KAPAO (pronounced "Ka-Pow"), for **K**eypoints **A**nd **P**oses **A**s **O**bjects. KAPAO is applied to the problem of single-stage multi-person human pose estimation by simultaneously detecting human pose and keypoint objects and fusing the detections to exploit the strengths of both object representations. In experiments we observe that KAPAO is faster and more accurate than previous methods, which suffer greatly from heatmap post-processing. The accuracy-speed trade-off is especially favourable in the practical setting when not using test-time augmentation. Source code: https://github.com/wmcnally/kapao.

Keywords: Human pose estimation · Object detection · YOLO

1 Introduction

Keypoint estimation is a computer vision task that involves localizing points of interest in images. It has emerged as one of the most highly researched topics in the computer vision literature [1,9,11,15,18,19,37–40,47,49,55,60,63,67,70]. The most common method for estimating keypoint locations involves generating target fields, referred to as *heatmaps*, that center 2D Gaussians on the target keypoint coordinates. Deep convolutional neural networks [26] are then used to regress the target heatmaps on the input images, and keypoint predictions are made via the arguments of the maxima of the predicted heatmaps [57].

While strong empirical results have positioned heatmap regression as the *de facto* standard method for detecting and localizing keypoints [3,5–7,12,24, 35,37,43,54,57,66,68], there are several known drawbacks. First, these methods

ⓒ The Author(s), under exclusive license to Springer Nature Switzerland AG 2022
S. Avidan et al. (Eds.): ECCV 2022, LNCS 13666, pp. 37–54, 2022.
https://doi.org/10.1007/978-3-031-20068-7_3

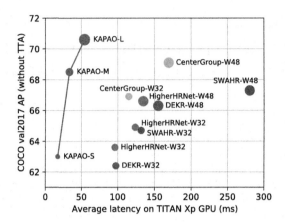

Fig. 1. Accuracy vs. Inference Speed: KAPAO compared to state-of-the-art single-stage multi-person human pose estimation methods DEKR [12], HigherHRNet [7], HigherHR-Net + SWAHR [35], and CenterGroup [3] without test-time augmentation (TTA), *i.e.*, excluding multi-scale testing and horizontal flipping. The raw data are provided in Table 1. The circle size is proportional to the number of model parameters.

suffer from quantization error: the precision of a keypoint prediction is inherently limited by the spatial resolution of the output heatmap. Larger heatmaps are therefore advantageous, but require additional upsampling operations and costly processing at higher resolution [3,7,12,35,37]. Even when large heatmaps are used, special post-processing steps are required to refine keypoint predictions, slowing down inference [6,7,35,43]. Second, when two keypoints of the same type (*i.e.*, class) appear in close proximity to one another, the overlapping heatmap signals may be mistaken for a single keypoint. Indeed, this is a common failure case [5]. For these reasons, researchers have started to investigate alternative, *heatmap-free* keypoint detection methods [27,29,30,38,67].

In this paper, we introduce a new heatmap-free keypoint detection method and apply it to single-stage multi-person human pose estimation. Our method builds on recent research showing how keypoints can be modeled as objects within a dense anchor-based detection framework by representing keypoints at the center of small *keypoint bounding boxes* [38]. In preliminary experimentation with human pose estimation, we found that this keypoint detection approach works well for human keypoints that are characterized by local image features (*e.g.*, the eyes), but the same approach is less effective at detecting human key-points that require a more global understanding (*e.g.*, the hips). We therefore introduce a new *pose object* representation to help detect sets of keypoints that are spatially related. Furthermore, we detect keypoint objects and pose objects simultaneously and fuse the results using a simple matching algorithm to exploit the benefits of both object representations. By virtue of detecting pose objects, we unify person detection and keypoint estimation and provide a highly efficient single-stage approach to multi-person human pose estimation.

As a result of not using heatmaps, KAPAO compares favourably against recent single-stage human pose estimation models in terms of accuracy *and* inference speed, especially when not using test-time augmentation (TTA), which represents how such models are deployed in practice. As shown in Fig. 1, KAPAO achieves an AP of 70.6 on the Microsoft COCO Keypoints validation set without TTA while having an average latency of 54.4 ms (forward pass + post-processing time). Compared to the state-of-the-art single-stage model HigherHRNet + SWAHR [35], KAPAO is 5.1× faster and 3.3 AP more accurate when not using TTA. Compared to CenterGroup [3], KAPAO is 3.1× faster and 1.5 AP more accurate. The contributions of this work are summarized as follows:

– A new *pose object* representation is proposed that extends the conventional object representation by including a set of keypoints associated with the object.
– A new approach to single-stage human pose estimation is developed by simultaneously detecting *keypoint objects* and *pose objects* and fusing the detections. The proposed heatmap-free method is significantly faster and more accurate than state-of-the-art heatmap-based methods when not using TTA.

2   Related Work

Heatmap-free Keypoint Detection. DeepPose [58] regressed keypoint coordinates directly from images using a cascade of deep neural networks that iteratively refined the keypoint predictions. Shortly thereafter, Tompson *et al.* [57] introduced the notion of keypoint heatmaps, which have since remained prevalent in human pose estimation [5–7,12,24,37,43,54,65,66,68] and other keypoint detection applications [9,15,18,59,63]. Remarking the computational inefficiencies associated with generating heatmaps, Li *et al.* [30] disentangled the horizontal and vertical keypoint coordinates such that each coordinate was represented using a one-hot encoded vector. This saved computation and permitted an expansion of the output resolution, thereby reducing the effects of quantization error and eliminating the need for refinement post-processing. Li *et al.* [27] introduced the residual log-likelihood (RLE), a novel loss function for direct keypoint regression based on normalizing flows [53]. Direct keypoint regression has also been attempted using Transformers [29].

Outside the realm of human pose estimation, Xu *et al.* [67] regressed anchor templates of facial keypoints and aggregated them to achieve state-of-the-art accuracy in facial alignment. In sports analytics, McNally *et al.* [38] encountered the issue of overlapping heatmap signals in the development of an automatic scoring system for darts and therefore opted to model keypoints as objects using small square bounding boxes. This keypoint representation proved to be highly effective and serves as the inspiration for this work.

Single-stage Human Pose Estimation. Single-stage human pose estimation methods predict the poses of every person in an image using a single forward pass [5,7,12,14,25,42,44]. In contrast, two-stage methods [6,10,24,27,37,46,54,

66] first detect the people in an image using an off-the-shelf person detector (*e.g.*, Faster R-CNN [52], YOLOv3 [51], etc.) and then estimate poses for each detection. Single-stage methods are generally less accurate, but usually perform better in crowded scenes [28] and are often preferred because of their simplicity and efficiency, which becomes particularly favourable as the number of people in the image increases. Single-stage approaches vary more in their design compared to two-stage approaches. For instance, they may: (i) detect all the keypoints in an image and perform a *bottom-up* grouping into human poses [3, 5, 7, 16, 17, 22, 25, 35, 42, 48]; (ii) extend object detectors to unify person detection and keypoint estimation [14, 36, 64, 70]; or (iii) use alternative keypoint/pose representations (*e.g.*, predicting root keypoints and relative displacements [12, 44, 45]). We briefly summarize the most recent state-of-the-art single-stage methods below.

Cheng *et al.* [7] repurposed HRNet [54] for bottom-up human pose estimation by adding a transpose convolution to double the output heatmap resolution (HigherHRNet) and using associative embeddings [42] for keypoint grouping. They also implemented multi-resolution training to address the scale variation problem. Geng *et al.* [12] predicted person center heatmaps and $2K$ offset maps representing offset vectors for the K keypoints of a pose candidate centered on each pixel using an HRNet backbone. They also disentangled the keypoint regression (DEKR) using separate regression heads and adaptive convolutions. Luo *et al.* [35] used HigherHRNet as a base and proposed scale and weight adaptive heatmap regression (SWAHR), which scaled the ground-truth heatmap Gaussian variances based on the person scale and balanced the foreground/background loss weighting. Their modifications provided significant accuracy improvements over HigherHRNet and comparable performance to many two-stage methods. Again using HigherHRNet as a base, Brasó *et al.* [3] proposed CenterGroup to match keypoints to person centers using a fully differentiable self-attention module that was trained end-to-end together with the keypoint detector. Notably, all of the aforementioned methods suffer from costly heatmap post-processing and as such, their inference speeds leave much to be desired.

Extending Object Detectors for Human Pose Estimation. There is significant overlap between the tasks of object detection and human pose estimation. For instance, He *et al.* [14] used the Mask R-CNN instance segmentation model for human pose estimation by predicting keypoints using one-hot masks. Wei *et al.* [64] proposed Point-Set Anchors, which adapted the RetinaNet [32] object detector using pose anchors instead of bounding box anchors. Zhou *et al.* [70] modeled objects using heatmap-based center points with CenterNet and represented poses as a 2K-dimensional property of the center point. Mao *et al.* [36] adapted the FCOS [56] object detector with FCPose using dynamic filters [21]. While these methods based on object detectors provide good efficiency, their accuracies have not competed with state-of-the-art heatmap-based methods. Our work is most similar to Point-Set Anchors [64]; however, our method does not require defining data-dependent pose anchors. Moreover, we simultaneously detect individual keypoints and poses and fuse the detections to improve the accuracy of our final pose predictions.

3   KAPAO: Keypoints and Poses as Objects

KAPAO uses a dense detection network to simultaneously predict a set of keypoint objects $\{\hat{\mathcal{O}}^k \in \hat{\mathbf{O}}^k\}$ and a set of pose objects $\{\hat{\mathcal{O}}^p \in \hat{\mathbf{O}}^p\}$, collectively $\hat{\mathbf{O}} = \hat{\mathbf{O}}^k \bigcup \hat{\mathbf{O}}^p$. We introduce the concept behind each object type and the relevant notation below. All units are assumed to be in pixels unless stated otherwise.

A keypoint object $\mathcal{O}^k$ is an adaptation of the conventional object representation in which the coordinates of a keypoint are represented at the center (b_x, b_y) of a small bounding box $\mathbf{b}$ with equal width b_w and height b_h: $\mathbf{b} = (b_x, b_y, b_w, b_h)$. The hyperparameter b_s controls the keypoint bounding box size (i.e., $b_s = b_w = b_h$). There are K classes of keypoint objects, one for each type in the dataset [38].

Generally speaking, a pose object $\mathcal{O}^p$ is considered to be an extension of the conventional object representation that additionally includes a set of keypoints associated with the object. While we expect pose objects to be useful in related tasks such as facial and object landmark detection [20,67], they are applied herein to human pose estimation via detection of *human pose objects*, comprising a bounding box of class "person," and a set of keypoints $\mathbf{z} = \{(x_k, y_k)\}_{k=1}^K$ that coincide with anatomical landmarks.

Both object representations possess unique advantages. Keypoint objects are specialized for the detection of individual keypoints that are characterized by strong local features. Examples of such keypoints that are common in human pose estimation include the eyes, ears and nose. However, keypoint objects carry no information regarding the concept of a person or pose. If used on their own for multi-person human pose estimation, a bottom-up grouping method would be required to parse the detected keypoints into human poses. In contrast, pose objects are better suited for localizing keypoints with weak local features as they enable the network to learn the spatial relationships within a set of keypoints. Moreover, they can be leveraged for multi-person human pose estimation directly without the need for bottom-up keypoint grouping.

Recognizing that keypoint objects exist in a subspace of a pose objects, the KAPAO network was designed to simultaneously detect both object types with minimal computational overhead using a single shared network head. During inference, the more precise keypoint object detections are fused with the human pose detections using a simple tolerance-based matching algorithm that improves the accuracy of the human pose predictions without sacrificing any significant amount of inference speed. The following sections provide details on the network architecture, the loss function used to train the network, and inference.

3.1   Architectural Details

A diagram of the KAPAO pipeline is provided in Fig. 2. It uses a deep convolutional neural network $\mathcal{N}$ to map an RGB input image $\mathbf{I} \in \mathbb{R}^{h \times w \times 3}$ to a set of four output grids $\hat{\mathbf{G}} = \{\hat{\mathcal{G}}^s \mid s \in \{8, 16, 32, 64\}\}$ containing the object predictions $\hat{\mathbf{O}}$, where $\hat{\mathcal{G}}^s \in \mathbb{R}^{\frac{h}{s} \times \frac{w}{s} \times N_a \times N_o}$:

$$\mathcal{N}(\mathbf{I}) = \hat{\mathbf{G}}. \tag{1}$$

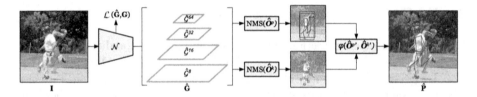

Fig. 2. KAPAO uses a dense detection network $\mathcal{N}$ trained using the multi-task loss $\mathcal{L}$ to map an RGB image $\mathbf{I}$ to a set of output grids $\hat{\mathbf{G}}$ containing the predicted pose objects $\hat{\mathbf{O}}^p$ and keypoint objects $\hat{\mathbf{O}}^k$. Non-maximum suppression (NMS) is used to obtain candidate detections $\hat{\mathbf{O}}^{p\prime}$ and $\hat{\mathbf{O}}^{k\prime}$, which are fused together using a matching algorithm φ to obtain the final human pose predictions $\hat{\mathbf{P}}$. The N_a and N_o dimensions in $\hat{\mathbf{G}}$ are not shown for clarity.

N_a is the number of anchor channels and N_o is the number of output channels for each object. $\mathcal{N}$ is a YOLO-style feature extractor that makes extensive use of Cross-Stage-Partial (CSP) bottlenecks [62] within a feature pyramid [31] macroarchitecture. To provide flexibility for different speed requirements, three sizes of KAPAO models were trained (*i.e.*, KAPAO-S/M/L) by scaling the number of layers and channels in $\mathcal{N}$.

Due to the nature of strided convolutions, the features in an output grid cell $\hat{\mathcal{G}}^s_{i,j}$ are conditioned on the image patch $\mathbf{I}_p = \mathbf{I}_{si:s(i+1),sj:s(j+1)}$. Therefore, if the center of a target object (b_x, b_y) is situated in $\mathbf{I}_p$, the output grid cell $\hat{\mathcal{G}}^s_{i,j}$ is responsible for detecting it. The receptive field of an output grid increases with s, so smaller output grids are better suited for detecting larger objects.

The output grid cells $\hat{\mathcal{G}}^s_{i,j}$ contain N_a anchor channels corresponding to anchor boxes $\mathbf{A}^s = \{(A_{w_a}, A_{h_a})\}_{a=1}^{N_a}$. A target object $\mathcal{O}$ is assigned to an anchor channel via tolerance-based matching of the object and anchor box sizes. This provides redundancy such that the grid cells $\hat{\mathcal{G}}^s_{i,j}$ can detect multiple objects and enables specialization for different object sizes and shapes. Additional detection redundancy is provided by also allowing the neighbouring grid cells $\hat{\mathcal{G}}^s_{i\pm1,j}$ and $\hat{\mathcal{G}}^s_{i,j\pm1}$ to detect an object in $\mathbf{I}_p$ [23,61].

The N_o output channels of $\hat{\mathcal{G}}^s_{i,j,a}$ contain the properties of a predicted object $\hat{\mathcal{O}}$, including the objectness $\hat{p}_o$ (the probability that an object exists), the intermediate bounding boxes $\hat{\mathbf{t}}' = (\hat{t}'_x, \hat{t}'_y, \hat{t}'_w, \hat{t}'_h)$, the object class scores $\hat{\mathbf{c}} = (\hat{c}_1, ..., \hat{c}_{K+1})$, and the intermediate keypoints $\hat{\mathbf{v}}' = \{(\hat{v}'_{xk}, \hat{v}'_{yk})\}_{k=1}^K$ for the human pose objects. Hence, $N_o = 3K + 6$.

Following [23,61], an object's intermediate bounding box $\hat{\mathbf{t}}$ is predicted in the grid coordinates and relative to the grid cell origin (i,j) using:

$$\hat{t}_x = 2\sigma(\hat{t}'_x) - 0.5 \qquad \hat{t}_y = 2\sigma(\hat{t}'_y) - 0.5 \tag{2}$$

$$\hat{t}_w = \frac{A_w}{s}(2\sigma(\hat{t}'_w))^2 \qquad \hat{t}_h = \frac{A_h}{s}(2\sigma(\hat{t}'_h))^2. \tag{3}$$

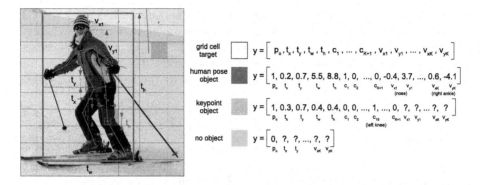

Fig. 3. Sample targets for training, including a human pose object (blue), keypoint object (red), and no object (green). The "?" values are not used in the loss computation. (Color figure online)

This detection strategy is extended to the keypoints of a pose object. A pose object's intermediate keypoints $\hat{\mathbf{v}}$ are predicted in the grid coordinates and relative to the grid cell origin (i, j) using:

$$\hat{v}_{xk} = \frac{A_w}{s}(4\sigma(\hat{v}'_{xk}) - 2) \qquad \hat{v}_{yk} = \frac{A_h}{s}(4\sigma(\hat{v}'_{yk}) - 2). \tag{4}$$

The sigmoid function σ facilitates learning by constraining the ranges of the object properties (*e.g.*, $\hat{v}_{xk}$ and $\hat{v}_{yk}$ are constrained to $\pm 2\frac{A_w}{s}$ and $\pm 2\frac{A_h}{s}$, respectively). To learn $\hat{\mathbf{t}}$ and $\hat{\mathbf{v}}$, losses are applied in the grid space. Sample targets $\mathbf{t}$ and $\mathbf{v}$ are shown in Fig. 3.

3.2 Loss Function

A target set of grids $\mathbf{G}$ is constructed and a multi-task loss $\mathcal{L}(\hat{\mathbf{G}}, \mathbf{G})$ is applied to learn the objectness $\hat{p}_o$ ($\mathcal{L}_{obj}$), the intermediate bounding boxes $\hat{\mathbf{t}}$ ($\mathcal{L}_{box}$), the class scores $\hat{\mathbf{c}}$ ($\mathcal{L}_{cls}$), and the intermediate pose object keypoints $\hat{\mathbf{v}}$ ($\mathcal{L}_{kps}$). The loss components are computed for a single image as follows:

$$\mathcal{L}_{obj} = \sum_s \frac{\omega_s}{n(G^s)} \sum_{G^s} \text{BCE}(\hat{p}_o, p_o \cdot \text{IoU}(\hat{\mathbf{t}}, \mathbf{t})) \tag{5}$$

$$\mathcal{L}_{box} = \sum_s \frac{1}{n(\mathcal{O} \in G^s)} \sum_{\mathcal{O} \in G^s} 1 - \text{IoU}(\hat{\mathbf{t}}, \mathbf{t}) \tag{6}$$

$$\mathcal{L}_{cls} = \sum_s \frac{1}{n(\mathcal{O} \in G^s)} \sum_{\mathcal{O} \in G^s} \text{BCE}(\hat{c}, c) \tag{7}$$

$$\mathcal{L}_{kps} = \sum_s \frac{1}{n(\mathcal{O}^p \in G^s)} \sum_{\mathcal{O}^p \in G^s} \sum_{k=1}^{K} \delta(\nu_k > 0)||\hat{\mathbf{v}}_k - \mathbf{v}_k||_2 \tag{8}$$

where ω_s is the grid weighting, BCE is the binary cross-entropy, IoU is the complete intersection over union (CIoU) [69], and ν_k are the keypoint visibility flags. When $\mathcal{G}^s_{i,j,a}$ represents a target object $\mathcal{O}$, the target objectness $p_o = 1$ is multiplied by the IoU to promote specialization amongst the anchor channel predictions [50]. When $\mathcal{G}^s_{i,j,a}$ is not a target object, $p_o = 0$. In practice, the losses are applied over a batch of images using batched grids. The total loss $\mathcal{L}$ is the weighted summation of the loss components scaled by the batch size N_b:

$$\mathcal{L} = N_b(\lambda_{obj}\mathcal{L}_{obj} + \lambda_{box}\mathcal{L}_{box} + \lambda_{cls}\mathcal{L}_{cls} + \lambda_{kps}\mathcal{L}_{kps}). \qquad (9)$$

3.3   Inference

The predicted intermediate bounding boxes $\hat{\mathbf{t}}$ and keypoints $\hat{\mathbf{v}}$ are mapped back to the original image coordinates using the following transformation:

$$\hat{\mathbf{b}} = s(\hat{\mathbf{t}} + [i, j, 0, 0]) \qquad \hat{\mathbf{z}}_k = s(\hat{\mathbf{v}}_k + [i, j]). \qquad (10)$$

$\hat{\mathcal{G}}^s_{i,j,a}$ represents a positive pose object detection $\hat{\mathcal{O}}^p$ if its confidence $\hat{p}_o \cdot \max(\hat{\mathbf{c}})$ is greater than a threshold τ_{cp} and $\arg\max(\hat{\mathbf{c}}) = 1$. Similarly, $\hat{\mathcal{G}}^s_{i,j,a}$ represents a positive keypoint object detection $\hat{\mathcal{O}}^k$ if $\hat{p}_o \cdot \max(\hat{\mathbf{c}}) > \tau_{ck}$ and $\arg\max(\hat{\mathbf{c}}) > 1$, where the keypoint object class is $\arg\max(\hat{\mathbf{c}}) - 1$. To remove redundant detections and obtain the candidate pose objects $\hat{\mathbf{O}}^{p\prime}$ and the candidate keypoint objects $\hat{\mathbf{O}}^{k\prime}$, the sets of positive pose object detections $\hat{\mathbf{O}}^p$ and positive keypoint object detections $\hat{\mathbf{O}}^p$ are filtered using non-maximum suppression (NMS) applied to the pose object bounding boxes with the IoU thresholds τ_{bp} and τ_{bk}:

$$\hat{\mathbf{O}}^{p\prime} = \text{NMS}(\hat{\mathbf{O}}^p, \tau_{bp}) \qquad \hat{\mathbf{O}}^{k\prime} = \text{NMS}(\hat{\mathbf{O}}^k, \tau_{bk}). \qquad (11)$$

It is noted that τ_{ck} and τ_{bk} are scalar thresholds used for all keypoint object classes. Finally, the human pose predictions $\hat{\mathbf{P}} = \{\hat{\mathbf{P}}_i \in \mathbb{R}^{K \times 3}\}$ for $i \in \{1...n(\hat{\mathbf{O}}^{p\prime})\}$ are obtained by fusing the candidate keypoint objects with the candidate pose objects using a distance tolerance τ_{fd}. To promote correct matches of keypoint objects to poses, the keypoint objects are only fused to pose objects with confidence $\hat{p}_o \cdot \max(\hat{\mathbf{c}}) > \tau_{fc}$:

$$\hat{\mathbf{P}} = \varphi(\hat{\mathbf{O}}^{p\prime}, \hat{\mathbf{O}}^{k\prime}, \tau_{fd}, \tau_{fc}). \qquad (12)$$

The keypoint object fusion function φ is defined in Algorithm 1, where the following notation is used to index an object's properties: $\hat{x} = \hat{\mathcal{O}}_x$ (e.g., a pose object's keypoints $\hat{\mathbf{z}}$ are referenced as $\hat{\mathcal{O}}^p_{\mathbf{z}}$).

3.4   Limitations

A limitation of KAPAO is that pose objects do not include individual keypoint confidences, so the human pose predictions typically contain a sparse set of keypoint confidences $\hat{\mathbf{P}}_i[:, 3]$ populated by the fused keypoint objects (see Algorithm 1 for details). If desired, a complete set of keypoint confidences can be induced by only using keypoint objects, which is realized when $\tau_{ck} \to 0$. Another limitation is that training requires a considerable amount of time and GPU memory due to the large input size used.

Algorithm 1: Keypoint object fusion (φ)

Input: $\hat{\mathbf{O}}^{p\prime}$, $\hat{\mathbf{O}}^{k\prime}$, τ_{fd}, τ_{fc}
Output: $\hat{\mathbf{P}}$
if $n(\hat{\mathbf{O}}^{p\prime}) > 0$ **then**
    $\hat{\mathbf{P}} \leftarrow \{0_{K \times 3} \mid \_ \in \{1...n(\hat{\mathbf{O}}^{p\prime})\}\}$ // initialize poses
    $\zeta \leftarrow \{0 \mid \_ \in \{1...n(\hat{\mathbf{O}}^{p\prime})\}\}$ // initialize pose confidences
    for $(i, \hat{\mathcal{O}}^p) \in$ **enumerate**$(\hat{\mathbf{O}}^{p\prime})$ **do**
        $\zeta_i = \hat{\mathcal{O}}^p_{p_o} \cdot \max(\hat{\mathcal{O}}^p_c)$
        for $k \in \{1...K\}$ **do**
            $\hat{\mathbf{P}}_i[k] \leftarrow (\hat{\mathcal{O}}^p_{x_k}, \hat{\mathcal{O}}^p_{y_k}, 0)$ // assign pose object keypoints
    $\hat{\mathbf{P}}^* \leftarrow \{\hat{\mathbf{P}}_i \in \hat{\mathbf{P}} \mid \zeta_i > \tau_{fc}\}$ // poses above confidence threshold
    if $n(\hat{\mathbf{P}}^*) > 0 \wedge n(\hat{\mathbf{O}}^{k\prime}) > 0$ **then**
        for $\hat{\mathcal{O}}^k \in \hat{\mathbf{O}}^{k\prime}$ **do**
            $k \leftarrow \arg\max(\hat{\mathcal{O}}^k_c) - 1$ // keypoint index
            $C_k \leftarrow \hat{\mathcal{O}}^k_{p_o} \max(\hat{\mathcal{O}}^k_c)$ // keypoint object confidence
            $\mathbf{d}_i \leftarrow \|\hat{\mathbf{P}}^*_i[k, [1,2]] - (\hat{\mathcal{O}}^k_{b_x}, \hat{\mathcal{O}}^k_{b_y})\|_2$ // distances
            $m \leftarrow \arg\min(\mathbf{d})$ // match index
            if $\mathbf{d}_m < \tau_{fd} \wedge \hat{\mathbf{P}}^*_m[k, 3] < C_k$ **then**
                $\hat{\mathbf{P}}^*_m[k] = (\hat{\mathcal{O}}^k_{b_x}, \hat{\mathcal{O}}^k_{b_y}, C_k)$ // assign keypoint object to pose
else
    $\hat{\mathbf{P}} = \emptyset$ // empty set

---

4 Experiments

We evaluate KAPAO on two multi-person human pose estimation datasets: COCO Keypoints [33] ($K = 17$) and CrowdPose [28] ($K = 14$). We report the standard AP/AR detection metrics based on Object Keypoint Similarity [33] and compare against state-of-the-art methods. All hyperparameters are provided in the source code.

4.1 Microsoft COCO Keypoints

Training. KAPAO-S/M/L were all trained for 500 epochs on COCO train2017 using stochastic gradient descent with Nesterov momentum [41], weight decay, and a learning rate decayed over a single cosine cycle [34] with a 3-epoch warm-up period [13]. The input images were resized and padded to 1280×1280, keeping the original aspect ratio. Data augmentation used during training included mosaic [2], HSV color-space perturbations, horizontal flipping, translations, and scaling. Many of the training hyperparameters were inherited from [23,61], including the anchor boxes $\mathbf{A}$ and the loss weights w, λ_{obj}, λ_{box}, and λ_{cls}. Others, including the keypoint bounding box size b_s and the keypoint loss weight λ_{kps}, were manually tuned using a small grid search. The models were trained on four V100 GPUs with 32 GB memory each using batch sizes of 128, 72, and

Table 1. Accuracy and speed comparison with state-of-the-art single-stage human pose estimation models on COCO `val2017`, including the forward pass (FP) and post-processing (PP). Latencies (Lat.) averaged over `val2017` using a batch size of 1 on a TITAN Xp GPU.

Method	TTA	Input Size(s)	Params (M)	FP (ms)	PP (ms)	Lat. (ms)	AP	AR
HigherHRNet-W32 [7]	N	512	28.6	46.1	50.1	96.2	63.6	69.0
+ SWAHR [35]	N	512	28.6	45.1	86.6	132	64.7	70.3
HigherHRNet-W32 [7]	N	640	28.6	52.4	71.4	124	64.9	70.3
HigherHRNet-W48 [7]	N	640	63.8	75.4	59.2	135	66.6	71.5
+ SWAHR [35]	N	640	63.8	86.3	194	280	67.3	73.0
DEKR-W32 [12]	N	512	29.6	62.6	34.9	97.5	62.4	69.6
DEKR-W48 [12]	N	640	65.7	109	45.8	155	66.3	73.2
CenterGroup-W32 [3]	N	512	30.3	98.9	16.0	115	66.9	71.6
CenterGroup-W48 [3]	N	640	65.5	155	14.5	170	69.1	74.0
KAPAO-S	N	1280	**12.6**	**14.7**	**2.80**	**17.5**	63.0	70.2
KAPAO-M	N	1280	35.8	30.7	2.88	33.5	68.5	75.5
KAPAO-L	N	1280	77.0	51.3	3.07	54.4	**70.6**	**77.4**
HigherHRNet-W32 [7]	Y	256, 512, 1024	28.6	365	372	737	69.9	74.3
+ SWAHR [35]	Y	256, 512, 1024	28.6	389	491	880	71.3	75.9
HigherHRNet-W32 [7]	Y	320, 640, 1280	28.6	431	447	878	70.6	75.0
HigherHRNet-W48 [7]	Y	320, 640, 1280	63.8	643	436	1080	72.1	76.1
+ SWAHR [35]	Y	320, 640, 1280	63.8	809	781	1590	73.0	77.6
DEKR-W32 [12]	Y	256, 512, 1024	29.6	552	137	689	70.5	76.2
DEKR-W48 [12]	Y	320, 640, 1280	65.7	1010	157	1170	72.1	77.8
CenterGroup-W32 [3]	Y	256, 512, 1024	30.3	473	13.8	487	71.9	76.1
CenterGroup-W48 [3]	Y	320, 640, 1280	65.5	1050	11.8	1060	**73.3**	77.6
KAPAO-S	Y	1024, 1280, 1536	**12.6**	**61.5**	**3.70**	**65.2**	64.4	71.5
KAPAO-M	Y	1024, 1280, 1536	35.8	126	3.67	130	69.9	76.8
KAPAO-L	Y	1024, 1280, 1536	77.0	211	3.70	215	71.6	**78.5**

48 for KAPAO-S, M, and L, respectively. Validation was performed after every epoch, saving the model weights that provided the highest validation AP.

Testing. The six inference parameters (τ_{cp}, τ_{ck}, τ_{bp}, τ_{bk}, τ_{fd}, and τ_{fc}) were manually tuned on the validation set using a coarse grid search to maximize accuracy. The results were not overly sensitive to the inference parameter values. When using TTA, the input image was scaled by factors of 0.8, 1, and 1.2, and the unscaled image was horizontally flipped. During post-processing, the multiscale detections were concatenated before running NMS. When not using TTA, rectangular input images were used (*i.e.*, 1280 px on the longest side), which marginally reduced the accuracy but increased the inference speed.

Results. Table 1 compares the accuracy, forward pass (FP) time, and post-processing (PP) time of KAPAO with state-of-the-art single-stage methods HigherHRNet [7], HigherHRNet + SWAHR [35], DEKR [12], and CenterGroup [3] on `val2017`. Two test settings were considered: (1) without any test-time augmentation (using a single forward pass of the network), and (2) with multi-scale and horizontal flipping test-time augmentation (TTA). It is noted that with the exception of CenterGroup, no inference speeds were reported in the original works. Rather, FLOPs were used as an indirect measure of computational efficiency. FLOPs are not only a poor indication of inference speed [8], but they are also only computed for the forward pass of the network and thus do not provide an indication of the amount of computation required for post-processing.

Due to expensive heatmap refinement, the post-processing times of HigherHRNet, HigherHRNet + SWAHR, and DEKR are at least an order of magnitude greater than KAPAO-L when not using TTA. The post-processing time of KAPAO depends less on the input size so it only increases by approximately 1 ms when using TTA. Conversely, HigherHRNet and HigherHRNet + SWAHR generate and refine large heatmaps during multi-scale testing and therefore require more than two orders of magnitude more post-processing time than KAPAO-L.

CenterGroup requires significantly less post-processing time than HigherHRNet and DEKR because it skips heatmap refinement and directly encodes pose center and keypoint heatmaps as embeddings that are fed to an attention-based grouping module. When not using TTA, CenterGroup-W48 provides an improvement of 2.5 AP over HigherHRNet-W48 and has a better accuracy-speed tradeoff. Still, KAPAO-L is 3.1× faster than CenterGroup-W48 and 1.5 AP more accurate due to its efficient network architecture and near cost-free post-processing. When using TTA, KAPAO-L is 1.7 AP less accurate than CenterGroup-W48, but 4.9× faster. KAPAO-L also achieves state-of-the-art AR, which is indicative of better detection rates.

We suspect that KAPAO is more accurate without TTA compared to previous methods because it uses larger input images; however, we emphasize that KAPAO consumes larger input sizes while still being faster than previous methods due to its well-designed network architecture and efficient post-processing. For the same reason, TTA (multi-scale testing in particular) doesn't provide as much of a benefit; input sizes >1280 are less effective due to the dataset images being limited to 640 px.

In Table 2, the accuracy of KAPAO is compared to single-stage and two-stage methods on `test-dev`. KAPAO-L achieves state-of-the-art AR and falls within 1.7 AP of the best performing single-stage method HigherHRNet-W48 + SWAHR while being 7.4× faster. Notably, KAPAO-L is more accurate than the early two-stage methods G-RMI [46] and RMPE [10] and popular single-stage methods like OpenPose [4,5], Associative Embeddings [42], and PersonLab [45]. Compared to other single-stage methods that extend object detectors for human pose estimation (Mask R-CNN [14], CenterNet [70], Point-Set Anchors [64], and FCPose [36]), KAPAO-L is considerably more accurate. Among all the single-stage methods, KAPAO-L achieves state-of-the-art AP at an OKS threshold of 0.50, which is indicative of better detection rates but less precise keypoint localization. This is an area to explore in future work.

Table 2. Accuracy comparison with two-stage (†) and single-stage methods on COCO `test-dev`. Best results reported (*i.e.*, including TTA). DEKR results use a model-agnostic rescoring network [12]. Latencies (Lat.) taken from Table 1. *Latencies reported in original papers [4,36] and measured using an NVIDIA GTX 1080Ti GPU.

Method	Lat. (ms)	AP	AP$^{.50}$	AP$^{.75}$	AP^M	AP^L	AR
G-RMI [46]†	-	64.9	85.5	71.3	62.3	70.0	69.7
RMPE [10]†	-	61.8	83.7	69.8	58.6	67.6	-
CPN [6]†	-	72.1	91.4	80.0	68.7	77.2	78.5
SimpleBaseline [66]†	-	73.7	91.9	81.1	70.3	80.0	79.0
HRNet-W48 [54]†	-	75.5	**92.5**	**83.3**	71.9	**81.5**	80.5
EvoPose2D-L [37]†	-	**75.7**	91.9	83.1	72.2	**81.5**	**81.7**
MIPNet [24]†	-	**75.7**	-	-	-	-	-
RLE [27]†	-	**75.7**	92.3	82.9	**72.3**	81.3	-
OpenPose [4,5]	74*	61.8	84.9	67.5	57.1	68.2	66.5
Mask R-CNN [14]	-	63.1	87.3	68.7	57.8	71.4	-
Associative Embeddings [42]	-	65.5	86.8	72.3	60.6	72.6	70.2
PersonLab [45]	-	68.7	89.0	75.4	64.1	75.5	75.4
SPM [44]	-	66.9	88.5	72.9	62.6	73.1	-
PifPaf [25]	-	66.7	-	-	62.4	72.9	-
HGG [22]	-	67.6	85.1	73.7	62.7	74.6	71.3
CenterNet [70]	-	63.0	86.8	69.6	58.9	70.4	-
Point-Set Anchors [64]	-	68.7	89.9	76.3	64.8	75.3	-
HigherHRNet-W48 [7]	1080	70.5	89.3	77.2	66.6	75.8	74.9
+ SWAHR [35]	1590	**72.0**	90.7	**78.8**	**67.8**	**77.7**	-
FCPose [36]	93*	65.6	87.9	72.6	62.1	72.3	-
DEKR-W48 [12]	1170	71.0	89.2	78.0	67.1	76.9	76.7
CenterGroup-W48 [3]	1060	71.4	90.5	78.1	67.2	77.5	-
KAPAO-S	**65.2**	63.8	88.4	70.4	58.6	71.7	71.2
KAPAO-M	130	68.8	90.5	76.5	64.3	76.0	76.3
KAPAO-L	215	70.3	**91.2**	77.8	66.3	76.8	**77.7**

4.2 CrowdPose

KAPAO was trained on the `trainval` split with 12k images and was evaluated on the 8k images in `test`. The same training and inference settings as on COCO were used except the models were trained for 300 epochs and no validation was performed during training. The final model weights were used for testing. Table 3 compares the accuracy of KAPAO against state-of-the-art methods. It was found that KAPAO excels in the presence of occlusion, achieving competitive results across all metrics compared to previous single-stage methods and state-of-the-

Table 3. Comparison with single-stage and two-stage (†) methods on CrowdPose `test`, including TTA. DEKR results use a model-agnostic rescoring network [12]. HigherHR-Net + SWAHR [35] not included due to issues reproducing the results reported in the paper using the source code. Latencies (Lat.) taken from Table 1. *Latency reported in original paper [4] and measured using NVIDIA GTX 1080Ti GPU on COCO.

Method	Lat. (ms)	AP	AP$^{.50}$	AP$^{.75}$	AP^E	AP^M	AP^H
Mask R-CNN [14]	-	57.2	83.5	60.3	69.4	57.9	45.8
AlphaPose [10]†	-	61.0	81.3	**66.0**	**71.2**	**61.4**	**51.1**
SimpleBaseline [66]†	-	60.8	81.4	65.7	71.4	61.2	51.2
SPPE [28]	-	66.0	84.2	71.5	75.5	66.3	57.4
MIPNet [24]†	-	**70.0**	-	-	-	-	-
OpenPose [5]	74*	-	-	-	62.7	48.7	32.3
HigherHRNet-W48 [7]	1080	67.6	87.4	72.6	75.8	68.1	58.9
DEKR-W48 [12]	1170	68.0	85.5	73.4	76.6	68.8	58.4
CenterGroup-W48 [3]	1060	**70.0**	88.9	**75.7**	**77.3**	**70.8**	**63.2**
KAPAO-S	65.2	63.8	87.7	69.4	72.1	64.8	53.2
KAPAO-M	130	67.1	88.8	73.4	75.2	68.1	56.9
KAPAO-L	215	68.9	**89.4**	75.6	76.6	69.9	59.5

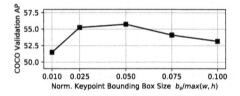
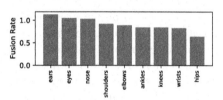

Fig. 4. Left: The influence of keypoint object bounding box size on learning. Each KAPAO-S model was trained for 50 epochs. Right: Keypoint object fusion rates for each keypoint type. Evaluated on COCO `val2017` using KAPAO-S without TTA.

art accuracy for AP$^{.50}$. The proficiency of KAPAO in crowded scenes is clear when analyzing AP^E, AP^M, and AP^H: KAPAO-L and DEKR-W48 [12] perform equally on images with easy Crowd Index (less occlusion), but KAPAO-L is 1.1 AP more accurate for both medium and hard Crowd Indices (more occlusion).

4.3 Ablation Studies

The influence of the keypoint bounding box size b_s, one of KAPAO's important hyperparameters, was empirically analyzed. Five KAPAO-S models were trained on COCO `train2017` for 50 epochs using normalized keypoint bounding box sizes $b_s/max(w, h) \in \{0.01, 0.025, 0.05, 0.075, 0.1\}$. The validation AP is plotted in Fig. 4 (left). The results are consistent with the prior work of McNally *et al.* [38]: $b_s/max(w, h) < 2.5\%$ destabilizes training leading to poor accuracy,

Table 4. Accuracy improvement when fusing keypoint object detections with human pose detections. Latencies averaged over each dataset using a batch size of 1 on a TITAN Xp GPU.

Method	TTA	Δ Lat. (ms) / ΔAP (COCO val2017)	Δ Lat. (ms) / ΔAP (CrowdPose test)
KAPAO-S	N	+1.2 / +2.4	+3.3 / +2.9
KAPAO-M	N	+1.2 / +1.1	+3.5 / +3.2
KAPAO-L	N	+1.7 / +1.2	+4.2 / +1.0
KAPAO-S	Y	+1.7 / +2.8	+3.9 / +3.2
KAPAO-M	Y	+1.6 / +1.5	+4.4 / +3.5
KAPAO-L	Y	+1.4 / +1.1	+4.5 / +1.0

and optimal $b_s/max(w, h)$ is observed around 5% (used for the experiments in previous section). In contrast to McNally *et al.*, the accuracy in this study degrades quickly for $b_s/max(w, h) > 5\%$. It is hypothesized that large b_s in this application interferes with pose object learning.

The accuracy improvements resulting from fusing the keypoint objects with the pose objects are provided in Table 4. Keypoint object fusion adds no less than 1.0 AP and over 3.0 AP in some cases. Moreover, keypoint object fusion is fast; the added post-processing time per image is ≤ 1.7 ms on COCO and ≤ 4.5 ms on CrowdPose. Relative to the time required for the forward pass of the network (see Table 1), these are small increases.

The fusion of keypoint objects by class is also studied. Figure 4 (right) plots the fusion rates for each keypoint type for KAPAO-S with no TTA on COCO val2017. The fusion rate is equal to the number of fused keypoint objects divided by the number of keypoints of that type in the dataset. Because the number of human pose predictions is generally greater than the actual number of person instances in the dataset, the fusion rate can be greater than 1. As originally hypothesized, keypoints that are characterized by distinct local image features (*e.g.*, the eyes, ears, and nose) have higher fusion rates as they are detected more precisely as keypoint objects than as pose objects. Conversely, keypoints that require a more global understanding (*e.g.*, the hips) are better detected using pose objects, as evidenced by lower fusion rates.

5 Conclusion

This paper presents KAPAO, a heatmap-free keypoint estimation method based on modeling keypoints and poses as objects. KAPAO is effectively applied to the problem of single-stage multi-person human pose estimation by detecting human pose objects. Moreover, fusing jointly detected keypoint objects improves the accuracy of the predicted human poses with minimal computational overhead. When not using test-time augmentation, KAPAO is significantly faster and more accurate than previous single-stage methods, which are impeded greatly by heatmap post-processing and bottom-up keypoint grouping. Moreover, KAPAO performs well in the presence of heavy occlusion as evidenced by competitive results on CrowdPose.

Acknowledgements. This work was supported in part by Compute Canada, the Canada Research Chairs Program, the Natural Sciences and Engineering Research Council of Canada, a Microsoft Azure Grant, and an NVIDIA Hardware Grant.

References

1. Andriluka, M., et al.: Posetrack: A benchmark for human pose estimation and tracking. In: CVPR (2018)
2. Bochkovskiy, A., Wang, C.Y., Liao, H.Y.M.: Yolov4: Optimal speed and accuracy of object detection. arXiv preprint arXiv:2004.10934 (2020)
3. Brasó, G., Kister, N., Leal-Taixé, L.: The center of attention: Center-keypoint grouping via attention for multi-person pose estimation. In: ICCV (2021)
4. Cao, Z., Hidalgo, G., Simon, T., Wei, S.E., Sheikh, Y.: Openpose: real-time multi-person 2d pose estimation using part affinity fields. arXiv preprint arXiv:1812.08008 (2018)
5. Cao, Z., Simon, T., Wei, S.E., Sheikh, Y.: Realtime multi-person 2d pose estimation using part affinity fields. In: CVPR (2017)
6. Chen, Y., Wang, Z., Peng, Y., Zhang, Z., Yu, G., Sun, J.: Cascaded pyramid network for multi-person pose estimation. In: CVPR (2018)
7. Cheng, B., Xiao, B., Wang, J., Shi, H., Huang, T.S., Zhang, L.: HigherHRNet: Scale-aware representation learning for bottom-up human pose estimation. In: CVPR (2020)
8. Ding, X., Zhang, X., Ma, N., Han, J., Ding, G., Sun, J.: RepVGG: Making VGG-style convnets great again. In: CVPR (2021)
9. Dong, X., Yan, Y., Ouyang, W., Yang, Y.: Style aggregated network for facial landmark detection. In: CVPR (2018)
10. Fang, H.S., Xie, S., Tai, Y.W., Lu, C.: RMPE: Regional multi-person pose estimation. In: ICCV (2017)
11. Gavrilyuk, K., Sanford, R., Javan, M., Snoek, C.G.: Actor-transformers for group activity recognition. In: CVPR (2020)
12. Geng, Z., Sun, K., Xiao, B., Zhang, Z., Wang, J.: Bottom-up human pose estimation via disentangled keypoint regression. In: CVPR (2021)
13. Goyal, P., et al.: Accurate, large minibatch sgd: Training imagenet in 1 hour. arXiv preprint arXiv:1706.02677 (2017)
14. He, K., Gkioxari, G., Dollár, P., Girshick, R.: Mask R-CNN. In: ICCV (2017)
15. Huang, W., Ren, P., Wang, J., Qi, Q., Sun, H.: Awr: Adaptive weighting regression for 3d hand pose estimation. In: AAAI (2020)
16. Insafutdinov, E., Pishchulin, L., Andres, B., Andriluka, M., Schiele, B.: DeeperCut: A deeper, stronger, and faster multi-person pose estimation model. In: Leibe, B., Matas, J., Sebe, N., Welling, M. (eds.) ECCV 2016. LNCS, vol. 9910, pp. 34–50. Springer, Cham (2016). https://doi.org/10.1007/978-3-319-46466-4_3
17. Iqbal, U., Gall, J.: Multi-person pose estimation with local joint-to-person associations. In: Hua, G., Jégou, H. (eds.) ECCV 2016. LNCS, vol. 9914, pp. 627–642. Springer, Cham (2016). https://doi.org/10.1007/978-3-319-48881-3_44

18. Iqbal, U., Molchanov, P., Breuel, T., Gall, J., Kautz, J.: Hand pose estimation via latent 2.5D heatmap regression. In: Ferrari, V., Hebert, M., Sminchisescu, C., Weiss, Y. (eds.) ECCV 2018. LNCS, vol. 11215, pp. 125–143. Springer, Cham (2018). https://doi.org/10.1007/978-3-030-01252-6_8

19. Jakab, T., Gupta, A., Bilen, H., Vedaldi, A.: Unsupervised learning of object landmarks through conditional image generation. In: NeurIPS (2018)

20. Jeon, S., Min, D., Kim, S., Sohn, K.: Joint learning of semantic alignment and object landmark detection. In: ICCV (2019)

21. Jia, X., De Brabandere, B., Tuytelaars, T., Gool, L.V.: Dynamic filter networks. In: NeurIPS (2016)

22. Jin, S., et al.: Differentiable hierarchical graph grouping for multi-person pose estimation. In: Vedaldi, A., Bischof, H., Brox, T., Frahm, J.-M. (eds.) ECCV 2020. LNCS, vol. 12352, pp. 718–734. Springer, Cham (2020). https://doi.org/10.1007/978-3-030-58571-6_42

23. Jocher, G., et al.: ultralytics/yolov5: v5.0 (Apr 2021). DOI: https://doi.org/10.5281/zenodo.4679653

24. Khirodkar, R., Chari, V., Agrawal, A., Tyagi, A.: Multi-hypothesis pose networks: Rethinking top-down pose estimation. In: ICCV (2021)

25. Kreiss, S., Bertoni, L., Alahi, A.: Pifpaf: Composite fields for human pose estimation. In: CVPR (2019)

26. LeCun, Y., Bengio, Y., et al.: Convolutional networks for images, speech, and time series. In: The Handbook of Brain Theory and Neural Networks, vol. 3361(10) (1995)

27. Li, J., et al.: Human pose regression with residual log-likelihood estimation. In: ICCV (2021)

28. Li, J., Wang, C., Zhu, H., Mao, Y., Fang, H.S., Lu, C.: Crowdpose: Efficient crowded scenes pose estimation and a new benchmark. In: CVPR (2019)

29. Li, K., Wang, S., Zhang, X., Xu, Y., Xu, W., Tu, Z.: Pose recognition with cascade transformers. In: CVPR (2021)

30. Li, Y., et al.: Is 2d heatmap representation even necessary for human pose estimation? arXiv preprint arXiv:2107.03332 (2021)

31. Lin, T.Y., Dollár, P., Girshick, R., He, K., Hariharan, B., Belongie, S.: Feature pyramid networks for object detection. In: CVPR (2017)

32. Lin, T.Y., Goyal, P., Girshick, R., He, K., Dollár, P.: Focal loss for dense object detection. In: ICCV (2017)

33. Lin, T.-Y., et al.: Microsoft COCO: Common objects in context. In: Fleet, D., Pajdla, T., Schiele, B., Tuytelaars, T. (eds.) ECCV 2014. LNCS, vol. 8693, pp. 740–755. Springer, Cham (2014). https://doi.org/10.1007/978-3-319-10602-1_48

34. Loshchilov, I., Hutter, F.: SGDR: Stochastic gradient descent with warm restarts. In: ICLR (2017)

35. Luo, Z., Wang, Z., Huang, Y., Wang, L., Tan, T., Zhou, E.: Rethinking the heatmap regression for bottom-up human pose estimation. In: CVPR (2021)

36. Mao, W., Tian, Z., Wang, X., Shen, C.: Fcpose: Fully convolutional multi-person pose estimation with dynamic instance-aware convolutions. In: CVPR (2021)

37. McNally, W., Vats, K., Wong, A., McPhee, J.: EvoPose2D: Pushing the boundaries of 2d human pose estimation using accelerated neuroevolution with weight transfer. IEEE Access (2021). https://doi.org/10.1109/ACCESS.2021.3118207

38. McNally, W., Walters, P., Vats, K., Wong, A., McPhee, J.: DeepDarts: Modeling keypoints as objects for automatic scorekeeping in darts using a single camera. In: CVPRW (2021)

39. McNally, W., Wong, A., McPhee, J.: Action recognition using deep convolutional neural networks and compressed spatio-temporal pose encodings. J. Comput. Vis. Imaging Syst. **4**(1), 3 (2018)

40. McNally, W., Wong, A., McPhee, J.: STAR-Net: Action recognition using spatio-temporal activation reprojection. In: CRV (2019)

41. Nesterov, Y.: A method for solving the convex programming problem with convergence rate o(1/k2). Proc. USSR Acad. Sci. **269**, 543–547 (1983)

42. Newell, A., Huang, Z., Deng, J.: Associative embedding: End-to-end learning for joint detection and grouping. In: NeurIPS (2017)

43. Newell, A., Yang, K., Deng, J.: Stacked hourglass networks for human pose estimation. In: Leibe, B., Matas, J., Sebe, N., Welling, M. (eds.) ECCV 2016. LNCS, vol. 9912, pp. 483–499. Springer, Cham (2016). https://doi.org/10.1007/978-3-319-46484-8_29

44. Nie, X., Feng, J., Zhang, J., Yan, S.: Single-stage multi-person pose machines. In: ICCV (2019)

45. Papandreou, G., Zhu, T., Chen, L.-C., Gidaris, S., Tompson, J., Murphy, K.: PersonLab: Person pose estimation and instance segmentation with a bottom-up, part-based, geometric embedding model. In: Ferrari, V., Hebert, M., Sminchisescu, C., Weiss, Y. (eds.) Computer Vision – ECCV 2018. LNCS, vol. 11218, pp. 282–299. Springer, Cham (2018). https://doi.org/10.1007/978-3-030-01264-9_17

46. Papandreou, G., Zhu, T., Kanazawa, N., Toshev, A., Tompson, J., Bregler, C., Murphy, K.: Towards accurate multi-person pose estimation in the wild. In: CVPR (2017)

47. Pavllo, D., Feichtenhofer, C., Grangier, D., Auli, M.: 3d human pose estimation in video with temporal convolutions and semi-supervised training. In: CVPR (2019)

48. Pishchulin, L., Insafutdinov, E., Tang, S., Andres, B., Andriluka, M., Gehler, P.V., Schiele, B.: DeepCut: Joint subset partition and labeling for multi person pose estimation. In: CVPR (2016)

49. Raaj, Y., Idrees, H., Hidalgo, G., Sheikh, Y.: Efficient online multi-person 2d pose tracking with recurrent spatio-temporal affinity fields. In: CVPR (2019)

50. Redmon, J., Divvala, S., Girshick, R., Farhadi, A.: You only look once: Unified, real-time object detection. In: CVPR (2016)

51. Redmon, J., Farhadi, A.: Yolov3: An incremental improvement. arXiv preprint arXiv:1804.02767 (2018)

52. Ren, S., He, K., Girshick, R., Sun, J.: Faster R-CNN: Towards real-time object detection with region proposal networks (2015)

53. Rezende, D., Mohamed, S.: Variational inference with normalizing flows. In: ICML (2015)

54. Sun, K., Xiao, B., Liu, D., Wang, J.: Deep high-resolution representation learning for human pose estimation. In: CVPR (2019)

55. Suwajanakorn, S., Snavely, N., Tompson, J., Norouzi, M.: Discovery of latent 3d keypoints via end-to-end geometric reasoning. In: NeurIPS (2018)

56. Tian, Z., Shen, C., Chen, H., He, T.: FCOS: Fully convolutional one-stage object detection. In: ICCV (2019)

57. Tompson, J.J., Jain, A., LeCun, Y., Bregler, C.: Joint training of a convolutional network and a graphical model for human pose estimation. In: NeurIPS (2014)

58. Toshev, A., Szegedy, C.: DeepPose: Human pose estimation via deep neural networks. In: CVPR (2014)

59. Vats, K., McNally, W., Dulhanty, C., Lin, Z.Q., Clausi, D.A., Zelek, J.: Puck-Net: Estimating hockey puck location from broadcast video. In: AAAI Workshops (2019)

60. Voeikov, R., Falaleev, N., Baikulov, R.: Ttnet: Real-time temporal and spatial video analysis of table tennis. In: CVPRW (2020)
61. Wang, C.Y., Bochkovskiy, A., Liao, H.Y.M.: Scaled-YOLOv4: Scaling cross stage partial network. arXiv preprint arXiv:2011.08036 (2020)
62. Wang, C.Y., Liao, H.Y.M., Wu, Y.H., Chen, P.Y., Hsieh, J.W., Yeh, I.H.: Cspnet: A new backbone that can enhance learning capability of cnn. In: CVPR (2020)
63. Wang, X., Bo, L., Fuxin, L.: Adaptive wing loss for robust face alignment via heatmap regression. In: ICCV (2019)
64. Wei, F., Sun, X., Li, H., Wang, J., Lin, S.: Point-set anchors for object detection, instance segmentation and pose estimation. In: Vedaldi, A., Bischof, H., Brox, T., Frahm, J.-M. (eds.) ECCV 2020. LNCS, vol. 12355, pp. 527–544. Springer, Cham (2020). https://doi.org/10.1007/978-3-030-58607-2_31
65. Wei, S.E., Ramakrishna, V., Kanade, T., Sheikh, Y.: Convolutional pose machines. In: CVPR (2016)
66. Xiao, B., Wu, H., Wei, Y.: Simple baselines for human pose estimation and tracking. In: Ferrari, V., Hebert, M., Sminchisescu, C., Weiss, Y. (eds.) ECCV 2018. LNCS, vol. 11210, pp. 472–487. Springer, Cham (2018). https://doi.org/10.1007/978-3-030-01231-1_29
67. Xu, Z., Li, B., Yuan, Y., Geng, M.: AnchorFace: An anchor-based facial landmark detector across large poses. In: AAAI (2021)
68. Yang, S., Quan, Z., Nie, M., Yang, W.: Transpose: Keypoint localization via transformer. In: ICCV (2021)
69. Zheng, Z., Wang, P., Liu, W., Li, J., Ye, R., Ren, D.: Distance-IoU loss: Faster and better learning for bounding box regression. In: AAAI (2020)
70. Zhou, X., Wang, D., Krähenbühl, P.: Objects as points. arXiv preprint arXiv:1904.07850 (2019)

VirtualPose: Learning Generalizable 3D Human Pose Models from Virtual Data

Jiajun Su[1,2], Chunyu Wang[5(✉)], Xiaoxuan Ma[2,3], Wenjun Zeng[6], and Yizhou Wang[2,3,4]

[1] Center for Data Science, Peking University, Beijing, China
sujiajun@pku.edu.cn
[2] Center on Frontiers of Computing Studies, Peking University, Beijing, China
{maxiaoxuan,yizhou.wang}@pku.edu.cn
[3] Department of Computer Science, Peking University, Beijing, China
[4] Institute for Artificial Intelligence, Peking University, Beijing, China
[5] Microsoft Research Asia, Beijing, China
chnuwa@microsoft.com
[6] EIT Institute for Advanced Study, Ningbo, China
zengw2011@hotmail.com

Abstract. While monocular 3D pose estimation seems to have achieved very accurate results on the public datasets, their generalization ability is largely overlooked. In this work, we perform a systematic evaluation of the existing methods and find that they get notably larger errors when tested on different cameras, human poses and appearance. To address the problem, we introduce *VirtualPose*, a two-stage learning framework to exploit the hidden "free lunch" specific to this task, *i.e.*generating infinite number of poses and cameras for training models at no cost. To that end, the first stage transforms images to abstract geometry representations (AGR), and then the second maps them to 3D poses. It addresses the generalization issue from two aspects: (1) the first stage can be trained on diverse 2D datasets to reduce the risk of over-fitting to limited appearance; (2) the second stage can be trained on diverse AGR synthesized from a large number of virtual cameras and poses. It outperforms the SOTA methods without using any paired images and 3D poses from the benchmarks, which paves the way for practical applications. Code is available at https://github.com/wkom/VirtualPose.

Keyword: Absolute 3D human pose estimation

1 Introduction

Monocular 3D pose estimation has attracted much attention since it can benefit many applications. Most works [4,5,17,19,24,25,32,38,39] focus on a simpler sub-task of *relative* 3D pose estimation where only relative joint positions are estimated. Absolute 3D pose estimation needs to estimate the depth of a person's *root* joint in the camera coordinate system. This is more challenging because it

© The Author(s), under exclusive license to Springer Nature Switzerland AG 2022
S. Avidan et al. (Eds.): ECCV 2022, LNCS 13666, pp. 55–71, 2022.
https://doi.org/10.1007/978-3-031-20068-7_4

is ill-posed and multiple entangled latent factors jointly determine the depth. As shown in Fig. 1, the relevant factors include at least the height of the person in neutral standing pose, its relative posture, its projection size in 2D, camera focal length, and camera view point. Some factors such as focal length may be assumed known in some cases but most others need to be implicitly estimated from images along with depth.

Many works [3,15,23,30,37,42,43,47] propose to brute-forcely learn the mapping from images to depth. Although they have got good results on the public datasets, they have poor generalization ability. We are aware that other tasks also face the issue but the situation is very different for pose estimation. First, the pose datasets [10,12,20,22,31] have extremely limited variations in terms of cameras, human poses and appearance. Second, many data augmentation techniques are not applicable, e.g., we can not change the view point neither the human poses in an image. So, addressing the generalization issue is non-trivial compared to other tasks. This was not identified as a serious issue previously because the current training and testing data [10,12] are similar. In fact, even for the cross-dataset experiment (train on MuCo-3DHP [22] and test on MuPoTS-3D [22]), the camera views are also similar.

In this paper, we address the challenges by introducing an intermediate representation, termed as Abstract Geometry Representation (AGR), into the 3D pose estimation network. It is a bundle of multiple geometry representations that satisfy three requirements: (1) they are helpful for recovering absolute 3D poses, (2) can be synthesized from 3D poses, and (3) can be robustly estimated from images even when the model is trained on wild images rather than mocap datasets. As shown in Fig. 2, AGR splits a 3D pose estimator into two successive modules. The first module maps a raw image to AGR which, in current implementation, consists of human detection and joint localization results. Since it only handles 2D tasks which are barely affected by 3D projection geometry, we can train the model on the diverse 2D datasets such as COCO [16], which covers a large number of camera views, human poses and backgrounds, and apply extensive data augmentation. As a result, the module is robust to different factors and achieves desirable results on wild data.

The second module learns to regress 3D pose from AGR. Different from the previous works, we propose a novel training strategy which synthesizes a large number of paired <AGR, Pose> data from diverse camera views, poses and person positions to learn a generalizable model. It is worth noting that AGR suffers less from domain gaps than raw images. In some cases when we want to deploy a model for a fixed environment, e.g.installing a camera at home for elderly care, we can even generate virtual training data specifically for the environment, which as shown in our experiment, gets more accurate results. Combining the two modules, we get an accurate yet generalizable 3D pose estimator. It not only outperforms the state-of-the-art methods on the benchmark datasets but also achieves good results on our own videos collected in retail stores with cluttered background and severe occlusion.

We implement the above idea following the architecture of VoxelPose [33], as shown in Fig. 2. Given an image as input, we first estimate bounding boxes and

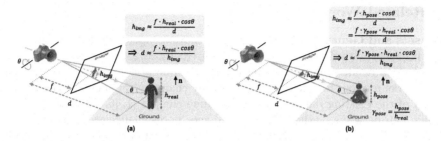

Fig. 1. Projection geometry of a pinhole camera model. (a) shows the case where a person is in a standing pose. (b) shows the case with a different pose.

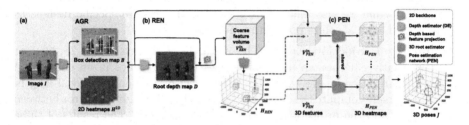

Fig. 2. Our 3D human pose estimation pipeline. (a) Given an image as input, it first estimates the AGR (*i.e.*bounding boxes and heatmaps) of all people. (b) Then, in Root Estimation Network (REN), it estimates the depth map of root joints from the AGR. The AGR and the depth map are integrated via depth based feature projection to estimate 3D root positions. (c) Finally, in Pose Estimation Network (PEN) for each root joint, we construct a feature volume around it to estimate a fine-grained 3D pose.

2D pose heatmaps as AGR using a CNN network. Then they are integrated into the 3D space to estimate the 3D positions of all persons in the image. Finally, for each person, we construct a feature volume around its position to estimate a fine-grained 3D pose.

In summary, our contributions are three-fold. First, we present the first systematic study on models' generalization ability which is largely overlooked in the previous works. We argue that it is important to purposely prevent models from over-fitting when designing and evaluating new models. Second, we present one possible way for learning generalizable models purely from virtual 3D poses and cameras which is made possible by AGR. Note that the decoupling strategy has been used in previous works [2,14,18,26,33,40] for different motivations. Our contribution lies in leveraging it in our training strategy for absolute 3D pose estimation with concrete designs. Finally, the method outperforms the existing methods without using paired images and 3D poses for training, which notably improves its applicability in practice.

2   Related Work

Datasets and Generalization. Collecting motion capture datasets is cumbersome because it either uses multiview systems [10,12,20,22,31] or wearable IMUs [18,45]. As a result, they usually have limited camera views, poses and actors. Some works propose to generate more data by changing the image backgrounds [22,23] of the existing datasets, or using game engines [1,46,50]. However, the domain gap between synthetic and real images poses challenges for neural networks. We find that the models trained on these datasets lack generalization capability. Some works [36,41,48] address the generalization problem in relative pose estimation but they cannot be extended to the absolute task. There are some works in other areas that also decouple a network into different stages [18,33,40]. While we also follow this general idea, we have specific designs to apply it to the 3D absolute pose estimation task.

Minimizing Projection Error. The methods of this class [6,7,28,29] first estimate relative 3D human poses with sizes from an image in an end-to-end manner. Then based on the estimated 2D projection size and the focal length, they can coarsely compute the depth of each pose by minimizing an error between the 2D pose and the projection of the estimated 3D pose. The results of these methods heavily rely on the accuracy of relative 3D pose estimation. Some later works [36,48] show that they have poor generalization results because they need to be trained on the (small) motion capture datasets [10,20].

Ground Plane Geometry. Some works such as [21] propose to analytically compute the real 3D size and depth from ground plane geometry. They assume that the camera is calibrated, people are standing on the ground and their feet are visible in the image. Then the absolute human height and depth can be calculated by projection geometry. However, these assumptions are not always true in practice which limits their applicability.

End-to-End Learning. Some works [15,23,37,47] directly estimate depth from images. We first explain why this is possible. Consider a simple case where a person with height h_{real} stands on the ground plane and a camera with focal length f is placed with pitch angle θ, as shown in Fig. 1(a). Then the height of the person in the image h_{img} is approximately $h_{img} \approx \frac{f \cdot h_{real} \cdot \cos\theta}{d}$. In general, people may be in various poses, $e.g.$ sitting on the ground as shown in Fig. 1(b). We define the height of the person perpendicular to the ground as h_{pose}, and a pose-dependent correction factor as $\gamma_{pose} = \frac{h_{pose}}{h_{real}}$, then we have $h_{img} \approx \frac{f \cdot \gamma_{pose} \cdot h_{real} \cdot \cos\theta}{d}$, from which the depth d of the person can be computed.

These methods usually assume f is known and estimate normalized depth $d^{norm} = \frac{d}{f}$. It is challenging to estimate h_{real} from a single image. But since there are only few actors in the benchmark datasets, they are implicitly learned by the network. The rest factors of γ_{pose}, θ and h_{img} can be estimated from images when the training data is large and diverse. However, since most benchmark datasets are small, $e.g.$ having limited camera poses, human poses and backgrounds, the depth estimation models may easily over-fit to these datasets but can not generalize well on unseen images.

3   Generalization Study

In this section, we systematically evaluate the robustness of the existing methods to the variations of the key factors. In Sect. 3.1, we first introduce three representative baselines for estimating depth which are most frequently used by the existing 3D pose estimators [8,15,23,34,37,47,49]. Then we evaluate their robustness to the three factors including camera pose, image background and human pose.

3.1   Baselines and Datasets

Top-down Box Size Based Method (TBS). Given an image as input, it first localizes all people by bounding boxes and then estimates depth for each people. They assume that the 3D sizes of all people are constant and known, and geometrically compute the depth based on the 2D size of the bounding box. However, as discussed in Fig. 1(b), the 2D size is also dependent on the human pose. So they learn a correction factor from images. The factor is used to refine the estimated depth. Multiple methods [8,23] follow this strategy. We choose RootNet [23] in our experiments.

Top-down Image Feature Based Method (TIF). It first detects all people in the input image. But instead of using the size of the detected bounding box to analytically compute depth, they use the estimated 2D heatmaps as attention masks to pool features from the image and directly predict the human depth. We choose HDNet [15] in our experiments.

Bottom-up Depth Regression Based Method (BDR). This method directly estimates a depth map from each image using a deep network. The depth of each joint can then be obtained from the depth map directly. Many works [34,37,47] follow this pipeline. We present a simple 3D pose estimator which has two branches for estimating 2D pose heatmaps and depth maps, respectively. The 3D pose can then be analytically computed from them.

Implementation Details. In order to mitigate the influence of detection results, we use the GT human bounding box in TBS and TIF methods. The backbone in the BDR method is ResNet-50 [9]. In order to mitigate the influence of 2D pose estimation, we use the GT 2D root position to obtain root depth from the depth maps in BDR method. We conduct experiments on the CMU Panoptic [12], MuCo-3DHP and MuPoTS-3D [22] datasets.

CMU Panoptic. [12] is a large-scale multi-person pose dataset captured in a studio with multiple cameras. We select data of four activities (Haggling, Mafia, Ultimatum, Pizza) as our training and test set. The training and testing splits are different in different ablative experiments and will be made clear as needed.

MuCo-3DHP. [22] is created by compositing randomly sampled 3D poses from single-person 3D human pose dataset MPI-INF-3DHP [20] to synthesize multi-person scenes. The images are synthesized by resizing and compositing the corresponding segmented images of each person according to their 3D positions.

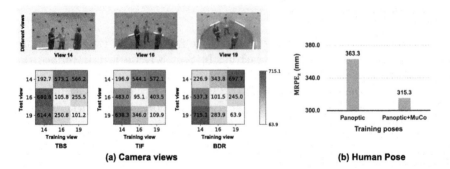

Fig. 3. (a) Cross-view results (MRPE$_z$) of the three models on the CMU Panoptic dataset. The x- and y-axes represent the camera index in training and test, respectively. (b) Depth estimation results (MRPE$_z$) when the training poses are from the CMU Panoptic dataset, or from the mixture of "Panoptic+MuCo" datasets. The MuPoTS-3D dataset is the test dataset.

We use the data provided by [23] which contains images with green screen background and images with augmented background using COCO [16] dataset.

MuPoTS-3D. [22] is a multi-person test set comprising 20 general real world scenes with GT 3D pose obtained with a multi-view marker-less motion capture system. It contains 5 indoor and 15 outdoor settings, varying human poses and camera poses, which is a commonly used test set to validate the models' generalization ability.

Table 1. Depth estimation results (MRPE$_z$) when we train the models on images with green-screen background (green) or with mixture of green-screen and augmented background (augmented), respectively.

Method	Training data	Test data	
		MuCo (green)	MuCo (augmented)
TBS	green	76.0	281.6
	augmented	73.3	82.5
TIF	green	57.3	168.8
	augmented	58.7	65.5
BDR	green	126.3	267.8
	augmented	141.7	148.9

Metrics. We focus on evaluating the quality of the estimated depth of root joint in this section. We use the metric of MRPE$_z$ (in mm) proposed in [23], which is the mean of the root position errors of all people in the z direction (*i.e.* the depth direction in the camera coordinate system).

3.2   Experimental Results

Camera Views. We conduct the cross-view experiment on the CMU Panoptic [12] dataset using cameras of 14, 16 and 19 as shown in Fig. 3(a). We train the three baseline models on one of the cameras and test them on the rest. The results are shown in Fig. 3(a). All methods get several times larger depth estimation errors when they are trained and tested on different cameras. The results are reasonable because (1) camera angle affects image appearance and image features; (2) camera angle also affects the 2D size of the people in the image. The results suggest that the models learned on few camera views are barely generalizable. It is helpful to train the models on as many views as possible.

Image Background. For each method, we train two models on the MuCo-3DHP [22] dataset, with the first on images with green screen background and the second with both green screen and augmented background. We select 70% of the dataset for training, and the rest for testing. Table 1 shows the results. When tested on the green screen subset of MuCo-3DHP, BDR (green) achieves a smaller error than BDR (augmented). It means that BDR probably learns some scene priors to reduce the ambiguity in estimation but it may also risk over-fitting. For example, BDR (green) gets a significantly larger error on the augmented subset of MuCo-3DHP. The results not only validate the limitations of those methods on small training datasets, but also suggest that we actually need a better evaluation protocol, *e.g.*training and testing on datasets with large differences, to convincingly evaluate the future works.

Human Pose. We train two models either using poses only from the CMU Panoptic dataset, or from the combined CMU Panoptic and MuCo-3DHP datasets. We test the models on the MuPoTS-3D dataset. To keep other factors such as human appearance the same, we modify BDR to take pose heatmaps as input and output the root depth map D (this is actually part of our method as will be described). The results are shown in Fig. 3(b). The model trained on CMU Panoptic poses achieves a larger error meaning that the model trained on limited poses may have poor generalization results. While the conclusion is not surprising, it actually points out an overlooked problem that relying on limited mocap datasets to train 3D pose estimators will probably fail in real-world applications.

4   VirtualPose

In this section, we present our *VirtualPose*. To address the challenges, we introduce an intermediate representation, termed as Abstract Geometry Representation (AGR, Sect. 4.1), into the 3D pose estimation network so that we can simultaneously leverage the diverse 2D datasets and large amounts of synthetic data. As shown in Fig. 2, AGR splits a 3D pose estimator into two successive modules. The first module maps a raw image to AGR which consists of human detection and joint localization results. Then the second module maps AGR to the corresponding 3D pose which is trained on synthesized <AGR, Pose> data.

In particular, we present Root Estimation Network (REN, Sect. 4.2) to estimate 3D positions of the persons. Then for each person, Pose Estimation Network (PEN, Sect. 4.3) is proposed to estimate the 3D pose.

4.1 Abstract Geometry Representation

AGR is a general concept representing a bundle of geometry representations that satisfy three requirements: (1) they are helpful for recovering absolute 3D poses, and (2) can be robustly estimated from images even when the model is only trained on the wild 2D datasets rather than the 3D motion capture datasets, and (3) can be synthesized or rendered from 3D poses. In current implementation, we only use 2D pose heatmaps and human detection bounding boxes in AGR for simplicity. But more cues such as ordinal depth, occlusion relationship or segmentation mask can also be leveraged.

We adopt a simple architecture for estimating AGR from images following CenterNet [49]. As shown in Fig. 2(a), given an image I as input, the 2D backbone outputs the corresponding 2D pose heatmaps $H^{2D} \in [0, 1]^{W \times H \times N}$ and box detection map $B \in \mathcal{R}^{W \times H \times 4}$ where the four channels encode the distances from the human root joint to the four edges of the human bounding box, respectively. Here, N indicates the number of human joints, and W, H are the width and height of the output maps. The 2D human pose estimation and detection network is trained by:

$$\mathcal{L}_{2D} = \mathcal{L}_{heat}^{2D} + \lambda_{bbox}\mathcal{L}_{bbox} \tag{1}$$

$$\mathcal{L}_{heat}^{2D} = ||H^{2D} - \widetilde{H}^{2D}||_2^2 \tag{2}$$

$$\mathcal{L}_{bbox} = \sum_{p \in \mathcal{P}} ||B_p - \widetilde{B}_p||_1, \tag{3}$$

where $\widetilde{H}^{2D}$ is the GT 2D pose heatmaps and λ_{bbox} is a hyper-parameter. The box supervision is only enforced at GT root joint locations $\mathcal{P}$ where B_p is the estimated box embedding for the p_{th} person and $\widetilde{B}_p \in \mathcal{R}^4$ is the GT box embedding.

4.2 Root Estimation Network

We first estimate a coarse depth map for the root joint as shown in Fig. 2, which will be used to reduce the ambiguity when projecting 2D heatmaps to the 3D space. To that end, the previously estimated 2D pose heatmaps H^{2D} are fed to the 2D CNN-based Depth Estimator (DE) to estimate a root depth map D. It is trained by minimizing:

$$\mathcal{L}_{depth} = \sum_{p \in \mathcal{P}} |D_p - \widetilde{D}_p|, \tag{4}$$

where D_p and $\widetilde{D}_p$ are the estimated and GT depth values of the root joint for the p_{th} person.

Then we estimate the 3D positions of the root joints by constructing a 3D representation. We discretize the 3D space in which people can freely move into $X \times Y \times Z$ voxels $\{G_{x,y,z}\}$, and construct a 3D feature volume $V_{REN}^{in} \in [0,1]^{X \times Y \times Z \times N}$ by inversely projecting 2D pose heatmaps of N body joints to the 3D space using camera parameters. Different from the previous works [33,44], for a heatmap vector at a pixel location within a bounding box, we only project it to a few voxels whose depths are similar to the estimated depth D_p of the root joint in the bounding box. For example, if a voxel $G_{x,y,z}$ whose projected 2D pixel location (u,v) is within the p_{th} human bounding box, then the feature of $G_{x,y,z}$ can be calculated as

$$V_{REN}^{in}(x,y,z) = H^{2D}(u,v)\exp(-\frac{(z-D_p)^2}{2\sigma^2}), \qquad (5)$$

where σ is empirically set to be 200. This is particularly important for monocular 3D pose estimation which helps reduce the ambiguity. The feature volume V_{REN}^{in} coarsely encodes the likelihood of each person's position in each voxel. We feed V_{REN}^{in} to a 3D network to estimate the corresponding 3D heatmaps $H_{REN} \in [0,1]^{X \times Y \times Z}$ indicating the confidence of each voxel containing a root joint as shown in Fig. 2(b). We select the voxels with large confidence values in the estimated H_{REN} with Non-Maximum Suppression (NMS). We train the 3D network by minimizing:

$$\mathcal{L}_{REN} = ||H_{REN} - \widetilde{H}_{REN}||_2^2, \qquad (6)$$

where $\widetilde{H}_{REN} \in [0,1]^{X \times Y \times Z}$ is the GT 3D heatmap for root joint. We set X, Y and Z to be 80, 80 and 24, respectively.

4.3 Pose Estimation Network

After estimating the root joint position for each person, we will estimate a complete 3D pose for it. As shown in Fig. 2(c), we first construct a finer-grained feature volume centered at the estimated root joint position by inversely projecting the estimated 2D pose heatmaps H^{2D}. The spatial size of the feature volume $V_{PEN}^{in} \in [0,1]^{X' \times Y' \times Z' \times N}$ is set to be $2m \times 2m \times 2m$ which is sufficiently large to cover people in arbitrary poses. We set $X' = Y' = Z' = 64$, so approximately each voxel has a size of 30 mm.

We feed V_{PEN}^{in} to a 3D Pose Estimation Network (PEN) to estimate 3D heatmaps $H_{PEN} \in [0,1]^{X' \times Y' \times Z' \times N}$ for N joints, including the root joint. For each joint k, the 3D location J_k can be obtained using the integration trick proposed in [32] to reduce quantization error:

$$J_k = \sum_{x=1}^{X'}\sum_{y=1}^{Y'}\sum_{z=1}^{Z'}(x,y,z) \cdot H_{PEN,k}(x,y,z). \qquad (7)$$

We train PEN using the L_1 loss as in [33]:

$$\mathcal{L}_{PEN} = \frac{1}{N} \sum_{k=1}^{N} ||\boldsymbol{J}_k - \widetilde{\boldsymbol{J}}_k||_1. \tag{8}$$

PEN has the same network structure as the 3D network in REN, and the weights are shared for different people. We find that by estimating the absolute 3D locations of all joints, it further improves the absolute position of the root joint compared to the REN output.

5   Experiments

5.1   Implementation Details

General Details. The 2D backbone for estimating boxes and 2D pose heatmaps is ResNet-152 [9]. The backbone for estimating depth map from heatmaps is ResNet-18 [9]. The input image is resized to 512×960 and the size of the resulting heatmap is 128×240. We adopt Adam [13] as optimizer, the learning rate is 1×10^{-4} and the batch size is 24. The 2D backbone network is trained for 40 epochs. The depth estimator, REN and PEN are trained end-to-end with synthetic heatmaps and their GT 3D poses for 20 epochs.

Training Data. For the experiments on CMU Panoptic [12], the backbone is trained on the combined COCO [16] and CMU Panoptic datasets. When synthesizing AGR training data, the absolute 3D poses and camera views are the same as the original training data in Panoptic dataset. For the MuPoTS-3D [22] experiment, the backbone is trained on the combined COCO and MuCo-3DHP [22] datasets. When synthesizing AGR training data, the relative 3D poses and camera views are from MuCo-3DHP, and we randomly place the poses in 3D space to enhance the diversity of the training data.

5.2   Comparison to the State-of-the-arts

CMU Panoptic [12]. Following [42], we use the video sequences of camera 16 and 30 as training and test data which consist of four activities, $i.e.$ Haggling, Mafia, Ultimatum, Pizza. We show the results in Table 2. We achieve better results than previous methods except for HMOR [37] which uses the GT depth when estimating the absolute 3D pose. Besides, our method achieves the best performance in the Pizza sequence which is not included in the training data. This partially validates the generalization ability of our method.

Table 2. Comparison to the state-of-the-art methods on the CMU Panoptic dataset. The metric is MPJPE (mm). [37]† uses the GT depth when estimating absolute 3D poses so it is not fairly comparable to other methods. Our method does not use paired images and poses data for training but it still achieves smaller errors than other methods.

Method	Haggling	Mafia	Ultimatum	Pizza	Mean ↓
Li et al.(**HMOR**) [37]†	50.9	50.5	50.7	68.2	55.1
PoPa et al.[27]	217.9	187.3	193.6	221.3	203.4
Zanfir et al.[42]	140.0	165.9	150.7	156.0	153.4
Moon et al.(**RootNet**) [23]	89.6	91.3	79.6	90.1	87.6
Zanfir et al.[43]	72.4	78.8	66.8	94.3	78.1
Zhen et al.(**SMAP**) [47]	<u>63.1</u>	**60.3**	<u>56.6</u>	<u>67.1</u>	<u>61.8</u>
Ours	**54.1**	<u>61.6</u>	**54.6**	**65.4**	**58.9**

MuPoTS-3D [22]. Our method is trained on the synthetic data where the 3D poses are from the MuCo-3DHP dataset. The rest methods are trained end-to-end on paired images and 3D poses from the MuCo-3DHP dataset. Following the standard practice on this dataset, the metric of percentage of correct keypoints (3DPCK) is used to measure the estimation results. The results are shown in Table 3. PCK_{abs} measures the accuracy of absolute pose and PCK_{root} measures the accuracy of the root joint. We can see that our method achieves significantly better depth and pose estimation results than the state-of-the-arts. It validates that our absolute 3D depth estimation method has strong generalization capability. We hope to emphasize the importance of the results because it means the method has the potential to be applied in the wild environments.

Table 3. Comparison to the state-of-the-art methods on MuPoTS-3D. *Matched people* only computes accuracy for GT poses which are matched to predictions and *All people* computes accuracy for all GT poses in the dataset. The methods are not strictly comparable because they may have different backbones.

Method	Matched people		All people
	PCK_{abs} ↑	PCK_{root} ↑	PCK_{abs} ↑
Moon et al.(**RootNet**) [23]	31.8	31.0	31.5
Lin et al.(**HDNet**) [15]	35.2	39.4	-
Zhen et al.(**SMAP**) [47]	38.7	45.5	35.4
Veges et al.[35]	39.6	-	37.3
Sarandi et al.[30]	40.5	-	38.4
Li et al.(**HMOR**) [37]	-	-	43.8
Guo et al.[8]	39.6	-	39.2
Ours	**47.0**	**53.5**	**44.0**

5.3   Ablation Study

In this section, we will evaluate the impact of our proposed modules and the training strategies to the estimation results of the root joint.

Root Estimation Network. We first introduce two baselines. Baseline (a) analytically computes the 3D root position based on the 2D position and the estimated depth map. The baseline (b) uses the 3D root estimator to estimate the 3D root position on top of (a). The results on the CMU Panoptic and MuPoTS-3D datasets are shown in Table 4. By comparing the results of (a) and (b), we can see that the root depth error has a significant reduction which validates the effectiveness of the 3D root estimator.

Pose Estimation Network. By comparing the results of (b) and (c) in Table 4, we can see that depth estimation can be notably improved by PEN, which leverages the rest of the body joints to refine the root joint. Another reason for the improvement is that the quantization error is reduced by computing continuous root locations via the integral trick.

Depth Based Feature Projection. As stated in Sect. 4.2, we construct the 3D feature volume by projecting 2D pose heatmaps based on the estimated depths and bounding boxes. We compare it to a baseline which naively projects the heatmaps to all voxels as in [11,33] and find that MRPE and $MRPE_z$ of our method are significantly better than the baseline (204.0 mm $vs.$ 253.2 mm, and 159.8 mm $vs.$ 210.5 mm) on the MuPoTS-3D dataset.

Table 4. Ablation study on Root Estimation Network (REN) and Pose Estimation Network (PEN) in our method. We report the MRPE and $MRPE_z$ (mm) on the test set of CMU Panoptic and MuPoTS-3D dataset.

Method	REN	PEN	CMU Panoptic		MuPoTS-3D	
			MRPE ↓	$MRPE_z$ ↓	MRPE ↓	$MRPE_z$ ↓
(a) DE	2D	✗	113.9	104.1	282.0	245.4
(b) REN	2D+3D	✗	115.7	93.6	217.5	165.0
(c) Ours	2D+3D	✓	**97.0**	**86.0**	**204.0**	**159.8**

Training Data Generation Strategies. We compare several training data generation strategies for different scenarios. First, when we have little knowledge about the testing camera view point, we can only uniformly sample camera views for the virtual camera to synthesize training data. The results are shown in Table 5. We can see that by training a universal model, our method achieves smaller depth estimation errors than the model trained on a single camera.

Second, if we know the camera view point in the testing environment, we can generate training data specifically for it. If we train a model for camera 19, then the testing error on camera 19 will be decreased significantly to 62.3 mm.

This is helpful when the camera is fixed, *e.g.* deployed at home for child or elderly care. In this case, we can get very accurate estimation results. We have similar observations for the pose factor. In particular, if we have the pose information for the people who are going to appear in the camera, then we can generate AGR using those poses. In that case, the testing accuracy will also be significantly improved. For example, if we train the model using the poses from the MuPoTS-3D dataset, then the PCK_{abs} will be improved from 44.0% to 50.4%.

Table 5. Impact of training data generation strategies. The metric is $MRPE_z$ (mm). We can see that by training a universal model, our method achieves smaller depth estimation errors than the model trained on a single camera.

Training Camera View	Test Camera view		
	14	16	19
14	-	170.3	294.6
16	454.6	-	198.6
19	621.3	385.1	-
Random	**273.8**	**134.0**	**155.2**

5.4   Qualitative Results

Figure 4(a) shows some estimation results for images from the COCO dataset and MuPoTS-3D dataset. Since the camera parameters are not provided in the COCO dataset, we choose a general focal length (*i.e.*1400) and assume the pitch angle of the camera is zero. We can see that our approach not only obtains accurate 3D pose for each person in the image but also estimates their absolute depth correctly in the 3D space. In particular, the model is robust to pose and background variations. For instance, in the baseball example, we get correct depth estimate for the person in sitting posture. Figure 4(b) and (c) show some typical failure cases. In Fig. 4(b), the man in the red circle is occluded and truncated, while in Fig. 4(c), the little girl is much shorter than the people in the training dataset. In the future, to address the second issue, we will study the possibility of adding another parallel branch in the 2D network to estimate a correction factor to refine the estimated depth of each person.

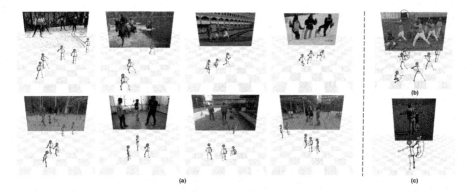

Fig. 4. (a) Some pose estimation results on the COCO (top) and MuPoTS-3D (bottom) datasets. (b) Typical failure cases due to occlusion and truncation. (c) Typical failure cases due to the person is shorter than those in the training dataset. As a result, the estimated depth is larger than GT.

6 Conclusion

In this work, we present a systematic study of the generalization problem of 3D pose estimation. We hope the study can inspire future works to consider the generalization aspect when designing and evaluating new models. Then we present *VirtualPose*, an approach for absolute 3D human pose estimation, which does not require paired images and 3D poses for training. In particular, part of the network is trained on abundant 2D datasets such as COCO and the rest are trained on synthetic datasets. The decoupling strategy helps the approach avoid over-fitting to small training data. As a result, it can be flexibly adapted to a new environment with minimal human effort. Our method achieves significantly better results than the existing methods on the benchmark datasets especially when the training and test datasets have different distributions.

6.1 Future Work

First, in the current implementation, AGR only consists of 2D joint heatmaps and person-level bounding boxes which are powerful to recover the absolute positions of the root joints. But we can actually explore finer-grained AGRs such as segmentation maps and occlusion relationship maps which can benefit more to relative pose estimation. Second, we only used the 3D poses from the Panoptic and MuCo-3DHP dataset for generating AGR training data. But we can actually generate more poses by manipulating joint angles which may further improve the results.

Acknowledgement. This work was supported in part by MOST-2018AAA0102004 and NSFC-62061136001.

References

1. Cao, Z., Gao, H., Mangalam, K., Cai, Q.-Z., Vo, M., Malik, J.: Long-term human motion prediction with scene context. In: Vedaldi, A., Bischof, H., Brox, T., Frahm, J.-M. (eds.) ECCV 2020. LNCS, vol. 12346, pp. 387–404. Springer, Cham (2020). https://doi.org/10.1007/978-3-030-58452-8_23
2. Chang, J.Y., Moon, G., Lee, K.M.: Absposelifter: absolute 3D human pose lifting network from a single noisy 2d human pose. CoRR (2019)
3. Cheng, Y., Wang, B., Tan, R.: Dual networks based 3d multi-person pose estimation from monocular video. IEEE Trans. Pattern Anal. Mach. Intell. (2022)
4. Ci, H., Ma, X., Wang, C., Wang, Y.: Locally connected network for monocular 3D human pose estimation. IEEE Trans. Pattern Anal. Mach. Intell. **44**, 1429–1442 (2020)
5. Ci, H., Wang, C., Ma, X., Wang, Y.: Optimizing network structure for 3D human pose estimation. In: ICCV, pp. 2262–2271 (2019)
6. Dabral, R., Gundavarapu, N.B., Mitra, R., Sharma, A., Ramakrishnan, G., Jain, A.: Multi-person 3D human pose estimation from monocular images. In: 3dv, pp. 405–414. IEEE (2019)
7. Fabbri, M., Lanzi, F., Calderara, S., Alletto, S., Cucchiara, R.: Compressed volumetric heatmaps for multi-person 3D pose estimation. In: CVPR, pp. 7204–7213 (2020)
8. Guo, Y., Ma, L., Li, Z., Wang, X., Wang, F.: Monocular 3d multi-person pose estimation via predicting factorised correction factors. In: Computer Vision and Image Understanding (CVIU), p. 103278 (2021)
9. He, K., Zhang, X., Ren, S., Sun, J.: Deep residual learning for image recognition. In: CVPR, pp. 770–778 (2016)
10. Ionescu, C., Papava, D., Olaru, V., Sminchisescu, C.: Human3. 6m: large scale datasets and predictive methods for 3D human sensing in natural environments. PAMI **36**(7), 1325–1339 (2013)
11. Iskakov, K., Burkov, E., Lempitsky, V., Malkov, Y.: Learnable triangulation of human pose. In: ICCV (2019)
12. Joo, H., et al.: Panoptic studio: a massively multiview system for social motion capture. In: ICCV, pp. 3334–3342 (2015)
13. Kingma, D.P., Ba, J.: Adam: a method for stochastic optimization. In: ICLR (2015)
14. Li, S., Ke, L., Pratama, K., Tai, Y.W., Tang, C.K., Cheng, K.T.: Cascaded deep monocular 3d human pose estimation with evolutionary training data. In: CVPR, pp. 6173–6183 (2020)
15. Lin, J., Lee, G.H.: HDNet: human depth estimation for multi-person camera-space localization. In: Vedaldi, A., Bischof, H., Brox, T., Frahm, J.-M. (eds.) ECCV 2020. LNCS, vol. 12363, pp. 633–648. Springer, Cham (2020). https://doi.org/10.1007/978-3-030-58523-5_37
16. Lin, T.-Y., et al.: Microsoft COCO: common objects in context. In: Fleet, D., Pajdla, T., Schiele, B., Tuytelaars, T. (eds.) ECCV 2014. LNCS, vol. 8693, pp. 740–755. Springer, Cham (2014). https://doi.org/10.1007/978-3-319-10602-1_48
17. Ma, X., Su, J., Wang, C., Ci, H., Wang, Y.: Context modeling in 3D human pose estimation: a unified perspective. In: Proceedings of the IEEE/CVF Conference on Computer Vision and Pattern Recognition, pp. 6238–6247 (2021)
18. von Marcard, T., Henschel, R., Black, M.J., Rosenhahn, B., Pons-Moll, G.: Recovering accurate 3D human pose in the wild using IMUs and a moving camera. In: Ferrari, V., Hebert, M., Sminchisescu, C., Weiss, Y. (eds.) ECCV 2018. LNCS,

vol. 11214, pp. 614–631. Springer, Cham (2018). https://doi.org/10.1007/978-3-030-01249-6_37

19. Martinez, J., Hossain, R., Romero, J., Little, J.J.: A simple yet effective baseline for 3D human pose estimation. In: ICCV, pp. 2640–2649 (2017)

20. Mehta, D., et al.: Monocular 3d human pose estimation in the wild using improved CNN supervision. In: 3DV, pp. 506–516. IEEE (2017)

21. Mehta, D., et al.: Xnect: real-time multi-person 3D human pose estimation with a single RGB camera. TOG 39(4) (2020)

22. Mehta, D., et al.: Single-shot multi-person 3D pose estimation from monocular RGB. In: 3DV, pp. 120–130. IEEE (2018)

23. Moon, G., Chang, J.Y., Lee, K.M.: Camera distance-aware top-down approach for 3D multi-person pose estimation from a single RGB image. In: ICCV, pp. 10133–10142 (2019)

24. Moreno-Noguer, F.: 3D human pose estimation from a single image via distance matrix regression. In: CVPR, pp. 2823–2832 (2017)

25. Pavlakos, G., Zhou, X., Derpanis, K.G., Daniilidis, K.: Coarse-to-fine volumetric prediction for single-image 3D human pose. In: CVPR, pp. 7025–7034 (2017)

26. Pavllo, D., Feichtenhofer, C., Grangier, D., Auli, M.: 3D human pose estimation in video with temporal convolutions and semi-supervised training. In: CVPR, pp. 7753–7762 (2019)

27. Popa, A.I., Zanfir, M., Sminchisescu, C.: Deep multitask architecture for integrated 2D and 3D human sensing. In: CVPR, pp. 6289–6298 (2017)

28. Rogez, G., Weinzaepfel, P., Schmid, C.: LCR-net: localization-classification-regression for human pose. In: CVPR, pp. 3433–3441 (2017)

29. Rogez, G., Weinzaepfel, P., Schmid, C.: LCR-net++: multi-person 2D and 3D pose detection in natural images. PAMI 42(5), 1146–1161 (2019)

30. Sárándi, I., Linder, T., Arras, K.O., Leibe, B.: Metrabs: metric-scale truncation-robust heatmaps for absolute 3D human pose estimation. IEEE Trans. Biometr. Behav. Ident. Sci. 3(1), 16–30 (2020)

31. Sigal, L., Balan, A.O., Black, M.J.: Humaneva: synchronized video and motion capture dataset and baseline algorithm for evaluation of articulated human motion. IJCV 87(1–2), 4 (2010)

32. Sun, X., Xiao, B., Wei, F., Liang, S., Wei, Y.: Integral human pose regression. In: Ferrari, V., Hebert, M., Sminchisescu, C., Weiss, Y. (eds.) ECCV 2018. LNCS, vol. 11210, pp. 536–553. Springer, Cham (2018). https://doi.org/10.1007/978-3-030-01231-1_33

33. Tu, H., Wang, C., Zeng, W.: VoxelPose: towards multi-camera 3d human pose estimation in wild environment. In: Vedaldi, A., Bischof, H., Brox, T., Frahm, J.-M. (eds.) ECCV 2020. LNCS, vol. 12346, pp. 197–212. Springer, Cham (2020). https://doi.org/10.1007/978-3-030-58452-8_12

34. Véges, M., Lőrincz, A.: Absolute human pose estimation with depth prediction network. In: IJCNN, pp. 1–7. IEEE (2019)

35. Véges, M., Lőrincz, A.: Multi-person absolute 3D human pose estimation with weak depth supervision. In: Farkaš, I., Masulli, P., Wermter, S. (eds.) ICANN 2020. LNCS, vol. 12396, pp. 258–270. Springer, Cham (2020). https://doi.org/10.1007/978-3-030-61609-0_21

36. Wandt, B., Rosenhahn, B.: RepNet: weakly supervised training of an adversarial reprojection network for 3D human pose estimation. In: CVPR, pp. 7782–7791 (2019)

37. Wang, C., Li, J., Liu, W., Qian, C., Lu, C.: HMOR: hierarchical multi-person ordinal relations for monocular multi-person 3D pose estimation. In: Vedaldi, A., Bischof, H., Brox, T., Frahm, J.-M. (eds.) ECCV 2020. LNCS, vol. 12348, pp. 242–259. Springer, Cham (2020). https://doi.org/10.1007/978-3-030-58580-8_15

38. Wang, C., Wang, Y., Lin, Z., Yuille, A.L.: Robust 3d human pose estimation from single images or video sequences. IEEE Trans. Pattern Anal. Mach. Intell. **41**(5), 1227–1241 (2018)

39. Wang, C., Wang, Y., Lin, Z., Yuille, A.L., Gao, W.: Robust estimation of 3D human poses from a single image. In: Proceedings of the IEEE Conference on Computer Vision and Pattern Recognition, pp. 2361–2368 (2014)

40. Wu, J., et al.: 3D interpreter networks for viewer-centered wireframe modeling. Int. J. Comput. Vision **126**(9), 1009–1026 (2018)

41. Yang, W., Ouyang, W., Wang, X., Ren, J., Li, H., Wang, X.: 3D human pose estimation in the wild by adversarial learning. In: CVPR, pp. 5255–5264 (2018)

42. Zanfir, A., Marinoiu, E., Sminchisescu, C.: Monocular 3D pose and shape estimation of multiple people in natural scenes-the importance of multiple scene constraints. In: CVPR, pp. 2148–2157 (2018)

43. Zanfir, A., Marinoiu, E., Zanfir, M., Popa, A.I., Sminchisescu, C.: Deep network for the integrated 3d sensing of multiple people in natural images. NIPS **31**, 8410–8419 (2018)

44. Zhang, Y., Wang, C., Wang, X., Liu, W., Zeng, W.: Voxeltrack: multi-person 3D human pose estimation and tracking in the wild. T-PAMI (2022)

45. Zhang, Z., Wang, C., Qin, W., Zeng, W.: Fusing wearable Imus with multi-view images for human pose estimation: a geometric approach. In: CVPR, pp. 2200–2209 (2020)

46. Zhang, Z., Wang, C., Qiu, W., Qin, W., Zeng, W.: Adafuse: adaptive multiview fusion for accurate human pose estimation in the wild. IJCV **129**(3), 703–718 (2021)

47. Zhen, J., et al.: SMAP: single-shot multi-person absolute 3D pose estimation. In: Vedaldi, A., Bischof, H., Brox, T., Frahm, J.-M. (eds.) ECCV 2020. LNCS, vol. 12360, pp. 550–566. Springer, Cham (2020). https://doi.org/10.1007/978-3-030-58555-6_33

48. Zhou, X., Huang, Q., Sun, X., Xue, X., Wei, Y.: Towards 3D human pose estimation in the wild: a weakly-supervised approach. In: ICCV, pp. 398–407 (2017)

49. Zhou, X., Wang, D., Krähenbühl, P.: Objects as points. arXiv preprint arXiv:1904.07850 (2019)

50. Zhu, L., Rematas, K., Curless, B., Seitz, S.M., Kemelmacher-Shlizerman, I.: Reconstructing NBA players. In: Vedaldi, A., Bischof, H., Brox, T., Frahm, J.-M. (eds.) ECCV 2020. LNCS, vol. 12350, pp. 177–194. Springer, Cham (2020). https://doi.org/10.1007/978-3-030-58558-7_11

Poseur: Direct Human Pose Regression with Transformers

Weian Mao[1], Yongtao Ge[1], Chunhua Shen[3(✉)], Zhi Tian[1], Xinlong Wang[1], Zhibin Wang[2], and Anton van den Hengel[1]

[1] The University of Adelaide, Adelaide, Australia
[2] Alibaba Damo Academy, Hangzhou, China
[3] Zhejiang University, Hangzhou, China
Chhshen@gmail.com

Abstract. We propose a direct, regression-based approach to 2D human pose estimation from single images. We formulate the problem as a sequence prediction task, which we solve using a Transformer network. This network *directly* learns a regression mapping from images to the keypoint coordinates, without resorting to intermediate representations such as heatmaps. This approach avoids much of the complexity associated with heatmap-based approaches. To overcome the feature misalignment issues of previous regression-based methods, we propose an attention mechanism that adaptively attends to the features that are most relevant to the target keypoints, considerably improving the accuracy. Importantly, our framework is end-to-end differentiable, and naturally learns to exploit the dependencies between keypoints. Experiments on MS-COCO and MPII, two predominant pose-estimation datasets, demonstrate that our method significantly improves upon the state-of-the-art in regression-based pose estimation. More notably, ours is the first regression-based approach to perform favorably compared to the best heatmap-based pose estimation methods. Code is available at: https://github.com/aim-uofa/Poseur.

Keywords: 2d human pose estimation · Keypoint detection · Transformer

1 Introduction

Human pose estimation is one of the core challenges in computer vision, not least due to its importance in understanding human behaviour. It is also a critical pre-process to a variety of human-centered challenges including activity recognition, video augmentation, and human-robot interaction. Human pose estimation

---

WM and YG contributed equally. YG's contribution was in part made when visiting Alibaba. ZT is now with Meituan Inc.

Supplementary Information The online version contains supplementary material available at https://doi.org/10.1007/978-3-031-20068-7_5.

© The Author(s), under exclusive license to Springer Nature Switzerland AG 2022
S. Avidan et al. (Eds.): ECCV 2022, LNCS 13666, pp. 72–88, 2022.
https://doi.org/10.1007/978-3-031-20068-7_5

requires estimating the location of a set of keypoints in an image, in order that the pose of a simplified human skeleton might be recovered.

Existing methods for human pose estimation can be broadly categorized into heatmap-based and regression-based methods. Heatmap-based methods first predict a heatmap, or classification score map, that reflects the likelihood that each pixel in a region corresponds to a particular skeleton keypoint. The current state-of-the-art methods use a fully convolutional network (FCN) to estimate this heatmap. The final keypoint location estimate corresponds to the peak in the heatmap intensity. Most current pose estimation methods are heatmap-based because this approach has thus far achieved higher accuracy than regression-based approaches. Heatmap-based methods have their disadvantages, however. 1) The ground-truth heatmaps need to be manually designed and heuristically tuned. The noise inevitably introduced impacts on the final results [17,24,28]. 2) A post-processing operation is required to find a single maximum of the heatmap. This operation is often heuristic, and non-differentiable, which precludes end-to-end training-based approaches. 3) The resolution of heatmaps predicted by the FCNs is usually lower than the resolution of the input image. The reduced resolution results in a quantization error and limits the precision of keypoint localization. This quantization error might be ameliorated somewhat by various forms of interpolation, but this makes the framework less differentiable, more complicated and introduces some extra hyper-parameters.

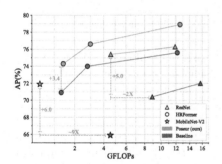

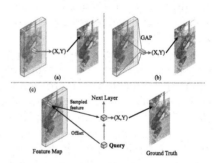

Fig. 1. Comparing the proposed Poseur against heatmap-based methods with various backbone networks on COCO *val.* set. Baseline refers to heatmap-based methods. Heatmap-based baseline of MobileNet-V2 and ResNet use the same deconvolutional head as SimpleBaseline [36].

Fig. 2. Comparison of Poseur and previous regression-based methods. 'GAP' indicates global average pooling. (a) shows the feature misalignment issue. (b) shows crucial spatial information is inevitably lost with GAP. We alleviate both issues with the design in (c).

Regression-based methods directly map the input image to the coordinates of body joints, typically using a fully-connected (FC) prediction layer, eliminating the need for heatmaps. The pipeline of regression-based methods is much more straightforward than heatmap-based methods, as pose estimation is naturally formulated as a process of predicting a set of coordinate values. A regression-based approach also alleviates the need for non-maximum suppression, heatmap generation, and quantization compensation, and is inherently end-to-end differentiable.

Regression-based pose-estimation has received less attention than heatmap-based methods due to its inferior performance. There are a variety of causes of this performance deficit. First, in order to reduce the number of parameters in the final FC prediction layer, models such as DeepPose [31] and RLE [18] employ a global average pooling that is applied to reduce the CNN feature map's resolution before the FC layers, as illustrated in Fig. 2(b). This global average pooling destroys the spatial structure of the convolutional feature maps, and has a significantly negative impact on performance. Next, as shown in Fig. 2(a), the convolutional features and predictions of some regression-based models (e.g. DirectPose [30] and SPM [26]) are misaligned, which consequently reduces localization precision. Lastly, regression-based methods only regress the coordinates of body joints and do not exploit the structured dependency between them [28].

Recently, Transformers have been applied to a range of tasks in computer vision, achieving impressive results [4,12,40]. This, and the fact that transformers were originally designed for sequence-to-sequence tasks, motivated our formulation of single person pose estimation as a sequence prediction problem. Specifically, we pose the problem as that of predicting a length-K sequence of coordinates, where K is the number of body joints for one person. This leads to a simple and novel regression-based pose estimation framework, that we label as **Poseur**.

As shown in Fig. 3, taking as inputs the feature maps of an encoder CNN, the transformer predicts K coordinate pairs. In doing so, Poseur alleviates the aforementioned difficulties of regression-based methods. First, it does not need global average pooling to reduce feature dimensionality (*cf.* RLE [18]). Second, Poseur eliminates the misalignment between the backbone features and predictions with the proposed efficient cross-attention mechanism. Third, since the self-attention module is applied across the keypoint queries, the transformer naturally captures the structured dependencies among the keypoints. Lastly, as shown in Fig. 1, Poseur outperforms heatmap-based methods with a variety of backbones. The improvement is more significant for the backbones using low-resolution representation, e.g., MobileNet V2 and ResNet. The results indicate that Poseur can be deployed with fast backbones of low-resolution representation without large performance drop, which is difficult to be achieved for heatmap-based methods. We refer readers to Sect. 4.4 for more details.

Our main contributions are as follows.

– We propose a transformer-based framework (termed **Poseur**) for directly human pose regression, which is lightweight and can work well with the backbones using low-resolution representation. For example, with 49% fewer FLOPs, ResNet-50 based Poseur outperforms the heatmap-based method SimpleBaseline [36] by 5.0 AP on the COCO *val* set.

- Poseur significantly improves the performance of regression-based methods, to the point where it is comparable to the state-of-the-art heatmap-based approaches. For example, it improves on the previously best regression-based method (RLE [18]) by 4.9 AP with the ResNet-50 backbone on the COCO *val* set and outperforms the previously best heatmap-based method UDP-Pose [27] by 1.0 AP with HRNet-W48 on the COCO *test-dev* set.
- Our proposed framework can be easily extended to an end-to-end pipeline without manual crop operation, for example, we integrate Poseur into Mask R-CNN [15], which is end-to-end trainable and can overcome many drawbacks of the heatmap-based methods. In this end-to-end setting, our method outperforms the previously best end-to-end top-down method PointSet Anchor [34] by 3.8 AP with the HRNet-W48 backbone on the COCO *val* set.

2 Related Work

Heatmap-Based Pose Estimation. Heatmap-based 2D pose estimation methods [2,3,6,7,15,21,25,27,36] estimate per-pixel likelihoods for each keypoint location, and currently dominate in the field of 2D human pose estimation. A few works [2,25,27] attempt to design powerful backbone networks which can maintain high-resolution feature maps for heatmap supervision. Another line of works [17,28,39] focus on alleviating biased data processing pipeline for heatmap-based methods. Despite the good performance, the heatmap representation bears a few drawbacks in nature, e.g. , non-differentiable decoding pipeline [29,30] and quantization errors [17,39] due to the down sampling of feature maps.

Regression-Based Pose Estimation. 2D human pose estimation is naturally a regression problem [29]. However, regression-based methods have historically not been as accurate as heatmap-based methods, and it has received less attention as a result [5,26,28–31]. Integral Pose [29] proposes integral regression, which shares the merits of both heatmap representation and regression approaches, to avoid non-differentiable post-processing and quantization error issues. However, integral regression is proven to have an underlying bias compared with direct regression according to [14]. RLE [18] develops a regression-based method using maximum likelihood estimation and flow models. RLE [18] is the first to push the performance of the regression-based method to a level comparable with that of the heatmap-based methods. However, it is trained on the backbone that pre-trained by the heatmap loss.

Transformer-Based Architectures. Transformers have been applied to the pose estimation task with some success. TransPose [37] and HRFormer [38] enhance the backbone via applying the Transformer encoder to the backbone; TokenPose [22] designs the pose estimation network in a ViT-style fashion by splitting image into patches and applying class tokens, which makes the pose estimation more explainable. These methods are all heatmap-based and use a heavy transformer encoder to improve the model capacity. In contrast, Poseur is

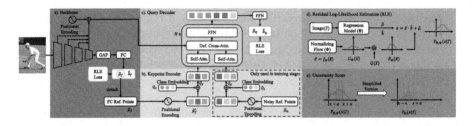

Fig. 3. The architecture of Poseur. The model directly predicts a sequence of keypoint coordinates in parallel by combining (a) backbone network with (b) keypoint encoder and (c) query decoder. (d) Residual Log-likelihood Estimation [18]. (e) The proposed uncertainty score for our method.

a regression-based method with a lightweight transformer decoder. Thus, Poseur is more computational efficient while can still achieve high performance.

PRTR [20] leverage the encoder-decoder structure in transformers to perform pose regression. PRTR is based on DETR [4], i.e., it uses Hungarian matching strategy to find a bipartite matching between non class-specific queries and ground-truth joints. It brings two issues: 1) heavy computational cost; 2) redundant queries for each instance. In contrast, Poseur can alleviate both issues while achieving much higher performance.

3 Method

3.1 Poseur Architecture

Our proposed pose estimator Poseur aims to predict K human keypoint coordinates from a cropped single person image. As shown in Fig. 2(c), The core idea of our method is to represent human keypoints with queries, i.e., each query corresponds to a human keypoint. The queries are input to the deformable attention module [40], which adaptively attends to the image features that most relevant to the query/keypoint. In this way, the information about a specific keypoint can be summarized and encoded into a single query, which is used to regress the keypoint coordinate later. As such, the issue of losing spatial information caused by the global average pooling in RLE [19] (As shown in Fig. 2(b)) is well addressed.

Specifically, in Poseur framework (shown in Fig. 3), two main components are added upon the backbone: a keypoint encoder and a query decoder. An input image is first encoded as dense feature maps with the backbone, which are followed by an FC layer to predict the rough keypoint coordinates, used as a set of rough proposals. We denote the proposal coordinates as $\hat{\boldsymbol{\mu}}_f \in \mathbb{R}^{K \times 2}$. Then, those proposals are used to initialize the keypoint-specific query $\mathbf{Q} \in \mathbb{R}^{K \times C}$ (where C is the embedding dimension) in the keypoint encoder. Finally, the feature maps from the backbone and $\mathbf{Q}$ are sent into the query decoder to obtain the final features for the keypoints, each of which is sent into a linear layer to predict the corresponding keypoint coordinates. In addition, unlike previous methods simply regressing the keypoint coordinates and applying the L_1 loss for supervision, Poseur, following RLE [19], predicts a probability distribution reflecting the probability of the ground truth appearing in each location and supervise the network by maximum the probability on the ground truth location. Specifically, a location parameter $\hat{\boldsymbol{\mu}}_q$ and a scale parameter $\hat{\boldsymbol{b}}_q$ are predicted by Poseur (Θ) for shifting and scaling the distribution generated by a flow model Φ (refer to Sect. 3.2). $\hat{\boldsymbol{\mu}}_q$ is the center of the distribution and can be regarded as the predicted keypoint coordinates.

Backbone. Our method is applicable to both CNN (e.g. ResNet [16], HRNet [27]) and transformer backbones (e.g. HRFormer [38]). Given the backbone, multi-level feature maps are extracted and then fed into the query decoder. At the same time, a global average pooling operation is conducted in the last stage of the backbone and followed by an FC layer to regress the coarse keypoint coordinates $\hat{\boldsymbol{\mu}}_f$ (normalized in $[0, 1]$) and the corresponding scale parameter $\hat{\boldsymbol{b}}_f$, supervised by Residual Log-Likelihood Estimation (RLE) process introduced in Sect. 3.2.

Keypoint Encoder. The keypoint encoder is used to initialize each query $\mathbf{Q}$ for the query decoder. For initializing the query better, two keypoints' attributes, location and category, are encoded into the query in the keypoint encoder. Specifically, first, for location attribute, we encode the rough x-y keypoint coordinates $\hat{\boldsymbol{\mu}}_f$ with the fixed positional encodings, transforming the x-y coordinates to the sine-cosine positional embedding following [32]. The obtained tensor is denoted by $\hat{\boldsymbol{\mu}}_f^* \in \mathbb{R}^{K \times C}$; second, for the category attribute, K learnable vectors $\mathbf{Q}_c \in \mathbb{R}^{K \times C}$, called class embedding, is used to represent K different categories separately. Finally, the initial queries $\mathbf{Q}_z \in \mathbb{R}^{K \times C}$ are generated by fusing the location and category attribute through element-wise addition of the positional and class embedding, i.e. $\mathbf{Q}_z = \mathbf{Q}_c + \hat{\boldsymbol{\mu}}_f^*$.

However, $\hat{\boldsymbol{\mu}}_f$ is just a coarse proposal, which sometimes goes wrong during inference. To make our model more robust for the wrong proposal, we introduce a query augmentation process, named *noisy reference points sampling strategy*, used only during training. The core idea of noisy reference points sampling strategy is to simulate the case that the coarse proposals $\hat{\boldsymbol{\mu}}_f$ goes wrong and force the decoder to located correct keypoint with wrong proposal. Specifically, during training, we construct two types of keypoint queries. The first type of keypoint query is initialized with the proposal $\hat{\boldsymbol{\mu}}_f$; the second type of keypoint query is initialized with normalized random coordinates $\hat{\boldsymbol{\mu}}_n$ (noisy proposal). And then, both of two types query are processed equally in all following training stages. Our experiment shows that training the decoder network with noisy proposal $\hat{\boldsymbol{\mu}}_n$ improves its robustness to errors introduced by coarse proposal $\hat{\boldsymbol{\mu}}_f$ during the inference stage. Note, that during inference randomly initialized keypoint queries are not used.

Query Decoder. In query decoder, query and feature map are mainly used to module the relationship between keypoints and input image. As shown in Fig. 3, the decoder follows the typical transformer decoder paradigm, in which, there are N identical layers in the decoder, each layer consisting of self-attention, cross-attention and feed-forward networks (FFNs). The query $\mathbf{Q}$ goes through these modules sequentially and generates an updated $\mathbf{Q}$ as the input to the next layer. As in DETR [4], the self-attention and FFNs are a multi-head self-attention [32] module and MLPs, respectively. For the cross-attention networks, we propose an efficient multi-scale deformable attention (EMSDA) module, based on MSDA proposed by Deformable DETR [40]. Similar to MSDA, in EMSDA, each query learns to sample relevant features from the feature maps by given the sampling offset around a reference point (a pair of coordinates, and which will be introduced later); and then, the sampled features are summarized by the attention mechanism to update the query. Different from MSDA, which applies a linear layer to the entire feature maps and thus is less efficient, we found that it is enough to only apply the linear layer to the sampled features after bilinear interpolation. Experiments show that the latter can have a similar performance while being much more efficient. Specifically, EMSDA can be written as

$$\text{EMSDA}(\mathbf{Q}_q, \hat{\mathbf{p}}_q, \{\mathbf{x}^l\}_{l=1}^L) = \text{Concat}(\text{head}_1, \ldots, \text{head}_M)\mathbf{W}^o$$
$$\text{where } \text{head}_i = (\sum_{l=1}^L \sum_{s=1}^S \mathbf{A}_{i,l,q,s} \cdot \mathbf{x}^l(\phi_l(\hat{\mathbf{p}}_q) + \Delta p_{i,l,q,s}))\mathbf{W}_i^v, \tag{1}$$

where $\mathbf{Q}_q \in \mathbb{R}^C$, $\hat{\mathbf{p}}_q \in \mathbb{R}^2$ and $\{\mathbf{x}^l\}_{l=1}^L$ are the q-th input query vector, the reference point offset of q-th query and l-th level of feature maps from the backbone; the dimension of each feature vector in $\mathbf{x}$ is C. head_i represents i-th attention head. L, M and S represent the number of feature map levels used in the decoder, the number of attention heads and the number of sampling points on each level feature map, respectively. $\mathbf{A}_{i,l,q,s} \in \mathbb{R}^1$ and $\Delta p_{i,l,q,s} \in \mathbb{R}^2$ represent the attention weights and the sampling offsets of the i-th head, l-th level, q-th query and s-th sampling point, respectively; The query feature $\mathbf{Q}_q$ is fed to a linear projection to generate $\mathbf{A}_{i,l,q,s}$ and $\Delta p_{i,l,q,s}$. $\mathbf{A}_{i,l,q,s}$ satisfies the limitation, $\sum_{l=1}^L \sum_{s=1}^S \mathbf{A}_{i,l,q,s} = 1$. $\phi_l(\cdot)$ is the function transforming the $\hat{\mathbf{p}}_q$ to the coordinate system of the l-th level features. $\mathbf{x}^l(\phi_l(\hat{\mathbf{p}}_q) + \Delta p_{i,l,q,s})$ represents sampling the feature vector located in offset $(\phi_l(\hat{\mathbf{p}}_q) + \Delta p_{i,l,q,s})$ on the feature map $\mathbf{x}^l$ by bilinear interpolation. $\mathbf{W}^o \in \mathbb{R}^{C \times C}$ and $\mathbf{W}_i^v \in \mathbb{R}^{C \times (C/M)}$ are two groups of trainable weights. The reference point $\hat{\mathbf{p}}_q$ will be updated at the end of each decoder layer by applying a linear layer on $\mathbf{Q}_q$. Note, the FC output $\hat{\boldsymbol{\mu}}_f$ is leveraged as reference point for the initial query $\mathbf{Q}_z$. For more details and computational complexity, we refer readers to our supplementary material.

To sum up, the relations between different keypoints are modeled through a self-attention module, and the relations between the input image and keypoints are modeled through EMSDA module. Notably, the problem of feature misalignment in fully-connected regression is solved by EMSDA.

3.2 Training Targets and Loss Functions

Following RLE [18], we calculate a probability distribution $P_{\Theta,\Phi}(\mathbf{x}|\mathcal{I})$ reflecting the probability of the ground truth appearing in the location $\mathbf{x}$ conditioning on the input image $\mathcal{I}$, where Θ is the parameters of Poseur and Φ is the parameters of a flow model. As shown in Fig. 3(d), The flow model f_ϕ is leveraged to reflect the deviation of the output from the ground truth μ_g by mapping a initial distribution $\bar{\mathbf{z}} \sim \mathcal{N}(0,\mathbf{I})$ to a zero-mean complex distribution $\bar{\mathbf{x}} \sim G_\phi(\bar{\mathbf{x}})$. Then $P_\phi(\bar{\mathbf{x}})$ is obtained by adding a zero-mean Laplace distribution $L(\bar{\mathbf{x}})$ to $G(\bar{\mathbf{x}})$. The regression model Θ predictions the center $\hat{\mu}$, and scale $\hat{b}$ of the distribution. Finally, the distribution $P_{\Theta,\Phi}(\mathbf{x}|\mathcal{I})$ is built upon $P_\phi(\bar{\mathbf{x}})$ by shifting and rescaling $\bar{\mathbf{x}}$ into $\mathbf{x}$, where $\mathbf{x} = \bar{\mathbf{x}} \cdot \hat{\sigma} + \hat{\mu}$. We refer readers to [18] for more details.

Different from RLE [18], we only use the proposal $(\hat{\mu}_f, \hat{b}_f)$ for coarse prediction. This prediction is then updated by the query-based approach described above to generate an improved estimate $(\hat{\mu}_q, \hat{b}_q)$. Both coarse proposal $(\hat{\mu}_f, \hat{b}_f)$ and query decoder preditions $(\hat{\mu}_q, \hat{b}_q)$ are supervised with the maximum likelihood estimation (MLE) process. The learning process of MLE optimizes the model parameters so as to make the observed ground truth μ_g most probable. The loss function of FC predictions $(\hat{\mu}_f, \hat{b}_f)$ can be defined as:

$$\mathcal{L}_{rle}^{fc} = -\log P_{\Theta_f,\Phi_f}(\mathbf{x}|\mathcal{I})\Big|_{\mathbf{x}=\mu_g}, \tag{2}$$

where Θ_f and Φ_f are the parameters of the backbone and flow model, respectively. Similarly, the loss of distribution associated with query decoder preditions $(\hat{\mu}_q, \hat{b}_q)$ can be defined as:

$$\mathcal{L}_{rle}^{dec} = -\log P_{\Theta_q,\Phi_q}(\mathbf{x}|\mathcal{I})\Big|_{\mathbf{x}=\mu_g}, \tag{3}$$

where Θ_q and Φ_q are the parameters of the query decoder and another flow model, respectively. Finally, we sum the two loss functions to obtain the total loss:

$$\mathcal{L}_{total} = \mathcal{L}_{rle}^{fc} + \lambda \mathcal{L}_{rle}^{dec}, \tag{4}$$

where λ is a constant and used to balance the two losses. We set $\lambda = 1$ by default.

3.3 Inference

Inference Pipeline. During the inference stage, Poseur predicts the $(\hat{\mu}_q, \hat{b}_q)$ for each keypoint as mentioned; $\hat{\mu}_q$ is taken as the predicted keypoint coordinates and $\hat{b}_q$ is used to calculate the keypoint confidence score.

Prediction Uncertainty Estimation. For heatmap-based methods, e.g. SimpleBaseline [36], the prediction score of each keypoint is combined with a bounding box score to enhance the final human instance score:

$$s^{inst} = s^{bbox} \frac{\sum_{i=1}^{k} s_i^{kp}}{K}, \tag{5}$$

where s^{inst} is the final prediction score of the instance; s^{bbox} is the bounding box score predicted by the person detector, s_i^{kp} is the i-th keypoint score predicted by the keypoint detector and K is the total keypoint number of each human. Most previous regression-based methods [29,31] ignore the importance of the keypoint score. As a result, compared to heatmap based methods, regression methods typically achieve higher recall but lower precision. Given the same well-trained Poseur model, adding the keypoint score brings 4.7 AP improvement (74.7 AP vs. 70.0 AP) due to the significantly reduced number of false positives, and both of the models achieve almost the same average recall (AR).

Our model predicts a probability distribution over the image coordinates for each human keypoint. We define the i-th keypoint prediction score s_i^{kp} to be the probability of the keypoint falling into the region ($[\hat{\boldsymbol{\mu}}_i - \mathbf{a}, \hat{\boldsymbol{\mu}}_i + \mathbf{a}]$) near the prediction coordinate $\hat{\boldsymbol{\mu}}_i$. In practise, the score s_i^{kp} are calculated separately on x-axis and y-axis and followed by a multiplication operation, i.e.

$$s_i^{kp} = \int_{\hat{\mu}_i^x - \mathbf{a}}^{\hat{\mu}_i^x + \mathbf{a}} P_{\Theta_q, \Phi_q}(\mathbf{x}|\mathcal{I}) dx \int_{\hat{\mu}_i^y - \mathbf{a}}^{\hat{\mu}_i^y + \mathbf{a}} P_{\Theta_q, \Phi_q}(\mathbf{x}|\mathcal{I}) dy, \qquad (6)$$

where $\mathbf{a}$ is a hyperparameter that controls the size of the $\boldsymbol{\mu}$-adjacent interval, and $(\hat{\boldsymbol{\mu}}_i^x, \hat{\boldsymbol{\mu}}_i^y)$ are the coordinates of the corresponding keypoint predicted by Poseur. In practice, running the normalization flow model during the inference stage would add more computational cost. We found that comparable performance can be achieved by shifting and re-scaling the zero-mean Laplace distribution $L(\bar{\mathbf{x}})$ with query decoder predictions $(\hat{\boldsymbol{\mu}}_q, \hat{\boldsymbol{b}}_q)$. So the probability density function can be rewritten as:

$$P_{\Theta_q, \Phi_q}(\mathbf{x}|\mathcal{I}) \approx f(\mathbf{x}|\hat{\boldsymbol{\mu}}_i, \hat{\boldsymbol{b}}_i) = \frac{1}{2\hat{\boldsymbol{b}}_i} \exp\left(-\frac{|\mathbf{x} - \hat{\boldsymbol{\mu}}_i|}{\hat{\boldsymbol{b}}_i}\right), \qquad (7)$$

where f is the probability density function for Laplace distribution. Finally, s_i^{kp} can be written as:

$$\begin{aligned} s_i^{kp} &\approx \int_{\hat{\mu}_i^x - \mathbf{a}}^{\hat{\mu}_i^x + \mathbf{a}} f(\mathbf{x}|\hat{\boldsymbol{\mu}}_i^x, \hat{\boldsymbol{b}}_i^x) dx \int_{\hat{\mu}_i^y - \mathbf{a}}^{\hat{\mu}_i^y + \mathbf{a}} f(\mathbf{x}|\hat{\boldsymbol{\mu}}_i^y, \hat{\boldsymbol{b}}_i^y) dy \\ &= \left(1 - \exp\left(-\frac{\mathbf{a}}{\hat{\boldsymbol{b}}_i^x}\right)\right) * \left(1 - \exp\left(-\frac{\mathbf{a}}{\hat{\boldsymbol{b}}_i^y}\right)\right), \end{aligned} \qquad (8)$$

where $(\hat{\boldsymbol{b}}_i^x, \hat{\boldsymbol{b}}_i^y)$ are the scale parameters predicted by the query decoder of Poseur.

4   Experiments

4.1   Implementation Details

Datasets. Our experiments are mainly conducted on COCO 2017 Keypoint Detection benchmark [33], which contains about $250K$ person instances with

17 keypoints. We report results on the *val* set for ablation studies and compare with other state-of-the-art methods on both of the *val* set and *test-dev* sets. The Average Precision (AP) based on Object Keypoint Similarity (OKS) is employed as the evaluation metric on COCO dataset. We also conduct experiments on MPII [1] dataset with Percentage of Correct Keypoint (PCK) as evaluation metric.

Model Settings. Unless specified, ResNet-50 [16] is used as the backbone in ablation study. The size of input image is 256×192. The weights pre-trained on ImageNet [9] are used to initialize the ResNet backbone. The rest parts of our network are initialized with random parameters. All the decoder embedding size is set as 256; 3 decoder layers are used by default.

Training. All the models are trained with batch size 256 (batch size 128 for HRFormer-B due to the limited GPU memory), and are optimized by AdamW [23] with a base learning rate of 1×10^{-3} decreased to 1×10^{-4} and 1×10^{-5} at the 255-th epoch and 310-th epoch and ended at the 325-th epoch; β_1 and β_2 are set to 0.9 and 0.999, respectively; Weight decay is set to 10^{-4}. Following Deformable DETR [40], the learning rate of the linear projections for sampling offsets and reference points are multiplied by a factor of 0.1. Following RLE [18], we adopt RealNVP [11] as the flow model. Other settings follow that of mmpose [8]. For HRNet-W48 and HRFormer-B, cutout [10] and color jitter augmentation are applied to avoid over-fitting.

Inference. Following conventional settings, we use the same person detector as in SimpleBaseline [36] for COCO evaluation. According to the bounding box generated by the person detector, the single person image patch is cropped out from the original image and resized to a fix resolution, e.g. 256×192. The flow model is removed during the inference. We set $\mathbf{a} = 0.2$ in Eq. (7) by default.

4.2 Ablation Study

Initialization of Keypoint Queries. We conduct experiments to verify the impact of initialization of keypoint queries. Deformable DETR [40] introduces reference points that represent the location information of object queries. In their paper, reference points are 2-d tensors predicted from the 256-d object queries via a linear projection. We set this configuration as our baseline model. As shown in Table 1a, the baseline model achieves 72.3 AP with 3 decoder layers, which is 0.6 AP lower than keypoint queries which initialized from coarse proposal $\hat{\mu}_f$. This indicates that coarse proposal $\hat{\mu}_f$ provide a good initialization for the keypoint queries.

Noisy Reference Points Sampling Strategy. As mentioned in Sect. 3.1, we apply the noisy reference points sampling strategy during the training. To validate its effectiveness, we perform ablation experiment on COCO, as show in Table 1b. The experiment result shows that the noisy reference points sampling strategy can improve the accuracy by 0.6 AP without adding any extra computational cost during inference.

Table 1. Ablation of proposed Poseur on COCO `val2017` split. "Ours": Using the fully convolutional layer at the end of backbone to regress the coarse proposal $\hat{\mu}_f$; "Noisy Reference Points": applying the noisy reference points sampling strategy in the keypoint encoder; "Res-i": i-th level feature map of ResNet; "N_d": the number of decoder layers

(a) Varying Initial Reference Points Methods

Initial Ref. Points	AP
Def. DETR[40]	72.3
Ours	72.9

(b) Varying the Noisy Reference Points

Noisy Ref. Points	AP
✗	73.7
✓	74.3

(c) Varying the Uncertainty Estimation

Uncertainty Esti.	AP
RLE [18]	73.6
Ours	74.7

(d) Varying the scale levels of input feature map for decoder

Res2	Res3	Res4	Res5	Params	GFLOPs	AP
			✓	28.3M	4.12	73.7
		✓	✓	28.7M	4.18	74.2
	✓	✓	✓	28.9M	4.28	74.4
✓	✓	✓	✓	29.0M	4.48	74.7

(e) Varying the numbers of decoder layers

N_d	Params	GFLOPs	AP	AP_{50}	AP_{75}
3	28.8M	4.48	74.7	90.2	81.6
4	30.2M	4.51	75.3	90.5	82.1
5	31.6M	4.54	75.4	90.3	82.2
6	33.1M	4.57	75.4	90.5	82.2

Varying the Levels of Feature Map. We explore the impact of feeding different levels of backbone features into the proposed query decoder. As shown in Table 1d, the performance grows consistently with more levels of feature maps, e.g., 73.7 AP, 74.2 AP, 74.4 AP, 74.7 AP for 1, 2, 3, 4 levels of feature maps, respectively.

Uncertainty Estimation. As mentioned in Sect. 3.3, we redesign the prediction confidence score proposed in [18]. To study the effectiveness of the proposed score s^{kp}, we compare it with predictions without re-score and predictions with RLE score [18] using the same model. As shown in Table 1c, the proposed method brings significant improvement (4.7 AP) to the model without uncertainty estimation, and outperforms the RLE score [18] by 1.0 AP.

Varying Decoder Layers. Here we study the effect of query decoder's depth. Specifically, we conduct experiments by varying the number of decoder layers in Transformer decoder. As shown in Table 1e, the performance grows at the first three layers and saturates at the sixth decoder layer.

Varying the Input Size. We conduct experiments to explore the robust of Poseur under different input resolutions. Table 2b compares Poseur with SimpleBaseline, showing that our method consistently outperforms SimpleBaseline in all input sizes. The results also indicate that heatmap-based method suffers larger performance drop with the low-resolution input. For example, the proposed method outperforms SimpleBaseline by 14.6 AP in 64 × 64 input resolution.

4.3   Extensions: End-to-End Pose Estimation

Our framework can easily extend to end-to-end human pose estimation, i.e., detecting multi-person poses without the manual crop operation. With Poseur as a plug-and-play scheme, end-to-end top-down keypoint detectors can obtain additional improvement. Here, we take Mask-RCNN as example to show the superiority of our method. The original keypoint head of Mask R-CNN is stacked

Table 2. Comparison with heatmap methods by varying the backbone and the input resolution on the COCO *val* set. "SimBa": SimpleBaseline [36]. For (a), the input resolution is 256×192 and the number of decoder layers is 5. For (b), we use ResNet-50 as backbone and the number of decoder layers is 3.

(a) Varying the backbone

Method	Backbone	GFLOPs	AP
SimBa.	MobileNet-V2	4.55	65.9
Poseur	MobileNet-V2	0.52	71.9
SimBa.	ResNet-50	8.27	72.4
Poseur	ResNet-50	4.54	75.4
HRNet	HRNet-W32	7.68	75.0
Poseur	HRNet-W32	7.95	76.9

(b) Varying the input resolution

Method	Input size	Params	GFLOPs	AP
SimBa. [36]	64×64	34.0M	0.69	31.4
Poseur	64×64	28.8M	0.49	**47.9**
SimBa. [36]	128×128	34.0M	2.76	59.3
Poseur	128×128	28.8M	1.55	**67.1**
SimBa. [36]	256×192	34.0M	8.26	71.0
Poseur	256×192	28.8M	4.48	**74.7**

Table 3. Comparison with **end-to-end top-down methods** on the COCO *val* set. [†] denote flipping and multi-sacle testing. Reg: regression-based approach; HM: heatmap-based approach

Method	Backbone	Type	AP	AP$_{50}$	AP$_{75}$
PRTR [20]	HRNet-W48	Reg	64.9	87.0	71.7
Mask R-CNN [15]	ResNet-101	HM	66.0	86.9	71.5
Mask R-CNN + RLE [18]	ResNet-101	Reg	66.7	86.7	72.6
PointSet Anchor[†] [34]	HRNet-W48	Reg	67.0	87.3	73.5
Mask R-CNN + Poseur	ResNet-101	Reg	68.6	87.5	74.8
Mask R-CNN + Poseur	HRNet-W48	Reg	70.1	**88.0**	76.5
Mask R-CNN + Poseur [†]	HRNet-W48	Reg	**70.8**	87.9	**77.0**

Table 4. Comparisons on MPII validation set (PCKh@0.5). SimBa: SimpleBaseline [36]. Reg: regression-base approach; HM: heatmap-based approach

Method	Backbone	Type	Mean
SimBa. [36]	ResNet-152	HM.	89.6
HRNet [27]	HRNet-W32	HM.	90.1
TokenPose [22]	L/D24	HM.	90.2
Integral [29]	ResNet-101	Reg.	87.3
PRTR [20]	HRNet-W32	Reg.	89.5
Poseur	HRNet-W32	Reg.	**90.5**

8 convolutional layers, followed by a deconv layer and 2× bilinear upscaling, producing an output resolution of 56×56. We replace the deconv layer by an average pooling layer and an FC layer like [18]. The output of the FC layer is used to produce initial coarse proposal $\hat{\boldsymbol{\mu}}_f$. Then coarse proposal $\hat{\boldsymbol{\mu}}_f$ is feed into the keypoint encoder and query decoder as described in Sect. 3.1. We randomly sample 600 queries per image for training efficiency. Note that we conduct EMSDA on multi-scale backbone feature maps, rather than on ROI features. The output of FC layer and transformer decoder are both supervised with RLE loss [18]. We perform scale jittering [13] with random crops during training. We train the entire network for 180,000 iterations, with a batchsize of 32 in total. Other parameters are the same as the Detectron2 [35]. As shown in Table 3, Poseur outperforms the heatmap-based Mask R-CNN with ResNet 101 by 1.9 AP. Poseur outperforms the state-of-the-art regression-based method, PointSet Anchor with HRNet-W48 by 3.8 AP.

Table 5. Comparisons with state-of-the-art methods on the COCO *val* set. Input size and the GFLOPs are calculated under top-down single person pose estimation setting. Unless specified, the number of decoder layers is set to 6. "3 Dec.": three decoder layers.

Method	Backbone/Type	Input Size	GFLOPs	AP^{kp}	AP^{kp}_{50}	AP^{kp}_{75}	AP^{kp}_{M}	AP^{kp}_{L}
Heatmap-based methods								
SimBa. [36]	ResNet-50	256 × 192	8.9	70.4	88.6	78.3	67.1	77.2
SimBa. [36]	ResNet-152	256 × 192	15.7	72.0	89.3	79.8	68.7	78.9
HRNet [27]	HRNet-W32	256 × 192	7.1	74.4	90.5	81.9	70.8	81.0
HRNet [27]	HRNet-W48	384 × 288	32.9	76.3	90.8	82.9	72.3	83.4
TransPose [37]	H-A6	256 × 192	21.8	75.8	–	–	–	–
TokenPose [22]	S-V2	256 × 192	11.6	73.5	89.4	80.3	69.8	80.5
TokenPose [22]	B	256 × 192	5.7	74.7	89.8	81.4	71.3	81.4
TokenPose [22]	L/D6	256 × 192	9.1	75.4	90.0	81.8	71.8	82.4
TokenPose [22]	L/D24	256 × 192	11.0	75.8	90.3	82.5	72.3	82.7
HRFormer [38]	HRFormer-T	256 × 192	1.3	70.9	89.0	78.4	67.2	77.8
HRFormer [38]	HRFormer-S	256 × 192	2.8	74.0	90.2	81.2	70.4	80.7
HRFormer [38]	HRFormer-B	256 × 192	12.2	75.6	90.8	82.8	71.7	82.6
HRFormer [38]	HRFormer-B	384 × 288	26.8	77.2	91.0	83.6	73.2	84.2
UDP-Pose [17]	HRNet-W32	256 × 192	7.2	76.8	91.9	83.7	73.1	83.3
UDP-Pose [17]	HRNet-W48	384 × 288	33.0	77.8	92.0	84.3	74.2	84.5
Regression-based methods								
PRTR [20]	ResNet-50	384 × 288	11.0	68.2	88.2	75.2	63.2	76.2
PRTR [20]	HRNet-W32	384 × 288	21.6	73.1	89.4	79.8	68.8	80.4
PRTR [20]	HRNet-W32	512 × 384	37.8	73.3	89.2	79.9	69.0	80.9
RLE [19]	ResNet-50	256 × 192	4.0	70.5	88.5	77.4	–	–
RLE [19]	HRNet-W32	256 × 192	7.1	74.3	89.7	80.8	–	–
Ours	MobileNet-v2	256 × 192	0.5	71.9	88.9	78.6	65.2	74.3
Ours	ResNet-50	256 × 192	4.6	75.4	90.5	82.2	68.1	78.6
Ours	ResNet-152	256 × 192	11.9	76.3	91.1	83.3	69.1	79.5
Ours	HRNet-W32	256 × 192	7.4	76.9	91.0	83.5	70.1	79.7
Ours	HRNet-W48	384 × 288	33.6	78.8	91.6	85.1	72.1	81.8
Ours (3 Dec.)	HRFormer-T	256 × 192	1.4	74.3	90.1	81.4	67.5	76.9
Ours (3 Dec.)	HRFormer-S	256 × 192	3.0	76.6	91.0	83.4	69.8	79.4
Ours	HRFormer-B	256 × 192	12.6	78.9	92.0	85.7	72.3	81.7
Ours	HRFormer-B	384 × 288	27.4	79.6	92.1	85.9	72.9	82.9

4.4 Main Results

Gains on Low-Resolution Backbone. In this part, we show the great improvement of Poseur on non-HRNet paradigm backbone which encode the input image as low-resolution representation. All models and training settings are tightly aligned. The input resolution of all models is 256 × 192.

Table 6. Comparison with top-down methods on the COCO *test-dev* set. The proposed paradigm outpeforms heatmap-based methods in various settings. The input resolution of all methods is 384×288.

Method	Backbone	AP^{kp}	AP^{kp}_{50}	AP^{kp}_{75}	AP^{kp}_{M}	AP^{kp}_{L}
Heatmap-based methods						
SimBa[†] [36]	ResNet-152	73.7	91.9	81.1	70.3	80.0
HRNet[†] [27]	HRNet-W32	74.9	92.5	82.8	71.3	80.9
HRNet[†] [27]	HRNet-W48	75.5	92.5	83.3	71.9	81.5
TokenPose [22]	L/D24	75.9	92.3	83.4	72.2	82.1
HRFormer [38]	HRFormer-B	76.2	92.7	83.8	72.5	82.3
UDP-Pose [17]	HRNet-W48	76.5	92.7	84.0	73.0	82.4
Regression-based methods						
PRTR [20]	ResNet-101	68.8	89.9	76.9	64.7	75.8
PRTR [20]	HRNet-W32	71.7	90.6	79.6	67.6	78.4
RLE [19]	ResNet-152	74.2	91.5	81.9	71.2	79.3
RLE [19]	HRNet-W48	75.7	92.3	82.9	72.3	81.3
Ours (6 Dec.)	HRNet-W48	77.6	92.9	85.0	74.4	82.7
Ours (6 Dec.)	HRFormer-B	**78.3**	**93.5**	**85.9**	**75.2**	**83.4**

In Table 2a, Poseur with ResNet-50 significantly outperforms SimpleBaseline, and *it is even higher than HRNet-W32*, while the computational cost is much lower. Apart from that, Poseur with the lightweight backbone MobileNet-V2 can achieve comparable performance with SimpleBaseline using ResNet-50 backbone. In contrast, the performance of the MobileNet-V2 based SimpleBaseline is much worse, 6.0 AP lower than our method with the same backbone. It is worth noting that the computational cost of Poseur with MobileNet-V2 is only about one-ninth that of SimpleBaseline with the same backbone.

Comparison with the State-of-the-Art Methods. We compare the proposed Poseur with state-of-the-art methods on COCO and MPII dataset. Poseur outperforms all regression-based and heatmap-based methods when using the same backbone, and achieves state-of-the-art performance with HRFormer-B backbone, i.e., 79.6 AP on the COCO *val* set and 78.3 AP on the COCO *test-dev* set. Poseur with HRFormer-B can even outperform the previous state-of-the-art UDP-Pose (384×288) by 1.1 AP on the COCO *val* set, when using lower input resolution (256×192). Quantitative results are reported in Table 5 and Sect. 6. On the MPII *val* set, Poseur with HRNet-W32 is 0.4 PCKh higher than heatmap-based method with HRNet-W32. Quantitative results are reported in Table 4.

5 Conclusion

We have proposed a novel pose estimation framework named Poseur built upon Transformers, which largely improves the performance of the regression-based pose estimation and bypasses the drawbacks of heatmap-based methods such as the non-differentiable post-processing and quantization error. Extensive experiments on the MS-COCO and MPII benchmarks show that Poseur can achieve state-of-the-art performance among both regression-based methods and heatmap-based methods.

References

1. Andriluka, M., Pishchulin, L., Gehler, P., Schiele, B.: 2D human pose estimation: new benchmark and state of the art analysis. In: IEEE Conference on Computer Vision and Pattern Recognition, pp. 3686–3693 (2014)
2. Cai, Y.: Learning delicate local representations for multi-person pose estimation. In: Vedaldi, A., Bischof, H., Brox, T., Frahm, J.-M. (eds.) ECCV 2020. LNCS, vol. 12348, pp. 455–472. Springer, Cham (2020). https://doi.org/10.1007/978-3-030-58580-8_27
3. Cao, Z., Hidalgo, G., Simon, T., Wei, S.E., Sheikh, Y.: Openpose: realtime multi-person 2d pose estimation using part affinity fields. IEEE Trans. Pattern Anal. Mach. Intell. **43**(1), 172–186 (2019)
4. Carion, N., Massa, F., Synnaeve, G., Usunier, N., Kirillov, A., Zagoruyko, S.: End-to-end object detection with transformers. In: Vedaldi, A., Bischof, H., Brox, T., Frahm, J.-M. (eds.) ECCV 2020. LNCS, vol. 12346, pp. 213–229. Springer, Cham (2020). https://doi.org/10.1007/978-3-030-58452-8_13
5. Carreira, J., Agrawal, P., Fragkiadaki, K., Malik, J.: Human pose estimation with iterative error feedback. In: Proceedings of the IEEE Conference on Computer Vision and Pattern Recognition, pp. 4733–4742 (2016)
6. Chen, Y., Wang, Z., Peng, Y., Zhang, Z., Yu, G., Sun, J.: Cascaded pyramid network for multi-person pose estimation. In: Proceedings of the IEEE Conference on Computer Vision and Pattern Recognition, pp. 7103–7112 (2018)
7. Cheng, B., Xiao, B., Wang, J., Shi, H., Huang, T.S., Zhang, L.: Higherhrnet: scale-aware representation learning for bottom-up human pose estimation. In: Proceedings of the IEEE Conference on Computer Vision and Pattern Recognition, pp. 5386–5395 (2020)
8. Contributors, M.: Openmmlab pose estimation toolbox and benchmark (2020). https://github.com/open-mmlab/mmpose
9. Deng, J., Dong, W., Socher, R., Li, L.J., Li, K., Fei-Fei, L.: Imagenet: a large-scale hierarchical image database. In: Proceedings of the IEEE Conference on Computer Vision and Pattern Recognition, pp. 248–255. IEEE (2009)
10. DeVries, T., Taylor, G.W.: Improved regularization of convolutional neural networks with cutout. arXiv: Comp. Res. Repository (2017)
11. Dinh, L., Sohl-Dickstein, J., Bengio, S.: Density estimation using real NVP. In: Proceedings of the International Conference on Learning Representations (2017)
12. Dosovitskiy, A., et al.: An image is worth 16x16 words: transformers for image recognition at scale. arXiv: Comp. Res. Repository (2020)
13. Ghiasi, G., et al.: Simple copy-paste is a strong data augmentation method for instance segmentation. In: Proceedings of the IEEE Conference on Computer Vision and Pattern Recognition, pp. 2918–2928 (2021)
14. Gu, K., Yang, L., Yao, A.: Removing the bias of integral pose regression. In: Proceedings of the IEEE Conference on Computer Vision, pp. 11067–11076 (2021)

15. He, K., Gkioxari, G., Dollár, P., Girshick, R.: Mask R-CNN. In: Proceedings of the IEEE Conference on Computer Vision, pp. 2961–2969 (2017)
16. He, K., Zhang, X., Ren, S., Sun, J.: Deep residual learning for image recognition. In: Proceedings of the IEEE Conference on Computer Vision and Pattern Recognition, pp. 770–778 (2016)
17. Huang, J., Zhu, Z., Guo, F., Huang, G.: The devil is in the details: delving into unbiased data processing for human pose estimation. In: Proceedings of the IEEE Conference on Computer Vision and Pattern Recognition, pp. 5700–5709 (2020)
18. Li, J., et al.: Human pose regression with residual log-likelihood estimation. In: Proceedings of the IEEE Conference on Computer Vision (2021)
19. Li, J., Bian, S., Zeng, A., Wang, C., Pang, B., Liu, W., Lu, C.: Human pose regression with residual log-likelihood estimation. In: Proceedings of the IEEE Conference on Computer Vision (2021)
20. Li, K., Wang, S., Zhang, X., Xu, Y., Xu, W., Tu, Z.: Pose recognition with cascade transformers. In: Proceedings of the IEEE Conference on Computer Vision and Pattern Recognition, pp. 1944–1953 (2021)
21. Li, W., et al.: Rethinking on multi-stage networks for human pose estimation. arXiv: Comp. Res. Repository (2019)
22. Li, Y., et al.: TokenPose: learning keypoint tokens for human pose estimation. In: Proceedings of the IEEE Conference on Computer Vision (2021)
23. Loshchilov, I., Hutter, F.: Decoupled weight decay regularization. In: Proceedings of the International Conference on Learning Representations (2019)
24. Luo, Z., Wang, Z., Huang, Y., Tan, T., Zhou, E.: Rethinking the heatmap regression for bottom-up human pose estimation. arXiv preprint arXiv:2012.15175 (2020)
25. Newell, A., Yang, K., Deng, J.: Stacked hourglass networks for human pose estimation. In: Leibe, B., Matas, J., Sebe, N., Welling, M. (eds.) ECCV 2016. LNCS, vol. 9912, pp. 483–499. Springer, Cham (2016). https://doi.org/10.1007/978-3-319-46484-8_29
26. Nie, X., Feng, J., Zhang, J., Yan, S.: Single-stage multi-person pose machines. In: Proceedings of the IEEE International Conference on Computing Vision, pp. 6951–6960 (2019)
27. Sun, K., Xiao, B., Liu, D., Wang, J.: Deep high-resolution representation learning for human pose estimation. In: Proceedings of the IEEE Conference on Computer Vision and Pattern Recognition, pp. 5693–5703 (2019)
28. Sun, X., Shang, J., Liang, S., Wei, Y.: Compositional human pose regression. In: Proceedings of the IEEE Conference on Computer Vision, pp. 2602–2611 (2017)
29. Sun, X., Xiao, B., Wei, F., Liang, S., Wei, Y.: Integral human pose regression. In: Proceedings of the IEEE Conference on Computer Vision, pp. 529–545 (2018)
30. Tian, Z., Chen, H., Shen, C.: Directpose: Direct end-to-end multi-person pose estimation. arXiv: Comp. Res. Repository (2019)
31. Toshev, A., Szegedy, C.: Deeppose: human pose estimation via deep neural networks. In: Proceedings of the IEEE Conference on Computer Vision and Pattern Recognition, pp. 1653–1660 (2014)
32. Vaswani, A., et al.: Attention is all you need. In: Proceedings of the Advances in Neural Information Processing System, pp. 5998–6008 (2017)
33. Wang, Z., et al.: MSCOCO keypoints challenge 2018. In: Proceedings of the European Conference on Computing Vision, vol. 5 (2018)
34. Wei, F., Sun, X., Li, H., Wang, J., Lin, S.: Point-set anchors for object detection, instance segmentation and pose estimation (2020)
35. Wu, Y., Kirillov, A., Massa, F., Lo, W.Y., Girshick, R.: Detectron2. https://github.com/facebookresearch/detectron2 (2019)

36. Xiao, B., Wu, H., Wei, Y.: Simple baselines for human pose estimation and tracking. In: Proceedings of the European Conference on Computing Vision, pp. 466–481 (2018)
37. Yang, S., Quan, Z., Nie, M., Yang, W.: TransPose: keypoint localization via Transformer. In: Proceedings of the IEEE International Conference on Computing Vision (2021)
38. Yuan, Y., et al.: HRFormer: high-resolution transformer for dense prediction. In: Proceedings of the Advances in Neural Information Processing System (2021)
39. Zhang, F., Zhu, X., Dai, H., Ye, M., Zhu, C.: Distribution-aware coordinate representation for human pose estimation. In: Proceedings of the IEEE Conference on Computer Vision and Pattern Recognition, June 2020
40. Zhu, X., Su, W., Lu, L., Li, B., Wang, X., Dai, J.: Deformable DETR: deformable Transformers for end-to-end object detection. In: Proceedings of the International Conference on Learning Representations (2021)

SimCC: A Simple Coordinate Classification Perspective for Human Pose Estimation

Yanjie Li[1], Sen Yang[2], Peidong Liu[1], Shoukui Zhang[3], Yunxiao Wang[1], Zhicheng Wang[4], Wankou Yang[2], and Shu-Tao Xia[1,5(✉)]

[1] Tsinghua Shenzhen International Graduate School, Tsinghua University, Beijing, China
`xiast@sz.tsinghua.edu.cn`
[2] Southeast University, Nanjing, China
[3] Meituan Inc., Beijing, China
[4] Nreal, Beijing, China
[5] Research Center of Artificial Intelligence, Peng Cheng Laboratory, Shenzhen, China

Abstract. The 2D heatmap-based approaches have dominated Human Pose Estimation (HPE) for years due to high performance. However, the long-standing quantization error problem in the 2D heatmap-based methods leads to several well-known drawbacks: 1) The performance for the low-resolution inputs is limited; 2) To improve the feature map resolution for higher localization precision, multiple costly upsampling layers are required; 3) Extra post-processing is adopted to reduce the quantization error. To address these issues, we aim to explore a brand new scheme, called *SimCC*, which reformulates HPE as two classification tasks for horizontal and vertical coordinates. The proposed SimCC uniformly divides each pixel into several bins, thus achieving *sub-pixel* localization precision and low quantization error. Benefiting from that, SimCC can omit additional refinement post-processing and exclude upsampling layers under certain settings, resulting in a more simple and effective pipeline for HPE. Extensive experiments conducted over COCO, CrowdPose, and MPII datasets show that SimCC outperforms heatmap-based counterparts, especially in low-resolution settings by a large margin. Code is now publicly available at https://github.com/leeyegy/SimCC.

Keywords: Human poes estimation · 2d heatmap · Coordinate classification

1 Introduction

2D Human Pose Estimation (HPE) aims to localize body joints from a single image, where 2D heatmap-based methods [2,3,6,7,17,18,20,23,29,38,40,43] has become the *de facto* standard in recent years. The 2D heatmap is generated as a 2-dimensional Gaussian distribution centering at the ground-truth joint position,

© The Author(s), under exclusive license to Springer Nature Switzerland AG 2022
S. Avidan et al. (Eds.): ECCV 2022, LNCS 13666, pp. 89–106, 2022.
https://doi.org/10.1007/978-3-031-20068-7_6

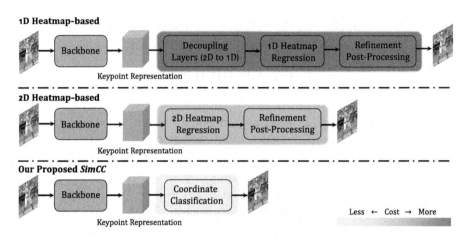

Fig. 1. Comparisons between the proposed SimCC and 2D/1D heatmap-based pipelines. The 2D heatmap-based scheme includes: 1) a backbone to extract keypoint representations; 2) a regression head to generate the 2D heatmap, which may consist of multiple time-consuming upsampling layers; 3) extra post-processing to refine the predictions, such as empirical shift and DARK [43]. The 1D heatmap regression [42] is introduced for facial landmark. Compared to the 2D heatmap-based scheme, The 1D heatmap regression [42] brings additional learnable decoupling layers consisting of multiple CNN layers and a co-attention module, to transform the 2D features to 1D heatmaps. Different from these heatmap-based schemes, the proposed SimCC is much simpler, which only needs two linear classifier heads for coordinate classification.

which inhibits the cases of false positive and smooths the training process by assigning a probability value to each position.

Despite its success, heatmap-based methods suffer seriously from the long-standing quantization error problem, which is caused by mapping the continuous coordinate values into discretized 2D downscaled heatmaps. The substantial quantization error further brings about several well-known shortcomings: 1) Costly upsampling layers (*e.g.*, deconvolution layers [38]) are used to increase the feature map resolution to alleviate the quantization error; 2) Extra post-processing is introduced to refine the predictions; 3) The performances are far from satisfactory for low-resolution inputs due to the serious quantization error. Considering obtaining high-resolution 2D heatmap brings heavy computation cost, a natural way to decrease the quantization error is to firstly decouple the 2D heatmap into 1D heatmap and then increase the resolution, which has been explored by Yin et al. [42] for facial landmark area. However, to realize that goal, Yin et al. [42] introduces additional decoupling layers and costly deconvolution modules, resulting in an even more complicated pipeline.

Therefore, in this work, we try to explore a brand-new scheme against heatmap-based methods for HPE. Specifically, we propose a simple yet effective coordinate classification pipeline, namely *SimCC*, which regards HPE as two classification tasks for horizontal and vertical coordinates. SimCC firstly employs a Convolutional Neural Network (CNN) or Transformer-based backbone to extract keypoint representations. Given the obtained keypoint representations, SimCC then performs coordinate classification for vertical and horizontal coordinates independently to yield the final predictions. To reduce the quantization error, SimCC uniformly divides each pixel into several bins, which achieves *sub-pixel* localization precision. Note that different from heatmap-based approaches which may introduce multiple deconvolution layers, SimCC only needs two lightweight classifier heads (*i.e.* only one linear layer for each head).

Figure 1 shows the comparisons between our proposed SimCC and 1D/2D heatmap-based approaches. Compared to the dominant 2D heatmap-based scheme, SimCC has three benefits: 1) It reduces quantization error by uniformly dividing each pixel into several bins; 2) SimCC omits upsampling layers under certain settings [38] and excludes the costly refinement post-processing, which is more friendly to real-world applications; 3) SimCC shows impressing performance even with low input sizes. Our contributions are summarized as follows:

- We propose a coordinate classification pipeline for human pose estimation called SimCC, reformulating the problem as two classification tasks for horizontal and vertical coordinates. SimCC serves as a general scheme and can be easily applied to existing CNN-based or Transformer-based HPE models.
- SimCC achieves high efficiency by omitting the extra time-consuming upsampling and post-processing in heatmap-based methods. In particular, applying SimCC reduces over 55% GFLOPs of SimBa-Res50 [38] and achieves higher model performance than heatmap-based counterpart.
- Comprehensive experiments over COCO, CrowdPose, and MPII datasets are conducted to verify the effectiveness of the proposed SimCC with different backbones and multiple input sizes.

It's our belief that the predominant 2D heatmap-based methods may not be the final solution for HPE due to its high computation cost, complicated post-processing and poor performance under low input resolutions. We hope that the exploration of SimCC could provide a new perspective for the potential research work and practical deployment for HPE.

2   Related Work

Regression-Based HPE. Regression-based methods [4,24,30,31,33,35] are explored more often in the early stage of 2D human pose estimation. Different from relying on 2D grid-like heatmap, this line of work directly regresses the keypoint coordinates in a computationally friendly framework. However, only a handful of existing methods adopt this scheme due to the unsatisfactory performance. Very recently, Li *et al.*. [14] introduce the residual log-likelihood (RLE), which utilizes the normalizing flows [27] to capture the underlying output distribution and makes regression-based methods match the accuracy of state-of-the-art heatmap-based methods. Our method focuses on the coordinate representation, while the core idea of RLE is to construct an adaptive loss based on the normalizing flows, which is complementary to our work.

2D Heatmap-Based HPE. Another line of work [2,3,6,7,11,17,18,20,23,29, 38,40,43] adopts two-dimensional Gaussian distribution (*i.e.*, *heatmap*) to represent joint coordinate. Each position on the heatmap is assigned with a probability to be the ground truth point. As one of the earliest uses of heatmap, Tompson *et al.* [34] propose a hybrid architecture consisting of a deep Convolutional Network and a Markov Random Field. Newell *et al.* [23] introduce hourglass-style architecture into HPE. Papandreou *et al.* [25] propose to aggregate the heatmap and offset prediction to improve the localization precision. Xiao *et al.* [38] propose a simple baseline that utilizes three deconvolutional layers following a backbone network to obtain the final predicted heatmap. Instead, Sun *et al.* [29] propose a novel network to maintain high-resolution representations through the whole process, achieving significant improvement. Owing to the involvement of spatial uncertainty, this kind of learning schema has the tolerance of mistakes of jitter. As a result, heatmap-based methods keep stable state-of-the-art performance for years. However, quantization error remains a significant problem of the heatmap-based methods, especially in low input resolutions. To address the large quantization error caused by the discretized 2D downscaled heatmaps, Zhang *et al.* [43] propose to comprehensively account for the distribution information of heatmap activation by adopting Taylor-expansion based distribution approximation as post-processing, which complicates the pipeline.

1D Heatmap Regression in Facial Landmark. Outside the realm of human pose estimation, 1D heatmap-based methods [39,42] have been explored for facial landmark detection. Among those, Yin *et al.* [42] propose an attentive 1D heatmap regression method, which adopts learnable decoupling layers to transform 2D heatmap to 1D heatmap and then uses additional deconvolution layers to alleviate the quantization error. To capture the joint distribution information between the decoupled 1D heatmaps, a co-attention module is introduced in the 1D heatmap regression [42].

Coordinate Classification. Concurrent to our work, Chen *et al.* [5] propose Pix2Seq to casts object detection as a language modeling task, where an object is described as sequences of five discrete tokens for further classification. In Pix2Seq, the Transformer decoder architecture is essential to "read out" each object (yield the predictions). By contrast, our proposed SimCC aims to explore a new path against heatmap-based methods for human pose estimation, which can be easily combined with CNN or Transformer-based HPE methods and does not rely on an additional Transformer decoder to generate the prediction.

3   SimCC: Reformulating HPE from Classification Perspective

The key idea of SimCC is to regards human pose estimation as two classification tasks for vertical and horizontal coordinates and to reduce quantization error by

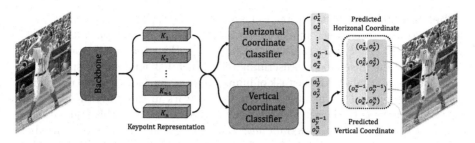

Fig. 2. The proposed SimCC pipeline for HPE. SimCC firstly extracts n keypoint representations via a backbone which can be either CNN-based or Transformer-based networks. For the CNN-based backbone, we simply flatten the obtained keypoint representations from (n, H', W') to $(n, H' \times W')$ for the subsequent classification. Based on the n keypoint representations, SimCC then performs coordinate classification for horizontal and vertical axes independently to yield the final predictions. Specifically, given i-th keypoint representation as input, the horizontal and vertical coordinate classifiers (*i.e.*, only one linear layer for each classifier) generate the i-th keypoint predictions o_x^i and o_y^i, respectively. Note that SimCC uniformly divides each pixel into multiple bins thus the quantization error is reduced and sub-pixel localization precision is achieved.

dividing each pixel to multiple bins. Figure 2 shows the schematic illustration of SimCC composed of a backbone network and two classifier heads. We will describe each components in this section in details.

Backbone. Given an input image of size $H \times W \times 3$, SimCC employs either CNN-based or Transformer-based network (*e.g.*, HRNet [29], TokenPose [18]) as the backbone to extract n keypoint representations for n corresponding keypoints.

Head. As shown in Fig. 2, horizontal and vertical classifiers (*i.e.*, only one linear layer for each classifier) are appended after the backbone to perform coordinate classification, respectively. For the CNN-based backbone, we simply flatten the outputted keypoint representations from (n, H', W') to $(n, H' \times W')$ for classification. Compared to heatmap-based approach [38] which uses multiple costly deconvolution layers as head, SimCC head is much more lightweight and simple.

Coordinate Classification. To achieve classification, we propose to uniformly discretize each continuous coordinate value into an integer as class label for model training: $c_x \in [1, N_x], c_y \in [1, N_y]$, where $N_x = W \cdot k$ and $N_y = H \cdot k$ represent the number of bins for horizontal and vertical axes, respectively. k is the splitting factor and set as ≥ 1 to reduce quantization error, resulting in *sub-pixel* localization precision. To yield the final prediction, SimCC performs vertical and horizontal coordinate classification independently based on the n keypoint representations learnt by the backbone. Concretely, given i-th keypoint representation as input, the i-th keypoint predictions o_x^i and o_y^i are generated by the horizontal and vertical coordinate classifiers, respectively. In addition, Kullback-Leibler divergence is used as loss function for training.

Label Smoothing. In traditional classification tasks, label smoothing [32] is widely utilized to enhance model performance. Hence, we adopt it for SimCC, which is called *equal label smoothing* in this paper. However, equal label smoothing punishes the false labels indiscriminately, which has ignored the spatial relevance of adjacent labels for the task of human pose estimation. A more reasonable solution is supposed to encourage the model to work in this way: the closer the output category is to the groundtruth, the better. To address this issue, we also explore to use *Laplace* or *Gaussian label smoothing*, resulting in smoothed labels following corresponding distribution. Unless noted otherwise, SimCC is used as the abbreviation for the variant with equal label smoothing .

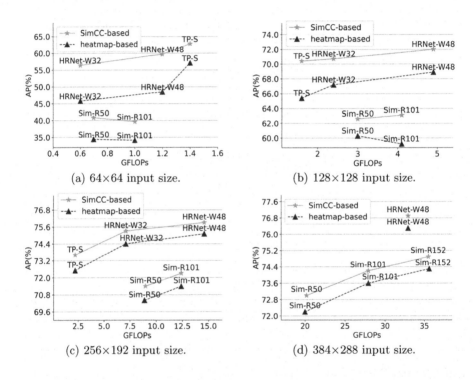

Fig. 3. Comparisons with 2D heatmap-based approaches on COCO2017 val set across various input sizes. 'TP-S' and 'Sim' represent TokenPose-S [18] and SimpleBaseline [38], respectively. Both CNN-based (*i.e.*, SimpleBaseline [38] and HRNet [29]) and Transformer-based (*i.e.*, TokenPose [18]) HPE models are chosen to verify the effectiveness of the proposed SimCC. SimCC shows clear gains compared to 2D heatmap-based counterparts across various input sizes, especially in low resolution.

3.1 Comparisons to 2D Heatmap-Based Approaches

In this part, we give a comprehensive investigation on the superiority of using SimCC scheme compared to the 2D heatmap-based approaches.

Quantization Error. Due to the computational cost of obtaining or maintaining high-resolution two-dimensional structure, 2D heatmap-based methods tend to output feature maps with $\lambda\times$ downscaled input resolution, which significantly enlarges the quantization error. On the contrary, SimCC uniformly divides each pixel into k (≥ 1) bins during discretization, which reduces the quantization error and obtains sub-pixel localization precision.

Refinement Post-Processing. Heatmap-based approaches rely heavily on extra post-processing (*e.g.*, empirical shift and DARK [43]) to reduce the quantization error. As shown in Table 1, the performance of heatmap-based methods drops significantly if without using post-processing for refinement. However, these post-processing strategies are usually computationally expensive and thus unfriendly to real-world applications. For example, DARK [43] uses Taylor-expansion and higher derivative needs to be calculated based on the obtained 2D heatmap. By contrast, the proposed SimCC omits refinement post-processing due to its sub-pixel localization precision, resulting in a simpler scheme for HPE.

Low/High Resolution Robustness. Figure 3 visualizes the comparison results. Benefiting from low quantization error, SimCC-based methods can easily outperform heatmap-based counterparts in various input sizes (*i.e.*, 64×64, 128×128, 256×192 and 384×288), demonstrating clear gains especially in low input resolutions. More specific quantitative results are discussed in Sect. 4.

Speed. SimCC makes methods like [38] get rid of time-consuming deconvolution modules, which can speed up the inference. It's worth noting that after removing the upsampling layers, SimpleBaseline-Res50 [38] with SimCC reduces **57.3%** GFLOPs, improves **23.5%** speed, and gains **+0.4** AP over heatmap-based counterpart. More comparisons are presented in Sect. 4.

4 Experiments

In the following sections, we empirically investigate the effectiveness of the proposed SimCC for 2D human pose estimation. We conduct experiments on three benchmark datasets: COCO [19], CrowdPose [15], and MPII [1].

4.1 COCO Keypoint Detection

As one of the largest and most challenging datasets for HPE, the COCO dataset [19] contains more than 200,000 images and 250,000 person instances labeling with 17 keypoints (*e.g.*, nose, left ear, etc.). The COCO dataset is divided into three parts: 57k images for the training set, 5k for val set and 20k for test-dev set. In this paper, we follow the data augmentation in [29].

Evaluation Metric. The standard average precision (AP) is used as our evaluation metric on the COCO dataset, which is calculated based on Object Keypoint Similarity (OKS):

$$OKS = \frac{\sum_i exp(-d_i^2/2s^2 j_i^2)\sigma(v_i > 0)}{\sum_i \sigma(v_i > 0)}, \tag{1}$$

where d_i is the Euclidean distance between the i-th predicted keypoint coordinate and its corresponding coordinate groundtruth, j_i is a constant, v_i is the visibilty flag, σ denotes indicator function and s is the object scale.

Table 1. Comparisons with 2D heatmap-based methods on COCO validation set. The results are provided with the same detected human boxes for fair comparison. 2D heatmap-based approaches adopt extra post-processing for refinement following their original paper, *i.e.*, DARK [43] for TokenPose [18] and empirical shift for HRNet [29] as well as SimpleBaseline [38]. SimCC brings significant gains in all input resolutions while omitting costly refinement post-processing. In particular, SimCC-based SimBa-R50 [38] achieves better results than 2D heatmap-based counterpart with over **55%** FLOPs reduction.

Method	Scheme	Input size	#Params	GFLOPs	Extra post.	AP	AR
TokenPose-S [18]	Heatmap	64 × 64	4.9M	1.4	w/o	35.9	47.0
	Heatmap	64 × 64	4.9M	1.4	DARK [43]	57.1	64.8
	SimCC	64 × 64	4.9M	1.4	**w/o**	**62.8**	**70.1**
	Heatmap	128 × 128	5.2M	1.6	w/o	57.6	64.9
	Heatmap	128 × 128	5.2M	1.6	DARK [43]	65.4	71.6
	SimCC	128 × 128	5.1M	1.6	**w/o**	**70.4**	**76.4**
	Heatmap	256 × 192	6.6M	2.2	w/o	69.9	75.8
	Heatmap	256 × 192	6.6M	2.2	DARK [43]	72.5	78.0
	SimCC	256 × 192	5.5M	2.2	**w/o**	**73.6**	**78.9**
SimBa-R50 [38]	Heatmap	64 × 64	34.0M	0.7	w/o	25.8	36.0
	Heatmap	64 × 64	34.0M	0.7	shift	34.4	43.7
	SimCC	64 × 64	24.7M	0.3	**w/o**	**39.3**	**48.4**
	Heatmap	128 × 128	34.0M	3.0	w/o	55.4	63.3
	Heatmap	128 × 128	34.0M	3.0	shift	60.3	67.6
	SimCC	128 × 128	25.0M	1.3	**w/o**	**62.6**	**69.5**
	Heatmap	256 × 192	34.0M	8.9	w/o	68.5	74.8
	Heatmap	256 × 192	34.0M	8.9	shift	70.4	76.3
	SimCC	256 × 192	25.7M	3.8	**w/o**	**70.8**	**76.8**
HRNet-W48 [29]	Heatmap	64 × 64	63.6M	1.2	w/o	36.9	47.8
	Heatmap	64 × 64	63.6M	1.2	shift	48.5	57.8
	SimCC	64 × 64	63.7M	1.2	**w/o**	**59.7**	**67.5**
	Heatmap	128 × 128	63.6M	4.9	w/o	63.3	70.5
	Heatmap	128 × 128	63.6M	4.9	shift	68.9	75.3
	SimCC	128 × 128	64.1M	4.9	**w/o**	**72.0**	**77.9**
	Heatmap	256 × 192	63.6M	14.6	w/o	73.1	78.7
	Heatmap	256 × 192	63.6M	14.6	shift	75.1	80.4
	SimCC	256 × 192	66.3M	14.6	**w/o**	**75.9**	**81.2**

Baselines. There are many *CNN-based* and recent *Transformer-based* methods for HPE. To show the superiority of the proposed SimCC, we choose two state-

Table 2. Comparisons on the COCO test-dev set. 'Trans.' represents Transformer [36] for short. "†" indicates that the Gaussian label smoothing is adopted. The proposed SimCC achieves state-of-the-art results, demonstrating clear performance improvements compared to 2D heatmap-based counterparts.

Method	Encoder	Input size	GFLOPs	AP	AP^{50}	AP^{75}	AP^M	AP^L	AR
2D Heatmap-based									
Mask-RCNN [9]	ResNet-50-FPN	–	–	63.1	87.3	68.7	57.8	71.4	–
CMU-Pose [3]	VGG-19 [28]	–	–	64.2	86.2	70.1	61.0	68.8	–
G-RMI [25]	ResNet-101 [10]	353×257	–	64.9	85.5	71.3	62.3	70.0	69.7
AE [22]	Hourglass [23]	512×512	–	65.5	86.8	72.3	60.6	72.6	70.2
MultiPoseNet [13]	–	480×480	–	69.6	86.3	76.6	65.0	76.3	73.5
RMPE [8]	PyraNet [41]	320×256	26.7	72.3	89.2	79.1	68.0	78.6	–
CPN [6]	ResNet-Inception	384×288	29.2	72.1	91.4	80.0	68.7	77.2	78.5
CFN [12]	–	–	–	72.6	86.1	69.7	78.3	64.1	–
SimBa [38]	ResNet-152	384×288	35.6	73.7	91.9	81.1	70.3	80.0	79.0
TransPose-H [40]	HRNet-W48+Trans.	256×192	21.8	75.0	92.2	82.3	71.3	81.1	80.1
HRNet-W32 [29]	HRNet-W32	384×288	16.0	74.9	92.5	82.8	71.3	80.9	80.1
SimBa [38]	ResNet-50	384×288	20.0	71.5	91.1	78.7	67.8	78.0	76.9
HRNet-W48 [29]	HRNet-W48	256×192	14.6	74.2	94.4	82.4	70.9	79.7	79.5
HRNet-W48 [29]	HRNet-W48	384×288	32.9	75.5	92.5	83.3	71.9	81.5	80.5
Regression-based									
SPM [24]	Hourglass [23]	–	–	66.9	88.5	72.9	62.6	73.1	–
DeepPose [35]	ResNet-101	256×192	7.7	57.4	86.5	64.2	55.0	62.8	–
DeepPose [35]	ResNet-152	256×192	11.3	59.3	87.6	66.7	56.8	64.9	–
CenterNet [44]	Hourglass [23]	–	–	63.0	86.8	69.6	58.9	70.4	–
DirectPose [33]	ResNet-50	–	–	62.2	86.4	68.2	56.7	69.8	–
PointSetNet [37]	HRNet-W48	–	–	68.7	89.9	76.3	64.8	75.3	–
Integral Pose [31]	ResNet-101	256×256	11.0	67.8	88.2	74.8	63.9	74.0	–
TFPose [21]	ResNet-50+Trans.	384×288	20.4	72.2	90.9	80.1	69.1	78.8	–
PRTR [16]	HRNet-W48+Trans	–	–	64.9	87.0	71.7	60.2	72.5	74.1
PRTR [16]	HRNet-W32+Trans	384×288	21.6	71.7	90.6	79.6	67.6	78.4	78.8
PRTR [16]	HRNet-W32+Trans	512×384	37.8	72.1	90.4	79.6	68.1	79.0	79.4
RLE [14]	HRNet-W48	–	–	75.7	92.3	82.9	72.3	81.3	–
SimCC-based									
SimBa (SimCC†)	ResNet-50	384×288	20.2	72.7	91.2	80.1	69.2	79.0	78.0
HRNet (SimCC†)	HRNet-W48	256×192	14.6	75.4	92.4	82.7	71.9	81.3	80.5
HRNet (SimCC†)	HRNet-W48	384×288	32.9	**76.0**	**92.4**	**83.5**	**72.5**	**81.9**	**81.1**

of-the-art methods (*i.e.*, SimpleBaseline [38] and HRNet [29]) from the former and one (*i.e.*, TokenPose [18]) from the latter as our baselines.

Implementation Details. For the selected baselines, we simply follow the original settings in their papers. Specifically, for SimpleBaseline [38], the base learning rate is set as $1e-3$, and is dropped to $1e-4$ and $1e-5$ at the 90-th and 120-th epochs respectively. For HRNet [29], the base learning rate is set as $1e-3$, and decreased to $1e-4$ and $1e-5$ at the 170-th and 200-th epochs.

The total training processes are terminated within 140 and 210 epochs respectively for SimpleBaseline [38] and HRNet [29]. Note that the training process of TokenPose-S follows [29]. In this paper, we use the two-stage [6,25,29,38] top-down human pose estimation pipeline: the person instances are firstly detected and then the keypoints are estimated. We adopt a popular person detector with 56.4% AP provided by [38] for COCO validation set. In addition, label smoothing is adopted in model training, which is commonly used in the task of classification for better generalization (equal smoothing sets the coefficient as 0.1 by default, following [32]). Experiments are conducted in 4 NVIDIA Tesla V100 GPUs.

Results on the COCO val Set. Extensive experiments are conducted on the COCO2017 validation set for comparing 2D heatmap-based and SimCC-based methods across various input resolutions (*i.e.*, 64×64, 128×128, 256×192, and 384×288). Note that the evaluation and network training are under the same input size. Some top-performed CNN-based and Transformer-based methods are chosen as our baselines. Results presented in Table 1 demonstrate that SimCC-based methods show consistent performance superiority over heatmap-based counterparts, especially in low-resolution input cases. For example, SimCC-based HRNet-W48 [29] outperforms heatmap-based counterpart by **+0.8** AP at the input size of 256×192. And under low input resolution as 64×64, our SimCC shows much larger performance gain, *i.e.*, **+11.2** AP on the COCO val dataset.

According to the results presented in Table 1, we can further draw the following conclusions: 1) Heatmap-based approaches rely seriously on post-processing for refinement, which brings extra computational cost and complicates the whole process. For example, TokenPose-S dramatically drops **21.2** AP at the input size of 64×64 if without the DARK [43] post-processing; 2) Our proposed SimCC works well without any refinement post-processing, leading to a more simple and efficient scheme compared to heatmap-based methods. For instance, our SimCC-based HRNet-W48 w/o extra post-processing outperforms heatmap-based counterpart (empirical shift is used) by 0.8 AP at the input size of 256×192.

Results on the COCO Test-Dev Set. We conduct comparisons on COCO test-dev set and present the results in Table 2. SimCC-based HRNet-W48 and SimpleBaseline-Res50 surpass heatmap-based counterparts by **+0.5** and **+1.2** AP respectively, at the input size of 384×288.

Inference Speed. We discuss the impact of our proposed SimCC to the inference speed for SimpleBaseline [38], TokenPose-S [18] and HRNet-W48 [29]. The 'inference speed' here refers to the average time consuming of model feedforward (we compute 300 samples with batchsize = 1). We adopt FPS to quantitatively illustrate the inference latency. The CPU implementation results are presented with the same machine: Intel(R) Xeon(R) Gold 6130 CPU @ 2.10 GHz.

1) *SimpleBaseline* Adopting SimCC allows one to remove the costly deconvolution layers of SimpleBaseline. We conduct experiments via SimpleBaseline-Res50 [38] on COCO val set with input size of 256×192. SimCC-based method w/o deconvolution modules can surpass 2D heatmap-based counterpart by **+0.4** AP (70.8 vs. 70.4) with **23.5%** faster speed (21 vs. 17 FPS). More specific ablation study of deconvolution modules is conducted in Sect. 4.2.

2) *TokenPose&HRNet* Due to that SimpleBaseline [38] uses an encoder-decoder architecture, we can replace its decoder part (deconvolutions) with classifier heads of SimCC. But for HRNet [29] and TokenPose [18], they have no extra independent modules as the decoder. To apply SimCC to them, we directly append the classifier heads to the original HRNet and replace the MLP head of TokenPose with ours, respectively. These are minor changes to the original architectures, thus only bringing little computation overhead for HRNet [29] and even reducing the model parameters for TokenPose [18], as shown in Table 1. Hence, SimCC only has a slight impact on the inference latency for HRNet and TokenPose. For instance, the FPS of HRNet-W48 using heatmap or SimCC is almost the same (4.5/4.8) at the input size of 256 × 192.

Is 1D Heatmap Regression a Promising Solution for HPE? We also study the performance of expanding the 1D heatmap [42] into the field of HPE, which is initially designed for facial landmark. Table 3 shows that the 1D heatmap regression [42] increases the model parameters and computational cost yet performs even worse than 2D heatmap-based counterpart. The potential reason might be that the core challenges of facial landmark and HPE are different: facial landmark possesses rigid deformation while human body joints have much higher degrees of freedom. Since the co-attention module as well as decoupling layers in [42] are only empirically verified to be effective for the task of facial landmark and their generalization to other fields (*e.g.*, HPE) remains unclear.

Table 3. Comparisons with the 1D heatmap regression [42] and 2D heatmap-based methods. Results achieved by SimBa-R50 [38] via different schemes (2D/1D heatmap, SimCC) on COCO val set with input size of 256×256. SimCC performs better than 2D/1D heatmap-based methods and requires **only 41.7%/34.7%** computation cost.

Scheme	Deconvolation	#Params	GFLOPs	Extra post.	AP
2D Heatmap	3	34.0M	12.0	shift	70.4
2D Heatmap	3	34.0M	12.0	w/o	68.8
1D Heatmap [42]	5	39.0M	14.4	w/o	68.5
SimCC	0	**26.3M**	**5.0**	w/o	**70.4**

4.2   Ablation Study

Splitting Factor k. The splitting factor k controls the how many bins per pixel in SimCC. Specifically, the larger k is, the smaller the quantization error of SimCC is. Nevertheless, model training becomes more difficult when k increases. Hence, there is a trade-off between the quantization error and the model performance. We test $k \in \{1, 2, 3, 4\}$ based on SimpleBaseline [38] and HRNet [29] under various input resolutions. As shown in Fig. 4, model performance tends to increase first and then decrease as k grows. For HRNet-W32 [29], the recommended settings are $k = 2$ for both 128×128 and 256×192 input size. For SimBa-Res50 [38], the recommended settings are $k = 3$ and $k = 2$ for 128×128 and 256×192 input size, respectively.

Upsampling Modules. Upsampling modules are usually computationally costly and substantially slow down the network's inference speed, however, indispensable for heatmap-based methods. Hence, it is of practical significance to explore if applying SimCC can reduce the dependence of upsampling modules in HPE. Notice that the upsampling modules[1] adopted in SimpleBaseline [38] is independent to the backbone and thus can be easily removed. Therefore we conduct ablation study of SimCC w/ and w/o deconvolution modules based on SimpleBaseline [38]. Table 4 show the results on the COCO2017 val dataset. It can be observed that compared to heatmap, SimCC allows one to remove the costly deconvolution layers of SimpleBaseline, resulting in consistent computational cost reduction across various input resolutions. For example, SimCC-based SimpleBaseline-Res50 w/o upsampling modules still outperform heatmap-based counterpart w/ upsampling modules by **+0.4** AP, with **57.3%** fewer GFLOPs at the input size of 256×192.

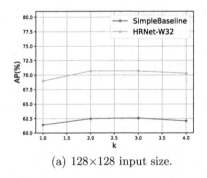
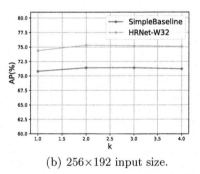

(a) 128×128 input size.   (b) 256×192 input size.

Fig. 4. Ablation study of splitting factor k value on the COCO validation set. SimpleBaseline [38] uses ResNet-50 as backbone. k controls how many bins per pixel in SimCC. Model performance increases first and then drops as k becomes larger.

---

[1] The upsampling modules used in SimpleBaseline [38] recover the feature map resolution from $1/32\times$ to $1/4\times$ input size, consisting of three deconvolution layers.

Table 4. Ablation study of upsampling modules. Results achieved by SimBa-R50 [38] on COCO val set. "Heatmap" represents 2D heatmap-based methods for short. Employing deconvolution improves SimCC-based methods yet the gains are slight. Even without any deconvolution layers, SimCC-based approaches surpass 2D heatmap-based counterparts, significantly reducing over 55% FLOPs.

Scheme	Input size	Deconvolution	#Params	GFLOPs	AP
Heatmap	64×64	✓	34.0M	0.7	34.4
SimCC	64×64	✓	34.1M	0.7	**40.8**
SimCC	64×64	✗	**24.7M**	**0.3**	39.3
Heatmap	128×128	✓	34.0M	3.0	60.3
SimCC	128×128	✓	34.8M	3.0	**62.6**
SimCC	128×128	✗	**25.0M**	**1.3**	**62.6**
Heatmap	256×192	✓	34.0M	8.9	70.4
SimCC	256×192	✓	36.8M	9.0	**71.4**
SimCC	256×192	✗	**25.7M**	**3.8**	70.8

Table 5. Ablation study of label smoothing. Results are achieved based on SimpleBaseline-Res50 [38] with the input size of 384×288 on COCO2017 val dataset. Employing label smoothing significantly improves the performance by 2.1 AP.

Label smoothing	AP	AP^{50}	AP^{75}	AP^M	AP^L	AR
w/o	71.3	88.8	78.2	67.8	78.2	77.3
Equal	73.0	89.3	79.7	69.5	79.9	78.6
Gaussian	73.4	89.2	80.0	69.7	80.6	78.8
Laplace	73.0	89.3	79.7	69.3	80.3	78.4

Label Smoothing. Label smoothing [32] is a commonly used strategy to improve generalization for the task of classification. To investigate its effect on our proposed method, we train SimpleBaseline-Res50 [38] based on SimCC with various label smoothing strategies: {*w/o, equal, Gaussian, Laplace*}. Table 5 demonstrates that label smoothing strategy does make a difference. Therefore, a promising way to further improve SimCC may be replacing the heuristic label smoothing strategy in a self-adaptive way. Further discussion is out the scope of this paper and we regard it as future work.

Table 6. Comparisons with 2D heatmap-based methods on CrowdPose test dataset. Results are achieved by HRNet-W32 [29] and "Heatmap" denotes 2D heatmap as an abbreviation. SimCC-based HRNet-W32 demonstrates consistent improvements compared to 2D heatmap-based methods.

Scheme	Input size	AP	AP^{50}	AP^{75}	AP^E	AP^M	AP^H
Heatmap	64×64	42.4	69.6	45.5	51.2	43.1	31.8
SimCC	64×64	**46.5**	**70.9**	**50.0**	**56.0**	**47.5**	**34.7**
Heatmap	256×192	66.4	81.1	71.5	74.0	67.4	55.6
SimCC	256×192	**66.7**	**82.1**	**72.0**	**74.1**	**67.8**	**56.2**

4.3 CrowdPose

One may concern about the performance of SimCC in dense pose scenes. Thus we further illustrate the effectiveness of the proposed SimCC on the CrowdPose [15] dataset, which contains much more crowded scenes than the COCO keypoint dataset. There are 20K images and 80K person instances in the CrowdPose. The training, validation and testing subset consist of about 10K, 2K, and 8K images respectively. Similar evaluation metric to that of COCO [19] is adopted here, with extra AP^E (AP scores on relatively easier samples) and AP^H (AP scores on harder samples). We follow the original paper [15] to adopt YoloV3 [26] as the human detector, and batch size is set as 64. We conduct comparison experiments on the CrowdPose test dataset, at the input size of 64×64 and 256×192 respectively. The results in Table 6 show that SimCC-based methods outperform heatmap-based counterparts.

4.4 MPII Human Pose Estimation

The MPII Human Pose dataset [1] contains 40K person samples with 16 joints labels. We point out that the data augmentation used on the MPII dataset is the same as that on COCO dataset.

Results on the Validatoin Set. We follow the evaluation procedure in HRNet [29]. The head-normalized probability of correct keypoint (PCKh) [1] score is used for model evaluation. The results are presented in Table 7. At the input size of 256×256, SimCC-based methods achieve competitive performances under PCKh@0.5, and show clear gains under the stricter measurement PCKh@0.1.

Table 7. Comparisons with 2D heatmap-based methods on the MPII validation set. Experiments are conducted based on HRNet-W32 [29] and "Heatmap" means 2D heatmap for short. "†" denotes that Gaussian label smoothing is utilized. Under stricter metric PCKh@0.1, SimCC shows clear gains across different input sizes.

Scheme	Input size	Hea	Sho	Elb	Wri	Hip	Kne	Ank	Mean
PCKh@0.5									
Heatmap	64×64	89.7	86.6	75.1	65.7	77.2	69.2	63.6	76.4
SimCC	64×64	**93.5**	**89.5**	**77.5**	**67.6**	**79.8**	**71.5**	**65.0**	**78.7**
Heatmap	256×256	97.1	95.9	90.3	**86.4**	89.1	**87.1**	**83.3**	**90.3**
SimCC	256×256	96.8	95.9	90.0	85.0	89.1	85.4	81.3	89.6
SimCC†	256×256	**97.2**	**96.0**	**90.4**	85.6	**89.5**	85.8	81.8	90.0
PCKh@0.1									
Heatmap	64×64	12.9	11.7	9.7	7.1	7.2	7.2	6.6	9.2
SimCC	64×64	**30.9**	**23.3**	**18.1**	**15.0**	**10.5**	**13.1**	**12.8**	**18.5**
Heatmap	256×256	44.5	37.3	37.5	36.9	15.1	25.9	27.2	33.1
SimCC	256×256	**50.1**	41.0	**45.3**	**42.4**	16.6	**29.7**	**30.3**	**37.8**
SimCC†	256×256	49.6	**41.9**	43.0	39.6	**17.0**	28.2	28.9	36.8

5 Limitation and Future Work

SimCC introduced in this paper works under the setting of top-down human pose estimation. When it comes to bottom-up multi-person pose estimation, the presence of multiple people brings the identification ambiguity. Potential future work may introduce extra embeddings in a similar way to AE [22], in order to address the matching problem between candidate coordinate x and y values.

6 Conclusion

In this paper, we explore a simple yet promising coordinate representation (namely SimCC). It regards the keypoint localization task as two independent sub-tasks of classification for horizontal and vertical axes. The experimental results empirically show that the 2D structure might not be a key ingredient for coordinate representation to sustain superior performance. The proposed SimCC shows advantages over heatmap-based representation at model performances. Moreover, it may also inspire new works on lightweight model design for HPE.

Acknowledgement. This work is supported in part by the National Natural Science Foundation of China under Grant 62171248, and the PCNL KEY project (PCL2021A07), and in part by the National Natural Science Foundation of China under Grant 61773117.

References

1. Andriluka, M., Pishchulin, L., Gehler, P., Schiele, B.: 2D human pose estimation: new benchmark and state of the art analysis. In: Proceedings of the IEEE Conference on Computer Vision and Pattern Recognition, pp. 3686–3693 (2014)

2. Cai, Y., et al.: Learning delicate local representations for multi-person pose estimation. In: Vedaldi, A., Bischof, H., Brox, T., Frahm, J.-M. (eds.) ECCV 2020. LNCS, vol. 12348, pp. 455–472. Springer, Cham (2020). https://doi.org/10.1007/978-3-030-58580-8_27

3. Cao, Z., Hidalgo, G., Simon, T., Wei, S.E., Sheikh, Y.: Openpose: realtime multi-person 2d pose estimation using part affinity fields. IEEE Trans. Pattern Anal. Mach. Intell. **43**(1), 172–186 (2019)

4. Carreira, J., Agrawal, P., Fragkiadaki, K., Malik, J.: Human pose estimation with iterative error feedback. In: Proceedings of the IEEE Conference on Computer Vision and Pattern Recognition, pp. 4733–4742 (2016)

5. Chen, T., Saxena, S., Li, L., Fleet, D.J., Hinton, G.: Pix2seq: a language modeling framework for object detection. arXiv preprint arXiv:2109.10852 (2021)

6. Chen, Y., Wang, Z., Peng, Y., Zhang, Z., Yu, G., Sun, J.: Cascaded pyramid network for multi-person pose estimation. In: Proceedings of the IEEE Conference on Computer Vision and Pattern Recognition, pp. 7103–7112 (2018)

7. Cheng, B., Xiao, B., Wang, J., Shi, H., Huang, T.S., Zhang, L.: Higherhrnet: scale-aware representation learning for bottom-up human pose estimation. In: Proceedings of the IEEE/CVF Conference on Computer Vision and Pattern Recognition, pp. 5386–5395 (2020)

8. Fang, H.S., Xie, S., Tai, Y.W., Lu, C.: Rmpe: regional multi-person pose estimation. In: Proceedings of the IEEE International Conference on Computer Vision, pp. 2334–2343 (2017)

9. He, K., Gkioxari, G., Dollár, P., Girshick, R.: Mask R-CNN. In: Proceedings of the IEEE International Conference on Computer Vision, pp. 2961–2969 (2017)

10. He, K., Zhang, X., Ren, S., Sun, J.: Deep residual learning for image recognition. In: Proceedings of the IEEE Conference on Computer Vision and Pattern Recognition, pp. 770–778 (2016)

11. Huang, J., Zhu, Z., Guo, F., Huang, G.: The devil is in the details: Delving into unbiased data processing for human pose estimation. In: Proceedings of the IEEE/CVF Conference on Computer Vision and Pattern Recognition, pp. 5700–5709 (2020)

12. Huang, S., Gong, M., Tao, D.: A coarse-fine network for keypoint localization. In: Proceedings of the IEEE International Conference on Computer Vision, pp. 3028–3037 (2017)

13. Kocabas, M., Karagoz, S., Akbas, E.: MultiPoseNet: fast multi-person pose estimation using pose residual network. In: Ferrari, V., Hebert, M., Sminchisescu, C., Weiss, Y. (eds.) ECCV 2018. LNCS, vol. 11215, pp. 437–453. Springer, Cham (2018). https://doi.org/10.1007/978-3-030-01252-6_26

14. Li, J., Bian, S., Zeng, A., Wang, C., Pang, B., Liu, W., Lu, C.: Human pose regression with residual log-likelihood estimation. In: Proceedings of the IEEE/CVF International Conference on Computer Vision, pp. 11025–11034 (2021)

15. Li, J., Wang, C., Zhu, H., Mao, Y., Fang, H.S., Lu, C.: Crowdpose: efficient crowded scenes pose estimation and a new benchmark. In: Proceedings of the IEEE/CVF Conference on Computer Vision and Pattern Recognition, pp. 10863–10872 (2019)

16. Li, K., Wang, S., Zhang, X., Xu, Y., Xu, W., Tu, Z.: Pose recognition with cascade transformers. arXiv preprint arXiv:2104.06976 (2021)
17. Li, W., et al.: Rethinking on multi-stage networks for human pose estimation. arXiv preprint arXiv:1901.00148 (2019)
18. Li, Y., et al.: Tokenpose: learning keypoint tokens for human pose estimation. arXiv preprint arXiv:2104.03516 (2021)
19. Lin, T.-Y., et al.: Microsoft COCO: common objects in context. In: Fleet, D., Pajdla, T., Schiele, B., Tuytelaars, T. (eds.) ECCV 2014. LNCS, vol. 8693, pp. 740–755. Springer, Cham (2014). https://doi.org/10.1007/978-3-319-10602-1_48
20. Luo, Z., Wang, Z., Huang, Y., Tan, T., Zhou, E.: Rethinking the heatmap regression for bottom-up human pose estimation. arXiv preprint arXiv:2012.15175 (2020)
21. Mao, W., Ge, Y., Shen, C., Tian, Z., Wang, X., Wang, Z.: Tfpose: direct human pose estimation with transformers. arXiv preprint arXiv:2103.15320 (2021)
22. Newell, A., Huang, Z., Deng, J.: Associative embedding: End-to-end learning for joint detection and grouping. In: Advances in Neural Information Processing Systems (2017)
23. Newell, A., Yang, K., Deng, J.: Stacked hourglass networks for human pose estimation. In: Leibe, B., Matas, J., Sebe, N., Welling, M. (eds.) ECCV 2016. LNCS, vol. 9912, pp. 483–499. Springer, Cham (2016). https://doi.org/10.1007/978-3-319-46484-8_29
24. Nie, X., Feng, J., Zhang, J., Yan, S.: Single-stage multi-person pose machines. In: Proceedings of the IEEE/CVF International Conference on Computer Vision, pp. 6951–6960 (2019)
25. Papandreou, G., et al.: Towards accurate multi-person pose estimation in the wild. In: Proceedings of the IEEE Conference on Computer Vision and Pattern Recognition, pp. 4903–4911 (2017)
26. Redmon, J., Farhadi, A.: Yolov3: An incremental improvement. arXiv preprint arXiv:1804.02767 (2018)
27. Rezende, D., Mohamed, S.: Variational inference with normalizing flows. In: International Conference on machine Learning, pp. 1530–1538. PMLR (2015)
28. Simonyan, K., Zisserman, A.: Very deep convolutional networks for large-scale image recognition. arXiv preprint arXiv:1409.1556 (2014)
29. Sun, K., Xiao, B., Liu, D., Wang, J.: Deep high-resolution representation learning for human pose estimation. In: Proceedings of the IEEE/CVF Conference on Computer Vision and Pattern Recognition, pp. 5693–5703 (2019)
30. Sun, X., Shang, J., Liang, S., Wei, Y.: Compositional human pose regression. In: Proceedings of the IEEE International Conference on Computer Vision, pp. 2602–2611 (2017)
31. Sun, X., Xiao, B., Wei, F., Liang, S., Wei, Y.: Integral human pose regression. In: Ferrari, V., Hebert, M., Sminchisescu, C., Weiss, Y. (eds.) ECCV 2018. LNCS, vol. 11210, pp. 536–553. Springer, Cham (2018). https://doi.org/10.1007/978-3-030-01231-1_33
32. Szegedy, C., Vanhoucke, V., Ioffe, S., Shlens, J., Wojna, Z.: Rethinking the inception architecture for computer vision. In: Proceedings of the IEEE Conference on Computer Vision and Pattern Recognition, pp. 2818–2826 (2016)
33. Tian, Z., Chen, H., Shen, C.: Directpose: direct end-to-end multi-person pose estimation. arXiv preprint arXiv:1911.07451 (2019)
34. Tompson, J., Jain, A., LeCun, Y., Bregler, C.: Joint training of a convolutional network and a graphical model for human pose estimation. arXiv preprint arXiv:1406.2984 (2014)

35. Toshev, A., Szegedy, C.: Deeppose: Human pose estimation via deep neural networks. In: Proceedings of the IEEE Conference on Computer Vision and Pattern Recognition, pp. 1653–1660 (2014)
36. Vaswani, A., et al.: Attention is all you need. arXiv preprint arXiv:1706.03762 (2017)
37. Wei, F., Sun, X., Li, H., Wang, J., Lin, S.: Point-set anchors for object detection, instance segmentation and pose estimation. In: Vedaldi, A., Bischof, H., Brox, T., Frahm, J.-M. (eds.) ECCV 2020. LNCS, vol. 12355, pp. 527–544. Springer, Cham (2020). https://doi.org/10.1007/978-3-030-58607-2_31
38. Xiao, B., Wu, H., Wei, Y.: Simple baselines for human pose estimation and tracking. In: Proceedings of the European Conference on Computer Vision, pp. 466–481 (2018)
39. Xiong, Y., Zhou, Z., Dou, Y., Su, Z.: Gaussian vector: an efficient solution for facial landmark detection. In: Proceedings of the Asian Conference on Computer Vision (2020)
40. Yang, S., Quan, Z., Nie, M., Yang, W.: Transpose: towards explainable human pose estimation by transformer. arXiv preprint arXiv:2012.14214 (2020)
41. Yang, W., Li, S., Ouyang, W., Li, H., Wang, X.: Learning feature pyramids for human pose estimation. In: proceedings of the IEEE International Conference on Computer Vision, pp. 1281–1290 (2017)
42. Yin, S., Wang, S., Chen, X., Chen, E.: Attentive one-dimensional heatmap regression for facial landmark detection and tracking (2020)
43. Zhang, F., Zhu, X., Dai, H., Ye, M., Zhu, C.: Distribution-aware coordinate representation for human pose estimation. In: Proceedings of the IEEE/CVF Conference on Computer Vision and Pattern Recognition, pp. 7093–7102 (2020)
44. Zhou, X., Wang, D., Krähenbühl, P.: Objects as points. arXiv preprint arXiv:1904.07850 (2019)

Regularizing Vector Embedding in Bottom-Up Human Pose Estimation

Haixin Wang[1,2(✉)], Lu Zhou[2], Yingying Chen[2], Ming Tang[1,2],
and Jinqiao Wang[1,2,3,4]

[1] School of Artificial Intelligence, University of Chinese Academy of Sciences,
Beijing, China
[2] National Laboratory of Pattern Recognition, Institute of Automation,
Chinese Academy of Sciences, Beijing, China
{haixin.wang,lu.zhou,yingying.chen,tangm,jqwang}@nlpr.ia.ac.cn
[3] Peng Cheng Laboratory, Shenzhen, China
[4] ObjectEye Inc., Beijing, China

Abstract. The embedding-based method such as Associative Embedding is popular in bottom-up human pose estimation. Methods under this framework group candidate keypoints according to the predicted identity embeddings. However, the identity embeddings of different instances are likely to be linearly inseparable in some complex scenes, such as crowded scene or when the number of instances in the image is large. To reduce the impact of this phenomenon on keypoint grouping, we try to learn a sparse multidimensional embedding for each keypoint. We observe that the different dimensions of embeddings are highly linearly correlated. To address this issue, we impose an additional constraint on the embeddings during training phase. Based on the fact that the scales of instances usually have significant variations, we utilize the scales of instances to regularize the embeddings, which effectively reduces the linear correlation of embeddings and makes embeddings being sparse. We evaluate our model on CrowdPose Test and COCO Test-dev. Compared to vanilla Associative Embedding, our method has an impressive superiority in keypoint grouping, especially in crowded scenes with a large number of instances. Furthermore, our method achieves state-of-the-art results on CrowdPose Test (74.5 AP) and COCO Test-dev (72.8 AP), outperforming other bottom-up methods. Our code and pretrained models are available at https://github.com/CR320/CoupledEmbedding.

Keywords: Human pose estimation · Bottom-up · Embedding

1 Introduction

Multi-person human pose estimation (HPE) is a fundamental task in computer vision. Current multi-person HPE methods are mainly split up into two paradigms: top-down and bottom-up. Top-down methods [3,25,28,30] first detect instances via human detector and then perform keypoint detection for

© The Author(s), under exclusive license to Springer Nature Switzerland AG 2022
S. Avidan et al. (Eds.): ECCV 2022, LNCS 13666, pp. 107–122, 2022.
https://doi.org/10.1007/978-3-031-20068-7_7

each detected instance. By contrast, bottom-up methods [2,14,22,24] first detect all identity-free keypoints and then group them into individual persons.

Judging the identities of candidate keypoint is a significant challenge of bottom-up methods. The part field-based methods [2,14] utilize limb information to construct connective intensity between keypoints. The human center regression-based methods [8,23,27] utilize a human center point to represent the instance and densely estimate keypoint offsets w.r.t. the center. The embedding-based methods [4,21,22] assign each candidate keypoint an identity embedding and group keypoints with a heuristic matching algorithm in post-processing. In recent years, the embedding-based methods are popular in human pose estimation.

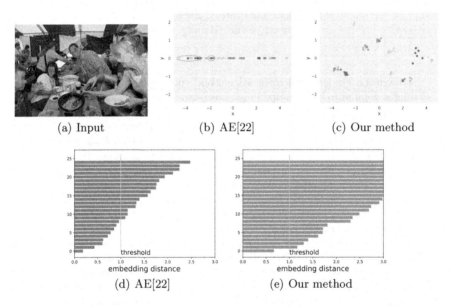

(a) Input   (b) AE[22]   (c) Our method

(d) AE[22]   (e) Our method

Fig. 1. (a) shows the input image in a typical complex scene. (b) and (c) show the embedding distribution in a 2-dimensional space (the original embedding dimensionality is set to 8, we adopt PCA to reduce the dimensionality to 2). (d) and (e) show the embedding distances between different instances (we only show the smallest 25 pairs) (Color figure online)

Despite the embedding-based methods achieve impressive results on some common benchmarks [1,20], they still suffer from precision degradation in some complex scenes. For example, in crowded scenes with a large number of instances, some predicted embeddings of different instances are likely to be linearly inseparable, resulting in incorrect keypoint grouping in the post-processing of the embedding-based methods. When the 1-D embeddings are replaced by multidimensional embeddings, they are still distributed on a line and the linear inseparability is not diminished. As shown in Fig. 1(b), the embeddings predicted by AE

[22] in red circle are linearly inseparable. To analyze the relationship between different dimensions of embeddings, we collect images with more than 3 instances in CrowdPose Test [18] and calculate the correlation coefficients between different dimensions of embeddings in one image. The histogram in Fig. 2(a) shows that all the mean correlation coefficients are really close to 1, which means different dimensions of embeddings predicted by AE [22] are highly linearly correlated.

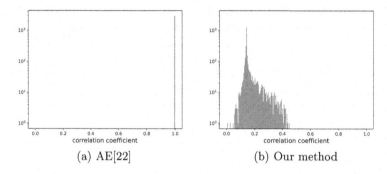

(a) AE[22]   (b) Our method

Fig. 2. Histogram of correlation coefficients. (a) shows the result of AE [22] and (b) shows the result of our method. The dimensionalities of embeddings are set to 8 in both methods. All samples are collected from CrowdPose Test [18].

To learn sparse multidimensional embeddings, we propose a novel method named Coupled Embedding (CE). Different from vanilla embedding-based methods, our method imposes an additional regularization on the embeddings. Based on the fact that the scales of instances usually have significant variations, we choose the scales as the supervised inforamtion for regularization. In our method, we convert the instance scales to a normalized vector which only has high values in one or two adjacent dimensions. Then we minimize the angle between the scale vector and the vector embedding. This constraint pushes the principal components of embeddings to be concentrated in certain dimensions. Figure 2(b) shows that our method significantly reduces the linear correlation of embeddings in an images.

To demonstrate the superiority of our method, we compare the embeddings of AE [22] with our method in a typical complex scene. Comparing the result in Fig. 1(a) and Fig. 1(b), it shows embeddings in AE [22] are almost distributed on a line but the embeddings in our methods are scattered. Some linearly inseparable embeddings predicted by AE [22] become linearly separable in our method. Figure 1(d) shows that some embedding distances between different instances in AE [22] are lower than grouping threshold, which will cause incorrect keypoint grouping. By contrast, Fig. 1(e) shows that the embedding distances increase apparently in our method, which means our method can efficiently improve keypoint grouping.

Recent SOTA embedding-based methods [4, 21] focus on improving heatmap regression to enhance keypoint detection. As keypoint grouping is based on the results of keypoint detection, for a fair comparison with current embedding-based methods, we further utilize learned scale information and adaptive loss weights to improve heatmap regression.

In conclusion, our contributions are mainly as follows:

- To our best knowledge, we are the first to probe the limitation of keypoint grouping in Associative Embedding. We find that different dimensions of embeddings in an image are highly linearly correlated.
- We propose a novel keypoint grouping method named Coupled Embedding for bottom-up human pose estimation. Our method imposes an additional constraint on embeddings to learn sparse multidimensional embeddings.
- Our method achieves new state-of-the-art results on CrowdPose Test (74.5 AP) and COCO Test-dev (72.8 AP), outperforming all existing bottom-up methods. We conduct a series of experiments and the results demonstrate that our model has significant advantages in crowded scenes compared with other bottom-up methods.

2   Related Work

2.1   Bottom-Up Methods

Bottom-up methods first detect all candidate keypoints in an image, then assemble them into each instance. Pioneering works such as DeepCut [26] and L-JPA [12] formulate the keypoint association problem as an integer linear program, which however takes longer processing time. In recent years, there are three popular types of bottom-up methods, including part field [2,14,17], human center regression [8,23,27] and identity embedding [4,21,22]. The part field-based methods produce a 2D vector field to construct connective intensity between keypoints. OpenPose [2] is a representative part field-based method that predicts the part affinity fields to construct the connective intensity and then utilizes a greedy algorithm to assemble different keypoints of the same instance. Inspired by OpenPose [2], PifPaf [14] utilizes the part intensity fields to localize body parts, and employs the part association fields to associate body parts with each other. The human center regression-based methods first locate a center position of each instance, then densely predict displacements w.r.t the center position for keypoints which belong to the instance. The method [23] proposes a single-stage multi-person pose machine that simultaneously regresses the center positions and body keypoint displacements, predicting multi-person poses within one stage. DEKER [8] utilizes a multi-branch structure for separate regression, where each branch learns a representation with dedicated adaptive convolutions and regresses one keypoint offset. Associative Embedding [22] is the first to predict identity embeddings for keypoint grouping. Later methods [4,21] focus on improving heatmap regression to enhance keypoint detection. Higherhrnet [4] utilize higher-resolution heatmaps to handle scale variation. The method [21] add a new branch to predict the uncertainty maps which adaptively adjust the standard deviation of the gaussian kernel for each keypoint, enabling the model to be more tolerant of various human scales and labeling ambiguities.

2.2   Vector Embedding

Prior works apply vector embedding to many tasks. The methods [6,29] in image retrieval utilize vector embedding to measure similarity between images. The methods [9,31] map visual features and text features to the same vector space to establish their connection in image classification or image captioning. Deep clustering method [7,11] utilize vector embedding to obtain a feasible feature space. Recently, many methods [4,21,22] in human pose estimation and object detection [16] apply vector embedding in keypoint grouping.

For multi-person human pose estimation, Associative Embedding [22] is the first to apply vector embedding for keypoint grouping and defines a loss function which prompts keypoints from the same instance to have similar embeddings and keypoints across different instances to have distinguishing embeddings. The authors of Associative Embedding [22] found there are little performance gap between 1-D embedding and multi-dimensional embedding, but they did not probe the reason further. In our paper, we find that the different dimensions of embeddings in an image are highly linearly correlated. Therefore, even in high-dimensional space, the embeddings are almost distributed on one line, which is the same as the 1-D case.

3   Our Method

3.1   Model Framework

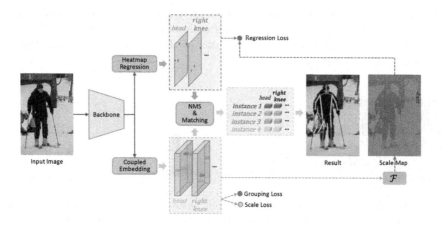

Fig. 3. An overview of our model. For each body keypoint, the model simultaneously predicts detection heatmaps (gray) and embedding maps (pink). Function $\mathcal{F}$ tranforms embedding maps into scale maps. Each location in scale maps represents a scale factor. We draw the valid scale factors with yellow color, where larger value corresponds to higher brightness. To make it easier to understand, locations in scale maps with low detection scores are masked. (Color figure online)

Figure 3 illustrates the framework of our model. There are two branches that produce detection heatmaps and embedding maps, respectively. During training, regression loss is employed to supervise detection heatmaps and grouping loss is employed to supervise the identity embeddings. The scale loss acts as a regularization item to constrain the embeddings. In addition, the vectors in embedding maps can be transformed into scale factors which adaptively adjust the ground truth heatmaps of detection branch. For a fair comparison with the baseline method, we choose the same post processing as AE [22]. We first utilize non-maximum suppression to get the peak detections for each keypoint. Then we retrieve their corresponding embeddings at the same pixel location in embedding maps. At last, we identify the group of detected keypoints across body parts by matching embeddings via Hungarian algorithm [15]. To verify the generality of our method, we further apply our method to HigherHRNet [4].

3.2   Coupled Embedding

Coupled Embedding predicts embedding maps $T \in \mathcal{R}^{H \times W \times K \times M}$ for K types of keypoint, where M denotes the dimensionality of embeddings, H and W denotes the height and width of embedding maps, respectively. Following AE [22], we adopt the grouping loss to prompt embeddings within an instance tend to have close distance, while embeddings across instances tend to be far apart. At the same time, we expect that the multi-dimensional embeddings can be sparse. Hence, we attempt to constrain the embeddings so that the principal components of embeddings are concentrated in certain dimensions, while keeping the values in other dimensions small. Based on the fact that the scales of instances usually have significant variations, we utilize the scales to generate vectors for embedding regularizing. In this paper, we define the scale of instance as $S_n = \sqrt{S_{box_n}}/L$, where S_{box_n} denotes the bounding box area of the nth instance and L denotes the short size of the input image.

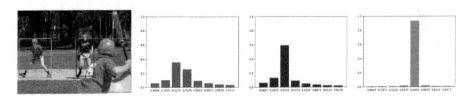

Fig. 4. Regularization vectors of three different instances in an image. The x-axis and y-axis denote scale level and the normalized component value, respectively.

Suppose s_n denotes the generated regularization vector of the nth instance, we compute s_n as:

$$s_n = \frac{(|S_n - d|)^{-1}}{\|(|S_n - d|)^{-1}\|_2}, \tag{1}$$

where S_n denotes the scale of the nth instance and the d is a constant vector which divides the normalized scale into multiple levels. The value of each dimension of d and can be written as:

$$d_i = \frac{0.5 + i}{M}(i = 0, 1, \cdots, M - 1) \tag{2}$$

There is an example of regularization vectors of three different instances in Fig. 4. As shown in Fig. 4, the principal components of different regularization vectors are different. The dimension with the highest value corresponds the scale level which is the closest to the scale of instance.

3.3   Improving Heatmap Regression with Coupled Embedding

The 2D gaussian activation functions of heatmap regression in previous methods are totally similar, which can be written as:

$$h_{n,k,i,j} = e^{\frac{-((i-x_{n,k})^2 + (j-y_{n,k})^2)}{2\sigma^2}}, \tag{3}$$

where $\{x_{n,k}, y_{n,k}\}$ denotes the coordinate of each keypoint and $\{i, j\}$ denotes the coordinate of each pixel in heatmap. σ is the standard deviation of gaussian kernel which is usually set as a constant in previous methods. However, fixing standard deviation is unreasonable because the model needs to handle a large variance of human scales. An intuitive approach to solve this problem is applying a scale factor to adaptively adjust the standard deviation of gaussian kernel, which can be written as:

$$h_{n,k,i,j}^{\gamma} = e^{\frac{-((i-x_{n,k})^2 + (j-y_{n,k})^2)}{2(\sigma \cdot \gamma_n)^2}} = (h_{n,k,i,j})^{1/\gamma_n^2}, \tag{4}$$

where γ_n denotes scale factor. And we define the scale factor as $\gamma_n = S_n/\theta$, where θ is a hyper-parameter to adjust the range of scale factor value.

Table 1. Comparison of training with fixed standard deviation and training with adjusted standard deviation. We apply associative embedding [22] as the baseline.

σ	Fixed	Adjusted					
θ	–	0.85	0.75	0.65	0.55	0.45	0.35
AP	64.8	59.8	60.8	63.9	61.6	61.4	61.7

We attempt to directly take the scale of instance as the scale factor to adjust the standard deviation, however we find it is inferior to prior fixed standard deviation. We conduct multiple experiments in different values of θ, and the results is shown in Table 1. We argue that the reason of the precision degradation is that complex pose, occlusion and partially labeling cause the scale of instance contains much noise. To tackle this problem, we utilize learned embedding to generate scale factor which eliminates the influence of scale noise and can been written as:

$$\gamma_{i,j} = \frac{1}{\theta} \sum_{m=0}^{M-1} \hat{t}_{i,j,m} d_m, \tag{5}$$

where $\hat{t}_{i,j}$ is the normalized value of $|t_{i,j}|$ and d_m is the constant vector defined in Eq. 2.

3.4 Loss Function

For Coupled Embedding, we simultaneously impose regularization loss and grouping loss on embedding maps. We denote regularization loss and grouping loss as $\mathcal{L}_s$ and $\mathcal{L}_g$, respectively. The regularization loss is written as:

$$\mathcal{L}_s = \frac{1}{NK} \sum_n \sum_k (1 - \langle \hat{t}_{n,k}, s_{n,k} \rangle), \tag{6}$$

where $\hat{t}_{n,k}$ is sampled in embedding maps and $s_{n,k}$ is the corresponding regularization vectors. The $\mathcal{L}_s$ maximizes the cosine similarity between $\hat{t}_{n,k}$ and $s_{n,k}$. Grouping loss encourages pairs of embeddings to be assigned similar values if the corresponding keypoints belong to the same instance or dissimilar values otherwise. The loss function can be written as:

$$\mathcal{L}_g = \frac{1}{NK} \sum_n \sum_k \|t_{n,k} - \bar{t}_n\|_2^2 + \frac{2}{N(N-1)} \sum_n \sum_m e^{-\|\bar{t}_n - \bar{t}_m\|_2^2/2}, \tag{7}$$

where $\bar{t}_n = \frac{1}{K} \sum_k t_{n,k}$.

In detection branch, distances between predicted heatmaps and target heatmaps are frequently measured by L2 loss [2,14,22,24]. In target heatmaps, background samples make up the vast majority, which leads to imbalanced training data. To tackle this problem, we adaptively decays the loss value of easy samples, which is similar to focal loss [19] in classification. In [16,21,32], this idea is also applied to improve heatmap regression. The regression loss can be written as:

$$\mathcal{L}_r = W \cdot \|H_p - H_g^{\sigma \cdot \Gamma}\|_2^2, \tag{8}$$

where H_p is the predicted heatmap and $H_g^{\sigma \cdot \Gamma}$ is the adaptively adjusted ground truth. W is the weight which can be defined as:

$$W = P \cdot |1 - H_p| + (1 - P) \cdot |H_p|, \tag{9}$$

$$P = (1 - log^{H_g^{\sigma \cdot \Gamma}})^{-\beta}, \tag{10}$$

where β is the hyper-parameter that controls the decay rate of the noncentral sample. In our practice, we set β to 0.01. The P defines the likelihood that a sample is positive. Equation (9) shows that positive samples which predict high activations are assigned low weights and negative samples which predict low activations are assigned low weights.

In conclusion, the total loss of our method can be written as:

$$\mathcal{L}_{total} = \mathcal{L}_r + \lambda_1 \mathcal{L}_g + \lambda_2 \mathcal{L}_s, \qquad (11)$$

where λ_1 and λ_2 are hyper-parameters. In practice, we set λ_1 to 1e-3 and λ_2 to 1e-4.

4   Experiments

4.1   Datasets and Implementation Details

Datasets. In this paper, we validate our method on CrowdPose [18] and COCO Keypoint [20] benchmarks. CrowdPose consists of three splits of *Train, Val, Test* with 10K, 2K, 8K images, respectively. COCO Keypoint has larger scale and includes three splits of *Train, Val, Test-dev* with 64K, 5K, 20K images, respectively. The images in COCO Keypoint are usually collected from daily life where crowded scenes only account for a small portion. CrowdPose defines an index to represent the crowding level of input images and sets up the benchmark that covers various scenes.

Implementation Details. Our models are trained with Adam optimizer [13] for a total of 300 epochs on both COCO [20] and CrowdPose [18]. The base learning rate is initialized to 1.5e-3 at the beginning, then dropped to 1.5e-4 and 1.5e-5 at the 200th and 260th epochs, respectively. Following previous works [4,21,22], we apply data augmentation with random scale ($[0.75, 1.5]$), random rotation ($[-30°, 30°]$), random translation ($[-40, 40]$) and random horizontal flipping in a probability of 0.5. During test, the short side of input image is resized to 512 (or 640) and the flip test is also performed in all experiments, which is the same as previous works [4,21,22]. When we perform multi-scale test, we resize the original image with multiple scale factors which are set to $\{0.5, 1.0, 1.5\}$.

4.2   Comparison with SOTA

CrowdPose Test. We compare our Coupled Embedding (CE) with state-of-the-art HPE methods on CrowdPose Test whose results are shown in Table 2. Our method achieves the best performance among all methods for both single and multi-scale test. Top-down methods do not perform well in crowded scenes and get lower AP scores than bottom-up methods. Compared with the SOTA embedding-based method [21] (this method is based on HigherHRNet [4]), when the model is not pre-trained on COCO, our method achieves 1.8 points gain in AP and 1.6 points gain in AP^H (highly crowded scenes). After pre-training on COCO, the AP gain reduces to 0.5 but our method still achieves 1.2 points gain in AP^H. Compared with other bottom-up methods, the superiority of our

Table 2. Comparisons on CrowdPose Test. Superscripts E, M and H of AP stand for easy, medium and hard. Superscript * means multi-scale test. Subscript $_\dagger$ means model is pretained on COCO

Method	AP	AP^{50}	AP^{75}	AP^E	AP^M	AP^H
Top-down methods						
Mask-RCNN [10]	57.2	83.5	60.3	69.4	57.9	45.8
AlphaPose [5]	61.0	81.3	66.0	71.2	61.4	51.1
SimpleBaseline [30]	60.8	84.2	71.5	71.4	61.2	51.2
SPPE [18]	60.0	84.2	71.5	75.5	66.3	57.4
Bottom-up methods						
OpenPose [2]	–	–	–	62.7	48.7	32.3
HigherHRNet-W48 [4]	65.9	86.4	70.6	73.3	66.5	57.9
HigherHRNet-W48* [4]	67.6	87.4	72.6	75.8	68.1	58.9
DEKR-W32 [8]	65.7	85.7	70.4	73.0	66.4	57.5
DEKR-W48 [8]	67.3	86.4	72.2	74.6	68.1	58.7
DEKR-W48* [8]	68.0	85.5	73.4	76.6	68.8	58.4
SWAHR-W32 [21]	66.7	86.9	71.7	74.3	67.3	58.9
SWAHR-W48 [21]	68.0	88.1	72.9	75.2	68.5	60.5
SWAHR-W48* [21]	69.7	89.0	75.1	77.2	70.4	61.6
CE-W32(HRNet)	68.9	89.0	74.2	76.3	69.5	60.8
CE-W48(HRNet)	70.1	89.8	75.5	77.5	70.8	62.2
CE-W32(HigherHRNet)	69.6	89.7	74.9	76.9	70.3	61.6
CE-W48(HigherHRNet)	70.5	89.9	76.0	77.7	71.1	62.4
CE-W48*(HigherHRNet)	**71.6**	**90.1**	**77.3**	**79.0**	**72.2**	**63.3**
Bottom-up methods pre-trained on COCO						
SWAHR-W48$_\dagger$ [21]	71.6	88.5	77.6	78.9	72.4	63.0
SWAHR-W48$^*_\dagger$ [21]	73.8	90.5	79.9	81.2	74.7	64.7
CE-W48$_\dagger$(HigherHRNet)	72.9	89.5	78.8	79.6	73.7	64.5
CE-W48$^*_\dagger$(HigherHRNet)	**74.5**	**91.1**	**80.2**	**81.3**	**75.4**	**66.2**

method is more apparent. Overall, the strong results on CrowdPose Test especially for AP^H demonstrate that our method is excellent at handling images in crowded scenes.

COCO Test-dev. As shown in Table 3, we make comparisons with the state-of-the-art HPE methods on COCO Test-dev which is dominated by top-down methods. Compared with the performance on CrowdPose Test, our method has lower AP gain on COCO Test-dev since there are less images in complex scenes. However, our method still outperforms other bottom-up methods. And when we evaluate the model with multi-scale test, we can get the highest AP score at 72.8. This achieves a new state-of-the-art result. Compared with top-down methods, our best result has an advantage in AP score over early methods [3,10,25] and is comparable with recent top-down methods [3,30].

Table 3. Comparisons on COCO Test-dev. AE(HRNet-W32) means a implemention of associative embedding in [4], where the model replaces the backbone with HRNet. Superscripts M and L of AP stand for medium and large. Superscript * means multi-scale test

Method	AP	AP^{50}	AP^{75}	AP^{M}	AP^{L}
Top-down methods					
Mask-RCNN [10]	63.1	87.3	68.7	57.8	71.4
G-RMI [25]	64.9	85.5	71.3	62.3	70.0
CPN [3]	72.1	91.4	80.0	68.7	77.2
SimpleBaseline [30]	73.7	91.9	81.1	70.3	80.0
HRNet-W48 [28]	75.5	92.5	83.3	71.9	81.5
Bottom-up methods					
OpenPose [2]	61.8	84.9	67.5	57.1	68.2
AE(HRNet-W32) [4]	64.1	86.3	70.4	57.4	73.9
PersonLab [24]	66.5	88.0	72.6	62.4	72.3
PersonLab* [24]	68.7	89.0	75.4	64.1	75.5
PifPaf [14]	66.7	–	–	62.4	72.9
SPM [23]	66.9	88.5	72.9	62.6	73.1
HigherHRNet-W32 [4]	66.4	87.5	72.8	61.2	74.2
HigherHRNet-W48 [4]	68.4	88.2	75.1	64.4	74.2
HigherHRNet-W48* [4]	70.5	89.3	77.2	66.6	75.8
DEKR-W32 [8]	67.3	87.9	74.1	61.5	76.1
DEKR-W48 [8]	70.0	89.4	77.3	65.7	76.9
DEKR-W48* [8]	71.0	89.2	78.0	67.1	76.9
SWAHR-W32 [21]	67.9	88.9	74.5	62.4	75.5
SWAHR-W48 [21]	70.2	89.9	76.9	65.2	77.0
SWAHR-W48* [21]	72.0	90.7	78.8	67.8	77.7
CE-W32(HRNet)	67.0	88.9	73.7	60.4	76.4
CE-W48(HRNet)	68.4	88.7	75.5	63.8	75.9
CE-W32(HigherHRNet)	68.8	90.3	75.2	62.9	77.1
CE-W48(HigherHRNet)	71.1	90.8	77.8	66.4	78.0
CE-W48*(HigherHRNet)	**72.8**	**91.2**	**79.9**	**68.3**	**79.3**

4.3   Group Margin

In order to measure the keypoint grouping competence of embedding-based methods without AP, we introduce an index named group margin which is defined as the minimum embedding distance minus grouping threshold. Then we evaluate images on CrowdPose Test [18] and collect group margins of each image for above two methods. At last, we calculate the mean group margin of test images.

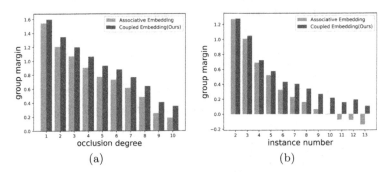

Fig. 5. (a) shows the group margins in 10 different occlusion degrees. (b) shows the group margins corresponding to number of instances from 2 to 13. In (b), the negative group margin indicates the embedding distance is lower than grouping threshold.

Comparing the group margin in Fig. 5(b), we observe that AE [22] is sensitive to number variation of instances in an image. When the number of instances is higher than ten, the embedding distance is lower than grouping threshold. Compared with AE [22], our method achieves larger group margin in each occlusion degree and number of instances. It indicates our model has more powerful grouping capacity in crowded scenes. In Fig. 5(a), we observe that our advantages in different occlusion degrees are relatively stable. In Fig. 5(b), our advantage is overwhelming when number of instances is large. Large number of instances in image means large number of clustering centers in embedding space. This experiment result illustrates that if the number of clustering centers is large, some embeddings could be assigned to the wrong group, where the embeddings of different instances are likely to be linearly inseparable.

4.4   Comparison of Keypoint Grouping

Our method has obvious advantages in keypoint grouping, but it only indicates in some complex scenes such as high occlusion degree or large number of instances. However, many test samples are in simple scenes in our test sets. Hence, to explore the superiority of our method in keypoint grouping, we sample 4 subsets from the CrowdPose Test according to different occlusion degrees and instance numbers. To eliminate the influence of keypoint detection, all methods in the experiments apply naive heatmap regression.

All the results are shown in Table 4. Subset1 has small number of instances but high occlusion degree. In this scene, embedding-based methods indicate obvious advantage and our method has larger superiority. Subset2 has small number

Table 4. Comparisons on 4 different subsets. We apply 3 methods in this experiment. DEKR belongs to dense regression methods and AE [22] is the vanilla embedding-based method. The backbone and the input resolution are the same in all the methods.

		Subset1	Subset2	Subset3	Subset4
Number of instances		$2 \sim 5$	$2 \sim 5$	> 6	> 6
Occlusion degree		Top 20%	Last 20%	Top 20%	Last 20%
AP	DEKR	61.8	78.7	50.3	**62.5**
	AE	64.4	**78.8**	49.8	60.3
	Ours(AE + scale loss)	**65.9**	78.7	**52.0**	62.2

of instances and low occlusion degree, which is a common simple scene. In this scene, all the methods achieve similar AP scores. Subset3 has high occlusion degree and large number of instances which is a pretty complex scene. In this scene, our method performs much better than other methods. Subset4 has low occlusion degree but large number of instances. In this scene, vanilla embedding-based method has noticeable performance degradation but our method alleviates this negative influence. The above results show the superiority of our method in keypoint grouping when the occlusion degree is high or number of instances is large.

4.5   Ablation Study

Table 5. Ablation study of different strategies. We apply AE [22] with the backbone of HRNet-W32 as our baseline.

Baseline	√	√	√	√	√
Embedding regularization		√	√	√	√
Adjusted heatmap				√	√
Weighted L2-loss			√		√
AP	64.8	66.0	67.6	67.6	**68.9**
AP^{hard}	57.5	58.2	59.6	59.8	**60.8**

We perform a series of ablation experiments on CrowdPose Test to study the effects of our strategies. As we can see in Table 5, all of our designs lead to obvious increases in AP. Eventually, our method gets around +4 AP gain over the baseline. Compared to the baseline, the embedding regularization achieve a gain of +1.2 AP. The adjusting for ground truth heatmaps and weighted L2-loss brings both bring apparent improvement. As keypoint grouping is based on the results of keypoint detection, we utilize these two strategies to improve heatmap regression for a fair comparison with current SOTA embedding-based methods. Besides mean AP, all of our strategies bring improvements on AP^{hard}.

4.6   Hyper-parameter Study

Table 6. Study of M and θ. The results are reported on CrowdPose Test and COCO Val with single-scale test. Detection heatmap in each model is trained by standard L2-loss.

(a) $\theta = 0.55$

M	4	8	12	16
AP	67.1	**67.6**	67.6	67.3

(b) $M = 8$

	CrowdPose Test					COCO Val				
θ	0.45	0.50	0.55	0.60	0.65	0.30	0.35	0.40	0.45	0.50
AP	66.8	67.5	**67.6**	67.2	66.9	65.1	66.1	**66.4**	66.0	61.8

For Coupled Embedding, we study two significant hyper-parameters in Eq. 5 including M and θ which denote the dimensionality of embeddings and the coefficient of scale factors, respectively. As shown in Table 6(a), we can get the best result when M is set to 8 or 12. Considering both efficiency and accuracy, we finally set M to 8. The θ is a coefficient that controls the scaling amplitudes of scale factors. To explore an appropriate θ, we perform experiments with different values of θ on CrowdPose and COCO. Considering results in Table 6(b), we set θ to 0.55 and 0.4 when we experiment on CrowdPose and COCO, respectively.

5   Conclusions

In this paper, we probe the limitation of keypoint grouping in Associative Embedding [22] and find that different dimensions of embeddings in an image are highly linearly correlated. To address this issue, we propose a novel keypoint grouping method named Coupled Embedding for bottom-up human pose estimation. Our method imposes an additional constraint on embeddings to learn sparse multidimensional embeddings. Our method creates new state-of-the-art results on CrowdPose Test (74.5 AP) and COCO Test-dev (72.8 AP), outperforming all existing bottom-up methods. We conduct a series of experiments and the results show that our model has significant advantages in complex scenes.

Acknowledgment. This work was supported by Key-Area Research and Development Program of Guangdong Province (No. 2019B010153001). This work is being sponsored by Zhejiang Lab (No. 2021KH0AB07). This work was also supported by National Natural Science Foundation of China under Grants 62006230, 62076235.

References

1. Andriluka, M., Pishchulin, L., Gehler, P., Schiele, B.: 2D human pose estimation: new benchmark and state of the art analysis. In: CVPR 2014 Proceedings of the 2014 IEEE Conference on Computer Vision and Pattern Recognition, pp. 3686–3693 (2014)
2. Cao, Z., Hidalgo, G., Simon, T., Wei, S.E., Sheikh, Y.: Openpose: real-time multi-person 2d pose estimation using part affinity fields. arXiv preprint arXiv:1812.08008 (2018)
3. Chen, Y., Wang, Z., Peng, Y., Zhang, Z., Yu, G., Sun, J.: Cascaded pyramid network for multi-person pose estimation. In: 2018 IEEE/CVF Conference on Computer Vision and Pattern Recognition, pp. 7103–7112 (2018)
4. Cheng, B., Xiao, B., Wang, J., Shi, H., Huang, T.S., Zhang, L.: HigherHRNet: scale-aware representation learning for bottom-up human pose estimation. In: 2020 IEEE/CVF Conference on Computer Vision and Pattern Recognition (CVPR), pp. 5386–5395 (2020)
5. Fang, H.S., Xie, S., Tai, Y.W., Lu, C.: RMPE: regional multi-person pose estimation. In: 2017 IEEE International Conference on Computer Vision (ICCV), pp. 2353–2362 (2017)
6. Frome, A., et al.: Devise: a deep visual-semantic embedding model. In: Advances in Neural Information Processing Systems 26, vol. 26, pp. 2121–2129 (2013)
7. Frome, A., Singer, Y., Sha, F., Malik, J.: Learning globally-consistent local distance functions for shape-based image retrieval and classification. In: 2007 IEEE 11th International Conference on Computer Vision, pp. 1–8 (2007)
8. Geng, Z., Sun, K., Xiao, B., Zhang, Z., Wang, J.: Bottom-up human pose estimation via disentangled keypoint regression. arXiv preprint arXiv:2104.02300 (2021)
9. Gong, Y., Wang, L., Hodosh, M., Hockenmaier, J., Lazebnik, S.: Improving image-sentence embeddings using large weakly annotated photo collections. In: Fleet, D., Pajdla, T., Schiele, B., Tuytelaars, T. (eds.) ECCV 2014. LNCS, vol. 8692, pp. 529–545. Springer, Cham (2014). https://doi.org/10.1007/978-3-319-10593-2_35
10. He, K., Gkioxari, G., Dollar, P., Girshick, R.: Mask R-CNN. IEEE Trans. Pattern Anal. Mach. Intell. **42**(2), 386–397 (2020)
11. Huang, P., Huang, Y., Wang, W., Wang, L.: Deep embedding network for clustering. In: ICPR 2014 Proceedings of the 2014 22nd International Conference on Pattern Recognition, pp. 1532–1537 (2014)
12. Iqbal, U., Gall, J.: Multi-person pose estimation with local joint-to-person associations. In: Hua, G., Jégou, H. (eds.) ECCV 2016. LNCS, vol. 9914, pp. 627–642. Springer, Cham (2016). https://doi.org/10.1007/978-3-319-48881-3_44
13. Kingma, D.P., Ba, J.L.: Adam: a method for stochastic optimization. In: ICLR 2015: International Conference on Learning Representations 2015 (2015)
14. Kreiss, S., Bertoni, L., Alahi, A.: PifPaf: composite fields for human pose estimation. In: 2019 IEEE/CVF Conference on Computer Vision and Pattern Recognition (CVPR), pp. 11969–11978 (2019)
15. Kuhn, H.W.: The hungarian method for the assignment problem. Naval Res. Logist. Quart. **2**(1), 83–97 (1955)
16. Law, H., Deng, J.: CornerNet: detecting objects as paired keypoints. International Journal of Computer Vision **128**(3), 642–656 (2019). https://doi.org/10.1007/s11263-019-01204-1
17. Li, J., Su, W., Wang, Z.: Simple pose: rethinking and improving a bottom-up approach for multi-person pose estimation. In: Proceedings of the AAAI conference on artificial intelligence, vol. 34, pp. 11354–11361 (2020)

18. Li, J., Wang, C., Zhu, H., Mao, Y., Fang, H.S., Lu, C.: CrowdPose: efficient crowded scenes pose estimation and a new benchmark. In: 2019 IEEE/CVF Conference on Computer Vision and Pattern Recognition (CVPR), pp. 10863–10872 (2019)

19. Lin, T.Y., Goyal, P., Girshick, R., He, K., Dollar, P.: Focal loss for dense object detection. IEEE Trans. Pattern Anal. Mach. Intell. **42**(2), 318–327 (2020)

20. Lin, T.-Y., et al.: Microsoft COCO: common objects in context. In: Fleet, D., Pajdla, T., Schiele, B., Tuytelaars, T. (eds.) ECCV 2014. LNCS, vol. 8693, pp. 740–755. Springer, Cham (2014). https://doi.org/10.1007/978-3-319-10602-1_48

21. Luo, Z., Wang, Z., Huang, Y., Tan, T., Zhou, E.: Rethinking the heatmap regression for bottom-up human pose estimation. arXiv preprint arXiv:2012.15175 (2020)

22. Newell, A., Huang, Z., Deng, J.: Associative embedding: end-to-end learning for joint detection and grouping. In: 31st Annual Conference on Neural Information Processing Systems, NIPS 2017, vol. 30, pp. 2278–2288 (2017)

23. Nie, X., Feng, J., Zhang, J., Yan, S.: Single-stage multi-person pose machines. In: 2019 IEEE/CVF International Conference on Computer Vision (ICCV), pp. 6951–6960 (2019)

24. Papandreou, G., Zhu, T., Chen, L.-C., Gidaris, S., Tompson, J., Murphy, K.: PersonLab: person pose estimation and instance segmentation with a bottom-up, part-based, geometric embedding model. In: Ferrari, V., Hebert, M., Sminchisescu, C., Weiss, Y. (eds.) Computer Vision – ECCV 2018. LNCS, vol. 11218, pp. 282–299. Springer, Cham (2018). https://doi.org/10.1007/978-3-030-01264-9_17

25. Papandreou, G., et al.: Towards accurate multi-person pose estimation in the wild. In: 2017 IEEE Conference on Computer Vision and Pattern Recognition (CVPR), pp. 3711–3719 (2017)

26. Pishchulin, L., et al.: DeepCut: joint subset partition and labeling for multi person pose estimation. In: 2016 IEEE Conference on Computer Vision and Pattern Recognition (CVPR), pp. 4929–4937 (2016)

27. Sun, K., et al.: Bottom-up human pose estimation by ranking heatmap-guided adaptive keypoint estimates. arXiv preprint arXiv:2006.15480 (2020)

28. Sun, K., Xiao, B., Liu, D., Wang, J.: Deep high-resolution representation learning for human pose estimation. In: 2019 IEEE/CVF Conference on Computer Vision and Pattern Recognition (CVPR), pp. 5693–5703 (2019)

29. Weinberger, K.Q., Saul, L.K.: Distance metric learning for large margin nearest neighbor classification. J. Mach. Learn. Res. **10**(9), 207–244 (2009)

30. Xiao, B., Wu, H., Wei, Y.: Simple baselines for human pose estimation and tracking. In: Ferrari, V., Hebert, M., Sminchisescu, C., Weiss, Y. (eds.) ECCV 2018. LNCS, vol. 11210, pp. 472–487. Springer, Cham (2018). https://doi.org/10.1007/978-3-030-01231-1_29

31. Yang, B., Fu, X., Sidiropoulos, N.D., Hong, M.: Towards k-means-friendly spaces: simultaneous deep learning and clustering. In: ICML2017 Proceedings of the 34th International Conference on Machine Learning - vol. 70. pp. 3861–3870 (2017)

32. Zhou, X., Wang, D., Krähenbühl, P.: Objects as points. arXiv preprint arXiv:1904.07850 (2019)

A Visual Navigation Perspective for Category-Level Object Pose Estimation

Jiaxin Guo[1,2], Fangxun Zhong[2], Rong Xiong[1], Yunhui Liu[2], Yue Wang[1(✉)], and Yiyi Liao[1(✉)]

[1] Zhejiang University, Hangzhou, China
{rxiong,ywang24,yiyi.liao}@zju.edu.cn
[2] The Chinese University of Hong Kong, Hong Kong, China
{jxguo,fxzhong,yhliu}@mae.cuhk.edu.hk

Abstract. This paper studies category-level object pose estimation based on a single monocular image. Recent advances in pose-aware generative models have paved the way for addressing this challenging task using analysis-by-synthesis. The idea is to sequentially update a set of latent variables, e.g., pose, shape, and appearance, of the generative model until the generated image best agrees with the observation. However, convergence and efficiency are two challenges of this inference procedure. In this paper, we take a deeper look at the inference of analysis-by-synthesis from the perspective of visual navigation, and investigate what is a good navigation policy for this specific task. We evaluate three different strategies, including gradient descent, reinforcement learning and imitation learning, via thorough comparisons in terms of convergence, robustness and efficiency. Moreover, we show that a simple hybrid approach leads to an effective and efficient solution. We further compare these strategies to state-of-the-art methods, and demonstrate superior performance on synthetic and real-world datasets leveraging off-the-shelf pose-aware generative models.

Keywords: Category-level object pose estimation · Analysis-by-synthesis

1 Introduction

Object pose estimation is a fundamental research problem that aims to estimate the 6 DoF pose of an object from a given observation. To enable broad applications in augmented reality and robotics, it is essential that the object pose estimation methods allow for generalizing to unseen objects and being applicable to widely used sensors, e.g., monocular cameras. Thus, there is a growing

---

Supplementary Information The online version contains supplementary material available at https://doi.org/10.1007/978-3-031-20068-7_8.

© The Author(s), under exclusive license to Springer Nature Switzerland AG 2022
S. Avidan et al. (Eds.): ECCV 2022, LNCS 13666, pp. 123–141, 2022.
https://doi.org/10.1007/978-3-031-20068-7_8

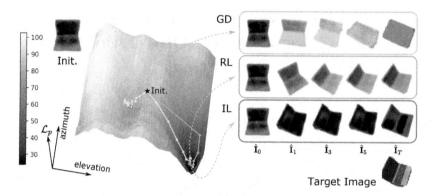

Fig. 1. Inference of Analysis-by-Synthesis. We illustrate the perceptual loss between the synthesized image and the target image, calculated over a grid of azimuth and elevation. We further show the navigation trajectory of gradient descent (GD), reinforcement learning (RL) and imitation learning (IL) given the same initialization, including the synthesized images generated at multiple steps. Note that GD converges to a local minimum due to the non-convex loss landscape. RL and IL converge in the correct direction while IL converges faster.

interest in the challenging task of category-level object pose estimation based on a single monocular image [8].

As a classic idea in computer vision, analysis-by-synthesis has recently shown competitive performance in object pose estimation [8,25,46,54]. This line of approaches leverages a forward synthesis model that can be controlled by a low-dimensional input, e.g., object pose, and infers the pose via render-and-compare. Given an observation image, multiple images can be synthesized under different object poses, and the one that best matches the observation is selected. While earlier methods only apply to instances of known CAD models taking a graphics renderer as the forward model [25,46], recent works extend this idea to category-level object pose estimation leveraging pose-aware generative models and demonstrate superior performance compared to direct pose regression [8,54].

In this paper, we advocate analysis-by-synthesis but identify a major limitation of existing approaches: it is non-trivial to efficiently retrieve the pose that best reproduces the target observation. Figure 1 illustrates that existing methods based on gradient descent (GD) are sensitive to initialization and are prone to convergence problems. This is due to the fact that the objective function, i.e., the difference between the synthesized image and the observation, is highly non-convex. Leveraging multiple initial poses is a common remedy for this problem [8,38]. However, this is time-consuming and computationally expensive.

Intending to analyze and improve the *inference* process of analysis-by-synthesis, we view the inference as a visual navigation task, where an agent uses visual input to take a sequence of actions to reach its own goal [58]. This perspective allows us to take inspirations from the visual navigation literature and compare different navigation policies. This formulation leads to our main question: *what is a good navigation policy for category-level object pose estimation?*

To answer this question, we systematically compare different navigation policies. Taking the pose-aware generative model as a *simulator*, we explore common strategies in visual navigation, including reinforcement learning (RL) [33,41,58] and imitation learning (IL) [24,43]. We also study the behavior of GD as a one-step greedy strategy within the same framework. Specifically, we first investigate how design choices, i.e., planning horizon and loss function, affect the behavior of navigation policies. Next, we compare all strategies wrt. convergence, robustness, and efficiency and make the following observations: 1) Both RL and IL remarkably alleviate convergence problems compared to GD as shown in Fig. 1. Despite easily getting stuck in local minima, GD yields a more precise prediction given a good initialization; 2) GD tends to be more robust against disturbance of brightness and shift on the target image; 3) Both RL and IL are more efficient than GD during inference. Compared to RL, IL requires less training time but is less competitive when trained with off-policy data. However, IL achieves similar or even better performance than RL when augmented with on-policy data. Based on these observations, we suggest to combine IL's convergence and efficiency with GD's precision and robustness. We demonstrate that this simple hybrid approach achieves superior performance on category-level pose estimation.

We summarize our contributions as follows: i) We propose to view the inference process of analysis-by-synthesis as a visual navigation task, leveraging the pose-aware generative model as a simulator to provide training data without manual labeling. ii) We conduct thorough comparisons between GD, RL, and IL in terms of convergence, robustness and efficiency. Based on our observations we suggest a simple combination of IL and GD that is effective and efficient. iii) We compare different strategies to state-of-the-art methods on category-level object pose estimation on synthetic and real-world datasets. Our hybrid approach shows competitive performance and consistently improves the inference process of different pose-aware generative models. Our code is released at https://github.com/wrld/visual_navigation_pose_estimation.git.

2   Related Work

Object Pose Estimation. Extensive studies have been conducted for object pose estimation of known *instances* [10,12,19,22,26–28,35,39,40,53]. Only recently, there has been a growing interest in a more general task of *category-level* 6 DoF object pose estimation for unseen instances in a specific category [6,7,44,49–51]. These methods achieve promising results via establishing correspondences across different objects [49–51] or direct regression [6]. In this paper, we are interested in category-level object pose estimation leveraging a pose-aware generative model, eliminating the need for intermediate correspondences compared to [49–51]. In contrast to direct regression methods [6], we model the problem as a long-horizon navigation task to approach the goal sequentially via a set of relative updates. Moreover, all aforementioned methods for category-level object pose estimation are applied to RGB-D images while we focus on a single RGB image-based solution.

Analysis-by-Synthesis for Object Pose Estimation. It is a classical idea to analyze a signal by reproducing it using a synthesis model, which is referred to as analysis-by-synthesis [55]. It has been successfully applied to many tasks, including human pose estimation [31], object recognition [16], and scene understanding [20,34]. A few methods leverage this idea for instance-level object pose estimation [25,46], but are not applicable to unseen instances.

With the rapid progress of pose-aware generative models that allow for generating 2D images under controllable object poses [5,18,29,36,37,45], analysis-by-synthesis approaches are extended to category-level object pose estimation recently [8,38,54]. Among them, a few works demonstrate promising results using a single RGB image [8,54]. As the generative models are differentiable, all these approaches leverage gradient descent to infer the object pose. Due to the non-convex objective function, gradient-based optimization suffers from convergence problems. While iNeRF [54] constrains the initialization range during inference, LatentFusion [38] and Chen et al. [8] start from multiple pose candidates and keep the one that best aligns with the observation. However, it is computationally expensive, and the computing time increases wrt. the number of initial poses. Another idea is to leverage an encoder to provide a better initialization [8,13]. Note that the common underlying idea of these methods is to improve the initialization. In contrast, we focus on analyzing and improving the policy for updating the pose.

Visual Navigation. By sufficiently interacting with the simulation environment, RL has demonstrated superior performance in long-horizon decision tasks in visual navigation [33,41,58]. IL is also commonly adopted when expert demonstrations are available [4,24,43]. In contrast to all aforementioned methods, we propose to adopt a pose-aware generative model as a simulator, where the agent navigates in the input space of a pose-aware generative model for category-level pose estimation. Exploiting RL/IL to learn the gradient is similar to meta gradient descent methods [2]. Compared to existing meta-GD methods, we utilize the simulator to provide explicit supervision towards the global optimum.

Inversion of Generative Models. The idea of analysis-by-synthesis is also closely related to inversion of generative models [1,47,57], see [52] for a detailed survey. While all these works focus on enabling the editing of a real image by searching its corresponding latent code, we leverage pose-aware generative models to estimate category-level object poses. In our task, the inverting process is more sensitive to initialization and prone to convergence problems.

3   Object Pose Estimation as Visual Navigation

Our goal is to improve the inference procedure of the analysis-by-synthesis pipeline for category-level object pose estimation. In the following, we first formulate the problem as a visual navigation task in Sect. 3.1. Next, we present several navigation policies, including gradient descent (Sect. 3.2), reinforcement learning (Sect. 3.3) and imitation learning (Sect. 3.4).

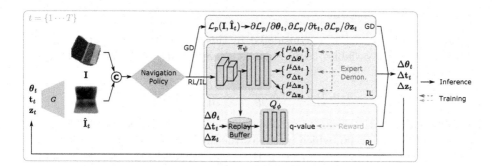

Fig. 2. Category-Level Object Pose Estimation as Visual Navigation. We illustrate the visual navigation pipeline, where an agent uses visual input (the synthesized image $\hat{\mathbf{I}}$) to reach a target state $\boldsymbol{\theta}^*, \mathbf{t}^*, \mathbf{z}^*$ via iteratively taking T steps of actions. At a time step t, the navigation policy takes as input the synthesized image $\hat{\mathbf{I}}_t = G(\boldsymbol{\theta}_t, \mathbf{t}_t, \mathbf{z}_t)$ and the target image $\mathbf{I}$, to update the state $\boldsymbol{\theta}_t, \mathbf{t}_t, \mathbf{z}_t$ via $\Delta \mathbf{R}_t, \Delta \mathbf{t}_t, \Delta \mathbf{z}_t$. We evaluate and compare three different strategies as the navigation policy, including gradient descent (GD), reinforcement learning (RL) and imitation learning (IL). Note that G is fixed and the GD policy does not contain any trainable parameters. Both RL and IL learn the policy via a network parameterized by ψ, while supervised by different signals.

3.1   Problem Formulation

We aim for 6 DoF category-level object pose estimation from a single image via analysis-by-synthesis. The idea is to sequentially update a set of input variables, e.g., object pose, shape and appearance, of a forward synthesis model, until the generated image best matches the target. The corresponding pose is then selected as the prediction. We view this sequential procedure as a long-horizon visual navigation task as illustrated in Fig. 2. Formally, we model this problem as a Markov decision process (MDP). Let $\mathbf{I}$ denote the target image, and $\hat{\mathbf{I}} = G(\boldsymbol{\theta}, \mathbf{t}, \mathbf{z})$ denote a synthesized image generated by a pose-aware generative model G. Here, G takes as input the object's rotation $\mathbf{R}_\theta \in SO(3)$, which is parametrized using Euler angles $\boldsymbol{\theta} = [\boldsymbol{\theta}_x, \boldsymbol{\theta}_y, \boldsymbol{\theta}_z]$, translation $\mathbf{t} \in \mathbb{R}^3$, and a latent code $\mathbf{z}$ for its shape and appearance. Note that G is fixed during the navigation process. The state at a step $t \in [0, T]$ is $\boldsymbol{\theta}_t, \mathbf{t}_t, \mathbf{z}_t$ with a linear state transition:

$$\boldsymbol{\theta}_{t+1} = \boldsymbol{\theta}_t + \Delta \boldsymbol{\theta}_t, \ \mathbf{t}_{t+1} = \mathbf{t}_t + \Delta \mathbf{t}_t, \ \mathbf{z}_{t+1} = \mathbf{z}_t + \Delta \mathbf{z}_t \tag{1}$$

We further consider the forward synthesis model as the observation function, and the observation $\mathbf{o}_t$ at a step t is the synthesized image $\hat{\mathbf{I}}_t$ combined with the target $\mathbf{I}$. Given an initial state $\boldsymbol{\theta}_0, \mathbf{t}_0, \mathbf{z}_0$, the agent iteratively takes T steps of actions towards reaching the goal state $\boldsymbol{\theta}^*, \mathbf{t}^*, \mathbf{z}^*$ that can best reproduce $\mathbf{I}$. At each step, an action $\mathbf{a}_t := \Delta\boldsymbol{\theta}_t, \Delta\mathbf{t}_t, \Delta\mathbf{z}_t$ is taken following the policy $\pi(\mathbf{a}_t|\mathbf{o}_t)$. This formulation leads to a key question: what is a good navigation policy $\pi(\mathbf{a}_t|\mathbf{o}_t)$? We now briefly discuss three different strategies in this unified pipeline.

3.2   Gradient Descent

When G is differentiable as considered in this paper, it is straightforward to update the input variables using gradient descent (GD) [8,38,54], yielding the following policy:

$$\pi(\mathbf{a}_t|\mathbf{o}_t) = -\lambda\frac{\partial\mathcal{L}_p}{\partial\boldsymbol{\theta}_t}, -\lambda\frac{\partial\mathcal{L}_p}{\partial\mathbf{t}_t}, -\lambda\frac{\partial\mathcal{L}_p}{\partial\mathbf{z}_t} \tag{2}$$

where λ controls the speed of gradient descent. $\mathcal{L}_p$ is the perceptual loss [21] following Chen et al. [8], which measures the discrepancy between the observed image $\mathbf{I}$ and the synthesized image $\hat{\mathbf{I}}$. Here, the policy $\pi(\mathbf{a}_t|\mathbf{o}_t)$ does not contain any trainable parameters, thus can be directly applied without training. On the other hand, the agent may easily get stuck in a local minimum due to the non-convex loss landscape as shown in Fig. 1. Thus, the final performance highly depends on the initial state $\boldsymbol{\theta}_0, \mathbf{t}_0, \mathbf{z}_0$. The main reason is that the agent cannot look into the future to plan for a long-term reward.

3.3   Reinforcement Learning

In contrast to GD, RL allows the agent to explore the environment to maximize an accumulated reward over multiple steps. The RL policy is inspired by [46], where RL is adopted for instance-level pose estimation. While this requires a known CAD model, we apply RL for category-level object pose estimation and recover both the object and its pose simultaneously.

Specifically, we apply Soft Actor-Critic to train the RL agent [15]. As illustrated in Fig. 2, it consists of a policy network $\pi_\psi(\mathbf{a}_t|\mathbf{o}_t)$ to produce a stochastic policy and a Q-value function $Q_\phi(\mathbf{o}_t, \mathbf{a}_t)$ to inform how good the policy is, with ψ and ϕ denoting the parameters of the networks, respectively. The policy network is trained to maximize the expected sum of future discounted rewards $\mathbb{E}[\sum_{t=0}^{T}\gamma^t r_t]$ approximated by $Q_\phi(\mathbf{o}_t, \mathbf{a}_t)$, where T is the number of steps, γ is a discount factor and r_t is a reward at each step:

$$r_t = -\lambda_1\|\mathbf{q}(\boldsymbol{\theta}^* - \boldsymbol{\theta}_t) - \mathbf{q}(\Delta\boldsymbol{\theta}_t)\|_2^2 - \lambda_2\|(\mathbf{t}^* - \mathbf{t}_t) - \Delta\mathbf{t}_t\|_2^2$$
$$- \lambda_3\|(\mathbf{z}^* - \mathbf{z}_t) - \Delta\mathbf{z}_t\|_2^2 \tag{3}$$

where $\mathbf{q}(\boldsymbol{\theta})$ denotes the quaternion of Euler angles $\boldsymbol{\theta}$, and the weight parameters $\lambda_1 = 10.0, \lambda_2 = 5.0, \lambda_3 = 1.0$ are set to balance the contributions of each term. Here, we assume the target state $\boldsymbol{\theta}^*, \mathbf{t}^*, \mathbf{z}^*$ is available when training the policy network. For example, it can be obtained by randomly sampling a target image from the simulator as $\mathbf{I} = G(\boldsymbol{\theta}^*, \mathbf{t}^*, \mathbf{z}^*)$.

There are two major differences comparing RL to GD. Firstly, the reward in (3) provides cues for global convergence through direct comparison to the best possible action, while the perception loss in (2) does not necessarily lead to an update towards reaching the global optimum. Secondly, the RL policy aims to maximize the predicted accumulated reward in future steps, while the GD policy greedily minimizes a one-step loss. Therefore, the RL policy is expected to be less prone to local minima.

Training Efficiency. The training of the Soft Actor-Critic is based on an experience replay buffer that stores a set of state-action reward pairs. During early training, unconverged policies can lead an agent to random locations, filling the experience replay buffer with low-reward samples and causing inefficient learning. We improve the training efficiency of RL in two ways. Following the relabeling strategy [3], we first relabel the final synthesized image of a failure trial as the target image, turning it into a successful trial. We further manually sample successful trials. Adding both, the relabeled and the manually sampled trajectories, to the experience replay buffer allows for speeding up the training. We refer to the supplementary for ablation study of the training efficiency.

3.4 Imitation Learning

As expert demonstrations are easily accessible from the simulator, an alternative is to directly learn a policy network via imitation learning.

Behavior Cloning. Taking the same network structure in RL, we directly train a policy network $\pi_\psi(\mathbf{a}_t|\mathbf{o}_t)$ via Behavior Cloning (BC) [4], see Fig. 2. In this supervised setting, the policy network is trained with one-step supervision, forcing it to reach the goal in one update. The loss can be formulated as follow:

$$
\begin{aligned}
\mathcal{L}_{IL} = {} & \lambda_1 \|\mathbf{q}(\boldsymbol{\theta}^* - \boldsymbol{\theta}_t) - \mathbf{q}(\Delta\boldsymbol{\theta}_t)\|_2^2 + \lambda_2 \|(\mathbf{t}^* - \mathbf{t}_t) - \Delta\mathbf{t}_t\|_2^2 \\
& + \lambda_3 \|(\mathbf{z}^* - \mathbf{z}) - \Delta\mathbf{z}\|_2^2
\end{aligned}
\tag{4}
$$

where the weight parameters $\lambda_1 = 10.0, \lambda_2 = 5.0, \lambda_3 = 1.0$ are the same as (3). Again, we assume the target state $\boldsymbol{\theta}^*, \mathbf{t}^*, \mathbf{z}^*$ is available during training. Although the agent is supervised by the one-step update, it can be applied iteratively to reach the goal during inference.

DAgger. One disadvantage of BC compared to RL is that the i.i.d. assumption of BC is violated when applied iteratively during inference, as the synthesized image at step $t + 1$ depends on previous predictions at step t. Therefore, BC suffers from drift when supervised by off-policy data only. This can be avoided by Dataset Aggregation (DAgger) [42], which extends the training dataset on-the-fly by collecting data under the current policy. Specifically, given a predicted action $\Delta\boldsymbol{\theta}, \Delta\mathbf{t}, \Delta\mathbf{z}$, the synthesized image $G(\boldsymbol{\theta} + \Delta\boldsymbol{\theta}, \mathbf{t} + \Delta\mathbf{t}, \mathbf{z} + \Delta\mathbf{z})$ and its corresponding action label are aggregated to the training set. While differing in the training set, the same loss as BC (4) is adopted. Note that DAgger usually requires an expert to annotate such on-policy data. However, in our case, the pose-aware generative model can provide labeled on-policy data for free.

4   Implementation Details

4.1   Pose-Aware Generative Model

In principle, our navigation framework is compatible with any pose-aware generative model, and we provide two examples in this paper. For both, we use trained networks by the authors and fix them throughout our work.

Voxel-based Generative Model. Chen et al. [8] propose a pose-aware generative model using a voxel-based structure. This model is trained in a supervised manner, taking images of single objects and corresponding poses as supervision. Once trained, it could generate images by controlling the camera/object pose and a latent code $\mathbf{z}$.

GRAF. Generative Radiance Fields (GRAF) [45] is a generative model for radiance fields [32] for high-resolution 3D-aware image synthesis. In contrast to the voxel-based generative model, it learns from *unposed* 2D images using the adversarial loss [14]. GRAF can generate images conditioned on the camera/object pose and two latent codes for object shape and appearance, respectively. We consider these two latent codes jointly as our $\mathbf{z}$. Note that adopting unsupervised generative models such as GRAF means that the pose estimation can be achieved without collecting posed images. Neither the generative model nor the navigation agent requires real-world posed images for training.

4.2   Navigation Policy

Architecture. Following Chen et al. [8], we define the rotation Euler angles $\boldsymbol{\theta}$ by azimuth, elevation and in-plane rotation. The translation $\mathbf{t}$ is represented by horizontal and vertical shifts in the image plane, and the scale factor along the z-axis which aligns with the principle axis of the camera. Following the official implementations, we set the dimension of $\mathbf{z}$ to 16 for the voxel-based generator [8] and 256 for GRAF [45]. More details about the network architecture of our RL and IL policies can be found in the supplementary.

Inference. For GD, we set the number of update steps $T = 50$ and leverage the Adam optimizer [23] using the same learning rate with Chen et al. [8]. For RL and IL, we observe that they converge faster and thus use update steps $T = 10$. We initialize $\boldsymbol{\theta}_0, \mathbf{t}_0$ as the mean pose of all objects within one category. For the latent code, we set $\mathbf{z}_0 = \mathbf{0}$ for all strategies when using the voxel-based generative model, meaning that the agent starts from the mean appearance. We experimentally observe that $\mathbf{z}$ is harder to estimate for GRAF due to its higher dimension. Thereby we initialize $\mathbf{z}$ using an encoder similar to Chen et al. [8]. Note that GRAF relies on volumetric rendering and is memory intensive when calculating gradients on high-resolution images. Inspired by the patch-discriminator used in GRAF, we use image patches as inputs to the GD policy. RL and IL policies are applied to the full image as both do not back-propagate through the GRAF generator and thus are more memory efficient.

5 Experiments

In this section, we first analyze how design choices affect the performance of the navigation strategies in Sect. 5.1. Next, we systematically compare all three strategies in terms of convergence, robustness and efficiency in Sect. 5.2. Finally, we compare these strategies to state-of-the-art approaches for category-level pose estimation in Sect. 5.3 on both synthetic and real-world datasets.

Dataset. We first evaluate on *REAL275* [50], a standard dataset for benchmarking category-level object pose estimation. We follow the official split of [50] to evaluate on 2760 real-world images, including 6 categories (camera, can, bottle, bowl, laptop and mug). Here, we use the voxel-based generative model provided by Chen et al. [8] as our simulator. Note that this voxel-based generator is trained on synthetic images only. To investigate the performance gap between synthetic and real, we also test on synthetic images in one category (laptop) used for training the generator.

Additionally, we evaluate on *Cars* [11] and *Faces* [30] used in GRAF when using GRAF as the pose-aware generative model. As the poses of the Cars dataset are available, we evaluate on 2000 images used for training GRAF. For the real-world Faces dataset where poses are not available, we sample 2000 images from GRAF as target images for quantitative evaluation and show qualitative evaluation using real-world face images.

We train an RL/IL policy network on each category individually. Since RL and IL are well-known to be sensitive to different random seeds [17], we apply 10 random seeds and report the standard variation for experiments in Sect. 5.1 and Sect. 5.2. For REAL275, we train on synthetic images used for training the voxel-based generator as their poses are available. As for Cars and Faces, we randomly generate samples from GRAF for training.

Metrics. We follow the evaluation protocol of NOCS [50] to evaluate average precision (AP) at different error thresholds. For the REAL275 dataset where original images contain multiple objects with background, NOCS considers object detection, classification and pose estimation jointly. Following Chen et al. [8], we use the trained Mask-RCNN network provided by NOCS to detect and segment objects, such that a single-object target image without background is provided to our visual navigation pipeline. This ensures fair comparison to Chen et al. [8] and NOCS as all methods rely on the same network for pre-processing. Following Chen et al. [8], the rotation and translation errors are evaluated as:

$$e_{\mathbf{R}} = arccos\frac{Tr(\mathbf{R}^* \cdot \mathbf{R}_T^{-1}) - 1}{2}, \quad e_{\mathbf{t}} = \|\mathbf{t}^* - \mathbf{t}_T\|_2 \tag{5}$$

where Tr represents the trace of a matrix, $\mathbf{R}_T$ and $\mathbf{t}_T$ denote the final prediction. Following NOCS [50], the rotation along the axis of symmetry is not penalized for symmetric object categories, i.e., bottle, bowl and can.

5.1 How Are Policies Affected by Design Choices?

When adopting a trainable policy such as RL or IL, there are several open questions to design choices: Is it necessary to reach the goal in multi-steps? Is it important to recover the latent code $\mathbf{z}^*$ while we are interested in pose estimation only? We first investigate these questions on the laptop category in REAL275 and its corresponding synthetic images for training the voxel-based generator.

Multi-Step v.s. Single-Step. We investigate whether it is beneficial to perform sequential updates during inference when adopting a trainable policy. Specifically, we compare two variants of IL, behavior cloning (IL$_{BC}$) and DAgger (IL$_{DA}$). Both variants are supervised by one-step demonstrations during training, while applied for one step or multiple steps during inference. In this comparison, we refer to multi-step as using $T = 10$ steps. As for RL that is usually applied for making sequential decisions, we observe a degenerated performance when using single-step and report results in the supplementary.

Figure 3a shows rotation AP on both synthetic and real-world target images. Interestingly, IL$_{BC}$ and IL$_{DA}$ perform similar at single-step inference. However, their behaviors diverge when taking multiple steps: IL$_{BC}$ is degraded while IL$_{DA}$ is improved. As IL$_{BC}$ is trained with off-policy data, it diverges when applied iteratively. In contrast, IL$_{DA}$ overcomes this problem by adding on-policy data. Furthermore, the gap between single-step and multiple-step becomes more prominent when transferred to the real world. It suggests that the multi-step inference helps to overcome the synthetic-to-real gap when leveraging proper training data.

Prediction of Latent Code. Taking the simple single-step IL$_{BC}$ as an example, we study whether it makes a difference to recover $\mathbf{z}^*$ or not. Specifically, we train another IL$_{BC}$ policy using the same network architecture but omitting $\|(\mathbf{z}^* - \mathbf{z}) - \Delta\mathbf{z}\|_2^2$ in (4). Figure 3b compares the rotation AP of IL$_{BC}$ trained with and without loss on $\Delta\mathbf{z}$. Surprisingly, adding the loss on $\Delta\mathbf{z}$ improves the pose estimation accuracy, especially when the target is real-world images. This finding is interesting as iterative update is not applied here, i.e., $\Delta\mathbf{z}$ does not directly affect the final prediction of $\mathbf{R}, \mathbf{t}$. We hypothesize that recovering $\mathbf{z}^*$ acts as an auxiliary task which can boost the performance of related tasks [56], i.e., the prediction of $\Delta\mathbf{R}$ and $\Delta\mathbf{t}$.

Discussions. We observe that the long-horizon navigation policy can be beneficial despite the trainable policy making reasonable predictions in a single step. However, it is important to take the multi-step inference into account during training, e.g., via on-policy training data in IL. Further, recovering $\mathbf{z}^*$ acts as a multi-task constraint that helps to improve the performance of pose estimation.

5.2   What Is a Good Navigation Policy?

We now compare all strategies, GD, RL and $\mathrm{IL_{BC}}$ and $\mathrm{IL_{DA}}$. Based on previous analysis, we adopt single-step inference for $\mathrm{IL_{BC}}$ and multi-step for $\mathrm{IL_{DA}}$.

Convergence. We first evaluate GD, RL, $\mathrm{IL_{BC}}$ and $\mathrm{IL_{DA}}$ in how the initialization affects the pose estimation. To this goal, we manually control the relative pose between the initial state and the target. We evaluate on Cars where the variation of the target poses is the largest. Specifically, we keep the relative translation fixed, and increase the relative azimuth angle from $10°$ to $180°$ with an interval of $10°$. We compare the rotation precision $AP_{10°}$ and $AP_{30°}$ in Fig. 4a. As can be seen, GD achieves the best precision in the range $[10°, 40°]$, demonstrating that GD is more precise given a good initialization. This is because that GD is guaranteed to converge to the global optimum of L_p given a good initialization. However, the precision of GD degrades significantly when the initialized angle deviates further from the target. In contrast, RL, $\mathrm{IL_{BC}}$ and $\mathrm{IL_{DA}}$ are not affected, maintaining almost the same performance in different initialization conditions. Further note that $\mathrm{IL_{DA}}$ trained with on-policy data achieves superior performance compared to RL while $\mathrm{IL_{BC}}$ is less competitive (at $AP_{30°}$).

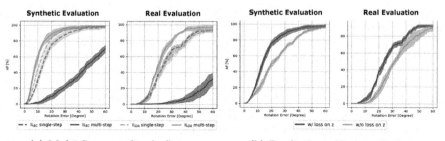

(a) Multi-Step v.s. Single-Step.   (b) Prediction of Latent Code.

Fig. 3. Effect of Design Choices. (a) We compare $\mathrm{IL_{BC}}$ and $\mathrm{IL_{DA}}$ on the laptop category on synthetic and real-world images. (b) We compare single-step $\mathrm{IL_{BC}}$ on the laptop category with and without loss on $\Delta\mathbf{z}$ on both synthetic and real-world target images.

Robustness. Inspired by Chen et al. [8], we compare the robustness of GD, RL, $\mathrm{IL_{BC}}$ and $\mathrm{IL_{DA}}$ against variations of brightness, occlusion and shift in the target image. This is evaluated on the synthetic images of the laptop category.

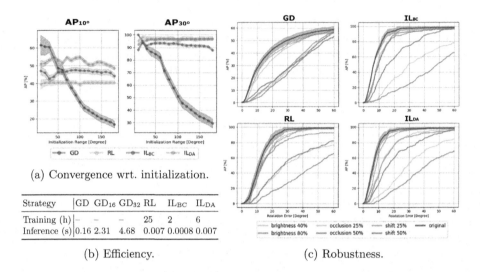

(a) Convergence wrt. initialization.

Strategy	GD	GD$_{16}$	GD$_{32}$	RL	IL$_{BC}$	IL$_{DA}$
Training (h)	–	–	–	25	2	6
Inference (s)	0.16	2.31	4.68	0.007	0.0008	0.007

(b) Efficiency.

(c) Robustness.

Fig. 4. Convergence, Robustness and Efficiency of different navigation policies. (a) Rotation $AP_{10°}$ and $AP_{30°}$ given different initial states. (b) Total training time and averaged inference time on a single image, both evaluated using the voxel-based generative model at the image resolution of 64 × 64. (c) Rotation AP of navigation policies against disturbance in brightness, occlusion and shift.

As shown in Fig. 4c, GD is more robust against disturbance in brightness and shift compared to other strategies. One possible explanation is that the perceptual loss is more robust, as it is calculated based on VGG [48] pretrained on ImageNet [9]. In contrast, both RL and IL policy networks are trained on synthetic images only, thus being less robust against the domain shift. All methods struggle to some extent in terms of occlusions, which can be a disadvantage of the analysis-by-synthesis pipeline. Note that neither RL nor IL policy is trained with data augmentation regarding brightness, occlusion, or shift. We expect better robustness when trained with augmentation against these disturbances.

Efficiency. Figure 4b shows the training and inference time of different strategies on the same device NVIDIA RTX 3090. For GD, we further evaluate the inference time using multiple different initial states. This strategy is used in Chen et al. [8] to avoid converging to local minima. Despite that GD does not require training, its inference takes longer compared to RL, IL$_{BC}$ and IL$_{DA}$. Furthermore, the time cost of GD increases wrt. the number of initial states. Taking 32 initial states as used in Chen et al. [8] requires almost 7 s for one target image. For trainable policies, the training time of both IL variants is less compared to the RL policy thanks to the direct supervision. During inference, IL$_{BC}$ is the most efficient method as we take only a single-step update when using IL$_{BC}$. RL and IL$_{DA}$ take longer, but the overhead is acceptable.

Discussions. Our analysis shows that GD achieves the best precision given a good initialization and better robustness against brightness and shift. However, it easily gets stuck in local minima when the initial state is far from the target. Solving this problem by adopting multiple initial states sacrifices efficiency. On the other hand, RL and IL policies are efficient and less prone to local minima. When augmented with on-policy data, IL_{DA} performs similar or even better compared to RL while requiring less training time. Therefore, we suggest to combine GD's precision and robustness with the convergence and efficiency of IL_{DA} by applying a few steps of GD (e.g., $T = 10$) after IL_{DA}. We show results of this simple hybrid method in the next section.

5.3 Comparison to the State-of-the-Art

Baselines. We now compare different strategies to baselines for category-level object pose estimation. We first evaluate a simple baseline following Chen et al. [8], where a VGG16 [48] is adopted to regress the object pose from an RGB image directly. We then compare to state-of-the-art analysis-by-synthesis approaches, including iNeRF [54] and Chen et al. [8]. Both approaches follow the principle of the GD policy but improve from different aspects: iNeRF samples image patches in interested regions to calculate the loss while [8] starts from 32 different initial states. We also consider NOCS [50] as a reference on the REAL275 dataset. Note that NOCS does not apply to Cars and Faces due to the lack of supervision. Moreover, NOCS is trained jointly on synthetic and real-world RGB-D images, while our method is trained on synthetic RGB images only.

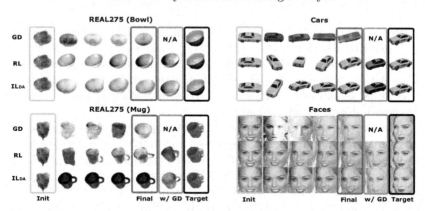

Fig. 5. Qualitative Comparison of different strategies, including the initialization, the optimization process, the final image and the target image. For RL and IL_{DA}, we further show the synthesized image after adding 10 steps of GD.

Results. The quantitative results are shown in Table 1. Firstly, we observe that VGG is outperformed by other methods, suggesting that it is difficult to regress the pose from a single RGB image directly. For iNeRF, it is interesting that it

Table 1. Quantitative Comparison of category-level pose estimation on different datasets.

Dataset	Metric	NOCS* [50]	VGG [48]	iNeRF [54]	Chen [8]	GD	RL	IL$_{DA}$	RL w/ GD	IL$_{DA}$ w/ GD
REAL275	$AP_{10°}$	32.8	6.4	21.0	24.0	20.5	18.6	21.6	<u>24.8</u>	**25.0**
Dataset	$AP_{30°}$	66.5	34.8	88.7	92.1	86.2	91.7	<u>93.6</u>	92.5	94.2
(Symmetry)	$AP_{60°}$	99.3	76.3	97.1	**99.9**	96.7	98.8	<u>99.6</u>	<u>99.6</u>	99.9
	AP_{5cm}	93.4	7.8	11.9	12.7	11.9	11.8	12.4	<u>13.2</u>	14.6
	AP_{10cm}	95.0	23.7	26.1	27.4	24.5	23.9	**29.1**	27.2	<u>28.8</u>
	AP_{15cm}	97.3	38.1	43.8	**46.9**	41.4	39.5	42.3	42.6	<u>46.4</u>
REAL275	$AP_{10°}$	20.5	0.6	5.1	**6.9**	5.0	5.1	4.8	6.5	<u>6.8</u>
Dataset	$AP_{30°}$	55.5	12.4	43.1	<u>59.5</u>	21.1	51.6	53.5	58.7	**60.0**
(Asymmetry)	$AP_{60°}$	93.3	35.1	62.8	79.2	35.0	74.5	<u>80.6</u>	76.3	**82.3**
	AP_{5cm}	87.7	10.3	7.7	12.1	9.8	9.7	**17.5**	<u>12.8</u>	12.5
	AP_{10cm}	98.2	38.1	33.2	42.4	27.7	41.7	**52.2**	42.2	<u>46.8</u>
	AP_{15cm}	99.5	61.8	48.7	<u>73.1</u>	50.6	71.6	**75.8**	73.0	72.8
Cars	$AP_{10°}$	\	5.6	31.7	51.8	21.3	42.4	47.6	<u>62.9</u>	**65.3**
Dataset	$AP_{30°}$	\	15.4	45.4	85.5	33.7	92.8	93.5	<u>93.8</u>	**94.1**
	$AP_{60°}$	\	32.8	56.6	93.7	37.4	94.2	<u>98.2</u>	97.7	**98.8**
	AP_{1cm}	\	8.9	12.4	<u>35.7</u>	9.6	27.2	35.5	29.1	**36.7**
	AP_{3cm}	\	35.2	41.6	<u>75.8</u>	32.7	71.8	**76.3**	72.5	75.6
	AP_{6cm}	\	52.1	68.3	85.7	60.1	91.8	<u>92.0</u>	91.4	**92.9**
Faces	$AP_{5°}$	\	5.3	4.6	24.8	2.0	17.3	**25.8**	15.4	<u>23.1</u>
Dataset	$AP_{15°}$	\	32.8	42.6	88.7	35.9	84.2	<u>89.5</u>	88.4	**90.8**
	$AP_{30°}$	\	71.1	80.9	92.5	81.2	98.6	98.3	**99.5**	<u>99.1</u>
	AP_{1cm}	\	11.0	18.2	<u>27.4</u>	14.3	**27.9**	25.9	26.7	25.3
	AP_{3cm}	\	41.0	59.6	**92.6**	53.8	86.3	90.1	87.8	<u>91.5</u>
	AP_{6cm}	\	72.9	85.7	<u>98.5</u>	82.3	97.2	97.7	<u>98.5</u>	**99.5**
Mean	AP_{rot}	\	27.4	48.3	66.6	39.7	64.2	67.2	<u>68.0</u>	**70.0**
	AP_{tran}	\	33.4	38.1	52.5	34.9	50.0	**53.9**	51.4	<u>53.6</u>

*NOCS is based on RGB-D while the others are based on RGB images.

outperforms GD based on interest region sampling, even when GD is applied to the full image on REAL275. However, it struggles to overcome the convergence problem given the uncurated initialization range as in this paper, particularly on the Cars dataset where the initial azimuth is within the range of $[-180°, 180°]$. Chen et al. [8] significantly outperforms GD by leveraging 32 initial states, but is time-consuming as shown in Fig. 4b.

In contrast, RL and IL$_{DA}$ achieve competitive performance compared to [8] but are remarkably more efficient. Moreover, the simple hybrid approaches, RL w/ GD and IL$_{DA}$ w/ GD, often lead to better performance. As RL/IL$_{DA}$ provides a fairly good start, the subsequent GD converges in only a few steps. This reduces the required steps of "w/ GD" to $T = 10$ in contrast to $T = 50$ in the standard GD, and the inference time of RL, IL$_{BC}$, IL$_{DA}$ change to 0.033s, 0.027s, 0.033s respectively. The hybrid approach is still much more efficient compared to [8] (0.033s v.s. 4.68s). Note that IL$_{DA}$ w/ GD yields the best performance among all RGB based approaches and sometimes even achieves comparable performance to NOCS based on RGB-D input. Interestingly, the hybrid approach sometimes worsens the translation performance, e.g., on the asymmetry categories of REAL275. This might be due to the scale ambiguity of the generative model. Here, NOCS achieves superior performance in translation leveraging depth maps. Lastly, it is worth noting that our learned policies consistently improve the inference of different pose-aware generators. This brings hope to apply our method to more advanced synthesis models for more challenging tasks.

We further show the qualitative comparison of different navigation strategies in Fig. 5. Note that RL and IL both allow for converging to the correct pose starting from a bad initialization, e.g., the car example. Furthermore, adding 10 steps of GD helps to refine the object pose, see the mug category of REAL275. More qualitative comparisons are provided in the supplementary.

6 Conclusions

In this paper, we formulate the category-level object pose estimation problem as a long-horizon visual navigation task. We experimentally analyze three different navigation policies in terms of convergence, robustness and efficiency. Based on our analysis, we come up with a simple yet effective hybrid approach that enhances the convergence of existing analysis-by-synthesis approaches without sacrificing the efficiency. We further show that it improves the inference of different pose-aware generative models. However, the scale ambiguity of monocular images remains unsolved, thus estimating correct translation is particularly challenging. We plan to tackle these challenges in the future.

Acknowledgement. This work is supported in NSFC under grant U21B2004, and partially supported by Shenzhen Portion of Shenzhen-Hong Kong Science and Technology Innovation Cooperation Zone under HZQB-KCZYB-20200089, the HK RGC under T42-409/18-R and 14202918, the Multi-Scale Medical Robotics Centre, InnoHK, and the VC Fund 4930745 of the CUHK T Stone Robotics Institute.

References

1. Abdal, R., Qin, Y., Wonka, P.: Image2stylegan: how to embed images into the styleGAN latent space? In: Proceedings of the IEEE International Conference on Computer Vision (ICCV) (2019)
2. Andrychowicz, M., et al.: Learning to learn by gradient descent by gradient descent. In: Advances in Neural Information Processing Systems 29 (2016)
3. Andrychowicz, M., et al.: Hindsight experience replay. In: Advances in Neural Information Processing Systems (NeurIPS) (2017)
4. Bojarski, M., et al.: End to end learning for self-driving cars. arXiv.org 1604.07316 (2016)
5. Chan, E.R., Monteiro, M., Kellnhofer, P., Wu, J., Wetzstein, G.: Pi-GAN: Periodic implicit generative adversarial networks for 3D-aware image synthesis. In: Proceedings IEEE Conference on Computer Vision and Pattern Recognition (CVPR) (2021)
6. Chen, D., Li, J., Wang, Z., Xu, K.: Learning canonical shape space for category-level 6D object pose and size estimation. In: Proceedings IEEE Conference on Computer Vision and Pattern Recognition (CVPR) (2020)
7. Chen, W., Jia, X., Chang, H.J., Duan, J., Shen, L., Leonardis, A.: FS-Net: fast shape-based network for category-level 6d object pose estimation with decoupled rotation mechanism. In: Proceedings IEEE Conference on Computer Vision and Pattern Recognition (CVPR) (2021)

8. Chen, X., Dong, Z., Song, J., Geiger, A., Hilliges, O.: Category level object pose estimation via neural analysis-by-synthesis. In: Vedaldi, A., Bischof, H., Brox, T., Frahm, J.-M. (eds.) ECCV 2020. LNCS, vol. 12371, pp. 139–156. Springer, Cham (2020). https://doi.org/10.1007/978-3-030-58574-7_9

9. Deng, J., Dong, W., Socher, R., Li, L., Li, K., Fei-Fei, L.: Imagenet: a large-scale hierarchical image database. In: Proceedings IEEE Conference on Computer Vision and Pattern Recognition (CVPR) (2009)

10. Do, T., Pham, T., Cai, M., Reid, I.: LieNet: real-time monocular object instance 6D pose estimation. In: Proceedings of the British Machine Vision Conference (BMVC) (2018)

11. Dosovitskiy, A., Ros, G., Codevilla, F., Lopez, A., Koltun, V.: Carla: An open urban driving simulator. In: Proceedings Conference on Robot Learning (CoRL) (2017)

12. Drost, B., Ulrich, M., Navab, N., Ilic, S.: Model globally, match locally: efficient and robust 3d object recognition. In: Proceedings IEEE Conference on Computer Vision and Pattern Recognition (CVPR) (2010)

13. Duggal, S., et al.: Secrets of 3D implicit object shape reconstruction in the wild. arXiv.org 2101.06860 (2021)

14. Goodfellow, I.J., et al.: Generative adversarial nets. In: Advances in Neural Information Processing Systems (NeurIPS) (2014)

15. Haarnoja, T., Zhou, A., Abbeel, P., Levine, S.: Soft actor-critic: Off-policy maximum entropy deep reinforcement learning with a stochastic actor. In: Proceedings of the International Conference on Machine Learning (ICML) (2018)

16. Hejrati, M., Ramanan, D.: Analysis by synthesis: 3D object recognition by object reconstruction. In: Proc. IEEE Conference on Computer Vision and Pattern Recognition (CVPR) (2014)

17. Henderson, P., Islam, R., Bachman, P., Pineau, J., Precup, D., Meger, D.: Deep reinforcement learning that matters. In: Proceedings of the AAAI Conference on Artificial Intelligence, vol. 32 (2018)

18. Henzler, P., Mitra, N.J., Ritschel, T.: Escaping plato's cave: 3D shape from adversarial rendering. In: Proceedings of the IEEE International Conference on Computer Vision (ICCV) (2019)

19. Hu, Y., Hugonot, J., Fua, P., Salzmann, M.: Segmentation-driven 6D object pose estimation. In: Proceedings IEEE Conference on Computer Vision and Pattern Recognition (CVPR) (2019)

20. Isola, P., Liu, C.: Scene collaging: analysis and synthesis of natural images with semantic layers. In: Proceedings of the IEEE International Conference on Computer Vision (ICCV) (2013)

21. Johnson, J., Alahi, A., Fei-Fei, L.: Perceptual losses for real-time style transfer and super-resolution. In: Leibe, B., Matas, J., Sebe, N., Welling, M. (eds.) ECCV 2016. LNCS, vol. 9906, pp. 694–711. Springer, Cham (2016). https://doi.org/10.1007/978-3-319-46475-6_43

22. Kehl, W., Manhardt, F., Tombari, F., Ilic, S., Navab, N.: SSD-6D: making RGB-based 3D detection and 6d pose estimation great again. In: Proceedings of the IEEE International Conference on Computer Vision (ICCV) (2017)

23. Kingma, D.P., Ba, J.: Adam: a method for stochastic optimization. In: Bengio, Y., LeCun, Y. (eds.) Proceedings of the International Conference on Learning Representations (ICLR) (2015)

24. Kretzschmar, H., Spies, M., Sprunk, C., Burgard, W.: Socially compliant mobile robot navigation via inverse reinforcement learning. Int. J. Robot. Res. (IJRR) **35**(11), 1289–1307 (2016)

25. Krull, A., Brachmann, E., Michel, F., Yang, M.Y., Gumhold, S., Rother, C.: Learning analysis-by-synthesis for 6d pose estimation in RGB-D images. In: Proceedings of the IEEE International Conference on Computer Vision (ICCV) (2015)
26. Krull, A., Brachmann, E., Nowozin, S., Michel, F., Shotton, J., Rother, C.: PoseAgent: budget-constrained 6d object pose estimation via reinforcement learning. In: Proceedings IEEE Conference on Computer Vision and Pattern Recognition (CVPR) (2017)
27. Li, Y., Wang, G., Ji, X., Xiang, Yu., Fox, D.: DeepIM: deep iterative matching for 6D pose estimation. In: Ferrari, V., Hebert, M., Sminchisescu, C., Weiss, Y. (eds.) ECCV 2018. LNCS, vol. 11210, pp. 695–711. Springer, Cham (2018). https://doi.org/10.1007/978-3-030-01231-1_42
28. Li, Z., Wang, G., Ji, X.: CDPN: coordinates-based disentangled pose network for real-time rgb-based 6-dof object pose estimation. In: Proceedings of the IEEE International Conference on Computer Vision (ICCV) (2019)
29. Liao, Y., Schwarz, K., Mescheder, L.M., Geiger, A.: Towards unsupervised learning of generative models for 3D controllable image synthesis. In: Proceedings IEEE Conference on Computer Vision and Pattern Recognition (CVPR) (2020)
30. Liu, Z., Li, X., Luo, P., Loy, C.C., Tang, X.: Semantic image segmentation via deep parsing network. In: Proceedings of the IEEE International Conference on Computer Vision (ICCV) (2015)
31. Loper, M.M., Black, M.J.: OpenDR: an approximate differentiable renderer. In: Fleet, D., Pajdla, T., Schiele, B., Tuytelaars, T. (eds.) ECCV 2014. LNCS, vol. 8695, pp. 154–169. Springer, Cham (2014). https://doi.org/10.1007/978-3-319-10584-0_11
32. Mildenhall, B., Srinivasan, P.P., Tancik, M., Barron, J.T., Ramamoorthi, R., Ng, R.: NeRF: representing scenes as neural radiance fields for view synthesis. In: Vedaldi, A., Bischof, H., Brox, T., Frahm, J.-M. (eds.) ECCV 2020. LNCS, vol. 12346, pp. 405–421. Springer, Cham (2020). https://doi.org/10.1007/978-3-030-58452-8_24
33. Mirowski, P., et al.: Learning to navigate in complex environments. In: Proceedings of the International Conference on Learning Representations (ICLR) (2017)
34. Moreno, P., Williams, C.K.I., Nash, C., Kohli, P.: Overcoming occlusion with inverse graphics. In: Hua, G., Jégou, H. (eds.) ECCV 2016. LNCS, vol. 9915, pp. 170–185. Springer, Cham (2016). https://doi.org/10.1007/978-3-319-49409-8_16
35. Muñoz, E., Konishi, Y., Murino, V., Del Bue, A.: Fast 6D pose estimation for texture-less objects from a single RGB image. In: Proceedings IEEE International Conference on Robotics and Automation (ICRA) (2016)
36. Nguyen-Phuoc, T., Li, C., Theis, L., Richardt, C., Yang, Y.L.: HoloGAN: unsupervised learning of 3D representations from natural images. In: Proceedings of the IEEE International Conference on Computer Vision (ICCV) (2019)
37. Niemeyer, M., Geiger, A.: GIRAFFE: representing scenes as compositional generative neural feature fields. In: Proceedings IEEE Conference on Computer Vision and Pattern Recognition (CVPR) (2021)
38. Park, K., Mousavian, A., Xiang, Y., Fox, D.: LatentFusion: end-to-end differentiable reconstruction and rendering for unseen object pose estimation. In: Proceedings IEEE Conference on Computer Vision and Pattern Recognition (CVPR) (2020)
39. Park, K., Patten, T., Vincze, M.: Pix2pose: pixel-wise coordinate regression of objects for 6d pose estimation. In: Proceedings of the IEEE International Conference on Computer Vision (ICCV) (2019)

40. Peng, S., Liu, Y., Huang, Q., Zhou, X., Bao, H.: PVNet: pixel-wise voting network for 6D of pose estimation. In: Proceedings IEEE Conference on Computer Vision and Pattern Recognition (CVPR) (2019)
41. Pfeiffer, M., et al.: Reinforced imitation: sample efficient deep reinforcement learning for mapless navigation by leveraging prior demonstrations. IEEE Robot. Autom. Lett. (RA-L) **3**(4), 4423–4430 (2018)
42. Ross, S., Gordon, G.J., Bagnell, D.: A reduction of imitation learning and structured prediction to no-regret online learning. In: Conference on Artificial Intelligence and Statistics (AISTATS) (2011)
43. Ross, S., et al.: Learning monocular reactive UAV control in cluttered natural environments. In: Proceedings IEEE International Conf. on Robotics and Automation (ICRA) (2013)
44. Sahin, C., Kim, T.-K.: Category-level 6D object pose recovery in depth images. In: Leal-Taixé, L., Roth, S. (eds.) ECCV 2018. LNCS, vol. 11129, pp. 665–681. Springer, Cham (2019). https://doi.org/10.1007/978-3-030-11009-3_41
45. Schwarz, K., Liao, Y., Niemeyer, M., Geiger, A.: GRAF: generative radiance fields for 3d-aware image synthesis. In: Advances in Neural Information Processing Systems (NeurIPS) (2020)
46. Shao, J., Jiang, Y., Wang, G., Li, Z., Ji, X.: PFRL: pose-free reinforcement learning for 6D pose estimation. In: Proceedings IEEE Conference on Computer Vision and Pattern Recognition (CVPR) (2020)
47. Shen, Y., Gu, J., Tang, X., Zhou, B.: Interpreting the latent space of GANs for semantic face editing. In: Proceedings IEEE Conference on Computer Vision and Pattern Recognition (CVPR) (2020)
48. Simonyan, K., Zisserman, A.: Very deep convolutional networks for large-scale image recognition. In: Proceedings of the International Conference on Learning Representations (ICLR) (2015)
49. Tian, M., Ang, M.H., Lee, G.H.: Shape prior deformation for categorical 6d object pose and size estimation. In: Vedaldi, A., Bischof, H., Brox, T., Frahm, J.-M. (eds.) ECCV 2020. LNCS, vol. 12366, pp. 530–546. Springer, Cham (2020). https://doi.org/10.1007/978-3-030-58589-1_32
50. Wang, H., Sridhar, S., Huang, J., Valentin, J., Song, S., Guibas, L.J.: Normalized object coordinate space for category-level 6D object pose and size estimation. In: Proceedings IEEE Conference on Computer Vision and Pattern Recognition (CVPR) (2019)
51. Wang, J., Chen, K., Dou, Q.: Category-level 6D object pose estimation via cascaded relation and recurrent reconstruction networks. In: Proceedings IEEE International Conference on Intelligent Robots and Systems (IROS) (2021)
52. Xia, W., Zhang, Y., Yang, Y., Xue, J., Zhou, B., Yang, M.: GAN inversion: a survey. arXiv.org 2101.05278 (2021)
53. Xiang, Y., Schmidt, T., Narayanan, V., Fox, D.: PoseCNN: a convolutional neural network for 6d object pose estimation in cluttered scenes. In: Proceedings Robotics: Science and Systems (RSS) (2018)
54. Yen-Chen, L., Florence, P., Barron, J.T., Rodriguez, A., Isola, P., Lin, T.Y.: INeRF: inverting neural radiance fields for pose estimation. In: Proceedings IEEE International Conference on Intelligent Robots and Systems (IROS) (2021)
55. Yuille, A., Kersten, D.: Vision as Bayesian inference: analysis by synthesis? Trends Cogn. Sci. **10**(7), 301–308 (2006)
56. Zamir, A.R., Sax, A., Shen, W.B., Guibas, L.J., Malik, J., Savarese, S.: Taskonomy: disentangling task transfer learning. In: Proceedings IEEE Conference on Computer Vision and Pattern Recognition (CVPR) (2018)

57. Zhu, J.-Y., Krähenbühl, P., Shechtman, E., Efros, A.A.: Generative visual manipulation on the natural image manifold. In: Leibe, B., Matas, J., Sebe, N., Welling, M. (eds.) ECCV 2016. LNCS, vol. 9909, pp. 597–613. Springer, Cham (2016). https://doi.org/10.1007/978-3-319-46454-1_36
58. Zhu, Y., et al.: Target-driven visual navigation in indoor scenes using deep reinforcement learning. In: Proc. IEEE International Conference on Robotics and Automation (ICRA) (2017)

Faster VoxelPose: Real-time 3D Human Pose Estimation by Orthographic Projection

Hang Ye[1], Wentao Zhu[2,3], Chunyu Wang[4(✉)], Rujie Wu[2,3],
and Yizhou Wang[2,3,5]

[1] Yuanpei College, Peking University, Beijing, China
`yehang@pku.edu.cn`
[2] Center on Frontiers of Computing Studies, Peking University, Beijing, China
`{wtzhu,wu_rujie,yizhou.wang}@pku.edu.cn`
[3] School of Computer Science, Peking University, Beijing, China
[4] Microsoft Research Asia, Beijing, China
`chnuwa@microsoft.com`
[5] Institute for Artificial Intelligence, Peking University, Beijing, China

Abstract. While the voxel-based methods have achieved promising results for multi-person 3D pose estimation from multi-cameras, they suffer from heavy computation burdens, especially for large scenes. We present *Faster VoxelPose* to address the challenge by re-projecting the feature volume to the three two-dimensional coordinate planes and estimating X, Y, Z coordinates from them separately. To that end, we first localize each person by a 3D bounding box by estimating a 2D box and its height based on the volume features projected to the xy-plane and z-axis, respectively. Then for each person, we estimate partial joint coordinates from the three coordinate planes separately which are then fused to obtain the final 3D pose. The method is free from costly 3D-CNNs and improves the speed of VoxelPose by ten times and meanwhile achieves competitive accuracy as the state-of-the-art methods, proving its potential in real-time applications.

Keywords: 3D human pose estimation · Multi-view multi-person

1 Introduction

Estimating 3D human pose from RGB images is a fundamental problem in computer vision. It not only paves the way for some important downstream tasks such as action recognition [36,39,42,43,50] and human-computer interaction [1,18],

---

H. Ye and W. Zhu—Equal contribution.

Supplementary Information The online version contains supplementary material available at https://doi.org/10.1007/978-3-031-20068-7_9.

ⓒ The Author(s), under exclusive license to Springer Nature Switzerland AG 2022
S. Avidan et al. (Eds.): ECCV 2022, LNCS 13666, pp. 142–159, 2022.
https://doi.org/10.1007/978-3-031-20068-7_9

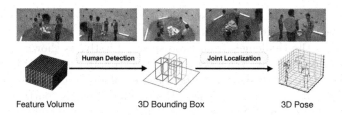

Fig. 1. Multi-view 3D Pose Estimation. Given multi-view images and camera parameters, the task aims to estimate the 3D poses of all people in the world coordinates. Similar to [38], our approach is based on the volumetric representation and detects 3D box as an intermediate step.

but also enables a wide range of applications, *e.g.* sports analysis [5,29] and virtual avatar animation [46,63].

While many works [8,24,27,40,41,59,61] address monocular 3D pose estimation, their application in serious scenarios is limited because of the degraded accuracy [20,34]. In addition, monocular human pose estimation struggles when occlusion occurs which is ubiquitous in natural images [7,10]. As a result, the state-of-the-art 3D human pose estimation results are usually obtained via multi-camera systems which consist of a group of synchronized and calibrated wide-baseline cameras [2,9,22,38,47,55,57,58].

Simple triangulation [14,51] can achieve accurate 3D pose estimates if the 2D poses in all views are accurate. However, 2D pose estimates may have errors in practice especially when occlusion occurs. To address the problem, voxel-based methods [17,28,31,38,47,54] have been proposed which inversely project 2D features or heatmaps in each view to the 3D space and then fuse the multi-view features. The resulting feature volume is more robust to occlusions in individual cameras. Then they apply a 3D-CNN to estimate the 3D positions of the body joints from the feature volume. While these methods achieve very accurate results, the computation complexity increases cubically with space size. As a result, they cannot support real-time inference for large scenes such as sports stadiums or retail stores.

In this work, we present Faster VoxelPose which is about ten times faster than VoxelPose on the common benchmarks and more importantly scales gracefully to large spaces. Inspired by technical drawing where a 3D object is often unambiguously represented by three 2D orthographic projections, *i.e.* plan, elevation and section, we re-project the previously fused 3D volumetric features to the three 2D coordinate planes by orthographic projection and estimate partial coordinates, *e.g.* xy, xz and yz, of a 3D pose from each of the 2D planes, which are then fused by a tiny network to predict xyz. The main advantage of the method is that we can replace the expensive 3D-CNNs with 2D-CNNs which reduces the computation cost from $O(n^3)$ to $O(n^2)$ where n is the spatial resolution. However, the factorization brings two new challenges. First, people that are far away in the 3D space could overlap in some planes after re-projection, which may bring severe ambiguity to the corresponding features. Second, the estimation results may be inconsistent across planes so we need a strategy to aggregate the contradictory predictions.

We address the challenges from two aspects. Firstly, as shown in Fig. 1, we present *Human Detection Networks* (HDN) to estimate a *tight* 3D box for each person which is used to filter out the features of other people. By contrast, VoxelPose [38] use a loose fixed-size 3D bounding box. In particular, we re-project the 3D feature volume to the xy plane by max-pooling along the z axis (bird's-eye view), and apply a 2D-CNN to localize people by a 2D box in the xy plane. Then, for each bounding box, we obtain a 1D "column" feature representation from the volume at the box center along the z axis, and apply a 1D-CNN to estimate the vertical position of the box center.

Then we present *Joint Localization Networks* to estimate a 3D pose for each 3D box. We first mask out the features in the volume which are outside the box to reduce the impact of other people, obtaining *person-specific* feature volume. We re-project the masked volume to the three coordinate planes and estimate the X, Y and Z coordinates, respectively. For each coordinate, we have two predictions from two planes. It is probable that the two predictions are contradictory so we propose a fusion network to learn a weight for each prediction and aggregate them to obtain the final 3D pose.

Our approach achieves competing results as the baseline method which uses 3D-CNN. But ours is about 10 times faster than it (speed improvement is larger for larger scenes). Our contributions are four-fold: 1) We design a lightweight framework for efficient training and inference of the multi-view multi-person 3D pose estimation problem. Our approach demonstrates that 3D human detection and pose estimation can be resolved on the re-projected 2D feature maps with careful design. 2) We propose a novel 3D human detector that disentangles ground plane localization and height estimation. 3) We utilize 3D bounding box for feature masking, which contributes to person-specific feature volume and improves joint localization accuracy. 4) We deploy the confidence regression networks to adaptively fuse the estimates on the re-projected planes to compensate for their individual accuracy loss. While we focus on pose estimation in this work, the idea may also benefit other voxel-based tasks such as object detection [23,33,60] and shape completion [45].

2   Related Work

2.1   Multi-view 3D Pose Estimation

For the single-person case, the key is to handle 2D pose estimation errors in individual planes. Iskakov *et al.* [17] designed differentiable triangulation which uses joint detection confidence in each camera view to learn the optimal triangulation weights. Pavlakos *et al.* [26] applied CNN with 3D PSM for markerless motion capture. Qiu *et al.* [28] used epipolar lines to guide cross-view feature fusion followed by a recurrent PSM. Epipolar transformer [15] extended [28] to handle dynamic cameras. Generally speaking, single-person 3D pose estimation has achieved satisfactory results when there are sufficient cameras to guarantee that every body joint can be seen from at least two cameras.

Multi-person 3D human pose estimation is more challenging because it needs to solve two additional sub-tasks: 1) Identifying joint-to-person association in different views. 2) Handling mutual occlusions among the crowd. To address the first challenge, various association strategies are proposed based on re-id features [9], dynamic matching [2], 4D graph cut [56], and plane sweep stereo [22]. However, in crowded scenes, noisy 2D pose estimates would harm their accuracy. To address the second challenge, Belagiannis et al. [2] extended PSM for multi-person. Wang et al. [44] propose a transformer-based direct regression model with projective attention.

Recently, voxel-based methods [30,38,47,54] are proposed to avoid making decisions in each camera view. Instead, they fuse multi-view features in the 3D space and only make the decision there. Such methods are free from pairwise reasoning of camera views and enable learning human posture knowledge in a data-driven way. However, the computation-intensive 3D convolutions prevent these approaches from being real-time and applicable to large spaces. Our method enjoys the benefit of volumetric feature aggregation, meanwhile being significantly faster and more scalable.

2.2 Efficient Human Pose Estimation

Designing efficient human pose estimators has been intensively studied for practical usage. For extracting 2D pose from images, state-of-the-art methods [21,25,35,49,52] have achieved real-time inference speed. In terms of multi-view 3D pose estimation, Bultman et al. [6] explores an efficient system using edge sensors. Remelli et al. [32] and Fabbri et al. [12] adopt encoder-decoder networks to reduce computation, but they are not applicable to the multi-person setting. Most recently, Lin et al. [22] and Wang et al. [44] present alternative solutions to volumetric methods [38,47,54] and show some speed improvement. Nevertheless, these methods are capped in terms of scalability, which prevents them from being deployed to large scenes. Our method is complementary to state-of-the-art lightweight 2D pose estimators, and can further improve the speed of other volumetric methods [12,30,47].

3 Method

3.1 Overview

Without loss of generality, we explain our motivation with a simple case in which there is only one person. As shown in Fig. 2 (A), the input to our approach is a 3D feature volume $\mathbf{V} \in \mathbb{R}^{K \times L \times W \times H}$ which is constructed by back-projecting the 2D pose heatmaps in multiple cameras to the 3D voxel space [38]. The 2D pose heatmaps are extracted from the images using an off-the-shelf pose estimation model [37]. $L \times W \times H$ represents the number of voxels that are used to discretize

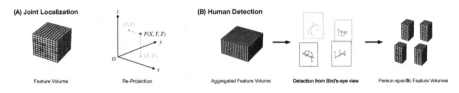

Fig. 2. Problem Decomposition. (A): Considering a single person, we re-project its feature volume to the coordinate planes with orthographic projection. The partial coordinates can be estimated by 2D CNN and assembled to 3D estimation. (B): Multi-person brings the extra challenge of ambiguity and occlusion. Nonetheless, people can be easily isolated on the bird's-eye view of the aggregated feature volume. Based on the intuitive ideas, we develop the lightweight *Joint Localization Networks* and *Human Detection Networks* respectively.

the space and K represents the number of joint types. The volume approximately encodes the per-voxel likelihood of body joints.

In Fig. 2 (A), we show a 3D joint of interest, *e.g.* a shoulder joint, as $P = (X, Y, Z)$. In general, the corresponding feature volume should have a distinctive pattern around P so that it can be localized by expensive 3D-CNNs [38]. To reduce the computation cost, we re-project the volume to the three coordinate planes (*i.e.* the xy, yz, xz planes), respectively, resulting in three 2D feature maps. We can imagine that there are also distinctive patterns at the corresponding locations of each 2D feature map, *e.g.* (X, Y) at the xy plane, which can be similarly detected by 2D-CNNs. Then the 3D position of P can be assembled from the estimated coordinates in the three planes.

However, when we apply the idea to the multi-person scenario, we are confronted with new challenges. The features of different people may be mixed together after being projected to the coordinate planes even when they are far away from each other in the 3D space. This may corrupt the pose estimation accuracy. Inspired by top-down 2D pose estimation [13], the problem can be alleviated by "cropping" the person from the overall 3D space and only projecting features belonging to the person to the planes. So the remaining task is to detect each person in the 3D space efficiently. We utilize the prior that people barely overlap along the z axis, therefore they can be easily detected in the bird's-eye view as shown in Fig. 2 (B).

We take a two-phase approach to address the challenges. In the first phase, we present *Human Detection Networks* (Sect. 3.2) which efficiently detects all people from bird's-eye view by 3D bounding boxes, ensuring that only the person-of-interest features are passed to the next phase. The second phase conducts fine-grained pose estimation for each person with *Joint Localization Networks* (Sect. 3.3), which is greatly eased since occlusion and distraction are mostly eliminated in the first phase. Importantly, all the operators in the networks are on 2D and 1D features, which boosts the speed.

3.2   Human Detection Networks

We first apply HRNet [37] to estimate 2D pose heatmaps from the multiview images, and construct an aggregated feature volume $\mathbf{V} \in \mathbb{R}^{K \times L \times W \times H}$ by back-projecting the heatmaps to the 3D voxel space. Since people are usually on the ground plane and it is less probable that one person is right on top of another, it inspires us to construct a 2D bird's-eye view representation from the feature volume for efficiently detecting people.

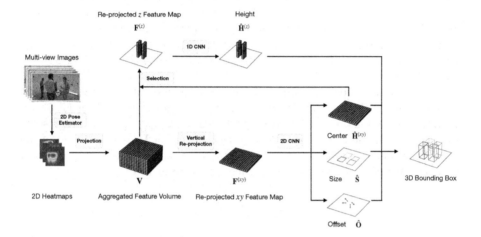

Fig. 3. Human Detection Networks. We first construct the feature volume $\mathbf{V}$ from the multi-view images. It is then projected to the xy plane to obtain the feature map $\mathbf{F}^{(xy)}$ (bird's-eye view). A Multi-branch 2D CNN estimates three feature maps encoding each person's center position, bounding box size, and center offset, respectively. We then select the 1D columns feature $\mathbf{F}^{(z)}$ from the positions with high confidence values on $\hat{\mathbf{H}}^{(xy)}$. Then a 1D CNN estimates the heatmap $\hat{\mathbf{H}}^{(z)}$ of the vertical position of the 3D box center. Finally, HDN outputs the combined 3D bounding box.

Detection in xy Plane. We re-project the aggregated feature volume to the ground plane (xy) by performing max-pooling along the z direction and obtain $\mathbf{F}^{(xy)} \in \mathbb{R}^{K \times L \times W}$. Then we feed $\mathbf{F}^{(xy)}$ to a 2D fully convolutional network to detect the locations of people in the xy plane. The positions of all people in the plane are encoded by a 2D confidence map $\hat{\mathbf{H}}^{(xy)} \in [0,1]^{L \times W}$ whose value $\hat{\mathbf{H}}_{i,j}^{(xy)}$ represents the likelihood of human presence at the location (i,j). For training supervision, we generate the ground-truth (GT) 2D confidence map $\mathbf{H}^{(xy)}$. Its values are computed by the distance between the GT center point and each grid point using a Gaussian kernel. Specifically, the confidence value of grid point (i,j) is computed by:

$$\mathbf{H}_{i,j}^{(xy)} = \max_{1 \le n \le N} \exp\{-\frac{(i - \tilde{i}_n)^2 + (j - \tilde{j}_n)^2}{2\sigma^2}\}$$

where N denotes the number of persons and $(\tilde{i}_n, \tilde{j}_n)$ represents the corresponding GT position for person n. We just keep the largest scores in the presence of multiple people. The mean squared error (MSE) loss is computed by:

$$\mathcal{L}_{2d} = \sum_{i=1}^{L} \sum_{j=1}^{W} \| \mathbf{H}_{i,j}^{(xy)} - \hat{\mathbf{H}}_{i,j}^{(xy)} \|_2 \tag{1}$$

We further estimate a 2D box size for each person instead of assuming a loose constant size as in the previous work [38]. The height of the box is simply set to be 2000 mm. This is critical to isolate the interference of multiple people, especially in crowded scenes. Our model generates a box size embedding at all grid points, denoted as $\hat{\mathbf{S}} \in \mathbb{R}^{2 \times L \times W}$. But only those at the locations with large confidences are meaningful. We compute a ground-truth size embedding $\mathbf{S}$ based on box annotations.

During training, we only compute losses on the grid points which are adjacent to the ground-truth box centers. Specifically, for a 2D GT box center $(\tilde{x}, \tilde{y})$, we only add supervision on the discretized grid points $(\lfloor \frac{\tilde{x}}{l} \rfloor, \lfloor \frac{\tilde{y}}{w} \rfloor)$, where l represents the length of a single voxel and w denotes the width. Let $\mathbf{U}$ denote the set of the neighboring points mentioned above and suppose N is the number of persons in the image. We compute an L_1 loss at each center point in $\mathbf{U}$:

$$\mathcal{L}_{size} = \frac{1}{N} \sum_{(i,j) \in \mathbf{U}} \| \mathbf{S}_{i,j} - \hat{\mathbf{S}}_{i,j} \|_1 \tag{2}$$

In addition, to reduce the quantization error, we estimate the local offset for each root joint on the horizontal plane. Similar to size estimation, the model outputs a offset prediction at each grid point, denoted as $\hat{\mathbf{O}} \in \mathbb{R}^{2 \times L \times W}$. We also generate a GT offset prediction $\mathbf{O}$ and use an L_1 loss on the neighboring points:

$$\mathcal{L}_{off} = \frac{1}{N} \sum_{(i,j) \in \mathbf{U}} \| \mathbf{O}_{i,j} - \hat{\mathbf{O}}_{i,j} \|_1 \tag{3}$$

Inspired by [62], we use a simple network structure with three parallel branches to estimate the heatmap, offset and size respectively. As shown in Fig. 3, the 2D bird's-eye features are passed through a fully-convolutional backbone network and then fed into three separate branches with identical designs, which consist of a 3×3 convolution, ReLU, and another 1×1 convolution.

Detection in z Axis. The remaining task is to estimate the center height for each proposal. Firstly, we obtain the proposals with P largest confidences on the 2D heatmap $\hat{\mathbf{H}}^{(xy)}$ after applying non-maximum suppression (NMS). We set $P = 10$ in all the experiments. Subsequently, we extract the corresponding 1D "columns" for each proposal from the aggregated feature volume $\mathbf{V}$, denoted as $\mathbf{F}^{(z)} \in \mathbb{R}^{P \times K \times H}$, which is then fed into a 1D fully convolutional network to regress the height. Similar to 2D detection, our model generates 1D heatmap estimation $\hat{\mathbf{H}}^{(z)} \in [0,1]^{P \times H}$, indicating the likelihood of human presence at every possible height. We compute a GT 1D heatmap $\mathbf{H}^{(z)}$ for each proposal based on its center height using the Gaussian distribution. Likewise, we use an MSE loss here:

$$\mathcal{L}_{1d} = \frac{1}{P} \sum_{p=1}^{P} \sum_{k=1}^{H} \|\mathbf{H}_{p,k}^{(z)} - \hat{\mathbf{H}}_{p,k}^{(z)}\|_2 \tag{4}$$

Finally, we select the height with the maximum confidence and by combining it with the 2D box center, offset and size, we can obtain the 3D bounding box. The overall confidence score for each box is computed by multiplying the scores of 2D heatmap and 1D outputs. According to the exponential property of the Gaussian function, it can be regarded as an approximate of the 3D Gaussian distribution. We set a threshold for confidence scores to select the valid proposals. To sum up, the overall training objective is as follows:

$$\mathcal{L}_{HDN} = \mathcal{L}_{2d} + \lambda_{size}\mathcal{L}_{size} + \lambda_{off}\mathcal{L}_{off} + \lambda_{1d}\mathcal{L}_{1d} \tag{5}$$

where we set $\lambda_{size} = 0.02$, $\lambda_{off} = 0.1$ and $\lambda_{1d} = 1$.

3.3   Joint Localization Networks

Person-specific Feature Volume. With the bounding box of each person, we construct its fine-grained feature volume to predict the final 3D pose. We first crop a smaller feature volume $\mathbf{V}'$ from $\mathbf{V}$ centered at the box center with a fixed size (*i.e.* 2m × 2m × 2m). It suffices to cover arbitrary poses and maintains the relative scale of the motion space. The space is then divided into $L' \times W' \times H'$ voxels. Now the key step is to **zero out** the features outside the estimated bounding box to get the person-specific feature volume $\mathbf{V_s}$. This masking mechanism reduces the distraction of other people and enables safe volume re-projection in the following stage.

Joint Localization. To reduce the computational cost, we re-project $\mathbf{V_s}$ onto three orthogonal 2D planes, *i.e.* the xy plane, xz plane and yz planes in the world coordinate systems. Let $\mathbf{P}^{(xy)} \in \mathbb{R}^{K \times L' \times W'}$, $\mathbf{P}^{(xz)} \in \mathbb{R}^{K \times L' \times H'}$ and $\mathbf{P}^{(yz)} \in \mathbb{R}^{K \times W' \times H'}$ denote the re-projected feature maps corresponding to the three planes, respectively. Again, we use max-pooling for feature projection.

Subsequently, they are concatenated as a batch and fed to a 2D CNN for joint localization, as shown in Fig. 4. Note that we set the same granularity of voxels on different axes to enable parallel estimation, *i.e.* $L' = W' = H'$. The 2D CNN produces a joint-wise heatmap estimation for each re-projection plane, denoted as $\hat{\mathbf{H}}^{(t)}(t \in \{xy, xz, yz\})$ in the same shape of $\mathbf{P}^{(t)}$. To reduce the quantization error, we compute the center of mass of $\hat{\mathbf{H}}^{(t)}$ instead of taking the maximum responses. Specifically, the estimated positions $\hat{\mathbf{J}}^{(t)} \in \mathbb{R}^{K \times 2}$ are computed by:

$$\hat{\mathbf{J}}^{(xy)} = \sum_{i=1}^{L} \sum_{j=1}^{W} (i,j) \cdot \hat{\mathbf{H}}_{i,j}^{(xy)}, \hat{\mathbf{J}}^{(xz)} = \sum_{i=1}^{L} \sum_{k=1}^{H} (i,k) \cdot \hat{\mathbf{H}}_{i,k}^{(xz)}, \hat{\mathbf{J}}^{(yz)} = \sum_{j=1}^{W} \sum_{k=1}^{H} (j,k) \cdot \hat{\mathbf{H}}_{j,k}^{(yz)} \tag{6}$$

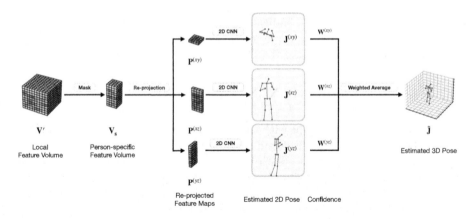

Fig. 4. Joint Localization Networks. For each person, we first construct its local feature volume $\mathbf{V}'$. The person-specific feature volume $\mathbf{V_s}$ is obtained by masking $\mathbf{V}'$ with the detected 3D box. We re-project $\mathbf{V_s}$ to three orthogonal coordinate planes to get the 2D feature maps $\mathbf{P}^{(t)}$. A shared 2D pose estimator regresses the joint locations $\mathbf{J}^{(t)}$ for each plane, and a confidence network computes the corresponding weights $\mathbf{W}^{(t)}$. Finally, the 3D pose $\tilde{\mathbf{J}}$ is computed by weighting $\mathbf{J}^{(t)}$ with $\mathbf{W}^{(t)}$ in a pairwise manner. ($t \in \{xy, xz, yz\}$)

We supervise the estimations with the ground-truth 2D location $\mathbf{J}^{(t)} \in \mathbb{R}^{K \times 2}$ on each plane. An L_1 loss is computed by:

$$\mathcal{L}_{hm} = \sum_t \sum_{k=1}^{K} \|\mathbf{J}_k^{(t)} - \hat{\mathbf{J}}_k^{(t)}\|_1 \tag{7}$$

Adaptive Weighted Fusion. The quality of $\mathbf{P}^{(t)}$ and the difficulty of pose estimation naturally vary with the re-projection plane and human pose, thus we hope the model could learn to discriminate and balance the estimations from different planes automatically. To achieve this, we introduce a lightweight confidence regression network. We assume that the pattern of $\hat{\mathbf{H}}^{(t)}$ could reflect the quality of 2D pose estimation. Therefore, the estimated heatmaps $\hat{\mathbf{H}}^{(t)}$ are fed into a shared confidence regression network. Inspired by [58], we adopt a simple design for the confidence regression network, consisting of a convolutional layer, a global average pooling layer and one fully-connected layer.

The network generates joint-wise fusion weight for each plane, denoted as $\mathbf{W}^{(t)} \in \mathbb{R}^{K}$. We then use the Softmax function for normalization in a pair-wise manner and obtain the final 3D prediction $\tilde{\mathbf{J}} \in \mathbb{R}^{K \times 3}$. Specifically, for the joint k, the final estimations can be computed by:

$$\tilde{\mathbf{J}}_{k,1} = \text{softmax}(\mathbf{W}_k^{(xy)}, \mathbf{W}_k^{(xz)}) \cdot (\hat{\mathbf{J}}_{k,1}^{(xy)}, \hat{\mathbf{J}}_{k,1}^{(xz)})$$
$$\tilde{\mathbf{J}}_{k,2} = \text{softmax}(\mathbf{W}_k^{(xy)}, \mathbf{W}_k^{(yz)}) \cdot (\hat{\mathbf{J}}_{k,2}^{(xy)}, \hat{\mathbf{J}}_{k,1}^{(yz)}) \qquad (8)$$
$$\tilde{\mathbf{J}}_{k,3} = \text{softmax}(\mathbf{W}_k^{(xz)}, \mathbf{W}_k^{(yz)}) \cdot (\hat{\mathbf{J}}_{k,2}^{(xz)}, \hat{\mathbf{J}}_{k,2}^{(yz)})$$

where $\hat{\mathbf{J}}_{k,1}^{(xy)}$ denotes taking the first component of the 2D estimated coordinates of $\hat{\mathbf{J}}_k^{(xy)}$, namely the component on the x-axis, and the other notations have similar interpretations. Let $\mathbf{J}$ denote the GT 3D pose, we use an L_1 loss to train the confidence regression network:

$$\mathcal{L}_{conf} = \sum_{k=1}^{K} \|\mathbf{J}_k - \tilde{\mathbf{J}}_k\|_1 \qquad (9)$$

Now we get the overall training objective of JLN as follows. In our experiments, we set $\lambda_{conf} = 1$.

$$\mathcal{L}_{JLN} = \mathcal{L}_{hm} + \lambda_{conf}\mathcal{L}_{conf} \qquad (10)$$

4   Experiments

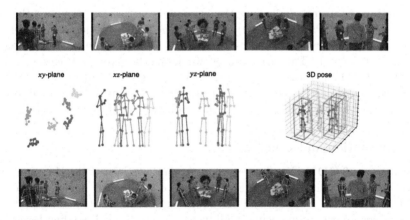

Fig. 5. Qualitative Results on the CMU Panoptic Dataset. The first row illustrates the estimated root joints in HDN. The second row shows the estimated 2D poses on the three orthogonal re-projection planes and the fused 3D pose in JLN. The last row shows the 2D back-projection of the estimated 3D pose to each camera view.

4.1   Setup

Datasets. The Shelf [2] dataset captures four people disassembling a shelf using five cameras. We select the frames of test set following previous works [22,38]. The Campus [2] dataset captures multiple people interacting with each other in an outdoor environment shot by three cameras. The CMU Panoptic [19] dataset captures multiple people engaging in social activities. We use the same training and testing sequences captured by five HD cameras as in [22,38].

Training Strategies. Due to incomplete annotations of Shelf and Campus, we use synthetic 3D poses to train the model for the two datasets, following [22,38]. For the Panoptic dataset, we first finetune the 2D heatmap estimation network. Then we fix the 2D network and train the 3D networks following [38].

Table 1. Quantitative Evaluation of HDN. We measure the mean center error, precision and recall rate to evaluate the quality of human center detection and offset regression. The IoU score is computed between the estimated horizontal bounding box and GT, which additionally reflects the precision of bounding box size estimation.

Mean Center Error (mm)	Precision	Recall	IoU
53.73	0.9982	0.9985	0.757

Evaluation Metrics. Following the common practice, we compute the Percentage of Correct Parts (PCP3D) metric on Shelf and Campus. Specifically, we pair each GT pose with the closest estimation and calculate the percentage of correct parts. For the Panoptic dataset, we adopt the Average Precision (AP_K) and Mean Per Joint Position Error (MPJPE) as metrics, which reflect the quality of multi-person 3D pose estimation more comprehensively. In addition, we measure the inference time and frame per second (FPS) on the Panoptic dataset.

4.2   Evaluation and Comparison

Evaluation of HDN. We first evaluate the performance of the Human Detection Networks qualitatively. As Fig. 5 shows, our model is able to detect the human centers and estimate the 3D bounding boxes as intended, despite the fact that severe occlusion occurs in all views. Accurate 3D bounding boxes help to isolate the persons for the fine-grained joint localization. In addition, we quantitatively measure the performance of HDN in terms of both center position and bounding box. As Table 1 shows, our HDN localizes the root joint well, and the regressed bounding boxes overlap with GT mostly. The mean center error is larger than the MPJPE of JLN because JLN involves detailed pose estimation on a finer voxel granularity. Still, the center precision suffices to provide a reasonable 3D bounding box for joint localization.

Table 2. Comparison with SOTA on Campus and Shelf. We compute the PCP3D (Percentage of Correct Parts) metrics following previous work. A part is considered correct if its distance with GT is at most half of the limb length.

Method	Shelf				Campus			
	Actor1	Actor2	Actor3	Average	Actor1	Actor2	Actor3	Average
Belagiannis *et al.* [2]	66.1	65.0	83.2	71.4	82.0	72.4	73.7	75.8
Belagiannis *et al.* [4]	75.0	67.0	86.0	76.0	83.0	73.0	78.0	78.0
Belagiannis *et al.* [3]	75.3	69.7	87.6	77.5	93.5	75.7	84.4	84.5
Ershadi-Nasab *et al.* [11]	93.3	75.9	94.8	88.0	94.2	92.9	84.6	90.6
Dong *et al.* [9]	98.8	94.1	97.8	96.9	97.6	93.3	98.0	96.3
Huang *et al.* [16]	98.8	96.2	97.2	97.4	98.0	94.8	97.4	96.7
Tu *et al.* [38]	99.3	94.1	97.6	97.0	97.6	93.8	98.8	96.7
Lin *et al.* [22]	99.3	96.5	98.0	97.9	98.4	93.7	99.0	97.0
Wang *et al.* [44]	99.3	95.1	97.8	97.4	98.2	94.1	97.4	96.6
Ours	99.4	96.0	97.5	97.6	96.5	94.1	97.9	96.2

Table 3. Comparison with SOTA on Panoptic. For efficiency metrics, We measure the average per-sample inference time on Panoptics test set (5 camera views, 3.41 person per frame). The measurement is done on a Linux machine with GPU GeForce RTX 2080 Ti and CPU Intel(R) Xeon(R) CPU E5-2699A v4 @ 2.40 GHz. Batch size is set to be 1 for all methods.

Method	AP_{25}	AP_{50}	AP_{100}	AP_{150}	MPJPE	Time	FPS
VoxelPose [38]	83.59	98.33	99.76	99.91	17.68 mm	316.0 ms	3.2
PlaneSweepPose [22]	92.12	98.96	99.81	99.84	16.75 mm	234.3 ms	4.3
MvP [44]	92.28	96.60	97.45	97.69	15.76 mm	278.8 ms	3.6
Ours	85.22	98.08	99.32	99.48	18.26 mm	32.2 ms	31.1

Evaluation of JLN. We compare the 3D pose estimation performance with the state-of-the-art (SOTA) multi-view multi-person 3D pose estimation methods on Shelf and Campus [2]. While the proposed method is primarily optimized for inference efficiency and makes several approximations, it performs competitively with SOTA as shown in Table 2. On the Shelf dataset, it outperforms the SOTA volumetric approach VoxelPose [38] which features fully 3D convolutional architecture. We also train and test on the Panoptic [19] dataset following the most recent works [22,38]. As shown in Table 3, our method receives an extra per-joint error of about 2mm. We argue that the error margin is within an acceptable range given the speed-accuracy trade-off in real-time applications.

Efficiency. We first compare the inference speed of our method to the SOTA methods, and then conduct an in-depth efficiency analysis. The speed results of other methods are obtained using their official codes on the same hardware as ours. For a fair comparison, we set the batch size to be one for all methods during inference following [44] to simulate the real-time use case where data arrives frame by frame. The batch size of PlaneSweepPose [22] was set to be 64 in the original paper so their reported speed is different from the one reported in this paper. For all the methods, the off-the-shelf 2D pose estimator time is not measured following [22,44]. The results on the Panoptic dataset are shown in Table 3. Our approach shows a considerable advantage in terms of inference speed and supports real-time inference.

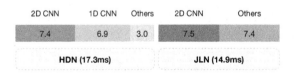

Fig. 6. Time Cost Visualization. We visualize the average inference time cost for each module on the Panoptic test set in milliseconds (ms). It takes 32.2 ms in total.

The inference time broken down per module is shown in Fig. 6. The "others" parts mainly consist of data preparation and feature volume construction. For HDN, the time cost is independent of the number of cameras and persons. For JLN, the theoretical computation complexity is linear to the number of persons. In practice, feature maps of different persons are concatenated as a batch and inferred in a single feedforward. As we only use the re-projected 2D feature maps, the batch size could be large enough to cover very crowded scenes. In general, the time cost of our method is mainly determined by voxel granularity. By using $2\times$ coarser voxel, its computation complexity could be reduced to $\frac{1}{4}$. The voxel granularity selection serves as a trade-off between speed and accuracy.

Finally, we analyze the scalability of our method and compare it with the existing methods. Consider applying the algorithms to a challenging scenario that is much larger and more crowded than the current datasets [2,19]. In order to retain a reasonable coverage, the number of cameras needs to grow proportionally [48,53]. VoxelPose [38] uses massive 3D convolution operations that are computation-intensive, and its efficiency disadvantage would be enlarged when scaling. PlaneSweepPose [22] needs to enumerate the depth planes for every pair of camera views and persons. As a result, the computation complexity increases in polynomials regarding the number of cameras and persons. For example, simply shifting from Campus (3 persons, 3 cameras) to Shelf (4 persons, 5 cameras) slows PlaneSweepPose by $2.6\times$ according to [22] ($1.3\times$ for our method). MvP [44] uses projective attention to integrate the multi-view information, and its time cost also grows quadratically as camera number increases. As previously analyzed, our method does not involve explicit view-person association, and its speed is mainly affected by the granularity of space division. We argue that the above characteristics make our method more scalable to large, crowded scenes than the previous methods. We deployed our model to a basketball court and a retail store where the space size is 16m×16m with 12 cameras and 10 people. Our inference time increases by 28.8% compared to that on Panoptic (8m × 8m, 5 cameras, 3.4 person).

4.3   Ablation Study

Table 4. Ablation Study Results. Our full approach is (a). From (b) to (e), we study the effect of volume feature masking, weighted fusion and camera views respectively.

Method	#Views	Mask	Weighted	AP_{25}	AP_{50}	AP_{100}	AP_{150}	MPJPE
(a)	5	✓	✓	85.22	98.08	99.32	99.48	18.26 mm
(b)	5		✓	72.05	96.75	99.10	99.39	21.07 mm
(c)	5	✓		77.23	97.61	99.18	99.48	20.11 mm
(d)	4	✓	✓	73.95	97.02	99.21	99.35	21.12 mm
(e)	3	✓	✓	53.68	91.89	97.40	98.30	26.13 mm

Table 5. Influence of Voxel Granularity. We additionally report the MACs (Multiply-Accumulate Operations) and number of parameters of the networks.

JLN Voxels	AP_{25}	AP_{50}	AP_{100}	AP_{150}	MPJPE	MACs	Parameters
$64 \times 64 \times 64$	85.22	98.08	99.32	99.48	18.26 mm	8.670G	1.236 M
$48 \times 48 \times 48$	78.76	97.14	98.99	99.14	19.66 mm	4.877G	1.210 M
$32 \times 32 \times 32$	73.20	97.37	98.93	99.08	20.47 mm	2.167G	1.190 M

We train some ablated models to study the impact of the individual factors. All the ablation experiments are evaluated on CMU Panoptic [19], and the results are shown in Table 4.

Feature Masking. In (b), we remove the masking step and directly use the local feature volume $\mathbf{V}'$ in JLN. This is equivalent to using a fixed bounding box size as [38]. The degraded performance indicates that the masking mechanism indeed reduces the ambiguity and helps joint localization.

Adaptive Weighted Fusion. In (c), we simply take the mean of the estimated coordinates from different planes to compute the final result. The performance gap suggests that the learned confidence weights emphasize the more reliable estimations as intended.

Number of Cameras. In (d)-(e), we compare the performance under different camera numbers. The accuracy drops with fewer camera views as the feature volume coverage is weakened.

Granularity of Voxels. We study the impact of voxel granularity on both efficiency and accuracy. Table 5. shows models trained with different JLN voxel sizes. By reducing the number of voxels (effectively increasing the individual voxel size), the error increases slightly, while the inference efficiency additionally improves. It inspires us to balance the trade-off between speed and accuracy in real usage.

5 Conclusion

In this paper, we present a novel method for 3D human pose estimation from multi-view images. Our pipeline uniquely integrates the feature volume reprojection to both human detection and joint localization, which substitutes the computation-intensive 3D convolutions. Experiment results prove the effectiveness of the proposed HDN and JLN. The accelerated inference demonstrates the potential of our method in real-time applications, especially for large scenes.

Acknowledgement. This work was supported in part by MOST-2018AAA0102004 and NSFC-62061136001.

References

1. Ahuja, K., Ofek, E., Gonzalez-Franco, M., Holz, C., Wilson, A.D.: Coolmoves: user motion accentuation in virtual reality. In: IMWUT (2021)
2. Belagiannis, V., Amin, S., Andriluka, M., Schiele, B., Navab, N., Ilic, S.: 3D pictorial structures for multiple human pose estimation. In: CVPR (2014)
3. Belagiannis, V., Amin, S., Andriluka, M., Schiele, B., Navab, N., Ilic, S.: 3D pictorial structures revisited: Multiple human pose estimation. IEEE Transactions on Pattern Analysis and Machine Intelligence (2015)
4. Belagiannis, V., Wang, X., Schiele, B., Fua, P., Ilic, S., Navab, N.: Multiple human pose estimation with temporally consistent 3D pictorial structures. In: Agapito, L., Bronstein, M.M., Rother, C. (eds.) ECCV 2014. LNCS, vol. 8925, pp. 742–754. Springer, Cham (2015). https://doi.org/10.1007/978-3-319-16178-5_52
5. Bridgeman, L., Volino, M., Guillemaut, J.Y., Hilton, A.: Multi-person 3D pose estimation and tracking in sports. In: CVPR Workshops (2019)
6. Bultmann, S., Behnke, S.: Real-time multi-view 3D human pose estimation using semantic feedback to smart edge sensors. In: RSS (2021)
7. Cheng, Y., Yang, B., Wang, B., Yan, W., Tan, R.T.: Occlusion-Aware networks for 3D human pose estimation in video. In: ICCV (2019)
8. Ci, H., Wang, C., Ma, X., Wang, Y.: Optimizing network structure for 3D human pose estimation. In: ICCV (2019)
9. Dong, J., Jiang, W., Huang, Q., Bao, H., Zhou, X.: Fast and robust multi-person 3D pose estimation from multiple views (2019)
10. Dong, J., Shuai, Q., Zhang, Y., Liu, X., Zhou, X., Bao, H.: Motion capture from internet videos. In: Vedaldi, A., Bischof, H., Brox, T., Frahm, J.-M. (eds.) ECCV 2020. LNCS, vol. 12347, pp. 210–227. Springer, Cham (2020). https://doi.org/10.1007/978-3-030-58536-5_13

11. Ershadi-Nasab, S., Noury, E., Kasaei, S., Sanaei, E.: Multiple human 3D pose estimation from multiview images. Multimed. Tools Appl. **77**(12), 15573–15601 (2017). https://doi.org/10.1007/s11042-017-5133-8
12. Fabbri, M., Lanzi, F., Calderara, S., Alletto, S., Cucchiara, R.: Compressed volumetric heatmaps for multi-person 3D pose estimation. In: CVPR (2020)
13. Fang, H.S., Xie, S., Tai, Y.W., Lu, C.: RMPE: regional multi-person pose estimation. In: ICCV (2017)
14. Hartley, R., Zisserman, A.: Multiple view geometry in computer vision, 2nd edn. Cambridge University Press, USA (2003)
15. He, Y., Yan, R., Fragkiadaki, K., Yu, S.I.: Epipolar transformers. In: CVPR, pp. 7779–7788 (2020)
16. Huang, C., et al.: End-to-end dynamic matching network for multi-view multi-person 3D pose estimation. In: Vedaldi, A., Bischof, H., Brox, T., Frahm, J.-M. (eds.) ECCV 2020. LNCS, vol. 12373, pp. 477–493. Springer, Cham (2020). https://doi.org/10.1007/978-3-030-58604-1_29
17. Iskakov, K., Burkov, E., Lempitsky, V., Malkov, Y.: Learnable triangulation of human pose (2019)
18. Jansen, Y., Hornbæk, K.: How relevant are incidental power poses for HCI? In: CHI (2018)
19. Joo, H., et al.: Panoptic studio: a massively multiview system for social motion capture. In: ICCV (2015)
20. Li, C., Lee, G.H.: Generating multiple hypotheses for 3D human pose estimation with mixture density network. In: CVPR (2019)
21. Li, Z., Ye, J., Song, M., Huang, Y., Pan, Z.: Online knowledge distillation for efficient pose estimation. In: ICCV (2021)
22. Lin, J., Lee, G.H.: Multi-view multi-person 3D pose estimation with plane sweep stereo. In: CVPR (2021)
23. Liu, F., Liu, X.: Voxel-based 3D detection and reconstruction of multiple objects from a single image. In: NeurIPS (2021)
24. Ma, X., Su, J., Wang, C., Ci, H., Wang, Y.: Context modeling in 3D human pose estimation: a unified perspective. In: CVPR (2021)
25. Mehta, D., et al.: VNect: real-time 3D human pose estimation with a single RGB camera (2017)
26. Pavlakos, G., Zhou, X., Derpanis, K.G., Daniilidis, K.: Harvesting multiple views for marker-less 3D human pose annotations. In: CVPR (2017)
27. Pavllo, D., Feichtenhofer, C., Grangier, D., Auli, M.: 3D human pose estimation in video with temporal convolutions and semi-supervised training. In: CVPR (2019)
28. Qiu, H., Wang, C., Wang, J., Wang, N., Zeng, W.: Cross view fusion for 3D human pose estimation. In: ICCV (2019)
29. Ramanathan, V., Huang, J., Abu-El-Haija, S., Gorban, A., Murphy, K., Fei-Fei, L.: Detecting events and key actors in multi-person videos. In: CVPR (2016)
30. Reddy, N.D., Guigues, L., Pischulini, L., Eledath, J., Narasimhan, S.: Tessetrack: end-to-end learnable multi-person articulated 3D pose tracking. In: CVPR (2021)
31. Reddy, N.D., Guigues, L., Pishchulin, L., Eledath, J., Narasimhan, S.G.: Tessetrack: End-to-end learnable multi-person articulated 3d pose tracking. In: Proceedings of the IEEE/CVF Conference on Computer Vision and Pattern Recognition, pp. 15190–15200 (2021)
32. Remelli, E., Han, S., Honari, S., Fua, P., Wang, R.: Lightweight multi-view 3D pose estimation through camera-disentangled representation. In: CVPR (2020)

33. Rukhovich, D., Vorontsova, A., Konushin, A.: ImvoxelNet: image to voxels projection for monocular and multi-view general-purpose 3d object detection. In: WACV (2022)

34. Sharma, S., Varigonda, P.T., Bindal, P., Sharma, A., Jain, A.: Monocular 3D human pose estimation by generation and ordinal ranking. In: ICCV (2019)

35. Shen, X., et al.: Towards fast and accurate multi-person pose estimation on mobile devices. In: IJCAI (2021)

36. Shi, L., Zhang, Y., Cheng, J., Lu, H.: Skeleton-based action recognition with directed graph neural networks. In: CVPR (2019)

37. Sun, K., Xiao, B., Liu, D., Wang, J.: Deep high-resolution representation learning for human pose estimation. In: CVPR (2019)

38. Tu, H., Wang, C., Zeng, W.: VoxelPose: towards multi-camera 3D human pose estimation in wild environment. In: Vedaldi, A., Bischof, H., Brox, T., Frahm, J.-M. (eds.) ECCV 2020. LNCS, vol. 12346, pp. 197–212. Springer, Cham (2020). https://doi.org/10.1007/978-3-030-58452-8_12

39. Wang, C., Flynn, J., Wang, Y., Yuille, A.: Recognizing actions in 3D using action-snippets and activated simplices. In: Thirtieth AAAI Conference on Artificial Intelligence (2016)

40. Wang, C., Wang, Y., Lin, Z., Yuille, A.L.: Robust 3D human pose estimation from single images or video sequences. IEEE Trans. Pattern Anal. Mach. Intell. **41**(5), 1227–1241 (2018)

41. Wang, C., Wang, Y., Lin, Z., Yuille, A.L., Gao, W.: Robust estimation of 3D human poses from a single image. In: Proceedings of the IEEE Conference on Computer Vision and Pattern Recognition, pp. 2361–2368 (2014)

42. Wang, C., Wang, Y., Yuille, A.L.: An approach to pose-based action recognition. In: Proceedings of the IEEE Conference on Computer Vision and Pattern Recognition, pp. 915–922 (2013)

43. Wang, C., Wang, Y., Yuille, A.L.: Mining 3D key-pose-motifs for action recognition. In: Proceedings of the IEEE Conference on Computer Vision and Pattern Recognition, pp. 2639–2647 (2016)

44. Wang, T., Zhang, J., Cai, Y., Yan, S., Feng, J.: Direct multi-view multi-person 3D human pose estimation. In: Advances in Neural Information Processing Systems (2021)

45. Wang, X., Ang, M.H., Lee, G.H.: Voxel-based network for shape completion by leveraging edge generation. In: ICCV (2021)

46. Weng, C.Y., Curless, B., Kemelmacher-Shlizerman, I.: Photo wake-up: 3D character animation from a single photo. In: CVPR (2019)

47. Wu, S., et al.: Graph-Based 3D Multi-Person pose estimation using Multi-View images. In: ICCV (2021)

48. Xu, J., Zhong, F., Wang, Y.: Learning multi-agent coordination for enhancing target coverage in directional sensor networks. In: Advances in Neural Information Processing Systems (2020)

49. Xu, L., et al.: ViPNAS: efficient video pose estimation via neural architecture search. In: CVPR (2021)

50. Yan, S., Xiong, Y., Lin, D.: Spatial temporal graph convolutional networks for skeleton-based action recognition. In: AAAI (2018)

51. Yu, Z., et al.: HUMBI: a large multiview dataset of human body expressions. In: CVPR (2020)

52. Zhang, F., Zhu, X., Ye, M.: Fast human pose estimation. In: CVPR (2019)

53. Zhang, S., Staudt, E., Faltemier, T., Roy-chowdhury, A.K.: A camera network tracking (camnet) dataset and performance baseline. In: WACV (2015)

54. Zhang, Y., Wang, C., Wang, X., Liu, W., Zeng, W.: Voxeltrack: multi-person 3D human pose estimation and tracking in the wild. arXiv preprint arXiv:2108.02452
55. Zhang, Y., Wang, C., Wang, X., Liu, W., Zeng, W.: Voxeltrack: multi-person 3D human pose estimation and tracking in the wild. IEEE Transactions on Pattern Analysis and Machine Intelligence (2022)
56. Zhang, Y., An, L., Yu, T., Li, x., Li, K., Liu, Y.: 4D association graph for realtime multi-person motion capture using multiple video cameras. In: CVPR (2020)
57. Zhang, Z., Wang, C., Qin, W., Zeng, W.: Fusing wearable IMUs with multi-view images for human pose estimation: a geometric approach. In: Proceedings of the IEEE/CVF Conference on Computer Vision and Pattern Recognition, pp. 2200–2209 (2020)
58. Zhang, Z., Wang, C., Qiu, W., Qin, W., Zeng, W.: AdaFuse: adaptive multiview fusion for accurate human pose estimation in the wild. Int. J. Comput. Vision **129**(3), 703–718 (2021)
59. Zheng, C., Zhu, S., Mendieta, M., Yang, T., Chen, C., Ding, Z.: 3D human pose estimation with spatial and temporal transformers. In: ICCV (2021)
60. Zhong, Y., Zhu, M., Peng, H.: VIN: voxel-based implicit network for joint 3D object detection and segmentation for lidars (2021)
61. Zhou, K., Han, X., Jiang, N., Jia, K., Lu, J.: Hemlets pose: learning part-centric heatmap triplets for accurate 3D human pose estimation. In: ICCV (2019)
62. Zhou, X., Wang, D., Krähenbühl, P.: Objects as points. In: CVPR (2019)
63. Zhu, L., Rematas, K., Curless, B., Seitz, S.M., Kemelmacher-Shlizerman, I.: Reconstructing NBA players. In: Vedaldi, A., Bischof, H., Brox, T., Frahm, J.-M. (eds.) ECCV 2020. LNCS, vol. 12350, pp. 177–194. Springer, Cham (2020). https://doi.org/10.1007/978-3-030-58558-7_11

Learning to Fit Morphable Models

Vasileios Choutas[1,2]([✉]), Federica Bogo[2], Jingjing Shen[2], and Julien Valentin[2]

[1] Max Planck Institute for Intelligent Systems, Tübingen, Germany
vchoutas@tue.mpg.de
[2] Microsoft, Redmond, USA
fbogo@fb.com, {jinshen,valentin,julien}@microsoft.com

Abstract. Fitting parametric models of human bodies, hands or faces to sparse input signals in an accurate, robust, and fast manner has the promise of significantly improving immersion in AR and VR scenarios. A common first step in systems that tackle these problems is to regress the parameters of the parametric model directly from the input data. This approach is fast, robust, and is a good starting point for an iterative minimization algorithm. The latter searches for the minimum of an energy function, typically composed of a data term and priors that encode our knowledge about the problem's structure. While this is undoubtedly a very successful recipe, priors are often hand defined heuristics and finding the right balance between the different terms to achieve high quality results is a non-trivial task. Furthermore, converting and optimizing these systems to run in a performant way requires custom implementations that demand significant time investments from both engineers and domain experts. In this work, we build upon recent advances in learned optimization and propose an update rule inspired by the classic Levenberg-Marquardt algorithm. We show the effectiveness of the proposed neural optimizer on three problems, 3D body estimation from a head-mounted device, 3D body estimation from sparse 2D keypoints and face surface estimation from dense 2D landmarks. Our method can easily be applied to new model fitting problems and offers a competitive alternative to well-tuned 'traditional' model fitting pipelines, both in terms of accuracy and speed.

1 Introduction

Fitting parametric models [3,19,31,51,54,71] to noisy input data is one of the most common tasks in computer vision. Notable examples include fitting 3D body [8,13,21,36,38,51,68], face [19], and hands [4,9,25,59].

Direct regression using neural networks is the de facto default tool to estimate model parameters from observations. While the obtained predictions are robust

---

V. Choutas—Work performed at Microsoft.
F. Bogo—Now at Meta Reality Labs Research.

Supplementary Information The online version contains supplementary material available at https://doi.org/10.1007/978-3-031-20068-7_10.

© The Author(s), under exclusive license to Springer Nature Switzerland AG 2022
S. Avidan et al. (Eds.): ECCV 2022, LNCS 13666, pp. 160–179, 2022.
https://doi.org/10.1007/978-3-031-20068-7_10

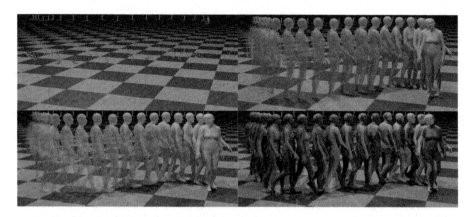

Fig. 1. Top: Head and hand tracking signals from AR/VR devices (left) and the corresponding body model fit obtained from regression followed by iterative mathematical optimization. Bottom: Body model fit obtained from our learned optimizer (left), overlaid with the ground-truth (right). Learned optimizers are fast, able to tightly fit the input data and require significantly less manual labor to achieve this result. All results are estimated independently per-frame.

and accurate to a large extent, they often fail to tightly fit the observations [78] and require large quantities of annotated data. Classic optimization methods, e.g. the Levenberg-Marquardt (LM) algorithm [40,46], can tightly fit the parametric model to the data by iteratively minimizing a hand-crafted energy function, but are prone to local minimas and require good starting points for fast convergence. Hence, practitioners combine these two approaches to benefit from their complementary strengths, initializing the model parameters from a regressor, followed by energy minimization using a classic optimizer.

If we look one level deeper, optimization-based model fitting methods have another disadvantage of often requiring hand-crafted energy functions that are difficult to define and non-trivial to tune. Besides the data terms, each fitting problem effectively requires the definition of their own prior terms and regularization terms. Besides the work required to formulate these terms and train the priors, domain experts needs to spend significant amounts of time to balance the effect of each term. Since these priors are often hand-defined or assumed to follow distributions that are tractable/easy to optimize, the resulting fitting energy usually contains biases that can limit the accuracy of the resulting fits.

To get the best of both regression using deep learning and classical numerical optimization, we turn to the field of machine learning based continuous optimization [2,14,56,57,60,77]. Here, instead of updating the model parameters using a first or second order model fitter, a network learns to iteratively update the parameters that minimize the target loss, with the added benefit of optimized ML back-ends for fast inference. End-to-end network training removes the need for hand-crafted priors, since the model learns them directly from data.

Inspired by the properties of the popular Levenberg-Marquardt and Adam [34] algorithms, our main contribution extends the system presented in [60] with an iterative machine learning solver which (i) keeps information from previous iterations, (ii) controls the learning rate of each variable independently and (iii) combines updates from gradient descent and from a network that is capable of swiftly reducing the fitting energy, for robustness and convergence speed. We evaluate our approach on different challenging scenarios: full-body tracking from head and hand inputs only, e.g. given by a device like the HoloLens 2, body estimation from 2D keypoints and face tracking from 2D landmarks, demonstrating both high quality results and versatility of the proposed framework.

2   Related Work

Learning to Optimize [2,56,57] is a field that, casts optimization as a learning problem. The goal is to create models that learn to exploit the problem structure, producing faster and more effective energy minimizers. In this way, we can remove the need for hand-designed parameter update rules and priors, since we can learn them directly from the data. This approach has been used for image denoising and depth-from-stereo estimation [66], rigid motion estimation [43], view synthesis [22], joint estimation of motion and scene geometry [14], nonlinear tomographic inversion problem with simulated data [1], face alignment [70] and object reconstruction from a single image [37].

Parametric Human Model Fitting: The seminal work of Blanz and Vetter [7] introduced a parametric model of human faces and a user-assisted method to fit the model to images. Since then, the field has evolved and produced better face models and faster, more accurate and more robust estimation methods [19]. With the introduction of SMPL [42], the field of 3D body pose and shape estimation has been rapidly progressing. The community has created large motion databases [44] from motion capture data, as well as datasets, both real and synthetic, with images and corresponding 3D body ground-truth [24,45,50]. Thanks to these, we can now train neural network regressors that can reliably predict SMPL parameters from images [30,32,38,39,41,78] and videos [12,35]. With the introduction of expressive models [31,51,71], the latest regression approaches [13,21,55] can now predict the 3D body, face and hands. However, one common issue, present in all regression scenarios, is the misalignment of the predictions and the input data [58,78]. Thus, they often serve as the initial point for an optimization-based method [8,51,68], which refines the estimated parameters until some convergence criterion is met. This combination produces system that are effective, robust and able to work in real-time and under challenging conditions [47,59,62]. These hybrid regression-optimization systems are also effective pseudo annotators for in-the-wild images [38], where standard capture technologies are not applicable. However, formulating the correct energy terms and finding the right balance between them is a challenging and time-consuming task. Furthermore, adapting the optimizer to run in real-time is a non-trivial operation, even when using popular algorithms such as the Levenberg-Marquardt algorithm [28,40,46] which has a cubic complexity. Thus, explicitly computing the Jacobian [14,43] is often prohibitive in practice, either in terms of memory or runtime. The most common and practical way to speedup the optimization is to utilize the sparsity of the problem or make certain assumptions to simplify it [20]. Learned optimizers promise to overcome these issues, by learning the parametric model priors directly from the data and taking more aggressive steps, thus converging in fewer iterations. The effectiveness of these approaches has been demonstrated in different scenarios, such as fitting a body model [42,71] to images [60,77] and videos [75], to sparse sensor data from electromagnetic sensors [33] and multi-body estimation from multi-view images [17].

We propose a new update rule, computed as a weighted combination of the gradient descent step and the network update [60], where their relative weights are a function of the residuals. Many popular optimizers have an internal memory, such as Adam's [34] running averages, Clark et al.'s [14] and Neural Descent's [77] RNN. We adopt this insight, using an RNN to predict the network update and the combination weights. The network can choose to follow either the gradient or the network direction more, using both current and past residual values.

Estimating 3D human pose from a head-mounted device is a difficult problem, due to self-occlusions caused by the position of the headset and the sparsity of the input signals [72]. Yuan and Kitani [73,74] cast this as a control problem, where a model learns to produce target joint angles for a Proportional-Derivative (PD) controller. Other methods [64,65] tackle this as a learning problem, where a neural network learns to predict the 3D pose from the cameras mounted on the HMD. Guzov et al. [23] use sensor data from IMUs placed on the subject's body and combine them with camera self-localization. They formulate an optimization problem with scene constraints, enabling the capture of long-term motions that respect scene constraints, such as foot contact with the ground. Finally, Dittadi et al. [16] propose a likelihood model that maps head and hand signals to full body poses. In our work, we focus on this scenario and empirically show that the proposed optimizer rule is competitive, both with a classic optimization baseline and a state-of-the-art likelihood model [16].

3   Method

3.1   Neural Fitter

Levenberg-Marquardt (LM) [28,40,46] and Powell's dog leg method (PDL) [52] are examples of popular iterative optimization algorithms used in applications that fit either faces or full human body models to observations. These techniques employ the Gauss-Newton algorithm for both its convergence rate approaching the quadratic regime and its computational efficiency, enabling real-time model fitting applications, e.g. generative face [63,81] and hand [59,62] tracking. For robustness, LM and PDL both combine the Gauss-Newton algorithm and gradient descent, leading to implicit and explicit trust region being used when calculating updates, respectively. In LM, the relative contribution of the approximate Hessian and the identity matrix is weighted by a single scalar that is changing over iterations with its value carried over from one iteration to the next. Given an optimization problem over a set of parameters Θ, LM computes the parameter update $\Delta\Theta$ as the solution of the system $(J^T J + \lambda \mathrm{diag}(J^T J))\Delta\Theta = J^T \mathcal{R}$, where J is the Jacobian and $\mathcal{R}$ are the current residual values. It is interesting to note that several popular optimizers, including ADAGRAD [18] and Adam [34], also carry over information about previous iteration(s), in this case to help control the learning rate for each parameter.

Inspired by the success of these algorithms, we aim at constructing a novel neural optimizer that (a) is easily applicable to different fitting problems, (b) can run at interactive rates without requiring significant efforts, (c) does not require hand crafted priors. (d) carries over information about previous iterations of the solve, (e) controls the learning rate of each parameter independently, (f) for robustness and convergence speed, combines updates from gradient descent and from a method capable of very quickly reducing the fitting energy. Note that the Learned Gradient Descent (LGD) proposed in [60] achieves (a), (b), and (c), but does not consider (d), (e), and (f). As demonstrated experimentally in Sect. 4, each of these additional properties leads to improved results compared to [60], and the best results are achieved when combined together.

Algorithm 1. Neural fitting

Require: Input data D
$\quad \Theta_0 = \Phi(D)$
$\quad h_0 = \Phi_h(D)$
$\quad$**while** not converged **do**
$\quad\quad \Delta\Theta_n, h_n \leftarrow f([g_{n-1}, \Theta_{n-1}], D, h_{n-1})$
$\quad\quad \Theta_n \leftarrow \Theta_{n-1} + u(\Delta\Theta_n, g_{n-1}, \Theta_{n-1})$
$\quad$**end while**

Our proposed neural fitter estimates the values of the parameters Θ by iteratively updating an initial estimate Θ_0, see Algorithm 1. While the initial estimate Θ_0 obtained from a deep neural network Φ might be sufficiently accurate for some applications, we will show that a careful construction of the update rule ($u(.)$ in Algorithm 1) leads to significant improvements after only a few iterations. It is important to note that we do not focus on building the best possible initializer Φ for the fitting tasks at hand, which is the focus of e.g. VIBE [35] and SPIN [38]. That being said, note that these regressors could be leveraged to provide Θ_0 from Algorithm 1. h_0 and h_n are the hidden states of the optimization process. At the n-th iteration in the loop of Algorithm 1, we use a neural network f to predict $\Delta\Theta_n$, and then apply the following update rule:

$$u(\Delta\Theta_n, g_{n-1}, \Theta_{n-1}) = \lambda\Delta\Theta_n + (-\gamma g_{n-1}) \tag{1}$$

$$\lambda, \gamma = f_{\lambda,\gamma}(\mathcal{R}(\Theta_{n-1}), \mathcal{R}(\Theta_{n-1} + \Delta\Theta_n)), \lambda, \gamma \in \mathbb{R}^{|\Theta|} \tag{2}$$

Note that LGD [60] is a special case of Eq. 1, with $\lambda = 1, \gamma = 0$, and with no knowledge preserved across fitting iterations. g_n is the gradient of the target data term w.r.t. to the problem parameters: $g_n = \nabla\mathcal{L}^D$.

The proposed neural fitter satisfies the requirements (a), (b) and (c) in a similar fashion to LGD [60]. In the following, we describe how the properties (d), (e), and (f) outlined earlier in this section are satisfied.

(d): Keeping Track of Past Iterations. The functions $f, f_{\lambda,\gamma}$ are implemented with a Gated Recurrent Unit (GRU) [11]. Unlike previous work, where the learned optimizer only stores past parameter values and the total loss [77], leveraging GRUs allows to learn an abstract representation of the knowledge that is important to use and forget about the previous iteration(s), and of the knowledge about the current iteration that should be preserved.

(e): independent learning rate. When fitting face or body models to data, the variables being optimized over are of different nature. For instance, rotations might be expressed in Euler angles while translation in meters. Since each of these parameter has a different scale and/or unit, it is useful to have per-parameter step size values. Here, we propose to predict vectors λ and γ independently to scale the relative contribution of $\Delta\Theta_n$ and g_n to the update applied to each entry of Θ_n. It is interesting to note that f_λ having knowledge about the current value of residuals at Θ_n and the residual at $\Theta_n + \Delta\Theta_n$, effectively makes use of an estimate of the step direction before setting a step size which is analogous to how line-search operates. Motivated by this observation we tried a few learned versions of line search which yielded similar or inferior results to what we propose here. The alternatives we tried are described in the **Sup. Mat.**.

(f): combining gradient descent and network updates. LM interpolates between Gradient Descent (GD) and Gauss-Newton (GN) using an iteration dependent scalar. LM combines the benefits of both approaches, namely fast convergence near the minimum like GN and large descent steps away from the minimum like GD. In this work, we replace the GN direction, which is often prohibitive to compute, with a network-predicted update, described in Eq. (1). The neural optimizer should learn the optimal descent direction and the relative weights to minimize the data term in as few steps as possible. In the **Sup. Mat.** we provide alternative combinations, e.g. via convex combination, which yielded inferior results in our experiments.

3.2   Human Body Model and Fitting Tasks

Fig. 2. Left to right: 1) Input 6-DoF transformations T_H, T_L, T_R and fingertip positions $P_{i=1,...5}^L, P_{i=1,...5}^R$, given by the head-mounted device, 2) ground-truth mesh, 3) half-space visibility, everything behind the headset is not visible.

We represent the human body using SMPL [42]/SMPL+H [54], a differentiable function that computes mesh vertices $M(\theta, \beta) \in \mathbb{R}^{V \times 3}$, $V = 6890$, from pose θ and shape β, using standard linear blend skinning (LBS). The 3D joints, $\mathcal{J}(\beta)$, of a kinematic skeleton are computed from the shape parameters. The pose parameters $\theta \in \mathbb{R}^{J \times D + 3}$ contain the parent-relative rotations of each joint and the root translation, where D is the dimension of the rotation representation and J is the number of skeleton joints. We represent rotations using the 6D rotation parameterization of Zhou et al. [80], thus $\theta \in \mathbb{R}^{J \times 6 + 3}$. The world transformation $T_j(\theta) \in SE(3)$

of each joint j is computed by following the transformations of its parents in the kinematic tree: $T_j(\boldsymbol{\theta}) = T_{p(j)}(\boldsymbol{\theta}) * T(\boldsymbol{\theta}_j, \mathcal{J}_j(\boldsymbol{\beta}))$, where $p(j)$ is the index of the parent of joint j and $T(\boldsymbol{\theta}_j, \mathcal{J}_j(\boldsymbol{\beta}))$ is the rigid transformation of joint j relative to its parent. Variables with a *hat* denote observed quantities.

We focus on two 3D human body estimation problems: 1) fitting a body model [42] to 2D keypoints and 2) inferring the body, including hand articulation [54], from head and hand signals returned by AR/VR devices, shown in Fig. 2. The first is by now a standard problem in the Computer Vision community. The second, which uses only head and hand signals in the AR/VR scenario, is a significantly harder task which requires strong priors, in particular to produce plausible results for the lower body and hands. The design of such priors is not trivial, requires expert knowledge and a significant investment of time.

2D Keypoint Fitting: We follow the setup of Song et al. [60], computing the projection of the 3D SMPL joints $\mathcal{J}$ with a weak-perspective camera Π with scale $s \in \mathbb{R}$, translation $\boldsymbol{t} \in \mathbb{R}^2$: $\mathsf{j} = \Pi_o(\mathcal{J}(\boldsymbol{\theta}, \boldsymbol{\beta}), s, \boldsymbol{t})$. Our goal is to estimate SMPL and camera parameters $\boldsymbol{\Theta}^B = \{\boldsymbol{\theta}, \boldsymbol{\beta}\}$, $\mathsf{K}^B = \{s, \boldsymbol{t}\}$, such that the projected joints j match the detected keypoints $D^B = \{\hat{\mathsf{j}}\}$, e.g. from OpenPose [10]. **Fitting SMPL+H to AR/VR device signals:** We make the following assumptions: 1. the device head tracking system provides a 6-DoF transformation $\hat{T}^H$, that contains the position and orientation of the *headset* in the world coordinate frame. 2. the device hand tracking system gives us the orientation and position of the left and right wrist, $\hat{T}^L, \hat{T}^R \in SE(3)$, and the positions of the fingertips $\hat{P}^L_{1,...,5}, \hat{P}^R_{1,...,5} \in \mathbb{R}^3$ in the world coordinate frame, if and when they are in the field of view (FOV) of the HMD. In order to estimate the SMPL+H parameters that best fit the above observations, we compute the estimated headset position and orientation from the SMPL+H world transformations as $T^H(\boldsymbol{\Theta}) = T^{\mathrm{HMD}} T_{j_H}(\boldsymbol{\Theta})$, where j_H is the index of the head joint of SMPL+H. T^{HMD} is a fixed transform from the SMPL+H head joint to the headset, obtained from an offline calibration phase.

Visibility is represented by $v_L, v_R \in \{0, 1\}$ for the left and right hand respectively. We examine two scenarios: 1. full visibility, where the hands are always visible, 2. half-space visibility, where only the area in front of the HMD is visible. Specifically, we transform the points into the coordinate frame of the headset, using T^H. All points with $z \geq 0$ are behind the headset and thus invisible. Figure 2 right visualizes the plane that defines what is visible or not.

To sum up, the sensor data are: $D^{\mathrm{HMD}} = \{\hat{T}^H, \hat{T}^L, \hat{T}^R, \hat{P}^L_{i=1,...,5}, \hat{P}^R_{i=1,...,5}, v_L, v_R\}$. The goal is to estimate the parameters $\boldsymbol{\Theta}^{\mathrm{HMD}} = \{\boldsymbol{\theta}\} \in \mathbb{R}^{315}$, that best fit D^{HMD}. Note that we assume we are given body shape $\boldsymbol{\beta}$ for the HMD fitting scenario.

3.3 Human Face Model and Fitting Task

We represent the human face using the parametric face model proposed by Wood et al. [67]. It is a blendshape model [19], with $V = 7667$ vertices, 4 skeleton joints (head, neck and two eyes), with their rotations and translations denoted with θ, identity $\beta \in \mathbb{R}^{256}$ and expression $\psi \in \mathbb{R}^{233}$ blendshapes. The deformed face mesh is obtained with standard linear blend skinning.

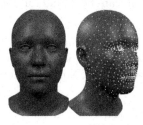

Fig. 3. Blue: The face model template of Wood et al. [67]. White: 669 dense landmarks.

For face fitting, we select a set of mesh vertices as the face landmarks $\mathcal{P}(\theta, \psi, \beta) \in \mathbb{R}^{P \times 3}$, P = 669 (see Fig. 3 right). The input data are the corresponding 2D face landmarks $\hat{p} \in \mathbb{R}^P \times 2$, detected using the landmark neural network proposed by Wood et al. [67].

For this task, our goal is to estimate translation, joint rotations, expression and identity coefficients $\Theta^F = \{\theta, \psi, \beta\} \in \mathbb{R}^{516}$ that best fit the 2D landmarks $D^F = \hat{p}$. We assume we are dealing with calibrated cameras and thus have access to the camera intrinsics K. $\Pi_p(\mathcal{P}; K)$ is the perspective camera projection function used to project the 3D landmarks $\mathcal{P}$ onto the image plane.

3.4 Data Terms

The data term is a function $\mathcal{L}^D(\Theta; D)$ that measures the discrepancy between the observed inputs D and the parametric model evaluated at the estimated parameters Θ.

At the n-th iteration of the fitting process, we compute both 1) the array $\mathcal{R}(\Theta_n)$ that contains all the corresponding residuals of the data term $\mathcal{L}^D$ for the current set of parameters Θ_n, and 2) the gradient $g_n = \nabla \mathcal{L}^D(\Theta_n)$.

Let $[\![\,]\!]$ by any metric appropriate for $SE(3)$ [16] and $\|\,\|\|_\psi$ a robust norm [5]. To compute residuals, we use the Frobenius norm for $[\![\,]\!]$ and $\|\,\|\|_\psi$ Note that any other norm choice can be made compatible with LM [76].

Body Fitting to 2D Keypoints: We employ the re-projection error between the detected joints and those estimated from the model as the data term:

$$\mathcal{L}^D(\Theta^B; D^B) = \|\hat{j} - \Pi_p\left(\mathcal{J}(\Theta^B), K^B\right)\|_\psi \tag{3}$$

Here $\mathcal{J}(\Theta^B)$ denotes the "posed" joints.

Body Fitting to HMD Signals: We measure the discrepancy between the observed data D^{HMD} and the estimated model parameters Θ^{HMD} with the following data term:

$$\mathcal{L}^D(\Theta^{\text{HMD}}; D^{\text{HMD}}) = [\![\hat{T}^{\text{H}}, T^{\text{H}}(\Theta^{\text{HMD}})]\!] +$$
$$\sum_{w \in \text{L,R}} v_w \left([\![\hat{T}^w, T^w(\Theta^{\text{HMD}})]\!] + \sum_{i=1}^{5} \|\hat{P}_i^w - P_i^w(\Theta^{\text{HMD}})\|_\psi\right) \tag{4}$$

Face Fitting to 2D Landmarks: The data term is the landmark re-projection error:

$$\mathcal{L}^D(\Theta^F; D^F) = \|\hat{p} - \Pi_p\left(\mathcal{P}(\Theta^F); K^F\right)\|_\psi \tag{5}$$

3.5   Training Details

Training Losses: We train our learned fitter using a combination of model parameter and mesh losses. Their precise formulation can be found in the **Sup. Mat.**

Model Structure: Unless otherwise specified, $f, f_{\lambda, \gamma}$ (in Algorithm 1, (2)) use a stack of two GRUs with 1024 units each. The initialization Φ, Φ_h in Algorithm 1 are MLPs with two layers of 256 units, ReLU [48] and Batch Normalization [29].

Datasets: For the body fitting tasks, we use AMASS [44] to train and test our fitters. When fitting SMPL to 2D keypoints, we use 3DPW's [45] test set to evaluate the learned fitter's accuracy, using the detected OpenPose [10] keypoints as the target. The face fitter is trained and evaluated on synthetic data . Please see the **Sup. Mat.** for more details on the datasets.

4   Experiments

4.1   Metrics

Metrics with a *PA* prefix are computed after undoing rotation, scale and translation, i.e. Procrustes alignment. Variables with a *tilde* are ground-truth values.

Vertex-to-Vertex (V2V): As we know the correspondence between ground-truth $\tilde{M}$ and estimated vertices M, we are able to compute the mean per-vertex error: $\text{V2V}(\tilde{M}, M) = \frac{1}{V}\sum_{i=1}^{V}\|\tilde{M}_i - M_i\|_2$. For SMPL+H, in addition to the full mesh error (FB), we report error values for the head (H) and hands (L, R). A visualization of the selected parts is included in the **Sup. Mat.** The **3D per-joint error (JntErr)** is equal to: $\text{JntErr}(\tilde{\mathcal{J}}, \mathcal{J}) = \frac{1}{J}\sum_{i=1}^{J}\|\tilde{\mathcal{J}}_i - \mathcal{J}_i\|_2$.

Ground Penetration (GrPe.): We report the average distance to the ground plane for all vertices below ground [75]: $\text{GrPe.}(M) = \frac{1}{|S|}\sum_{n\in S}|d_{\text{gnd}}(M_i)|$, where $d_{\text{gnd}}(M_i) = M_i \cdot n_{\text{gnd}}$ and $S = \{i \mid d_{\text{gnd}}(M_i) < 0\}$.

Face Landmark Error (LdmkErr): We report the mean distance between estimated and ground-truth 3D landmarks $\text{LdmkErr}(\tilde{\mathcal{P}}, \mathcal{P}) = \frac{1}{P}\sum_{i=1}^{P}\|\tilde{\mathcal{P}}_i - \mathcal{P}_i\|_2$.

4.2   Quantitative Evaluation

Fitting the Body to 2D Keypoints: We compare our proposed update rule with existing regressors, classic and learned optimization methods on 3DPW [45]. For a fairer comparison with Song et al. [60], we train two versions of our proposed fitter, one where we change the update rule of LGD with Eq. 1, and our full system which also has network architecture changes. Table 1 shows that just by changing the update rule (Ours, LGD + Eq. 1), we outperform all baselines.

Table 1. Using 3DPW [45] to compare different approaches that estimate SMPL from images, 2D keypoints and part segmentation masks. Replacing LGD's [60] update rule with ours leads to a 2 mm PA-MPJPE improvement. Our full system, that uses GRUs, leads to a further 1.6 mm improvement. "O/R" denotes Optimization/Regression.

Method	Type	Image	2D keypoints	Part segmentation	PA-MPJPE
SMPLify [8]	O	✗	✓	✗	106.1
SCOPE [20]	O	✗	✓	✗	68.0
SPIN [38]	R	✓	✗	✗	59.6
VIBE [35]	R	✓	✗	✗	55.9
Neural Descent [77]	R+O	✓	✓	✓	57.5
LGD [60]	R+O	✗	✓	✗	55.9
Ours, LGD + Eq. 1	R+O	✗	✓	✗	53.9
Ours (full)	R+O	✗	✓	✗	**52.2**

Fitting the Body to HMD Data: In Table 2 we compare our proposed learned optimizer with a standard optimization pipeline, a variant of SMPLify [8,51] adapted to the HMD fitting task (first 3 rows), and two neural network regressors (a VAE predictor [16] in the 4th row and our initializer Φ of Algorithm 1 in the 5th row), on the task of fitting SMPL+H to sparse HMD signals, see Sect. 3.2 . The optimization baseline minimizes the energy with data term ($\mathcal{L}^D$ in Eq. (4)), gravity term $\mathcal{L}^{\mathcal{G}}$, prior term $\mathcal{L}^{\theta}_{\text{prior}}$, without/with temporal term $\mathcal{L}^T$ (first/second row of Table 2) to estimate the parameters $\Theta_{1,...,T}$ of a sequence of length T:

$$\mathcal{L}^O(\Theta^{\text{HMD}}) = \mathcal{L}^D(\Theta^{\text{HMD}}; D^{\text{HMD}}) + \mathcal{L}^{\mathcal{G}} + \mathcal{L}^{\theta}_{\text{prior}} + \mathcal{L}^T$$

$$\mathcal{L}^{\mathcal{G}}(\Theta^{\text{HMD}}) = 1 - \frac{T_{\text{pelvis}}(1,:3) \cdot \mathbf{u}}{\|T_{\text{pelvis}}(1,:3)\|_2 \|\mathbf{u}\|_2}, \ \mathbf{u} = (0,1,0) \tag{6}$$

$$\mathcal{L}^T(\Theta^{\text{HMD}}) = \sum_{t=1}^{T-1} [\![T_{t+1}(\Theta^{\text{HMD}}_{t+1}) - T_t(\Theta^{\text{HMD}}_t)]\!]$$

We use two different pose priors, a GMM [8] and a VAE encoder $\mathcal{E}(*)$ [51]:

$$\mathcal{L}^{\theta}_{\text{GMM}} = -\min_j \log \left(w_j \mathcal{N}(\theta; \mu_{\theta,j}, \Sigma_{\theta,j}) \right) \tag{7}$$

$$\mathcal{L}^{\theta}_{\text{VAE}} = \text{Neg. Log-Likelihood}(\mathcal{N}(\mathcal{E}(\theta), \mathcal{I})) \tag{8}$$

We minimize the loss above using L-BFGS [49, Ch. 7.2] for 120 iterations on the test split of the MoCap data. We choose L-BFGS instead of Levenberg-Marquardt, since PyTorch currently lacks the feature to efficiently compute jacobians, without having to resort to multiple backward passes for derivative computations. We report the results for both full and half-space visibility in Table 2 using the metrics of Sect. 4.1. Our method outperforms the baselines in terms of full-body and penetration metrics, and shows competitive performance w.r.t. to

Table 2. Fitting SMPL+H to simulated sequences of HMD data. Our proposed fitter outperforms the classical optimization baselines (L-BFGS prefix) on the full body and ground penetration metrics, with similar or better performance on the part metrics, and the regressor baselines (the VAE predictor [16] and the regressor Φ), on all metrics. "F/H" denotes full/half-plane visibility.

Method	Vertex-to-vertex (mm) ↓						JntErr		GrPe.	
	Full body		Head		L/R hand		(mm) ↓		(mm) ↓	
	F	H	F	H	F	H	F	H	F	H
L-BFGS, GMM	73.1	116.2	2.9	3.4	3.2/3.0	5.6/5.3	49.7	137.26	70.8	74.0
L-BFGS, GMM, Tempo	72.6	113.3	2.9	3.4	3.3/3.1	6.8/6.5	49.4	132.1	70.7	73.5
L-BFGS, VAE Enc.	76.1	119.3	3.9	4.1	5.3 /4.7	8.7/7.6	52.6	140.5	63.6	66.7
Dittadi et al. [16]	n/a		n/a		n/a		43.3	n/a	n/a	
Ours Φ, $(N = 0)$	44.2	69.7	19.1	22.7	27.8/25.9	32.1/29.9	38.9	84.9	16.1	20.1
Ours $(N = 5)$	**26.1**	**49.9**	**2.2**	**3.2**	**3.0/3.3**	**3.1/3.7**	**18.1**	**62.1**	**12.5**	**15.5**

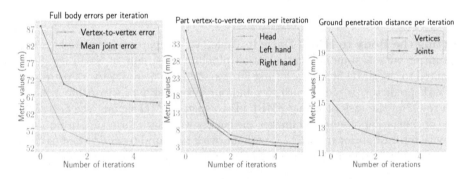

Fig. 4. Errors per iteration when fitting SMPL+H to HMD data for the half-space visibility scenario, see **Sup. Mat.** for full visibility. Left to right: 1) full body vertex and joint errors, 2) head, left and right hand V2V errors and 3) vertex and joint ground distance, computed on the set of points below ground.

the part metrics. Regression-only methods [16] cannot tightly fit the data, due to the lack of a feedback mechanism.

Runtime: Our method (PyTorch) runs at *150 ms* per frame on a P100 GPU, while the baseline L-BFGS method (PyTorch) above requires *520 ms*, on the same hardware. We are aware that a highly optimized real-time version of the latter exists and runs at *0.8 ms* per frame, performing at most 3 LM iterations, but it requires investing significant effort into a problem specific C++ codebase.

Figure 4 contains the metrics per iteration of our method, averaged across the entire test dataset. It shows that our learned fitter is able to aggressively optimize the target data term and converge quickly.

Table 3. Using per-step network weights reduces head and ground penetration errors, albeit at an N-folder parameter increase.

Weights	V2V (mm) ↓			JntErr	GrPe.
	FB	H	L/R	(mm) ↓	(mm)↓
Shared	52.3	3.5	3.6/**3.7**	64.1	18.2
Per-step	**49.9**	**3.2**	**3.1**/**3.7**	**62.1**	**15.5**

Table 4. GRU vs a residual feed-forward network [26,61]. GRU's memory makes it more effective. Multiple layers bring further benefits, but increase runtime.

Network	V2V (mm) ↓			JntErr	GrPe.
Structure	FB	H	L/R	(mm) ↓	(mm)↓
ResNet	65.3	6.8	7.3/7.6	73.1	16.2
GRU (1024)	53.6	3.7	3.4/4.0	66.1	**15.1**
GRU (1024, 1024)	**49.9**	**3.2**	**3.1/3.7**	**62.1**	15.5

Table 5. Comparison of our update rule (Eq. 1) with the pure network update $\Delta\Theta_n$. Our proposed combination improves the results for all metrics.

Update	V2V (mm) ↓			JntErr	GrPe.
Rule	FB	H	L/R	(mm) ↓	(mm)↓
$+\Delta\Theta_n$	53.8	14.7	7.8/7.9	66.3	15.8
+Eq. 1	**49.9**	**3.2**	**3.1/3.7**	**62.1**	**15.5**

Table 6. Learning to predict γ is better than a constant, with performance degrading gracefully, providing an option for a lowercomputational cost.

Learning	V2V (mm) ↓			JntErr	GrPe.
rate γ	FB	H	L/R	(mm) ↓	(mm)↓
1e-4	51.9	3.5	3.8/4.6	64.2	**15.5**
Learned	**49.9**	**3.2**	**3.1/3.7**	**62.1**	**15.5**

Ablation Study: We perform our ablations on the problem of fitting SMPL+H to HMD signals, using the half-space visibility setting. Unless otherwise stated, we report the performance of regression and 5 iterations of the learned fitter.

We first compare two variants of the fitter, one with shared and the other with separate network weights per optimization step. Table 3 shows that the latter can help reduce the errors, at the cost of an N-fold increase in memory.

Secondly, we investigate the effect of the type and structure of the network, replacing the GRU with a feed-forward network with skip connections, i.e., ResNet [26,61]. We also train a version of our fitter with a single GRU with 1024 units. Table 4 shows that the GRU is better suited to this type of problem, thanks to its internal memory. This is very much in line with many popular continuous optimizer work [77].

Thirdly, we compare the update rule of Eq. 1 with a learned fitter that only uses the network update, i.e. $\gamma = 0, \lambda = 1$ in Eq. 1. This is an instantiation of LGD [60], albeit with a different network and task. Table 5 shows that the proposed weighted combination is better than the pure network update.

Fourthly, we investigate whether we need to learn the step size γ or if a constant value is enough. Table 6 shows that performance gracefully degrades when using a constant learning value. Therefore, it is an option for decreasing the computational cost, without a significant performance drop.

Finally, we present some qualitative results in Fig. 6. Notice how the learned fitter corrects the head pose and hand articulation of the initial predictions.

Face Fitting to 2D Landmarks: We compare our proposed learned optimizer with a C++ production grade solution that uses LM to solve the face fitting problem described in Sect. 3.3. Given the per-image 2D landmarks as input, the optimization baseline minimizes the energy with data term ($\mathcal{L}^D$ in Eq. 5) and a simple regularization term to estimate $\boldsymbol{\Theta}^F = \{\boldsymbol{\theta}, \boldsymbol{\psi}, \boldsymbol{\beta}\}$:

Table 7. Face fitting to 2D landmarks.

Method	V2V (mm) ↓				LdmkErr (mm) ↓	
	Face		Head			
	–	PA	–	PA	–	PA
LM	34.4	3.7	33.8	5.3	33.8	**3.4**
Ours	**7.9**	**3.5**	**8.5**	**4.1**	**8.0**	3.7

$$\mathcal{L}^O(\boldsymbol{\Theta}^F) = \mathcal{L}^D(\boldsymbol{\Theta}^F; D^F) + \mathbf{w} * \|\boldsymbol{\Theta}^F\|_2 \tag{9}$$

$\mathbf{w}$ contains the different regularization weights for $\boldsymbol{\theta}, \boldsymbol{\psi}, \boldsymbol{\beta}$, which are tuned manually for the best baseline result.

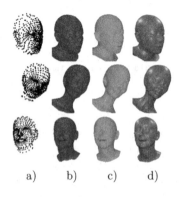

a)   b)   c)   d)

Fig. 5. Face model [67] fitting to dense 2D landmarks a) target 2D landmarks, b) LM fitter, c) ours, d) ground-truth.

The quantitative comparison in Table 7 shows that our proposed fitter outperforms the LM baseline on almost all metrics. The large value in absolute errors ("-" columns) is due to the wrong estimation of the depth of the mesh. After alignment (*PA* columns), the gap is much smaller. See Fig. 5 for a qualitative comparison.

Runtime: Here, the baseline optimization is in C++ and thus for a fair comparison, we only compare the time it takes to compute the parameter update given the residuals and jacobians (per-iteration). Computing the values of the learned parameter update (ours, using PyTorch) takes *12 ms* on a P100 GPU, while computing the LM update (baseline, C++) requires *34.7 ms* (504 free variables). Note that the LM update only requires *0.8 ms* on a laptop CPU when optimizing over 100 free variables. The difference is due to the cubic complexity of LM w.r.t. the number of free variables of the problem.

4.3   Discussion

If we apply the proposed method to a sequence of data, we will get plausible per-frame results, but the overall motion will be implausible. Since the model is trained on a per-frame basis and lacks temporal context, it cannot learn the proper dynamics present in temporal data. Thus, limbs in successive frames will move unnaturally, with large jumps or jitter. Future extensions of this work should therefore explore how to best use past frames and inputs. This could be coupled with a physics based approach, either as part of a controller [75] or using explicit physical losses [53,69,79] in $\mathcal{L}^D$. Another interesting direction is the use of more effective parameterizations for the per-step weights [15,27].

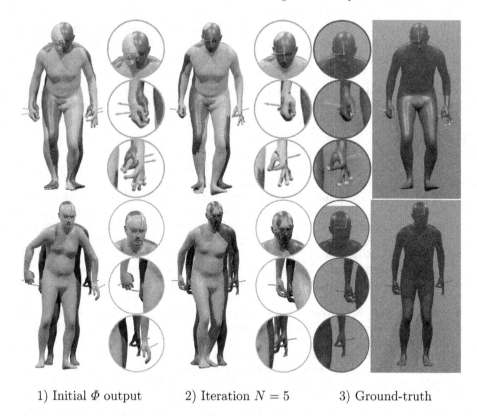

1) Initial Φ output   2) Iteration $N = 5$ 3) Ground-truth

Fig. 6. Estimates in yellow, ground-truth in blue, best viewed in color. Our learned optimizer successfully fits the target data and produces plausible poses for the full 3D body. Points that are greyed out are outside of the field of view, e.g. the hands in the second row, and thus not perfectly fitted. (Color figure online)

While all the problems we tackle here are under-constrained and could thus have multiple solutions, the current system returns only one. Therefore, combining the proposed system with multi-modal regressors [6, 39] is another possible extension.

5   Conclusion

In this work, we propose a learned parameter update rule inspired from classic optimization algorithms that outperforms the pure network update and is competitive with standard optimization baselines. We demonstrate the utility of our algorithm on three different problem sets, estimating the 3D body from 2D keypoints, from sparse HMD signals and fitting the face to dense 2D landmarks. Learned optimizers combine the advantages of classic optimization and regression approaches. They greatly simplify the development process for new problems, since the parameter priors are directly learned from the data, without manual specification and tuning, and they run at interactive speeds, thanks to the development of specialized software for neural network inference. Thus, we believe that our proposed optimizer will be useful for any applications that involve generative model fitting.

Acknowledgement. We thank Pashmina Cameron, Sadegh Aliakbarian, Tom Cashman, Darren Cosker and Andrew Fitzgibbon for valuable discussions and proof reading.

References

1. Adler, J., Öktem, O.: Solving ill-posed inverse problems using iterative deep neural networks. Inverse Problems **33**(12), 124007 (2017)
2. Andrychowicz, M., Denil, M., Gómez, S., Hoffman, M.W., Pfau, D., Schaul, T., Shillingford, B., de Freitas, N.: Learning to learn by gradient descent by gradient descent. In: NeurIPS. vol. 29. Curran Associates, Inc. (2016), https://proceedings. neurips.cc/paper/2016/file/fb87582825f9d28a8d42c5e5e8b23d-Paper.pdf
3. Anguelov, D., Srinivasan, P., Koller, D., Thrun, S., Rodgers, J., Davis, J.: SCAPE: Shape Completion and Animation of People. ACM Transactions on Graphics **24**(3), 408–416 (July 2005) 10.1145/1073204.1073207, https://doi.org/10.1145/1073204. 1073207
4. Baek, S., Kim, K.I., Kim, T.K.: Pushing the envelope for RGB-based dense 3D hand pose estimation via neural rendering. In: Computer Vision and Pattern Recognition (CVPR). pp. 1067–1076 (June 2019)
5. Barron, J.T.: A general and adaptive robust loss function. Computer Vision and Pattern Recognition (CVPR) pp. 4326–4334 (June 2019)
6. Biggs, B., Novotny, D., Ehrhardt, S., Joo, H., Graham, B., Vedaldi, A.: 3D Multi-bodies: Fitting Sets of Plausible 3D Human Models to Ambiguous Image Data. In: NeurIPS. vol. 33, pp. 20496–20507. Curran Associates, Inc. (2020), https://proceedings.neurips.cc/paper/2020/file/ebf99bb5df6533b6dd9180a590346 98d-Paper.pdf
7. Blanz, V., Vetter, T.: A morphable model for the synthesis of 3D faces. In: ACM Transactions on Graphics (Proceedings of SIGGRAPH). pp. 187–194 (1999)
8. Bogo, F., Kanazawa, A., Lassner, C., Gehler, P., Romero, J., Black, M.J.: Keep it SMPL: Automatic estimation of 3D human pose and shape from a single image. In: European Conference on Computer Vision (ECCV). pp. 561–578. Lecture Notes in Computer Science, Springer International Publishing (October 2016)
9. Boukhayma, A., Bem, R.d., Torr, P.H.: 3D hand shape and pose from images in the wild. In: Computer Vision and Pattern Recognition (CVPR). pp. 10843–10852 (June 2019)
10. Cao, Z., Hidalgo, G., Simon, T., Wei, S.E., Sheikh, Y.: OpenPose: Realtime Multi-Person 2D Pose Estimation using Part Affinity Fields. Transactions on Pattern Analysis and Machine Intelligence (TPAMI) **43**(1), 172–186 (2021)
11. Cho, K., van Merriënboer, B., Gulcehre, C., Bahdanau, D., Bougares, F., Schwenk, H., Bengio, Y.: Learning phrase representations using RNN encoder-decoder for statistical machine translation. In: Proceedings of the 2014 Conference on Empirical Methods in Natural Language Processing (EMNLP). pp. 1724–1734. Association for Computational Linguistics, Doha, Qatar (Oct 2014). DOI: https://doi. org/10.3115/v1/D14-1179,https://aclanthology.org/D14-1179
12. Choi, H., Moon, G., Lee, K.M.: Beyond Static Features for Temporally Consistent 3D Human Pose and Shape from a Video. In: Computer Vision and Pattern Recognition (CVPR). pp. 1964–1973 (June 2021)

13. Choutas, V., Pavlakos, G., Bolkart, T., Tzionas, D., Black, M.J.: Monocular Expressive Body Regression through Body-Driven Attention. In: European Conference on Computer Vision (ECCV). pp. 20–40 (August 2020)
14. Clark, R., Bloesch, M., Czarnowski, J., Leutenegger, S., Davison, A.J.: Learning to Solve Nonlinear Least Squares for Monocular Stereo. In: European Conference on Computer Vision (ECCV). pp. 291–306 (September 2018)
15. Dehesa, J., Vidler, A., Padget, J., Lutteroth, C.: Grid-Functioned Neural Networks. In: ICML. Proceedings of Machine Learning Research, vol. 139, pp. 2559–2567. PMLR (July 2021), https://proceedings.mlr.press/v139/dehesa21a.html
16. Dittadi, A., Dziadzio, S., Cosker, D., Lundell, B., Cashman, T.J., Shotton, J.: Full-Body Motion From a Single Head-Mounted Device: Generating SMPL Poses From Partial Observations. In: International Conference on Computer Vision (ICCV). pp. 11687–11697 (October 2021)
17. Dong, Z., Song, J., Chen, X., Guo, C., Hilliges, O.: Shape-aware Multi-Person Pose Estimation from Multi-View Images. In: International Conference on Computer Vision (ICCV). pp. 11158–11168 (October 2021)
18. Duchi, J., Hazan, E., Singer, Y.: Adaptive Subgradient Methods for Online Learning and Stochastic Optimization. Journal of Machine Learning Research 12(7), 2121–2159 (2011)
19. Egger, B., Smith, W.A.P., Tewari, A., Wuhrer, S., Zollhoefer, M., Beeler, T., Bernard, F., Bolkart, T., Kortylewski, A., Romdhani, S., Theobalt, C., Blanz, V., Vetter, T.: 3D Morphable Face Models - Past, Present and Future. ACM Transactions on Graphics 39(5) (August 2020). DOI: https://doi.org/10.1145/3395208
20. Fan, T., Alwala, K.V., Xiang, D., Xu, W., Murphey, T., Mukadam, M.: Revitalizing Optimization for 3D Human Pose and Shape Estimation: A Sparse Constrained Formulation. In: International Conference on Computer Vision (ICCV). pp. 11457–11466 (October 2021)
21. Feng, Y., Choutas, V., Bolkart, T., Tzionas, D., Black, M.J.: Collaborative regression of expressive bodies using moderation. In: International Conference on 3D Vision (3DV). pp. 792–804 (2021)
22. Flynn, J., Broxton, M., Debevec, P., DuVall, M., Fyffe, G., Overbeck, R., Snavely, N., Tucker, R.: DeepView View Synthesis with Learned Gradient Descent. In: Computer Vision and Pattern Recognition (CVPR). pp. 2367–2376 (June 2019)
23. Guzov, V., Mir, A., Sattler, T., Pons-Moll, G.: Human POSEitioning System (HPS): 3D Human Pose Estimation and Self-Localization in Large Scenes From Body-Mounted Sensors. In: Computer Vision and Pattern Recognition (CVPR). pp. 4318–4329 (June 2021)
24. Hassan, M., Choutas, V., Tzionas, D., Black, M.J.: Resolving 3D human pose ambiguities with 3D scene constraints. In: International Conference on Computer Vision (ICCV). pp. 2282–2292 (October 2019), https://prox.is.tue.mpg.de
25. Hasson, Y., Varol, G., Tzionas, D., Kalevatykh, I., Black, M.J., Laptev, I., Schmid, C.: Learning Joint Reconstruction of Hands and Manipulated Objects. In: Computer Vision and Pattern Recognition (CVPR). pp. 11807–11816 (June 2019)
26. He, K., Zhang, X., Ren, S., Sun, J.: Deep residual learning for image recognition. In: Computer Vision and Pattern Recognition (CVPR). pp. 770–778 (June 2016)
27. Holden, D., Komura, T., Saito, J.: Phase-Functioned Neural Networks for Character Control. ACM Transactions on Graphics 36(4) (July 2017). DOI: https://doi.org/10.1145/3072959.3073663,https://doi.org/10.1145/3072959.3073663
28. Igel, C., Toussaint, M., Weishui, W.: Rprop using the natural gradient. In: Trends and Applications in Constructive Approximation. pp. 259–272. Birkhäuser Basel, Basel (2005)

29. Ioffe, S., Szegedy, C.: Batch normalization: Accelerating deep network training by reducing internal covariate shift. In: ICLR. pp. 448–456. PMLR (2015)
30. Joo, H., Neverova, N., Vedaldi, A.: Exemplar Fine-Tuning for 3D Human Pose Fitting Towards In-the-Wild 3D Human Pose Estimation. In: International Conference on 3D Vision (3DV). pp. 42–52 (2021)
31. Joo, H., Simon, T., Sheikh, Y.: Total capture: A 3D deformation model for tracking faces, hands, and bodies. In: Computer Vision and Pattern Recognition (CVPR). pp. 8320–8329 (June 2018)
32. Kanazawa, A., Black, M.J., Jacobs, D.W., Malik, J.: End-to-end recovery of human shape and pose. In: Computer Vision and Pattern Recognition (CVPR). pp. 7122–7131 (June 2018)
33. Kaufmann, M., Zhao, Y., Tang, C., Tao, L., Twigg, C., Song, J., Wang, R., Hilliges, O.: EM-POSE: 3D Human Pose Estimation From Sparse Electromagnetic Trackers. In: International Conference on Computer Vision (ICCV). pp. 11510–11520 (October 2021)
34. Kingma, D.P., Ba, J.: Adam: A method for stochastic optimization. In: ICLR (2015), https://arxiv.org/abs/1412.6980
35. Kocabas, M., Athanasiou, N., Black, M.J.: VIBE: Video inference for human body pose and shape estimation. In: Computer Vision and Pattern Recognition (CVPR). pp. 5252–5262 (June 2020)
36. Kocabas, M., Huang, C.H.P., Hilliges, O., Black, M.J.: PARE: Part attention regressor for 3D human body estimation. In: International Conference on Computer Vision (ICCV). pp. 11127–11137 (October 2021)
37. Kokkinos, F., Kokkinos, I.: To The Point: Correspondence-driven monocular 3D category reconstruction. In: NeurIPS (2021), https://openreview.net/forum?id=AWMU04iXQ08
38. Kolotouros, N., Pavlakos, G., Black, M.J., Daniilidis, K.: Learning to reconstruct 3D human pose and shape via Model-Fitting in the loop. In: International Conference on Computer Vision (ICCV). pp. 2252–2261 (October 2019)
39. Kolotouros, N., Pavlakos, G., Jayaraman, D., Daniilidis, K.: Probabilistic modeling for human mesh recovery. In: International Conference on Computer Vision (ICCV). pp. 11585–11594 (October 2021)
40. Levenberg, K.: A method for the solution of certain non-linear problems in least squares. Quarterly of applied mathematics **2**(2), 164–168 (1944)
41. Li, J., Xu, C., Chen, Z., Bian, S., Yang, L., Lu, C.: HybrIK: A Hybrid Analytical-Neural Inverse Kinematics Solution for 3D Human Pose and Shape Estimation. In: Computer Vision and Pattern Recognition (CVPR). pp. 3383–3393 (June 2021)
42. Loper, M., Mahmood, N., Romero, J., Pons-Moll, G., Black, M.J.: SMPL: A Skinned Multi-Person Linear Model. ACM Transactions on Graphics (Proceedings of SIGGRAPH Asia) 34(6), 248:1–248:16 (October 2015)
43. Lv, Z., Dellaert, F., Rehg, J.M., Geiger, A.: Taking a deeper look at the inverse compositional algorithm. In: Computer Vision and Pattern Recognition (CVPR). pp. 4581–4590 (June 2019)
44. Mahmood, N., Ghorbani, N., Troje, N.F., Pons-Moll, G., Black, M.J.: AMASS: Archive of motion capture as surface shapes. In: International Conference on Computer Vision (ICCV). pp. 5442–5451 (October 2019)
45. von Marcard, T., Henschel, R., Black, M., Rosenhahn, B., Pons-Moll, G.: Recovering Accurate 3D Human Pose in The Wild Using IMUs and a Moving Camera. In: European Conference on Computer Vision (ECCV). pp. 614–631 (September 2018)

46. Marquardt, D.W.: An algorithm for least-squares estimation of nonlinear parameters. Journal of the society for Industrial and Applied Mathematics **11**(2), 431–441 (1963)
47. Mueller, F., Davis, M., Bernard, F., Sotnychenko, O., Verschoor, M., Otaduy, M.A., Casas, D., Theobalt, C.: Real-time pose and shape reconstruction of two interacting hands with a single depth camera. ACM Transactions on Graphics 38(4) (July 2019). DOI: https://doi.org/10.1145/3306346.3322958,https://doi.org/10.1145/3306346.3322958
48. Nair, V., Hinton, G.E.: Rectified linear units improve restricted boltzmann machines. In: ICML (2010)
49. Nocedal, J., Wright, S.J.: Numerical Optimization. USA, second edn, Springer, New York, NY (2006)
50. Patel, P., Huang, C.H.P., Tesch, J., Hoffmann, D.T., Tripathi, S., Black, M.J.: AGORA: Avatars in geography optimized for regression analysis. In: Computer Vision and Pattern Recognition (CVPR). pp. 13463–13473 (June 2021)
51. Pavlakos, G., Choutas, V., Ghorbani, N., Bolkart, T., Osman, A.A.A., Tzionas, D., Black, M.J.: Expressive body capture: 3D hands, face, and body from a single image. In: Computer Vision and Pattern Recognition (CVPR). pp. 10975–10985 (June 2019)
52. Powell, M.J.D.: A hybrid method for nonlinear equations. In: Numerical Methods for Nonlinear Algebraic Equations. Gordon and Breach (1970)
53. Rempe, D., Birdal, T., Hertzmann, A., Yang, J., Sridhar, S., Guibas, L.J.: HuMoR: 3D Human Motion Model for Robust Pose Estimation. In: International Conference on Computer Vision (ICCV). pp. 11468–11479 (October 2021)
54. Romero, J., Tzionas, D., Black, M.J.: Embodied hands: Modeling and capturing hands and bodies together. ACM Transactions on Graphics (Proceedings of SIGGRAPH Asia) 36(6) (November 2017)
55. Rong, Y., Shiratori, T., Joo, H.: FrankMocap: A Monocular 3D Whole-Body Pose Estimation System via Regression and Integration. In: International Conference on Computer Vision Workshops (ICCVw) (October 2021)
56. Schmidhuber, J.: Learning to control fast-weight memories: An alternative to dynamic recurrent networks. Neural Computation **4**(1), 131–139 (1992)
57. Schmidhuber, J.: A neural network that embeds its own meta-levels. In: IEEE International Conference on Neural Networks. pp. 407–412. IEEE (1993)
58. Seeber, M., Poranne, R., Polleyfeyes, M., Oswald, M.: RealisticHands: A Hybrid Model for 3D Hand Reconstruction. In: International Conference on 3D Vision (3DV). pp. 22–31 (December 2021)
59. Shen, J., Cashman, T.J., Ye, Q., Hutton, T., Sharp, T., Bogo, F., Fitzgibbon, A.W., Shotton, J.: The Phong Surface: Efficient 3D Model Fitting using Lifted Optimization. In: European Conference on Computer Vision (ECCV). pp. 687–703. Springer (August 2020)
60. Song, J., Chen, X., Hilliges, O.: Human Body Model Fitting by Learned Gradient Descent. In: European Conference on Computer Vision (ECCV). pp. 744–760 (August 2020)
61. Srivastava, R.K., Greff, K., Schmidhuber, J.: Training very deep networks. In: NeurIPS. vol. 28. Curran Associates, Inc. (2015), https://proceedings.neurips.cc/paper/2015/file/215a71a12769b056c3c32e7299f1c5ed-Paper.pdf

62. Taylor, J., Bordeaux, L., Cashman, T., Corish, B., Keskin, C., Sharp, T., Soto, E., Sweeney, D., Valentin, J., Luff, B., Topalian, A., Wood, E., Khamis, S., Kohli, P., Izadi, S., Banks, R., Fitzgibbon, A., Shotton, J.: Efficient and precise interactive hand tracking through joint, continuous optimization of pose and correspondences. ACM Transactions on Graphics 35(4) (July 2016). DOI: https://doi.org/10.1145/2897824.2925965,https://doi.org/10.1145/2897824.2925965
63. Thies, J., Zollhofer, M., Stamminger, M., Theobalt, C., Nießner, M.: Face2Face: Real-time Face Capture and Reenactment of RGB Videos. In: Computer Vision and Pattern Recognition (CVPR). pp. 2387–2395 (June 2016)
64. Tomè, D., Alldieck, T., Peluse, P., Pons-Moll, G., Agapito, L., Badino, H., la Torre, F.D.: SelfPose: 3D Egocentric Pose Estimation from a Headset Mounted Camera. Transactions on Pattern Analysis and Machine Intelligence (TPAMI) pp. 1–1 (2020). DOI: https://doi.org/10.1109/TPAMI.2020.3029700
65. Tome, D., Peluse, P., Agapito, L., Badino, H.: xR-EgoPose: Egocentric 3D Human Pose from an HMD Camera. In: International Conference on Computer Vision (ICCV). pp. 7728–7738 (October 2019)
66. Vogel, C., Pock, T.: A primal dual network for low-level vision problems. In: Pattern Recognition. pp. 189–202. Springer International Publishing, Cham (2017)
67. Wood, E., Baltrušaitis, T., Hewitt, C., Dziadzio, S., Johnson, M., Estellers, V., Cashman, T.J., Shotton, J.: Fake It Till You Make It: Face Analysis in the Wild Using Synthetic Data Alone. In: International Conference on Computer Vision (ICCV). pp. 3681–3691 (October 2021)
68. Xiang, D., Joo, H., Sheikh, Y.: Monocular Total Capture: Posing Face, Body, and Hands in the Wild. In: Computer Vision and Pattern Recognition (CVPR). pp. 10965–10974 (June 2019)
69. Xie, K., Wang, T., Iqbal, U., Guo, Y., Fidler, S., Shkurti, F.: Physics-Based Human Motion Estimation and Synthesis From Videos. In: International Conference on Computer Vision (ICCV). pp. 11532–11541 (October 2021)
70. Xiong, X., De la Torre, F.: Supervised descent method and its applications to face alignment. In: Computer Vision and Pattern Recognition (CVPR). pp. 532–539 (June 2013)
71. Xu, H., Bazavan, E.G., Zanfir, A., Freeman, W.T., Sukthankar, R., Sminchisescu, C.: GHUM & GHUML: Generative 3D human shape and articulated pose models. In: Computer Vision and Pattern Recognition (CVPR). pp. 6183–6192 (June 2020)
72. Yang, D., Kim, D., Lee, S.H.: LoBSTr: Real-time Lower-body Pose Prediction from Sparse Upper-body Tracking Signals. Computer Graphics Forum (2021). https://doi.org/10.1111/cgf.142631
73. Yuan, Y., Kitani, K.: Ego-Pose Estimation and Forecasting as Real-Time PD Control. In: International Conference on Computer Vision (ICCV). pp. 10082–10092 (October 2019)
74. Yuan, Y., Kitani, K.M.: 3D Ego-Pose Estimation via Imitation Learning. In: European Conference on Computer Vision (ECCV). pp. 763–778 (September 2018)
75. Yuan, Y., Wei, S.E., Simon, T., Kitani, K., Saragih, J.: SimPoE: Simulated Character Control for 3D Human Pose Estimation. In: Computer Vision and Pattern Recognition (CVPR). pp. 7159–7169 (June 2021)
76. Zach, C.: Robust bundle adjustment revisited. In: European Conference on Computer Vision (ECCV). pp. 772–787. Springer International Publishing, Cham (September 2014)
77. Zanfir, A., Bazavan, E.G., Zanfir, M., Freeman, W.T., Sukthankar, R., Sminchisescu, C.: Neural Descent for Visual 3D Human Pose and Shape. In: Computer Vision and Pattern Recognition (CVPR). pp. 14484–14493 (June 2021)

78. Zhang, H., Tian, Y., Zhou, X., Ouyang, W., Liu, Y., Wang, L., Sun, Z.: PyMAF: 3D human pose and shape regression with pyramidal mesh alignment feedback loop. In: International Conference on Computer Vision (ICCV). pp. 11446–11456 (October 2021)
79. Zhang, S., Zhang, Y., Bogo, F., Marc, P., Tang, S.: Learning Motion Priors for 4D Human Body Capture in 3D Scenes. In: International Conference on Computer Vision (ICCV). pp. 11343–11353 (October 2021)
80. Zhou, Y., Barnes, C., Lu, J., Yang, J., Li, H.: On the continuity of rotation representations in neural networks. In: Computer Vision and Pattern Recognition (CVPR). pp. 5738–5746 (June 2019)
81. Zollhöfer, M., Thies, J., Garrido, P., Bradley, D., Beeler, T., Pérez, P., Stamminger, M., Nießner, M., Theobalt, C.: State of the art on monocular 3D face reconstruction, tracking, and applications. In: Computer Graphics Forum. vol. 37, pp. 523–550. Wiley Online Library (2018)

EgoBody: Human Body Shape and Motion of Interacting People from Head-Mounted Devices

Siwei Zhang[1]([✉]), Qianli Ma[1], Yan Zhang[1], Zhiyin Qian[1], Taein Kwon[1], Marc Pollefeys[1,2], Federica Bogo[2], and Siyu Tang[1]

[1] ETH Zürich, Zürich, Switzerland
{siwei.zhang,qianli.ma,yan.zhang,taein.kwon,marc.pollefeys, siyu.tang}@inf.ethz.ch, zhqian@ethz.ch
[2] Microsoft, Zurich, Switzerland
fbogo@fb.com

Abstract. Understanding social interactions from *egocentric* views is crucial for many applications, ranging from assistive robotics to AR/VR. Key to reasoning about interactions is to understand the body pose and motion of the interaction partner from the egocentric view. However, research in this area is severely hindered by the lack of datasets. Existing datasets are limited in terms of either size, capture/annotation modalities, ground-truth quality, or interaction diversity. We fill this gap by proposing EgoBody, a novel large-scale dataset for human pose, shape and motion estimation from egocentric views, during interactions in complex 3D scenes. We employ Microsoft HoloLens2 headsets to record rich egocentric data streams (including RGB, depth, eye gaze, head and hand tracking). To obtain accurate 3D ground truth, we calibrate the headset with a multi-Kinect rig and fit expressive SMPL-X body meshes to multi-view RGB-D frames, reconstructing 3D human shapes and poses relative to the scene, over time. We collect 125 sequences, spanning diverse interaction scenarios, and propose the first benchmark for 3D full-body pose and shape estimation of the interaction partner from egocentric views. We extensively evaluate state-of-the-art methods, highlight their limitations in the egocentric scenario, and address such limitations leveraging our high-quality annotations. Data and code are available at https:// sanweiliti.github.io/egobody/egobody.html.

Keywords: Pose estimation · Egocentric view · Motion capture · Dataset

1 Introduction

Humans constantly interact and communicate with each other; understanding our social interaction partners' motions, intentions and emotions is almost

---

F. Bogo—Now at Meta Reality Labs Research.

Supplementary Information The online version contains supplementary material available at https://doi.org/10.1007/978-3-031-20068-7_11.

© The Author(s), under exclusive license to Springer Nature Switzerland AG 2022
S. Avidan et al. (Eds.): ECCV 2022, LNCS 13666, pp. 180–200, 2022.
https://doi.org/10.1007/978-3-031-20068-7_11

Fig. 1. EgoBody is a large-scale dataset capturing ground-truth 3D human motions during social interactions in 3D scenes. Given two interacting subjects, we leverage a lightweight multi-camera rig to reconstruct their 3D shape and pose over time (top row). One of the subjects (blue) wears a head-mounted device, synchronized with the rig, capturing egocentric multi-modal data like eye gaze tracking (red circles in first two rows) and RGB images (bottom). (Color figure online)

instinctive for us. However, the same does not hold for machines. A first step towards automated human interaction understanding is the estimation of the 3D body pose, shape and motion of the social interaction partner (*"interactee"*) from egocentric views, *e.g.* from head-mounted devices (HMD). Addressing this challenging problem is crucial for many applications, ranging from assistive robotics to Augmented and Virtual Reality (AR/VR), where sensors typically perceive the interactee from the egocentric view. Despite its importance, the problem has received little attention in the literature so far. While there are a large number of methods for full-body pose (and sometimes also shape) estimation from RGB(D) frames [14,20,30,39,40,44,47,59,72,81,90,93,98–101], they tend to perform poorly on data captured with an HMD (see Sect. 5). Indeed, this setup brings its own unique challenges, which most methods have not explicitly addressed so far. Any method aiming at understanding the pose and shape of the interactee must deal with severe body truncations, motion blur (exacerbated by the embodied movement of the HMD), people entering/exiting the field of view, to name a few.

A reason for such limited attention is the lack of data. On one hand, most human motion datasets are captured by *third-person-view* cameras without egocentric frames [23,30,33,36,37,64,85,102], which do not faithfully replicate AR/VR scenarios; most capture only one subject at a time, without interactions [30,33]. On the other hand, existing *egocentric* datasets are limited in terms of annotation modalities, scale and interaction diversity. They either focus on coarse-level interaction/action labels [21,55,66,74,79], or provide only the camera wearer's pose without considering [83,84,92,97], or with very limited data involving [29], the interactee. You2Me [67] collects egocentric RGB frames of two-people interactions, annotated with 3D skeletons, without 3D scene context, nor the body shape. Recently, Ego4D [27] collects a large amount of egocentric

Table 1. Comparison with existing image-based datasets with 3D human pose annotations. "Fr.#" denotes frame numbers. "3rd-PV" and "Ego" refers to the third-person-view and egocentric view, respectively. "Mesh" refers to the body mesh. "Interact" refers to social interactions. "Global-Cfg." refers to global translation and rotation.

Dataset	Fr.#	Sub.#	3rd-PV	Ego	Mesh	Gaze	3D-Scene	Interact	Global-Cfg
TNT15 [63]	13k	4	✓		✓				✓
3DPW [62]	51k	7	✓		✓*			✓	
PROX [30]	100k	20	✓		✓*		✓		✓
Panoptic [37]	297k	180+	✓				✓		✓
HUMBI [96]	380k	772	✓		✓*	✓			✓
TotalCapture [85]	1,900k	5	✓						✓
Human3.6M [33]	3,600k	11	✓		✓				✓
Mo2Cap2 [92]	15k	5		✓					
You2Me [67]	150k	10	✓					✓	
HPS [29]	300k	7		✓	✓*		✓		✓
Ours	220k	36	✓	✓	✓*	✓	✓	✓	✓

* Body Mesh defined by parametric body models.

videos for various tasks including action and social interaction understanding, but without 3D ground truth for human pose, shape and motions.

To fill this gap, we propose EgoBody, a unique, large-scale egocentric dataset capturing high-quality 3D human motions during social interactions. We focus on 2-people interaction cases, and define interaction scenarios based on the social interaction categories studied in sociology [8]. Unlike most existing datasets that only provide RGB streams, EgoBody collects egocentric multi-modal data, with accurate 3D human shape, pose and motion ground-truth for both interacting subjects, accompanied by eye gaze tracking for the camera wearer. Furthermore, EgoBody includes accurate 3D scene reconstructions, providing a holistic and consistent 3D understanding of the physical world around the camera wearer.

The egocentric data is captured with a Microsoft HoloLens2 headset [3], which provides rich multi-modal streams: RGB, depth, head, hand and eye gaze tracking, correlated in space and time. In particular, eye gaze carries vital information about human attention during interactions. By providing eye gaze tracking synchronized with other modalities, EgoBody opens the door to study relationships between human attention, interactions and motions. We obtain high-quality 3D human shape and motion annotations in an automated way, by leveraging a marker-less motion capture approach. Namely, we utilize a multi-camera rig consisting of multiple Azure Kinects [1] as our motion capture system.

However, combining raw data streams from the egocentric- and the third-person-view remains highly challenging due to hardware limitations. Specifically, the Kinect-HoloLens2 calibration exhibit inaccuracies due to not perfectly accurate factory calibration and tracking drift. We address this by proposing a refinement scheme based on body keypoints. With carefully calibrated data, we further build an efficient motion capture pipeline based on [101] to fit the SMPL-X body model [72] to multi-view and egocentric RGB-D data, reconstructing accurate 3D full-body meshes for both the camera wearer and the interactee. In this way, we get accurate and well calibrated ground truth across all sensor coordinates, as well as the world coordinate, which is not available in most existing datasets. The setup is lightweight and easy to deploy in various environments.

With EgoBody we propose the first benchmark for 3D human pose and shape estimation (3DHPS) of the interactee, in interactions captured by the HMD. By evaluating state-of-the-art 3DHPS methods on the EgoBody's test set, we carefully analyze and highlight the limitations of existing methods in this egocentric setup. We show the usefulness of EgoBody by fine-tuning three recent methods [35,47,56] on its training set, obtaining significantly improved performance on our *test set*. Finally, in a cross-dataset evaluation we show how models fine-tuned on EgoBody also achieve a better performance on the *You2Me* dataset [67].

Contributions. In summary, we: **(1)** provide the first large-scale egocentric dataset, EgoBody, comprising both egocentric- and third-person-view multi-modal data, annotated with high-quality 3D ground-truth motions for *both* interacting people and 3D scene reconstructions; **(2)** extensively evaluate state-of-the-art 3DHPS methods on our test set, showing their shortcomings in this egocentric setup and providing insights for future methods in this direction; **(3)** show the usefulness of our training set: a simple fine-tuning on it significantly improves existing methods' performance and robustness on both our test set *and a different egocentric dataset*; **(4)** provide the first benchmark for 3DHPS estimation of the interactee in the egocentric view during social interactions.

2 Related Work

Datasets for 3D Human Pose, Motion and Interactions. A large number of datasets focus on 3D human pose and motion from *third-person-views* [23,30,33,36,37,51,62–64,71,85,96,102]. For example, Human3.6M [33] and AMASS [61] use optical marker-based motion capture to collect large amounts of high-quality 3D motion sequences; they are limited to constrained studio setups and images – when available – are polluted by markers. PROX [30] performs marker-less capture of people moving in 3D scenes from monocular RGB-D, without human-human interactions. The quality of the reconstructed motion is further improved by LEMO [101]. The Panoptic Studio datasets [36–38,91] capture interactions between people using a multi-view camera system, annotated with body and hand 3D joints plus facial landmarks. CHI3D [23] focuses on close human-human contacts, using a motion capture system to extract ground-truth 3D skeletons. 3DPW [62] reconstructs the 3D shape and motion of people by fitting SMPL [58] to IMU data and RGB images captured with a hand-held camera, without 3D environment reconstruction. None of these datasets provides egocentric data.

Among datasets for *egocentric* vision, a lot of attention has been put on hand-object interactions and action recognition, often without 3D ground-truth [10,16,17,22,41–43,50,55,66,69,74,76,79,95,103]. Mo2Cap2 [92] and xR-EgoPose [83,84] provide image-3D skeleton pairs for egocentric body pose prediction of the camera wearer, without the interactee involved. HPS [29] reconstructs the body pose and shape of the camera wearer moving in large 3D scenes; only a few frames include interactions with an interactee. You2Me [67] provides 3D skeletons for both interacting people paired with images captured with a chest-mounted camera plus external cameras; there are no body shape or 3D scene annotations. EgoMoCap [57] analyzes the interactee body shape and pose in outdoor social scenarios capturing only the egocentric RGB stream.

Table 1 compares EgoBody with the most related human motion datasets. EgoBody is the first motion capture dataset that collects calibrated egocentric- and third-person-view images, with various interaction scenarios, multi-modal data and rich 3D ground-truth. Additionally, EgoBody provides the camera wearer's eye gaze to facilitate potential social interaction studies which jointly analyze human attention and motion.

3D Human Pose Estimation. The problem of estimating 3D human pose from *third-person-view* RGB(D) images has been extensively studied in the literature – either from single frames [5,9,12,15,20,26,28,30,39,45–49,54,56,65,70,72,80, 82,86,88,90,93,100,104], monocular videos [14,40,44,59,81,98,99,101] or multi-view camera sequences [19,24,32,38,77,89]. SPIN [47] estimates SMPL [58] parameters from single RGB images by combining deep learning with optimization frameworks. METRO [56] reconstructs human meshes without relying on parametric body models. Most methods require "full-body" images and therefore lack robustness when parts of the body are occluded or truncated, as it is the case with the interactee in egocentric videos. EFT [35] injects crop augmentations at training time to better reconstruct highly truncated people. PARE [45] explicitly learns to predict body-part-guided attention masks. However, these methods exhibit a significant performance drop when applied to egocentric data. Our dataset helps fill this performance gap, as we show in Sect. 5.

The problem of *egocentric* pose estimation is receiving growing attention. Most methods estimate the *camera wearer*'s 3D skeleton, based on images, IMU data, scene cues or body-object interactions [29,34,60,78,83,84,97]. You2Me [67] estimates the camera wearer's pose given the interactee's pose as an additional cue. Liu et al. [57] estimate 3D human pose and shape of the interactee given egocentric videos in outdoor scenes, with limited interaction diversity.

Egocentric Social Interaction Learning. Egocentric videos provide a unique way to study social interactions. Most methods focus on social interaction recognition [6,7,18,21,53,66,76,94,95]. Lee et al. [52] produce a storyboard summary of the camera wearer's day given egocentric videos. Northcutt et al. [68] collect an egocentric communication dataset focusing on conversations. Recently Ego4D [27] dataset collects massive egocentric videos for various tasks including hand-object and social interaction understanding, making significant advances in stimulating future research in the egocentric domain. EgoBody is unique in that we are the first egocentric dataset that provides rich 3D annotations including accurate 3D human pose and shape for all interacting subjects.

3 Building the EgoBody Dataset

EgoBody collects sequences capturing subjects performing diverse social inter-actions in various indoor scenes. For each sequence, two subjects are involved in one or more interaction scenarios (Sect. 3.1). Their performance is captured from both egocentric- and third-person-views. One subject (the camera wearer) wears a HoloLens2 headset [3], capturing multi-modal egocentric data (RGB, depth, head, hand and eye gaze tracking streams). Their interaction partner, *i.e.* inter-actee, does not wear any device. The camera wearer's HoloLens2 is calibrated and synchronized with three to five Azure Kinect cameras [1] which capture the interaction from different viewpoints (Sect. 3.2). Based on this multi-view data, we acquire rich ground-truth annotations for all frames, including 3D full-body pose and shape for both interacting subjects and the reconstructed 3D scene (Sect. 3.3). Statistics for EgoBody are reported in Sect. 4.

Table 2. EgoBody interaction scenarios.

Category	Interaction scenarios
Cooperation	Guess by Action game, catching and tossing, searching for items, etc.
Social exchange	Teaching to dance/workout, giving a presentation, etc.
Conflict	Arguing about a specific topic
Conformity	One subject instructs the other to perform a task
Others	Haggling, negotiation, promotion, self-introduction, casual chat, etc.
Action Types	Sitting, standing, walking, dancing, exercising, bending, lying,
	Grasping, squatting, drinking, passing objects, catching, throwing, etc.

3.1 Interaction Scenarios

To guide the subjects and obtain rich, diverse body motions, we define mul-tiple interaction scenarios within five major interaction categories in sociology studies [8]: *cooperation, social exchange, conflict, conformity* and *others*, span-ning diverse action types (Table 2) and body poses (Fig. 5). For each sequence, we pre-define one or more interaction scenarios and ask the two participants to interact accordingly. We allow the subjects to improvise within each interaction scenario to ensure intra-class variation. The motion diversity is further increased with various human-scene interactions by capturing in 3D scenes.

3.2 Data Acquisition Setup

As mentioned above, EgoBody collects egocentric- and third-person-view multi-modal data, plus 3D scene reconstructions. Figure 2 illustrates our system setup.

Egocentric-View Capture. We use a Microsoft Hololens2 [3] headset to record egocentric data. Using the Research Mode API [87], we capture RGB videos (1920×1080) at 30 FPS, long-throw depth frames (512×512) at 1–5 FPS, as well as eye gaze, hand and head tracking at 60 FPS. Note that we do not record depth at a higher framerate (AHAT) due to the "depth aliasing" described in [87]. We

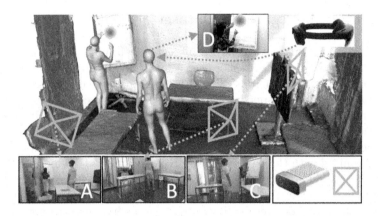

Fig. 2. Capture setup. Multiple Azure Kinects capture the interactions from different views (A, B, C), and a synchronized HoloLens2 worn by one subject captures the egocentric view image (D), as well as the eye gaze (red circle) of the camera wearer. (Color figure online)

observe that captures exhibit typical challenges for limited power-devices, like frame drops and blurry images.

Third-Person Multi-view Capture. We use three to five Azure Kinect cameras [1] (denoted by $Cam1 \sim Cam5$) to capture multi-view, synchronized RGB-D videos of interacting subjects. Having multi-view data helps our motion reconstruction pipeline for ground-truth acquisition (Sect. 3.3). The cameras are fixed during recording. They capture synchronized RGB frames (1920×1080) and depth frames (640×576) at 30 FPS.

3D Scene Representation. We pre-scan the environment using an iPhone12 Pro Max running the 3D Scanner app [2]. Scene reconstructions are stored as 3D triangulated meshes, each with $10^5 \sim 10^6$ vertices. We choose this procedure for its efficiency and reconstruction quality.

Calibration and Synchronization. For each Kinect, we extract its camera parameters via the Azure Kinect DK [1]. For the HoloLens2, we get its camera parameters as exposed by Research Mode [87]. We synchronize the Kinects via hardware, using audio cables. Since it is not possible to synchronize HoloLens2 and Kinect in a similar way, we use a flashlight visible to all devices as signal for the first frame. Kinect-Kinect and Kinect-HoloLens2 cameras are spatially calibrated using a checkerboard and refined by rigid alignment steps (ICP [11]).

The Kinect-HoloLens2 calibration is further optimized based on body keypoints (Sect. 3.3). We use $Cam1$ to define our world coordinate frame origin. Once we calibrate the HoloLens2 coordinate frame with $Cam1$'s world origin, we can track the headset position, and therefore its cameras, by relying on its built-in head tracker [87]. We also register the 3D scene into the coordinate frame of $Cam1$, and reconstruct the human body in this space (see details in Supp. Mat.).

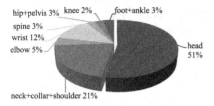

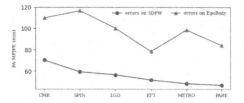

Fig. 3. **Which body part attracts more attention?** For each joint group, % of the occurrences it is the closest to the 2D gaze point in the image.

Fig. 4. Accuracy of SoTAs on 3DPW and EgoBody with the advance of the 3DHPS field.

3.3 Ground-truth Acquisition

Given the RGB-D frames captured with the multi-Kinect rig and the egocentric frames, our motion reconstruction pipeline estimates, for each frame and each subject, the corresponding SMPL-X body parameters [72], including the global translation $\gamma \in \mathbb{R}^3$, body shape $\beta \in \mathbb{R}^{10}$, pose $\theta \in \mathbb{R}^{96}$ (body and hand) and facial expression $\phi \in \mathbb{R}^{10}$. To address the challenges posed by not perfectly accurate factory calibration of HoloLens2 depth, which further leads to inaccurate Kinect-HoloLens2 calibration, we propose a keypoint-based refinement scheme to better leverage observations from the HoloLens2. We introduce the first solution to reconstruct accurate 3D human pose, shape and motions with multi-view Kinect cameras and an embodied HMD. Thanks to the refined Kinect-HoloLens2 calibration, this provides accurate per-frame pose, natural human motion dynamics and realistic human-scene interactions for both egocentric-and third-person-view frames. Note that we estimate the body in the coordinate frame of *Cam1*.

Data Preprocessing. We use OpenPose [13] to detect 2D body joints in all (Kinect and HoloLens2) RGB frames. OpenPose identifies people in the same image by assigning a body index to each detected person. In general, this works well, but gives false positives which we process afterwards. To extract human body point clouds from Kinect depth frames, we use Mask-RCNN [31] and DeepLabv3 [31]. We manually inspect the data to remove spurious detections (*e.g.* irrelevant people in the background, and scene objects misdetected as people). We also ensure consistent subject identification across frames and views, and manually fix inaccurate 2D joint detections, mostly due to body-body and body-scene occlusions. See Supp. Mat. for more details.

Per-frame Fitting. As in [101], given Kinect depth and 2D joints, we first optimize the SMPL-X parameters for each subject/frame separately, minimizing an objective function similar to that defined in [30]:

$$E(\beta, \gamma, \theta, \phi) = E_J + \lambda_D E_D + E_{prior} + \lambda_{contact} E_{contact} + \lambda_{coll} E_{coll}, \qquad (1)$$

where β, γ, θ, ϕ are optimized SMPL-X parameters.

Given the preprocessed OpenPose 2D joints J_{OP}^v from n views ($v \in \{1, ..., n\}$), the multi-view joint error term E_J minimizes the sum of 2D distances between J_{OP}^v and the 2D projection of SMPL-X joints onto camera view v for all views:

$$E_J(\boldsymbol{\beta}, \boldsymbol{\gamma}, \boldsymbol{\theta}, \boldsymbol{\phi}) = \sum_{view\ v} E_{J_v}(\boldsymbol{\beta}, \boldsymbol{\gamma}, \boldsymbol{\theta}, \boldsymbol{\phi}, J_{OP}^v, K_v, T_v), \qquad (2)$$

where K_v denotes the intrinsics parameters of camera v, and T_v denotes the extrinsics between *Cam v* and *Cam 1*. The depth term E_D penalizes discrepancies between the estimated body surface and body depth point clouds for all views; E_{prior} represents body pose, shape and expression priors; $E_{contact}$ encourages scene-body contacts; and E_{coll} penalizes scene-body collisions. The λ_is weight the contribution of each term. We refer the reader to [30,101] for more details.

Kinect-HoloLens2 Calibration Refinement. The Kinect-Hololens2 calibration is represented by the extrinsics T between Kinect *Cam1*, and the HoloLens2 coordinate system's origin. For each capture session, this origin is fixed in the world [87]; as the HMD moves, its head tracker provides the transformation between this origin and each egocentric frame t, denoted by T_t^{ego}. To address the inaccurate initial Kinect-HoloLens2 calibration T_{init} caused by imperfect HoloLens2 depth factory calibration, we propose a keypoint-based scheme to refine it. For each frame t, we project the 3D SMPL-X joints $J_{3D,t}$ (obtained from per-frame fitting, in *Cam1*'s coordinate) onto the egocentric image. We minimize the 2D error between the projected 2D joints and the OpenPose joint detections $J_{OP,t}^{ego}$ of the egocentric frame t, and optimize the transformation T:

$$E_T(T) = \sum_t ||K^{ego}T_t^{ego}TJ_{3D,t} - J_{OP,t}^{ego}||_2^2 + \lambda ||T - T_{init}||_2^2, \qquad (3)$$

where K^{ego} denotes the HoloLens2 RGB camera intrinsic parameters, and λ weights the regularizer.

Temporally Consistent Fitting. Per-frame fitting gives us a set of reasonable, initial pose estimates, which however are jittery and inconsistent over time. We therefore run a second optimization stage based on LEMO priors [101] to obtain smooth, realistic human motions. Furthermore, to improve consistency between egocentric- and third-person-view estimates, we consider also egocentric data given the refined Kinect-HoloLens2 calibration. We take OpenPose 2D joint estimations from HoloLens2 RGB frames and use them as further constraints. Still, we optimize for each subject separately. The resulting objective function minimized in the temporal fitting stage is:

$$E(\boldsymbol{\gamma}, \boldsymbol{\theta}, \boldsymbol{\phi}) = E_J + E_{J_{ego}} + E_{prior} + \lambda_{smooth}E_{smooth} + \lambda_{fric}E_{fric}, \qquad (4)$$

where E_{fric} is the contact friction term defined in [101] to prevent body sliding, E_{smooth} and E_{prior} denote temporal and static priors as in [101]. $E_{J_{ego}}$ is the 2D projection term which minimizes the error between OpenPose detections on egocentric view frames and the 2D projections of SMPL-X joints onto the egocentric view; $E_{J_{ego}}$ is only enabled for the interactee when they are visible in the egocentric frames. The λ_is weight balance the contribution of each term.

4   EgoBody Dataset

EgoBody collects 125 sequences from 36 subjects (18 male and 18 female) performing diverse social interactions in 15 indoor scenes. In total, there are 219,731 synchronized frames captured from Azure Kinects, from multiple third-person-views. We refer to this as the "Multi-view (MV)Set". For each MV frame, we provide 3D human full-body pose and shape annotations (as SMPL-X parameters) for both interacting subjects together with the 3D scene mesh. Furthermore, we have 199,111 egocentric RGB frames (the "EgoSet"), captured from HoloLens2, calibrated and synchronized with Kinect frames. Given the camera wearer's head motion, the interactee is not visible in every egocentric frame; in total, we have 175,611 frames with the interactee visible in the egocentric view ("EgoSet-interactee"). Figure 5 shows example images. For EgoSet, we also collect the head, hand and eye tracking data, plus the depth frames from the HoloLens2. We also provide SMPL [58] body annotations via the official transfer tool [4]. Below we provide dataset statistics; for more detailed analysis and ground truth annotation quality please refer to the Supp. Mat.

Fig. 5. Reconstructed ground-truth bodies overlaid on third-person-view images from 3 Kinects (row 1–3), and the corresponding egocentric view image (row 4). Left/middle/right shows three different frames. Row 5 shows more examples from the egocentric view. Blue denotes the camera wearer, and pink denotes the interactee. Eye gaze of the camera wearer are in red circles. (Color figure online)

Training/Validation/Test Splits. We split data into training, validation and test sets such that they have no overlapping subjects. The EgoBody training set contains 116,630 MVSet frames, 105,388 EgoSet frames and 90,124 EgoSet-interactee frames. The EgoBody validation set contains 29,140 MVSet frames, 25,416 EgoSet frames and 23,332 EgoSet-interactee frames. The test set contains 73,961 MV frames, 68,307 EgoSet frames and 62,155 Ego-interactee frames.

Joint Visibility. The camera wearer's motion, the headset's field of view and the close distance between the interacting subjects cause the interactee to be often truncated in the egocentric view. To quantify the occurrences of truncations, we project the fitted 3D body joints onto the HoloLens2 images, and deem a projected 2D joint as "visible" if it lies inside the image. As shown in Fig. 6 (2nd row, right), the lower body parts are more frequently truncated in the images. Please refer to Sect. 5 for the impact of joint visibility on 3DHPS estimation performance.

Eye Gaze and Attention. We can combine the HoloLens2 eye gaze tracking with our 3D reconstruction of the scene/people to estimate the 3D location the user looks at, and project it on the egocentric images (interpreted as where the user's "attention" is focused), thereby obtaining valuable data to understand interactions. We observe that the camera wearer's attention is highly focused on the interactee during interactions. and tends to be closer to the upper body joints (Fig. 3), which in turn results in lower visibility for the lower body parts.

5   Experiments

We leverage EgoBody to introduce the first benchmark for 3D human pose and shape (3DHPS) estimation from egocentric images. Given a single RGB image of a target subject, the goal of a 3DHPS method is to estimate a human body mesh and a set of camera parameters, which best explain the image data. State-of-the-art (SoTA) 3DHPS methods are mostly trained and evaluated on third-person-view data, and their performance is starting to saturate on common third-person-view datasets [33,62] (see Fig. 4); yet, their capabilities to generalize to real-world scenarios (*e.g.* cropped or blurry images) are still limited [71]. With EgoBody, we can test their capabilities on egocentric images.

We define a benchmark for 3DHPS methods on our EgoSet-interactee test set. Within the social interaction scenarios, the input will be an egocentric view image of the interactee. We evaluate SoTA methods and show that their performance significantly drops on our data. We expose limitations of existing methods by in-depth analysis (Sect. 5.2), given that the egocentric view brings considerable challenges that are rarely present in existing third-person-view datasets.

We also provide valuable insights to boost their performance for egocentric scenarios. In particular, we show that our EgoSet-interactee training set can help address the challenges brought by egocentric view data: using it, we fine-tune three recent methods, SPIN [47], METRO [56] and EFT [35], achieving significantly improved accuracy and robustness on both our test set (Sect. 5.3) and over a cross-dataset evaluation on the You2Me [67] dataset (Sect. 5.4).

5.1   Benchmark Evaluation Metrics

We employ two common metrics: **Mean Per-Joint Position Error (MPJPE)** and **Vertex-to-Vertex (V2V)** errors. We use two types of alignments before computing the accuracy for each metric: (1) translation-only alignment (aligns the bodies at the pelvis joint [71]) and (2) Procrustes Alignment [25] ("PA", solves for scale, translation and rotation). Results are by default reported with translation-only alignment unless specified with the "PA-" prefix. **MPJPE** is the mean Euclidean distance between predicted and ground-truth 3D joints, evaluated on 24 SMPL body joints. **V2V** error is the mean Euclidean distance over all body vertices, computed between two meshes.

Table 3. Evaluation of SoTA 3DHPS estimation methods on our test set. All metrics are in mm. "PA-" stands for Procrustes alignment. "SPIN-ft", "METRO-ft" and "EFT-ft" denote results of fine-tuning SPIN, METRO and EFT on our training set.

Method	MPJPE ↓	PA-MPJPE ↓	V2V ↓	PA-V2V ↓
CMR [48]	200.7	109.6	218.7	136.8
SPIN [47]	182.8	116.6	187.3	123.7
LGD [80]	158.0	99.9	168.3	106.0
METRO [56]	153.1	98.4	164.6	106.4
PARE [45]	123.0	83.8	131.5	89.7
EFT [35]	123.9	78.4	134.9	86.0
SPIN-ft (Ours)	106.5	67.1	120.9	78.3
METRO-ft (Ours)	**98.5**	70.0	**110.5**	76.8
EFT-ft (Ours)	102.1	**64.8**	116.1	**74.8**

5.2   Baseline Evaluation

Table 3 summarizes the evaluation of SoTA 3DHPS methods from different categories: (1) fitting-based method [80]; and regression-based methods that (2) predict parameters of a parametric body model [35,45,47,48] or (3) predict non-parametric body meshes [56]. For each baseline method, we use the best performing model provided by the authors (trained with the optimal training data).

In Fig. 4 we plot the PA-MPJPE error of these methods on our dataset and on an existing major third-person-view benchmark[1], On average, the methods yield a 77% higher 3D joint error on EgoBody than on 3DPW. More importantly, while the accuracy curve drives towards saturation on 3DPW, different SoTA methods still show largely varying performance on our dataset. This suggests that current datasets are not sufficient to train models that can handle egocentric view images well. Below we discuss two key challenging factors that impact performance.

---

[1] The results on 3DPW are taken from the respective original papers.

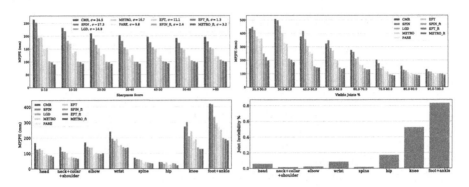

Fig. 6. First Row: Impact of motion blur (left) / joint visibility (right) on SoTA method accuracies. Second Row: 3D joint error analysis by body parts (left) / ratio of each joint group being *in*visible (truncated) from the images in our test set (right).

Motion Blur. Motion blur is common in the egocentric view images due to the motion of the camera wearer. To study how motion blur influences 3DHPS estimation accuracy, we plot in Fig. 6 (1st row, left) the MPJPE of all methods vs. the image sharpness score. The sharpness score is defined as the variance of the Laplacian of an image [73], upper-thresholded at 60; higher scores mean sharper images. We observe that, surprisingly, most methods are insensitive to blurriness, except for heavily blurred cases (score <10). However, our fine-tuned models (SPIN-ft / METRO-ft / EFT-ft) are more robust against motion blur: among all methods, they achieve the lowest standard deviation over the seven image sharpness levels; see the number next to each method in the legend of Fig. 6 (1st row, left).

Joint Visibility. While most 3DHPS methods assume that the target body is (almost) fully visible in the image as in existing third-person-view datasets such as 3DPW [62], this is seldom the case in egocentric view images. To assess the importance of this issue, we analyze the performance of each baseline with respect to the portion of visible body joints ("visibility", see Sect. 4) in the images from our test set. The result is summarized in Fig. 6 (row 1, right). Note that our definition of a joint's visibility is related to, but differs from, the concept of *occlusion*: both measure how much pixel information is missing for a body part, but visibility focuses on how much of the body is *truncated* from the image. A joint that is occluded by an object can still be considered visible by our definition.

Overall, all methods yield a lower error when there is less body truncation. Two recent methods, PARE [45] and EFT [35], achieve the best results. PARE is designed to be robust against occlusions by explicitly employing a body part attention mechanism, whereas EFT handles body truncation "implicitly" by aggressively cropping images as training data augmentation.

We further plot the MPJPE and the *in*visibility ratio of each joint group in Fig. 6 (2nd row). Overall the two are in accordance: the lesser a joint is visible, the higher the error it exhibits. An exception is on the wrist joints: despite good visibility, their error remains relatively high. As observed also in [45], high errors on the extremities are a common problem with existing 3DHPS models, possibly because most current models only use a single, global feature from the input image for regression. This points to potential future work that deploys local image features, which has been shown effective in recent 3DHPS models [28,45].

5.3   Baseline Improvement

To evaluate the effectiveness of the EgoBody training set, we use it to fine-tune three of the baseline methods: two model-based methods, SPIN [47] and EFT [35], as they both use the same architecture (HMR [39] network) that is the backbone for many other recent models [39,44,75]; a model-free method METRO [56] which directly predicts the body mesh. The pre-trained EFT differs from SPIN majorly in that it is trained with extended 3D pseudo ground-truth data (from the EFT-dataset) and uses aggressive image cropping as data augmentation. We use the same hyperparameters provided by the authors and select the fine-tuned model with the best validation score.

As shown in Table 3, after fine-tuning, the error is largely reduced for all three methods on all metrics: SPIN-ft/METRO-ft/EFT-ft has 42%/36%/18% lower MPJPE, and 35%/33%/14% V2V than their corresponding original models.

The improvement can also be seen for all blurriness/visibility categories in Figs. 6. For the motion blur specifically, the fine-tuned models not only achieve a lower error at every image sharpness level, but also show increased robustness. This is shown by the standard deviations of each method across the sharpness levels, dropping from 27.3 to 2.4 for SPIN, from 16.7 to 3.2 for METRO, and from 11.1 to 1.3 for EFT, respectively, after fine-tuning. The results show that our training set can serve as an effective source to adapt existing 3DHPS methods to the egocentric setting.

5.4   Cross-dataset Evaluation on You2Me

Is the effect of our training set only specific to our capture scenario, or does it generalize to other egocentric pose estimation datasets? To verify this, we evaluate SPIN, EFT and METRO against their fine-tuned counterparts on the You2Me [67] dataset. Here we report the PA-MPJPE for pose errors (in mm): SPIN (152.8) vs. SPIN-ft (87.9); EFT (95.8) vs. EFT-ft (85.6), and METRO (117.7) vs. METRO-ft (88.2). Again, fine-tuning on our training set improves all models' performance; see Supp. Mat. for more details. These results suggest that our data empowers existing models with the ability to address challenges faced in the generic egocentric view setup.

6   Conclusion

We presented EgoBody, a dataset capturing human pose, shape and motions of interacting people in diverse environments. EgoBody collects multi-modal egocentric- and third-person-view data, accompanied by ground-truth 3D human pose and shape for all interacting subjects. With this dataset, we introduced a benchmark on egocentric-view 3D human body pose and shape (3DHPS) estimation, systematically evaluated and analyzed limitations of state-of-the-art methods on the egocentric setting, and demonstrated a significant, generalizable performance gain in them with the help of our annotations. This paper has shown EgoBody's unique value for the 3DHPS estimation task, and we see its great potential in moving the fields towards a better understanding of egocentric human motions, behaviors, and social interactions. In the future, adding more participants and even richer data modalities (*e.g.* audio recordings and motion annotations by natural language descriptions) could further enrich the dataset.

Acknowledgements. This work was supported by the SNF grant 200021 204840 and Microsoft Mixed Reality & AI Zurich Lab PhD scholarship. Qianli Ma is partially funded by the Max Planck ETH Center for Learning Systems.

References

1. Azure Kinect. https://docs.microsoft.com/en-us/azure/kinect-dk/
2. LAAN Labs 3D Scanner app. https://apps.apple.com/us/app/3d-scanner-app/id1419913995
3. Microsoft Hololens2. https://www.microsoft.com/en-us/hololens
4. SMPL model transfer. https://github.com/vchoutas/smplx/tree/master/transfer_mode
5. Agarwal, A., Triggs, B.: Recovering 3d human pose from monocular images. IEEE Trans. Pattern Anal. Mach. Intell. **28**(1), 44–58 (2005)
6. Aghaei, M., Dimiccoli, M., Ferrer, C.C., Radeva, P.: Towards social pattern characterization in egocentric photo-streams. Comput. Vis. Image Underst. **171**, 104–117 (2018)
7. Aghaei, M., Dimiccoli, M., Radeva, P.: With whom do i interact? Detecting social interactions in egocentric photo-streams. In: 2016 23rd International Conference on Pattern Recognition (ICPR), pp. 2959–2964. IEEE (2016)
8. A. Nisbet, R.: The Social Bond: An Introduction to the Study of Society (1970)
9. Bălan, A.O., Black, M.J.: The naked truth: estimating body shape under clothing. In: Forsyth, D., Torr, P., Zisserman, A. (eds.) ECCV 2008. LNCS, vol. 5303, pp. 15–29. Springer, Heidelberg (2008). https://doi.org/10.1007/978-3-540-88688-4_2
10. Bambach, S., Lee, S., Crandall, D.J., Yu, C.: Lending a hand: detecting hands and recognizing activities in complex egocentric interactions. In: Proceedings of the IEEE International Conference on Computer Vision, pp. 1949–1957 (2015)
11. Besl, P., McKay, N.D.: A method for registration of 3-d shapes. IEEE Trans. Pattern Anal. Mach. Intell. **14**(2), 239–256 (1992)
12. Bogo, F., Kanazawa, A., Lassner, C., Gehler, P., Romero, J., Black, M.J.: Keep it SMPL: automatic estimation of 3d human pose and shape from a single image. In: Leibe, B., Matas, J., Sebe, N., Welling, M. (eds.) ECCV 2016. LNCS, vol. 9909, pp. 561–578. Springer, Cham (2016). https://doi.org/10.1007/978-3-319-46454-1_34
13. Cao, Z., Hidalgo Martinez, G., Simon, T., Wei, S., Sheikh, Y.A.: Openpose: Real-time multi-person 2d pose estimation using part affinity fields. In: IEEE Transactions on Pattern Analysis and Machine Intelligence (2019)

14. Choi, H., Moon, G., Chang, J.Y., Lee, K.M.: Beyond static features for temporally consistent 3d human pose and shape from a video. In: Proceedings of the IEEE/CVF Conference on Computer Vision and Pattern Recognition, pp. 1964–1973 (2021)
15. Choi, H., Moon, G., Lee, K.M.: Pose2Mesh: graph convolutional network for 3d human pose and mesh recovery from a 2d human pose. In: Vedaldi, A., Bischof, H., Brox, T., Frahm, J.-M. (eds.) ECCV 2020. LNCS, vol. 12352, pp. 769–787. Springer, Cham (2020). https://doi.org/10.1007/978-3-030-58571-6_45
16. Doughty, D., et al.: Scaling egocentric vision: the dataset. In: Ferrari, V., Hebert, M., Sminchisescu, C., Weiss, Y. (eds.) ECCV 2018. LNCS, vol. 11208, pp. 753–771. Springer, Cham (2018). https://doi.org/10.1007/978-3-030-01225-0_44
17. Damen, D., et al.: Rescaling egocentric vision: collection, pipeline and challenges for epic-kitchens-100. Int. J. Comput. Vision 130(1), 33–55 (2022)
18. Dhand, A., Dalton, A.E., Luke, D.A., Gage, B.F., Lee, J.M.: Accuracy of wearable cameras to track social interactions in stroke survivors. J. Stroke Cerebrovasc. Dis. 25(12), 2907–2910 (2016)
19. Dong, J., Shuai, Q., Zhang, Y., Liu, X., Zhou, X., Bao, H.: Motion capture from internet videos. In: Vedaldi, A., Bischof, H., Brox, T., Frahm, J.-M. (eds.) ECCV 2020. LNCS, vol. 12347, pp. 210–227. Springer, Cham (2020). https://doi.org/10.1007/978-3-030-58536-5_13
20. Fang, Q., Shuai, Q., Dong, J., Bao, H., Zhou, X.: Reconstructing 3d human pose by watching humans in the mirror. In: Proceedings of the IEEE/CVF Conference on Computer Vision and Pattern Recognition, pp. 12814–12823 (2021)
21. Fathi, A., Hodgins, J.K., Rehg, J.M.: Social interactions: a first-person perspective. In: 2012 IEEE Conference on Computer Vision and Pattern Recognition, pp. 1226–1233. IEEE (2012)
22. Fathi, A., Farhadi, A., Rehg, J.M.: Understanding egocentric activities. In: 2011 International Conference on Computer Visio, pp. 407–414. IEEE (2011)
23. Fieraru, M., Zanfir, M., Oneata, E., Popa, A.I., Olaru, V., Sminchisescu, C.: Three-dimensional reconstruction of human interactions. In: Proceedings of the IEEE/CVF Conference on Computer Vision and Pattern Recognition, pp. 7214–7223 (2020)
24. Gall, J., Rosenhahn, B., Brox, T., Seidel, H.P.: Optimization and filtering for human motion capture. Int. J. Comput. Vision 87(1–2), 75 (2010)
25. Gower, J.C.: Generalized Procrustes analysis. Psychometrika 40(1), 33–51 (1975)
26. Grauman, K., Shakhnarovich, G., Darrell, T.: Inferring 3d structure with a statistical image-based shape model. In: ICCV, vol. 3, p. 641 (2003)
27. Grauman, K., et al.: Ego4D: Around the world in 3000 hours of egocentric video. arXiv preprint arXiv:2110.07058 (2021)
28. Guler, R.A., Kokkinos, I.: Holopose: Holistic 3d human reconstruction in-the-wild. In: Proceedings of the IEEE Conference on Computer Vision and Pattern Recognition, pp. 10884–10894 (2019)
29. Guzov, V., Mir, A., Sattler, T., Pons-Moll, G.: Human positioning system (HPS): 3d human pose estimation and self-localization in large scenes from body-mounted sensors. In: Proceedings of the IEEE/CVF Conference on Computer Vision and Pattern Recognition, pp. 4318–4329 (2021)
30. Hassan, M., Choutas, V., Tzionas, D., Black, M.J.: Resolving 3d human pose ambiguities with 3d scene constraints. In: Proceedings of the IEEE/CVF International Conference on Computer Vision, pp. 2282–2292 (2019)
31. He, K., Gkioxari, G., Dollár, P., Girshick, R.: Mask R-CNN. In: Proceedings of the IEEE International Conference on Computer Vision, pp. 2961–2969 (2017)

32. Huang, Y., Bogo, F., Lassner, C., Kanazawa, A., Gehler, P.V., Romero, J., Akhter, I., Black, M.J.: Towards accurate marker-less human shape and pose estimation over time. In: 2017 International Conference on 3D Vision (3DV), pp. 421–430. IEEE (2017)

33. Ionescu, C., Papava, D., Olaru, V., Sminchisescu, C.: Human3. 6m: large scale datasets and predictive methods for 3d human sensing in natural environments. IEEE Trans. Pattern Anal. Mach. Intell. **36**(7), 1325–1339 (2013)

34. Jiang, H., Grauman, K.: Seeing invisible poses: estimating 3d body pose from egocentric video. In: 2017 IEEE Conference on Computer Vision and Pattern Recognition (CVPR), pp. 3501–3509. IEEE (2017)

35. Joo, H., Neverova, N., Vedaldi, A.: Exemplar fine-tuning for 3d human pose fitting towards in-the-wild 3d human pose estimation (2021)

36. Joo, H., Simon, T., Cikara, M., Sheikh, Y.: Towards social artificial intelligence: nonverbal social signal prediction in a triadic interaction. In: Proceedings of the IEEE/CVF Conference on Computer Vision and Pattern Recognition, pp. 10873–10883 (2019)

37. Joo, H., et al.: Panoptic studio: a massively multiview system for social interaction capture. IEEE Trans. Pattern Anal. Mach. Intell. **41**(1), 190–204 (2017)

38. Joo, H., Simon, T., Sheikh, Y.: Total capture: a 3d deformation model for tracking faces, hands, and bodies. In: Proceedings of the IEEE Conference on Computer Vision and Pattern Recognition, pp. 8320–8329 (2018)

39. Kanazawa, A., Black, M.J., Jacobs, D.W., Malik, J.: End-to-end recovery of human shape and pose. In: Proceedings of the IEEE Conference on Computer Vision and Pattern Recognition, pp. 7122–7131 (2018)

40. Kanazawa, A., Zhang, J.Y., Felsen, P., Malik, J.: Learning 3d human dynamics from video. In: Proceedings of the IEEE Conference on Computer Vision and Pattern Recognition, pp. 5614–5623 (2019)

41. Kay, W., et al.: The kinetics human action video dataset. arXiv preprint arXiv:1705.06950 (2017)

42. Kazakos, E., Nagrani, A., Zisserman, A., Damen, D.: Epic-fusion: audio-visual temporal binding for egocentric action recognition. In: Proceedings of the IEEE/CVF International Conference on Computer Vision, pp. 5492–5501 (2019)

43. Kitani, K.M., Okabe, T., Sato, Y., Sugimoto, A.: Fast unsupervised ego-action learning for first-person sports videos. In: CVPR 2011, pp. 3241–3248. IEEE (2011)

44. Kocabas, M., Athanasiou, N., Black, M.J.: Vibe: video inference for human body pose and shape estimation. In: Proceedings of the IEEE/CVF Conference on Computer Vision and Pattern Recognition, pp. 5253–5263 (2020)

45. Kocabas, M., Huang, C.H.P., Hilliges, O., Black, M.J.: PARE: part attention regressor for 3D human body estimation. In: Proceedings International Conference on Computer Vision (ICCV), pp. 11127–11137. IEEE, October 2021

46. Kocabas, M., Huang, C.H.P., Tesch, J., Müller, L., Hilliges, O., Black, M.J.: SPEC: Seeing people in the wild with an estimated camera. In: Proceedings of International Conference on Computer Vision (ICCV), pp. 11035–11045, October 2021

47. Kolotouros, N., Pavlakos, G., Black, M.J., Daniilidis, K.: Learning to reconstruct 3d human pose and shape via model-fitting in the loop. In: Proceedings of the IEEE International Conference on Computer Vision, pp. 2252–2261 (2019)

48. Kolotouros, N., Pavlakos, G., Daniilidis, K.: Convolutional mesh regression for single-image human shape reconstruction. In: CVPR (2019)

49. Kolotouros, N., Pavlakos, G., Jayaraman, D., Daniilidis, K.: Probabilistic modeling for human mesh recovery. In: ICCV (2021)
50. Kwon, T., Tekin, B., Stuhmer, J., Bogo, F., Pollefeys, M.: H2O: two hands manipulating objects for first person interaction recognition. In: International Conference on Computer Vision (ICCV) (2021)
51. Lab, C.G.: CMU Graphics Lab Motion Capture Database (2000). https://mocap. cs.cmu.edu/
52. Lee, Y.J., Ghosh, J., Grauman, K.: Discovering important people and objects for egocentric video summarization. In: 2012 IEEE Conference on Computer Vision and Pattern Recognition, pp. 1346–1353. IEEE (2012)
53. Li, H., Cai, Y., Zheng, W.S.: Deep dual relation modeling for egocentric interaction recognition. In: Proceedings of the IEEE/CVF Conference on Computer Vision and Pattern Recognition, pp. 7932–7941 (2019)
54. Li, J., Xu, C., Chen, Z., Bian, S., Yang, L., Lu, C.: Hybrik: a hybrid analytical-neural inverse kinematics solution for 3d human pose and shape estimation. In: Proceedings of the IEEE/CVF Conference on Computer Vision and Pattern Recognition, pp. 3383–3393 (2021)
55. Li, Y., Liu, M., Rehg, J.M.: In the eye of beholder: joint learning of gaze and actions in first person video. In: Ferrari, V., Hebert, M., Sminchisescu, C., Weiss, Y. (eds.) ECCV 2018. LNCS, vol. 11209, pp. 639–655. Springer, Cham (2018). https://doi.org/10.1007/978-3-030-01228-1_38
56. Lin, K., Wang, L., Liu, Z.: End-to-end human pose and mesh reconstruction with transformers. In: CVPR (2021)
57. Liu, M., Yang, D., Zhang, Y., Cui, Z., Rehg, J.M., Tang, S.: 4D human body capture from egocentric video via 3D scene grounding. In: 2021 International Conference on 3D Vision (3DV) (2021)
58. Loper, M., Mahmood, N., Romero, J., Pons-Moll, G., Black, M.J.: SMPL: a skinned multi-person linear model. ACM Trans. Graph. (TOG) 34(6), 1–16 (2015)
59. Luo, Z., Golestaneh, S.A., Kitani, K.M.: 3d human motion estimation via motion compression and refinement. In: Proceedings of the Asian Conference on Computer Vision (2020)
60. Luo, Z., Hachiuma, R., Yuan, Y., Iwase, S., Kitani, K.M.: Kinematics-guided reinforcement learning for object-aware 3d ego-pose estimation. arXiv preprint arXiv:2011.04837 (2020)
61. Mahmood, N., Ghorbani, N., Troje, N.F., Pons-Moll, G., Black, M.J.: Amass: archive of motion capture as surface shapes. In: Proceedings of the IEEE/CVF International Conference on Computer Vision. pp. 5442–5451 (2019)
62. von Marcard, T., Henschel, R., Black, M.J., Rosenhahn, B., Pons-Moll, G.: Recovering accurate 3d human pose in the wild using IMUs and a moving camera. In: Ferrari, V., Hebert, M., Sminchisescu, C., Weiss, Y. (eds.) ECCV 2018. LNCS, vol. 11214, pp. 614–631. Springer, Cham (2018). https://doi.org/10.1007/978-3-030-01249-6_37
63. von Marcard, T., Pons-Moll, G., Rosenhahn, B.: Human pose estimation from video and IMUs. Trans. Pattern Anal. Mach. Intell. 38(8), 1533–1547 (2016)
64. Mehta, D., et al.: Monocular 3d human pose estimation in the wild using improved CNN supervision. In: 2017 International Conference on 3D Vision (3DV), pp. 506–516. IEEE (2017)
65. Moon, G., Lee, K.M.: I2L-MeshNet: image-to-lixel prediction network for accurate 3d human pose and mesh estimation from a single RGB image. In: Vedaldi, A., Bischof, H., Brox, T., Frahm, J.-M. (eds.) ECCV 2020. LNCS, vol. 12352, pp. 752–768. Springer, Cham (2020). https://doi.org/10.1007/978-3-030-58571-6_44

66. Narayan, S., Kankanhalli, M.S., Ramakrishnan, K.R.: Action and interaction recognition in first-person videos. In: Proceedings of the IEEE Conference on Computer Vision and Pattern Recognition Workshops, pp. 512–518 (2014)
67. Ng, E., Xiang, D., Joo, H., Grauman, K.: You2me: Inferring body pose in egocentric video via first and second person interactions. In: Proceedings of the IEEE/CVF Conference on Computer Vision and Pattern Recognition, pp. 9890–9900 (2020)
68. Northcutt, C., Zha, S., Lovegrove, S., Newcombe, R.: EgoCom: a multi-person multi-modal egocentric communications dataset. In: IEEE Transactions on Pattern Analysis and Machine Intelligence (2020)
69. Ogaki, K., Kitani, K.M., Sugano, Y., Sato, Y.: Coupling eye-motion and ego-motion features for first-person activity recognition. In: 2012 IEEE Computer Society Conference on Computer Vision and Pattern Recognition Workshops, pp. 1–7. IEEE (2012)
70. Omran, M., Lassner, C., Pons-Moll, G., Gehler, P., Schiele, B.: Neural body fitting: unifying deep learning and model based human pose and shape estimation. In: 2018 international conference on 3D vision (3DV), pp. 484–494. IEEE (2018)
71. Patel, P., Huang, C.H.P., Tesch, J., Hoffmann, D.T., Tripathi, S., Black, M.J.: AGORA: avatars in geography optimized for regression analysis. In: Proceedings IEEE/CVF Conference on Computer Vision and Pattern Recognition (CVPR), June 2021
72. Pavlakos, G., et al.: Expressive body capture: 3d hands, face, and body from a single image. In: Proceedings of the IEEE Conference on Computer Vision and Pattern Recognition, pp. 10975–10985 (2019)
73. Pech-Pacheco, J.L., Cristóbal, G., Chamorro-Martinez, J., Fernández-Valdivia, J.: Diatom autofocusing in bright field microscopy: a comparative study. In: Proceedings 15th International Conference on Pattern Recognition. ICPR-2000, vol. 3, pp. 314–317. IEEE (2000)
74. Pirsiavash, H., Ramanan, D.: Detecting activities of daily living in first-person camera views. In: 2012 IEEE Conference on Computer Vision and Pattern Recognition, pp. 2847–2854. IEEE (2012)
75. Rong, Y., Shiratori, T., Joo, H.: FrankMocap: a monocular 3d whole-body pose estimation system via regression and integration. In: IEEE International Conference on Computer Vision Workshops (2021)
76. Ryoo, M.S., Matthies, L.: First-person activity recognition: What are they doing to me? In: Proceedings of the IEEE Conference on Computer Vision and Pattern Recognition, pp. 2730–2737 (2013)
77. Saini, N., et al.: MarkerLess outdoor human motion capture using multiple autonomous micro aerial vehicles. In: Proceedings of the IEEE/CVF International Conference on Computer Vision, pp. 823–832 (2019)
78. Shiratori, T., Park, H.S., Sigal, L., Sheikh, Y., Hodgins, J.K.: Motion capture from body-mounted cameras. In: ACM SIGGRAPH 2011 Papers, pp. 1–10 (2011)
79. Sigurdsson, G.A., Gupta, A., Schmid, C., Farhadi, A., Alahari, K.: Actor and observer: joint modeling of first and third-person videos. In: Proceedings of the IEEE Conference on Computer Vision and Pattern Recognition, pp. 7396–7404 (2018)
80. Song, J., Chen, X., Hilliges, O.: Human body model fitting by learned gradient descent. In: Vedaldi, A., Bischof, H., Brox, T., Frahm, J.-M. (eds.) ECCV 2020. LNCS, vol. 12365, pp. 744–760. Springer, Cham (2020). https://doi.org/10.1007/978-3-030-58565-5_44

81. Sun, Y., Ye, Y., Liu, W., Gao, W., Fu, Y., Mei, T.: Human mesh recovery from monocular images via a skeleton-disentangled representation. In: Proceedings of the IEEE International Conference on Computer Vision, pp. 5349–5358 (2019)

82. Tan, J.K.V., Budvytis, I., Cipolla, R.: Indirect deep structured learning for 3d human body shape and pose prediction (2017)

83. Tome, D., et al.: SelfPose: 3d egocentric pose estimation from a headset mounted camera. arXiv preprint arXiv:2011.01519 (2020)

84. Tome, D., Peluse, P., Agapito, L., Badino, H.: XR-EgoPose: EgoCentric 3d human pose from an HMD camera. In: Proceedings of the IEEE/CVF International Conference on Computer Vision, pp. 7728–7738 (2019)

85. Trumble, M., Gilbert, A., Malleson, C., Hilton, A., Collomosse, J.: Total capture: 3d human pose estimation fusing video and inertial sensors. In: 2017 British Machine Vision Conference (BMVC) (2017)

86. Tung, H.Y., Tung, H.W., Yumer, E., Fragkiadaki, K.: Self-supervised learning of motion capture. In: Advances in Neural Information Processing Systems, pp. 5236–5246 (2017)

87. Ungureanu, D., et al.: HoloLens 2 Research Mode as a Tool for Computer Vision Research. arXiv:2008.11239 (2020)

88. Wandt, B., Rudolph, M., Zell, P., Rhodin, H., Rosenhahn, B.: CanonPose: self-supervised monocular 3d human pose estimation in the wild. In: Proceedings of the IEEE/CVF Conference on Computer Vision and Pattern Recognition, pp. 13294–13304 (2021)

89. Wang, Y., Liu, Y., Tong, X., Dai, Q., Tan, P.: Outdoor markerless motion capture with sparse handheld video cameras. IEEE Trans. Visual Comput. Graph. 24(5), 1856–1866 (2017)

90. Weng, Z., Yeung, S.: Holistic 3d human and scene mesh estimation from single view images. In: Proceedings of the IEEE/CVF Conference on Computer Vision and Pattern Recognition, pp. 334–343 (2021)

91. Xiang, D., Joo, H., Sheikh, Y.: Monocular total capture: posing face, body, and hands in the wild. In: Proceedings of the IEEE/CVF Conference on Computer Vision and Pattern Recognition (2019)

92. Xu, W., et al.: Mo2Cap2: real-time mobile 3D motion capture with a cap-mounted fisheye camera. IEEE Trans. Visual Comput. Graph. 25(5), 2093–2101 (2019)

93. Xu, Y., Zhu, S.C., Tung, T.: DenseRaC: joint 3d pose and shape estimation by dense render-and-compare. In: Proceedings of the IEEE/CVF International Conference on Computer Vision, pp. 7760–7770 (2019)

94. Yang, J.A., Lee, C.H., Yang, S.W., Somayazulu, V.S., Chen, Y.K., Chien, S.Y.: Wearable social camera: egocentric video summarization for social interaction. In: 2016 IEEE International Conference on Multimedia & Expo Workshops (ICMEW), pp. 1–6. IEEE (2016)

95. Yonetani, R., Kitani, K.M., Sato, Y.: Recognizing micro-actions and reactions from paired egocentric videos. In: Proceedings of the IEEE Conference on Computer Vision and Pattern Recognition, pp. 2629–2638 (2016)

96. Yu, Z., et al.: HUMBI: a large multiview dataset of human body expressions. In: Proceedings of the IEEE/CVF Conference on Computer Vision and Pattern Recognition, pp. 2990–3000 (2020)

97. Yuan, Y., Kitani, K.: Ego-pose estimation and forecasting as real-time PD control. In: Proceedings of the IEEE/CVF International Conference on Computer Vision, pp. 10082–10092 (2019)

98. Yuan, Y., Wei, S.E., Simon, T., Kitani, K., Saragih, J.: SimPoe: simulated character control for 3d human pose estimation. In: Proceedings of the IEEE/CVF Conference on Computer Vision and Pattern Recognition, pp. 7159–7169 (2021)
99. Zanfir, A., Bazavan, E.G., Xu, H., Freeman, B., Sukthankar, R., Sminchisescu, C.: Weakly supervised 3d human pose and shape reconstruction with normalizing flows. arXiv preprint arXiv:2003.10350 (2020)
100. Zhang, J., Yu, D., Liew, J.H., Nie, X., Feng, J.: Body meshes as points. In: Proceedings of the IEEE/CVF Conference on Computer Vision and Pattern Recognition, pp. 546–556 (2021)
101. Zhang, S., Zhang, Y., Bogo, F., Marc, P., Tang, S.: Learning motion priors for 4d human body capture in 3d scenes. In: International Conference on Computer Vision (ICCV), October 2021
102. Zhang, Y., An, L., Yu, T., Li, X., Li, K., Liu, Y.: 4d association graph for realtime multi-person motion capture using multiple video cameras. In: Proceedings of the IEEE/CVF Conference on Computer Vision and Pattern Recognition, pp. 1324–1333 (2020)
103. Zhang, Z., Crandall, D., Proulx, M., Talathi, S., Sharma, A.: Can gaze inform egocentric action recognition? In: 2022 Symposium on Eye Tracking Research and Applications, pp. 1–7 (2022)
104. Zhou, Y., Habermann, M., Habibie, I., Tewari, A., Theobalt, C., Xu, F.: Monocular real-time full body capture with inter-part correlations. In: Proceedings of the IEEE/CVF Conference on Computer Vision and Pattern Recognition, pp. 4811–4822 (2021)

Grasp'D: Differentiable Contact-Rich Grasp Synthesis for Multi-Fingered Hands

Dylan Turpin[1,2,3(✉)], Liquan Wang[1,2,3], Eric Heiden[3], Yun-Chun Chen[1,2], Miles Macklin[3], Stavros Tsogkas[4], Sven Dickinson[1,2,4], and Animesh Garg[1,2,3]

[1] University of Toronto, Toronto, Canada
dylanturpin@cs.toronto.edu
[2] Vector Institute, Toronto, Canada
[3] Nvidia, Santa Clara, USA
[4] Samsung AI Centre Toronto, Toronto, Canada

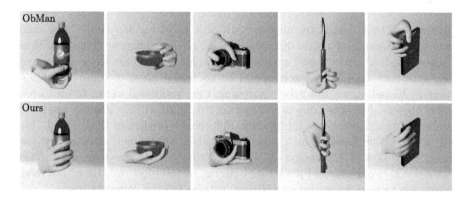

Fig. 1. Multi-finger grasp synthesis with Differentiable Simulation. Analytically synthesized grasps, such as in ObMan [39] based on the GraspIt! [63], plan sparse contacts at the fingertips. Our method (Grasp'D) for grasp synthesis discovers stable, contact-rich grasps that conform to detailed object surface geometry. Grasp'D creates larger contact-areas that better match the contact distribution of real human grasps.

Abstract. The study of hand-object interaction requires generating viable grasp poses for high-dimensional multi-finger models, often relying on analytic grasp synthesis which tends to produce brittle and unnatural results. This paper presents Grasp'D, an approach to grasp synthesis by differentiable contact simulation that can work with both known models and visual inputs. We use gradient-based methods as an alternative to sampling-based grasp synthesis, which fails without simplifying assumptions, such as pre-specified contact locations and eigengrasps. Such assumptions limit grasp discovery and, in particular, exclude high-contact power grasps. In contrast, our simulation-based approach allows for stable, efficient, physically realistic, high-contact grasp synthesis,

---

Supplementary Information The online version contains supplementary material available at https://doi.org/10.1007/978-3-031-20068-7_12.

© The Author(s), under exclusive license to Springer Nature Switzerland AG 2022
S. Avidan et al. (Eds.): ECCV 2022, LNCS 13666, pp. 201–221, 2022.
https://doi.org/10.1007/978-3-031-20068-7_12

even for gripper morphologies with high-degrees of freedom. We identify and address challenges in making grasp simulation amenable to gradient-based optimization, such as non-smooth object surface geometry, contact sparsity, and a rugged optimization landscape. Grasp'D compares favorably to analytic grasp synthesis on human and robotic hand models, and resultant grasps achieve over 4× denser contact, leading to significantly higher grasp stability. Video and code available at: graspd-eccv22.github.io.

Keywords: Multi-finger grasping · Grasp synthesis · Vision-Based grasping

1   Introduction

Humans use their hands to interact with objects of varying shape, size, and material thousands of times throughout a single day. Despite being effortless – almost instinctive – these interactions employ a complex visuomotor system, with components that correspond to dedicated areas of computer vision research. Visual inputs from the environment are processed in our brain to recognize objects of interest (object recognition [16,22,26,34,85]), identify modes of interaction to achieve a certain function (affordance prediction [7,20,53,72,76]), and position our hand(s) in a way that enables that function (pose estimation [2,6,32,37,80,91], grasping [25,51,82]). Proficiency in this task comes from accumulated experience in interacting with the same object over time, and readily extends to new categories or different instances of the same category.

This is an intriguing observation: humans can leverage accumulated knowledge from previous interactions, to quickly infer how to successfully manipulate an unknown object, *purely from visual input*. Granting machines the same ability to directly translate visual cues into plausible grasp predictions can have significant practical implications in the way robotic manipulators interact with novel objects [25,77] or in virtual environments in AR/VR [18,30].

Grasp prediction has previously been considered in the context of computer vision [42,45,67,89] and robotics [69]. It amounts to predicting the base pose (position and rotation) and joint angles of a robotic or human hand that is stably grasping a given object. This prediction is usually conditioned on visual inputs, such as RGB(D) images, point clouds, etc., and is typically performed online for real-time applications. Predicting grasps from visual inputs can be naturally posed as a learning problem, using paired visual data with their respective grasp annotations. However, capturing and annotating human grasps is laborious and not applicable to robotic grasping, so researchers often rely on datasets of synthetically generated grasps instead (see Table 1 for a list of recent works). Consequently, high-quality datasets of plausible, diverse grasps are crucial for any modern vision system performing grasp prediction, motivating the development of better methods for grasp synthesis.

Table 1. Modern vision-based grasp prediction for multi-finger hands relies on datasets created by human capture or analytic synthesis. Human capture is expensive and does not address the need for robotic grasp datasets. Analytic synthesis is only practical under significant limiting assumptions that exclude key grasp types [15,39].

Year	Name	Hand Model(s)	Analytic (A) or Human Capture (HC)
2019	ObMan [39]	MANO	A (GraspIt! [63])
2019	ContactDB [7]	MANO	HC
2020	Hope-net [21]	MANO	A (ObMan [39])
2020	UniGrasp [78]	Various	A (FastGrasp [71])
2020	ContactPose [9]	MANO	HC
2020	GANHand [15]	MANO	Other (manual)
2020	Grasping Field [49]	MANO	A (ObMan)
2020	GRAB [81]	MANO	HC
2021	Multi-Fin GAN [56]	Barrett	A (GraspIt!)
2021	DDGC [57]	Barrett	A (GraspIt!)
2021	Contact-Consistency [46]	MANO	A (ObMan)

Grasp synthesis assumes that the complete object geometry (e.g., mesh) is known, and is usually achieved by optimizing over a grasping metric which can be computed analytically or through simulation. *Analytic metrics* are handcrafted measures of a grasp's quality. For example, the epsilon metric [27] measures the magnitude of the smallest force that can break a grasp, computed as a function of the contact positions and normals that the grasp induces. While analytic metrics can be computationally faster, they often transfer poorly to the real world. *Simulation-based metrics* [24,48,90] measure grasp quality by running a simulation to test grasp effectiveness, e.g., by shaking the object and checking whether it is dropped. These can achieve a higher degree of physical fidelity, but require more computation. In both cases, optimization is usually black box, as neither the analytic metric or simulator is differentiable. Black box optimization can find good grasps in a reasonable number of steps as long as the search space is low-dimensional, e.g., when searching the pose space of parallel-jaw grippers [19,23,24,66,84]. However, when the number of degrees of freedom becomes larger, as in the case of multi-finger grippers, black box optimization over a grasping metric (whether analytic or simulation-based) becomes infeasible. Simplifying assumptions can be made to reduce the dimensionality of the search space, but they often reduce the plausibility of generated grasps.

To address these shortcomings, we propose Grasp'D, a grasp synthesis pipeline based on *differentiable simulation* which can generate contact-rich grasps that realistically conform to object surface geometry without any simplifying assumptions. A metric based on differentiable simulation admits gradient-based optimization, which is sample-efficient, even in high-dimensional spaces, and affords all the benefits of simulation-based metrics, i.e., physical plausibility, scalability, and extendability. Differentiable grasping simulation, however, also

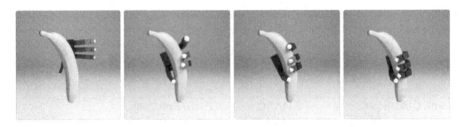

Fig. 2. Our method can synthesize grasps for both human and robotic hands, such as the four-finger Allegro hand in this figure. After hand initialization, we run gradient-based optimization to iteratively improve the grasp, in terms of stability and contact area. We include additional examples in Appendix B.

presents new challenges. Non-smooth object geometry (e.g., at the edges or corners of a cube) results in discontinuities in the contact forces and, subsequently, our grasping metric, complicating gradient-based optimization. Adding to that, if the hand and the object are not touching, small perturbations to the hand pose do not generate any additional force, resulting in vanishing gradients. Finally, the optimization landscape is rugged, making optimization challenging. Once the hand is touching the object, small changes to the hand pose may result in large changes to contact forces (and our metric).

We address these challenges as follows: (1) At the start of each optimization, we simulate contact between the hand and a smoothed, padded version of the object surface that gradually resolves to the true, detailed surface geometry, using a coarse-to-fine approach. This smoothing softens discontinuities in surface normals, allowing gradient-based optimization to smoothly move from one continuous surface area to another. This is enabled by our signed-distance function (SDF) approach to collision detection, which lets us freely recover a rounded object surface as the radius r level set of the SDF. (2) We allow gradients to *leak* through force computations for contact points that are not yet in the collision, introducing a biased gradient that can be followed to create new contacts. The intuition behind this choice is similar to the one for using LeakyReLU activations to prevent the phenomenon of "dying neurons" in deep neural networks [58]. (3) Inspired by Contact-Invariant Optimization (CIO) [64,65], we relax the problem formulation by introducing additional force variables that allow physics violations to be treated as a cost rather than a constraint. In effect, this decomposes the problem into finding contact forces that solve the task (of keeping the object stably in place) and finding a hand pose that provides those forces. We evaluate our method on synthetic object models from ShapeNet [11] and object meshes reconstructed from the YCB RGB-D dataset [10]. Experimental results show that our method generates contact-rich grasps with physical realism and with favorable performance against an existing analytic method [39].

Figure 1 displays example grasps generated by our method side-by-side with grasps from [39]. Because we do not make assumptions about contact locations or reduce the dimensionality of the search space, our method can discover contact-rich grasps that are more stable and more plausible than the fingertip-only grasps usually discovered by analytic synthesis. The same procedure works equally for robotic hands. Figure 2 displays snapshots of an optimization trajectory for an Allegro hand. As optimization progresses and our simulated metric decreases, the grasp becomes increasingly stable, plausible, and high-contact.

Summary of contributions:

1. We propose a differentiable simulation-based protocol for generating synthetic grasps from visual data. Unlike other simulation-based approaches, our method can scale to tens of thousands of dense contacts, and discover plausible, contact-rich grasps, without any simplifying assumptions.
2. We address challenges arising from the differentiable nature of our scheme, using a coarse-to-fine SDF collision detection approach, defining leaky gradients for contact points that are not yet in collision, and integrating physics violations as additional terms to our cost function.
3. We show that our method finds grasps with better stability, lower interpenetration, and higher contact area when compared to analytic grasp synthesis baselines, and justify our design choices through extensive evaluations.

2   Related Work

Grasp Synthesis. Although analytic metrics have been successfully applied to parallel-jaw gripper grasp synthesis (based on grasp wrench space analysis [27,35,63], robust grasp wrench space analysis [60,86], or caging [62,74]), more recent works [19,24,48,66] have focused on simulation-based synthesis. While they are more computationally costly, simulation-based metrics for parallel-jaw grasps better align with human judgement [48] and with real world performance [17,24,61,66]. In contrast to parallel-jaw grippers, multi-finger grasp synthesis is still largely analytic, with many recent works in multi-finger robotic grasping [56,57,78], grasp affordance prediction [49], and hand-object pose estimation [21,39,46] relying on datasets of analytically synthesized grasps (see Table 1). Notably, [21,39,46,49,56,57] all use datasets synthesized with the GraspIt! [63] simulator, which is widely used for both multi-finger robotic and human grasp synthesis. The ObMan dataset [39] for hand-object pose estimation (also used in [46,49]) is constructed by performing grasp synthesis with the MANO hand [75] in the GraspIt! Eigengrasp planner, and rendering the synthesized grasps against realistic backgrounds. The GraspIt! Eigengrasp planner optimizes analytic metrics based on grasp wrench space analysis. Dimensionality reduction [13] in the hand joint space, or using pre-specified contact locations for each hand link can be used to make the problem more tractable, but this limits the space of discoverable grasps and requires careful tuning. Our approach can successfully operate in the full grasp space, eschewing such simplifying assumptions while excelling in terms of physical fidelity over analytic synthesis for multi-finger grippers.

Human Grasp Capture. To estimate human grasps from visual inputs, existing methods train models on large-scale datasets [7,9,31,38,83]. Collecting these datasets puts humans in a lab with precise, calibrated cameras, lidar, and special gloves for accurately capturing human grasp poses. A human in the loop may also be needed for collecting annotations. All these requirements make the data collection process expensive and laborious. In addition, the captured grasps are only appropriate for human hands and not for robotic ones (which are important for many applications [1,12]). Some works [8,52] aim to transfer human grasps to robotic hands by matching contact patterns, but these suffer from important limitations, since the same contacts may not be achievable by human and robotic hands, given differences in their morphology and articulation constraints (e.g., see Fig. 8 of [52]). Our method provides a procedural way of generating high quality grasps for any type of hand – human or robotic.

Vision-Based Grasp Prediction. Whereas grasp synthesis is useful for generating grasps when full object geometry is available (i.e., a mesh or complete SDF is given), practical scenarios require predicting grasps from visual input. GAN-Hand [15] learns to predict human grasp affordances (as poses of a MANO [75] hand model) from input RGBD images using GANs. Since analytic synthesized datasets do not include many high-contact grasps, the authors also released the YCB Affordance dataset of 367 fine-grained grasps of the YCB object set [10], created by manually setting MANO hand joint angles in the GraspIt! simulator's GUI. Rather than predicting joint angles, Grasping Field [49] takes an implicit approach to grasp representation by learning to jointly predict signed distances for the MANO hand and the object to be grasped. For parallel-jaw grippers, most recent works [47,61,66,79] learn from simulation-based datasets (e.g., [24,48]). In contrast, multi-finger grasp prediction systems are still trained on either analytically synthesized datasets or datasets of captured human grasps (see Table 1). [21,39,46,49,56,57] all use analytically synthesized datasets from the GraspIt! simulator [63], whereas [7,9,81] use datasets of captured human grasps. [36,46] use captured human grasps to train a contact model, then refine grasps at test-time by optimizing hand pose to match predicted contacts. The higher quality training data generated by our grasp synthesis pipeline can lead to improved performance for any of these vision-based grasping prediction systems. Our system can also be used directly for vision-based grasp prediction, by running simulations with reconstructed objects (see Sect. 4.3).

Differentiable Grasping. We know of two works that have created differentiable grasp metrics in order to take advantage of gradient-based optimization for multi-finger grasp synthesis. [54] formulates a differentiable version of the epsilon metric [27] and uses it to synthesize grasps with the shadow robotic hand. They formulate the epsilon metric computation as a semidefinite programming (SDP) problem. Sensitivity analysis on this problem can then provide the gradient of the solution with respect to the problem parameters, including gripper pose. They manually label 45 potential contact points on the gripper. In contrast, we are able to scale to tens of thousands of contact points. Since the gripper may not yet be in contact with the object, they use an exponential weighting of points. Liu et al. [55] formulate a differentiable force closure metric and use gradient-based optimization to synthesize grasps with the MANO [75] hand model. Their formulation assumes zero friction and that the magnitude of all contact forces is uniform across contact points (although an error term allows both of these constraints to be slightly violated). Our method requires neither of these assumptions: the user can specify varying friction coefficients, and contact forces at different points are free to vary realistically. Their optimization problem involves finding a hand pose and a subset of candidate contact points on the hand that minimize an energy function. They find that the algorithm performs better with a smaller number of contact points and candidates. Selecting 3 contact points from the 773 candidate vertices of the MANO hand, it takes about 40 min to find 5 acceptable grasps. In contrast, our method is able to scale to tens of thousands of contact points while synthesizing an acceptable grasp in about 5 min. Notably, both of these prior works aim to take an analytic metric (the epsilon metric [27]) and make a differentiable variant. In contrast, we are presenting a differentiable simulation-based metric, which prior work on parallel-jaw grippers suggests will have greater physical fidelity [17,24,66] and better match human judgements [48] than analytic metrics.

Differentiable Physics. There has been significant progress in the development of differentiable physics engines [28,33,40,41,43,44,73,87,88]. However, certain limitations in recent approaches render them inadequate. Brax [28] and the Tiny Differentiable Simulator [41] only support collision primitives and cannot model general collisions between objects. Nimblephysics [87] supports mesh-to-mesh collision, but cannot handle cases where the gradient of contact normals with respect to position is zero (e.g., on a mesh face). While its analytic computation of gradients is fast, Nimblephysics requires manually writing forward and backward passes in C++, and only runs on CPU. Our work presents a new class of differentiable physics simulators to addresses many of these shortcomings. Further, Grasp'D supports GPU parallelism, enabling us to scale to tens of thousands of contacts, effectively approximating surface contacts.

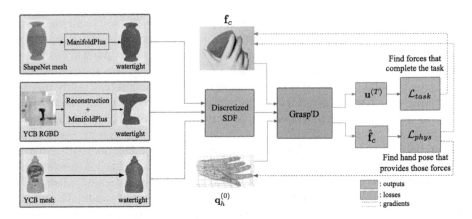

Fig. 3. Method overview. Grasp'D takes as input the discretized-SDF of an object (computed from a mesh or reconstructed from RGB-D) and synthesizes a stable grasp that can hold the object static as we vary the object's initial velocity. We optimize jointly over a hand pose $\mathbf{u}^{(T)}$ and the stabilizing forces $\hat{\mathbf{f}}_c$ provided by its contacts.

3   Grasp'D: Differentiable Contact-rich Grasp Synthesis

We present a method for solving the grasp synthesis problem (Fig. 3). From an input object and hand model (represented respectively by a signed-distance function and an articulation chain with mesh links), we generate a physically-plausible stable grasp, as a base pose and joint angles of the hand. This is achieved by iterative gradient-based optimization over a metric computed by differentiable simulation. The final grasp is dependent on the pose initialization of the hand, so different grasps can be recovered by sampling different starting poses. We detail our method below, but first outline the challenges that motivate our design.

Non-smooth Object Geometry. When optimizing the location of contacts between a hand and a sphere, the gradient of contact normals with respect to contact positions is well-defined and continuous, allowing gradient-based optimization to smoothly adjust contact positions along the sphere surface. But most objects are not perfectly smooth. Discontinuities in surface normals (e.g., at the edges or corners of a cube) result in discontinuities in contact normals and their gradients with respect to contact positions. Gradient-based optimization cannot effectively optimize across these discontinuities (e.g., cannot follow the gradient to move contact locations from one face of a cube to another). We address this with a coarse-to-fine smoothing approach, optimizing against a smoothed and padded version of the object surface that gradually resolves to the true surface as optimization continues (see Sect. 3.2).

Contact Sparsity. Of all possible contacts between the hand and object, only a sparse subset is active at any given time. If a particular point on the hand is inactive (not in contact with the object), then an infinitesimal perturbation of the hand pose will not change its status (make it touch the object). The gradient of the force applied by any inactive contact (with respect to hand pose) will be exactly zero. This means that gradient-based optimization can not effectively create new contacts, since contacts that are not already active do not contribute to the gradient. We address this by allowing gradient to *leak* through the force computations of inactive contacts (see Sect. 3.3).

Rugged Optimization Landscape. When many contacts are active (i.e., hand touching the object), small changes to hand pose may result in large changes to contact forces and, subsequently, large changes to our grasp metric. This makes gradient-based optimization challenging. We address this with a problem relaxation inspired by Contact-Invariant Optimization [64,65] (see Sect. 3.4).

3.1 Rigid Body Dynamics

In the interest of speed and simplicity, we limit ourselves to simple rigid body dynamics. Let $\mathbf{q}$ and $\mathbf{u}$ be the joint and spatial coordinates, respectively, with first and second time derivatives $\dot{\mathbf{q}}$, $\ddot{\mathbf{q}}$, $\dot{\mathbf{u}}$, $\ddot{\mathbf{u}}$. Let $\mathbf{M}$ be the mass matrix. The kinematic map $\mathbf{H}$ maps joint coordinate time derivatives to spatial velocities as $\dot{\mathbf{q}} = \mathbf{H}(\mathbf{q})\mathbf{u}$, and is related to contact and external forces ($\mathbf{f}_c$ and $\mathbf{f}_{ext}$) through the following motion equation: $\mathbf{H}\mathbf{M}\mathbf{H}^\top \ddot{\mathbf{q}} = \mathbf{f}_c + \mathbf{f}_{ext}$, which yields the semi-implicit Euler update used for discrete time stepping [5]:

$$\dot{\mathbf{q}}^{(t+1)} \leftarrow \dot{\mathbf{q}}^{(t)} + \Delta t \mathbf{M}^{-1}(\mathbf{f}_c + \mathbf{f}_{ext}) \tag{1}$$

$$\mathbf{q}^{(t+1)} \leftarrow \mathbf{q}^{(t)} + \Delta t \dot{\mathbf{q}}^{(t+1)}. \tag{2}$$

3.2 Object Model with Coarse-to-fine Surface Smoothing

SDF Representation. For the purpose of collision detection, the hand is represented by a set of surface points $\mathbf{X}_h$, and the object to grasp is represented by its Signed Distance Function (SDF), $\phi(\mathbf{x})$ (similar to [4,29,59]). The SDF maps a spatial position $\mathbf{x} \in \mathbb{R}^3$ to its distance to the closest point on the surface of the object, with a negative or positive sign for interior and exterior points, respectively [68]. The object surface can be recovered as the zero level-set of the SDF: $\{\mathbf{x}|\phi(\mathbf{x}) = 0\}$. The gradient of the SDF $\nabla\phi(\mathbf{x})$ is always of unit magnitude, corresponds to the surface normal for $\mathbf{x}$ on the object surface, and yields the closest point on the object as $\mathbf{x} - \phi(\mathbf{x})\nabla\phi(\mathbf{x})$. SDF representations are well-suited to differentiable collision detection [59], since contact forces can be written in terms of a penetration depth (ϕ) and normal direction ($\nabla\phi$), for which gradients can be computed as $\nabla\phi$ and $\nabla^2\phi$, respectively.

Whereas primitive objects (e.g., a sphere or box) admit an analytic SDF, this is not the case for complex objects, for which an SDF representation is not readily available. We model the object to be grasped by a discretized SDF which we extract from ground truth meshes (easier to come by for most object sets [10,11]), yielding a 3D grid. Given a query point $\mathbf{x}$, to compute $\phi(\mathbf{x})$ based on the grid, we first convert $\mathbf{x}$ to local shape coordinates (where the object is in canonical pose: unrotated and centered at the origin), yielding $\mathbf{x}_{\text{local}}$. If $\mathbf{x}_{\text{local}}$ falls within the bounds of the grid, we map it to grid indices and compute $\phi(\mathbf{x}_{\text{local}})$ by tri-linear interpolation of neighbouring grid cells. If $\mathbf{x}_{\text{local}}$ falls outside the grid, we clamp it to the grid bounds, yielding $\mathbf{x}_{\text{clamp}}$, and compute $\phi(\mathbf{x}) := \phi(\mathbf{x}_{\text{clamp}}) + \|\mathbf{x} - \mathbf{x}_{\text{clamp}}\|$.

Coarse-To-Fine Smoothing. To successfully optimize contact locations over non-smooth object geometry we employ surface smoothing in a coarse-to-fine way. At the start of each optimization, we define the object surface *not* as the zero level-set of the SDF, but as the radius r level-set: $\{\mathbf{x}|\phi(\mathbf{x}) = r > 0\}$, which gives a smoothed and padded version of the original surface. As optimization continues, we decrease r on a linear schedule until it reaches 0, yielding the original surface. This coarse-to-fine smoothing allows gradient-based optimization to effectively move contact points across discontinuities and prevents the optimization from quickly overfitting to local geometric features. We set r to approximately 10cm at the start of each optimization. Details are in Appendix A.2.

3.3   Contact Dynamics with Leaky Gradient

Contact Forces. We use a primal (penalty-based) formulation of contact forces, which allows us to compute derivatives with autodiff [3] and keep a consistent memory footprint. For a given point $\mathbf{x} \in \mathbf{X}_{\text{h}}$, the resultant contact force is

$$\mathbf{f}_c = \mathbf{f}_n + \mathbf{f}_t \tag{3}$$

$$\mathbf{f}_n = k_n \min(\phi(\mathbf{x}),\, 0)\nabla\phi(\mathbf{x}) \tag{4}$$

$$\mathbf{f}_t = -\min(k_f\|\mathbf{v}_t\|,\, \mu\|\mathbf{f}_n\|)\mathbf{v}_t, \tag{5}$$

where $\mathbf{f}_n$ is the normal component, proportional to penetration depth $\phi(\mathbf{x})$, and $\mathbf{f}_t$ is the frictional component, computed using a Coulomb friction model. k_n and k_f are the normal and frictional stiffness coefficients, respectively, μ is the friction coefficient, and $\mathbf{v}_t$ is the component of relative velocity between hand and object at the contact point $\mathbf{x}$ that is tangent to the contact normal $\nabla\phi(\mathbf{x})$.

Leaky Gradients. At any one time, most possible hand-object contacts are inactive – a property we refer to as *contact sparsity*. Since an infinitesimal perturbation to hand pose will not activate these contacts (i.e., will not make them touch the object), the gradient of their contact forces with respect to hand pose is zero, i.e., $\partial\mathbf{f}_c/\partial\mathbf{q} = \partial\mathbf{f}_c/\partial\dot{\mathbf{q}} = \partial\mathbf{f}_c/\partial\ddot{\mathbf{q}} = 0$. When the hand is not touching the object, all contacts are inactive and gradient-based optimization can get stuck in a plateau. We work around this by computing a *leaky* gradient for the normal force term. From equation (4), we have $\frac{\partial \|\mathbf{f}_n\|}{\partial \mathbf{q}} = 0$ if $\phi(\mathbf{x}) \geq 0$ but we instead set

$$
\frac{\partial \|\mathbf{f}_n\|}{\partial \mathbf{q}} := \begin{cases} k_n \frac{\partial \phi}{\partial \mathbf{q}} & \text{if } \phi(\mathbf{x}) < 0 \\ \alpha k_n \frac{\partial \phi}{\partial \mathbf{q}} & \text{otherwise} \end{cases}, \tag{6}
$$

where $\alpha \in [0, 1]$ controls how much gradient leaks through the minimum. We set $\alpha = 0.1$ in our experiments.

3.4   Grasping Metric and Problem Relaxation

Simulation Setup. To compute the grasp metric, we simulate the rigid-body interaction between a hand and an object. The hand is kinematic (does not react to contact forces), while the object is dynamic (thus subject to contact forces). The simulator state is given by the configuration vector $\mathbf{q}$ and its first and second time derivatives $\dot{\mathbf{q}}, \ddot{\mathbf{q}}$. $\mathbf{q}$ is composed of hand and object components $\mathbf{q} = (\mathbf{q}_h, \mathbf{q}_o)$ with corresponding spatial coordinates $\mathbf{u} = (\mathbf{u}_h, \mathbf{u}_{obj})$. The object is always initialized with the same configuration $\mathbf{q}_o^{(0)}$: unrotated and untranslated at the origin. Given a state $\mathbf{q}^{(t)}$, following equations (1) and (2), our simulator uses a semi-implicit Euler update scheme to compute subsequent state $\mathbf{q}^{(t+1)}$.

Computing the Grasp Metric by Simulation. To measure the quality of a candidate grasp $\mathbf{q}_h$, we test its ability to withstand forces applied to the object. Given an initial state $\mathbf{q}^{(0)} = (\mathbf{q}_h, \mathbf{q}_o^{(0)})$, we apply an initial velocity $\dot{\mathbf{q}}_o^{(0)}$ to the object. The hand is kept static, with $\dot{\mathbf{u}}_h = 0$. We run forward simulation to compute the object's final velocity $\dot{\mathbf{u}}_o^{(T)}$. A stable grasp will produce contact forces that resist the object velocity, so lower $\|\dot{\mathbf{u}}_o^{(T)}\|$ indicates a more stable grasp. In fact, a stable grasp should be able to resist object velocities in *any* direction, so we perform multiple simulations with different initial velocities and average the results. This suggests the following basic grasp metric: for each set of M simulations, indexed by $m = \{1, \ldots, M\}$, we set a different initial object velocity, run the simulation, and record $L_m = \|\dot{\mathbf{u}}_o^{(T)}\|$. Then, averaging, we have

$$
\mathcal{L}_{\text{grasp}} = \sum_{m=1}^{M} \frac{L_m}{M}. \tag{7}
$$

Since $\mathcal{L}_{\text{grasp}}$ is a differentiable function of the output of a differentiable simulation, it is itself differentiable with respect to $\mathbf{q}_h$, and we can compute loss gradients $\partial \mathcal{L}_{\text{grasp}} / \partial \mathbf{q}_h$ and use gradient-based optimization to find stable grasps.

Unfortunately, in practice, this basic procedure does not succeed. As explained at the beginning of Sect. 3, the grasp optimization landscape is extremely rugged, with sharp and narrow ridges, peaks, and valleys. Our leaky contact force gradients (see Sect. 3.3) provide some help in escaping plateaus, but once the hand is in contact with the object, small changes in hand configuration still cause large jumps in contact forces by making/breaking contacts and shifting contact normals. However, differentiability alone does not resolve this issue.

Problem Relaxation. Inspired by Contact-Invariant Optimization [64,65] we relax the problem making it more forgiving to gradient-based optimization. Specifically, we introduce additional *desired* or *prescribed* contact force variables. This allows us to model physics violations as a cost rather than a constraint. For each surface point on the hand $\mathbf{x}^i \in \mathbf{X}_h$, we introduce a 6-dimensional vector $\widehat{\mathbf{f}}_c^i$ representing the desired hand-object contact wrench arising from contact at $\mathbf{x}^i$.

Our overall loss now has two components. The task loss $\mathcal{L}_{\text{task}}(\widehat{\mathbf{f}}_c)$ measures whether the prescribed forces $\widehat{\mathbf{f}}_c$ successfully resist initial object velocities. This is computed identically to the previous $\mathcal{L}_{\text{grasp}}$, except that instead of computing contact forces according to equations (3), (4) and (5), contact forces are simply set equal to $\widehat{\mathbf{f}}_c$. The physics violation loss $\mathcal{L}_{\text{phys}}(\mathbf{q}_h, \widehat{\mathbf{f}}_c)$ measures whether the hand configuration $\mathbf{q}_h$ actually provides the desired forces $\widehat{\mathbf{f}}_c$. It is computed as

$$\mathcal{L}_{\text{phys}}(\mathbf{q}_h, \widehat{\mathbf{f}}_c) = \|f_c(\mathbf{q}_h) - \widehat{\mathbf{f}}_c\|, \tag{8}$$

where $f_c(\mathbf{q}_h)$ is the contact force arising from the hand pose $\mathbf{q}_h$ according to equations (3), (4) and (5).

Intuitively, minimizing these losses corresponds to finding a set of desired forces (as close as possible to the actual contact forces arising from the current hand configuration) that complete the task, and finding a hand configuration that provides those forces. We expect problem formulations derived from and inspired by Contact-Invariant Optimization [13,14] to be a fruitful area of research as they are made newly attractive by advances in differentiable simulation.

Additional Heuristic Losses. We include some additional losses that improve the plausibility of resulting grasps. Most hand models have defined joint range limits. Let $\mathbf{q}_h^{\text{low}}$ and $\mathbf{q}_h^{\text{up}}$ be the lower and upper joint limits respectively. $\mathcal{L}_{\text{range}}$ encourages hand joints to be near the middle of their ranges. $\mathcal{L}_{\text{limit}}$ penalizes hand joints outside of their range. $\mathcal{L}_{\text{inter}}$ penalizes self intersections of the hand.

$$\mathcal{L}_{\text{range}}(\mathbf{q}_h) = \left\| \mathbf{q}_h - \frac{\mathbf{q}_h^{\text{up}} + \mathbf{q}_h^{\text{low}}}{2} \right\| \tag{9}$$

$$\mathcal{L}_{\text{limit}}(\mathbf{q}_h) = \max(\mathbf{q}_h - \mathbf{q}_h^{\text{up}}, 0) + \max(\mathbf{q}_h^{\text{low}} - \mathbf{q}_h, 0) \tag{10}$$

$$\mathcal{L}_{\text{inter}}(\mathbf{q}_h) = \|\mathbf{f}_{\text{link}}\|. \tag{11}$$

The hand is kinematic, so it is not subject to contact forces. However, we still compute forces arising from contact between the hand links, for use in this loss term, as $\mathbf{f}_{\text{link}}$. We ignore contacts between neighbouring links in the chain. For the purpose of computing $\mathbf{f}_{\text{link}}$, we represent each hand link as both a point set and an SDF and compute $\mathbf{f}_{\text{link}}$ according to equations (3), (4), and (5).

3.5   Optimization

We use the Modified Differential Multiplier Method [70], treating $\mathcal{L}_{\text{task}} < C_{\text{task}}$ and $\mathcal{L}_{\text{limit}} < C_{\text{limit}}$ as constraints, while minimizing $\mathcal{L}_{\text{phys}}$, $\mathcal{L}_{\text{limit}}$ and $\mathcal{L}_{\text{inter}}$. We update our parameters $\widehat{\mathbf{f}}_c$ and $\mathbf{q}_h$ using the Adamax [50] optimizer. Details of learning rates, C_{task} and C_{limit} can be found in Appendix A.7.

4   Experiments

Our evaluations and analysis of Grasp'D answer the following questions:

1. How well does Grasp'D perform compared to analytic methods? (Sect. 4.2)
2. Can Grasp'D generalize to objects reconstructed from real-world RGBD images? (Sect. 4.3)
3. How much do coarse-to-fine SDF collision and the problem relaxation contribute to final performance? (Sect. 4.4)

4.1   Experimental Setup

For each experiment, we synthesize grasps following the procedure described in Sect. 3. We compute the metric with $M = 3$ simulations: each setting a different initial velocity on the hand: $(0, 0, 0)$, $(0.01, 0.01, 0.01)$ or $(-0.01, -0.01, -0.01)\text{m/s}$. Each simulation is run for a single timestep of length $1 \times 10^{-5}\text{s}$.

Evaluation Metrics. We follow [39] and use contact area (CA), intersection volume (IV), and the ratio between contact area and intersection volume ($\frac{\text{CA}}{\text{IV}}$). We compute evaluation metrics that measure grasp stability and contact area. In addition, we measure the contact area each grasp creates and the volume of hand-object interpenetration. We compute two analytic measures of stability – the Ferrari-Canny (epsilon ϵ) [27] and the volume metric (Vol) – and one simulated measure: the simulation displacement (SD) metric introduced in [39].

Hand Parameterization. We use a differentiable PyTorch layer [39] to compute the 773 vertices of the MANO hand [75] model. The input is a set of weights for principal components extracted from the MANO dataset of human scans [75]. We find that this PCA parameterization provides a useful prior for human-like hand poses. We use the maximum number of principal components (44).

Table 2. Experimental results. We synthesize MANO hand grasps for ShapeNet objects. Our grasps achieve over 4× denser contact (as measured by contact surface area - CA) than an analytic synthesis baseline [39], leading to significantly higher grasp stability (4× lower simulation displacement - SD). Higher contact does result in higher interpenetration, but we keep a similar ratio of contact area to interpenetration volume.

Method	CA ↑	IV ↓	$\frac{CA}{IV}$ ↑	ϵ ↑	Vol ↑	SD ↓
Scale (Unit)	cm²	cm³	cm⁻¹	×10⁻¹	×10¹	cm
ObMan [39] (top2)	9.4	1.28	7.37	4.70	1.36	1.95
ObMan [39] (top5)	7.8	**1.05**	7.37	4.52	1.36	2.22
Grasp'D (top2)	**43.0**	5.70	**7.55**	5.01	1.44	**0.59**
Grasp'D (top5)	41.4	5.48	**7.55**	**5.02**	**1.46**	1.04

4.2   Grasp Synthesis with ShapeNet Models

We compare to baseline grasps from the ObMan [39] dataset, which generates grasps with the GraspIt! [63] simulator using an analytic metric. We report these metrics over the top-2 and top-5 grasps per scaled object, with ranking decided by simulation displacement for our method and by ObMan's heuristic measure (detailed in Appendix C.2 of [39]) for theirs. Further details in Appendix A.6.

Data. We evaluate our approach to grasp synthesis by generating grasps with the MANO human hand [75] model for 57 ShapeNet [11] objects that span 8 categories (bottles, bowls, cameras, cans, cellphones, jars, knives, remote controls), and are each considered at 5 different scales (as in ObMan). See the Appendix A for details of mesh pre-processing, initialization, simulation, and optimization.

Results. Results are presented in Table 2. Grasps generated by our method (both top-2 and top-5) have a contact area of around 42cm². This is higher than the ∼ 20cm² area achieved with fingertip only grasps [7] and about 4× higher than grasps from the ObMan dataset (top-2 or top-5). These contact-rich grasps achieve modest improvements in analytic measures of stability, and a significant reduction in simulation displacement (∼ 3× for top-2 grasps). Visualizations of our generated grasps in Fig. 1 confirm that these grasps achieve larger areas of contact by closely conforming to object surface geometry, whereas the analytically generated grasps largely make use of fingertip contact only. These higher contact grasps have accordingly higher interpenetration, but the ratio between contact area and intersection volume is similar to the ObMan baseline.

Fig. 4. Grasp synthesis from RGB-D. We use RGB-D captures from the YCB dataset [10] (top row) to reconstruct object models from which we synthesize grasps (bottom row). Our method can synthesize plausible grasps not just from ground truth object models, but also from imperfect reconstructions.

4.3 Grasp Synthesis from RGB-D Input of Unknown Objects

Setting. One possible application of our method is to direct grasp prediction from RGB-D images by simulation on reconstructed object models. Currently, our method is too slow to be used online (about 5 min per grasp), but as simulation speeds increase and recent works in implicit fields push reconstruction accuracy higher and higher, we believe that grasp prediction by simulation models will become increasingly viable. To validate the plausibility of using our method with reconstructed object models, we present results from running our system on meshes reconstructed from RGB-D inputs. We synthesize grasps based on RGB-D (with camera pose) inputs from the YCB object dataset [10]. In addition to reconstructed meshes, the YCB dataset provides the original RGB-D captures the meshes are based on. Each object was captured from 5 different cameras at 120 different angles for a total of 600 images. To confirm that our method can work with reconstructions done under more realistic assumptions, we limit our reconstructions to using 5 different angles from 3 cameras (2.5% of captures).

Data. For a subset of the YCB objects, we generate Poisson surface reconstructions and use our method to synthesize MANO hand grasps. Since the inputs are from cameras with a known pose, the object reconstruction is in the world frame. Details in the Appendix A.4.

Results. Our results confirm the viability of using simulation to synthesize grasps on reconstructed object models. Qualitative results are presented in Fig. 4; additional results can be found in Appendix D. Although synthesis does not perform as well as with ground-truth models, plausible human grasps are discovered for many objects and the grasps appear well-aligned with the real-world object poses. Future work could take advantage of learning-based reconstruction methods to achieve grasp synthesis with fewer input images.

Table 3. Ablation study. We validate our design choices with an ablation study. Our relaxed problem formulation has a large positive impact on all metrics. The quantitative impact of coarse-to-fine smoothing is more limited, but we observe a qualitative difference in grasps generated with and without smoothing.

Method	CA ↑	IV ↓	$\frac{CA}{IV}$ ↑	ϵ ↑	Vol ↑	SD ↓
Scale/Unit	cm^2	cm^3	cm^{-1}	$\times 10^{-1}$	$\times 10^1$	cm
Grasp'D	42.6	2.83	15.1	2.38	20.6	0.41
Grasp'D w/o coarse-to-fine	43.2	2.84	15.2	2.37	20.7	0.55
Grasp'D w/o problem relaxation	6.1	0.40	15.2	0.52	4.0	3.82

4.4   Ablation Study

We investigate the impact of our coarse-to-fine smoothing (Sect. 3.2), leaky contact force gradients (Sect. 3.3), and relaxed problem formulation (Sect. 3.4). We generate MANO hand grasps on 21 objects from the YCB dataset [10]. *Grasp'D w/o coarse-to-fine* does not pad or smooth the object. *Grasp'D w/o problem relaxation* attempts to solve the problem without introducing additional force variables or a relaxed objective. This amounts to the "basic procedure" described in Sect. 3.4, i.e., directly optimize over hand pose to minimize $\mathcal{L}_{grasp}$ and the heuristic losses.

Results. We adopt the same data as in Sect. 4.2. Table 3 presents the results. Our relaxed problem formulation is key to our method's success, and without it, performance greatly degrades by all measures, with discovered grasps creating very little contact (low contact area and intersection volume). Coarse-to-fine smoothing has a modest impact, with all metrics comparable with or without smoothing, except for simulation displacement, which is about 25% higher without smoothing. We did not include a variant without leaky gradient, since this variant would never make contact with the object (if the hand is not touching the object at initialization, there will be no gradient to follow and optimization will immediately be stuck in a plateau).

5   Conclusions

We presented a simulation-based grasp synthesis pipeline capable of generating large datasets of plausible, high-contact grasps. By being differentiable, our simulator is amenable to gradient-based optimization, allowing us to produce high-quality grasps, even for multi-finger grippers, while scaling to thousands of dense contacts. Our experiments have shown that we outperform the existing classical grasping algorithm both quantitatively and qualitatively. Our approach is compatible with PyTorch and can be easily integrated into existing pipelines.

More importantly, the produced grasps can directly benefit any vision pipeline that learns grasp prediction from synthetic data.

Acknowledgements. DT was supported in part by a Vector research grant. The authors appreciate the support of NSERC, Vector Institute and Samsung AI. AG was also supported by NSERC Discovery Grant, NSERC Exploration Grant, CIFAR AI Chair, XSeed Discovery Grant from University of Toronto.

References

1. Allshire, A., et al.:Transferring dexterous manipulation from gpu simulation to a remote real-world trifinger. arXiv preprint arXiv:2108.09779 (2021)
2. Baek, S., Kim, K.I., Kim, T.K.: Pushing the envelope for rgb-based dense 3d hand pose estimation via neural rendering. In: CVPR (2019)
3. Baydin, A.G., Pearlmutter, B.A., Radul, A.A., Siskind, J.M.: Automatic differentiation in machine learning: a survey. JMLR (2018)
4. Bender, J., Duriez, C., Jaillet, F., Zachmann, G.: Continuous collision detection between points and signed distance fields. In: Workshop on Virtual Reality Interaction and Physical Simulation (2014)
5. Bender, J., Erleben, K., Trinkle, J.: Interactive simulation of rigid body dynamics in computer graphics. Comput. Graph. Forum **33**(1), 246–270 (2014)
6. Boukhayma, A., Bem, R.d., Torr, P.H.: 3d hand shape and pose from images in the wild. In: CVPR (2019)
7. Brahmbhatt, S., Ham, C., Kemp, C.C., Hays, J.: Contactdb: Analyzing and predicting grasp contact via thermal imaging. In: CVPR (2019)
8. Brahmbhatt, S., Handa, A., Hays, J., Fox, D.: Contactgrasp: Functional multi-finger grasp synthesis from contact. In: IROS (2019)
9. Brahmbhatt, S., Tang, C., Twigg, C.D., Kemp, C.C., Hays, J.: Contactpose: A dataset of grasps with object contact and hand pose. In: ECCV (2020)
10. Calli, B., et al.: Yale-cmu-berkeley dataset for robotic manipulation research. Int. J. Robot. Res. **36**(3), 027836491770071 (2017)
11. Chang, A.X., et al.: Shapenet: An information-rich 3d model repository. arXiv preprint arXiv:1512.03012 (2015)
12. Chen, T., Xu, J., Agrawal, P.: A system for general in-hand object re-orientation. In: CoRL (2022)
13. Ciocarlie, M., Goldfeder, C., Allen, P.: Dexterous grasping via eigengrasps: A low-dimensional approach to a high-complexity problem. In: RSS (2007)
14. Ciocarlie, M.T., Allen, P.K.: Hand posture subspaces for dexterous robotic grasping. Int. J. Robot. Res. **28**(7), 851–867 (2009)
15. Corona, E., Pumarola, A., Alenya, G., Moreno-Noguer, F., Rogez, G.: Ganhand: Predicting human grasp affordances in multi-object scenes. In: CVPR (2020)
16. Dalal, N., Triggs, B.: Histograms of oriented gradients for human detection. In: CVPR (2005)
17. Danielczuk, M., Xu, J., Mahler, J., Matl, M., Chentanez, N., Goldberg, K.: Reach: Reducing false negatives in robot grasp planning with a robust efficient area contact hypothesis model. In: International Symposium of Robotic Research (2019)
18. De Giorgio, A., Romero, M., Onori, M., Wang, L.: Human-machine collaboration in virtual reality for adaptive production engineering. Procedia Manufacturing (2017)

19. Depierre, A., Dellandréa, E., Chen, L.: Jacquard: A large scale dataset for robotic grasp detection. In: IROS (2018)
20. Do, T.T., Nguyen, A., Reid, I.: Affordancenet: An end-to-end deep learning approach for object affordance detection. In: ICRA (2018)
21. Doosti, B., Naha, S., Mirbagheri, M., Crandall, D.J.: Hope-net: A graph-based model for hand-object pose estimation. In: CVPR (2020)
22. Duan, K., Bai, S., Xie, L., Qi, H., Huang, Q., Tian, Q.: Centernet: Keypoint triplets for object detection. In: ICCV (2019)
23. Eppner, C., Mousavian, A., Fox, D.: A billion ways to grasp: An evaluation of grasp sampling schemes on a dense, physics-based grasp data set. arXiv preprint arXiv:1912.05604 (2019)
24. Eppner, C., Mousavian, A., Fox, D.: Acronym: A large-scale grasp dataset based on simulation. In: ICRA (2021)
25. Fang, K., Zhu, Y., Garg, A., Kurenkov, A., Mehta, V., Fei-Fei, L., Savarese, S.: Learning task-oriented grasping for tool manipulation from simulated self-supervision. Int. J. Robot. Research (IJRR) 39(2–3), 202–216 (2019)
26. Felzenszwalb, P.F., Girshick, R.B., McAllester, D., Ramanan, D.: Object detection with discriminatively trained part-based models. TPAMI (2009)
27. Ferrari, C., Canny, J.F.: Planning optimal grasps. In: ICRA (1992)
28. Freeman, C.D., Frey, E., Raichuk, A., Girgin, S., Mordatch, I., Bachem, O.: Brax - a differentiable physics engine for large scale rigid body simulation (2021). https://github.com/google/brax
29. Fuhrmann, A., Sobotka, G., Groß, C.: Distance fields for rapid collision detection in physically based modeling. In: Proceedings of GraphiCon (2003)
30. Gammieri, L., Schumann, M., Pelliccia, L., Di Gironimo, G., Klimant, P.: Coupling of a redundant manipulator with a virtual reality environment to enhance human-robot cooperation. Procedia Cirp (2017)
31. Garcia-Hernando, G., Yuan, S., Baek, S., Kim, T.K.: First-person hand action benchmark with rgb-d videos and 3d hand pose annotations. In: CVPR (2018)
32. Ge, L., Ren, Z., Li, Y., Xue, Z., Wang, Y., Cai, J., Yuan, J.: 3d hand shape and pose estimation from a single rgb image. In: CVPR (2019)
33. Geilinger, M., Hahn, D., Zehnder, J., Bächer, M., Thomaszewski, B., Coros, S.: Add: Analytically differentiable dynamics for multi-body systems with frictional contact. ACM Trans. Graph. 39(6), 1–15 (2020)
34. Girshick, R., Donahue, J., Darrell, T., Malik, J.: Rich feature hierarchies for accurate object detection and semantic segmentation. In: CVPR (2014)
35. Goldfeder, C., Ciocarlie, M., Dang, H., Allen, P.K.: The columbia grasp database. In: ICRA (2009)
36. Grady, P., Tang, C., Twigg, C.D., Vo, M., Brahmbhatt, S., Kemp, C.C.: Contactopt: Optimizing contact to improve grasps. In: CVPR (2021)
37. Hamer, H., Schindler, K., Koller-Meier, E., Van Gool, L.: Tracking a hand manipulating an object. In: ICCV (2009)
38. Hampali, S., Rad, M., Oberweger, M., Lepetit, V.: Honnotate: A method for 3d annotation of hand and object poses. In: CVPR (2020)
39. Hasson, Y., Varol, G., Tzionas, D., Kalevatykh, I., Black, M.J., Laptev, I., Schmid, C.: Learning joint reconstruction of hands and manipulated objects. In: CVPR (2019)
40. Heiden, E., Macklin, M., Narang, Y.S., Fox, D., Garg, A., Ramos, F.: DiSECt: A Differentiable Simulation Engine for Autonomous Robotic Cutting. In: RSS (2021)
41. Heiden, E., Millard, D., Coumans, E., Sheng, Y., Sukhatme, G.S.: NeuralSim: Augmenting differentiable simulators with neural networks. In: ICRA (2021)

42. Heumer, G., Amor, H.B., Weber, M., Jung, B.: Grasp recognition with uncalibrated data gloves-a comparison of classification methods. In: IEEE Virtual Reality Conference (2007)
43. Hu, Y., Anderson, L., Li, T.M., Sun, Q., Carr, N., Ragan-Kelley, J., Durand, F.: Difftaichi: Differentiable programming for physical simulation. In: ICLR (2020)
44. Hu, Y, et al.: Chainqueen: A real-time differentiable physical simulator for soft robotics. In: ICRA (2019)
45. Huang, D.A., Ma, M., Ma, W.C., Kitani, K.M.: How do we use our hands? discovering a diverse set of common grasps. In: CVPR (2015)
46. Jiang, H., Liu, S., Wang, J., Wang, X.: Hand-object contact consistency reasoning for human grasps generation. In: ICCV (2021)
47. Jiang, Z., Zhu, Y., Svetlik, M., Fang, K., Zhu, Y.: Synergies between affordance and geometry: 6-dof grasp detection via implicit representations. arXiv preprint arXiv:2104.01542 (2021)
48. Kappler, D., Bohg, J., Schaal, S.: Leveraging big data for grasp planning. In: ICRA (2015)
49. Karunratanakul, K., Yang, J., Zhang, Y., Black, M.J., Muandet, K., Tang, S.: Grasping field: Learning implicit representations for human grasps. In: 3DV (2020)
50. Kingma, D.P., Ba, J.: Adam: A method for stochastic optimization. In: ICLR (2014)
51. Kokic, M., Kragic, D., Bohg, J.: Learning task-oriented grasping from human activity datasets. IEEE Robotics and Automation Letters (2020)
52. Lakshmipathy, A., Bauer, D., Bauer, C., Pollard, N.S.: Contact transfer: A direct, user-driven method for human to robot transfer of grasps and manipulations. In: 2022 International Conference on Robotics and Automation (ICRA), pp. 6195–6201. IEEE (2022)
53. Lau, M., Dev, K., Shi, W., Dorsey, J., Rushmeier, H.: Tactile mesh saliency. ACM Trans. Graph. **35**(4), 1–11 (2016)
54. Liu, M., Pan, Z., Xu, K., Ganguly, K., Manocha, D.: Deep differentiable grasp planner for high-dof grippers. arXiv preprint arXiv:2002.01530 (2020)
55. Liu, T., Liu, Z., Jiao, Z., Zhu, Y., Zhu, S.C.: Synthesizing diverse and physically stable grasps with arbitrary hand structures using differentiable force closure estimator. IEEE Robotics and Automation Letters (2021)
56. Lundell, J., et al.: Multi-fingan: Generative coarse-to-fine sampling of multi-finger grasps. arXiv preprint arXiv:2012.09696 (2020)
57. Lundell, J., Verdoja, F., Kyrki, V.: Ddgc: Generative deep dexterous grasping in clutter. IEEE Robot. Autom. Lett. **6**(4), 6599–6906 (2021)
58. Maas, A.L., Hannun, A.Y., Ng, A.Y., et al.: Rectifier nonlinearities improve neural network acoustic models. In: ICML (2013)
59. Macklin, M., Erleben, K., Müller, M., Chentanez, N., Jeschke, S., Corse, Z.: Local optimization for robust signed distance field collision. ACM Comput. Graph. Interact. Tech. **3**(1), 1–17 (2020)
60. Mahler, J., et al.: Dex-net 2.0: Deep learning to plan robust grasps with synthetic point clouds and analytic grasp metrics. arXiv preprint arXiv:1703.09312 (2017)
61. Mahler, J., et al.: Learning ambidextrous robot grasping policies. Sci. Robot. **4**(26), eaau4984 (2019)
62. Mahler, J., Pokorny, F.T., McCarthy, Z., van der Stappen, A.F., Goldberg, K.: Energy-bounded caging: Formal definition and 2-d energy lower bound algorithm based on weighted alpha shapes. IEEE Robotics and Automation Letters (2016)
63. Miller, A.T., Allen, P.K.: Graspit! a versatile simulator for robotic grasping. IEEE Robot. Autom. Mag. **11**(4), 110–122 (2004)

64. Mordatch, I., Popović, Z., Todorov, E.: Contact-invariant optimization for hand manipulation. In: ACM SIGGRAPH/Eurographics Symposium on Computer Animation (2012)
65. Mordatch, I., Todorov, E., Popović, Z.: Discovery of complex behaviors through contact-invariant optimization. ACM Trans. Graph. **31**(4), 1–8 (2012)
66. Mousavian, A., Eppner, C., Fox, D.: 6-dof graspnet: Variational grasp generation for object manipulation. In: ICCV (2019)
67. Nakamura, Y.C., Troniak, D.M., Rodriguez, A., Mason, M.T., Pollard, N.S.: The complexities of grasping in the wild. In: International Conference on Humanoid Robotics (2017)
68. Osher, S., Fedkiw, R.: Level Set Methods and Dynamic Implicit Surfaces. AMS, vol. 153. Springer, New York (2003). https://doi.org/10.1007/b98879
69. Pirk, S., et al.: Understanding and exploiting object interaction landscapes. ACM Trans. Graphi. **36**(4), 1 (2017)
70. Platt, J.C., Barr, A.H.: Constrained differential optimization. In: NeurIPS (1987)
71. Pokorny, F.T., Kragic, D.: Classical grasp quality evaluation: New algorithms and theory. In: IROS (2013)
72. Porzi, L., Bulo, S.R., Penate-Sanchez, A., Ricci, E., Moreno-Noguer, F.: Learning depth-aware deep representations for robotic perception. IEEE Robot. Autom. Lett. **2**(2), 468–475 (2016)
73. Qiao, Y.L., Liang, J., Koltun, V., Lin, M.C.: Efficient differentiable simulation of articulated bodies. In: ICML (2021)
74. Rodriguez, A., Mason, M.T., Ferry, S.: From caging to grasping. International J. Robot. Res. **31**(7), 889–900 (2012)
75. Romero, J., Tzionas, D., Black, M.J.: Embodied hands: Modeling and capturing hands and bodies together. ACM Trans. Graph. **36**(6) (2017)
76. Roy, A., Todorovic, S.: A multi-scale CNN for affordance segmentation in RGB images. In: Leibe, B., Matas, J., Sebe, N., Welling, M. (eds.) ECCV 2016. LNCS, vol. 9908, pp. 186–201. Springer, Cham (2016). https://doi.org/10.1007/978-3-319-46493-0_12
77. Saxena, A., Driemeyer, J., Kearns, J., Ng, A.: Robotic grasping of novel objects. In: Advances in Neural Information Processing Systems, vol. 19 (2006)
78. Shao, L., et al.: Unigrasp: Learning a unified model to grasp with multifingered robotic hands. IEEE Robot. Autom. Lett. **5** 2286–2293 (2020)
79. Sundermeyer, M., Mousavian, A., Triebel, R., Fox, D.: Contact-graspnet: Efficient 6-dof grasp generation in cluttered scenes. In: ICRA (2021)
80. Supančič, J.S., Rogez, G., Yang, Y., Shotton, J., Ramanan, D.: Depth-based hand pose estimation: methods, data, and challenges. IJCV (2018)
81. Taheri, O., Ghorbani, N., Black, M.J., Tzionas, D.: GRAB: a dataset of whole-body human grasping of objects. In: Vedaldi, A., Bischof, H., Brox, T., Frahm, J.-M. (eds.) ECCV 2020. LNCS, vol. 12349, pp. 581–600. Springer, Cham (2020). https://doi.org/10.1007/978-3-030-58548-8_34
82. Turpin, D., Wang, L., Tsogkas, S., Dickinson, S., Garg, A.: GIFT: Generalizable Interaction-aware Functional Tool Affordances without Labels. In: Robotics: Systems and Science (RSS) (2021)
83. Tzionas, D., Ballan, L., Srikantha, A., Aponte, P., Pollefeys, M., Gall, J.: Capturing hands in action using discriminative salient points and physics simulation. IJCV (2016)
84. Veres, M., Moussa, M., Taylor, G.W.: An integrated simulator and dataset that combines grasping and vision for deep learning. arXiv preprint arXiv:1702.02103 (2017)

85. Viola, P., Jones, M.: Rapid object detection using a boosted cascade of simple features. In: CVPR (2001)
86. Weisz, J., Allen, P.K.: Pose error robust grasping from contact wrench space metrics. In: ICRA (2012)
87. Werling, K., Omens, D., Lee, J., Exarchos, I., Liu, C.K.: Fast and feature-complete differentiable physics for articulated rigid bodies with contact. arXiv preprint arXiv:2103.16021 (2021)
88. Xu, J., Makoviychuk, V., Narang, Y., Ramos, F., Matusik, W., Garg, A., Macklin, M.: Accelerated Policy Learning with Parallel Differentiable Simulation. In: International Conference on Learning Representations (ICLR) (2022)
89. Yang, Y., Fermuller, C., Li, Y., Aloimonos, Y.: Grasp type revisited: A modern perspective on a classical feature for vision. In: CVPR (2015)
90. Zhou, Y., Hauser, K.: 6dof grasp planning by optimizing a deep learning scoring function. In: RSS (2017)
91. Zimmermann, C., Brox, T.: Learning to estimate 3d hand pose from single rgb images. In: ICCV (2017)

AutoAvatar: Autoregressive Neural Fields for Dynamic Avatar Modeling

Ziqian Bai[1,2(✉)], Timur Bagautdinov[2], Javier Romero[2], Michael Zollhöfer[2], Ping Tan[1], and Shunsuke Saito[2]

[1] Simon Fraser University, Burnaby, Canada
ziqian_bai@sfu.ca
[2] Reality Labs Research, Pittsburgh, USA

Abstract. Neural fields such as implicit surfaces have recently enabled avatar modeling from raw scans without explicit temporal correspondences. In this work, we exploit autoregressive modeling to further extend this notion to capture dynamic effects, such as soft-tissue deformations. Although autoregressive models are naturally capable of handling dynamics, it is non-trivial to apply them to implicit representations, as explicit state decoding is infeasible due to prohibitive memory requirements. In this work, for the first time, we enable autoregressive modeling of implicit avatars. To reduce the memory bottleneck and efficiently model dynamic implicit surfaces, we introduce the notion of articulated observer points, which relate implicit states to the explicit surface of a parametric human body model. We demonstrate that encoding implicit surfaces as a set of height fields defined on articulated observer points leads to significantly better generalization compared to a latent representation. The experiments show that our approach outperforms the state of the art, achieving plausible dynamic deformations even for unseen motions. https://zqbai-jeremy.github.io/autoavatar.

1 Introduction

Animatable 3D human body models are key enablers for various applications ranging from virtual try-on to social telepresence [4]. While modeling of human avatars from 3D scans without surface registration is gaining more and more attention in recent years [8,24,25,42,47], complex temporal dynamics are often completely ignored and the resulting deformations are often treated exclusively as a function of the pose parameters. However, the body shape is not uniquely determined by the current pose of the human, but also depends on the history of shape deformations due to secondary motion effects. The goal of our work is to realistically model these history-dependent dynamic effects for human bodies without requiring precise surface registration (Fig. 1).

To this end, we propose AutoAvatar, a novel autoregressive model for dynamically deforming human bodies. AutoAvatar models body geometry implicitly - using a signed

---

Z. Bai—Work done while He was an intern at Reality Labs Research, Pittsburgh, PA, USA.

Supplementary Information The online version contains supplementary material available at https://doi.org/10.1007/978-3-031-20068-7_13.

ⓒ The Author(s), under exclusive license to Springer Nature Switzerland AG 2022
S. Avidan et al. (Eds.): ECCV 2022, LNCS 13666, pp. 222–239, 2022.
https://doi.org/10.1007/978-3-031-20068-7_13

Fig. 1. AutoAvatar. Given raw 4D scans with self-intersections, holes, and noise (grey meshes) and fitted SMPL models (blue meshes), AutoAvatar automatically learns highly detailed animatable body models with plausible secondary motion dynamics without requiring a personalized template or surface registration (right). (Color figure online)

distance field (SDF) - and is able to directly learn from raw scans without requiring temporal correspondences for supervision. In addition, akin to physics-based simulation, AutoAvatar infers the complete shape of an avatar given history of shape and motion. The aforementioned properties lead to a generalizable method that models complex dynamic effects including inertia and elastic deformations without requiring a personalized template or precise temporal correspondences across training frames.

To model temporal dependencies in the data, prior work has typically resorted to autoregressive models [22,27,38,44]. While the autoregressive framework naturally allows for incorporation of temporal information, combining it with neural implicit surface representations [9,28,35] for modeling human bodies is non-trivial. Unlike explicit shape representations, such neural representations implicitly encode the shape in the parameters of the neural network and latent codes. Thus, in practice, producing the actual shape requires expensive neural network evaluation at each voxel of a dense spatial grid [35]. This aspect is particularly problematic for autoregressive modeling, since most of the successful autoregressive models rely on rollout training [19,27] to ensure stability of both training and inference. Unfortunately, rollout training requires multiple evaluations of the model for each time step, and thus becomes prohibitively expensive both in terms of memory and compute as the resolution of the spatial grid grows. Another approach would be learning an autoregressive model using latent embeddings that encode dynamic shape information [15]. However, it is infeasible to observe the entire span of possible surface deformations from limited real-world scans, which makes the model prone to overfitting and leads to worse generalization at test time.

By addressing these limitations, we, for the first time, enable autoregressive training of a full-body geometry model represented by a neural implicit surface. To tackle the scalability issues of rollout training for implicit representations, we introduce the novel notion of articulated observer points. Intuitively, articulated observer points are temporally coherent locations on the human body surface which store the dynamically changing state of the implicit function. In practice, we parameterize the observer points using the underlying body model [22], and then represent the state of the implicit surface as signed heights with respect to the vertices of the pose-dependent geometry produced by the articulated model (see Fig. 3a). The number of query points is significantly lower than the number of voxels in a high-resolution grid, which allows for a significant reduction in terms of memory and compute requirements, making rollout training tractable for implicit surfaces. In addition, we demonstrate that explicitly encoding shapes as signed height fields is less prone to overfitting compared to latent embeddings, a common way to represent autoregressive states [19,51].

Our main contributions are the following:

- The first autoregressive approach for modeling history-dependent implicit surfaces of human bodies,
- Articulated observer points to enable autoregressive training of neural fields, and
- Comprehensive experiments that provide insights on the design decisions for modeling dynamic effects with neural fields.

2 Related Work

Parametric Human Models. Since the anatomical structure of humans is shared across identities, various methods have been proposed to parameterize shape and pose of human bodies from large-scale 3D scan data [1,3,13,22,32,53]. SCAPE [3,13] learns statistical human model models using triangle deformations. The pioneering work by Allen et al. [2] used a vertex-based representation enhanced with pose-dependent deformations, but the model was complex and trained with insufficient data, resulting in overfitting. SMPL [22] improved the generalizability of [2] by training on more data and removing the shape dependency in the pose-dependent deformations. More recent works show that sparsity in the pose correctives reduces spurious correlations [32], and that non-linear deformation bases parameterized by neural networks achieve better modeling accuracy [53]. While most works focus on modeling static human bodies under different poses, Dyna [38] and DMPL (Dynamic SMPL) [22] enable parametric modeling of dynamic deformations by learning a linear autoregressive model. Kim et al. [16] combine a volumetric parametric model, VSMPL, with an external layer driven by the finite element method to enable soft tissue dynamics. SoftSMPL [44] learns a more powerful recurrent neural network to achieve better generalization to unseen subjects. Xiang et al. [51] model dynamically moving clothing from a history of poses. Importantly, the foundation of the aforementioned works is accurate surface registration of a template body mesh [6,7], which remains non-trivial. Habermann et al. [12] also model dynamic deformations from a history of poses. While they relax the need of registration by leveraging image-based supervision, a personalized template is still required as a preprocessing step.

Recently, neural networks promise to enable the modeling of animatable bodies without requiring surface registration or a personalized template [8,10,24,42,47]. These methods leverage structured point clouds [24,25,55] or 3D neural fields [52] to learn animatable avatars. Approaches based on neural fields parameterize human bodies as compositional articulated occupancy networks [10] or implicit surface in canonical space with linear blend skinning [8,29,42,50] and deformation fields [34,47]. Since implicit surfaces do not require surface correspondences for training, avatars can be learned from raw scans. Similarly, neural radiance fields [30] have been applied to body

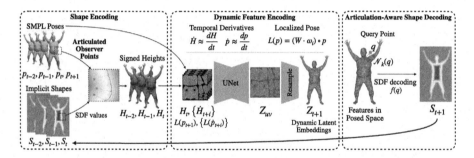

Fig. 2. Overview. AutoAvatar learns a pose-driven animatable human body model with plausible dynamics including secondary motions. Notice that our approach takes the history of implicit shapes in an autoregressive manner for learning dynamics.

modeling to build animatable avatars from multi-view images [20,36]. However, these approaches represent avatars as a function of only pose parameters, and thus are unable to model dynamics. While our approach is also based on 3D neural fields to eliminate the need for surface registration, our approach learns not only pose-dependent deformations but also history-dependent dynamics by enabling autoregressive training of neural implicit surfaces.

Learning Dynamics. Traditionally, physics-based simulation [45] is used to model dynamics of objects. While material parameters of physics simulation can be estimated from real data [5,46,49,54], accurately simulating dynamic behavior of objects remains an open question. In addition, authenticity of physics-based simulation is bounded by the underlying model, and complex anisotropic materials such as the human body are still challenging to model accurately. For this reason, several works attempt to substitute a deterministic physics-based simulation with a learnable module parameterized by neural networks [14,37,43,56]. Such approaches have been applied to cloth simulation [14,37], fluid [43], and elastic bodies [56]. Subspace Neural Physics [14] learns a recurrent neural network from offline simulation to predict the simulation state in a subspace. Deep Emulator [56] first learns an autoregressive model to predict deformations using a simple primitive (sphere), and applies the learned function to more complex characters. While we share the same spirit with the aforementioned works by learning dynamic deformations in an autoregressive manner, our approach fundamentally differs from them. The aforementioned approaches all assume that physical quantities such as vertex positions are observable with perfect correspondence in time, and thus results are only demonstrated on synthetic data. In contrast, we learn dynamic deformations from real-world observation while requiring only coarse temporal guidance by the fitted SMPL models. This property is essential to model faithful dynamics of real humans.

3   Method

Our approach is an autoregressive model, which takes as inputs human poses and a shape history and produces the implicit surface for a future frame. Figure 2 shows

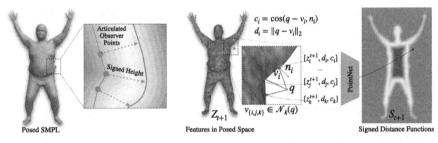

(a) Shape Encoding.   (b) Articulation-Aware SDF Decoding.

Fig. 3. Shape Encoding/Decoding. Our novel shape encoding via articulated observer points and articulated-aware SDF decoding lead to faithful modeling of dynamics.

the overview of our approach. Given a sequence of T implicitly encoded shapes $\{S_{t-T+1}, ..., S_t\}$ and $T + 1$ poses $\{p_{t-T+1}, ..., p_{t+1}\}$ with t being the current time frame, our model predicts the implicit surface S_{t+1} of the future frame $t + 1$.

The output shape S_{t+1} is then passed as an input to the next frame prediction in an autoregressive manner. Our model is supervised directly with raw body scans, and requires a training dataset of 4D scans (sequences of 3D scans) along with fitted SMPL body models [22]. Unfortunately, explicitly representing shapes S_t as levelsets of implicit surface is prohibitively expensive for end-to-end training. To this end, we introduce the concept of *articulated observer points* - vertex locations on the underlying articulated model - which are used as a local reference for defining the full body geometry. The underlying implicit surface is encoded as a height field with respect to the articulated observer points (Sect. 3.1). Given a history of height fields and pose parameters, we convert those to dynamic latent feature maps in UV space (Sect. 3.2). Finally, we map the resulting features to SDFs by associating continuous 3D space with the learned features on the SMPL vertices, which are directly supervised by point clouds with surface normals (Sect. 3.3).

3.1 Shape Encoding via Articulated Observer Points

The core of our approach is an autoregressive model that operates on implicit neural surfaces, allowing us to incorporate temporal shape information necessary for modeling challenging dynamics. The key challenge that arises when training such autoregressive models is finding a way to encode the shape - parameterized implicitly as a neural field - into a representation that can be efficiently computed and fed back into the model. The most straightforward way is to extract an explicit geometry representation by evaluating the neural field on a dense spatial grid and running marching cubes [23]. However, in practice this approach is infeasible due to prohibitive memory and computational costs, in particular due to the cubic scaling with respect to the grid dimensions. Instead, we propose to encode the state of the implicit surface into a set of observer points.

Encoding geometry into discrete point sets has been shown to be efficient and effective for learning shape representations from point clouds [39]. Prokudin et al. [39] relies on a fixed set of randomly sampled observer points in global world coordinates, which is not suitable for modeling dynamic humans due to the articulated nature of human motion. Namely, a model relying on observer points with a fixed 3D location needs to account for extremely large shape variations including rigid transformations, making the learning task difficult. Moreover, associating randomly sampled 3D points with a parametric human body is non-trivial. To address these limitations, we further extend the notion of observer points to an articulated template represented by the SMPL model [22], which provides several advantages for modeling dynamic articulated geometries. In particular, soft-tissue dynamic deformations appear only around the minimally clothed body, and we can rely on this notion as an explicit prior to effectively allocate observer points only to the relevant regions. In addition, the SMPL model provides a mapping of 3D vertices to a common UV parameterization, allowing us to effectively process shape information using 2D CNNs in a temporally consistent manner.

More specifically, to encode the neural implicit surface into the articulated observer points, we compute "signed heights" $H = \{h_j\}_{j=1}^M \in \mathbb{R}^M$ from M vertices on a fitted SMPL model. For each vertex, the signed height h_j is the signed distance from the vertex to the zero-crossing of the implicit surface along the vertex normal (see Fig. 3a). We use the iterative secant method as in [31] to compute the zero-crossings. Note that there can be multiple valid signed heights per vertex since the line along the normal can hit the zero-crossing multiple times. Based on the observation that the SMPL vertices are usually close to the actual surface with their normals roughly facing into the same direction, we use the minimum signed height within a predefined range $[h_{min}, h_{max}]$ (in our experiments, we use $h_{min} = -2\,\text{cm}, h_{max} = 8\,\text{cm}$). If no zero-crossing is found inside this range, we set the signed height to h_{min}. Note that the computed heights are signed because the fitted SMPL can go beyond the actual surface due to its limited expressiveness and inaccuracy in the fitting stage.

3.2 Dynamic Feature Encoding

The essence of AutoAvatar is an animatable autoregressive model. In other words, a reconstructed avatar is driven by pose parameters, while secondary dynamics is automatically synthesized from the history of shapes and poses. To enable this, we learn a mapping that encodes the history of shape and pose information to latent embeddings containing the shape information of the future frame. More specifically, denoting the current time frame as t, we take as input $T + 1$ poses $\{p_{t-T+1}, ..., p_{t+1}\}$ and T signed heights vectors $\{H_{t-T+1}, ..., H_t\}$, and produce dynamic features $Z_{t+1} \in \mathbb{R}^{M \times C}$. Given these inputs, we also compute the temporal derivatives of poses $\{\dot{p}_{t+i}\}_{i=-T+2}^1$ and signed heights $\{\dot{H}_{t+i}\}_{i=-T+2}^0$ as follows:

$$\dot{p}_k = p_k p_{k-1}^{-1}$$
$$\dot{H}_k = H_k - H_{k-1}, \tag{1}$$

where p_* are represented as quaternions. To emphasize small values in $\dot{H}$, we apply the following transformation $g(x) = \text{sign}(x) \cdot \ln(\alpha|x| + 1) \cdot \beta$, where $\alpha = 1000$ and $\beta = 0.25$. Following prior works [4,42], we also localize pose parameters to reduce long range spurious correlations as follows:

$$L(\boldsymbol{p}) = (W \cdot \omega_j) \circ \boldsymbol{p}, \tag{2}$$

where $\circ$ denotes the element-wise product, j is the vertex index, $W \in \mathbb{R}^{J \times J}$ is an association matrix of J joints, and $\omega_j \in \mathbb{R}^{J \times 1}$ is the skinning weights of the j-th vertex. We set $W_{n,m} = 1$ if the n-th joint is within the 1-ring neighborhood of the m-th joint (otherwise $W_{n,m} = 0$). Note that the derivative of the root transformation is included in $\{L(\dot{\boldsymbol{p}}_{t+i})\}$ without localization. Finally, we map $\boldsymbol{H}_t$, $\{\dot{\boldsymbol{H}}_{t+i}\}$, $L(\boldsymbol{p}_{t+1})$, and $\{L(\dot{\boldsymbol{p}}_{t+i})\}$ to UV space using barycentric interpolation. The concatenated features are fed into a UNet [41] to generate a feature map $\boldsymbol{Z}_{uv}$. We then resample $\boldsymbol{Z}_{uv}$ on the UV coordinates corresponding to SMPL vertices to obtain the per-vertex dynamic latent embeddings $\boldsymbol{Z}$. We empirically found that incorporating temporal derivatives further improves the realism of dynamics (see Supp. Mat. video for comparison).

3.3   Articulation-Aware Shape Decoding

Given the dynamic feature $\boldsymbol{Z}_{t+1} = \{\boldsymbol{z}_1^{t+1}, ..., \boldsymbol{z}_M^{t+1}\}$ and a query point $\boldsymbol{q}$, we decode signed distance fields $f(\boldsymbol{q})$ to obtain the surface geometry of the dynamic avatar. Several methods model the implicit surface in canonical space by jointly learning a warping function from the posed space to the canonical space [8,42]. However, we observe that the canonicalization step is very sensitive to small fitting error in the SMPL model, and further amplifies the error in the canonical space, making it difficult to learn dynamics (see discussion in Sect. 4). Therefore, we directly model the implicit surface in a posed space while being robust to pose changes. Inspired by Neural Actor [20], we associate a queried 3D point with a human body model and pose-agnostic spatial information. Specifically, Neural Actor uses height from the closest surface point on the SMPL model to the query location together with a feature vector sampled on the same surface point. However, we find that their approach based on the single closest point leads to artifacts around body joints (e.g., armpits) for unseen poses. To better distinguish regions with multiple body parts, we instead use k-nearest neighbor vertices. Figure 3b shows the illustration of our SDF decoding approach. Given a query point $\boldsymbol{q}$, we first compute the k-nearest SMPL vertices $\{\boldsymbol{v}_j\}_{j \in \mathcal{N}_k(\boldsymbol{q})}$, where $\mathcal{N}_k(\boldsymbol{q})$ is a set of indices of k-nearest neighbor vertices. To encode pose-agnostic spatial information, we use rotation-invariant features. Specifically, we compute the distance $d_j = \|\boldsymbol{q} - \boldsymbol{v}_j\|_2$ and cosine value $c_j = \cos(\boldsymbol{x}_j, \boldsymbol{n}_j)$, where $\boldsymbol{x}_j$ is the vertex-to-query vector $\boldsymbol{x}_j = \boldsymbol{q} - \boldsymbol{v}_j$, and $\boldsymbol{n}_j$ is the surface normal on $\boldsymbol{v}_j$. We feed the concatenated vector $\left[\boldsymbol{z}_j^{t+1}, d_j, c_j\right]$ into a PointNet-like [40] architecture to compute the final SDFs with the max pooling replaced by a weighted average pooling based on jointly predicted weights for better continuity.

As in [42], we employ implicit geometric regularization (IGR) [11] to train our model directly from raw scans without requiring watertight meshes. Note that in contrast, other methods [8,29,47] require watertight meshes to compute ground-truth occupancy or signed distance values for training. Our final objective function L is the following:

$$L = L_s + L_n + \lambda_{igr} L_{igr} + \lambda_o L_o, \tag{3}$$

where $\lambda_{igr} = 1.0$, $\lambda_o = 0.1$. L_s promotes SDFs which vanish on the ground truth surface, while L_n encourages that its normal align with the ones from data: $L_s = \sum_{q \in Q_s} |f(q)|$, $L_n = \sum_{q \in Q_s} \|\nabla_q f(q) - n(q)\|_2$, where Q_s is the surface of the input raw scans. L_{igr} is the Eikonal regularization term [11] that encourages the function f to satisfy the Eikonal equation: $L_{igr} = \mathbb{E}_q (\|\nabla_q f(q)\|_2 - 1)^2$, and L_o prevents off-surface SDF values from being too close to the zero-crossings as follows: $L_o = \mathbb{E}_q (\exp(-\gamma \cdot |f(q)|))$, where $\gamma = 50$.

3.4 Implementation Details

Network Architectures. In our experiments, we use a UV map of resolution 256×256, $T = 3$, and $k = 20$. Before the k-nearest neighbor (k-NN) query in Sect. 3.3, we subsample 3928 vertices by poisson-disk sampling on the SMPL mesh, and only use these subsampled vertices for k-NN computation. This subsampling ensures that vertices are distributed uniformly, leading to consistent area coverage by k-NN selection. Please see Supp. Mat. for more discussions and architecture details.

Training. Our training consists of two stages. First, we train our model using ground-truth signed heights without rollout for 90000 iterations. Then, we finetune the model using a rollout of 2 frames for another 7500 iterations to reduce error accumulation for both training and inference. We use the Adam optimizer with a learning rate of 1.0×10^{-4} (1.0×10^{-5}) at the first (second) stage. To compute L_n, we sample $10000(1000)$ points on the scan surface. Similarly, for L_{igr}, we sample $10000(1000)$ points around the scan surface by adding Gaussian noise with standard deviation of 10cm to uniformly sampled surface points, and sample $2000(500)$ points within the bounding box around the raw scans. The points uniformly sampled inside the bounding box are also used to compute L_o. Both stages are trained with a batch size of 1.

Inference. At the beginning of the animations, we assume ground-truth raw scans are available for the previous T frames for initialization. If no ground truth initial shape is available, we initialize the first T frames with our baseline model conditioned only on pose parameters. Note that the scan data is extremely noisy around the hand and foot areas, and the SMPL fitting of the head region is especially inaccurate. Therefore, we fix the dynamic features on the face, hands, and feet to the ones of the first frame.

4 Experimental Results

4.1 Datasets and Metrics

Datasets. We use the DFaust dataset [7] for both training and quantitative evaluation, and AIST++ [18,48] for qualitative evaluation on unseen motions. For the DFaust dataset, we choose 2 subjects (50002 and 50004), who exhibit the most soft-tissue deformations. The interpolation test evaluates the fidelity of dynamics under the same type of motions as in training but at different time instance, and the extrapolation test evaluates performance on unseen motion. For 50002, we use the 2nd half of chicken_wings and running_on_spot for the interpolation test, one_leg_jump for the extrapolation test, and the rest for training. For 50004, we use the 2nd half of chicken_wings and `running_on_spot` for interpolation, `one_leg_loose` for extrapolation, and the rest for training. The fitted SMPL parameters in DFaust are provided by the AMASS [26] dataset that uses sparse points on the registered data as approximated mocap marker locations and computes the parameters using MoSh [21]. Note that more accurate pose can be obtained by using all the registration vertices (see Supp. Mat.), but this is not required by our method to recover soft-tissue deformation.

Metrics. For evaluation, we extract the 0-level set surface at each time step using Marching Cubes [23] with a resolution of 256^3. We also use simplified scans with around 10000 vertices and outlier points (distance to the nearest SMPL vertex larger than 10cm) have been removed. We evaluate the accuracy of the predicted surface in terms of its position and dynamics accuracy. The surface position accuracy is measured by averaging the distance from each simplified scan vertex to the closest prediction surface point. Evaluating the dynamics accuracy of the implicit surface efficiently is more challenging. We approximate the local occupied volume as a scalar per registration vertex representing the ratio of surrounding points contained in the interior of the (ground-truth or inferred) surface. We use 10 points uniformly sampled inside a 5cm cube centered at the vertex. When computing the per-vertex scalars, the head, hands and feet vertices are ignored due to their high noise levels. The temporal difference of this scalar across adjacent frames can be interpreted as a dynamic measure of the local volume evolution. We report the mean square difference between this dynamic descriptor as computed with the ground truth simplified scan and the inferred implicit surface. Since a small phase shift in dynamics may lead to large cumulative error, reporting only the averaged errors from the entire frames can be misleading. Therefore, we report errors along the progression of rollout predictions. For each evaluation sequence, we start prediction every 20 frames (i.e., 20th frame, 40th frame, ...), and use the ground truth pose and shape history only for the first frame, followed by the autoregressive predictions for the error computation. In Table 1, we report the averaged errors for both metrics after 1, 2, 4, 8, 16, and 30 rollouts. The errors for small number of rollouts evaluate the accuracy of future shape prediction given the ground-truth shape history, whereas the errors with longer rollouts evaluate the accumulated errors by autoregressively taking as input the predictions of previous frames. We discuss the limitation of error metrics with longer rollouts in Sect. 4.2.

4.2   Evaluation

In this section, we provide comprehensive analysis to validate our design choices and highlight the limitations of alternative approaches and SoTA methods based on both implicit and explicit shape representations. Note that all approaches use the same training set, and are trained with the same number of iterations as our method for fair comparison.

Effectiveness of Autoregressive Modeling. While autoregressive modeling is a widely used technique for learning dynamics [37,38,56], several recent methods still employ only the history of poses for modeling dynamic avatars [12,51]. Thus, to evaluate the effectiveness of autoregressive modeling we compare AutoAvatar with pose-dependent

Table 1. Quantitative Comparison with Baseline Methods. Our method produces the most accurate predictions of the future frames given the ground-truth shape history among all baseline methods (see rollout 1–4). For longer rollouts, more dynamic predictions lead to higher error than less dynamic results due to high sensitivity to initial conditions in dynamic systems [33] (see discussion in Sect. 4.2).

(a) Mean Scan-to-Prediction Distance (mm) ↓ on DFaust.

		Rollout (# of frames)					
		1	2	4	8	16	30
	Interpolation Set						
Non-Autoregressive	SNARF [8]	7.428	7.372	7.337	7.476	7.530	7.656
	Pose	4.218	4.202	4.075	4.240	4.409	4.426
	PoseTCN	4.068	4.118	4.086	4.228	4.405	4.411
	Pose + dPose	3.852	3.841	3.764	3.972	4.164	4.156
Autoregressive	G-embed	2.932	3.006	3.131	3.462	3.756	3.793
	L-embed	1.784	2.138	2.863	4.250	5.448	5.916
	Ours	1.569	1.914	2.587	3.627	4.736	5.255
	Extrapolation Set						
Non-Autoregressive	SNARF [8]	7.264	7.287	7.321	7.387	7.308	7.251
	Pose	4.303	4.306	4.308	4.299	4.385	4.398
	PoseTCN	4.090	4.091	4.105	4.119	4.233	4.257
	Pose + dPose	3.984	3.991	4.017	4.063	4.162	4.190
Autoregressive	G-embed	2.884	2.926	3.043	3.258	3.577	3.787
	L-embed	1.329	1.539	2.079	3.326	4.578	5.192
	Ours	1.150	1.361	1.834	2.689	3.789	4.526

(b) Mean Squared Error of Volume Change ↓ on DFaust.

		Rollout (# of frames)				
		2	4	8	16	30
	Interpolation Set					
Non-Autoregressive	SNARF [8]	0.01582	0.01552	0.01610	0.01658	0.01682
	Pose	0.01355	0.01305	0.01341	0.01367	0.01387
	PoseTCN	0.01364	0.01323	0.01350	0.01399	0.01416
	Pose + dPose	0.01288	0.01247	0.01273	0.01311	0.01321
Autoregressive	G-embed	0.01179	0.01168	0.01199	0.01248	0.01265
	L-embed	0.01003	0.01180	0.01466	0.01716	0.01844
	Ours	0.00902	0.01053	0.01258	0.01456	0.01565
	Extrapolation Set					
Non-Autoregressive	SNARF [8]	0.01178	0.01194	0.01251	0.01228	0.01206
	Pose	0.01027	0.01039	0.01074	0.01052	0.01039
	PoseTCN	0.01020	0.01038	0.01064	0.01040	0.01029
	Pose + dPose	0.00992	0.01014	0.01048	0.01029	0.01013
Autoregressive	G-embed	0.00936	0.00959	0.00995	0.00996	0.00998
	L-embed	0.00648	0.00821	0.01100	0.01308	0.01402
	Ours	0.00567	0.00715	0.00915	0.01039	0.01107

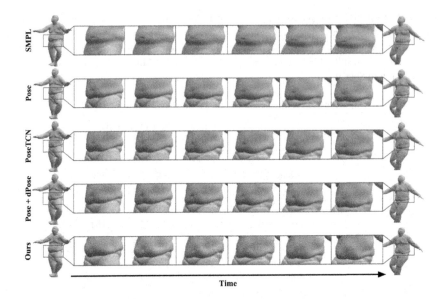

Fig. 4. Qualitative Comparison with Non-Autoregressive Baselines. As the belly region is highly non-rigid, it exhibits fluid-like dynamic deformations asynchronously with the skeletal motion. Our method successfully models this non-rigid dynamics, while other methods fail at modeling this as if the belly is rigidly attached to the rest of the body parts.

alternatives that use neural implicit surfaces. More specifically, we design the following 3 non-autoregressive baselines:

1. Pose: We only feed pose parameters of the next frame $L(p_{t+1})$ in our architecture. Prior avatar modeling methods based on neural fields employ this pose-only parameterization [8,42,47].
2. PoseTCN: Temporal convolutional networks (TCN) [17] support the incorporation of a long-range history for learning tasks, and have been used in several avatar modeling methods [12,51]. Thus, we use a TCN that takes as input the sequence of poses with the length of 16. We first compute localized pose parameters, as in our method, for each frame and apply the TCN to obtain 64-dim features for each SMPL vertex. The features are then fed into the UNet and SDF decoders identical to our method.
3. Pose+dPose: Our approach without autoregressive components $(H_t, \{\dot{H}_{t+i}\})$.

Table 1 shows that our approach outperforms the baseline methods for the first 8 frames for interpolation, and first 16 frames for extrapolation. In particular, there is a significantly large margin for the first 4–8 frames, indicating that our method achieves the most accurate prediction of the future frames given the ground-truth shape history. We also observe that the non-autoregressive methods tend to collapse to predicting the "mean" shape under each pose without faithful dynamics for unseen motions (see Fig. 4 and Supp. Mat. video). Since the accumulation of small errors in each frame may lead to large deviations from the ground-truth due to high sensitivity to initial conditions in

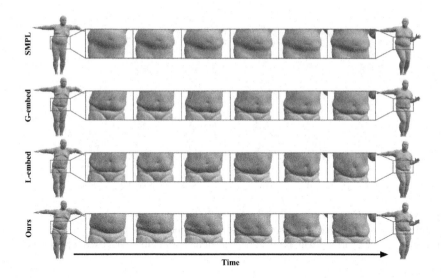

Fig. 5. Qualitative Comparison with Latent-space Autoregression. While the latent space-based autoregression approaches suffer either from overfitting to pose parameters (G-embed) or instability (L-embed, see Supp. Mat. video), our approach based on a physically meaningful quantity (signed height) achieves the most stable and expressive synthesis of dynamics.

dynamic systems [33], for longer rollouts mean predictions without any dynamics can produce lower errors than more dynamic predictions. In fact, although our method leads to slightly higher errors on longer rollouts, Fig. 4 clearly shows that our approach produces the most visually plausible dynamics on the AIST++ sequences. Importantly, we do not observe any instability or explosions in our autoregressive model for longer rollouts, as can be seen from the error behavior shown in Fig. 7. We also highly encourage readers to see Supp. Mat. video for qualitative comparison in animation. In summary, our results confirm that autoregressive modeling plays a critical role for generalization to unseen motions and improving the realism of dynamics.

Explicit Shape Encoding vs. Latent Encoding. Efficiently encoding the geometry of implicit surfaces is non-trivial. While our proposed approach encodes the geometry via signed heights on articulated observer points, prior approaches have demonstrated shape encoding based on a learned latent space [4,35]. Therefore, we also investigate different encoding methods for autoregressive modeling with the following 2 baselines:

1. G-embed: Inspired by DeepSDF [35], we first learn per-frame global embeddings $l_g \in \mathbb{R}^{512}$ with the UNet and SDF decoder by replacing H_t, $\{\dot{H}_{t+i}\}$, $\{L(\dot{p}_{t+i})\}$ with repeated global embeddings. Then, we train a small MLP with three 512-dim hidden layers using Softplus except for the last layer, taking as input p_{t+1}, $\{\dot{p}_{t+i}\}$, and 3 embeddings of previous frames to predict the global embedding at time $t+1$.
2. L-embed: For modeling mesh-based body avatars, localized embeddings are shown to be effective [4]. Inspired by this, we also train a model with localized embeddings $l_l \in \mathbb{R}^{16 \times 64 \times 64}$. We first learn per-frame local embeddings l_l together with

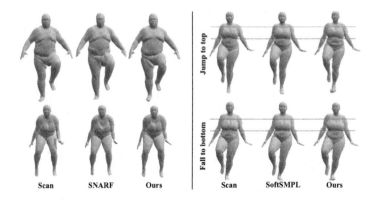

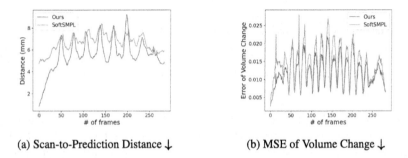

Fig. 6. Qualitative Comparison with SoTA Methods. Our approach produces significantly more faithful shapes and dynamics than the state-of-the-art implicit avatar modeling method [8], and shows comparable dynamics with prior art dependent on registrations with fixed topology [44].

(a) Scan-to-Prediction Distance ↓   (b) MSE of Volume Change ↓

Fig. 7. Comparison with SoftSMPL [44]. We plot the errors on the sequence of one_leg_loose for subject 50004. Surprisingly, our registration-free approach mostly outperforms this baseline that has to rely on registered data with fixed topology.

the UNet and SDF decoder by replacing H_t, $\{\dot{H}_{t+i}\}$, $\{L(\dot{p}_{t+i})\}$ with bilinearly upsampled l_l. Then we train another UNet that takes as input $L(p_{t+1})$, $\{L(\dot{p}_{t+i})\}$, and 3 embeddings of previous frames to predict the localized embeddings at time $t+1$.

Note that for evaluation, we optimize per-frame embeddings for test sequences using Eq. (3) such that the baseline methods can use the best possible history of embeddings for autoregression. Table 1 shows that our method outperforms L-embed in all cases because L-embed becomes unstable for the test sequences. For G-embed, we observe the same trend as for the non-autoregressive baselines: our approach achieves significantly more accurate predictions of the future frames given the ground-truth trajectories (see the errors for 1–4 rollouts), and G-embed tends to predict "mean" shapes without plausible dynamics. The qualitative comparison in Fig. 5 confirms that our approach produces more plausible dynamics. Please refer to Supp. Mat. video for detailed visual comparison in animation. We summarize that physically meaningful shape encodings (e.g., signed heights) enable more stable learning of dynamics via autoregression than methods relying on latent space.

Comparison to SoTA Methods. We compare our approach with state-of-the-art methods for both implicit surface representations and mesh-based representations. As a method using neural implicit surfaces, we choose SNARF [8], which jointly learns a pose-conditioned implicit surface in a canonical T-pose and a forward skinning network for reposing. Similar to ours, SNARF does not require temporal correspondences other than the fitted SMPL models. We use the training code released by the authors using the same training data and the fitted SMPL parameters as in our method. Note that in the DFaust experiment in [8], SNARF is trained using only the fitted SMPL models to DFaust as ground-truth geometry, which do not contain any dynamic deformations. Table 1 shows that our approach significantly outperforms SNARF for any number of rollouts. Interestingly, SNARF can produce dynamic effects for training data by severely overfitting to the pose parameters, but this does not generalize to unseen poses as the learned dynamics is the results of spurious correlations. As mentioned in Sect. 3.3, we also observe that the performance of SNARF heavily relies on the accuracy of the SMPL fitting for canonicalization, and any small alignment errors in the underlying SMPL registration deteriorates their test-time performance (see Fig. 6). Therefore, this experiment demonstrates not only the importance of autoregressive dynamic avatar modeling, but also the efficacy of our articulation-aware shape decoding approach given the quality of available SMPL fitting for real-world scans.

We also compare against SoftSMPL [44], a state-of-the-art mesh-based method that learns dynamically deforming human bodies from registered meshes. The authors of SoftSMPL kindly provide their predictions on the sequence of one_leg_loose for subject 50004, which is excluded from training for both our method and SoftSMPL for fair comparison. To our surprise, Fig. 7 show that our results are slightly better on both metrics for the majority of frames, although we tackle a significantly harder problem because our approach learns dynamic bodies directly from raw scans, whereas Soft-SMPL learns from the carefully registered data. We speculate that the lower error may be mainly attributed to the higher resolution of our geometry using implicit surfaces in contrast to their predictions on the coarse SMPL topology (see Fig. 6). Nevertheless, this result is highly encouraging as our approach achieves comparable performance on dynamics modeling without having to rely on surface registration.

5   Conclusion

We have introduced AutoAvatar, an autoregressive approach for modeling high-fidelity dynamic deformations of human bodies directly from raw 4D scans using neural implicit surfaces. The reconstructed avatars can be driven by pose parameters, and automatically incorporate secondary dynamic effects that depend on the history of shapes. Our experiments indicate that modeling dynamic avatars without relying on accurate registrations is made possible by choosing an efficient representation for our autoregressive model.

Limitations and Future Work. While our method has shown to be effective in modeling the elastic deformations of real humans, we observe that it remains challenging, yet promising, to model clothing deformations that involve high-frequency wrinkles (see Supp. Mat. for details). Our evaluation also suggests that ground-truth comparison with longer rollouts may not reliably reflect the plausibility of dynamics. Quantitative metrics that handle the high sensitivity to initial conditions in dynamics could be further investigated. Currently, AutoAvatar models subject-specific dynamic human bodies, but generalizing it to multiple identities, as demonstrated in registration-based shape modeling [22,38,44], is an interesting direction for future work. The most exciting venue for future work is to extend the notion of dynamics to image-based avatars [20,36]. In contrast to implicit surfaces, neural radiance fields [30] do not have an explicit "surface" as they model geometry using density fields. While this remains an open question, we believe that our contributions in this work such as efficiently modeling the state of shapes via articulated observer points might be useful to unlock this application.

References

1. Alldieck, T., Xu, H., Sminchisescu, C.: imGHUM: implicit generative models of 3D human shape and articulated pose. In: Proceedings of International Conference on Computer Vision (ICCV), pp. 5461–5470 (2021)
2. Allen, B., Curless, B., Popović, Z., Hertzmann, A.: Learning a correlated model of identity and pose-dependent body shape variation for real-time synthesis. In: Proceedings of the 2006 ACM SIGGRAPH/Eurographics Symposium on Computer Animation, pp. 147–156 (2006)
3. Anguelov, D., Srinivasan, P., Koller, D., Thrun, S., Rodgers, J., Davis, J.: SCAPE: shape completion and animation of people. ACM Trans. Graph. (TOG) **24**(3), 408–416 (2005)
4. Bagautdinov, T., et al.: Driving-signal aware full-body avatars. ACM Trans. Graph. (TOG) **40**(4), 1–17 (2021)
5. Bhat, K.S., Twigg, C.D., Hodgins, J.K., Khosla, P., Popovic, Z., Seitz, S.M.: Estimating cloth simulation parameters from video (2003)
6. Bogo, F., Romero, J., Loper, M., Black, M.J.: Faust: dataset and evaluation for 3D mesh registration. In: Proceedings of Computer Vision and Pattern Recognition (CVPR), pp. 3794–3801 (2014)
7. Bogo, F., Romero, J., Pons-Moll, G., Black, M.J.: Dynamic faust: registering human bodies in motion. In: Proceedings of Computer Vision and Pattern Recognition (CVPR), pp. 6233–6242 (2017)
8. Chen, X., Zheng, Y., Black, M.J., Hilliges, O., Geiger, A.: Snarf: differentiable forward skinning for animating non-rigid neural implicit shapes. In: Proceedings of International Conference on Computer Vision (ICCV) (2021)
9. Chen, Z., Zhang, H.: Learning implicit fields for generative shape modeling. In: Proceedings of Computer Vision and Pattern Recognition (CVPR), pp. 5939–5948. Computer Vision Foundation/IEEE (2019)
10. Deng, B., et al.: NASA neural articulated shape approximation. In: Vedaldi, A., Bischof, H., Brox, T., Frahm, J.-M. (eds.) ECCV 2020. LNCS, vol. 12352, pp. 612–628. Springer, Cham (2020). https://doi.org/10.1007/978-3-030-58571-6_36
11. Gropp, A., Yariv, L., Haim, N., Atzmon, M., Lipman, Y.: Implicit geometric regularization for learning shapes. In: Proceedings of the 37th International Conference on Machine Learning (ICML). Proceedings of Machine Learning Research, vol. 119, pp. 3789–3799. PMLR (2020)
12. Habermann, M., Liu, L., Xu, W., Zollhoefer, M., Pons-Moll, G., Theobalt, C.: Real-time deep dynamic characters. ACM Trans. Graph. (TOG) **40**(4), 1–16 (2021)

13. Hasler, N., Stoll, C., Sunkel, M., Rosenhahn, B., Seidel, H.: A statistical model of human pose and body shape. Comput. Graph. Forum **28**(2), 337–346 (2009)
14. Holden, D., Duong, B.C., Datta, S., Nowrouzezahrai, D.: Subspace neural physics: fast data-driven interactive simulation. In: Proceedings of the 18th Annual ACM SIG-GRAPH/Eurographics Symposium on Computer Animation, pp. 1–12 (2019)
15. Kanazawa, A., Zhang, J.Y., Felsen, P., Malik, J.: Learning 3D human dynamics from video. In: Proceedings of Computer Vision and Pattern Recognition (CVPR) (2019)
16. Kim, M., et al.: Data-driven physics for human soft tissue animation. ACM Trans. Graph. (TOG) **36**(4), 54:1–54:12 (2017)
17. Lea, C., Vidal, R., Reiter, A., Hager, G.D.: Temporal convolutional networks: a unified approach to action segmentation. In: Hua, G., Jégou, H. (eds.) ECCV 2016. LNCS, vol. 9915, pp. 47–54. Springer, Cham (2016). https://doi.org/10.1007/978-3-319-49409-8_7
18. Li, R., Yang, S., Ross, D.A., Kanazawa, A.: AI choreographer: music conditioned 3D dance generation with AIST++. In: Proceedings of International Conference on Computer Vision (ICCV), pp. 13401–13412 (2021)
19. Ling, H.Y., Zinno, F., Cheng, G., Van De Panne, M.: Character controllers using motion VAEs. ACM Trans. Graph. (TOG) **39**(4), 40–1 (2020)
20. Liu, L., Habermann, M., Rudnev, V., Sarkar, K., Gu, J., Theobalt, C.: Neural actor: neural free-view synthesis of human actors with pose control. ACM Trans. Graph. (TOG) **40**(6), 1–16 (2021)
21. Loper, M., Mahmood, N., Black, M.J.: Mosh: motion and shape capture from sparse markers. ACM Trans. Graph. (TOG) **33**(6), 1–13 (2014)
22. Loper, M., Mahmood, N., Romero, J., Pons-Moll, G., Black, M.J.: SMPL: a skinned multi-person linear model. ACM Trans. Graph. (TOG) **34**(6), 248:1–248:16 (2015)
23. Lorensen, W.E., Cline, H.E.: Marching cubes: a high resolution 3D surface construction algorithm. ACM Siggraph Comput. Graph. **21**(4), 163–169 (1987)
24. Ma, Q., Saito, S., Yang, J., Tang, S., Black, M.J.: SCALE: modeling clothed humans with a surface codec of articulated local elements. In: Proceedings of Computer Vision and Pattern Recognition (CVPR), June 2021
25. Ma, Q., Yang, J., Tang, S., Black, M.J.: The power of points for modeling humans in clothing. In: Proceedings of International Conference on Computer Vision (ICCV), October 2021
26. Mahmood, N., Ghorbani, N., Troje, N.F., Pons-Moll, G., Black, M.J.: AMASS: archive of motion capture as surface shapes. In: Proceedings of International Conference on Computer Vision (ICCV), pp. 5442–5451 (2019)
27. Martinez, J., Black, M.J., Romero, J.: On human motion prediction using recurrent neural networks. In: Proceedings of Computer Vision and Pattern Recognition (CVPR), pp. 2891–2900 (2017)
28. Mescheder, L.M., Oechsle, M., Niemeyer, M., Nowozin, S., Geiger, A.: Occupancy networks: learning 3D reconstruction in function space. In: Proceedings of Computer Vision and Pattern Recognition (CVPR), pp. 4460–4470. Computer Vision Foundation/IEEE (2019)
29. Mihajlovic, M., Zhang, Y., Black, M.J., Tang, S.: LEAP: learning articulated occupancy of people. In: Proceedings of Computer Vision and Pattern Recognition (CVPR), June 2021
30. Mildenhall, B., Srinivasan, P.P., Tancik, M., Barron, J.T., Ramamoorthi, R., Ng, R.: NeRF: representing scenes as neural radiance fields for view synthesis. In: Vedaldi, A., Bischof, H., Brox, T., Frahm, J.-M. (eds.) ECCV 2020. LNCS, vol. 12346, pp. 405–421. Springer, Cham (2020). https://doi.org/10.1007/978-3-030-58452-8_24
31. Niemeyer, M., Mescheder, L., Oechsle, M., Geiger, A.: Differentiable volumetric rendering: learning implicit 3D representations without 3D supervision. In: Proceedings of Computer Vision and Pattern Recognition (CVPR) (2020)

32. Osman, A.A.A., Bolkart, T., Black, M.J.: STAR: sparse trained articulated human body regressor. In: Vedaldi, A., Bischof, H., Brox, T., Frahm, J.-M. (eds.) ECCV 2020. LNCS, vol. 12351, pp. 598–613. Springer, Cham (2020). https://doi.org/10.1007/978-3-030-58539-6_36

33. Ott, E., Grebogi, C., Yorke, J.A.: Controlling chaos. Phys. Rev. Lett. **64**(11), 1196 (1990)

34. Palafox, P., Božič, A., Thies, J., Nießner, M., Dai, A.: NPMS: neural parametric models for 3D deformable shapes. In: Proceedings of International Conference on Computer Vision (ICCV), pp. 12695–12705 (2021)

35. Park, J.J., Florence, P., Straub, J., Newcombe, R.A., Lovegrove, S.: DeepSDF: learning continuous signed distance functions for shape representation. In: Proceedings of Computer Vision and Pattern Recognition (CVPR), pp. 165–174. Computer Vision Foundation/IEEE (2019)

36. Peng, S., et al.: Neural body: implicit neural representations with structured latent codes for novel view synthesis of dynamic humans. In: Proceedings of Computer Vision and Pattern Recognition (CVPR), pp. 9054–9063 (2021)

37. Pfaff, T., Fortunato, M., Sanchez-Gonzalez, A., Battaglia, P.: Learning mesh-based simulation with graph networks. In: International Conference on Learning Representations (2021)

38. Pons-Moll, G., Romero, J., Mahmood, N., Black, M.J.: Dyna: a model of dynamic human shape in motion. ACM Trans. Graph. (TOG) **34**(4), 1–14 (2015)

39. Prokudin, S., Lassner, C., Romero, J.: Efficient learning on point clouds with basis point sets. In: Proceedings of International Conference on Computer Vision (ICCV), pp. 4332–4341 (2019)

40. Qi, C.R., Su, H., Mo, K., Guibas, L.J.: Pointnet: deep learning on point sets for 3D classification and segmentation. In: Proceedings of Computer Vision and Pattern Recognition (CVPR), pp. 652–660 (2017)

41. Ronneberger, O., Fischer, P., Brox, T.: U-Net: convolutional networks for biomedical image segmentation. In: Navab, N., Hornegger, J., Wells, W.M., Frangi, A.F. (eds.) MICCAI 2015. LNCS, vol. 9351, pp. 234–241. Springer, Cham (2015). https://doi.org/10.1007/978-3-319-24574-4_28

42. Saito, S., Yang, J., Ma, Q., Black, M.J.: SCANimate: weakly supervised learning of skinned clothed avatar networks. In: Proceedings of Computer Vision and Pattern Recognition (CVPR), June 2021

43. Sanchez-Gonzalez, A., Godwin, J., Pfaff, T., Ying, R., Leskovec, J., Battaglia, P.: Learning to simulate complex physics with graph networks. In: International Conference on Machine Learning, pp. 8459–8468. PMLR (2020)

44. Santesteban, I., Garces, E., Otaduy, M.A., Casas, D.: SoftSMPL: data-driven modeling of nonlinear soft-tissue dynamics for parametric humans. In: Computer Graphics Forum, vol. 39, pp. 65–75. Wiley Online Library (2020)

45. Sifakis, E., Barbic, J.: Fem simulation of 3D deformable solids: a practitioner's guide to theory, discretization and model reduction. In: ACM SIGGRAPH 2012 Courses, pp. 1–50 (2012)

46. Srinivasan, S.G., Wang, Q., Rojas, J., Klár, G., Kavan, L., Sifakis, E.: Learning active quasistatic physics-based models from data. ACM Trans. Graph. (TOG) **40**(4), 1–14 (2021)

47. Tiwari, G., Sarafianos, N., Tung, T., Pons-Moll, G.: Neural-gif: neural generalized implicit functions for animating people in clothing. In: Proceedings of International Conference on Computer Vision (ICCV), pp. 11708–11718 (2021)

48. Tsuchida, S., Fukayama, S., Hamasaki, M., Goto, M.: AIST dance video database: multigenre, multi-dancer, and multi-camera database for dance information processing. In: ISMIR, vol. 1, p. 6 (2019)

49. Wang, H., O'Brien, J.F., Ramamoorthi, R.: Data-driven elastic models for cloth: modeling and measurement. ACM Trans. Graph. (TOG) **30**(4), 1–12 (2011)

50. Wang, S., Mihajlovic, M., Ma, Q., Geiger, A., Tang, S.: Metaavatar: learning animatable clothed human models from few depth images. In: Proceedings of Advances in Neural Information Processing Systems (NeurIPS), vol. 34 (2021)
51. Xiang, D., et al.: Modeling clothing as a separate layer for an animatable human avatar. ACM Trans. Graph. (TOG) **40**(6), 1–15 (2021)
52. Xie, Y., et al.: Neural fields in visual computing and beyond. arXiv preprint arXiv:2111.11426 (2021)
53. Xu, H., Bazavan, E.G., Zanfir, A., Freeman, W.T., Sukthankar, R., Sminchisescu, C.: GHUM & GHUML: generative 3D human shape and articulated pose models. In: Proceedings of Computer Vision and Pattern Recognition (CVPR), pp. 6183–6192. IEEE (2020)
54. Yang, S., Liang, J., Lin, M.C.: Learning-based cloth material recovery from video. In: Proceedings of International Conference on Computer Vision (ICCV), pp. 4393–4403. IEEE Computer Society (2017)
55. Zakharkin, I., Mazur, K., Grigorev, A., Lempitsky, V.: Point-based modeling of human clothing. In: Proceedings of International Conference on Computer Vision (ICCV), pp. 14718–14727 (2021)
56. Zheng, M., Zhou, Y., Ceylan, D., Barbic, J.: A deep emulator for secondary motion of 3D characters. In: Proceedings of Computer Vision and Pattern Recognition (CVPR), pp. 5932–5940 (2021)

Deep Radial Embedding for Visual Sequence Learning

Yuecong Min[1,2], Peiqi Jiao[1,2], Yanan Li[3], Xiaotao Wang[3], Lei Lei[3],
Xiujuan Chai[4], and Xilin Chen[1,2]

[1] Key Lab of Intelligent Information Processing of Chinese Academy of Sciences
(CAS), Institute of Computing Technology, CAS, Beijing 100190, China
{yuecong.min,peiqi.jiao}@vipl.ict.ac.cn, xlchen@ict.ac.cn
[2] University of Chinese Academy of Sciences, Beijing 100049, China
[3] Xiaomi Inc., Beijing, China
{liyanan3,wangxiaotao,leilei1}@xiaomi.com
[4] Agricultural Information Institute, Chinese Academy of Agricultural Sciences,
Beijing 100081, China
chaixiujuan@caas.cn

Abstract. Connectionist Temporal Classification (CTC) is a popular objective function in sequence recognition, which provides supervision for unsegmented sequence data through aligning sequence and its corresponding labeling iteratively. The blank class of CTC plays a crucial role in the alignment process and is often considered responsible for the peaky behavior of CTC. In this study, we propose an objective function named RadialCTC that constrains sequence features on a hypersphere while retaining the iterative alignment mechanism of CTC. The learned features of each non-blank class are distributed on a radial arc from the center of the blank class, which provides a clear geometric interpretation and makes the alignment process more efficient. Besides, RadialCTC can control the peaky behavior by simply modifying the logit of the blank class. Experimental results of recognition and localization demonstrate the effectiveness of RadialCTC on two sequence recognition applications.

Keywords: Deep feature embedding · Visaul sequence learning · Sign language recognition · Scene text recognition

1 Introduction

Sequence data (*e.g.*, text, audio, and video) are present everywhere in daily life. Automatically analyzing and understanding sequences is a challenging yet fascinating field. As a fundamental task in sequence learning, sequence recognition aims to recognize occurred events from the data stream in a weakly supervised manner. Due to the continuity of the event, it is hard to identify its beginning and end points, which brings difficulties to both data annotation and analysis.

Supplementary Information The online version contains supplementary material available at https://doi.org/10.1007/978-3-031-20068-7_14.

© The Author(s), under exclusive license to Springer Nature Switzerland AG 2022
S. Avidan et al. (Eds.): ECCV 2022, LNCS 13666, pp. 240–256, 2022.
https://doi.org/10.1007/978-3-031-20068-7_14

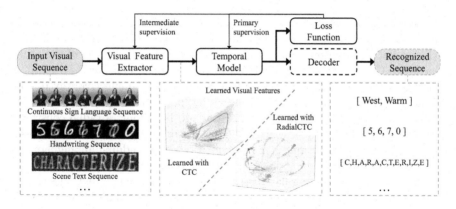

Fig. 1. The typical framework for visual sequence recongnition. **Best view in color**

Recent years have witnessed the great success of deep learning in sequence learning tasks [2, 37]. To achieve automatic alignment between sequence data and its corresponding labeling, Connectionist Temporal Classification (CTC) [10] leverages the natural monotonicity constraint that exists in sequence learning and adopts an extra 'blank' class to maximize the posterior probability of all feasible alignment paths. The typical framework is presented in Fig. 1, and CTC has been successfully adopted in many sequence learning applications [3, 11, 12, 29] to provide intermediate or primary supervision.

One of the most interesting and controversial issues about CTC is its peaky behavior [10]: networks trained with CTC will conservatively predict a series of spikes. This peaky behavior helps the sequence recognition model quickly converge and fast decode. On the other hand, some works [4, 23, 43] regard the peaky behavior as a symptom of overfitting, which will deteriorate the performance dramatically when data are insufficient. Although CTC can achieve outstanding performance, its peaky behavior makes it unable to provide clear boundaries like some traditional statistical models (e.g., Hidden Markov Model) do.

Many works [13, 14, 22, 23, 43, 44] provide interesting insights and possible solutions about the peaky behavior of CTC. Hu *et al.* [23] propose an entropy-based regularization term, which maximizes the entropy of feasible paths and penalizes the peaky distribution. Some works [14, 22] try to improve the generalization ability of the model by extending the peaky prediction as frame-wise supervision. However, simply extending the peaky prediction may break the continuity of features and not take full advantage of CTC. Earlier works [13, 43] show that CTC can be regarded as an iterative alignment process, which provides supervision via the Expectation-Maximization. Recent work [29] shows that training with CTC also makes feature norm peaky, which makes it easier to overfit when combined with powerful temporal models.

Inspired by the iterative alignment mechanism of CTC, we proposed an objective function named RadialCTC that constrains sequence features on a hypersphere. RadialCTC adopts several constraints and enforces the model to learn angularly discriminative features compared to the less constrained features in the inner space. As shown in Fig. 1, the proposed RadialCTC constrains features of non-blank classes to distribute on radial arcs from the center of the blank class. Such a radial distribution provides a clear geometric interpretation of the peaky behavior of CTC and makes the alignment process more efficient.

Besides, the radial distribution of features provides an effective way to control the peaky behavior. Different from adding path-wise regularization [23] or modifying the peaky predictions [14,22], RadialCTC adopts a radial constraint to control the peaky behavior with the help of the iterative alignment mechanism of CTC. The radial constraint is implemented by simply adding an angular perturbation term on the blank logit. This term is dominated by a global non-blank ratio and sequence-wise angular distribution, providing consistent supervision for all sequence data. With the help of this constraint, RadialCTC can provide controllable event boundaries while achieving competitive recognition accuracy.

To show the effectiveness of RadialCTC, we conduct thoughtful experiments on a simulated sequence recognition dataset and two public benchmarks. Experimental results of recognition and localization demonstrate the effectiveness of RadialCTC. The major contributions are summarized as follows:

- Proposing the RadialCTC for sequence feature learning, which constrains sequence features on a hypersphere while retaining the iterative alignment mechanism of CTC. Features of non-blank classes are distributed on radial arcs from the center of the blank class.
- Proposing a simple angular perturbation term to control the peaky behavior, which can provide consistent supervision for all sequence data considering sequence-wise angular distribution.
- Conducting thoughtful experiments about the relationship between recognition and localization. Experimental results show the effectiveness of RadialCTC, which achieves competitive results on two sequence recognition applications and can also provide controllable event boundaries.

2   Related Work

2.1   Connectionist Temporal Classification

CTC [10] is proposed to provide supervision for unsegmented sequence data, which has shown advantages in many sequence recognition tasks (e.g.handwriting recognition [12], speech recognition [11], and sign language recognition [1,21, 29]). Compared to other attention-based methods [2,37], CTC satisfies the monotonous nature of sequence recognition, and the CNN-LSTM-CTC model becomes a popular framework in sequence recognition tasks [5,35]. A controversial characteristic of CTC is its spike phenomenon [10]: networks trained with CTC will conservatively predict a series of spikes. The spike phenomenon can accelerate the decoding process but is also regarded as a symptom of overfitting [23,29]. Liu et al. [23] propose a entropy-based regularization method to penalize the peaky distribution and encourage exploration. Min et al. [29] propose a visual alignment constraint to enhance feature extraction before the powerful temporal module. Adding constraints on the CTC-based framework can alleviate the overfitting problem. However, the peaky behavior still exists, and it is hard to provide clear event boundaries.

Many works [13,14,22,43,44] try to understand the peaky behavior of CTC. Earlier speech recognition works [13,43] interpret CTC as a special kind of Hidden Markov Model [33], which is trained with the Baum-Welch soft alignment algorithm, and the alignment result is updated at each iteration. Some recent works [14,22] leverage this iterative fitting characteristic and extend the spiky activations to get better recognition performance. However, these methods change the pseudo label at each iteration manually and may break the continuity of the sequence feature. Similar work to ours is [44], where the authors find that the peaky behavior is a property of local convergence, and the peaky behavior can be suboptimal. Different to [44], we constrain sequence features on a hypersphere and control the peaky behavior with an angular perturbation term.

2.2 Deep Feature Learning

The main goal of deep feature learning is to learn discriminative feature space with proper supervision. In some fine-grained image classification tasks (*e.g.*, face recognition), an important technical route is to learn strong discriminative features by improving the conventional softmax loss. Several margin-based losses [8,25,26,39] are proposed to learn more separable feature space. Wen *et al.* [41] propose to learn a center for each class and minimize the distance between deep features and their corresponding class centers, which can reduce intra-class variance. L-softmax [26] ignores the bias term in the classifier and adopts an angle-based margin to constrain the angles between learned features and their corresponding weights. SphereFace [25] further normalizes the weights of the classifier and constrains the learned feature on the unit hypersphere. On the other hand, several works [31,34] observe that the L_2-norm of the feature is informative to its quality and adopt the feature normalization to overcome sample distribution bias. Wang *et al.* [38] show the necessity of normalization and normalizing both features and weights, which become a common strategy in the following works [8,39]. Several angular-margin based losses [8,28,39] are proposed to further improve the recognition results.

3   Method

3.1   A Toy Sequence Recognition Example

To better illustrate the proposed method, we first build a simulated sequence recognition dataset named Seq-MNIST. Each sequence of Seq-MNIST is generated with four keyframes sampled from the MNIST database [19]. The transition clip from the former keyframe to the next is generated by interpolating α frames between them: the next keyframe fades in, and the former keyframe fades out. An example of the generation process is visualized in Fig. 2. The Seq-MNIST has 15,000 training sequences and 2500 testing sequences, and each sequence

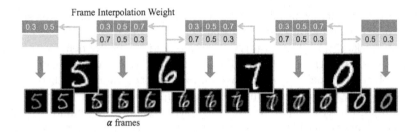

Frame Interpolation Weight

α frames

Fig. 2. An illustration of the data generation process of Seq-MNIST

contains 41 frames ($\alpha = 9$ and 5 additional transition frames at the beginning and the end). The proposed Seq-MNIST can be used to explore the design of the sequence recognition model, which is expected to recognize numbers from the generated sequence (*e.g.*, [5, 6, 7, 0] for the sequence in Fig. 2).

We adopt the modified version of LeNet [41] as the *frame-wise feature extractor* (FFE) and set the dimension of output features to 3 for visualization. The feature extractor takes the image sequence of T frames $x = (x_1, \cdots, x_T)$ and abstracts frame-wise features $v = (v_1, \cdots, v_T)$. To clearly illustrate the relationship between frames, no temporal module is adopted in this sequence recongnition model. The output features are fed to the *fully-connected* (FC) layer with $n+1$ output neurons (the vocubulary $\mathcal{V}$ contains n non-blank classes and one extra 'blank' class) for recognition. The whole process is formulated as:

$$v = \text{FFE}(x), \quad y_i^t = \frac{e^{W_i^{\mathsf{T}} v_t + b_i}}{\sum_{j=1}^{N} e^{W_j^{\mathsf{T}} v_t + b_j}}, \tag{1}$$

where $v \in \mathbb{R}^{T \times d}$ and d is the dimension of features. $W \in \mathbb{R}^{d \times (n+1)}$ and $b \in \mathbb{R}^{n+1}$ are the weight matrix and the bias term of the FC layer.

As a widely-used loss function for weakly-supervised sequence recognition, CTC provides supervision by considering all possible alignments and maximizing the sum of their probabilities. With the help of an extra 'blank' class, CTC defines a many-to-one mapping $\mathcal{B} : \mathcal{V}^T \to \mathcal{V}^{\leq T}$ to align the alignment path π and its corresponding labeling l. This mapping is achieved by successively removing the repeated labels and blanks in the path. For example, $\mathcal{B}(\text{-}aaa\text{--}aabbb\text{-}) = \mathcal{B}(\text{-}a\text{-}ab\text{-}) = aab$. The posterior probability of the labeling can be calculated by:

$$p(l|v) = \sum_{\pi} p(\pi|l, v) = \sum_{\pi \in \mathcal{B}^{-1}(l)} p(\pi|v)$$
$$p(\pi|v) = \prod_{t=1}^{T} p(\pi_t|v) = \prod_{t=1}^{T} y_{\pi_t}^t \tag{2}$$

The frame-wise features v abstracted by the trained model are visualized in Fig. 3(a). Although we adopt a small feature dimension for visualization, it can reflect some characteristics of feature space and inspire us to optimize the design

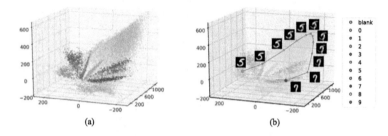

Fig. 3. Visualization of (a) the distribution of frame-wise features and (b) an example of transition trajectory in the test set of Seq-MNIST. Points with different colors are corresponding to different classes. **Best view in color** (Color figure online)

of loss function, which can also be extended to the high-dimensional case. From Fig. 3 we can observe that: (1) after training with CTC, the frame-wise features are separable among non-blank classes, but the decision boundary between non-blank classes and the blank class is pretty complicated, (2) over half of the features are classified to the blank class, which is corresponding to the peaky behavior of CTC, and features of the blank class have a large intra-class variance, and (3) although some transition frames are pretty similar to the keyframe, they are classified to the blank class as Fig. 3(b) shown.

3.2 The Design of Loss Function for Sequence Recognition

Many efforts have been devoted to learning discriminative features for fine-grained image classification, and we briefly summarize relevant designs as:

$$
\min \sum_{i=1}^{N} \Big(\underbrace{-\log p(l_i|v_i, m)}_{\text{margin-based loss}} + \underbrace{\frac{1}{2} \|v_i - c_{l_i}\|_2}_{\text{center regularization}} \Big)
$$
$$
\text{s.t.} \quad \underbrace{\tilde{v}_i = \frac{sv_i}{\|v_i\|_2}, \quad i = 1, \cdots, N, \quad \tilde{W}_j = \frac{W_j}{\|W_j\|_2}, \quad j = 1, \cdots, C}_{\text{normalization}}, \quad (3)
$$

where v_i and l_i are visual feature of sample i and its label, and c_k is the center vector of class k. s controls the feature scale to ensure the convergence. The center constraint aims to reduce intra-class variance [41], the normalization constraint can provide a geometric interpretation [25,38] and reduce the training data imbalance issue [25], and the margin-based loss [8,25,26,28,39] can enforce intra-class compactness and inter-class separation.

Like fine-grained image classification, sequence recognition needs a *discriminative* yet *steady* feature space. Inspired by the design of loss function in Eq. (3), we propose several constraints in the context of sequence learning.

Normalization. Different from image classification, sequence recognition not only needs to learn steady feature space but also needs to learn a generalized

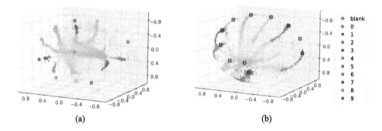

Fig. 4. The distribution of frame-wise features with (a) normalization and (b) normalization, angle and center constraints in the test set of Seq-MNIST, Points with different colors correspond to different classes. **Best view in color** (Color figure online)

feature space from weakly supervised labeling. As shown in Fig. 3, the learned features with supervision from CTC have large intra-class variance, especially on the blank class, and the decision boundary between the blank class and non-blank classes is not clear. The vanilla CTC takes the inner distance between features and weights as input and provides little constraint on the alignment process. To learn a more separable feature space, we normalize both the features and weights and constrain the learned features on a hypersphere, which has been proven a practical approach in face recognition [25,38]. Fig. 4(a) shows the learned feature distribution after normalization. *After constraining all features on the hypersphere, the search space of the alignment process is reduced considerably, and features are distributed along several disjoint paths from the center of the blank class.* Besides, these features are not equally distributed among different classes and tend to distribute near the decision boundary rather than its class center. We further propose angle and center constraints to relieve these problems and make the features more discriminative.

Angle Regularization. The blank class plays a unique role in CTC that the model trained with CTC will predict blank labels at uncertain frames. In other words, any frames between two non-blank keyframes can be classified into the blank class. Therefore, any transition trajectory between two non-blank keyframes will go through the decision region of the blank class as shown in Fig. 3(b). The data distribution and the recognition difficulty will affect the angle between the blank and non-blank classes. To enhance the discriminative and the generalization ability of the model, we propose an angle regularization term to minimize the distance between $\tilde{W}_b^\mathsf{T} \tilde{W}_{nb}$ and a given value $\cos(\beta)$.

Center Regularization. As shown in Fig. 4(a), features are likely to be near the decision boundary of the blank class. CTC provides supervision by considering all possible alignments and has no explicit constraint on the separability of frame-wise features. Inspired by the pioneering work [38] that reduces intra-class variance by minimizing the distance between the deep feature and its corresponding class center, we assume that it is also helpful for sequence recognition. However, sequence recognition generally does not require frame-wise labels, and sequences often have many uncertain frames. Indiscriminately applying center regularization on all frames will affect the representation steadiness and generalization ability of the model. Therefore, we only apply center regularization on keyframes set $KF(v)$, which is implemented by first estimating the alignment path $\hat{\pi} = \arg\max_\pi p(\pi|v,l;\theta)$ with the maximal probability as previous work [7] does and then minimizing the distance between features of keyframes in $\hat{\pi}$ and their corresponding classes.

Figure 4(b) visualizes the learned feature distribution with the above constraints. These constraints provide a clear geometric interpretation for the sequence recognition with CTC supervision: the blank class plays a central role in the sequence recognition and the features of transition frames distributed on the disjoint arcs between centers of the blank class and non-blank classes.

The conservative supervision from CTC only classified a small ratio of frames to non-blank classes, but we can observe from Fig. 4(b) that features of the blank class are also clustered into several groups, which are distributed along the disjoint arcs to the centers of non-blank classes. This observation raises two questions: *(1) can we obtain accurate localization information from CTC, and (2) what is the relationship between the recognition and localization abilities of the model trained with CTC?*

The Role of the Angular Margin. Adopting an angular/cosine-margin-based constraint is popular in deep feature learning, which can make learned features more discriminative by adding a margin term in softmax loss. Different from fully-supervised learning, sequence recognition does not require frame-wise annotation generally. It is hard to generate reliable frame-wise labels to apply a margin-based constraint on the sequence recognition model, but, *what will happen if we directly add an angular margin on a frame of the blank class?*

Several previous works [13,43] regard the CTC method as a special case of HMM, which is trained with Baum-Welch soft alignment at each iteration, and its optimization process can be interpreted via Expectation-Maximization. The gradient of $p(l|x)$ with regard to the logit a_k^t [10] is:

$$\frac{\partial \ln p(l|v)}{\partial a_k^t} = y_k^t - \hat{y}_k^t, \tag{4}$$

where $\hat{y}_k^t$ is the conditional expected predictions calculated based on the *Forward-Backward* Algorithm *(FB)* [10]:

$$\hat{y}_k^t = FB(t,k,y,l) = \frac{1}{p(l|v;\theta)} \sum_{\pi \in \mathcal{B}^{-1}(l), \pi_t = k} p(\pi|v;\theta). \tag{5}$$

The frame-wise gradient of CTC has the same formulation as the Cross-Entropy (CE) loss, and the optimization of CTC is equivalent to iterative fitting [22]. However, the pseudo label $\hat{y}_k^t$ is calculated by considering probabilities of all feasible paths. In other words, changes in the logit also influence the probabilities of relevant paths, and *adding a margin term on one frame also changes the pseudo labels of its neighboring frames.*

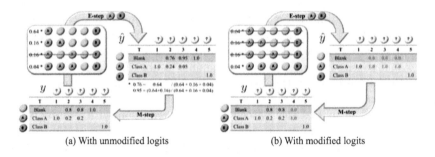

Fig. 5. An illustration of the iterative alignment mechanism of CTC

Figure 5 presents an example to illustrate this characteristic of CTC. For a sequence with five frames and labeling AB, the pseudo label $\hat{y}_k^t$ is calculated by filtering out infeasible alignments and then calculating the expectation values. When adopting a large margin term in softmax operation to change the output of the fourth frame in Fig. 5(a) from $(1.0, 0.0, 0.0)$ to $(0.0, 1.0, 0.0)$, the pseudo labels of 2–4th frames changes from the blank class to class A. In this example, the angular margin plays a role in perturbation and provides a way to change the pseudo label while retaining the iterative alignment mechanism of CTC.

3.3 RadialCTC

Adopting an angular perturbation term can change the pseudo label, which provides a valuable tool to control the peaky behavior. However, it is hard to choose reliable frames to add this term, and a pre-defined term is hardly suitable for all sequences. Therefore, we try to control the peaky behavior of CTC by perturbing blank logits of all frames with a sequence-dependent term.

As the decision boundaries between the blank class and non-blank classes are similar, we look into the decision criteria of softmax in the binary case. After normalizing both features and weights and ignoring the bias term, the decision boundary between the blank class b and a non-blank class nb is $\theta_1 = \theta_2$, where $\theta_1 = \arccos(\tilde{W}_b^\mathsf{T}\tilde{v})$ and $\theta_2 = \arccos(\tilde{W}_{nb}^\mathsf{T}\tilde{v})$. A frame is recognized as the blank class when it lies on the hyperarc-like region ω_1 with $\theta_1 < \theta_2$, and Fig. 6 provides both 2D and 3D examples for better understanding. We can shrink the constrained region of the blank class from $\theta_1 < \theta_2$ to $\theta_1 + m < \theta_2$ by adding an angular perturbation term m on the blank frame. However, the prediction will soon become peaky again when training the model with this term and CTC because the learned features tend to evolve along with the decision boundary.

To control the peaky behavior flexibly, we propose a radial constraint that is implemented by adding an angular perturbation term $m(\eta, \boldsymbol{\theta}, \boldsymbol{l})$ between $\tilde{v}$ and $\tilde{W}_b$ and adopt *the pseudo label of the perturbed logits* to provide supervision for *the original logits*. Unlike adopting a global perturbation term, we search for a proper frame within the sequence and move the decision boundary based on its feature to satisfy a pre-defined non-blank ratio η. Specially, given visual features $\boldsymbol{v} = (v_1, \cdots, v_T)$ and its corresponding labeling $\boldsymbol{l} = (l_1, \cdots, l_U)$, we find

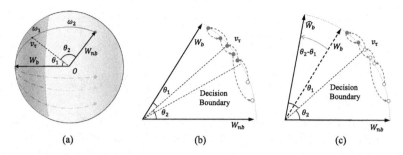

Fig. 6. The geometric interpretation of the angluar perturbation process. Visualization of the decision boundaries of (a) CTC on hypersphere, (b) CTC in binary case and (c) RadialCTC in binary case

the frame v_τ which has the kth ($k = U + 1 + \lfloor (T - U) * \eta \rfloor$) largest angular difference between the blank class and the class with the highest probability that has appeared in the labeling. This process can be formulated as:

$$\boldsymbol{\theta} = \arccos(\tilde{W}^\mathsf{T}\tilde{\boldsymbol{v}})$$
$$m(\eta, \boldsymbol{\theta}, \boldsymbol{l}), \tau = \text{topk}(\max_{c \in l} \boldsymbol{\theta}_c - \boldsymbol{\theta}_b), \tag{6}$$

where topk returns the kth largest value and its corresponding index. Then we add this angular perturbation term between $\tilde{v}$ and $\hat{W}_b$ and calculate the perturbed prediction z, which is calculated by:

$$z_i = \begin{cases} \dfrac{e^{s\cos(\theta_b + m(\eta,\theta,l))}}{e^{s\cos(\theta_b + m(\eta,\theta,l))} + \sum_{j=1, j \neq b}^{n+1} e^{s\cos(\theta_j)}}, & \text{if } i = b \\[3ex] \dfrac{e^{s\cos(\theta_i)}}{e^{s\cos(\theta_b + m(\eta,\theta,l))} + \sum_{j=1, j \neq b}^{n+1} e^{s\cos(\theta_j)}}, & \text{otherswise} \end{cases} \tag{7}$$

Figure 6(b) and (c) provide the geometric interpretation of $m(\eta, \boldsymbol{\theta}, \boldsymbol{l})$ in the binary-class case. The original prediction of CTC is peaky, and only two frames are classified to label nb. To adjust the blank ratio, the 5th largest angular difference ($\theta_2 - \theta_1$) is selected as $m(\eta, \boldsymbol{\theta}, \boldsymbol{l})$. The prediction calculation process of Eq. 7 is equivalent to rotating the weight vector of the blank class from W_b to the virtual weight vector $\hat{W}_b$. The decision boundary will move to the angular bisector of $\hat{W}_b$ and W_i and change the ratio of blanks as expected. The position of $\hat{W}_b$ is adjusted by the non-blank ratio η and the sequence-wise angular distribution, which is more flexible than a fixed global margin.

It seems like applying CTC to this modified prediction can adjust the ratio of non-blank supervision from CTC. However, the modified process leverages the labeling information, which is unknown during inference. A feasible solution is adopting the modified prediction as the pseudo label and iteratively narrowing the gap between it and the original prediction, which is similar to the iterative soft alignment mechanism of CTC. With the help of the FB Algorithm of CTC, we can calculate pseudo labels with higher quality and provide supervision for the original prediction:

$$\hat{z}_k^t = FB(t, k, \boldsymbol{z}, \boldsymbol{l})$$

$$L = -\log p\Big(l_i | \boldsymbol{v}_i, m(\eta, \boldsymbol{\theta}, \boldsymbol{l})\Big) = -\sum_{t=1}^{T} \sum_{k=1}^{N} \hat{z}_k^t \log y_k^{t^.} \tag{8}$$

The only difference between Eq. 8 and the original CTC (Eq. 4 and Eq. 5) is that the prediction used for pseudo label calculation is modified from the original prediction, which can flexibly adjust the blank ratio while retaining the iterative alignment mechanism of CTC. As the proposed method adjust the blank ratio based on 'radial' feature distribution, we named this method RadialCTC. The entire process can be formulated as:

$$\min \quad \underbrace{\sum_{i=1}^{N} \Big(-\log p\Big(l_i | \boldsymbol{v}_i, m(\eta, \boldsymbol{\theta}, \boldsymbol{l})\Big)}_{\text{radial constraint}} + \lambda_1 \underbrace{\sum_{j=1, j\neq b}^{C} \Big(\tilde{W}_b^{\mathsf{T}} \tilde{W}_j - \cos(\beta)\Big)^2}_{\text{angle regularization}}$$

$$+ \lambda_2 \underbrace{\sum_{t_i \in KF(v)} \Big\| \tilde{\boldsymbol{v}}_{t_i} - \tilde{W}_{y_{t_i}} \Big\|_2}_{\text{center regularization}} \Big) \qquad , \tag{9}$$

$$\text{s.t.} \quad \underbrace{\tilde{\boldsymbol{v}}_i = \frac{s\boldsymbol{v}_i}{\|\boldsymbol{v}_i\|_2}, \quad i = 1, \cdots, N, \quad \tilde{W}_j = \frac{W_j}{\|W_j\|_2}, \quad j = 1, \cdots, C}_{\text{normalization}}$$

where λ_1 and λ_2 are hyperparameters to control the strength of regularization.

4   Experiments

This section conducts ablation studies on the Seq-MNIST and evaluates the recognition and localization results. To show the generalization ability of the proposed method, we exemplify it for sequence recognition with two applications: *continuous sign language recognition* (CSLR) and scene text recognition.

4.1   Datasets

Seq-MNIST. Seq-MNIST maintains the distribution balance from MNIST [19]. We also simulate an unbalanced training set by sampling images at the rate of 0.1 for classes 0 to 4 and remaining unchanged for others.

Phoenix14. As a popular CSLR dataset, Phoenix14 [17] contains about 12.5 h of video data collected from weather forecast broadcast and is divided into three parts: 5,672 sentence for training, 540 for *development* (Dev), and 629 for *testing* (Test). It also provides a signer-independent setting where data of 8 signers are chosen for training and leave out data of signer05 for evaluation.

Table 1. Experimental results (%) on Seq-MNIST (dim = 3)

Setting				Balanced			Unbalanced		
Constraint				Train	Test		Train	Test	
Norm	Angle	Center	Radial	Acc.	Acc.	mAP	Acc.	Acc.	mAP
				99.5	95.1	**30.7**	99.9	**87.8**	33.0
✓				99.6	94.8	24.6	98.8	79.5	42.7
✓	✓			99.5	95.2	25.9	98.7	79.5	36.1
✓		✓		99.7	**95.6**	26.9	98.1	74.2	**44.8**
✓	✓	✓		98.5	93.6	25.6	98.2	73.6	42.2
✓	✓	✓	$\eta = 0.0$	96.7	90.4	22.7	98.9	**81.5**	19.7
✓	✓	✓	$\eta = 0.2$	99.8	**93.7**	40.5	97.3	72.3	41.5
✓	✓	✓	$\eta = 0.4$	97.9	88.7	62.8	86.1	31.4	50.7
✓	✓	✓	$\eta = 0.6$	96.6	84.2	78.7	75.7	22.7	56.7
✓	✓	✓	$\eta = 0.8$	94.5	80.8	**87.9**	61.3	23.4	**60.9**

Scene Text Recognition Datasets. Following the standard experimental setting, we use the synthetic Synth90k [15] as training data and test our methods on four real-world benchmarks (*ICDAR-2003*(IC03) [27], *ICDAR-2013*(IC13) [16], *IIIT5k-word*(IIIT5k) [30] and *Street View Text*(SVT) [40]) without fine-tuning.

For Seq-MNIST and scene text recognition datasets, we use sequence accuracy as the evaluation metric. *Word error rate* (WER) is adopted as the evaluation metric of CSLR as previous work does [29]. We adopt the *mean Average Precious* (mAP) [9] to evaluate the localization performance. Other implementation details can be found in the Supplementary.

4.2 Experimental Results

Ablation on RadialCTC Design. We adopt the modified LeNet [41] mentioned in Sect. 3.1 as baseline and present ablation results of RadialCTC on Seq-MNIST in Table 1. To better illustrate the effect of different constraints, we set the dimension of output features to 3. We can observe that adopting either angle or center regularization can improve the recognition results. However, the combined use of them leads to a performance drop. We assume this is because this constraint is too strong to learn separable features in this low-dimensional space, and it achieves better performance when the dimension increases to 128. We can also observe that RadialCTC performs worse on the extremely unbalanced setting, which tends to make more predictions (mAP increases from 33.0% to 42.2%) but also brings more errors. Visualization of learned features and more results can be found in the Supplementary.

Localization Ability of RadialCTC. We adopt the class with a larger interpolation weight as its label for each frame in the sequence and calculate the mAP of different settings to show their localization ability. As η increases, the

Table 2. Performance comparison (%) on Phoenix14 dataset under multi-signer setting

	Dev		Test	
	del/ins	WER	del/ins	WER
Re-Sign [18]	-	27.1	-	26.8
DNF [6]	7.8/3.5	23.8	7.8/3.4	24.4
CMA [32]	7.3/2.7	21.3	7.3/2.4	21.9
STMC [45]	7.7/3.4	21.1	7.4/2.6	20.7
SMKD [14]	6.8/**2.5**	20.8	6.3/**2.3**	21.0
Baseline [29]	7.3/2.6	21.0	7.6/3.0	22.6
RadialCTC	**6.5**/2.7	**19.4**	**6.1**/2.6	**20.2**

Table 3. Performance comparison (%) on Phoenix14 dataset under signer-independent setting

	Dev		Test	
	del/ins	WER	del/ins	WER
Re-Sign [18]	-	45.1	-	44.1
DNF [6]	**9.2**/4.3	36.0	**9.5**/4.6	35.7
CMA [32]	11.1/**2.4**	34.8	11.4/3.3	34.3
Baseline [29]	11.6/3.6	36.7	9.8/3.5	33.8
RadialCTC	10.5/2.9	**33.8**	9.7/**2.9**	**32.2**

Table 4. Performance comparison (%) on scene text recognition datasets

Method	IIIT5K	SVT	IC03	IC13
R2AM [20]	78.4	80.7	88.7	90.0
STAR-Net [24]	**83.3**	**83.6**	89.9	89.1
RARE [36]	81.9	81.9	90.1	88.6
CRNN [35]	78.2	80.8	89.4	86.7
EnEsCTC [23]	82.0	80.6	92.0	90.6
ACE(1D, Cross Entropy) [42]	82.3	82.6	92.1	89.7
Reinterpreting CTC [22]	81.1	82.2	91.2	87.7
Baseline [35]	79.8	80.4	89.9	87.3
RadialCTC	83.2	82.1	**92.3**	**90.7**

localization performance significantly improves (from 22.7% to 87.9%) in Table 1. Although the sequence accuracy drops as η increases, we find this mainly because model trained with larger η tends to merge repeated labels into one (e.g., predicting 567 rather than 5567). After ignoring this case, the recognition accuracy of the $\eta = 0.8$ setting improves from 80.8% to 94.6%, which indicates the proposed RadialCTC can provide accurate boundaries while achieving competitive recognition results. Besides, we can conclude that the localization ability of vanilla CTC is between $\eta = 0.0$ and $\eta = 0.2$ settings.

Limitations of RadialCTC. Experimental results on the unbalanced setting in Table 1 show some limitations of the RadialCTC. When the dataset is extremely unbalanced, prematurely adding center regularization will reduce intra-class variance before the class centers are sufficiently separable and damage the generalization ability of the model. Besides, the distribution of data also affects the localization ability of the model. RadialCTC controls the peaky behavior through a sequence-dependent term. Therefore, the model is more likely to predict the dominant sequence class and limits its localization ability on classes with fewer samples. This conclusion is reflected in the slower growth of mAP.

Continuous Sign Language Recognition. As a typical visual sequence recognition task, visual features play an essential role in CSLR. Recent work [29] has shown that adding an extra CTC on visual features can efficiently improve the recognition results. Therefore, we replace this extra CTC with RadialCTC to show its effectiveness as intermediate supervision without using the distillation loss for simplicity. As shown in Table 2, the proposed RadialCTC improves the recognition results and achieves sota results, which indicates that RadialCTC can learn more discriminative features even if the dataset has limited data. Similar conclusions can be drawn from the signer-independent setting in Table 3.

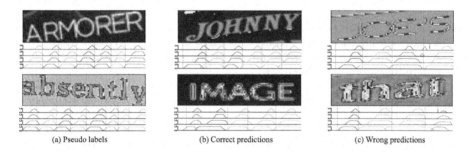

(a) Pseudo labels   (b) Correct predictions   (c) Wrong predictions

Fig. 7. Scene text recognition examples with different non-blank ratios ($\eta = 0.2$, 0.4, 0.6, 0.8 from top to bottom)

Scene Text Recognition. As a classical framework for scene text recognition, modified versions of CTC [22,23,42] adopt CRNN [35] as the baseline and evaluate the performance on a standard benchmark. We follow this experimental setting and present results in Table 4. By changing the primary supervision from CTC to the proposed RadialCTC, the scene text recognition model achieves more than 1.7% improvement on four real-world test sets. The proposed method outperforms other modified versions of CTC on almost all test sets and is competitive with other methods. Previous works [22,23] are also driven by designing a proper method to relieve the peaky behavior. However, we have not found that improving localization ability is helpful for recognition, and the performance gain is obtained without using the radial constraint.

To better show the localization ability of RadialCTC, we visualize pseudo labels and predictions of different non-blank ratios in Fig. 7. RadialCTC can provide confident and accurate pseudo labels and predictions as η increases.

5   Conclusion

As a popular objective function in sequence recognition, CTC provides supervision for unsegmented sequences through an iterative alignment mechanism. In this study, we propose a RadialCTC that constrains sequence features on a hypersphere while retaining the iterative alignment mechanism of CTC. RadialCTC provides a clear geometric interpretation of the distribution of sequence features. Besides, an efficient constraint is proposed to control the peaky behavior of vanilla CTC. Experimental results show that RadialCTC can effectively improve recognition results and provide reliable localization results. We hope the proposed RadialCTC can be a useful tool in sequence recognition, and the geometric interpretation of CTC can inspire other sequence learning tasks.

Acknowledgement. This study was partially supported by the Natural Science Foundation of China under contract No. 61976219.

References

1. Albanie, S., et al.: BSL-1K: scaling up co-articulated sign language recognition using mouthing cues. In: Vedaldi, A., Bischof, H., Brox, T., Frahm, J.-M. (eds.) ECCV 2020. LNCS, vol. 12356, pp. 35–53. Springer, Cham (2020). https://doi.org/10.1007/978-3-030-58621-8_3
2. Bahdanau, D., Cho, K.H., Bengio, Y.: Neural machine translation by jointly learning to align and translate. In: International Conference on Learning Representations (2015)
3. Camgoz, N.C., Hadfield, S., Koller, O., Bowden, R.: Subnets: end-to-end hand shape and continuous sign language recognition. In: Proceedings of the IEEE International Conference on Computer Vision, pp. 3075–3084 (2017)
4. Cheng, K.L., Yang, Z., Chen, Q., Tai, Y.-W.: Fully convolutional networks for continuous sign language recognition. In: Vedaldi, A., Bischof, H., Brox, T., Frahm, J.-M. (eds.) ECCV 2020. LNCS, vol. 12369, pp. 697–714. Springer, Cham (2020). https://doi.org/10.1007/978-3-030-58586-0_41
5. Cihan Camgoz, N., Hadfield, S., Koller, O., Bowden, R.: Subnets: end-to-end hand shape and continuous sign language recognition. In: Proceedings of the IEEE International Conference on Computer Vision, pp. 3056–3065 (2017)
6. Cui, R., Liu, H., Zhang, C.: Recurrent convolutional neural networks for continuous sign language recognition by staged optimization. In: Proceedings of the IEEE Conference on Computer Vision and Pattern Recognition, pp. 7361–7369 (2017)
7. Cui, R., Liu, H., Zhang, C.: A deep neural framework for continuous sign language recognition by iterative training. IEEE Trans. Multimedia **21**(7), 1880–1891 (2019)
8. Deng, J., Guo, J., Xue, N., Zafeiriou, S.: Arcface: additive angular margin loss for deep face recognition. In: Proceedings of the IEEE Conference on Computer Vision and Pattern Recognition, pp. 4690–4699 (2019)
9. Everingham, M., Van Gool, L., Williams, C.K., Winn, J., Zisserman, A.: The pascal visual object classes (VOC) challenge. Int. J. Comput. Vision **88**(2), 303–338 (2010)
10. Graves, A., Fernández, S., Gomez, F., Schmidhuber, J.: Connectionist temporal classification: labelling unsegmented sequence data with recurrent neural networks. In: Proceedings of International Conference on Machine Learning, pp. 369–376 (2006)
11. Graves, A., Jaitly, N.: Towards end-to-end speech recognition with recurrent neural networks. In: Proceedings of the International Conference on Machine Learning, pp. 1764–1772. PMLR (2014)
12. Graves, A., Liwicki, M., Fernández, S., Bertolami, R., Bunke, H., Schmidhuber, J.: A novel connectionist system for unconstrained handwriting recognition. IEEE Trans. Pattern Anal. Mach. Intell. **31**(5), 855–868 (2008)

13. Hadian, H., Sameti, H., Povey, D., Khudanpur, S.: End-to-end speech recognition using lattice-free mmi. In: Interspeech, pp. 12–16 (2018)
14. Hao, A., Min, Y., Chen, X.: Self-mutual distillation learning for continuous sign language recognition. In: Proceedings of the IEEE International Conference on Computer Vision, pp. 11303–11312 (2021)
15. Jaderberg, M., Simonyan, K., Vedaldi, A., Zisserman, A.: Synthetic data and artificial neural networks for natural scene text recognition. arXiv preprint arXiv:1406.2227 (2014)
16. Karatzas, D., et al.: ICDAR 2013 robust reading competition. In: 2013 12th International Conference on Document Analysis and Recognition, pp. 1484–1493. IEEE (2013)
17. Koller, O., Forster, J., Ney, H.: Continuous sign language recognition: towards large vocabulary statistical recognition systems handling multiple signers. Comput. Vis. Image Underst. **141**, 108–125 (2015)
18. Koller, O., Zargaran, S., Ney, H.: Re-sign: re-aligned end-to-end sequence modelling with deep recurrent CNN-HMMs. In: Proceedings of the IEEE Conference on Computer Vision and Pattern Recognition, pp. 4297–4305 (2017)
19. LeCun, Y., Bottou, L., Bengio, Y., Haffner, P.: Gradient-based learning applied to document recognition. Proc. IEEE **86**(11), 2278–2324 (1998)
20. Lee, C.Y., Osindero, S.: Recursive recurrent nets with attention modeling for OCR in the wild. In: Proceedings of the IEEE Conference on Computer Vision and Pattern Recognition, pp. 2231–2239 (2016)
21. Li, D., Rodriguez, C., Yu, X., Li, H.: Word-level deep sign language recognition from video: a new large-scale dataset and methods comparison. In: Proceedings of the IEEE Winter Conference on Applications of Computer Vision, pp. 1459–1469 (2020)
22. Li, H., Wang, W.: Reinterpreting CTC training as iterative fitting. Pattern Recogn. **105**, 107392 (2020)
23. Liu, H., Jin, S., Zhang, C.: Connectionist temporal classification with maximum entropy regularization. Adv. Neural. Inf. Process. Syst. **31**, 831–841 (2018)
24. Liu, W., Chen, C., Wong, K.Y.K., Su, Z., Han, J.: Star-net: a spatial attention residue network for scene text recognition. In: Proceedings of the British Machine Vision Conference, vol. 2, p. 7 (2016)
25. Liu, W., Wen, Y., Yu, Z., Li, M., Raj, B., Song, L.: Sphereface: deep hypersphere embedding for face recognition. In: Proceedings of the IEEE Conference on Computer Vision and Pattern Recognition, pp. 212–220 (2017)
26. Liu, W., Wen, Y., Yu, Z., Yang, M.: Large-margin softmax loss for convolutional neural networks. In: Proceedings of the International Conference on Machine Learning, vol. 2, p. 7 (2016)
27. Lucas, S.M., Panaretos, A., Sosa, L., et al.: ICDAR 2003 robust reading competitions: entries, results, and future directions. Int. J. Doc. Anal. Recognit. **7**(2), 105–122 (2005)
28. Meng, Q., Zhao, S., Huang, Z., Zhou, F.: Magface: a universal representation for face recognition and quality assessment. In: Proceedings of the IEEE Conference on Computer Vision and Pattern Recognition, pp. 14225–14234 (2021)
29. Min, Y., Hao, A., Chai, X., Chen, X.: Visual alignment constraint for continuous sign language recognition. In: Proceedings of the IEEE International Conference on Computer Vision, pp. 11542–11551 (2021)

30. Mishra, A., Alahari, K., Jawahar, C.: Scene text recognition using higher order language priors. In: Proceedings of the British Machine Vision Conference (2012)
31. Parde, C.J., et al.: Deep convolutional neural network features and the original image. arXiv preprint arXiv:1611.01751 (2016)
32. Pu, J., Zhou, W., Hu, H., Li, H.: Boosting continuous sign language recognition via cross modality augmentation. In: Proceedings of the 28th ACM International Conference on Multimedia, pp. 1497–1505 (2020)
33. Rabiner, L.R.: A tutorial on hidden Markov models and selected applications in speech recognition. Proc. IEEE **77**(2), 257–286 (1989)
34. Ranjan, R., Castillo, C.D., Chellappa, R.: L2-constrained softmax loss for discriminative face verification. arXiv preprint arXiv:1703.09507 (2017)
35. Shi, B., Bai, X., Yao, C.: An end-to-end trainable neural network for image-based sequence recognition and its application to scene text recognition. IEEE Trans. Pattern Anal. Mach. Intell. **39**(11), 2298–2304 (2016)
36. Shi, B., Wang, X., Lyu, P., Yao, C., Bai, X.: Robust scene text recognition with automatic rectification. In: Proceedings of the IEEE Conference on Computer Vision and Pattern Recognition, pp. 4168–4176 (2016)
37. Vaswani, A., et al.: Attention is all you need. In: Advances in Neural Information Processing Systems, vol. 30 (2017)
38. Wang, F., Xiang, X., Cheng, J., Yuille, A.L.: Normface: L2 hypersphere embedding for face verification. In: Proceedings of the 25th ACM International Conference on Multimedia, pp. 1041–1049 (2017)
39. Wang, H., et al.: Cosface: large margin cosine loss for deep face recognition. In: Proceedings of the IEEE Conference on Computer Vision and Pattern Recognition, pp. 5265–5274 (2018)
40. Wang, K., Babenko, B., Belongie, S.: End-to-end scene text recognition. In: Proceedings of the IEEE International Conference on Computer Vision, pp. 1457–1464. IEEE (2011)
41. Wen, Y., Zhang, K., Li, Z., Qiao, Yu.: A discriminative feature learning approach for deep face recognition. In: Leibe, B., Matas, J., Sebe, N., Welling, M. (eds.) ECCV 2016. LNCS, vol. 9911, pp. 499–515. Springer, Cham (2016). https://doi.org/10.1007/978-3-319-46478-7_31
42. Xie, Z., Huang, Y., Zhu, Y., Jin, L., Liu, Y., Xie, L.: Aggregation cross-entropy for sequence recognition. In: Proceedings of the IEEE Conference on Computer Vision and Pattern Recognition, pp. 6538–6547 (2019)
43. Zeyer, A., Beck, E., Schlüter, R., Ney, H.: CTC in the context of generalized full-sum hmm training. In: Interspeech, pp. 944–948 (2017)
44. Zeyer, A., Schlüter, R., Ney, H.: Why does CTC result in peaky behavior? arXiv preprint arXiv:2105.14849 (2021)
45. Zhou, H., Zhou, W., Zhou, Y., Li, H.: Spatial-temporal multi-cue network for continuous sign language recognition. In: Proceedings of the Association for the Advancement of Artificial Intelligence, pp. 13009–13016 (2020)

SAGA: Stochastic Whole-Body Grasping with Contact

Yan Wu[1](✉), Jiahao Wang[2], Yan Zhang[1], Siwei Zhang[1], Otmar Hilliges[1],
Fisher Yu[1], and Siyu Tang[1]

[1] ETH Zürich, Zürich, Switzerland
yan.wu@vision.ee.ethz.ch,
{yan.zhang,siwei.zhang,otmar.hilliges,siyu.tang}@inf.ethz.ch, i@yf.io
[2] Max Planck Institute for Informatics, Saarbrücken, Germany
jiwang@mpi-inf.mpg.de

Abstract. The synthesis of human grasping has numerous applications
including AR/VR, video games and robotics. While methods have been
proposed to generate realistic hand–object interaction for object grasping
and manipulation, these typically only consider interacting hand alone.
Our goal is to **synthesize whole-body grasping motions**. Starting
from an arbitrary initial pose, we aim to generate diverse and natural
whole-body human motions to approach and grasp a target object in
3D space. This task is challenging as it requires modeling both whole-
body dynamics and dexterous finger movements. To this end, we propose
SAGA (StochAstic whole-body Grasping with contAct), a framework
which consists of two key components: (a) Static whole-body grasping
pose generation. Specifically, we propose a multi-task generative model,
to jointly learn static whole-body grasping poses and human-object contacts. (b) Grasping motion infilling. Given an initial pose and the generated whole-body grasping pose as the start and end of the motion respectively, we design a novel contact-aware generative motion infilling module
to generate a diverse set of grasp-oriented motions. We demonstrate the
effectiveness of our method, which is a novel generative framework to synthesize realistic and expressive whole-body motions that approach and
grasp randomly placed unseen objects. Code and models are available at
https://jiahaoplus.github.io/SAGA/saga.html.

Keywords: Motion generation · Whole-body grasping synthesis ·
Human-object interaction

1 Introduction

A fully automated system that synthesizes realistic 3D human bodies approaching and grasping a target object in 3D space will be valuable in various fields,

---

Y. Wu and J. Wang—Equal contribution.

Supplementary Information The online version contains supplementary material
available at https://doi.org/10.1007/978-3-031-20068-7_15.

© The Author(s), under exclusive license to Springer Nature Switzerland AG 2022
S. Avidan et al. (Eds.): ECCV 2022, LNCS 13666, pp. 257–274, 2022.
https://doi.org/10.1007/978-3-031-20068-7_15

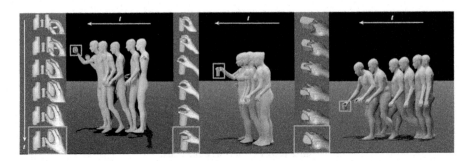

Fig. 1. Generated whole-body grasping motion sequences (in beige) starting from a given pose (in white) to approach and grasp randomly placed unseen objects. For each sample, we present hand motion details in the last few frames on the left column.

from robotics and animation to computer vision. Although remarkable progress has been made towards synthesizing realistic hand–object interactions, most existing works only focus on hand pose synthesis without considering whole-body movements [22,24,50]. Meanwhile, whole-body motion synthesis [17,19,37,60] largely ignores the presence of objects in the scene (Fig. 1).

Modeling and synthesizing realistic whole-body grasping motions are challenging and remain unsolved due to a number of reasons. Firstly, whole-body grasping motions involve both full-body dynamics and dexterous finger movements [50], while the high dimensional degrees of freedom make the synthesis of grasping motions complicated. Secondly, a whole-body grasping sequence exhibits complex and frequent body–scene and hand–object contacts which are challenging to synthesize in a perceptually realistic way. For example, the hand's surface should conform naturally to the object and there should be no foot-skating artifacts in the whole-body motion. Thirdly, given only a starting pose and a target object in 3D space, there could be an infinite number of ways for the person to approach and grasp the object. The diversity of plausible grasping motions is further amplified by the large potential variation in object shape and pose. How to build an effective generative model that can capture this diversity and synthesize diverse realistic motions to grasp various 3D objects is an unsolved question.

To address these challenges, we propose **SAGA** (**S**toch**A**stic whole-body **G**rasping with cont**A**ct), a novel whole-body grasping generation framework that can synthesize stochastic motions of a 3D human body approaching and grasping 3D objects. Our solution consists of two components: (1) a novel 3D body generator that synthesizes diverse static whole-body grasping end poses, and (2) a novel human motion generator that creates diverse and plausible motions between given start and end poses. We present two key insights on both components. First, instead of directly using parametric body models (e.g. SMPL [38]) to represent 3D bodies, we employ the markers-based representation [60] which captures 3D human shape and pose information with a set of sparse markers on the human body surface. As demonstrated in [60], the markers-based representation is easier for neural networks to learn than the latent parameters of the parametric body models, yielding more realistic motion. We show that the markers-based representation is especially advantageous to the latent body parameters for learning whole-body grasping, as the accumulation of errors along the kinematic chain has a significant impact on the physical plausibility of generated hand grasps, resulting in severe hand–object interpenetration. Second, *contact* plays a central role in our pipeline. As the human moves in 3D space and grasps a 3D object, physical contact is key for modeling realistic motions and interactions. For both components of our method, we learn contact representations from data and use them to guide interaction synthesis, greatly improving the realism of the generated motion.

For the static grasping pose generation, we built a multi-task conditional variational autoencoder (CVAE) to jointly learn whole-body marker positions and fine-grained marker–object contact labels. During inference, given a target object in 3D space, our model jointly generates a diverse set of consistent full-body marker locations and the contact labels on both the body markers and the object surface. A contact-aware pose optimization module further recovers a parametric body mesh from the predicted markers, while explicitly enforcing the hand–object contact by leveraging the predicted contact labels. Next, given the generated static whole-body grasping pose as the end pose, and an initial pose as a start pose, we propose a novel generative motion infilling network to capture motion uncertainty and generate diverse motions in between. We design a CVAE-based architecture to generate both the diverse in-between motion trajectories and the diverse in-between local pose articulations. In addition, contacts between feet and the ground are also predicted as a multi-task learning objective to enforce a better foot-ground interaction. Furthermore, leveraging the predicted human–object contacts, we design a contact-aware motion optimization module to produce realistic grasp-oriented whole-body motions from the generated marker sequences. By leveraging the GRAB [50] and AMASS [34] datasets to learn our generative models, our method can successfully generate realistic and diverse whole-body grasping motion sequences for approaching and grasping a variety of 3D objects.

Contributions. In summary, we provide (1) a novel generative framework to synthesize diverse and realistic whole-body motions approaching and grasping various unseen objects for 3D humans that exhibit various body shapes, (2) a novel multi-task learning model to jointly learn the static whole-body grasping poses and the body–object interactions, (3) a novel generative motion infilling model that can stochastically infill both the global trajectories and the local pose articulations, yielding diverse and realistic full-body motions between a start pose and end pose. We perform extensive experiments to validate technical contributions. Experimental results demonstrate both the efficacy of our full pipeline and the superiority of each component to existing solutions.

2   Related Work

Human Grasp Synthesis is a challenging task and has been studied in computer graphics [23,27,30,39,42,58] and robotics [9,20,26,30,33,46]. With the advancement in deep learning, recent works also approach the realistic 3D human grasp synthesis task by leveraging large-scale datasets [3,22,24,50,58], however they only focus on hand grasp synthesis.

Grasping Field [24] proposes an implicit representation of hand–object interaction and builds a model to generate plausible human grasps. GrabNet [50] proposes a CVAE to directly sample the MANO [43] hand parameters, and additionally train a neural network to refine the hand pose for a more plausible hand–object contact. GraspTTA [22] suggests using consistent hand–object interactions to synthesize realistic hand grasping poses. It sequentially generates coarse hand grasping poses and estimates consistent object contact maps, and using the estimated object contact maps, the produced hand pose is further optimized for realistic hand–object interactions. Similarly, ContactOpt [11] proposes an object contact map estimation network and a contact-based hand pose optimization module to produce realistic hand–object interaction. Different from GraspTTA and ContactOpt, which predict consistent hand pose and hand–object contacts sequentially in two stages, we build a multi-task generative model that generates consistent whole-body pose and the mutual human-object contacts jointly to address a more complicated whole-body grasping pose learning problem. Going beyond the static grasp pose generation, provided the wrist trajectory and object trajectory, ManipNet [58] generates dexterous finger motions to manipulate objects using an autoregressive model. Nonetheless, to our best knowledge, none of the previous works studied 3D human whole-body grasp learning and synthesis.

3D Human Motion Synthesis. In recent years, human motion prediction has received a lot of attention in computer vision and computer graphics [4,8,10,18, 21,31,32,36,48,53,60,61]. Existing motion prediction models can also be split into two categories: deterministic [17,19,25,37,55] and stochastic [2,5,28,56]. For deterministic motion prediction, [25] adopt convolutional models to provide spatial or temporal consistent motions, and [37] propose an RNN with residual connections and sampling-based loss to model human motion represented by joints. For stochastic motion prediction, recently, Li et al. [28] and Cai et al. [5] use VAE-based models to address general motion synthesis problems. While these methods make great contributions to human motion understanding, they do not study the interaction with the 3D environment.

There are several works predict human motion paths or poses in scene context [1,6,12,13,15,16,29,35,41,44,45,47,51,52,54,59]. Cao et al. [6] estimate goals, 3D human paths, and pose sequences given 2D pose histories and an image of the scene. However, the human is represented in skeletons, thus it is hard to accurately model body–scene contacts, which limits its application. Recently, Wang et al. [54] propose a pipeline to infill human motions in 3D scenes, which first synthesizes sub-goal bodies, then fills in the motion between these sub-goals, then refines the bodies. However, the generated motion appears unnatural especially in the foot–ground contact. [15] presents an RNN-based network with contact loss and adversarial losses to handle motion in-betweening problems. They use the humanoid skeleton as the body representation and require 10 start frames and one end frame as input. [41] adopts a conditional variational autoencoder to correct the pose at each timestamp to address noise and occlusions. They also use a test-time optimization to get more plausible motions and human–ground contacts. [59] propose a contact-aware motion infiller to generate the motion of unobserved body parts. They predict motion with better foot–ground contact, but their deterministic model does not capture the nature of human motion diversity. Unlike the methods mentioned above, our generative motion infilling model, when given the first and the last frame, captures both the global trajectory diversity in between and the diversity of local body articulations.

Concurrent Work. GOAL [49] builds a similar two-stage pipeline to approach the whole-body grasping motion generation, producing end pose first and then infilling the in-between motion. Unlike our work which captures both the diversity of grasping ending poses and in-between motions, however, GOAL builds a deterministic auto-regressive model to in-paint the in-between motion, which does not fully explore the uncertainty of grasping motions.

3   Method

Preliminaries. (a) 3D human body representation. (1) SMPL-X [38] is a parametric human body model which models body mesh with hand details. In this work, the SMPL-X body parameters $\boldsymbol{\Theta}$ include the shape parameters $\boldsymbol{\beta} \in \mathbb{R}^{10}$, the body global translation $\boldsymbol{t} \in \mathbb{R}^3$, the 6D continuous representation [62] of the body rotation $\boldsymbol{R} \in \mathbb{R}^6$, and full-body pose parameters $\boldsymbol{\theta} = [\boldsymbol{\theta}_b, \boldsymbol{\theta}_h, \boldsymbol{\theta}_e]$, where $\boldsymbol{\theta}_b \in \mathbb{R}^{32}$, $\boldsymbol{\theta}_h \in \mathbb{R}^{48}$, $\boldsymbol{\theta}_e \in \mathbb{R}^6$ are the body pose in the Vposer latent space [38], the hands pose in the MANO [43] PCA space and the eyes pose, respectively; (2) Markers-based representation [60] captures the body shape and pose information with the 3D locations $\boldsymbol{M} \in \mathbb{R}^{N \times 3}$ of a set of sparse markers on the body surface, where N is the number of markers. We learn the markers representation in our neural networks, from which we further recover SMPL-X body mesh. **(b) 3D objects** are represented with centered point cloud data $\boldsymbol{O}$ and the objects height $t_O \in \mathbb{R}^1$. We sample 2048 points on the object surface and each point has 6 features (3 XYZ positions + 3 normal features).

Notations. For clarity, in the following text, $\tilde{X}$ and $\hat{X}$ denote the CVAE reconstruction result of X, and random samples of X from CVAE, respectively.

3.1   Overview

Given an initial human pose and a 3D object randomly placed in front of the human within a reasonable range, our goal is to generate realistic and diverse whole-body motions, starting from the given initial pose and approaching to grasp the object. As presented in Fig. 2, we propose a two-stage grasping motion generation pipeline to approach this task.

Stage 1: Stochastic whole-body grasping ending pose generation (Sect. 3.2). We first build an object-conditioned multi-task CVAE which synthesizes whole-body grasping ending poses in markers and the explicit human–object contacts. We further perform contact-aware pose optimization to produce

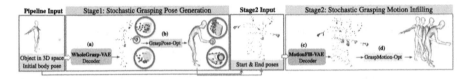

Fig. 2. Illustration of our two-stage pipeline. Given an object in 3D space and a human start pose, our method produces diverse human whole-body grasping motions. In stage 1, (a) taking the given 3D object information as inputs, our WholeGrasp-VAE (Sect. 3.2) decoder generates whole-body grasping poses represented by marker locations and mutual marker–object contact probabilities (green markers and red areas on the object surface indicate a high contact probability); (b) GraspPose-Opt (Sect. 3.2) further recovers body mesh from predicted markers. We use the generated grasping pose as the targeted end pose. Then in stage 2, (c) we feed in the start pose and the end pose into the MotionFill-VAE decoder (Sect. 3.3) to generate the in-between motions in markers representation, and (d) and GraspMotion-Opt (Sect. 3.4) further recovers smooth and realistic whole-body grasping motions. (Color figure online)

3D body meshes with realistic interactions with objects by leveraging the contacts information.

Stage 2: Stochastic grasp-oriented motion infilling. We build a novel generative motion infilling model (Sect. 3.3) which takes the provided initial pose and the generated end pose in stage 1 as inputs, and outputs diverse intermediate motions. We further process the generated motions via a contact-aware optimization step (Sect. 3.4) to produce realistic human whole-body grasping motions.

3.2   Whole-Body Grasping Pose Generation

To synthesize diverse whole-body poses to grasp a given object, we propose a novel multi-task WholeGrasp-VAE to learn diverse yet consistent grasping poses and mutual contacts between human and object. The explicit human–object contacts provide fine-grained human–object interaction information which helps to produce realistic body meshes with high-fidelity interactions with the object.

Model Architecture. We visualize the multi-task WholeGrasp-VAE design in Fig. 3. The encoder takes the body markers' positions $M \in \mathbb{R}^{N \times 3}$, body markers contacts $C_M \in \{0, 1\}^N$ and object contacts $C_O \in \{0, 1\}^{2048}$ as inputs, where N is the number of markers, and learns a joint Gaussian latent space $\mathbf{z_j}$. We use PointNet++ [40] to encode the object feature.

Training. The overall training objective is given by $\mathcal{L}_{train} = \mathcal{L}_{rec} + \lambda_{KL}\mathcal{L}_{KL} + \lambda_c\mathcal{L}_c$, where λ_{KL}, λ_c are hyper-parameters.

Reconstruction loss includes the L1 reconstruction loss of body markers' positions and the binary cross-entropy (BCE) loss of contact probabilities:

$$\mathcal{L}_{rec} = |M - \tilde{M}| + \lambda_M \mathcal{L}_{bce}(C_M, \tilde{C}_M) + \lambda_O \mathcal{L}_{bce}(C_O, \tilde{C}_O). \tag{1}$$

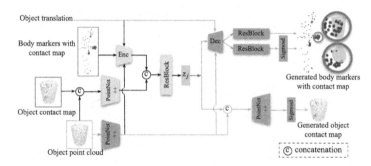

Fig. 3. The WholeGrasp-VAE design. WholeGrasp-VAE jointly learns the (1) body markers' locations; (2) body marker contacts (markers with high contact probability are shown in green); (3) Object contact map (the area with high contact probability is shown in red). The red arrow indicates sampling from the latent space. At inference time, activated modules are shown in orange. (Color figure online)

KL-divergence Loss. We employ the robust KL-divergence term [60] to avoid the VAE posterior collapse:

$$\mathcal{L}_{KL} = \Psi(D_{KL}(q(\mathbf{z_j}|M,C_M,C_O,t_O,O)||\mathcal{N}(\mathbf{0},\mathbf{I}))), \tag{2}$$

where $\Psi(s) = \sqrt{s^2+1}-1$ [7]. This function automatically penalizes the gradient to update the above KLD term, when the KL-divergence is small.

Consistency Loss. We use a consistency loss to implicitly encourage consistent predictions of marker positions and mutual marker–object contacts:

$$\mathcal{L}_c = \sum_{m\in M, \tilde{m}\in\tilde{M}} \tilde{C}_m|d(\tilde{m},O) - d(m,O)| + \sum_{o\in O} \tilde{C}_o|d(o,\tilde{M}) - d(o,M)|, \tag{3}$$

$d(x,\mathcal{Y}) = \min_{y\in\mathcal{Y}}||x-y||_2^2$ is the minimum distance from point x to point cloud $\mathcal{Y}$.

Inference. During inference, we feed the provided target object information into the WholeGrasp-VAE decoder to generate plausible body markers $\hat{M}$ and marker–object contact labels $\hat{C}_M$, $\hat{C}_O$. We design a contact-aware pose optimization algorithm, GraspPose-Opt, to generate a realistic body mesh from markers and refine body pose for high-fidelity human–object interaction by leveraging the fine-grained human–object contacts. Specifically, by optimizing SMPL-X parameters Θ, the overall optimization objective is given by:

$$E_{opt}(\Theta) = E_{fit} + E_{colli}^o + E_{cont}^o + E_{cont}^g. \tag{4}$$

Marker Fitting Loss. To project the predicted markers to a valid body mesh, we minimize the L1 distance between the sampled markers $\hat{M}$ and the queried markers $M(\Theta)$ on the SMPL-X body mesh:

$$E_{fit}(\Theta) = |\hat{M} - M(\Theta)| + \alpha_\theta|\theta|^2, \tag{5}$$

where α_θ is the pose parameters regularization weight.

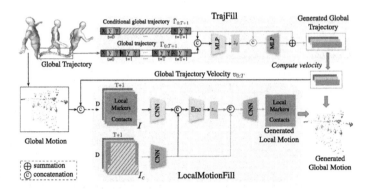

Fig. 4. MotionFill-VAE consists of two concatenated CVAEs: (1) TrajFill outputs the infilled global root trajectory when the start root and the end root are given; (2) LocalMotionFill takes the global trajectory information from TrajFill as one of the inputs, and it outputs the infilled local motion when the start pose, the end pose, and the global trajectory are given. We reconstruct the global motion from the generated global trajectory and the local motion. The red arrow indicates sampling from the latent space. The dash arrow indicates the input processing step for building the four-channel motion image (one local motion channel with contact states and three root velocity channels). At inference time, activated modules are shown in orange (Color figure online).

Object Contact Loss. By leveraging sampled contact maps, we propose a mutual contact loss to encourage body markers and object points with high contact probabilities to contact the object surface and body surface, respectively.

$$E^o_{cont}(\boldsymbol{\Theta}) = \alpha^o_{cont} \sum_{o \in O} \hat{C}_o d(o, \mathcal{V}_B(\boldsymbol{\Theta})) + \alpha^m_{cont} \sum_{m \in M(\Theta)} \hat{C}_m d(m, \boldsymbol{O}). \qquad (6)$$

where $\mathcal{V}_B(\boldsymbol{\Theta})$ denotes the SMPL-X body vertices.

Collision Loss. We employ a signed-distance based collision loss to penalize the body–object interpenetration:

$$E_{colli}(\boldsymbol{\Theta}) = \alpha^B_{colli} \sum_{b \in \mathcal{V}^h_B(\boldsymbol{\Theta})} \max(-\mathcal{S}(b, \boldsymbol{O}), \sigma_b) + \alpha^O_{colli} \sum_{o \in O} \max(-\mathcal{S}(o, \mathcal{V}^h_B(\boldsymbol{\Theta})), \sigma_o)$$

$$(7)$$

where $\mathcal{S}(x, \mathcal{y})$ is the signed-distance from point x to point cloud $\mathcal{y}$, $\mathcal{V}^h_B(\boldsymbol{\Theta})$ denotes the hand vertices, and σ_b, σ_o are small interpenetration thresholds.

Ground contact loss is given by $E^g_{cont}(\boldsymbol{\Theta}) = \alpha_{cont} \sum_{v \in \mathcal{V}^f_B} |h(v)|$, where we penalize the heights of feet vertices $\mathcal{V}^f_B$ to enforce a plausible foot–ground contact.

3.3 Generative Motion Infilling

Given body markers on the start and end poses produced by GraspPose-Opt, *i.e.*, M_0 and M_T, many in-between motions are plausible. To model such uncertainty, we build a novel generative motion infilling model, namely MotionFill-VAE, to capture both the uncertainties of intermediate global root (pelvis joint) trajectories and intermediate root-related local body poses. Specifically, given motion $M_{0:T}$ represented in a sequence of markers positions, following [19,25,59], we represent the global motion $M_{0:T}$ with a hierarchical combination of global root velocity $v_{0:T}$ (where $v_t = \Gamma_{t+1} - \Gamma_t, t \in [0,T]$, Γ and v denote the root trajectory and root velocity respectively) and the trajectory-conditioned local motion $M_{0:T}^l$. Accordingly, we build the MotionFill-VAE to capture both the conditional global trajectory distribution $P(\Gamma_{0:T+1}|\Gamma_0, \Gamma_T)$ and the conditional local motion distribution $P(M_{0:T}^l|v_{0:T}, M_0^l, M_T^l)$.

Model Architecture. As shown in Fig. 4, the MotionFill-VAE consists of two concatenated CVAEs: **(1) TrajFill** learns the conditional intermediate global root trajectory latent space z_t. Taking the root states Γ_0 and Γ_T as inputs, which are derived from the given start and end pose, our goal is to get the trajectory $\Gamma_{0:T+1}$. Instead of directly learning $\Gamma_{0:T+1}$, we build TrajFill to learn the trajectory deviation $\Delta\Gamma_{0:T+1} = \Gamma_{0:T+1} - \overline{\Gamma}_{0:T+1}$, where $\overline{\Gamma}_{0:T+1}$ is a straight trajectory which is a linear interpolation and one-step extrapolation of the given Γ_0 and Γ_T. We further compute the velocity $v_{0:T}$ from the predicted trajectory $\Gamma_{0:T+1}$. **(2) LocalMotionFill** learns the conditional intermediate local motion latent space z_m. Taking the TrajFill output $v_{0:T}$ and the given M_0, M_T as inputs, LocalMotionFill generates the trajectory-conditioned local motion sequence. Specifically, following [59], we build a four-channel image I, which is a concatenation of local motion information with foot–ground contact labels and root velocity, and we use it as the input to our CNN-based LocalMotionFill architecture. Similarly, we build the four-channel conditional image I_c with the unknown motion in between filled with all 0.

Training. The training loss is $\mathcal{L}_M = \mathcal{L}_{rec} + \lambda_{KL}\mathcal{L}_{KL}$, and λ_{KL} is hyper-parameter.

Reconstruction loss $\mathcal{L}_{rec}$ contains the global trajectory reconstruction, local motion reconstruction and foot–ground contact label reconstruction losses:

$$\mathcal{L}_{rec} = \sum_{t=0}^{T+1} |\Gamma_t - \tilde{\Gamma}_t| + \lambda_1 \sum_{t=0}^{T} |v_t^\Gamma - \tilde{v}_t^\Gamma| + \lambda_2 \mathcal{L}_{bce}(C_F, \tilde{C}_F)$$
$$+ \lambda_3 \sum_{t=0}^{T} |M_t^l - \tilde{M}_t^l| + \lambda_4 \sum_{t=0}^{T-1} |v_t^{M^l} - \tilde{v}_t^{M^l}|, \tag{8}$$

where $v_t^{(*)} = (*)_{t+1} - (*)_t$ denotes the velocity, and $\lambda_1 - \lambda_4$ are hyper-parameters.

KL-divergence Loss. We use the robust KL-divergence loss for both TrajFill and LocalMotionFill:

$$\mathcal{L}_{KL} = \Psi(D_{KL}(q(z_t|\Gamma_{0:T+1}, \overline{\Gamma}_{0:T+1})||\mathcal{N}(0, I))) + \Psi(D_{KL}(q(z_m|I, I_c)||\mathcal{N}(0, I))). \tag{9}$$

Inference. At inference time, given the start and end body markers M_0, M_T with known root states Γ_0, Γ_T, by first feeding the initial interpolated trajectory $\overline{\Gamma}_{0:T+1}$ into the decoder of TrajFill, we generate stochastic in-between global motion trajectory $\hat{\Gamma}_{0:T+1}$. Next, with the given M_0, M_T and the generated $\hat{\Gamma}_{0:T+1}$, we further build the condition input image I_c as the input to the LocalMotion-Fill decoder, from which we can generate infilled local motion sequences $\hat{M}^l_{0:T}$ and also the foot–ground contact probabilities $\hat{C}_{F_{0:T}}$. Finally, we reconstruct the global motion sequences $\hat{M}_{0:T}$ from the generated $\hat{\Gamma}_{0:T}$ and $\hat{M}^l_{0:T}$.

3.4   Contact-Aware Grasping Motion Optimization

With the generated marker sequences $\hat{M}_{0:T}$, foot–ground contacts $\hat{C}_F$ from MotionFill-VAE, and the human–object contacts $\hat{C}_M, \hat{C}_O$ from WholeGrasp-VAE, we design GraspMotion-Opt, a contact-aware motion optimization algorithm, to recover smooth motions $B_{0:T}$ with natural interactions with the scene.

Similar to GraspPose-opt, we propose the contact-aware marker fitting loss:

$$E_{basic}(\Theta_{0:T}) = \sum_{t=0}^{T}(E_{fit}(\Theta_t) + E^o_{colli}(\Theta_t)) + \sum_{t=T-4}^{T} E^o_{cont}(\Theta_t), \tag{10}$$

where $E_{fit}, E^o_{cont}, E^o_{colli}$ are formulated in Eq. 5–7, and we only apply object contact loss E^o_{colli} on the last 5 frames.

We design the following loss to encourage a natural hand grasping motion by encouraging the palm to face the object's surface on approach.

$$E_g(\Theta_{0:T}) = \sum_{t=0}^{T} \alpha_t \sum_{m \in \mathcal{V}^p_B(\Theta_t)} \mathbb{1}(d(m, O) < \sigma)(\cos\gamma_m - 1)^2, \tag{11}$$

where $\alpha_t = 1 - (\frac{t}{T})^2$, $\mathcal{V}^p_B(\Theta)$ denotes the selected vertices on palm, and γ_m is the angle between the palm normal vector and the vector from palm vertices to the closest object surface points. We only apply this constraint when palm vertices are close to the object's surface (within radius $\sigma = 1cm$).

Inspired by [59], we enforce smoothness on the motion latent space to yield smoother motion, and we also reduce the foot skating artifacts by leveraging the foot–ground contact labels $\hat{C}_F$. For more details, please refer to the Appendix.

4   Experiments

Datasets. (1) We use **GRAB** [50] dataset to train and evaluate our Whole Grasp-VAE and also finetune the MotionFill-VAE. For WholeGrasp-VAE training and evaluation, following [50], we take all frames with right-hand grasps and have the same train/valid/test set split. For MotionFill-VAE training, we downsample the motion sequences to 30fps and clip 62 frames per sequence, with last frames being in stable grasping poses. (2) We use the **AMASS** [34] dataset to pretrain our LocalMotionFill-CVAE. We down-sample the sequences to 30 fps and cut them into clips with 61 frames. (3) We take unseen objects from **HO3D** [14] dataset to test the generalization ability of our method.

Table 1. Comparisons with the extended GrabNet baseline and ablation study result on the multi-task WholeGrasp-VAE design. Numbers in **bold**/blue indicates the **best**/second-best respectively.

Method	APD ($\uparrow$)	Contact Ratio ($\uparrow$)	Inter. Vol. $[cm^3]$ ($\downarrow$)	Inter. Depth $[cm]$ ($\downarrow$)
GrabNet [50]-SMPLX	0.33	0.65	14.15	0.78
WholeGrasp-single w/o opt.*	**2.94**	0.90	11.44	0.78
WholeGrasp-single w/ heuristic opt		0.81	**0.21**	**0.12**
WholeGrasp w/o opt.*	2.92	**0.96**	12.20	0.85
WholeGrasp w/ opt. (**Ours**)		0.94	0.48	0.16

* Body meshes are recovered from sampled markers with only E_{fit} in Eq. 5.

We conduct extensive experiments to study the effectiveness of each stage in our pipeline. In Sect. 4.1 and Sect. 4.2, we study our static grasping pose generator and the stochastic motion infilling model respectively. In Sect. 4.3, we evaluate the entire pipeline performance for synthesizing stochastic grasping motions. We encourage readers to watch the video of generated grasping poses and motions.

4.1   Stochastic Whole-Body Grasp Pose Synthesis

We evaluate our proposed stochastic whole-body grasp pose generation module on GRAB dataset. We also conduct ablation studies to study the effectiveness of several proposed components, including the multi-task CVAE design and the contact-aware optimization module design.

Baseline. GrabNet [50] builds a CVAE to generate the MANO hand parameters for grasping a given object, and we extend GrabNet to whole-body grasp synthesis by learning the whole-body SMPL-X parameters. We compare our method against the extended GrabNet (named as GrabNet-SMPLX)[1].

Evaluation Metrics. *(1) Contact Ratio.* To evaluate the grasp stability, we measure the ratio of body meshes being in minimal contact with object meshes. *(2) Interpenetration Volume and Depth.* We measure the interpenetration volumes and depths between the body and object mesh. Low interpenetration volume and depth with a high contact ratio are desirable for perceptually realistic body–object interactions. *(3) Diversity.* We follow [57] to employ the Average L2 Pairwise Distance (**APD**) to evaluate the diversity within random samples.

Results. In Table 1, we compare our method against the extended GrabNet baseline. Because the extended GrabNet baseline does not include an additional body mesh refinement step, we compare it to our results without GraspPose-Opt optimization (WholeGrasp w/o. opt. in Table 1). Our method w/o optimization outperforms the extended GrabNet baseline in the sample diversity (APD)

---

[1] Please refer to the Appendix for experimental setup and implementation details..

Table 2. Ablation studies on different optimization losses (E_{fit}, E_{colli}, E^o_{cont} in Eq. 5–Eq. 6). We fit ground truth markers (GT columns) and sampled markers (Samples columns), and numbers in **bold**/blue indicate the **best**/second-best respectively.

	Contact Ratio($\uparrow$)		Inter. Vol.($\downarrow$)		Inter. Depth($\downarrow$)	
	GT	Samples	GT	Samples	GT	Samples
GT Mesh	0.99	-	2.04	-	0.45	-
$E_{fit} + E^g_{cont}$	**0.99**	**0.96**	2.21	12.20	0.46	0.85
$E_{fit} + E^g_{cont} + E_{colli}$	0.25	0.24	**0.12**	**0.12**	**0.04**	**0.07**
$E_{fit} + E^g_{cont} + E_{colli} + E^o_{cont}$	0.94	0.94	0.52	0.48	0.17	0.16

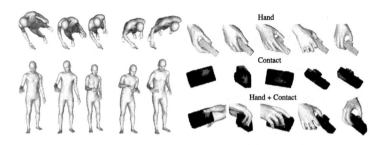

Fig. 5. Five **random** samples for an unseen object placed at the same positions. Left side: top view and front view of generated whole-body poses. Right side: hand grasping details and generated object contact maps (red areas indicate high contact probability). (Color figure online)

and achieves higher contact ratio and smaller intersection. The extended Grab-Net experiment demonstrates the challenges in learning the whole-body pose parameters for a plausible human–object interaction, with marker representation appearing to be more favorable for learning human grasping pose. Nevertheless, the derived body meshes from markers without pose optimization still have human–object interpenetration, and our contact-aware pose optimization (WholeGrasp w/ opt. in Table 1) drastically reduces the human–object collision issue while maintaining a high contact ratio.

Figure 5 presents 5 **random** samples together with the generated object contact maps and hand grasping details for an unseen object. We can see that our models generate natural grasping poses with diverse body shapes and whole-body poses.

Ablation Study. *(1) Multi-task WholeGrasp design:* To study the effect of learning human–object contact labels, we build a single-task WholeGrasp-VAE architecture which only learns the markers' positions (WholeGrasp-single in Table 1). A similar pose optimization step as our GraspPose-opt further refines the grasping pose (WholeGrasp-single w/ heuristic opt. in Table 1), but we replace the mutual contact loss E_{cont} in Eq. 6 with a heuristic contact loss which is based on a pre-defined hand contact pattern. Both the single-task and multi-task WholeGrasp experiments demonstrate the benefit of using contact to refine the human–object interaction, and our multi-task WholeGrasp with

Table 3. Comparisons with motion infilling baselines. Best results are in boldface.

	Methods	ADE (↓)	Skat (↓)	PSKL-J (↓)	
				(P, GT)	(GT, P)
Local motion infilling*	CNN-AE [25]	0.091	0.245	0.804	0.739
	LEMO [59]	0.083	0.152	0.507	0.447
	PoseNet [54]	0.090	0.236	0.611	0.668
	Ours-Local†	**0.079**	**0.137**	**0.377**	**0.327**
Traj + local motion infilling	Route+PoseNet [54]	0.219	0.575	0.955	0.884
	Ours†	**0.083**	**0.394**	**0.772**	**0.609**

* Ground truth trajectories are used in the local motion infilling experiments.
† Generative models. And all the other methods are deterministic models.

explicit mutual contact learning outperforms the single-task setup with the pre-defined hand contact pattern. *(2) Study of GraspPose-Opt* (see Table 2): We evaluate recovered body meshes from both the ground truth markers and the randomly sampled markers, and also the ground truth body mesh. By fitting the body mesh to ground truth markers, our proposed GraspPose-Opt with only E_{fit} can recover an accurate body mesh with the human–object interaction metrics comparable to the ground truth mesh. The proposed E_{colli} and E_{cont} help to recover realistic human–object interaction significantly.

4.2 Stochastic Motion Infilling

We evaluate our motion infilling model on AMASS and GRAB datasets. To our best knowledge, we are the first generative model to learn both the global trajectory and the local motion infilling given only one start pose and end pose. We compare our method with several representative motion infilling models.

Baselines. Wang *et al.* [54] proposed two sequential yet separate LSTM-based deterministic networks to first predict global trajectory (RouteNet) and then the local pose articulations (PoseNet) to approach the motion infilling task, and we take this sequential network (named as Route+PoseNet) as a baseline to our end-to-end generative global motion infilling model. There are some existing works which take the ground truth trajectory, start pose and end poses as inputs to predict the intermediate local poses, and following the same task setup, we also compare the generative local motion infilling component in our network against these baselines, including the convolution autoencoder network (CNN-AE) in [25], LEMO [59] and PoseNet [54]. We have chosen these baselines as they are the closest ones compared with our setting. For fair comparisons, we use the same body markers and the trajectory representation in all experiments (see footnote 1).

Evaluation Metrics. *(1) 3D marker accuracy.* For deterministic models, we measure the marker prediction accuracy by computing the Average L2 Distance Error (ADE) between the predicted markers and ground truth. For our generative model, we follow [57] to measure the sample accuracy by computing the minimal error between the ground truth and 10 random samples. *(2) Motion smoothness.* We follow [59] to use PSKL-J to measure the Power Spectrum KL divergence between the acceleration distribution of synthesized and ground truth joint motion sequences. PSKL-J being non-symmetric, we show the results of both direction, *i.e.*, (Predicted, Ground Truth) and (Ground Truth, Predicted). *(3) Foot skating.* Following [60], we measure the foot skating artifacts during motion and define skating as when the heel is within 5cm of the ground and the heel speed of both feet exceeds 75mm/s. *(4) foot–ground collision.* We also use a non-collision score, defined as the number of body mesh vertices above the ground divided by the total number of vertices.

Results. In Table 3, we compare our generative motion infilling model with the deterministic Route+PoseNet baseline [54], and both methods can infill the global trajectory and local pose motion. The results show that our generative model can yield much lower average 3D marker distance error (ADE). Also, our method has less foot skating and lower PSKL-J scores in both directions, which demonstrates that our method can generate more natural motions. We also compare our stochastic local motion infilling component (**Ours**-Local) against other deterministic local motion infilling baselines in Table 3. Our method outperforms all the other baselines in ADE, foot skating and PSKL-J, demonstrating that the our generative model can better capture human motion patterns and generate more natural motions. The motion sequences from the GRAB dataset and our generated motions have non-collision score of 0.9771 and 0.9743, respectively, showing that our method can effectively prevent foot–ground interpenetration.

4.3   Whole-Body Grasp Motion Synthesis

Experiment Setup. We test our grasping motion generation pipeline on 14 unseen objects from GRAB and HO3D dataset, and we generate 2 s motions to grasp the object. Given different initial human poses, we place objects in front of the human at different heights (0.5 m–1.7 m) with various orientations (0–360° around the gravity axis) and different distances from start point to objects (5 cm– 1.1 m). We conduct user studies on Amazon Mechanical Turk (AMT) for both ground truth grasping motion sequences from GRAB and our generated samples. On a five-point scale, three users are asked to rate the realism of presented motions, ranging from *strongly disagree* (score 0) to *strongly agree* (score 5) (see footnote 1).

Results. The perceptual scores for ground truth sequences and our synthesized sequences are 4.04 (around *agree*) and 3.15 (above *slightly agree*) respectively, showing that our proposed pipeline can synthesize high-fidelity grasping motions.

5   Conclusion and Discussion

In this work, we address an important task on how to synthesize realistic whole-body grasping motion. We propose a new approach consisting of two stages:

(a) a WholeGrasp-VAE to generate static whole-body grasping poses; (b) a MotionFill-VAE to infill the grasp-oriented motion, given an initial pose and the predicted end pose. Our method, SAGA, is able to generate diverse motion sequences that have realistic interactions with the ground and random objects. We believe SAGA makes progress towards synthesizing human–object interaction, and provides a useful tool for computer graphics and robotics applications. However, in this work, we focus on the human motion synthesis task where a virtual human approaches to grasp an object without further hand–object manipulation. A future work is to synthesize the hand–object manipulation, while taking the object affordance, physics and the goal of the interaction into account.

Acknowledgement. This work was supported by the SNF grant 200021 204840 and Microsoft Mixed Reality & AI Zurich Lab PhD scholarship.

References

1. Alahi, A., Ramanathan, V., Fei-Fei, L.: Socially-aware large-scale crowd forecasting. In: Proceedings of the IEEE Conference on Computer Vision and Pattern Recognition, pp. 2203–2210 (2014)
2. Barsoum, E., Kender, J., Liu, Z.: HP-GAN: probabilistic 3D human motion prediction via GAN. In: Proceedings of the IEEE Conference on Computer Vision and Pattern Recognition Workshops, pp. 1418–1427 (2018)
3. Brahmbhatt, S., Handa, A., Hays, J., Fox, D.: ContactGrasp: functional multifinger grasp synthesis from contact. In: 2019 IEEE/RSJ International Conference on Intelligent Robots and Systems (IROS) (2019)
4. Cai, Y., et al.: Learning progressive joint propagation for human motion prediction. In: Vedaldi, A., Bischof, H., Brox, T., Frahm, J.-M. (eds.) ECCV 2020. LNCS, vol. 12352, pp. 226–242. Springer, Cham (2020). https://doi.org/10.1007/978-3-030-58571-6_14
5. Cai, Y., et al.: A unified 3D human motion synthesis model via conditional variational auto-encoder. In: Proceedings of the IEEE/CVF International Conference on Computer Vision, pp. 11645–11655 (2021)
6. Cao, Z., Gao, H., Mangalam, K., Cai, Q.-Z., Vo, M., Malik, J.: Long-term human motion prediction with scene context. In: Vedaldi, A., Bischof, H., Brox, T., Frahm, J.-M. (eds.) ECCV 2020. LNCS, vol. 12346, pp. 387–404. Springer, Cham (2020). https://doi.org/10.1007/978-3-030-58452-8_23
7. Charbonnier, P., Blanc-Feraud, L., Aubert, G., Barlaud, M.: Two deterministic half-quadratic regularization algorithms for computed imaging. In: Proceedings of 1st International Conference on Image Processing, vol. 2, pp. 168–172 (1994)
8. Chiu, H.k., Adeli, E., Wang, B., Huang, D.A., Niebles, J.C.: Action-agnostic human pose forecasting. In: 2019 IEEE Winter Conference on Applications of Computer Vision (WACV), pp. 1423–1432. IEEE (2019)
9. Detry, R., Kraft, D., Buch, A.G., Krüger, N., Piater, J.: Refining grasp affordance models by experience. In: 2010 IEEE International Conference on Robotics and Automation, pp. 2287–2293 (2010)
10. Fragkiadaki, K., Levine, S., Felsen, P., Malik, J.: Recurrent network models for human dynamics. In: Proceedings of the IEEE International Conference on Computer Vision, pp. 4346–4354 (2015)

11. Grady, P., Tang, C., Twigg, C.D., Vo, M., Brahmbhatt, S., Kemp, C.C.: ContactOpt: optimizing contact to improve grasps. In: Conference on Computer Vision and Pattern Recognition (CVPR) (2021)
12. Gupta, A., Satkin, S., Efros, A.A., Hebert, M.: From 3D scene geometry to human workspace. In: CVPR 2011, pp. 1961–1968. IEEE (2011)
13. Gupta, A., Johnson, J., Fei-Fei, L., Savarese, S., Alahi, A.: Social GAN: socially acceptable trajectories with generative adversarial networks. In: Proceedings of the IEEE Conference on Computer Vision and Pattern Recognition, pp. 2255–2264 (2018)
14. Hampali, S., Rad, M., Oberweger, M., Lepetit, V.: Honnotate: a method for 3D annotation of hand and object poses. In: Proceedings of the IEEE/CVF Conference on Computer Vision and Pattern Recognition, pp. 3196–3206 (2020)
15. Harvey, F.G., Yurick, M., Nowrouzezahrai, D., Pal, C.: Robust motion in-betweening. ACM Trans. Graph. (TOG) $39(4)$, 60–1 (2020)
16. Helbing, D., Molnar, P.: Social force model for pedestrian dynamics. Phys. Rev. E $51(5)$, 4282 (1995)
17. Hernandez, A., Gall, J., Moreno-Noguer, F.: Human motion prediction via spatio-temporal inpainting. In: Proceedings of the IEEE/CVF International Conference on Computer Vision, pp. 7134–7143 (2019)
18. Holden, D., Komura, T., Saito, J.: Phase-functioned neural networks for character control. ACM Trans. Graph. (TOG) $36(4)$, 1–13 (2017)
19. Holden, D., Saito, J., Komura, T.: A deep learning framework for character motion synthesis and editing. ACM Trans. Graph. (TOG) $35(4)$, 1–11 (2016)
20. Hsiao, K., Lozano-Perez, T.: Imitation learning of whole-body grasps. In: 2006 IEEE/RSJ International Conference on Intelligent Robots and Systems, pp. 5657–5662. IEEE (2006)
21. Jain, A., Zamir, A.R., Savarese, S., Saxena, A.: Structural-RNN: deep learning on spatio-temporal graphs. In: Proceedings of the IEEE Conference on Computer Vision and Pattern Recognition, pp. 5308–5317 (2016)
22. Jiang, H., Liu, S., Wang, J., Wang, X.: Hand-object contact consistency reasoning for human grasps generation. In: Proceedings of the International Conference on Computer Vision (2021)
23. Kalisiak, M., Van de Panne, M.: A grasp-based motion planning algorithm for character animation. J. Vis. Comput. Animat. $12(3)$, 117–129 (2001)
24. Karunratanakul, K., Yang, J., Zhang, Y., Black, M., Muandet, K., Tang, S.: Grasping field: learning implicit representations for human grasps. In: 8th International Conference on 3D Vision, pp. 333–344. IEEE, November 2020
25. Kaufmann, M., Aksan, E., Song, J., Pece, F., Ziegler, R., Hilliges, O.: Convolutional autoencoders for human motion infilling. In: 2020 International Conference on 3D Vision (3DV), pp. 918–927. IEEE (2020)
26. Krug, R., Dimitrov, D., Charusta, K., Iliev, B.: On the efficient computation of independent contact regions for force closure grasps. In: 2010 IEEE/RSJ International Conference on Intelligent Robots and Systems, pp. 586–591 (2010)
27. Kry, P.G., Pai, D.K.: Interaction capture and synthesis. ACM Trans. Graph. $25(3)$, 872–880 (2006)
28. Li, J., et al.: Task-generic hierarchical human motion prior using VAEs. In: 2021 International Conference on 3D Vision (3DV), pp. 771–781. IEEE (2021)
29. Li, X., Liu, S., Kim, K., Wang, X., Yang, M.H., Kautz, J.: Putting humans in a scene: learning affordance in 3D indoor environments. In: Proceedings of the IEEE Conference on Computer Vision and Pattern Recognition, pp. 12368–12376 (2019)

30. Li, Y., Fu, J.L., Pollard, N.S.: Data-driven grasp synthesis using shape matching and task-based pruning. IEEE Trans. Visual Comput. Graphics **13**(4), 732–747 (2007)
31. Ling, H.Y., Zinno, F., Cheng, G., Van De Panne, M.: Character controllers using motion VAEs. ACM Trans. Graph. (TOG) **39**(4), 40–1 (2020)
32. Liu, L., Hodgins, J.: Learning basketball dribbling skills using trajectory optimization and deep reinforcement learning. ACM Trans. Graph. (TOG) **37**(4), 1–14 (2018)
33. Liu, M., Pan, Z., Xu, K., Ganguly, K., Manocha, D.: Generating grasp poses for a high-DOF gripper using neural networks. In: 2019 IEEE/RSJ International Conference on Intelligent Robots and Systems (IROS), pp. 1518–1525. IEEE (2019)
34. Mahmood, N., Ghorbani, N., Troje, N.F., Pons-Moll, G., Black, M.J.: AMASS: archive of motion capture as surface shapes. In: International Conference on Computer Vision, pp. 5442–5451 (2019)
35. Makansi, O., Ilg, E., Cicek, O., Brox, T.: Overcoming limitations of mixture density networks: a sampling and fitting framework for multimodal future prediction. In: Proceedings of the IEEE Conference on Computer Vision and Pattern Recognition, pp. 7144–7153 (2019)
36. Mao, W., Liu, M., Salzmann, M., Li, H.: Learning trajectory dependencies for human motion prediction. In: Proceedings of the IEEE International Conference on Computer Vision, pp. 9489–9497 (2019)
37. Martinez, J., Black, M.J., Romero, J.: On human motion prediction using recurrent neural networks. In: Proceedings of the IEEE Conference on Computer Vision and Pattern Recognition, pp. 2891–2900 (2017)
38. Pavlakos, G., et al.: Expressive body capture: 3D hands, face, and body from a single image. In: Proceedings IEEE Conference on Computer Vision and Pattern Recognition (CVPR), pp. 10975–10985 (2019)
39. Pollard, N.S., Zordan, V.B.: Physically based grasping control from example. In: Proceedings of the 2005 ACM SIGGRAPH/Eurographics Symposium on Computer Animation, pp. 311–318 (2005)
40. Qi, C.R., Yi, L., Su, H., Guibas, L.J.: Pointnet++: deep hierarchical feature learning on point sets in a metric space. In: Advances in Neural Information Processing Systems, vol. 30 (2017)
41. Rempe, D., Birdal, T., Hertzmann, A., Yang, J., Sridhar, S., Guibas, L.J.: Humor: 3D human motion model for robust pose estimation. In: Proceedings of the IEEE/CVF International Conference on Computer Vision, pp. 11488–11499 (2021)
42. Rijpkema, H., Girard, M.: Computer animation of knowledge-based human grasping. ACM Siggraph Comput. Graph. **25**(4), 339–348 (1991)
43. Romero, J., Tzionas, D., Black, M.J.: Embodied hands: modeling and capturing hands and bodies together. ACM Trans. Graph. (Proc. SIGGRAPH Asia) **36**(6) (2017)
44. Sadeghian, A., Kosaraju, V., Sadeghian, A., Hirose, N., Rezatofighi, H., Savarese, S.: Sophie: an attentive GAN for predicting paths compliant to social and physical constraints. In: Proceedings of the IEEE Conference on Computer Vision and Pattern Recognition, pp. 1349–1358 (2019)
45. Savva, M., Chang, A.X., Hanrahan, P., Fisher, M., Nießner, M.: Pigraphs: learning interaction snapshots from observations. ACM Trans. Graph. (TOG) **35**(4), 1–12 (2016)
46. Seo, J., Kim, S., Kumar, V.: Planar, bimanual, whole-arm grasping. In: 2012 IEEE International Conference on Robotics and Automation, pp. 3271–3277 (2012)

47. Starke, S., Zhang, H., Komura, T., Saito, J.: Neural state machine for character-scene interactions. ACM Trans. Graph. **38**(6), 209-1 (2019)
48. Starke, S., Zhao, Y., Komura, T., Zaman, K.: Local motion phases for learning multi-contact character movements. ACM Trans. Graph. (TOG) **39**(4), 54-1 (2020)
49. Taheri, O., Choutas, V., Black, M.J., Tzionas, D.: Goal: generating 4D whole-body motion for hand-object grasping. arXiv preprint arXiv:2112.11454 (2021)
50. Taheri, O., Ghorbani, N., Black, M.J., Tzionas, D.: GRAB: a dataset of whole-body human grasping of objects. In: Vedaldi, A., Bischof, H., Brox, T., Frahm, J.-M. (eds.) ECCV 2020. LNCS, vol. 12349, pp. 581–600. Springer, Cham (2020). https://doi.org/10.1007/978-3-030-58548-8_34
51. Tai, L., Zhang, J., Liu, M., Burgard, W.: Socially compliant navigation through raw depth inputs with generative adversarial imitation learning. In: 2018 IEEE International Conference on Robotics and Automation (ICRA), pp. 1111–1117. IEEE (2018)
52. Tan, F., Bernier, C., Cohen, B., Ordonez, V., Barnes, C.: Where and who? Automatic semantic-aware person composition. In: 2018 IEEE Winter Conference on Applications of Computer Vision (WACV), pp. 1519–1528. IEEE (2018)
53. Wang, B., Adeli, E., Chiu, H.k., Huang, D.A., Niebles, J.C.: Imitation learning for human pose prediction. In: Proceedings of the IEEE International Conference on Computer Vision, pp. 7124–7133 (2019)
54. Wang, J., Xu, H., Xu, J., Liu, S., Wang, X.: Synthesizing long-term 3D human motion and interaction in 3D scenes. In: Proceedings of the IEEE/CVF Conference on Computer Vision and Pattern Recognition, pp. 9401–9411 (2021)
55. Yan, S., Li, Z., Xiong, Y., Yan, H., Lin, D.: Convolutional sequence generation for skeleton-based action synthesis. In: Proceedings of the IEEE/CVF International Conference on Computer Vision, pp. 4394–4402 (2019)
56. Yan, X., et al.: MT-VAE: learning motion transformations to generate multimodal human dynamics. In: Proceedings of the European Conference on Computer Vision (ECCV), pp. 265–281 (2018)
57. Yuan, Y., Kitani, K.: Dlow: diversifying latent flows for diverse human motion prediction. In: Proceedings of the European Conference on Computer Vision (ECCV) (2020)
58. Zhang, H., Ye, Y., Shiratori, T., Komura, T.: Manipnet: neural manipulation synthesis with a hand-object spatial representation. ACM Trans. Graph. **40**, 121:1–121:14 (2021)
59. Zhang, S., Zhang, Y., Bogo, F., Pollefeys, M., Tang, S.: Learning motion priors for 4D human body capture in 3D scenes. In: IEEE/CVF International Conference on Computer Vision (ICCV 2021) (2021)
60. Zhang, Y., Black, M.J., Tang, S.: We are more than our joints: predicting how 3D bodies move. In: Proceedings of the IEEE/CVF Conference on Computer Vision and Pattern Recognition, pp. 3372–3382 (2021)
61. Zhang, Y., Yu, W., Liu, C.K., Kemp, C., Turk, G.: Learning to manipulate amorphous materials. ACM Trans. Graph. (TOG) **39**(6), 1–11 (2020)
62. Zhou, Y., Barnes, C., Lu, J., Yang, J., Li, H.: On the continuity of rotation representations in neural networks. In: Proceedings of the IEEE/CVF Conference on Computer Vision and Pattern Recognition (CVPR) (2019)

Neural Capture of Animatable 3D
Human from Monocular Video

Gusi Te[1,2], Xiu Li[2,3], Xiao Li[2], Jinglu Wang[2], Wei Hu[1(✉)], and Yan Lu[2(✉)]

[1] Peking Univh Asia, Beijing, China
[2] Microsoft Research Asia, Beijing, China
yanlu@microsoft.com, forhuwei@pku.edu.cn
[3] Tencent, Shenzhen, China

Abstract. We present a novel paradigm of building an animatable 3D human representation from a monocular video input, such that it can be rendered in any unseen poses and views. Our method is based on a dynamic Neural Radiance Field (NeRF) rigged by a mesh-based parametric 3D human model serving as a geometry proxy. Previous methods usually rely on multi-view videos or accurate 3D geometry information as additional inputs; besides, most methods suffer from degraded quality when generalized to unseen poses. We identify that the key to generalization is a good input embedding for querying dynamic NeRF: A good input embedding should define an injective mapping in the full volumetric space, guided by surface mesh deformation under pose variation. Based on this observation, we propose to embed the input query with its relationship to local surface regions spanned by a set of geodesic nearest neighbors on mesh vertices. By including both position and relative distance information, our embedding defines a distance-preserved deformation mapping and generalizes well to unseen poses. To reduce the dependency on additional inputs, we first initialize per-frame 3D meshes using off-the-shelf tools and then propose a pipeline to jointly optimize NeRF and refine the initial mesh. Extensive experiments show our method can synthesize plausible human rendering results under unseen poses and views.

1 Introduction

The problem of digital reconstruction, modeling and photo-realistic synthesis of humans from a video sequence such that it can be rendered with any pose from any viewpoint is important, which enables various applications ranging from character animation for games and movies to immersive experience for virtual conferencing. This problem is extremely challenging due to the complicated joint space of human geometry, appearance, and dynamic motion given only RGB videos as observation, especially for monocular videos where multi-view concurrency is unavailable.

G. Te and X. Li—Work done during an internship at Microsoft Research Asia.

Supplementary Information The online version contains supplementary material available at https://doi.org/10.1007/978-3-031-20068-7_16.

© The Author(s), under exclusive license to Springer Nature Switzerland AG 2022
S. Avidan et al. (Eds.): ECCV 2022, LNCS 13666, pp. 275–291, 2022.
https://doi.org/10.1007/978-3-031-20068-7_16

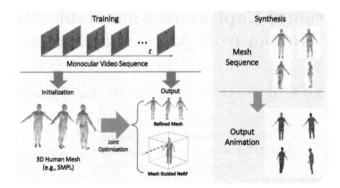

Fig. 1. Left: given a monocular video sequence of human performance with initial posed 3D human with off-the-shelf tools, our method jointly reconstructs a mesh-guided neural radiance field (NeRF) and refined per-frame human mesh. Right: our trained mesh-guided NeRF is rigged with 3D mesh model and enables novel pose and view synthesis.

Because of the difficulty in jointly modeling shape, pose and appearance of 3D humans from monocular videos, many previous approaches focus on solving part of the problem only, such as skeleton-based human pose estimation [4, 10] or parametric 3D model [3,18] based human shape reconstruction [14,32]. These methods exploit sophisticated pose and shape priors and are thus able to partially counteract the geometry ambiguity; however, due to the lack of appearance information, the obtained results might not perfectly align with the input observations in certain frames. Extracted texture based on the estimated surface is usually blurry and cannot be used for photo-realistic synthesis (Fig. 1).

Recently proposed volumetric neural rendering methods, *i.e.* NeRF and its variants [2,19,28], have shown great advances in high-quality free-view synthesis for static objects. NeRF models static objects by an implicit radiance field function with multi-layer perceptron (MLP) networks. Inspired by NeRF, recent works [17,21,24,25] attempt to model 3D humans by conditioning the radiance field on 3D poses/parametric meshes. While promising human reconstruction and view synthesis results have been achieved, these methods only focus on the modeling of conditional radiance field itself and require accurate 3D poses or meshes as a prior. This assumption is often too strong to be fulfilled in practical capture setups, especially with monocular video only.

To this end, we propose a novel paradigm of modeling an animatable 3D human representation from a monocular video sequence of a single person. Our goal is to build a reconstruction pipeline with few non-trivial requirements such as accurate 3D human poses and/or geometry. To achieve this goal, we propose to jointly optimize per-frame human mesh reconstruction and a dynamic neural radiance field (NeRF) which is conditional on mesh information. Given a monocular video sequence as input observations, the optimization process is driven by the re-rendering error on the neural rendering output corresponding to both the NeRF and human poses, which are updated via back-propagation. To constrain

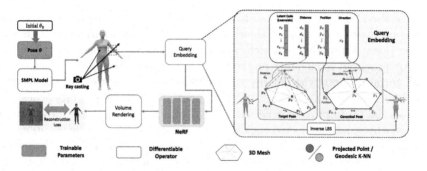

Fig. 2. Our pipeline. A 3D mesh is generated from SMPL model with target pose θ, followed with a mesh-guided NeRF which takes query embedding of 3D points and renders image via volume rendering. The query embedding encodes both surface deformation constraint with information of nearest mesh vertices under rest pose, as well as distance-preserve prior with distance to mesh vertices in a local region under target pose. During training the pose is initialized with off-the-shelf tools and are jointly refined with mesh-guided NeRF.

the optimization space of human mesh, we exploit the widely-used parametric human body model [3], and initialize the optimization with poses provided by monocular pose estimation solutions [14,32] as a starting point. Our joint optimization strategy connects the (previously mangled) 3D geometry estimation problem and NeRF-based appearance optimization problem, and eliminates the requirement of accurate 3D geometry information as a priori, making the modeling pipeline more applicable under monocular video scenarios.

A key property of a good neural representation of humans is that it should have good generalization under unseen human poses after training on limited observations. This is a non-trivial task as previous NeRF-based works for human modeling [24,25] suffer from degraded quality more or less when generalized to unseen human poses. Our observation is that the key for better pose generalization lies in the embedding method of input for querying NeRF. Intrinsically, the dynamic NeRF-based representation of humans can be regarded as a static NeRF under rest pose equipped with 3D volume deformation that is conditioned on the mesh deformation from rest pose to any arbitrary target pose. Thus, a good embedding for querying a dynamic NeRF input under arbitrary poses should "reverse" the pose deformation in an injective way to find the correct point at the static NeRF. As the "correct" deformation mapping is only available on the surface mesh, the reverse deformation at any off-surface region in the space should be constrained with additional priors. Otherwise, the deformation mapping will be distorted and collapsed, thus failing to generalize to unseen poses.

Based on this observation, we propose a new embedding method for querying mesh-guided dynamic NeRF by encoding the input position with its relationship to local nearby surface regions. Specifically, given a query point and a human mesh corresponding to a target pose, we project the query point onto the mesh and find a set of nearest neighbor mesh vertices locally; we then construct the input embedding with distances to these vertices in the **target** space as well as the normalized position of these vertices in the **canonical** space with **rest** human pose, eliminating pose deformation and view transformation.

Out proposed embedding method is able to guide the volume deformation at off-surface points with nearby surface deformation (as we give the inverse-transformed nearest neighbor vertices on mesh). It has two key properties that are essential for improving generalization. First, the embedding is locally based on a nearby small connected region on the guided mesh. The local priors are crucial because they prevent the network from inadvertently relating the output to irrelevant articulated parts, which is known to hurt model generalization to poses unseen during training [21,34]. Second, since we give the distances to all nearest neighboring vertices in the target space, the embedding will encourage a locally distance-preserve prior to restrain the deformation from collapse.

Our method requires only the monocular video of a single person with a fixed camera, which does not rely on dedicated capture devices and/or accurate human pose information. Extensive experimental results demonstrate the superiority of our model on a variety of data that exhibit various human shapes and poses. To summarize, our contributions are as follows:

- We propose a novel paradigm for building a neural human representation that can be rendered in unseen poses and views with monocular video inputs.
- We propose a novel input embedding representation for querying mesh-guided NeRF which improves the generalization ability on novel poses.
- We develop a pipeline for joint optimization of 3D human meshes and mesh-guided dynamic NeRF supervised by the reconstruction loss only.

2   Related Works

Human Reconstruction. The problem of digital reconstruction of humans is a long-standing problem in computer vision and computer graphics. Traditional methods usually achieve high quality with complicated capture setups such as multi-view capture studio [8,35,36] or RGB-D camera arrays [30,33]. To reduce capture efforts, recent methods leverage deep neural networks to directly reconstruct 3d humans from even single images [7,14,20,27]. These methods often estimate output coefficients of parametric models of 3D human shape and poses [18]. The parametric model of 3D humans is often constructed from a large database of scanned shapes of different humans in a variety of poses and the rigged with a pre-defined skeleton to animate the human mesh.

Neural 3D Representations. Recently, neural representation of 3D scenes has attracted considerable attention in the literature [2,5,6,19,22,28]. These methods exploit a neural network (usually multi-layer perceptrons) to represent implicit fields such as signed distance functions for surface or volumetric radiance fields, thus inherently encoding 3D information in a view-consistent manner. Among those neural representations, NeRF [19] (and its variants) has surpassed previous state-of-the-art methods on novel view synthesis tasks for static objects. Some works also extended NeRF to handle general space-time dynamic scenes [23,26,31]. Our method targets extending NeRF to model dynamic representation of 3D humans with the help of parametric 3D body mesh models.

Rigging NeRF. A prevalent approach for representing dynamic humans with NeRF is to rig NeRF with articulated models. Common articulation choices are 3D pose skeletons [21,29] and parametric 3D mesh models [9,17,24,25]. Our method utilizes a parametric 3D mesh model [3] for articulation. While we are similar to previous and concurrent works [17,21,24,29] by sharing the same goal of modeling dynamic human body with articulated NeRF representation, our method differs them in two aspects. First, we attempts to simplify the input to monocular video input as opposed to multi-view video inputs [17,24] and relax the dependence on accurate 3D geometry input [21] a priori. Second, we propose a new embedding method for querying articulated dynamic NeRF with locality and distance-preserving constraints. Noguchi et al. [21] proposed to learn a most relevant articulated part for any given query point. The concurrent work of Su et al. [29] propose a similar framework with joint-optimization of NeRF and human pose, using the skeleton as the human shape representation and directly relates the input query to all articulated skeleton joints. We focus on improving the generalization ability for NeRF-based animatable 3D human reconstruction with novel embedding designs. Our method preserves locality via nearest-neighbor projection, and encourages locality distance-preserving to avoid collapse of deformation in the whole volume.

3   Method

Given a monocular video sequence $\{\mathbf{I}_i\}_{i=1}^{K}$ as input, we aim to construct a neural human representation that encodes both appearance and geometry knowledge and can be rendered under an arbitrary pose θ. In particular, we model our representation with a neural radiance field (NeRF). Our NeRF is dynamically controlled by an underlying parametric mesh model (Sect. 3.1). Given an observation-space pose, the mesh surface is deformed from its rest pose correspondingly. We design a novel query embedding (Sect. 3.2) for the input which encodes both information of surface deformation and addition constraints. Based on the proposed mesh-guided NeRF, we propose an analysis-by-synthesis method to jointly estimate pre-frame 3D mesh from the input video and train NeRF (Sect. 3.3), using off-the-shelf tools for mesh initialization.

3.1   Mesh-Guided NeRF

In NeRF, the rendered color $\bar{\mathbf{C}}(u, v)$ at image pixel (u, v) is generated by querying and blending the radiance along the corresponding camera ray according to the volume density value:

$$\bar{\mathbf{C}}(u, v) = \sum_{i=1}^{N} T_i(1 - \exp(-\sigma_i \delta_i))\mathbf{c}_i, \tag{1}$$

where

$$T_i = \exp(-\sum_{j=1}^{i-1}(-\sigma_j \delta_j))), \tag{2}$$

and

$$(\mathbf{c}_i, \sigma_i) = F(\mathbf{x}_i). \tag{3}$$

$\mathbf{c}_i \in \mathcal{R}^3$ and σ_i are the color and volume density of the i-th sampled point $\mathbf{x}_i$ along the ray direction. $F(\mathbf{x})$ is usually parameterized with an MLP network.

We extend NeRF to handle the dynamic, articulated human body with a mesh-based parametric 3D model SMPL [18]. An SMPL model $S(\theta, \beta)$ takes a human 3D pose θ of skeleton joint rotations as well as a low-dimensional feature vector of human shape as input and outputs a 3D mesh. As we mainly focus on synthesizing humans under different poses, we omit the shape β afterwards.

Formally, given a pose input θ, the radiance color $\mathbf{c}(\mathbf{x})$ and volume density of our mesh-guided NeRF at point x is computed as follows:

$$(\mathbf{c}(\mathbf{x}), \sigma(\mathbf{x})) = F_\Phi(q(\mathbf{x}, S(\theta))), \tag{4}$$

where the query embedding q is the most important part as it directly relates the output of NeRF with the underlay deformable mesh, as we will discuss next.

3.2   Query Embedding for NeRF

The input of NeRF for querying radiance value at point $\mathbf{x}$ is given by its 3D location (x, y, z) and 2D viewing direction θ, ϕ in the world space. A natural extension of input querying for the dynamic scene is to define a deformation field that transforms observation-space points to rest space. Directly estimating a general deformation field together with the NeRF, as in [23,26,31], is highly ill-posed and prone to local minima. Inspired by [17,24], we leverage the deformable SMPL model as the human prior to guide our transformation for input queries. The underlay SMPL model defines reasonable deformation fields on its surface; however, a radiance field from NeRF is defined on full 3D volume, and we still need to determine the deformation on unconstrained off-surface points. Naively projecting off-surface points to its nearest vertex point on the mesh is not optimal because the off-surface deformation will be collapsed, as illustrated in Fig. 3.

We address this issue from another perspective: instead of inputting an inverse-transformed point with an explicitly defined deformation field for querying NeRF, we construct a query embedding of the input point which encodes two types of information: (1) information that guides how the deformation field should roughly be (denoted as *Deformation Guidance*), and (2) priors that prevent the deformation field from collapsed local minima (denoted as *Deformation Priors*). The NeRF then implicitly learns a radiance field based on the input embedding. Figure 2 illustrates our design of query embedding.

Deformation Guidance. Our deformation guidance is based on the underlay SMPL model. For the SMPL model, the transformation relationship between a

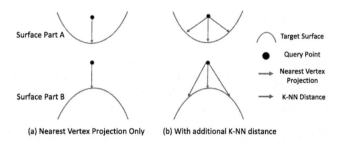

Surface Part A

Surface Part B

(a) Nearest Vertex Projection Only   (b) With additional K-NN distance

Target Surface

Query Point

Nearest Vertex Projection

K-NN Distance

Fig. 3. An illustration of our distance-preserved query embedding. (a) Naively embedding the query with nearest neighbor vertex on mesh (the red line), leads to indistinguishable embedding of different surface deformation patterns. (b) With additional geometric K-NN distance information (purple lines), different deformation patterns are clearly separated.

canonical-space surface point $\mathbf{v}$ and its observation space counterpart $\mathbf{v}'$ is given by the linear blend skinning (LBS) algorithm [15]:

$$\mathbf{v}' = (\sum_{k=1}^{K} w(\mathbf{v})_k G_k)\mathbf{v}, \tag{5}$$

where K is the number of human parts, $G_k \in SE(3)$ is the transformation matrix of the k-th part on the human skeleton, and $w(\mathbf{v})$ is the blend weight.

Intuitively, the guidance information from the SMPL model should neither be too global such that the network inadvertently relates the output to irrelevant articulated parts [21,34], nor collapse to a single nearest neighboring point as the deformation field will remain unconstrained (Fig. 3). To this end, we build the deformation guidance part of the input query with the nearest projected vertex on the mesh as well as the k-nearest adjacent vertices of the projected vertex in rest space via inverse LBS as:

$$q_g(\mathbf{x}) = (\mathbf{x}_{dir}, \mathbf{v}_0, \mathbf{v}_1, ..., \mathbf{v}_k), \tag{6}$$

where $\mathbf{v}_k = (\sum_{l=1}^{L} w(\mathbf{v}_k)_l G_l)^{-1}\mathbf{v}'_k$ and $\mathbf{v}'_k$ is the k-th nearest neighboring mesh point in the observation space. Note that, we additionally give the relative direction from query point $\mathbf{x}$ to its projected point $\mathbf{v}_0$:

$$\mathbf{x}_{dir} = \mathcal{R}((\sum_{k=1}^{K} w(\mathbf{v})_k G_k)^{-1}) \frac{\mathbf{v}_0 - \mathbf{x}}{\|\mathbf{v}_0 - \mathbf{x}\|_2}. \tag{7}$$

Here $\mathcal{R}$ denotes the rotational part of the transformation matrix.

Deformation Priors. Our deformation guidance embedding q_g itself is based on mesh surface only and insufficient to ensure a well-defined deformation field in the whole volume. We therefore provide an additional part to the query embedding by equipping the input query with the Euclidean distances to its nearest points in the observation space:

$$q_p(\mathbf{x}) = (d_0, d_1, ..., d_k),   \tag{8}$$

where $d_k = \|\mathbf{v}'_k - \mathbf{x}\|_2$. Using the distance in the observation space is important as such information preserves the local difference under different poses and leads to a distance-preserved deformation field.

Appearance Latent Code. To better capture the geometry and appearance detail which cannot be captured by surface mesh deformation, we additionally provide a learnable latent code l_k defined on each mesh vertex:

$$q_a(\mathbf{x}) = (\mathbf{l}_0, \mathbf{l}_1, ..., \mathbf{l}_k).   \tag{9}$$

The complete query embedding for the NeRF input is generated by feeding the concatenation vectors into a tiny 3-layer MLP network ψ:

$$q(\mathbf{x}) = \psi(\gamma(q_g(\mathbf{x})), \gamma(q_p(\mathbf{x})), q_a(\mathbf{x})),   \tag{10}$$

where γ denotes positional encoding as used in the original NeRF [19].

3.3   Joint Mesh Estimation and NeRF Training

Training the mesh-guided NeRF from monocular video input requires paired data of input frames $\{\mathbf{I}_i\}$ and human mesh $\{\mathbf{M}_i\}$. State-of-the-art monocular video based human mesh reconstruction methods such as [13,14] produce plausible results for human mesh estimation; however, they are still not accurate enough for training our NeRF as non-aligned mesh part to the image will give incorrect guidance and make the NeRF over-fitting to misaligned training poses. Hence we opt to use the plausible mesh estimates provided by prior solutions as initialization, and jointly fine-tune the mesh with NeRF training. Practically, we choose to optimize the pose parameter θ^i for each training frame instead of per-vertex mesh offset, as it gives us enough capability to refine mesh-image misalignment without too much flexibility that overfits to local minima.

Training Objective. Our training is guided by the reconstruction error between the mesh-guided NeRF and the ground-truth frames over the whole video sequence as well as a regularization term penalizing too large deviation from the initial pose estimation θ_0:

$$L = \sum_i \sum_{u,v} L_i(u,v) + \lambda_p \sum_i \|\theta^i - \theta_0^i\|_2^2,   \tag{11}$$

and

$$L_i(u,v) = \|\bar{\mathbf{C}}(u,v) - \mathbf{I}_i(u,v)\|_2^2,   \tag{12}$$

where $\mathbf{I}_i(u,v)$ is the ground truth pixel value at (u,v) from the i-th frame. $\bar{\mathbf{C}}(u,v)$ is computed using Eq. 1, Eq. 4 and the proposed query embedding (Eq. 10).

4   Experiments

4.1   Experimental Setup

Datasets. We conduct experiments on different datasets as follows:

- People-Snapshot [1]: This dataset contains 24 subjects with monocular videos performing turning around. Among them, we choose female-1-casual, female-3-casual, male-1-sport and male-9-plaza for training. We remove the background of the video frames with ground truth silhouettes provided and resize the video to half-size (1080p → 540p). An initial mesh is provided in the data.
- DoubleFusion [33]: This dataset contains only a sequence of one man, where the actor performs more complex actions while turning around. Thus, we consider it not suitable for a quantitative benchmark and only use it to show qualitative comparisons on novel pose synthesis. The initial mesh is provided in the dataset using additional depth information.
- ZJU-MoCap [25]: This dataset contains multi-view video sequences of 9 objects with 21 cameras. We choose a single view (subject 313 and subject 386 from camera 7) for training.
- Human3.6M [11]: This dataset consists of a large number of 3D human poses and corresponding multi-view video sequences. We follow the same protocol as [29], extracting every 64th frame of the videos. We train the model on the subject 9 and subject 11. For each video, we select camera 2 as the input view and employ SPIN [14] to estimate the initial mesh from video frames.

Network Structure. The network ψ in the query embedding module is implemented with a 3-layer MLP with 128 channels. The NeRF network ϕ is composed of an 8-layer MLP with 256 channels. In the position embedding module, we implement the tiny 3-layer MLP ψ with 128 channels, and the NeRF module ϕ for rendering is composed of 8-layer MLP with 256 channels. We apply a positional encoding of 10 frequencies to query embedding features except latent codes.

Training Details. We utilize Adam optimizer [12] with learning rate of $1e-4$ for optimizing NeRF and latent code. The learning rate of body poses is set to $5e-4$ and λ_p is set to 2.0. For volumetric rendering we employ the coarse-to-fine ray sampling strategy of [19]. We also constrain the sampled rays to be more focused on the human part in the image by sampling rays within the 1.2× padding bounding box of 2D keypoints with 70% probability, and randomly sampled in the whole image with 30% probability. Each sampled ray is discreted within $[z_{near} - 0.04, z_{far} + 0.04]$, where z_{near} and z_{far} denote the nearest and farthest ray-point intersection with body mesh, respectively. Our model is trained with a single Nvidia Tesla V100 32 GB GPU, and the training approximately takes 60 h to converge. For datasets without background mask available, we either apply an off-the-shelf matting algorithm [16] or jointly model the background during training. Please check the supplemental materials for details.

Evaluation Metrics. Peak-Signal-to-Noise Ratio (PSNR) and Structural Similarity Index Measure (SSIM) are used to evaluate image quality.

Table 1. Ablation studies on (a) type of direction, (b) type of distances and (c) type of neighborhood selection for embedding construction.

	SSIM ↑		PSNR ↑	
	Training	Novel	Training	Novel
w/o distance	0.935	0.906	29.18	27.51
canonical distance	0.926	0.916	29.06	27.48
observation distance	**0.980**	**0.973**	**35.87**	**34.75**

(a) Impact of distance embedding.

	SSIM ↑		PSNR ↑	
	Training	Novel	Training	Novel
w/o direction	0.942	0.923	30.52	28.15
w/o inverse	0.959	0.921	32.14	28.12
full	**0.980**	**0.972**	**35.87**	**34.75**

(b) Impact of direction embedding.

	SSIM ↑		PSNR ↑	
	Training	Novel	Training	Novel
Euclidean, 2 neighbors	0.950	0.935	32.35	30.69
Geodesic, 2-hop neighbors	0.962	0.954	32.74	31.97
Geodesic, only nearest neighbor	0.961	0.938	31.87	30.07
Geodesic 1-hop neighbors	**0.980**	**0.972**	**35.87**	**34.75**

(c) Impact of neighborhood selection.

4.2 Ablation Studies

To validate the influence of our proposed query embedding, we conduct the ablation study on the People-Snapshot dataset and report quantitative results on both training and test (unseen) poses, from the following aspects:

Neighborhood Range: As we have discussed in Sect. 3.2, the deformation guidance from the SMPL model should be neither too global nor too local. We verified this by conducting training with different ranges of mesh neighborhood. The results are shown in Table 1c. Either increasing range (*2-hop neighbors*) or *only nearest neighbor* projected point leads to degraded performance, both for training and novel poses. We also test a variant of our method by sampling K-NN point based on Euclidean distance (*spatial K-NN*) instead of geodesic distance. The results are also degraded as it fails to aware human part connectivity (*i.e.* two adjacent points in Euclidean space might belong to distinct human parts).

Distance Prior: We validate the importance of distance information in Table 1a. We remove the distance feature in the *w/o distance* model, and substitute rest-pose distance for observation-pose distance in the *canonical distance* model. Obviously, without distance information, the results are significantly degraded and the difference between training and novel poses is increased.

Relative Direction: The impact of relative direction embedding is demonstrated in Table 1b, where *w/o direction* denotes embedding without direction, and *w/o inverse* denotes embedding direction in observation space. It is worth noting that the *w/o inverse* greatly reduces the generalization on novel poses.

Pose Refinement: Our joint pose refinement with NeRF training is crucial when the initial mesh is not accurate enough. To validate this, we conduct experiments on both Human3.6M and People-Snapshot dataset. The People-Snapshot dataset has provided an initial mesh that is rather reasonable; yet, we

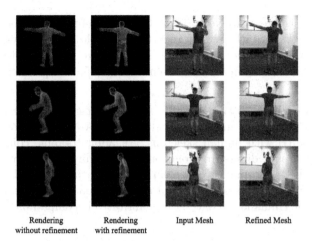

Rendering without refinement   Rendering with refinement   Input Mesh   Refined Mesh

Fig. 4. Qualitative comparison between original and optimized mesh. The final result corrects the initial human mesh, e.g., the alignment error on the arms.

Table 2. The effect of using joint pose refinement.

Dataset	Method	SSIM ↑	PSNR ↑
Human3.6M	w/ refinement	**0.978**	**31.51**
	w/o refinement	0.951	29.04
People-Snapshot	w/ refinement	**0.972**	**34.75**
	w/o refinement	0.969	32.99

Table 3. Quantitative comparison with AniNeRF and A-NeRF.

	ZJU-Mocap		Human3.6M			People-snapshot	
	AniNeRF	Ours	AniNeRF	A-NeRF	Ours	AniNeRF	Ours
SSIM ↑	0.758	**0.768**	0.865	**0.928**	0.912	0.948	**0.973**
PSNR ↑	23.75	**25.01**	23.44	**27.45**	27.11	29.11	**34.75**

still observe minor artifacts without pose refinement and our joint training further improves the result, both quantitatively (Table 2) and qualitatively (Fig 4 and Fig. 5).

4.3 Comparsions

As there is very few (formally peer-reviewed and published) NeRF-based work that shares the same succinct **monocular** inputs with **mesh-based** geometry proxy as ours, we compare with the following methods:

AniNeRF (ICCV 2021). AniNeRF [24] is NeRF-based method for dynamic human modeling. AniNeRF also uses mesh as geometry guidance but requires more strict input requirements of multi-view video input. It produces high quality results with typically 3 to 4 synchronized views. For a fair comparison, we follow the same single view setting and training data to re-train AniNeRF, and report the comparison results in Fig. 7. We emphasize that this experiment setup with monocular input is **not** for producing best-quality results, but to demonstrate the challenge of monocular video scenario as well as the benefit of our proposed method. Compared with AniNeRF, our method generates complete skin and cloth, whereas AniNeRF is unable to model the whole body with limited view. The quantitative result reported in Table 3 also shows our method outperforms AniNeRF under the same settings. We also refer to the supplemental material for a comparsion to NeuralBody [25], the precursor method of AniNeRF.

A-NeRF (NeurIPS 2021). A-NeRF [29] is a recent work for modeling 3D human with NeRF using monocular video input. A-NeRF exploits joint optimization of NeRF with human skeletons. An apple-to-apple comparsion with A-NeRF is hard as it differs from our method in many implementation aspects which affects the result quality, e.g., from the underly parametric body representation (skeleton-based v.s. mesh-based) to the backbone capacities. Nevertheless, our result on the Human3.6M dataset is quantitatively comparable with A-NeRF (Table 3).

Non-NeRF methods. Regarding non-NeRF methods, we also compare our method with a SMPL-model based method, VideoAvatar [1]. The qualitative results are shown in Fig. 6. Given the same monocular video as input, the NeRF-based method generates results with more natural and realistic color effects.

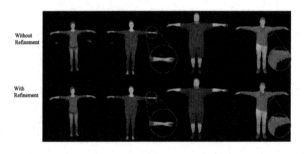

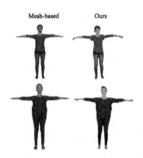

Fig. 5. The effect of pose refinement on People-Snapshot dataset. Jointly refinement contributes to clearer geometry and eliminates outliers. The improvement brought by refinement is enlarged in red.

Fig. 6. A qualitative comparison with mesh-based method VideoAvatar.

4.4   Applications

Novel Pose Synthesis. Our trained representation enables character animation from novel unseen poses. We evaluate our generalization ability by comparing testing data and our rendering driven by the same set of unseen poses on the People-Snapshot and DoubleFusion dataset. The qualitative result is depicted in Fig. 8a. Our model successfully disentangles background and foreground pixels and veritably reconstructs the human body in the Doublefusion dataset (First row). As for side and back view, our model still generates images of high quality

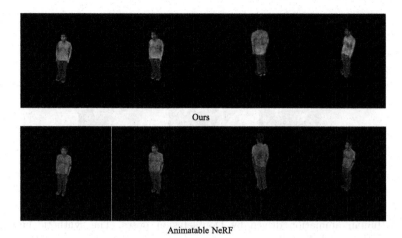

Ours

Animatable NeRF

Fig. 7. Qualitative comparison of Ani-NeRF [24] and ours under novel view. Both methods are trained with single view sequence.

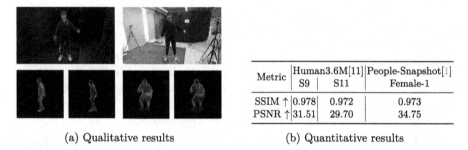

| Metric | Human3.6M[11] | | People-Snapshot[1] |
	S9	S11	Female-1
SSIM ↑	0.978	0.972	0.973
PSNR ↑	31.51	29.70	34.75

(a) Qualitative results   (b) Quantitative results

Fig. 8. Qualitative and quantitative results of **novel** pose synthesis on multiple datasets. (a) Top row: novel pose rendering (left) and ground truth (right) on DoubleFusion. Bottom row: rendering (odd column) and ground truth (even column) on Human3.6M. (b) Quantitative results of novel pose synthesis on Human3.6M and People-Snapshot dataset.

as shown in the Human3.6M dataset (Second row). We also provide quantitative results in Fig. 8b on the People-Snapshot and Human3.6m datasets.

Pose Retargeting. The generalization ability of our model is further evaluated by pose retargeting experiments. The results are shown in Fig. 9, where the driven poses derive from the Doublefusion dataset and training body comes from the People-snapshot dataset. We observe that our model generates realistic human bodies with various poses, which demonstrates the generalization of the proposed methods. We refer to the supplemental material for more novel pose synthesis results, including animation videos.

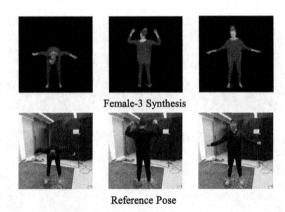

Female-3 Synthesis

Reference Pose

Fig. 9. Human animation driven by Doublefusion poses. The synthetic human is trained on the People-Snapshot dataset.

5   Conclusion

We presented a new method for building animatable neural 3D human representations from only monocular video inputs. Our representation is based on dynamic Neural Radiance Field guided by parametric 3D human meshes. We designed a novel input query embedding of the mesh-guided NeRF. We train the representation by we first initialize per-frame 3D meshes using off-the-shelf tools and then joint optimizing the 3D mesh and dynamic NeRF. The learned neural representation can generalize well to unseen views and poses.

Limitations. Our method is not without limitations. The input embedding of our querying is related to a local region on the mesh surface with a restricted reception field; thus the joint optimization might fail if the initial pose has deviated too much from the ground truth. Due to resolution constraint and the expressiveness of the mesh model we used, our method is still straggling at recovering high-resolution details such as human faces.

Future Work. For future works, we plan to explore different kinds of deformation priors and their effects on rigging dynamic NeRF, improving our performance with sharp details, and extending to general, non-articulated dynamic objects.

Acknowledgements. We would like to thank all the reviewers for their constructive feedback.

References

1. Alldieck, T., Magnor, M., Xu, W., Theobalt, C., Pons-Moll, G.: Video based reconstruction of 3D people models. In: IEEE/CVF Conference on Computer Vision and Pattern Recognition (CVPR), pp. 8387–8397, June 2018. https://doi.org/10.1109/CVPR.2018.00875. CVPR Spotlight Paper

2. Barron, J.T., Mildenhall, B., Tancik, M., Hedman, P., Martin-Brualla, R., Srinivasan, P.P.: Mip-NeRF: a multiscale representation for anti-aliasing neural radiance fields. arXiv preprint arXiv:2103.13415 (2021)
3. Bogo, F., Kanazawa, A., Lassner, C., Gehler, P., Romero, J., Black, M.J.: Keep it SMPL: automatic estimation of 3D human pose and shape from a single image. In: Leibe, B., Matas, J., Sebe, N., Welling, M. (eds.) ECCV 2016. LNCS, vol. 9909, pp. 561–578. Springer, Cham (2016). https://doi.org/10.1007/978-3-319-46454-1_34
4. Cao, Z., Hidalgo, G., Simon, T., Wei, S.E., Sheikh, Y.: Openpose: realtime multi-person 2D pose estimation using part affinity fields. IEEE Trans. Pattern Anal. Mach. Intell. 43(1), 172–186 (2019)
5. Chen, X., Zheng, Y., Black, M.J., Hilliges, O., Geiger, A.: SNARF: differentiable forward skinning for animating non-rigid neural implicit shapes. In: International Conference on Computer Vision (ICCV) (2021)
6. Deng, Y., Yang, J., Tong, X.: Deformed implicit field: modeling 3D shapes with learned dense correspondence. In: Proceedings of the IEEE/CVF Conference on Computer Vision and Pattern Recognition, pp. 10286–10296 (2021)
7. Deng, Y., Yang, J., Xu, S., Chen, D., Jia, Y., Tong, X.: Accurate 3D face reconstruction with weakly-supervised learning: from single image to image set. In: Proceedings of IEEE Computer Vision and Pattern Recognition Workshop on Analysis and Modeling of Faces and Gestures (2019)
8. Dou, M., et al.: Fusion4D: real-time performance capture of challenging scenes. ACM Trans. Graph. (ToG) 35(4), 1–13 (2016)
9. Guo, Y., Chen, K., Liang, S., Liu, Y., Bao, H., Zhang, J.: AD-NeRF: audio driven neural radiance fields for talking head synthesis. arXiv preprint arXiv:2103.11078 (2021)
10. He, Y., Yan, R., Fragkiadaki, K., Yu, S.I.: Epipolar transformers. In: Proceedings of the IEEE/CVF Conference on Computer Vision and Pattern Recognition, pp. 7779–7788 (2020)
11. Ionescu, C., Papava, D., Olaru, V., Sminchisescu, C.: Human3. 6m: large scale datasets and predictive methods for 3D human sensing in natural environments. IEEE Trans. pattern Anal. Mach. Intell. 36(7), 1325–1339 (2013)
12. Kingma, D.P., Ba, J.: Adam: a method for stochastic optimization. arXiv preprint arXiv:1412.6980 (2014)
13. Kocabas, M., Athanasiou, N., Black, M.J.: Vibe: video inference for human body pose and shape estimation. In: Proceedings of the IEEE/CVF Conference on Computer Vision and Pattern Recognition, pp. 5253–5263 (2020)
14. Kolotouros, N., Pavlakos, G., Black, M.J., Daniilidis, K.: Learning to reconstruct 3D human pose and shape via model-fitting in the loop. In: Proceedings of the IEEE/CVF International Conference on Computer Vision, pp. 2252–2261 (2019)
15. Lewis, J.P., Cordner, M., Fong, N.: Pose space deformation: a unified approach to shape interpolation and skeleton-driven deformation. In: Proceedings of the 27th Annual Conference on Computer Graphics and Interactive Techniques, pp. 165–172 (2000)
16. Lin, S., Yang, L., Saleemi, I., Sengupta, S.: Robust high-resolution video matting with temporal guidance. arXiv preprint arXiv:2108.11515 (2021)
17. Liu, L., Habermann, M., Rudnev, V., Sarkar, K., Gu, J., Theobalt, C.: Neural actor: Neural free-view synthesis of human actors with pose control. arXiv preprint arXiv:2106.02019 (2021)
18. Loper, M., Mahmood, N., Romero, J., Pons-Moll, G., Black, M.J.: SMPL: a skinned multi-person linear model. ACM Trans. Graph. (Proc. SIGGRAPH Asia) 34(6), 248:1–248:16 (2015)

19. Mildenhall, B., Srinivasan, P.P., Tancik, M., Barron, J.T., Ramamoorthi, R., Ng, R.: NeRF: representing scenes as neural radiance fields for view synthesis. In: Vedaldi, A., Bischof, H., Brox, T., Frahm, J.-M. (eds.) ECCV 2020. LNCS, vol. 12346, pp. 405–421. Springer, Cham (2020). https://doi.org/10.1007/978-3-030-58452-8_24

20. Natsume, R., et al.: SiCloPe: silhouette-based clothed people. In: Proceedings of the IEEE/CVF Conference on Computer Vision and Pattern Recognition, pp. 4480–4490 (2019)

21. Noguchi, A., Sun, X., Lin, S., Harada, T.: Neural articulated radiance field. arXiv preprint arXiv:2104.03110 (2021)

22. Park, J.J., Florence, P., Straub, J., Newcombe, R., Lovegrove, S.: DeepSDF: learning continuous signed distance functions for shape representation. In: Proceedings of the IEEE/CVF Conference on Computer Vision and Pattern Recognition, pp. 165–174 (2019)

23. Park, K., et al.: Nerfies: deformable neural radiance fields. In: Proceedings of the IEEE/CVF International Conference on Computer Vision, pp. 5865–5874 (2021)

24. Peng, S., et al.: Animatable neural radiance fields for human body modeling. arXiv preprint arXiv:2105.02872 (2021)

25. Peng, S., et al.: Neural body: implicit neural representations with structured latent codes for novel view synthesis of dynamic humans. In: CVPR (2021)

26. Pumarola, A., Corona, E., Pons-Moll, G., Moreno-Noguer, F.: D-NeRF: neural radiance fields for dynamic scenes. In: Proceedings of the IEEE/CVF Conference on Computer Vision and Pattern Recognition, pp. 10318–10327 (2021)

27. Saito, S., Huang, Z., Natsume, R., Morishima, S., Kanazawa, A., Li, H.: PIFu: Pixel-aligned implicit function for high-resolution clothed human digitization. In: Proceedings of the IEEE/CVF International Conference on Computer Vision, pp. 2304–2314 (2019)

28. Sitzmann, V., Martel, J., Bergman, A., Lindell, D., Wetzstein, G.: Implicit neural representations with periodic activation functions. In: Advances in Neural Information Processing Systems 33 (2020)

29. Su, S.Y., Yu, F., Zollhoefer, M., Rhodin, H.: A-NeRF: surface-free human 3D pose refinement via neural rendering. arXiv preprint arXiv:2102.06199 (2021)

30. Su, Z., Xu, L., Zheng, Z., Yu, T., Liu, Y., Fang, L.: RobustFusion: human volumetric capture with data-driven visual cues using a RGBD camera. In: Vedaldi, A., Bischof, H., Brox, T., Frahm, J.-M. (eds.) ECCV 2020, Part IV. LNCS, vol. 12349, pp. 246–264. Springer, Cham (2020). https://doi.org/10.1007/978-3-030-58548-8_15

31. Xian, W., Huang, J.B., Kopf, J., Kim, C.: Space-time neural irradiance fields for free-viewpoint video. In: Proceedings of the IEEE/CVF Conference on Computer Vision and Pattern Recognition, pp. 9421–9431 (2021)

32. Xiang, D., Joo, H., Sheikh, Y.: Monocular total capture: posing face, body, and hands in the wild. In: Proceedings of the IEEE/CVF Conference on Computer Vision and Pattern Recognition, pp. 10965–10974 (2019)

33. Yu, T., et al.: DoubleFusion: real-time capture of human performances with inner body shapes from a single depth sensor. In: Proceedings of the IEEE Conference on Computer Vision and Pattern Recognition, pp. 7287–7296 (2018)

34. Zeng, A., Sun, X., Huang, F., Liu, M., Xu, Q., Lin, S.: SRNet: improving generalization in 3D human pose estimation with a split-and-recombine approach. In: Vedaldi, A., Bischof, H., Brox, T., Frahm, J.-M. (eds.) ECCV 2020. LNCS, vol. 12359, pp. 507–523. Springer, Cham (2020). https://doi.org/10.1007/978-3-030-58568-6_30

35. Zhang, Y., Li, Z., An, L., Li, M., Yu, T., Liu, Y.: Lightweight multi-person total motion capture using sparse multi-view cameras. In: Proceedings of the IEEE/CVF International Conference on Computer Vision, pp. 5560–5569 (2021)
36. Zheng, Y., et al.: DeepMultiCap: performance capture of multiple characters using sparse multiview cameras. arXiv preprint arXiv:2105.00261 (2021)

General Object Pose Transformation Network from Unpaired Data

Yukun Su[1,2], Guosheng Lin[2(✉)], Ruizhou Sun[1], and Qingyao Wu[1,3(✉)]

[1] School of Software Engineering, South China University of Technology,
Guangzhou, China
qyw@scut.edu.cn
[2] Nanyang Technological University, Singapore, Singapore
gslin@ntu.edu.sg
[3] Pazhou Lab, Guangzhou, China

Abstract. Object pose transformation is a challenging task. Yet, most existing pose transformation networks only focus on synthesizing humans. These methods either rely on the keypoints information or rely on the manual annotations of the paired target pose images for training. However, collecting such paired data is laboring and the cue of keypoints is inapplicable to general objects. In this paper, we address a problem of novel general object pose transformation from unpaired data. Given a source image of an object that provides appearance information and a desired pose image as reference in the absence of paired examples, we produce a depiction of the object in that specified pose, retaining the appearance of both the object and background. Specifically, to preserve the source information, we propose an adversarial network with **S**patial-**S**tructural (SS) block and **T**exture-**S**tyle-**C**olor (TSC) block after the correlation matching module that facilitates the output to be semantically corresponding to the target pose image while contextually related to the source image. In addition, we can extend our network to complete multi-object and cross-category pose transformation. Extensive experiments demonstrate the effectiveness of our method which can create more realistic images when compared to those of recent approaches in terms of image quality. Moreover, we show the practicality of our method for several applications.

Keywords: Pose transformation · Adversarial network · Semantically · Contextually

1 Introduction

Image-to-image translation tasks include image colorization [4], image super-resolution [20,64], style transfer [13], domain adaptation [35] and pose transformation [31,51], *etc.* Among them, we are interested in pose transformation, which has huge potential applications in re-enactment, character animation, movie or game making and so on. However, most recent approaches [2,23,32]

Supplementary Information The online version contains supplementary material available at https://doi.org/10.1007/978-3-031-20068-7_17.

© The Author(s), under exclusive license to Springer Nature Switzerland AG 2022
S. Avidan et al. (Eds.): ECCV 2022, LNCS 13666, pp. 292–310, 2022.
https://doi.org/10.1007/978-3-031-20068-7_17

Fig. 1. Illustrative examples of different general objects pose transformation.
Given the desired pose image (1st row) and the appearance image (2nd row) in the
absence of paired examples, we produce the output image (3rd row) in that pose and
retain the appearance of object and background. We can obtain high-quality images
and apply the network to different object posture modalities. The generated samples
are not cherry-picked, more samples are provided in supplementary material.

merely explore human pose transformation, and such methods require abundant
keypoints information [5,55] or paired data, $e.g.$, they collect the same person
of different target poses for training. With these in mind, we argue that the
previous works suffer from some **limitations**: (1) In addition to human, some
other general objects should also be able to conduct pose transformation, which
is helpful for wider applications. (2) As for the general objects, such human
keypoints [5] and body mesh [15] information will not be suitable. (3) In real
life, it is difficult for us to collect different postures of the same object, which is
laborious and time-costly.

To address the issues mentioned above, we propose a **U**nified **F**ramework for
general **O**bject **P**ose **T**ransformation with unpaired data, termed as **UFO-PT**.
As shown in Fig. 1, given the unpaired images that provide pose and appearance
information, respectively, we can yield the output images in that pose while
keeping the appearance of objects and background unchanged. Our method can
be applied not only to human body pose transformation, but also to non-rigid
objects such as mammals ($i.e.$, cow, sheep, horse, $etc.$) and birds, and even rigid
objects such as vehicles.

In this paper, we propose a network which comprises four sub-blocks as shown
in Fig. 2: (1) The correlation matching block is introduced to align the unpaired
images and warp the appearance image into the target pose. Specifically, we
estimate two types of warpings inspired by [66] in different level: (i) Dense warping. (ii) Thin Plate Spline (TPS) warping [59]. The former has a high degree of
freedom, which can be utilized to map pixels to be well-aligned with the target
pose. While the latter roughly transfers the images into the desired pose but
with well-preserved details, which can be utilized to retain the appearance information. (2) The **S**patial-**S**tructural (SS) block employs the information from the
output of dense warping in the form of spatially-variant de-normalization [43]
to progressively inject the spatial details to the generated network. (3) The
Texture-**S**tyle-**C**olor (TSC) block employs the information from the output of

TPS warping to preserve the appearance details when synthesizing the results. (4) The generating block is responsible to combine the transformed foreground object and background to produce the output, which is semantically aligned to the target pose image while contextually related to the source appearance image. Moreover, our proposed method can be applied to some practical applications such as data augmentation and video imitation. Our contribution can be summarized as follows:

- We address the problem of general object pose transformation and propose a unified framework with unpaired data, which to our best knowledge, has not been well explored.
- With the proposed four sub-blocks in the network, we can generate more realistic transformed images in the desired pose preserving the original appearance and background compared to recent methods.
- Quantitative comparisons against several prior methods demonstrate the superiority of our approach, which can also be applied to several practical applications.

2 Related Work

Pose-Guided Human Image Generation: Skeletal pose cues [5,53,54] provide strong information and most previous methods are based on conditioned generative adversarial networks (CGAN) [34]. Ma *et al.* [31] generates human images conditioned on pose utilizing a two-stage network. Siarohin *et al.* [51] introduces deformable skip connections to spatially transform the features. Si *et al.* [49] proposes a multistage adversarial loss and separately generates the foreground and background. Zhu *et al.* [71] designs a progressive pose-attention transfer block to avoid the issues of capturing the complex structure of the global manifold. Some other works like [2,32,38,49,50] all combine target image along with source pose (2D keypoints) as inputs or use video optical flow [7] information to generate images by GANs. Liu *et al.* [23] later suggests to use SMPL [27] to disentangle the pose and shape, which can help to promote the transformed results. However, the above mentioned methods only focus on synthesizing humans, and they require paired data and keypoints information for training. It is difficult to collect such data and they fail to conduct general objects pose transformation, which will weaken their practicality. These shortcomings might limit their wide applications.

View Synthesis: View synthesis is a task in computer vision in which unseen camera views or poses of objects are synthesized given a prior image. Most view synthesis work has focused on simple rigid objects such as cars [14,19,42,44,69]. These methods rely on camera viewpoints and underlying 3D models. Recently, HoloGan [41], Graf [47] and π-GAN [6] propose to correctly inject 3D priors into the GAN framework to transform the 3D pose of 2D objects, while our proposed technique in this paper treats the problem as a 2D one and attempts to replace pixels of one object with another one. Lv *et al.* [29] later addresses the problem

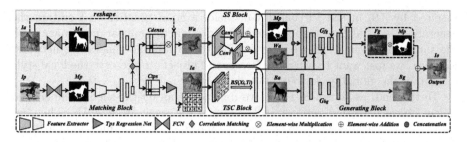

Fig. 2. The Overview of the UFO-PT architecture. For simplicity, we take *"horse"* as an example for input. Given the unpaired images I_a and I_p providing appearance and pose information, the matching block first aligns them and establishes the two types of warpings. Then, the generating block yield the transformed output I_o based on the different injected warped intermediates from SS block and TSC block, respectively.

of novel view synthesis for vehicles without exploiting additional 3D details but using stack hourglass [39] to obtain keypoint polygon. Likewise, some of these methods depend on the paired target pose data for training and the objects they work with are relatively easy and have a simple background.

Example-Guided Image Synthesis: Recently, a few works [3,30] propose to synthesize photorealistic images from semantic layout under the guidance of exemplars. Wang *et al.* [60] and Zhang *et al.* [68] both can readily be applied to human pose transformation that semantically consistent to the label maps. However, these methods require to constitute style consistency image pairs or generate images from abstract semantic label maps such as pixel-wise segmentation maps or sparse landmarks, which makes it unsuitable for general image translation and it is difficult to obtain instance-level labels.

Content-Style Image Translation: Unpaired image-to-image translation aims to map an image from a source domain to a target domain. Such methods as [16,17,70] encourage the translated domain to be faithfully reconstructed when mapping back to the original domain with cycle loss. Lorenz *et al.* [28] proposes an part-based disentangling method for object shape and TransGaGa [65] introduces geometry-aware technique for image translation. However, they either focus on human animation or object faces. More recently, Liu *et al.* [21] and Saito *et al.* [46] introduce more powerful methods to preserve the structure of the input image while emulating the appearance of the unseen domain. However, these methods fail to delicately control the output since this content-style translation will break the global information of the image in the pose transformation task.

3   Method

Correspondence Matching Block. To synthesize the transfer results, one of the main challenges is to establish the correlation between the input I_a and I_p.

Inspired by [59] in the Virtual Try-on field, a good practice to facilitate the generation is to utilize warping methods to align the appearance image with the target pose image first before feeding them into the generating network. However, we just want to warp the foreground objects to preserve the local style but retain the global background details.

To this end, as shown in Fig.2, we first adopt an off-the-shelf unsupervised salient object detection network [40] to obtain the mask M_a and M_p. Then, we employ two separate feature extractors F_A and F_B to extract high-level features f_a and f_p of I_a and M_p, where $f_a = F_A(I_a, \theta_a)$ and $f_p = F_B(M_p, \theta_p)$. The merit of this is that when conducting warping, it only pays attention to the foreground objects and will not be interfered by the background. After that, we estimate the correspondence matrices $C_{dense} \in \mathbb{R}^{\frac{HW}{4} \times \frac{HW}{4}}$ using a sliding kennel size = 1, stride = 1 and padding = 0, while $C_{tps} \in \mathbb{R}^{\frac{HW}{16} \times \frac{HW}{16}}$ by utilizing a sliding kennel size = 4, stride = 4 and padding = 0 for spatial reduction, where H and W indicate the spatial size of the original input image.

As for dense correspondence warping, we propose to match the features of f_a and f_p by using cosine similarity as follows:

$$C_{dense} = \frac{(f_a - \mu_a)^T (f_p - \mu_p)}{||f_a - \mu_a|| ||f_p - \mu_p||}, \tag{1}$$

where μ_a and μ_p represent the mean vectors. We then calculate the weighted average to estimate the dense correspondence warping in the form as [68]:

$$W_a = \sum \text{Softmax}(\alpha C_{dense} \cdot I_a, \text{dim} = 1), \tag{2}$$

where α is a hyper-parameter that controls the sharpness of the softmax function. To force the network to learn a reasonable dense semantic warping, we introduce a geometric loss as follows:

$$\mathcal{L}_{geo} = ||I_p - W_a||_1. \tag{3}$$

Although dense warping is capable to handle high degree of geometric changes, it fails to preserve the detailed style and texture information. To tackle this drawback, we further involve TPS warping, which can roughly transform the objects but with little information loss.

As for TPS warping, after obtaining C_{tps} matrix like C_{dense}, then we employ a regression net [59] to predict the corresponding control points and calculate the flow parameters T. Concretely, we use the following loss to restrict the transformation flow:

$$\mathcal{L}_{tps} = ||BS(I_a, T) - I_p||_1 + \mathcal{L}_{cst}, \tag{4}$$

where BS indicates the bilinear sampler operation. $\mathcal{L}_{cst}$ is a constraint loss [67] that restricts the warp distance and amplitude to prevent the internal patterns from losing natural information.

SS and TSC Block. (i) SS block utilizes the information from the output of the dense warping. Specifically, we employ the spatially-adaptive denormalization block [43] to project the spatially variant style to different activation decoder layers in the generating network as shown in Fig.2. Formally, let $F^i \in \mathbb{R}^{h \times w}$ denote the activations of the i-th layer of a deep convolutional network, we inject the dense warping information as follows:

$$\hat{F}^i = \gamma^i W_a \times \frac{F^i - \mu^i}{\sigma^i} + \beta^i W_a, \tag{5}$$

where $\sigma^i = \sqrt{\frac{1}{nhw} \sum ((F^i)^2 - (\mu^i)^2)}$ and $\mu^i = \frac{1}{nhw} \sum F^i$, where n is batch sample number. We implement the functions γ^i and β^i by using a simple two-layer convolutional network. (ii) TSC block employs the information from the output of TPS warping and project the appearance details to different activation encoder layers in the generating network. Formally, let X^i denote the activations of the i-th layer of the network, we inject the TPS warping information as follows:

$$\hat{X}^i = \varphi^i(BS(I_a, T)) + X^i, \tag{6}$$

where we use a simple plain convolutional layer to obtain φ^i.

Generating Block. For G_{Fg}, we combine W_a and M_p as input. For G_{Bg}, we take $B_a = I_a \otimes (1 - M_a)$ as input, and they do not share parameters. The final output can be obtained as: $I_o = Fg \otimes M_p + Bg$. More details about network architectures are provided in supplementary material.

End-to-end Training. To encourage the training of different blocks benefit from each other, we train our model in a joint style, and we combine several different losses to produce high-quality transferred output images:

Perceptual-Loss: The final output should be semantically consistent with the desired pose image, we then minimize the semantic discrepancy between them as follow:

$$\mathcal{L}_{perc} = ||\phi_l(I_o) - \phi_l(I_p)||_2, \tag{7}$$

where ϕ_l are the activation after relu4_2 layer in the VGG-19 network.

Contextual-Loss: To encourage our network to preserve more details from source appearance image, we employ the loss proposed in [33] as follow:

$$\mathcal{L}_{cont} = \sum_l \zeta_l [-log(\frac{1}{n_l} \sum_i \max_j A^l(\phi_l(I_o), \phi_l(I_a)))], \tag{8}$$

where i and j index the feature map of layer ϕ_l that contains n_l features, and ζ_l controls the relative importance of different layers. A_l denotes the pairwise affinities between features. We use relu2_2 up to relu5_2 layers for ϕ_l.

Style-Loss: In order to obtain the more realistic output, we penalize the statistic error between high-level features as follow:

$$\mathcal{L}_{style} = \sum_l ||G_l(I_o) - G_l(I_a)||_2, \tag{9}$$

where G_l denotes the Gram matrix estimated from ϕ_l form relu2_2 to relu4_2.

Self-Loss: To fully utilize the data under self-supervision, we construct pseudo paired data by apply random geometry transformations to I_a to obtain its desired pose image I'_a. In this way, the output I_o should be the same as I'_o, we then penalize the loss as follow:

$$\mathcal{L}_{self} = \sum_l ||\phi_l(I_o) - \phi_l(I'_a)||_1, \tag{10}$$

where ϕ_l denotes the activation of layer form relu2_2 to relu5_2.

Regularization-Loss: In the matching block, since we align the image and mask from two domains, we here apply a $\mathcal{L}_1$ regularization to encourage them to be closer as follow:

$$\mathcal{L}_{reg} = ||f_a - f_p||_1. \tag{11}$$

Adversarial-Loss: To force the generator to generate realistic images, we deploy a discriminator like in [61] to discriminate the generated fake images. The adversarial objectives of D and G are respectively formulated as follow:

$$\begin{aligned}
\mathcal{L}^D_{adv} &= -\mathbb{E}[(D(I_a))] - \mathbb{E}[-D(G(I_a, I_p))], \\
\mathcal{L}^G_{adv} &= -\mathbb{E}[D(G(I_a, I_p))].
\end{aligned} \tag{12}$$

Finally, we optimize the total loss as follow:

$$\begin{aligned}
\mathcal{L}_{total} = \lambda_1 \mathcal{L}_{geo} + \lambda_2 \mathcal{L}_{tps} + \lambda_3 \mathcal{L}_{perc} + \lambda_4 \mathcal{L}_{cont} \\
+ \lambda_5 \mathcal{L}_{style} + \lambda_6 \mathcal{L}_{self} + \lambda_7 \mathcal{L}_{reg} + \lambda_8 \mathcal{L}_{adv},
\end{aligned} \tag{13}$$

where $\lambda_1 \sim \lambda_8$ are hyper-parameters controlling the weights to balance the objectives.

4   Experiment

Implementation. We adopt Adam [18] with $\beta_1 = 0.1$, $\beta_2 = 0.999$ as the optimizer in our all experiments using PyTorch library. Our model is jointly trained for 200 epochs with input-size $= 256 \times 256$. We set the learning rates to 0.0001 and 0.0004 respectively, for the generator and discriminator. We set $\alpha = 100$, $\lambda_1 = \lambda_2 = 1$, $\lambda_3 = 0.1$, $\lambda_4, \lambda_6 = 1$, $\lambda_5 = 0.01$, $\lambda_7, \lambda_8 = 10$. Let $C_{k_i S_j}$ denote a convolution layer with kernel size of i and a stride of j, followed by InstanceNorm2d Normalization [57] and ReLu activation function [36]. Let ResBlock denote the

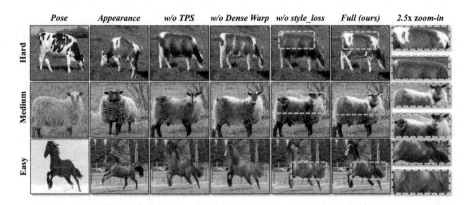

Fig. 3. Visual comparisons of our ablation methods.

Table 1. Exploration of different components of our method. ↔ denotes the position change of **SS** and **TSC** blocks where they inject to.

Methods	Human		Mammals		Birds		Cars	
	mFID ↓	mSSIM ↑	mFID ↓	mSSIM ↑	mFID ↓	mSSIM ↑	mFID ↓	mSSIM ↑
w/o $\mathcal{L}_{perc}$	63.1	0.255	68.4	0.193	57.6	0.211	71.4	0.132
w/o $\mathcal{L}_{cont}$	52.8	0.406	58.5	0.394	49.2	0.301	62.2	0.267
w/o $\mathcal{L}_{self}$	40.6	0.601	36.6	0.521	30.7	0.528	43.1	0.452
w/o $\mathcal{L}_{reg}$	38.8	0.649	35.0	0.533	29.5	0.538	41.6	0.464
w/o Tps	38.9	0.645	35.0	0.547	29.3	0.527	41.6	0.459
w/o Dense Warp	38.7	0.651	34.8	0.554	28.9	0.539	41.3	0.464
w/o $\mathcal{L}_{style}$	39.1	0.635	35.2	0.523	29.8	0.517	41.9	0.448
TPS (TSC) ↔ Dense Warp (SS)	38.2	0.655	34.3	0.543	29.1	0.542	41.3	0.468
Ours (full)	**37.6**	**0.676**	**33.9**	**0.576**	**28.3**	**0.571**	**40.8**	**0.491**

Residual Block structure proposed by [10], in which the BatchNorm2d Normalization is replaced by InstanceNorm2d Normalization [57]. Similar to [68], the two separate feature extractors F_A and F_B share the same structure but without sharing weight in the form of $\{C_{k_3S_1}, C_{k_4S_2}, C_{k_3S_1}, C_{k_4S_2}, C_{k_3S_1}, \text{ResBlock} * 3\}$, which will output two different features. Note that we perform different $C_{k_1S_1}$ and $C_{k_4S_4}$ operations to estimate the C_{dense} and C_{tps}, and thus these two matrices are in different shapes. Let L denote a linear function output m dimensions. As for the TPS warping regression network, we follow [59] and adopt the structure in the form of $\{C_{k_4S_2}, C_{k_4S_2}, C_{k_3S_1}, C_{k_3S_1}, L_{18}\}$. The foreground generator is in a encoder-decoder like network and the background generator network can be in arbitrary Unet [37] structure for reconstruction. More network architecture can be referred to supplementary material.

Datasets. We evaluate our method on several challenging datasets that contain large variations in terms of pose and category. Specifically, to illustrate that our framework can conduct pose transformation for general objects, we benchmark our method using four datasets: (i) *Human*: We perform training on the DeepFashion dataset provided by [26]. Note that we do not use the skeleton information and the ground-truth targeted pose images for training. (ii) *Mam-*

mals: We collect 5 classes of animals images including *horse, cow, sheep, dog* and *lion* from ImageNet [45] and WebDataset [48]. We then combine them to build the Mammals dataset. In total, it consists of ~5k images, and we split them into training/testing set at the ratio of 8:2 on each subject separately. (iii) *Birds*: We use the Caltech-UCSD Birds-200–2011 [58] as our Birds dataset. We follow the setting as the original list for training and testing. (iv) *Cars*: We use VeRi [25] dataset as our Cars dataset which contains many categories with diverse poses, and we strictly follow the training and testing set as in the original paper.

Evaluation Metrics. We use the mean Fréchet Inception Score (mFID) [11] and mean Structural Similarity (mSSIM) [63] to measure the distance between the distributions of transferred synthesized images and original real images. We also conduct a user study to compute user preference (UP) scores on the translation results. Specifically, given 30 images from each method randomly, we interviewed 1,00 participants and asked them to rate their favorite works. Note that the participants are unaware of the specific algorithm that produce the transferred images, and we finally report the proportion of the results they prefer.

4.1   Ablation Studies

Table 1 reports all the results of our ablation experiments. Specifically, in four datasets, our full model outperforms others by different degrees. It shows that removing some kinds of blocks and loss functions, it will make the network learn less detailed appearance or spatial information. In addition, changing SS and TSC position can not yield better results. We conjecture that the encoder can retain the underlying appearance information, while the decoder is responsible for incorporating the high-semantic spatial transformation information. We further visualize some examples and make qualitative comparison, as shown in Fig. 3. We show three cases including *cow, sheep* and *horse*, and we define them as hard, medium, easy examples according to their pose and appearance difficulties. *w/o* $\mathcal{L}_{style}$ and *w/o* Tps will cause the network to miss some detailed appearance information such as textures, style and colour, *i.e.*, the skin of cow, which makes the output results less realistic. Besides, although the visual performance of *w/o* Dense warp is close to the full model due to the powerful loss functions driven, it fails to achieve the satisfactory results in terms of mFID and mSSIM metrics.

4.2   Qualitative Comparison

Since general object pose transformation has not been extensively studied, therefore, we re-implement and compare with some existing generative models which can be applied to our task. Specifically, for *Mammals* and *Birds* datasets, we compare our method with CoCosNet [68], FUNIT [21] and COCO-FUNIT [46], where the former one aims to synthesize realistic images given the examplar images while the latter two focus on style-content translation. They both can be readily applied to our tasks, and we retrain the methods with the same training

Fig. 4. Qualitative comparison of different methods on *Mammals* and *Birds* dataset.

Fig. 5. Qualitative comparison of different methods on *Human* and *Cars* datasets.

set as ours to keep the fairness. For *Human* dataset, we use the state-of-the-art method Liquid-GAN [23] and Liquid++ [24] for comparisons. For *Cars* dataset, we compare our method with PAGM [29] and HoloGan [41], which can be applied to car view-synthesis. Note that all the re-implement results are produced by using the open-source code.

As shown in Fig. 4, it shows that our model synthesizes more convincing results with well-preserved characteristics of objects. To be specific, Although CoCosNet [68] yields the transferred outputs, it fails to preserve the same appearance details from the source images. For instance, the output *"horse"* should be in brown body and with a little white on head rather than in the whole black body. Moreover, it can not fix the original background information, making the output images unsatisfactory. Likewise, FUNIT [21] and COCO-FUNIT [46] also fail to predict high-quality results since it transfers the style from one image to another globally, which will also break the background information. As for the foreground object characteristics, it cannot well deal with the issue of retaining the content from the source appearance images. Compared to these methods, our proposed method can successfully yield the output in the desired pose retaining the appearance of both objects and background due to the proposed sub-blocks and loss functions. Table 2 shows the detailed quantitative metrics comparison between these methods, among which, our method outperform them by a large margin and achieve the top user preference.

Table 2. Quantitative comparisons of our method with other methods on *Mammals* and *Birds* dataset.

Methods	Mammals			Birds		
	mFID ↓	mSSIM ↑	UP ↑	mFID ↓	mSSIM ↑	UP ↑
FUNIT [21]	78.5	0.138	4%	80.4	0.182	3%
COCO-FUNIT [46]	70.7	0.141	7%	78.8	0.186	4%
CoCosNet [68]	81.6	0.156	6%	64.5	0.211	6%
Ours	**33.9**	**0.576**	**83%**	**28.3**	**0.571**	**87%**

Table 3. Quantitative comparisons of our method with other methods on *Human* and *Cars* dataset.

Methods	Human			Cars		
	mFID ↓	mSSIM ↑	UP ↑	mFID ↓	mSSIM ↑	UP ↑
Liquid [23]	44.6	0.559	20%	–	–	–
Liquid++ [24]	41.4	0.567	30%	–	—	–
HoloGan [41]	–	–	–	51.8	0.251	18%
PAGM [29]	—	–	—	46.7	0.284	28%
Ours	**37.6**	**0.676**	**50%**	**40.8**	**0.491**	**54%**

For *Human* dataset, Fig. 5 (left) shows that our method can produce more reasonable results. Note that our method is a generic general object pose transformation framework but not specially designed for human. In other words, we do not employ Face-Loss [22] and some keypoints or body mesh [27] information to train our network as in [23,24]. Therefore, the transferred output images we yield are acceptable and make it convenient to conduct human pose transformation without using auxiliary information. More quantitative comparisons can be seen in Table 3.

For *Cars* dataset, our method outperforms the recent state-of-the-art PAGM [29] and HoloGan [41] as shown in Table 3. More specifically, Fig. 5 (right) shows us some examples that the previous methods fail to retain the color of the car (upper) or abortively transfer the view of the vehicle (bottom). As for our proposed framework, we successfully synthesize the new view of vehicle given the unpaired data, which illustrates the effectiveness of our approach.

4.3   Multi-object Pose Transformation

To further illustrate the generality of our framework, we conduct experiments and visualize some multi-object examples. As shown in Fig. 6 (left), given the same number of objects in appearance and desired pose images, we can transfer all the objects in the same pose, which broadens the usefulness of our framework. It's worth mentioning that we do not advocate transferring images with mismatched number of objects between appearance and pose images. This is

Fig. 6. Qualitative results of multi-object pose transformation and cross-category object pose transformation.

Table 4. Different baselines performance with data augmentation by our framework in mIoU on PASCAL VOC dataset. **+DA** denotes conducting data augmentation.

Network	CAM	Pseudo-Masks	Seg. Masks (val)	Seg. Masks (test)
IRNet [1]	48.3	65.9	63.5	64.8
+DA	$49.6_{+1.3}$	$66.8_{+0.9}$	$64.6_{+1.1}$	$65.8_{+1.0}$
SEAM [62]	55.4	63.4	64.5	65.7
+DA	$56.4_{+1.0}$	$64.4_{+1.1}$	$65.7_{+1.2}$	$66.5_{+0.8}$

because asymmetrical quantities will lead to ambiguity in object pose transformation.

4.4 Cross-Category Pose Transformation

Under some extreme circumstances, some species often have only a few images, and it is difficult to construct unpaired pairs. Take *"horse"* as an example, in real life, we may only observe the standing horses, and there is no other reference data. However, there are many other similar animals in nature, such as cow and sheep, which they all have limbs. Based on cross-category observations, we humans have the ability to imitate *"horse"* to an unknown posture based on references from other categories. With this in mind, we conduct experiments on cross-category pose transformation. As shown in Fig. 6 (right), our proposed method can address this issue and produce reasonable images, which will not miss the original appearance details. This finding will encourage wider applications in the future.

4.5 Applications

Data Augmentation. In the weakly supervised semantic segmentation (WSSS) task [1,56], it aims to leverage the class-activation-maps [52] to find out the

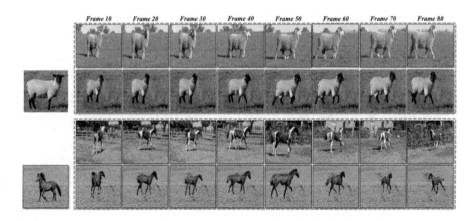

Fig. 7. Illustrative examples of objects video imitation. The reference pose videos are sampled from Got-10k [12] dataset. For more examples, please refer to supplemental material.

objects' potential regions and yield the pseudo masks with only class-level labels. In order to improve the class-activation-maps, object diversity is of great significance in weakly supervised semantic segmentation. In this setup, our goal is to expand the object images in different poses so as to provide more realistic images for training. We here choose IRNet [1] and SEAM [62] as baseline models to conduct experiments on PASCAL VOC dataset [8] to verify the quality of the images we produce. Note that we train our **UFO-PT** using PASCAL VOC dataset without extra data. Specifically, we produce more training images in different poses by our method, including *"horse"*, *"cow"*, *"sheep"*, *"dog"*, *"cat"*, *"person"* and *"vehicle"*. Table 4 shows that compared to the baseline model, our method can help both the baselines boost the performance, which demonstrates the practicality of our method.

Video Imitation. Moreover, we can apply our method to video imitation. As shown in Fig. 7, given a static image providing appearance and a dynamic sequential video, we can yield an unseen video of that object. This intriguing study has a wide range of applications, which can synthesize more action videos of objects to reduce the burden of collecting data artificially.

4.6   Failure Case

While our approach effectively addresses the general object pose transformation problem, it still has several failure modes. Fig. 8 illustrates some failure cases generated by our method. When the body part of the image is hard to localize, the model generates unsatisfactory results. However, this is a common problem in deep learning, such as object occlusions and pose extraction of hard examples. We will try to alleviate this issue in future work to further improve our method.

| Pose | Appearance | Ours | Pose | Appearance | Ours |

Fig. 8. Failure cases visualization.

5   More-In-Depth Discussion

This paper pushes the frontier of the general object pose transformation that is beneficial to many applications in computer vision tasks. The final generation might be upper-bounded by the quality of the saliency mask, however, most of the previous works also adopt off-the-shelf methods like Densepose [9] or SMPL [27] to segment out the object for transformation. Segmenting out the foreground is not the main focus of our method. We take the early step to conduct general pose transformation, and we use the unsupervised saliency to highlight the foreground objects and conduct warping and generating images, which is acceptable.

6   Conclusion

Unlike the previous works that only focus on whether humans or some mammals in isolation, we introduce a unified framework for general object pose transformation with unpaired data. We propose to align and match two input images semantically using SS block and TSC block to inject spatial and detailed style information into the generating block. Experiments on different datasets show the superiority of our approach. Moreover, we can apply our framework to several applications such as data augmentation and video imitation, which can further show its practicality.

Acknowledgment. This work was supported by National Natural Science Foundation of China (NSFC) 61876208, Key-Area Research and Development Program of Guangdong Province 2018B010108002, and the National Research Foundation, Singapore under its AI Singapore Programme (AISG Award No: AISG-RP-2018-003), the Ministry of Education, Singapore, under its Academic Research Fund Tier 2 (MOE-T2EP20220-0007) and Tier 1 (RG95/20).

References

1. Ahn, J., Cho, S., Kwak, S.: Weakly supervised learning of instance segmentation with inter-pixel relations. In: Proceedings of the IEEE Conference on Computer Vision and Pattern Recognition, pp. 2209–2218 (2019)
2. Balakrishnan, G., Zhao, A., Dalca, A.V., Durand, F., Guttag, J.: Synthesizing images of humans in unseen poses. In: Proceedings of the IEEE Conference on Computer Vision and Pattern Recognition, pp. 8340–8348 (2018)
3. Bansal, A., Sheikh, Y., Ramanan, D.: Shapes and context: in-the-wild image synthesis & manipulation. In: Proceedings of the IEEE/CVF Conference on Computer Vision and Pattern Recognition, pp. 2317–2326 (2019)
4. Cao, Y., Zhou, Z., Zhang, W., Yu, Y.: Unsupervised diverse colorization via generative adversarial networks. In: Ceci, M., Hollmén, J., Todorovski, L., Vens, C., Džeroski, S. (eds.) ECML PKDD 2017. LNCS (LNAI), vol. 10534, pp. 151–166. Springer, Cham (2017). https://doi.org/10.1007/978-3-319-71249-9_10
5. Cao, Z., Hidalgo, G., Simon, T., Wei, S.E., Sheikh, Y.: Openpose: realtime multi-person 2d pose estimation using part affinity fields. IEEE Trans. Pattern Anal. Mach. Intell. **43**(1), 172–186 (2019)
6. Chan, E.R., Monteiro, M., Kellnhofer, P., Wu, J., Wetzstein, G.: pi-gan: periodic implicit generative adversarial networks for 3d-aware image synthesis. In: Proceedings of the IEEE/CVF Conference on Computer Vision and Pattern Recognition, pp. 5799–5809 (2021)
7. Dosovitskiy, A., et al: Flownet: learning optical flow with convolutional networks. In: Proceedings of the IEEE International Conference on Computer Vision, pp. 2758–2766 (2015)
8. Everingham, M., Eslami, S.M.A., Van Gool, L., Williams, C.K.I., Winn, J., Zisserman, A.: The PASCAL Visual Object Classes Challenge: a Retrospective. Int. J. Comput. Vis. **111**(1), 98–136 (2014). https://doi.org/10.1007/s11263-014-0733-5
9. Güler, R.A., Neverova, N., Kokkinos, I.: Densepose: dense human pose estimation in the wild. In: Proceedings of the IEEE Conference on Computer Vision and Pattern Recognition, pp. 7297–7306 (2018)
10. He, K., Zhang, X., Ren, S., Sun, J.: Deep residual learning for image recognition. In: Proceedings of the IEEE Conference on Computer Vision and Pattern Recognition, pp. 770–778 (2016)
11. Heusel, M., Ramsauer, H., Unterthiner, T., Nessler, B., Hochreiter, S.: Gans trained by a two time-scale update rule converge to a local nash equilibrium. arXiv preprint. arXiv:1706.08500 (2017)
12. Huang, L., Zhao, X., Huang, K.: Got-10k: a large high-diversity benchmark for generic object tracking in the wild. IEEE Trans. Pattern Anal. Mach. Intell. **43**(5), 1562–1577 (2019)
13. Isola, P., Zhu, J.Y., Zhou, T., Efros, A.A.: Image-to-image translation with conditional adversarial networks. In: Proceedings of the IEEE Conference on Computer Vision and Pattern Recognition, pp. 1125–1134 (2017)
14. Ji, D., Kwon, J., McFarland, M., Savarese, S.: Deep view morphing. In: Proceedings of the IEEE Conference on Computer Vision and Pattern Recognition, pp. 2155–2163 (2017)
15. Kanazawa, A., Black, M.J., Jacobs, D.W., Malik, J.: End-to-end recovery of human shape and pose. In: Proceedings of the IEEE Conference on Computer Vision and Pattern Recognition, pp. 7122–7131 (2018)

16. Karras, T., Laine, S., Aila, T.: A style-based generator architecture for generative adversarial networks. In: Proceedings of the IEEE/CVF Conference on Computer Vision and Pattern Recognition, pp. 4401–4410 (2019)
17. Kim, T., Cha, M., Kim, H., Lee, J.K., Kim, J.: Learning to discover cross-domain relations with generative adversarial networks. In: International Conference on Machine Learning, pp. 1857–1865. PMLR (2017)
18. Kingma, D.P., Ba, J.: Adam: a method for stochastic optimization. arXiv preprint. arXiv:1412.6980 (2014)
19. Kulkarni, T.D., Whitney, W., Kohli, P., Tenenbaum, J.B.: Deep convolutional inverse graphics network. arXiv preprint. arXiv:1503.03167 (2015)
20. Ledig, C., et al.: Photo-realistic single image super-resolution using a generative adversarial network. In: Proceedings of the IEEE Conference on Computer Vision and Pattern Recognition, pp. 4681–4690 (2017)
21. Liu, M.Y., et al.: Few-shot unsupervised image-to-image translation. In: Proceedings of the IEEE/CVF International Conference on Computer Vision, pp. 10551–10560 (2019)
22. Liu, W., Wen, Y., Yu, Z., Li, M., Raj, B., Song, L.: Sphereface: deep hypersphere embedding for face recognition. In: Proceedings of the IEEE Conference on Computer Vision and Pattern Recognition, pp. 212–220 (2017)
23. Liu, W., Piao, Z., Min, J., Luo, W., Ma, L., Gao, S.: Liquid warping gan: a unified framework for human motion imitation, appearance transfer and novel view synthesis. In: Proceedings of the IEEE/CVF International Conference on Computer Vision, pp. 5904–5913 (2019)
24. Liu, W., Piao, Z., Tu, Z., Luo, W., Ma, L., Gao, S.: Liquid warping GAN with attention: a unified framework for human image synthesis. IEEE Trans. Pattern Anal. Mach. Intell. **44**, 5114–5132 (2021)
25. Liu, X., Liu, W., Mei, T., Ma, H.: Provid: progressive and multimodal vehicle reidentification for large-scale urban surveillance. IEEE Trans. Multimedia **20**(3), 645–658 (2018)
26. Liu, Z., Luo, P., Qiu, S., Wang, X., Tang, X.: Deepfashion: powering robust clothes recognition and retrieval with rich annotations. In: Proceedings of the IEEE Conference on Computer Vision and Pattern Recognition, pp. 1096–1104 (2016)
27. Loper, M., Mahmood, N., Romero, J., Pons-Moll, G., Black, M.J.: Smpl: a skinned multi-person linear model. ACM Trans. Graphics (TOG) **34**(6), 1–16 (2015)
28. Lorenz, D., Bereska, L., Milbich, T., Ommer, B.: Unsupervised part-based disentangling of object shape and appearance. In: Proceedings of the IEEE/CVF Conference on Computer Vision and Pattern Recognition, pp. 10955–10964 (2019)
29. Lv, K., Sheng, H., Xiong, Z., Li, W., Zheng, L.: Pose-based view synthesis for vehicles: a perspective aware method. IEEE Trans. Image Process. **29**, 5163–5174 (2020)
30. Ma, L., Jia, X., Georgoulis, S., Tuytelaars, T., Van Gool, L.: Exemplar guided unsupervised image-to-image translation with semantic consistency. arXiv preprint. arXiv:1805.11145 (2018)
31. Ma, L., Jia, X., Sun, Q., Schiele, B., Tuytelaars, T., Van Gool, L.: Pose guided person image generation. arXiv preprint. arXiv:1705.09368 (2017)
32. Ma, L., Sun, Q., Georgoulis, S., Van Gool, L., Schiele, B., Fritz, M.: Disentangled person image generation. In: Proceedings of the IEEE Conference on Computer Vision and Pattern Recognition, pp. 99–108 (2018)

33. Mechrez, R., Talmi, I., Zelnik-Manor, L.: The contextual loss for image transformation with non-aligned data. In: Ferrari, V., Hebert, M., Sminchisescu, C., Weiss, Y. (eds.) Computer Vision – ECCV 2018. LNCS, vol. 11218, pp. 800–815. Springer, Cham (2018). https://doi.org/10.1007/978-3-030-01264-9_47

34. Mirza, M., Osindero, S.: Conditional generative adversarial nets. arXiv preprint. arXiv:1411.1784 (2014)

35. Murez, Z., Kolouri, S., Kriegman, D., Ramamoorthi, R., Kim, K.: Image to image translation for domain adaptation. In: Proceedings of the IEEE Conference on Computer Vision and Pattern Recognition, pp. 4500–4509 (2018)

36. Nair, V., Hinton, G.E.: Rectified linear units improve restricted boltzmann machines. In: ICML (2010)

37. Nazeri, K., Ng, E., Joseph, T., Qureshi, F., Ebrahimi, M.: Edgeconnect: structure guided image inpainting using edge prediction. In: The IEEE International Conference on Computer Vision (ICCV) Workshops (2019)

38. Neverova, N., Alp Güler, R., Kokkinos, I.: Dense pose transfer. In: Ferrari, V., Hebert, M., Sminchisescu, C., Weiss, Y. (eds.) ECCV 2018. LNCS, vol. 11207, pp. 128–143. Springer, Cham (2018). https://doi.org/10.1007/978-3-030-01219-9_8

39. Newell, A., Yang, K., Deng, J.: Stacked hourglass networks for human pose estimation. In: Leibe, B., Matas, J., Sebe, N., Welling, M. (eds.) ECCV 2016. LNCS, vol. 9912, pp. 483–499. Springer, Cham (2016). https://doi.org/10.1007/978-3-319-46484-8_29

40. Nguyen, D.T., et al.: Deepusps: deep robust unsupervised saliency prediction with self-supervision. arXiv preprint. arXiv:1909.13055 (2019)

41. Nguyen-Phuoc, T., Li, C., Theis, L., Richardt, C., Yang, Y.L.: Hologan: unsupervised learning of 3d representations from natural images. In: Proceedings of the IEEE/CVF International Conference on Computer Vision, pp. 7588–7597 (2019)

42. Park, E., Yang, J., Yumer, E., Ceylan, D., Berg, A.C.: Transformation-grounded image generation network for novel 3d view synthesis. In: Proceedings of the IEEE Conference on Computer Vision and Pattern Recognition, pp. 3500–3509 (2017)

43. Park, T., Liu, M.Y., Wang, T.C., Zhu, J.Y.: Semantic image synthesis with spatially-adaptive normalization. In: Proceedings of the IEEE/CVF Conference on Computer Vision and Pattern Recognition, pp. 2337–2346 (2019)

44. Rematas, K., Nguyen, C.H., Ritschel, T., Fritz, M., Tuytelaars, T.: Novel views of objects from a single image. IEEE Trans. Pattern Anal. Mach. Intell. **39**(8), 1576–1590 (2016)

45. Russakovsky, O., et al.: ImageNet large scale visual recognition challenge. Int. J. Comput. Vis. **115**(3), 211–252 (2015). https://doi.org/10.1007/s11263-015-0816-y

46. Saito, K., Saenko, K., Liu, M.Y.: Coco-funit: few-shot unsupervised image translation with a content conditioned style encoder. arXiv preprint. arXiv:2007.07431 2 (2020)

47. Schwarz, K., Liao, Y., Niemeyer, M., Geiger, A.: Graf: generative radiance fields for 3d-aware image synthesis. arXiv preprint. arXiv:2007.02442 (2020)

48. Shen, T., Lin, G., Shen, C., Reid, I.: Bootstrapping the performance of webly supervised semantic segmentation. In: Proceedings of the IEEE Conference on Computer Vision and Pattern Recognition, pp. 1363–1371 (2018)

49. Si, C., Wang, W., Wang, L., Tan, T.: Multistage adversarial losses for pose-based human image synthesis. In: Proceedings of the IEEE Conference on Computer Vision and Pattern Recognition, pp. 118–126 (2018)

50. Siarohin, A., Lathuilière, S., Tulyakov, S., Ricci, E., Sebe, N.: First order motion model for image animation. Adv. Neural. Inf. Process. Syst. **32**, 7137–7147 (2019)

51. Siarohin, A., Sangineto, E., Lathuiliere, S., Sebe, N.: Deformable gans for pose-based human image generation. In: Proceedings of the IEEE Conference on Computer Vision and Pattern Recognition, pp. 3408–3416 (2018)
52. Su, Y., Lin, G., Hao, Y., Cao, Y., Wang, W., Wu, Q.: Self-supervised object localization with joint graph partition. In: Proceedings of the AAAI Conference on Artificial Intelligence, vol. 36, pp. 2289–2297 (2022)
53. Su, Y., Lin, G., Sun, R., Hao, Y., Wu, Q.: Modeling the uncertainty for self-supervised 3d skeleton action representation learning. In: Proceedings of the 29th ACM International Conference on Multimedia, pp. 769–778 (2021)
54. Su, Y., Lin, G., Wu, Q.: Self-supervised 3d skeleton action representation learning with motion consistency and continuity. In: Proceedings of the IEEE/CVF International Conference on Computer Vision, pp. 13328–13338 (2021)
55. Su, Y., Lin, G., Zhu, J., Wu, Q.: Human interaction learning on 3d skeleton point clouds for video violence recognition. In: Vedaldi, A., Bischof, H., Brox, T., Frahm, J.-M. (eds.) ECCV 2020. LNCS, vol. 12349, pp. 74–90. Springer, Cham (2020). https://doi.org/10.1007/978-3-030-58548-8_5
56. Su, Y., Sun, R., Lin, G., Wu, Q.: Context decoupling augmentation for weakly supervised semantic segmentation. In: Proceedings of the IEEE/CVF International Conference on Computer Vision, pp. 7004–7014 (2021)
57. Ulyanov, D., Vedaldi, A., Lempitsky, V.: Instance normalization: the missing ingredient for fast stylization. arXiv preprint. arXiv:1607.08022 (2016)
58. Wah, C., Branson, S., Welinder, P., Perona, P., Belongie, S.: The caltech-UCSD birds-200-2011 dataset. Technical reports CNS-TR-2011-001, California Institute of Technology (2011)
59. Wang, B., Zheng, H., Liang, X., Chen, Y., Lin, L., Yang, M.: Toward characteristic-preserving image-based virtual try-on network. In: Ferrari, V., Hebert, M., Sminchisescu, C., Weiss, Y. (eds.) ECCV 2018. LNCS, vol. 11217, pp. 607–623. Springer, Cham (2018). https://doi.org/10.1007/978-3-030-01261-8_36
60. Wang, M., et al.: Example-guided style-consistent image synthesis from semantic labeling. In: Proceedings of the IEEE/CVF Conference on Computer Vision and Pattern Recognition, pp. 1495–1504 (2019)
61. Wang, T.C., Liu, M.Y., Zhu, J.Y., Tao, A., Kautz, J., Catanzaro, B.: High-resolution image synthesis and semantic manipulation with conditional gans. In: Proceedings of the IEEE Conference on Computer Vision and Pattern Recognition, pp. 8798–8807 (2018)
62. Wang, Y., Zhang, J., Kan, M., Shan, S., Chen, X.: Self-supervised equivariant attention mechanism for weakly supervised semantic segmentation. In: Proceedings of the IEEE/CVF Conference on Computer Vision and Pattern Recognition, pp. 12275–12284 (2020)
63. Wang, Z., Bovik, A.C., Sheikh, H.R., Simoncelli, E.P.: Image quality assessment: from error visibility to structural similarity. IEEE Trans. Image Process. **13**(4), 600–612 (2004)
64. Wu, B., Duan, H., Liu, Z., Sun, G.: Srpgan: perceptual generative adversarial network for single image super resolution. arXiv preprint. arXiv:1712.05927 (2017)
65. Wu, W., Cao, K., Li, C., Qian, C., Loy, C.C.: Transgaga: geometry-aware unsupervised image-to-image translation. In: Proceedings of the IEEE/CVF Conference on Computer Vision and Pattern Recognition, pp. 8012–8021 (2019)
66. Yang, F., Lin, G.: Ct-net: Complementary transfering network for garment transfer with arbitrary geometric changes. arXiv preprint. arXiv:2105.05497 (2021)

67. Yang, H., Zhang, R., Guo, X., Liu, W., Zuo, W., Luo, P.: Towards photo-realistic virtual try-on by adaptively generating-preserving image content. In: Proceedings of the IEEE/CVF Conference on Computer Vision and Pattern Recognition, pp. 7850–7859 (2020)

68. Zhang, P., Zhang, B., Chen, D., Yuan, L., Wen, F.: Cross-domain correspondence learning for exemplar-based image translation. In: Proceedings of the IEEE/CVF Conference on Computer Vision and Pattern Recognition, pp. 5143–5153 (2020)

69. Zhou, T., Tulsiani, S., Sun, W., Malik, J., Efros, A.A.: View synthesis by appearance flow. In: Leibe, B., Matas, J., Sebe, N., Welling, M. (eds.) ECCV 2016. LNCS, vol. 9908, pp. 286–301. Springer, Cham (2016). https://doi.org/10.1007/978-3-319-46493-0_18

70. Zhu, J.Y., Park, T., Isola, P., Efros, A.A.: Unpaired image-to-image translation using cycle-consistent adversarial networks. In: Proceedings of the IEEE International Conference on Computer Vision, pp. 2223–2232 (2017)

71. Zhu, Z., Huang, T., Shi, B., Yu, M., Wang, B., Bai, X.: Progressive pose attention transfer for person image generation. In: Proceedings of the IEEE/CVF Conference on Computer Vision and Pattern Recognition, pp. 2347–2356 (2019)

Compositional Human-Scene Interaction Synthesis with Semantic Control

Kaifeng Zhao[1]([✉]), Shaofei Wang[1], Yan Zhang[1], Thabo Beeler[2], and Siyu Tang[1]

[1] ETH Zürich, Zürich, Switzerland
{kaifeng.zhao,shaofei.wang,yan.zhang,siyu.tang}@inf.ethz.ch
[2] Google, Zurich, Switzerland

Abstract. Synthesizing natural interactions between virtual humans and their 3D environments is critical for numerous applications, such as computer games and AR/VR experiences. Recent methods mainly focus on modeling geometric relations between 3D environments and humans, where the high-level semantics of the human-scene interaction has frequently been ignored. Our goal is to synthesize humans interacting with a given 3D scene controlled by high-level semantic specifications as pairs of action categories and object instances, e.g., "sit on the chair". The key challenge of incorporating interaction semantics into the generation framework is to learn a joint representation that effectively captures heterogeneous information, including human body articulation, 3D object geometry, and the intent of the interaction. To address this challenge, we design a novel transformer-based generative model, in which the articulated 3D human body surface points and 3D objects are jointly encoded in a unified latent space, and the semantics of the interaction between the human and objects are embedded via positional encoding. Furthermore, inspired by the compositional nature of interactions that humans can simultaneously interact with multiple objects, we define interaction semantics as the composition of varying numbers of atomic action-object pairs. Our proposed generative model can naturally incorporate varying numbers of atomic interactions, which enables synthesizing compositional human-scene interactions without requiring composite interaction data. We extend the PROX dataset with interaction semantic labels and scene instance segmentation to evaluate our method and demonstrate that our method can generate realistic human-scene interactions with semantic control. Our perceptual study shows that our synthesized virtual humans can naturally interact with 3D scenes, considerably outperforming existing methods. We name our method **COINS**, for **CO**mpositional **IN**teraction Synthesis with Semantic Control. Code and data are available at https://github.com/zkf1997/COINS.

Keywords: Human-scene interaction synthesis · Semantic composition · Virtual humans

Supplementary Information The online version contains supplementary material available at https://doi.org/10.1007/978-3-031-20068-7_18.

© The Author(s), under exclusive license to Springer Nature Switzerland AG 2022
S. Avidan et al. (Eds.): ECCV 2022, LNCS 13666, pp. 311–327, 2022.
https://doi.org/10.1007/978-3-031-20068-7_18

1   Introduction

People constantly interact with their surroundings, and such interactions have semantics, specifically as combinations of actions and object instances, e.g., "sit on the chair" or "lie on the bed". Incorporating and controlling such interaction semantics is critical for creating virtual humans with realistic behavior. An effective solution for semantic-aware virtual human generation could advance existing technologies in AR/VR, computer games, and synthetic data generation to train machine learning perception algorithms. However, existing methods focus on modeling geometric relationships between virtual humans and their 3D environments [11,45,46], and thus are not able to synthesize body-scene interactions with semantic control of human actions and specific interaction objects. This heavily limits their use in practice.

In this paper, we aim to incorporate semantic control into the synthesis of human-scene interactions. This is a challenging task due to the following reasons. First, semantic-aware human-scene interactions are characterized by body articulation, 3D object geometry, and the intent of the interaction. It is challenging to

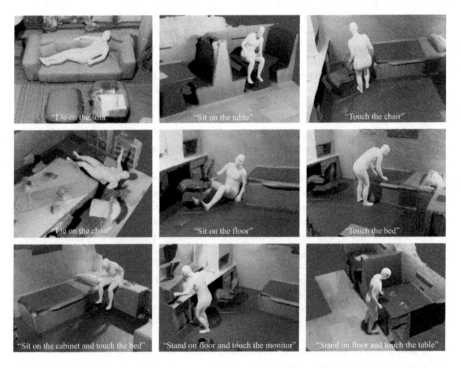

Fig. 1. Given a pair of action and object instance as the semantic specification, our method generates virtual humans naturally interacting with the object (*first row*). Furthermore, our method retargets interactions on unseen action-object combinations (*second row*) and synthesizes composite interactions without requiring any corresponding composite training data (*third row*).

learn a generalizable representation to capture such heterogeneous information. Second, given a 3D scene, the space for plausible human-scene interactions is enormous, and obtaining sufficiently diverse training data remains challenging.

To address these challenges, we introduce a novel interaction synthesis approach that leverages transformer-based generative models and can synthesize realistic 3D human bodies, given a 3D scene and a varying number of action-object pairs. These pairs can specify the intent of the interactions and the interacting objects. The key advantages of our models are two-fold: First, we represent human body articulation and 3D object geometry as tokens in the proposed transformer network, and the interaction semantics are embedded via positional encoding. Combined with a conditional variational auto-encoder (VAE) [16,33], we learn a unified latent space that captures the distribution of human articulation conditioned on the given 3D objects and the interaction semantics. Second, our models can be used to synthesize composite interactions, as they can naturally incorporate a varying number of 3D objects and interaction semantics. By training only on irreducible atomic interactions (e.g., "sit on the sofa", "touch the table"), our model can generate novel composite interactions (e.g., "sit on the sofa *and* touch the table") in unseen 3D scenes without requiring composite training data (Fig. 1). Furthermore, we decompose the interaction synthesis task into three stages. First, we infer plausible global body locations and orientations given pairs of actions and objects. Second, we generate detailed body articulation and body-scene contact that aligns with the object geometry and interaction semantics. Lastly, we further refine the local body-scene contact by leveraging the inferred contact map.

To train and evaluate our method, we extend the PROX dataset [10] to the PROX-S dataset, which includes 3D instance segmentation, SMPL-X body estimation, and per-frame annotation of interaction semantics. Since there are no existing methods working on the same task of populating scenes with semantic control, we adapt PiGraph [31] and POSA [11] to this new task, and train their modified versions on the PROX-S dataset as baselines. Our perceptual study shows that our proposed method can generate realistic 3D human bodies in a 3D scene with semantic control, significantly outperforming those baselines.

In summary, our contributions are: (1) a novel compositional representation for interaction with semantics; (2) a generative model for synthesizing diverse and realistic human-scene interactions from semantic specifications; (3) a framework for composing atomic interactions to generate composite interactions; and (4) the extended human-scene interaction dataset PROX-S containing scene instance segmentation and per-frame interaction semantic annotation.

2 Related Work

Human-Scene Interaction Synthesis. Synthesizing human-scene interactions has been a challenging problem in the computer vision and graphics community. Various methods have been proposed to analyze object affordances and generate static human-scene interactions [6,8,12,15,17,30,31]. However, the realism of synthesized interactions from these methods is often limited by their oversimplified human body representations. The recently published PSI [46] uses the parametric body model SMPL-X [23] to put 3D human bodies into scenes, conditioned on scene semantic segmentation and depth map. In addition, geometric constraints are applied to resolve human-scene contact and penetration problems. PLACE [45] learns the human-scene proximity and contact in interactions to infer physically plausible humans in 3D scenes. POSA [11] proposes an egocentric contact feature map that encodes per-vertex contact distance and semantics information. A stochastic model is trained to predict contact feature maps given body meshes, with the predicted contact features guiding the body placement optimization in scenes. Wang et al. [40] generate human bodies at specified locations and orientations, conditioning on the point cloud of the scene and implicitly modeling the scene affordance. Concurrent work [41] first generates scene-agnostic body poses from actions and then places body into scene using POSA, which is similar to the POSA-I baseline we implement.

Apart from being realistic, semantic control is another important goal in synthesizing interactions. PiGraph [31] learns a probabilistic distribution for each annotated interaction category and synthesizes interactions by selecting the highest scoring samples of fitted categorical distribution. Conditional action synthesis methods [1,2,24] generate human motion conditioned on action categories or text descriptions while ignoring human-scene interaction. NSM [34] uses a mixture of experts modulated by the action category to generate human motion of seven predefined categories. SAMP [9] extends NSM by incorporating stochastic motion modeling and a GoalNet predicting possible interaction goals given scene objects and action categories. NSM and SAMP are limited in interaction semantics modeling since they can only model interactions with one single object or the surrounding environment as a whole. Our work, in contrast, models the compositional nature of interaction semantics and can generate composite interactions involving multiple objects simultaneously.

Human Behavior Semantics Modelling. Understanding human behavior is an important problem that has long received a significant amount of attention. Action recognition [13,14,32,37] classifies human activities into predefined action categories. Language driven pose and motion generation [1,2,35] incorporates natural languages that can represent more expressive and fine-grained action semantics. Human-object interaction detection [5,7,42] models interactions as triplets of (human, action, object), detecting humans and objects from images along with the relations between them.

One key observation is that humans can perform multiple actions simultaneously and such behaviors have composite semantics. Composite semantics are often modeled as the combination of basic semantic units, like how phrases are composed by words in natural languages. Semantic composition is termed as compound in linguistics [18,25] and studied in natural language processing [21,22,43]. PiGraph [31] describes composite human-scene interaction semantics with a set of (verb, noun) pairs. BABEL [26] uses natural language labels to annotate human motion capture data [3, 19, 20, 36, 38] and allow multiple descriptions existing in a single frame to model composite semantics. These works model semantics on the object category level and ignore the differences among instances of the same category. Our work goes beyond this limitation to model interaction semantics with specific object instances, which is critical for solving ambiguity in scenes with multiple objects of the same category.

3   Method

3.1   Preliminaries

Body Representation. We represent the 3D human body using a simplified SMPL-X model, consisting of vertex locations, triangle faces, and auxiliary per-vertex binary contact features, denoted as $\mathbf{B} = (\mathbf{V}, \mathbf{F}, \mathbf{C})$. For computational efficiency, we downsample the original SMPl-X mesh to have 655 vertices $\mathbf{V} \in \mathbb{R}^{655 \times 3}$ and 1296 faces $\mathbf{F} \in \{1 \cdots 655\}^{1296 \times 3}$ using the sampling method of [28]. The binary contact features $\mathbf{C} \in \{0, 1\}^{655}$ indicate whether each body vertex is in contact with scene objects [11]. Specifically, we consider a body vertex is in contact if its distance to scene objects is below a threshold value. We introduce the auxiliary contact features because human-object contact is a strong cue for interaction semantics, e.g., "touch" implies contact on hands. We use the contact features to further refine human-scene interaction in post-optimization.

3D Scene Representation. We represent a 3D scene as a set of object instances, denoted as $\mathbf{S} = \{o^i\}_{i=1}^{O}$ where O is the number of object instances. Each object instance $o^i \in \mathbb{R}^{8192 \times 9}$ is an oriented point cloud of 8192 points with attributes of location, color, and normal. We represent objects as point clouds to incorporate the geometry information and enable generalization to open-set objects that do not belong to predefined object categories, unlike previous works [11, 31, 46] that only use object category information. Moreover, the effect of intra-class object variance on interactions can be learned from the object geometry to improve fine-grained human-scene contacts.

Compositional Interaction Representation. Human-scene interactions involve three types of components: human bodies, actions, and objects. Inspired by the observation that humans can perform multiple interactions at the same time, we propose a compositional interaction representation $\mathbf{I} = (\mathbf{B}, \{(a^i, o^i)\}_{i=1}^{M})$, where $\mathbf{B}$ denotes the human body, and $\{(a^i, o^i)\}_{i=1}^{M}$ is a set of atomic interactions. We use the term atomic interaction to refer to the basic, irreducible building block for interaction semantics, and each atomic interaction (a^i, o^i) is a pair of a one-hot encoded action and an object instance, e.g., "sit on a chair". In addition, interactions can comprise more than one such atomic interaction unit, since one can simultaneously interact with multiple objects, e.g., "sit on a chair and type on a keyboard". We refer to such interactions consisting of more than one atomic interaction as composite interactions.

"Sit on the chair and touch the table"

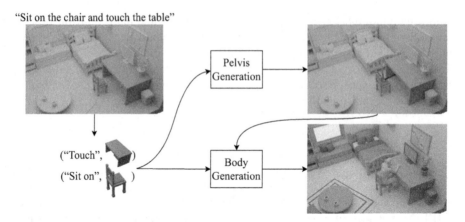

Fig. 2. Illustration of our COINS method for human-scene interaction synthesis with semantic control. Given a 3D scene and semantic specifications of actions (e.g., "sit on", "touch") paired with object instances (highlighted with color), COINS first generates a plausible human pelvis location and orientation and then generates the detailed body.

3.2 Interaction Synthesis with Semantic Control

Synthesizing interactions with semantic control requires generating human bodies interacting with given scene objects in a natural and semantically correct way. Specifically, given a scene S and interaction semantics specified as $\{(a^i, o^i)\}_{i=1}^{M}$, the task is to generate a human body $\mathbf{B}$ that perceptually satisfies the constraints of performing action a^i with object o^i.

We propose a multi-stage method for interaction synthesis with semantic control as illustrated in Fig. 2. Given interaction semantics specified as action-object pairs, we first infer possible pelvis locations and orientations. Then we transform objects to the generated pelvis coordinate frame and sample body and contact map in the local space. We separately train two transformer-based conditional VAE (cVAE) [16,33] models for pelvis and body generation, and name them as PelvisVAE and BodyVAE respectively. Lastly, we apply an interaction-based optimization that is guided by contact features to refine the generated interactions.

Architecture. We propose a transformer-based conditional variational auto-encoder (cVAE) architecture that can handle the heterogeneous inputs of our compositional interaction representation containing body mesh vertices, object points without predefined topology, and interaction semantics. Specifically, object points and body vertices are represented as token inputs to the transformer, and learnable action embeddings are added to paired object tokens as positional encoding.

The BodyVAE architecture is illustrated in Fig. 3. The PelvisVAE shares a similar architecture and we refer readers to the Supp. Mat. for illustration.

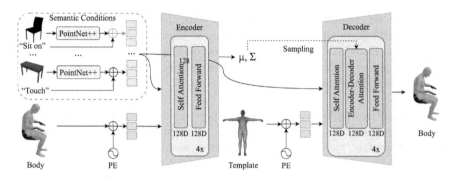

Fig. 3. Illustration of BodyVAE architecture. Human body and objects are represented as tokens of the transformers while each action category is mapped to a learnable embedding and added to the corresponding object tokens. Modules within the dashed box are the semantic conditions of a varying number of action-object pairs. We denote addition with $\oplus$ and positional encoding with "PE". We visualize vertices with positive contact features as blue on the body mesh.

Our cVAE networks take varying numbers of action-object pairs as conditional inputs. Each action category is mapped to a learnable embedding, and each object point cloud is first converted to 256 local keypoints using PointNet++ [27]. The action embedding is then added to the tokens of the paired object as positional encoding. Compared to treating actions as separate tokens [24], encoding actions into the positional encoding for object tokens can regulate each action to only affect the paired object, e.g., the action "sit on" is only related to the sofa, but not the table, in the example of Fig. 3. The human body input comprises mesh vertices with location and auxiliary contact features. We apply a linear layer to map vertices to tokens and vertex index based positional encoding to encode body topology.

The transformer encoder maps input interactions into a latent space and the decoder predicts human bodies with contact features from conditional action-object pairs and the sampled latent code. On top of the encoder transformer network, we apply average pooling on the output human tokens followed by a linear layer to predict the latent normal distribution. At the decoder, we use a template body with person-dependent shape parameters for body tokens. Using the personalized template body makes our model generalize to different body shapes and enables explicit control of the body shape. The sampled latent code is used for keys and values of the encoder-decoder attention layers [39].

BodyVAE shares the same transformer-based architecture and the same conditional input of action-object pairs as PelvisVAE. There are mainly two differences between BodyVAE and PelvisVAE. First, BodyVAE represents a human as a body mesh with contact features, while PelvisVAE represents a human as the pelvis joint location and orientation. Second, all input objects are in the scene coordinate frame in PelvisVAE while input objects are transformed to the local pelvis coordinate frame in BodyVAE.

To make our sampled bodies compatible with the SMPL-X body model and ensure a valid body shape, we jointly train a Multi-Layer Perceptron (MLP) [29] with the BodyVAE to regress the corresponding SMPL-X body parameters from the sampled body meshes. We refer to the Supp. Mat. for more details on architecture and the training losses.

Interaction-Based Optimization. Our model is trained with the pseudo ground truth body estimation [10,44], which does not guarantee natural human-scene contact. Therefore, the generated interactions can also be unnatural. We follow [11,45,46] to apply interaction-based optimization to refine the interactions. We use generated SMPL-X parameters as initialization and optimize body translation t, global orientation R and pose θ. The optimization objective is given by:

$$E(t, R, \theta) = \mathcal{L}_{interaction} + \mathcal{L}_{coll} + \mathcal{L}_{reg}, \tag{1}$$

where $\mathcal{L}_{interaction}$ encourages body vertices with positive contact features to have zero distance to objects, $\mathcal{L}_{coll}$ is the scene SDF based collision term defined in [46], and the $\mathcal{L}_{reg}$ term penalizes t, R and θ deviating from the initialization. We refer to the Supp. Mat. for detailed definitions.

3.3   Compositional Interaction Generation

Compositional interaction generation aims to generate composite interactions using models trained only on atomic interactions. Compositional interaction generation reflects the compositional nature of interaction semantics and can save the need to collect composite interaction data. Although our transformer-based generative model can synthesize bodies given composite interaction semantics, e.g. "sit on the sofa and touch the wall", it requires collecting data and training for all composite interactions we want to synthesize. However, collecting composite interaction data is exponentially more expensive than atomic interactions considering the vast possible combinations of atomic interactions. Therefore, it is desirable to have an automatic way to generate composite interactions requiring only atomic interaction data.

To that end, we propose a simple yet effective two-step approach to generating composite interactions using models trained only on atomic interactions: (1) Compositional pelvis generation, where we formulate the task of generating pelvis frames given composite interaction semantics as finding the intersection of pelvis distributions of atomic interactions. (2) Compositional body generation, where we leverage attention masks derived from contact statistics in transformer inference to compose atomic interactions at the body parts level.

Compositional Pelvis Generation. We formulate compositional pelvis generation as finding the intersection of pelvis distributions of component atomic interactions. Using our PelvisVAE trained for atomic interactions, we can decode the prior standard Gaussian distribution to distributions of plausible pelvis frames given atomic interaction semantics. Each component atomic interaction of a composite interaction determines a pelvis frame distribution in scenes, and intuitively the plausible pelvis of the composite interaction should lie in the intersection of all pelvis distributions. Therefore, we propose a compositional pelvis generation method where we sample pelvis frames for each atomic interaction, optimize all pelvis frames to be close in space, and average the optimized pelvis frames as the generated composite pelvis frame.

Specifically, we denote the decoder of the PelvisVAE as a function $\mathcal{G}(z^i|a^i, o^i)$ mapping a latent code z^i to a pelvis frame conditioned on the action-object pair of (a^i, o^i), we obtain the final pelvis frame from the composition of M atomic interactions from the following optimization problem:

$$\tilde{Z} = \underset{Z=\{z^i\}_{i=1}^M}{\arg\min} \sum_{1 \leq i < M} \sum_{i < j \leq M} \left| \mathcal{G}(z^i|a^i, o^i) - \mathcal{G}(z^j|a^j, o^j) \right| - \lambda \sum_{1 \leq i \leq M} log(p(z^i)),$$

(2)

Z denotes the set of M randomly sampled latent codes for M component atomic interactions, and λ is a tunable weight. The initial values of the latent codes are randomly sampled from the prior distribution. The motivation is to optimize the latent codes of M component atomic interactions to make their decoded pelvis frames as close as possible in the scene while maintaining high probabilities in each component pelvis distribution. We take the average of the M optimized component pelvis frames as the sampled composite pelvis frame.

Compositional Body Generation. For compositional body generation, we use the attention mechanism of transformer networks to compose atomic interactions at body part level. Although we use BodyVAE trained only on atomic interaction data, we can input more than one atomic interaction and achieve compositional body generation with additional attention masks derived from contact statistics.

Our method is inspired by the observation from contact probability statistics that interaction semantics can often be determined by contact on certain body parts instead of the whole body, e.g., sitting is characterized by contact around the hip area. Specifically, we calculate the per-vertex contact probability for each action using training data. The vertex contact probability for one action is defined as the ratio of the number of positive contact features of the vertex and the number of all contact features of the vertex in the interaction data of the specified action. Heatmap visualization of such categorical contact statistics is shown in Fig. 4. High contact probability indicates a high correlation between the body vertex area and action semantics.

Inspired by the observed action-part correlation, we propose leveraging the attention mechanism to compose atomic interactions according to three body parts: upper limbs, lower limbs, and torso. Given composite interaction semantics for body generation, we calculate the sum of contact probability at each part for each action. If the sum of contact probability of one action at one body part exceeds those of other actions by a threshold, we mask the attention between the

"Lie on"-Side   "Lie on"-Bottom   "Sit on"-Side   "Sit on"-Bottom

Fig. 4. Visualization of per-vertex contact probability for two actions from the side and bottom views. Brighter colors indicate higher contact probability with objects. We randomly sample a pose within the action category for visualization.

Fig. 5. Illustration of the PROX-S dataset. From left to right, it shows the RGB image, 3D scene reconstruction with instance segmentation, and the fitted SMPL-X human body with per-frame interaction semantic labels.

part and all other atomic interactions to be zero. Taking the composite interaction "sit on chair and touch table" as an example, touching has a significantly greater sum of contact probability on upper limbs so the attention between upper limb tokens and chair (objects not paired with touching) tokens will be masked as zero.

We input such attention masks and component atomic interactions to the transformer for compositional body generation. The derived attention masks can naturally compose the component atomic interactions via BodyVAE.

4   Experiments

4.1   Dataset

We annotate a new dataset called PROX-S on top of the PROX [10] dataset to evaluate interaction synthesis with semantic control since there is no existing dataset suitable for this task. The PROX-S dataset contains (1) 3D instance segmentation of all 12 PROX scenes; (2) 3D human body reconstructions within the scenes; and (3) per-frame interaction semantic labels in the form of action-object pairs, as shown in Fig. 5. We refer to the Supp. Mat. for the detailed process description and statistics.

4.2   Evaluation Metrics

Semantic Contact. Compared to the semantics-agnostic body-scene contact score used in [46], we propose a semantic contact score to evaluate whether the generated interactions adhere to the semantic specifications characterized by proper body-scene contact. Using the action-specific body vertex contact probability introduced in Sect. 3.3 as weights, we calculate a weighted sum of binary contact features for each body in the training data and name the sum as the semantic contact score. This action-dependent semantic contact score reflects how body contact features align with the semantics of one action. We use the 20 percentile semantic contact score of training data bodies as the threshold score for each action to filter low-quality training interaction data with inaccurate contact. When evaluating a generated interaction sample, we calculate the weighted sum of contact features and compare it to the action-specific threshold score. The semantic contact score is one if the sum is higher than the threshold and zero otherwise.

Physical Plausibility. We evaluate the physical plausibility of generated interactions using the non-collision metric from [4,11,45,46]. It is calculated as the ratio of the number of body vertices with non-negative scene SDF values and the number of all body vertices.

Diversity. Following [46], we perform K-Means clustering to cluster the SMPL-X parameters of generated bodies into 50 clusters and evaluate the diversity using the entropy of the cluster ID histogram and the mean distance to cluster centers.

Perceptual Study. We evaluate the perceptual realism and semantic accuracy of generated human-scene interactions by conducting perceptual studies on Amazon Mechanical Turk (AMT). We perform a binary-choice perceptual study where samples of the same interaction semantics from different sources are shown and the turkers are asked to choose the more natural one. For semantic accuracy, we instruct the turkers to rate the consistency between shown interaction samples and semantic labels from 1 (strongly disagree) to 5 (strongly agree). For more details regarding the perceptual studies, please refer to the Supp. Mat.

4.3   Baselines

There is no existing method that directly applies to the problem of generating 3D human bodies given a 3D scene and interaction semantics. Therefore, we modify two state-of-the-art interaction synthesis methods for our tasks and train their models using the same PROX-S dataset.

PiGraph-X. PiGraph [31] is the most related work to our knowledges, which simultaneously generates scene placement and human skeletons from interaction category specifications. We remove the scene placement step of the original paper and replace the skeleton body representation with the more realistic SMPL-X

Table 1. Binary realism perceptual study.

(a) Interaction Synthesis with Semantic Control.

% users rated as "more realistic"	
Ours	POSA-I
63.8 %	36.2 %
Ours	PiGraph-X
79.7 %	20.3 %
Ours	PseudoGT
45.3 %	**54.7** %

(b) Interaction Synthesis via Semantic Composition.

% users rated as "more realistic"	
Ours-C	PiGraph-X-C
81.2 %	18.2 %
Ours-C	PseudoGT
42.4 %	**57.6** %

body model. We refer to this modified PiGraph variant as PiGraph-X. For compositional interaction generation, we extend PiGraph by sampling basic bodies from all comprised atomic interactions and using the average similarity score to those atomic interactions. We denote this PiGraph extension as PiGraph-X-C.

POSA-I. POSA [11] generates human-scene interactions using optimization guided by per-vertex contact features. However, POSA lacks global control of the generated contact features and cannot generate human bodies conditioned on interaction semantics. To incorporate global semantics of human-scene interaction, we modify POSA to generate human bodies with vertex-level contact features from interaction semantics in the format of action-noun pairs. We denote the semantic-controllable POSA variant as POSA-I.

4.4   Interaction Synthesis with Semantic Control

We evaluate the synthesized interactions in terms of perceptual realism, perceptual semantic accuracy, semantic contact, physical plausibility, and diversity. Table 1 and 2 show the results of the perceptual studies on binary realism and other quantitative metrics, respectively. Our method significantly outperforms the baselines in the binary realism study and even comes close to the body poses reconstructed from the real human-scene interactions, which we consider as the pseudo ground truth. Our method also achieves higher perceptual semantic ratings than all the baselines. Quantitatively, our method achieves the highest semantic contact score (0.93) which significantly outperforms the baselines. Our method performs comparably on physical plausibility as POSA-I and significantly better than PiGraph-X. For diversity metrics, our method has a larger cluster entropy and smaller cluster size compared to the baselines. We observe more frequent unnatural interaction samples from PiGraph-X and POSA-I, which accounts for their larger cluster sizes. Note that our method is a generative pipeline where we evaluate every randomly sampled result, while both baselines need to search thousands of samples of global placement in scenes.

We show the qualitative comparison of interactions generated from ours and two baselines in Fig. 6. PiGraph-X naively models the human body as independent joints and therefore suffers from unnatural body poses, poor human-scene contact, and penetration. POSA-I generates bodies with physically plausible

Table 2. Evaluation of semantics, physical plausibility and diversity.

	Semantic accuracy	Semantic contact	Non-collision	Entropy	Cluster size	Samples
PiGraph-X	3.90 ± 0.93	0.84	0.85	3.67	1.07	25K
POSA-I	4.03 ± 0.85	0.67	**0.98**	3.75	**1.08**	$> 1K$
Ours	**4.17 ± 0.71**	**0.93**	0.97	**3.77**	0.83	1

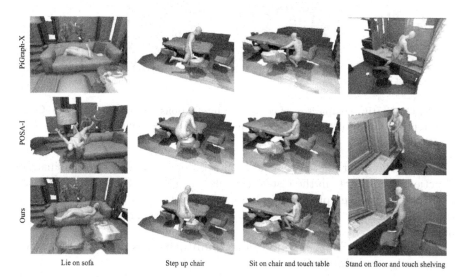

Lie on sofa   Step up chair   Sit on chair and touch table   Stand on floor and touch shelving

Fig. 6. Qualitative comparison of interactions generated with our method and two baselines. Each row shows interactions generated from one method. From left to right, the columns correspond to different interaction semantics of "lying on the sofa", "stepping up on the chair", "sitting on the chair and touching the table", and "standing on the floor and touching the shelving".

interactions, but since it needs to find plausible body placement in the scene, its optimization can easily get stuck at local minimums that are not semantically accurate and have inferior human-scene contact. In contrast, our method learns how humans interact with objects given different interaction semantics and generates realistic interactions that are both physically plausible and human-like.

4.5   Compositional Interaction Generation

We conduct the same evaluation for novel composite interaction generation as introduced in Sect. 4.4. We compare our method to the PiGraph-X-C extension for compositional interaction generation. POSA-I is not included in this part since it can not be easily extended for semantic composition. In the forced-alternative-choice (binary-choice) perceptual study (Table 1 (b)), our method significantly outperforms the baseline. The semantic accuracy, semantic contact, non-collision and diversity comparisons are shown in Table 3. Our method achieves significantly better semantic accuracy, physical plausibility, and sample

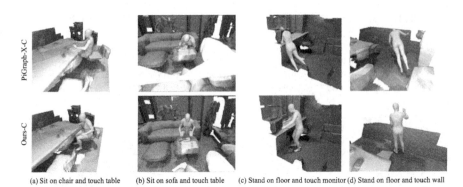

(a) Sit on chair and touch table   (b) Sit on sofa and touch table   (c) Stand on floor and touch monitor (d) Stand on floor and touch wall

Fig. 7. Qualitative comparison of composite interactions generated using ours-C and PiGraph-X-C. Each row shows interactions generated from one method.

efficiency. The slight inferior semantic contact score is because the combinations of actions and objects in the test scenes may not always afford natural contact, like touching an incomplete wall in Fig. 7 (d). Touching the wall and floor simultaneously generates higher contact scores but perceptually unnatural poses to humans.

We refer to the Supp. Mat. for **more qualitative results, failures, ablation study, and limitations.**

Table 3. Evaluation of semantics, physical plausibility and diversity for novel compositional interaction generation.

	Semantic accuracy	Semantic contact	Non-collision	Entropy	Cluster size	Samples
PiGraph-X-C	3.88 ± 1.15	**0.80**	0.84	3.72	**1.09**	25K
Ours-C	**3.95 ± 1.18**	0.76	**0.98**	**3.80**	0.68	1

5   Conclusion

In this paper, we introduce a method to generate humans interacting with 3D scenes given interaction semantics as action-object pairs. We propose a compositional interaction representation and transformer-based VAE models to stochastically generate human-scene interactions. We further explored generating composite interactions by composing atomic interactions, which does not demand training on composite interaction data. Our method is a step towards creating virtual avatars interacting with 3D scenes.

Acknowledgements. We sincerely acknowledge the anonymous reviewers for their insightful suggestions. We thank Francis Engelmann for help with scene segmentation and proofreading, and Siwei Zhang for providing body fitting results. This work was supported by the SNF grant 200021 204840

References

1. Ahn, H., Ha, T., Choi, Y., Yoo, H., Oh, S.: Text2action: generative adversarial synthesis from language to action. In: Proceedings of ICRA. IEEE (2018)
2. Ahuja, C., Morency, L.P.: Language2pose: natural language grounded pose forecasting. In: Proceedings of 3DV. IEEE (2019)
3. Akhter, I., Black, M.J.: Pose-conditioned joint angle limits for 3d human pose reconstruction. In: Proceedings of CVPR (2015)
4. Engelmann, F., Rematas, K., Leibe, B., Ferrari, V.: From points to multi-object 3D reconstruction. In: Proceedings of CVPR (2021)
5. Gkioxari, G., Girshick, R., Dollár, P., He, K.: Detecting and recognizing human-object interactions. In: Proceedings of CVPR (2018)
6. Grabner, H., Gall, J., Van Gool, L.: What makes a chair a chair? In: Proceedings of CVPR. IEEE (2011)
7. Gupta, A., Kembhavi, A., Davis, L.S.: Observing human-object interactions: using spatial and functional compatibility for recognition. IEEE Trans. Pattern Anal. Mach. Intell. **31**, 1775–1789 (2009)
8. Gupta, A., Satkin, S., Efros, A.A., Hebert, M.: From 3d scene geometry to human workspace. In: Proceedings of CVPR. IEEE (2011)
9. Hassan, M., et al.: Stochastic scene-aware motion prediction. In: Proceedings of ICCV (2021)
10. Hassan, M., Choutas, V., Tzionas, D., Black, M.J.: Resolving 3D human pose ambiguities with 3D scene constraints. In: Proceedings of ICCV (2019)
11. Hassan, M., Ghosh, P., Tesch, J., Tzionas, D., Black, M.J.: Populating 3D scenes by learning human-scene interaction. In: Proceedings of CVPR (2021)
12. Hu, R., et al.: Predictive and generative neural networks for object functionality. arXiv preprint. arXiv:2006.15520 (2020)
13. Ji, S., Xu, W., Yang, M., Yu, K.: 3d convolutional neural networks for human action recognition. IEEE Trans. Pattern Anal. Mach. Intell. **35**(1), 221–231 (2012)
14. Kay, W., et al.: The kinetics human action video dataset. arXiv preprint. arXiv:1705.06950 (2017)
15. Kim, V.G., Chaudhuri, S., Guibas, L.J., Funkhouser, T.: Shape2pose: human-centric shape analysis. In: ACM Transactions on Graphics, (Proceedings SIGGRAPH) (2014)
16. Kingma, D.P., Welling, M.: Auto-encoding variational bayes. arXiv preprint. arXiv:1312.6114 (2013)
17. Li, X., Liu, S., Kim, K., Wang, X., Yang, M.H., Kautz, J.: Putting humans in a scene: learning affordance in 3d indoor environments. In: Proceedings of CVPR (2019)
18. Lieber, R., Stekauer, P.: The Oxford Handbook of Compounding (2011)
19. Mahmood, N., Ghorbani, N., Troje, N.F., Pons-Moll, G., Black, M.J.: AMASS: archive of motion capture as surface shapes. In: Proceedings of ICCV (2019)
20. Mandery, C., Terlemez, O., Do, M., Vahrenkamp, N., Asfour, T.: The kit whole-body human motion database. In: Proceedings of ICAR (2015)
21. Mineshima, K., Martínez-Gómez, P., Miyao, Y., Bekki, D.: Higher-order logical inference with compositional semantics. In: Proceedings of the 2015 Conference on Empirical Methods in Natural Language Processing (2015)
22. Mitchell, J., Lapata, M.: Vector-based models of semantic composition. In: Proceedings of ACL (2008)

23. Pavlakos, G., et al.: Expressive body capture: 3d hands, face, and body from a single image. In: Proceedings of CVPR (2019)
24. Petrovich, M., Black, M.J., Varol, G.: Action-conditioned 3d human motion synthesis with transformer vae. In: Proceedings of ICCV (2021)
25. Plag, I.: Word-formation in English. Cambridge University Press, Cambridge (2018)
26. Punnakkal, A.R., Chandrasekaran, A., Athanasiou, N., Quiros-Ramirez, A., Black, M.J.: BABEL: bodies, action and behavior with english labels. In: Proceedings of CVPR (2021)
27. Qi, C.R., Yi, L., Su, H., Guibas, L.J.: Pointnet++: deep hierarchical feature learning on point sets in a metric space. arXiv preprint. arXiv:1706.02413 (2017)
28. Ranjan, A., Bolkart, T., Sanyal, S., Black, M.J.: Generating 3D faces using convolutional mesh autoencoders. In: Ferrari, V., Hebert, M., Sminchisescu, C., Weiss, Y. (eds.) ECCV 2018. LNCS, vol. 11207, pp. 725–741. Springer, Cham (2018). https://doi.org/10.1007/978-3-030-01219-9_43
29. Rumelhart, D.E., Hinton, G.E., Williams, R.J.: Learning internal representations by error propagation. California Univ San Diego La Jolla Inst for Cognitive Science. Technical report (1985)
30. Savva, M., Chang, A.X., Hanrahan, P., Fisher, M., Nießner, M.: Scenegrok: inferring action maps in 3d environments. In: ACM Transactions on Graphics (TOG), (Proceedings SIGGRAPH), vol. 33, no. 6, pp. 1–10 (2014)
31. Savva, M., Chang, A.X., Hanrahan, P., Fisher, M., Nießner, M.: PiGraphs: learning interaction snapshots from observations. In: ACM Transactions on Graphics, (Proceedings SIGGRAPH), vol. 35, no. 4 (2016)
32. Simonyan, K., Zisserman, A.: Two-stream convolutional networks for action recognition in videos. In: Proceedings of NeurIPS (2014)
33. Sohn, K., Lee, H., Yan, X.: Learning structured output representation using deep conditional generative models. In: Proceedings of NeurIPS (2015)
34. Starke, S., Zhang, H., Komura, T., Saito, J.: Neural state machine for character-scene interactions. In: ACM Transactions Graphics (ACM SIGGRAPH Asia) (2019)
35. Tevet, G., Gordon, B., Hertz, A., Bermano, A.H., Cohen-Or, D.: Motionclip: exposing human motion generation to clip space. arXiv preprint. arXiv:2203.08063 (2022)
36. De la Torre, F., Hodgins, J., Bargteil, A., Martin, X., Macey, J., Collado, A., Beltran, P.: Guide to the carnegie mellon university multimodal activity (cmu-mmac) database (2009)
37. Tran, D., Wang, H., Torresani, L., Ray, J., LeCun, Y., Paluri, M.: A closer look at spatiotemporal convolutions for action recognition. In: Proceedings of CVPR (2018)
38. Troje, N.F.: Decomposing biological motion: a framework for analysis and synthesis of human gait patterns. J. Vis. **2**, 371–387 (2002)
39. Vaswani, A., et al.: Attention is all you need. In: Proceedings of NeurIPS (2017)
40. Wang, J., Xu, H., Xu, J., Liu, S., Wang, X.: Synthesizing long-term 3d human motion and interaction in 3d scenes. In: Proceedings of CVPR (2021)
41. Wang, J., Rong, Y., Liu, J., Yan, S., Lin, D., Dai, B.: Towards diverse and natural scene-aware 3d human motion synthesis. In: Proceedings of CVPR (2022)
42. Yao, B., Fei-Fei, L.: Modeling mutual context of object and human pose in human-object interaction activities. In: Proceedings of CVPR (2010)

43. Yin, D., Meng, T., Chang, K.W.: Sentibert: a transferable transformer-based architecture for compositional sentiment semantics. arXiv preprint. arXiv:2005.04114 (2020)
44. Zhang, S., Zhang, Y., Bogo, F., Marc, P., Tang, S.: Learning motion priors for 4d human body capture in 3d scenes. In: Proceedings of ICCV (2021)
45. Zhang, S., Zhang, Y., Ma, Q., Black, M.J., Tang, S.: PLACE: Proximity learning of articulation and contact in 3D environments. In: Proceedings of 3DV (2020)
46. Zhang, Y., Hassan, M., Neumann, H., Black, M.J., Tang, S.: Generating 3d people in scenes without people. In: Proceedings of CVPR (2020)

PressureVision: Estimating Hand Pressure from a Single RGB Image

Patrick Grady[1]($\boxtimes$) ⓘ, Chengcheng Tang[2] ⓘ, Samarth Brahmbhatt[3] ⓘ,
Christopher D. Twigg[2] ⓘ, Chengde Wan[2] ⓘ, James Hays[1] ⓘ,
and Charles C. Kemp[1] ⓘ

[1] Georgia Institute of Technology, Atlanta, USA
patrick.grady@gatech.edu
[2] Meta Reality Labs, San Francisco, USA
[3] Intel Labs, Santa Clara, USA

Abstract. People often interact with their surroundings by applying pressure with their hands. While hand pressure can be measured by placing pressure sensors between the hand and the environment, doing so can alter contact mechanics, interfere with human tactile perception, require costly sensors, and scale poorly to large environments. We explore the possibility of using a conventional RGB camera to infer hand pressure, enabling machine perception of hand pressure from uninstrumented hands and surfaces. The central insight is that the application of pressure by a hand results in informative appearance changes. Hands share biomechanical properties that result in similar observable phenomena, such as soft-tissue deformation, blood distribution, hand pose, and cast shadows. We collected videos of 36 participants with diverse skin tone applying pressure to an instrumented planar surface. We then trained a deep model (PressureVisionNet) to infer a pressure image from a single RGB image. Our model infers pressure for participants outside of the training data and outperforms baselines. We also show that the output of our model depends on the appearance of the hand and cast shadows near contact regions. Overall, our results suggest the appearance of a previously unobserved human hand can be used to accurately infer applied pressure.

1 Introduction

Humans often interact with their surroundings by applying pressure with their hands. Given the importance of hand pressure, methods that enable the machine perception of this quantity could have broad applications. Traditionally, measuring the pressure a hand exerts has been accomplished with physical sensors that sit between the hand and contact surface. This includes sensors worn on the hand, such as pressure-sensitive gloves, and sensors mounted to the environment, such as arrays of pressure sensors (Fig. 1).

Data, code, and models are available online (https://github.com/facebookresearch/pressurevision).

Supplementary Information The online version contains supplementary material available at https://doi.org/10.1007/978-3-031-20068-7_19.

ⓒ The Author(s), under exclusive license to Springer Nature Switzerland AG 2022
S. Avidan et al. (Eds.): ECCV 2022, LNCS 13666, pp. 328–345, 2022.
https://doi.org/10.1007/978-3-031-20068-7_19

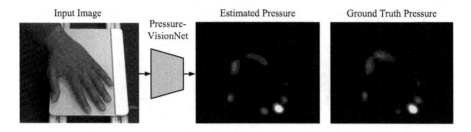

Fig. 1. PressureVisionNet takes an RGB image as input and outputs a pressure image with estimates of pressure applied by the hand to a planar surface. Each pixel of the pressure image is an estimate of hand pressure for the corresponding pixel in the RGB image. Black, purple, and yellow represent zero, low, and high pressure.

While physical sensors are accurate and robust, they have drawbacks. Sensors between the hand and the environment alter surface properties, changing appearance and interfering with contact mechanics relevant to human manipulation and tactile sensing. Sensors attached to hands can also be uncomfortable. Sensors mounted to environments require large numbers of sensing elements to cover modest areas, such tabletops, at high resolution and can be difficult to apply to varied surfaces.

Cameras have the potential to economically cover surfaces with virtual pressure sensors at high spatial resolution and do so without requiring the application of cumbersome instrumentation. Much like markerless pose estimation has enabled new applications by inferring human kinematics from RGB images, *visual hand pressure estimation* has the potential to be widely applied. For example, modern augmented and virtual reality headsets have cameras that could be used to perceive hand pressure, turning a wall into a giant touchscreen, or a tabletop into piano keyboard.

As a first step towards general visual hand pressure estimation, we investigate the feasibility of estimating hand pressure from RGB images under controlled conditions. To the best of our knowledge, our work is the first to demonstrate the feasibility of this approach. In particular, we address two critical questions: 1) Can appearance-based inference estimate hand pressure? 2) Can visual hand pressure inference generalize to previously unseen hands from a diverse population? We use a planar pressure sensing array to measure ground truth pressure during natural interactions from 36 participants with diverse skin tones.

We developed PressureVisionNet to infer hand pressure from a single RGB image. PressureVisionNet performed well with unseen participants, providing evidence that the visual signals used for pressure estimation are shared across people. Our sensitivity analysis also indicates that PressureVisionNet relies on the appearance of the hand close to regions of contact, where we expect applied pressure to most influence hand appearance. Similarly, PressureVisionNet performs poorly at estimating pressure for visually occluded parts of the hand. We also provide a demonstration of PressureVisionNet inferring plausible pressure given conditions outside of the training data. Our demonstrations involve a

No Contact   Low Force   High Force

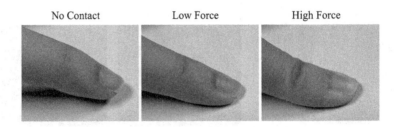

Fig. 2. Fingers display visible cues indicative of applied pressure. In the no-contact case, shadows are diffuse and the finger can be less sharp due to motion blur. As the finger makes contact, the skin at the fingertip loses color, the distal joint hyperextends, the texture of the skin changes, and the finger pad expands.

smartphone camera observing an uninstrumented tabletop with ambient office lighting being contacted by people outside of the training set.

Our central insight is that hands display subtle visual cues that indicate the presence of pressure. As the hand applies pressure to a surface, the surface applies equal and opposite pressure to the hand. As such, the hand itself can serve as a physical probe that changes in predictable ways when pressure is applied to it, and the camera can observe this probe from a distance to infer the associated pressure. The shape of the hand can also result in informative shadows cast on the surface.

Hands are complex, non-rigid appendages with multiple types of soft tissues and fluids surrounding an interior skeleton that is often modeled as having 27 degrees of freedom. Pressure applied to the hand deforms tissues, moves fluids, and changes the configuration of the joints. The active application of pressure also involves contraction of hand muscles and tensile force applied by muscles in the forearm via tendons. These biomechanical processes result in changes to the appearance of the hand in visible light, including changes to surface geometry, color, and texture (Fig. 2).

In summary, our paper makes the following contributions:

– We propose a novel task, *visual hand pressure estimation.*
– We present PressureVisionNet and show that it can infer hand pressure from a single RGB image and generalize to new people.
– We release PressureVisionDB, a dataset of 36 participants with paired pressure and image data.
– We release our trained models and code.

2   Related Work

Physical Sensors for Force Measurement. Sensors to directly measure the force that a hand exerts generally fall into two categories: sensors on the hand and sensors on the surface being touched. Gloves instrumented with flexible force sensors can directly measure the force that the hand exerts [7,54]. While sensors on the hand work for a wide range of objects, they can inhibit natural manipulation, reduce the person's tactile sensation, and often do not cover the entire hand. Commercially available systems are also expensive [46,56].

Alternatively, objects can be instrumented to capture force information [2, 6, 39, 45]. While these methods can accurately measure pressure, they change the properties of the surfaces they cover, can be challenging to mount on curved surfaces, and scale poorly to larger surfaces.

A variety of fingertip pressure sensors have been developed for robotic grippers. These internal sensors sometimes observe the deformation of a soft exterior [58,65] or monitor an internal fluid [59].

Inferring Contact and Force from Vision. One class of methods uses physics to infer the contact forces given the contact points and object trajectory. Methods proposed to determine the contact points include neural networks [17,34] or by combining markerless tracking of the hands with mesh-object intersection [44,45,47]. These methods complement our own because they can infer contact that is occluded or out-of-view, but methods that rely on the accelerations of hand-held objects cannot generalize to interactions with relatively immobile surfaces like tables.

Additional work studies force application in general human-environment interactions such as sitting and standing [52,68,69]. Clever *et al.* use depth data to regress the amount of pressure between a human at rest and a mattress [12]. They use a neural network to estimate the pose of a body on the bed in addition to pressure.

Predicting Pressure Using Hand and Surface Appearance. As the hand applies force, blood in the surrounding tissue is displaced. This effect is visible at the fingertip and underneath the fingernail, where a whitening of the tissue can be observed. Various techniques have been proposed to estimate fingertip force using optical sensors focused on this effect [9,36,37].

The soft tissue in the palm and pads of the fingers deforms under applied force [43]. This deformation is accompanied by expansion in other areas, often visible as a widening of the pads of the fingers. Hwang *et al.* [30] use surface deformation to infer contact force, but support only unoccluded point contacts. Johnson *et al.* [31] use the deformation of the hand to perform a high-resolution reconstruction of the object surface.

Cast shadows provide important cues in human perception of depth in a 3D scene [26,27,29]. Researchers have used visual observations of shadows for closed-loop control of a robot [18].

It has additionally been demonstrated that videos of faces can be used to identify if participants are squeezing an object tightly [1].

Amplifying Imperceptible Visual Cues. Various techniques have been presented to extract subtle cues from images or video which are typically not noticed by the human eye. Wu *et al.* present Eulerian Video Magnification [60]. They magnify periodic signals to make them clearly visible, including minute changes in skin color due to bloodflow. Davis *et al.* [14] are able to amplify tiny subpixel vibrations in videos to reconstruct audio from visual data.

Contact for Grasping and Pose Estimation. Contact between hands and objects is important for grasping and manipulation. Estimating where contact should occur is often a first step for planning a robotic grasp [4,10,50,51] or creating anthropomorphic animation [32,64,67]. For pose estimation during hand-object interaction [19,21], using contact to enforce consistency between hands and objects improves pose plausibility and accuracy [20,22,23,48,57]. In a broader context, contact is used when reasoning about people interacting with the surrounding environment [11,25,40,53,68].

Contact for Human-Computer Interaction. Detecting contact with ordinary surfaces can be useful for building human-computer interfaces. MRTouch [61] uses depth data to identify touches on flat surfaces for the Microsoft HoloLens. The method first fits a 3D plane to the wall or tabletop surface and thresholds the distance between the plane and the fingertip. TapID [38] uses subtle accelerations from a pair of IMU sensors on the wrist to detect contact between fingers and surfaces. TouchAnywhere [41] detects touch via heuristics by estimating the intersection between finger and its shadow, but only detects binary contact and does not include pressure ground truth.

Table 1. Datasets for contact between hands and surfaces: GRAB [55] infers dynamic contact via geometric models and marker-based motion capture. TactileGloves [54] measures dynamic pressure with a sensorized glove. ContactDB [3] and ContactPose [5] measure static contact via thermal imaging. Ours, PressureVisionDB, measures pressure with a sensorized plane and provides registered and synchronized RGB images.

	Diverse surfaces	Bare hands	Images	Pressure
GRAB [55]	✓	✗	✗	✗
TactileGloves [54]	✓	✗	✗	✓
ContactDB [3]	✓	✓	✗	✗
ContactPose [5]	✓	✓	✓	✗
PressureVisionDB (Ours)	✗	✓	✓	✓

Hand-Object Contact Datasets. GRAB [55] uses optical motion capture to capture hand and object pose and indirectly infers contact using mesh proximity. ContactDB [3] measures high-resolution contact on a variety of objects. After participants grasp an object, the thermal imprint from the hand is measured from the object surface using a thermal camera. ContactPose [5] adds paired images, object poses, and hand poses to ContactDB. ContactDB and ContactPose do not provide pressure measurements and only provide contact for static grasps.

As shown in Table 1, our dataset is unique compared with these datasets, providing RGB images paired with high-resolution, dynamic pressure images.

3   The PressureVisionDB Dataset

We collected PressureVisionDB, a novel dataset of bare hands interacting with a pressure-sensitive object. The dataset includes 16 h of data collected from 36 participants with pressure data and RGB images from four synchronized cameras, totalling 64 h of RGB video data.

3.1   The Capture Setup

We assemble a rigid frame to which we attached cameras, lights, and a pressure sensing surface (Fig. 3a). Participants reached through one side of the cube-shaped frame to place their hands on the planar sensing surface.

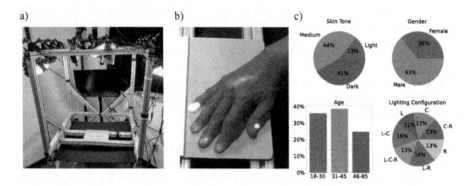

Fig. 3. a) The data capture rig used to collect PressureVisionDB. Participants reach into the front opening to make contact with the elevated pressure sensor. b) The sensorized plane records a pressure image, which is projected into image space for training and evaluation. Pressure is visualized as bright blue regions. c) PressureVisionDB includes participants with diverse skin tones, ages, and genders under varied lighting conditions.

Pressure Sensor. To measure hand pressure, we used a Sensel Morph [39] (Fig. 3b). The sensor is a planar surface featuring a grid of force-sensitive resistor (FSR) pixels. The sensor produces a 185×105 "pressure image", with each pixel having a pitch of 1.25 mm. The sensor produces diffuse readings below 0.5 kPa, which we use as the minimum effective pressure, and the 99th percentile pressure recorded in the dataset is 82 kPa.

We covered the sensor surface with a white vinyl overlay for most participants, and covered it with a wood-textured overlay for seven participants. We mounted the sensor above the table surface to allow participants to reach underneath the sensor for pinching and grasping actions (Fig. 3a). PressureVisionDB only measures pressure across this single planar surface, and we leave the capture of hand pressure on more diverse shapes to future work. Additionally, the sensor measures pressure normal to the plane, so we only consider this component of pressure.

Cameras. The capture setup uses four synchronized and calibrated OptiTrack Prime Color cameras to capture 1080p RGB frames. We mounted the cameras to provide overhead views of the scene along with three OptiTrack eStrobe light sources. Each light can be turned on or off to achieve 8 different lighting conditions. The lighting condition was changed after each participant.

Participants. PressureVisionDB was collected from a diverse set of adults (Fig. 4) with a range of skin tones, ages, and genders (Fig. 3c). Participants self-reported their age and gender, and their skin tone were measured objectively. A Pantone RM200 colorimeter was used to classify the participant's skin tone in the Pantone SkinTone Guide [42]. These skin tones were then divided into three categories: light, medium, and dark.

Protocol. We developed a protocol to capture a variety of hand-surface interactions. Participants were asked to perform 36 different actions with one hand and then the other. Prior to each action, participants were shown a text description and an image of the action. The list of actions includes pressing with a single finger (index, thumb, or other), pressing with the whole hand, applying tangential force, grasping the edge of the sensor, and drawing with a finger. For many actions, participants were prompted to use one of three force levels: high force, low force, and no contact. For the no contact condition, participants moved their hand very close to the sensor, as if they intended to touch the sensor, but did not make contact.

Ethics. Participants gave informed consent and were compensated for their time. The data was captured by a third-party corporation that specializes in data collection with human participants. The capture rig was designed so that no images of the participants' torsos or faces were collected. The third-party did not provide personally identifiable information to the research team.

At the inception of our project, we were concerned about the potential for darker skin tones to reduce performance [8,13,33]. Melanin and hemoglobin both influence skin color in visible light and melanin concentration varies widely across people [70]. As such, we prioritized recruiting participants with a wide range of skin tones (Fig. 3c).

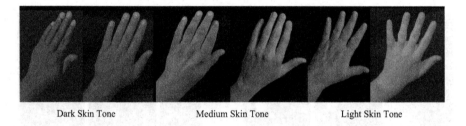

Dark Skin Tone   Medium Skin Tone   Light Skin Tone

Fig. 4. PressureVisionDB includes data from participants with diverse skin tones.

4   Estimating Pressure and Contact from RGB

We designed a deep network to infer hand contact and pressure. From an input RGB image, the network estimates a pressure image of the same size. The pressure image provides a pressure estimate for each pixel of the RGB image.

4.1   Network Architecture

We designed PressureVisionNet to estimate the location and magnitude of pressure between a hand and surface. The network is an encoder-decoder architecture which inputs a single RGB image, I, and outputs a pressure map, $\hat{P} = f(I)$. During training and evaluation, the ground truth pressure data from the sensor is projected into image space (Fig. 3b). Consequently, the network estimates hand pressure for each pixel of the input image, which results in an output pressure image that is the same size as the input image.

Pressure estimation is treated as a classification problem. The pressure range is divided into nine bins placed in logarithmic space [15]. The network infers the pressure bin for each pixel of the output pressure image. We experimented with direct regression of pressure scalars, but found that this was outperformed by the classification approach.

We cropped images from each camera to include a margin around the pressure sensor and resized the images to 480×384 pixels. PressureNet uses a SE-ResNeXt50 [24,28,62] encoder, with weights from pretraining on ImageNet [16]. A feature pyramid network (FPN) [35,63] decoder produces the output image. A cross-entropy loss was used during training. During inference, the network runs at 53 FPS using an RTX 3090 GPU.

4.2   Evaluation Metrics

We considered four types of contact and pressure metrics. Contact is a binary quantity that describes if the hand and sensor are touching, while pressure is a scalar describing how hard the hand and sensor are pressing against each other. Contact maps C are generated by thresholding the pressure map P at a low value, $P_{th} = 1.0$ kPa. Values greater than this are marked as *in contact*.

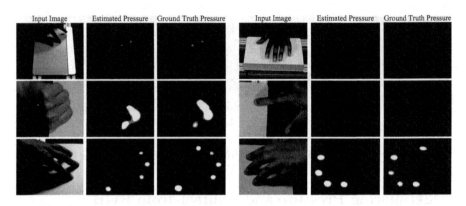

Fig. 5. Results from PressureVisionNet on held-out participants. Some images have been magnified for clarity. PressureVisionNet can accurately infer the location and magnitude of pressure from an RGB image. PressureVisionNet correctly identifies the lack of contact in "no-contact" actions (right, top two). The bottom row illustrates a common failure mode: no pressure is estimated for parts of the hand that are occluded.

– **Temporal Accuracy** To evaluate the *temporal* accuracy with which the onset and termination of contact are estimated, if *any* contact is present in the estimated and ground truth contact maps, $\hat{C}$ and C, the frame is marked as in contact. A frame is marked correct if the presence of contact is consistent in estimated and ground truth frames.

– **Contact IoU** To evaluate the *spatial* and *temporal* accuracy of estimated contact, we computed the intersection over union (IoU) between the the binary contact images. This metric does not consider the magnitude of the estimated pressure, and is an upper bound on Volumetric IoU.

– **Volumetric IoU** We propose the Volumetric IoU (Fig. 6), a novel metric that extends Contact IoU to evaluate the *magnitudes* of pressure estimates in addition to their *spatial* and *temporal* accuracy. Each 2D pressure image is converted into a 3D "pressure volume", where the height of the volume is equal to the amount of pressure at that pixel. The Volumetric IoU can be calculated as:

$$IoU_{vol} = \frac{\sum^{i,j} min(P_{i,j}, \hat{P}_{i,j})}{\sum^{i,j} max(P_{i,j}, \hat{P}_{i,j})} \tag{1}$$

– **Mean Absolute Error** To evaluate the accuracy of estimated pressure in *physical units*, we calculate mean absolute error (MAE) over each pixel. As most of the dataset pressure images consist of zeros, these numbers are close to zero.

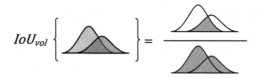

Fig. 6. Volumetric IoU quantifies the agreement between two pressure images by treating them as pressure volumes.

4.3 Dataset Splits

The dataset consists of 36 participants. Prior to using the dataset to develop PressureVisionNet, we selected 6 participants spanning skin tone and demographics for a held-out test set. We used data from the remaining 30 participants for training and validation.

5 Results

Our primary goal was to investigate the potential to infer hand pressure from a single RGB image. In addition to characterizing overall performance, we focused on three questions. First, we considered how well performance can generalize to people outside of the training set, since feasibility depends on the existence of shared properties across hands and human behavior. Second, we considered whether the appearance of the hand and its cast shadows were used for inference. Third, we considered whether a trained model can produce reasonable estimates for images captured in an unseen environment.

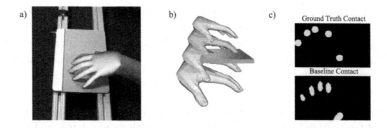

Fig. 7. a) A 3D pose estimator is used to estimate hand pose. b) As monocular pose estimators have difficulty in estimating true hand scale, hand scale is swept through a range of values (selected scales are visualized, optimal scale is colored). c) Ground truth contact is compared to contact calculated by mesh intersection.

5.1   Baseline Models

Since inferring hand pressure from an RGB image is a new task, there were no existing methods available for direct comparison. To provide context for our numeric results, we created a baseline model for comparison.

3D models of the human body have been used to infer contact and pressure in other contexts [12,20,55]. Our use of a single RGB image makes this approach more challenging. Prior work used multiple cameras, depth cameras, and motion capture systems to obtain high fidelity 3D models. We used FrankMocap [49] to produce a 3D pose estimate with a free parameter for the scale of the hand. As the true hand scale is not known, for each sequence we swept the hand scale with a discretization that corresponds to sub-millimeter adjustment in depth, and find the scale that maximizes the Contact IoU with respect to ground truth (Fig. 7). Contact was estimated by finding intersection between the hand and sensor meshes.

5.2   Can Inference Succeed with New People?

Table 2. PressureVisionNet outperforms the 3D Pose Baseline on a test set of unseen participants.

Method	Temporal acc	Contact IoU	Vol. IoU	MAE
Zero guesser	53.7%	0.0%	0.0%	51.9 Pa
3D pose baseline [49]	78.1%	13.0%	–	–
PressureVisionNet	96.2%	55.8%	41.3%	39.9 Pa

Table 2 shows performance on the ≈490k images in our test set, which includes frames from all four cameras, five distinct lighting conditions, and 6 participants performing 36 actions. None of the participants in our test set were in our training set, so performance indicates how well our approach generalizes to new people.

Table 3. Participants were prompted to perform actions with various force levels. Estimated forces from PressureVisionNet correlate with ground truth (GT).

Force requested to participant	Mean GT force	Mean Est force
High force	8.16 N	5.73 N
Low force	3.24 N	3.63 N
No contact	0.00 N	0.04 N

PressureVisionNet outperformed our baseline model. Its discretized representation for pressure limits its best possible Volumetric IoU to 81% and MAE to 10.9 Pa. The *Zero Guesser* always outputs a zero-pressure image. It achieved 53.7% temporal accuracy since no pressure was recorded for the majority of frames in the dataset. The *3D Pose Estimator* had generally low performance. PressureVisionNet performed well with non-contact images and inferred higher pressures on average when participants were instructed to apply more force (Table 3 and Fig. 5).

Skin Tone. Skin tone is a significant source of variability across people. Due to the limited number of participants in each skin tone category, we used cross-validation. The training set is split into five folds, and the model is trained with one rotating fold left out for testing. As shown Table 4, the highest performance was with dark skin tones. We performed a two-sample Kolmogorov-Smirnov test between each pair of skin tone categories, and did not find a statistically significant difference.

Table 4. Performance across skin tones is found via cross validation. We did not find a statistically significant difference between categories.

Skin tone	Vol. IoU
Light	38.5%
Medium	37.2%
Dark	39.0%

5.3 Is Hand-Related Appearance Used for Inference?

We expected the appearance of the hand and cast shadows to provide visual cues for pressure inference. Our results suggest that this is the case. In addition to providing evidence for the underlying information used for inference, these results reduce the likelihood that PressureVisionNet is exploiting information specific to our data that would not be generalizable, such as unintended sensor artifacts.

Sensitivity Analysis. We conducted a sensitivity analysis to identify spatial regions that strongly influence PressureVisionNet's output. Our method is similar to the Occlusion Sensitivity method from Zieler and Fergus [66]. We divide the input RGB image into a 48×48 grid of cells. For each cell i, j, we create a new image $\mathbf{B}_{i,j}(I)$ replacing the cell contents with its average color. We provide this image as an input to the network and calculate how much the output pressure changes. We create a sensitivity image by normalizing the following image, S, to be between 0 and 1.

$$S_{i,j} = ||f(\mathbf{B}_{i,j}(I)) - f(I)||_2 \tag{2}$$

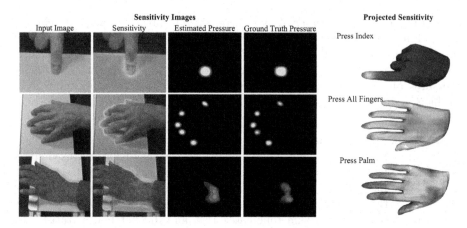

Fig. 8. Left: PressureVisionNet is sensitive to the appearance of the hand and shadows near regions of contact. Right: Results of projecting sensitivity images onto hand meshes and averaging over many frames for selected actions.

Figure 8 shows examples of resulting sensitivity images that indicate the model uses the appearance of the hand and cast shadows near regions of contact. To show this objectively, we also projected the sensitivity images from multiple frames onto the hand meshes generated for the 3D Pose Baseline. Figure 8 shows the results for three different actions that confirm that PressureVisionNet is highly sensitive to blurring of the hand near regions of contact.

We also found a common failure mode that corroborates this result. As shown in the bottom row of Fig. 5, PressureVisionNet typically guesses zero pressure for parts of the hand that are occluded from view.

Dependence on Actions. We found that PressureVisionNet's performance depended on the participant's action. For example, performance was highest with a single index finger action and lower with actions that apply pressure with the palm (Table 5). Two relevant factors are likely the visibility of the part of the hand near the region of contact and the tendency for larger areas of ground truth pressure to result in larger errors.

Table 5. The performance of PressureVisionNet on selected actions. Actions with lower visibility and larger contact areas tend to result in lower performance.

Action name	Vol. IoU
Press index, pull towards	59.4%
Press all fingers	42.1%
Press all fingers and palm	35.4%
Press palm	33.2%

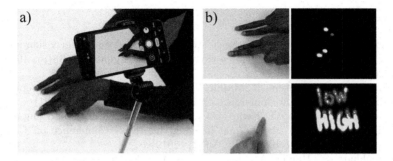

Fig. 9. PressureVisionNet may generalize to new environments. Results shown in b) were captured with a smartphone camera in unaltered office lighting on a tabletop. Pressure estimates can be accumulated over time to allow writing with a finger.

5.4   Is Inference Reasonable with New Conditions?

We considered whether PressureVisionNet can produce reasonable estimates when given new RGB images acquired with conditions that differ from Pressure-VisionDB. For this question, we provide preliminary evidence based on images of hands not included in the dataset. We captured additional data with a smartphone camera in unaltered office lighting. The smartphone camera had different focal length, resolution, and color characteristics than the dataset cameras. The smartphone was mounted with a tripod to observe a normal white tabletop.

Figure 9 demonstrates that PressureVisionNet has some ability to generalize to new environments. The system can generalize to images with multiple hands, and can run over multiple frames in a video while accumulating inferred pressure estimates. In the bottom image, an author used the system to write with their index finger first with low pressure, then with high pressure. This illustrates a potential application and provides evidence that PressureVisionNet is not overly sensitive to the camera, the illumination, or the contact surface.

6   Conclusion

We collected a novel dataset, PressureVisionDB, and developed a deep model, PressureVisionNet, to infer hand pressure from a single RGB image. Using this model, we provided evidence that hand pressure can be accurately inferred from a single RGB image of a hand from a previously unobserved person. Our results suggest that the appearance of regions of the hand near regions of contact are especially informative when inferring pressure.

Acknowledgements. We thank Kevin Harris, Steve Miller, and Steve Olsen for their help in data collection, and Robert Wang, Minh Vo, Tomas Hodan, Amy Zhao, Kenrick Kin, Mark Richardson, and Cem Keskin for their advice.

References

1. Asadi, H., Zhou, G., Lee, J.J., Aggarwal, V., Yu, D.: A computer vision approach for classifying isometric grip force exertion levels. Ergonomics **63**(8), 1010–1026 (2020)
2. Bhirangi, R., Hellebrekers, T., Majidi, C., Gupta, A.: ReSkin: versatile, replaceable, lasting tactile skins. In: Conference on Robot Learning (CoRL) (2021)
3. Brahmbhatt, S., Ham, C., Kemp, C.C., Hays, J.: ContactDB: analyzing and predicting grasp contact via thermal imaging. In: IEEE Conference on Computer Vision and Pattern Recognition (CVPR) (2019)
4. Brahmbhatt, S., Handa, A., Hays, J., Fox, D.: ContactGrasp: functional multi-finger grasp synthesis from contact. In: 2019 IEEE/RSJ International Conference on Intelligent Robots and Systems (IROS), pp. 2386–2393. IEEE (2019)
5. Brahmbhatt, S., Tang, C., Twigg, C.D., Kemp, C.C., Hays, J.: ContactPose: a dataset of grasps with object contact and hand pose. In: Vedaldi, A., Bischof, H., Brox, T., Frahm, J.-M. (eds.) ECCV 2020. LNCS, vol. 12358, pp. 361–378. Springer, Cham (2020). https://doi.org/10.1007/978-3-030-58601-0_22
6. Brahmbhatt, S.M.: Grasp contact between hand and object: capture, analysis, and applications. Ph.D. thesis, Georgia Institute of Technology (2020)
7. Büscher, G.H., Kõiva, R., Schürmann, C., Haschke, R., Ritter, H.J.: Flexible and stretchable fabric-based tactile sensor. Robot. Auton. Syst. **63**, 244–252 (2015)
8. Cavazos, J.G., Phillips, P.J., Castillo, C.D., O'Toole, A.J.: Accuracy comparison across face recognition algorithms: where are we on measuring race bias? IEEE Trans. Biometrics Behav. Identity Sci. **3**(1), 101–111 (2020)
9. Chen, N., Westling, G., Edin, B.B., van der Smagt, P.: Estimating fingertip forces, torques, and local curvatures from fingernail images. Robotica **38**(7), 1242–1262 (2020)
10. Chu, F.J., Xu, R., Vela, P.A.: Real-world multiobject, multigrasp detection. IEEE Robot. Autom. Lett. **3**(4), 3355–3362 (2018)
11. Clever, H.M., Erickson, Z., Kapusta, A., Turk, G., Liu, C.K., Kemp, C.C.: Bodies at rest: 3D human pose and shape estimation from a pressure image using synthetic data. In: IEEE Conference on Computer Vision and Pattern Recognition (CVPR). IEEE (2020)
12. Clever, H.M., Grady, P., Turk, G., Kemp, C.C.: BodyPressure - inferring body pose and contact pressure from a depth image. IEEE Trans. Pattern Anal. Mach. Intell. (2021). https://ieeexplore.ieee.org/document/9743547
13. Cook, C.M., Howard, J.J., Sirotin, Y.B., Tipton, J.L., Vemury, A.R.: Demographic effects in facial recognition and their dependence on image acquisition: an evaluation of eleven commercial systems. IEEE Trans. Biometrics Behav. Identity Sci. **1**(1), 32–41 (2019)
14. Davis, A., Rubinstein, M., Wadhwa, N., Mysore, G.J., Durand, F., Freeman, W.T.: The visual microphone: passive recovery of sound from video. ACM Trans. Graph. **33**(4), 1–10 (2014)
15. Dehaene, S.: The neural basis of the weber-fechner law: a logarithmic mental number line. Trends Cogn. Sci. **7**(4), 145–147 (2003)
16. Deng, J., Dong, W., Socher, R., Li, L.J., Li, K., Fei-Fei, L.: ImageNet: a large-scale hierarchical image database. In: IEEE Conference on Computer Vision and Pattern Recognition (CVPR), pp. 248–255. IEEE (2009)
17. Ehsani, K., Tulsiani, S., Gupta, S., Farhadi, A., Gupta, A.: Use the force, Luke! Learning to predict physical forces by simulating effects. In: IEEE Conference on Computer Vision and Pattern Recognition (CVPR), pp. 224–233 (2020)

18. Fitzpatrick, P.M., Torres-Jara, E.R.: The power of the dark side: using cast shadows for visually-guided touching. In: 2004 4th IEEE/RAS International Conference on Humanoid Robots, vol. 1, pp. 437–449. IEEE (2004)
19. Garcia-Hernando, G., Yuan, S., Baek, S., Kim, T.K.: First-person hand action benchmark with RGB-D videos and 3D hand pose annotations. In: IEEE Conference on Computer Vision and Pattern Recognition (CVPR), pp. 409–419 (2018)
20. Grady, P., Tang, C., Twigg, C.D., Vo, M., Brahmbhatt, S., Kemp, C.C.: ContactOpt: Optimizing contact to improve grasps. In: IEEE Conference on Computer Vision and Pattern Recognition (CVPR), pp. 1471–1481 (2021)
21. Hampali, S., Rad, M., Oberweger, M., Lepetit, V.: HOnnotate: a method for 3D annotation of hand and object poses. In: IEEE Conference on Computer Vision and Pattern Recognition (CVPR), pp. 3196–3206 (2020)
22. Hasson, Y., Tekin, B., Bogo, F., Laptev, I., Pollefeys, M., Schmid, C.: Leveraging photometric consistency over time for sparsely supervised hand-object reconstruction. In: The IEEE Conference on Computer Vision and Pattern Recognition (CVPR), pp. 571–580 (2020)
23. Hasson, Y., et al.: Learning joint reconstruction of hands and manipulated objects. In: The IEEE Conference on Computer Vision and Pattern Recognition (CVPR), pp. 11807–11816 (2019)
24. He, K., Zhang, X., Ren, S., Sun, J.: Deep residual learning for image recognition. In: IEEE Conference on Computer Vision and Pattern Recognition (CVPR), pp. 770–778 (2016)
25. Holden, D., Kanoun, O., Perepichka, M., Popa, T.: Learned motion matching. ACM Trans. Graph. 39(4), 1–12 (2020)
26. Hu, H.H., Gooch, A.A., Creem-Regehr, S.H., Thompson, W.B.: Visual cues for perceiving distances from objects to surfaces. Presence: Teleoper. Virtual Environ. 11(6), 652–664 (2002)
27. Hu, H.H., Gooch, A.A., Thompson, W.B., Smits, B.E., Rieser, J.J., Shirley, P.: Visual cues for imminent object contact in realistic virtual environments. In: 2000 Proceedings Visualization, pp. 179–185. IEEE (2000)
28. Hu, J., Shen, L., Sun, G.: Squeeze-and-excitation networks. In: IEEE Conference on Computer Vision and Pattern Recognition (CVPR), pp. 7132–7141 (2018)
29. Hubona, G.S., Wheeler, P.N., Shirah, G.W., Brandt, M.: The relative contributions of stereo, lighting, and background scenes in promoting 3D depth visualization. ACM Trans. Comput. Human Interact. 6(3), 214–242 (1999)
30. Hwang, W., Lim, S.: Inferring interaction force from visual information without using physical force sensors. Sensors 17(11), 2455 (2017)
31. Johnson, M.K., Adelson, E.H.: Retrographic sensing for the measurement of surface texture and shape. In: IEEE Conference on Computer Vision and Pattern Recognition (CVPR), pp. 1070–1077. IEEE (2009)
32. Karunratanakul, K., Yang, J., Zhang, Y., Black, M.J., Muandet, K., Tang, S.: Grasping field: learning implicit representations for human grasps. In: 8th International Conference on 3D Vision, pp. 333–344. IEEE (2020)
33. Krishnapriya, K., Albiero, V., Vangara, K., King, M.C., Bowyer, K.W.: Issues related to face recognition accuracy varying based on race and skin tone. IEEE Transa. Technol. Soc. 1(1), 8–20 (2020)
34. Li, Z., Sedlár, J., Carpentier, J., Laptev, I., Mansard, N., Sivic, J.: Estimating 3D motion and forces of person-object interactions from monocular video. In: IEEE Conference on Computer Vision and Pattern Recognition (CVPR), pp. 8640–8649 (2019)

35. Lin, T.Y., Dollár, P., Girshick, R., He, K., Hariharan, B., Belongie, S.: Feature pyramid networks for object detection. In: IEEE Conference on Computer Vision and Pattern Recognition (CVPR), pp. 2117–2125 (2017)
36. Mascaro, S.A., Asada, H.H.: Photoplethysmograph fingernail sensors for measuring finger forces without haptic obstruction. IEEE Trans. Robot. Autom. 17(5), 698–708 (2001)
37. Mascaro, S.A., Asada, H.H.: Measurement of finger posture and three-axis fingertip touch force using fingernail sensors. IEEE Trans. Robot. Autom. 20(1), 26–35 (2004)
38. Meier, M., Streli, P., Fender, A., Holz, C.: TapID: rapid touch interaction in virtual reality using wearable sensing. In: 2021 IEEE Virtual Reality and 3D User Interfaces (VR), pp. 519–528. IEEE (2021)
39. Morph: sensel morph haptic sensing tablet, www.sensel.com/pages/the-sensel-morph. Accessed 25 Feb 2020
40. Narasimhaswamy, S., Nguyen, T., Nguyen, M.H.: Detecting hands and recognizing physical contact in the wild. In: Advances in Neural Information Processing Systems, vol. 33 (2020)
41. Niikura, T., Watanabe, Y., Ishikawa, M.: Anywhere surface touch: utilizing any surface as an input area. In: Proceedings of the 5th Augmented Human International Conference, pp. 1–8 (2014)
42. Pantone LLC: pantone skintone guide (2012)
43. Pérez-González, A., Vergara, M., Sancho-Bru, J.L.: Stiffness map of the grasping contact areas of the human hand. J. Biomech. 46(15), 2644–2650 (2013)
44. Pham, T.H., Kheddar, A., Qammaz, A., Argyros, A.A.: Towards force sensing from vision: observing hand-object interactions to infer manipulation forces. In: IEEE Conference on Computer Vision and Pattern Recognition (CVPR), pp. 2810–2819 (2015)
45. Pham, T.H., Kyriazis, N., Argyros, A.A., Kheddar, A.: Hand-object contact force estimation from markerless visual tracking. IEEE Trans. Pattern Anal. Mach. Intell. 40(12), 2883–2896 (2017)
46. Pressure Profile Systems: PPS TactileGlove. www.pressureprofile.com/body-pressure-mapping/tactile-glove
47. Rogez, G., Supancic, J.S., Ramanan, D.: Understanding everyday hands in action from RGB-D images. In: IEEE International Conference on Computer Vision (ICCV), pp. 3889–3897 (2015)
48. Romero, J., Kjellström, H., Kragic, D.: Hands in action: real-time 3D reconstruction of hands in interaction with objects. In: 2010 IEEE International Conference on Robotics and Automation, pp. 458–463. IEEE (2010)
49. Rong, Y., Shiratori, T., Joo, H.: FrankmoCap: a monocular 3D whole-body pose estimation system via regression and integration. In: IEEE International Conference on Computer Vision Workshops (2021)
50. Rosales, C., Porta, J.M., Ros, L.: Global optimization of robotic grasps. In: Proceedings of Robotics: Science and Systems VII (2011)
51. Saxena, A., Driemeyer, J., Ng, A.Y.: Robotic grasping of novel objects using vision. The Int. J. Robot. Res. 27(2), 157–173 (2008)
52. Scott, J., Ravichandran, B., Funk, C., Collins, R.T., Liu, Y.: From image to stability: learning dynamics from human pose. In: Vedaldi, A., Bischof, H., Brox, T., Frahm, J.-M. (eds.) ECCV 2020. LNCS, vol. 12368, pp. 536–554. Springer, Cham (2020). https://doi.org/10.1007/978-3-030-58592-1_32

53. Starke, S., Zhao, Y., Komura, T., Zaman, K.: Local motion phases for learning multi-contact character movements. ACM Trans. Graph. **39**(4), 1–13 (2020). https://doi.org/10.1145/3386569.3392450
54. Sundaram, S., Kellnhofer, P., Li, Y., Zhu, J.Y., Torralba, A., Matusik, W.: Learning the signatures of the human grasp using a scalable tactile glove. Nature **569**(7758), 698–702 (2019)
55. Taheri, O., Ghorbani, N., Black, M.J., Tzionas, D.: GRAB: a dataset of whole-body human grasping of objects. In: Vedaldi, A., Bischof, H., Brox, T., Frahm, J.-M. (eds.) ECCV 2020. LNCS, vol. 12349, pp. 581–600. Springer, Cham (2020). https://doi.org/10.1007/978-3-030-58548-8_34
56. TekScan: TekScan Grip System. www.tekscan.com
57. Tzionas, D., Ballan, L., Srikantha, A., Aponte, P., Pollefeys, M., Gall, J.: Capturing hands in action using discriminative salient points and physics simulation. Int. J. Comput. Vis. **118**(2), 172–193 (2016)
58. Ward-Cherrier, B., et al.: The TacTip family: soft optical tactile sensors with 3D-printed biomimetic morphologies. Soft Rob. **5**(2), 216–227 (2018)
59. Wettels, N., Santos, V.J., Johansson, R.S., Loeb, G.E.: Biomimetic tactile sensor array. Adv. Robot. **22**(8), 829–849 (2008)
60. Wu, H., Rubinstein, M., Shih, E., Guttag, J.V., Durand, F., Freeman, W.T.: Eulerian video magnification for revealing subtle changes in the world. ACM Trans. Graph. **31**(4), 1–8 (2012)
61. Xiao, R., Schwarz, J., Throm, N., Wilson, A.D., Benko, H.: MRTouch: adding touch input to head-mounted mixed reality. IEEE Trans. Visual Comput. Graphics **24**(4), 1653–1660 (2018)
62. Xie, S., Girshick, R.B., Dollár, P., Tu, Z., He, K.: Aggregated residual transformations for deep neural networks. In: IEEE Conference on Computer Vision and Pattern Recognition (CVPR), pp. 5987–5995 (2017)
63. Yakubovskiy, P.: Segmentation models pytorch (2020)
64. Ye, Y., Liu, C.K.: Synthesis of detailed hand manipulations using contact sampling. ACM Trans. Graph. (TOG) **31**(4), 41 (2012)
65. Yuan, W., Dong, S., Adelson, E.H.: GelSight: high-resolution robot tactile sensors for estimating geometry and force. Sensors **17**(12), 2762 (2017)
66. Zeiler, M.D., Fergus, R.: Visualizing and understanding convolutional networks. In: Fleet, D., Pajdla, T., Schiele, B., Tuytelaars, T. (eds.) ECCV 2014. LNCS, vol. 8689, pp. 818–833. Springer, Cham (2014). https://doi.org/10.1007/978-3-319-10590-1_53
67. Zhang, H., Ye, Y., Shiratori, T., Komura, T.: ManipNet: neural manipulation synthesis with a hand-object spatial representation. ACM Trans. Graph. (TOG) **40**(4), 1–14 (2021)
68. Zhang, Y., Hassan, M., Neumann, H., Black, M.J., Tang, S.: Generating 3D people in scenes without people. In: IEEE Conference on Computer Vision and Pattern Recognition (CVPR), pp. 6193–6203 (2020)
69. Zhu, Y., Jiang, C., Zhao, Y., Terzopoulos, D., Zhu, S.C.: Inferring forces and learning human utilities from videos. In: IEEE Conference on Computer Vision and Pattern Recognition (CVPR), pp. 3823–3833 (2016)
70. Zonios, G., Bykowski, J., Kollias, N.: Skin melanin, hemoglobin, and light scattering properties can be quantitatively assessed in vivo using diffuse reflectance spectroscopy. J. Invest. Dermatol. **117**(6), 1452–1457 (2001)

PoseScript: 3D Human Poses from Natural Language

Ginger Delmas[1,2(✉)], Philippe Weinzaepfel[2], Thomas Lucas[2],
Francesc Moreno-Noguer[1], and Grégory Rogez[2]

[1] Institut de Robòtica i Informàtica Industrial, CSIC-UPC, Barcelona, Spain
`gdelmas@iri.upc.edu`
[2] NAVER LABS Europe, Meylan, France

Abstract. Natural language is leveraged in many computer vision tasks such as image captioning, cross-modal retrieval or visual question answering, to provide fine-grained semantic information. While human pose is key to human understanding, current 3D human pose datasets lack detailed language descriptions. In this work, we introduce the PoseScript dataset, which pairs a few thousand 3D human poses from AMASS with rich human-annotated descriptions of the body parts and their spatial relationships. To increase the size of this dataset to a scale compatible with typical data hungry learning algorithms, we propose an elaborate captioning process that generates automatic synthetic descriptions in natural language from given 3D keypoints. This process extracts low-level pose information – the *posecodes* – using a set of simple but generic rules on the 3D keypoints. The posecodes are then combined into higher level textual descriptions using syntactic rules. Automatic annotations substantially increase the amount of available data, and make it possible to effectively pretrain deep models for finetuning on human captions. To demonstrate the potential of annotated poses, we show applications of the PoseScript dataset to retrieval of relevant poses from large-scale datasets and to synthetic pose generation, both based on a textual pose description. Code and dataset are available at https://europe.naverlabs.com/research/computer-vision/posescript/.

1 Introduction

'*The pose has the head down, ultimately touching the floor, with the weight of the body on the palms and the feet. The arms are stretched straight forward, shoulder width apart; the feet are a foot apart, the legs are straight, and the hips are raised as high as possible.*'. The text above describes the downward dog yoga pose[1], and a reader is able to picture such a pose from this natural language description. Being able to automatically map natural language descriptions and accurate 3D human poses would open the door to a number of applications such

---

[1] https://en.wikipedia.org/wiki/Downward_Dog_Pose.

Supplementary Information The online version contains supplementary material available at https://doi.org/10.1007/978-3-031-20068-7_20.

© The Author(s), under exclusive license to Springer Nature Switzerland AG 2022
S. Avidan et al. (Eds.): ECCV 2022, LNCS 13666, pp. 346–362, 2022.
https://doi.org/10.1007/978-3-031-20068-7_20

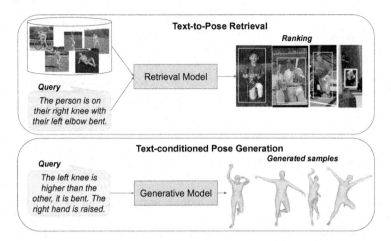

Fig. 1. Illustration of possible applications using PoseScript. The top figure illustrates text-to-pose retrieval where the goal is to retrieve poses in a large-scale database given a text query. This can be applied to databases of images with associated SMPL fits. The bottom figure shows an example of text-conditioned pose generation.

as helping image annotation when the deployment of Motion Capture (MoCap) systems is not practical; performing semantic searches in large-scale datasets (see Fig. 1 top), which are currently only based on high-level metadata such as the action being performed [14,25,34]; complex pose or motion data generation in digital animation (see Fig. 1 bottom); or teaching basic posture skills to visually impaired individuals [41].

While the problem of combining language and images or videos has attracted significant attention [10,17,20,42], in particular with the impressive results obtained by the recent multimodal neural networks CLIP [35] and DALL-E [36], the problem of linking text and 3D geometry is largely unexplored. There have been a few recent attempts at mapping text to rigid 3D shapes [8], and at using natural language for 3D object localization [7] or 3D object differentiation [1]. More recently, Fieraru *et al.* [11] introduce AIFit, an approach to automatically generate human-interpretable feedback on the difference between a reference and a target motion. There have also been a number of attempts to model humans using various forms of text. Attributes have been used for instance to model body shape [40] and face images [15]. Other approaches [2,3,12,30] leverage textual descriptions to generate motion, but without fine-grained control of the body limbs. More related to our work, Pavlakos *et al.* [28] exploit the relation between two joints along the depth dimension, and Pons-Moll *et al.*. [33] describe 3D human poses through a series of *posebits*, which are binary indicators for different types of questions such as 'Is the right hand above the hips?'. However, these types of Boolean assertions have limited expressivity and remain far from the natural language descriptions a human would use.

In this paper, we propose to map 3D human poses with arbitrarily complex structural descriptions, in natural language, of the body parts and their spatial relationships. To that end, we first introduce the *PoseScript* dataset,

The person is kneeling on their left knee and has their right arm touching the ground, with the left arm being held straight out and almost parallel to their back.

The person is standing while bending backwards, as if they are dodging bullets in The Matrix. Both legs are bent backwards, and their arms are at their sides while not touching the ground.

Data collection on AMT

Automatic Captioning Pipeline

The person is in a crouching pose and is touching the ground. The left hand is backwards, spread apart from the right hand. The right hand is beside the right foot, below the right hip, then the left elbow is bent at right angle, the left upper arm and the right thigh are parallel to the floor and the right arm is in front of the left arm, both knees are almost completely bent. The person is kneeling on their left leg and is bent forward.

The figure is doing backwards movements and is in a inclined pose. The right knee is forming a L shape and the left foot is stretched forwards, the right elbow is barely bent, then the left shoulder is further down than the right. The subject is inclined backward and to the left of the pelvis. The left hand is further down than the left hip and behind the right hand and wide apart from the right hand, the right leg is behind the other. The right upper arm is parallel to the ground.

Fig. 2. Examples of pose descriptions from PoseScript, produced by human annotators (left) and by our automatic captioning pipeline (right).

which consists of captions written by human annotators for about 4,000 poses from the AMASS dataset [25]. To scale-up this dataset, we additionally propose an automatic captioning pipeline for human-centric poses that makes it possible to annotate thousands of human poses in a few minutes. Our pipeline is built on (a) low-level information obtained via an extension of posebits [33] to finer-grained categorical relations of the different body parts (*e.g.*'the knees are slightly/relatively/completely bent'), units that we refer to as *posecodes*, and on (b) higher-level concepts that come either from the action labels annotated by the BABEL dataset [34], or combinations of posecodes. We define rules to select and aggregate posecodes using linguistic aggregation principles, and convert them into sentences to produce textual descriptions. As a result, we are able to automatically extract human-like captions for a normalized input 3D pose. Importantly, since the process is randomized, we can generate several descriptions per pose, as different human annotators would do. We used this procedure to describe 20,000 poses extracted from the AMASS dataset. Figure 2 shows examples of human-written and automatic captions.

Using the PoseScript dataset, we propose to tackle two tasks, see Fig. 1. The first is a cross-modal retrieval task where the goal is to retrieve from a database the poses that are most similar to a given text query; this can also be applied to RGB images by associating them with 3D human fits. The second task consists in generating human poses conditioned on a textual description. In both cases, our experiments demonstrate that it is beneficial to pretrain models using the automatic captions before finetuning them on real captions.

In summary, our contributions are threefold:

o We introduce the PoseScript dataset (Sect. 3). It associates human poses and structural descriptions in natural language, either obtained through human-written annotations or using our automatic captioning pipeline.
o We then study the task of text-to-pose retrieval (Sect. 4).
o We finally present the task of text-conditioned pose generation (Sect. 5).

2 Related Work

Text for Humans in Images. Some previous works have used attributes as semantic-level representation to edit body shapes [40] or image faces [15]. In contrast, our approach focuses on body poses and leverages natural language, which has the advantage of being unconstrained and more flexible. Closer to our work, [6,45] focus on generating human 2D poses, SMPL parameters or even images from captions. However, they use MS Coco [23] captions, which are generally simple image-level statements on the activity performed by the human, and which sometimes relate to the interaction with other elements from the scene, e.g.'A soccer player is running while the ball is in the air'. In contrast, we focus on fine-grained detailed captions about the pose only. FixMyPose [18] provides manually annotated captions about the difference between human poses in two synthetic images. These captions also mention objects from the environment, e.g.'carpet' or 'door'. Similarly, AIFit [11] proposes to automatically generate text about the discrepancies between a reference motion and a performed one, based on differences of angles and positions. We instead focus on describing one single pose without relying on any other visual element.

Text for Human Motion. We deal with static poses, whereas several existing methods have mainly studied 3D action (sequence) recognition or text-based 2D [2] or 3D motion synthesis. They either condition their model on action labels [13,24,30], or descriptions in natural language [3,12,22,32,44]. Yet, even if motion descriptions effectively constrain *sequences* of poses, they do not specifically inform about individual poses. What if an animation studio looks for a sequence of 3D body poses where 'the man is running with his hands on his hips'? The model used by the artists to initialize the animation should have a deep understanding of the relations between the body parts. To this end, it is important to learn about specific pose semantics, beyond global pose sequence semantics.

Pose Semantic Representations. Our captioning generation process relies on posecodes that capture relevant information about the pose semantics. Posecodes are inspired from posebits [33] where images showing a human are annotated with various binary indicators. This data is used to reduce ambiguities in 3D pose estimation. Conversely, we automatically extract posecodes from normalized 3D poses in order to generate descriptions in natural language. Ordinal depth [28] can be seen as a special case of posebits, focusing on the depth relationship between two joints. They obtain annotations on some training images to improve a human mesh recovery model by adding extra constraints. Poselets [5] can also be seen as another way to extract discriminative pose information, but are not easily interpreted. In contrast to these representations, we propose to generate pose descriptions in natural language, which have the advantage (a) of being a very intuitive way to communicate ideas, and (b) of providing greater flexibility.

In summary, our proposed PoseScript dataset differs from existing datasets in that it focuses on single 3D poses instead of motion [31], and provides direct descriptions in natural language instead of simple action labels [13,14,21,34,39], binary relations [28,33] or modifying texts [11,18]. To the best of our knowledge, this is the first attempt at associating static 3D poses and descriptions in natural language.

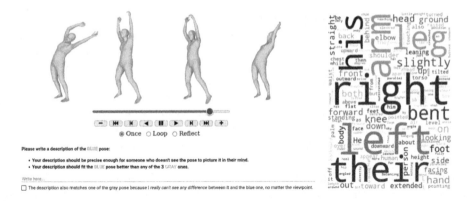

Fig. 3. Left: Interface presented to the AMT annotators in order to collect discriminative descriptions of the blue pose. **Right: Wordcloud** of the most frequent words in the human-written descriptions.

3   The PoseScript Dataset

The PoseScript dataset is composed of static 3D human poses, together with fine-grained semantic annotations in natural language. We provide **H**uman-written annotated descriptions (PoseScript-H), and further increase the amount of data with **A**utomatically generated captions (PoseScript-A). The crowd-sourced data collection process is described in Sect. 3.1, and the automatic captioning pipeline in Sect. 3.2. Finally, aggregated statistics over the PoseScript dataset are provided in Sect. 3.3.

3.1   Dataset Collection

We collect human-written captions for 3D human poses extracted from the AMASS dataset [25], using Amazon Mechanical Turk[2] (AMT), a crowd-sourced annotation platform. The interface, displayed in Fig. 3 (left), presents the annotators with the mesh of the human pose to annotate (in blue), and a slider to control the viewpoint. To encourage discriminative captions, we additionally display 3 discriminator poses (in gray), which are semantically close to the pose to annotate. The task is to provide a description of the blue pose which is precise enough to distinguish it from the three others. We detail the discriminator selection, the complete task instructions and annotator information in the supplementary material. Some PoseScript-H examples are shown in Fig. 2 (left).

3.2   Automatic Captioning Pipeline

We now describe the process used to generate synthetic textual descriptions for 3D human poses. As depicted in Fig. 4, it relies on the extraction, selection and aggregation of elementary pieces of pose information, called *posecodes*, that are eventually converted into sentences to produce a description.

---

[2] https://www.mturk.com.

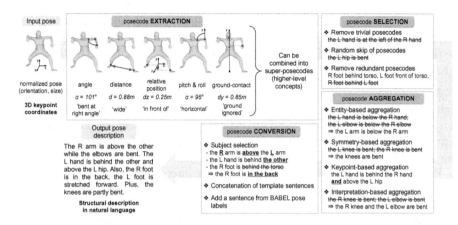

Fig. 4. Overview of our captioning pipeline. Given a normalized 3D pose, we use posecodes to extract semantic pose information. These posecodes are then selected, merged or combined (when relevant) before being converted into a structural pose description in natural language. Letters 'L' and 'R' stand for 'left' and 'right' respectively.

The process takes 3D keypoint coordinates of human-centric poses as input. These are inferred with the SMPL-H body model [37] using the default shape coefficients and a normalized global orientation along the y-axis.

1. Posecode extraction. A posecode describes a relation between a specific set of joints. We capture five kinds of elementary relations: angles, distances and relative positions (as in [33]), but also pitch, roll and ground-contacts.

○ *Angle posecodes* describe how a body part 'bends' at a given joint, *e.g.*the left elbow. Depending on the angle, the posecode is assigned one of the following attributes: 'straight', 'slightly bent', 'partially bent', 'bent at right angle', 'almost completely bent' and 'completely bent'.

○ *Distance posecodes* categorize the $L2$-distance between two keypoints (*e.g.*the two hands) into 'close', 'shoulder width apart', 'spread' or 'wide' apart.

○ *Posecodes on relative position* compute the difference between two keypoints along a given axis. The possible categories are, for the x-axis: 'at the right of', 'x-ignored', 'at the left of'; for the y-axis: 'below', 'y-ignored', 'above'; and for the z-axis: 'behind', 'z-ignored' and 'in front of'. In particular, comparing the x-coordinate of the left and right hands allows to infer if they are crossed (*i.e.*, the left hand is 'at the right' of the right hand). The 'ignored' interpretations are ambiguous configurations which will not be described.

○ *Pitch & roll posecodes* assess the verticality or horizontality of a body part defined by two keypoints (*e.g.*the left knee and hip together define the left thigh). A body part is 'vertical' if it is approximately orthogonal to the y-hyperplane, and 'horizontal' if it is in it. Other configurations are 'pitch-roll-ignored'.

○ *Ground-contact posecodes*, used for intermediate computation only, denote whether a keypoint is 'on the ground' (*i.e.*, vertically close to the keypoint of minimal height in the body, considered as the ground) or 'ground-ignored'.

Handling ambiguity in posecode categorization. Posecode categorizations are obtained using predefined thresholds. As these values are inherently subjective, we randomize the binning step by also defining a noise level applied to the measured angles and distances values before thresholding.

Higher-level concepts. We additionally define a few *super-posecodes* to extract higher-level pose concepts. These posecodes are binary (they either apply or not to a given pose configuration), and are expressed from elementary posecodes. For instance, the super-posecode 'kneeling' can be defined as having both knees 'on the ground' and 'completely bent'.

2. Posecode selection aims at selecting an interesting subset of posecodes among those extracted, to obtain a concise yet discriminative description. First, we remove trivial settings (*e.g.*'the left hand is at the left of the right hand'). Next, based on a statistical study over the whole set of poses, we randomly skip a few non-essential –*i.e.*, non-trivial but non highly discriminative – posecodes, to account for natural human oversights. We also set highly-discriminative posecodes as unskippable. Finally, we remove redundant posecodes based on statistically frequent pairs and triplets of posecodes, and transitive relations between body parts. Details are provided in the supplementary material.

3. Posecode aggregation consists in merging together posecodes that share semantic information. This reduces the size of the caption and makes it more natural. We propose four specific aggregation rules:

○ *Entity-based aggregation* merges posecodes that have similar categorizations while describing keypoints that belong to a larger entity (*e.g.*the arm or the leg). For instance 'the left hand is below the right hand' + 'the left elbow is below the right hand' is combined into 'the left arm is below the right hand'.

○ *Symmetry-based aggregation* fuses posecodes that share the same categorization, and operate on joint sets that differ only by their side of the body. The joint of interest is hence put in plural form, *e.g.*'the left elbow is bent' + 'the right elbow is bent' becomes 'the elbows are bent'.

○ *Keypoint-based aggregation* brings together posecodes with a common keypoint. We factor the shared keypoint as the subject and concatenate the descriptions. The subject can be referred to again using *e.g.*'it' or 'they'. For instance, 'the left elbow is above the right elbow' + 'the left elbow is close to the right shoulder' + 'the left elbow is bent' is aggregated into 'The left elbow is above the right elbow, and close to the right shoulder. It is bent.'.

○ *Interpretation-based aggregation* merges posecodes that have the same categorization, but apply on different joint sets (that may overlap). Conversely to entity-based aggregation, it does not require that the involved keypoints belong to a shared entity. For instance, 'the left knee is bent' + 'right elbow is bent' becomes 'the left knee and the right elbow are bent'.

Aggregation rules are applied at random when their conditions are met. In particular, joint-based and interpretation-based aggregation rules may operate on the same posecodes. To avoid favouring one rule over the other, merging options are first listed together and then applied at random.

4. Posecode conversion into sentences is performed in two steps. First, we select the subject of each posecode. For symmetrical posecodes – which involve two joints that only differ by their body side – the subject is chosen at random between the two keypoints, and the other is randomly referred to by its name, its side or 'the other' to avoid repetitions and provide more varied captions. For asymmetrical posecodes, we define a 'main' keypoint (chosen as subject) and 'support' keypoints, used to specify pose information (*e.g.*the 'head' in 'the left hand is raised above the head'). For the sake of flow, in some predefined cases, we omit to name the support keypoint (*e.g.*'the left hand is raised above the head' is reduced to 'the left hand is raised'). Second, we combine all posecodes together in a final aggregation step. We obtain individual descriptions by plugging each posecode information into one template sentence, picked at random in the set of possible templates for a given posecode category. Finally, we concatenate the pieces in random order, using random pre-defined transitions. Optionally, for poses extracted from annotated sequences in BABEL [34], we add a sentence based on the associated high-level concepts (*e.g.*'the person is in a yoga pose').

Some automatic captioning examples are presented in Fig. 2 (right). The captioning process is highly modular; it allows to simply define, select and aggregate the posecodes based on different rules. Design of new kinds of posecodes (especially super-posecodes) or additional aggregation rules, can yield further improvements in the future. Importantly, randomization has been included at each step of the pipeline which makes it possible to generate different captions for the same pose, as a form of data augmentation, see supplementary material.

3.3 Dataset Statistics

The PoseScript dataset contains a total of 20,000 human poses sampled from the AMASS dataset using a farthest-point sampling algorithm to maximize the variability. Specifically, we first infer the joint positions for each pose in a normalized way, using the neutral body model with the default shape coefficients and the global orientation set to 0. Then, starting from one random pose in the dataset, we iteratively select the pose with the maximum MPJE (mean per-joint error) to the set of poses that were already selected.

We collected 3.893 human annotations on AMT (PoseScript-H). We semi-automatically clean the descriptions by manually correcting the spelling of words that are not in the English dictionary, by removing one of two identical consecutive words, and by checking the error detected by a spell checker, namely NeuSpell [26]. Human-written descriptions have an average length of 55.1 tokens (51.4 words, plus punctuation). An overview of the most frequent words, among a vocabulary of 1664, is presented in Fig. 3 (right).

We used the automatic captioning pipeline to increase the number of pose descriptions in the dataset (PoseScript-A). We designed a total of 87 posecodes, and automatically generated 6 captions for each of the 20,000 poses, in less than 6 min. Overall, automatic descriptions were produced using a posecode skipping rate of 15%, and an aggregation probability of 95%. Further details about the posecodes and other dataset statistics are provided in the supplementary.

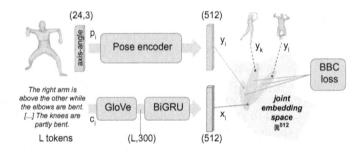

Fig. 5. Overview of the training scheme of the retrieval model. The input pose and caption are fed to a pose encoder and a text encoder respectively to map them into a joint embedding space. The loss encourages the pose embedding y_i and its caption embedding x_i to be close in this latent space, while being pulled apart from features of other poses in the same training batch (*e.g.* y_k and y_l).

We split the dataset into roughly 70% for training, 10% for validation and 20% for testing while ensuring that poses from the same AMASS sequence belong to the same split. When considering the automatic captions, we obtain 14,004 poses for training, 2,025 for validation and 3,971 for testing. When considering the human-written captions, each split respectively includes 2,713 (train), 400 (validation) and 780 (test) human-annotated poses.

4   Application to Text-to-Pose Retrieval

In this section, we study the problem of *text-to-pose retrieval*, which consists in ranking a large collection of poses by relevance to a given textual query (and likewise for pose-to-text retrieval). In such cross-modal retrieval task, it is standard to encode the multiple modalities into a common latent space.

Problem Formulation. Let $S = \{(c_i, p_i)\}_{i=1}^{N}$ be a set of caption-and-pose pairs. By construction, p_i is the most relevant pose for caption c_i, which means that $p_{j \neq i}$ should be ranked after p_i for text-to-pose retrieval. In other words, the retrieval model aims to learn a similarity function $s(c, p) \in \mathbb{R}$ such that $s(c_i, p_i) > s(c_i, p_{j \neq i})$. As a result, a set of relevant poses can be retrieved for a given text query by computing and ranking the similarity scores between the query and each pose from the collection (the same goes for pose-to-text retrieval).

Since poses and captions are from two different modalities, we first use modality-specific encoders to embed the inputs into a joint embedding space, where the two representations will be compared to produce the similarity score.

Let $\theta(\cdot)$ and $\phi(\cdot)$ be the textual and pose encoders respectively. We denote as $x = \theta(c) \in \mathbb{R}^d$ and $y = \phi(p) \in \mathbb{R}^d$ the $L2$-normalized representations of a caption c and of a pose p in the joint embedding space (see Fig. 5).

Encoders. The tokenized caption is embedded by a bi-GRU [9] taking pretrained GloVe word embeddings [29] as input. The pose is first encoded as a matrix of size $(24, 3)$, consisting of the rotation of the main 22 body joints with

Table 1. Text-to-pose and pose-to-text retrieval results on the test split of the PoseScript dataset. For human-written captions (PoseScript-H), we evaluate models trained on each specific caption set alone, and one pretrained on automatic captions (PoseScript-A) then finetuned (FT) on human captions.

	mRecall↑	pose-to-text			text-to-pose		
		R@1↑	R@5↑	R@10↑	R@1↑	R@5↑	R@10↑
test on PoseScript-A (3,971 samples)							
trained on PoseScript-A	**69.1**	41.8	72.6	82.3	50.1	80.0	87.7
test on PoseScript-H (780 samples)							
trained on PoseScript-A	7.6	2.3	9.7	13.9	1.4	6.8	11.5
trained on PoseScript-H	12.4	3.7	13.6	20.7	3.6	13.2	19.4
trained on PoseScript-A, FT on PoseScript-H	**30.4**	11.5	32.1	42.7	12.6	35.4	48.0

2 more representing the hands in axis-angle representation. The pose is then flattened and fed as input to the pose encoder, chosen as the VPoser encoder [27]: it consists of a 2-layer MLP with 512 units, batch normalization and leaky-ReLU, followed by a fully-connected layer of 32 units. We add a ReLU and a final projection layer to produce an embedding of the same size d as the text encoding.

Training. Given a batch of B training pairs (x_i, y_i), we use the Batch-Based Classification (BBC) loss which is common in cross-modal retrieval [43]:

$$\mathcal{L}_{\text{BBC}} = -\frac{1}{B}\sum_{i=1}^{B} \log\frac{\exp\big(\gamma\sigma(x_i, y_i)\big)}{\sum_j \exp\big(\gamma\sigma(x_i, y_j)\big)}, \tag{1}$$

where γ is a learnable temperature parameter and σ is the cosine similarity function $\sigma(x, y) = x^\top y/\big(\|x\|_2 \times \|y\|_2\big)$.

Evaluation Protocol. Text-to-pose retrieval is evaluated by ranking the whole set of poses for each of the query texts. We then compute the recall@K ($R@K$), which is the proportion of query texts for which the corresponding pose is ranked in the top-K retrieved poses. We proceed similarly to evaluate pose-to-text retrieval. We use K = 1, 5, 10 and additionally report the mean recall (mRecall) as the average over all recall@K values from both retrieval directions.

Quantitative Results. We report results on the test set of PoseScript in Table 1, both on automatic and human-written captions. Our model trained on automatic captions obtains a mean recall of 69.1%, with a R@1 above 40% and a R@10 above 80% on automatic captions. However, the performance degrades on human captions, as many words from the richer human vocabulary are unseen during training on automatic captions. When trained on human captions, the model obtains a higher – but still rather low – performance. Using human captions to finetune the initial model trained on automatic ones brings an improvement of a factor 2 and more, with a mean recall (resp. R@10 for text-to-pose) of 30.4% (resp. 48.0%) compared to 12.4% (resp. 19.4%) when training from scratch. This experiment clearly shows the benefit of using the automatic captioning pipeline to scale-up the PoseScript dataset. In particular, this suggests

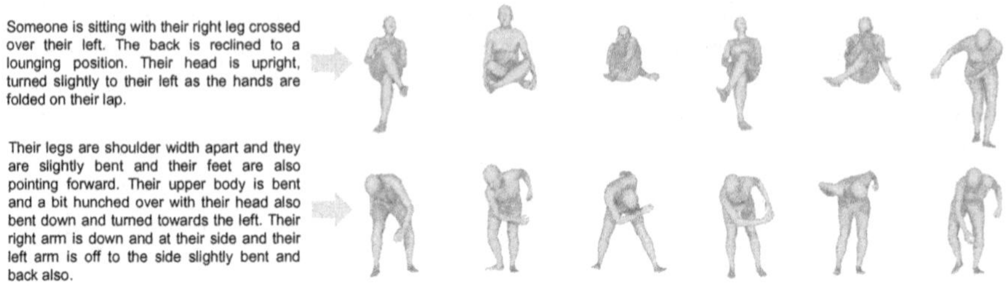

Someone is sitting with their right leg crossed over their left. The back is reclined to a lounging position. Their head is upright, turned slightly to their left as the hands are folded on their lap.

Their legs are shoulder width apart and they are slightly bent and their feet are also pointing forward. Their upper body is bent and a bit hunched over with their head also bent down and turned towards the left. Their right arm is down and at their side and their left arm is off to the side slightly bent and back also.

Fig. 6. Text-to-pose retrieval results for human-written captions from the PoseScript dataset. Directions such as 'left' and 'right' are relative to the body.

that the model is able to derive new concepts in human-written captions from non-trivial combination of existing posecodes in automatic captions.

Qualitative Retrieval Results. Examples of text-to-pose retrieval results are presented in Fig. 6. It appears that the model is able to encode several pose concepts concurrently and to distinguish between the left and right body parts.

Retrieval in Image Databases. MS Coco [23] is one of several real-world datasets that have been used for human mesh recovery. We resort to the 74,834 pseudo-ground-truth SMPL fits provided by EFT [16], on which we apply our text-to-pose retrieval model trained with PoseScript. We then retrieve 3D poses among this MS Coco-EFT set, and display the corresponding images with the associated bounding box around the human body. Results are shown in Fig. 7. We observe that overall, the constraints specified in the query text are satisfied in the images. Retrieval is based on the poses and not on the context, hence the third image of the first row where the pose is close to an actual kneeling one. This shows one application of a retrieval model trained on the PoseScript dataset: specific pose retrieval in images. Our model can be applied to any dataset of images containing humans, as long as SMPL fits are also available.

5   Application to Text-Conditioned Pose Generation

We next study the problem of *text-conditioned human pose generation, i.e.,* generating possible matching poses for a given text query. Our proposed model is based on Variational Auto-Encoders (VAEs) [19].

Training. Our goal is to generate a pose $\hat{p}$ given its caption c. To this end, we train a conditional VAE model that takes a tuple (p, c) composed of a pose p and its caption c at training time. Figure 8 gives an overview of our model. A pose encoder maps the pose p to a posterior over latent variables by producing the mean $\mu(p)$ and variance $\Sigma(p)$ of a normal distribution $\mathcal{N}_p = \mathcal{N}(\cdot|\mu(p), \Sigma(p))$. Another encoder is used to obtain a prior distribution $\mathcal{N}_c$, independent of p but conditioned on c. A latent variable $z \sim \mathcal{N}_p$ is sampled from $\mathcal{N}_p$ and decoded into a reconstructed pose $\hat{p}$. The training loss combines a reconstruction term $\mathcal{L}_R(p, \hat{p})$

The person is kneeling down like they are at the starting line of a race. The right knee is slightly off of the ground and the right hand is in front of it touching the ground.

Legs crossed, head facing forward.

The person is striding forward with the right leg in front of the left. The right heel is on the ground with the toes pointing up. The left knee is bent. The upper body is hunched forward slightly. Both arms are bent, with the left arm reaching in front of the upper body.

The person is leaning slightly forward with both arms stretched out behind them level with shoulders. The left foot is forward as if taking a step.

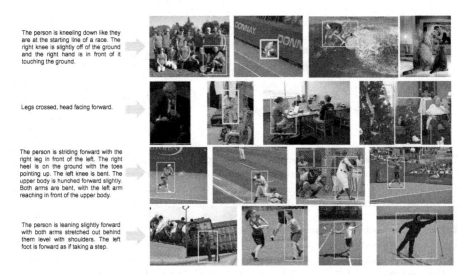

Fig. 7. Retrieval results in image databases. We use our text-to-pose retrieval model trained on human captions from PoseScript to retrieve 3D poses from SMPL fits on MS Coco, for some given text queries. We display the corresponding pictures for the top retrieved poses, along with the bounding boxes around the pose.

between the original and reconstructed poses, p and $\hat{p}$ and a regularization term, the Kullback-Leibler (KL) divergence between $\mathcal{N}_p$ and the prior $\mathcal{N}_c$:

$$\mathcal{L} = \mathcal{L}_R(p, \hat{p}) + \mathcal{L}_{KL}(\mathcal{N}_p, \mathcal{N}_c). \tag{2}$$

We also experiment with an additional loss term, $\mathcal{L}_{KL}(\mathcal{N}_p, \mathcal{N}(\cdot|0, I))$ which is a KL divergence between the posterior and the standard Gaussian $\mathcal{N}_0 = \mathcal{N}(\cdot|0, I)$. It can be seen as another regularizer and it also allows to sample poses from the model without conditioning on captions. We treat the variance of the decoder as a learned constant [38] and use a negative log likelihood (nll) as reconstruction loss, either from a Gaussian – which corresponds to an L2 loss and a learned variance term – or a Laplacian density, which corresponds to an L1 loss. Following VPoser, we use SMPL inputs, with the axis-angle representation, and output joint rotations with the continuous 6D representation of [46]. Our reconstruction loss $\mathcal{L}_R(p, \hat{p})$ is a sum of the reconstruction losses between the rotation matrices – evaluated with a Gaussian log-likelihood – the position of the joints and the position of the vertices, both evaluated with a Laplacian log-likelihood.

Text-Conditioned Generation. At test time, a caption c is encoded into $\mathcal{N}_c$, from which z is sampled and decoded into a generated pose $\hat{p}$.

Evaluation Metrics. We evaluate sample quality following the principle of the Fréchet inception distance: we compare the distributions of features extracted using our retrieval model (see Sect. 4), using real test poses and poses generated from test captions. This is denoted FID with an abuse of notation. We also report

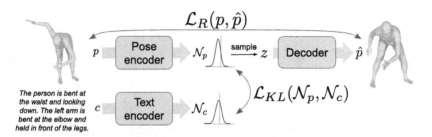

Fig. 8. Overview of the text-conditioned generative model. During training, it follows a VAE but where the latent distribution $\mathcal{N}_p$ from the pose encoder has a KL divergence term with the prior distribution $\mathcal{N}_c$ given by the text encoder. At test time, the sample z is drawn from the distribution $\mathcal{N}_c$.

Table 2. Evaluation of the text-conditioned generative model on PoseScript-A for a model without or with $\mathcal{L}_{KL}(\mathcal{N}_p, \mathcal{N}_0)$ (top) and on PoseScript-H without or with pretraining on PoseScript-A (bottom). For comparison, the mRecall when training and testing on real poses is 69.1 with PoseScript-A and 30.4 on PoseScript-H.

	FID↓	ELBO jts↑	ELBO vert.↑	ELBO rot.↑	mRecall R/G↑	mRecall G/R↑
evaluation on automatic captions (PoseScript-A)						
without $\mathcal{L}_{KL}(\mathcal{N}_p, \mathcal{N}_0)$	0.10	1.18	1.49	0.30	24.7	14.4
with $\mathcal{L}_{KL}(\mathcal{N}_p, \mathcal{N}_0)$	**0.08**	**1.23**	**1.52**	**0.33**	**29.2**	**17.3**
evaluation on human captions (PoseScript-H) for the model with $\mathcal{L}_{KL}(\mathcal{N}_p, \mathcal{N}_0)$						
without pretraining	0.14	-0.42	0.92	-0.64	4.8	2.7
with pretraining	**0.11**	**0.50**	**1.30**	**-0.17**	**15.4**	**16.2**

the mean-recall of retrieval models trained on real poses and evaluated on generated poses (mR R/G), and vice-versa (mR G/R). Both metrics are sensitive to sample quality: the retrieval model will fail if the data is unrealistic. The second metric is also sensitive to diversity: missing parts of the data distribution hinder the retrieval model trained on samples. Finally, we report the Evidence Lower Bound (ELBO) computed on joints, vertices or rotation matrices, normalized by the target dimension.

Results. We present quantitative results in Table 2. We first study the impact of adding the extra-regularization loss $\mathcal{L}_{KL}(\mathcal{N}_p, \mathcal{N}_0)$ to the model trained and evaluated on automatic captions. It improves all metrics (FID, ELBO and mRecall), thus we keep this configuration and evaluate it when (a) training on human captions and (b) pretraining on automatic captions and finetuning on human captions. Pretraining improves all metrics, in particular retrieval testing and ELBOs improve substantially: pretraining helps to yield realistic and diverse samples. We display generated samples in Fig. 9; the poses are realistic and generally correspond to the query. There are some variations, especially when the caption allows it, for instance with the position of the left arm in the top example or the

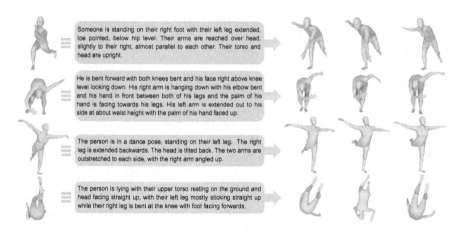

Fig. 9. Examples of generated samples. We show several generated samples (in grey) obtained for the human-written captions presented in the middle. For reference, we also show in blue the pose for which this annotation was originally collected.

Fig. 10. Example of potential application to SMPL fitting in images. Using the text-conditional pose prior (right) yields a more accurate 3D pose than a generic pose prior (left) when running the optimization-based SMPL fitting method SMPLify.

height of the right leg in the third row. Failure cases can happen; in particular rare words like 'lying' in the bottom row lead to higher variance in the generated samples; some of them are nevertheless close to the reference.

Application to SMPL Fitting in Image. We showcase the potential of leveraging text data for 3D tasks on a challenging example from SMPLify [4], in Fig. 10. We use our text-conditional prior instead of the generic VPoser prior [27] to initialize to a pose closer to the ground truth and to better guide the in-the-loop optimization, which helps to avoid bad local minima traps.

6   Conclusion

We introduced PoseScript, the first dataset to map 3D human poses and structural descriptions in natural language. We provided applications to text-to-pose retrieval and to text-conditioned human pose generation. For both tasks, performance is improved by pretraining on the automatic captions. Future avenues on this topic include generating images from the generated poses or exploring motion generation conditioned on complex textual description.

Acknowledgements. This work is supported in part by the Spanish government with the project MoHuCo PID2020-120049RB-I00.

References

1. Achlioptas, P., Fan, J., Hawkins, R., Goodman, N., Guibas, L.J.: ShapeGlot: learning language for shape differentiation. In: ICCV (2019)
2. Ahn, H., Ha, T., Choi, Y., Yoo, H., Oh, S.: Text2Action: generative adversarial synthesis from language to action. In: ICRA (2018)
3. Ahuja, C., Morency, L.P.: Language2Pose: natural language grounded pose forecasting. 3DV (2019)
4. Bogo, F., Kanazawa, A., Lassner, C., Gehler, P., Romero, J., Black, M.J.: Keep It SMPL: automatic estimation of 3D human pose and shape from a single image. In: Leibe, B., Matas, J., Sebe, N., Welling, M. (eds.) ECCV 2016. LNCS, vol. 9909, pp. 561–578. Springer, Cham (2016). https://doi.org/10.1007/978-3-319-46454-1_34
5. Bourdev, L., Malik, J.: Poselets: body part detectors trained using 3D human pose annotations. In: ICCV (2009)
6. Briq, R., Kochar, P., Gall, J.: Towards better adversarial synthesis of human images from text. arXiv preprint arXiv:2107.01869 (2021)
7. Chen, D.Z., Chang, A.X., Nießner, M.: ScanRefer: 3D object localization in RGB-D scans using natural language. In: Vedaldi, A., Bischof, H., Brox, T., Frahm, J.-M. (eds.) ECCV 2020. LNCS, vol. 12365, pp. 202–221. Springer, Cham (2020). https://doi.org/10.1007/978-3-030-58565-5_13
8. Chen, K., Choy, C.B., Savva, M., Chang, A.X., Funkhouser, T., Savarese, S.: Text2Shape: generating shapes from natural language by learning joint embeddings. In: Jawahar, C.V., Li, H., Mori, G., Schindler, K. (eds.) ACCV 2018. LNCS, vol. 11363, pp. 100–116. Springer, Cham (2019). https://doi.org/10.1007/978-3-030-20893-6_7
9. Cho, K., et al.: Learning phrase representations using RNN encoder-decoder for statistical machine translation. In: EMNLP (2014)
10. Feng, F., Wang, X., Li, R.: Cross-modal retrieval with correspondence autoencoder. In: ACMMM (2014)
11. Fieraru, M., Zanfir, M., Pirlea, S.C., Olaru, V., Sminchisescu, C.: AIFit: automatic 3D human-interpretable feedback models for fitness training. In: CVPR (2021)
12. Ghosh, A., Cheema, N., Oguz, C., Theobalt, C., Slusallek, P.: Synthesis of compositional animations from textual descriptions. In: ICCV (2021)
13. Guo, et al.: Action2Motion: conditioned generation of 3D human motions. In: ACMMM (2020)
14. Ionescu, C., Papava, D., Olaru, V., Sminchisescu, C.: Human3.6M: large scale datasets and predictive methods for 3D human sensing in natural environments. IEEE Trans. PAMI **36**, 1325–1339 (2014)
15. Jiang, Y., Huang, Z., Pan, X., Loy, C.C., Liu, Z.: Talk-to-edit: fine-grained facial editing via dialog. In: ICCV (2021)
16. Joo, H., Neverova, N., Vedaldi, A.: Exemplar fine-tuning for 3D human model fitting towards in-the-wild 3D human pose estimation. In: 3DV (2020)
17. Karpathy, A., Fei-Fei, L.: Deep visual-semantic alignments for generating image descriptions. In: CVPR (2015)
18. Kim, H., Zala, A., Burri, G., Bansal, M.: FixMyPose: pose correctional captioning and retrieval. In: AAAI (2021)

19. Kingma, D.P., Welling, M.: Auto-encoding variational bayes. In: ICLR (2014)
20. Li, S., Xiao, T., Li, H., Yang, W., Wang, X.: Identity-aware textual-visual matching with latent co-attention. In: ICCV (2017)
21. Li, W., Zhang, Z., Liu, Z.: Action recognition based on a bag of 3D points. In: CVPR Workshops (2010)
22. Lin, A.S., Wu, L., Corona, R., Tai, K.W.H., Huang, Q., Mooney, R.J.: Generating animated videos of human activities from natural language descriptions. In: NeurIPS workshops (2018)
23. Lin, T.-Y., et al.: Microsoft COCO: common objects in context. In: Fleet, D., Pajdla, T., Schiele, B., Tuytelaars, T. (eds.) ECCV 2014. LNCS, vol. 8693, pp. 740–755. Springer, Cham (2014). https://doi.org/10.1007/978-3-319-10602-1_48
24. Lucas, T., Baradel, F., Weinzaepfel, P., Rogez, G.: PoseGPT: quantization-based 3D human motion generation and forecasting. In: ECCV (2022)
25. Mahmood, N., Ghorbani, N., Troje, N.F., Pons-Moll, G., Black, M.J.: AMASS: archive of motion capture as surface shapes. In: ICCV (2019)
26. Muralidhar Jayanthi, S., Pruthi, D., Neubig, G.: NeuSpell: a neural spelling correction toolkit. In: EMNLP (2020)
27. Pavlakos, G., et al.: Expressive body capture: 3D hands, face, and body from a single image. In: CVPR (2019)
28. Pavlakos, G., Zhou, X., Daniilidis, K.: Ordinal depth supervision for 3D human pose estimation. In: CVPR (2018)
29. Pennington, J., Socher, R., Manning, C.D.: Glove: global vectors for word representation. In: EMNLP (2014)
30. Petrovich, M., Black, M.J., Varol, G.: Action-conditioned 3D human motion synthesis with transformer VAE. In: ICCV (2021)
31. Plappert, M., Mandery, C., Asfour, T.: The kit motion-language dataset. Big Data 4, 236–252 (2016)
32. Plappert, M., Mandery, C., Asfour, T.: Learning a bidirectional mapping between human whole-body motion and natural language using deep recurrent neural networks. Robot. Auton. Syst. 109, 13–26 (2018)
33. Pons-Moll, G., Fleet, D.J., Rosenhahn, B.: Posebits for monocular human pose estimation. In: CVPR (2014)
34. Punnakkal, A.R., Chandrasekaran, A., Athanasiou, N., Quiros-Ramirez, A., Black, M.J.: BABEL: bodies, action and behavior with English labels. In: CVPR (2021)
35. Radford, A., et al.: Learning transferable visual models from natural language supervision. In: ICML (2021)
36. Ramesh, A., et al.: Zero-shot text-to-image generation. In: ICML (2021)
37. Romero, J., Tzionas, D., Black, M.J.: Embodied hands: modeling and capturing hands and bodies together. In: SIGGRAPH Asia (2017)
38. Rybkin, O., Daniilidis, K., Levine, S.: Simple and effective VAE training with calibrated decoders. In: ICML (2021)
39. Shahroudy, A., Liu, J., Ng, T.T., Wang, G.: NTU RGB+D: a large scale dataset for 3D human activity analysis. In: CVPR (2016)
40. Streuber, S., et al.: Body talk: crowdshaping realistic 3D avatars with words. ACM TOG 35, 1–14 (2016)
41. Suveren-Erdogan, C., Suveren, S.: Teaching of basic posture skills in visually impaired individuals and its implementation under aggravated conditions. J. Educ. Learn. 7, 109–116 (2018)
42. Vinyals, O., Toshev, A., Bengio, S., Erhan, D.: Show and tell: a neural image caption generator. In: CVPR (2015)

43. Vo, N., et al.: Composing text and image for image retrieval-an empirical odyssey. In: CVPR (2019)
44. Yamada, T., Matsunaga, H., Ogata, T.: Paired recurrent autoencoders for bidirectional translation between robot actions and linguistic descriptions. IEEE RAL **3**, 3441–3448 (2018)
45. Zhang, Y., Briq, R., Tanke, J., Gall, J.: Adversarial synthesis of human pose from text. In: Akata, Z., Geiger, A., Sattler, T. (eds.) DAGM GCPR 2020. LNCS, vol. 12544, pp. 145–158. Springer, Cham (2021). https://doi.org/10.1007/978-3-030-71278-5_11
46. Zhou, Y., Barnes, C., Lu, J., Yang, J., Li, H.: On the continuity of rotation representations in neural networks. In: CVPR (2019)

DProST: Dynamic Projective Spatial Transformer Network for 6D Pose Estimation

Jaewoo Park[1,2] and Nam Ik Cho[1,2,3(✉)]

[1] Department of ECE and INMC, Seoul National University, Seoul, Korea
[2] SNU-LG AI Research Center, Seoul, Korea
{bjw0611,nicho}@snu.ac.kr
[3] IPAI, Seoul National University, Seoul, Korea

Abstract. Predicting the object's 6D pose from a single RGB image is a fundamental computer vision task. Generally, the distance between transformed object vertices is employed as an objective function for pose estimation methods. However, projective geometry in the camera space is not considered in those methods and causes performance degradation. In this regard, we propose a new pose estimation system based on a projective grid instead of object vertices. Our pose estimation method, dynamic projective spatial transformer network (DProST), localizes the region of interest grid on the rays in camera space and transforms the grid to object space by estimated pose. The transformed grid is used as both a sampling grid and a new criterion of the estimated pose. Additionally, because DProST does not require object vertices, our method can be used in a mesh-less setting by replacing the mesh with a reconstructed feature. Experimental results show that mesh-less DProST outperforms the state-of-the-art mesh-based methods on the LINEMOD and LINEMOD-OCCLUSION dataset, and shows competitive performance on the YCBV dataset with mesh data. The source code is available at https://github.com/parkjaewoo0611/DProST.

Keywords: 6D pose estimation · Spatial transformer network · 3D reconstruction

1 Introduction

Single image object pose estimation attempts to predict the transformation from the object space to the camera space based on an observed RGB image. Because the transformation can be expressed as rotation and translation, each having three degrees of freedom (DoF), it is also called the 6-DoF pose estimation. Finding the pose is commonly required in augmented reality (AR) [23], robot grasping problems [6,38,39,46], and autonomous driving [4,43].

Supplementary Information The online version contains supplementary material available at https://doi.org/10.1007/978-3-031-20068-7_21.

© The Author(s), under exclusive license to Springer Nature Switzerland AG 2022
S. Avidan et al. (Eds.): ECCV 2022, LNCS 13666, pp. 363–379, 2022.
https://doi.org/10.1007/978-3-031-20068-7_21

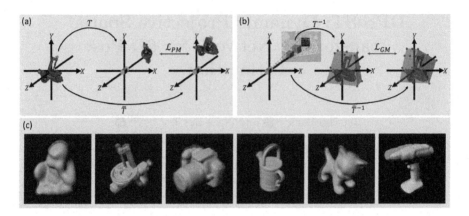

Fig. 1. Key idea and perspective effect: (a) Point matching loss is based on the distance between object vertices in camera space. The estimated pose is represented by T, while the ground-truth pose is denoted by $\bar{T}$. (b) Grid matching loss is based on the distance between cone-beam grid in object space. The region of interest grid is localized in camera space and transformed to object space by inverse transformation T^{-1}. We colorize the grid in blue and brown for each prediction and ground-truth. (c) The superimposed examples of each perspective and orthographic projection visualize the shape variance due to projective geometry.

Recently, deep learning-based methods have shown outstanding performance in complex computer vision problems. Therefore, researchers have proposed methods for applying deep learning to the object pose estimation problem with great performance [2,8,14,15,19,21,22,26,28,31,32,37,40,41]. Some of these state-of-the-art methods use the point matching (PM) loss for pose estimation [19,21]. In particular, they used the pair-wise distance of the transformed object vertices by predicted pose and ground-truth pose in camera space. The PM loss is a trivial approach in the camera space. However, although the PM-based methods assume the camera's focal length and principal point available, the perspective effect is ignored because they only consider the vertices on the rigid object as shown in Fig. 1(a). Consequently, the perspective effect is treated as a noisy shape variance as shown in Fig. 1(c) that degrades the pose estimation performance. On the other hand, image-space representation based methods [5,22,28,29,31,41] may learn the perspective effect implicitly by the projected image. However, they also fail to address the projective geometry in their loss function and suffer from z-direction translation error because of 3D information loss.

Meanwhile, projective spatial transformer (ProST) network has been proposed in [9], which first considered the projective geometry in spatial transformer network [17] to reflect the perspective effect. As the target of ProST is CT/radiograph registration, it dealt with only the limited camera pose, where the distance from the camera to the view frustum is fixed. However, since the region-of-interest (RoI) on camera space is vastly distributed in the object pose estimation, the ProST approach is not directly applicable because of memory and computation issues. In other words, to apply ProST on the object pose estimation, dynamically focusing the grid on the localized RoI is necessary.

In this regard, we propose a dynamic projective spatial transformer network (DProST) that estimates object pose based on the localized RoI cone-beam grid covering the object in object space. This grid leverages the 3D information while considering the projective geometry, as shown in Fig. 1(b). Additionally, we propose the grid distance (GD) loss and the grid matching (GM) loss to train the model based on grid correspondence. The grid-based approach has four major advantages. First, the shape of the cone-beam grid reflects the projective geometry. Second, because the grid has 3D coordinates, grid matching shows accurate z-axis translation estimation. Third, because the grid is uniformly distributed, it is relatively free from the object shape biases. Finally, since it does not use object vertices, it can be applied in mesh-less settings and shows excellent performance even with a simple space carving-based voxel feature instead of mesh. We confirm that our method shows state-of-the-art performance in LINEMOD [12], LINEMOD-OCCLUSION [1], and comparable performance in YCBV [42] datasets.

Our contributions are summarized as follows:

- We propose DProST based on a localized grid in the object space for pose estimation.
- We propose GM loss and GD loss considering projective geometry.
- We confirm that our method can be used in a mesh-less environment based on space-carving feature that was extracted from reference images and masks.
- We confirm that our method shows state-of-the-art performance on LINEMOD, LINEMOD-OCCLUSION, and competitive performance on YCBV benchmarks.

2   Related Work

Recently proposed deep learning-based single image object pose estimation methods can be divided into three types. The first is to estimate the 3D intermediate representation and then find the matching pose using the perspective-n-point (PnP) algorithm [20]. For example, [15,32] used the corners of a 3D bounding box, [31,37] detected projected 3D keypoints of an object, and [28] used 2D-3D coordinates to train the network.

The second type used gradient updates to minimize the difference between latent features or projected texture. For example, [5,16] updated the pose by minimizing the difference between 2D reconstruction result and the observed image. Furthermore, as sophisticated novel view synthesis methods like [24, 25,36] are proposed, pose estimation methods based on 3D view projection such as [27,44] are also suggested, which also use the gradient update over the view projection models. In particular, [27] shows both RGB-based and RGBD-based results, and considers mesh-less unseen object scenario. However, view projection-based methods require a lot of computation overhead to learn the

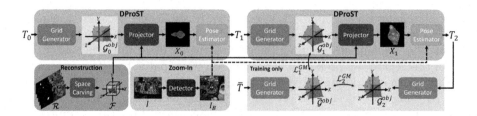

Fig. 2. Overview of DProST: Space carving extracts a reference feature from images and masks. Given the reference feature and detected object, the object's pose is iteratively refined by DProST. Grid generator converts the pose to the object space grid visualized in red dots. The projector outputs estimated appearance based on the grid and the reference feature. Then, the pose estimator refines the pose based on appearance. Grid is also used as a comparison target for GM loss during the training phase.

3D feature. Additionally, although an unseen and mesh-less scenario in [27] has great generalizability, it is not as accurate as the state-of-the-art methods based on mesh-based seen object. Considering the pros and cons of the above-referenced methods, to improve the generalizability without compromising the performance, we focus on mesh-less seen object scenario by replacing the mesh with the reference feature. Additionally, to reduce the computation overhead of 3D reconstruction, we use a simple space-carving method instead of a deep learning model.

The last type directly estimates the pose from the network. For example, [8,22,40,45] proposed a learning method to use both 2D-3D coordinate representation and direct pose regression. [21] used the rendered object image and the observed object image as inputs to iteratively refine the pose. Also, in this method, the disentangled representation of rotation and translation greatly improved the performance. Based on an iterative fashion and disentangled representation similar to [21], the single view method in [19] showed the most superior performance in the object pose estimation challenge [13] using a large synthetic image dataset. However, because these methods are based on point matching loss, they fail to address the projective geometry in objective function. We combine the iterative pose refining configuration with ProST [9] to consider both projective geometry and the performance.

3 Method

3.1 Framework Overview

The overall process of DProST is shown in Fig. 2. We follow the zoom-in setting used in [19,21,22]. Hence, the off-the-shelf detector is first used to find the bounding box area of the object I_B from the overall image I, where the bounding box is $B = (x, y, w, h)$.

Then, the space-carving-based reconstruction stage generates a reference feature $\mathcal{F}$ in the object space's unit sphere based on the reference set $\mathcal{R} =$

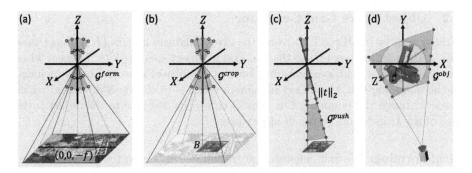

Fig. 3. Substeps in grid generator: (a) The grid inside a unit sphere is generated in camera space on the ray to the 3D image plane. (b) The RoI grid is extracted based on the bounding box. (c) The grid is pushed by $\|t\|_2$ along the ray to cover the object in camera space. (d) The grid is transformed by T^{-1} from camera space to object space.

$\left\{ \left(I_k^{\mathcal{R}}, M_k^{\mathcal{R}}, \bar{T}_k^{\mathcal{R}}, K_k^{\mathcal{R}} \right) | k \in [1, N^{\mathcal{R}}] \right\}$ consists of $N^{\mathcal{R}}$ tuples of images $I_k^{\mathcal{R}}$ and masks $M_k^{\mathcal{R}}$ with known poses $\bar{T}_k^{\mathcal{R}}$ and intrinsic matrices $K_k^{\mathcal{R}}$ sampled from training set, which can be written as

$$\mathcal{F} = f_{carv}(\mathcal{R}). \tag{1}$$

We will discuss the details about the reconstruction stage in Sect. 3.3.

Subsequently, we iteratively refine the initial pose T_0 based on the $\mathcal{F}$ and I_B. Each pose refinement iteration i consists of three submodules. First, based on a bounding box B, object pose $T_i = \{R_i, t_i\}$, and intrinsic camera parameter K, grid generator extracts a localized RoI grid as

$$\mathcal{G}_i^{obj} = f_{grid}(B, T_i, K) \tag{2}$$

on the rays from the camera to the image plane in object space. Grid generator is composed of four sub-steps, grid forming, grid cropping, grid pushing, and grid transformation, and we will discuss the details of each step in Sect. 3.2.

The projector renders object appearance X_i of each iteration by sampling features from $\mathcal{F}$ based on $\mathcal{G}_i^{obj}$ that can be written as

$$X_i = f_{proj}(\mathcal{G}_i^{obj}, \mathcal{F}). \tag{3}$$

The projection stage plays a similar role to mesh rendering in [19, 21]. It can also be replaced with mesh rendering methods when the reference pose is not diverse enough to carve the object shape in the reconstruction stage.

Finally, to refine the pose, the pose estimator network of the i-th iteration with parameter θ_i predicts the relative pose ΔT_i between X_i and I_B as

$$\Delta T_i = f_{\theta_i}(X_i, I_B). \tag{4}$$

The details of the projection stage and pose estimator are discussed in Sect. 3.4. Finally, we will address the overall objective function in Sect. 3.5.

3.2   Object Space Grid Generator

Grid generator in DProST converts the given intrinsic matrix (K), object pose (T), and bounding box (B) to the RoI grid in object space $(\mathcal{G}^{obj})$. Two key ideas are used for RoI grid localization. First, as the object's projection is included in the bounding box, the object in camera space is in the ray's direction, which passes through the bounding box area. Second, the distance to the object is the size of the translation vector in object pose.

Grid Forming: We first generate the grid on the rays from the camera (origin) to the image plane pixel's 3D location $\mathcal{I} \in \mathbb{R}^{H \times W \times 3}$ in the camera space and match the principal point to $(0, 0, -f)$ as shown in Fig. 3(a). The initialized grid with the given the focal length f and principal point $\mathbf{p} = (p_x, p_y)$ can be written as follows:

$$\mathcal{I}(l, m) = (l - p_x, m - p_y, -f), \tag{5}$$

$$\mathcal{G}^{form}(l, m, n) = \frac{\mathcal{I}(l, m)}{\|\mathcal{I}(l, m)\|_2} \left(\frac{2n}{N_z} - 1 \right), \tag{6}$$

where (l, m) is the (x, y) index of a pixel in $\mathcal{I}$, the $\mathcal{G}^{form} \in \mathbb{R}^{H \times W \times N_z \times 3}$ is formed grid, N_z is the number of points in the grid on each ray, and $n \in [0, N_z - 1]$ is the index of the points on each ray, respectively.

Grid Cropping: Bounding box is used as a direction indicator from camera to object in camera space. As shown in Fig. 3(b), we used the RoI align [10] method to extract the grid on the rays that are projected into the bounding box $B = (x, y, w, h)$ to focus the grid near the object, which can be written as

$$\mathcal{G}^{crop} = RoI\,Align\left(\mathcal{G}^{form}, B \right), \tag{7}$$

where $\mathcal{G}^{crop} \in \mathbb{R}^{h \times w \times N_z \times 3}$ is the extracted RoI grid.

Grid Pushing: We then push the grid on the rays as much as the distance to object $\|t\|_2$ towards the $\mathcal{I}$ to cover the object in camera space, as shown in Fig. 3(c), which can be written as

$$\mathcal{G}^{push} = \{ g - \|t\|_2 \frac{g}{\|g\|_2} sign\left((g)_z \right) | g \in \mathcal{G}^{crop}(l, m, n) \}, \tag{8}$$

where $\mathcal{G}^{push} \in \mathbb{R}^{h \times w \times N_z \times 3}$ is the pushed grid in camera space, and the $sign$ function is used to invert the pushing direction of grid in $+Z$ to $-Z$ direction.

Grid Transformation: Finally, to cover the $\mathcal{F}$ in object space with the grid, as shown in Fig. 3(d), we transform the pushed grid from camera space to object space with inverse of pose transformation as

$$\mathcal{G}^{obj} = T^{-1}\left(\mathcal{G}^{push} \right), \tag{9}$$

where $\mathcal{G}^{obj} \in \mathbb{R}^{h \times w \times N_z \times 3}$ is the RoI grid that tightly wraps around the $\mathcal{F}$. Note that unlike point matching-based and render-and-compare-based methods [19, 21], which require transformation twice for each loss computation and rendering, $\mathcal{G}^{obj}$ can be used for both grid sampling in projector and loss function in our method.

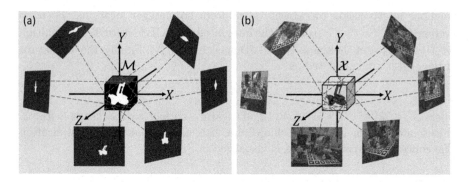

Fig. 4. 3D feature reconstruction: We visualize the object shaping and coloring process of generating reference feature. (a) Only the voxels projected into each reference object mask remain positive, while others are cut off. (b) The values in reference images are averaged to extract the RGB value of reference voxels.

3.3   3D Feature Reconstruction

In this section, we present a non-learning-required and a simple space-carving-based reference feature generation method. To generate the reference feature $\mathcal{F}$ in the unit sphere of the object space, we use pose-known reference images $\{X^k | k \in [1, N^{\mathcal{R}}]\}$ and corresponding masks $\{M^k | k \in [1, N^{\mathcal{R}}]\}$ sampled from the training set. The reference quality is improved when the various views and fine details are included. Hence, we set the first reference image as the sample with the largest object mask in the training set. Then, based on the geodesic distance of the rotation matrix, we use the farthest point sampling (FPS) algorithm in [31] to select the other reference images. We generate a 3D canvas as a normalized voxel grid $\mathcal{A} \in \mathbb{R}^{S \times S \times S \times 3}$, which is divided uniformly into S^3 voxels, and each contains the coordinates of itself. Then, for each reference mask and image, $\mathcal{A}$ is projected with the given K and the pose of the k-th reference $\bar{T}^k$ to find the region where the canvas grid is projected. Hence, we assign the projected canvas location in A^k as

$$A^k = \pi \left(\bar{T}^k \left(\mathcal{A} \right), K \right), \tag{10}$$

where $\pi(p, K)$ represents the projection of the point p with the intrinsic matrix K in the pinhole camera model. Then, using A^k as a grid, we apply the grid sampling method proposed in [17] to generate a 3D RGB feature $\mathcal{X}^k \in \mathbb{R}^{S \times S \times S \times 3}$

from X^k and a 3D mask feature $\mathcal{M}^k \in \mathbb{R}^{S \times S \times S \times 1}$ from M^k as follows:

$$\mathcal{X}^k = X^k \left(\left(a^k \right)_x, \left(a^k \right)_y \right), \tag{11}$$

$$\mathcal{M}^k = M^k \left(\left(a^k \right)_x, \left(a^k \right)_y \right), \tag{12}$$

where $\left(a^k \right)_x$ and $\left(a^k \right)_y$ are (x, y) coordinates in A^k. Note that we use nearest-neighbor interpolation to extract values from non-integer locations. Then, we average the $\mathcal{X}^{k \in [1, N^{\mathcal{R}}]}$'s to obtain the integrated 3D RGB feature $\mathcal{X}$, and multiply $\mathcal{M}^{k \in [1, N^{\mathcal{R}}]}$'s to get the shape-carved 3D mask feature $\mathcal{M}$. Finally, the 3D features of the object are calculated as

$$\mathcal{F} = \mathcal{M} \odot \mathcal{X}, \tag{13}$$

where $\mathcal{F} \in \mathbb{R}^{S \times S \times S \times 3}$ is an RGB 3D feature with a carved shape with the object information in voxel fashion, and $\odot$ is an element-wise multiplication. The concept of carving process is visualized in Fig. 4.

3.4   Projector and Pose Estimator

With the $\mathcal{G}^{obj}$ obtained from grid generator and the reference feature $\mathcal{F}$, we apply the grid sampling [9], which can be written as

$$\mathcal{F}^{interp} = interp(\mathcal{F}, \mathcal{G}^{obj}), \tag{14}$$

where $\mathcal{F}^{interp} \in \mathbb{R}^{h \times w \times N_z \times 3}$ is the sampled feature of the object and $interp$ is the trilinear interpolation-based grid sampling function.

Then, to compare the estimated pose and I_B, we project $\mathcal{F}^{interp}$ into a 2D feature $F \in \mathbb{R}^{h \times w \times 3}$ by choosing the closest valid point to the camera on each ray as

$$F = \mathcal{F}^{interp} \left(l, m, \min_n \{ \delta(l, m) \} \right), \tag{15}$$

where $\delta(l, m) = \{ n | \mathcal{F}^{interp}(l, m, n) \neq 0 \}$.

For each iteration i, we use a ResNet34 [11] based pose estimator to refine the pose T_{i-1} to T_i to match the projected reference F_{i-1} to the detected object image I_B. The last layer of ResNet34 is replaced with a fully connected layer that outputs nine values, each of which is image space translation, scale factor, and two axis-based relative rotation representation as in [19]. See the supplementary materials for more details about the pose estimator's output format.

3.5   Objective Functions

Instead of PM loss based on the mesh vertices of the object, we propose GM loss for mesh-less training. For each iteration i, we use the Euclidean distance of the object space grid as the GM loss, which can be written as

$$\mathcal{L}_i^{GM} = \frac{1}{|\mathcal{G}_i^{obj}|} \sum \left\| \bar{\mathcal{G}}^{obj} - \mathcal{G}_i^{obj} \right\|_2, \tag{16}$$

where $|\mathcal{G}_i^{obj}|$ is the number of points in the grid, $\bar{\mathcal{G}}^{obj}$ is a grid from the ground-truth pose $\bar{T}$, and $\mathcal{G}_i^{obj}$ is the predicted object space grid. Note that, as the DProST module is based on fully differentiable operations, the i-th GM loss is used as an objective function for the i-th pose estimator, as shown in Fig. 2.

Additionally, to help the pose estimator determine the distance from the camera to the object in the grid pushing step, we use an auxiliary loss called GD loss as

$$\mathcal{L}_i^{GD} = \left|\|\bar{t}\|_2 - \|t_i\|_2\right|_1, \tag{17}$$

which is the absolute difference between the predicted distance and ground-truth distance in the grid pushing step.

Finally, the overall loss $\mathcal{L}_i$ for training our network on each iteration i is the combination of the above two losses as

$$\mathcal{L}_i = \mathcal{L}_i^{GM} + \lambda^{GD}\mathcal{L}_i^{GD}, \tag{18}$$

where λ^{GD} is the balance factor. The $\mathcal{L}_i$ is applied to outputs of each iterations' pose estimator.

4 Experiments

4.1 Datasets and Evaluation Metrics

The performance is tested on LINEMOD (LM) [12], LINEMOD-OCCLUSION (LMO) [1], and YCB-video (YCBV) dataset [42]. The LM consists of 13 objects with approximately 1.2K images per object. We follow the settings described in [2], which uses 15% of the data for training and the rest for testing. The LMO dataset is a subset of the LM dataset consisting of eight objects in more cluttered scenes. The YCBV dataset consists of 21 objects with between 10k and 20k real images per object. The YCBV dataset is very hard compared to the LM dataset because of the hard occluded samples. Also, the views in YCBV dataset are not as various as the LM dataset. We used the official pbr dataset from the BOP challenge [13] in training along with the real image training set. For the LM dataset, we also report the performance trained on the synthetic training dataset introduced from [21].

The $ADD(\text{-}S)$ score [12] is used to measure the performance, which is the most widely employed metric in the object pose estimation [16,21,37,37,40,42]. In particular, we use the ADD score for non-symmetric objects, which computes the pair-wise distance of vertices transformed by the predicted pose and ground-truth pose. And we use the $ADD\text{-}S$ score for symmetric objects, which measures the nearest distance of transformed vertices by predicted pose and ground-truth pose. The predicted pose is considered correct if the mean distance is less than the threshold ratio thr of the object diameter in the $ADD(\text{-}S)^{thr}$ metric. The area-under-curve of the $ADD(\text{-}S)$ metric [42] is additionally used for the YCBV dataset.

We also compare the projection error $Proj2D$ [21], which measures the pixel-level discrepancy of the projected vertices in the image space.

4.2   Experiment Setup

Implementation Details. Our pipeline is implemented based on the Pytorch [30] and Pytorch3d [33] framework. We used the ADAM optimizer [18] with a learning rate of 0.0001. Because the number of real training images is much smaller than the number of synthetic training images, we construct half of each mini-batch from real images and the other half from synthetic images to focus on the real dataset. The pose estimator is trained for 3,000 epochs based on the real dataset, and we divide the learning rate by ten on the 2,000th epoch for the LM and LMO dataset. Similarly, we train on the YCBV dataset for 300 epochs and divide the learning rate on the 200th epoch.

The pretrained ResNet34 [11] on ImageNet [7] is used as the backbone of the pose estimator. To prevent the object from being out of sight in the initial pose, we set the initial translation vector to fit the projection of the 3D reference feature into the bounding box with the identity matrix as the initial pose's rotation as implemented in [19]. For more details about the initial pose, check the supplementary materials. Additionally, we use distinct weights for the pose estimator in each iteration to teach the models to work in a cascade fashion [3], that shows better performance than that of iterative models. We use $\lambda^{GD} = 1$ in Eq. (18).

In the reconstruction stage, we use eight reference images ($N^{\mathcal{R}} = 8$) to generate reference features for each object and the number of voxels along the axis is 128 ($S = 128$) because we used a 128×128 image size for the pose estimator. In the grid generator, 64-grid points ($N_z = 64$) per ray are used and confirmed that the quality of the projection is saturated when N_z is greater than 64. Details about hyperparameter experiments are given in the ablation study.

Object Zoom-In. We zoom in [19,21,22,40] the detected object to a fixed size 128×128, while keeping the aspect ratio of the image. In particular, we follow the dynamic zoom-in setting suggested in [22], where noisy ground-truth bounding boxes are used in the training phase and off-the-shelf detectors [34,35] are used in the test phase.

4.3   Comparison with the State-of-the-Art

Table 1 presents the results on the LM dataset. As shown in the table, our method shows state-of-the-art accuracy on the LM dataset even without mesh data. Compared to a point matching-based method [21], which uses mesh vertices, our method shows more accurate results for almost every object.

Also, the accuracy of the LMO dataset is described in Table 2, and our method shows state-of-the-art performance. Some qualitative results on the LMO dataset are shown in Fig. 5. The figure shows that even the low-quality texture reference from the simple space-carving is enough for most samples.

However, we confirm that the reference feature-based projection is vulnerable to some conditions. For example, when the overall training view is similar, such as a video-based training set, or when majority of the samples are occluded,

Table 1. Results on the LM dataset. A comparison of other baseline methods and our method in terms of the $ADD(\text{-}S)^{0.1d}$ score. Objects annotated with ($*$) indicate symmetric pose ambiguity. A.O represents a pose estimator trained on all objects.

Method	PoseCNN [42]	DeepIM [21]	HybridPose [37]	GDR-Net [40]	SO-Pose [8]	RePOSE [16]	DProST	DProST	DProST	DProST
	w/ Mesh						w/o Mesh			
A.O	✓	✓		✓	✓			✓		✓
Training set	real +syn	real +syn	real +syn	real +syn	real +syn	real +syn	real +syn	real +syn	real +pbr	real +pbr
ape	–	77.0	77.6	–	–	79.5	91.4	91.5	91.1	**91.6**
benchwise	–	97.5	99.6	–	–	100.0	100.0	99.9	100.0	99.7
cam	–	93.5	95.9	–	–	99.2	98.8	98.4	99.1	98.2
can	–	96.5	93.6	–	–	99.8	99.5	99.5	**99.9**	99.6
cat	–	82.1	93.5	–	–	97.9	98.0	98.1	97.9	**98.2**
driller	–	95.0	97.2	–	–	99.0	**99.5**	97.0	99.2	98.4
duck	–	77.7	87.0	–	–	80.3	88.5	**91.0**	89.2	90.8
eggbox*	–	97.1	99.6	–	–	100.0	99.9	99.8	100.0	99.8
glue*	–	99.4	98.7	–	–	98.3	99.8	100.0	100.0	99.9
holepuncher	–	52.8	92.5	–	–	96.9	97.0	97.0	96.4	**97.6**
iron	–	98.3	98.1	–	–	100.0	99.5	98.8	100.0	99.1
lamp	–	97.5	96.9	–	–	99.8	99.6	99.7	100.0	99.8
phone	–	87.7	98.3	–	–	**98.9**	95.8	98.2	97.4	97.7
Average	62.7	88.6	94.5	93.7	96.0	96.1	97.5	97.6	**97.7**	**97.7**

the shape of the reference quality is degraded. Because the YCBV has these characteristics, our reconstruction module fails to generate a plausible shape of the reference feature of some objects as shown in Fig. 6(a), therefore we used the mesh-based renderer in pytorch3d instead of our projector in the YCBV dataset. As stated in Table 3, our model shows comparable performance to other state-of-the-art methods on the YCBV dataset. We also visualize some qualitative results of the YCBV dataset in Fig. 6(b). More qualitative results and comparisons with the other state-of-the-art methods are included in the supplementary material.

4.4 Ablation Studies

We conduct several ablation studies on the LM dataset. First, we test our method with the number of iterations as shown in Table 4 *left*. The result shows that the performance is improved in the second iteration but saturates in more iterations. We visualize an example of iterative refinement in Fig. 6(c).

We also visualize $\mathcal{G}^{obj}$s of the qualitative results in Fig. 6(b), (c). As shown in the figure, the difference of the grid area toward the camera and the opposite is caused by projective geometry. And since the ratio of two areas is inversely proportional to the object's distance, the shape of the $\mathcal{G}^{obj}$ reflects the object distance information. Consequently, as the GM loss leverages the shape of the $\mathcal{G}^{obj}$ to learn the distance, training even without GD loss is successful, as shown in Table 4 *middle*. In other words, projective geometry helps our method to learn the distance to the object. We also confirm that L^{GD} improves the performance, especially on the $ADD(\text{-}S)$ score, since it helps estimate more accurate distance of the grid in camera space. Additionally, the effect of GM loss compared to PM loss and image matching loss is reported in the supplementary material.

Table 2. Results on the LMO dataset. The accuracy of baseline methods and our method in terms of the $ADD(\text{-}S)^{0.1d}$ score. Objects annotated with ($*$) indicate symmetric pose ambiguity. A.O represents a pose estimator trained on all objects.

Method	PoseCNN [42]	DeepIM [21]	PVNet [31]	S.Stage [14]	HybridPose [37]	GDR-Net [40]	GDR-Net [40]	SO-Pose [8]	RePOSE [16]	DProST	DProST
	w/ Mesh									w/o Mesh	
A.O	✓	✓					✓	✓			✓
Training set	real +syn	real +syn	real +syn	real +syn	real +syn	real +pbr	real +pbr	real +pbr	real +syn	real +pbr	real +pbr
ape	9.6	59.2	15.8	19.2	20.9	46.8	44.9	48.4	31.1	50.9	**51.4**
can	45.2	63.5	63.3	65.1	75.3	**90.8**	79.7	85.8	80.0	87.2	78.7
cat	0.9	26.2	16.7	18.9	24.9	40.5	30.6	32.7	25.6	46.0	**48.1**
driller	41.4	55.6	25.2	69.0	70.2	82.6	67.8	77.4	73.1	**86.1**	77.4
duck	19.6	52.4	**65.7**	25.3	27.9	46.9	40.0	48.9	43.0	47.7	45.4
eggbox*	22.0	**63.0**	50.2	52.0	52.4	54.2	49.8	52.4	51.7	46.9	55.3
glue*	38.5	71.7	49.6	51.4	53.8	75.8	73.7	**78.3**	54.3	68.5	76.9
holepuncher	22.1	52.5	39.7	45.6	54.2	60.1	62.7	**75.3**	53.6	65.4	67.4
Average	24.9	55.5	40.8	43.3	47.5	62.2	56.1	62.4	51.6	62.3	**62.6**

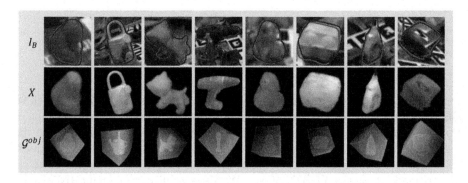

Fig. 5. Qualitative results of LMO dataset. The contours of projection by both label pose and predicted pose are represented as green and blue, respectively. The second row shows the projection by the estimated pose, and the third row shows the predicted grid, unit sphere, and the reference feature $\mathcal{F}$ in the object space. (Color figure online)

The performance about the number of points per ray (N_z) is in Table 4 *right*, and $N_z = 64$ shows the best in both $ADD(\text{-}S)$ and $Proj2D$ score.

Table 5 *left* shows the experiment on the source of projection and view sampling method in reference feature. As demonstrated, a simple space-carving-based reference feature can replace the mesh without significant performance degradation, and FPS outperforms the random sampling of reference.

Finally, we conduct an ablation study of the number of views ($N^{\mathcal{R}}$) for the reference image in Table 5 *right*. As shown in the table, eight reference images show the best performance. Note that because each voxel value of the reference feature is the average of the reference image, if there are too many references, the texture becomes blurry, and performance suffer. The quality of the reference feature depending on the number of views is demonstrated in the supplementary material.

Table 3. Results on the YCBV dataset. The score of the baseline methods and our method in terms of $ADD(\text{-}S)^{0.1d}$ and AUC of $ADD(\text{-}S)$. A.O represents a pose estimator trained on all objects.

Method	PoseCNN [42]	PVNet [31]	DeepIM [21]	Cosypose [19]	GDR-Net [40]	SO-Pose [8]	RePOSE [16]	DProST	DProST
A.O	✓		✓	✓		✓			✓
$ADD(\text{-}S)^{0.1d}$	21.3	–	53.6	–	60.1	56.8	49.6	**65.1**	43.8
AUC of $ADD(\text{-}S)$	61.3	73.4	81.9	**84.5**	84.4	83.9	77.2	77.4	69.2

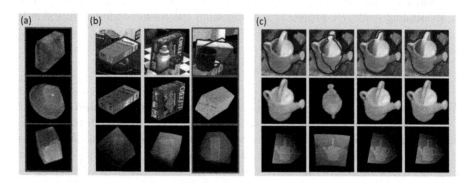

Fig. 6. Qualitative results. We visualize the contour of the projection by label pose in green, the prediction pose in blue, and error cases in a red box. (a) Space-carving failure cases in the YCBV dataset. (b) Qualitative results of the YCBV dataset. We demonstrate the rendered mesh images in the second row and superimposed $\mathcal{G}^{obj}$ of label and prediction in the third row. (c) Qualitative result of each iteration in the LM dataset. The first column shows the label, and each column from the second to the fourth indicates the initial pose and the predicted pose from each iteration. (Color figure online)

Table 4. Ablation studies of the pose estimator. *left*: Ablation of the number of iterations. *middle*: Ablation of the loss function. *right*: Ablation of the N_z.

Iter	$ADD(\text{-}S)$ 0.02d	0.05d	0.10d	$Proj2D$ 2pix	5pix
1	22.6	68.9	93.2	62.4	97.6
2	48.1	85.8	**97.7**	89.3	**99.2**
3	**50.8**	**86.3**	**97.7**	**90.8**	99.1

Loss	$ADD(\text{-}S)$ 0.02d	0.05d	0.10d	$Proj2D$ 2pix	5pix
$\mathcal{L}^{GM}$	35.5	75.8	94.5	86.6	99.0
$\mathcal{L}^{GM} + \mathcal{L}^{GD}$	**48.1**	**85.8**	**97.7**	**89.3**	**99.2**

N_z	$ADD(\text{-}S)$ 0.02d	0.05d	0.10d	$Proj2D$ 2pix	5pix
32	46.3	85.4	97.6	88.0	99.1
64	**48.1**	**85.8**	**97.7**	**89.3**	**99.2**
128	47.1	85.4	97.5	88.8	99.1

Table 5. Ablation studies of the 3D feature. *left*: Ablation of the projection source and reference generation method. *right*: Ablation of the number of references.

Source	Sampling	$ADD(\text{-}S)$ 0.02d	0.05d	0.10d	$Proj2D$ 2pix	5pix
Mesh		**51.6**	**87.8**	**98.3**	**91.5**	99.1
Reference	Random	45.9	84.7	97.5	88.8	99.1
Reference	FPS	48.1	85.8	97.7	89.3	**99.2**

$N^{\mathcal{R}}$	$ADD(\text{-}S)$ 0.02d	0.05d	0.10d	$Proj2D$ 2pix	5pix
4	44.1	84.2	97.5	87.5	98.9
8	**48.1**	**85.8**	**97.7**	**89.3**	**99.2**
16	45.6	84.9	97.6	87.8	99.1

4.5 Runtime Analysis

The experiments is conducted on an AMD Ryzen 9 3900X 12-Core CPU with an NVIDIA Geforce RTX 2080Ti GPU. In addition to the 1.21 s for space carving and 15 ms in detection, our method takes 0.22 ms in grid generator, 2.06 ms in the projector, and 3.86 ms in the pose estimator for each step. Note that, since our method focuses on the seen object scenario, the reference feature is created only once for each object in training phase and used repeatedly without additional generation. Because the grid from the grid generator is directly used as a sampling grid, our projector is faster than the mesh rendering function in pytorch3d, which takes 3.14 ms.

5   Conclusion

We have proposed a new 6D object pose estimation method based on a grid of the object space. To accomplish this, we have designed the DProST model that elaborately considers the projective geometry, while reducing the number of computations by focusing the grid on object space RoI. Additionally, we have introduced new objective functions, GM and GD, which can be used to train the pose estimator based on the object space grid. We also have proposed a simple space-carving-based reference feature generation method, which can replace the mesh data in the projection stage. Experiments have shown that DProST outperforms the state-of-the-art pose estimation method even without mesh data on the LM and LMO datasets and shows competitive performance on the YCBV dataset with mesh data. We plan to apply other 3D reconstruction methods based on deep learning to the DProST in the future. Also, applying our method to unseen or categorical objects would be one area for future research.

Acknowledgement. This research was supported in part by LG AI Research, in part by Institute of Information & Communications Technology Planning & Evaluation (IITP) Grant funded by the Korea government(MSIT) [NO.2021-0-01343, Artificial Intelligence Graduate School Program (Seoul National University)], and partially by the BK21 FOUR program of the Education and Research Program for Future ICT Pioneers, Seoul National University in 2022.

References

1. Brachmann, E., Krull, A., Michel, F., Gumhold, S., Shotton, J., Rother, C.: Learning 6D object pose estimation using 3D object coordinates. In: Fleet, D., Pajdla, T., Schiele, B., Tuytelaars, T. (eds.) ECCV 2014. LNCS, vol. 8690, pp. 536–551. Springer, Cham (2014). https://doi.org/10.1007/978-3-319-10605-2_35
2. Brachmann, E., Michel, F., Krull, A., Yang, M.Y., Gumhold, S., et al.: Uncertainty-driven 6D pose estimation of objects and scenes from a single RGB image. In: Proceedings of the IEEE Conference on Computer Vision and Pattern Recognition, pp. 3364–3372 (2016)

3. Cai, Z., Vasconcelos, N.: Cascade R-CNN: delving into high quality object detection. In: Proceedings of the IEEE Conference on Computer Vision and Pattern Recognition, pp. 6154–6162 (2018)
4. Chen, X., Ma, H., Wan, J., Li, B., Xia, T.: Multi-view 3D object detection network for autonomous driving. In: Proceedings of the IEEE Conference on Computer Vision and Pattern Recognition, pp. 1907–1915 (2017)
5. Chen, X., Dong, Z., Song, J., Geiger, A., Hilliges, O.: Category level object pose estimation via neural analysis-by-synthesis. In: Vedaldi, A., Bischof, H., Brox, T., Frahm, J.-M. (eds.) ECCV 2020. LNCS, vol. 12371, pp. 139–156. Springer, Cham (2020). https://doi.org/10.1007/978-3-030-58574-7_9
6. Cheng, Y., et al.: 6D pose estimation with correlation fusion. In: 2020 25th International Conference on Pattern Recognition (ICPR), pp. 2988–2994. IEEE (2021)
7. Deng, J., Dong, W., Socher, R., Li, L.J., Li, K., Fei-Fei, L.: ImageNet: a large-scale hierarchical image database. In: 2009 IEEE Conference on Computer Vision and Pattern Recognition, pp. 248–255. IEEE (2009)
8. Di, Y., Manhardt, F., Wang, G., Ji, X., Navab, N., Tombari, F.: So-pose: exploiting self-occlusion for direct 6D pose estimation. In: Proceedings of the IEEE/CVF International Conference on Computer Vision, pp. 12396–12405 (2021)
9. Gao, C., et al.: Generalizing spatial transformers to projective geometry with applications to 2D/3D registration. In: Martel, A.L., et al. (eds.) MICCAI 2020. LNCS, vol. 12263, pp. 329–339. Springer, Cham (2020). https://doi.org/10.1007/978-3-030-59716-0_32
10. He, K., Gkioxari, G., Dollár, P., Girshick, R.: Mask R-CNN. In: Proceedings of the IEEE International Conference on Computer Vision, pp. 2961–2969 (2017)
11. He, K., Zhang, X., Ren, S., Sun, J.: Deep residual learning for image recognition. In: Proceedings of the IEEE Conference on Computer Vision and Pattern Recognition, pp. 770–778 (2016)
12. Hinterstoisser, S., et al.: Model based training, detection and pose estimation of texture-less 3D objects in heavily cluttered scenes. In: Lee, K.M., Matsushita, Y., Rehg, J.M., Hu, Z. (eds.) ACCV 2012. LNCS, vol. 7724, pp. 548–562. Springer, Heidelberg (2013). https://doi.org/10.1007/978-3-642-37331-2_42
13. Hodaň, T., et al.: BOP challenge 2020 on 6D object localization. In: Bartoli, A., Fusiello, A. (eds.) ECCV 2020. LNCS, vol. 12536, pp. 577–594. Springer, Cham (2020). https://doi.org/10.1007/978-3-030-66096-3_39
14. Hu, Y., Fua, P., Wang, W., Salzmann, M.: Single-stage 6D object pose estimation. In: Proceedings of the IEEE/CVF Conference on Computer Vision and Pattern Recognition, pp. 2930–2939 (2020)
15. Hu, Y., Hugonot, J., Fua, P., Salzmann, M.: Segmentation-driven 6D object pose estimation. In: Proceedings of the IEEE/CVF Conference on Computer Vision and Pattern Recognition, pp. 3385–3394 (2019)
16. Iwase, S., Liu, X., Khirodkar, R., Yokota, R., Kitani, K.M.: Repose: fast 6D object pose refinement via deep texture rendering. In: Proceedings of the IEEE/CVF International Conference on Computer Vision, pp. 3303–3312 (2021)
17. Jaderberg, M., Simonyan, K., Zisserman, A., et al.: Spatial transformer networks. Adv. Neural. Inf. Process. Syst. **28**, 2017–2025 (2015)
18. Kingma, D.P., Ba, J.: Adam: a method for stochastic optimization. arXiv preprint arXiv:1412.6980 (2014)
19. Labbé, Y., Carpentier, J., Aubry, M., Sivic, J.: CosyPose: consistent multi-view multi-object 6D pose estimation. In: Vedaldi, A., Bischof, H., Brox, T., Frahm, J.-M. (eds.) ECCV 2020. LNCS, vol. 12362, pp. 574–591. Springer, Cham (2020). https://doi.org/10.1007/978-3-030-58520-4_34

20. Lepetit, V., Moreno-Noguer, F., Fua, P.: EPnP: an accurate O(n) solution to the PnP problem. Int. J. Comput. Vision **81**(2), 155 (2009)
21. Li, Y., Wang, G., Ji, X., Xiang, Y., Fox, D.: DeepIM: deep iterative matching for 6D pose estimation. In: Proceedings of the European Conference on Computer Vision (ECCV), pp. 683–698 (2018)
22. Li, Z., Wang, G., Ji, X.: CDPN: coordinates-based disentangled pose network for real-time RGB-based 6-DOF object pose estimation. In: Proceedings of the IEEE/CVF International Conference on Computer Vision, pp. 7678–7687 (2019)
23. Marchand, E., Uchiyama, H., Spindler, F.: Pose estimation for augmented reality: a hands-on survey. IEEE Trans. Visual Comput. Graph. **22**(12), 2633–2651 (2015)
24. Mildenhall, B., Srinivasan, P.P., Tancik, M., Barron, J.T., Ramamoorthi, R., Ng, R.: NeRF: representing scenes as neural radiance fields for view synthesis. In: Vedaldi, A., Bischof, H., Brox, T., Frahm, J.-M. (eds.) ECCV 2020. LNCS, vol. 12346, pp. 405–421. Springer, Cham (2020). https://doi.org/10.1007/978-3-030-58452-8_24
25. Nguyen-Phuoc, T., Li, C., Balaban, S., Yang, Y.L.: RenderNet: a deep convolutional network for differentiable rendering from 3D shapes. In: Advances in Neural Information Processing Systems, vol. 31 (2018)
26. Oberweger, M., Rad, M., Lepetit, V.: Making deep heatmaps robust to partial occlusions for 3D object pose estimation. In: Ferrari, V., Hebert, M., Sminchisescu, C., Weiss, Y. (eds.) ECCV 2018. LNCS, vol. 11219, pp. 125–141. Springer, Cham (2018). https://doi.org/10.1007/978-3-030-01267-0_8
27. Park, K., Mousavian, A., Xiang, Y., Fox, D.: LatentFusion: end-to-end differentiable reconstruction and rendering for unseen object pose estimation. In: Proceedings of the IEEE/CVF Conference on Computer Vision and Pattern Recognition, pp. 10710–10719 (2020)
28. Park, K., Patten, T., Vincze, M.: Pix2Pose: pixel-wise coordinate regression of objects for 6d pose estimation. In: Proceedings of the IEEE/CVF International Conference on Computer Vision, pp. 7668–7677 (2019)
29. Park, K., Patten, T., Vincze, M.: Neural object learning for 6D pose estimation using a few cluttered images. In: Vedaldi, A., Bischof, H., Brox, T., Frahm, J.-M. (eds.) ECCV 2020. LNCS, vol. 12349, pp. 656–673. Springer, Cham (2020). https://doi.org/10.1007/978-3-030-58548-8_38
30. Paszke, A., et al.: PyTorch: an imperative style, high-performance deep learning library. Adv. Neural. Inf. Process. Syst. **32**, 8026–8037 (2019)
31. Peng, S., Liu, Y., Huang, Q., Zhou, X., Bao, H.: PVNet: pixel-wise voting network for 6Dof pose estimation. In: Proceedings of the IEEE/CVF Conference on Computer Vision and Pattern Recognition, pp. 4561–4570 (2019)
32. Rad, M., Lepetit, V.: BB8: a scalable, accurate, robust to partial occlusion method for predicting the 3D poses of challenging objects without using depth. In: Proceedings of the IEEE International Conference on Computer Vision, pp. 3828–3836 (2017)
33. Ravi, N., et al.: Accelerating 3D deep learning with pytorch3D. arXiv preprint arXiv:2007.08501 (2020)
34. Redmon, J., Farhadi, A.: YOLOv3: an incremental improvement. arXiv preprint arXiv:1804.02767 (2018)
35. Ren, S., He, K., Girshick, R., Sun, J.: Faster R-CNN: towards real-time object detection with region proposal networks. Adv. Neural. Inf. Process. Syst. **28**, 91–99 (2015)

36. Sitzmann, V., Thies, J., Heide, F., Nießner, M., Wetzstein, G., Zollhofer, M.: DeepVoxels: learning persistent 3D feature embeddings. In: Proceedings of the IEEE/CVF Conference on Computer Vision and Pattern Recognition, pp. 2437–2446 (2019)

37. Song, C., Song, J., Huang, Q.: HybridPose: 6D object pose estimation under hybrid representations. In: Proceedings of the IEEE/CVF Conference on Computer Vision and Pattern Recognition, pp. 431–440 (2020)

38. Tremblay, J., To, T., Sundaralingam, B., Xiang, Y., Fox, D., Birchfield, S.: Deep object pose estimation for semantic robotic grasping of household objects. In: Conference on Robot Learning, pp. 306–316. PMLR (2018)

39. Wang, C., et al.: DenseFusion: 6D object pose estimation by iterative dense fusion. In: Proceedings of the IEEE/CVF Conference on Computer Vision and Pattern Recognition, pp. 3343–3352 (2019)

40. Wang, G., Manhardt, F., Tombari, F., Ji, X.: GDR-Net: geometry-guided direct regression network for monocular 6D object pose estimation. In: Proceedings of the IEEE/CVF Conference on Computer Vision and Pattern Recognition, pp. 16611–16621 (2021)

41. Wang, H., Sridhar, S., Huang, J., Valentin, J., Song, S., Guibas, L.J.: Normalized object coordinate space for category-level 6d object pose and size estimation. In: Proceedings of the IEEE/CVF Conference on Computer Vision and Pattern Recognition, pp. 2642–2651 (2019)

42. Xiang, Y., Schmidt, T., Narayanan, V., Fox, D.: PoseCNN: a convolutional neural network for 6D object pose estimation in cluttered scenes. In: Proceedings of Robotics: Science and Systems. Pittsburgh, Pennsylvania (2018). https://doi.org/10.15607/RSS.2018.XIV.019

43. Xu, D., Anguelov, D., Jain, A.: PointFusion: deep sensor fusion for 3D bounding box estimation. In: Proceedings of the IEEE Conference on Computer Vision and Pattern Recognition, pp. 244–253 (2018)

44. Yen-Chen, L., Florence, P., Barron, J.T., Rodriguez, A., Isola, P., Lin, T.Y.: INeRF: inverting neural radiance fields for pose estimation. In: 2021 IEEE/RSJ International Conference on Intelligent Robots and Systems (IROS), pp. 1323–1330. IEEE (2021)

45. Zakharov, S., Shugurov, I., Ilic, S.: DPOD: 6D pose object detector and refiner. In: Proceedings of the IEEE/CVF International Conference on Computer Vision, pp. 1941–1950 (2019)

46. Zhu, M., et al.: Single image 3D object detection and pose estimation for grasping. In: 2014 IEEE International Conference on Robotics and Automation (ICRA), pp. 3936–3943. IEEE (2014)

3D Interacting Hand Pose Estimation by Hand De-occlusion and Removal

Hao Meng[1,3], Sheng Jin[2,3(✉)], Wentao Liu[3,4], Chen Qian[3],
Mengxiang Lin[1], Wanli Ouyang[4,5], and Ping Luo[2]

[1] Beihang University, Beijing, China
linmx@buaa.edu.cn
[2] The University of Hong Kong, Pok Fu Lam, Hong Kong
pluo@cs.hku.hk
[3] SenseTime Research and Tetras.AI, Beijing, China
{jinsheng,liuwentao,qianchen}@tetras.ai
[4] Shanghai AI Lab, Shanghai, China
[5] The University of Sydney, Sydney, Australia
wanli.ouyang@sydney.edu.au

Abstract. Estimating 3D interacting hand pose from a single RGB image is essential for understanding human actions. Unlike most previous works that directly predict the 3D poses of two interacting hands simultaneously, we propose to decompose the challenging interacting hand pose estimation task and estimate the pose of each hand separately. In this way, it is straightforward to take advantage of the latest research progress on the single-hand pose estimation system. However, hand pose estimation in interacting scenarios is very challenging, due to (1) severe hand-hand occlusion and (2) ambiguity caused by the homogeneous appearance of hands. To tackle these two challenges, we propose a novel Hand De-occlusion and Removal (HDR) framework to perform hand de-occlusion and distractor removal. We also propose the first large-scale synthetic amodal hand dataset, termed Amodal InterHand Dataset (AIH), to facilitate model training and promote the development of the related research. Experiments show that the proposed method significantly outperforms previous state-of-the-art interacting hand pose estimation approaches. Codes and data are available at https://github.com/MengHao666/HDR.

Keywords: 3D interacting hand pose estimation · De-occlusion · Removal · Amodal InterHand Dataset

---

H. Meng and S. Jin—Equal Contribution.

Supplementary Information The online version contains supplementary material available at https://doi.org/10.1007/978-3-031-20068-7_22.

© The Author(s), under exclusive license to Springer Nature Switzerland AG 2022
S. Avidan et al. (Eds.): ECCV 2022, LNCS 13666, pp. 380–397, 2022.
https://doi.org/10.1007/978-3-031-20068-7_22

1   Introduction

Estimating the 3D hand pose from a monocular RGB image is critical in many real-world applications, *e.g.* human-computer interaction, augmented and virtual reality (AR/VR), and sign language recognition. Although significant progress has been made for single-hand pose estimation, analysis of hand-hand interactions remains challenging. Estimating 3D interacting hand pose from a single RGB image has attracted increasing research attention in recent years.

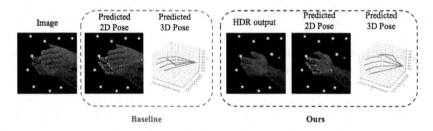

Fig. 1. State-of-the-art hand pose estimation models often struggle to estimate the 3D poses of interacting hands, due to severe hand-hand occlusion and appearance ambiguity of two hands. In this example, we observe erroneous pose estimation of the occluded part and significant uncertainty between the left and right wrist. Our HDR framework tackles these two challenges via hand de-occlusion (recovering the appearance content of the occluded part) and removal (removing the other distracting hand). It transforms the challenging interacting hand image into a simple single-hand image, which can be easily handled by the hand pose estimator.

In this paper, we propose to decompose the challenging interacting hand pose estimation task, and predict the pose of the left and the right hand separately. However, solving single-hand pose estimation in close two-hand interaction cases is non-trivial, because of two major challenges. One of the main challenges is the severe hand-hand occlusion. Considering hands in close interactions, the occlusion patterns are complex. Many areas of the target hand can be occluded, making it very challenging to infer the pose of the invisible parts. Another challenge is that the homogeneous and self-similar appearance of hands (*i.e.* the left and the right hand) may cause ambiguities. And the hand pose estimator may be confused by the other visually similar distracting hand.

To tackle these challenges, we propose a simple yet effective Hand De-occlusion and Removal (HDR) framework. Specifically, our HDR framework comprises three parts, Hand Amodal Segmentation Module (HASM), Hand De-occlusion and Removal Module (HDRM), and the Single Hand Pose Estimator (SHPE). HAS segments both the complete (amodal) and visible parts for both two hands. The resulting segmentation masks not only contain information to localize the rough position of the two hands, but also provide cues for subsequent de-occlusion and removal process by HDRM. *De-occlusion* targets at predicting the appearance content of the occluded part. *Removal* targets at removing the distracting part in the image. In our case, when estimating the pose of the right hand, the left hand becomes the distracting part and should be removed. As shown in Fig. 1, recent state-of-the-art hand pose estimation methods suffer from severe hand-hand occlusion and the homogeneous appearance of two hands, resulting in inferior pose estimation results. Thanks to our proposed HDR framework, we can transform the challenging scenario of hand-hand interactions into a common single-hand scenario, which can be easily handled by an off-the-shelf SHPE.

However, to the best of our knowledge, there exist no datasets that contain both the amodal segmentation and appearance content ground-truths of interactive hands. To fill in this blank, we synthetically generate a large-scale Amodal InterHand dataset, namely AIH dataset. The dataset contains over 3 million interacting hand images along with ground-truth amodal and modal segmentation, de-occlusion and removal ground-truths. The dataset consists of two parts, *i.e.* AIH_Syn and AIH_Render. AIH_Syn is obtained by simple random copy-and-paste. It retains detailed and realistic appearance information. However, it may generate implausible interacting hand poses that violate the biomechanical structure of the human body. AIH_Render is generated by rendering the textured 3D interacting hand mesh to the image plane. The inter-dependencies between two hands are fully considered to avoid physically implausible configurations, *e.g.* intersecting fingers. However, it may suffer from the appearance gap because the rendered texture is synthetic. Combining the advantages of both, we make a large-scale 3D hand-hand interaction dataset with large pose and appearance variety. We empirically validate the effectiveness of the synthetic dataset through extensive experiments. We envision that our proposed dataset will foster the development of the related research, *e.g.* interacting hand pose estimation, amodal or modal instance segmentation, de-occlusion, etc.

Our proposed Hand De-occlusion and Removal (HDR) framework is simple, flexible, and effective. Extensive experiments on the well-known InterHand2.6M benchmark [21] show that our method significantly outperforms the state-of-the-art 3D interacting hand pose estimation systems. Our framework builds upon the latest research progress of amodal segmentation [33], de-occlusion [19, 36, 38], and 3D single-hand pose estimation [39]. Note that, we do not perform complete comparisons with previous amodal segmentation, de-occlusion, and SHPE approaches. We also do not claim any algorithmic superiority concerning model architecture design. Because our aim is to propose a framework to solve the challenges of 3D interacting hand pose estimation. And designing powerful modules to improve the performance of amodal segmentation, de-occlusion, and SHPE is not the focus of this paper.

Our contributions are summarized as follows:

- We propose a novel Hand De-occlusion and Removal (HDR) framework to tackle the challenging task of 3D interacting hand pose estimation.
- We propose to explicitly handle the challenges of self-occlusion by hand de-occlusion and the homogeneous appearance ambiguity by distractor removal.

To the best of our knowledge, we are the first to apply de-occlusion techniques to improve the downstream pose estimation accuracy.

– We propose the first large-scale synthetic Amodal InterHand Dataset (AIH) to settle the task of hand de-occlusion and removal. We envision that AIH will foster the development of the related research.

2   Related Work

2.1   Amodal Instance Segmentation and De-occlusion

Amodal Instance Segmentation. Unlike modal instance segmentation, which aims at assigning labels to visible parts of instances, amodal instance segmentation targets at producing the amodal (integrated) masks of each object instance involving its occluded parts. Li and Malik [16] proposed the first amodal instance segmentation model which iteratively expands the bounding boxes and recomputes the heatmaps. Zhu *et al.* [40] proposed COCOA dataset for amodal instance segmentation and presented AmodalMask model as the baseline. Zhan *et al.* [36] propose a method to reason about the underlying occlusion ordering and recover the invisible parts in a self-supervised manner.

De-occlusion. De-occlusion aims at recovering the appearance content of the invisible occluded parts. SeGAN [6] adopts a residual network based model for mask completion and inferring the appearance of the invisible parts of indoor objects. Yan *et al.* [34] presented an iterative multi-task framework for amodal mask completion and de-occlusion of vehicles. Zhou *et al.* [38] built upon a well-known inpainting approach [19] and proposed to reason about the occluded regions and recover the appearance content of humans. Baek *et al.* [2] presents a weakly-supervised method to adapt from hand-object domain to single hand-only domain. However, its image generation module and the pose estimator are deeply coupled together, limiting its generalization ability to adapt to different hand pose estimators and resulting in low-quality restored image.

Our approach differs from previous works in three major aspects. First, previous works mostly focus on improving the quality of image content recovery, while we aim to improve the performance of the downstream task, *i.e.* 3D interactive hand pose estimation. Second, compared with common rigid objects, recovering the appearance content of the interacting hands is more challenging because of larger pose variations, severe hand-hand occlusion, and self-similar appearance of hands and fingers. Third, besides de-occlusion, our proposed HDR framework also performs distracting hand removal to reduce the ambiguities caused by the homogeneous appearance of hands.

2.2   Monocular RGB-Based Hand Pose Estimation

Isolated Hand Pose Estimation. RGB-based single (isolated) hand pose estimation has made significant progress in the past few years. Zimmermann *et al.*

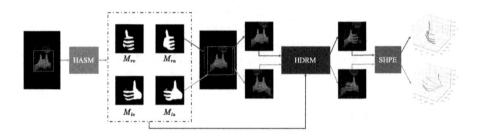

Fig. 2. Illustration of our Hand De-occlusion and Removal (HDR) framework for the task of 3D interacting hand pose estimation. We first employ **HASM** (Hand Amodal Segmentation Module) to segment the amodal and modal masks of the left and the right hand in the image. Given the predicted masks, we locate and crop the image patch centered at each hand. Then, for every cropped image, the **HDRM** (Hand De-occlusion and Removal Module) recovers the appearance content of the occluded part of one hand and removes the other distracting hand simultaneously. In this way, the interacting two-hand image is transformed into a single-hand image, and can be easily handled by **SHPE** (Single Hand Pose Estimation) to get the final 3D hand poses.

[41] introduced one of the first deep learning models to estimate hand poses from monocular RGB images. It first uses HandSegNet to localize hand regions, then uses PoseNet to estimate 2D hand poses, and finally maps 2D poses into 3D space. Iqbal *et al.* [11] proposed to encode hand joint locations with 2.5D heatmap representation to address the depth ambiguity problems and improve localization precision. Spurr *et al.* [29] proposed a VAE-based generative model to regress 3D hand joint locations. Zhou *et al.* [39] proposed to fully exploit non-image MoCap data to improve model generalization and robustness. Recently, many works also attempt to estimate 3D hand meshes from monocular RGB images. Most of them [1,4,35] are model-based, which train a convolutional neural network to estimate the MANO parameters [26]. Others are model-free, which directly regress 3D vertices of the human hand using mesh convolution [15], graph neural networks [5], or transformers [18].

Interacting Hand Pose Estimation. Most works conduct interacting two-hand pose estimation by utilizing multi-view RGB images [3,9], depth data [22,23,30], and tracking strategy [23,28,31]. Only a few existing works have considered estimating 3D poses of two hands from a single RGB image, which is challenging due to severe occlusion and close interactions. Lin *et al.* [17] employed a synthetic egocentric hand dataset to learn to estimate two-hand poses from a single RGB image. Moon *et al.* proposed a large-scale interacting hand dataset, termed InterHand2.6M dataset [21], and designed the InterNet model to predict 2.5D hand poses. Zhang *et al.* [37] designed a hand pose-aware attention module to address the self-similarity ambiguities and leveraged a context-aware cascaded refinement module to improve pose accuracy. Kim *et al.* [13] introduced an end-to-end trainable framework to jointly perform interacting hand pose estimation. Rong *et al.* [27] presented a two-stage framework to generate precise 3D hand poses and meshes with minimal collisions from monocular single RGB images. Fan *et al.* [7] proposed DIGIT (DIsambiGuating hands in InTeraction) to explicitly leverage the per-pixel probabilities to reduce the ambiguities caused by self-similarity of hands.

In this work, we empirically show that existing hand pose estimators often suffer from extreme self-occlusions and appearance ambiguity. To this end, we propose a novel Hand De-occlusion and Removal (HDR) framework to explicitly handle these two challenges, which significantly outperforms prior arts.

3   Method

3.1   Overview

As shown in Fig. 2, we propose a three-stage framework for interactive hand pose estimation. The first stage segments the complete and visible part for both two hands. The second stage recovers the RGB values of the occluded hand and the background behind the distracting hand at the same time. The third stage predicts the 3D pose of each hand separately.

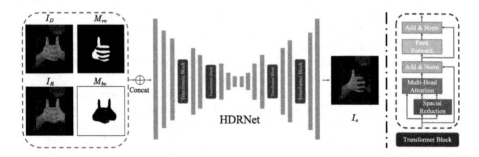

Fig. 3. Illustration of the HDRNet. The input of HDRNet includes 4 kinds of data: (a) the image erased on occluded portion of the right hand I_D, (b) the modal mask of the right hand M_{rv}, (c) the image erased on redundant portion of the distracting hand I_R, and (d) the modal mask of background M_{bv}. HDRNet recovers the appearance content of the occluded parts and inpaints the distracting hand to avoid ambiguity.

3.2   Hand Amodal Segmentation Module (HASM)

As shown in Fig. 2, given an interacting two-hand image, we first obtain the modal and amodal masks of both hands using the Hand Amodal Segmentation Module (HASM). We simply adapt the off-the-shelf instance segmentation model, *i.e.* SegFormer [33], to fit in our two-hand amodal segmentation tasks. Specifically, we increase the number of decode heads from one to four to predict four kinds of segmentation masks, namely the right hand amodal mask M_{ra}, the right hand visible mask M_{rv}, the left hand amodal mask M_{la} and the left hand visible mask M_{lv}. These segmentation masks contain (1) spatial localization information to roughly localize the left/right hand, and (2) rich cues about the occluded regions for de-occlusion and the distractor regions for removal.

We apply the binary cross entropy losses $\mathcal{L}_{BCE}(*)$ to supervise the segmentation model. The final segmentation loss functions are formulated as follows:

$$
\begin{aligned}
\mathcal{L}_{HAS} = \ &\mathcal{L}_{BCE}\left(M_{ra}, M_{ra}^*\right) + \mathcal{L}_{BCE}\left(M_{lv}, M_{lv}^*\right) \\
+ \ &\mathcal{L}_{BCE}\left(M_{la}, M_{la}^*\right) + \mathcal{L}_{BCE}\left(M_{lv}, M_{lv}^*\right),
\end{aligned}
\tag{1}
$$

where M_{ra}, M_{lv}, M_{la}, and M_{lv} are predicted segmentation masks; M_{ra}^*, M_{lv}^*, M_{la}^*, and M_{lv}^* are the corresponding ground-truth masks.

3.3 Hand De-occlusion and Removal Module (HDRM)

Hand De-occlusion and Removal Module (HDRM) aims at transforming a previously challenging case of hand-hand interactions into a common single-hand case, which can be easily solved by an off-the-shelf single-hand pose estimator. Specifically, given amodal and modal masks, *De-occlusion* is responsible for recovering the appearance content or RGB values of the occluded regions, while *Removal* targets at inpainting the distracting regions in the image, reducing the ambiguities caused by the homogeneous appearance of two hands.

For clarity, in the following sections, we will focus on the right hand only and regard the left hand as the distractor. Note that, the left-hand centered image can be flipped horizontally before performing hand de-occlusion, removal, and pose estimation, thus following the same pipeline.

As shown in Fig. 2, for the right hand, we first use the amodal mask M_{ra} to locate the right hand. Then we crop the original image and the segmentation masks at the center of the right hand. The newly cropped image and masks are denoted as I_s^{crop}, M_{ra}^{crop}, M_{rv}^{crop}, M_{la}^{crop} and M_{lv}^{crop} respectively. We will omit the superscript *crop* in subsequent sections for simplicity.

We use M_D to denote the region where the target hand is occluded by the other hand and M_R to denote the region where the distracting hand occupies. They are computed as follows:

$$
\begin{aligned}
M_D &= M_{ra} \cdot (1 - M_{rv}), \\
M_R &= (1 - M_{ra}) \cdot M_{lv}.
\end{aligned}
\tag{2}
$$

I_D and I_R are the original image I_s erased by the mask M_D and M_R respectively. They can inform the HDRNet where to focus and how to inpaint these two regions with partial convolution [19]. In addition, the modal mask of the right hand M_{rv} and the modal mask of the background M_{bv} point out where the HDRNet can refer to for de-occlusion and removal respectively. Formally, I_D, I_R and M_{bv} are computed as follows:

$$
\begin{aligned}
I_D &= I_s \cdot (1 - M_D), \\
I_R &= I_s \cdot (1 - M_R), \\
M_{bv} &= (1 - M_{ra}) \cdot (1 - M_{la}).
\end{aligned}
\tag{3}
$$

I_D, M_{rv}, I_R and M_{bv} are concatenated together as the input, as shown in Fig. 3. HDRNet then uses these data to recover the appearance content of the occluded parts and inpaints the distracting hand to avoid ambiguity. For model architecture choice, we follow [36,38] to adopt the network of Liu *et al.* [19] and further improve it by adding a few transformer blocks [32]. The transformer block enhances image feature interactions, enlarges the receptive fields, and focuses more on important image regions. Finally, the HDRNet outputs a recovered image I_o. We follow [38] to employ an image discriminator [12] D to enhance the image recovery quality through adversarial training. The loss function of HDRNet is as follows:

$$\mathcal{L}_{HDR} = \lambda_1(\mathbb{E}_{I_o}[\log(1 - D(I_o))] + \mathbb{E}_{I_o^*}[\log(D(I_o^*))]) \\ + \lambda_2\mathcal{L}_{\ell 1}(I_o, I_o^*) + \lambda_3\mathcal{L}_{prec}(I_o, I_o^*) + \lambda_4\mathcal{L}_{style}(I_o, I_o^*), \quad (4)$$

where $\mathcal{L}_{prec}(*)$ denotes the perceptual loss [8], and $\mathcal{L}_{style}(*)$ denotes the style loss [19]. I_o is the recovered image, while I_o^* is its corresponding ground truth. λ_1, λ_2, λ_3, and λ_4 are hyper-parameters to balance the losses.

3.4   3D Single Hand Pose Estimation (SHPE)

Our de-occlusion and removal framework can be applied to any off-the-shelf pose estimators. However, designing a more powerful hand pose estimation network architecture is not the focus of this paper. In this work, we choose the DetNet of MinimalHand [39] as our baseline SHPE for its simplicity and good performance. MinimalHand [39] comprises two modules, *i.e.* DetNet and IKNet. DetNet predicts the 2D and 3D hand joint positions. IKNet then takes as input the predicted 3D hand joint positions and maps them to the joint angles. In our implementation, we simply discard the IKNet and re-train the DetNet on the InterHand2.6M dataset [21]. The loss function of SHPE is as follows:

$$\mathcal{L}_{SHPE} = \mathcal{L}_{heat} + \mathcal{L}_{loc} + \mathcal{L}_{delta} + \mathcal{L}_{reg}, \quad (5)$$

where $\mathcal{L}_{heat}$ is the 2D heatmap loss. $\mathcal{L}_{loc}$ and $\mathcal{L}_{delta}$ are location map loss and delta map loss respectively. $\mathcal{L}_{reg}$ is a ℓ_2 weight regularizer to avoid overfitting. Please refer to Zhou *et al.* [39] for more training details.

4   Amodal InterHand (AIH) Dataset

Existing amodal perception datasets [10,24,40] mostly focus on amodal segmentation of common objects (*e.g.* , vehicles, buildings, and indoor objects). To the best of our knowledge, there exists no dataset that targets at amodal segmentation and appearance content recovery of interactive hands. To fill in this blank, we synthetically generate the first large-scale Amodal InterHand dataset, namely AIH dataset. We envision that the proposed dataset will boost the related research, *e.g.* amodal perception, de-occlusion, and hand pose estimation.

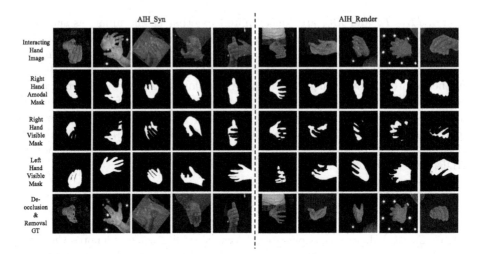

Fig. 4. Visualization of our proposed Amodal InterHand (AIH) dataset. AIH_Syn is obtained by simple 2D copy-and-paste, while AIH_Render is generated by rendering the textured 3D interacting hand mesh to the image plane.

Our AIH dataset is constructed based on the well-known InterHand2.6M V1.0 dataset [21]. As shown in Fig. 4, our proposed Amodal InterHand (AIH) dataset consists of two parts: AIH_Syn and AIH_Render. In total, AIH dataset consists of about 3 million images, where AIH_Syn contains 2.2M samples and AIH_Render contains over 0.7M samples. AIH_Syn is generated by simple 2D image-level copy and paste, *i.e.* copy the left single-hand image and paste it on the right single-hand image; AIH_Render is obtained by rendering the textured interacting hand mesh to the image plane. Both AIH_Syn and AIH_Render contain the amodal and modal segmentation masks as well as the appearance content ground-truths.

AIH_Syn. We first get the hand mesh with the ground-truth MANO parameters of the single-hand samples from the InterHand2.6M V1.0 dataset, and then project it into the 2D image plane to get the amodal segmentation mask. Then, we filter out some bad samples in which MANO parameters or the corresponding image are not valid. As a result, we get over 250K cropped single-hand images with masks for each side hand. To generate the interacting two-hand samples, we randomly pick two hands with similar texture from both sides. Then we crop the left hand region given its amodal mask and paste it on the right hand image. Random scaling, rotation, and color jittering are applied to increase diversity.

AIH_Render. Although AIH_Syn provides plenty of amodal data, such 2D level copy-and-paste can not generate mutual occlusion cases which are very common for interacting hands. Therefore, based on MANO parameters of InterHand2.6M V1.0 dataset, we decorate the corresponding hand mesh with random hand texture [25], augment it with random translation and rotation, and finally render it to a random background image from the dataset.

5 Experiments

5.1 Implementation Details

All experiments are conducted on 8 NVIDIA Tesla V100 GPUs. Training mini-batch size is set as 48 and Adam [14] is adopted for model parameter tuning. **Details of HASM.** Our HASM is trained for 200k iterations with a learning rate of 2.5×10^{-3} following the training setting of SegFormer [33]. **Details of HDRM.** Our HDRM has an input resolution of 256×256. And the loss weights are set as $\lambda_1 = 0.1$, $\lambda_2 = 3.0$, $\lambda_3 = 0.1$, $\lambda_4 = 250.0$. We first train HDRM with ground-truth masks for 100k iteration, and then fine-tune it with segmentation masks for another 100k iteration. The learning rate of these two stages are 1.5×10^{-3} and 1×10^{-3} respectively. **Details of SHPE.** Our SHPE has an input resolution of 256×256. We train the network for 300k iterations with an initial learning rate of 1×10^{-3}. The learning rate is decayed to 1×10^{-4} and 1×10^{-5} at the 100k and 200k iterations respectively. Other training settings are kept the same as those of MinimalHand [39].

5.2 Datasets and Evaluation Metrics

Datasets. The experiments are conducted on InterHand2.6M V1.0 [21] dataset and Tzionas dataset [30]. *InterHand2.6M V1.0 dataset* [21] is a publicly available large-scale realistic pose estimation dataset for two-hand interactions. The dataset provides RGB images with semi-automatically annotated 3D poses, and MANO [26] parameters obtained from NeuralAnnot [20]. In the experiments, we follow the common practice [21] to use the downsized 512×334 image resolution at 5 frames-per-second (FPS) version of the released dataset. Following the official configurations, the dataset is split into three branches, namely 'H' for the human annotation branch, 'M' for the machine annotation branch, and 'ALL' for all data. The 'M' branch data contains many unseen poses and more diverse sequences, which makes it more similar to real-world scenarios. Moreover, we notice that the 'H' branch data contains missing or incomplete mesh annotations. In the experiments, we majorly conduct experiments on the 'M' branch, but also report the results on 'ALL' branch for comparisons. To focus on the interacting hands, the original dataset [21] divides the whole dataset (IH26M-ALL) into single-hands subset (IH26M-SH) and interacting-hands subset (IH26M-IH). Following [27], we further select samples from the original "IH26M-IH" test set, and generate a more challenging subset called "IH26M-Inter". "IH26M-Inter" contains samples with more than 30 valid 'ground-truth' 3D hand keypoints. Since InterHand2.6M [21] is captured in a lab environment, its background diversity is relatively limited. To evaluate the generalization ability, we perform qualitative and quantitative experiments on the *Tzionas dataset* [30]. Since Tzionas dataset does not provide a separate training set, we directly use it as the testing set to evaluate the model trained on the InterHand2.6M dataset [21].

Evaluation Metrics. For InterHand2.6M [21], we report 3D Mean Per Joint Position Error (MPJPE). MPJPE is defined as the mean Euclidean distance between ground truth and predicted 3D joint locations, calculated after aligning the root joint for each left and right hand separately. The measurements are reported in millimeters (mm). For Tzionas dataset [30], we follow the common practice [4,13,21] to use 2D end point error (EPE) for evaluation.

5.3   Comparisons with State-of-the-Art Methods

We compare with previous state-of-the-art pose estimation methods on the 'ALL' branch and the 'machine_annot (M)' branch of InterHand2.6M V1.0 dataset [21]. MPJPE (mm) is adopted to evaluate the 3D hand pose estimation accuracy. For fair comparisons, the AIH dataset is only used to train HASM and HDRM for amodal segmentation and de-occlusion. No pose annotations in AIH are used to train the pose estimator (SHPE). Table 1 summarizes the experimental results.

Table 1. Comparisons with state-of-the-art methods on the 'ALL' branch and the 'machine_annot (M)' branch of InterHand2.6M V1.0 Dataset. MPJPE (mm) is adopted to evaluate the 3D joint estimation accuracy. The results marked with '*' are from [27].

Methods	InterHand2.6M - ALL branch				InterHand2.6M - M branch		
	IH26M-SH	IH26M-IH	IH26M-ALL	IH26M-Inter	IH26M-SH	IH26M-IH	IH26M-ALL
*Boukhayma et al. [4]	–	–	27.14	31.46	–	–	–
*Pose2Mesh [5]	–	–	27.10	32.11	–	–	–
*BiHand [35]	–	–	25.10	28.23	–	–	–
*Rong et al. [27]	–	–	17.12	20.66	–	–	–
DIGIT [7]	–	14.27	–	–	–	–	–
InterNet [21]	12.16	16.02	14.21	18.04	12.52	18.04	15.28
HDR (Ours)	**8.51**	**13.12**	**10.97**	**14.74**	**8.52**	**14.98**	**11.74**

We first compare performances of three single-hand methods, i.e. Boukhayma et al. [4], Pose2Mesh [5] and BiHand [35]. Our approach significantly outperforms all the state-of-the-art single-hand approaches. On the "IH26M-ALL" split, compared with BiHand [35], our model reduces MPJPE from 25.10 mm to 10.97 mm, resulting in as much as 56% error reduction. And in the more challenging "IH26M-Inter" split, our approach obtains about 47% accuracy improvement. This shows existing single-hand pose estimators do not handle heavy hand-hand occlusions and are easily confused by the other distracting hand.

We also compare with recent two-hand pose estimation approaches, i.e. Inter-Net [21], Rong et al. [27], and DIGIT [7]. We show superior performance over these 3D interacting hand pose estimation systems. For example, our approach significantly improves upon Moon et al. [21]'s state-of-the-art results from 14.21mm to 10.97mm (about 23% error reduction) on the "IH26M-ALL" split. The clear performance gap validates the effectiveness of our framework. Overall, our approach consistently ranks the first across all evaluation protocols.

Table 2. Comparisons with state-of-the-art methods on Tzionas dataset [30]. The results of other algorithms are from [13]. 2D EPE is adopted to evaluate pose results.

Model	Boukhayma et al. [4]	Wang et al. [31]	InterNet [21]	Kim et al. [13]	SHPE	SHPE+HDR
EPE↓	12.91	13.31	17.61	12.42	14.88	**8.70**

We also follow [13] to report hand pose estimation results (EPE) on Tzionas dataset [30] in Table 2. Our method (SHPE+HDR in the table) significantly improves upon the baseline SHPE, and outperforms the prior arts.

5.4   Effect of Hand De-occlusion and Removal (HDR) Framework

As shown in Table 3, and Table 4, we conduct experiments on the 'machine_annot (M)' branch and the 'ALL' branch of InterHand2.6M V1.0 dataset respectively. We compare the results with or without using our HDR framework. We notice that the recent state-of-the-art single-hand pose estimation (SHPE) method (MinimalHand [39]) struggles with occlusions and appearance ambiguity in interacting hand scenarios (IH26M-IH). To tackle these challenges, we propose a novel Hand De-occlusion and Removal (HDR) framework to perform hand de-occlusion and distractor removal. In Table 3, we show that our approach significantly improves upon the SHPE baseline in interacting hand scenarios, e.g. from 40.98 mm to 25.45 mm (M, IH26M-IH). We find that adding AIH dataset for training will further improve the performance of SHPE, which validates the effect of AIH dataset. Experiments on the 'ALL' branch have a similar phenomenon.

Table 3. Effect of HDR framework. Experiments are conducted on the 'machine_annot (M)' branch of InterHand2.6M V1.0 dataset. MPJPE (mm) is adopted to evaluate the 3D joint estimation accuracy.

Methods	Train (M, IH26M-SH)		Train (M, IH26M-SH +AIH)	
	IH26M-IH	IH26M-ALL	IH26M-IH	IH26M-ALL
SHPE [39]	40.98	25.78	32.27	21.66
+HDR (Ours)	25.45	17.98	24.59	17.80

Table 4. Effect of HDR framework. Experiments are conducted on the 'ALL' branch of InterHand2.6M V1.0 dataset. MPJPE (mm) is adopted to evaluate the 3D joint estimation accuracy.

Methods	Train (ALL, IH26M-SH)		Train (ALL, IH26M-SH +AIH)	
	IH26M-IH	IH26M-ALL	IH26M-IH	IH26M-ALL
SHPE [39]	39.96	25.90	30.23	20.93
+HDR (Ours)	25.93	18.39	23.99	17.58

5.5   Ablation Study

In this section, we conduct ablation studies to evaluate the effectiveness of the key components of our approach on the 'machine annot (M)' branch of Inter-Hand2.6M V1.0 dataset [21]. For fair comparisons, in all the ablation experiments, we use the same SHPE [39] trained on the IH26M-SH set.

Analysis of Hand De-occlusion and Removal (HDR) Module. There are two major challenges of hand pose estimation in interacting scenarios, *i.e.* severe self-occlusion, and ambiguity caused by the homogeneous appearance of hands. As shown in Table 5, #1, #2, #3, and #8, we conduct ablative experiments to quantitatively evaluate the effect of De-occlusion and Removal. Comparing #2 and #8, we observe that disabling 'Removal' will dramatically increase the MPJPE by 34.4%. Comparing #3 and #8, we see that disabling 'De-occlusion' increases the MPJPE by 9.5%. If we only apply SHPE [39] without HDR, the errors are further increased. These results clearly show that (1) state-of-the-art SHPE [39] is sensitive to self-occlusions and inter-hand ambiguities (2) HDRM is effective in handling the aforementioned two major challenges.

Analysis of Model Design Choices. We empirically validate the model design choice of HDRNet, especially *Discriminator* and the *Transformer* block. Discriminator is applied to enhance the image recovery quality by adversarial training. Comparing #4 and #8 in Table 5, we observe that although Discriminator helps in improving the quality of the recovered image, its influence on the final results is only marginal (0.7%). The Transformer block enhances image feature interactions, enlarges the receptive fields, and focuses more on important image regions. Comparing #5 and #8 in Table 5, we see that without using the Transformer block impacts the final results by a clear margin (4.8%).

Table 5. Ablation studies. Experiments are conducted on the 'machine_annot (M)' branch of InterHand2.6M V1.0 dataset. We use MPJPE (mm) to evaluate the 3D joint estimation accuracy. Δ means the absolute (and relative) difference compared with our final model #8. 'w/o' is short for 'without'.

	Methods	MPJPE (mm)	Δ
#1	SHPE [39] only	25.78	+7.80 (43.4%)
#2	w/o Removal	24.16	+6.18 (34.4%)
#3	w/o De-occlusion	19.69	+1.71 (9.5%)
#4	w/o Discriminator	18.11	+0.13 (0.7%)
#5	w/o Transformer Block	18.85	+0.87 (4.8%)
#6	AIH_Render only	18.10	+0.12 (0.7%)
#7	AIH_Syn only	18.35	+0.37 (2.1%)
#8	Ours	**17.98**	–

Analysis of AIH_Syn and AIH_Render. Our proposed AIH dataset is composed of two subsets, namely AIH_Syn and AIH_Render. Both have their own advantages and disadvantages. AIH_Syn retains more detailed and realistic appearance features, while AIH_Render considers the inter-dependencies between two hands to avoid physically implausible configurations. Using a combination of these two sets to train the HDRNet will achieve the best performance. In Table 5, comparing #6, #7, and #8, we compare different training settings for HDRNet. We notice that it already achieves reasonably good results even if we only use one of the two sets. For example, using "AIH_Render only" to train HDRNet, we can achieve 18.10 MPJPE (mm), which is only marginally worse than the final model #8. We also empirically find that "AIH_Render" seems to have a larger impact on the final results than "AIH_Syn" does.

5.6   Time Complexity Analysis

We analyze the time cost on one Tesla P40 GPU in a single thread. On average, HASM, HDRM, and SHPE take 12.6 ms, 0.6 ms, and 34.0 ms per frame (including two hands) respectively. The time cost of HDRM (our major contribution) is only a small proportion of the total time cost (0.6 vs 47.2 ms).

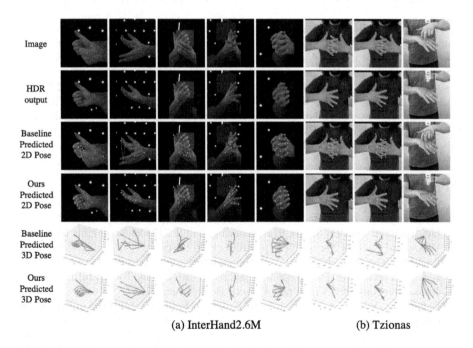

(a) InterHand2.6M   (b) Tzionas

Fig. 5. Qualitive results of how HDR helps in handling severe hand-hand occlusion and appearance ambiguities of two hands. Best viewed in color. (Color figure online)

5.7 Qualitative Results

In Fig. 5, we provide qualitative analysis on InterHand2.6M [21] and Tzionas dataset [30] to illustrate how HDR helps in handling severe hand-hand occlusion and the homogeneous appearance of hands. We see that HDR recovers the appearance in the occluded region and removes the distractor in challenging hand-hand occlusion cases. The results on Tzionas dataset [30] further validates the generalization ability of our proposed framework.

6 Conclusions and Limitations

Interacting hand pose estimation is important but challenging due to severe hand-to-hand occlusion and ambiguity caused by the other distracting hand. In this paper, we propose to decompose the task into two relatively simple subtasks, *i.e.* (1) Hand De-occlusion and Removal (HDR), (2) Single Hand Pose Estimation (SHPE). Through HDR, we can simplify the case, which an off-the-shelf SHPE can handle. We empirically verified the effectiveness of our HDR framework on the InterHand2.6M and Tzionas dataset. Our limitations mainly lie in artifacts produced by HDRM. Improving the image recovery quality requires efforts in various research fields, which we will explore in the future.

Acknowledgement. We would like to thank Wentao Jiang, Wang Zeng, Neng Qian, Yumeng Hu, Lixin Yang, Yu Rong, Qiang Zhou and Jiayi Wang for their helpful discussions and feedback. Mengxiang Lin is supported by State Key Laboratory of Software Development Environment under Grant No SKLSDE 2022ZX-06. Ping Luo is supported by the General Research Fund of HK No.27208720, No.17212120, and No.17200622. Wanli Ouyang is supported by the Australian Research Council Grant DP200103223, Australian Medical Research Future Fund MRFAI000085, CRC-P Smart Material Recovery Facility (SMRF) - Curby Soft Plastics, and CRC-P ARIA - Bionic Visual-Spatial Prosthesis for the Blind.

References

1. Baek, S., Kim, K.I., Kim, T.K.: Pushing the envelope for RGB-based dense 3D hand pose estimation via neural rendering. In: IEEE Conference on Computer Vision and Pattern Recognition, pp. 1067–1076 (2019)
2. Baek, S., Kim, K.I., Kim, T.K.: Weakly-supervised domain adaptation via GAN and mesh model for estimating 3D hand poses interacting objects. In: IEEE Conference on Computer Vision and Pattern Recognition (2020)
3. Ballan, L., Taneja, A., Gall, J., Van Gool, L., Pollefeys, M.: Motion capture of hands in action using discriminative salient points. In: Fitzgibbon, A., Lazebnik, S., Perona, P., Sato, Y., Schmid, C. (eds.) ECCV 2012. LNCS, vol. 7577, pp. 640–653. Springer, Heidelberg (2012). https://doi.org/10.1007/978-3-642-33783-3_46
4. Boukhayma, A., Bem, R.d., Torr, P.H.: 3D hand shape and pose from images in the wild. In: IEEE Conference on Computer Vision and Pattern Recognition, pp. 10843–10852 (2019)

5. Choi, H., Moon, G., Lee, K.M.: Pose2Mesh: graph convolutional network for 3D human pose and mesh recovery from a 2D human pose. In: Vedaldi, A., Bischof, H., Brox, T., Frahm, J.-M. (eds.) ECCV 2020. LNCS, vol. 12352, pp. 769–787. Springer, Cham (2020). https://doi.org/10.1007/978-3-030-58571-6_45

6. Ehsani, K., Mottaghi, R., Farhadi, A.: SeGAN: segmenting and generating the invisible. In: IEEE Conference on Computer Vision and Pattern Recognition, pp. 6144–6153 (2018)

7. Fan, Z., Spurr, A., Kocabas, M., Tang, S., Black, M., Hilliges, O.: Learning to disambiguate strongly interacting hands via probabilistic per-pixel part segmentation. In: International Conference on 3D Vision (3DV) (2021)

8. Gatys, L.A., Ecker, A.S., Bethge, M.: Image style transfer using convolutional neural networks. In: IEEE Conference on Computer Vision and Pattern Recognition, pp. 2414–2423 (2016)

9. Han, S., et al.: MEgATrack: monochrome egocentric articulated hand-tracking for virtual reality. ACM Trans. Graph. **39**(4), 1–87 (2020)

10. Hu, Y.T., Chen, H.S., Hui, K., Huang, J.B., Schwing, A.G.: Sail-VOS: semantic Amodal instance level video object segmentation-a synthetic dataset and baselines. In: IEEE Conference on Computer Vision and Pattern Recognition, pp. 3105–3115 (2019)

11. Iqbal, U., Molchanov, P., Breuel, T., Gall, J., Kautz, J.: Hand pose estimation via latent 2.5D heatmap regression. In: Ferrari, V., Hebert, M., Sminchisescu, C., Weiss, Y. (eds.) ECCV 2018. LNCS, vol. 11215, pp. 125–143. Springer, Cham (2018). https://doi.org/10.1007/978-3-030-01252-6_8

12. Isola, P., Zhu, J.Y., Zhou, T., Efros, A.A.: Image-to-image translation with conditional adversarial networks. In: IEEE Conference on Computer Vision and Pattern Recognition, pp. 1125–1134 (2017)

13. Kim, D.U., Kim, K.I., Baek, S.: End-to-end detection and pose estimation of two interacting hands. In: International Conference on Computer Vision, pp. 11189–11198 (2021)

14. Kingma, D.P., Ba, J.: Adam: a method for stochastic optimization. arXiv preprint arXiv:1412.6980 (2014)

15. Kulon, D., Guler, R.A., Kokkinos, I., Bronstein, M.M., Zafeiriou, S.: Weakly-supervised mesh-convolutional hand reconstruction in the wild. In: IEEE Conference on Computer Vision and Pattern Recognition, pp. 4990–5000 (2020)

16. Li, K., Malik, J.: Amodal instance segmentation. In: Leibe, B., Matas, J., Sebe, N., Welling, M. (eds.) ECCV 2016. LNCS, vol. 9906, pp. 677–693. Springer, Cham (2016). https://doi.org/10.1007/978-3-319-46475-6_42

17. Lin, F., Wilhelm, C., Martinez, T.: Two-hand global 3D pose estimation using monocular RGB. In: Proceedings of the IEEE/CVF Winter Conference on Applications of Computer Vision, pp. 2373–2381 (2021)

18. Lin, K., Wang, L., Liu, Z.: End-to-end human pose and mesh reconstruction with transformers. In: IEEE Conference on Computer Vision and Pattern Recognition, pp. 1954–1963 (2021)

19. Liu, G., Reda, F.A., Shih, K.J., Wang, T.-C., Tao, A., Catanzaro, B.: Image inpainting for irregular holes using partial convolutions. In: Ferrari, V., Hebert, M., Sminchisescu, C., Weiss, Y. (eds.) ECCV 2018. LNCS, vol. 11215, pp. 89–105. Springer, Cham (2018). https://doi.org/10.1007/978-3-030-01252-6_6

20. Moon, G., Lee, K.M.: NeuralAnnot: neural annotator for in-the-wild expressive 3D human pose and mesh training sets. arXiv preprint arXiv:2011.11232 (2020)

21. Moon, G., Yu, S.-I., Wen, H., Shiratori, T., Lee, K.M.: InterHand2.6M: a dataset and baseline for 3D interacting hand pose estimation from a single RGB image. In: Vedaldi, A., Bischof, H., Brox, T., Frahm, J.-M. (eds.) ECCV 2020. LNCS, vol. 12365, pp. 548–564. Springer, Cham (2020). https://doi.org/10.1007/978-3-030-58565-5_33

22. Mueller, F., Davis, M., Bernard, F., Sotnychenko, O., Verschoor, M., Otaduy, M.A., Casas, D., Theobalt, C.: Real-time pose and shape reconstruction of two interacting hands with a single depth camera. ACM Trans. Graph. **38**(4), 1–13 (2019)

23. Oikonomidis, I., Kyriazis, N., Argyros, A.A.: Tracking the articulated motion of two strongly interacting hands. In: IEEE Conference on Computer Vision and Pattern Recognition, pp. 1862–1869. IEEE (2012)

24. Qi, L., Jiang, L., Liu, S., Shen, X., Jia, J.: Amodal instance segmentation with KINS dataset. In: IEEE Conference on Computer Vision and Pattern Recognition, pp. 3014–3023 (2019)

25. Qian, N., Wang, J., Mueller, F., Bernard, F., Golyanik, V., Theobalt, C.: HTML: a parametric hand texture model for 3D hand reconstruction and personalization. In: Vedaldi, A., Bischof, H., Brox, T., Frahm, J.-M. (eds.) ECCV 2020. LNCS, vol. 12356, pp. 54–71. Springer, Cham (2020). https://doi.org/10.1007/978-3-030-58621-8_4

26. Romero, J., Tzionas, D., Black, M.J.: Embodied hands: modeling and capturing hands and bodies together. arXiv preprint arXiv:2201.02610 (2022)

27. Rong, Y., Wang, J., Liu, Z., Loy, C.C.: Monocular 3D reconstruction of interacting hands via collision-aware factorized refinements. In: International Conference on 3D Vision (2021)

28. Smith, B.: Constraining dense hand surface tracking with elasticity. ACM Trans. Graph. **39**(6), 1–14 (2020)

29. Spurr, A., Song, J., Park, S., Hilliges, O.: Cross-modal deep variational hand pose estimation. In: IEEE Conference on Computer Vision and Pattern Recognition, pp. 89–98 (2018)

30. Tzionas, D., Ballan, L., Srikantha, A., Aponte, P., Pollefeys, M., Gall, J.: Capturing hands in action using discriminative salient points and physics simulation. Int. J. Comput. Vis. **118**(2), 172–193 (2016). https://doi.org/10.1007/s11263-016-0895-4

31. Wang, J., et al.: RGB2hands: real-time tracking of 3D hand interactions from monocular RGB video. ACM Trans. Graph. **39**(6), 1–16 (2020)

32. Wang, W., et al.: PVTv 2: improved baselines with pyramid vision transformer. Computational Visual Media **8**(3), 1–10 (2022). https://doi.org/10.1007/s41095-022-0274-8

33. Xie, E., Wang, W., Yu, Z., Anandkumar, A., Alvarez, J.M., Luo, P.: SegFormer: simple and efficient design for semantic segmentation with transformers. Adv. Neural Inform. Process. Syst. **34**, 12077–12090 (2021)

34. Yan, X., et al.: Visualizing the invisible: occluded vehicle segmentation and recovery. In: International Conference on Computer Vision, pp. 7618–7627 (2019)

35. Yang, L., Li, J., Xu, W., Diao, Y., Lu, C.: BiHand: recovering hand mesh with multi-stage bisected hourglass networks. In: The British Machine Vision Conference (2020)

36. Zhan, X., Pan, X., Dai, B., Liu, Z., Lin, D., Loy, C.C.: Self-supervised scene de-occlusion. In: IEEE Conference on Computer Vision and Pattern Recognition, pp. 3784–3792 (2020)

37. Zhang, B., et al.: Interacting two-hand 3D pose and shape reconstruction from single color image. In: International Conference on Computer Vision, pp. 11354–11363 (2021)

38. Zhou, Q., Wang, S., Wang, Y., Huang, Z., Wang, X.: Human DE-occlusion: invisible perception and recovery for humans. In: IEEE Conference on Computer Vision and Pattern Recognition, pp. 3691–3701 (2021)
39. Zhou, Y., Habermann, M., Xu, W., Habibie, I., Theobalt, C., Xu, F.: Monocular real-time hand shape and motion capture using multi-modal data. In: IEEE Conference on Computer Vision and Pattern Recognition, pp. 5346–5355 (2020)
40. Zhu, Y., Tian, Y., Metaxas, D., Dollár, P.: Semantic Amodal segmentation. In: IEEE Conference on Computer Vision and Pattern Recognition, pp. 1464–1472 (2017)
41. Zimmermann, C., Brox, T.: Learning to estimate 3D hand pose from single RGB images. In: International Conference On Computer Vision, pp. 4903–4911 (2017)

Pose for Everything: Towards Category-Agnostic Pose Estimation

Lumin Xu[1,2](✉) [ID], Sheng Jin[3,4] [ID], Wang Zeng[1,2] [ID], Wentao Liu[4,5] [ID],
Chen Qian[4] [ID], Wanli Ouyang[5,6] [ID], Ping Luo[3] [ID], and Xiaogang Wang[1] [ID]

[1] The Chinese University of Hong Kong, Shatin, Hong Kong
{luminxu,zengwang}@link.cuhk.edu.hk, xgwang@ee.cuhk.edu.hk
[2] SenseTime Research, Beijing, China
[3] The University of Hong Kong, Pok Fu Lam, Hong Kong
js20@connect.hku.hk, pluo@cs.hku.hk
[4] SenseTime Research and Tetras.AI, Beijing, China
{liuwentao,qianchen}@sensetime.com
[5] Shanghai AI Laboratory, Shanghai, China
wanli.ouyang@sydney.edu.au
[6] The University of Sydney, Sydney, Australia

Abstract. Existing works on 2D pose estimation mainly focus on a
certain category, *e.g.* human, animal, and vehicle. However, there are
lots of application scenarios that require detecting the poses/keypoints
of the unseen class of objects. In this paper, we introduce the task of
Category-Agnostic Pose Estimation (CAPE), which aims to create a pose
estimation model capable of detecting the pose of any class of object
given only a few samples with keypoint definition. To achieve this goal, we
formulate the pose estimation problem as a keypoint matching problem
and design a novel CAPE framework, termed POse Matching Network
(POMNet). A transformer-based Keypoint Interaction Module (KIM)
is proposed to capture both the interactions among different keypoints
and the relationship between the support and query images. We also
introduce Multi-category Pose (MP-100) dataset, which is a 2D pose
dataset of 100 object categories containing over 20K instances and is
well-designed for developing CAPE algorithms. Experiments show that
our method outperforms other baseline approaches by a large margin.
Codes and data are available at https://github.com/luminxu/Pose-for-
Everything.

Keywords: 2D pose estimation · Class-agnostic · Few-shot · MP-100
dataset

L. Xu and S. Jin—Equal contribution.

Supplementary Information The online version contains supplementary material
available at https://doi.org/10.1007/978-3-031-20068-7_23.

© The Author(s), under exclusive license to Springer Nature Switzerland AG 2022
S. Avidan et al. (Eds.): ECCV 2022, LNCS 13666, pp. 398–416, 2022.
https://doi.org/10.1007/978-3-031-20068-7_23

1   Introduction

2D pose estimation (also referred to as keypoint localization) aims to predict the locations of the pre-defined semantic parts of an instance. It has received great attention in the computer vision community in recent years because of its broad application scenarios in both academia and industry. For example, human pose estimation [2] has been widely used in virtual reality (VR) and augmented reality (AR); animal pose estimation [67] is of great significance in zoology and wildlife conservation; vehicle pose estimation [44] is critical for autonomous driving.

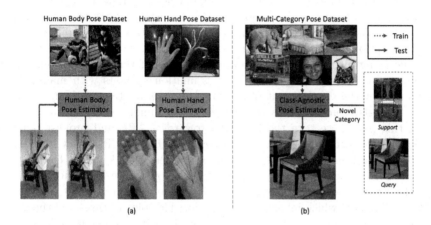

Fig. 1. Category-Specific Pose Estimation vs Class-Agnostic Pose Estimation (CAPE). (a) Traditional pose estimation task is category-specific. Pose estimators are trained on the dataset containing objects of a single category, and can only predict the poses of that category. (b) CAPE task requires the pose estimator to detect poses of arbitrary category given the keypoint definition. After training on the pose dataset containing multi-category objects, the pose estimators can generalize to novel categories given one or a few support images.

The real-world applications from different fields often involve detecting the poses of a variety of novel objects of interest. For example, biologists may study the plant growth by analyzing the poses of plants. However, traditional pose estimators are category-specific and can only be applied to the category that they are trained on. In order to detect poses of novel objects, users have to collect a huge amount of labeled data and design category-specific pose estimation models, which is time-consuming and laborious. To make matters worse, data collection for rare objects (*e.g.* endangered animals) and semantic keypoint annotation for cases that need domain knowledge (*e.g.* medical images) are extremely challenging. Therefore, there is increasing demand for developing pose estimation approaches that can generalize across different categories.

In this paper, we introduce an important yet challenging task, termed Category-Agnostic Pose Estimation (CAPE). As shown in Fig. 1, unlike traditional pose estimation methods that can only predict the poses of a specific category, CAPE aims at using a single model for detecting poses of any category. Given a support image of a novel category and the corresponding keypoint definition, the class-agnostic pose estimator predicts the pose of the same category in the query image. In this way, the pose of any object of interest can be generated according to the arbitrary keypoint definition. The huge cost of data collection, model training and parameter tuning for each novel class is greatly reduced.

There are several challenges preventing the computer vision community from designing systems capable of predicting the poses of a large number of object categories. First, most pose estimation approaches [50] treat it as a supervised regression task, requiring thousands of labeled images to learn to map an input image to keypoint locations. Second, different objects may have different keypoint definition and unknown number of keypoints. It is non-trivial to learn the unique output representations and utilize the structural information. Third, there are few to none large-scale pose estimation datasets with many visual categories for the development of a general pose estimation method. Previous datasets mostly consist of only one category (*e.g.* human body).

In this paper, we take the first step towards CAPE and propose a novel framework, termed POse Matching Network (POMNet). POMNet formulates the 2D pose estimation task as a matching problem. The keypoint features are extracted from the support images based on the reference keypoint definition, and the image features are extracted from the query image. Matching Head (MH) is designed, which integrates the support keypoint features and the query image features, to estimate the keypoint positions with the maximal possibility. In this way, the model is agnostic to the object category and can be used for any number of keypoints. A transformer-based Keypoint Interaction Module (KIM) is also proposed to capture both the connections among different keypoints and the relationship between the support and query images. The features of different keypoints mutually interact with each other to learn their inherent structure for the given object category. The keypoint features are further aligned with the query image features for better matching. Experimental results show that our model significantly outperforms the other baseline models by a large margin.

In order to train and evaluate the class-agnostic pose estimators, we collect a large-scale pose dataset called Multi-category Pose (MP-100) dataset. The dataset contains over 20K instances, covering 100 sub-categories (*e.g.* vinegar fly body, sofa, suv, and skirt) and 8 super-categories (*e.g.* animal face, furniture, vehicle, and clothes). To our best knowledge, it is the first benchmark that contains the pose annotation of multiple visual (super-)categories.

The main contributions of our work are three-folds.

- We introduce an important yet challenging task termed Category-Agnostic Pose Estimation (CAPE). CAPE requires the model to predict the poses of any objects given a few support images with keypoint definition.
- We propose the novel CAPE framework, namely POse Matching Network (POMNet), and formulate the keypoint detection task as a matching problem.

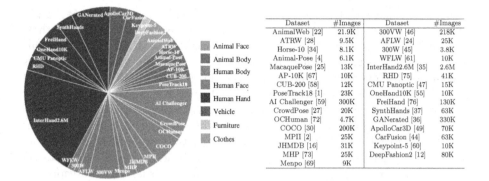

Dataset	#Images	Dataset	#Images
AnimalWeb [22]	21.9K	300VW [46]	218K
ATRW [28]	9.5K	AFLW [24]	25K
Horse-10 [34]	8.1K	300W [45]	3.8K
Animal-Pose [4]	6.1K	WFLW [61]	10K
MacaquePose [25]	13K	InterHand2.6M [35]	2.6M
AP-10K [67]	10K	RHD [75]	41K
CUB-200 [58]	12K	CMU Panoptic [47]	15K
PoseTrack18 [1]	23K	OneHand10K [55]	10K
AI Challenger [59]	300K	FreiHand [76]	130K
CrowdPose [27]	20K	SynthHands [37]	63K
OCHuman [72]	4.7K	GANerated [36]	330K
COCO [30]	200K	ApolloCar3D [49]	70K
MPII [2]	25K	CarFusion [44]	63K
JHMDB [16]	31K	Keypoint-5 [60]	10K
MHP [73]	25K	DeepFashion2 [12]	80K
Menpo [69]	9K		

Animal Face
Animal Body
Human Body
Human Face
Human Hand
Vehicle
Furniture
Clothes

Fig. 2. Categories and image numbers for popular 2D pose estimation datasets.

Keypoint Interaction Module (KIM) is proposed to capture both the keypoint-level relationship and the support-query relationship.
– We build the first large-scale multi-(super-)category dataset for the task of CAPE, termed Multi-category Pose (MP-100), to boost the related research.

2   Related Works

2.1   2D Pose Estimation

There are two types of keypoints in computer vision community. Semantic points are points with clear semantic meanings (*e.g.* the left eye), while interest points are low-level points (*e.g.* corner points). 2D pose estimation focuses on predicting the semantic points of objects, *e.g.* human body parts [10,21,30], facial landmarks [3], hand keypoints [75], and animal poses [4]. However, current pose estimation methods and datasets [12,30,67] only focus on keypoints of a single super-category and can not support cross-category/unseen pose estimation.

2D Pose Estimation Method. Existing methods can be classified into two categories: regression-based methods [26,40,51,52] and heatmap-based methods [6–8,18–20,27,39,50,57,62]. Regression-based approaches directly map the image to keypoint coordinates. Such methods are flexible and efficient for real-time applications. However, they are vulnerable to occlusion and motion blur, resulting in inferior performance. Heatmap-based approaches use likelihood heatmaps to encode the keypoint location. Because of excellent localization precision, heatmap-based methods are dominant in the field of 2D pose estimation. Recent works on pose estimation mostly focus on designing powerful convolutional neural networks [6,8,39,50,57,62,63] or transformer-based architectures [29,33,65,68,70]. However, they only focus on detecting the keypoints of object categories that appear during training. In comparison, our model is capable of detecting the keypoints of arbitrary objects of unseen classes.

2D Pose Estimation Benchmark. Existing 2D pose estimation datasets only focus on a single super-category. As shown in Fig. 2, most attentions have been focused on human-related categories (*e.g.* human body [1,2,16,27,30,59,72,73], human face [24,45,46,61,69], and human hand [35–37,47,55,75,76]), and there are numerous large-scale datasets for these classes. For other long-tailed categories, the datasets are relatively limited in terms of both the dataset sizes and diversity. Nevertheless, analyzing these long-tailed object categories is of great significance in both academia and industry. For example, vehicle pose estimation [44,49] is important for autonomous driving. Animal pose estimation [4,25,28,34,58,67] is of great significance in zoology and wildlife conservation. Indoor furniture pose estimation [60] is important for developing household robots. In this paper, we build the first large-scale benchmark (MP-100 dataset) that contains the pose annotations of a wide range of visual super-categories.

2.2   Category-Agnostic Estimation

Category-agnostic estimation has been applied to many computer vision tasks, including detection [17], segmentation [71], object counting [31,66] and viewpoint estimation [74]. Our work is mostly related to StarMap [74], which proposes category-agnostic 3D keypoint representations encoded with canonical view locations. However, StarMap is only applicable for rigid objects (*e.g.* furniture), and relies on several expensive 3D CAD models of the target category to identify the predicted keypoint proposals. In comparison, CAPE aims at predicting 2D poses of any object category (both rigid and flexible) according to any manual keypoint definition given by one or a few support images.

2.3   Few-Shot Learning

Few-shot learning [32] aims at learning novel classes using only a few examples. Recent few-shot learning approaches can be roughly classified into three categories, *i.e.* metric-learning-based approaches [48,54,64], meta-learning-based approaches [11,43], and data-augmentation-based approaches [14]. *Metric-learning-based Approaches.* Prototypical networks [48] learn the prototype (embedding features) of each class in the support data and then classify query data as the class whose prototype is the "nearest". *Meta-learning-based Approaches.* Model-agnostic meta-learning [11] and LSTM-based meta-learner [43] aim at searching for a set of good initialization weights, such that the classifier can rapidly generalize to novel tasks by fine-tuning on only a few support samples. *Data-augmentation-based Approaches.* [14,56] generate synthetic examples of novel classes to improve the performance by using these synthetic examples for retraining. Our approach belongs to metric-learning-based approaches. It is the first framework towards CAPE. Besides, Keypoint Interaction Module (KIM) is specifically designed for CAPE to capture both the relationship among different keypoints and the relationship between support and query images.

3   Class-Agnostic Pose Estimation (CAPE)

3.1   Problem Definition

This paper introduces a novel task, termed class-agnostic pose estimation (CAPE). Unlike existing pose estimation tasks that predict keypoints of a single *known/seen* (super-)category, CAPE requires a single model to detect keypoints of arbitrary category. More specifically, given one or a few support samples with keypoint definition of an *unseen* category, object keypoints of this category can be detected without labeling large-scale supervisions and retraining models, significantly reducing the cost of data annotation and parameter tuning.

In order to validate the generalization capacity of CAPE models on unseen categories, they are trained on the *base* categories but evaluated on *novel* categories. The base categories and the novel categories are mutually exclusive, where the novel categories on the test set do not appear in the training data. During testing, CAPE models are provided with K labeled support samples of an unseen category. The models are required to detect the poses of the query samples that are of the same category as the support samples. In this sense, CAPE task can be viewed as a K-shot pose estimation problem. Especially, when $K = 1$, it is one-shot pose estimation.

3.2   POse Matching Network (POMNet)

Traditional pose estimators can be applied to neither the unseen object categories nor different keypoint definitions of the same class (*e.g.* 19-keypoint human face definition and 68-keypoint human face definition). To achieve CAPE, we formulate the task as a matching problem and propose a novel framework termed POse Matching Network (POMNet). POMNet works by computing the matching similarity between the reference support keypoint features and the query image features at each location. Therefore, POMNet is capable of handling various categories with different keypoint numbers and definitions. As shown in Fig. 3, POMNet consists of three parts, *i.e.* the feature extractors (Θ_S and Θ_Q), Keypoint Interaction Module (KIM), and Matching Head (MH).

Feature Extractor. We employ two parallel feature extractors to extract the support keypoint features and the query image features. In our implementation, ResNet-50 [15] pre-trained on ImageNet dataset is used as the backbone.

For the support image I_S, the feature extractor Θ_S is utilized to extract the support image features $\mathcal{F}_S = \Theta_S(I_S)$. The keypoint annotations of the support sample are provided in the heatmap representations. We denote the ground-truth heatmaps of the support sample as H_S^*, and $H_S^{*j} \in \mathbb{R}^{H \times W \times 1}$ represents the heatmap of the j_{th} keypoint. Given the support image features and the ground-truth heatmaps of the support sample, we can obtain the corresponding keypoint features as follows.

$$\hat{\mathcal{F}}_S^j = AvgPool(Upsample(\mathcal{F}_S) \otimes H_S^{*j}), \quad j = 1, 2, ..., J \tag{1}$$

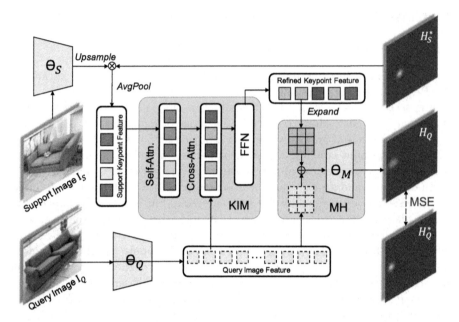

Fig. 3. Overview of POse Matching Network (POMNet). Feature extractors Θ_S and Θ_Q extract the support keypoint features and the query image features respectively. Keypoint Interaction Module (KIM) refines the keypoint features by message passing among keypoints and capturing the relationship between the query and support images. Matching Head (MH) integrates the refined keypoint features and the query image features to predict the keypoint localization in the query image. MSE loss is applied to supervise the model.

where $\mathcal{F}_S \in \mathbb{R}^{h \times w \times c}$ and $\hat{\mathcal{F}}_S^j \in \mathbb{R}^{1 \times 1 \times c}$ denote the support image features and the j_{th} keypoint features respectively. $Upsample()$ is the up-sampling operation that reshapes the support image features to the same size of the corresponding heatmaps. $\otimes$ denotes pixel-wise multiplication. $AvgPool()$ is the average pooling operation that aggregates the support image features around the ground-truth keypoint position via weighted mean. J is the number of reference keypoints.

For the query image I_Q, we follow a similar pipeline and apply the feature extractor Θ_Q to extract the query image features $\mathcal{F}_Q = \Theta_Q(I_Q)$. We collapse the spatial dimensions of the query image features and reshape them into a sequence. The extracted image features are then used to refine the support keypoint features in Keypoint Interaction Module (KIM) and to predict the keypoint localization in Matching Head (MH).

Keypoint Interaction Module (KIM). KIM targets at enhancing the support keypoint features through efficient attention mechanisms. We first reduce the channel dimension of support keypoint features by a fully-connected layer and input the features of different keypoints as a sequence. As the keypoint numbers of different categories are different, several dummy features with padding mask are added at the end to keep a fixed number L of input features ($L = 100$ in our implementation), which enables KIM to adapt to various keypoint numbers. KIM has three transformer blocks, each of which consists of two major components, *i.e.* Self-Attn. and Cross-Attn. *Self-Attn.* The self-attention layer [53] learns to exchange information among keypoints and utilize inherent object structures. It allows the keypoint features to interact with each other, and aggregate these interactions using the attention weights. *Cross-Attn.* The keypoint features also interact with the query image features to align the feature representations and mitigate the representation gap. Specifically, a cross-attention layer [5] is applied to aggregate useful information in the query image. The keypoint features are input as query, and the flattened query image features are input as the key and the value. The channel dimension of the query image features are reduced to match the channel dimension of the keypoint features, and the sinusoidal position embedding [41,53] is supplemented to the query image features. A feed forward network (FFN) is also included following the common practice [53]. As a result, the support keypoint features are processed and refined by KIM, $\{\mathcal{F}_S^j\}_{j=1}^L = \text{KIM}(\{\mathcal{F}_S^j\}_{j=1}^L, \mathcal{F}_Q)$. We exclude the dummy padding ones and obtain the refined keypoint features $\{\bar{\mathcal{F}}_S^j\}_{j=1}^J$ by selecting the first J valid keypoint features, where $J \leq L$.

Matching Head (MH). Given the refined keypoint features as the reference, Matching Head (MH) targets at seeking the best matching positions in the query image that are encoded with heatmaps.

We expand the refined keypoint features to the same spatial shape as the query image features $\mathcal{F}_Q$. The expanded features are then concatenated with the query image features. Finally, a decoder Θ_M is employed to estimate the keypoint heatmaps. This procedure can be formulated as follows.

$$H_Q^j = \Theta_M(Expand(\bar{\mathcal{F}}_S^j) \oplus \mathcal{F}_Q), \quad j = 1, 2, ..., J. \tag{2}$$

where $\oplus$ refers to the channel-wise concatenation. $Expand()$ denotes the spatial expansion operation, *i.e.* copying the refined keypoint features spatially to fit in the spatial size of the query image features. H_Q^j is the predicted heatmap of the j_{th} keypoint. The decoder Θ_M consists of one 3×3 convolutional layer, followed by deconvolutional layers for higher resolution as the common practice [62]. Pixel-wise mean squared error (MSE) loss is applied to supervise POMNet.

$$\mathcal{L}_{MSE} = \frac{1}{JHW} \sum_{j=1}^{J} \sum_{p} \|H_Q^j(p) - H_Q^{*j}(p)\|_2^2, \tag{3}$$

where H and W refer to the height and width of heatmaps. $H_Q^j(p)$ and $H_Q^{*j}(p)$ are the predicted and the ground-truth pixel intensity at the position p.

Extension to K-Shot. When K ($K > 1$) support images are available, we first extract the support keypoint features for each sample individually, and then calculate the mean among the K samples. The subsequent pipeline (including

KIM and MH) is exactly the same as that of the 1-shot setting. With more support images, POMNet is able to capture more robust keypoint features to handle the intra-category variance and the ambiguity of the keypoint definition.

4 Mulit-category Pose (MP-100) Dataset

Previous pose estimation datasets only consist of objects of one (super-)category and there are no existing datasets for CAPE task. We therefore construct the first large-scale pose dataset containing objects of multiple super-categories, termed Multi-category Pose (MP-100). In total, MP-100 dataset covers 100 sub-categories and 8 super-categories (human hand, human face, human body, animal body, animal face, clothes, furniture, and vehicle) as shown in Fig. 4.

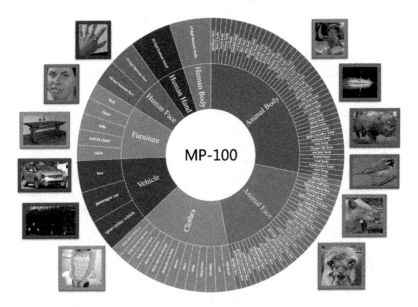

Fig. 4. MP-100 dataset covers 100 sub-categories and 8 super-categories (human hand & face & body, animal face & body, clothes, furniture, and vehicle).

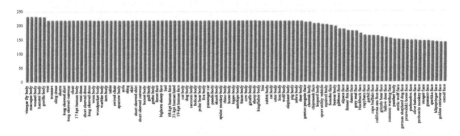

Fig. 5. Histogram for instance number of each category on MP-100 dataset.

Over 18K images and 20K annotations are collected from several popular 2D pose datasets, including COCO [30], 300W [45], AFLW [24], OneHand10K [55], DeepFasion2 [12], AP-10K [67], MacaquePose [25], Vinegar Fly [42], Desert Locust [13], CUB-200 [58], CarFusion [44], AnimalWeb [22], and Keypoint-5 [60]. Keypoint numbers are diverse across different categories, ranging from 8 to 68.

We split the collected 100 categories into train/val/test sets (70 for train, 10 for val, and 20 for test). Following the common settings, we form five splits whose test sets are non-overlapping and evaluate the average model performance on the five splits. In this case, each category is tested as novel one on different splits and the category bias is avoided. Moreover, to treat all categories equally, we try our best to balance the number of instances among different categories.

For the test set on each split, 2K samples are selected with 100 instances in each category. And for train/val set, 14K/2K samples are chosen for 70/10 categories respectively. As the number of instances available for different categories are extremely diverse and there are rare categories with less than 200 instances, we minimize the standard deviation of the instance number of all the categories. During sample selection, for each category, we give preference to the instances with more valid keypoints labeled and larger image resolution. In Fig. 5, we demonstrate the histogram plot for the number of instances of each category on MP-100 dataset. The number of instances for each category is roughly balanced.

5   Experiments

5.1   Implementation Details

For each split on MP-100 dataset, we train POMNet on the train set, validate the performance on the val set, and finally evaluate the model on the test set. Note that the categories of the train/val/test set are mutually exclusive. During training, the support images and the query images of the same category are randomly paired. Each object of interest is cropped according to the bounding box and is resized to 256×256. Data augmentation with random scaling ($[-15\%, 15\%]$) and random rotation ($[-15°, 15°]$) is applied to improve the model generalization ability. The training is conducted on 8 GPUs with a batch size of 16 in each GPU for 210 epochs. We follow MMPose [9] to adopt Adam optimizer [23] with the base learning rate of $1e-3$ and decay the learning rate to $1e-4$ and $1e-5$ respectively at the 170th and 200th epochs. During testing, we sample 3,000 random episodes for each novel category. Since there are 20 test categories for each split, we construct a total of 60,000 episodes for evaluation.

PCK (Probability of Correct Keypoint) is a popular metric for pose estimation. If the normalized distance between the predicted keypoint and the ground-truth keypoint is less than a certain threshold (σ), it is considered correct.

$$\text{PCK} = \frac{1}{N} \sum_{i=1}^{N} \mathbf{1} \left(\frac{\|p_i - p_i^*\|_2}{d} \leq \sigma \right), \tag{4}$$

Table 1. Comparisons with the baseline methods on MP-100 dataset under both 5-shot and 1-shot settings. POMNet significantly outperforms other approaches.

5-Shot	Split1	Split2	Split3	Split4	Split5	Mean (PCK)
ProtoNet [48]	60.31	53.51	61.92	58.44	58.61	58.56
MAML [11]	70.03	55.98	63.21	64.79	58.47	62.50
Fine-tune [38]	71.67	57.84	66.76	66.53	60.24	64.61
POMNet (Ours)	**84.72**	**79.61**	**78.00**	**80.38**	**80.85**	**80.71**

1-Shot	Split1	Split2	Split3	Split4	Split5	Mean (PCK)
ProtoNet [48]	46.05	40.84	49.13	43.34	44.54	44.78
MAML [11]	68.14	54.72	64.19	63.24	57.20	61.50
Fine-tune [38]	70.60	57.04	66.06	65.00	59.20	63.58
POMNet (Ours)	**84.23**	**78.25**	**78.17**	**78.68**	**79.17**	**79.70**

where p_i and p_i^* are predicted and ground-truth keypoint locations respectively. $1(\cdot)$ is the indicator function. d is the longest side of the ground-truth bounding box, which is used as the normalization term. The correct ratio of the overall N keypoints is calculated. In the experiments, we report the average PCK@0.2 ($\sigma = 0.2$) of all the categories in each split. In order to minimize the category bias, the mean PCK result of all the 5 splits is also reported.

5.2 Benchmark Results on MP-100 Dataset

Class-Agnostic Pose Estimation (CAPE) is a new task that has not been tackled before. We tailor the existing few-shot learning baseline approaches, including Prototypical Networks [48], Finetune [38], and MAML [11] to address this new task. For fair comparisons, all baselines employ the same backbone network architecture (ResNet-50 [15]) as ours.

Prototypical Networks (ProtoNet) [48]. ProtoNet is a popular few-shot image classification approach, which constructs a prototype for each class and the query example is assigned to the class whose prototype is the "nearest". To solve CAPE, we adapt ProtoNet to construct a prototype for each keypoint and find the location whose features are closest to the prototype in the query image. Unlike image classification, both the receptive fields and the spatial resolution of the features are critical for pose estimation. We empirically find that the features from Stage-3 achieve a good balance of these two factors among all the 4 stages.

Fine-Tune [38]. The model is first pre-trained using a combination of all base categories on the train set. During testing, the model is fine-tuned on the support images of the novel category before estimating the pose of the query images. To handle the problem of various number of keypoints, the model is designed to output the maximum number of keypoints among all the categories, *i.e.* 68 on MP-100 dataset, and only the few valid keypoints are supervised for each particular category during training and fine-tuning.

Table 2. Cross super-category evaluation (PCK). POMNet outperforms other methods. But there is still large room for improvement on the rare categories.

Method	Human body	Human face	Vehicle	Furniture
ProtoNet [48]	37.61	57.80	28.35	42.64
MAML [11]	51.93	25.72	17.68	20.09
Fine-tune [38]	52.11	25.53	17.46	20.76
POMNet (Ours)	**73.82**	**79.63**	**34.92**	**47.27**

Model-Agnostic Meta-Learning (MAML) [11]. Through meta training, the MAML model is explicitly trained to search for a good initialization such that its parameters can quickly adapt to the given category by fine-tuning on several support images. Similar to Fine-tune [38], the number of keypoints of the model is set as 68. During meta testing, the model can rapidly adapt to the novel categories given a few support images.

As shown in Table 1, our proposed POMNet shows superiority over the existing few-shot learning based approaches on the task of Class-Agnostic Pose Estimation (CAPE). We first conduct experimental comparisons under the 5-shot setting. We observe that ProtoNet [48] mostly relies on low-level appearance features and encounters difficulties in constructing a reliable prototype using only 5 samples for all the keypoints. It processes each type of keypoint individually and does not utilize the structural information, restricting its upper bound performance. MAML [11] and Fine-tune [38] adapt to the novel object category by fine-tuning on a few samples during testing. However, the limited number of samples makes it hard for the model to achieve good performance on the novel categories due to severe over-fitting or under-fitting problems. Our proposed POMNet considers the CAPE task as a matching problem, decoupling the model from the object category and the number of keypoints. In the meanwhile, KIM explicitly captures the relationship among keypoints and the structure of the object of interest. As a result, POMNet achieves 80.71 PCK on the novel categories under 5-shot settings, and outperforms the baseline methods by a large margin (over 25% improvement).

When the number of sample images decreases to one, the degeneration of our POMNet is only 1.3% (79.70 vs 80.71 PCK). This is presumably because POMNet captures the relationship among semantic keypoints and is more robust to occlusion and visual ambiguity. In comparison, ProtoNet requires building the prototype based on a single keypoint, thus is more sensitive to the appearance variation, resulting in a larger performance drop (44.78 vs 58.46 PCK).

5.3 Cross Super-Category Pose Estimation

In order to further evaluate the generalization ability, we conduct the cross super-category pose estimation evaluation with the "Leave-One-Out" strategy. That is, we train the model on all but one super-categories on MP-100 dataset, and

Table 3. Ablation study of proposed components on MP-100 Split1 under 1-shot setting. KIM and MH significantly improve the model performance.

	Self-atten.	Cross-atten.	Matching head	PCK
#1			√	74.40
#2	√	√		79.19
#3		√	√	80.76
#4	√		√	82.92
#5	√	√	√	84.23

evaluate the performance on the remaining one super-category. The super-categories to be evaluated include human body, human face, vehicle, and furniture.

As shown in Table 2, our proposed POMNet outperforms the baseline methods on all the super-categories, demonstrating stronger generalization ability. However, super-category generalization is challenging and there is still a large room for improvement. We notice that all the methods perform poorly on the super-categories of vehicle and furniture. This is possibly because these categories are very different from the training ones and the extracted features are not discriminative enough. There are a great number of invisible keypoints for vehicle, and the intra-class variation between images is large for furniture, making these two super-categories more challenging. Solving CAPE requires to handle occlusion and intra-class appearance variation, and extract more discriminative features for unseen categories. We will explore these directions in the future.

5.4   Ablation Study

Effect of Model Components. Table 3 shows the effect of Keypoint Interaction Module (KIM) and Matching Head (MH). Comparing #1 and #5, we find that KIM significantly improves the CAPE model performance (13.2% improvement). #3 and #4 show the effect of self-attention and cross-attention design, respectively. Especially, the 11.5% gain from #1 to #4 shows that message passing among keypoints by self-attention greatly benefits keypoint localization. Comparison between #2 and #5 verifies the necessity of MH. #2 replaces MH by matrix multiplication between support keypoint features and query image

Table 4. Left: Effect of training category number ("#Train") under 1-shot setting. Evaluation is conducted on a novel category ("human body"). **Right:** Both training and testing are on "human body" only.

#Train	1	9	49	99	Oracle	SBL-Res50 [60]
PCK	39.32	55.74	70.46	73.82	89.79	89.76

features. It collapses the channel dimension to 1 for each keypoint, causing undesirable information loss required for precise localization.

Effect of Training Category Number. As shown in Table 4 **Left**, more training categories leads to better generalizability to the novel category, which validates the necessity of MP-100 dataset and the rationality of our experiments.

Sanity Check. We perform traditional one class pose estimation as a sanity check. In Table 4 **Right**, "Oracle" means POMNet trained and tested on the same category ("human body") only. It performs comparable with SBL-Res50 [15], which demonstrates the correctness of our design choices.

5.5   Qualitative Results

In Fig. 6, we qualitatively evaluate the generalization ability of POMNet to the novel categories on MP-100 test sets. Our method is robust to perspective variation and appearance diversity. Typical failure cases include appearance ambiguity (the first two examples) and severe occlusion (the 3rd example).

Fig. 6. Qualitative results of POMNet on unseen categories. The first column shows the manually annotated support samples, and the others are the predicted query samples. The last column shows some failure cases (in RED circles). (Color figure online)

6   Conclusions and Limitations

This paper introduces a novel task, termed Category-Agnostic Pose Estimation (CAPE). The idea of CAPE can benefit a wide range of application scenarios. It would not only promote the development of pose estimation (*e.g.* pseudo-labeling for novel categories), but also enable the researchers in the other fields to detect keypoints of objects they are interested in (*e.g.* plants). Besides, it may also make broader positive impacts for other computer vision tasks. For example, CAPE models can be developed for keypoint-based object tracking, contour-based instance segmentation, and graph matching. To achieve this goal, we propose the first CAPE framework, POse Matching Network (POMNet), and the first dataset for CAPE task, Multi-category Pose (MP-100). Experiments show that POMNet significantly outperforms the other approaches on MP-100 dataset. However, there are still many remaining challenges, *e.g.* the generalization performance on rare categories, intra-class appearance variation, self-occlusion, and appearance ambiguity. In conclusion, CAPE, as an important yet challenging task, is worth more research attention and further exploration.

Acknowledgement. This work is supported in part by the General Research Fund through the Research Grants Council of Hong Kong under Grants (Nos. 14202217, 14203118, 14208619), in part by Research Impact Fund Grant No. R5001-18. Ping Luo is supported by the General Research Fund of HK No. 27208720, No. 17212120, and No. 17200622. Wanli Ouyang is supported by the Australian Research Council Grant DP200103223, Australian Medical Research Future Fund MRFAI000085, CRC-P Smart Material Recovery Facility (SMRF) - Curby Soft Plastics, and CRC-P ARIA - Bionic Visual-Spatial Prosthesis for the Blind.

References

1. Andriluka, M., et al.: PoseTrack: a benchmark for human pose estimation and tracking. In: IEEE Conference on Computer Vision and Pattern Recognition (2018)
2. Andriluka, M., Pishchulin, L., Gehler, P., Schiele, B.: 2D human pose estimation: new benchmark and state of the art analysis. In: IEEE Conference on Computer Vision and Pattern Recognition (2014)
3. Bulat, A., Tzimiropoulos, G.: How far are we from solving the 2D & 3D face alignment problem? In: International Conference on Computer Vision (2017)
4. Cao, J., Tang, H., Fang, H.S., Shen, X., Lu, C., Tai, Y.W.: Cross-domain adaptation for animal pose estimation. In: International Conference on Computer Vision (2019)
5. Carion, N., Massa, F., Synnaeve, G., Usunier, N., Kirillov, A., Zagoruyko, S.: End-to-end object detection with transformers. In: Vedaldi, A., Bischof, H., Brox, T., Frahm, J.-M. (eds.) ECCV 2020. LNCS, vol. 12346, pp. 213–229. Springer, Cham (2020). https://doi.org/10.1007/978-3-030-58452-8_13
6. Chen, Y., Wang, Z., Peng, Y., Zhang, Z., Yu, G., Sun, J.: Cascaded pyramid network for multi-person pose estimation. In: IEEE Conference on Computer Vision and Pattern Recognition (2018)
7. Cheng, B., Xiao, B., Wang, J., Shi, H., Huang, T.S., Zhang, L.: HigherHRNet: scale-aware representation learning for bottom-up human pose estimation. In: IEEE Conference on Computer Vision and Pattern Recognition (2020)
8. Chu, X., Yang, W., Ouyang, W., Ma, C., Yuille, A.L., Wang, X.: Multi-context attention for human pose estimation. In: IEEE Conference on Computer Vision and Pattern Recognition (2017)
9. Contributors, M.: OpenMMlab pose estimation toolbox and benchmark. https://github.com/open-mmlab/mmpose (2020)

10. Duan, H., Lin, K.Y., Jin, S., Liu, W., Qian, C., Ouyang, W.: TRB: a novel triplet representation for understanding 2D human body. In: International Conference on Computer Vision (2019)

11. Finn, C., Abbeel, P., Levine, S.: Model-agnostic meta-learning for fast adaptation of deep networks. In: ICML (2017)

12. Ge, Y., Zhang, R., Wang, X., Tang, X., Luo, P.: DeepFashion2: a versatile benchmark for detection, pose estimation, segmentation and re-identification of clothing images. In: IEEE Conference on Computer Vision and Pattern Recognition (2019)

13. Graving, J.M., et al.: DeepPoseKit, a software toolkit for fast and robust animal pose estimation using deep learning. Elife **8**, e47994 (2019)

14. Hariharan, B., Girshick, R.: Low-shot visual recognition by shrinking and hallucinating features. In: International Conference on Computer Vision (2017)

15. He, K., Zhang, X., Ren, S., Sun, J.: Deep residual learning for image recognition. In: IEEE Conference on Computer Vision and Pattern Recognition (2016)

16. Jhuang, H., Gall, J., Zuffi, S., Schmid, C., Black, M.J.: Towards understanding action recognition. In: International Conference on Computer Vision (2013)

17. Jiang, S., Liang, S., Chen, C., Zhu, Y., Li, X.: Class agnostic image common object detection. IEEE Trans. Image Process. **28**(6), 2836–2846 (2019)

18. Jin, S., Liu, W., Ouyang, W., Qian, C.: Multi-person articulated tracking with spatial and temporal embeddings. In: IEEE Conference on Computer Vision and Pattern Recognition (2019)

19. Jin, S., et al.: Differentiable hierarchical graph grouping for multi-person pose estimation. In: Vedaldi, A., Bischof, H., Brox, T., Frahm, J.-M. (eds.) ECCV 2020. LNCS, vol. 12352, pp. 718–734. Springer, Cham (2020). https://doi.org/10.1007/978-3-030-58571-6_42

20. Jin, S., et al.: Towards multi-person pose tracking: bottom-up and top-down methods. In: International Conference on Computer Vision Workshop (2017)

21. Jin, S., et al.: Whole-body human pose estimation in the wild. In: Vedaldi, A., Bischof, H., Brox, T., Frahm, J.-M. (eds.) ECCV 2020. LNCS, vol. 12354, pp. 196–214. Springer, Cham (2020). https://doi.org/10.1007/978-3-030-58545-7_12

22. Khan, M.H., et al.: AnimalWeb: a large-scale hierarchical dataset of annotated animal faces. In: IEEE Conference on Computer Vision and Pattern Recognition (2020)

23. Kingma, D.P., Ba, J.: Adam: a method for stochastic optimization. In: International Conference on Learning Representations (2015)

24. Kostinger, M., Wohlhart, P., Roth, P., Bischof, H.: Annotated facial landmarks in the wild: a large-scale, real-world database for facial landmark localization. In: International Conference on Computer Vision Workshop (2011)

25. Labuguen, R., et al.: MacaquePose: a novel "in the wild" macaque monkey pose dataset for markerless motion capture. Front. Behav. Neurosci. **14**, 581154 (2021)

26. Li, J., Bian, S., Zeng, A., Wang, C., Pang, B., Liu, W., Lu, C.: Human pose regression with residual log-likelihood estimation. In: International Conference on Computer Vision (2021)

27. Li, J., Wang, C., Zhu, H., Mao, Y., Fang, H.S., Lu, C.: CrowdPose: efficient crowded scenes pose estimation and a new benchmark. In: IEEE Conference on Computer Vision and Pattern Recognition (2019)

28. Li, S., Li, J., Tang, H., Qian, R., Lin, W.: ATRW: a benchmark for amur tiger re-identification in the wild. In: ACM International Conference on Multimedia (2020)

29. Li, Y., et al.: TokenPose: learning keypoint tokens for human pose estimation. arXiv preprint arXiv:2104.03516 (2021)

30. Lin, T.-Y., et al.: Microsoft COCO: common objects in context. In: Fleet, D., Pajdla, T., Schiele, B., Tuytelaars, T. (eds.) ECCV 2014. LNCS, vol. 8693, pp. 740–755. Springer, Cham (2014). https://doi.org/10.1007/978-3-319-10602-1_48

31. Lu, E., Xie, W., Zisserman, A.: Class-agnostic counting. In: Jawahar, C.V., Li, H., Mori, G., Schindler, K. (eds.) ACCV 2018. LNCS, vol. 11363, pp. 669–684. Springer, Cham (2019). https://doi.org/10.1007/978-3-030-20893-6_42

32. Lu, J., Gong, P., Ye, J., Zhang, C.: Learning from very few samples: a survey. arXiv preprint arXiv:2009.02653 (2020)

33. Mao, W., Ge, Y., Shen, C., Tian, Z., Wang, X., Wang, Z.: TFPose: direct human pose estimation with transformers. arXiv preprint arXiv:2103.15320 (2021)

34. Mathis, A., et al.: Pretraining boosts out-of-domain robustness for pose estimation. In: Proceedings of the IEEE/CVF Winter Conference on Applications of Computer Vision (2021)

35. Moon, G., Yu, S.-I., Wen, H., Shiratori, T., Lee, K.M.: InterHand2.6M: a dataset and baseline for 3D interacting hand pose estimation from a single RGB image. In: Vedaldi, A., Bischof, H., Brox, T., Frahm, J.-M. (eds.) ECCV 2020. LNCS, vol. 12365, pp. 548–564. Springer, Cham (2020). https://doi.org/10.1007/978-3-030-58565-5_33

36. Mueller, F., et al.: Ganerated hands for real-time 3D hand tracking from monocular RGB. In: IEEE Conference on Computer Vision and Pattern Recognition (2018)

37. Mueller, F., Mehta, D., Sotnychenko, O., Sridhar, S., Casas, D., Theobalt, C.: Real-time hand tracking under occlusion from an egocentric RGB-D sensor. In: International Conference on Computer Vision (2017)

38. Nakamura, A., Harada, T.: Revisiting fine-tuning for few-shot learning. arXiv preprint arXiv:1910.00216 (2019)

39. Newell, A., Yang, K., Deng, J.: Stacked hourglass networks for human pose estimation. In: Leibe, B., Matas, J., Sebe, N., Welling, M. (eds.) ECCV 2016. LNCS, vol. 9912, pp. 483–499. Springer, Cham (2016). https://doi.org/10.1007/978-3-319-46484-8_29

40. Nie, X., Feng, J., Zhang, J., Yan, S.: Single-stage multi-person pose machines. In: International Conference on Computer Vision (2019)

41. Parmar, N., et al.: Image transformer. In: ICML (2018)

42. Pereira, T.D., et al.: Fast animal pose estimation using deep neural networks. Nat. Methods 16, 117–125 (2019)

43. Ravi, S., Larochelle, H.: Optimization as a model for few-shot learning. In: International Conference on Learning Representations (2017)

44. Reddy, N.D., Vo, M., Narasimhan, S.G.: CarFusion: combining point tracking and part detection for dynamic 3D reconstruction of vehicles. In: IEEE Conference on Computer Vision and Pattern Recognition (2018)

45. Sagonas, C., Antonakos, E., Tzimiropoulos, G., Zafeiriou, S., Pantic, M.: 300 faces in-the-wild challenge: database and results. Image Vision Comput. 47, 3–18 (2016)

46. Shen, J., Zafeiriou, S., Chrysos, G.G., Kossaifi, J., Tzimiropoulos, G., Pantic, M.: The first facial landmark tracking in-the-wild challenge: Benchmark and results. In: International Conference on Computer Vision Workshop (2015)

47. Simon, T., Joo, H., Matthews, I., Sheikh, Y.: Hand keypoint detection in single images using multiview bootstrapping. In: IEEE Conference on Computer Vision and Pattern Recognition (2017)

48. Snell, J., Swersky, K., Zemel, R.: Prototypical networks for few-shot learning. In: Advance Neural Information and Processing Systems (2017)

49. Song, X., et al.: ApolloCar3D: a large 3D car instance understanding benchmark for autonomous driving. In: IEEE Conference on Computer Vision and Pattern Recognition (2019)
50. Sun, K., Xiao, B., Liu, D., Wang, J.: Deep high-resolution representation learning for human pose estimation. In: IEEE Conference on Computer Vision and Pattern Recognition (2019)
51. Sun, X., Shang, J., Liang, S., Wei, Y.: Compositional human pose regression. In: International Conference on Computer Vision (2017)
52. Toshev, A., Szegedy, C.: DeepPose: human pose estimation via deep neural networks. In: IEEE Conference on Computer Vision and Pattern Recognition (2014)
53. Vaswani, A., et al.: Attention is all you need. In: Advance Neural Information and Processing Systems (2017)
54. Vinyals, O., Blundell, C., Lillicrap, T., Wierstra, D., et al.: Matching networks for one shot learning. In: Advance Neural Information and Processing Systems (2016)
55. Wang, Y., Peng, C., Liu, Y.: Mask-pose cascaded CNN for 2D hand pose estimation from single color image. IEEE Trans. Circ. Syst. Video Technol. **29**, 3258–3268 (2018)
56. Wang, Y.X., Girshick, R., Hebert, M., Hariharan, B.: Low-shot learning from imaginary data. In: IEEE Conference on Computer Vision and Pattern Recognition (2018)
57. Wei, S.E., Ramakrishna, V., Kanade, T., Sheikh, Y.: Convolutional pose machines. In: IEEE Conference on Computer Vision and Pattern Recognition (2016)
58. Welinder, P., et al.: Caltech-UCSD Birds 200. Technical report CNS-TR-2010-001, California Institute of Technology (2010)
59. Wu, J., et al.: AI challenger: a large-scale dataset for going deeper in image understanding. arXiv preprint arXiv:1711.06475 (2017)
60. Wu, J., et al.: Single image 3D interpreter network. In: Leibe, B., Matas, J., Sebe, N., Welling, M. (eds.) ECCV 2016. LNCS, vol. 9910, pp. 365–382. Springer, Cham (2016). https://doi.org/10.1007/978-3-319-46466-4_22
61. Wu, W., Qian, C., Yang, S., Wang, Q., Cai, Y., Zhou, Q.: Look at boundary: a boundary-aware face alignment algorithm. In: IEEE Conference on Computer Vision and Pattern Recognition (2018)
62. Xiao, B., Wu, H., Wei, Y.: Simple baselines for human pose estimation and tracking. In: Ferrari, V., Hebert, M., Sminchisescu, C., Weiss, Y. (eds.) ECCV 2018. LNCS, vol. 11210, pp. 472–487. Springer, Cham (2018). https://doi.org/10.1007/978-3-030-01231-1_29
63. Xu, L., et al.: ViPNAS: efficient video pose estimation via neural architecture search. In: IEEE Conference on Computer Vision and Pattern Recognition (2021)
64. Yang, F.S.Y., Zhang, L., Xiang, T., Torr, P.H., Hospedales, T.M.: Learning to compare: relation network for few-shot learning. In: IEEE Conference on Computer Vision and Pattern Recognition (2018)
65. Yang, S., Quan, Z., Nie, M., Yang, W.: TransPose: towards explainable human pose estimation by transformer. arXiv preprint arXiv:2012.14214 (2020)
66. Yang, S.D., Su, H.T., Hsu, W.H., Chen, W.C.: Class-agnostic few-shot object counting. In: Proceedings of the IEEE/CVF Winter Conference on Applications of Computer Vision (2021)
67. Yu, H., Xu, Y., Zhang, J., Zhao, W., Guan, Z., Tao, D.: AP-10k: a benchmark for animal pose estimation in the wild. arXiv preprint arXiv:2108.12617 (2021)
68. Yuan, Y., et al.: HRFormer: high-resolution transformer for dense prediction. arXiv preprint arXiv:2110.09408 (2021)

69. Zafeiriou, S., Trigeorgis, G., Chrysos, G., Deng, J., Shen, J.: The Menpo facial landmark localisation challenge: a step towards the solution. In: IEEE Conference on Computer Vision and Pattern Recognition Workshop (2017)

70. Zeng, W., et al.: Not all tokens are equal: human-centric visual analysis via token clustering transformer. In: IEEE Conference on Computer Vision and Pattern Recognition (2022)

71. Zhang, C., Lin, G., Liu, F., Yao, R., Shen, C.: CANet: class-agnostic segmentation networks with iterative refinement and attentive few-shot learning. In: IEEE Conference on Computer Vision and Pattern Recognition, pp. 5217–5226 (2019)

72. Zhang, S.H., et al.: Pose2Seg: detection free human instance segmentation. In: IEEE Conference on Computer Vision and Pattern Recognition (2019)

73. Zhao, J., Li, J., Cheng, Y., Sim, T., Yan, S., Feng, J.: Understanding humans in crowded scenes: Deep nested adversarial learning and a new benchmark for multi-human parsing. In: ACM International Conference on Multimedia (2018)

74. Zhou, X., Karpur, A., Luo, L., Huang, Q.: StarMap for category-agnostic keypoint and viewpoint estimation. In: European Conference on Computer Vision, pp. 318–334 (2018)

75. Zimmermann, C., Brox, T.: Learning to estimate 3D hand pose from single RGB images. In: International Conference on Computer Vision (2017)

76. Zimmermann, C., Ceylan, D., Yang, J., Russell, B., Argus, M., Brox, T.: FreiHAND: a dataset for markerless capture of hand pose and shape from single RGB images. In: International Conference on Computer Vision (2019)

PoseGPT: Quantization-Based 3D Human Motion Generation and Forecasting

Thomas Lucas[(✉)], Fabien Baradel, Philippe Weinzaepfel, and Grégory Rogez

NAVER LABS Europe, Meylan, France
thomas.lucas@naverlabs.com
https://europe.naverlabs.com/research/computer-vision/posegpt

Abstract. We address the problem of action-conditioned generation of human motion sequences. Existing work falls into two categories: forecast models conditioned on observed past motions, or generative models conditioned on action labels and duration only. In contrast, we generate motion conditioned on observations of arbitrary length, including none. To solve this generalized problem, we propose PoseGPT, an auto-regressive transformer-based approach which internally compresses human motion into quantized latent sequences. An auto-encoder first maps human motion to latent index sequences in a discrete space, and vice-versa. Inspired by the Generative Pretrained Transformer (GPT), we propose to train a GPT-like model for next-index prediction in that space; this allows PoseGPT to output distributions on possible futures, with or without conditioning on past motion. The discrete and compressed nature of the latent space allows the GPT-like model to focus on long-range signal, as it removes low-level redundancy in the input signal. Predicting discrete indices also alleviates the common pitfall of predicting averaged poses, a typical failure case when regressing continuous values, as the average of discrete targets is not a target itself. Our experimental results show that our proposed approach achieves state-of-the-art results on HumanAct12, a standard but small scale dataset, as

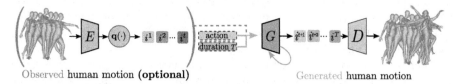

Observed human motion (**optional**)   Generated human motion

Fig. 1. Method Overview. PoseGPT generates a human motion sequence, conditioned on an action label, a duration T, and optionally on an observed past human motion. A GPT-like [52] model G sequentially predicts discrete latent indices, which are decoded using a decoder D into a generated human motion. When conditioning also on past human motion, the input human motion is encoded with E and quantized using $q(.)$ into the discrete latent space.

T. Lucas and F. Baradel—Equal contribution.

Supplementary Information The online version contains supplementary material available at https://doi.org/10.1007/978-3-031-20068-7_24.

© The Author(s), under exclusive license to Springer Nature Switzerland AG 2022
S. Avidan et al. (Eds.): ECCV 2022, LNCS 13666, pp. 417–435, 2022.
https://doi.org/10.1007/978-3-031-20068-7_24

well as on BABEL, a recent large scale MoCap dataset, and on GRAB, a human-object interactions dataset.

1   Introduction

Generating realistic and controllable human motion is still an open research question despite decades of efforts in this domain [5,6]. In this work, we tackle the task of action-conditioned generation of realistic human motion sequences of varying length, with or without observation of past motion. Most of the effort in human motion synthesis has been focused on future motion prediction, typically conditioned on a sequence of past frames [4,9,29,69,70]; however, this requirement is a limiting constraint. In particular applications to virtual reality or character control [31,59] ideally should not require real world observations. And indeed, recent works [27,49] have shown that deep models can handle the highly multi-modal nature of human motion sequences, without conditioning on the past to narrow it down. Nevertheless, many possible applications of human motion modeling do require conditioning. In particular, vision based human-robot interactions may require robots to observe humans and predict likely future movements to successfully avoid them or interact with them. Therefore, we propose a class of models flexible enough to approach the more general problem of motion generation conditioned on observations of *arbitrary length*, including none.

Auto-regressive generative models [45,46] are natural candidates to handle this task. By factorizing distributions over the time dimension, they can be conditioned on past sequences of arbitrary length. However when applied to human motion sequences their potential is limited in at least two ways by the nature of the data. First, they are costly and inefficient to train on data captured at high frame rates, *e.g.* 30 frames per second (fps), in particular when using state-of-the-art transformer architectures. Second, long-term future is highly multi-modal; in a continuous target space this leads to average unrealistic predictions and, in turn, to error drift when sampling from auto-regressive models. Indeed, related previous works that have proposed auto-regressive approaches (based on LSTMs [22] and GRUs [43]), have shown that they are subject to error drift and prone to regress unrealistic average poses.

Therefore, we propose to compress human motion into a space that is lower dimensional and *discrete*, to reduce input redundancy. This allows training an auto-regressive model using discrete targets rather than to regress in a continuous space, such that the average of targets is not a valid output itself. We propose an auto-encoder transformer-based network which maps the human motion to a low dimensional space, discretized using a quantization bottleneck [47], and vice versa. Importantly, we ensure that the causal structure of the time dimension is kept in the latent representations such that it *respects the arrow of the time* (i.e. only the past influences the present). To do so we rely on causal attention in the encoder. This is crucial to enable conditioning of our model on observed past motions of arbitrary length, unlike in [49].

Then, we employ an auto-regressive GPT-like model to capture human motion directly in the learned discrete space. Transformer models have become the de-facto architecture for language tasks [51,52,65] and are increasingly adopted in computer vision [15,20]. This requires adaptations to deal with continuous and locally redundant data, which is not well suited to the quadratic computational cost induced by the lack of inductive prior in transformers. The input data used in this work falls into this category: we employ parametric 3D models [40,48] which represent human motion as a sequence of human 3D meshes, a continuous, high-dimensional and redundant representation. Our proposed discretization of the human motion alleviates the need for the auto-regressive model to capture low-level signal and enables it to concentrate on long-range relations. Indeed, while the space of human body model parameters [48] is high-dimensional and sparse – random samples are unlikely to be realistic – the quantization step concentrates useful regions into a finite set of points. In particular, random sequences in that space produce locally realistic sequences that lack temporal coherence. The GPT-like component of our method, called PoseGPT, is trained to predict a distribution over the next index in the discrete space. This allows probabilistic modeling of possible futures, with or without conditioning on past motion.

Motion capture (MoCap) datasets with action labels are costly to create [32,62]. We have been able to learn models from several orders of magnitude more data than prior art [27,49], owing to the recent availability of the BABEL [50] dataset, and also relying on the smaller HumanAct12 for fair comparison with previous works. In addition, we propose an evaluation protocol which we believe aggregates the best practices from prior art [49] and from the generative image modeling literature [8,41,44,57]. It is based on three principles; first, sample quality is evaluated using metrics based on classifiers, inspired from the GAN literature. Second, we strive to account for over-fitting together with sample quality. Indeed, sample quality metrics typically compare synthetic data to train data, without employing a validation set, which rewards over-fitting. While this is harmless when working with plentiful and complex data that deep models are unlikely to over-fit, we show that is not the case with small human motion datasets such as HumanAct12. Finally, we report likelihood based metrics to evaluate mode coverage. Indeed, while it is notoriously difficult to measure diversity from samples alone [44,57], that is in principle not the case for models that allow likelihood computations on test data. Using these principles we show that our proposed approach outperforms existing ones while being more flexible.

2   Related Work

Human Motion Forecasting. Predicting future human poses given a past motion is a topic of interest in human motion analysis [5,6]. The first successful methods were based on statistical models [11,23], with most recent work relying on deep learning based methods [26,34]. In particular image generation methods such as GANs [26] and VAEs [34] have been extended to human motion forecasting [9,28,39]. In DLow [69], a pretrained model is employed to enforce diversity in the predicted motions. In Cao *et al.* [14], the scene context is also taken into account to predict future human motion. However they both show limitations when it comes to predicting long-term future horizons; in particular they tend to predict average poses, which is a known issue for methods trained by predicting continuous values [25]. In contrast, we propose a method able to predict future motion without error drift by quantizing motions.

Human Motion Synthesis. The task of human motion synthesis, given a class query, was first tackled with a focus on simple and cyclic human actions such as walking [61,63]. More recently, a lot of focus has been devoted to human pose and motion generation conditioned on a rich query representation such as a short textual description [2,3,19,24,38,39] or an audio representation such as music [36,37]. Class labels can be seen as a coarse case of textual descriptions; they bring less information about the motion than detailed descriptions, but are simpler to acquire and use. A few recent propositions have tackled 3D human motion generation given action classes [27,49,54], and in particular ACTOR [49] shows impressive results at generating human motion for non-periodic actions. However only small scale-datasets were available at the time [27,73,74]. The generated human motions are always front view, and the trajectories in the training data lack diversity. In [54], action sequences are modeled by conditioning predictions at each time frame on the last; this performs well for short sequences but does not allow conditioning on observations of arbitrary length. To go beyond these limitations, we develop a method trained on large-scale datasets, with long-tailed class distributions such as the recently released BABEL [50]. Our method can optionally be conditioned on past observations of arbitrary length, and obtains state-of-the-art performance. Most similar to ours, the concurrent work in [58] also relies on a quantization step and a GPT model for successfully learning dance motion conditioned on music.

Pose Representation. Human body representations are often expressed as skeleton representations, where a known kinematic structure is available. Most work in human modeling, ranging from human pose estimation [1,56,67,71] to human pose modeling [25,30], have used this type of representations for a while. However recent works are moving toward 3D body shape models [7,35,40,48] which are more realistic and enable more powerful applications such as augmented and virtual reality. Representing the 3D human body, and in particular the pose, is not straightforward. One can express a human pose as a set of 3D joint locations in the Euclidean space or as a set of bone angles encoding the rotations necessary to obtain the pose. However the lack of continuity in the space of rotation representations is a commonly observed issue [12,72] for deep learning methods. There has not been convergence towards a unified human pose representation format so far. In this work, we do not explicitly enforce any human pose representation but rather propose a model that can learn to embed and quantize any representation to a discrete latent space learned by the model.

Generative Modeling. Deep generative models can be broadly classified in two categories: maximum-likelihood based models, trained to maximize the like-

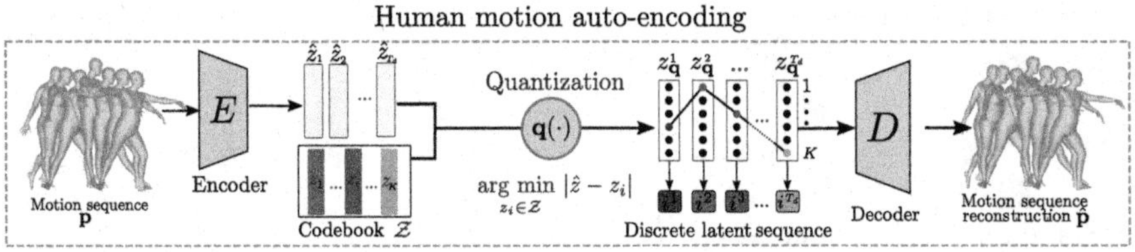

Human motion auto-encoding

Fig. 2. Discrete latent representation for human motion. The encoder E maps a human motion p to a latent representation $\hat{z}$ which is then quantized using a codebook $\mathcal{Z}$. The decoder D reconstructs the human motion $\hat{p}$ from the quantized latent sequence $z_{\mathbf{q}}$.

lihood of generating training data, and adversarial models [26] trained to maximize the quality of generated images as evaluated by a discriminator model. In the maximum-likelihood based literature, which is most relevant to our work, there are two dominant paradigms to handle the highly multi-modal nature of perceptual data. The first family is that of variational auto-encoders (VAEs) [34,55], which relies on an encoder, and the second that of autoregressive models [16,46] which relies on the chain rule decomposition of high-dimensional data. Both paradigms are leveraged in our work: in the first stage of our approach we adapt a flavour of auto-encoders called VQVAEs [64], which uses quantized latent variables, to our problem. In the second stage, we train a transformer based auto-regressive model to sequentially predict discrete latent sequences. Similar recipes have been applied to high-resolution image generation in [18,21,53], to video prediction [66,68] and to speech modeling in [17]. Note that while GANs generally display an impressive aptitude to generate high quality samples [13], they are not well suited to the task of human future pose/motion prediction. Indeed, they suffer from mode-collapse [57], *i.e.*, the inability to cover the full variability of the training data. This ability is critical for example for applications such as human-robot interactions where likely modes of the distribution of possible futures must not be ignored. Thus, this class of models is not a good candidate on its own.

3   The PoseGPT Model

In this section we describe PoseGPT, our proposed approach for generative modeling of human pose sequences. First, we present how we compress human motion to a discrete space, and reconstruct motion from it (Sect. 3.1). Second, we introduce a GPT-like model trained for next-index probabilistic prediction in that space (Sect. 3.2).

3.1   Learning a Discrete Latent Space Representation

Human actions defined by body-motions can be characterized by the rotations of body parts, disentangled from the body shape. This allows the generation

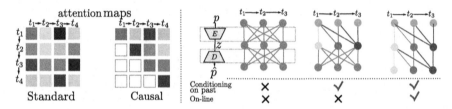

Fig. 3. Conditioning on past with causal attention. Masking attention maps in the encoder leads to models that can be conditioned on past observations. Masking the attention maps in the decoder as well allows models that can make on-line predictions.

of motions with actors of different morphology. For this, we rely on parametric differential body models – SMPL [40] and SMPL-X [48] – which disentangle body parts rotations from body shape; a human motion p of length T is represented as a sequence of body poses and translations of the root joints: $p = \{(\theta_1, \delta_1), \dots, (\theta_T, \delta_T)\}$ where θ and δ represent the body pose and the translation respectively. We use an encoder E and a quantization operator $\mathbf{q}$ to encode pose sequences and a decoder D to reconstruct $\hat{p} = D(\mathbf{q}(E(p)))$. We use causal attention mechanisms to maintain a temporally coherent latent space and neural discrete representation learning [47] for quantization. An overview of the training procedure is shown in Fig. 2.

Causal Latent Space. The encoder first represents human motion sequences as a latent sequence representation $\hat{z} = \{\hat{z}^1, \dots, \hat{z}^{T_d}\} = E(p)$ where $T_d \leq T$ is the temporal dimension of the latent sequence. By default, we require that our latent representation respects the arrow of time, *i.e.*, that for any $t \leq T_d$, $\{\hat{z}_1, \dots, \hat{z}_t\}$ depends only on $\{p_1, \dots, p_{\lfloor t \cdot T/T_d \rfloor}\}$; such as illustrated in Fig. 3. For this, we rely on transformers with causal attention; it avoids any inductive prior besides causality, by modeling interactions between all inputs using self-attention [65], modified to respect the arrow of time. Intermediate representations are mapped using three feature-wise linear projections, into query $Q \in \mathbb{R}^{N \times d_k}$, key $K \in \mathbb{R}^{N \times d_k}$ and value $V \in \mathbb{R}^{N \times d_v}$; in addition, a causal mask is defined as $C_{i,j} = -\infty \cdot [\![i > j]\!] + [\![i \leq j]\!]$, and the output is computed as:

$$\text{Attn}(Q, K, V) = \text{softmax}\left(\frac{QK^\top \cdot C}{\sqrt{d_k}}\right) V \in \mathbb{R}^{N \times d_v}. \tag{1}$$

The causal mask ensures that all entries below the diagonal of the attention matrix do not contribute to the final output and thus that the arrow of time is respected. This is crucial to allow conditioning on past observations when sampling from the model: if latent variables depend on the full sequence, they are impossible to compute from past observations alone.

Quantizing the Latent Space. To build an efficient latent representation of human motion sequences, we then rely on a discrete codebook of learned temporal representations; more precisely a latent space sequence $\hat{z} \in \mathbb{R}^{T_d \times n_z}$

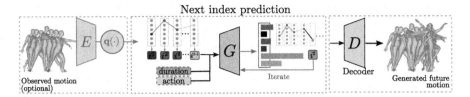

Fig. 4. Future motion prediction. In the discrete latent space, an auto-regressive transformer model G predicts the next latent index given previous ones. We condition on a human action label, a sequence duration and optionally on an observed motion.

is mapped to a sequence of codebook entries $z_\mathbf{q} \in \mathcal{Z}^{T_d}$, where $\mathcal{Z}$ is a set of C codes of dimension n_z. Equivalently, this can be summarized as a sequence of T_d indices corresponding to the code entries in the codebook. A given sequence $\boldsymbol{p}$ is approximately reconstructed by $\hat{\boldsymbol{p}} = D(z_\mathbf{q})$ where $z_\mathbf{q}$ is obtained by encoding $\hat{z} = E(x) \in \mathbb{R}^{T_d \times n_z}$ and mapping each temporal element of this tensor with $\mathbf{q}(\cdot)$ to its closest codebook entry z_k:

$$z_\mathbf{q} = \mathbf{q}(\hat{z}) := \left(\arg\min_{z_k \in \mathcal{Z}} \|\hat{z}_t - z_k\| \right) \in \mathbb{R}^{T_d \times n_z} \tag{2}$$

$$\hat{\boldsymbol{p}} = D(z_\mathbf{q}) = D\left(\mathbf{q}(E(\boldsymbol{p}))\right). \tag{3}$$

Equation (3) is non differentiable; the standard way to backpropagate through it is to rely on the straight-through gradient estimator, which during the backward pass simply approximates the quantization step as an identity function by copying the gradients from the decoder to the encoder [10]. Thus the encoder, decoder and codebook can be trained by optimizing:

$$\mathcal{L}_{\mathrm{VQ}}(E, D, \mathcal{Z}) = \|\boldsymbol{p} - \hat{\boldsymbol{p}}\|^2 + \|\mathrm{sg}[E(\boldsymbol{p})] - z_\mathbf{q}\|_2^2 + \beta\|\mathrm{sg}[z_\mathbf{q}] - E(\boldsymbol{p})\|_2^2, \tag{4}$$

with $\mathrm{sg}[\cdot]$ the stop-gradient operator. The term $\|\mathrm{sg}[z_\mathbf{q}] - E(\boldsymbol{p})\|_2^2$, dubbed the "commitment loss" [47], has been shown necessary to stable training.

Product Quantization. To increase the flexibility of the discrete representations learned by the encoder E, we propose using product quantization [33]: each element $\hat{z}_i \in \mathbb{R}^{n_z}$ in the sequence of latent representation is cut into K chunks $(\hat{z}_i^1, \ldots, \hat{z}_i^K) \in \mathbb{R}^{n_z/K \times K}$, and each chunk is discretized separately using K different codebooks $\{\mathcal{Z}_1, \ldots, \mathcal{Z}_K\}$. The size of the discrete space learned increases exponentially with K, for a total of $C^{T_d \cdot K}$ combinations. We empirically validate the utility of using product quantization in our experiments. Instead of one index target per time step, product quantization produces K targets. To capture relations between them, we propose a prediction head that models the K factors sequentially rather than in parallel, called 'auto-regressive' head and evaluated in Sect. 3.2; see the supplementary material for more details.

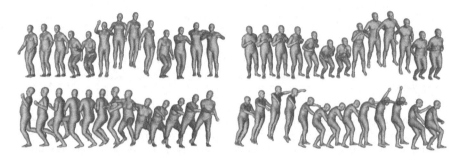

Fig. 5. Samples generated from scratch. Samples generated without any observed motion for the action labels 'jumping' (top) and for the action 'dancing' (bottom). Note: Times flows from left to right (*i.e.*, the blue texture corresponds to the first frame and the red texture to the last frame).

3.2   Learning a Density Model in the Discrete Latent Space

The latent representation $z_{\mathbf{q}} = \mathbf{q}(E(\boldsymbol{p})) \in \mathbb{R}^{T_d \times n_z}$ produced by composing the encoder E and the quantization operator $\mathbf{q}(\cdot)$ can be represented as the sequence of codebook indices of the encodings, $\boldsymbol{i} \in \{0, \ldots, |\mathcal{Z}| - 1\}^{T_d}$, by replacing each code by its index in the codebook $\mathcal{Z}$, *i.e.*, $i_t = k$ such that $(z_{\mathbf{q}})_t = z_k$. Indices of $\boldsymbol{i}$ can be mapped back to the corresponding codebook entries and decoded to a sequence $\hat{\boldsymbol{p}} = D(z_{i_1}, \ldots, z_{i_{T_d}})$.

Learning to Predict Next Pose Index. As a second step to our method, we propose to learn a prior distribution over learned latent code sequences. A motion sequence $\boldsymbol{p}$ of the human action a is encoded into $(i_t)_{1..T_d}$. We then formulate the problem of latent sequence generation as auto-regressive index prediction; for this we keep the natural temporal ordering, which can be interpreted as time due to the use of causal attention in the encoder. We train a transformer model [65] denoted G – well suited to discrete sequential data – using maximum-likelihood estimation, similar in spirit to GPT [52].

Given $\boldsymbol{i}_{<j}$, the action a and the sequence length T, the transformer outputs a softmax distribution over the next indices, *i.e.*, $p_G(i_j|\boldsymbol{i}_{<j}, a, T)$, the likelihood of the latent sequence is $p_G(\boldsymbol{i}) = \prod_j p_G(\mathbf{i}_j|\mathbf{i}_{<j}, a, T)$ and the model is trained to minimize:

$$\mathcal{L}_{\text{GPT}} = \mathbb{E}_{\boldsymbol{i}} \left[-\sum_j \log p_G(i_j|\boldsymbol{i}_{<j}, a, T) \right]. \tag{5}$$

An overview of the training procedure is shown in Fig. 4 and, in the supplementary material, we discuss different input sequence embeddings for processing by the GPT.

Sampling Human Motion. Human motion is generated sequentially by sampling from $p(s_i|\boldsymbol{s}_{<i}, a, T)$ to obtain a sequence of pose indices $\tilde{\boldsymbol{z}}$ given an action

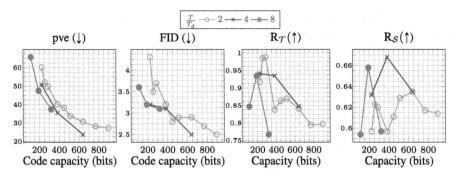

Fig. 6. Latent space design. We define models for $T/T_d \in \{2, 4, 8\}$ by varying K and C and present results as a function of the capacity of latent sequence.

and sequence length, and decoding it into a sequence of pose $\tilde{p} = D(\tilde{z})$ (see Fig. 5 for samples).

4   Experiments

We experiment with two parametric 3D models: SMPL [40] for comparison to state-of-the-art approaches, and SMPL-X [48] to enable control of the face and hands. We now present the three datasets considered for evaluation; architectural and implementation details are in the supplementary material.

HumanAct12 allows comparison to prior art [27,49], but its small size and the absence of train/val/test splits are limiting. It contains 1191 videos and SMPL pose parameters, 12 action classes and a single action per video. The poses, automatically optimized from estimated 3D joints, are noisier than annotations from capture environments.

BABEL [50] is a subset of AMASS [42], a large collection of MoCap data captured in controlled environments for high quality annotations. It contains 28K sequences (43 hours of motion in total); sequence length varies from 3 s to several minutes and there are 120 manually annotated human actions in total. The action distribution is very long-tailed so we use only the 60 most common actions as proposed by the authors. In short, BABEL is over 40 times bigger than HumanAct12, has a train/val/test split, no noise in the SMPL parameters and a rich variety of human actions; we believe this makes it a dataset of choice to move forward.

GRAB [60] contains whole-body SMPL-X of people grasping objects, with 11 persons performing 29 motions with 51 different rigid objects, for a total of 1500 sequences of 8 seconds on average, with 7 persons for training and 2 for testing.

4.1   Evaluation Metrics

Generative models can be evaluated through generated data; a perfect set of samples contains data that is *as realistic* and *as diverse* as real *unseen* test data. These aspects are not always trivial to quantify, and we now discuss how they are measured in practice.

Sample Quality Evaluation. The dominant approach [27,49] to measure sample quality relies on pretrained classifiers. In particular the Frechet Inception Distance (FID), which we report, measures a distance between distributions of classifier features obtained from a set of samples D_{samples} and real data. Following [49], we also rely on a classifier T pre-trained on train data and report the ratio between accuracies on sampled and test data:

$$R_T(D_{\text{samples}}, D_{\text{test}}) = \frac{|D_{\text{samples}}|}{|D_{\text{test}}|} \cdot \frac{\sum_{x \in D_{\text{test}}} \text{acc}_T(x)}{\sum_{x \in D_{\text{samples}}} \text{acc}_T(x)}. \tag{6}$$

This metric is not sensitive to diversity – the model can drop modes as long as the rest is very well classified. The ratio normalizes values that otherwise depend on choices orthogonal to sample quality; we refer to the supplementary material for details on the action classifier.

Diversity Evaluation. First, we evaluate sample diversity by training a classifier S on *samples* and evaluating it on unseen *test data*, following [57]. Intuitively, for S to perform as well as T, samples need to be as diverse and as realistic as real data; we measure it with:

$$R_S(D_{\text{test}}) = \sum_{x \in D_{\text{test}}} \frac{\text{acc}_S(x)}{\text{acc}_T(x)}. \tag{7}$$

This metric is sensitive to diversity as real data modalities not captured by the generator will not be seen by S and misclassified, but not by T, which will degrade the ratio. The pair (R_S, R_T) is best considered together [57]: if R_S is close to one, we consider sample quality to be high, and gains in R_T can be attributed to diversity [44]. Note that S and T have the same architecture and are trained with the same hyper parameters. More classically, we also report likelihood based metrics; dropped modes will lead to data points with very low likelihood, so they are sensitive to mode coverage [8]. In particular, we report the test reconstruction error of the auto-encoder using the Per-Vertex Error (pve), and the test likelihood of the GPT on encoded test sequences. As these metrics do not guarantee realistic samples, we consider them together with classifier based quality metrics.

Over-Fitting. Sample quality metrics typically used – standard FID or classification accuracy [49] – measure differences between train data and generated data, without involving a test set. This does not account for over-fitting and rewards models that perfectly copy train data: on small datasets, all metrics will monotonically improve with model capacity. To remedy this, we keep unseen data on BABEL and compute the FID, R_S ratio and maximum-likelihood based metrics using that test data. Our only metric not sensitive to over-fitting is R_T; we rely on the others to detect over-fitting.

Table 1. Impact of latent space capacity on BABEL for $T/T_d = 2$ (left) and for $C = 256$ (right). **bold** denotes best in column (across K); <u>underlined</u> denotes best in row (across C).

K (nb. codebooks)	pve↓	R_T↑	R_S↑	FID↓	pve↓	R_T↑	R_S↑	FID↓	pve↓	R_T↑	R_S↑	FID↓
		$C = 128$				$C = 256$				$C = 512$		
1	60.1	**0.91**	0.60	4.3	52.1	**0.98**	0.61	<u>3.5</u>	49.7	**<u>0.99</u>**	<u>0.62</u>	3.7
2	40.2	0.84	0.60	3.2	38.3	0.86	0.61	<u>2.8</u>	33.8	<u>0.87</u>	<u>0.63</u>	2.9
4	30.6	<u>0.84</u>	<u>0.64</u>	2.9	28.2	0.79	0.62	**2.7**	27.3	0.80	0.61	**<u>2.5</u>**
8	27.2	<u>0.48</u>	<u>0.49</u>	**3.0**	23.7	0.49	0.46	4.4	26.7	0.41	0.47	4.3

$(T/T_d = 2)$

K (nb. codebooks)	pve↓	R_T↑	R_S↑	FID↓	pve↓	R_T↑	R_S↑	FID↓
		$T/T_d = 4$				$T/T_d = 8$		
2	50.7	**0.94**	0.63	3.2	47.5	**0.93**	0.66	3.2
4	35.5	0.93	0.67	3.1	37.5	0.77	0.60	3.1
8	28.8	0.64	0.54	**2.5**	65.6	0.85	0.59	3.6

$(C = 256)$

4.2   Ablative Study of Design Choices

We now ablate the main design choices made in PoseGPT. The first is the design of the discrete latent space, in particular the quantization bottleneck and its capacity. The second regards the GPT component, trained for next index prediction; in particular we ablate the choice of input embedding method and prediction head. Finally, we evaluate the impact of using causal attention in the auto-encoder. Note that as there is no test split on HumanAct12; because it is too small to define one of reasonable size without severely degrading performance, we compute the FID using train data on this dataset.

Latent Sequence Space Design. The main design choice regarding the latent sequence space is the quantization bottleneck. We now study the impact of its capacity, mostly controlled by T_d (latent sequence length), K (nb. of product quantization factor) and C (total number of centroids). More capacity yields lower reconstruction errors at the cost of less compressed representations. In our case, that means more indices to predict for the GPT, which impacts sampling, and we now explore this trade-off.

In Table 1 (left), models trained on BABEL show that as expected, pve goes down monotonously with both K and C, but not the R_S and R_T ratios, as also shown in Fig. 6. Models with $K = 1$ obtain high sample classification accuracy but poor reconstruction on test data and lower R_S; this suggests insufficient

Table 2. Latent space design on HumanAct12. **Bold** denotes best value.

K (nb. codebooks)	FID ↓	R_S(↑)	FID ↓	R_S(↑)
	$C = 256$		$C = 512$	
8	0.12	93.8	0.11	93.7
16	0.11	94.5	0.10	94.9
32	**0.09**	**95.1**	**0.08**	**95.2**

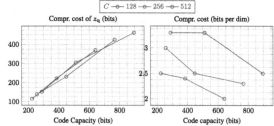

Fig. 7. Cost of compressing z_q using the GPT, in bits and bits per dimension.

Table 3. GPT design on BABEL and Human-Act12. **Bold** text denotes best value. ar denotes auto-regressive.

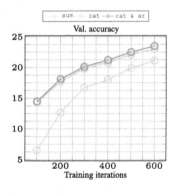

Val. accuracy

t^0: extra token at $t = 0$. $+$: sum at all t. $::$ concat at all t.								
Input tokens		**Prediction head**		**BABEL**			**HumanAct12**	
a	T	mlp	ar	$R_S(\uparrow)$	$R_T(\uparrow)$	gpt-acc.($\uparrow$)	FID($\downarrow$)	$R_T(\uparrow)$
t^0	✗	✗	✗	0.65	0.51	22.4 (20.8)	0.56	0.74
$+$	✗	✗	✗	0.79	0.55	23.1 (16.3)	0.19	0.91
$+$	$+$	✗	✗	0.79	0.57	23.9 (16.2)	**0.10**	0.94
$::$	$::$	✗	✗	**0.86**	**0.61**	24.9 (22.9)	0.22	0.86
$+$	$+$	✓	✗	-	-	-	**0.09**	95.1
$::$	$::$	✓	✗	0.86	0.61	25.1 (22.7)	-	-
$::$	$::$	✓	✓	**0.98**	**0.64**	25.9 (22.6)	-	-

Fig. 8. Index pred. accuracy using concatenation $vs.$ summation.

capacity to capture the full diversity of the data. On the other hand, models with the most capacity (*e.g.*, $K = 8$) yield sub-par performance. The best trade-offs are achieved with $(K, C) \in \{(2, 256), (2, 512), (4, 128), (4, 256)\}$. The table on the right shows that the model can handle decreased temporal resolution. Note that using $K = 8$ works better at coarser resolutions, as it compensates for the loss of information. In Table 2, all metrics improve monotonically with K and C; this is expected as over-fitting is not factored out by the metrics and the dataset is small enough to over-fit. Finally, in Fig. 7, we report the cost of compressing z_q using the GPT model. We observe that the absolute compression cost in bits (left) increases, *i.e.*, z_q contains more information, while the cost per dimension decreases: each sequence index is easier to predict individually.

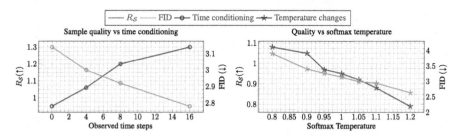

Fig. 9. Sample quality with our best model for different amounts of observed motion, and different temperatures, measure with the FID and R_S metrics.

Ablations on Next Index Prediction. We now study two design choices made in the GPT component of PoseGPT: the choices of input embedding and predictions head. Using the proper input embedding has a strong impact on the performance of transformer architectures [52], and depends on the input data. In Table 3, we study this impact when working with human motion. For this ablation, we fix the latent sequence space, *i.e.*, the auto-encoder hyper-parameters and weights, and train our GPT model with different input embeddings. We measure sample quality, and the accuracy of the GPT model at predicting discrete sequence indices. Note that this accuracy is directly comparable across models, as the latent space is frozen and identical.

In the first row, we observe that embedding the action at each timestep, rather than as an extra transformer input, has significant positive impact. Conditioning on the sequence length is also beneficial (Row 3 *vs.*Row 4); this is expected, as it relieves the model from having to predict when to stop generating new poses. As an added benefit, it also allows extra control at inference time. We also see that a concatenation of the embedded information, followed by a linear projection – which can be seen as a learned weighted sum – is better than simple summation on BABEL. On the other hand this extra model capacity is not beneficial on HumanAct12, which may be due to the size of the dataset. In Fig. 8, we also observe that models using concatenation rather than summation train significantly faster.

Having determined the best input configuration for both datasets, we further experiment with more expressive output layers for the model; we show that having a MLP head rather than a single fully-connected layer is beneficial, and we obtain further gains using an auto-regressive layer (see Sect. 3.2). This can be explained by the fact that with product quantization, several codebook indices are extracted simultaneously from a single input vector, but are not independent, and using an MLP and/or an auto-regressive layer better captures the correlations between them.

Causal Attention. In Table 4, we study the impact of using causal attention in the auto-encoder, for $K \in \{2, 4\}$ and $C = 256$. Causal attention is a restriction on model flexibility, as it limits the inputs used by features in the encoder. Empirically, we observe that adding causal attention indeed degrades performance. Adding it to the encoder, which is mandatory to create a model that can be conditioned on past observations, causes only a mild degradation. Adding it in the decoder as well allows to run the model on-line, *i.e.*, make observations and predictions in parallel, but strongly degrades performance.

Conditioning and Temperature. Conditioning the model on past observation is expected to improve the quality of generated samples. In Fig. 9 (left), we see that indeed both R_S and the FID improve monotonically as the length of observations increases. In the right plot, we see that increasing or decreasing the softmax temperature leads to a trade-off between the two metrics; this behaviour can be expected: decreasing the temperature improves sample quality by concentrating the mass on major modes of the distribution, and thus increases mode-dropping.

Table 4. Impact of causal attention in the encoder and decoder for $C = 256$.

K (nb. codebooks)	Causal E	Causal D	pve ($\downarrow$)
2	✗	✗	**35.7**
2	✓	✗	38.3
2	✓	✓	50.2
4	✗	✗	**25.3**
4	✓	✗	28.2
4	✓	✓	38.6

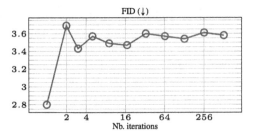

Fig. 10. Evaluation of error drift. Model iteratively conditioned on last predictions made.

Error-Drift in Long-Term Horizon Generation. In Fig. 10, we study the robustness of PoseGPT to error drift, a typical failure case of models that make auto-regressive predictions in continuous space. To this end, we sample from our model several times consecutively, by conditioning the last pose generated by the model. To initiate this process, the first motion is generated without temporal conditioning. Empirically, we observe that in this setting, PoseGPT is robust to long-term error drift: the FID initially degrades but remains stable even when we repeat the generation process many times.

4.3   Comparison to the State of the Art

In Table 5, we compare PoseGPT against the state-of-the-art results. For fair comparison, these metrics are computed without conditioning on past observations. We find that PoseGPT outperforms the state-of-the-art method, namely ACTOR [49], when looking at the FID metric with a relative gain of 33% (0.12 $vs.$0.08) on HumanAct12 and over 50% on BABEL. The performance in diversity and the multimodality indicates that PoseGPT covers the human motion distribution of this dataset. On BABEL, the gains are around 50% in terms of both FID and classification accuracy. The gains in classification accuracy indicate both higher quality samples, and a richer distribution.

Table 5. State-of-the-art comparison. On HumanAct12 (left), PoseGPT obtains better FID and comparable classification accuracy. On BABEL (center) and on GRAB (right), PoseGPT obtains substantial gains for all metrics. * means trained by us based on official code. Note that the FID of real data is not 0 due to data augmentations. For consistency with [27,49], we report diversity and multimodality metrics on Human-Act12; these metrics are considered good when close to the values obtained on real data.

Model	FID$\downarrow$	R_T (%).$\uparrow$	Div.	Multimod.
Real	0.02	99.4	6.86	2.60
Action2Motion [27]	2.46	92.3	7.03	2.87
ACTOR [49]	0.12	95.5	6.84	2.53
PoseGPT	0.08	95.8	6.85	2.82

Model	action cond.	length cond.	future pred.	$R_S(\uparrow)$	FID$\downarrow$	$R_T(\uparrow)$
Real	-	-	-	1.0	0.01	1.0
ACTOR*	✓	✓	X	0.35	9.5	0.56
PoseGPT	✓	✓	✓	**0.64**	**2.7**	**0.98**

Model	FID $\downarrow$	$Acc_S(D)\uparrow$	$Acc_D(S)\uparrow$
Real	0.01	0.99	-
ACTOR*	20.7	0.20	-
PoseGPT	5.1	0.86	-

Fig. 11. Samples conditioned on past observation. On the left in green, we show an observed initial pose, then we sample two different future human motions that we show side by side. The top row corresponds to the human action 'jumping' and the bottom row is sampled from the human action 'stretching'.

Fig. 12. Samples conditioned on an initial pose and with four different actions. Given an initial pose shown in green, we generate four different human motions conditioned on four different actions. What are these actions?[1]

Qualitative Examples. Finally, we show samples of human motions generated by PoseGPT. In Fig. 5, we show samples of human motion generated by conditioning on a human action only. We observe that human motions are realistic and diverse for both actions. Then in Fig. 11, we display two possible future motions given an initial pose and an action. The generated human motions are diverse which demonstrates that PoseGPT is able to handle the multimodal nature of the future. Finally in Fig. 12, given a initial pose, we generate four human motions with four different actions[1]. This demonstrates that the action information is taken into account and impacts the human motion generation. We provide more visualizations in the supplementary material.

5   Conclusion

This work introduces PoseGPT, an auto-regressive transformer-based approach which quantizes human motion into latent sequences. Given a human action, a duration and an arbitrarily long past observation, it outputs realistic and diverse 3D human motions. We provide quantitative and qualitative experiments to show the strengths of our proposed method. In particular, ablations demonstrate that

---

[1] From left to right and top to bottom: 'turning', 'touching face', 'walking', 'sitting'.

quantization is a key component, and we study each part of our approach in detail. PoseGPT reaches state-of-the-art performance on three different benchmarks and is able to generate human motions given an action label, conditioned on observed past motion of arbitrary length.

References

1. Agarwal, A., Triggs, B.: Recovering 3D human pose from monocular images. IEEE Trans. Pattern Anal. Mach. Intell. **28**(1), 44–58 (2005)
2. Ahn, H., Ha, T., Choi, Y., Yoo, H., Oh, S.: Text2Action: generative adversarial synthesis from language to action. In: ICRA, pp. 5915–5920 (2018)
3. Ahuja, C., Morency, L.: Language2Pose: natural language grounded pose forecasting. In: 3DV, pp. 719–728 (2019)
4. Aksan, E., Kaufmann, M., Hilliges, O.: Structured prediction helps 3D human motion modelling. In: ICCV, pp. 7144–7153 (2019)
5. Badler, N.: Temporal scene analysis: conceptual descriptions of object movements. PhD thesis, University of Toronto (1975)
6. Badler, N.I., Phillips, C.B., Webber, B.L.: Simulating Humans: Computer Graphics Animation and Control. Oxford University Press, NY (1993)
7. Baradel, F., Groueix, T., Weinzaepfel, P., Brégier, R., Kalantidis, Y., Rogez, G.: Leveraging mocap data for human mesh recovery. In: 3DV, pp. 586–595 (2021)
8. Barratt, S., Sharma, R.: A note on the inception score. arXiv preprint arXiv:1801.01973 (2018)
9. Barsoum, E., Kender, J., Liu, Z.: HP-GAN: probabilistic 3D human motion prediction via GAN. In: CVPRW, pp. 1418–1427 (2018)
10. Bengio, Y., Léonard, N., Courville, A.: Estimating or propagating gradients through stochastic neurons for conditional computation. arXiv preprint arXiv:1308.3432 (2013)
11. Bowden, R.: Learning statistical models of human motion. In: CVPRW (2000)
12. Brégier, R.: Deep regression on manifolds: a 3D rotation case study. In: 3DV, pp. 166–174 (2021)
13. Brock, A., Donahue, J., Simonyan, K.: Large scale GAN training for high fidelity natural image synthesis. In: ICLR (2019)
14. Cao, Z., Gao, H., Mangalam, K., Cai, Q.-Z., Vo, M., Malik, J.: Long-term human motion prediction with scene context. In: Vedaldi, A., Bischof, H., Brox, T., Frahm, J.-M. (eds.) ECCV 2020. LNCS, vol. 12346, pp. 387–404. Springer, Cham (2020). https://doi.org/10.1007/978-3-030-58452-8_23
15. Chen, M., et al.: Generative pretraining from pixels. In: ICML, pp. 1691–1703 (2020)
16. Chen, X., Mishra, N., Rohaninejad, M., Abbeel, P.: PixelSNAIL: an improved autoregressive generative model. In: ICML, pp. 864–872 (2018)
17. Chorowski, J., Weiss, R.J., Bengio, S., Van Den Oord, A.: Unsupervised speech representation learning using WaveNet autoencoders. IEEE/ACM Trans. Audio Speech Lang. Process. **27**(12), 2041–2053 (2019)
18. De Fauw, J., Dieleman, S., Simonyan, K.: Hierarchical autoregressive image models with auxiliary decoders. arXiv preprint arXiv:1903.04933 (2019)
19. Delmas, G., Weinzaepfel, P., Lucas, T., Moreno-Noguer, F., Rogez, G.: PoseScript: 3D human poses from natural language. In: ECCV (2022)

20. Dosovitskiy, A., et al.: An image is worth 16x16 words: transformers for image recognition at scale. In: ICLR (2021)
21. Esser, P., Rombach, R., Ommer, B.: Taming transformers for high-resolution image synthesis. In: CVPR, pp. 12873–12883 (2021)
22. Fragkiadaki, K., Levine, S., Felsen, P., Malik, J.: Recurrent network models for human dynamics. In: ICCV, pp. 4346–4354 (2015)
23. Galata, A., Johnson, N., Hogg, D.: Learning variable-length Markov models of behavior. Comput. Vis. Image Underst. **81**(3), 398–413 (2001)
24. Ghosh, A., Cheema, N., Oguz, C., Theobalt, C., Slusallek, P.: Synthesis of compositional animations from textual descriptions. In: CVPR, pp. 1396–1406 (2021)
25. Ghosh, P., Song, J., Aksan, E., Hilliges, O.: Learning human motion models for long-term predictions. In: 3DV, pp. 458–466 (2017)
26. Goodfellow, I., et al.: Generative adversarial nets. Commun. ACM **63**(11), 139–144 (2014)
27. Guo, C., et al.: Action2Motion: conditioned generation of 3D human motions. In: ACMMM, pp. 2021–2029 (2020)
28. Gupta, A., Johnson, J., Fei-Fei, L., Savarese, S., Alahi, A.: Social GAN: socially acceptable trajectories with generative adversarial networks. In: CVPR, pp. 2255–2264 (2018)
29. Habibie, I., Holden, D., Schwarz, J., Yearsley, J., Komura, T.: A recurrent variational autoencoder for human motion synthesis. In: BMVC (2017)
30. Herda, L., Fua, P., Plankers, R., Boulic, R., Thalmann, D.: Skeleton-based motion capture for robust reconstruction of human motion. In: Proceedings Computer Animation 2000, pp. 77–83 (2000)
31. Holden, D., Komura, T., Saito, J.: Phase-functioned neural networks for character control. ACM Trans. Graph. **36**(4), 1–13 (2017)
32. Ionescu, C., Papava, D., Olaru, V., Sminchisescu, C.: Human3.6M: large scale datasets and predictive methods for 3D human sensing in natural environments. IEEE Trans. Pattern Anal. Mach. Intell. **36**(7), 1325–1339 (2014)
33. Jegou, H., Douze, M., Schmid, C.: Product quantization for nearest neighbor search. IEEE Trans. Pattern Anal. Mach. Intell. **33**(1), 117–128 (2010)
34. Kingma, D.P., Welling, M.: Auto-encoding variational bayes. arXiv preprint arXiv:1312.6114 (2013)
35. Kocabas, M., Athanasiou, N., Black, M.J.: VIBE: video inference for human body pose and shape estimation. In: CVPR, pp. 5253–5263 (2020)
36. Lee, H.Y., et al.: Dancing to music. Adv. Neural Inf. Process. Syst. **32** (2019)
37. Li, R., Yang, S., Ross, D.A., Kanazawa, A.: Learn to dance with AIST++: music conditioned 3D dance generation. arXiv preprint arXiv:2101.08779 (2021)
38. Lin, A.S., Wu, L., Rodolfo, C., Kevin Tai, Q.H.R.J.M.: Generating animated videos of human activities from natural language descriptions. In: Proceedings of the Visually Grounded Interaction and Language Workshop at NeurIPS (2018)
39. Lin, X., Amer, M.R.: Human motion modeling using DVGANs. arXiv preprint arXiv:1804.10652 (2018)
40. Loper, M., Mahmood, N., Romero, J., Pons-Moll, G., Black, M.J.: SMPL: a skinned multi-person linear model. ACM Trans. Graph. **34**(6), 1–16 (2015)
41. Lucas, T., Shmelkov, K., Alahari, K., Schmid, C., Verbeek, J.: Adaptive density estimation for generative models. Adv. Neural Inf. Process. Syst. **32** (2019)
42. Mahmood, N., Ghorbani, N., Troje, N.F., Pons-Moll, G., Black, M.J.: AMASS: archive of motion capture as surface shapes. In: ICCV, pp. 5442–5451 (2019)
43. Martinez, J., Black, M.J., Romero, J.: On human motion prediction using recurrent neural networks. In: CVPR, pp. 2891–2900 (2017)

44. Naeem, M.F., Oh, S.J., Uh, Y., Choi, Y., Yoo, J.: Reliable fidelity and diversity metrics for generative models. In: ICML, pp. 7176–7185 (2020)
45. Van den Oord, A., et al.: Conditional image generation with PixelCNN decoders. Adv. Neural Inf. Process. Syst. **29** (2016)
46. van den Oord, A., Kalchbrenner, N., Kavukcuoglu, K.: Pixel recurrent neural networks. In: ICML, pp. 1747–1756 (2016)
47. van den Oord, A., Oriol, V., Kavukcuoglu, K.: Neural discrete representation learning. In: ICML (2018)
48. Pavlakos, G., et al.: Expressive body capture: 3D hands, face, and body from a single image. In: CVPR, pp. 10975–10985 (2019)
49. Petrovich, M., Black, M.J., Varol, G.: Action-conditioned 3D human motion synthesis with transformer VAE. In: ICCV, pp. 10985–10995 (2021)
50. Punnakkal, A.R., Chandrasekaran, A., Athanasiou, N., Quiros-Ramirez, A., Black, M.J.: BABEL: bodies, action and behavior with English labels. In: CVPR, pp. 722–731 (2021)
51. Radford, A., Wu, J., Child, R., Luan, D., Amodei, D., Sutskever, I.: Language models are unsupervised multitask learners. OpenAI blog **1**(8), 9 (2019)
52. Radford, A., Narasimhan, K., Salimans, T., Sutskever, I., et al.: Improving language understanding by generative pre-training (2018)
53. Razavi, A., Van den Oord, A., Vinyals, O.: Generating diverse high-fidelity images with VQ-VAE-2. Adv. Neural Inf. Process. Syst. **32** (2019)
54. Rempe, D., Birdal, T., Hertzmann, A., Yang, J., Sridhar, S., Guibas, L.J.: HuMoR: 3D human motion model for robust pose estimation. ICCV, pp. 11488–11499 (2021)
55. Rezende, D.J., Mohamed, S., Wierstra, D.: Stochastic backpropagation and approximate inference in deep, generative models. In: ICML, pp. 1278–1286 (2014)
56. Rogez, G., Weinzaepfel, P., Schmid, C.: LCR-Net++: multi-person 2D and 3D pose detection in natural images. IEEE Trans. Pattern Anal. Mach. Intell. **42**(5), 1146–1161 (2019)
57. Shmelkov, K., Schmid, C., Alahari, K.: How good is my GAN? In: ECCV, pp. 213–229 (2018)
58. Siyao, L., et al.: Bailando: 3D dance generation by actor-critic GPT with choreographic memory. In: CVPR, pp. 11050–11059 (2022)
59. Starke, S., Zhang, H., Komura, T., Saito, J.: Neural state machine for character-scene interactions. ACM Trans. Graph. **38**(6), 1–14 (2019)
60. Taheri, O., Ghorbani, N., Black, M.J., Tzionas, D.: GRAB: a dataset of whole-body human grasping of objects. In: Vedaldi, A., Bischof, H., Brox, T., Frahm, J.-M. (eds.) ECCV 2020. LNCS, vol. 12349, pp. 581–600. Springer, Cham (2020). https://doi.org/10.1007/978-3-030-58548-8_34
61. Taylor, G.W., Hinton, G.E., Roweis, S.: Modeling human motion using binary latent variables. Adv. Neural Inf. Process. Syst. **19** (2006)
62. Carnegie Mellon University: CMU graphics lab motion capture database. http://mocap.cs.cmu.edu/
63. Urtasun, R., Fleet, D.J., Lawrence, N.D.: Modeling human locomotion with topologically constrained latent variable models. In: Elgammal, A., Rosenhahn, B., Klette, R. (eds.) HuMo 2007. LNCS, vol. 4814, pp. 104–118. Springer, Heidelberg (2007). https://doi.org/10.1007/978-3-540-75703-0_8
64. Van Den Oord, A., Vinyals, O., et al.: Neural discrete representation learning. Adv. Neural Inf. Process. Syst. **30** (2017)
65. Vaswani, A., et al.: Attention is all you need. Adv. Neural Inf. Process. Syst. **30** (2017)

66. Walker, J., Razavi, A., Oord, A.V.D.: Predicting video with VQVAE. arXiv preprint arXiv:2103.01950 (2021)
67. Weinzaepfel, P., Brégier, R., Combaluzier, H., Leroy, V., Rogez, G.: DOPE: distillation of part experts for whole-body 3D pose estimation in the wild. In: Vedaldi, A., Bischof, H., Brox, T., Frahm, J.-M. (eds.) ECCV 2020. LNCS, vol. 12371, pp. 380–397. Springer, Cham (2020). https://doi.org/10.1007/978-3-030-58574-7_23
68. Weissenborn, D., Täckström, O., Uszkoreit, J.: Scaling autoregressive video models. In: ICLR (2020)
69. Yuan, Y., Kitani, K.: DLow: diversifying latent flows for diverse human motion prediction. In: Vedaldi, A., Bischof, H., Brox, T., Frahm, J.-M. (eds.) ECCV 2020. LNCS, vol. 12354, pp. 346–364. Springer, Cham (2020). https://doi.org/10.1007/978-3-030-58545-7_20
70. Zhang, Y., Black, M.J., Tang, S.: We are more than our joints: predicting how 3D bodies move. In: CVPR, pp. 3372–3382 (2021)
71. Zheng, C., et al.: Deep learning-based human pose estimation: a survey. arXiv preprint arXiv:2012.13392 (2020)
72. Zhou, Y., Barnes, C., Lu, J., Yang, J., Li, H.: On the continuity of rotation representations in neural networks. In: CVPR, pp. 5745–5753 (2019)
73. Zou, S., et al.: Polarization human shape and pose dataset. arXiv preprint arXiv:2004.14899 (2020)
74. Zou, S., et al.: 3D human shape reconstruction from a polarization image. In: Vedaldi, A., Bischof, H., Brox, T., Frahm, J.-M. (eds.) ECCV 2020. LNCS, vol. 12359, pp. 351–368. Springer, Cham (2020). https://doi.org/10.1007/978-3-030-58568-6_21

DH-AUG: DH Forward Kinematics Model Driven Augmentation for 3D Human Pose Estimation

Linzhi Huang, Jiahao Liang, and Weihong Deng$^{(\boxtimes)}$

Beijing University of Posts and Telecommunications, Beijing, China
{huanglinzhi,jiahao.liang,whdeng}@bupt.edu.cn

Abstract. Due to the lack of diversity of datasets, the generalization ability of the pose estimator is poor. To solve this problem, we propose a pose augmentation solution via DH forward kinematics model, which we call DH-AUG. We observe that the previous work is all based on single-frame pose augmentation, if it is directly applied to video pose estimator, there will be several previously ignored problems: (i) angle ambiguity in bone rotation (multiple solutions); (ii) the generated skeleton video lacks movement continuity. To solve these problems, we propose a special generator based on DH forward kinematics model, which is called DH-generator. Extensive experiments demonstrate that DH-AUG can greatly increase the generalization ability of the video pose estimator. In addition, when applied to a single-frame 3D pose estimator, our method outperforms the previous best pose augmentation method. The source code has been released at https://github.com/hlz0606/DH-AUG-DH-Forward-Kinematics-Model-Driven-Augmentation-for-3D-Human-Pose-Estimation.

Keywords: Pose augmentation · Video · Forward kinematics · Human pose estimation

1 Introduction

3D pose estimation is the task of estimating 3D human pose from images. It is a fundamental task in action recognition [19,22,38,50], human tracking [30], etc. It is difficult to obtain a 3D label, so the existing 3D data is very limited and the diversity is seriously insufficient. This also leads to poor generalization ability of the 2D-to-3D model.

Recently, a work [23] enhanced data by randomly exchanging limbs, locally rotating limbs, and randomly changing bone length. This method is dependent on the random seed, and the result is unstable. PoseAug [11] uses GAN [12] to solve the above problems. However, PoseAug is also designed for a single-frame 3D pose estimator. There are some problems that can not be ignored in

Supplementary Information The online version contains supplementary material available at https://doi.org/10.1007/978-3-031-20068-7_25.

© The Author(s), under exclusive license to Springer Nature Switzerland AG 2022
S. Avidan et al. (Eds.): ECCV 2022, LNCS 13666, pp. 436–453, 2022.
https://doi.org/10.1007/978-3-031-20068-7_25

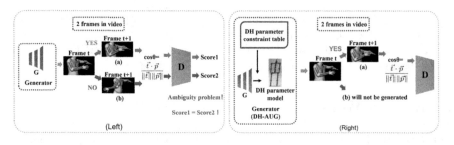

Fig. 1. Angle ambiguity (multiple solutions). Left: Pose augmentation of ordinary GAN framework. **Right**: DH-AUG. **(a)**: Elbow rotates normally (angle is about 90°). **(b)**: Elbow rotates abnormally (angle is about −90°). Although the rotation directions of (a) and (b) are different, the cosine angle values calculated by vector inner product are the same. Both of them will make the discriminator output the same score, resulting in ambiguity. To weaken the ambiguity problem, we improve the generator by adding DH forward kinematics model (DH parameter model) and constraints. t and p are a pair of adjacent bone vectors. SMPL [25] is only used for visualization.

pose augmentation in video 3D human pose estimation: angle ambiguity and angle continuity. Most pose discriminators [5,11,47] calculates the cosine angle value through the inner product of two bone vectors for constraint. But this is a problem of multiple solutions (angle ambiguity) as shown in Fig. 1 (Left). The value calculated by the inner product corresponds to multiple angles. For example, 0 corresponds to 90° and −90°, which makes the discriminator unable to distinguish between elbow 90° internal rotation and 90° external rotation. Both of them will make the discriminator output the same score, and the data distribution of the generator will contain the angle value of abnormal rotation. What's more, there will be discontinuous actions in the skeleton video because of angle ambiguity. So it is not enough to use the discriminator for constraints. We try to modify the generator to weaken this problem. Specifically, we use DH parameters to build a human kinematics model (DH parameter model). This model allows us to obtain a new pose directly by changing the joint angle, and we can easily constrain the rotation direction of the joint. We introduce this model into the generator and constrain the DH parameters so that the generator will not produce an unreasonable pose as shown in Fig. 1 (Right). Inspired by some previous work [5,39,45], we also add timing information to the discriminator to increase the continuity of the generated skeleton video.

Our contributions are as follows:

- We propose DH-AUG: a pose augmentation framework for 3D human pose estimation. It consists of DH-Generator, DH parameter model, single-frame pose discriminator and multi-stream motion discriminator.
- We use DH parameters to design a human kinematics model, called DH parameter model. By adding DH parameter model and constraints to the generator, the angle ambiguity is successfully weakened and the possibility of generating unreasonable pose is reduced.
- Extensive experiments demonstrate that DH-AUG can greatly increase the generalization ability of the video pose estimator. In addition, when applied

to a single-frame 3D pose estimator, our method outperforms the previous best pose augmentation method.
- We release a new dataset (DH-3DP) synthesized with DH-AUG, which can be used in the 2D-to-3D network.

2   Related Work

3D Human Pose Estimation. There are two mainstream monocular 3D human pose estimation methods, one is to obtain 3D pose end-to-end [33,43,44], and the other is through the multi-stage method, first obtain 2D pose from the images [6,40,42], and then further obtain 3D pose from 2D pose [5,20,28,48]. The second method is more common. We do not pay too much attention to the model structure. We focus on pose augmentation for 2D-to-3D networks and produce 2D-3D pairs. According to the input mode, it can be divided into single-frame input and video input. Video input can weaken the depth ambiguity problem [2,34,52]. We design a pose augmentation scheme for single-frame pose estimation and video pose estimation.

Kinematic Model. The kinematic model is widely used in the field of the robot [9], hand pose estimation [18,32], and games. Recent work [21] uses forward and inverse kinematics to make up for the shortcomings of 3D pose estimation and mesh parameter models. Inspired by this, we use the DH parameter [8] to build a 3D human forward kinematics model to weaken the angle ambiguity. DH parameter is a method to describe the coordinate system of connecting links.

Pose Augmentation for 3D Human Pose Estimation. Due to the high cost of 3D data acquisition and insufficient data diversity, the 2D-to-3D model is difficult to have good generalization ability. In some works, pose augmentation of 3D pose estimation is carried out by synthesizing images [35,36,46]. It is worth noting that there is another way to obtain new data pairs by synthesizing 2D and 3D data. The recently proposed evolutionary algorithm [23] uses random exchange, local rotation to generate data. The data generated in this way has great randomness, depending on the preset parameters. PoseAug [11] proposes to use GAN with a feedback mechanism to generate data, which is more effective than the former. However, this method has insufficient constraints on joint rotation. This is not conducive to being extended to video pose estimation. Therefore, we propose a combination of the DH parameter model and GAN for pose augmentation.

3   Method

3.1   Overview

There are multiple solutions for mapping the coordinates of 3D keypoints to the angle value, so it is not enough to use the discriminator for constraints. To weaken the angle ambiguity problem and further improve the effect of pose

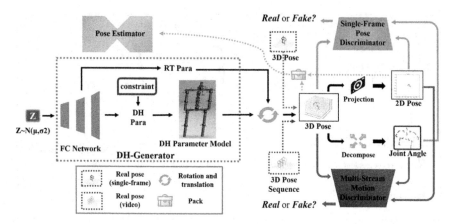

Fig. 2. Overview of the overall framework of DH-AUG. 128-dimensional vectors are sampled from the normal distribution and input into the fully connected network to obtain DH parameters, global rotation and translation parameters. Then, the 3D pose is obtained through DH parameter model. **1) Single-frame**: The 3D pose, 2D pose and joint angle are transmitted to the single-frame pose discriminator for training. **2) Video**: Input 3D pose sequence, 2D pose sequence, bone rotation trajectory (joint angle) into single-frame pose discriminator and multi-stream motion discriminator. Finally, the newly generated 2D-3D data pair is packaged into a new dataset and transmitted to the pose estimator for training.

augmentation, we introduce DH parameters into GAN framework, as shown in Fig. 2. We use the fully connected network to generate DH parameters, etc., and transfer them into the DH parameter model to obtain the corresponding 3D pose. In addition, we also use discriminators to force the generator to generate more reasonable and diversified 3D pose. It is worth noting that we add constraints to the DH parameter model to avoid generating unreasonable pose and weaken the angle ambiguity. More specific contents will be introduced in this section.

3.2　DH Parameter Model

Human Kinematics Model Based on DH Parameters. DH parameter [8] is a method to describe the coordinate system of connecting links. The schematic diagram of the DH parameter can be seen in the right part of Fig. 4, where a is the link length, d is the link offset, α is the twist angle, θ is the joint angle. These four parameters are DH parameters. Each degree of freedom (DOF) has a set of DH parameters. We use DH parameters to establish the human kinematics model as shown in Fig. 3. Some parameters of the model are fixed, which determines the connection relationship between bones, while others determines the rotation relationship between bones and the length of bones. In the DH parameter table in Fig. 3, those marked with red triangles are variable parameters, and others are preset fixed parameters. See Algorithm 1 for the process of building a human kinematics model (DH parameter model) with DH parameters. Δa, Δd, $\Delta\alpha$, $\Delta\theta$

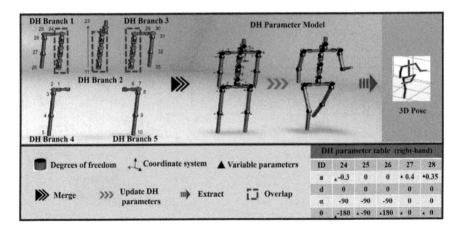

Fig. 3. DH parameter model. There are 33°C of freedom (DOF) and 48 changeable DH parameters. 5 DOF in the figure are not drawn (head, ankle, and wrist). We built 5 DH branches. The root node is the hip, and the overlapping parts share DH parameters. The part sharing DH parameters combines 5 branches into a complete human kinematics model. Then the new transformation matrix is obtained by updating the DH parameters. Finally, a new 3D pose is extracted from the transformation matrix. (See Algorithm 1 for the process of building a human kinematics model with DH parameters. The complete DH parameter table is in the supplementary material.)

are the change in DH parameters. R_x, R_y, R_z are the global rotation parameters. T_x, T_y, T_z are the global translation parameters. In addition, they are the values output by the fully connected network. Output P_{new} is a new 3D pose. The value of N_{branch} is 5, which is the number of DH branches. $N_{Dof(i)}$ is the number of degrees of freedom (DOF) per branch. First, the DH parameters are converted into the transformation matrix:

$$M_{DH} = \begin{bmatrix} cos(\theta) & -sin(\theta) & 0 & a \\ sin(\theta)cos(\alpha) & cos(\theta)cos(\alpha) & -sin(\alpha) & -dsin(\alpha) \\ sin(\theta)sin(\alpha) & cos(\theta)sin(\alpha) & cos(\alpha) & dcos(\alpha) \\ 0 & 0 & 0 & 1 \end{bmatrix} \quad (1)$$

where a is the link length, d is the link offset, α is the twist angle, θ is the joint angle. Next, The inner product is used to update the transformation matrix:

$$M'_{DH(i,k+1)} = M_{DH(i,k)}M_{DH(i,k+1)} \quad (2)$$

where i is the index of the branch, and k is the index of the degree of freedom in $branch_i$. Then, a new 3D pose is extracted from M_{DH}. Finally, we globally rotate and translate the new 3D pose. Other details are illustrated in Fig. 3.

Constraints on DH Parameter Model. We implemented two constraints on the DH parameter model. **1)** We removed the redundant degrees of freedom

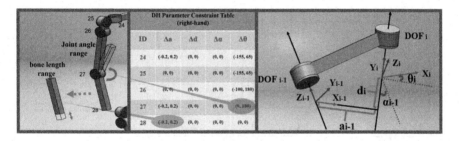

Fig. 4. Left: The constraint diagram of the elbow. **Middle**: DH parameter constraint table. **Right**: The schematic diagram of DH parameter [8]. a is link length, d is link offset, α is twist angle, θ is the joint angle. $\Delta a, \Delta d, \Delta \alpha, \Delta \theta$ is the change in the DH parameter. **(The complete DH parameter constraint table can be seen in the supplementary material.)**

Algorithm 1. DH parameter model

Input:$\Delta a, \Delta d, \Delta \alpha, \Delta \theta, R_x, R_y, R_z, T_x, T_y, T_z$
Output:P_{new}

  for i in N_{branch} **do**

  for k in $N_{Dof(i)}$ **do**
    $A = a_{i,k} + \Delta a_{i,k}$; $B = d_{i,k} + \Delta d_{i,k}$; $C = \alpha_{i,k} + \Delta \alpha_{i,k}$; $D = \theta_{i,k} + \Delta \theta_{i,k}$;
    $M_{DH(i,k)} = $ Get_Matrix(A, B, C, D); **See Eq.1**

  for k in $N_{Dof(i)}$ - 1 **do**
    $M_{DH(i,k+1)} = $ Update_MDH($M_{DH(i,k)}, M_{DH(i,k+1)}$); **See Eq.2**

  for i in N_{branch} **do**
  for k in $N_{Dof(i)}$ **do**
    $x_{i,k} = M_{DH(i,k,0,3)}$; $y_{i,k} = M_{DH(i,k,1,3)}$; $z_{i,k} = M_{DH(i,k,2,3)}$;
    $P_{new(i,k)} = R_x R_y R_z(x_{i,k}, y_{i,k}, z_{i,k}) + (T_x, T_y, T_z)$;

  return P_{new}

(DOF). For example, we only set 1 DOF for the elbow and knee instead of 3, and the number of DOF is changed from 48 to 33 (the number of key points is 16). For details, see the human skeleton in Fig. 3. This operation not only greatly reduces the parameters that the GAN needs to learn, but also prevents the generator from producing a human skeleton with unreasonable rotation direction. **2)** We designed a DH parameter constraint table to limit the value of DH parameters. We list the constraint table of the right-hand branch, as shown in Fig. 4. The left side of Fig. 4 is the constraint diagram of the elbow, and the middle side is the DH parameter constraint table of the whole right-hand branch. DH parameter constraint table is added to the last layer of fully connected network:

$$P_{DH} = (1 + \tanh(O_{FC})) \frac{T_{DH(max)} - T_{DH(min)}}{2} \tag{3}$$

where P_{DH} is the DH parameter, O_{FC} is the output of the fully connected network, T_{DH} is the DH parameter constraint table (Fig. 4).

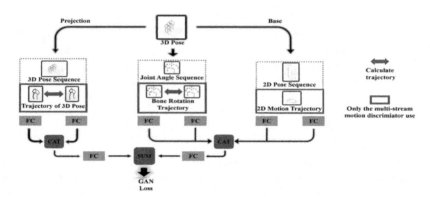

Fig. 5. Multi-stream motion discriminator (MSMD). It has 3 two-stream branches. **Left**: 3D pose two-stream branch. **Middle**: Bone rotation two-stream branch. **Right**: 2D pose two-stream branch. When we remove the branch in the blue box, it becomes a single-frame pose discriminator.

3.3 Architecture

Figure 2 shows the overall framework of DH-AUG. Here we will describe various components of DH-AUG.

DH-Generator. We combine the DH parameter model and fully connected network (FC) to form a new generator called DH-generator. The fully connected network first samples the 128-dimensional vector z from the normal distribution as the input then generates DH parameters: Δa, Δd, $\Delta \alpha$, $\Delta \theta$ (48 in total, includes bone length), global rotation parameters: R_x, R_y, R_z, and global translation parameters: T_x, T_y, T_z. These parameters are input into the DH parameter model. After a series of operations described in Sect. 3.2, a new 3D pose will be generated. Finally, the 3D pose is projected [14] to a 2D pose through camera parameters (from the original dataset). When DH-generator is used in single-frame pose estimation, only one 3D pose is generated by sampling one vector. However, when DH-generator is used in video pose estimation, a vector is sampled to generate a 3D pose sequence.

Multi-Stream Motion Discriminator (MSMD). To generate a skeleton video with motion continuity, we add timing information to the discriminator, as shown in Fig. 5. It has 3 two-stream branches. 1) 3D pose two-stream branch. We input the 3D pose sequence and the trajectory of the 3D pose into this two-stream branch. The trajectory of the 3D pose is calculated as follows:

$$D_{3D} = \sum_{t=1}^{T} \sum_{i=0}^{I} (P_{3D_{(t,i)}} - P_{3D_{(t-1,i)}}) \tag{4}$$

where $P_{3D_{(t,i)}}$ is the 3D coordinate of the ith key point in frame t. 2) Bone rotation two-stream branch. We calculate the joint angle between adjacent bones, and the formula is as follows:

$$A_{(t,i)} = \frac{V_{t,i} \cdot V_{t,i-1}}{L_{t,i} L_{t,i-1}} \tag{5}$$

where $V_{t,i}$ is the ith bone vector in frame t, $L_{t,i}$ is the ith bone length in frame t. i and $i-1$ are a pair of adjacent bones. Another input to this two-stream branch is the bone rotation trajectory:

$$D_{Angle} = \sum_{t=1}^{T} \sum_{i=0}^{I} (A_{t,i} - A_{t-1,i}) \tag{6}$$

where $A_{t,i}$ is the ith joint angle in frame t. 3) 2D pose two-stream branch. We input the 2D pose sequence and 2D motion trajectory into this two-stream branch. This branch mainly guides the generator to produce the correct viewpoint. The calculation formula of 2D motion trajectory is as follows:

$$D_{2D} = \sum_{t=1}^{T} (P_{2D_{(t,root)}} - P_{2D_{(t-1,root)}}) \tag{7}$$

where $P_{2D_{(t,root)}}$ is the 2D coordinate of the root key point in frame t, $root$ represents the key point of the hip.

Single-Frame Pose Discriminator. The single-frame pose discriminator we use is a simplified version of the MSMD. Its structure is the content after removing the components in the blue box in Fig. 5.

Training Loss. Loss used by our GAN is the objective function in improved Wasserstein GAN [13]. The loss we finally use is as follows:

$$\gamma = \begin{cases} 1 & epoch >= \beta \\ 0 & epoch < \beta \end{cases} \tag{8}$$

$$L = E[D_s(X_f)] - E[D_s(X_r)] + \alpha E[(\left\|\nabla_{\hat{X}} D_s(\hat{X})\right\|_2 - 1)^2] \\ + \gamma(E[D_m(X_f)] - E[D_m(X_r)] + \alpha E[(\left\|\nabla_{\hat{X}} D_m(\hat{X})\right\|_2 - 1)^2]) \tag{9}$$

where D_s represents the output of single-frame pose discriminator, D_m represents the output of multi-stream motion discriminator, α represents the weight of gradient penalty, γ represents whether to turn on the multi-stream motion discriminator, X_f is fake data, X_r is real data, $\hat{X}$ is randomly sampled data, β is the epoch that turns on the multi-stream motion discriminator. In our experiment, α is 10, β is 4.

Pose Estimator. In this paper, we use SemGCN [51], SimpleBaseline [28] and VPose [34] as single-frame 3D pose estimators, VPose [34] and PoseFormer [52] as video 3D pose estimators, and Det [10], CPN [4], HR [41] and ground truth as 2D pose estimators.

About the Use of Synthetic Data. Each epoch generates the same number of data pairs as the training set and packs them into a new dataset. Then in the next epoch, we will train the 3D pose estimator on the new dataset and the original dataset.

4   Experiments

4.1   Implementation Details

We use the fully connected network as the backbone network. See supplementary material for the specific structure of generator and discriminator. When pose augmentation is performed for the video pose estimator, we first train the single-frame pose discriminator for 4 epochs and then turn on the multi-stream motion discriminator. Single-frame: batch size is 1024, video: batch size is 512. The pose estimator uses the Adam optimizer with a learning rate of 1e-4, 1e-3, or 2e-3. The first 50 epochs use linear attenuation, and the subsequent epochs attenuate each epoch by 5% to 10%. Both generator and discriminator use Adam optimizer, and the learning rate remains 1e-4 unchanged. The training is carried out on one 1080ti GPU. Training about 100 to 140 epochs. The data used to train 2D-3D pose lifting network and DH-AUG are consistent. For example, In the weakly-supervised settings, both the pose lifting network and DH-AUG are trained using S1 in H36M. See supplementary material for DH parameter constraint table, model structure, etc.

4.2   Datasets

Human3.6M [15] is the largest benchmark dataset. Subjects 1, 5, 6, 7, 8 are used as the training set, and subjects 9, 11 are used as the test set. In case of weak supervision, S1 or S1, S5 shall be used for training, and S9, S11 shall be used for evaluation. MPJPE was used as evaluation criteria.

   MPI-INF-3DHP [30] and **3DPW** [27] are large 3D datasets containing complex outdoor scenes. Instead of using them for training, we use their test sets to evaluate the model's generalization ability to unseen environments. Evaluation criteria: PCK, AUC, MPJPE (MPI) and PA-MPJPE (3DPW).

   LSP [16] and **MPII** [1] are two 2D pose datasets containing a large number of outdoor scenes. We selected several difficult pictures for qualitative experiments.

   DH-3DP: We synthesized a dataset with more than 1 million 2D-3D data pairs using DH-AUG. The synthesis method of this dataset is: S15678 of H36M is used as the training set to train DH-AUG, with a total of 110 epochs. We use the pretrained DH-AUG to generate more than 1 million 2D-3D data pairs. See the supplementary materials for more details.

4.3   Pose Augmentation in Video Pose Estimation

We use VPose [34] and PoseFormer [52] as the 3D pose estimators and Det [10], CPN [4], HR [41], and ground truth as the 2D pose estimators. Experiments were carried out with 9 and 27 frames. Because H36M is large, we choose to use 10 times of downsampling data for training. The results are shown in Table 1. It can be seen that DH-AUG can greatly increase the generalization ability of the video pose estimator. It is worth noting that PoseAug [11] is designed for a single-frame pose estimator. It can not be directly used in a video pose estimator. Table 2 is the result on H36M and MPI. It can be seen that our method outperforms other SOTA methods.

Table 1. Results of using DH-AUG in video 3D pose estimation. f represents the number of input frames. The evaluation criteria uses MPJPE. We downsample the frames used by a factor of 10. We use VPose [34] and Poseformer [52] as 3D pose estimators. And DET [10], CPN [4], HR [41] and GT are used as 2D pose estimators. (It is worth noting that PoseAug [11] is designed for single-frame pose estimator.)

	MPI-3DHP (↓)				H36M (↓)			
	DET	CPN	HR	GT	DET	CPN	HR	GT
VPose [34] (f = 9)	97.56	94.26	90.83	90.7	61.47	55.74	53.79	42.14
Vpose+DH-AUG (f = 9)	**84.23**	**84.76**	**82.57**	**80.39**	**60.81**	**55.66**	**53.04**	**41.21**
VPose [34] (f = 27)	101.99	97.33	94.62	91.76	61.84	56.57	52.89	42.18
Vpose + DH-AUG (f = 27)	**86.34**	**88.38**	**84.37**	**80.85**	**61.19**	**56.07**	**52.57**	**41.52**
PoseFormer [52] (f = 9)	95.09	88.01	82.38	85.28	63.28	56.47	54.24	42.02
PoseFormer + DH-AUG (f = 9)	**81.99**	**81.13**	**76.07**	**76.25**	**63.13**	**55.73**	**53.32**	**39.29**
PoseFormer [52] (f = 27)	92.71	86.38	83.16	84.67	62.26	55.00	53.34	39.63
PoseFormer + DH-AUG (f = 27)	**81.04**	**77.13**	**72.18**	**75.36**	**62.26**	**54.95**	**52.46**	**37.92**

Table 2. Results on H36M and MPI. Evaluation criteria: MPJPE. Best in bold.

Method	3DHP (↓)	H36M (↓)
VPose [34] (f = 27)	91.76	42.18
Liu et al [24] (f = 243)	91.86	42.70
Anatomy [3] (f = 27)	86.01	39.98
PoseFormer [52] (f = 27)	84.67	39.63
PoseFormer (f = 27) + **DH-AUG (Ours)**	**75.36**	**37.92**

4.4   Pose Augmentation in Single-Frame Pose Estimation

To be consistent with other methods, we use HR [41] as the 2D pose estimator and VPose [34] as the 3D pose estimator. Table 3 is the result on H36M. It can be seen that our method outperforms other SOTA methods (fully-supervised).

To evaluate the model's generalization ability, we only use H36M for training and use MPI and 3DPW as test sets. Moreover, we use ground truth as 2D data and VPose [34] as the 3D pose estimator. See Table 4 for MPI test results. See

Table 3. Results on H36M (fully supervised). Evaluation criteria: MPJPE. Best in bold. * denotes the SOTA pose augmentation method.

Method	MPJPE (↓)
SemGCN (CVPR'19) [51]	57.60
Sharma (CVPR'19) [37]	58.00
Moon (ICCV'19) [31]	54.40
VPose (CVPR'19) [34]	52.70
*Li (CVPR'20) [23]	50.90
*VPose + PoseAug (CVPR'21) [11]	50.20
VPose + DH-AUG	**49.81**

Table 4. Results on MPI (fully supervised). The evaluation criteria were PCK, AUC and MPJPE. CE means evaluation across datasets. Best in bold. * represents SOTA pose augmentation method. **S1 + S5**: Use S1 and S5 for training.

Method	CE	MPJPE (↓)	PCK (↑)	AUC (↑)
Mehta [29]		117.60	76.50	40.80
VNect [30]		124.70	76.60	40.40
Multi Person [6]		122.20	75.20	37.80
OriNet [26]		89.40	81.80	45.20
LCN [7]	✓	−	74.00	36.70
HMR [17]	✓	113.20	77.10	40.70
SRNet [49]	✓	−	77.60	43.80
RepNet [47]	✓	92.50	81.80	54.80
*Li [23]	✓	99.70	81.20	46.10
VPose [34]	✓	86.60	−	−
*VPose+PoseAug [11]	✓	73.00	88.60	57.30
VPose+DH-AUG (S1+S5)	✓	72.93	88.60	57.65
VPose+DH-AUG	✓	**71.17**	**89.45**	**57.93**

Table 5. Results on H36M and MPI (weakly supervised). Evaluation criteria:MPJPE. Best in bold.

Train Set	S1		S1 + S5	
Method	MPI	H36M	MPI	H36M
VPose [34]	116.4	65.2	93.5	57.9
VPose+PoseAug [11]	90.3	56.7	77.9	51.3
VPose+DH-AUG	**86.72**	**52.15**	**72.93**	**46.99**

the right part of Table 6 for 3DPW test results. We can observe that our method achieves the best performance under all the metrics.

The effect of our method is more obvious when it is weakly-supervised. Consistent with other pose augmentation methods, we used S1 or S1, S5 in H36M dataset for training and evaluated on H36M and MPI. In addition, we use ground truth as 2D data and VPose [52] as the 3D pose estimator. The results are shown in Table 5. It can be seen that DH-AUG outperforms the previous best method.

To further prove the generality of our method. We use SemGCN [51], SimpleBaseline [28] and, VPose [34] as the 3D pose estimator and Det [10], CPN [4], HR [41], and ground truth as the 2D pose estimator. The results are shown in Table 6. It can be seen that our method outperforms the previous best pose augmentation method.

Table 6. Results on H36M, MPI and 3DPW. Different 2D and 3D pose estimators were used to evaluate the results before and after using DH-AUG. Consistent with previous experiments, DET [10], CPN [4], HR [41] and GT are used as 2D pose estimators, SemGCN [51], SimpleBaseline [28] and VideoPose [34] are used as 3D pose estimators, and +PoseAug denotes the result of the recent SOTA pose augmentation method [11]. The evaluation criteria is MPJPE (MPI, H36M) and PA-MPJPE (3DPW).

Method	MPI-3DHP (↓)				H36M (↓)				3DPW (↓)
	DET	CPN	HR	GT	DET	CPN	HR	GT	GT
SemGCN [51]	101.90	98.70	95.60	97.40	67.50	64.70	57.50	44.40	102.00
SemGCN + PoseAug [11]	89.90	89.30	89.10	86.10	65.20	60.00	55.00	41.50	82.20
SemGCN + DH-AUG	**79.68**	**76.67**	**72.99**	**71.31**	**63.16**	**56.93**	**54.04**	**40.00**	**79.07**
SimpleBaseline [28]	91.10	88.80	86.40	85.30	60.50	55.60	53.00	43.30	89.40
SimpleBaseline + PoseAug [11]	78.70	78.70	76.40	76.20	58.00	53.40	51.30	39.40	**78.10**
SimpleBaseline + DH-AUG	**77.99**	**75.87**	**72.97**	**72.28**	**57.86**	**53.13**	**50.06**	**38.89**	80.52
VPose [34] (1-frame)	92.60	89.80	85.60	86.60	60.00	55.20	52.70	41.80	94.60
VPose + PoseAug [11]	78.30	78.40	73.20	73.00	57.80	52.90	50.20	38.20	81.60
VPose + DH-AUG (1-frame)	**76.70**	**74.82**	**71.07**	**71.17**	**57.66**	**52.52**	**49.81**	**37.01**	**79.28**

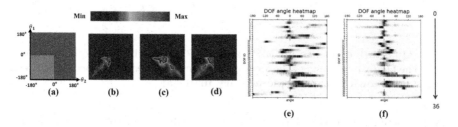

Fig. 6. Data distribution. (b), (c), (d) is the data distribution of left knee and right knee joint angles. The normal rotation range of the knee is $-180°$ to $0°$. (e), (f) is the data distribution of all joint angles. The amount of data in the (b), (c), (d) is the same. **(a):** The green area is the normal area. The red area is the area where ambiguity occurs. θ_1: Left knee joint angle. θ_2: Right knee joint angle. **(b):** Data distribution of H36M datasets (before pose augmentation). **(c):** Pose augmentation (no constraints). **(d):** Pose augmentation (add constraints). **(e):** Pose augmentation (no constraints). **(f):** Pose augmentation (add constraints).

Analysis of the Data Distribution. To further verify the diversity of the data we generated, we visualized the data distribution of the left knee and right knee. Distribution of H36M (before augmentation) form a small and concentrated cluster, also showing a limited diversity (Fig. 6 (b)). However, our method (DH-AUG) obtains a huge and decentralized cluster as shown in Fig. 6 (d). This shows that DH-AUG generates more diverse pose, and also proves why our method can greatly enhance the generalization ability. The comparison of distribution before and after adding constraints will be introduced in Sect. 4.6. In addition, we provide the distribution of all joint angles, as shown in Fig. 6 (e) and (f).

4.5   Qualitative Results

We select difficult figures from several datasets for estimation, as shown in Fig. 7. The pose estimator enhanced with DH-AUG can get results with more correct action, better scale matching, and higher accuracy. **More qualitative results are shown in the supplementary material.**

We selected 2 frames of data close to the camera and found that DH-AUG can solve the scale problem shown in Fig. 8. The reason for the scale mismatch is that the human motion in H36M is concentrated in one range, which makes the model unable to fully learn the relationship between bone length and distance.

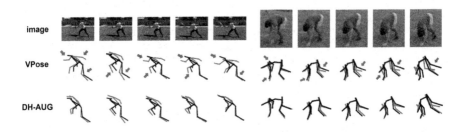

Fig. 7. Qualitative results on MPI and 3DPW. The black pose is the ground truth. The blue arrow points to the location of the main correction. **More qualitative results are shown in the supplementary material.**

Table 7. Ablation study. DHG: DH-generator. **BR:** Bone rotate two-stream module. **2DP:** 2D Pose two-stream. **DHT:** DH parameter constraint table.

Method	3DHP (↓)	H36M (↓)
Baseline	90.70	42.14
+ DHG + BR	88.97	43.65
+ DHG + BR + 2DP	84.12	41.31
+ DHG + BR + 2DP + 3DP	82.86	41.20
+ DHG + BR + 2DP + 3DP + DHT	80.39	41.21

4.6   Ablation Study

BR, 2DP, 3DP. BR is the bone rotation two-stream branch, which is used to constrain the joint angle parameters produced by the generator. **2DP** is the 2D pose two-stream branch, which is mainly used to constrain global translation parameters and motion trajectories. **3DP** is the 3D pose two-stream branch, which is mainly used to constrain global rotation parameters and enable the model to learn bone length information.

Effect of DH Parameter Constraint Table. DHT is the DH parameter constraint table. Figure 6 is the data distribution of the left knee and right knee. The normal rotation range is about −180° to 0°. Before adding the DHT (Fig. 6 (c)), the data distribution is asymmetric and unreasonable. Figure 6 (c) has a lot of outward rotation values (between 0° and 180°, the knee cannot be external rotation), which indicates that the generator has learned the wrong human kinematics information. This causes the generator to produce the skeleton video shown in Fig. 9 (a). However, by observing Fig. 6 (d), it will be found that the distribution is symmetrical and reasonable. After adding constraints, the skeleton video generated by DH-AUG is shown in Fig. 9 (b).

By observing the Table 7, we can see that the performance is improved by gradually adding **BR**, **2DP**, **3DP**, and **DHT** modules, which verifies the effectiveness of these modules.

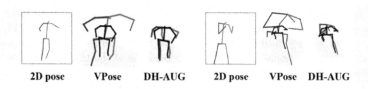

2D pose   **VPose**   **DH-AUG**   **2D pose**   **VPose**   **DH-AUG**

Fig. 8. Scale problem. Columns 1, 4 are 2D poses, columns 2, 5 are the results before pose augmentation, and columns 3, 6 are the results of using DH-AUG. The black pose is the ground truth.

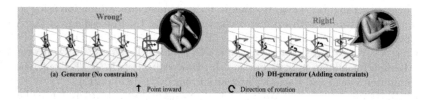

Fig. 9. Skeleton video generated by DH-AUG. (a) No constraints. (b) Adding constraints. SMPL is only used for visualization. **See the supplementary material for more skeleton videos**.

4.7   Limitation Analysis

Although our method increases the generalization ability of 3D human pose estimation, our method still has some limitations. The DH parameter constraint table we use is manually set according to personal experience. This increases the number of hyper-parameters that need to be adjusted. Although it will not have a great impact on the final result, it increases some workload.

5　Conclusion

In this paper, we propose a pose augmentation solution, which we call DH-AUG. DH-AUG has a special kinematics model called the DH parameter model, which weakens the angle ambiguity (multiple solutions). We use 3 common single-frame 3D pose estimators and 2 video 3D pose estimators to experiment. Extensive experiments demonstrate that DH-AUG can greatly increase the generalization ability of the pose estimator.

Acknowledgements. This work was supported in part by the National Natural Science Foundation of China under Grant 62192784 and Grant 61871052.

References

1. Andriluka, M., Pishchulin, L., Gehler, P., Schiele, B.: 2D human pose estimation: new benchmark and state of the art analysis. In: Proceedings of the IEEE Conference on Computer Vision and Pattern Recognition, pp. 3686–3693 (2014)
2. Cai, Y., et al.: Exploiting spatial-temporal relationships for 3D pose estimation via graph convolutional networks. In: Proceedings of the IEEE/CVF International Conference on Computer Vision, pp. 2272–2281 (2019)
3. Chen, T., Fang, C., Shen, X., Zhu, Y., Chen, Z., Luo, J.: Anatomy-aware 3D human pose estimation with bone-based pose decomposition. IEEE Trans. Circuits Syst. Video Technol. **32**(1), 198–209 (2021)
4. Chen, Y., Wang, Z., Peng, Y., Zhang, Z., Yu, G., Sun, J.: Cascaded pyramid network for multi-person pose estimation. In: Proceedings of the IEEE Conference on Computer Vision and Pattern Recognition, pp. 7103–7112 (2018)
5. Cheng, Y., Yang, B., Wang, B., Tan, R.T.: 3D human pose estimation using spatio-temporal networks with explicit occlusion training. In: Proceedings of the AAAI Conference on Artificial Intelligence, vol. 34, pp. 10631–10638 (2020)
6. Chu, X., Yang, W., Ouyang, W., Ma, C., Yuille, A.L., Wang, X.: Multi-context attention for human pose estimation. In: Proceedings of the IEEE Conference on Computer Vision and Pattern Recognition, pp. 1831–1840 (2017)
7. Ci, H., Wang, C., Ma, X., Wang, Y.: Optimizing network structure for 3D human pose estimation. In: Proceedings of the IEEE/CVF International Conference on Computer Vision, pp. 2262–2271 (2019)
8. Craig, J.J.: Introduction to robotics: mechanics and control, 3/E. Pearson Education India (2009)
9. Csiszar, A., Eilers, J., Verl, A.: On solving the inverse kinematics problem using neural networks. In: 2017 24th International Conference on Mechatronics and Machine Vision in Practice (M2VIP), pp. 1–6. IEEE (2017)
10. Girshick, R., Radosavovic, I.G.G.D.P., Kaiming, H.: Detectron (2018). https://github.com/facebookresearch/detectron
11. Gong, K., Zhang, J., Feng, J.: PoseAug: a differentiable pose augmentation framework for 3D human pose estimation. In: Proceedings of the IEEE/CVF Conference on Computer Vision and Pattern Recognition, pp. 8575–8584 (2021)
12. Goodfellow, I., et al.: Generative adversarial nets. Adv. Neural Inf. Process. Syst. **27** (2014)
13. Gulrajani, I., Ahmed, F., Arjovsky, M., Dumoulin, V., Courville, A.: Improved training of Wasserstein GANs. arXiv preprint arXiv:1704.00028 (2017)

14. Hartley, R., Zisserman, A.: Multiple View Geometry in Computer Vision, 2nd edn. Cambridge University Press, NY (2003)

15. Ionescu, C., Papava, D., Olaru, V., Sminchisescu, C.: Human3.6m: large scale datasets and predictive methods for 3D human sensing in natural environments. IEEE Trans. Pattern Anal. Mach. Intell. **36**(7), 1325–1339 (2014)

16. Johnson, S., Everingham, M.: Clustered pose and nonlinear appearance models for human pose estimation. In: bmvc, vol. 2, p. 5. Citeseer (2010)

17. Kanazawa, A., Black, M.J., Jacobs, D.W., Malik, J.: End-to-end recovery of human shape and pose. In: Proceedings of the IEEE Conference on Computer Vision and Pattern Recognition, pp. 7122–7131 (2018)

18. Kokic, M., Kragic, D., Bohg, J.: Learning to estimate pose and shape of hand-held objects from RGB images. In: 2019 IEEE/RSJ International Conference on Intelligent Robots and Systems (IROS), pp. 3980–3987. IEEE (2019)

19. Li, B., Li, X., Zhang, Z., Wu, F.: Spatio-temporal graph routing for skeleton-based action recognition. In: Proceedings of the AAAI Conference on Artificial Intelligence, vol. 33, pp. 8561–8568 (2019)

20. Li, C., Lee, G.H.: Generating multiple hypotheses for 3D human pose estimation with mixture density network. In: Proceedings of the IEEE/CVF Conference on Computer Vision and Pattern Recognition, pp. 9887–9895 (2019)

21. Li, J., Xu, C., Chen, Z., Bian, S., Yang, L., Lu, C.: HybrIK: a hybrid analytical-neural inverse kinematics solution for 3D human pose and shape estimation. In: Proceedings of the IEEE/CVF Conference on Computer Vision and Pattern Recognition, pp. 3383–3393 (2021)

22. Li, M., Chen, S., Chen, X., Zhang, Y., Wang, Y., Tian, Q.: Actional-structural graph convolutional networks for skeleton-based action recognition. In: Proceedings of the IEEE/CVF Conference on Computer Vision and Pattern Recognition, pp. 3595–3603 (2019)

23. Li, S., Ke, L., Pratama, K., Tai, Y.W., Tang, C.K., Cheng, K.T.: Cascaded deep monocular 3D human pose estimation with evolutionary training data. In: Proceedings of the IEEE/CVF Conference on Computer Vision and Pattern Recognition, pp. 6173–6183 (2020)

24. Liu, R., Shen, J., Wang, H., Chen, C., Cheung, S.C., Asari, V.: Attention mechanism exploits temporal contexts: real-time 3D human pose reconstruction. In: Proceedings of the IEEE/CVF Conference on Computer Vision and Pattern Recognition, pp. 5064–5073 (2020)

25. Loper, M., Mahmood, N., Romero, J., Pons-Moll, G., Black, M.J.: SMPL: a skinned multi-person linear model. ACM Trans. Graph. **34**(6), 1–16 (2015)

26. Luo, C., Chu, X., Yuille, A.: OriNet: a fully convolutional network for 3D human pose estimation. arXiv preprint arXiv:1811.04989 (2018)

27. von Marcard, T., Henschel, R., Black, M.J., Rosenhahn, B., Pons-Moll, G.: Recovering accurate 3D human pose in the wild using IMUs and a moving camera. In: Proceedings of the European Conference on Computer Vision (ECCV), pp. 601–617 (2018)

28. Martinez, J., Hossain, R., Romero, J., Little, J.J.: A simple yet effective baseline for 3D human pose estimation. In: Proceedings of the IEEE International Conference on Computer Vision, pp. 2640–2649 (2017)

29. Mehta, D., et al.: Monocular 3D human pose estimation in the wild using improved CNN supervision. In: 2017 International Conference on 3D Vision (3DV), pp. 506–516. IEEE (2017)

30. Mehta, D., et al.: VNect: real-time 3D human pose estimation with a single RGB camera. ACM Trans. Graph. **36**(4), 1–14 (2017)

31. Moon, G., Chang, J.Y., Lee, K.M.: Camera distance-aware top-down approach for 3D multi-person pose estimation from a single RGB image. In: Proceedings of the IEEE/CVF International Conference on Computer Vision, pp. 10133–10142 (2019)
32. Mueller, F., Mehta, D., Sotnychenko, O., Sridhar, S., Casas, D., Theobalt, C.: Real-time hand tracking under occlusion from an egocentric RGB-D sensor. In: Proceedings of the IEEE International Conference on Computer Vision, pp. 1154–1163 (2017)
33. Pavlakos, G., Zhou, X., Derpanis, K.G., Daniilidis, K.: Coarse-to-fine volumetric prediction for single-image 3D human pose. In: Proceedings of the IEEE Conference on Computer Vision and Pattern Recognition, pp. 7025–7034 (2017)
34. Pavllo, D., Feichtenhofer, C., Grangier, D., Auli, M.: 3D human pose estimation in video with temporal convolutions and semi-supervised training. In: Proceedings of the IEEE/CVF Conference on Computer Vision and Pattern Recognition, pp. 7753–7762 (2019)
35. Peng, X., Tang, Z., Yang, F., Feris, R.S., Metaxas, D.: Jointly optimize data augmentation and network training: adversarial data augmentation in human pose estimation. In: Proceedings of the IEEE Conference on Computer Vision and Pattern Recognition, pp. 2226–2234 (2018)
36. Rogez, G., Schmid, C.: MoCap-guided data augmentation for 3D pose estimation in the wild. arXiv preprint arXiv:1607.02046 (2016)
37. Sharma, S., Varigonda, P.T., Bindal, P., Sharma, A., Jain, A.: Monocular 3D human pose estimation by generation and ordinal ranking. In: Proceedings of the IEEE/CVF International Conference on Computer Vision, pp. 2325–2334 (2019)
38. Shi, L., Zhang, Y., Cheng, J., Lu, H.: Two-stream adaptive graph convolutional networks for skeleton-based action recognition. In: Proceedings of the IEEE/CVF Conference on Computer Vision and Pattern Recognition, pp. 12026–12035 (2019)
39. Shi, M., et al.: MotioNet: 3D human motion reconstruction from monocular video with skeleton consistency. ACM Trans. Graph. **40**(1), 1–15 (2020)
40. Su, Z., Ye, M., Zhang, G., Dai, L., Sheng, J.: Cascade feature aggregation for human pose estimation. arXiv preprint arXiv:1902.07837 (2019)
41. Sun, K., Xiao, B., Liu, D., Wang, J.: Deep high-resolution representation learning for human pose estimation. In: Proceedings of the IEEE/CVF Conference on Computer Vision and Pattern Recognition, pp. 5693–5703 (2019)
42. Tang, W., Yu, P., Wu, Y.: Deeply learned compositional models for human pose estimation. In: Proceedings of the European Conference on Computer Vision (ECCV), pp. 190–206 (2018)
43. Tekin, B., Katircioglu, I., Salzmann, M., Lepetit, V., Fua, P.: Structured prediction of 3D human pose with deep neural networks. arXiv preprint arXiv:1605.05180 (2016)
44. Tekin, B., Rozantsev, A., Lepetit, V., Fua, P.: Direct prediction of 3D body poses from motion compensated sequences. In: Proceedings of the IEEE Conference on Computer Vision and Pattern Recognition, pp. 991–1000 (2016)
45. Tripathi, S., Ranade, S., Tyagi, A., Agrawal, A.: PoseNet3D: learning temporally consistent 3D human pose via knowledge distillation. In: 2020 International Conference on 3D Vision (3DV), pp. 311–321. IEEE (2020)
46. Varol, G., et al.: Learning from synthetic humans. In: Proceedings of the IEEE Conference on Computer Vision and Pattern Recognition, pp. 109–117 (2017)
47. Wandt, B., Rosenhahn, B.: RepNet: weakly supervised training of an adversarial reprojection network for 3D human pose estimation. In: Proceedings of the IEEE/CVF Conference on Computer Vision and Pattern Recognition, pp. 7782–7791 (2019)

48. Xu, J., Yu, Z., Ni, B., Yang, J., Yang, X., Zhang, W.: Deep kinematics analysis for monocular 3D human pose estimation. In: Proceedings of the IEEE/CVF Conference on Computer Vision and Pattern Recognition, pp. 899–908 (2020)
49. Zeng, A., Sun, X., Huang, F., Liu, M., Xu, Q., Lin, S.: SRNet: improving generalization in 3D human pose estimation with a split-and-recombine approach. In: Vedaldi, A., Bischof, H., Brox, T., Frahm, J.-M. (eds.) ECCV 2020. LNCS, vol. 12359, pp. 507–523. Springer, Cham (2020). https://doi.org/10.1007/978-3-030-58568-6_30
50. Zhang, X., Xu, C., Tao, D.: Context aware graph convolution for skeleton-based action recognition. In: Proceedings of the IEEE/CVF Conference on Computer Vision and Pattern Recognition, pp. 14333–14342 (2020)
51. Zhao, L., Peng, X., Tian, Y., Kapadia, M., Metaxas, D.N.: Semantic graph convolutional networks for 3D human pose regression. In: Proceedings of the IEEE/CVF Conference on Computer Vision and Pattern Recognition, pp. 3425–3435 (2019)
52. Zheng, C., Zhu, S., Mendieta, M., Yang, T., Chen, C., Ding, Z.: 3D human pose estimation with spatial and temporal transformers. arXiv preprint arXiv:2103.10455 (2021)

Estimating Spatially-Varying Lighting in Urban Scenes with Disentangled Representation

Jiajun Tang[1], Yongjie Zhu[2], Haoyu Wang[1], Jun Hoong Chan[1], Si Li[2], and Boxin Shi[1,3(✉)]

[1] NERCVT, School of Computer Science, Peking University, Beijing, China
{jiajun.tang,wanghaoyu,shiboxin}@pku.edu.cn, junhoong95@stu.pku.edu.cn
[2] School of Artificial Intelligence, Beijing University of Posts
and Telecommunications, Beijing, China
yongjie.zhu.96@gmail.com, lisi@bupt.edu.cn
[3] Peng Cheng Laboratory, Shenzhen, China

Abstract. We present an end-to-end network for spatially-varying outdoor lighting estimation in urban scenes given a single limited field-of-view LDR image and any assigned 2D pixel position. We use three disentangled latent spaces learned by our network to represent sky light, sun light, and lighting-independent local contents respectively. At inference time, our lighting estimation network can run efficiently in an end-to-end manner by merging the global lighting and the local appearance rendered by the local appearance renderer with the predicted local silhouette. We enhance an existing synthetic dataset with more realistic material models and diverse lighting conditions for more effective training. We also capture the first real dataset with HDR labels for evaluating spatially-varying outdoor lighting estimation. Experiments on both synthetic and real datasets show that our method achieves state-of-the-art performance with more flexible editability.

Keywords: Spatially-varying lighting · Disentangled representation · Lighting estimation · Urban scenes

1 Introduction

Single image based outdoor illumination estimation, aiming at estimating lighting from a single limited field-of-view (FoV) image, takes a crucial role in many computer vision applications, such as object relighting, scene understanding, and augmented reality (AR). Unlike indoor scenarios, outdoor lighting contains rich high-frequency and high-intensity components. In early works, several low-dimensional parametric models are proposed to fit a distant global lighting, such as the Hošek-Wilkie (HW) sky model [13,14] and the Lalonde-Matthews

Supplementary Information The online version contains supplementary material available at https://doi.org/10.1007/978-3-031-20068-7_26.

© The Author(s), under exclusive license to Springer Nature Switzerland AG 2022
S. Avidan et al. (Eds.): ECCV 2022, LNCS 13666, pp. 454–469, 2022.
https://doi.org/10.1007/978-3-031-20068-7_26

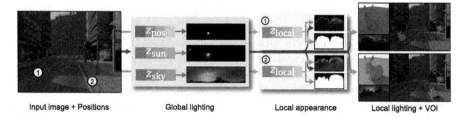

Input image + Positions   Global lighting   Local appearance   Local lighting + VOI

Fig. 1. We propose an end-to-end network for spatially-varying outdoor lighting estimation. Given a limited-FoV LDR image and the 2D pixel positions, the spatially-uniform global lighting is first estimated as the sun position, sun light, and sky light. The spatially-varying local content at each position is then estimated respectively. The spatially-varying local appearance is rendered with both local content information and global lighting condition, and the spatially-varying lighting at each position is finally obtained by merging the local appearance with the global lighting using the predicted local silhouette mask. Realistic virtual object insertion (VOI) can be conducted using the predicted local lighting (panoramas are shown in tone-mapped HDR).

(LM) sky model [17]. However, the capacities of those parametric models are not sufficient for real-world outdoor lighting, which often leads to unrealistic rendering results. Recent data-driven approaches start using latent spaces learned by autoencoders to represent outdoor lighting conditions to serve as the target of global lighting estimation [11]. Methods combining merits of latent space representation ability and interpretable parameters have also been proposed [26].

However, these methods all treat the outdoor lighting as a single *spatially-uniform (global)* lighting, *i.e.*, the light probe is surrounded by an environment map that casts rays from infinitely far away. Extending outdoor lighting estimation to support *spatially-varying (local)* prediction is of important practicability, especially for urban scenes where many buildings occlude the light path making the spatially-uniform representation rather unrealistic. Only until very recently, such a problem has been demonstrated to be solvable via intrinsic decomposition and panoramic environment map completion [28].

Although the first trial for outdoor spatially-varying lighting estimation [28] has shown its impressive performance, there still remains room for improvement: 1) The direct usage of panoramic environment maps is a less compact representation compared to latent parametric models [11]. 2) The estimated lightings in the form of panoramic maps have limited editability (horizontal rotation and scaling). 3) The SOLID-Img [28] synthetic dataset are with limited diversity (only default object materials in Blender SceneCity [2] and sunny environment maps) and there lacks a real-captured outdoor spatially-varying dataset with ground truth HDR lightings to more comprehensively evaluate the performance.

In this paper, we propose the *SOLD-Net* for *Spatially-varying Outdoor Lighting estimation with Disentangled representation*, which consists of the end-to-end *spatially-varying lighting estimator* for non-uniform lighting estimation on disentangled latent spaces and the *global lighting encoder-decoder* together with *local content encoder-renderer* for learning spatially-varying lighting representation. As shown in Fig. 1, the global lighting encoder-decoder learns to disentangle global lighting as two different latent spaces for sky light and sun light with separate parameters such as the sun position; the lighting-dependent spatially-varying local appearances are rendered given global lighting conditions and the lighting-independent local content information learned by the local content encoder-renderer. Our method achieves state-of-the-art performance on spatially-varying outdoor lighting estimation with the following contributions:

- using disentangled latent spaces to compactly represent global lighting conditions and local contents;
- designing an end-to-end network architecture to infer spatially-varying lighting with flexible editability;
- enhancing spatially-varying outdoor lighting estimation datasets by increasing material diversity and weather diversity for the synthetic dataset and capturing the first real dataset with HDR ground truth labels.

2   Related Work

Our method targets at lighting estimation from a single image for the outdoor urban scenario with local lighting effects being considered. In this section, we briefly review relevant works for outdoor lighting estimation first and then discuss how existing methods consider local lighting estimation.

Outdoor Lighting Estimation. The most direct way to obtain outdoor lighting representation is to capture HDR images with multiple exposures that include the sun and sky [25]. However, estimating illumination conditions from images is always desired for practical consideration. This is feasible since an outdoor image provides useful cues that could reveal the surrounding environment. Lalonde *et al.* [15] for the first time infer illumination from shadows, shading, and sky appearance variations observed in the image. A convolutional neural network [7] is used to process the symmetric view of pairwise photos captured from rear and front cameras of mobile devices, and to estimate the outdoor lighting represented by low-frequency spherical harmonic (SH) coefficients. However, it has a difficulty in dealing with high-frequency information. A physics-based Hošek-Wilkie (HW) sky model [13,14] is better tailored to recover HDR parameters for deep outdoor illumination estimation [12], but it is sensitive to cloud patches data. This issue is solved by using a more robust sky model, the Lalonde-Matthews (LM) model [17,27], which covers more comprehensive lighting conditions in the outdoor environment. More recently, a novel SkyNet autoencoder [11] is designed to learn a latent sky model from a large sky panorama dataset [16] and successfully estimates outdoor lighting from limited-FoV images. An encoder-decoder framework is further proposed [18] to learn a mapping from a limited-FoV LDR image to HDR lighting and a mobile phone camera equipped with three spheres of different reflectance is used to capture ground truth training data. HDSky [26] makes several physically meaningful attributes of global outdoor lighting estimation editable by hierarchically training autoencoders with different supervisions.

Local Lighting Estimation. Different from global illumination representation, the local illumination is related to the position where the light probe is placed, *i.e.*, to capture the lighting intensity at a target position using a mirror sphere in the scene [8]. However, calibrations of objects are not always available, so local lighting estimates from images attract researchers' attention. Earlier works infer intrinsic properties from a single RGBD image, and a noisy depth image is used to improve spherical harmonic estimation [5], but such an approach does not capture abrupt changes in ambient lighting caused by local geometry. Estimating spatially-varying indoor lighting from a single RGB image could be conducted in real-time [10], by using high-order SH representations learned by deep neural networks. After the first usage of spherical Gaussian (SG) in deep indoor lighting estimation [9], an inverse rendering network [19] is proposed to estimate indoor spatially-varying spherical Gaussian coefficients for scene editing. NeurIllum [23] recovers high-frequency local lighting with warped color image according to recovered geometry, which shows promising texture details, but the lighting estimations are sometimes imprecise due to the errors in the estimated geometry and the light which is not directly observed in the input. Lighthouse [24] achieves a spatially-coherent (varies smoothly in 3D) and spatially-varying indoor lighting estimation from stereo images using the 3D volumetric RGBA lighting model.

Spatially-varying lighting estimation for outdoor scenarios has not been demonstrated until the proposing of SOLID-Net [28], which is the most relevant work to ours. SOLID-Net relies on decomposing scene intrinsics first for global illumination and then 'warp and complete' a panoramic environment map to include local information. Our method uses only a few parameters in disentangled latent spaces to encode sky, sun, and local information compactly, and the local lighting can be estimated in an end-to-end manner at inference time.

3   Problem Formulation

As aforementioned, the outdoor lighting, especially in urban scenes, is spatially-varying and consists of two parts: 1) the *spatially-uniform (global)* part which can be approximately seen as light sources from infinitely far away and doesn't change with the view point, such as lights from far background objects in the sky-dome. 2) the *spatially-varying (local)* part whose changes with the view point are not eligible, mainly the lights come from or occluded by nearby ground, buildings or plants.

Accordingly, when using panoramic environment maps to present lighting, the global part of outdoor lighting corresponds to the global lighting map P_{global}. Since the sun light and the sky light are two different types of light sources, P_{global} can be further approximately decomposed into the ambient lighting from the sky P_{sky} and the distant lighting from the sun P_{sun}:

$$P_{\text{global}} = P_{\text{sky}} + z_{\text{vis}}(P_{\text{sun}} \odot M_{\text{sun}}), \tag{1}$$

where M_{sun} is the binary panoramic mask indicating the position of the sun, and $z_{\text{vis}} \in [0, 1]$ indicates the visibility of the sun under different conditions.

Note that in daytime, natural light is dominant over artificial light, thus the local part of outdoor lighting can be treated as the illuminated local appearance P_{app} by global lights from P_{global}:

$$P_{\text{app}} = \Phi(z_{\text{local}}, P_{\text{global}}), \tag{2}$$

where Φ denotes the lighting (or rendering) process, and z_{local} is the local content information containing *lighting-independent* properties (such as implicit albedo, normal, and silhouette) of forground objects. Here by indicating *local*, we mean *from the panoramic view* centered at the view point (x, y, z) in the 3D space corresponding to the pixel position (u, v) in a limited-FoV image.

Finally, we can get the spatially-varying local lighting map P_{local} by:

$$P_{\text{local}} = P_{\text{global}} \odot (1 - M_{\text{sil}}) + P_{\text{app}} \odot M_{\text{sil}}, \tag{3}$$

where M_{sil} is the panoramic silhouette of local content (foreground objects).

An intuitive illustration of the advantages of our disentangled lighting representation is shown in Fig. 2. Spherical harmonics (SH) [21] is ineffective to model high-frequency sun light resulting in soft shadows in the relighting, optimized spherical Gaussian (SG) [19] and our lighting representation both give a realistic relighting, while our lighting representation provides better editability by disentangling different types of lighting (ambient sky light, distant sun light, and illuminated local appearance). Based on this lighting representation, we design an end-to-end network (in Sect. 4) to estimate spatially-uniform global lighting P_{global} and spatially-varying local lighting P_{local} at the same time.

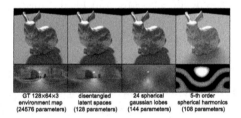

Fig. 2. The relighting results and corresponding environment maps of ground truth, our disentangled lighting representation, optimized spherical Gaussian [19], and spherical harmonics [21]. Our representation gives both realistic relighting and better editability.

4   Method

This section introduces the datasets we use (in Sect. 4.1), the design methodology (in Sect. 4.2), the training (in Sect. 4.3) and inference (in Sect. 4.4) procedures of our method, whose pipeline is shown in Fig. 3.

4.1   Dataset

As far as we know, the SOLID-Img dataset [28] is the only suitable one for spatially-varying outdoor lighting estimation. However, its synthetic and real-

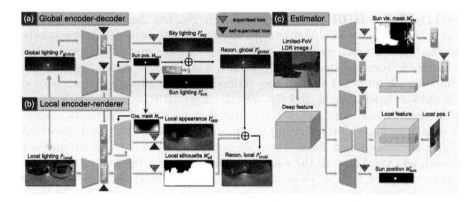

Fig. 3. Overview of our SOLD-Net. Our method uses (a) a global lighting encoder-decoder and (b) a local content encoder-renderer to learn disentangled latent spaces for global (sky, sun) and local information respectively, then (c) a spatially-varying lighting estimator predicts the spatially-varying lighting in disentangled lighting components from a single limited-FoV LDR image with a given pixel position.

world counterparts have limitations in terms of material diversity and ground truth quality. We expand both parts as our training and testing datasets.

Synthetic Dataset Enhancement. The SOLID-Img [28] dataset is rendered using a 3D city model from Blender SceneCity [2] and 70 HDR environment maps for different global lighting conditions and has 38,000 images. It only uses 12 default materials in Blender SceneCity [2], which are less realistic diffuse materials and might lead to insufficient generalization ability of trained models on real data. To make a dataset with greater diversity, we use a set of 30 open physically based rendering (PBR) materials [1] which contain color maps, normal maps, roughness maps, and displacement maps of the Disney principled BRDF model [6]. As shown in Fig. 4, we randomly apply different materials in the 3D city model according to the specific object type, and the issues of repetitive buildings and unrealistic grounds are solved. To cover more diverse lighting conditions, we select 108 representative outdoor HDR environment maps from Poly Haven [3] (including 75 sunny, 15 cloudy, and 18 partly-cloudy panoramas). By this way, we narrow the data gap and make the trained model more robust on real data. Moreover, we render paired local lighting maps of the same local content with different global lighting conditions for our self-supervised cross rendering loss (in Sect. 4.3). Finally, we render 151,632 images in total.

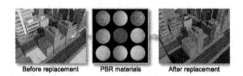

Fig. 4. An example of rendered 3D city model (bird view) before and after we randomly replacing the materials in the model with PBR materials in the same object category.

Real Data with HDR Local Lightings. The real test data in SOLID-Net [28] only have LDR panoramic environment maps as ground truth labels of spatially-varying lighting, which prevents us quantitatively measure the performance and qualitatively compare the relighting results. To provide a more comprehensive evaluation of outdoor local lighting estimation, we capture a test dataset of real outdoor urban scenes and the corresponding HDR spatially-varying local environment maps. The scenes are captured by a Sony ILCE-7RM3 camera. To obtain unclipped HDR capture of the sun intensity, we first capture a basic HDR panorama using a Ricoh Theta Z1 camera in which only the sun pixels is clipped, and then capture the sun region directly using the Sony ILCE-7RM3 camera equipped with a 3.0 neutral density (ND) filter; the final unclipped HDR panoramic environment maps are stitched by aligning the sun positions in panoramic maps and perspective images (warping the perspective images into panoramic coordinates). To compensate for the color shift caused by the ND filter and different cameras, we follow Stumpfel et al. [25] to compute the color correction matrix (CCM) and align captured intensities across different settings using an X-rite classic 24 patch colorchecker. In total, our real test dataset includes 20 outdoor scenes and 40 unclipped HDR local lighting environment maps. There are 17 sunny scenes and 3 partly-cloudy scenes of roads, buildings, bridges and parks, and the sun azimuths and elevations are scattered and diverse.

4.2   Network Architecture

We model three types of lighting: ambient sky light, distant sun light, and illuminated local appearances separately in disentangled parametric spaces. To this end, SOLD-Net consists of three parts: (a) a global encoder-decoder to encode sky light and sun light separately, (b) a local encoder-renderer to encode lighting-independent local properties, i.e., local contents, in the latent space and render local appearances given the global lighting conditions, and (c) a spatially-varying lighting estimator to estimate local lightings represented as disentangled components in an end-to-end manner.

Global Lighting Encoder-Decoder. Our global lighting encoder-decoder (Fig. 3(a)) takes a global lighting panorama P_{global} as input and disentangles sky light and sun light by using two encoders to encode z_{sky} and z_{sun} in two latent spaces respectively. The sun position M_{sun} is also made explicit from the latent space of sun light for the editability of the sun position [26]. The reconstructed global lighting panorama P'_{global} is composed of reconstructed sky light P'_{sky} and reconstructed sun light P'_{sun} following Eq. (1).

Local Content Encoder-Renderer. As shown in Fig. 3(b), the local content encoder takes a local lighting panorama P_{local} as input and extracts the lighting-independent component of local content encoded in z_{local}, which is achieved by local identity loss and cross rendering loss (in Sect. 4.3). To get the rendered local appearance P'_{app}, the local appearance renderer takes z_{local}, z_{sky}, z_{sun}, and a panoramic cosine mask M_{cos} as input to function as Eq. (2), where z_{sky} and z_{sun} are the encodings of sky light and sun light in the global lighting condition of

P_global corresponding to the local lighting panorama P_local. The cosine mask M_cos is derived from the sun position M_sun indicating the shading on a hypothesized Lambertian sphere in the panoramic coordinate. Since the silhouette is a lighting-independent property, we use a silhouette decoder to estimate the silhouette mask M'_sil of the local content from z_local as only input. The reconstruction of spatially-varying local lighting P'_local is then derived following Eq. (3).

Spatially-Varying Lighting Estimator. Since we model the outdoor lighting in three disentangled latent spaces, our spatially-varying lighting estimator predicts lighting components as latent codes instead of directly estimating panoramic lighting maps. Our estimator is a single-in-multi-out network (Fig. 3(c)), which only takes a limited-FoV LDR image I of the outdoor scene as input. After extracting deep features using a shared network backbone, the sun position M'_sun, sky light code z'_sky, and sun light code z'_sun of global lighting are estimated in different output branches. Here we estimate the sun position as an 8×32 classification task. To estimate spatially-varying sun visibility z_vis caused by occlusions or weather at each pixel position, we also use a branch to predict a sun visibility mask M'_vis to approximately indicate whether the object on the given pixel position can be directly illuminated by the sun. For local content estimation, the stacked hourglass network [20] is used to capture the pixel-aligned features in multiple scales. Given the pixel position $l(u, v)$ on the input image, the local features at the same position in the image coordinate are extracted [22], then the local content code z'_local at the corresponding 3D point $L(x, y, z)$ is estimated from the extracted pixel-aligned local features. Our local lighting estimator runs in an end-to-end manner and estimates local lighting as editable disentangled lighting components.

4.3   Training

As illustrated in Fig. 3, our full pipeline is trained with both supervised and self-supervised signals.

Supervised Losses. Since we are using rendered synthetic dataset, we can get the direct supervisions for many components in the pipeline. During the training of global lighting and local appearance encoding, we use the ℓ_1 reconstruction loss for P'_sky, P'_app, M'_sil, and the ℓ_2 reconstruction loss for P'_sun. Once our global and local encoders are trained, we run them on our synthetic dataset to get the disentangled codes as training targets. When training the estimator, we use the ℓ_2 reconstruction loss for M'_vis, z'_sky, z'_sun, and z'_local, and the cross-entropy loss (CE) for M'_sun. Please refer to the supplemental materials for more details.

Self-supervised Losses. In our formulation, local content have spatially-varying and lighting-independent properties. Therefore, the local content codes should also be lighting-independent. That is to say: 1) local lighting maps with different global lighting conditions and the same local content should have the same local content codes; 2) the local content codes encoded from the local lighting maps with the same local content should produce the same local appearance renderings with the same global lighting conditions. The constraints can be added by the local identity loss (ID) $\mathcal{L}_{id}$ and the cross rendering loss (CR) $\mathcal{L}_{cr}$. As said in Sect. 4.1, our synthetic dataset has paired local lighting maps $\{P_{local}^1, P_{local}^2\}$ with the same local content but different global lighting conditions, and let $\{z_{local}'^1, z_{local}'^2\}$ be the local content codes encoded by our local encoder, then we define:

$$\mathcal{L}_{id} = ||z_{local}'^1 - z_{local}'^2||_1, \tag{4}$$

and

$$\mathcal{L}_{cr} = ||P_{local}^1 \odot M_{sil} - P_{local}'^1(z_{local}'^2) \odot M_{sil}||_1 + \\ ||P_{local}^2 \odot M_{sil} - P_{local}'^2(z_{local}'^1) \odot M_{sil}||_1, \tag{5}$$

where $P_{local}'^i$ denotes rendering the local appearance map from local content codes using the global lighting condition of P_{local}^i. We also adopt the info loss (IF) $\mathcal{L}_{info}$ in HDSky [26] to ensure a better disentanglement of sky light and sun light.

4.4 Inference

At inference time, the inputs are a limited-FoV image and a designated pixel position. As shown in Fig. 3(c), the global lighting codes of sun light and sky light, sun position and sun visibility mask are predicted. Then local content code and local sun visibility are predicted at the given pixel position. The codes are further used to decode and render global and local lighting map predictions by trained global decoder and local renderer following the formulation in Sect. 3. To estimate local lighting at multiple pixel positions, only local feature extraction, local content code estimation and local appearance rendering are needed, which means our method is of high re-usability of network predictions.

5   Experiments

In this section, we perform detailed network analysis and present qualitative and quantitative results on both synthetic data and real data, we also show relighted bunny results and virtual object insertion results to validate our methods qualitatively.

Baseline Methods. To compare with spatially-varying local lighting estimation methods, we choose the latest **SOLID-Net** [28] as the baseline. To compare with global lighting estimation methods, we use **SkyNet** [11] as the baseline. To compare with fully parametric lighting models, we set two baseline **Ours_SH** and **Ours_SG** that use the same network architecture as our estimator to predict spatially-varying local lighting represented using 5-th order SH coefficients (108 parameters in total) and 24 SG lobes following [19] (144 parameters in total). All baselines are trained on the same synthetic dataset proposed with our method, and the implementation details can be found in supplemental materials.

Metrics. To measure the accuracy of predicted global lighting maps P_{global}', local appearance maps P_{app}', local lighting maps P_{local}', and the relighted objects, we use mean absolute error (MAE) and root mean square error (RMSE) as error metrics. To measure the sun position prediction, we use angular error, azimuth error, and elevation error as error metrics.

Table 1. Quantitative evaluation of our local encoder-renderer on our enhanced synthetic dataset. 'Reconstruction' and 'Cross Rendering' denote the errors of reconstructed and cross-rendered panoramic HDR lighting maps respectively before tone mapping.

Method	Reconstruction		Cross rendering	
	MAE	RMSE	MAE	RMSE
Ours	**0.028**	**0.075**	**0.031**	**0.079**
Ours w/o $M_{\cos}$	0.034	0.083	0.036	0.085
Ours w/o $\mathcal{L}_{cr}$	0.029	0.083	0.048	0.101
Ours w/o $\mathcal{L}_{id}$	0.032	0.087	0.035	0.089

5.1 Ablation Study

Effectiveness of Local Content Encoder-Renderer. To validate that our local content encoder-renderer learns the lighting-independent local content instead of the lighting-dependent local appearance in z_{local}, we design an experiment of cross rendering: A pair of local lighting maps $\{P_{\text{local}}^1, P_{\text{local}}^2\}$ (same local content, different global lighting) is encoded to z_{local}^1 and z_{local}^2 respectively, then the local codes are swapped and the cross-rendered local appearances are obtained using the swapped local codes and the original global lighting conditions. The cross-rendered results are expected be close to ground truth local appearances.

As shown in Table 1, our local content encoder-renderer achieves a good performance[1] in cross rendering, as well as reconstruction. Without panoramic cosine mask $M_{\cos}$ (Ours w/o $M_{\cos}$), the direction of sun light becomes unclear and the rendering performance is damaged both in reconstruction and cross rendering. Without local identity loss $\mathcal{L}_{id}$ in Eq. (4) (Ours w/o $\mathcal{L}_{id}$) or cross rendering loss $\mathcal{L}_{cr}$ in Eq. (5) (Ours w/o $\mathcal{L}_{cr}$), the cross rendering performance is heavily downgraded, indicating that the local encoder would fail to encode lighting-independent information into z_{local} without $\mathcal{L}_{cr}$ or $\mathcal{L}_{id}$.

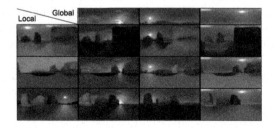

Fig. 5. Cross-rendered results of local lighting under different combinations of local contents and global lighting conditions on our enhanced synthetic dataset (shown in tone-mapped HDR). Different rows and columns indicate different local content information and global lighting conditions respectively.

---

[1] Errors are calculated on the masked region by the (predicted) local silhouette masks.

Table 2. Quantitative evaluation of spatially-uniform global lighting estimation on our enhanced synthetic dataset. 'Panorama' denotes the errors of panoramic HDR lighting maps before tone mapping. 'Relighting' denotes the errors of rendered HDR images using predicted lighting maps.

Method	Panorama		Relighting	
	MAE	RMSE	MAE	RMSE
Ours	0.439	7.607	**0.098**	**0.119**
SkyNet [11]	0.431	8.357	0.226	0.253
SOLID-Net [28]	**0.384**	**6.360**	0.153	0.174

Editability of Disentangled Lighting Representation. To illustrate the editability of our disentangled lighting representation, Fig. 5 shows the cross rendering results under different combinations of local contents and global lighting conditions. The first row and the first column show the reconstructed global lighting maps and local lighting maps from our network respectively. These maps correspond to different encoded global lighting and local content information. Here we use different combinations of global lighting information and local content information to cross-render corresponding local lighting maps. In each row, the same local content code z_{local} is shared and the layouts of local content are basically the same, which further validates that the lighting-independent local content information is indeed encoded into z_{local}. Given global lighting codes z_{sky} and z_{sun} in each column, local appearances are correctly rendered, such as blocking of the sun light by the buildings and reflection of the sun light on the ground when the sun is at a low elevation angle. The results show our method's editability of the local lighting. Our disentangled lighting representation also allows the editing of the global lighting since the sun light, sky light and sun position are represented in separate spaces (please refer to supplemental material).

Importance of Sun Visibility Mask. In our method, a predicted sun visibility mask M'_{vis} is used to indicate the effects of the weather and the spatially-varying occlusion of the sun, since whether an object is directly illuminated by the distant sun light will affect its appearance significantly. Such a design is verified by removing the prediction branch of M_{vis} in our lighting estimator and fix $z_{vis} = 1$ (Ours w/o M_{vis}). As we can see from Table 3, without using the information from the predicted sun visibility mask M'_{vis} to constrain the predicted distant sun light component in local lighting, the accuracy of both reconstructed environment maps and relighting results will be degraded.

5.2   Experimental Results

Spatially-Uniform Global Lighting Estimation. We compare global lighting estimation performance of our method (Ours), SkyNet [11], and SOLID-Net [28].

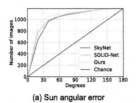 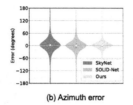 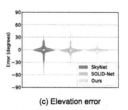

(a) Sun angular error   (b) Azimuth error   (c) Elevation error

Fig. 6. Quantitative evaluation of sun position estimation on our enhanced synthetic dataset. (a) Cumulative curves of the sun angular error of baseline methods and ours. (b) Azimuth errors and (c) elevation errors of the sun position estimation are displayed as 'violin plots', where the envelope of each bin represents the percentile, the gray line represents the percentile of 25% to 75%, and the white point represents the median.

Table 3. Quantitative evaluation of spatially-varying local lighting estimation on our enhanced synthetic dataset. 'Panorama' denotes the errors of panoramic HDR lighting maps before tone mapping. 'Relighting' denotes the errors of rendered HDR images using predicted lighting maps.

Method	Panorama		Relighting	
	MAE	RMSE	MAE	RMSE
Ours	**0.128**	2.394	**0.075**	0.145
Ours w/o M_{vis}	0.140	2.814	0.081	0.159
Ours$_{SH}$	0.190	**1.943**	0.081	**0.139**
Ours$_{SG}$	0.170	2.785	0.093	0.179
SOLID-Net [28]	0.308	3.384	0.186	0.337

To evaluate the sun position estimation, we compute sun angular error, azimuth error, and elevation error on our test set, as shown in Fig. 6. The sun position is calculated as the centroid of the largest connected component of the global lighting panorama above a threshold (98%) [28]. We can see that by treating sun position estimation as a disentangled task, our method achieves favorable improvement over other baseline methods in sun position estimation.

For quantitative evaluation, we calculate the errors on estimated global lighting of the sky-dome represented in panoramic maps (only the upper half of the predicted global environment maps by SOLID-Net [28] are used for calculation). The panoramas are rotated before evaluation to move the sun to its center [11]. Furthermore, we evaluate the rendering errors[2] on the relighting of a glossy Stanford Bunny [4] using predicted global lighting maps. For panoramic errors in global lighting map estimation, we can see from Table 2 that our method is on par with SkyNet [11] and SOLID-Net [28]. However, our method performs significantly better on relighting results. This is because metrics on outdoor lighting maps are sensitive to even a slight misalignment of high-intensity pixels, while metrics on relighting results are more robust and close to human perception.

---

[2] We calculate rendering errors on pixels belonging to the bunny body.

From the practical point of view, the relighting performance is of more concern. As shown in Fig. 7, our method better preserves the high-frequency information in sun light and our relighting results look more realistic than those of SkyNet [11] and SOLID-Net [28], which predict less high-frequency lighting component resulting in lower errors of panoramic lighting maps.

Spatially-Varying Local Lighting Estimation. We compare local lighting estimation performance of our method (Ours), Ours w/o M_{vis}, Ours$_{\text{SG}}$, Ours$_{\text{SH}}$, and SOLID-Net [28].

A quantitative evaluation of estimated panoramic local lighting maps and the relighting results by the estimated local lighting maps on our test set is shown in Table 3. Our method significantly outperforms the non-parametric method SOLID-Net [28] in both reconstruction and relighting results. The fully parametric methods Ours$_{\text{SH}}$ and Ours$_{\text{SG}}$ generally perform well, which shows the effectiveness of our local feature extraction network allowing spatially-varying prediction in both SH and SG models. Overall, our method achieves state-of-the-art performance with more flexible editability than other methods.

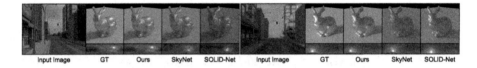

Fig. 7. Relighting results with global lighting maps on our enhanced synthetic dataset.

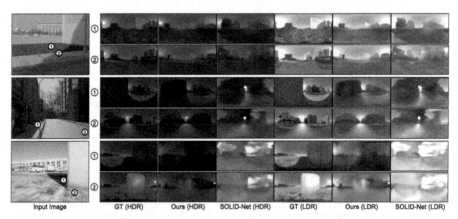

Fig. 8. Qualitative comparison of local lighting estimation results. Column 1 shows the input image and two selected pixel positions. Column 2 and column 5 show the ground truth local lighting environment map in HDR and LDR respectively. Columns 3–4 and columns 6–7 show the estimated local lighting by our method and SOLID-Net [28] in HDR and LDR respectively. The first two rows are from our enhanced synthetic dataset and the last row is from our captured real data.

As shown in the qualitative comparison of local lighting estimation (Fig. 8), our method can recover the major layout of local lighting maps, render local appearances given estimated global lighting conditions, and correctly predict sun visibility, while SOLID-Net [28] suffers from the accumulated errors of the scene geometry estimation and the lack of explicit constraint of sun visibility. Our method does not rely on explicitly estimating accurate geometry and can recover a cleaner environment map with fewer high-frequency artifacts.

We also show relighted bunny results in Fig. 9 for further qualitative comparison of estimated local lighting on our captured real data, which is more challenging due to the dataset shift. We can see that though Ours$_{SH}$ performs well on pixel average, the relighting results are visually unrealistic due to the lack of hard shadows. Ours$_{SG}$ is not as robust as Ours$_{SH}$ on real data. SOLID-Net [28] is misled by inaccurately estimating the complex geometry and shadow clues. Our method performs better visually on both dark and bright regions.

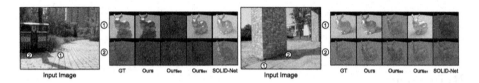

Fig. 9. Qualitative comparison of relighting results on our captured real data.

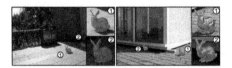

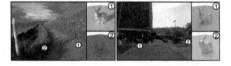

Fig. 10. Examples of virtual object insertion on our captured real data.

Fig. 11. Examples of local lighting estimation on in-the-wild data.

Virtual Object Insertion. A useful application of spatially-varying local lighting estimation is to insert a virtual object into the scene. As shown in Fig. 10, the inserted objects can be realistically relit at the positions of insertions.

Generalization Ability. Although our pipeline is trained on fully synthetic dataset of urban scenes, the spatially-varying properties of lighting in natural scenes can also be captured. Besides, thanks to the synthetic dataset enhancement, our pipeline can work for non-sunny weather, as shown in Fig. 11.

6   Conclusion

In this paper, we propose a novel parametric lighting model with disentangled spaces and formulate lighting estimation on outdoor scenes as an end-to-end learning problem. The major benefit of the proposed method is that it learns a flexible lighting representation that is user-friendly to manipulate. In addition, neither explicit intrinsic estimations nor time-consuming optimization procedures for traditional parametric lighting models are not needed. From extensive experiments and qualitative demonstrations, the effectiveness of the proposed method is verified and the proposed method achieves state-of-the-art performance compared with previous work on both synthetic and real data.

Limitations and Future Work. While our method performs well in estimating at bright regions, it may fail to handle the sharp lighting change near the boundary pixels. Exploring more spatially-coherent local lighting estimation [24] is also an interesting direction for our future work. Besides, our lighting editing only faithfully modifies disentangled components, and automatic harmonization to make the edited lighting more natural will benefit user interaction in the future. A large-scale dataset for spatially-varying lighting in more diverse outdoor scenes will be helpful to boost the training of learning-based methods.

Acknowledgements. This work is supported by National Natural Science Foundation of China under Grant No. 62136001, 61872012.

References

1. ambientCG, public domain materials for physically based rendering. [licensed under CC0 1.0 universal]. https://ambientcg.com
2. Blender SceneCity. https://www.cgchan.com/store/scenecity
3. Poly Haven, The Public 3D Asset Library. [licensed under CC0 1.0 universal]. https://polyhaven.com
4. The Stanford 3D Scanning Repository. http://graphics.stanford.edu/data/3Dscanrep/
5. Barron, J.T., Malik, J.: Intrinsic scene properties from a single RGB-D image. In: Proceedings of Computer Vision and Pattern Recognition (2013)
6. Burley, B.: Physically-based shading at Disney. In: SIGGRAPH Course: Practical Physically Based Shading in Film and Game Production (2012)
7. Cheng, D., Shi, J., Chen, Y., Deng, X., Zhang, X.: Learning scene illumination by pairwise photos from rear and front mobile cameras. Comput. Graph. Forum, **37**(7), 213–221 (2018)
8. Debevec, P.: Rendering synthetic objects into real scenes: bridging traditional and image-based graphics with global illumination and high dynamic range photography. In: Proceedings of ACM SIGGRAPH (1998)
9. Gardner, M.A., Hold-Geoffroy, Y., Sunkavalli, K., Gagné, C., Lalonde, J.F.: Deep parametric indoor lighting estimation. In: Proceedings of International Conference on Computer Vision (2019)
10. Garon, M., Sunkavalli, K., Hadap, S., Carr, N., Lalonde, J.F.: Fast spatially-varying indoor lighting estimation. In: Proceedings of Computer Vision and Pattern Recognition (2019)
11. Hold-Geoffroy, Y., Athawale, A., Lalonde, J.F.: Deep sky modeling for single image outdoor lighting estimation. In: Proceedings of Computer Vision and Pattern Recognition (2019)

12. Hold-Geoffroy, Y., Sunkavalli, K., Hadap, S., Gambaretto, E., Lalonde, J.F.: Deep outdoor illumination estimation. In: Proceedings of Computer Vision and Pattern Recognition (2017)
13. Hosek, L., Wilkie, A.: An analytic model for full spectral sky-dome radiance. ACM Trans. Graph. (TOG) **31**(4), 1–9 (2012)
14. Hosek, L., Wilkie, A.: Adding a solar-radiance function to the Hošek-Wilkie skylight model. IEEE Comput. Graphics Appl. **33**(3), 44–52 (2013)
15. Lalonde, J.F., Efros, A.A., Narasimhan, S.G.: Estimating the natural illumination conditions from a single outdoor image. Int. J. Comput. Vision **98**(2), 123–145 (2012)
16. Lalonde, J.F., et al.: The laval HDR sky database. [free license for academic or government-sponsored researchers] (2016). http://sky.hdrdb.com
17. Lalonde, J.F., Matthews, I.: Lighting estimation in outdoor image collections. In: Proceedings of International Conference on 3D Vision (2014)
18. LeGendre, C., et al.: DeepLight: learning illumination for unconstrained mobile mixed reality. In: Proceedings of Computer Vision and Pattern Recognition (2019)
19. Li, Z., Shafiei, M., Ramamoorthi, R., Sunkavalli, K., Chandraker, M.: Inverse rendering for complex indoor scenes: shape, spatially-varying lighting and SVBRDF from a single image. In: Proceedings of Computer Vision and Pattern Recognition (2020)
20. Newell, A., Yang, K., Deng, J.: Stacked hourglass networks for human pose estimation. In: Leibe, B., Matas, J., Sebe, N., Welling, M. (eds.) ECCV 2016. LNCS, vol. 9912, pp. 483–499. Springer, Cham (2016). https://doi.org/10.1007/978-3-319-46484-8_29
21. Ramamoorthi, R., Hanrahan, P.: An efficient representation for irradiance environment maps. In: Proceedings of ACM SIGGRAPH (2001)
22. Saito, S., Huang, Z., Natsume, R., Morishima, S., Kanazawa, A., Li, H.: PIFu: pixel-aligned implicit function for high-resolution clothed human digitization. In: Proceedings of International Conference on Computer Vision (2019)
23. Song, S., Funkhouser, T.: Neural illumination: lighting prediction for indoor environments. In: Proceedings of Computer Vision and Pattern Recognition (2019)
24. Srinivasan, P.P., Mildenhall, B., Tancik, M., Barron, J.T., Tucker, R., Snavely, N.: Lighthouse: predicting lighting volumes for spatially-coherent illumination. In: Proceedings of Computer Vision and Pattern Recognition (2020)
25. Stumpfel, J., Jones, A., Wenger, A., Tchou, C., Hawkins, T., Debevec, P.: Direct HDR capture of the sun and sky. In: Proceedings of ACM SIGGRAPH (2004)
26. Yu, P., et al.: Hierarchical disentangled representation learning for outdoor illumination estimation and editing. In: Proceedings of International Conference on Computer Vision (2021)
27. Zhang, J., Sunkavalli, K., Hold-Geoffroy, Y., Hadap, S., Eisenmann, J., Lalonde, J.F.: All-weather deep outdoor lighting estimation. In: Proceedings of Computer Vision and Pattern Recognition (2019)
28. Zhu, Y., Zhang, Y., Li, S., Shi, B.: Spatially-varying outdoor lighting estimation from intrinsics. In: Proceedings of Computer Vision and Pattern Recognition (2021)

Boosting Event Stream Super-Resolution with a Recurrent Neural Network

Wenming Weng⬭, Yueyi Zhang$^{(\boxtimes)}$⬭, and Zhiwei Xiong⬭

University of Science and Technology of China, Hefei, China
wmweng@mail.ustc.edu.cn, {zhyuey,zwxiong}@ustc.edu.cn

Abstract. Existing methods for event stream super-resolution (SR) either require high-quality and high-resolution frames or underperform for large factor SR. To address these problems, we propose a recurrent neural network for event SR without frames. First, we design a temporal propagation net for incorporating neighboring and long-range event-aware contexts that facilitates event SR. Second, we build a spatiotemporal fusion net for reliably aggregating the spatiotemporal clues of event stream. These two elaborate components are tightly synergized for achieving satisfying event SR results even for 16× SR. Synthetic and real-world experimental results demonstrate the clear superiority of our method. Furthermore, we evaluate our method on two downstream event-driven applications, i.e., object recognition and video reconstruction, achieving remarkable performance boost over existing methods.

Keywords: Event camera · Super-resolution · Recurrent network

1 Introduction

Event cameras, the novel bio-inspired imaging sensors, have accelerated the innovation in machine vision-enabled systems [4,13,43]. By taking a clue from human vision system, event cameras release a new form of vision capture enabling a promising ability to support diverse operating requirements such as stringent power consumption, demanding memory needs, high speed motion perception, and high dynamic range (HDR) scene imaging [13]. Therefore, the use of event cameras has fast gained wide acceptance recently [1,3,9,14,15,20,22,27,30,37–42,44–47,52–55,59,68–71,73].

In spite of many advantages, the spatial resolution of most commercial event cameras is relatively low due to the physical limitation [43]. Although some high-resolution (HR) devices, such as Prophesee Gen4 CD event cameras, have been developed, they are inevitably limited by low speed and high power consumption. To reconcile this problem, some works have been proposed to approach the event super-resolution (SR) task. Duan et al. [12] and Wang et al. [58]

Supplementary Information The online version contains supplementary material available at https://doi.org/10.1007/978-3-031-20068-7_27.

ⓒ The Author(s), under exclusive license to Springer Nature Switzerland AG 2022
S. Avidan et al. (Eds.): ECCV 2022, LNCS 13666, pp. 470–488, 2022.
https://doi.org/10.1007/978-3-031-20068-7_27

attempted to directly predict a super-resolved event count map via deep learning techniques or optimization frameworks for restoring HR event streams. Li et al. [34] and Li et al. [33] performed event SR by simultaneously estimating the spatiotemporal distribution using either a sparse signal representation [64] with a non-homogeneous poisson process or spiking neural networks (SNNs) [18]. However, these methods still have two major limitations: **1)** Joint filtering with intensity frames for restoring the HR event stream relies heavily on the quality of HR frames and the accuracy of optical flow estimation, which is computationally expensive [58]. **2)** Super-resolving event streams by large factors i.e., 8×, 16×, is rather comprehensively unexplored due to tough network training [12,34] or inaccurate spatiotemporal distribution estimation [33].

This work aims to address the above two challenges. Ideally, frame-assisted event SR strongly demands high-quality HR frames. However, the capture of RGB cameras is susceptible to deterioration caused by harsh environments, e.g., high speed motion and HDR scenes, leading to blurry and over(under)-exposure frames that may harm event SR due to the lack of sharp edges. Moreover, further processing of frames for accurate optical flow is typically time-consuming [58]. In this paper, we demonstrate the feasibility of achieving event SR solely with pure events, which is practical for real-world capture without RGB cameras. On the other hand, for large factor event SR, 3D UNet and SNNs used in existing works [12,34] to build an LR-HR projection are intractable to train due to unaccessible memory requirement. It thus calls for multiple times of small-factor SR to obtain large factor SR results, which leads to inevitable performance degradation while sacrificing the running time. In this paper, we make an attempt to use the recurrent neural network for event SR. Without the assistance of frames, we demonstrate that the proposed method is able to achieve the state-of-the-art results in one forward pass, even for 16× SR.

Specifically, we design our recurrent network by constructing two novel components, i.e., a temporal propagation net ($TPNet$) and a spatiotemporal fusion net ($STFNet$). In order to effectively relate and model the sequential temporal correlation of event stream, we devise the $TPNet$ by jointly embedding a local temporal correlation module implemented by the attention mechanism and a global temporal correlation module built upon the recursive state update mechanism. With these two elaborate modules, we can adaptively incorporate the event-aware contexts from both a local range and a global range, favorably promoting event SR. Moreover, for reliably aggregating the local and global temporal correlations captured by the $TPNet$, we build the $STFNet$ that contains a gated temporal fusion module and an adaptive spatiotemporal fusion module, which are tightly collaborated for reliable aggregation.

We summarize our main contributions as four-fold: **1)** We propose an advanced solution using a recurrent neural network to approach event SR, which gets rid of dependence on high-quality and HR frames and suits for large factor SR (even 16×); **2)** We design two novel components, i.e., a temporal propagation net and a spatiotemporal fusion net, for effectively relating and aggregating the sequential spatiotemporal clues of event stream; **3)** Synthetic and real-world

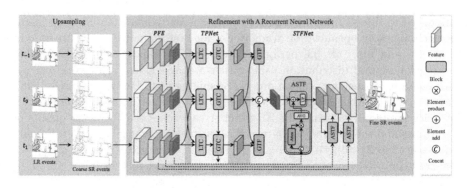

Fig. 1. Overall pipeline. First, the input LR event stream is spatially enlarged by upsampling tools to generate the coarse SR event stream. Then, the recurrent neural network is employed for the fine SR event stream. Three components, i.e., pyramidal feature extractor (PFE), temporal propagation net ($TPNet$) and spatiotemporal fusion net ($STFNet$) are tightly integrated in our recurrent network. The blocks with the same color are sharing weights.

experimental results demonstrate the clear superiority of our method over existing methods for event SR; **4)** Superior performance on two downstream event-driven applications, i.e., object recognition and video reconstruction, reconfirms the effectiveness of our method.

2 Related Work

Frame SR. The frame SR task has been investigated for many years and achieved significant progresses. Classic methods aim to super-resolve images by exploiting the statistical image priors to build a regression function from LR to HR images, which can be achieved by neighbor embedding [2,7], sparse coding [49,50,65,67] and internal patch recurrence [19,24]. The recent deep learning based SR methods have shown excellent performance and dominated the field of frame SR. For single image SR (SISR), Dong et al. [11] first applied convolutional neural networks (CNNs) to build an end-to-end LR-HR mapping for SISR. The works with advanced neural network architectures [32,36,51] are further reported, significantly promoting performance of SISR. For video SR (VSR), VESCP [5] is the pioneering work for approaching VSR by jointly training optical flow estimation and spatiotemporal networks. Recently, more works [6,25,26,28,48,57,61,62] have been proposed by investigating more sophisticated components to address the propagation and alignment problems.

Event SR. Compared with natural images, the event stream, captured by sensing the intensity changes, is essentially a kind of spatiotemporal data. To super-resolve the event stream, accurate spatial and temporal distributions need to be estimated. A few works [12,33,34,58] have been developed to approach event SR.

Similar to hybrid imaging [23,31,56,66], Wang et al. [58] developed a novel optimization framework termed as GEF, which took advantages of both frame-based and event-based sensing, to achieve the HR and noise-robust event stream. However, GEF is severely deteriorated when the auxiliary frame is visually blurry or the optical flow is inaccurately estimated. Duan et al. [12] proposed a novel network based on 3D U-Net with an event-to-image (E2I) module to learn the correspondence between the LR event stream and the HR event stream. Li et al. [33] utilized a sparse signal representation method [64] to acquire the spatial distribution of the event stream and then modeled a spatiotemporal filter to generate the temporal rate function. They finally used a non-homogeneous poisson process to simulate the per-pixel events. To build an end-to-end projection in the event domain, Li et al. [34] proposed a novel learning-based method with SNNs to achieve the HR event stream. The spatiotemporal constraint learning enables SNNs to learn the spatial and temporal distribution simultaneously. These works [12,33,34,58] are pioneers in the field of event SR, however, they either strongly depend on extra frames or fail in dealing with large factor event SR. This paper presents a new method to super-resolve the event stream even by a large factor, without the auxiliary of high-quality and HR frames.

3   Method

3.1   Problem Definition

The output of event cameras can be represented as a sparse stream $\mathcal{E} = \{e_k\}_{k=1}^{N_e}$, where N_e is the number of events. Each event $e_k \in \mathcal{E}$ is denoted as a four-element tuple (x_k, y_k, t_k, p_k), representing spatial coordinates, timestamp and polarity respectively. The problem of event SR is to predict HR event stream based on LR event stream. Specifically, we denote LR event stream as $\mathcal{E}^L = \{e_k^L(x_k^L, y_k^L)\}$ (timestamp and polarity are omitted here for brevity), where $x_k^L \in [1, W^L], y_k^L \in [1, H^L]$. The goal of event SR is to obtain HR event stream $\mathcal{E}^H = \{e_k^H(x_k^H, y_k^H)\}$ using LR event stream $\mathcal{E}^L$. The spatial coordinates of e_k^H are subject to $x_k^H \in [1, W^H], y_k^H \in [1, H^H]$.

The event stream is essentially sparse and spatiotemporal data that is different from natural images. Usually, a three-stage solution [12,58] is utilized to super-resolve the event stream. First, the temporal dimension of LR event stream is reduced by counting the event number to get a 2D LR Event Count Map (ECM), which describes the spatial distribution. Then the LR ECM is further processed by the designed algorithm, generating the HR ECM. Finally, the temporal distribution can be restored by randomly or uniformly assigning the timestamps according to the HR ECM, yielding the final HR event stream.

3.2   Overall Pipeline

In this paper, we construct an upsampling-refinement pipeline for event SR. Specifically, we first upsample LR ECM^L by counting the event number of LR event stream $\mathcal{E}^{\mathrm{L}}$ to acquire coarse SR ECM: $ECM^{\mathrm{SR}}_{coarse} = \mathrm{Upsample}(ECM^{\mathrm{L}})$. Then the refinement is performed on coarse $ECM^{\mathrm{SR}}_{coarse}$ for producing fine ECM: $ECM^{\mathrm{SR}}_{fine} = \mathrm{Refine}(ECM^{\mathrm{SR}}_{coarse})$, which is then redistributed for HR sparse event stream. We illustrate the overview of upsampling-refinement pipeline in Fig. 1.

The commonly-used upsampling tool in frame-based vision, bicubic, can be a natural choice for the operator $\mathrm{Upsample}(\cdot)$. However, bicubic as an interpolation method derives a new value for a new coordinate, inevitably introducing interpolation noise that may be harmful for event SR as shown in Fig. 4. As an alternative, we develop a simpler yet effective upsampling tool tailored for event data, named coordinate relocation. In contrast to bicubic, coordinate relocation is directly performed in event domain, which is noise-free and preserves the spatiotemporal distribution of the input event stream. Specifically, coordinate relocation is used to convert LR event stream $\mathcal{E}^{\mathrm{L}}$ to SR event stream: $\mathcal{E}^{\mathrm{SR}}_{cr} = \mathrm{CoordinateRelocate}(\mathcal{E}^{\mathrm{L}})$. The spatial coordinates of $\mathcal{E}^{\mathrm{SR}}_{cr}$ can be calculated as: $x^{\mathrm{SR}}_{cr} = \mathrm{Round}\left(\frac{x^{\mathrm{L}}}{W^{\mathrm{L}}} \cdot W^{\mathrm{H}}\right)$, $y^{\mathrm{SR}}_{cr} = \mathrm{Round}\left(\frac{y^{\mathrm{L}}}{H^{\mathrm{L}}} \cdot H^{\mathrm{H}}\right)$. The operator $\mathrm{Round}(\cdot)$ is employed to convert the derived coordinates x^{SR}_{cr}, y^{SR}_{cr} to integer values. We then convert $\mathcal{E}^{\mathrm{SR}}_{cr}$ to the coarse SR $ECM^{\mathrm{SR}}_{coarse}$ by counting the event number, which is further enhanced by the refinement network. We provide experimental comparisons between bicubic and coordinate relocation in Sect. 5.

3.3   Recurrent Neural Network for Event SR

Through upsampling operation, we obtain the coarse SR $ECM^{\mathrm{SR}}_{coarse}$. As shown in Fig. 1, $ECM^{\mathrm{SR}}_{coarse}$ is still severely corrupted, calling for further detail restoration to approach the ground-truth ECM^{GT}. To achieve this, we propose a **Rec**urrent neural network for **Ev**ent stream **S**uper-**R**esolution, termed as **RecEvSR**, to model the internal spatiotemporal correlation of event stream. We demonstrate the overview network in Fig. 1. Our RecEvSR consists of three elaborately designed components, i.e., pyramidal feature extractor, temporal propagation net and spatiotemporal fusion net. In the following, we elaborate the motivations of designing these network components.

Pyramidal Feature Extractor (PFE). After upsampling the LR event stream $\mathcal{E}^{\mathrm{L}}$, we consider the sequence of $ECM^{\mathrm{SR}}_{coarse}$ as the input to the pyramidal feature extractor. The potential reason of choosing a sequence is related to the balance between expensive computation of event-by-event processing and temporal correlation loss of event-by-count processing. As aforementioned in Sect. 3.2, producing ECM is computationally tractable, yet inevitably introduces temporal correlation loss. Therefore, all $ECM^{\mathrm{SR}}_{coarse}$ in a sequence are utilized as a remedy for partially recovering the lost temporal correlation in a single ECM. The number of ECM in a sequence is 3 for all experiments (as in Fig. 1), which can be increased for better results but with high training cost.

Specifically, our pyramidal feature extractor consists of a head and three stacked convolutional blocks. The head is employed to transform each $ECM^{\mathrm{SR}}_{coarse}$ in a sequence to a high-dimensional feature while keeping the spatial resolution. Subsequently, three stacked convolutional blocks further embed

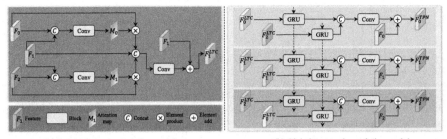

(a) Local temporal correlation module (b) Global temporal correlation module

Fig. 2. The details of temporal propagation net, which consists of a local temporal correlation module and a global temporal correlation module. Zoom in for best view.

the sequence of high-dimensional features while reducing the spatial resolution by $2\times$ step by step. In such a way, we finally obtain the deep pyramidal features at different timestamps, forming a feature sequence

$$Seq[F_{PFE}] = PFE(Seq[ECM^{SR}_{coarse}]), \tag{1}$$

where $Seq[\cdot]$ denotes a sequence of specified components. We omit the timestamp for brevity.

Notably, the pyramidal feature sequence generated by PFE implies two kinds of hidden clues: the temporal clues encoded by the same-scale features at different timestamps and the spatial clues encoded by the different-scale features at the same timestamp. We need to answer two questions here: **1)** how to excavate the temporal clues? **2)** how to aggregate the spatiotemporal clues?

Temporal Propagation Net (TPNet). At the beginning, let's take the first question into account. As discussed above, PFE is utilized to embed the input sequence of ECM^{SR}_{coarse} to acquire the deep pyramidal features at each timestamp. However, the temporal correlation among the deep pyramid features over different timestamps are not considered explicitly or implicitly, inevitably resulting in loss of intersected temporal event-aware information that favorably promotes event SR. To solve this problem, we build a temporal propagation net to further recover the lost intersected temporal clues.

Inspired by [60,63], we design the temporal propagation net by constructing two separated modules: local temporal correlation module (LTC) for locally modeling short-term temporal clues, and global temporal correlation module (GTC) for globally modeling long-term temporal clues. As shown in Fig. 2, for each timestamp, LTC take as input the feature sequence $Seq[F_{PFE}]$: $\{F_0, F_1, F_2\}$ generated by PFE. For efficient processing, we only utilize the features with the smallest scale. We then use two convolutional blocks to produce two spatial attention maps $\{M_0, M_1\}$, which describe the spatial reliability of $\{F_0, F_2\}$. The rectified boundary features and central feature are concatenated and fused with a residual connection to obtain the final output F_1^{LTC}. For GTC, we choose the bidirectional temporal propagation [60,63] built upon

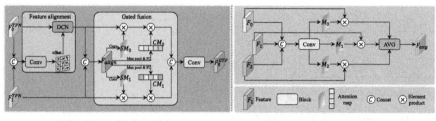

(a) Gated temporal fusion module   (b) Adaptive spatiotemporal fusion module

Fig. 3. The details of spatiotemporal fusion net, which consists of a gated temporal fusion module and an adaptive spatiotemporal module. Zoom in for best view.

GRU [8], for fully exploring the global temporal information of event streams. First bidirectional local temporal feature sequences: $\{F_0^{LTC}, F_1^{LTC}, F_2^{LTC}\}$ and $\{F_2^{LTC}, F_1^{LTC}, F_0^{LTC}\}$ are generated, which are then fed into GRU. We concatenate the outputs of GRU at each timestamp and then embed them before adding the original central feature sequence $\{F_0, F_1, F_2\}$ to obtain the final output $Seq[F_{TPN}] : \{F_0^{TPN}, F_1^{TPN}, F_2^{TPN}\}$. The forward process of $TPNet$ can be formulated as

$$Seq[F_{TPN}] = GTC(LTC(Seq[F_{PFE}])). \tag{2}$$

The designed LTC module implemented by attention mechanism is responsible for adaptively incorporating the neighboring event-aware contexts, which facilitates event SR from a local range. Exploiting recursive state update mechanism, GTC module is capable of implicitly embedding spatiotemporal clues of event stream into internal memories of the model for effective propagation in a long-range event sequence, thus favorably boosting event SR from a global range. The resultant F_{TPN} preserves the local and global temporal correlation simultaneously, capable of recovering fine-grained event-aware details.

Spatiotemporal Fusion Net (STFNet). We then answer the second question. As aforementioned, the feature sequence $Seq[F_{TPN}]$ generated by $TPNet$ captures intersected temporal clues both locally and globally. Nevertheless, each F_{PFE} in $Seq[F_{PFE}]$ maintains the unique spatiotemporal context details from currently fired events that are not included in other F_{PFE}. In order to acquire the embedded representation at the central timestamp, we design a spatiotemporal fusion net, which consists of a gated temporal fusion module (GTF) and an adaptive spatiotemporal fusion module ($ASTF$). Particularly, GTF aggregates the $Seq[F_{TPN}]$ by $TPNet$ using feature alignment and attention-based gated fusion for producing reliable output, while $ASTF$ is responsible for progressively aligning pyramidal sequence $Seq[F_{PFE}]$ by PFE using adaptive selection, meanwhile forming a skip connection for favoring network training (see Fig. 1).

As shown in Fig. 3, for GTF, we fuse the outputs by $TPNet$: $\{F_0^{TPN}, F_1^{TPN}\}$ via a two-stage process. First, we align the feature F_0^{TPN} to the central timestamp using the deformable neural network (DCN) [10,72]. Then, we concatenate the output of DCN with the central feature F_1^{TPN} to further produce the spatial attention maps $\{SM_0, SM_1\}$ and channel attention maps $\{CM_0, CM_1\}$ for fusing features in both spatial and channel dimensions. For $ASTF$, we use the skip connection to aggregate the outputs of PFE and $TPNet$. Specifically, for each scale (three scales in PFE), the feature sequence generated by PFE is first concatenated and then embedded by a convolutional block to produce three spatial attention maps $\{M_0, M_1, M_2\}$, representing the reliability of input features at different timestamps. We then average the weighted features before adding the aligned feature by GTF for final output as shown in Fig. 1. Mathematically, the central feature can be derived as

$$F_C = STFNet(Seq[F_{PFE}], Seq[F_{TPN}]). \tag{3}$$

The resultant F_C is then employed to reconstruct the ECM_{fine}^{SR}, which is further redistributed to the final sparse event stream.

Objective Function. We train our RecEvSR in a sequence clip, of which the length is further investigated in Sect. 5. Given the reconstructed $ECM_{fine,t}^{SR}$ and its ground-truth ECM_t^{GT} at timestamp t, we define the loss function $\mathcal{L}$ as

$$\mathcal{L} = \sum_{t=1}^{T} MSE(ECM_{fine,t}^{SR}, ECM_t^{GT}), \tag{4}$$

where T denotes the number of ECM_{fine}^{SR} in a sequence clip and $MSE(\cdot)$ represents the mean square error function.

4 Experimental Results

To validate the effectiveness of our proposed method, we conduct comprehensive experiments on both synthetic and real-world datasets, and evaluate the performance in both quantitative and qualitative ways.

Datasets and Settings. ENFS-real [12] is the first real-world dataset involving multi-scale LR-HR pairs for event SR, captured by a display-camera system. However, the resolution of this dataset is limited by the capturing devices and $8(16)\times$ data pairs are not developed. As a remedy, based on NFS [29], we first generate multi-scale frames and then convert them to events using the event simulator [16] for building a new synthetic dataset, termed as ENFS-syn, which involves $2(4, 8, 16)\times$ LR-HR pairs for training and testing. Our ENFS-syn contains 161 sequences for 65 scenes. The duration of each sequence is no more than 30 s. The maximum resolution is 1280×720, while the minimum resolution is 80×45. Moreover, we also utilize the HR frames from RGB-DAVIS [58] to synthesize another synthetic dataset called RGB-DAVIS-syn. Each aforementioned dataset is randomly splitted for training and testing. Following [12,58], we use RMSE as the evaluation metric. We also apply random horizontal, vertical and polarity flip for data augmentation in training. Please see the supplementary document for details of synthetic datasets and more experimental settings.

Baselines. We make comparisons with EventZoom [12], the first learning-based method for approaching event SR. We use the code provided by the project to

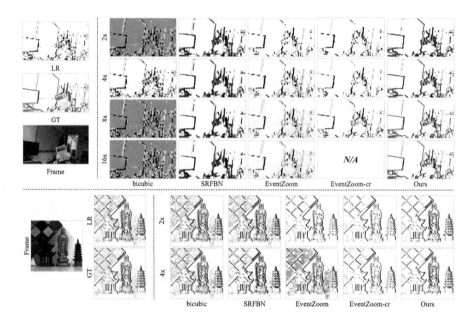

Fig. 4. Visual comparisons on synthetic datasets among bicubic, SRFBN [35], Event-Zoom [12], EventZoom-cr and ours. The first case (upper) is from ENFS-syn and the second case (below) is from RGB-DAVIS-syn. The 16× SR results of EventZoom-cr are not provided due to high training cost. Blue/red regions denote positive/negative events. Obviously for large factor SR, with severely corrupted LR events as the input, our method still recovers perceptually fine details. Bicubic introduces interpolation noise. SRFBN [35] cannot estimate the visual-satisfying results and EventZoom [12] fires wrong events. Zoom in for best view. (Color figure online)

Table 1. Quantitative comparisons among bicubic, SRFBN [35], EventZoom [12], EventZoom-cr and ours on synthetic and real-world datasets in terms of RMSE. Best in bold.

Methods	2×	4×	8×	16×	2×	4×	2×	4×
	ENFS-syn				RGB-DAVIS-syn		ENFS-real	
bicubic	0.821	0.784	0.791	0.764	0.387	0.378	0.899	0.969
SRFBN	0.694	0.690	0.708	0.678	0.366	0.362	0.669	0.753
EventZoom	0.843	1.036	2.385	5.970	0.583	1.100	0.773	0.910
EventZoom-cr	0.844	0.833	0.823	-	0.604	0.614	0.775	0.828
Ours	**0.686**	**0.653**	**0.617**	**0.582**	**0.352**	**0.329**	**0.663**	**0.663**

conduct all experiments. We retrained the E2I module in EventZoom to construct the whole architecture as suggested. For large factor SR, we run the EventZoom-2× model multiple times, which is also adopted in [12]. We have tried to train a single EventZoom for large factor SR but failed due to expen-

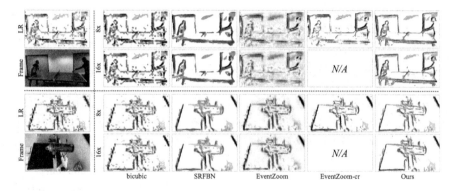

Fig. 5. Visual comparisons for large factor SR (8(16) ×) on real-world dataset (ENFS-real) among bicubic, SRFBN [35], EventZoom [12], EventZoom-cr and ours. The 16× SR results of EventZoom-cr are not provided due to high training cost. Obviously, we achieve superior performance for large factor SR compared with baselines, though our network is trained using synthetic datasets, which demonstrates our outstanding generalization ability against baselines. Zoom in for best view.

sive training cost of 3D-UNet. Moreover, we construct a variant of EventZoom, termed as EventZoom-cr, by combining EventZoom-1x [12] and coordinate relocation upsampling. As for other event SR methods [33,34,58], they either need frames as an auxiliary or only fit simple scenes, posing a challenge to make a fair comparison with them. We also make comparisons with the representative methods of frame-based SR, i.e., bicubic and SRFBN [35], which are omitted in [12]. It should be noted that directly applying the framed-based SR methods to super-resolve event streams may fail. For example, we found it hard to train the representative video SR method, RBPN [21], for the event SR task. We attribute it to two reasons: 1) value of ECM represents spatial distribution that is unlimited, while value of frame is typically no more than 255; 2) ECM is sparse and primarily contains edge information, while frame is dense and reflects more conceptual contexts. The essential discrepancy of event data and frame data motivates us to design the specific algorithm for event SR instead of direct adoption of existing frame-based SR methods.

Results on Synthetic Datasets. We present the quantitative comparison results on the synthetic datasets, i.e., ENFS-syn and RGB-DAVIS-syn, in Table 1. Compared with EventZoom, in terms of RMSE, our method achieves near 30% performance boost on average for 2(4)× SR on two datasets. For 8(16)× SR, our method presents clear superiority over EventZoom, yielding over 80% average RMSE gain on ENFS-syn. Compared with frame-based methods, our method still performs favorably against bicubic and SRFBN especially for 8(16)× SR, achieving a relative gain of over 19% in terms of RMSE on ENFS-syn. Furthermore, EventZoom-cr with coordinate relocation upsampling is able to significantly boost EventZoom for large factor SR, achieving 65.49% and 44.18% RMSE gain for 8× SR on ENFS-syn and 4× SR on RGB-DAVIS-syn, respec-

Table 2. Quantitative results of additive noise evaluation in terms of RMSE.

Methods	0	10%	20%	30%
bicubic	0.784	0.797	0.812	0.827
SRFBN	0.689	0.692	0.696	0.701
EventZoom	1.036	1.063	1.082	1.093
EventZoom-cr	0.833	0.830	0.829	0.831
Ours	**0.653**	**0.659**	**0.667**	**0.676**

Table 3. Ablation on upsampling method and recurrent neural network. "bi" means bicubic, "cr" means coordinate relocation.

Methods	2×	4×	8×
	RMSE ↓		
EventZoom	0.843	1.036	2.385
EventZoom-bi	0.845	0.833	0.838
EventZoom-cr	0.844	0.833	0.823
RecEvSR-bi	0.694	0.655	0.619
RecEvSR-cr (Ours)	**0.686**	**0.653**	**0.617**
	Upsampling time (ms)		
bicubic	57.6	217.3	892.2
coordinate relocation	**0.2**	**0.2**	**0.2**

Table 4. Ablation on network components. RMSE value is reported.

Variants	LTC	GTC	GTF	ASTF	RMSE
model#A	×	✓	✓	✓	0.704
model#B	✓	×	✓	✓	0.697
model#C	✓	✓	×	✓	0.701
model#D	✓	✓	✓	×	0.698
model#E	✓	✓	✓	✓	**0.695**

Table 5. Ablation on training settings. RMSE value is reported.

Metrics	Sequence length				Augmentation	
	3	6	9	12	w/o aug	w/ aug
RMSE	0.699	0.691	0.689	**0.687**	0.693	**0.688**

tively. For qualitative comparison, we visualize the super-resolved event streams of all methods in Fig. 4. We can see that our method can restore perceptually better texture details and sharper edges from the severely corrupted LR event stream, accurately presenting the complex scene motion variation, especially for $8(16)\times$ SR. The interpolation noise of bicubic can be obviously observed in Fig. 4, leading to harmful interference for event SR. Notably, although the numerical results in Table 1 show that EventZoom underperforms bicubic, the visual results of EventZoom in Fig. 4 are better than those of bicubic. We present more visual results in the supplementary document.

Results on Real-World Dataset. For real-world evaluation on ENFS-real [12], we give the quantitative results in Table 1. In terms of RMSE for $2(4)\times$ SR, our method achieves performance boost on average of 20% over EventZoom (EventZoom-cr) and 17% over frame-based methods. For $8(16)\times$ SR, we cannot provide the quantitative comparisons due to no ground-truth data in the ENFS-real. Therefore, we only exhibit the visual results in Fig. 5, using the pre-trained models on our synthetic ENFS-syn to super-resolve the LR event streams in ENFS-real. It can be clearly observed from Fig. 5 that, although with the severely-corrupted LR event stream as the input, we achieve the visually-satisfying real-world 8(16)× SR results with fine-grained textures against base-lines, presenting the strong generalization over baselines. More real-world visual results can be found in the supplementary document.

Results of Noise Robustness Evaluation. We also conduct noise robustness evaluation on ENFS-syn by adding the extra random noise into input event stream. We manually control the noise level, the percentage of input event number, to investigate the effect of noise for different methods. We conduct 4× SR for this experiment. Table 2 presents the numerical results. As can be seen, our method achieves best results compared with others, demonstrating the satisfying noise robustness of our method.

5   Ablation Study

In this section, we present more experimental analysis of our method from four aspects: upsampling method, recurrent neural network, recurrent network components and training settings. Before presenting the detailed results, we describe a nomenclature for the variants. The names of variants follow the pattern "A-B", where "B" represents the upsampling method to spatially zooming LR events and "A" represents the backbone network for further refinement. We conduct the ablation experiments on ENFS-syn.

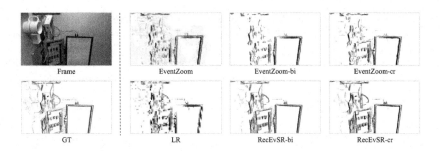

Fig. 6. Visual comparisons of ablation on upsampling method and recurrent network. "bi" means bicubic, "cr" means coordinate relocation. 4× SR results on ENFS-syn are presented. Zoom in for best view.

Ablation on Upsampling Method. Compared with bicubic upsampling, here we investigate how well our coordinate relocation behaves from two perspectives: 1) Can coordinate relocation perform better than bicubic? For fair comparisons, we keep the same refinement network except upsampling method. We choose EventZoom and our proposed RecEvSR as refinement network to explore how these two upsampling tools perform. As shown in Table 3, EventZoom-cr/RecEvSR-cr perform favorably against EventZoom-bi/RecEvSR-bi for 2(4, 8)× SR in terms of RMSE, reinforcing the effectiveness of coordinate relocation. Particularly, coordinate relocation is more efficient than bicubic in terms of upsampling time, as shown in Table 3. The visual results in Fig. 6 show that refinement network with coordinate relocation is able to provide more edges that are suppressed by with bicubic. **2)** Can coordinate relocation be combined with other methods and boost them? In order to validate the generality of coordinate relocation and if it synthesizes well with other methods, we choose "A" as EventZoom. We show the quantitative results in Table 3. As can be seen, EventZoom-cr shows favorable performance against EventZoom especially for $4(8)\times$ SR, demonstrating the generality of coordinate relocation to boost other methods. The visual results in Fig. 6 further present that EventZoom-cr provides more perceptually-satisfying details against EventZoom.

Ablation on Recurrent Neural Network. As aforementioned in Sect. 3.3, we build a recurrent neural network to model the internal spatiotemporal correlation of event stream by exploiting the recursive state update mechanism. In order to validate the effectiveness of our RecEvSR, we keep the same upsampling method "A". In such a way, the only different part is the choice of refinement network. It can be clearly observed from Table 3 that, RecEvSR-bi/RecEvSR-cr consistently surpasses EventZoom-bi/EventZoom-cr in terms of RMSE, demonstrating the superiority of our RecEvSR. The results in Fig. 6 also provide visual supports.

Ablation on Recurrent Network Components. In order to validate the effectiveness of the designed components of our recurrent neural network, we

Table 6. Quantitative results of downstream applications among bicubic, SRFBN [35], EventZoom [12], EventZoom-cr and ours on NCars [47] for object recognition and on ENFS-syn for video reconstruction. We evaluate object recognition using area under curve (AUC) and recognition accuracy (ACC). For video reconstruction, we show SSIM and LPIPS values. Best in bold, the runner up with underline.

Methods	Object recognition					
	$2\times$		$4\times$		$8\times$	
	AUC↑	ACC↑	AUC↑	ACC↑	AUC↑	ACC↑
bicubic	57.25	56.46	56.46	55.66	51.11	50.08
SRFBN	57.39	56.54	56.64	55.82	<u>51.32</u>	<u>50.29</u>
EventZoom	55.98	54.99	50.91	49.92	49.93	48.85
EventZoom-cr	<u>60.24</u>	<u>59.44</u>	<u>57.74</u>	<u>56.94</u>	50.59	49.58
Ours	**63.65**	**62.85**	**62.94**	**62.24**	**53.30**	**52.23**
Ref	85.29	85.23	93.20	93.38	95.33	95.31
Methods	Video reconstruction					
	SSIM↑	LPIPS↓	SSIM↑	LPIPS↓	SSIM↑	LPIPS↓
bicubic	0.562	0.399	0.615	0.516	<u>0.607</u>	0.577
SRFBN	<u>0.596</u>	0.397	0.605	0.493	0.602	<u>0.534</u>
EventZoom	0.555	0.413	0.586	0.480	0.582	0.563
EventZoom-cr	0.583	<u>0.393</u>	**0.657**	<u>0.434</u>	0.593	0.548
Ours	**0.609**	**0.375**	<u>0.643</u>	**0.422**	**0.626**	**0.473**

ablate each sub-network to form different variants to conduct the experiments on ENFS-syn. As shown in Table 4, our network with all sub-networks (model#E) achieves the best performance compared with other variants for 2× SR.

Ablation on Training Settings. 1) Sequence length. In order to investigate the influence of length of training sequence clip, we conduct ablation experiments on ENFS-syn and show the 2× SR results in Table 5. Obviously, the longer the training sequence is, the better results we can achieve. It implies that a longer training sequence may provide more reliable hidden states, which can be exploited by our recurrent network. However, longer training sequences result in high training cost, thus we choose 9 as the sequence length in all our experiments. **2)** Data augmentation. We also conduct the ablation experiments on the data augmentation as discussed in Sect. 4. As shown in Table 5, when disabling the data augmentation, the network shows the performance drop for 2× SR.

6   Downstream Event-Driven Applications

Object Recognition. We investigate the performance of bicubic, SRFBN [35], EventZoom [12], EventZoom-cr and our method on object recognition application. One popular event-based dataset: NCars [47] are utilized for experiments. We utilize the coordinate relocation reverse operation to down-sample the original event stream for 8×. After that, we perform different SR methods to up-sample the LR event stream for 2(4, 8)×. Then we conduct object recognition using the benchmark classifier proposed in [17]. Table 6 presents the evaluation results. We report area under curve (AUC) and accuracy (ACC) for evaluation. The row "Ref." means using the event stream directly down-sampled from the original event stream, which is the upper-bound. It can be observed from row "Ref." that AUC (ACC) intensifies as the resolution of the input event stream increases, demonstrating that higher resolution gives rise to better performance. As for the performance of different SR methods, we can see that our RecEvSR achieves the best performance compared with other methods. Furthermore, EventZoom-cr outperforms EventZoom by a large margin especially for 4(8)× SR, validating the effectiveness of upsampling with coordinate relocation.

Video Reconstruction. We also evaluate bicubic, SRFBN [35], Event-Zoom [12], EventZoom-cr and our method on video reconstruction application. ENFS-syn is employed for this task, because it provides the synchronized ground-truth frames for comparison. The E2VID [45] is chosen as the benchmark algorithm for event-to-video reconstruction with the evaluation metrics of SSIM and LPIPS. Table 6 shows the numerical results. Obviously, our method achieves the best result in terms of SSIM and LPIPS for 2(4, 8)× SR except that EventZoom-cr shows best SSIM for 4× SR. Comparing EventZoom with EventZoom-cr, we can see the significant performance boost achieved by EventZoom-cr, further validating the superiority of the combination of EventZoom and coordinate relocation on video reconstruction. The visual results in Fig. 7 clearly show that our method achieves perceptually fine details, in contrast to the artifacts produced

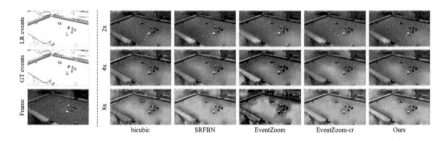

Fig. 7. Visual comparisons of video reconstruction among bicubic, SRFBN [35], EventZoom [12], EventZoom-cr and ours on ENFS-syn. Zoom in for best view.

by bicubic and EventZoom. We present more visual results in the supplementary document.

7   Conclusion

In this paper, we propose a recurrent neural network for event SR without assistance of frames, which suits for large factor SR. Two elaborate components, i.e., a temporal propagation net and a spatiotemporal fusion net, are built, leading to effective correlation and aggregation of event-aware contexts that enhance event SR. We demonstrate the visually-satisfying event SR results even up to $16\times$ both on synthetic and real-world datasets and validate the superiority of our method against the state-of-the-art methods with extensive experiments, quantitatively and qualitatively. Superior performance is also achieved by our method on two downstream event-driven tasks.

Acknowledgements. We acknowledge funding from National Key R&D Program of China under Grant 2017YFA0700800, National Natural Science Foundation of China under Grants 61901435, 62131003 and 62021001.

References

1. Amir, A., et al.: A low power, fully event-based gesture recognition system. In: CVPR (2017)
2. Bevilacqua, M., Roumy, A., Guillemot, C., Alberi-Morel, M.L.: Low-complexity single-image super-resolution based on nonnegative neighbor embedding (2012)
3. Bi, Y., Chadha, A., Abbas, A., Bourtsoulatze, E., Andreopoulos, Y.: Graph-based object classification for neuromorphic vision sensing. In: ICCV (2019)
4. Brandli, C., Berner, R., Yang, M., Liu, S.C., Delbruck, T.: A 240× 180 130 db 3 μs latency global shutter spatiotemporal vision sensor. IEEE J. Solid-State Circuits **49**(10), 2333–2341 (2014)
5. Caballero, J., et al.: Real-time video super-resolution with spatio-temporal networks and motion compensation. In: CVPR (2017)
6. Chan, K.C., Wang, X., Yu, K., Dong, C., Loy, C.C.: Basicvsr: the search for essential components in video super-resolution and beyond. In: CVPR (2021)

7. Chang, H., Yeung, D.Y., Xiong, Y.: Super-resolution through neighbor embedding. In: CVPR (2004)
8. Cho, K., et al.: Learning phrase representations using rnn encoder-decoder for statistical machine translation. arXiv preprint arXiv:1406.1078 (2014)
9. Choi, J., Yoon, K.J., et al.: Learning to super resolve intensity images from events. In: CVPR (2020)
10. Dai, J., et al.: Deformable convolutional networks. In: ICCV (2017)
11. Dong, C., Loy, C.C., He, K., Tang, X.: Learning a deep convolutional network for image super-resolution. In: Fleet, D., Pajdla, T., Schiele, B., Tuytelaars, T. (eds.) ECCV 2014. LNCS, vol. 8692, pp. 184–199. Springer, Cham (2014). https://doi.org/10.1007/978-3-319-10593-2_13
12. Duan, P., Wang, Z.W., Zhou, X., Ma, Y., Shi, B.: Eventzoom: learning to denoise and super resolve neuromorphic events. In: CVPR (2021)
13. Gallego, G., et al.: Event-based vision: a survey. IEEE Trans. Pattern Anal. Mach. Intell. (2020). https://doi.org/10.1109/TPAMI.2020.3008413
14. Gallego, G., Lund, J.E., Mueggler, E., Rebecq, H., Delbruck, T., Scaramuzza, D.: Event-based, 6-DOF camera tracking from photometric depth maps. IEEE Trans. Pattern Anal. Mach. Intell. 40(10), 2402–2412 (2017)
15. Gallego, G., Rebecq, H., Scaramuzza, D.: A unifying contrast maximization framework for event cameras, with applications to motion, depth, and optical flow estimation. In: CVPR (2018)
16. Gehrig, D., Gehrig, M., Hidalgo-Carrió, J., Scaramuzza, D.: Video to events: recycling video datasets for event cameras. In: CVPR (2020)
17. Gehrig, D., Loquercio, A., Derpanis, K.G., Scaramuzza, D.: End-to-end learning of representations for asynchronous event-based data. In: ICCV (2019)
18. Gerstner, W., Kistler, W.M.: Spiking Neuron Models: Single Neurons, Populations, Plasticity. Cambridge University Press, Cambridge (2002)
19. Glasner, D., Bagon, S., Irani, M.: Super-resolution from a single image. In: ICCV (2009)
20. Gu, C., Learned-Miller, E., Sheldon, D., Gallego, G., Bideau, P.: The spatio-temporal poisson point process: a simple model for the alignment of event camera data. In: ICCV (2021)
21. Haris, M., Shakhnarovich, G., Ukita, N.: Recurrent back-projection network for video super-resolution. In: CVPR (2019)
22. He, W., et al.: Timereplayer: unlocking the potential of event cameras for video interpolation. In: CVPR (2022)
23. Heist, S., Zhang, C., Reichwald, K., Kühmstedt, P., Notni, G., Tünnermann, A.: 5D hyperspectral imaging: fast and accurate measurement of surface shape and spectral characteristics using structured light. Opt. Express 26(18), 23366–23379 (2018)
24. Huang, J.B., Singh, A., Ahuja, N.: Single image super-resolution from transformed self-exemplars. In: CVPR (2015)
25. Isobe, T., Jia, X., Gu, S., Li, S., Wang, S., Tian, Q.: Video super-resolution with recurrent structure-detail network. In: Vedaldi, A., Bischof, H., Brox, T., Frahm, J.-M. (eds.) ECCV 2020. LNCS, vol. 12357, pp. 645–660. Springer, Cham (2020). https://doi.org/10.1007/978-3-030-58610-2_38
26. Isobe, T., Zhu, F., Jia, X., Wang, S.: Revisiting temporal modeling for video super-resolution. In: BMVC (2020)
27. Jiang, Z., Zhang, Y., Zou, D., Ren, J., Lv, J., Liu, Y.: Learning event-based motion deblurring. In: CVPR (2020)

28. Jo, Y., Oh, S.W., Kang, J., Kim, S.J.: Deep video super-resolution network using dynamic upsampling filters without explicit motion compensation. In: CVPR (2018)

29. Kiani Galoogahi, H., Fagg, A., Huang, C., Ramanan, D., Lucey, S.: Need for speed: a benchmark for higher frame rate object tracking. In: ICCV (2017)

30. Kim, H., Leutenegger, S., Davison, A.J.: Real-time 3D reconstruction and 6-DoF tracking with an event camera. In: Leibe, B., Matas, J., Sebe, N., Welling, M. (eds.) ECCV 2016. LNCS, vol. 9910, pp. 349–364. Springer, Cham (2016). https://doi.org/10.1007/978-3-319-46466-4_21

31. Kim, M.H., et al.: 3D imaging spectroscopy for measuring hyperspectral patterns on solid objects. ACM Trans. Graph. (TOG) **31**(4), 1–11 (2012)

32. Ledig, C., et al.: Photo-realistic single image super-resolution using a generative adversarial network. In: CVPR (2017)

33. Li, H., Li, G., Shi, L.: Super-resolution of spatiotemporal event-stream image. Neurocomputing **335**, 206–214 (2019)

34. Li, S., Feng, Y., Li, Y., Jiang, Y., Zou, C., Gao, Y.: Event stream super-resolution via spatiotemporal constraint learning. In: ICCV (2021)

35. Li, Z., Yang, J., Liu, Z., Yang, X., Jeon, G., Wu, W.: Feedback network for image super-resolution. In: CVPR (2019)

36. Lim, B., Son, S., Kim, H., Nah, S., Mu Lee, K.: Enhanced deep residual networks for single image super-resolution. In: CVPRW (2017)

37. Lin, S., et al.: Learning event-driven video deblurring and interpolation. In: Vedaldi, A., Bischof, H., Brox, T., Frahm, J.-M. (eds.) ECCV 2020. LNCS, vol. 12353, pp. 695–710. Springer, Cham (2020). https://doi.org/10.1007/978-3-030-58598-3_41

38. Liu, D., Parra, A., Chin, T.J.: Globally optimal contrast maximisation for event-based motion estimation. In: CVPR (2020)

39. Messikommer, N., Gehrig, D., Loquercio, A., Scaramuzza, D.: Event-based asynchronous sparse convolutional networks. In: Vedaldi, A., Bischof, H., Brox, T., Frahm, J.-M. (eds.) ECCV 2020. LNCS, vol. 12353, pp. 415–431. Springer, Cham (2020). https://doi.org/10.1007/978-3-030-58598-3_25

40. Orchard, G., Meyer, C., Etienne-Cummings, R., Posch, C., Thakor, N., Benosman, R.: Hfirst: a temporal approach to object recognition. IEEE Trans. Pattern Anal. Mach. Intell. **37**(10), 2028–2040 (2015)

41. Pan, L., Scheerlinck, C., Yu, X., Hartley, R., Liu, M., Dai, Y.: Bringing a blurry frame alive at high frame-rate with an event camera. In: CVPR (2019)

42. Paredes-Vallés, F., Scheper, K.Y., de Croon, G.C.: Unsupervised learning of a hierarchical spiking neural network for optical flow estimation: from events to global motion perception. IEEE Trans. Pattern Anal. Mach. Intell. **42**(8), 2051–2064 (2019)

43. Patrick, L., Posch, C., Delbruck, T.: A 128x 128 120 db 15μs latency asynchronous temporal contrast vision sensor. IEEE J. Solid-State Circuits **43**, 566–576 (2008)

44. Rebecq, H., Gallego, G., Scaramuzza, D.: EMVS: event-based multi-view stereo. In: BMVC (2016)

45. Rebecq, H., Ranftl, R., Koltun, V., Scaramuzza, D.: High speed and high dynamic range video with an event camera. IEEE Trans. Pattern Anal. Mach. Intell. **43**(6), 1964–1980 (2019)

46. Schaefer, S., Gehrig, D., Scaramuzza, D.: AEGNN: asynchronous event-based graph neural networks. In: CVPR (2022)

47. Sironi, A., Brambilla, M., Bourdis, N., Lagorce, X., Benosman, R.: HATS: histograms of averaged time surfaces for robust event-based object classification. In: CVPR (2018)
48. Tian, Y., Zhang, Y., Fu, Y., Xu, C.: TDAN: temporally-deformable alignment network for video super-resolution. In: CVPR (2020)
49. Timofte, R., De Smet, V., Van Gool, L.: Anchored neighborhood regression for fast example-based super-resolution. In: ICCV (2013)
50. Timofte, R., De Smet, V., Van Gool, L.: A+: adjusted anchored neighborhood regression for fast super-resolution. In: ACCV (2014)
51. Tong, T., Li, G., Liu, X., Gao, Q.: Image super-resolution using dense skip connections. In: ICCV (2017)
52. Tulyakov, S., Bochicchio, A., Gehrig, D., Georgoulis, S., Li, Y., Scaramuzza, D.: Time lens++: event-based frame interpolation with parametric non-linear flow and multi-scale fusion. In: CVPR (2022)
53. Wang, B., He, J., Yu, L., Xia, G.-S., Yang, W.: Event enhanced high-quality image recovery. In: Vedaldi, A., Bischof, H., Brox, T., Frahm, J.-M. (eds.) ECCV 2020. LNCS, vol. 12358, pp. 155–171. Springer, Cham (2020). https://doi.org/10.1007/978-3-030-58601-0_10
54. Wang, L., Ho, Y.S., Yoon, K.J., et al.: Event-based high dynamic range image and very high frame rate video generation using conditional generative adversarial networks. In: CVPR (2019)
55. Wang, L., Kim, T.K., Yoon, K.J.: Eventsr: from asynchronous events to image reconstruction, restoration, and super-resolution via end-to-end adversarial learning. In: CVPR (2020)
56. Wang, T.C., Zhu, J.Y., Kalantari, N.K., Efros, A.A., Ramamoorthi, R.: Light field video capture using a learning-based hybrid imaging system. ACM Trans. Graph. (TOG) **36**(4), 1–13 (2017)
57. Wang, X., Chan, K.C., Yu, K., Dong, C., Change Loy, C.: EDVR: video restoration with enhanced deformable convolutional networks. In: CVPRW (2019)
58. Wang, Z.W., Duan, P., Cossairt, O., Katsaggelos, A., Huang, T., Shi, B.: Joint filtering of intensity images and neuromorphic events for high-resolution noise-robust imaging. In: CVPR (2020)
59. Weng, W., Zhang, Y., Xiong, Z.: Event-based video reconstruction using transformer. In: ICCV (2021)
60. Xiang, X., Tian, Y., Zhang, Y., Fu, Y., Allebach, J.P., Xu, C.: Zooming slow-mo: fast and accurate one-stage space-time video super-resolution. In: CVPR (2020)
61. Xiao, Z., Fu, X., Huang, J., Cheng, Z., Xiong, Z.: Space-time distillation for video super-resolution. In: CVPR (2021)
62. Xiao, Z., Xiong, Z., Fu, X., Liu, D., Zha, Z.J.: Space-time video super-resolution using temporal profiles. In: ACM MM (2020)
63. Xu, G., Xu, J., Li, Z., Wang, L., Sun, X., Cheng, M.M.: Temporal modulation network for controllable space-time video super-resolution. In: CVPR (2021)
64. Yang, J., Wright, J., Huang, T., Ma, Y.: Image super-resolution as sparse representation of raw image patches. In: CVPR (2008)
65. Yang, J., Wright, J., Huang, T.S., Ma, Y.: Image super-resolution via sparse representation. IEEE Trans. Image Process. **19**(11), 2861–2873 (2010)
66. Yao, M., Xiong, Z., Wang, L., Liu, D., Chen, X.: Spectral-depth imaging with deep learning based reconstruction. Opt. Express **27**(26), 38312–38325 (2019)
67. Zeyde, R., Elad, M., Protter, M.: On single image scale-up using sparse-representations. In: Boissonnat, J.-D., et al. (eds.) Curves and Surfaces 2010.

LNCS, vol. 6920, pp. 711–730. Springer, Heidelberg (2012). https://doi.org/10.1007/978-3-642-27413-8_47

68. Zhang, X., Liao, W., Yu, L., Yang, W., Xia, G.S.: Event-based synthetic aperture imaging with a hybrid network. In: CVPR (2021)

69. Zhang, X., Yu, L.: Unifying motion deblurring and frame interpolation with events. In: CVPR (2022)

70. Zhou, Y., Gallego, G., Rebecq, H., Kneip, L., Li, H., Scaramuzza, D.: Semi-dense 3D reconstruction with a stereo event camera. In: ECCV (2018)

71. Zhu, A.Z., Yuan, L., Chaney, K., Daniilidis, K.: Unsupervised event-based learning of optical flow, depth, and egomotion. In: CVPR (2019)

72. Zhu, X., Hu, H., Lin, S., Dai, J.: Deformable convnets V2: more deformable, better results. In: CVPR (2019)

73. Zihao Zhu, A., Atanasov, N., Daniilidis, K.: Event-based visual inertial odometry. In: CVPR (2017)

Projective Parallel Single-Pixel Imaging to Overcome Global Illumination in 3D Structure Light Scanning

Yuxi Li[1] , Huijie Zhao[2], Hongzhi Jiang[1(✉)], and Xudong Li[1]

[1] School of Instrumentation and Optoelectronic Engineering,
Beihang University (BUAA), Beijing, China
{jhz1862,xdli}@buaa.edu.cn

[2] Institute of Artificial Intelligence, Beihang University (BUAA), Beijing, China
hjzhao@buaa.edu.cn

Abstract. We consider robust and efficient 3D structure light scanning method in situations dominated by global illumination. One typical way of solving this problem is via the analysis of 4D light transport coefficients (LTCs), which contains complete information for a projector-camera pair, and is a 4D data set. However, the process of capturing LTCs generally takes long time. We present projective parallel single-pixel imaging (pPSI), wherein the 4D LTCs are reduced to multiple projection functions to facilitate a highly efficient data capture process. We introduce local maximum constraint, which provides necessary condition for the location of correspondence matching points when projection functions are captured. Local slice extension method is introduced to further accelerate the capture of projection functions. We study the influence of scan ratio in local slice extension method on the accuracy of the correspondence matching points, and conclude that partial scanning is enough for satisfactory results. Our discussions and experiments include three typical kinds of global illuminations: inter-reflections, subsurface scattering, and step edge fringe aliasing. The proposed method is validated in several challenging scenarios.

Keywords: Global illumination · 3D reconstruction · Single-pixel imaging

1 Introduction

A common assumption in structure light scanning (SLS) methods, such as fringe projection profilometry (FPP) [8,34,35] and grey coding [12], is that light ray only travels along a direct path when transmitting through a scene. Therefore, SLS methods are susceptible to systematic distortions and random errors when global illumination exists between projector pixels and a camera pixel [13,16,

Supplementary Information The online version contains supplementary material available at https://doi.org/10.1007/978-3-031-20068-7_28.

© The Author(s), under exclusive license to Springer Nature Switzerland AG 2022
S. Avidan et al. (Eds.): ECCV 2022, LNCS 13666, pp. 489–504, 2022.
https://doi.org/10.1007/978-3-031-20068-7_28

31–33]. Global illumination can occur when the investigated objects embody complicated surfaces and materials. For instance, inter-reflections, as shown in Fig. 1(a), dominate between highly glossy reflective surfaces. In these surfaces, the light beams received by camera pixels contain not only directly reflected light, but also inter-reflected light between surfaces. Subsurface scattering effects, as shown in Fig. 1(b), arise at translucent surfaces when light penetrates the surface and exits at different positions around the incident point. Fringe aliasing occurs at positions with discontinued structures, such as step edge, wherein a camera pixel can simultaneously observe the foreground and background when the edge slice exactly passes through the pixel, as shown in Fig. 1(c). Analyzing and decomposing the influences caused by global illuminations through modern cameras is a challenging and open problem [22].

Light transport equation describes the complex transport behavior between projector pixels and camera pixels. The path between the projector and camera pixels can be determined by capturing and analyzing light transport coefficients (LTCs) [13], which denote the light radiance between every possible projector and camera positions combinations; this process enables correspondence matching because the direct path can be identified. However, LTCs are a 4D dataset, which parameterizes light rays in terms of a 2D camera and 2D projector coordinates. Thus, LTCs involve huge data volume, and capturing them takes long time. LTCs can be visualized by a 2D image with projector resolutions, given a camera pixel. We refer to the 2D image with projector resolutions as pixel transport image.

As a step toward a robust and efficient analysis of light transport behavior, we develop projective parallel single-pixel imaging (pPSI) to separate the influences of lights caused by global illumination in 3D scanning. Provided that only the correspondence point is the ultimate goal in 3D reconstruction, LTCs contains over-complete information because only the direct correspondence point is extracted and stored. In the present paper, we show that the correspondence matching position can be obtained when the projection function(s) of the pixel transport image is captured, through the local maximum constraint.

1.1   Contributions

We introduce pPSI, which is a robust, efficient and comprehensive method of 3D reconstruction in the presence of global illumination. Rather than capturing complete 4D LTCs, pPSI captures multiple projection functions, thereby enabling highly efficient data capture procedure. The local maximum constraint is proven, which states that the correspondence matched point (direct illumination point) on the pixel transport image is retained as the local maximum on the projection function(s). We introduce oblique sinusoidal pattern illumination mode to capture projection functions, and correspondence point can be calculated by intersecting the lines that satisfy the local maximum constraint. Local slice extension method, which involves a "coarse to fine" localization procedure, is introduced for highly efficient projective function capture. Experimental results show that partial frequency scanning can obtain satisfactory results, which enables 3D reconstruction under global illumination with a few hunderds patterns. Three kinds of global illuminations are discussed, namely inter-reflections, subsurface scattering and step edge fringe aliasing (Fig. 1). For step edge fringe aliasing, the upper edge illumination is referred to as direct illumination, and the lower edge illumination as global illumination.

The present paper offers the following contributions.

1. We develop pPSI, which is a robust, efficient and comprehensive model for analyzing and solving global illumination effects. Local slice extension method is introduced for highly efficient capture of projection functions.
2. The relationship between projection functions and LTCs is demonstrated theoretically, and the oblique sinusoidal pattern illumination mode is proposed.
3. The local maximum constraint is introduced for candidate calculation, and the fundamental principle is proven both theoretically and experimentally.

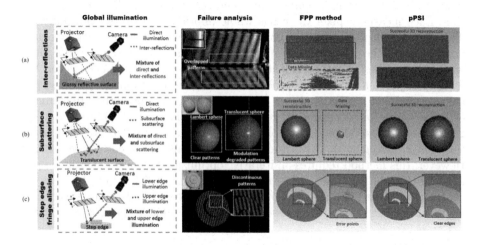

Fig. 1. Global illumination problems discussed in this study. Typical global illumination effects include (a) inter-reflections, (b) subsurface scattering, and (c) step edge fringe aliasing. Inter-reflections incurs overlapped pattern. Subsurface scattering degrades the modulation of the patterns, and step edges cause discontinuous patterns. Global illumination effects cause failure in traditional SLS methods, such as FPP. However, our method (pPSI) can solve these problems both robustly and efficiently.

2   Related Work

2.1   3D Reconstruction Under Global Illumination

Several methods are developed to solve 3D reconstruction under global illuminations; these methods include high-frequency projection methods [2,9,10,21], regional projection methods [11,17,29,30], and polarization projection methods [1,4]. However, these methods are based on specific assumptions that may not be satisfied in real applications. For example, high frequency projection methods such as modulated phase-shifting [2] and mircro-phase shifting [10] are mainly to suppress lower frequency inter-reflections. These methods used high frequency patterns and are based on an assumption: only low frequency global illumination exist, which fails in practical situations. O'Tool et al. [22] introduced structured light transport (SLT) method for 3D reconstruction under global illumination. However, non-epipolar assumption was made in SLT, which assumes that epipolar indirect illumination is not strong. In many real world applications, this assumption can be broken when epipolar plane reflection is strong. On the contrary, pPSI makes no explicit assumption and handles inter-reflections (espically specular inter-reflections) and strong subsurface scattering simultaneously.

Recently, several 3D reconstruction methods that assume no explicit assumption to overcome global illumination are introduced. Park et al. [24] proposed multipeak range imaging. However, this method requires long capture time, since each projector stripe line has to be illuminated in turn. In pPSI, each camera pixel is treated as an independent unit, and reconstructs a 1D projection function. Each measured pixel value has whole information of projection function. Thus, the excellent compressive propority of Fourier single-pixel imaging can be explored, and the projection number can be reduced largely. Recently, Diezu et al. [6] proposed a method called frequency shift triangulation. However, this method requires a calibration process to determine the minimal phase step of the measurement system, and uses a dynamic programming method to eliminate erroneous data for successful 3D reconstruction. Zhang et al. [32] introduced a general mathematical model to solve 3D reconstruction under global illumination. Later, Zhang et al. [31] introduced a sparse multi-path correction method. However, this method requires an iterative optimization process, which can prolong the calculation time and is not suitable for parallel computing. On the contrary, pPSI requires no additional calibration stage, and the reconstruction algorithm requires no iterative process, which is suitable for parallel computing.

2.2   Light Transport Coefficients Capture

Light transport is important for computer vision and graphics. Debevec et al. [5] introduced the capture of a simplified 4D light transport function by a light stage. Masselus et al. [20] proposed the use of a projector-camera system to capture a 6D slice of the full light transport function. These early methods directly capture LTCs, which results in a relatively low capture speed.

Adaptive methods, such as dual photography [26] and symmetric photography [7], and compressive imaging methods [3,25,27] are introduced for highly efficient light transport capture. However, these methods either require a complex illumination mode or a complex reconstruction algorithm. Primal-dual coding [23] and SLT [22] are developed, wherein both the illumination and camera pixels are controlled simultaneously to manipulate different components in the light transport between the projector and the camera. However, this method requires special optical design and hardware.

A single-pixel imaging method is developed for LTCs capture [15,16]. Jiang et al. [13] introduced parallel single-pixel imaging (PSI) for efficient LTCs capture using the local region extension (LRE) method. A compressive PSI [19] is also introduced for highly efficient LTCs capture. PSI is extended to paraxial systems [28], and for separating higher order inter-reflections [14]. This work is an extension to the work by Jiang et al. [13].

In the present paper, we aim to achieve robust and efficient correspondence matching under strong global illumination for 3D scanning. The most outstanding feature of pPSI is that pPSI provides good balance between robustness and efficiency in 3D reconstruction under global illumination. The robustnesss means that pPSI makes no explicit assumption and handles inter-reflections (specular) and strong subsurface scattering simultaneously. The efficiency means that pPSI captures projection functions rather than LTCs. This makes pPSI more efficient than the methods that capture LTCs to solve 3D reconstruction under global illumination. In the present paper, we take advantage of the excellent compressive property of Fourier spectrum, and achieve 3D reconstruction with a few hundreds patterns (336 pattterns).

3   Background

PSI captures LTCs $h(u', v'; u, v)$, which are a 4D dataset, between projector pixel (u', v') and camera pixel (u, v). LTCs describe the image forming process, which is expressed as

$$I(u,v) = O(u,v) + \sum_{v'=0}^{N-1} \sum_{u'=0}^{M-1} h(u',v';u,v)P(u',v'), \tag{1}$$

where $I(u,v)$ is the radiance captured by camera pixel (u,v), $O(u,v)$ is the environment illumination, $P(u',v')$ is the illuminated radiance of projector pixel (u',v'). M and N are the horizontal and vertical resolution of the projector, respectively.

Jiang et al. [13] introduced the LRE method to accelerate the capture efficiency of PSI; this method assumes that the visible region of each pixel is confined in a local region; they proved the perfect reconstruction property of LRE. Reference [13] provides detailed information on PSI. In the present paper, we refer to the visible region as reception field.

4   Projective Parallel Single-Pixel Imaging for Efficient Separation of Direct and Global Illumination

4.1   Local Maximum Constraint Proposition

This section provides the basics for obtaining direct illumination point (correspondence matched point) via projection functions. PSI requires complete LTCs capture. However, in the case of 3D reconstruction, LTCs contain over-complete information because only the direct correspondence point is extracted and stored. The key observation underlying pPSI is that the direct illumination point can be recovered if the 1D projection function(s) of the pixel transport image is captured (Fig. 2(a))

$$
\begin{aligned}
f_\theta^{Radon}(\rho; u, v) &= \Re_\theta[h(u', v'; u, v)] \\
&= \sum_{v'=0}^{N-1} \sum_{u'=0}^{M-1} \cdot h(u', v'; u, v) \cdot \delta(\rho - u' \cos \theta - v' \sin \theta),
\end{aligned} \tag{2}
$$

where $\Re_\theta[h(u', v'; u, v)]$ is the discrete Radon transform of LTCs along direction θ, which is the angle between the integral direction of the projection function and horizontal axis, ρ is the coordinate of the projection function, $\delta(\cdot)$ is the Dirac delt function. When each camera pixel is considered, $f_\theta(\rho; u, v)$ forms a 3D data cube.

We provide some definitions that are useful in following description. Angle θ defines the direction line to which the pixel transport image is projected. The direction line is obtained through counter-clockwise rotation of the horizontal axis by θ, as shown in Fig. 2(a). Given a direction line and a point (u', v'), projection line is defined as the line passing through point (u', v') and vertical to the direction line. Thus, the projection position of (u', v') to the direction line is the intersection of the projection line and the direction line, as shown in Fig. 2(a).

The fundamental principle for recovering direct illumination points given the projection functions is the local maximum constraint proposition, which provides constraint for the location of the correspondence matched point (direct illumination point) in the pixel transport image (Fig. 2(b)).

Theorem 1. *Local Maximum Constraint Proposition. The direct illumination point on the pixel transport image is a local maximum point on the projection functions, if the corresponding projection line does not pass through any speckles caused by global illumination.*

Proof of Local Maximum Constraint Proposition can be found in supplementary material.   □

Local maximum constraint proposition provides a necessary condition for the location of correspondence matched points. Figures 2(a) and (b) provide an intuitive explanation of local maximum constraint proposition. Suppose multiple projection functions $f_\theta(\rho; u, v)$ with D directions are obtained, with the direction angle of d-th projection at θ_d. The d-th projection function has a total of T_d local maximums. The j-th local maximum of the d-th projection function is denoted as ρ_d^j. A grayscale centroid subpixel matching processing is introduced in [16] and [15], which should be applied to obtain ρ_d^j. The candidate correspondence matched points are calculated by solving the following linear equations

$$
\begin{pmatrix}
\cos \theta_1 & \sin \theta_1 & -\rho_1^m \\
\cos \theta_2 & \sin \theta_2 & -\rho_2^n \\
& \vdots & \\
\cos \theta_D & \sin \theta_D & -\rho_D^p
\end{pmatrix}
\begin{pmatrix}
u' \\
v' \\
1
\end{pmatrix}
=
\begin{pmatrix}
0 \\
0 \\
\vdots \\
0
\end{pmatrix}, \tag{3}
$$

where m, n, p are integers, and take any combination that satisfy $m \in [0, T_1)$, $n \in [0, T_2)$, and $p \in [0, T_D)$. Each possible combination of local maximum in every projection line is formed and intersected according to Eq. (3), which can be solved by singular value decomposition (SVD). Not intersected combinations are eliminated by check of the rank. The ultimate correspondence matched points are then determined by the epipolar constraint between the projector and camera, as conducted in [13–16, 19, 28, 33].

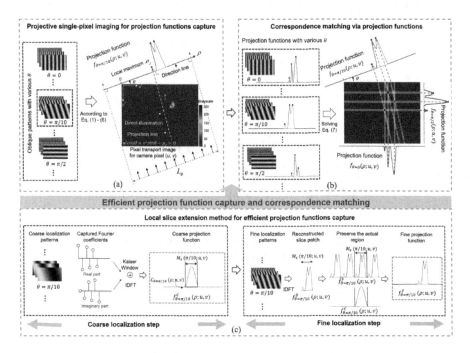

Fig. 2. Fundamental principles of pPSI. (a) Projective single-pixel imaging for projection functions capture. The illumination of oblique patterns is equivalent to the application of Radon transform to pixel transport image. The correspondence matching points of pixel transport image are retained in the projection functions (red spots). (b) Correspondence matching via projection functions. The red spots are local maximum. (c) Local slice extension method for efficient projection functions capture. (Color figure online)

4.2 Projective Single-Pixel Imaging for Projection Functions Capture

In this section, we show that illuminating oblique sinusoidal patterns is equivalent to applying Radon transform to the pixel transport image. Figure 2(a) provides the basic idea.

If the oblique S-step ($S \geq 3$) sinusoidal patterns with following form are illuminated

$$P_i(u', v'; k, \theta) = a + b \cdot \cos[\frac{2\pi k}{L_\theta}(u' \cos \theta + v' \sin \theta) + \frac{2\pi i}{S}], \tag{4}$$

where i denotes the phase step, and take values of $i = 0, 1, \ldots S - 1$. a and b are the average and contrast of the patterns. k is the discrete frequency samples, and take values of $k = 0, 1 \ldots K$, and $K \leq L_\theta$. L_θ is the equivalent projector resolution in the projector range for the directional projection function with an angle of θ (Fig. 2(a)), which can be calculated as

$$L_\theta = \begin{cases} \lceil M \cdot \cos \theta + N \cdot \sin \theta \rceil & 0 \leq \theta \leq \pi/2 \\ \lceil -M \cdot \cos \theta + N \cdot \sin \theta \rceil & \pi/2 < \theta < \pi \end{cases} \tag{5}$$

where $\lceil \cdot \rceil$ is the ceiling function.

According to Eq. (1), the captured intensity for camera pixel (u, v) can be calculated as

$$I_i(u, v; k, \theta) = O(u, v) + \sum_{v'=0}^{N-1} \sum_{u'=0}^{M-1} a \cdot h(u', v'; u, v)$$

$$+ \sum_{v'=0}^{N-1} \sum_{u'=0}^{M-1} b \cdot h(u', v'; u, v) \cdot \cos[\frac{2\pi k}{L_\theta}(u' \cos \theta + v' \sin \theta) + \frac{2\pi i}{S}]. \tag{6}$$

Supposed that all of phase step i is captured, given a frequency sample k and an direction θ, we can obtain the following quantity

$$F_\theta(k; u, v) = \sum_{i=0}^{S-1} I_i(u, v; k, \theta) \cos(2\pi i/S) + j \sum_{i=0}^{S-1} I_i(u, v; k, \theta) \sin(2\pi i/S)$$

$$= \frac{S}{2} \cdot \sum_{v'=0}^{N-1} \sum_{u'=0}^{M-1} b \cdot h(u', v'; u, v) \cdot \exp[-\frac{2\pi k}{L_\theta}(u' \cos \theta + v' \sin \theta)]. \tag{7}$$

Equation (7) holds because the Lagrange's trigonometric identities. The product-to-sum formulas of trigonometric identities and the Euler's formula can then be applied.

When patterns with $k = 0, 1 \ldots L_\theta - 1$ are illuminated, and $F_\theta(k; u, v)$ are calculated as Eq. (7), then, by taking IDFT to $F_\theta(k; u, v)$, the projection function $f_\theta(\rho; u, v)$, shown in Fig. 2, is obtained as

$$f_\theta(\rho; u, v) = IDFT\{\frac{Sb}{2} \cdot \sum_{v'=0}^{N-1} \sum_{u'=0}^{M-1} \cdot h(u', v'; u, v) \cdot \exp[-\frac{2\pi k}{L_\theta}(u' \cos \theta + v' \sin \theta)]\}$$

$$= \frac{Sb}{2} \cdot \sum_{r=-\infty}^{+\infty} \sum_{v'=0}^{N-1} \sum_{u'=0}^{M-1} \cdot h(u', v'; u, v) \cdot \delta(\rho - u' \cos \theta - v' \sin \theta - rL_\theta)$$

$$= \frac{Sb}{2} \cdot \Re_\theta[h(u', v'; u, v)], \tag{8}$$

where r are integers. Although $f_\theta(\rho; u, v)$ contains an infinite sum term, the pixel transport image has nonzero values only in one continuous region with length of L_θ. Thus, Eq. (8) is precisely applying discrete Radon transform to the pixel transport image along direction θ, with a scale factor. In the present paper, we use three-step sinusoidal oblique patterns for projection functions capture.

4.3 Local Slice Extension Method for Efficient Projection Functions Capture

Local slice extension method, which is implemented by a "coarse to fine" localization procedure, is introduced for highly efficient projection functions capture (Fig. 2(c)). The fundamental basis of local slice extension method can be proven by reducing the LRE reconstruction theorem [13] to 1D case. Compared with the LRE method, local slice extension method captures projection functions with different orientations. Thus, in local slice extension method, concepts equivalent to the size and location of the reception field in LRE method are the size and location of the reception field projected along projection direction with θ. We refer to them as the size and location of θ projected reception field (Fig. 2(c)). For implementation, focus should be on this section. Figure 2(c) illustrates local slice extension method.

Coarse Localization Step. This step has a two-fold goal, namely, detecting and obtaining the coarse location and size of the projected reception field. Oblique patterns with the form of Eq. (4) are projected. The obtained intensities are arranged as Eq. (7), and 1D IDFT is applied to the resulting quantities. A Kaiser window [18], wherein the shape parameter β is set as 5, is applied on the sampled low frequency samples to eliminate ringing effect. Coarse projection functions $f_\theta^C(\rho; u, v)$ can then be obtained. The coarse location of the projected reception field $C_\theta(\rho; u, v)$ can be determined, which is a mask that has a value of one when the reconstructed coarse projection functions are greater than the noise threshold, and zero otherwise. The size of the projected reception field $M_s(\theta; u, v)$ is determined between the length in the first position greater than the noise threshold and the last position greater than the noise threshold. The number of frequencies for coarse localization is set as 10 in the present paper. Refer to supplementary material for a theoretical analysis of the relationship between localization accuracy and frequency number in the coarse localization step, and how the number of frequencies for coarse localization is chosen.

Fine Localization Step. The fine projection patterns are in fact the 1D case of the periodic extension patterns introduced in reference [13]. Refer to supplementary material for detailed information on theoretical aspect of local slice extension method. Fine localization step contains three sub-steps.

First, the fine location patterns with the following form are projected

$$\tilde{P}_i(u', v'; k, \theta) = a + b \cdot \cos\left[\frac{2\pi k_\theta}{M_\theta}(u' \cos\theta + v' \sin\theta) + \frac{2\pi i}{S}\right], \qquad (9)$$

where θ is the angle between the integral direction of the projection function and horizontal axis. i denotes the phase step, and take values of $i = 0, 1, \ldots S - 1$. a and b are the average and contrast of the patterns. k is the discrete frequency samples, and takes the value of $k_\theta = 0, 1 \ldots M_\theta - 1$. M_θ is the size of the maximum of θ projected reception field for each camera pixel, and is defined by

$$M_\theta = \max_{(u,v)} [M_s(\theta; u, v)]. \tag{10}$$

Due to the excellent compressive property of Fourier spectrum, partial frequencies can be used to obtain a satisfactory result. We tested the subpixel matched error with respect to different ratio of sampled frequencies, and chose a scan ratio of 25% in the present paper. This means that only the first 25% frequencies are required to be captured. The unscanned frequencies are filled with zeros. Refer to supplementary material for detailed information.

Second, the captured intensities when each pattern is projected are arranged as Eq. (7), and 1D IDFT is applied to reconstruct slice patch $f_\theta^B(\rho; u, v)$. This reconstructed slice patch is then extended periodically for the projection functions with resolution of L_θ, and can be expressed by

$$\tilde{f}_\theta^F(\rho; u, v) = \sum_{r=0}^{\left\lceil \frac{L_\theta}{M_\theta} \right\rceil} f_\theta^B(\rho - rM_\theta; u, v), \tag{11}$$

where r is integer, and $\rho = 0, 1 \ldots L_\theta - 1$.

Finally, the fine projection functions are reconstructed by preserving the nonzero region of $C_\theta(\rho; u, v)$ obtained from coarse localization step, as expressed by

$$f_\theta^r(\rho; u, v) = \tilde{f}_\theta^F(\rho; u, v) \cdot C_\theta(\rho; u, v), \tag{12}$$

where $\cdot$ denote the element-wise product.

Compared with PSI, the capture complexity of pPSI is reduced from $O(M_s{}^2)$ to $O(M_s)$, where M_s is the size of the reception field.

5   Experiments and Evaluations

The experimental setup consisted of a camera and a projector (Fig. 1). The resolutions of the camera and projector are 1600×1200 and 1920×1080, respectively. The frame rate of the projector is synchronized with the frame rate of the camera. The capture rate of the system was 165 frames per second (fps). Several challenging scenarios were validated by pPSI. Refer to supplementary material for comparision of pPSI with micro-phase shifting.

5.1   Compound Scene

A compound scene, which contains a triangular groove and a candle, is used to compare pPSI and PSI. The image of the investigated scene is shown in Fig. 3(a).

Oblique patterns with four orientations of $\theta = 0°, 45°, 90°, 135°$ are projected. The length of the reception field for each direction was 150 according to the coarse localization step, which results in a total number of 336 patterns by pPSI. The steps for choosing the number of slices and the calculation of pattern number required by pPSI are provided in the supplementary material. Total acquisition time was 2 s. The reconstructed 3D shape is shown in Fig. 3(b). The number of patterns required by PSI is 51,000. Total acquisition time is about 5 min. Thus, pPSI provids about 150-fold improvement in the present experiment. The error map between pPSI and PSI is shown in Fig. 3(c). The root-mean-square (RMS) error is 0.023 (mm). This experiment illustrates that pPSI is both efficient and robust for 3D reconstruction in situations dominated by global illumination.

The LTCs for three typical points are shown in Figs. 3(e), (g) and (i). The coordinate of each correspondence point is also shown. We provided the coordinate of each correspondence point calculated by pPSI in Figs. 3(d), (f) and (h). These correspondence points are calculated as intersection points of the projection lines, as shown in Figs. 3(d), (f) and (h). The differences of these correspondence point calculated by pPSI and PSI are also shown.

5.2   Inter-reflections

In this subsection, pPSI is tested in situations dominated by inter-reflections. In the first scene, a gypsum bear was placed near a mirror (Fig. 4(a)). High-frequency inter-reflections result in overlapped patterns, which is challenging for FPP. In the second scene (Fig. 4(b)), two metal blades were measured. The specular reflection also incurs overlapped patterns, which results in large data missing areas.

Oblique patterns with four orientations of $\theta = 0°, 45°, 90°, 135°$ are projected for these two scenes. The length of the reception field for each direction was 150 according to the coarse localization step, which results in a total number of 336 patterns by pPSI. Total acquisition time was 2 s. Compared to PSI, pPSI achieved about 150-fold improvement in terms of acquisition time.

The accuracy of pPSI in situations dominated by inter-reflections is analyzed by a V-Groove that contains two metal gauge blocks (Fig. 5(a)). A plane was fitted for the upper and lower plane separately. The RMS error between the fitted planes and data points of the upper plane and lower plane was 0.021 (mm) and 0.015 (mm), respectively.

5.3   Subsurface Scattering

In this subsection, pPSI is tested in situations dominated by subsurface scattering. In the first scene, a jade horse was investigated (Fig. 4(c)). Strong subsurface scattering results in degraded patterns, which is challenging for FPP. In the second scene, a white onion and a pear was investigated. FPP method still failed to reconstruct satisfactory 3D shape. pPSI and PSI are able to reconstruct high quality 3D shapes for these two challenging scenes.

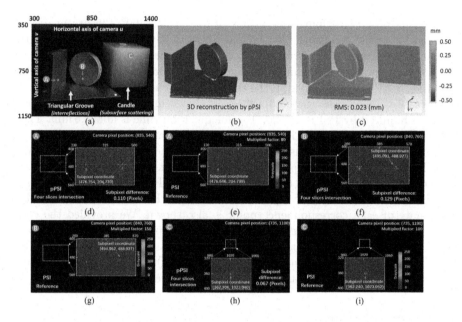

Fig. 3. Comparison between pPSI and PSI using the compound scene. (a) The compound scene contains inter-reflections and subsurface scattering. The camera coordinates are depicted. The positions of three points, namely points A, B, and C, are indicated by red circles. The intersection positions by pPSI and LTCs by PSI of these three points are shown in (d) - (i). (b) 3D shape reconstructed by pPSI. (c) Error map of the point cloud data between pPSI and PSI. RMS error was 0.023 mm. (d), (f) and (h) are the intersection points calculated by pPSI. The camera positions are indicated on the upper right corner. On the upper left corner of each of these subfigures, a circle with a letter inside indicates the point that corresponds to the subfigure. (e), (g) and (i) are the light transport coefficients and the subpixel matched positions calculated by PSI. The difference of the subpixel matched positions between pPSI and PSI are shown in (d), (f) and (h). (Color figure online)

The measurement parameters are the same to that in Sect. 5.2. The number of projected patterns is 336. The difference between pPSI and PSI is negligible, but pPSI achieved about 150-fold improvement in terms of acquisition time.

The accuracy of pPSI in situations dominated by subsurface scattering is analyzed by a polyamide sphere with diameter of 25.449 (mm) (Fig. 5(b)). A sphere was fitted by the reconstructd points. The RMS error between the fitted sphere and the reconstructed data points was 0.031 (mm), and the diameter of the fitted sphere was 25.432 (mm). Thus, the absolut reconstruction error of pPSI was 0.017 mm, and the uncertainty of the measurement was 0.031 mm.

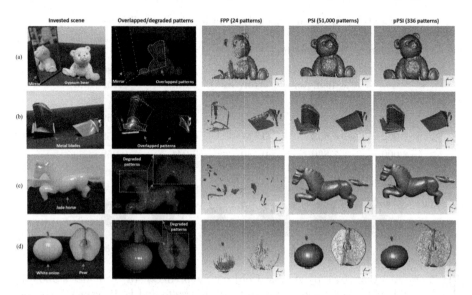

Fig. 4. Comparison of 3D shape reconstruction results among FPP, PSI and pPSI. The overlapped/degraded patterns are shown. (a) Gypsum bear. A mirror was placed near the bear such that high frequency strong inter-reflections dominate. (b) Metal blades. (c) Jade horse. (d) White onion and pear.

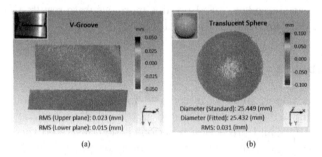

Fig. 5. Accuracy analysis of pPSI. (a) Accuracy analysis using V-Groove when inter-reflections are present. (b) Accuracy analysis using translucent sphere when subsurface scattering is present.

5.4   Step Edges

Fringe aliasing that occurs at step edges causes the missing data at step edges. We used three standard metal cylinder objects with diameters of 6.000 (mm), 7.000 (mm) and 8.000 (mm), as shown in Fig. 6(a), to test accuracy at step edges. The accuracy of the reconstructed diameter reflects the effect of the method used because the data points reconstructed by FPP tend to disappear near the step edges. The reconstructed results by FPP and pPSI are shown in Figs. 6(b)–(d). The black regions are the results reconstructed by FPP. The blue rings correspond to the area reconstructed by pPSI that were missed by FPP due to

Table 1. Accuracy analysis data on metal cylinders.

Diameter (mm)	FPP method		pPSI method	
	Measured diameter (mm)	Absolute error (mm)	Measured diameter (mm)	Absolute error (mm)
6.000	5.827	0.173	5.941	0.059
7.000	6.853	0.147	6.942	0.058
8.000	7.860	0.140	7.941	0.059

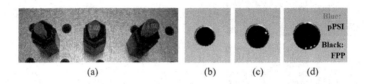

(a)   (b)   (c)   (d)

Fig. 6. Accuracy analysis by standard objects (step edges). (a) Cylinder standards. (b–d) The 3D data of the end surface. The pPSI results and FPP results are shown together. Black points correspond to FPP results, while blue points are pPSI results. (Color figure online)

fringe aliasing at step edges. pPSI obtains more accurate results than FPP. The experimental data are summarized in Table 1.

6   Conclusion

In the present paper, pPSI is introduced for efficient and robust correspondence matching in instances dominated by global illumination. The relationship between LTCs and projection functions is demonstrated theoretically. The oblique sinusoidal pattern illumination mode is proposed. The local maximum constraint is introduced to identify the candidate correspondence points by intersecting the region that satisfies the local maximum constraint. Local slice extension method is introduced to further accelerate capture efficiency. Several challenging scenes are measured and compared, which validates that pPSI achieves efficient and robust 3D shape measurement in the presence of global illumination.

References

1. Chen, T., Lensch, H.P., Fuchs, C., Seidel, H.P.: Polarization and phase-shifting for 3D scanning of translucent objects. In: 2007 IEEE Conference on Computer Vision and Pattern Recognition, pp. 1–8. IEEE (2007)
2. Chen, T., Seidel, H.P., Lensch, H.P.: Modulated phase-shifting for 3D scanning. In: 2008 IEEE Conference on Computer Vision and Pattern Recognition, pp. 1–8. IEEE (2008)

3. Chiba, N., Hashimoto, K.: 3D measurement by estimating homogeneous light transport (HLT) matrix. In: 2017 IEEE International Conference on Mechatronics and Automation (ICMA), pp. 1763–1768. IEEE (2017)

4. Clark, J., Trucco, E., Wolff, L.B.: Using light polarization in laser scanning. Image Vis. Comput. **15**(2), 107–117 (1997)

5. Debevec, P., Hawkins, T., Tchou, C., Duiker, H.P., Sarokin, W., Sagar, M.: Acquiring the reflectance field of a human face. In: Proceedings of the 27th Annual Conference on Computer Graphics and Interactive Techniques, pp. 145–156 (2000)

6. Dizeu, F.B.D., Boisvert, J., Drouin, M.A., Godin, G., Rivard, M., Lamouche, G.: Frequency shift triangulation: a robust fringe projection technique for 3D shape acquisition in the presence of strong interreflections. In: 2019 International Conference on 3D Vision (3DV), pp. 194–203. IEEE (2019)

7. Garg, G., Talvala, E.V., Levoy, M., Lensch, H.P.: Symmetric photography: exploiting data-sparseness in reflectance fields. In: Rendering Techniques, pp. 251–262 (2006)

8. Gorthi, S.S., Rastogi, P.: Fringe projection techniques: whither we are? Opt. Lasers Eng. **48**(ARTICLE), 133–140 (2010)

9. Gu, J., Kobayashi, T., Gupta, M., Nayar, S.K.: Multiplexed illumination for scene recovery in the presence of global illumination. In: International Conference on Computer Vision (2011)

10. Gupta, M., Nayar, S.K.: Micro phase shifting. In: 2012 IEEE Conference on Computer Vision and Pattern Recognition, pp. 813–820. IEEE (2012)

11. Hu, Q., Harding, K.G., Du, X., Hamilton, D.: Shiny parts measurement using color separation. Proc. SPIE Int. Soc. Opt. Eng. **6000**, 125–132 (2005)

12. Inokuchi, S.: Range imaging system for 3-D object recognition. In: ICPR 1984, pp. 806–808 (1984)

13. Jiang, H., Li, Y., Zhao, H., Li, X., Xu, Y.: Parallel single-pixel imaging: a general method for direct-global separation and 3d shape reconstruction under strong global illumination. Int. J. Comput. Vision **129**(4), 1060–1086 (2021)

14. Jiang, H., Yan, Y., Li, X., Zhao, H., Li, Y., Xu, Y.: Separation of interreflections based on parallel single-pixel imaging. Opt. Express **29**(16), 26150–26164 (2021)

15. Jiang, H., Yang, Q., Li, X., Zhao, H., Xu, Y.: 3D shape measurement in the presence of strong interreflections by using single-pixel imaging in a camera-projector system. Opt. Express **29**(3), 3609–3620 (2021)

16. Jiang, H., Zhai, H., Xu, Y., Li, X., Zhao, H.: 3D shape measurement of translucent objects based on fourier single-pixel imaging in projector-camera system. Opt. Express **27**(23), 33564–33574 (2019)

17. Jiang, H., Zhou, Y., Zhao, H.: Using adaptive regional projection to measure parts with strong reflection. In: AOPC 2017: 3D Measurement Technology for Intelligent Manufacturing, vol. 10458, p. 104581A. International Society for Optics and Photonics (2017)

18. Kaiser, J.F.: Nonrecursive digital filter design using the i_0-sinh window function. In: Proceedings of 1974 IEEE International Symposium on Circuits & Systems, San Francisco DA, April, pp. 20–23 (1974)

19. Li, Y., Jiang, H., Zhao, H., Li, X., Wang, Y., Xu, Y.: Compressive parallel single-pixel imaging for efficient 3D shape measurement in the presence of strong interreflections by using a sampling fourier strategy. Opt. Express **29**(16), 25032–25047 (2021)

20. Masselus, V., Peers, P., Dutre, P., Willems, Y.D.: Relighting with 4D incident light fields. ACM Trans. Graph. **22**(3), 613–620 (2003)

21. Nayar, S.K., Krishnan, G., Grossberg, M.D., Raskar, R.: Fast separation of direct and global components of a scene using high frequency illumination. In: ACM SIGGRAPH 2006 Papers, pp. 935–944 (2006)
22. O'Toole, M., Mather, J., Kutulakos, K.N.: 3D shape and indirect appearance by structured light transport. In: Proceedings of the IEEE Conference on Computer Vision and Pattern Recognition, pp. 3246–3253 (2014)
23. O'Toole, M., Raskar, R., Kutulakos, K.N.: Primal-dual coding to probe light transport. ACM Trans. Graph. 31(4), 39–1 (2012)
24. Park, J., Kak, A.: 3D modeling of optically challenging objects. IEEE Trans. Visual Comput. Graphics 14(2), 246–262 (2008)
25. Peers, P., et al.: Compressive light transport sensing. ACM Trans. Graph. (TOG) 28(1), 1–18 (2009)
26. Sen, P., et al.: Dual photography. ACM Trans. Graph. 24(3), 745–755 (2005)
27. Sen, P., Darabi, S.: Compressive dual photography. In: Computer Graphics Forum, vol. 28, pp. 609–618. Wiley Online Library (2009)
28. Wang, Y., Zhao, H., Jiang, H., Li, X., Li, Y., Xu, Y.: Paraxial 3D shape measurement using parallel single-pixel imaging. Opt. Express 29(19), 30543–30557 (2021)
29. Xu, Y., Aliaga, D.G.: Robust pixel classification for 3D modeling with structured light. In: Proceedings of Graphics Interface 2007, pp. 233–240 (2007)
30. Xu, Y., Aliaga, D.G.: An adaptive correspondence algorithm for modeling scenes with strong interreflections. IEEE Trans. Visual Comput. Graphics 15(3), 465–480 (2009)
31. Zhang, Y., Lau, D., Wipf, D.: Sparse multi-path corrections in fringe projection profilometry. In: Proceedings of the IEEE/CVF Conference on Computer Vision and Pattern Recognition, pp. 13344–13353 (2021)
32. Zhang, Y., Lau, D.L., Yu, Y.: Causes and corrections for bimodal multi-path scanning with structured light. In: Proceedings of the IEEE/CVF Conference on Computer Vision and Pattern Recognition, pp. 4431–4439 (2019)
33. Zhao, H., Xu, Y., Jiang, H., Li, X.: 3D shape measurement in the presence of strong interreflections by epipolar imaging and regional fringe projection. Opt. Express 26(6), 7117–7131 (2018)
34. Zuo, C., Feng, S., Huang, L., Tao, T., Yin, W., Chen, Q.: Phase shifting algorithms for fringe projection profilometry: a review. Opt. Lasers Eng. 109, 23–59 (2018)
35. Zuo, C., Huang, L., Zhang, M., Chen, Q., Asundi, A.: Temporal phase unwrapping algorithms for fringe projection profilometry: a comparative review. Opt. Lasers Eng. 85, 84–103 (2016)

Semantic-Sparse Colorization Network for Deep Exemplar-Based Colorization

Yunpeng Bai[1], Chao Dong[2,3], Zenghao Chai[1]📷, Andong Wang[1], Zhengzhuo Xu[1], and Chun Yuan[1,4(✉)]

[1] Tsinghua Shenzhen International Graduate School, Shenzhen, China
{byp20,wad20,xzz20}@mails.tsinghua.edu.cn,
yuanc@sz.tsinghua.edu.cn
[2] Shenzhen Institutes of Advanced Technology, Chinese Academy of Sciences, Shenzhen, China
chao.dong@siat.ac.cn
[3] Shanghai AI Laboratory, Shanghai, China
[4] Peng Cheng National Laboratory, Shenzhen, China

Abstract. Exemplar-based colorization approaches rely on reference image to provide plausible colors for target gray-scale image. The key and difficulty of exemplar-based colorization is to establish an accurate correspondence between these two images. Previous approaches have attempted to construct such a correspondence but are faced with two obstacles. First, using luminance channel for the calculation of correspondence is inaccurate. Second, the dense correspondence they built introduces wrong matching results and increases the computation burden. To address these two problems, we propose Semantic-Sparse Colorization Network (SSCN) to transfer both the global image style and detailed semantic-related colors to the gray-scale image in a coarse-to-fine manner. Our network can perfectly balance the global and local colors while alleviating the ambiguous matching problem. Experiments show that our method outperforms existing methods in both quantitative and qualitative evaluation and achieves state-of-the-art performance.

Keywords: Image colorization · Sparse attention · Exemplar-based colorization

1 Introduction

Image colorization is a classic and appealing task that predicts the vivid colors from a gray-scale image. As there is no unique correct color for a given pixel, three classes of methods are proposed to constrain the output color space. The first one is called automatic colorization, such as [5,40]. These methods generally rely on

---

Supplementary Information The online version contains supplementary material available at https://doi.org/10.1007/978-3-031-20068-7_29.

© The Author(s), under exclusive license to Springer Nature Switzerland AG 2022
S. Avidan et al. (Eds.): ECCV 2022, LNCS 13666, pp. 505–521, 2022.
https://doi.org/10.1007/978-3-031-20068-7_29

the powerful convolutional networks and learn a direct mapping from a large-scale image dataset. The second class introduces additional human intervention, such as user-guided scribbles [7,28,41] and text [1,25]. They require users to provide reliable color/text labels for more dedicated colorization. While the third class, denoted as exemplar-based method [2,6,10,11,19,21,23,33,35,36], is a trade-off between fully automatic and human intervention strategies. It adopts a reference image as guidance and generates a similar color-style image. These three kinds of methods have different applications and prior information, thus cannot be compared side-by-side. In this work, we study exemplar-based image colorization, due to its large flexibility and excellent performance (Fig. 1).

| Target | Reference | Result | Target | Reference | Result |

Fig. 1. Overview colorization results of the proposed method. Our method can commendably build correspondence between the target and reference images and has the capability to generate a plausible colorization of gray-scale images. (Color figure online)

The difficulty of exemplar-based image colorization is to build an accurate correspondence between the gray-scale image and the color reference. Some works regard colorization as a style transfer problem [35], and usually transfer the global color tones. As a result, they lack detailed color matching between semantically similar objects/parts. Other researchers [19,23,36,38,39] propose to construct a dense correspondence with a correlation matrix, whose elements characterize pairwise similarity between different image features. Although they have achieved considerable progress, they are still facing two obstacles. First, the correspondence is calculated using the luminance channel of the input image. However, as gray-scale images do not contain enough semantic information as color images (a common knowledge in image classification [11]), the correspondence based on the luminance channel [23,36,38,39] is inaccurate. Second, the dense correspondence itself will also bring in unavoidable drawbacks. It not only introduces wrong matching results for semantically unrelated objects, but also increases the computation burden.

To address the above mentioned problems, we propose a new coarse-to-fine colorization framework – Semantic-Sparse Colorization Network – to transfer both the global image style and the detailed semantic-related colors to the gray-scale image. Specifically, in the coarse colorization stage, we adopt an image transfer network to obtain a preliminary colorized result. The color information of the reference image is encoded as a vector, which is then migrated to the gray-scale image by an AdaIN [12] operation. In the fine colorization stage, we will first calculate the semantic correspondence between the coarse result and the reference image. Specially, only the semantic-significant parts and some background regions are reserved for calculation, leading to a sparse correlation matrix. Then the attention mechanism will be used to re-weight the reference image and help generate the final color result. The proposed method can perfectly balance the global and local colors while alleviating the ambiguous matching problem caused by dense correspondence. Extensive experiments have shown the superiority of our network towards other state-of-the-art methods. To facilitate numerical evaluation, we also propose a unified evaluation pipeline for all exemplar-based colorization methods. Our code will be publicly available for research purpose.

Our main contributions are summarized as follows:

- We propose to build a more accurate correspondence between a coarse-colorized result and the reference image. It not only minimizes the information gap between the gray-scale input and the color reference, but also achieves better performance on details.
- We propose a sparse attention mechanism to make the model focus on the semantically significant regions in the reference image. It could produce more detailed results with lower computation cost.
- We collect a new test dataset from ImageNet to solve the problem of fair comparison. We also design a new quantitative evaluation metric to evaluate exemplar-based colorization methods.

2   Related Work

Because image colorization plays an essential role in image processing tasks such as old photo restoration and image editing, this subject has been studied for a long time [2,4,13,24,26]. Recently, many studies have used learning-based methods to solve this ill-posed problem. These approaches can be roughly grouped into three classes.

The first one is called automatic colorization, which directly maps gray-scale images to color images, such as [5] and [40]. They are the earliest methods to use convolutional networks to learn the mapping from a large-scale image dataset. MemoPainter [37] uses a memory network to "memorize" rare examples, which can avoid the interference of dominant color in the dataset and make the model perform well even without sufficient data. More recently, Transformer has also been applied to address this task [18]. Some works [3,31,32] take advantage of generative models to promote the diversity of results. For instance, [32] leverages the rich and diverse color priors encapsulated in a pretrained StyleGAN [15] to recover vivid colors. The variational autoencoder (VAE) architecture has also been used in [9]. However, the colorization process of these methods are lack of controllability.

The second class introduces additional human intervention, such as user-guided scribbles and text. They require users to provide reliable color/text labels for more dedicated colorization. Traditional scribble-based colorization methods [20,34] usually propagate the local user hints to the whole image via an optimization approach, while learning-based methods [7,28,41] will combine color prior learned from large-scale image dataset with user's intervention for colorization. Recently, some researchers [16] have found that leveraging user interactions would be a promising approach for reducing color-breeding artifacts. These methods require a certain amount of human effort, and the quality of results depends on the user's skills. Text-based methods usually adopt image captions [25] or palettes converted from the text [1] as means of intervention. However, the color represented by text is challenging to transfer to the image accurately.

The third class, denoted as exemplar-based method, is a trade-off between fully automatic and human intervention strategies. Compared to the above two classes, it adopts sample reference images to provide rich colors without requiring the user to do too much manual work. The key and difficulty of exemplar-based colorization is to establish an accurate correspondence between these two images. DEPN [33] uses a pyramid structure to exploit multi-scale color information, but it only captures the global tones because no semantic correspondence is established. Some works [35] regard exemplar-based colorization as a style transfer problem, but cannot guarantee the correctness of semantics because they also lack a correspondence. Deep Image Analogy [22] was used in [11] to make the target and reference luminance channels aligned to get a coarse chrominance map for further refinement. [23] uses features extracted from the luminance channel of the target and reference images to obtain dense correspondence. However, inaccuracies caused by using luminance channels to calculate correspondence and wrong matching problems introduced by dense correspondence will lead to unsatisfactory results. A general attention based framework is proposed in [36] to fuse colors from the database when the correspondence is not established. However, this method sometimes will mistakenly use the colors from the database when the selected two images are highly semantically related, resulting in the final results looking different from the reference image.

3   Methods

3.1   Overview of the Proposed Method

The task of exemplar-based colorization can be formulated as follows. Given a gray-scale image I_g, which only contains the luminance channel l, our goal is to predict the corresponding a and b color channels in the CIE Lab color space, according to the reference color image I_r. The main challenge is to build an appropriate correspondence between the gray-scale image and the color reference. In order to make full use of the color information in the reference image, we will utilize the reference image twice in a coarse-to-fine manner during the whole colorization process. The proposed framework, namely Semantic-Sparse

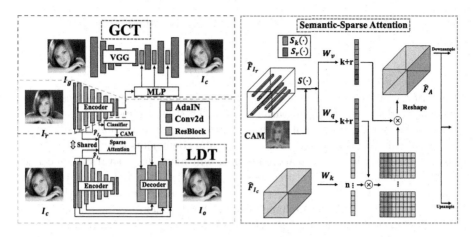

Fig. 2. The illustration of the proposed two-stage image colorization framework. Our method uses a coarse-colorized image to build more accurate correspondence, which is completely different from previous works. The right part shows our proposed sparse attention mechanism in detail. With the help of the semantic information provided by CAM, the model can accurately use the critical parts of the reference image and reduce the complex computation caused by the attention mechanism.

Colorization Network (SSCN), consists of two auxiliary modules, which transfer global and local colors in the reference image, respectively.

The overall pipeline of SSCN is illustrated in Fig. 2. Specifically, taking the reference image I_r as input, our model will first encode it into features F_{I_r}. These features will be used in both global and local coloring modules. In the coarse colorization stage, the Global Color Transfer (GCT) module will use F_{I_r} to preliminarily color the gray-scale image I_g, and get a coarse-colorized result I_c, which has similar global tones as I_r. Then the coarse output I_c will be further encoded into features F_{I_c} with the same encoder as F_{I_r}. In the fine colorization stage, the Local Details Transfer (LDT) module will use F_{I_r} and F_{I_c} to construct a correspondence that focuses on the semantically relevant regions of I_r. Note that these regions are sparsely selected according to their semantic levels. Based on the predicted mappings from LDT, the reference features F_{I_r} are reorganized and fused with F_{I_c} at different scales. Finally, the decoder takes the fused color features to produce the a and b channels of the input image I_g.

3.2 Global Color Transfer

We will first introduce the encoder of I_r, which is shared in both GCT and LDT modules. The encoder consists of six residual blocks. The last layer of F_{I_r} is passed through an MLP to form the style vector, which will be used in the GCT module for global style transfer. In GCT, the gray-scale image I_g will first be encoded into features $\{x_1, x_2, ..., x_n\}$. Then, we perform coarse colorization in the feature space by changing feature statistics with AdaIN operation as:

$$AdaIN(x_i, y) = y_{s,i} \frac{x_i - \mu(x_i)}{\sigma(x_i)} + y_{b,i} \; , \tag{1}$$

where $\mu(x_i)$ and $\sigma(x_i)$ represent the ith feature map's mean and variance, respectively. y_s and y_b are the affine parameters of the style vector, which is obtained from F_{I_r} via MLP transformation. Each feature map x_i is normalized separately and then scaled/biased using the corresponding coefficients from $y(y_s, y_b)$. After affine transformation, each feature channel will have the activation for certain color information. These features can be inverted to the Lab space by a convolutional decoder. We finally get the coarse colorized result I_c of the coarse colorization stage. In our implementation, the encoder uses sub-layers of the VGG19 [29], and the decoder is symmetric structure. AdaIN are added after CNN layers of the decoder.

3.3   Local Details Transfer

The target of the LDT module is to build a more detailed and accurate correspondence between the coarse-colorized result I_c and the reference image I_r. To begin with, we encode I_c into the corresponding features F_{I_c}, with the same encoder as F_{I_r}. To find their correspondence, we extract features from the first four layers of F_{I_r} and F_{I_c}, and resize them to the same spatial size of $1/4$ input image. Then these features are concatenated to form features $\hat{F}_{I_r}$ and $\hat{F}_{I_c}$, corresponding to the latent states of coarse and reference image, respectively. Their spatial size is both $d \times H/4 \times W/4$, where d is the number of feature maps. To facilitate computation, they are further flattened in the last two directions, and form features of size $d \times HW/16$. In this way, we segment the input image into $HW/16$ regions and represent each region with a d dimensional vector.

Based on the obtained features $\hat{F}_{I_r}$ and $\hat{F}_{I_c}$, the LDT module will calculate a correlation matrix A via attention mechanism, whose element is computed by the scaled dot product [30] illustrated as Formula 2:

$$\alpha_{ij} = \underset{j}{softmax} \left(\frac{(W_q f_i^c) \cdot (W_k f_j^r)}{\sqrt{d}} \right). \tag{2}$$

Here, α_{ij} represents the similarity between the i-th region of $\hat{F}_{I_c}$ and the j-th region of $\hat{F}_{I_r}$. $\hat{F}_{I_c}$ is used to retrieve relevant local details from $\hat{F}_{I_r}$. Then, we can re-weight the features $\hat{F}_{I_r}$ to obtain the attended feature $\hat{F}_a$ through a weighted sum operation as Formula 3:

$$f_i^a = \sum_j \alpha_{ij} W_v f_j^r \; , \tag{3}$$

where W_q, W_k and W_v represent the linear transformation matrix into *query*, *key*, and *value* vectors, respectively. The attended features $\hat{F}_a$ will be reshaped

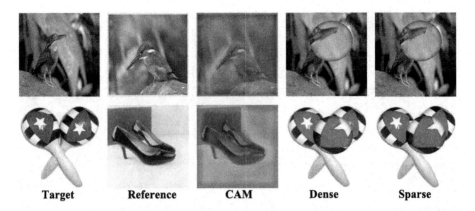

| Target | Reference | CAM | Dense | Sparse |

Fig. 3. Comparison results of dense and sparse correspondence strategies. The output results will be disturbed by the re-weighting process using dense correspondence. Sparse attention focusing on semantically important areas can solve this problem.

to the size of $d \times H/4 \times W/4$ and further resized into a suitable shape, fused with the features F_{I_c} at different scales and fed into the U-Net [27] decoder for the final detailed result of the fine colorization stage.

Semantic-Sparse Correspondence. In the above description, we use a standard attention mechanism to calculate the dense correspondence between coarse and reference images. We further propose a semantically sparse correspondence for better results with less computation cost. To be specific, the reference features $\hat{F}_{I_r}$ will go through a selection operation. First, the fifth layer of F_{I_r} will be fed into a classifier and get a class activation map (CAM) [42], which is used as the reference for selection. The CAM is flattened to $C = \{c_1, c_2, ..., c_{HW/16}\} \in \mathbb{R}^{HW/16}$. The selection operation $S(\cdot)$ contains the top-k selection $S_k(\cdot)$ and random selection $S_r(\cdot)$ implemented upon C. The $S_k(\cdot)$ selects the k largest elements of C and records their indexes $\mathbf{T}_k$. This encourages the attention mechanism to focus more on semantically significant areas and reduce the interference caused by insignificant parts. At the same time, the coloring of the background areas also needs reference. Thus $S_r(\cdot)$ randomly selects r more indexes $\mathbf{T}_r$. Finally, we obtain $S(C) = \mathbf{T}_k \cup \mathbf{T}_r$ and the semantic-sparse features $\hat{F}_{I_r}[S(C)]$. To calculate the new correspondence map, we can simply replace the features $\hat{F}_{I_r}$ with $\hat{F}_{I_r}[S(C)]$ in Formula 2, 3. The other steps remain the same as above.

3.4 Discussion

Dense Correspondence vs. Sparse Correspondence. Dense correspondence will be easily affected by irrelevant regions, especially when the reference is completely different from the gray-scale image. Even if the target region has low similarity with most reference regions, the re-weighting process will still disturb the final result. In contrast, sparse correspondence can overcome this difficulty by focusing only on semantically important regions, which can reduce

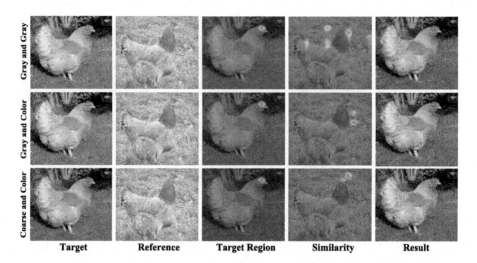

Fig. 4. Comparison results of using three different data types to build the correspondence. The coarse-colorized result we proposed to use can establish more accurate correspondence than the other two common types.

the interference of other regions. Moreover, the computational complexity goes from $\mathcal{O}\left((HW)^2\right)$ to $\mathcal{O}\left((k+r)HW\right)$, while $(k+r)$ is generally 8 to 16 times smaller than HW. The comparison results of these two strategies are shown in Fig. 3. It can be observed that some details are more accurately colorized after reducing the interference.

Coarse-colorized vs. Gray-Scale. In this work, we propose to use a coarse-colorized image to build the correspondence with the reference, which is completely different from previous works [23,36,38,39]. The coarse result is already consistent with the reference's global color style, thus can produce more dedicated correspondence than directly using the gray-scale image. Moreover, the correspondence between color images is more accurate than that between gray-scale images (luminance channels). To verify this comment, we build a correlation matrix for three data types with the same operations. Figure 4 shows the comparison results of the similarity between one target region and all reference regions. It is clear that the chicken comb is correctly matched between two color images, even with different colors.

3.5   Objective Functions

Smooth-L1 Loss. To avoid simply using the average scheme for solving the ambiguity colorization problem, a widely used loss function Smooth-L1 loss is adopted in image colorization tasks. This loss is added to the results of both two stages in our architecture as L_{stage1} and L_{stage2}. The following Formula 4 can calculate the Smooth-L1 loss between T_{ab} and $\hat{T}_{ab}$:

$$L_{stage1,2}(T_{ab}, \hat{T}_{ab}) = \begin{cases} \dfrac{1}{2}(T_{ab} - \hat{T}_{ab})^2 & for \left| T_{ab} - \hat{T}_{ab} \right| \leq \delta \\ \delta \left| T_{ab} - \hat{T}_{ab} \right| - \dfrac{1}{2}\delta^2 & otherwise. \end{cases} \quad (4)$$

Classification Loss. There is a classification loss L_{cls} in the classifier to get a CAM as a reference for $S(\cdot)$. This loss can also improve the encoder's ability of extracting color features. When F_{I_r} is fed into the classifier, its label vector is predicted. L_{cls} is defined as the cross-entropy between the classification vector $\hat{y}$ and its ground truth one-hot label.

Color Histogram Loss. To transfer the color distribution of the reference image to the target image accurately, we also add a histogram loss to the final output as Formula 5. Similar to the previous work [40], we treat the problem as multinomial classification. We quantify $\hat{T}_{ab}$ output space into bins with $gridsize = 10$ and keep the in-gamut $Q = 313$. The mapping to predicted color distribution $\hat{Z} \in [0,1]^{H \times W \times Q}$ is also learned with the decoder. The L_{his} is defined as a cross-entropy loss for every pixel to measure the distance between predicted distribution $\hat{Z}$ and ground truth Z, and sum over all pixels.

$$L_{his}(\hat{Z}, Z) = -\sum_{h,w}\sum_{q} Z_{h,w,q} \log(\hat{Z}_{h,w,q}) . \quad (5)$$

TV Regularization. To encourage spatial smoothness in the output result $\hat{T}_{ab}$, we follow previous work [14] and apply the total variation regularization $L_{TV}(\hat{T}_{ab})$ to the output of the fine colorization stage.

In summary, the overall loss function for the entire network is defined as:

$$L_{total} = \lambda_{stage1}L_{stage1} + \lambda_{stage2}L_{stage2} + \lambda_{TV}L_{TV} + \lambda_{cls}L_{cls} + \lambda_{his}L_{his} , \quad (6)$$

where λ_{stage1}, λ_{stage2}, λ_{TV}, λ_{cls} and λ_{his} are hyperparameters to constrain different loss terms.

4   Experiments

4.1   Implementation Details

We use ImageNet's [8] total training set to train the entire network with 5 epochs and set mini-batch size as 8. During training, the input image will be resized to 256×256. We use Adam [17] for optimization with $\beta_1 = 0.9, \beta_2 = 0.999$. The learning rate is set to 0.0001. We set the coefficients for each loss function as follows: $\lambda_{stage1} = 100$, $\lambda_{stage2} = 100$, $\lambda_{cls} = 0.1$, $\lambda_{TV} = 10$, and $\lambda_{his} = 1$. For the $S(\cdot)$, both k and r are set to 256.

Fig. 5. Qualitative comparison of colorizing results with previous methods. The target image, reference image, and each method's colorized images are displayed from top to bottom. The proposed method outperforms other models and achieves state-of-the-art performance.

For the exemplar-based colorization method, it is impossible to find enough source-reference pairs to train the network. We adopt a scheme similar to [19]. The reference is generated from the original image by geometric distortion, which can provide complete color information for the target image. The geometric distortion is realized by thin plate splines (TPS) transformation. The distortion is randomly applied to each image. In the training process, we apply violent transformation to some images to simulate semantically unrelated reference images.

4.2   Comparison with Previous Methods

Visual Comparison. We compare the results of our method with previous exemplar-based colorization approaches [11,23,33,35,36]. We run all 6 models on 230 pairs of images collected from ImageNet validation set and show several representative results. All comparison results are obtained by public available codes. We show the qualitative comparison in Fig. 5. See our supplementary materials for more results.

Content Different Reference   **Palette Reference**

Target   Reference   Result   Target   Reference   Result

Fig. 6. Colorization results of using content different references and palettes. Visually satisfactory results can also be obtained using these two types of references.

The 4th column of Fig. 5 shows the results of colorizing objects with unusual or artistic colors. Compared with method [11] constrained by the perceptual loss, the proposed method can appropriately colorize the target image according to the user's requirement. Since [23] tends to make the color histograms of the two images consistent, resulting in the wrong spatial distribution of colors.

In the 6th column, when there are large regions with less semantics in the image, our method can pay more attention to the semantically relevant areas, e.g., the pink area, while other methods fail to colorize the object or simply get a smooth result. In the 2nd column, the parrots in two input images are highly semantically related, while [36] uses the colors in the database, resulting in an unsatisfactory final result.

When the reference image is semantically unrelated to the target image (shown as 1st column in Fig. 5), due to the dependence on prior color knowledge, [11] will ignore the colors from the reference image. Histogram-based methods [33] can get plausible results by transferring global tones, whereas our method can yield better results. For some images with many details, [23] cannot properly colorize these details due to the inappropriate correspondence constructed with two gray-scale images, while the proposed method allows the target image to be colored correctly, e.g., 5th and 7th columns in Fig. 5.

These experimental results show that the proposed method can transfer color information for different image pairs accurately and effectively. We also show some results of using content different references and palettes in Fig. 6. Even when the semantics of the reference image are irrelevant or have no semantics, our method can also get satisfactory results.

Self-Augmentation PSNR/SSIM. Unlike automatic colorization, in exemplar-based colorization setting, when given a target-reference pair, there is no ground truth that has both the target's shape and the reference's color. The histogram intersection similarity (HIS) used in previous work [23,36] is not a suitable index. Mismatches may also occur in the spatial color distribution of the result with high histogram similarity with the reference image. In order to

Fig. 7. Comparison results of using random cropping reference image to colorize the target image. The results obtained by other methods are not satisfactory even when using such a suitable reference.

Table 1. Quantitative comparisons of self-augmentation PSNR/SSIM. A higher value indicates a better preference, while the proposed method outperforms other models.

Methods	TPS	RR	RC	Mean
He et al. (2018) [11]	28.51/0.902	28.67/0.903	27.57/0.898	28.25/0.901
Xiao et al. (2020) [33]	25.17/0.912	25.30/0.913	24.98/0.910	25.15/0.911
Xu et al. (2020) [35]	22.46/0.873	21.65/0.846	21.55/0.862	21.88/0.860
Lu et al. (2020) [23]	27.93/0.913	29.80/0.931	27.12/0.907	28.28/0.917
Yin et al. (2021) [36]	31.87/0.948	34.24/0.952	29.85/0.939	31.98/0.946
Ours	**36.32/0.969**	**35.49/0.966**	**32.39/0.958**	**34.73/0.964**

make a quantitative evaluation of the colorization results, similar to the training process, we use the augmentation of a color image as the reference to colorize its luminance channel, so that the original color image can be used as ground truth. With ground truth available for comparison, some existing evaluation metrics, such as peak signal-to-noise ratio (PSNR) and structural similarity (SSIM), can be used for evaluation.

We select 5000 images from the validation set of ImageNet to do three different data augmentation, including TPS, random rotation (RR), and random cropping (RC) as references to get different results. The quantitative comparisons of three different augmentation are reported in Table 1. Figure 7 shows an example of using a RC reference and comparing the results with other methods. We will release this test dataset for future comparison.

User Evaluation. We conduct user evaluation to verify the proposed method's effectiveness subjectively. In this part, we randomly select 50 groups from the above results. Semantically dependent pairs and semantically unrelated pairs are distributed in half. Eventually, all 6×50 color images are distributed anonymously and randomly to 30 college participants.

For fairness, the images with the same reference are shown simultaneously in a random order. All participants were asked to observe the images for no more than 5 s and choose the image that better matches the reference. As shown in Fig. 8, we show the percentage of votes for each method in the form of pie chart. It shows that images of our method are mostly preferred.

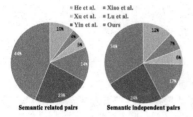

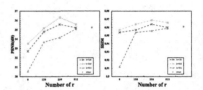

Fig. 8. The users' preferences for six different methods. Under two different image pairs, our results have been the most selected by users.

Fig. 9. The picture shows how the numerical changes of k and r affect the final result. Larger or smaller k and r will reduce the quality.

5 Ablation Studies

Ablation Study of $S_k\,(\cdot)$ and $S_r\,(\cdot)$. The use of sparse correspondence will lead to the question: how to select an appropriate number of regions in the process? Then we further study the effect of k and r, and use TPS reference to evaluate results quantitatively as described above. When the resolution of the reference image is 256×256, there are 4096 features available for selection. We increase k and r gradually from 128 and 0, respectively. The comparison results are shown in Fig. 9. Without random selection, the value of PNSR/SSIM will be much lower because some areas of the background are incorrectly colored. Increasing r gradually can improve the results, but increasing r further will cause the result deteriorate again. In addition, it can be seen from the comparison of the three broken lines that a larger or smaller k will reduce the quality.

Ablation Study of Two-Stage Architecture. To illustrate the importance of the two-stage structure in our model, we conduct ablation study on $k = 256, r = 256$ version. First, we evaluate the first stage results with PSNR and SSIM values of 30.02 and 0.937. There is a huge gap between them and the final results, thus illustrating the importance of LDT. To further validate the importance of preliminary coloring, we remove GCT from the whole architecture for comparison. Instead, we use another network with a similar structure to the encoder of I_r but with one channel input to extract the features of gray-scale image and calculate the correspondence in the same way. Due to the lack of information in the gray-scale image, the PSNR and SSIM values will decrease by 3.30 and 0.014. We also analyze the relationship between the results of the two stages in the encoder feature space. The similarity of features is shown in the form of heat map in Fig. 10. We can see that the differences between the two are mainly concentrated in some semantic details, which are completed in the second stage.

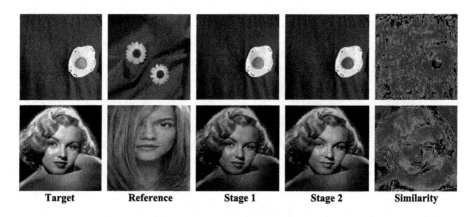

| Target | Reference | Stage 1 | Stage 2 | Similarity |

Fig. 10. Ablation study on the relationship between the results of the two stages. The bluer the part in the heat map, the less similar the features. The main differences are concentrated in some semantic details.

Ablation Study of Loss Functions. In order to verify that the classifier does not only provide a CAM but also help the encoder extract color features, we ablate the classification loss on the dense version. After this loss is removed, the corresponding PSNR and SSIM values are 33.73 and 0.952, while the PSNR and SSIM values of the dense version are 35.25 and 0.961. In addition, we also ablate color histogram loss of the best version ($k = 256, r = 256$) to analyze its effect. The PSNR and SSIM values will decrease by 1.28 and 0.009. Removing either of these losses will reduce the model's performance, especially in the L_{cls}.

6   Conclusions

This paper proposes a colorization framework named Semantic-Sparse Colorization Network (SSCN) to colorize the target image in a coarse-to-fine manner. Specifically, an image transfer network is adopted in the coarse colorization stage to obtain a preliminary colorized result. In the fine colorization stage, semantically related areas of the reference image will be selected to color the details of the target image. Thus, SSCN can adequately transfer a reference image's global color and local details onto a gray-scale image. It provides a way to obtain different levels of color information from the reference image hierarchically and accurately. Extensive experiments show that the proposed method outperforms previous state-of-the-art approaches by a large margin.

Acknowledgment. This work was supported by SZSTC Grant No. JCYJ201908 09172201639 and WDZC20200820200655001, Shenzhen Key Laboratory ZDSYS 20210623092001004.

References

1. Bahng, H., et al.: Coloring with words: guiding image colorization through text-based palette generation. In: Ferrari, V., Hebert, M., Sminchisescu, C., Weiss, Y. (eds.) ECCV 2018. LNCS, vol. 11216, pp. 443–459. Springer, Cham (2018). https://doi.org/10.1007/978-3-030-01258-8_27

2. Bugeau, A., Ta, V., Papadakis, N.: Variational exemplar-based image colorization. IEEE Trans. Image Process. **23**(1), 298–307 (2014)

3. Cao, Y., Zhou, Z., Zhang, W., Yu, Y.: Unsupervised diverse colorization via generative adversarial networks. In: Ceci, M., Hollmén, J., Todorovski, L., Vens, C., Džeroski, S. (eds.) ECML PKDD 2017. LNCS (LNAI), vol. 10534, pp. 151–166. Springer, Cham (2017). https://doi.org/10.1007/978-3-319-71249-9_10

4. Charpiat, G., Hofmann, M., Schölkopf, B.: Automatic image colorization via multimodal predictions. In: Forsyth, D., Torr, P., Zisserman, A. (eds.) ECCV 2008. LNCS, vol. 5304, pp. 126–139. Springer, Heidelberg (2008). https://doi.org/10.1007/978-3-540-88690-7_10

5. Cheng, Z., Yang, Q., Sheng, B.: Deep colorization. In: ICCV 2015, pp. 415–423. IEEE Computer Society (2015)

6. Chia, A.Y.S., et al.: Semantic colorization with internet images. ACM Trans. Graph. **30**(6), 156 (2011)

7. Ci, Y., Ma, X., Wang, Z., Li, H., Luo, Z.: User-guided deep anime line art colorization with conditional adversarial networks. In: MM 2018, pp. 1536–1544. ACM (2018)

8. Deng, J., Dong, W., Socher, R., Li, L., Li, K., Li, F.: Imagenet: a large-scale hierarchical image database. In: CVPR 2009, pp. 248–255. IEEE Computer Society (2009)

9. Deshpande, A., Lu, J., Yeh, M., Chong, M.J., Forsyth, D.A.: Learning diverse image colorization. In: CVPR 2017, pp. 2877–2885. IEEE Computer Society (2017)

10. Gupta, R.K., Chia, A.Y.S., Rajan, D., Ng, E.S., Huang, Z.: Image colorization using similar images. In: MM 2012, pp. 369–378. ACM (2012)

11. He, M., Chen, D., Liao, J., Sander, P.V., Yuan, L.: Deep exemplar-based colorization. ACM Trans. Graph. **37**(4), 47:1–47:16 (2018)

12. Huang, X., Belongie, S.J.: Arbitrary style transfer in real-time with adaptive instance normalization. In: IEEE International Conference on Computer Vision, ICCV 2017, Venice, Italy, 22–29 October 2017, pp. 1510–1519. IEEE Computer Society (2017)

13. Huang, Y., Tung, Y., Chen, J., Wang, S., Wu, J.: An adaptive edge detection based colorization algorithm and its applications. In: MM 2005, pp. 351–354. ACM (2005)
14. Johnson, J., Alahi, A., Fei-Fei, L.: Perceptual losses for real-time style transfer and super-resolution. In: Leibe, B., Matas, J., Sebe, N., Welling, M. (eds.) ECCV 2016. LNCS, vol. 9906, pp. 694–711. Springer, Cham (2016). https://doi.org/10.1007/978-3-319-46475-6_43
15. Karras, T., Laine, S., Aila, T.: A style-based generator architecture for generative adversarial networks. In: IEEE Conference on Computer Vision and Pattern Recognition, CVPR 2019, Long Beach, CA, USA, 16–20 June 2019, pp. 4401–4410. Computer Vision Foundation/IEEE (2019)
16. Kim, E., Lee, S., Park, J., Choi, S., Seo, C., Choo, J.: Deep edge-aware interactive colorization against color-bleeding effects. CoRR (2021)
17. Kingma, D.P., Ba, J.: Adam: a method for stochastic optimization. In: ICLR 2015 (2015)
18. Kumar, M., Weissenborn, D., Kalchbrenner, N.: Colorization transformer. CoRR arXiv:2102.04432 (2021)
19. Lee, J., Kim, E., Lee, Y., Kim, D., Chang, J., Choo, J.: Reference-based sketch image colorization using augmented-self reference and dense semantic correspondence. In: CVPR 2020, pp. 5800–5809. IEEE Computer Society (2020)
20. Levin, A., Lischinski, D., Weiss, Y.: Colorization using optimization. ACM Trans. Graph. **23**(3), 689–694 (2004)
21. Li, H., Sheng, B., Li, P., Ali, R., Chen, C.L.P.: Globally and locally semantic colorization via exemplar-based broad-GAN. IEEE Trans. Image Process. **30**, 8526–8539 (2021)
22. Liao, J., Yao, Y., Yuan, L., Hua, G., Kang, S.B.: Visual attribute transfer through deep image analogy. ACM Trans. Graph. **36**(4), 120:1–120:15 (2017)
23. Lu, P., Yu, J., Peng, X., Zhao, Z., Wang, X.: Gray2colornet: transfer more colors from reference image. In: MM 2020, pp. 3210–3218. ACM (2020)
24. Luan, Q., Wen, F., Cohen-Or, D., Liang, L., Xu, Y., Shum, H.: Natural image colorization. In: Proceedings of the Eurographics Symposium on Rendering Techniques 2007, pp. 309–320. Eurographics Association (2007)
25. Manjunatha, V., Iyyer, M., Boyd-Graber, J.L., Davis, L.S.: Learning to color from language. In: NAACL-HLT 2018, pp. 764–769. Association for Computational Linguistics (2018)
26. Qu, Y., Wong, T., Heng, P.: Manga colorization. ACM Trans. Graph. **25**(3), 1214–1220 (2006)
27. Ronneberger, O., Fischer, P., Brox, T.: U-Net: convolutional networks for biomedical image segmentation. In: Navab, N., Hornegger, J., Wells, W.M., Frangi, A.F. (eds.) MICCAI 2015. LNCS, vol. 9351, pp. 234–241. Springer, Cham (2015). https://doi.org/10.1007/978-3-319-24574-4_28
28. Sangkloy, P., Lu, J., Fang, C., Yu, F., Hays, J.: Scribbler: controlling deep image synthesis with sketch and color. In: CVPR 2017, pp. 6836–6845. IEEE Computer Society (2017)
29. Simonyan, K., Zisserman, A.: Very deep convolutional networks for large-scale image recognition. In: ICLR 2015 (2015)
30. Vaswani, A., et al.: Attention is all you need. In: Advances in Neural Information Processing Systems 30: Annual Conference on Neural Information Processing Systems 2017, pp. 5998–6008 (2017)
31. Vitoria, P., Raad, L., Ballester, C.: Chromagan: adversarial picture colorization with semantic class distribution. In: WACV 2020, pp. 2434–2443. IEEE (2020)

32. Wu, Y., Wang, X., Li, Y., Zhang, H., Zhao, X., Shan, Y.: Towards vivid and diverse image colorization with generative color prior. CoRR (2021)
33. Xiao, C., et al.: Example-based colourization via dense encoding pyramids. Comput. Graph. Forum **39**(1), 20–33 (2020)
34. Xu, K., Li, Y., Ju, T., Hu, S., Liu, T.: Efficient affinity-based edit propagation using K-D tree. ACM Trans. Graph. **28**(5), 118 (2009)
35. Xu, Z., Wang, T., Fang, F., Sheng, Y., Zhang, G.: Stylization-based architecture for fast deep exemplar colorization. In: CVPR 2020, pp. 9360–9369. IEEE (2020)
36. Yin, W., Lu, P., Zhao, Z., Peng, X.: Yes, "attention is all you need", for exemplar based colorization. In: MM 2021: ACM Multimedia Conference, Virtual Event, China, 20–24 October 2021, pp. 2243–2251. ACM (2021)
37. Yoo, S., Bahng, H., Chung, S., Lee, J., Chang, J., Choo, J.: Coloring with limited data: few-shot colorization via memory augmented networks. In: CVPR 2019, pp. 11283–11292. Computer Vision Foundation/IEEE (2019)
38. Zhang, B., et al.: Deep exemplar-based video colorization. In: CVPR 2019, pp. 8052–8061. Computer Vision Foundation/IEEE (2019)
39. Zhang, J., et al.: Scsnet: an efficient paradigm for learning simultaneously image colorization and super-resolution. CoRR (2022)
40. Zhang, R., Isola, P., Efros, A.A.: Colorful image colorization. In: Leibe, B., Matas, J., Sebe, N., Welling, M. (eds.) ECCV 2016. LNCS, vol. 9907, pp. 649–666. Springer, Cham (2016). https://doi.org/10.1007/978-3-319-46487-9_40
41. Zhang, R., et al.: Real-time user-guided image colorization with learned deep priors. ACM Trans. Graph. **36**(4), 119:1–119:11 (2017)
42. Zhou, B., Khosla, A., Lapedriza, À., Oliva, A., Torralba, A.: Learning deep features for discriminative localization. In: CVPR 2016, pp. 2921–2929. IEEE Computer Society (2016)

Practical and Scalable Desktop-Based High-Quality Facial Capture

Alexandros Lattas[2], Yiming Lin[1], Jayanth Kannan[1], Ekin Ozturk[1,2], Luca Filipi[1], Giuseppe Claudio Guarnera[1,3], Gaurav Chawla[1], and Abhijeet Ghosh[1,2(✉)]

[1] Lumirithmic Ltd., London, UK
{yiming.lin,jay,luca,gaurav.chawla}@lumirithmic.com
[2] Imperial College London, London, UK
{a.lattas,ekin.ozturk17,ghosh}@imperial.ac.uk
[3] University of York, York, UK
claudio.guarnera@york.ac.uk

Abstract. We present a novel desktop-based system for high-quality facial capture including geometry and facial appearance. The proposed acquisition system is highly practical and scalable, consisting purely of commodity components. The setup consists of a set of displays for controlled illumination for reflectance capture, in conjunction with multiview acquisition of facial geometry. We additionally present a novel set of modulated binary illumination patterns for efficient acquisition of reflectance and photometric normals using our setup, with diffuse-specular separation. We demonstrate high-quality results with two different variants of the capture setup – one entirely consisting of portable mobile devices targeting static facial capture, and the other consisting of desktop LCD displays targeting both static and dynamic facial capture.

Keywords: Facial capture · Active illumination · Reflectance · Photometric normals · Diffuse-specular separation · Dynamic capture

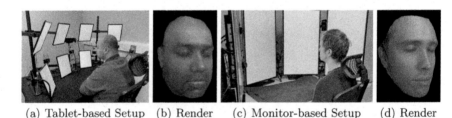

(a) Tablet-based Setup   (b) Render   (c) Monitor-based Setup   (d) Render

Fig. 1. Two proposed novel desktop-based setups (a, c) for high-quality facial capture (b, d). Left: setup consisting of a set of portable mobile devices – tablets and smartphones, for static facial capture. Right: setup consisting of a set desktop LCD displays for static and dynamic facial capture.

Supplementary Information The online version contains supplementary material available at https://doi.org/10.1007/978-3-031-20068-7_30.

© The Author(s), under exclusive license to Springer Nature Switzerland AG 2022

S. Avidan et al. (Eds.): ECCV 2022, LNCS 13666, pp. 522–537, 2022.
https://doi.org/10.1007/978-3-031-20068-7_30

1   Introduction

Realistic reconstruction and rendering of human faces has been a long standing goal in computer vision and graphics. It has wide ranging applications in well known sectors such as entertainment, advertising, AR/VR, training systems, etc., as well novel applications of digital avatars in social media, and virtual presence in the envisioned *metaverse*. Great strides have been made towards achieving this goal over the last two decades, both in terms of development of photo-realistic rendering algorithms, as well as realistic modeling of facial shape and appearance. The latter has been revolutionized with the development of acquisition techniques for high-quality 3D facial capture. However, creation of realistic digital characters from acquired data requires very high-quality data capture typically acquired using custom designed and expensive capture systems such as the Lightstage [4,10,21,29]. This usually restricts the application of such acquisition techniques in practice to big-budget film and games VFX, and/or to organizations that can either afford to access such setups at specific locations or to construct such capture systems in-house. Also, statistical [27] and deep-learning methods [9,19,20] still lack in quality compared to the above. This limits the accessibility of such 3D acquisition technology for wider applications.

Instead, this work aims to make acquisition of high quality facial geometry and appearance of a subject much more practical and accessible, thereby democratizing the creation of realistic virtual humans for various applications. Specifically, we propose a practical and scalable desktop-based setup for high-quality facial capture. The setup consists of a set of displays for active control of illumination for facial appearance capture, in conjunction with multiview acquisition of facial geometry. We present two different variants of the capture setup constructed entirely using commodity components – a highly portable setup consisting of a set of mobile devices (tablets and smartphones) targeting static facial capture, and a setup consisting of a set of desktop LCD displays targeting both static and dynamic facial capture (see Fig. 1). We additionally present a novel set of modulated binary illumination patterns emitted by the display panels in our setup for efficient acquisition of diffuse-specular separated reflectance and photometric normals. We present high-quality results of facial capture using both the proposed setups, and demonstrate the results to be qualitatively competitive with those obtained using dedicated, expensive capture setups. To summarize, this work introduces:

1. Two novel, scalable desktop setups for reflectance and shape capture, comprising only of commodity components.
2. A novel photometric acquisition pipeline with diffuse-specular separation employing modulated binary illumination that achieves high-quality results with the proposed desktop setups.
3. Novel design of spectral multiplexing for binary illumination that enables high-quality two-shot capture and estimation of spatially-varying specular roughness.
4. Demonstration of applicability of proposed setup and spectral multiplexing for dynamic facial appearance capture.

2   Related Work

Here we limit the discussion to the most related works on facial capture. For a broader discussion, we refer the reader to an excellent surveys on the topic [18,28].

2.1   Active Illumination

Photometric stereo systems have traditionally been popular in computer vision for estimating surface normals, in conjunction with color-multiplexed illumination for dynamic capture [14,17]. Debevec et al. [4] first proposed a specialized light stage setup to acquire a dense reflectance field of a human face for photo-realistic image-based relighting applications. They also fit microfacet-BRDF based reflectance using the acquired data. Weyrich et al. [29] instead employed an LED sphere and multiple cameras to densely record facial reflectance and computed view-independent estimates of spatially varying facial reflectance from the acquired data for driving a microfacet BRDF model-based rendering. Subsequently, Ma et al. [21] introduced polarized spherical gradient illumination (using an LED sphere) for efficient acquisition of the separated diffuse and specular albedos and photometric normals of a face, and demonstrated high quality facial geometry including skin mesostructure as well as realistic rendering with the acquired data.

Ghosh et al. [11] further extended the acquisition method to acquire layered facial reflectance using a combination of polarization and structured lighting, and further extended the view-dependent solution of Ma et al. for multi-view facial acquisition with polarized spherical gradient illumination [10]. These techniques have had significant impact in film VFX. Fyffe et al. [8] employed the method of [30] for temporal alignment of spherical gradient illumination for dynamic performance capture. Their method involves a heuristic based separation of reflectance which is not accurate and the capture process requires high speed cameras. Fyffe & Debevec [6] further proposed a single-shot method using a complex setup of a polarized RGB LED sphere for color-multiplexed spherical gradients that are further polarized using the method of [10] for diffuse-specular separation.

Closer to our work, Kampouris et al. [16] have employed binary spherical gradient illumination using an LED sphere for facial appearance capture including diffuse-specular separation of albedo and photometric normals. We employ a similar analysis of binary illumination in our work for diffuse-specular separation. However, we demonstrate our lighting patterns in conjunction with our illumination setup to result in fewer measurements for facial capture, even enabling high-quality results with spectral multiplexing which is not achieved by [16]. More recently, Guo et al. [13] have employed complementary pair of color-multiplexed spherical gradient illumination patterns using a spectral LED sphere for estimating diffuse and specular reflectance and surface normals for full-body volumetric capture. Unlike their approach, we employ a much simpler acquisition setup and estimate a broader set of spatially-varying reflectance parameters from each camera viewpoint using our spectral multiplexing approach.

An alternate approach that does not require an LED sphere is the work of Fyffe et al. [7] on static facial appearance capture employing off-the-shelf photography hardware. However, the approach does not extend to dynamic facial appearance capture and still requires quite a complex hardware setup consisting of 24 cameras and 6 flashes that are triggered in sequence within a few milliseconds. Our approach is inspired by these previous works. However, we aim to significantly simplify the capture process using commodity components and propose highly scalable desktop-based active illumination systems for high-quality facial capture. Very related to our approach is the recent work of Sengupta et al. [26] who employ a single desktop monitor to illuminate a face using a regular video sequence in order to learn a facial reflectance field with limited angular coverage. However, the goal of this work is to support facial relighting for video conferencing applications. Our desktop setup with brighter and wider illumination coverage is much more suitable for high-quality multiview capture, and we propose lighting patterns for direct acquisition of reflectance and photometric normals instead of learning based inference.

2.2   Passive Capture

Researchers have also investigated approaches for passive acquisition of faces and full-body. Such acquisition is particularly well suited for performance capture since active approaches usually require time-multiplexed illumination, imposing requirements of high frame rate acquisition, lighting control and synchronization. A popular approach has been to employ uniform constant illumination for multi-view facial capture [1,3]. Such an approach enables estimation of an albedo texture under flat lit illumination for rendering purposes besides facial geometry reconstruction based on multi-view stereo. High-frequency mesostructure is further embossed on the base-geometry using a high-pass filter on the diffuse texture [1]. The approach has been extended for reconstructing facial performances with drift-free tracking over long sequences using anchor frames [2]. While producing very good qualitative results for facial geometry, the estimated albedo is not completely diffuse and contains a small amount of specular reflectance baked into the texture and the embossed mesostructure is plausible rather than accurate.

More recent works have extended passive capture systems for achieving facial reflectance estimation using inverse rendering in conjunction with view-multiplexing [12,22]. However, while achieving impressive results for passive capture, the quality of acquired reflectance maps is not quite at par with active illumination systems. Gotardo et al. [12] are also able to acquire dynamic facial appearance like our monitor-based setup. However, their method requires initialization of neutral facial appearance through dense multiview capture in conjunction with measurement of person-specific change in skin color due to blood flow to constrain the optimization under passive illumination. Our method does not require any initialization or person-specific measurements and directly estimates high-quality appearance maps for each frame of dynamic capture.

3   Desktop-Based Capture System

We propose two desktop-based setups for facial capture in this work. Both setups employ specific types of display panels for controlled illumination, while employing a set of cameras for multiview acquisition. Both setups have been designed to provide controlled illumination over a frontal hemispherical zone of directions spanning $\beta < \pm 90°$ along the longitudinal directions ϕ, while spanning $\alpha < \pm 45°$ along the latitudinal directions θ (see supplemental material). Such a zone has previously been shown to include majority of facial surface normals [7].

3.1   Tablet-Based Setup

Our first desktop setup consists purely of a set of mobile devices – eight tablets and five smartphones, that are mounted on a desk as shown in Fig. 1(a). The tablets are arranged in two rows (latitudes) of four devices and oriented longitudinally so as to cover a significant zone of the frontal hemisphere around a subject's face. The screens of the tablets are oriented towards the subject and provide controlled piece-wise continuous illumination for acquiring facial reflectance. The selfie cameras on the tablets are employed to capture facial photometric response due to illumination during a capture sequence. These cameras are typically lower in resolution so they mostly serve to provide data for multiview 3D reconstruction (e.g., using structure-from-motion (SFM) [23]). We also place five smartphones in the setup along the equatorial plane, one between each column of the tablets, and employ their high-resolution back cameras (zoom lens) for acquiring facial reflectance and photometric normals. The tablets and the smartphones are mounted on a desk using appropriate table mounts. In this work, we employed iPad Air devices (4th generation) for the tablets and iPhone 12 Pro devices as the smartphones in our setup. Other types of tablets and smartphones (e.g., Android based) could also be used instead for the setup.

The devices are all controlled in synchronization during a capture process where one device acts as the master and the other devices act as slaves and they wirelessly communicate with each other over wifi. Once a capture command is initiated by an operator on the master device, the master broadcasts the start time for the capture process to all slave devices. All devices in the setup pool the global GPS clock-time from the GPS signal, and having received the capture instruction and start-time from the master device, then execute their own individual capture processes. Each device has a pre-built capture process that for the tablets includes illuminating a sequence of patterns from the device screen and simultaneously recording images using the selfie-camera, while for the smartphones involves capturing high-resolution images using the back zoom camera. All devices start and end their capture processes together in synchronized fashion in a few seconds due to pre-set capture/illumination timings. Afterwards, the acquired data from all devices is transferred to a single machine for off-line processing. The data transfer is also done wirelessly once initiated by an operator. The entire setup is highly portable since it consists of only the mobile devices and their table mounts. Hence, it can be easily moved from one location to another and quickly re-assembled for use without having to deal with any custom electronics and wiring.

3.2   Monitor-Based Setup

Our second setup consists of four desktop LCD monitors that we mount together on a desk in portrait mode as shown in Fig. 1(c). We employ four 27" 4K monitors with 16:9 aspect ratio (Asus ProArt PA279CV) in our setup. The monitors are arranged longitudinally facing the subject to cover a similar frontal hemispherical zone of directions with screen illumination. The four monitors are all controlled by single workstation (running Windows 10) via HDMI and display ports. The workstation includes a high-end graphics card (Nvidia RTX 3070 Ti) which is employed to drive the four monitors. We additionally mount stereo pairs of digital cameras within the vertical gaps between the monitors for multiview capture. Eight cameras are mounted using small desk-tripods and we chose mirrorless cameras with small form factor (Canon EOS M200) for ease of mounting in the setup. During acquisition, the workstation controls the monitors and the set of cameras in synchronization to rapidly capture a sequence of images under a set of controlled illumination patterns for 3D shape and reflectance capture. The monitor-based setup has the advantage over the tablet-based setup of much more fine-grained synchronization between multiple displays supporting much faster capture, even supporting video rate capture required for acquiring dynamic facial performance.

3.3   Modulated Binary Illumination

We employ horizontally and vertically aligned binary illumination patterns in this work, over the hemispherical zone of illumination of the proposed capture setups, for acquiring albedo and photometric normals with diffuse-specular separation. While this is similar to the approach of Kampouris et al. [16], our patterns require additional form-factor modulation due to being near-field with limited angular extent. Furthermore, we make the crucial observation that over the zone of hemispherical illumination covered by the displays in our setup, we do *not* need all three axis aligned (X, Y, Z) binary illumination conditions and their complements employed by [16]. Specifically, when we illuminate a subject with the horizontally aligned binary pattern and its complement (H and H' respectively), the lit portion of the zone does not have its centroid aligned with X-axis but is actually centered around $+45°$ and $-45°$ directions respectively in the XZ plane (with $0°$ corresponding to the +Z axis). This results in the complementary pair of horizontal binary patterns H and H' to have their centroids orthogonal to each other in the XZ plane (albeit with a $45°$ in-plane rotation), and hence sufficient for determining the x and z components of a photometric normal. We additionally only need measurement of the vertically aligned binary pattern V and its complement V' to determine the y component of the photometric normal. This reduces the number of measurements to only four photographs under the horizontal and vertical binary illumination patterns (see Fig. 2a).

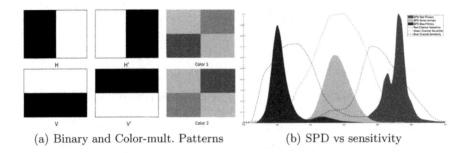

(a) Binary and Color-mult. Patterns   (b) SPD vs sensitivity

Fig. 2. (a) Four binary illumination patterns (H, H', V, V'), and color-multiplexed patterns used for 2-shot acquisition. (b) Display illumination SPD (solid fill) plotted against the spectral sensitivity of iPhone 12 Pro camera (dashed lines). The color patterns are designed to avoid cross-talk between green and red channels. (Color figure online)

Spectral Multiplexing. For faster acquisition, we further reduce the number of measurements to only two photographs by employing spectral multiplexing of the binary patterns using the R, G and B color channels of the display panels. While this is similar to the spectral multiplexing approach of [16], we demonstrate much higher quality results for faces with our spectral multiplexing scheme which are almost at par with results obtained using four measurements under binary white illumination. Unlike previous work employing spectral multiplexing for photometric measurements, we observe that typical RGB illumination observed by standard RGB cameras can suffer from a bit of spectral cross-talk between neighboring wavelengths. Specifically, depending on the spectral power distribution (SPD) of the RGB source and the spectral sensitivity of the camera, this can result in some cross-talk between the blue and green channels, or the green and red channels sensed by the camera. Both our setups employ LCD displays with DCI P3 color gamut. We measured the SPD of our displays using a spectrometer (Sekonic SpectoMaster C700) and camera spectral sensitivity (using the procedure of [15]), and found the green and red illumination emitted by the displays to be spectrally closer to each other due to an amber peak in the red illumination spectrum. This causes the green channel of the cameras we employ to be sensitive to red illumination emitted by the displays, and hence causes some spectral cross-talk between these two color channels (Fig. 2(b), see supplemental material for details).

In order to deal with this spectral cross-talk, we exploit our horizontal and vertical binary patterns to design two novel complementary spectral multiplexing patterns for high-quality photometric measurements. Specifically, we ensure that the patterns do not have any overlap of green and red illumination and we spectrally encode the horizontal and vertical binary patterns and their complements in the two patterns shown in Fig. 2(a). Each pattern consists of both the horizontal pattern H and its complement H' encoded in the red and green channels respectively (or vice versa), while the blue channel encodes either the vertical pattern V or its complement V'. The two patterns are complementary and sum to uniform white illumination.

Form-Factor Modulation. As previously mentioned, we additionally need to modulate the intensity of the binary illumination patterns to compensate for the form-factor of the measurement setup. This is required since the illumination is restricted to a hemispherical zone and hence is not uniformly incident from all directions (unlike an LED sphere). Specifically, due to the limited extent of the zone in the vertical (latitudinal) direction compared to the horizontal (longitudinal) direction, we need to modulate the intensity along the vertical direction to create an even distribution of illumination. We do this by reducing the intensity nearer to the equator compared to latitudes near the top and bottom of the zone. This form-factor modulation also needs to account for any local effects of illumination due to the setup geometry. We pre-compute this vertical modulation function using inverse rendering a diffuse sphere lit by display panel arrangements of our two setups. We then apply this vertical modulation function to the binary illumination patterns during acquisition.

Multi-view Capture. The acquired patterns are axis-aligned with the global coordinates of the capture setup. We observe that the patterns form a steerable basis and rotate the corresponding pairs into the local coordinate frame of each camera before employing the photometric estimation process described in Sect. 4.

4   Reflectance and Shape Estimation

4.1   Acquisition Using White Illumination

Given the acquired set of photographs of a subject under the four binary patterns $\mathbf{H}, \mathbf{H}', \mathbf{V}, \mathbf{V}'$ (Fig. 2), we first rotate the $\mathbf{H}$ and $\mathbf{H}'$ patterns around the Y axis by $\pm 45°$ to additionally obtain the axis aligned patterns $\mathbf{X}, \mathbf{X}'$, and $\mathbf{Z}$. Each binary-complement pair can be added to acquire a full-on observation $\mathbf{F}$, e.g., $\mathbf{F} = \mathbf{X} + \mathbf{X}'$. These observations can then be used to estimate photometric normals and separated diffuse and specular albedo.

Photometric Normals. The set of acquired binary patterns can be used to compute mixed photometric normals following [16]. However, due to incomplete hemispherical illumination (limited to $< \pm 45°$ latitudinal span) employed in our setups, this would result in skewed normals. Instead, we employ Singular Value Decomposition (SVD) to extract photometric normals with more correct global orientation. We directly stack the flattened $\mathbf{H}, \mathbf{H}', \mathbf{V}, \mathbf{V}'$ measurements into a matrix $\mathbf{A} \in \mathbb{R}^{WH \times 4}$, where W, H are the width and height of each measurement. As shown by [31], the eigenvectors of the three largest eigenvalues of $\mathbf{A}\mathbf{A}^\top$ correspond to the normals components $\mathbf{N}^\mathbf{X}, \mathbf{N}^\mathbf{Y}, \mathbf{N}^\mathbf{Z}$.

The orientation and order of the components of normals is arbitrary with SVD. Therefore we order them in the following way: We create a facial mask $\mathbf{M}$ by using a face detector [5] on F, and design a function $\mathcal{A}(\mathbf{N}, \mathbf{M})$, that aligns the components with the $+\mathrm{X}, +\mathrm{Y}, +\mathrm{Z}$ axes. Specifically, we fit for each component a linear regression on the X and Y axes, and assign each component to the axis with the highest absolute trend, while using the sign of the trend to orient the component. For $\mathbf{N}^Z$, the regression is fit on half of the X axis. For an $\mathbf{USV}^\top$ SVD decomposition of $\mathbf{A}$ and $\mathbf{U}'$ including the first three vectors of $\mathbf{U}$:

$$\mathbf{N} = \mathcal{A}(\mathbf{U}', \mathbf{M}), \quad \mathbf{A} = \mathbf{USV}^\top \tag{1}$$

Diffuse Normals. Shorter-wavelength channels exhibit sharper normal details, because of the wavelength-dependent diffuse scattering of light [21]. Under white illumination, we observe that the different color channels share the same amount of specular reflectance, which is white, but different amounts of diffuse reflectance. We can therefore acquire pure diffuse signal using the spectral differencing between the brightest (red) and darkest channels (blue) of each pattern, i.e., $\mathbf{X}_D = \mathbf{X}^R - \mathbf{X}^B$. The pure diffuse patterns can be used with Eq. 1 to compute the diffuse normals $\mathbf{N}_D$.

Specular Normals. We follow the observation of [16] that the mixed normals are a mixture of diffuse and specular normals. However, we employ a simpler empirical signal processing step for estimating specular normals from the mixture. The calculation, although heuristic in nature, produces sharp specular normals, which are able to generate highly photorealistic shading. Formulating mixed photometric normals $\mathbf{N}$ as a combination of the diffuse normals $\mathbf{N}_D$ and a portion of the specular signal $\alpha\mathbf{S}$, we separate the specular signal using a Gaussian high-pass filter $g()$. We empirically set $\alpha = 0.5$ for our results. To obtain the final specular normals $\mathbf{N}_S$, we add the separated specular signal to the diffuse normals and re-normalize the normals.:

$$\mathbf{N}_S = \frac{\mathbf{N}_D + \frac{1}{\alpha}(\mathbf{N} - g(\mathbf{N}))}{|| \, \mathbf{N}_D + \frac{1}{\alpha}(\mathbf{N} - g(\mathbf{N})) \, ||} \tag{2}$$

Diffuse-Specular Albedo Separation. For separating the reflectance albedo into diffuse $\mathbf{A}_D$ and specular $\mathbf{A}_S$ components respectively, we employ the linear system in Eq. 3 originally proposed by [16] for color-multiplexed data. We find the linear system based separation to also be well suited for binary patterns with white illumination. Assuming the binary observation along X is brighter than its complement X', the linear system is expressed as:

$$\begin{bmatrix} \mathbf{X} \\ \mathbf{X}' \end{bmatrix} = \begin{bmatrix} \mathbf{N_D.x} & 1 \\ (1 - \mathbf{N_D.x}) & 0 \end{bmatrix} \begin{bmatrix} \mathbf{A}_D \\ \mathbf{A}_S \end{bmatrix}, \tag{3}$$

where $\mathbf{N_D.x}$ is the x component of the diffuse normal scaled to $[0, 1]$. Equation 3 can be solved separately for each binary-complement pair to acquire an estimate of $\mathbf{A}_S$. Instead of the median of three axis-aligned solutions proposed by Kampouris et al., we find the best estimate as the average $\mathbf{A}_{S_{avg}}$ of solutions for only the $\mathbf{X}$ and $\mathbf{Y}$ binary pairs. Finally, for computing the diffuse albedo $\mathbf{A}_D$, we solve the linear system independently for each color channel and then subtract the channel wise $\mathbf{A}_{S_{avg}}$ from full-on $\mathbf{F}$ to obtain $\mathbf{A}_D$.

4.2   Color-Multiplexed Illumination

We reduce measurements to a two-shot capture process using color multiplexed binary patterns shown in Fig. 2. These patterns yield two spectral pairs of horizontally aligned patterns $\mathbf{H_1}, \mathbf{H'_1}$, $\mathbf{H_2}, \mathbf{H'_2}$ and one pair of vertically aligned patterns $\mathbf{V}, \mathbf{V'}$. Similarly to the white pattern captures, the orthogonal horizontal patterns can be rotated to create two sets of X and Y axis-aligned patterns. We then follow a similar approach to Sect. 4.1, but with the following key differences:

Diffuse and Specular Normals. We acquire two horizontal pattern sets, using the green channel $\mathbf{H_1}, \mathbf{H'_1}$ and the red channel $\mathbf{H_2}, \mathbf{H'_2}$. Photometric normals from shorter-wavelength channels exhibit sharper normal details [21]. Hence, we use the SVD method (Eq. 1) to estimate the mixed photometric normals $\mathbf{N}$ using the green-channel set $\mathbf{H_1}, \mathbf{H'_1}$ which has substantial specular signal. Additionally, we use SVD to estimate the normals using the red-channel set $\mathbf{H_2}, \mathbf{H'_2}$, which exhibits weaker specular signal, and treat these as the diffuse normals $\mathbf{N_D}$. Finally, we use Eq. 2 to calculate the specular normals given $\mathbf{N}$ and refined $\mathbf{N_D}$.

Diffuse-Specular Separation. Similar to white illumination, we employ the linear system of Eq. 3 to estimate the specular albedo $\mathbf{A}_{S_{avg}}$ by averaging the solutions for the X and Y axes. However, unlike the case of white illumination, to estimate the diffuse albedo $\mathbf{A_D}$ we first scale the average $\mathbf{A}_{S_{avg}}$ by the ratio r_c of the respective channel wise solutions of $\mathbf{A_S}$ relative to red channel solution, before subtracting it from full-on image $\mathbf{F}$: $\mathbf{A_D} = \mathbf{F} - r_c * \mathbf{A}_{S_{avg}}$. Here, $\mathbf{F}$ is obtained by adding the two color-multiplexed patterns.

4.3   Specular Roughness Estimation

We further exploit the observations under the color-multiplexed patterns to estimate spatially varying specular roughness. We make the observation that the two color patterns illuminate a subject with four saturated colors and increasing specular roughness blurs these colors to make them less saturated. Hence, we employ normalized color as a novel metric to estimate spatially varying specular roughness using an inverse rendering process. We employ the estimated diffuse albedo $\mathbf{A_D}$ and diffuse normal $\mathbf{N_D}$ to relight the subject under the two color multiplexed lighting conditions and subtract these rendered diffuse components from the photographs to isolate their specular components. We then employ the estimated specular albedo $\mathbf{A_S}$ and specular normal $\mathbf{N_S}$ to render the specular response to these lighting patterns and compare the normalized color of the renderings with various roughness parameters (Cook-Torrance BRDF) to the isolated specular component in the photographs. The estimated specular roughness corresponds to the best matching normalized color (L1 norm). This way, we exploit color as an additional cue to separate specular albedo and roughness.

4.4   Dynamic Capture

The reflectance estimation approach using color-multiplexed patterns (Sect. 4.2) is well-suited for dynamic capture. As proof-of-concept, we employ our monitor-based setup for dynamic capture and synchronize a machine vision camera (FLIR Grasshopper 3) with the refresh rate of the monitors. Using this setup, we capture alternating color-multiplexed patterns at 60 fps. The monitors take 16ms to update the pattern on the screens. In order to handle this, we double up the alternating patterns for two frames at a time and use every other frame in the sequence while ignoring the in-between frames corresponding to the screen updates. This provides an effective capture rate of 30 fps for the alternating patterns. Each pattern can be used in conjunction with the next pattern in the sequence for reflectance estimation at the effective capture rate.

4.5   Base Geometry Acquisition

We reconstruct base geometry using multiview capture for our static capture examples. We employ widely used structure-from-motion software COLMAP [24, 25] for this purpose and provide it a full-on image $\mathbf{F}$ (computed as sum of a binary pair) from each camera viewpoint. Each camera's processed reflectance and normals are projected on to the reconstructed mesh.

5   Results

5.1   Evaluation

Figure 3 presents comparison of reflectance and photometric normal maps estimated using our 4-shot method employing white binary illumination (top-left), and maps estimated using our 2-shot method using spectral multiplexing (top-right), vs those estimated using the 6-shot method (bottom-left) and the 2-shot method (bottom-right) proposed by Kampouris et al. [16]. Here, all methods have been implemented on our tablet-based capture setup. Both our 4-shot and 2-shot method achieve high quality results that are quite comparable, while achieving results that are superior to those obtained with the 6-shot and the 2-shot method respectively of [16] for both albedo and photometric normals. We note that the method of [16] was designed for an LED sphere and hence it does not perform as optimally in our setup. Finally, Fig. 11 shows a comparison of our reconstruction with a single-image learning-based method [20].

5.2   Static Capture

Figure 4 presents qualitative comparisons of acquired reflectance and photometric normal maps for a subject using both our proposed desktop-based capture setups. As can be seen, both setups acquire high-quality data. Figure 5 presents

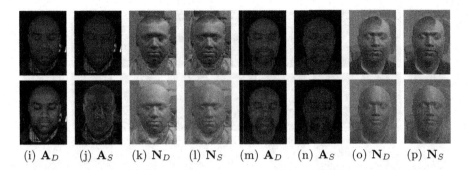

(i) $\mathbf{A}_D$ (j) $\mathbf{A}_S$ (k) $\mathbf{N}_D$ (l) $\mathbf{N}_S$ (m) $\mathbf{A}_D$ (n) $\mathbf{A}_S$ (o) $\mathbf{N}_D$ (p) $\mathbf{N}_S$

Fig. 3. Comparison of our results (top) with 4-shot white illumination (left), and 2-shot spectral multiplexing (right), against that of [16] (bottom) using 6-shot white illumination (left) and 2-shot spectral multiplexing (right).

maps of spatially varying specular roughness of a few subjects that were estimated using novel color cues given observations of the subjects under the two color multiplexed illumination conditions.

Figure 9 presents results of several subjects acquired using both of our proposed desktop-based capture setups. Here, we present results of our 2-shot capture process using spectral multiplexing. As can be seen, our estimated diffuse-specular separated reflectance and normals maps (c, d) enable camera-space renderings (b) that are a good qualitative match to the comparison photographs (a). The acquired data can be combined from multiple viewpoints for high quality renderings of 3D geometry (e), and appearance (f). We show multiview data projected to UV maps in Fig. 7. We compare the quantitative error between the validation photos (a) and our camera-space renderings (b) and report an average MSE of 0.0019 and PSNR of 27.205 across 7 subjects.

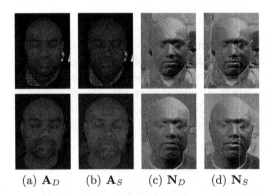

(a) $\mathbf{A}_D$ (b) $\mathbf{A}_S$ (c) $\mathbf{N}_D$ (d) $\mathbf{N}_S$

Fig. 4. Comparison of reflectance separation between the Tablet-based setup (top), and the monitor-based setup (down).

Fig. 5. Specular roughness maps, using novel color cues from the color multiplexed patterns.

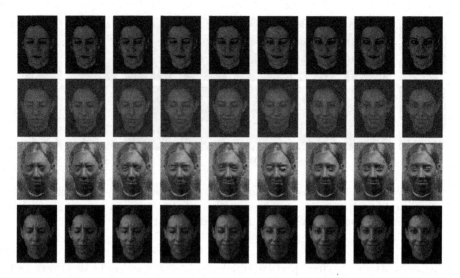

Fig. 6. Example of dynamic capture using our monitor-based setup, acquired at 60 FPS for results at 30 FPS. From top-to-bottom: diffuse albedo, specular albedo, specular normals and rendering in the Grace Cathedral environment.

(a) Diff. Alb   (b) Spec. Alb   (c) Sp. Norm   (a) Un.   (b) Pol.   (c) Ours

Fig. 7. Complete facial UV maps of our cap-tured reflectance, which shows the multi-view capabilities of our approach.

Fig. 8. Comparison between unpolarised, cross-polarized [10] and our albedo result.

5.3   Dynamic Capture

Figure 6 presents a few frames from a dynamic capture sequence of a female subject acquired at effective 30FPS (every other frame of a 60FPS capture pro-cess) using a machine vision camera. As can be seen, the monitor-based setup, in conjunction with our proposed color multiplexed patterns, is well suited for obtaining video-rate diffuse-specular separation and photometric normals of a dynamic capture sequence. We provide another example in the supplemental.

5.4   Limitations

Our proposed capture technique, while highly practical, has some limitations. The illumination is restricted to a frontal zone which may not be suitable for all object shapes, and limited illumination coverage can affect estimated pho-tometric maps at the extreme sides. We do not model any single scattering in skin [11]. Finally, dynamic capture rate is limited by monitor refresh rate.

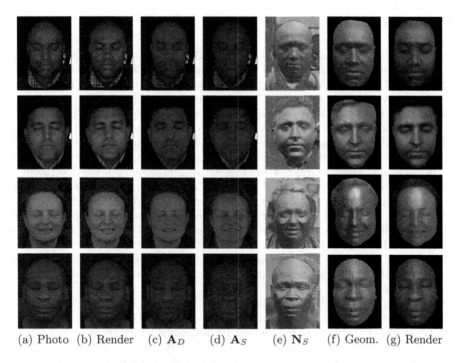

(a) Photo (b) Render   (c) $\mathbf{A}_D$ (d) $\mathbf{A}_S$ (e) $\mathbf{N}_S$ (f) Geom. (g) Render

Fig. 9. Various subjects acquired with our tablet-based setup (top two), and monitor-based setup (bottom two), captured using our 2-shot method.

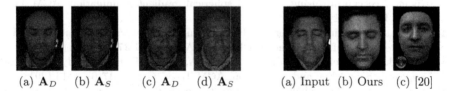

(a) $\mathbf{A}_D$ (b) $\mathbf{A}_S$ (c) $\mathbf{A}_D$ (d) $\mathbf{A}_S$ (a) Input (b) Ours   (c) [20]

Fig. 10. Comparison of albedo measurement and separation with our method using our setup (left), vs using a single screen (right).

Fig. 11. Our results compared with AvatarMe++, a deep-learning method [20].

6   Conclusions

We present two novel desktop-based setups for high quality facial capture, including reflectance and photometric normals, which are practical and scalable, consisting entirely of commodity components. We also present a novel analysis of binary illumination together with our setup, for efficient acquisition with reduced measurements. We achieve high-quality diffuse-specular separation with spectral multiplexing, exploit novel color cues for estimating specular roughness, and extend the two-shot capture for video-rate dynamic capture. Our proposed systems can make high-quality facial capture widely accessible.

References

1. Beeler, T., Bickel, B., Beardsley, P., Sumner, B., Gross, M.: High-quality single-shot capture of facial geometry. ACM Trans. Graph. (TOG) **29**(3), 40:1–40:9 (2010)
2. Beeler, T., et al.: High-quality passive facial performance capture using anchor frames. ACM Trans. Graph. (ACM) **30**, 75:1–75:10 (2011)
3. Bradley, D., Heidrich, W., Popa, T., Sheffer, A.: High resolution passive facial performance capture. ACM Trans. Graph. (TOG) **29**(4), 41 (2010)
4. Debevec, P., Hawkins, T., Tchou, C., Duiker, H.P., Sarokin, W., Sagar, M.: Acquiring the reflectance field of a human face. In: Proceedings of the 27th Annual Conference on Computer Graphics and Interactive Techniques, pp. 145–156 (2000)
5. Deng, J., Guo, J., Zhou, Y., Yu, J., Kotsia, I., Zafeiriou, S.: RetinaFace: single-stage dense face localisation in the wild. arXiv preprint arXiv:1905.00641 (2019)
6. Fyffe, G., Debevec, P.: Single-shot reflectance measurement from polarized color gradient illumination. In: International Conference on Computational Photography (ICCP). IEEE (2015)
7. Fyffe, G., Graham, P., Tunwattanapong, B., Ghosh, A., Debevec, P.: Near-instant capture of high-resolution facial geometry and reflectance. In: Computer Graphics Forum (2016)
8. Fyffe, G., Hawkins, T., Watts, C., Ma, W.C., Debevec, P.: Comprehensive facial performance capture. In: Computer Graphics Forum (CGF), vol. 30, no. 2 (2011)
9. Gecer, B., et al.: Synthesizing coupled 3D face modalities by trunk-branch generative adversarial networks. In: Vedaldi, A., Bischof, H., Brox, T., Frahm, J.-M. (eds.) ECCV 2020. LNCS, vol. 12374, pp. 415–433. Springer, Cham (2020). https://doi.org/10.1007/978-3-030-58526-6_25
10. Ghosh, A., Fyffe, G., Tunwattanapong, B., Busch, J., Yu, X., Debevec, P.: Multiview face capture using polarized spherical gradient illumination. ACM TOG **30**(6), 1–10 (2011)
11. Ghosh, A., Hawkins, T., Peers, P., Frederiksen, S., Debevec, P.: Practical modeling and acquisition of layered facial reflectance. ACM TOG **27**(5), 1–10 (2008)
12. Gotardo, P., Riviere, J., Bradley, D., Ghosh, A., Beeler, T.: Practical dynamic facial appearance modeling and acquisition. ACM Trans. Graph. **37**(6), 1–13 (2018)
13. Guo, K., et al.: The relightables: volumetric performance capture of humans with realistic relighting. ACM Trans. Graph. (TOG) **38**(6), 1–19 (2019)
14. Hernandez, C., Vogiatzis, G., Brostow, G.J., Stenger, B., Cipolla, R.: Non-rigid photometric stereo with colored lights. In: Proceedings of the IEEE/CVF International Conference on Computer Vision (2007)
15. Jiang, J., Liu, D., Gu, J., Süsstrunk, S.: What is the space of spectral sensitivity functions for digital color cameras? In: 2013 IEEE Workshop on Applications of Computer Vision (WACV), pp. 168–179. IEEE (2013)
16. Kampouris, C., Zafeiriou, S., Ghosh, A.: Diffuse-specular separation using binary spherical gradient illumination. In: EGSR (EI&I), pp. 1–10 (2018)
17. Klaudiny, M., Hilton, A.: High-detail 3D capture and non-sequential alignment of facial performance. In: Proceedings of 3DIMPVT (2012)
18. Klehm, O., et al.: Recent advances in facial appearance capture. In: Computer Graphics Forum (CGF), vol. 34, no. 2, pp. 709–733 (2015)
19. Lattas, A., et al.: AvatarMe: realistically renderable 3D facial reconstruction "in-the-wild". In: Proceedings of the IEEE/CVF Conference on Computer Vision and Pattern Recognition, pp. 760–769 (2020)

20. Lattas, A., Moschoglou, S., Ploumpis, S., Gecer, B., Ghosh, A., Zafeiriou, S.P.: AvatarMe++: facial shape and BRDF inference with rendering-aware GANs. TPAMI (2021). https://ieeexplore.ieee.org/abstract/document/9606538
21. Ma, W.C., Hawkins, T., Peers, P., Chabert, C.F., Weiss, M., Debevec, P.: Rapid acquisition of specular and diffuse normal maps from polarized spherical gradient illumination. In: Proceedings of the EGSR (2007)
22. Riviere, J., Gotardo, P., Bradley, D., Ghosh, A., Beeler, T.: Single-shot high-quality facial geometry and skin appearance capture. ACM Trans. Graph. **39**(4), 1–12 (2020)
23. Schonberger, J.L., Frahm, J.: Structure-from-motion revisited. In: 2016 IEEE Conference on Computer Vision and Pattern Recognition (CVPR), Los Alamitos, CA, USA, pp. 4104–4113. IEEE Computer Society, June 2016
24. Schönberger, J.L., Frahm, J.M.: Structure-from-motion revisited. In: Conference on Computer Vision and Pattern Recognition (CVPR) (2016)
25. Schönberger, J.L., Zheng, E., Frahm, J.-M., Pollefeys, M.: Pixelwise view selection for unstructured multi-view stereo. In: Leibe, B., Matas, J., Sebe, N., Welling, M. (eds.) ECCV 2016. LNCS, vol. 9907, pp. 501–518. Springer, Cham (2016). https://doi.org/10.1007/978-3-319-46487-9_31
26. Sengupta, S., Curless, B., Kemelmacher-Shlizerman, I., Seitz, S.M.: A light stage on every desk. In: Proceedings of the IEEE/CVF International Conference on Computer Vision, pp. 2420–2429 (2021)
27. Smith, W.A., Seck, A., Dee, H., Tiddeman, B., Tenenbaum, J.B., Egger, B.: A morphable face albedo model. In: Proceedings of the IEEE/CVF Conference on Computer Vision and Pattern Recognition, pp. 5011–5020 (2020)
28. Weyrich, T., Lawrence, J., Lensch, H., Rusinkiewicz, S., Zickler, T.: Principles of appearance acquisition and representation. Found. Trends Comput. Graph. Vis. **4**(2), 75–191 (2008)
29. Weyrich, T., et al.: Analysis of human faces using a measurement-based skin reflectance model. ACM Trans. Graph. (TOG) **25**(3), 1013–1024 (2006)
30. Wilson, C.A., Ghosh, A., Peers, P., Chiang, J.Y., Busch, J., Debevec, P.: Temporal upsampling of performance geometry using photometric alignment. ACM Trans. Graph. (TOG) **29**(2), 17 (2010)
31. Yuille, A.L., Snow, D., Epstein, R., Belhumeur, P.N.: Determining generative models of objects under varying illumination: shape and albedo from multiple images using SVD and integrability. Int. J. Comput. Vis. **35**(3), 203–222 (1999). https://doi.org/10.1023/A:1008180726317

FAST-VQA: Efficient End-to-End Video Quality Assessment with Fragment Sampling

Haoning Wu[1,2,3(✉)], Chaofeng Chen[1,2], Jingwen Hou[2], Liang Liao[1,2], Annan Wang[1,2], Wenxiu Sun[3], Qiong Yan[3], and Weisi Lin[2(✉)]

[1] S-Lab, Nanyang Technological University, Singapore, Singapore
haoning001@e.ntu.edu.sg
[2] School of Computer Science and Engineering, Nanyang Technological University, Singapore, Singapore
[3] Sensetime Research and Tetras AI, Hong Kong, China

Abstract. Current deep video quality assessment (VQA) methods are usually with high computational costs when evaluating high-resolution videos. This cost hinders them from learning better video-quality-related representations via end-to-end training. Existing approaches typically consider naive sampling to reduce the computational cost, such as *resizing* and *cropping*. However, they obviously corrupt quality-related information in videos and are thus not optimal to learn good representations for VQA. Therefore, there is an eager need to design a new quality-retained sampling scheme for VQA. In this paper, we propose Grid Mini-patch Sampling (GMS), which allows consideration of local quality by sampling patches at their raw resolution and covers global quality with contextual relations via mini-patches sampled in uniform grids. These mini-patches are spliced and aligned temporally, named as **fragments**. We further build the Fragment Attention Network (FANet) specially designed to accommodate **fragments** as inputs. Consisting of **fragments** and FANet, the proposed FrAgment Sample Transformer for VQA (**FAST-VQA**) enables efficient end-to-end deep VQA and learns effective video-quality-related representations. It improves state-of-the-art accuracy by around 10% while reducing 99.5% FLOPs on 1080P high-resolution videos. The newly learned video-quality-related representations can also be transferred into smaller VQA datasets, boosting the performance on these scenarios. Extensive experiments show that FAST-VQA has good performance on inputs of various resolutions while retaining high efficiency. We publish our code at https://github.com/timothyhtimothy/FAST-VQA.

Keywords: Video quality assessment, **fragments**

1 Introduction

More and more videos with a variety of contents are collected in-the-wild and uploaded to the Internet every day. With the growth of high-definition

© The Author(s), under exclusive license to Springer Nature Switzerland AG 2022
S. Avidan et al. (Eds.): ECCV 2022, LNCS 13666, pp. 538–554, 2022.
https://doi.org/10.1007/978-3-031-20068-7_31

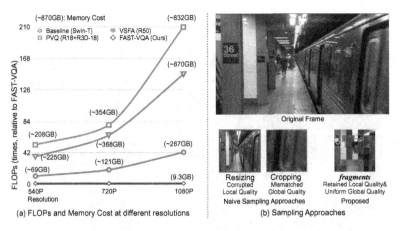

Fig. 1. Motivation for *fragments*: (a) The computational cost (FLOPs&Memory at Batch Size 4) for existing VQA methods is high especially on high-resolution videos. (b) Sampling approaches. Naive approaches such as *resizing* [17,45] and *cropping* [14,15] cannot preserve video quality well. Zoom in for clearer view.

video recording devices, a growing proportion of these videos are in high resolution (e.g. $\geq 1080P$). Classical video quality assessment (VQA) algorithms based on handcrafted features are difficult to handle these videos with diverse content and degradation. In recent years, deep-learning-based VQA methods [8,21,23,24,42,44] have shown better performance on in-the-wild VQA benchmarks [12,33,40,42]. However, the computational cost of deep VQA methods increases quadratically when applied to high resolution videos, and a video of size 1080×1920 would require **42.5×** floating point operations (FLOPs) than normal 224×224 inputs (as Fig. 1(a) shows), limiting these methods from practical applications. It is urgent to develop new VQA methods that are both effective and efficient.

Meanwhile, with high memory cost noted in Fig. 1(a), existing methods usually regress quality scores with fixed features extracted from pre-trained networks for classification tasks [10,11,34] to alleviate memory shortage problem on GPUs instead of end-to-end training, preventing them from learning *video-quality-related representations* that better represent quality information and limiting their accuracy. Existing approaches apply naive sampling on images or videos by resizing [17,45] or cropping [14,15] (as Fig. 1(b) shows) to reduce this cost and enable end-to-end training. However, they both cause artificial quality corruptions or changes during sampling, *e.g.*, resizing corrupts local textures that are significant for predicting video quality, while cropping causes mismatched global quality with local regions. Moreover, the severity of these problems increases with the raw resolution of the video, making them unsuitable for VQA tasks.

To improve the practical efficiency and the training effectiveness of deep VQA methods, we propose a new sampling scheme, Grid Mini-patch Sampling (GMS), to retain the sensitivity to original video quality. GMS cuts videos into spatially

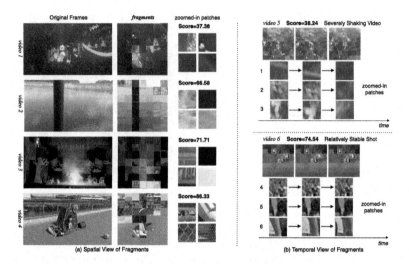

Fig. 2. *Fragments*, in spatial view (a) and temporal view (b). Zoom-in views of mini-patches show that *fragments* can retain spatial local quality information (a), and spot temporal variations such as shaking across frames (b). In (a), spliced mini-patches also keep the global scene information of original frames.

uniform non-overlapping grids, randomly sample a mini-patch from each grid, and then splice mini-patches together. In temporal view, we constrain the position of mini-patches to align across frames, in order to ensure the sensitivity on temporal variations. We name these temporally aligned and spatially spliced mini-patches as *fragments*. As shown in Fig. 2, The proposed fragments can well preserve the sensitivity on both spatial and temporal quality. First, it preserves the local texture-related quality information (*e.g.*, spot blurs happened in *video 1/2*) by retaining the original resolution in patches. Second, benefiting from the globally uniformly sampled grids, it covers the global quality even though different regions have different qualities (*e.g.*, *video 3*). Third, by splicing the mini-patches, *fragments* retains contextual relations of patches so that the model can learn global scene information of the original frames. At last, with temporal alignment, *fragments* preserve temporal quality sensitivity by retaining the inter-frame variations in mini-patches from raw resolution, so they can be used to spot temporal distortions in videos and distinguish between severely shaking videos (*e.g.*, *video 5*) from relatively stable shots (*e.g.*, *video 6*).

However, it is non-trivial to build a network using the proposed *fragments* as inputs. The network should follow two principles: 1) It should better extract the quality-related information preserved in *fragments*, including the retained local textures inside the raw resolution patches and the contextual relations between the spliced mini-patches; 2) It should distinguish the artificial discontinuity between mini-patches in *fragments* from the authentic quality degradation in the original videos. Based on these two principles, we propose a Fragment Attention Network (FANet) with Video Swin Transformer Tiny (Swin-T) [28] as the backbone. Swin-T has a hierarchical structure and processes inputs with patch-wise operations, which is naturally suitable for proceeding with proposed *fragments*.

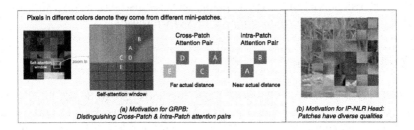

Fig. 3. Motivation for the two proposed modules in FANet: (a) Gated Relative Position Biases (GRPB); (b) Intra-Patch Non-Linear Regression (IP-NLR) head. The structures for the two modules are illustrated in Fig. 5. (Color figure online)

Furthermore, to avoid the negative impact of discontinuity between mini-patches on quality prediction, we propose two novel modules, *i.e.*, Gated Relative Position Biases (GRPB) and Intra-Patch Non-Linear Regression (IP-NLR), to correct for the self-attention computation and the final score regression in the FANet respectively. Specifically, considering that some pairs in the same attention window might have the same relative position (*e.g.*, Fig. 3(a) A–C, D–E, A–B), but the cross-patch attention pairs (A–C, D–E) are in far actual distances while intra-patch attention pairs (A–B) are in much nearer actual distances in the original video, we propose GRPB to explicitly distinguish these two kinds of attention pairs to avoid confusion of discontinuity between patches and authentic video artifacts. In addition, due to the discontinuity, different mini-patches contain diverse quality information (Fig. 3(b)), thus pooling operation before score regression applied in existing methods may confuse the information. To address this issue, we design IP-NLR as a quality-sensitive head, which first regresses the quality scores of mini-patches independently with non-linear layers and pools them after the regression.

In summary, we propose the FrAgment Sample Transformer for VQA (**FAST-VQA**), with the following contributions:

1. We propose *fragments*, a new sampling strategy for VQA that preserves both local quality and unbiased global quality with contextual relations via uniform Grid Mini-patch Sampling (GMS). The *fragments* can reduce the complexity of assessing 1080P videos by 97.6% and enables effective end-to-end training of VQA with quality-retained video samples.
2. We propose the Fragment Attention Network (FANet) to learn the local and contextual quality information from *fragments*, in which the Gated Relative Position Biases (GRPB) module is proposed to distinguish the intra-patch and cross-patch self-attention and the Intra-Patch Non-Linear Regression (IP-NLR) is proposed for better quality regression from *fragments*.

3. The proposed FAST-VQA can learn *video-quality-related representations* efficiently through end-to-end training. These quality features help FAST-VQA to be **10%** more accurate than the existing state-of-the-art approaches and **8%** better than full-resolution Swin-T baseline with fixed recognition features. Through transfer learning, these quality features also significantly improve the best benchmark performance for small VQA datasets.

2   Related Works

Classical VQA Methods. Classical VQA methods [20,26,30,32,36,37] handcrafted features to evaluate video quality. Among recent works, TLVQM [20] uses a combination of spatial high-complexity and temporal low-complexity handcraft features and VIDEVAL [36] ensembles different handcraft features to model the diverse authentic distortions. However, the reasons affecting the video quality are quite complicated and cannot be well captured with these handcrafted features.

Fixed-Feature-Based Deep VQA Methods. Due to the extremely high computational cost of deep networks on high resolution videos, existing deep VQA methods train only a feature regression network with fixed deep features. Among them, VSFA [23] uses the features extracted by pre-trained ResNet-50 [11] from ImageNet-1k [5] and GRU [4] for temporal regression. MLSP-FF [8] also uses heavier Inception-ResNet-V2 [34] for feature extraction. Some methods [42,43] use the features extractor pre-trained with IQA datasets [13,41]. Some recent methods [22,39,42] also extract features pretrained on action recognition dataset [16] for better perception on inter-frame distortion. These methods are limited by their high computational cost on high resolution videos. Additionally, without end-to-end training, fixed features pretrained by other tasks are not optimal for extracting quality-related information, which also limits their accuracy.

Vision Transformers. Vision transformers [1,6,19,27,35] have shown effective on computer vision tasks. They cut images or videos into non-overlapping patches as input and perform self-attention operations between them. The patch-wise operations in vision transformers naturally distinguish the edges of mini-patches and are suitable for handling with the proposed *fragments*.

3   Approach

In this section, we introduce the full pipeline of the proposed FAST-VQA method. An input video is first sampled into *fragments* via Grid Mini-patch Sampling (GMS, Sect. 3.1). After sampling, the resultant fragments are fed into the Fragment Attention Network (FANet, Sect. 3.2) to get the final prediction of the video's quality. We introduce both parts in the following subsections.

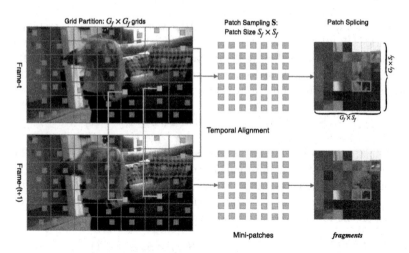

Fig. 4. The pipeline for sampling **fragments** with Grid Mini-patch Sampling (GMS), including grid partition, patch sampling, patch splicing, and temporal alignment. After GMS, the **fragments** are fed into the FANet (Fig. 5).

3.1 Grid Mini-patch Sampling (GMS)

To well preserve the original video quality after sampling, we follow several important principles when designing the sampling process for **fragments**. We will illustrate the process along with these principles below.

Preserving Global Quality: Uniform Grid Partition. To include each region for quality assessment and uniformly assess quality in different areas, we design the grid partition to cut video frames into uniform grids with each grid having the same size (as shown in Fig. 4). We cut the t-th video frame $\mathcal{V}_t$ into $G_f \times G_f$ uniform grids with the same sizes, denoted as $\mathcal{G}_t = \{g_t^{0,0}, ..g_t^{i,j}, ..g_t^{G_f-1,G_f-1}\}$, where $g_t^{i,j}$ denotes the grid in the i-th row and j-th column. The uniform grid partition process is formalized as follows.

$$g_t^{i,j} = \mathcal{V}_t[\frac{i \times H}{G_f} : \frac{(i+1) \times H}{G_f}, \frac{j \times W}{G_f} : \frac{(j+1) \times W}{G_f}] \quad (1)$$

where H and W denote the height and width of the video frame.

Preserving Local Quality: Raw Patch Sampling. To preserve the local textures (*e.g.* blurs, noises, artifacts) that are vital in VQA, we select raw resolution patches without any resizing operations to represent local textural quality in grids. We employ random patch sampling to select one mini-patch $\mathcal{MP}_t^{i,j}$ of size of $S_f \times S_f$ from each grid $g_t^{i,j}$. The patch sampling process is as follows.

$$\mathcal{MP}_t^{i,j} = \mathbf{S}_t^{i,j}(g_t^{i,j}) \quad (2)$$

where $\mathbf{S}_t^{i,j}$ is the patch sampling operation for frame t and grid i, j.

Preserving Temporal Quality: Temporal Alignment. It is widely recognized by early works [18,20,42] that inter-frame temporal variations are influential to video qualities. To retain the raw temporal variations in videos (with T frames), we strictly align the sample areas during patch sampling operations $\mathbf{S}$ in different frames, as the following constraint shows.

$$\mathbf{S}_t^{i,j} = \mathbf{S}_{\hat{t}}^{i,j} \qquad \forall\, 0 \leq t, \hat{t} < T,\ 0 \leq i,j < G_f \tag{3}$$

Preserving Contextual Relations: Patch Splicing. Existing works [8,23,25] have shown that the global scene information and contextual information affects quality predictions. To keep the global scene information of the original videos, we keep the contextual relations of mini-patches by splicing them into their original positions, as the following equation shows:

$$\begin{aligned} \mathcal{F}_t^{i,j} &= \mathcal{F}_t[i \times S_f : (i+1) \times S_f, j \times S_f : (j+1) \times S_f] \\ &= \mathcal{MP}_t^{i,j}, \qquad\qquad 0 \leq i,j < G_f \end{aligned} \tag{4}$$

where $\mathcal{F}$ denote the spliced and temporally aligned mini-patches after the Grid Mini-patch Sampling (GMS) pipeline, named as **fragments**.

3.2   Fragment Attention Network (FANet)

The Overall Framework. Figure 5 shows the overall framework of FANet. It uses a Swin-T with four hierarchical self-attention layers as backbone. We also design the following modules to adapt it to fragments well.

Gated Relative Position Biases. Swin-T adds relative position bias (RPB) that uses learnable Relative Bias Table ($\mathbf{T}$) to represent the relative positions of pixels in attention pairs (QK^T). For **fragments**, however, as discussed in Fig. 3(a), the cross-patch pairs have much large actual distances than intra-patch pairs and should not be modeled with the same bias table. Therefore, we propose the gated relative position biases (GRPB, Fig. 5(b)) that uses learnable real position bias table ($\mathbf{T}^{\mathrm{real}}$) and pseudo position bias table ($\mathbf{T}^{\mathrm{pseudo}}$) to replace $\mathbf{T}$. The mechanisms of them are the same as $\mathbf{T}$ but they are learnt separately and used for intra-patch and cross-patch attention pairs respectively. Denote $\mathbf{G}$ as the intra-patch gate ($\mathbf{G}_{i,j} = 1$ if i,j are in the same mini-patch else $\mathbf{G}_{i,j} = 0$), the self-attention matrix (M_A) with GRPB is calculated as:

$$B_{\mathrm{In},(i,j)} = \mathbf{T}^{\mathrm{real}}_{\mathrm{FRP}(i,j)};\, B_{\mathrm{Cr},(i,j)} = \mathbf{T}^{\mathrm{pseudo}}_{\mathrm{FRP}(i,j)} \tag{5}$$

$$M_A = QK^T + \mathbf{G} \otimes B_{\mathrm{In}} + (\mathbf{1} - \mathbf{G}) \otimes B_{\mathrm{Cr}} \tag{6}$$

where $\mathrm{FRP}(i,j)$ is the relative position of pair (i,j) in **fragments**.

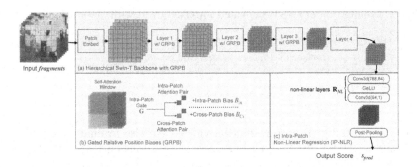

Fig. 5. The overall framework for FANet, including the Gated Relative Position Biases (GRPB) and Intra-Patch Non-Linear Regression (IP-NLR) modules. The input *fragments* come from Grid Mini-patch Sampling (Fig. 4). (Color figure online)

Intra-patch Non-linear Regression. As illustrated in Fig. 3(b), different mini-patches have diverse qualities due to discontinuity between them. If we pool features from different patches before regression, the quality representations of mini-patches will be confused with each other. To avoid this problem, we design the Intra-Patch Non-Linear Regression (IP-NLR, Fig. 5(c)) to regress the features via non-linear layers ($\mathbf{R}_{NL}$) first, and perform pooling following the regression. Denote features as f, output score as s_{pred}, pooling operation as $Pool(\cdot)$, the IP-NLR can be expressed as $s_{pred} = Pool(\mathbf{R}_{NL}(f))$.

4 Experiments

In the experiment part, we conduct several experiments to evaluate and analyze the performance of the proposed FAST-VQA model.

4.1 Evaluation Setup

Implementation Details. We use the Swin-T [28] pretrained on Kinetics-400 [16] dataset to initialize the backbone in FANet. As Table 1 shows, we implement two sampling densities for *fragments*: FAST-VQA (normal density) and FAST-VQA-M (lower density & higher efficiency), and accommodate window sizes in FANet to the input sizes. Without special notes, all ablation studies are on variants of FAST-VQA. We use PLCC (Pearson linear correlation coef.) and SRCC (Spearman rank correlation coef.) as metrics and use differentiable PLCC loss $l = \frac{(1-\mathrm{PLCC}(s_{pred}, s_{gt}))}{2}$ as loss function. We set the training batch size as 16.

Training and Benchmark Sets. We use the large-scale LSVQ$_{\text{train}}$ [42] dataset with 28,056 videos for training FAST-VQA. For evaluation, we choose 4 testing sets to test the model trained on LSVQ. The first two sets, LSVQ$_{\text{test}}$ and LSVQ$_{\text{1080p}}$ are official intra-dataset test subsets for LSVQ, while the LSVQ$_{\text{test}}$ consists of 7,400 various resolution videos from 240P to 720P, and LSVQ$_{\text{1080p}}$

Table 1. Comparison of FAST-VQA and FAST-VQA-M with lower sampling density.

Methods	Number of frames (T)	Patch size (S_f)	Number of grids (G_f)	Window size in FANet	FLOPs	Parameters
FAST-VQA	32	32	7	(8, 7, 7)	279G	27.7M
FAST-VQA-M	16	32	4	(4, 4, 4)	46G	27.5M

consists of 3,600 1080P high resolution videos. We also evaluate the generalization ability of FAST-VQA on cross-dataset evaluations on KoNViD-1k [12] and LIVE-VQC [33], two widely-recognized in-the-wild VQA benchmark datasets.

Table 2. Comparison with existing methods (classical and deep) and our baseline (Full-res Swin-T *features*). The 1st/2nd best scores are colored in red and **blue**, respectively.

Type/		Intra-dataset test sets				Cross-dataset test sets			
Testing set/		LSVQ$_{test}$		LSVQ$_{1080p}$		KoNViD-1k		LIVE-VQC	
Groups	Methods	SRCC	PLCC	SRCC	PLCC	SRCC	PLCC	SRCC	PLCC
Existing classical	BRISQUE [29]	0.569	0.576	0.497	0.531	0.646	0.647	0.524	0.536
	TLVQM [20]	0.772	0.774	0.589	0.616	0.732	0.724	0.670	0.691
	VIDEVAL [36]	0.794	0.783	0.545	0.554	0.751	0.741	0.630	0.640
Existing deep	VSFA [23]	0.801	0.796	0.675	0.704	0.784	0.794	0.734	0.772
	PVQ$_{wo/patch}$ [42]	0.814	0.816	0.686	0.708	0.781	0.781	0.747	0.776
	PVQ$_{w/patch}$ [42]	0.827	0.828	0.711	0.739	0.791	0.795	0.770	0.807
Full-res Swin-T [28] *features*		0.835	0.833	0.739	0.753	0.825	0.828	**0.794**	0.809
FAST-VQA-M (ours)		**0.852**	**0.854**	**0.739**	**0.773**	**0.841**	**0.832**	0.788	**0.810**
FAST-VQA (ours)		0.876	0.877	0.779	0.814	0.859	0.855	0.823	0.844
Improvement to PVQ$_{w/patch}$		*+6%*	*+6%*	*+10%*	*+10%*	*+9%*	*+8%*	*+7%*	*+5%*

4.2   Benchmark Results

In Table 2, we compare FAST-VQA with existing classical and deep VQA methods and our baseline, the full-resolution Swin-T with feature regression instead of end-to-end training (denoted as 'Full-res Swin-T *features*'). With its video-quality-related representations, FAST-VQA achieves at most 10% improvement to PVQ, the existing state-of-the-art on LSVQ$_{1080p}$. Even the efficient version FAST-VQA-M can outperform existing state-of-the-art. FAST-VQA also shows significant improvement to its fixed-feature-based baseline with the same backbone, demonstrating that the proposed new quality-retained sampling with end-to-end training scheme for VQA is not only much more efficient (with only 2.36% FLOPs required on 1080P videos, discussed in the next subsection) but also notably more accurate (with 8.10% improvement on PLCC metric for LSVQ$_{1080p}$) than the existing fixed-feature-based paradigm.

4.3   Efficiency of FAST-VQA

To demonstrate the efficiency of FAST-VQA, we compare the FLOPs and running times on CPU/GPU (average of ten runs per sample) of the proposed

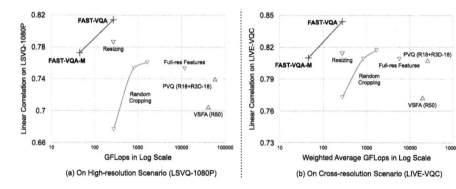

Fig. 6. The Performance-FLOPs curve of proposed **FAST-VQA** and baseline methods. (Color figure online)

Table 3. FLOPs and running time (on GPU/CPU, average of ten runs) comparison of FAST-VQA, state-of-the-art methods and our baseline on different resolutions. We **boldface** FLOPs $\leq$ 500G and running time $\leq$ 1 s.

Method	540P		720P		1080P	
	FLOPs (G)	Time (s)	FLOPs (G)	Time (s)	FLOPs (G)	Time (s)
VSFA [23]	$10249_{36.7\times}$	2.603/92.761	$18184_{65.2\times}$	3.571/134.9	$40919_{147\times}$	11.14/465.6
PVQ [42]	$14646_{52.5\times}$	3.091/97.85	$22029_{79.0\times}$	4.143/144.6	$58501_{210\times}$	13.79/538.4
Full-res Swin-T [28] *feat.*	$3032_{10.9\times}$	3.226/102.0	$5357_{19.2\times}$	5.049/166.2	$11852_{42.5\times}$	8.753/234.9
FAST-VQA (ours)	$\mathbf{279}_{1\times}$	**0.044/9.019**	$\mathbf{279}_{1\times}$	**0.043/9.530**	$\mathbf{279}_{1\times}$	**0.045/9.142**
FAST-VQA-M (ours)	$\mathbf{46}_{0.165\times}$	**0.019/0.729**	$\mathbf{46}_{0.165\times}$	**0.019/0.613**	$\mathbf{46}_{0.165\times}$	**0.019/0.714**

FAST-VQA with existing deep VQA approaches on different resolutions, see Table 3. We also draw the performance-FLOPs curve on LSVQ_{1080p} and LIVE-VQC in Fig. 6. As we can see, FAST-VQA reduces up to 210× FLOPs and 247× running time than PVQ while obtaining notably better performance. The more efficient version, FAST-VQA-M, only requires 1/1273 FLOPs of PVQ and 1/258 FLOPs of our full-resolution baseline while still achieving slightly better performance. Moreover, FAST-VQA (especially FAST-VQA-M) also runs very fast even on CPU, which reduces the hardware requirements for the applications of deep VQA methods. All these comparisons show the unprecedented efficiency of proposed FAST-VQA.[1]

4.4 Transfer Learning with Video-Quality-Related Representations

With *fragments*, FAST-VQA also *enables the pretrain-finetune scheme* on VQA with affordable computation resources. This is important as many VQA datasets [7,12,31,33,40] in specific scenarios are with much smaller scale than datasets for other video tasks [2,9,16] and it is relatively hard to learn robust quality representations on these small VQA datasets alone. With FAST-VQA, we

---

[1] Also, RAPIQUE [37] can also infer rapidly on CPU that requires **17.3 s** for 1080P videos. Yet, it is not compatible with GPU Inference due to its handcrafted branch.

Table 4. The finetune results on LIVE-VQC, KoNViD, CVD2014 and YouTube-UGC datasets, compared with existing classical and fixed-backbone deep VQA methods, and ensemble approaches of classical (C) and deep (D) branches.

Finetune dataset/		LIVE-VQC		KoNViD-1k		CVD2014		LIVE-Qualcomm		YouTube-UGC	
Groups	Methods	SRCC	PLCC	SRCC	PLCC	SRCC	PLCC	SRCC	PLCC	SRCC	PLCC
Existing classical	TLVQM [20]	0.799	0.803	0.773	0.768	0.83	0.85	0.77	0.81	0.669	0.659
	VIDEVAL [36]	0.752	0.751	0.783	0.780	NA	NA	NA	NA	0.779	0.773
	RAPIQUE [37]	0.755	0.786	0.803	0.817	NA	NA	NA	NA	0.759	0.768
Existing **fixed** deep	VSFA [23]	0.773	0.795	0.773	0.775	0.870	0.868	0.737	0.732	0.724	0.743
	PVQ [42]	**0.827**	**0.837**	0.791	0.786	NA	NA	NA	NA	NA	NA
	GST-VQA [3]	NA	NA	0.814	0.825	0.831	0.844	0.801	0.825	NA	NA
	CoINVQ [38]	NA	NA	0.767	0.764	NA	NA	NA	NA	**0.816**	0.802
Ensemble C+D	CNN+TLVQM [21]	0.825	0.834	0.816	0.818	0.863	0.880	**0.810**	0.833	NA	NA
	CNN+VIDEVAL [36]	0.785	0.810	0.815	0.817	NA	NA	NA	NA	0.808	**0.803**
Full-res Swin-T [28] *features*		0.799	0.808	0.841	0.838	0.868	0.870	0.788	0.803	0.798	0.796
FAST-VQA-M (ours)		0.803	0.828	**0.873**	**0.872**	**0.877**	**0.892**	0.804	**0.838**	0.768	0.765
FAST-VQA *w/o VQ-representations* (ours)		0.765	0.782	0.842	0.844	0.871	0.888	0.756	0.778	0.794	0.784
FAST-VQA (ours)		0.849	0.865	0.891	0.891	0.891	0.903	0.819	0.851	0.855	0.852
Improvements led by *VQ-representations*		+11.0%	+10.6%	+5.8%	+5.7%	+2.3%	+1.7%	+8.3%	+9.4%	+7.7%	+8.7%

can pretrain with large VQA datasets in end-to-end manner to learn quality related features, and then transfer to specific VQA scenarios where only small datasets are available. We use LSVQ as the large dataset and choose five small datasets representing diverse scenarios, including LIVE-VQC (real-world mobile photography, 240P–1080P), KoNViD-1k (various contents collected online, all 540P), CVD2014 (synthetic in-capture distortions, 480P–720P), LIVE-Qualcomm (selected types of distortions, all 1080P) and YouTube-UGC (user-generated contents, including computer graphic contents, 360P–2160P[2]). We divide each dataset into random splits for 10 times and report the average result on the test splits. As Table 4 shows, with video-quality-related representations, the proposed FAST-VQA outperforms the existing state-of-the-arts on all these scenarios while obtaining much higher efficiency. Note that YouTube-UGC contains 4K(2160P) videos but FAST-VQA still performs well. Even without video-quality-related representations, FAST-VQA also still achieves competitive performance, while these features steadily **improve performance on all cases**. It implies that the pretrained FAST-VQA could be able to serve as a strong backbone that boost further downstream tasks related to video quality.

4.5   Ablation Studies on *fragments*

For the first part of ablation studies, we prove the effectiveness of *fragments* by comparing with other common sampling approaches and different variants of fragments (Table 5). We keep the FANet structure fixed during this part.

Comparing with Resizing/Cropping. In Group 1 of Table 5, we compare the proposed fragments with two common sampling approaches: *bilinear resizing*

---

[2] Due to privacy reasons, the current public version of YouTube-UGC is incomplete and only with 1147 videos. The peer comparison is only for reference.

Table 5. Ablation study on *fragments*: comparison with resizing, cropping (Group 1) and different variants for fragments (Group 2).

Testing set/ Methods/metric	$\text{LSVQ}_{\text{test}}$		LSVQ_{1080p}		KoNViD-1k		LIVE-VQC	
	SRCC	PLCC	SRCC	PLCC	SRCC	PLCC	SRCC	PLCC
Group 1: Naive sampling approaches								
bilinear resizing	0.857	0.859	0.752	0.786	0.841	0.840	0.772	0.814
random cropping	0.807	0.812	0.643	0.677	0.734	0.776	0.740	0.773
- test with 3 crops	0.838	0.835	0.727	0.754	0.841	0.827	0.785	0.809
- test with 6 crops	0.843	0.844	0.734	0.761	0.845	0.834	0.796	0.817
Group 2: Variants of *fragments*								
random mini-patches	0.857	0.861	0.754	0.790	0.844	0.845	0.792	0.818
shuffled mini-patches	0.858	0.863	0.761	0.799	0.849	0.847	0.796	0.821
w/o temporal alignment	0.850	0.853	0.736	0.779	0.823	0.816	0.764	0.802
fragments (ours)	0.876	0.877	0.779	0.814	0.859	0.855	0.823	0.844

and *random cropping*. The proposed *fragments* are notably better than bilinear resizing on **high-resolution** (LSVQ_{1080p}) (+4%) and **cross-resolution** (LIVE-VQC) scenarios (+4%). Fragments still lead to non-trivial 2% improvements than resizing on lower-resolution scenarios where the problems of resizing is not that severe. This proves that keeping local textures is vital for VQA. Fragments also largely outperform single random crop as well as ensemble of multiple crops, suggesting that retaining the uniform global quality is also critical to VQA.

Comparing with Variants of Fragments. We also compare with three variants of *fragments* in Table 5, Group 2. We prove the effectiveness of uniform grid partition by comparing with *random mini-patches* (ignore grids while sampling), and the importance of retaining contextual relations by comparing with *shuffled mini-patches*. Fragments show notable improvements than both variants. Moreover, the proposed fragments show much better performance than the variant *without* temporal alignment especially on high resolution videos, suggesting that preserving the inter-frame temporal variations is necessary for fragments.

Table 6. Ablation study on FANet design: the effects for GRPB and IP-NLR modules.

Testing set/ Variants/metric	$\text{LSVQ}_{\text{test}}$		LSVQ_{1080p}		KoNViD-1k		LIVE-VQC	
	SRCC	PLCC	SRCC	PLCC	SRCC	PLCC	SRCC	PLCC
w/o GRPB	0.873	0.872	0.769	0.805	0.854	0.853	0.808	0.832
partial-GRPB on layer 1/2	0.873	0.875	0.772	0.809	0.856	0.851	0.812	0.838
linear regression	0.872	0.873	0.768	0.803	0.847	0.849	0.810	0.835
PrePool non-linear regression	0.873	0.874	0.771	0.805	0.851	0.850	0.813	0.834
FANet (ours)	0.876	0.877	0.779	0.814	0.859	0.855	0.823	0.844

4.6 Ablation Studies on FANet

Effects of GRPB and IP-NLR. In the second part of ablation studies, we analyze the effects of two important designs in FANet: the proposed Gated Relative Position Biases (GRPB) and Intra-Patch Non-Linear Regression (IP-NLR)

Table 7. Assessment stability and relative accuracy of single sampling of *fragments*.

Testing set/	LSVQ$_{test}$	LSVQ$_{1080p}$	KoNViD-1k	LIVE-VQC
Score range	0–100	0–100	1–5	0–100
std. dev. of single samplings	0.65	0.79	0.046	1.07
Normalized *std. dev.*	0.0065	0.0079	0.0115	0.0107
Relative pair accuracy compared with 6-samples	99.59%	99.40%	99.45%	99.52%

VQA Head as in Table 6. We compare the IP-NLR with two variants: the linear regression layer and the non-linear regression layers with pooling before regression (*PrePool*). Both modules lead to non-negligible improvements especially on high-resolution (LSVQ$_{1080p}$) or cross-resolution (LIVE-VQC) scenarios. As the discontinuity between mini-patches is more obvious in high-resolution videos, this result suggests that the corrected position biases and regression head are helpful on solving the problems caused by such discontinuity.

4.7   Reliability and Robustness Analyses

As FAST-VQA is based on samples rather than original videos while a single sample for *fragments* only keeps 2.4% spatial information in 1080P videos, it is important to analyze the reliability and robustness of FAST-VQA predictions.

Reliability of Single Sampling. We measure the reliability of single sampling in FAST-VQA by two metrics: 1) the assessment stability of different single samplings on the same video; 2) the relative accuracy of single sampling compared with multiple sample ensemble. As shown in Table 7, the normalized *std. dev.* of different sampling on a same video is only around 0.01, which means the sampled fragments are enough to make very stable predictions. Compared with 6-sample ensemble, sampling only once can already be 99.40% as accurate even on the pure high-resolution test set (LSVQ$_{1080P}$). They prove that a single sample of *fragments* is enough stable and reliable for quality assessment even though only a small proportion of information is kept during sampling.

Robustness on Different Resolutions. To analyze the robustness of FAST-VQA on different resolutions, we divide the cross-resolution VQA benchmark set LIVE-VQC into three resolution groups: (A) 1080P (110 videos); (B) 720P (316 videos); (C) ≤540P (159 videos) to see the performance of FAST-VQA on different resolutions, compared with several variants. As the results shown in Table 8, the proposed FAST-VQA shows good performance (≥ 0.80 SRCC&PLCC) on all resolution groups and most superior improvement than other variants on Group (A) with 1080P high-resolution videos, proving that FAST-VQA is robust and reliable on different resolutions of videos.

Table 8. Performance comparison on different resolution groups of LIVE-VQC dataset.

Resolution	(A): 1080P			(B): 720P			(C): ≤540P		
Variants	SRCC	PLCC	KRCC	SRCC	PLCC	KRCC	SRCC	PLCC	KRCC
Full-res Swin *features* (baseline)	0.771	0.774	0.584	0.796	0.811	0.602	0.810	0.853	0.625
bilinear resizing (sampling variant)	0.758	0.773	0.573	0.790	0.822	0.599	0.835	0.878	0.650
random cropping (sampling variant)	0.765	0.768	0.565	0.774	0.787	0.581	0.730	0.809	0.535
w/o GRPB (FANet variant)	0.796	0.785	0.598	0.802	0.820	0.608	0.834	0.883	0.649
FAST-VQA (ours)	0.807	0.806	0.610	0.803	0.825	0.610	0.840	0.885	0.654

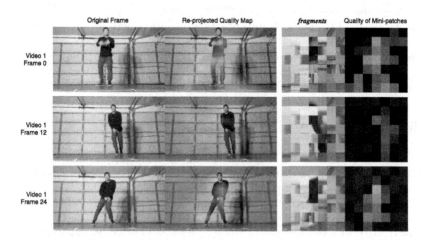

Fig. 7. Spatial-temporal patch-wise local quality maps, where red areas refer to low predicted quality and **green** areas refer to high predicted quality. This sample video is a 1080P video selected from LIVE-VQC [33] dataset. Zoom in for clearer view. (Color figure online)

4.8   Qualitative Results: Local Quality Maps

The proposed IP-NLR head with patch-wise independent quality regression enables FAST-VQA to generate patch-wise local quality maps, which helps us to qualitatively evaluate what quality information can be learned in FAST-VQA. We show the patch-wise local quality maps and the re-projected frame quality maps for a 1080P video (from LIVE-VQC [33] dataset) in Fig. 7. As the patch-wise quality maps and re-projected quality maps in Fig. 7 (column 2&4) shows, FAST-VQA is sensitive to textural quality information and distinguishes between clear (Frame 0) and blurry textures (Frame 12/24). It demonstrates that FAST-VQA with *fragments* (column 3) as input is sensitive to local texture quality. Furthermore, the qualities of the action-related areas are notably different from the background areas, showing that FAST-VQA effectively learns the global scene information and contextual relations in the video.

5   Conclusions

Our paper has shown that proposed *fragments* are effective samples for video quality assessment (VQA) that better retain quality information in videos than naive sampling approaches, to tackle the difficulties as results of high computing and memory requirements when high-resolution videos are to be evaluated. Based on *fragments*, the proposed end-to-end FAST-VQA achieves higher efficiency (−99.5% FLOPs) and accuracy (+10% PLCC) simultaneously than existing state-of-the-art method PVQ on 1080P videos. We hope that the FAST-VQA can bring deep VQA methods into practical use for videos in any resolutions.

Acknowledgment. This study is supported under the RIE2020 Industry Alignment Fund - Industry Collaboration Projects (IAF-ICP) Funding Initiative, as well as cash and in-kind contribution from the industry partner(s).

References

1. Arnab, A., Dehghani, M., Heigold, G., Sun, C., Lucic, M., Schmid, C.: ViViT: a video vision transformer. In: Proceedings of the IEEE/CVF International Conference on Computer Vision (ICCV), pp. 6836–6846, October 2021
2. Caba Heilbron, F., Escorcia, V., Ghanem, B., Carlos Niebles, J.: ActivityNet: a large-scale video benchmark for human activity understanding. In: Proceedings of the IEEE/CVF Conference on Computer Vision and Pattern Recognition (CVPR), June 2015
3. Chen, B., Zhu, L., Li, G., Lu, F., Fan, H., Wang, S.: Learning generalized spatial-temporal deep feature representation for no-reference video quality assessment. IEEE Trans. Circ. Syst. Video Technol. 32(4), 1903–1916 (2021)
4. Cho, K., et al.: Learning phrase representations using RNN encoder-decoder for statistical machine translation. In: Proceedings of the 2014 Conference on Empirical Methods in Natural Language Processing (EMNLP), pp. 1724–1734. ACL (2014)
5. Deng, J., Dong, W., Socher, R., Li, L.J., Li, K., Fei-Fei, L.: ImageNet: a large-scale hierarchical image database. In: Proceedings of the IEEE/CVF Conference on Computer Vision and Pattern Recognition (CVPR), pp. 248–255 (2009)
6. Fan, H., et al.: Multiscale vision transformers. In: Proceedings of the IEEE/CVF International Conference on Computer Vision (ICCV), pp. 6824–6835, October 2021
7. Ghadiyaram, D., Pan, J., Bovik, A.C., Moorthy, A.K., Panda, P., Yang, K.C.: In-capture mobile video distortions: a study of subjective behavior and objective algorithms. IEEE Trans. Circ. Syst. Video Technol. 28(9), 2061–2077 (2018)
8. Götz-Hahn, F., Hosu, V., Lin, H., Saupe, D.: KonVid-150k: a dataset for no-reference video quality assessment of videos in-the-wild. IEEE Access 9, 72139–72160 (2021)
9. Gu, C., et al.: AVA: a video dataset of spatio-temporally localized atomic visual actions. In: Proceedings of the IEEE/CVF Conference on Computer Vision and Pattern Recognition (CVPR), June 2018
10. Hara, K., Kataoka, H., Satoh, Y.: Learning spatio-temporal features with 3D residual networks for action recognition. In: Proceedings of the IEEE/CVF International Conference on Computer Vision (ICCV) Workshops, pp. 3154–3160 (2017)

11. He, K., Zhang, X., Ren, S., Sun, J.: Deep residual learning for image recognition. In: Proceedings of the IEEE/CVF Conference on Computer Vision and Pattern Recognition (CVPR), pp. 770–778 (2016)

12. Hosu, V., et al.: The Konstanz natural video database (KoNViD-1k). In: Ninth International Conference on Quality of Multimedia Experience (QoMEX), pp. 1–6 (2017)

13. Hosu, V., Lin, H., Sziranyi, T., Saupe, D.: KonIQ-10k: an ecologically valid database for deep learning of blind image quality assessment. IEEE Trans. Image Process. **29**, 4041–4056 (2020)

14. Kang, L., Ye, P., Li, Y., Doermann, D.: Convolutional neural networks for no-reference image quality assessment. In: Proceedings of the IEEE/CVF Conference on Computer Vision and Pattern Recognition (CVPR) (2014)

15. Kang, L., Ye, P., Li, Y., Doermann, D.: Simultaneous estimation of image quality and distortion via multi-task convolutional neural networks. In: IEEE International Conference on Image Processing (ICIP) (2015)

16. Kay, W., et al.: The kinetics human action video dataset. ArXiv abs/1705.06950 (2017)

17. Ke, J., Wang, Q., Wang, Y., Milanfar, P., Yang, F.: MUSIQ: multi-scale image quality transformer. In: Proceedings of the IEEE/CVF International Conference on Computer Vision (ICCV), pp. 5148–5157, October 2021

18. Kim, W., Kim, J., Ahn, S., Kim, J., Lee, S.: Deep video quality assessor: from spatio-temporal visual sensitivity to a convolutional neural aggregation network. In: Ferrari, V., Hebert, M., Sminchisescu, C., Weiss, Y. (eds.) ECCV 2018. LNCS, vol. 11205, pp. 224–241. Springer, Cham (2018). https://doi.org/10.1007/978-3-030-01246-5_14

19. Kolesnikov, A., et al.: An image is worth 16×16 words: transformers for image recognition at scale (2021)

20. Korhonen, J.: Two-level approach for no-reference consumer video quality assessment. IEEE Trans. Image Process. **28**(12), 5923–5938 (2019)

21. Korhonen, J., Su, Y., You, J.: Blind natural video quality prediction via statistical temporal features and deep spatial features. In: Proceedings of the 28th ACM International Conference on Multimedia, MM 2020, pp. 3311–3319. Association for Computing Machinery, New York (2020)

22. Li, B., Zhang, W., Tian, M., Zhai, G., Wang, X.: Blindly assess quality of in-the-wild videos via quality-aware pre-training and motion perception. IEEE Trans. Circ. Syst. Video Technol. **32**(9), 5944–5958 (2022)

23. Li, D., Jiang, T., Jiang, M.: Quality assessment of in-the-wild videos. In: Proceedings of the 27th ACM International Conference on Multimedia, MM 2019, pp. 2351–2359. Association for Computing Machinery, New York (2019)

24. Li, D., Jiang, T., Jiang, M.: Unified quality assessment of in-the-wild videos with mixed datasets training. Int. J. Comput. Vis. **129**(4), 1238–1257 (2021). https://doi.org/10.1007/s11263-020-01408-w

25. Li, D., Jiang, T., Lin, W., Jiang, M.: Which has better visual quality: the clear blue sky or a blurry animal? IEEE Trans. Multimedia **21**(5), 1221–1234 (2019)

26. Liao, L., et al.: Exploring the effectiveness of video perceptual representation in blind video quality assessment. In: Proceedings of the 30th ACM International Conference on Multimedia (ACM MM) (2022)

27. Liu, Z., et al.: Swin transformer: hierarchical vision transformer using shifted windows. arXiv preprint arXiv:2103.14030 (2021)

28. Liu, Z., et al.: Video swin transformer. arXiv preprint arXiv:2106.13230 (2021)

29. Mittal, A., Moorthy, A.K., Bovik, A.C.: No-reference image quality assessment in the spatial domain. IEEE Trans. Image Process. **21**(12), 4695–4708 (2012)
30. Mittal, A., Saad, M.A., Bovik, A.C.: A completely blind video integrity oracle. IEEE Trans. Image Process. **25**(1), 289–300 (2016)
31. Nuutinen, M., Virtanen, T., Vaahteranoksa, M., Vuori, T., Oittinen, P., Häkkinen, J.: CVD2014–a database for evaluating no-reference video quality assessment algorithms. IEEE Trans. Image Process. **25**(7), 3073–3086 (2016)
32. Saad, M.A., Bovik, A.C., Charrier, C.: Blind image quality assessment: a natural scene statistics approach in the DCT domain. IEEE Trans. Image Process. **21**(8), 3339–3352 (2012)
33. Sinno, Z., Bovik, A.C.: Large-scale study of perceptual video quality. IEEE Trans. Image Process. **28**(2), 612–627 (2019)
34. Szegedy, C., Ioffe, S., Vanhoucke, V., Alemi, A.A.: Inception-v4, inception-ResNet and the impact of residual connections on learning. In: Proceedings of the Thirty-First AAAI Conference on Artificial Intelligence, AAAI 2017, pp. 4278–4284. AAAI Press (2017)
35. Touvron, H., Cord, M., Douze, M., Massa, F., Sablayrolles, A., J'egou, H.: Training data-efficient image transformers & distillation through attention. In: Proceedings of the International Conference on Machine Learning (ICML) (2021)
36. Tu, Z., Wang, Y., Birkbeck, N., Adsumilli, B., Bovik, A.C.: UGC-VQA: benchmarking blind video quality assessment for user generated content. IEEE Trans. Image Process. **30**, 4449–4464 (2021)
37. Tu, Z., Yu, X., Wang, Y., Birkbeck, N., Adsumilli, B., Bovik, A.C.: RAPIQUE: rapid and accurate video quality prediction of user generated content. IEEE Open J. Sig. Process. **2**, 425–440 (2021)
38. Wang, Y., et al.: Rich features for perceptual quality assessment of UGC videos. In: Proceedings of the IEEE/CVF Conference on Computer Vision and Pattern Recognition (CVPR), pp. 13435–13444, June 2021
39. Wu, H., et al.: DisCoVQA: temporal distortion-content transformers for video quality assessment. arXiv preprint arXiv: 2206.09853 (2022)
40. Yim, J.G., Wang, Y., Birkbeck, N., Adsumilli, B.: Subjective quality assessment for YouTube UGC dataset. In: 2020 IEEE International Conference on Image Processing (ICIP), pp. 131–135 (2020)
41. Ying, Z.A., Niu, H., Gupta, P., Mahajan, D., Ghadiyaram, D., Bovik, A.: From patches to pictures (PaQ-2-PiQ): mapping the perceptual space of picture quality. arXiv preprint arXiv:1912.10088 (2019)
42. Ying, Z., Mandal, M., Ghadiyaram, D., Bovik, A.: Patch-VQ: 'patching up' the video quality problem. In: Proceedings of the IEEE/CVF Conference on Computer Vision and Pattern Recognition (CVPR), pp. 14019–14029, June 2021
43. You, J.: Long short-term convolutional transformer for no-reference video quality assessment. In: Proceedings of the 29th ACM International Conference on Multimedia, MM 2021, pp. 2112–2120. Association for Computing Machinery, New York (2021)
44. You, J., Korhonen, J.: Deep neural networks for no-reference video quality assessment. In: Proceedings of the IEEE International Conference on Image Processing (ICIP), pp. 2349–2353 (2019)
45. Zhang, W., Ma, K., Yan, J., Deng, D., Wang, Z.: Blind image quality assessment using a deep bilinear convolutional neural network. IEEE Trans. Circ. Syst. Video Technol. **30**(1), 36–47 (2020)

Physically-Based Editing of Indoor Scene Lighting from a Single Image

Zhengqin Li[1(✉)], Jia Shi[1,3], Sai Bi[1,2], Rui Zhu[1], Kalyan Sunkavalli[2],
Miloš Hašan[2], Zexiang Xu[2], Ravi Ramamoorthi[1], and Manmohan Chandraker[1]

[1] UC San Diego, San Diego, USA
lizhengqin2012@gmail.com
[2] Adobe Research, San Jose, USA
[3] Carnegie Mellon University, Pittsburgh, USA

Abstract. We present a method to edit complex indoor lighting from
a single image with its predicted depth and light source segmentation
masks. This is an extremely challenging problem that requires modeling
complex light transport, and disentangling HDR lighting from material
and geometry with only a partial LDR observation of the scene. We tackle
this problem using two novel components: 1) a holistic scene reconstruction method that estimates reflectance and parametric 3D lighting, and
2) a neural rendering framework that re-renders the scene from our predictions. We use physically-based light representations that allow for intuitive editing, and infer both visible and invisible light sources. Our neural
rendering framework combines physically-based direct illumination and
shadow rendering with deep networks to approximate global illumination.
It can capture challenging lighting effects, such as soft shadows, directional lighting, specular materials, and interreflections. Previous single
image inverse rendering methods usually entangle lighting and geometry
and only support applications like object insertion. Instead, by combining parametric 3D lighting estimation with neural scene rendering, we
demonstrate the first automatic method for full scene relighting from a
single image, including light source insertion, removal, and replacement.

1 Introduction

Light sources of various shapes, colors and types, such as lamps and windows,
play an important role in determining indoor scene appearances. Their influence
leads to several interesting phenomena such as light shafts through an open
window on a sunlit day, highlights on specular surfaces due to incandescent
lamps, interreflections from colored walls, or shadows cast by furniture in the
room. Correctly attributing those effects to individual visible or invisible light
sources in a single image enables abilities for photorealistic augmented reality
that have previously been intractable—virtual furniture insertion under varying
illuminations with consistent highlights and shadows, virtual try-on of wall paints

Supplementary Information The online version contains supplementary material
available at https://doi.org/10.1007/978-3-031-20068-7_32.

© The Author(s), under exclusive license to Springer Nature Switzerland AG 2022
S. Avidan et al. (Eds.): ECCV 2022, LNCS 13666, pp. 555–572, 2022.
https://doi.org/10.1007/978-3-031-20068-7_32

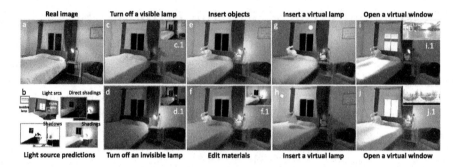

Fig. 1. We present the first method for globally consistent editing of indoor lighting from a single LDR image. Given the input (a), our framework first estimates physically-based light source parameters, for both visible and invisible lights, and then renders their direct contributions and interreflections through a neural rendering framework (b). Our framework can turn off visible and invisible light sources (c and d) with results closely matching the ground truths (c.1 and d.1). It can insert virtual objects (e) with consistent changes of highlight and shadow and edit materials with color bleeding being correctly rendered image (f) and shading (f.1). It can also insert virtual lamps (g and h) and open a virtual window (i and j) to let sunlight (i.1 and j.1) shine into the room.

with accurate global interreflections, or morphing a room under fluorescent lights into one reflecting the sunrise through a window (Fig. 1).

Several recent works estimate *lighting* in indoor scenes [12,25,41,44], but achieving the above outcomes requires estimating and editing *light sources*. While both are highly ill-posed for single-image inputs, we posit that the latter presents fundamentally different and harder challenges for computer vision. First, it requires disentangling the individual contributions of both visible and invisible light sources, independent of the effects of geometry and material. Second, it requires reasoning about long-range effects such as interreflections, shadows and highlights, while also being precise about highly localized 3D shapes, spectra, directions and bandwidths of light sources, where minor errors can lead to global artifacts due to the above distant interactions. Third, it requires photo-realistic re-rendering of the scene despite only partial observations of geometry and material, while handling complex light transport. Figure 2 illustrates a few such challenges.

We solve the above challenges by bringing together a rich set of insights across physically-based vision and neural rendering. Given a single LDR image of an indoor scene, with predicted depth map and masks for visible lights, we propose to estimate *parametric models* of both visible and invisible light sources, in addition to per-pixel reflectance. Beyond a 3D location, our modeling accurately supports physical properties such as geometry, color, directionality and fall-off. Next, we design a *neural differentiable renderer* that judiciously uses classical methods and learned priors to synthesize high-quality images from predicted reflectance and light sources. We accurately model long-range light trans-

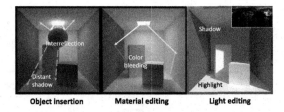

Fig. 2. Image editing must explicitly predict light sources to account for global effects such as distant shadows due to inserted objects, interreflections on far surfaces due to edited materials and light shafts by opening a window.

Table 1. Compared to prior works on inverse rendering, ours enables full scene relighting with global effects for inserted objects, edited materials or light sources. Also see Figs. 1 and 2.

	Input	Object insertion		Material editing		Light editing	
		Position	Non-local	Specular	Non-local	Lamp	Window
Auto, Karsch 14	Single	Any	✓	✗	✗	✓	✗
CGI, Li 18	Single	✗	✗	✗	✗	✗	✗
DeRenderNet, Zhu 21	Single	✗	✗	✗	✗	✗	✗
DeepPara, Gardner 19	Single	Any	✓	✗	✗	✗	✗
Invindoor, Li 20	Single	Surface	✗	✓	✗	✗	✗
Lighthouse, Srinivasan 20	Stereo	Any	✗	✗	✗	✗	✗
FreeView, Philip 21	Multi.	✗	✗	✗	✗	✓	✗
Ours	Single	Any	✓	✓	✓	✓	✓

port through a physically-based Monte Carlo ray tracer with a learned shadow denoiser to render direct illumination, and an indirect illumination network to infer non-local interreflection. Our neural renderer injects the inductive bias of physical image formation in training, while allowing rendering and editing of global light transport from partial observations, as well as optimization to refine predictions.

Our parametric light source estimation and physically-based neural renderer allow intuitive editing of lamps and windows, with their global effects handled explicitly. In Fig. 1(c, d), we turn off each visible and invisible lamps. Beyond standard object insertion of prior works (e), we visualize inserted objects by "turning on" a new lamp (g, h) or "opening" a window with incoming sunlight (i, j). In each case, global effects such as highlights, shadows and interreflections are accurately created for the entire scene by the neural renderer, and are also properly handled when we edit materials of scene surfaces (f). In the accompanying video, we show that these editing effects are consistent as we move virtual objects and light sources, or gradually change materials. These abilities significantly surpass prior methods for intrinsic decomposition or inverse rendering. As summarized in Table 1 and Sect. 2, our method is the first to allow a broad range of single image scene relighting abilities in the form of inserting objects, changing complex materials and editing light sources, with consistent global interactions.

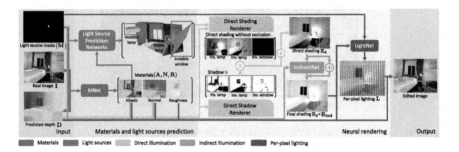

Fig. 3. Overview of our method. We start from a LDR RGB image, with depth map and visible light source masks estimated from the image or given as inputs. We first estimate per-pixel reflectance (albedo, normal, roughness) using a network (blue). Next, we estimate light sources (windows and lamps, visible and invisible) using four networks (green). To render the predictions back into an image, we use a neural renderer with three modules: direct shading, shadow (yellow), and indirect shading module (orange). The result is per-pixel shading (diffuse irradiance), which can be turned into per-pixel lighting (a grid of incoming radiance environment maps) using another network (red). (Color figure online)

2   Related Work

Inverse Rendering. Inverse rendering seeks to estimate factors of image formation (shape, materials and lighting) [30], which has traditionally required multiple images and controlled setups [7,9,14,45]. Several single-image works on material acquisition [22,26], or object-level shape and reflectance reconstruction use known [16,33] or semi-controlled lighting [27]. We consider a complex indoor scene under unknown illumination and jointly estimate its geometry, material and lighting from a single LDR image. Intrinsic decomposition [2–4,23,24,39] decomposes an image into Lambertian reflectance and diffuse shading. A recent work also predicts a shadow map [51]. Several deep learning methods estimate complex SVBRDFs and lighting [25,38]. But none of the above can estimate or edit light sources. We instead propose a novel physically-based 3D light source representation and neural rendering framework that estimates and edits individual light sources with distant shadows and global illumination being explicitly handled.

Lighting Estimation and Representation. Many single image approaches estimate lighting as a single environment map [10,11,21], which cannot express spatial variation of indoor illumination. Some recent works model spatial variations as per-pixel environment maps [1,13,25,50], or volumes [41,44]. However, these non-parametric representations can mainly be used for object insertion, while we estimate editable light sources with physically meaningful properties (position, geometry, direction, and intensity). Gardner et al. [12] predict a fixed number of spherical Gaussian lobes to approximate indoor light sources but do not handle light editing or its global effects. Zhang et al. recover geometry and radiance of an empty room but cannot handle furniture inside [49]. Karsch et al. reconstruct geometry, reflectance and lighting but do not model windows and invisible scene contributions, require extensive user inputs [18] or face artifacts from imperfect heuristics or optimization [19]. In contrast, our physically-based neural renderer synthesizes photorealistic images with complex light transport, to enable relighting, light source insertion and removal from a single image.

Neural Rendering and Relighting. NeRF [31] and other volumetric neural rendering approaches have achieved photo-realistic outputs, but usually limited to view synthesis [29,31,48]. A few recent works [5,6,8,40,46] handle relighting, but use a per-object optimization from a large set of images. Philip et al. [35] demonstrate relighting for outdoor scenes but require multiple images. Concurrent to our work, Philip et al. [36] consider indoor relighting, but require a large number of high-resolution RAW images, cannot reconstruct directional sunlight and do not support material editing and object insertion with their neural renderer. As shown in Fig. 2 and Table 1, our modeling and neural rendering enable applications not possible for prior works, such as light source insertion/removal, virtual objects insertion and editing materials with non-local effects, from a single image.

3   Material and Light Source Prediction

Our overall framework is summarized in Fig. 3. In this section, we describe our novel, physically meaningful and editable reflectance and light source representations, while Sect. 4 describes our neural renderer that is differentiable with respect to light sources to facilitate training and editing of complex light transport. For per-pixel reflectance, we train a U-net similar to [25] to predict material parameters: diffuse albedo ($\mathbf{A}$), normal ($\mathbf{N}$) and roughness ($\mathbf{R}$), following the SVBRDF model of [17]. The inputs are a 240×320 LDR image ($\mathbf{I}$) and its corresponding depth map ($\mathbf{D}$), which in our case can be predicted by a state-of-the-art monocular depth prediction network [37]. We predict the normals directly, instead of computing them as the normalized gradient of depth to avoid artifacts and discontinuities. Thus, our prediction is given by $\{\mathbf{A}, \mathbf{N}, \mathbf{R}\} = \mathbf{MNet}(\mathbf{I}, \mathbf{D})$.

3.1   Light Source Representation

To enable high-quality indoor scene relighting, we need lighting representations that are editable, expressive enough for different types of lighting and realistic enough for convincing rendering of complex scenes. We model radiance and geometry of two types of common light sources with very different properties: (a) *windows* that can cover large areas and may induce strong directional sunlight, and (b) *lamps* that tend to be small and with more complex geometry.

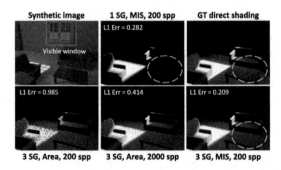

Fig. 4. Comparisons of direct shading rendered from different window representations with different sampling methods. We show that our 3 SGs models ambient lighting much better than a single SG, as shown in the green circle, and MIS sampling leads to much less noise compared to sampling window area uniformly. (Color figure online)

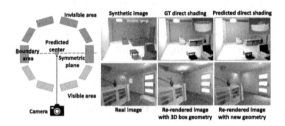

Fig. 5. A demonstration of our visible lamp geometry representation. Our representation for visible lamps is much less likely to cause highlight artifacts and wrong shadows compared to a standard 3D bounding box.

Radiance. The emitted radiance of lamps can be modeled by a standard Lambertian model, where every surface point with intensity $\mathbf{w}$ emits light uniformly. However, the radiance distribution of windows can be strongly directional due to sunlight coming through on a clear day, which is important for capturing realistic indoor lighting but often neglected by prior methods [36,41,42]. A recent work [44] models directional lighting with a single spherical Gaussian (SG), but as shown in Fig. 4, cannot recover ambient effects leading to sub-optimal rendering. Instead, we model the directional distribution of window radiance with 3 SGs corresponding to the sun, sky and ground. Each SG is defined by three parameters $\mathcal{G}_k = (\mathbf{w_k}, \lambda_k, \mathbf{d_k})$, for intensity, bandwidth and direction of lighting. For a ray in direction $\mathbf{l}$ that hits the window, its intensity is $\mathbf{L}_{\mathcal{W}}(\mathbf{l}) = \sum_k \mathbf{w_k} \exp\left(\lambda_k(\mathbf{d_k} \cdot \mathbf{l} - 1)\right)$, where $k \in \{\text{sun, sky, grnd}\}$. Figure 4 shows that our representation with multiple importance sampling leads to direct shading close to the ground-truth.

Geometry. Window geometry can be simply approximated by a rectangle $\{\mathbf{c}, \mathbf{x}, \mathbf{y}\}$, where $\mathbf{c}$ is the center and $\mathbf{x}, \mathbf{y}$ are the two axes. However, lamps present more diverse geometry. Naively representing a lamp with a 3D bounding box

$\{\mathbf{c}, \mathbf{x}, \mathbf{y}, \mathbf{z}\}$ works for invisible lamps, but it often leads to artifacts for visible lamps, as the imperfect shape generates incorrect highlights. Therefore, we carefully design a new visible lamp representation shown in Fig. 5. We first identify the visible surface based on the depth $\mathbf{D}$ and lamp segmentation mask $\mathbf{M}_{\mathcal{L}}$, reconstruct the invisible surface by reflecting the visible surface with respect to the lamp center $\mathbf{c}$ and then add the boundary area. As shown in Fig. 5, our new representation can effectively constrain the lamp geometry and achieve realistic rendering without highlight artifacts for difficult real world examples. More details are in the supp.

3.2   Light Source Prediction

We use four neural networks to predict visible and invisible light sources for the lamp and window categories. For visible light sources, the inputs include extra instance segmentation masks. We can obtain the mask by either fine-tuning a Mask R-CNN [15] for our dataset, combined with a graph-cut based post processing to refine the boundaries, or manually draw the masks. While this is not our main focus, we include both qualitative and quantitative analysis in the supp. Let $\mathbf{M}_{\mathcal{W}}$ be a mask for a window and $\mathbf{M}_{\mathcal{L}}$ be a mask for a lamp. We have

$$\{\mathbf{c}, \mathbf{w}\} = \mathbf{VisLampNet}(\mathbf{I}, \mathbf{A}, \mathbf{D}, \mathbf{M}_{\mathcal{L}}),$$
$$\{\mathbf{c}, \mathbf{x}, \mathbf{y}, \mathcal{G}_{\mathrm{sun}}, \mathcal{G}_{\mathrm{sky}}, \mathcal{G}_{\mathrm{grnd}}\} = \mathbf{VisWinNet}(\mathbf{I}, \mathbf{A}, \mathbf{D}, \mathbf{M}_{\mathcal{W}}).$$

We assume one invisible lamp and one invisible window. These are deliberate simplifications: while invisible lights can contribute significant illumination, they are hard to infer using only indirect cues. We limit the expressivity of the representation to account for this ill-posedness and find it to be a good choice in practice[1]. When a scene has no invisible light source, their predicted intensities

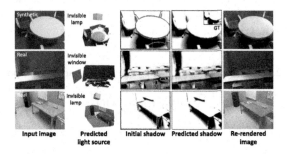

Input image   Predicted   Initial shadow   Predicted shadow   Re-rendered
               light source   image

Fig. 6. Direct rendering shadows with ray tracing leads to boundary artifacts as shown in red color in the third column. Our trained depth-based shadow renderer achieves high-quality shadows for both real and synthetic scenes, with re-rendered images closely matching the inputs. (Color figure online)

---

[1] The real scene in Fig. 1 has 4 invisible lamps and the last real scene in Fig. 6 has 2. In both cases, we achieve reasonable approximation with one invisible lamp.

are close to zero, as shown in Fig. 3 and Fig. 8. To learn a better separation of visible and invisible light sources, we provide a mask $\mathbf{M} = \sum_{\mathcal{W}} \mathbf{M}_{\mathcal{W}} + \sum_{\mathcal{L}} \mathbf{M}_{\mathcal{L}}$ of all visible sources to the invisible light sources estimation networks:

$$\{\mathbf{c}, \mathbf{x}, \mathbf{y}, \mathbf{z}\} = \mathbf{InvLampNet}(\mathbf{I}, \mathbf{A}, \mathbf{D}, \mathbf{M}),$$
$$\{\mathbf{c}, \mathbf{x}, \mathbf{y}, \mathcal{G}_{\text{sun}}, \mathcal{G}_{\text{sky}}, \mathcal{G}_{\text{grnd}}\} = \mathbf{InvWinNet}(\mathbf{I}, \mathbf{A}, \mathbf{D}, \mathbf{M}).$$

4   Neural Rendering Framework

To achieve photorealistic indoor light editing, we need a rendering framework that can handle complex light transport typical for indoor scenes, such as sharp directional lighting, hard and soft shadows and non-local interreflections. While existing differentiable path tracers can handle all these effects, they are computationally expensive. More importantly, they require the full reconstruction of reflectance and geometry of the entire scene, including its invisible parts.

To address these limitations, we introduce a neural rendering framework that combines the advantages of physically-based rendering and learning-based rendering. It works with our light source representations, does not require full scene reconstruction, achieves high performance, and is differentiable. Our framework, illustrated in Fig. 3 (right), has 4 modules: (1) a physically-based direct shading module that computes the direct irradiance from each light source through Monte Carlo sampling; (2) a hybrid shadow module that can render hard/soft shadows for each light source; (3) an indirect shading module that predicts non-local global illumination; (4) a per-pixel lighting module that predicts per-pixel environment map, which can be used to insert specular objects.

Our direct shading and shadows are computed based on ray tracing, while global illumination and per-pixel lighting are predicted by networks. The reason is that without full scene reconstruction, global illumination can only be computed heuristically (Fig. 7), which is suited for neural networks. Conversely, direct illumination and non-local shadowing can be efficiently computed by ray tracing, but remain tricky for neural methods.

Table 2. Shadow rendering error with or w/o network inpainting.

	Ray traced	Ours
L_2	0.011	0.005

4.1   Direct Shading Rendering Module

We use inspiration from physically-based rendering [34] to sample the surface of each light source and connect those samples to the scene points. Formally, let $\mathbf{p}$ be a shading point and $\mathbf{q}$ be a point uniformly sampled on the light surface, with $\mathbf{p} \rightarrow \mathbf{q}$ the unit vector from $\mathbf{p}$ to $\mathbf{q}$. The direct shading $\mathbf{E_j}$ caused by light source $\mathbf{j}$ is computed as:

$$\mathbf{E_j}(\mathbf{p}) = \frac{\text{area}(\mathbf{j})}{N_j} \sum_{\mathbf{q}} \frac{\mathbf{L_j}(\mathbf{q} \rightarrow \mathbf{p}) \max(\cos \theta_{\mathbf{p}} \cos \theta_{\mathbf{q}}, 0)}{\|\mathbf{q} - \mathbf{p}\|_2^2}, \tag{1}$$

where $\cos \theta_{\mathbf{p}} = \mathbf{p} \rightarrow \mathbf{q} \cdot \mathbf{N}(\mathbf{p})$, $\cos \theta_{\mathbf{q}} = \mathbf{q} \rightarrow \mathbf{p} \cdot \mathbf{N}(\mathbf{q})$ and N_j is the number of samples for light source $\mathbf{j}$. While our Monte Carlo estimation in (1) converges fast for lamps, it is not optimal for high-frequency directional sunlight coming through windows, since only when $\mathbf{q} \rightarrow \mathbf{p}$ aligns with the sun direction, will the $\mathbf{L}(\mathbf{q} \rightarrow \mathbf{p})$ return a significant contribution. To tackle this issue, with $\mathbf{Pr}(\mathbf{l})$ the probability of sampling direction $\mathbf{l}$ from $\mathcal{G}_{sun}$, we also generate samples according to the angular distribution of $\mathcal{G}_{\text{sun}}$:

$$\mathbf{E_j}(\mathbf{p}) = \sum_{\mathbf{l}} \frac{\mathbf{L_j}(\mathbf{l})\mathbf{I_j}(\mathbf{l}) \max(\cos \theta_{\mathbf{p}}, 0)}{N_j \mathbf{Pr}(\mathbf{l})}, \tag{2}$$

where $\mathbf{I_j}(\mathbf{l})$ is an indicator function to detect if ray $\mathbf{l}$ starting from $\mathbf{p}$ can hit the window plane. Note that both (1) and (2) are unbiased but with different variances, which we combine with multiple importance sampling (MIS) [43]. Details are in the supp. Figure 4 compares the direct shading of a window, where we observe that our MIS method can render high-quality direct shading with much fewer samples, which makes training with rendering loss possible.

4.2 Depth-Based Hybrid Shadow Rendering Module

Recall that in the above shading computation, $\mathbf{E}_{\mathbf{j}}, j \in \{\mathcal{W}\} \cup \{\mathcal{L}\}$ does not consider visibility and therefore cannot handle shadows. We could check visibility by ray tracing during the Monte Carlo sampling above, but this causes artifacts due to incomplete geometry, as shown in Fig. 6. We instead design a depth-based shadow rendering framework that combines Monte Carlo ray tracing with learning-based inpainting and denoising. Our shadow modules are not differentiable, as this is not necessary for our application: we train our network on a synthetic dataset, which provides the ground truth direct shading without the shadow effects, so back-propagation of error through the shadow renderer is not necessary.

Our approach first creates a mesh from the depth map, and then uses a GPU-based ray tracer to cast shadow rays from surfaces to light sources. To address the boundary artifacts, we first modify the renderer to detect the occlusion boundaries, then train a CNN to fill in the shadow at these regions. This hybrid approach outperforms both pure ray tracing and a CNN trained to clean up the entire ray traced shadow image. Formally, let $\mathbf{S}^{\text{Init}}$ be the initial shadow image rendered from depth map $\mathbf{D}$ and let $\mathbf{M}^{\mathbf{S}}$ be the mask for occlusion boundaries.

$$\mathbf{S} = \mathbf{M}^{\mathbf{S}} \cdot \mathbf{DShdNet}(\mathbf{S}^{\text{Init}}, \mathbf{D}, \mathbf{N}) + (1 - \mathbf{M}^{\mathbf{S}}) \cdot \mathbf{S}^{\text{Init}}. \tag{3}$$

The total direct shading from all sources is $\mathbf{E_d} = \sum_j \mathbf{E_j S_j}$. As seen in Fig. 1, 6 and 7, our framework can render higher quality soft and hard shadows that are

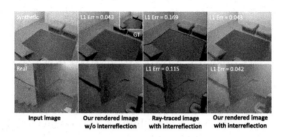

Input Image   Our rendered image   Ray-traced image   Our rendered image
                w/o interreflection   with interreflection   with interreflection

Fig. 7. Our neural renderer models both direct and indirect illumination accurately, while a ray tracer using only single-view predictions cannot model indirect illumination and has artifacts near occlusion boundaries.

closer to the ground-truths compared to a standard ray tracer. Table 2 shows that our CNN reduces the shadow error by more than 50%.

4.3 Indirect Shading Prediction

To render indirect illumination with a ray tracer, we would need full reconstruction of scene reflectance and geometry, which is infeasible from a single image. Instead, we train a 2D CNN to predict indirect shading in screen space. A similar idea was adopted by a recent work [47]. We use a network with large receptive field covering the entire image to model non-local inter-reflections. Our indirect shading is $\mathbf{E_{Ind}} = \mathbf{IndirectNet}(\mathbf{E_d}, \mathbf{D}, \mathbf{N}, \mathbf{A})$, which is added to the direct shading for the final shading prediction. In Fig. 7, we compare the indirect illumination rendered by our network and by a ray tracer using an incomplete textured mesh built from depth map and reflectance map predicted from a single image. Quantitative and qualitative results on real and synthetic examples show that our neural rendering layer renders both direct and indirect illumination accurately, while a ray tracer cannot handle indirect illumination with partial geometry and reflectance, leading to a darker image with similar intensity as the one with direct illumination only.

4.4 Predicting Lighting from Shading

The above framework cannot yet handle specular reflectance, which motivates us to add another network to infer spatially varying per-pixel lighting $\mathbf{L}$, taking the above shading (irradiance) $\mathbf{E}$ as input. We follow [25] to predict a grid of environment maps. We use a similar network architecture but replace the input image $\mathbf{I}$ with the shading $\mathbf{E}$ so that the predicted *local* lighting is a function of our lighting representation: $\mathbf{L} = \mathbf{LightNet}(\mathbf{E}, \mathbf{M}, \mathbf{A}, \mathbf{N}, \mathbf{R}, \mathbf{D})$. The predicted $\mathbf{L}$ can be used to render specular materials, shown in Fig. 11 and Fig. 12 in Sect. 5.

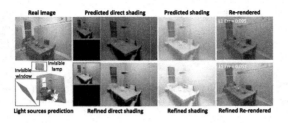

Fig. 8. Comparisons of light source prediction and rendering before and after the optimization on a real scene. Our neural renderer allows using the rendering loss to learn and refine light source intensity and direction

4.5   Implementation Details

Dataset. We train on OpenRooms [28] – a large-scale synthetic indoor dataset for inverse rendering – which is unique among currently available datasets in providing ground truths for all our outputs, such as light source geometry, per-light source shadings (with and without occlusion) and per-light source shadows. Thus, it allows to train each module separately, significantly simplifying training.

Optimized Light Source Parameters. We augment the OpenRooms dataset with optimized light source parameters $\{\mathcal{G}_{\mathrm{sun}}, \mathcal{G}_{\mathrm{sky}}, \mathcal{G}_{\mathrm{grd}}\}$ for windows, leading to sharper and more interpretable predictions. To compute those, we minimize the L_1 difference between the rendered direct shading without occlusion $\mathbf{E_j}$, $j \in \{\mathcal{W}\}$ and its corresponding ground truth, through our differentiable Monte Carlo rendering module (Sect. 4.1). More details are in the supp. The optimized direct shading is seen in Fig. 4 to closely match the ground truth.

Losses. We use L_2 loss to train **MNet**. The loss function for light source prediction is the sum of a rendering loss (**Loss$_{\mathrm{ren}}$**), a geometry loss (**Loss$_{\mathrm{geo}}$**), and a light source loss (**Loss$_{\mathrm{src}}$**). For **Loss$_{\mathrm{ren}}$**, we define it to be the L_1 distance between the rendered direct shading $\mathbf{E_j}$ and its ground-truth, without shadows applied. For **Loss$_{\mathrm{geo}}$**, we uniformly sample points $\{\mathbf{q}\}$ from the ground-truth and predicted light source geometry to compute their RMSE Chamfer distances and add an L_1 loss for its surface area to encourage sharper lighting. For **Loss$_{\mathrm{src}}$**, we use L_2 loss for direction $\mathbf{d}$, $\log L_2$ loss for intensity $\mathbf{w}$ and bandwidth λ. To train the shadow network, we use scale-invariant gradient loss proposed in [32] and find that it leads to many fewer artifacts compared to a simple L_2 loss. We supervise indirect shading with L_1 loss and per-pixel lighting with rendering loss and $\log L_2$ loss similar to [25]. More details are in the supp.

Training and Inference. We use Adam [20] with learning rate 10^{-4} and β (0.9, 0.999). We first train the **MNet** and then use its predictions as inputs to train **InvLampNet**, **InvWinNet**, **VisLampNet** and **VisWinNet** separately. We also train rendering modules independently by providing them with ground-truth $\mathbf{E_d}$ and $\mathbf{S}$. The typical inference time is less than 3s. More details are in the supp.

Fig. 9. Light source prediction on our synthetic dataset for four types of light sources. We visualize light source geometry and direct shading $\mathbf{E_j}$ without occlusion. Our method recovers both geometry and radiance of four types of light sources reasonably well.

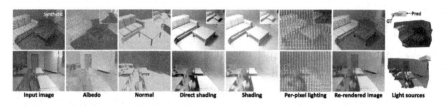

Fig. 10. Our reflectance, lighting and rendering results on a synthetic and a real example. Ground truths for the synthetic example are shown in the insets. We observe that even for invisible light sources, our framework accurately reconstructs their geometry and radiance, which enables realistic rendering of shadings, shadows, interreflections and per-pixel lighting and final images.

Refinement. While so far our framework can achieve high-quality light source prediction and indoor lighting editing in many cases, our differentiable neural renderer enables us to further refine the light source parameters by minimizing the rendering loss between the rendered and the input image. Figure 8 shows an example where we correct the intensity of an invisible lamp with our rendering loss-based refinement. Note that as this is an extremely ill-posed problem, good initialization from our network predictions is essential for the refinement to achieve good results. More discussions are in the supp. We only apply the refinement to real images shown in the paper, not to the synthetic images.

5   Experiments

We present light source estimation and neural rendering results on real and synthetic data, as well as various scene editing applications, especially light editing, on real data. For synthetic data, we test both ground-truth and predicted depths from DPT [37] w/o fine-tuning and use ground truth light source masks. For real data, we generate all depth predictions using DPT [37] and manually draw light source masks. While not being our main focus, we also evaluate a Mask RCNN [15] for light source detection in the supp.

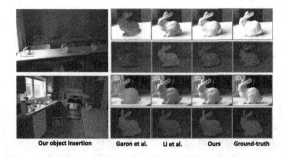

Our object insertion   Garon et al.   Li et al.   Ours   Ground-truth

Fig. 11. We achieve similar quality as prior state-of-the-art on Garon et al. [13] dataset for object insertion. Our method accurately reconstructs the complex lighting from windows to render more realistic highlights and shadows. See Fig. 12 for other editing tasks not possible for prior works.

Table 3. Light source prediction on OpenRooms with ground truth and predicted depth. We report RMSE chamfer loss and L_1 error of direct shading w/o shadows $\mathbf{E_j}$.

	Geometry		Rendering	
	Cham $(\mathbf{q_j}, \bar{\mathbf{q}}_j)$		$\mathbf{E_j}$	
	Gt.	Pred.	Gt.	Pred.
Vis. lamp	0.279	1.15	0.317	0.557
Vis. window	0.415	1.14	0.849	0.952
Inv. lamp	0.712	0.988	0.289	0.357
Inv. window	3.50	3.71	0.312	0.328

Table 4. Quantitative errors for our neural rendering framework on Open-Rooms with ground-truth and predicted depth. We report L_1 loss for the sum of direct shading with shadows $\mathbf{E_d}$ and shading with global illumination $\mathbf{E}$. We report $\log L_2$ loss for per-pixel lighting $\mathbf{L}$.

Direct shading		Shading		Perpix. envmap	
$\mathbf{E_d}$		$\mathbf{E}$		$\mathbf{L}$	
Gt.	Pred.	Gt.	Pred.	Gt.	Pred.
0.283	0.325	0.336	0.391	0.090	0.105

Light Source Predictions and Neural Rendering. Figure 9 shows qualitative results on synthetic images with ground truth depth. Qualitative synthetic results with predicted depth are in the supp. We observe that our method can recover both the geometry and radiance for all 4 types of light sources reasonably well, which enables us to render their direct shading quite close to the ground-truths. The major errors are global shifts of colors and intensities, while the locations of highlights are usually correct. This is reasonable given the ambiguities between materials and lighting. Table 3 reports the quantitative errors with both ground truth and predicted. The errors for windows are larger than those of lamps, since the outdoor lighting coming through windows is much more complicated compared to area lighting. In addition, the direct shading errors for invisible light sources are lower. This is because their overall contributions are usually lower since many of them are far away from the camera location. We observe that our method also achieves comparable rendering errors even with predicted depth, suggesting that it can generalize well to inaccurate geometry.

Table 5. User study on Garon et al. dataset.

Gardner et al. [11]	Garon et al. [13]	Li et al. [28]
72.4%	69.2%	52.0%

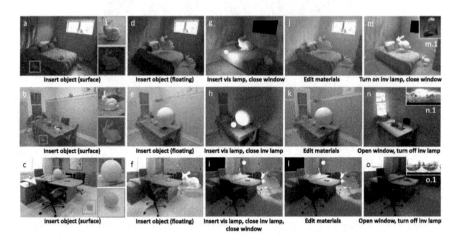

Fig. 12. Various editing applications demonstrated on 3 real examples. In addition to high-quality object insertion (a, b and c), our framework allows editing geometry, material and lighting of indoor scenes, with consistent non-local effects. This includes distant shadows projected to the bed, table and floor (d, e, f and i) or to the entire room when the object blocks the light source (g and h), changing color of walls that causes non-local color bleeding (j, k and l) and adding virtual light sources into the scene (g, h, i, l, m, n, o), such as turning on a lamp or opening a virtual window. (Color figure online)

Figure 10 shows our neural rendering results on a synthetic and a real example. Quantitative results are summarized in Table 4. For the synthetic example, our shadow prediction network combined with Monte-Carlo ray tracing can render distant shadows from a single depth map without boundary artifacts. Our indirect shading prediction network models non-local interreflections from only single-view reconstruction of geometry and materials. All the modules combined together lead to accurate reconstruction of shading and per-pixel lighting. For the real example, even though we do not have ground truths, we observe that the light source position, the highlight in the direct shading and shadows are all visually consistent. The re-rendered image closely matches the input, which further demonstrates that our framework can generalize well to real examples.

Comparisons with Prior Works. We reiterate that our method enables applications (e.g. light source editing) that are not possible with any prior work. While this makes direct comparisons challenging, we compare on a subset of tasks like object insertion that prior works support. We use Garon et al. dataset [13] for comparison, which is a widely-used, real dataset for spatially-varying lighting

Fig. 13. Our accurate reconstruction of visible/invisible light sources allows separating their contributions and turn them on and off. Our results closely match the ground-truth insets.

evaluation. We conduct a user study by requiring 200 users to compare our results with prior results and report the percentage of users who believes ours are better. Even though we are solving a harder problem, both qualitative and quantitative results in Fig. 11 and Table 5 show that our method achieves performance comparable to the prior state-of-the-arts which only handle local editing of the scene. Our per-pixel lighting prediction can be used to render specular objects realistically, with highlights, shadows and spatial consistency being correctly modeled. Specifically, our window representation and MIS based rendering layer can better handle high-frequency, complex sunlight, leading to rendering results closer to the ground truths, as presented in Fig. 11.

Novel Scene Editing Applications. In addition to object insertion (a, b, c) with realistic highlights and shadows, the true advantage of our framework is its ability to handle non-local effects in novel scene editing applications, which is only made possible by our accurate reconstruction of indoor light sources and high-quality neural rendering framework. These non-local effects include distant shadows and highlights, which is shown in (d, e, f) of Fig. 12 where the inserted virtual objects block the light coming from the visible window or the invisible lamp. This is further demonstrated in (g, h, i), where the inserted virtual lamp causes highlights on the nearby geometry and shadows that cover the whole wall behind the virtual bunny and sphere. Moreover, our framework can model non-local interreflection accurately. As shown in (j, k, l), as we change the color of walls to orange and blue, our indirect shading network paints the inserted white objects with correct color bleeding. In (m, n, o), we demonstrate our framework's ability to turn on an invisible lamp or open a virtual window. In n, o, we use the 3 SG approximation of the environment map shown in n.1 and o.1 respectively. Our representation combined with our neural renderer can render realistic directional sunlight. Our accurate reconstruction of indoor light sources further allows us to separate their contributions. As shown in both Fig. 1 and 13, our framework allows turning off visible and invisible, lamps or windows in the scene, with changed appearance similar to the ground-truth insets[2].

---

[2] The second example is from the internet so we do not have its ground truth.

Please see *supplementary material* for ablation studies, error distributions, failure cases, limitations and a video illustrating consistent scene editing effects as we move virtual objects and light sources, or gradually change the wall color.

6   Conclusions

We presented a method that enables full indoor scene relighting and other editing operations from a single LDR image with its predicted depth and light source segmentation masks. The first key innovation is our lighting representation; we estimate multiple global 3D parametric lights (lamps and windows), both visible and invisible. The second is our hybrid neural renderer, capable of producing high-quality images from our representations using a combination of Monte Carlo and neural techniques. We show that this careful combination can for the first time handle challenging scene editing applications including object insertion, material editing, light source insertion and editing, with realistic global effects.

Acknowledgment. We thank NSF CAREER 1751365, 2110409, 1703957, CHASE-CI, ONR N000142012529, N000141912293, a Google Award, gifts from Adobe, Ron L. Graham Chair, UCSD Center for Visual Computing and Qualcomm Fellowship.

References

1. Barron, J.T., Malik, J.: Shape, illumination, and reflectance from shading. PAMI **37**(8), 1670–1687 (2015)
2. Barrow, H.G., Tenenbaum, J.M.: Recovering intrinsic scene characteristics from images. Comput. Vis. Syst. 3–26 (1978)
3. Bell, S., Bala, K., Snavely, N.: Intrinsic images in the wild. ACM Trans. Graph. (TOG) **33**(4), 159 (2014)
4. Bi, S., Han, X., Yu, Y.: An l 1 image transform for edge-preserving smoothing and scene-level intrinsic decomposition. ACM Trans. Graph. (TOG) **34**(4), 1–12 (2015)
5. Bi, S., et al.: Neural reflectance fields for appearance acquisition. arXiv preprint arXiv:2008.03824 (2020)
6. Bi, S., et al.: Deep reflectance volumes: relightable reconstructions from multi-view photometric images. arXiv preprint arXiv:2007.09892 (2020)
7. Bi, S., Xu, Z., Sunkavalli, K., Kriegman, D., Ramamoorthi, R.: Deep 3D capture: geometry and reflectance from sparse multi-view images. In: Proceedings of the IEEE/CVF Conference on Computer Vision and Pattern Recognition, pp. 5960–5969 (2020)
8. Boss, M., Braun, R., Jampani, V., Barron, J.T., Liu, C., Lensch, H.: NeRD: neural reflectance decomposition from image collections. arXiv preprint arXiv:2012.03918 (2020)
9. Chandraker, M.: On shape and material recovery from motion. In: Fleet, D., Pajdla, T., Schiele, B., Tuytelaars, T. (eds.) ECCV 2014. LNCS, vol. 8695, pp. 202–217. Springer, Cham (2014). https://doi.org/10.1007/978-3-319-10584-0_14
10. Debevec, P.: Rendering synthetic objects into real scenes: bridging traditional and image-based graphics with global illumination and high dynamic range photography. In: SIGGRAPH, vol. 98, pp. 189–198 (1998)

11. Gardner, M.A., et al.: Learning to predict indoor illumination from a single image. ACM Trans. Graph. **9**(4) (2017)
12. Gardner, M.A., Hold-Geoffroy, Y., Sunkavalli, K., Gagne, C., Lalonde, J.F.: Deep parametric indoor lighting estimation. In: ICCV (2019)
13. Garon, M., Sunkavalli, K., Hadap, S., Carr, N., Lalonde, J.F.: Fast spatially-varying indoor lighting estimation. In: Proceedings of the IEEE Conference on Computer Vision and Pattern Recognition, pp. 6908–6917 (2019)
14. Goldman, D.B., Curless, B., Hertzmann, A., Seitz, S.M.: Shape and spatially-varying BRDFs from photometric stereo. PAMI **32**(6), 1060–1071 (2010)
15. He, K., Gkioxari, G., Dollár, P., Girshick, R.: Mask R-CNN. In: Proceedings of the IEEE International Conference on Computer Vision, pp. 2961–2969 (2017)
16. Johnson, M.K., Adelson, E.H.: Shape estimation in natural illumination. In: CVPR (2011)
17. Karis, B., Games, E.: Real shading in unreal engine 4. In: Proceedings of Physically Based Shading Theory Practice
18. Karsch, K., Hedau, V., Forsyth, D., Hoiem, D.: Rendering synthetic objects into legacy photographs. ACM Trans. Graph. **30**(6), 1 (2011)
19. Karsch, K., et al.: Automatic scene inference for 3d object compositing. ACM Trans. Graph. **33**, 32:1–32:15 (2014)
20. Kingma, D., Ba, J.: Adam: a method for stochastic optimization. arXiv preprint arXiv:1412.6980 (2014)
21. LeGendre, C., et al.: DeepLight: learning illumination for unconstrained mobile mixed reality. In: CVPR, pp. 5918–5928 (2019)
22. Li, X., Dong, Y., Peers, P., Tong, X.: Modeling surface appearance from a single photograph using self-augmented convolutional neural networks. ACM Trans. Graph. **36**(4), 1–11 (2017)
23. Li, Z., Snavely, N.: CGIntrinsics: better intrinsic image decomposition through physically-based rendering. In: ECCV, pp. 371–387 (2018)
24. Li, Z., Snavely, N.: Learning intrinsic image decomposition from watching the world. In: Proceedings of the IEEE Conference on Computer Vision and Pattern Recognition, pp. 9039–9048 (2018)
25. Li, Z., Shafiei, M., Ramamoorthi, R., Sunkavalli, K., Chandraker, M.: Inverse rendering for complex indoor scenes: shape, spatially-varying lighting and SVBRDF from a single image (2020)
26. Li, Z., Sunkavalli, K., Chandraker, M.: Materials for masses: SVBRDF acquisition with a single mobile phone image. In: Ferrari, V., Hebert, M., Sminchisescu, C., Weiss, Y. (eds.) ECCV 2018. LNCS, vol. 11207, pp. 74–90. Springer, Cham (2018). https://doi.org/10.1007/978-3-030-01219-9_5
27. Li, Z., Xu, Z., Ramamoorthi, R., Sunkavalli, K., Chandraker, M.: Learning to reconstruct shape and spatially-varying reflectance from a single image. In: SIGGRAPH Asia, p. 269. ACM (2018)
28. Li, Z., et al.: OpenRooms: an end-to-end open framework for photorealistic indoor scene datasets. In: CVPR (2021)
29. Liu, L., Gu, J., Lin, K.Z., Chua, T.S., Theobalt, C.: Neural sparse voxel fields. arXiv preprint arXiv:2007.11571 (2020)
30. Marschner, S.: Inverse rendering for computer graphics (1998)
31. Mildenhall, B., Srinivasan, P.P., Tancik, M., Barron, J.T., Ramamoorthi, R., Ng, R.: NeRF: representing scenes as neural radiance fields for view synthesis. In: Vedaldi, A., Bischof, H., Brox, T., Frahm, J.-M. (eds.) ECCV 2020. LNCS, vol. 12346, pp. 405–421. Springer, Cham (2020). https://doi.org/10.1007/978-3-030-58452-8_24

32. Niklaus, S., Mai, L., Yang, J., Liu, F.: 3D ken burns effect from a single image. ACM Trans. Graph. (TOG) **38**(6), 1–15 (2019)
33. Oxholm, G., Nishino, K.: Shape and reflectance from natural illumination. In: Fitzgibbon, A., Lazebnik, S., Perona, P., Sato, Y., Schmid, C. (eds.) ECCV 2012. LNCS, vol. 7572, pp. 528–541. Springer, Heidelberg (2012). https://doi.org/10.1007/978-3-642-33718-5_38
34. Pharr, M., Jakob, W., Humphreys, G.: Physically Based Rendering: From Theory to Implementation. Morgan Kaufmann (2016)
35. Philip, J., Gharbi, M., Zhou, T., Efros, A.A., Drettakis, G.: Multi-view relighting using a geometry-aware network. ACM Trans. Graph. (TOG) **38**(4), 1–14 (2019)
36. Philip, J., Morgenthaler, S., Gharbi, M., Drettakis, G.: Free-viewpoint indoor neural relighting from multi-view stereo. ACM Trans. Graph. **40**, 1–18 (2021)
37. Ranftl, R., Bochkovskiy, A., Koltun, V.: Vision transformers for dense prediction. In: ICCV, pp. 12179–12188 (2021)
38. Sengupta, S., Gu, J., Kim, K., Liu, G., Jacobs, D.W., Kautz, J.: Neural inverse rendering of an indoor scene from a single image. arXiv preprint arXiv:1901.02453 (2019)
39. Shen, J., Yang, X., Jia, Y., Li, X.: Intrinsic images using optimization. In: CVPR 2011, pp. 3481–3487. IEEE (2011)
40. Srinivasan, P.P., Deng, B., Zhang, X., Tancik, M., Mildenhall, B., Barron, J.T.: NeRV: neural reflectance and visibility fields for relighting and view synthesis. arXiv preprint arXiv:2012.03927 (2020)
41. Srinivasan, P.P., Mildenhall, B., Tancik, M., Barron, J.T., Tucker, R., Snavely, N.: Lighthouse: Predicting lighting volumes for spatially-coherent illumination. In: Proceedings of the IEEE/CVF Conference on Computer Vision and Pattern Recognition, pp. 8080–8089 (2020)
42. Straub, J., et al.: The Replica dataset: a digital replica of indoor spaces. arXiv preprint arXiv:1906.05797 (2019)
43. Veach, E.: Robust Monte Carlo methods for light transport simulation, vol. 1610. Stanford University Ph.D. thesis (1997)
44. Wang, Z., Philion, J., Fidler, S., Kautz, J.: Learning indoor inverse rendering with 3D spatially-varying lighting. In: ICCV (2021)
45. Xia, R., Dong, Y., Peers, P., Tong, X.: Recovering shape and spatially-varying surface reflectance under unknown illumination. ACM Trans. Graph. **35**(6), 187 (2016)
46. Xiang, F., Xu, Z., Hašan, M., Hold-Geoffroy, Y., Sunkavalli, K., Su, H.: NeuTex: neural texture mapping for volumetric neural rendering. arXiv preprint arXiv:2103.00762 (2021)
47. Xin, H., Zheng, S., Xu, K., Yan, L.Q.: Lightweight bilateral convolutional neural networks for interactive single-bounce diffuse indirect illumination. IEEE Ann. Hist. Comput. (01), 1 (2020)
48. Yu, A., Ye, V., Tancik, M., Kanazawa, A.: pixelNeRF: neural radiance fields from one or few images. arXiv preprint arXiv:2012.02190 (2020)
49. Zhang, E., Cohen, M.F., Curless, B.: Emptying, refurnishing, and relighting indoor spaces. ACM Trans. Graph. (TOG) **35**(6), 1–14 (2016)
50. Zhou, H., Yu, X., Jacobs, D.W.: GLoSH: global-local spherical harmonics for intrinsic image decomposition. In: Proceedings of the IEEE International Conference on Computer Vision, pp. 7820–7829 (2019)
51. Zhu, Y., Tang, J., Li, S., Shi, B.: DeRenderNet: intrinsic image decomposition of urban scenes with shape-(in) dependent shading rendering. In: 2021 IEEE International Conference on Computational Photography (ICCP), pp. 1–11. IEEE (2021)

LEDNet: Joint Low-Light Enhancement and Deblurring in the Dark

Shangchen Zhou, Chongyi Li, and Chen Change Loy

S-Lab, Nanyang Technological University, Singapore, Singapore
{s200094,chongyi.li,ccloy}@ntu.edu.sg
https://shangchenzhou.com/projects/LEDNet

Abstract. Night photography typically suffers from both low light and blurring issues due to the dim environment and the common use of long exposure. While existing light enhancement and deblurring methods could deal with each problem individually, a cascade of such methods cannot work harmoniously to cope well with joint degradation of visibility and sharpness. Training an end-to-end network is also infeasible as no paired data is available to characterize the coexistence of low light and blurs. We address the problem by introducing a novel data synthesis pipeline that models realistic low-light blurring degradations, especially for blurs in saturated regions, e.g., light streaks, that often appear in the night images. With the pipeline, we present the first large-scale dataset for joint low-light enhancement and deblurring. The dataset, **LOL-Blur**, contains 12,000 low-blur/normal-sharp pairs with diverse darkness and blurs in different scenarios. We further present an effective network, named **LEDNet**, to perform joint low-light enhancement and deblurring. Our network is unique as it is specially designed to consider the synergy between the two inter-connected tasks. Both the proposed dataset and network provide a foundation for this challenging joint task. Extensive experiments demonstrate the effectiveness of our method on both synthetic and real-world datasets.

1 Introduction

When capturing images at night, one would usually use a slow shutter speed (long exposure) to allow more available light to illuminate the image. Even so, the captured dark images may still suffer from low visibility and distorted color induced by insufficient light, which is constrained by minimum shutter speeds that are acceptable for handheld shooting in the dark. Annoyingly, long exposure inevitably causes motion blurs due to camera shake and dynamic scenes. Thus, both low light and motion blurs typically co-exist in the night images.

Prior methods address the two tasks independently, i.e., low-light enhancement [9,17,41] and image deblurring [5,11,16,30,36,47,50]. These methods made

Supplementary Information The online version contains supplementary material available at https://doi.org/10.1007/978-3-031-20068-7_33.

© The Author(s), under exclusive license to Springer Nature Switzerland AG 2022
S. Avidan et al. (Eds.): ECCV 2022, LNCS 13666, pp. 573–589, 2022.
https://doi.org/10.1007/978-3-031-20068-7_33

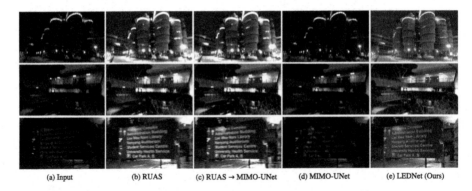

(a) Input   (b) RUAS   (c) RUAS → MIMO-UNet   (d) MIMO-UNet   (e) LEDNet (Ours)

Fig. 1. A comparison on the real-world night blurry images shows that existing low-light enhancement and deblurring methods fail in coping with the night blurry images. (a) Input images. (b) Motion blur in the saturated area is enlarged after performing light enhancement using a contemporary method RUAS [22] (indicated by red arrows). (c) Applying the deblurring network MIMO-UNet [7] after light enhancement still fails in blur removal. (d) MIMO-UNet trained on daytime GoPro dataset fails to remove blur in the nighttime images. (e) The proposed LEDNet trained with our LOL-Blur dataset yields satisfactory results through joint low-light enhancement and deblurring. (Color figure online)

independent assumptions in their specific problem. As a result, a forceful combination cannot solve the joint degradation caused by low light and motion blur. Specifically, existing low-light enhancement methods [22,41] perform intensity boosting and denoising, ignoring spatial degradation of motion blurs. Instead, motion blur is even enlarged in saturated regions due to over-exposing after performing light enhancement, as shown in Fig. 1(b). Low-light enhancement methods [41,53] also have the risk of removing informative clues for blur removal due to over-smoothing while denoising. Figure 1(c) shows that performing deblurring after light enhancement fails the blur removal. As for deblurring, existing methods [7,16,36,47] trained on the datasets that only contain daytime scenes, and thus, cannot be directly applied to the non-trivial night image deblurring. In particular, motion cues in dark regions are poorly visible and perceived due to the low dynamic range, posing a great challenge for these existing deblurring methods. Furthermore, night blurry images contain saturated regions (e.g., light streaks) in which the pixels do not conform to the blur model learned from daytime data [5,11]. As observed in Fig. 1(d), the deblurring network trained on daytime GoPro dataset fails to remove blur in the night images.

The solution to the aforementioned problems is to train a single network that addresses both types of degradations jointly. Clearly, the main obstacle is the availability of such data that come with low-light blurry and normal-light sharp image pairs. The collection is laborious and hard, if not impossible. Existing datasets for low-light enhancement, e.g., LOL [41] and SID [3], gather low-/normal-light pairs by changing exposure time and ISO in two shots. While deblurring datasets, e.g., RealBlur [32], need to capture paired blurry/sharp

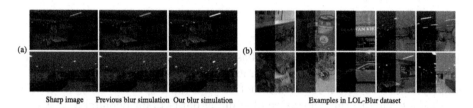

Sharp image   Previous blur simulation   Our blur simulation   Examples in LOL-Blur dataset

Fig. 2. (a) Comparison on blur simulation. The previous blur simulation [29,30,34], i.e., simple averaging of a sharp sequence, tends to weaken blurs in saturated pixels. By contrast, our simulation generates more realistic saturated blurs that maintain the saturated intensities during blur synthesis. (b) Paired images in the LOL-Blur dataset, containing diverse darkness and blurs (saturated and unsaturated) in the dark.

images under the long and short exposures using a dual-camera system. However, it is challenging to merge these two data collection processes harmoniously to capture paired data for this joint task. Moreover, the existing synthetic deblurring datasets [29,30,34] (e.g., GoPro) cannot simulate blurs of saturated regions for night images due to the lack of sequences that contain saturated scenes and their inappropriate blur simulation by simply averaging. As observed in Fig. 2(a) (middle), their blur simulation method tend to undesirably attenuate blurs of saturated areas, which do not resemble the real ones shown in Fig. 1(a).

This paper makes the first attempt to propose a novel data synthesis pipeline for joint low-light enhancement and deblurring. In particular, we circumvent the difficulty of obtaining dark and blurry images through a heuristic approach for simulating low-light degradation, and a new blur simulation method that pays special attention to model blurs in saturated regions correctly. Figure 2 shows that our blur simulation generates more realistic saturated blurs than the previous ones [29,30,34], maintaining saturated intensities during blur synthesis. The resulting dataset, **LOL-Blur**, contains 12,000 pairs of low-blur/normal-sharp pairs for training and testing. Examples of LOL-Blur are shown in Fig. 2(b).

Apart from the data, we show that it is beneficial to consider both low-light enhancement and deblurring in a single context. In particular, we demonstrate a novel encoder-decoder pipeline, **Low-light Enhancement and Deblurring Network (LEDNet)**, where the encoder is specialized in light enhancement and the decoder in deblurring. The encoder and decoder are linked with adaptive skip connections. This unique structure allows the passing of light enhanced features in the decoder for blur removal in the decoder.

The main contributions: 1) We introduce a novel data synthesis pipeline that models low-light blur degradation realistically, leading to the large-scale and diverse LOL-Blur dataset for joint low-light enhancement and deblurring. 2) We propose a unified network LEDNet with delicate designs to address low-light enhancement and deblurring jointly. 3) We present to aggregate hierarchical global prior that is crucial for stable training and artifacts suppression, as well as the learnable non-linear layer helps brighten dark areas without overexposing other regions. 4) Extensive experiments show that our method achieves superior results to prior arts on both synthetic and real-world datasets.

2   Related Work

Image Deblurring. Many CNN-based methods have been proposed for dynamic scene deblurring [7,16,30,36,47,48,50]. Most early studies [8,35] employ networks to estimate the motion blur kernels followed by non-blind methods. Owing to the emergence of training datasets for deblurring tasks [19, 29,30,32–34,57], end-to-end kernel-free networks become the dominant methods. To obtain a large receptive field, some networks [7,30,36] adopt a multi-scale strategy to handle large blurs Similarly, some multi-patch deblurring networks [10,46,50] employ the hierarchical structures without down-sampling. GAN-based deblurring methods [15,16] have been proposed to generate more details. To deal with spatially-varying blurs, Zhang *et al.* [48] propose spatially variant RNNs to remove blur via estimating RNN weights. Zhou *et al.* [56] propose the filter adaptive convolutional (FAC) layer to handle non-uniform blurs dynamically. In our paper, we built a filter adaptive skip connection between encoder and decoder using FAC layers.

Optimization-based approaches are proposed for low-light image deblurring [4–6,11]. Hu *et al.* [11] suggest the use of light streaks to estimate blur kernel. However, their method heavily relies on light streaks and tends to fail when the light sources are not available or too large beyond pre-designed blur kernel size. Chen *et al.* [5,6] process saturated regions specially and ensure smaller contributions of these pixels in optimization. Their results show few artifacts around saturated regions. While effective, all these methods are time-consuming, thus limiting their applicability.

Low-Light Enhancement. Deep networks have become the mainstream in low-light enhancement (LLE) [17]. The first CNN model LL-Net [23] employs an autoencoder to learn denoising and light enhancement simultaneously. Inspired by the Retinex theory, several LLE networks [22,38,41,43,53] are proposed. They commonly split a low-light input into reflectance and illumination maps, then adjust the illumination map to enhance the intensity. Most methods integrate a denoising module on the reflectance map for suppressing noise in the enhanced results. For example, Zheng *et al.* [55] propose an unfolding total variation network to estimate noise level for LLE. While the joint task of LLE and deblurring has not been investigated yet in the literature.

To improve the generalization capability, some unsupervised methods are proposed. EnlightenGAN [13] is an attention-based U-Net trained using adversarial loss. Zero-DCE [9] and Zero-DCE++ [18] formulate light enhancement as a task of image-specific curve estimation. Their training adopts several manually-defined losses on supervision of exposure or color, without limitation of paired or unpaired training data. Thus, Zero-DCE can be easily extended to generic lighting adjustments. Notably, due to the pixel-wise curve adjustment formulation, it can be used for spatially-varying light adjustment. In our data synthesis pipeline, we train an exposure conditioned Zero-DCE to darken images for low-light simulation. Given random low exposure degrees, we can generate low-light images of diverse darkness.

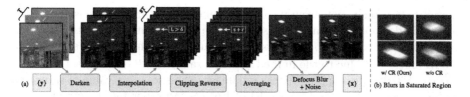

Fig. 3. (a) An overview of our data synthesis pipeline. (b) Comparisons on two blur simulations in the saturated regions. With the proposed Clipping Reverse (CR), we can generate realistic blurs with sharp boundaries in saturated regions, which better resembling real cases that are caused by the large light ratio in night photography.

3   LOL-Blur Dataset

Efforts have been made to collect real-world paired data for low-light enhancement [2,3,12,21,37,41] or image deblurring [32], but not both settings at the same time. The lack of such data is not surprising as (1) Paired images of low-light enhancement datasets and image deblurring datasets are commonly collected by different camera shot settings, and (2) The collection of both kinds of data is susceptible to geometric and photometric misalignment due to camera shake or dynamic environment during data acquisition.

In this work, inspired by the big success of data synthesis in the real-world super-resolution tasks [1,20,39,49], we introduce a synthesis pipeline that models low-light blur degradation jointly, hence allowing us to generate a large-scale dataset (LOL-Blur). We acquire a total of 170 videos for training and 30 videos for testing, each of which has 60 frames, amounting to 12,000 paired data.

3.1   Existing Synthesis Methods and Limitations

Low-Light Simulation. Prior works [23,25] use Gamma correction to simulate low-light images, defined by a nonlinearity power-law expression $I_{low} = \alpha I_{in}^{\gamma}, (\gamma > 1)$, where constant α is usually set to 1. This synthetic process tends to introduce large color deviation with noticeable warm tones [17], in contrast, our simulation method EC-Zero-DCE (refer to Sect. 3.2) produce more natural and realistic low-light images. A comparison is provided in the supplementary.

Blur Simulation. A standard synthesis pipeline of blurry data [19,29,30,34,57] is to average successive frames on high frame-rate sequences for approximating the blur model [30]. The process can be expressed as:

$$B = g\left(\frac{1}{T}\sum_{i=0}^{T-1} S[i]\right) = g\left(\frac{1}{T}\sum_{i=0}^{T-1} g^{-1}\left(\hat{S[i]}\right)\right), \tag{1}$$

where $g(\cdot)$ is CRF function (Gamma curve with $\gamma = 2.2$) that maps latent signal $S[i]$ into observed sRGB images $\hat{S[i]}$. This process can be used to generate blurry-sharp pairs for daytime scenes, assuming $\hat{S[i]} = g(S[i])$. This blur model, however, is usually not accurate to the regions of saturated pixels that often appear in dark blurry images. This is because the saturated intensities in latent signal $S[i]$ are clipped to the maximum value (255) when $S[i]$ is saved as an sRGB image $\hat{S}[i]$, due to the limited dynamic range of sRGB images, i.e., $\hat{S}[i] = Clip\,(g\,(S[i]))$. This clipping function damages the exceeding value of saturated regions, thus making the blur model of Eq. (1) improper for these regions [5]. Our simulation pipeline resolves this issue by recovering the clipped intensities in saturated regions (refer to Sect. 3.2), generating more realistic light blurs. As a visual comparison are shown in Fig. 2(a).

3.2   Data Generation Pipeline

The overview of our data generation pipeline is shown in Fig. 3. We use a Sony RX10 IV camera to record 200 high frame-rate videos at 250 fps. With the video sequences, we first downsize each frame to a resolution of 1120×640 to reduce noises. We then apply VBM4D [27] for further denoising and obtain the clean sequences. In our method, we take 7 or 9 frames as a sequence clip, as shown in Fig. 3. The mid-frame (with orange bounding box) among the sharp frames is treated as the ground truth image. Then, we process the following steps to generate low-light and blurred images.

Darkening with Conditional Zero-DCE. To simulate the degradation of low light, we reformulate the Zero-DCE [9] into an Exposure-Conditioned variant, EC-Zero-DCE. Contrary to Zero-DCE that is designed for improving the brightness of an image, EC-Zero-DCE simulates low light with controllable darkness levels, via implementing a reversed curve adjustment. Specifically, we modify the exposure control loss by replacing the fixed exposure value with a random parameter that represents darkness while other losses are kept in the same settings as Zero-DCE. Given different exposure levels, EC-Zero-DCE can generate realistic low-light images with diverse darkness. Note that EC-Zero-DCE performs pixel-wise and spatially-varying light adjustment, rather than uniform light degradation. We provide the luminance adjustment map in the supplementary to support this statement.

Frame Interpolation. To avoid discontinuous blurs in the synthetic blurry images, we increase the frame rate to 2000 fps fps using a high-quality frame interpolation network [31].

Clipping Reverse for Saturated Region. To restore the clipped intensity in saturated regions that were ignored by the previous blur simulation (i.e., Eq. (1)), a simple yet effective way is by adding a random supplementary value $r \sim \mathcal{U}(20, 100)$ to RGB channels in these regions. We first define the saturated regions where lightness channel $L > \delta$ in the Lab color space, the threshold δ is empirically set to 98 in our pipeline, where $L \in [0, 100]$. Then, we reformulate the blur model as a more general form for both saturated and unsaturated regions, as shown in Eq. (2):

$$B = g \left(\frac{1}{T} \sum_{i=0}^{T-1} Clip^{-1} \left(g^{-1} \left(\hat{S}[i] \right) \right) \right), \qquad (2)$$

where $Clip^{-1}(s) = s + r$ if s in the saturated regions, otherwise $Clip^{-1}(s) = s$. Figure 2(a) and Fig. 3(b) shows our blur simulation using clipping reverse (w/ CR) generates more realistic saturated blurs than the GoPro blur simulation (w/o CR) that is commonly used in previous datasets. Moreover, the modified blur simulation (w/ CR) indeed helps networks handle well on both unsaturated and saturated blurs, as indicated by the comparison in Fig. 8.

Frame Averaging. Next, we average 56 (7×8) or 72 (9×8) successive frames of 2000 fps fps videos to produce virtual blurry videos at around 24 fps.

Adding Defocus Blur and Noise. To generate more realistic low-light blurry images, our pipeline also considers defocus blurs by applying generalized Gaussian filters [39]. We also add realistic noises into low-blur images generated by CycleISP [44]. Both defocus blur and noise are added in a random fashion.

Discussion. Our dataset offers realism in low-light blur degradation and consists of 200 common dynamic dark scenarios (indoor and outdoor) with diverse darkness and motion blurs, as shown in Fig. 2(b). Compared to previous synthetic deblurring datasets (such as GoPro [30] and REDS [29]) that only contain daytime scenes and lacks the saturated regions, our dataset contains a total of 55 sequences with various sources of artificial lights that often appear in the night photography. Hence, our simulated data sufficiently covers hard cases with blurs in saturated areas, e.g., light streaks, which are indispensable for our joint task. Experimental results demonstrate that the networks trained using our dataset generalizes well on real-world dark blurred images.

4 LEDNet

We treat the joint task of low-light enhancement (LLE) and deblurring as a non-blind image restoration problem. The low-light blurry images $\{x\}$ contain the mixed degradations of visibility and texture. The two type degradations are spatially-varying due to local lighting conditions and dynamic scene blurs. To solve this issue, we specially design a network, LEDNet, to map low-light blurry images $\{x\}$ to its corresponding normal-light sharp images $\{y\}$. As shown in Fig. 4, LEDNet is built upon an encoder-decoder architecture with filter adaptive skip connections to solve this joint spatially-varying task.

4.1 Low-Light Enhancement Encoder

The encoder (LE-Encoder) is designed for Low-light Enhancement with the supervision of intermediate enhancement loss (see Sect. 4.4). It consists of three scale blocks, each of which contains one Residual Block, one Residual Downsampling Block [45], a Pyramid Pooling Module (PPM) [54], and a Curve Non-Linear Unit (CurveNLU), as shown in Fig. 4. To facilitate intermediate supervision, we

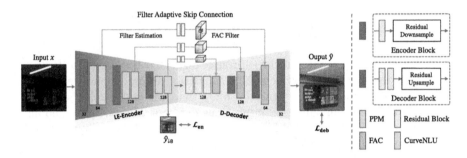

Fig. 4. An illustration of the proposed LEDNet. It contains an Encoder for Light Enhancement, LE-Encoder, and a Decoder for Deblurring, D-Decoder. They are connected by three Filter Adaptive Skip Connections. The PPM and CurveNLU layers are inserted in LE-Encoder, making light enhancement more stable and powerful. LEDNet applies spatially-adaptive transformation to D-Decoder using filters generated by FASC from enhanced features. CurveNLU and FASC enable LEDNet to perform spatially-varying feature transformation for both intensity enhancement and blur removal.

output an enhanced image by one convolution layer at the smallest scale. Our design gears LE-Encoder to embed the input image x into the feature space of normal-light images, allowing the subsequent decoder (D-Decoder) to pay more attention to the deblurring task.

Pyramid Pooling Module. The outputs of typical light enhancement networks are often prone to local artifacts, especially when the networks are fed with high-resolution inputs. We found that the problem can be significantly remedied by injecting global contextual prior into the networks. To achieve this goal, we introduce PPM into our LE-Encoder. The PPM extracts hierarchical global prior using multi-scale regional pooling layers and aggregates them in the last convolution layer. We adopt the original design of PPM that has four mean pooling branches with bin sizes of $1, 2, 3, 6$, respectively. The is the first time PPM is used in a low-light enhancement network. We show that it is crucial for suppressing artifacts that may be caused by the co-existence of other degradations of blur and noise (refer to a comparison shown in Fig. 9).

Curve Non-linear Unit. Local lighting such as light sources are often observed in the night environment. A global operator tends to over- or under-enhance these local regions. To solve this problem, Zero-DCE [9] applies pixel-wise curve parameters to the input image iteratively for light enhancement.

Inspired by Zero-DCE, we propose a learnable non-linear activation function, namely CurveNLU. The CurveNLU is designed for feature transformation using the estimated curve parameters, as shown in Fig. 5. Similar to Zero-DCE, we formulate the high-order curve in an iterative function:

$$C_n(p) = \begin{cases} A_1 F(p)(1 - F(p)) + F(p), & n = 1 \\ A_{n-1}(p)C_{n-1}(p)(1 - C_{n-1}(p)) + C_{n-1}(p), & n > 1 \end{cases} \quad (3)$$

where p denotes position coordinates of features, and A_{n-1} is the pixel-wise curve parameter for the n-*th* order of the estimated curve. Given an input

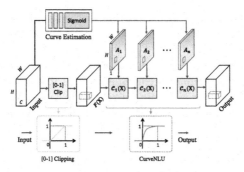

Fig. 5. An illustration of Curve Non-Linear Unit. This layer can be seen as a learnable non-linear activation function between 0 and 1. Based on Eq. 3, the learned function always follows concave down increasing curves to increase feature intensities.

feature $F \in \mathbb{R}^{H \times W \times C}$, Curve Estimation module estimates curve parameters $A \in \mathbb{R}^{H \times W \times n}$ that represent an $n+1$ order curve for different positions. Feature transformation is then achieved by Eq. 3 using the estimated curve parameters. Different from Zero-DCE that uses different curves for RGB channels, our CurveNLU applies the same curve to different channels in the feature domain. Note that the parameters A lay in $[0, 1]$, ensuring that CurveNLU always learns concave down increasing curves to increase the features of dark areas without overexposing other regions. To meet such a requirement, the input feature F of CurveNLU is needed to be clipped to the range of $[0, 1]$ at the beginning. The Curve Estimation module consists of three convolution layers followed by a Sigmoid function. We set the iteration number n to 3 in our experiments.

4.2 Deblurring Decoder

With the enhanced features from LE-Encoder, Deblurring Decoder (D-Decoder) is able to concentrate more on deblurring. It contains three convolutional blocks, each of which has two Residual Blocks, one Residual Upsampling Block [45], and a FAC Layer [56] that is used to bridge the LE-Encoder and the D-Decoder.

4.3 Filter Adaptive Skip Connection

Both low-light enhancement and deblurring in our task are spatially varying problems. Deblurring in the dynamic scenes is challenging due to its spatially variant blurs caused by object motion and depth variations. Though CurveNLU applies pixel-wise adjustment in the LE-Encoder, it is not enough for the deblurring task that usually needs dynamic spatial kernels to handle motion blurs. Filter Adaptive Convolutional (FAC) layer [56] has been proposed to apply dynamic convolution filters for each element in features. Built on the FAC layers, we design a Filter Adaptive Skip Connection (FASC) to solve the deblurring problem by exploiting the enhanced information from LE-Encoder. As shown in Fig. 4, given the enhanced features $E \in \mathbb{R}^{H \times W \times C}$ at different scales, FASC estimates the corresponding filter $K \in \mathbb{R}^{H \times W \times Cd^2}$ via three 3×3 convolution layers and a 1×1 convolution layer to expand the feature dimension. The filter K is then used by FAC layers to transform the features $D \in \mathbb{R}^{H \times W \times C}$ in D-Decoder. For each element of feature D, FAC applies a convolution operator using the corresponding $d \times d$ kernel from the filter K to obtain refined features. We set the kernel size d to 5 at the three scales, following the setting in Zhou *et al.* [56].

4.4 Loss Function

Low-Light Enhancement Losses. To provide intermediate supervision, we employ L1 loss and perceptual loss at $\times 8$ downsampled scale. Specifically, we predict the image $\hat{y}_{\downarrow 8}$ for the smallest scale of LE-Encoder, and then restrict it using scale-corresponding ground truth $y_{\downarrow 8}$, shown as Eq. (4):

$$\mathcal{L}_{en} = \|\hat{y}_{\downarrow 8} - y_{\downarrow 8}\|_1 + \lambda_{per} \|\phi(\hat{y}_{\downarrow 8}) - \phi(y_{\downarrow 8})\|_1, \tag{4}$$

where $\phi(\cdot)$ represents the pretrained VGG19 network. We adopt multi-scale feature maps from layer $\{conv1, \cdots, conv4\}$ following the widely-used setting [40]. Due to downsampling space, the enhancement loss $\mathcal{L}_{en}$ mainly supervises the exposure of intermediate output.

Deblurring Losses. We use the L1 loss and perceptual loss as our deblurring loss $\mathcal{L}_{deb}$, defined as follows:

$$\mathcal{L}_{deb} = \|\hat{y} - y\|_1 + \lambda_{per} \|\phi(\hat{y}) - \phi(y)\|_1. \tag{5}$$

The overall loss function is:

$$\mathcal{L} = \lambda_{en}\mathcal{L}_{en} + \lambda_{deb}\mathcal{L}_{deb}. \tag{6}$$

We set the loss weights of λ_{per}, λ_{en}, and λ_{deb} to 0.01, 0.8, and 1, respectively.

5   Experiments

Dataset and Experimental Settings. We train our network LEDNet and other baselines on LOL-Blur dataset. The 170 sequences (10,200 pairs) are used for training and 30 sequences (1,800 pairs) for test. We randomly crop 256×256 patches for training. The mini-batch size is set to 8. We train our network using Adam optimizer with $\beta_1 = 0.9, \beta_2 = 0.99$ for a total of 500k iterations. The initial learning rate is set to 10^{-4} and updated with cosine annealing strategy [24].

Table 1. Quantitative evaluation on our LOL-Blur dataset. PSNR/SSIM↑: the higher, the better; LPIPS↓: the lower, the better. The symbol '†' indicates that we use DeblurGAN-v2 trained on RealBlur dataset, and '*' indicates the network is retrained on our LOL-Blur dataset. The runtime and parameters are expressed in seconds and millions. All runtimes are evaluated on a 720p image using a GPU V100.

Methods	Enhancement → Deblurring		Deblurring → Enhancement			Training on LOL-Blur					
	Zero-DCE [9]	RUAS [22]	Chen [5]	DeblurGAN-v2† [16]	MIMO [7]	KinD++*	DRBN*	DeblurGAN-v2*	DMPHN*	MIMO*	Ours
	→ MIMO [7]	→ MIMO [7]	→ Zero-DCE [9]	→ Zero-DCE [9]	→ Zero-DCE [9]	[52]	[42]	[16]	[47]	[7]	
PSNR↑	17.68	17.81	17.02	18.33	17.52	21.26	21.78	22.30	22.20	22.41	**25.74**
SSIM↑	0.542	0.569	0.502	0.589	0.57	0.753	0.768	0.745	0.817	0.835	**0.850**
LPIPS↓	0.510	0.523	0.516	0.476	0.498	0.359	0.325	0.356	0.301	0.262	**0.224**
Runtime (s)	–	–	–	–	–	0.06	0.11	0.13	0.26	0.16	0.12
Params (M)	–	–	–	–	–	1.2	0.6	60.9	5.4	6.8	7.4

Fig. 6. Visual comparisons on the LOL-Blur dataset. The proposed method generates much sharper images with visually pleasing results. (**Zoom in for best view**)

5.1 Evaluation on LOL-Blur Dataset

We quantitatively and qualitatively evaluate the proposed LEDNet on our LOL-Blur Dataset. Since the joint task is newly-defined in this paper, there is no method available to make a comparison directly. We carefully choose and combine existing representative low-light enhancement and deblurring methods, providing three types of baselines for comparisons. Specifically, the baseline methods lay on following three categories:

1. **Enhancement → Deblurring.** We choose the recent representative light enhancement networks Zero-DCE [9] and RUAS [22] followed by a state-of-the-art deblurring network MIMO-UNet [7].
2. **Deblurring → Enhancement.** For deblurring, we include a recent optimization-based method [5] particularly designed for saturated image deblurring, a GAN-based network DeblurGAN-v2 [16] trained on RealBlur dataset, and a state-of-the-art deblurring network MIMO-UNet [7] trained on GoPro dataset. Since RUAS tends to produce overexposed results in the saturated regions that may cover up previous deblurring results, we employ Zero-DCE for light enhancement in this type of baseline.
3. **End-to-end training on LOL-Blur dataset.** We retrain some state-of-the-art baselines on our dataset using their released code. They include two light

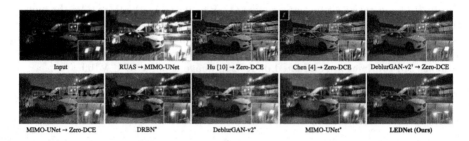

Fig. 7. Visual comparison on a real-world night blurred image. Our method achieves the best perceptual quality with more stable light enhancement and better deblurring performance, while other methods still leave large blurs in saturated regions and suffer from noticeable artifacts, as indicated by red arrows. (**Zoom in for best view**) (Color figure online)

enhancement networks KinD++ [52] and DRBN [42], and three deblurring networks of DeblurGAN-v2 [16], DMPHN [47], and MIMO-UNet [7].

Evaluation Metrics. We employ the PSNR and SSIM metrics for evaluation on the synthetic LOL-Blur dataset. To evaluate the perceptual quality of restored images, we also report the perceptual metric LPIPS [51] for references.

Quantitative Evaluations. Table 1 shows quantitative results on our LOL-Blur dataset. The proposed LEDNet performs favorably against other baseline methods. Notably, the better performance at a similar runtime cost and model size of other networks. The results suggest LEDNet is effective and particularly well-suited for this task due to the specially designed network and losses.

Qualitative Evaluations. Figure 6 compares the proposed LEDNet with baseline methods on LOL-Blur dataset. All compared methods produce unpleasing results and suffer from serious blur artifacts, especially in saturated regions. In contrast, LEDNet generates perceptually pleasant results with sharper textures.

5.2   Evaluation on Real Data

We also collected a real test dataset, named **Real-LOL-Blur**, that contains 240 captured low-light blurry images in the wild and 160 night blurry images from the RealBlur dataset [32].

Evaluation Metrics. As ground-truths are not available for real test images, We employ the recent image quality accessment method: MUSIQ [14], and two wildely-used ones: NRQM [26] and NIQE [28] as our perceptual metrics. We choose MUSIQ model trained on KonIQ-10k dataset, it focuses more on color contrast and sharpness assessment, which is more suitable for our task.

Quantitative Evaluations. As shown in Table 2, the proposed LEDNet achieves the highest MUSIQ score, indicating that our results are perceptually best in terms of color contrast and sharpness. LEDNet also obtains the best

NRQM and NIQE scores, showing our results have the best image qualities that are well in line with human perception.

Qualitative Evaluations. Figure 7 presents a visual comparison on a real-world night blurry image. The methods of Hu *et al.* [11] and Chen *et al.* [5] are particularly designed for saturated image deblurring, however, their cascading baselines still suffer from noticeable artifacts in the presence of large saturated regions. Besides, the end-to-end baseline networks trained on our LOL-Blur dataset are also less effective given the real-world inputs, as their architecture are not specially designed to handle this task. As shown in Fig. 7, their results usually suffer from undesired severe artifacts (red arrows) and blurs (yellow boxes) in their results. Overall, the proposed LEDNet shows the best visual quality, with fewer artifacts and blurs. The better performance is attributed to the CurveNLU and FASC, which enable LEDNet to perform spatially-varying feature transformation for both intensity enhancement and blur removal. The comparisons on real images strongly suggest the effectiveness of our dataset and network. Notably, benefiting from the noise simulation via CycleISP in the training dataset, our model handles real-world noises well.

Table 2. Evaluation on Real-LOL-Blur.

	RUAS → MIMO	MIMO → Zero-DCE	KinD++*	DRBN*	DMPHN*	MIMO*	Ours
MUSIQ↑	34.39	28.36	31.74	31.27	35.08	35.37	**39.11**
NRQM↑	3.322	3.697	3.854	4.019	4.470	5.140	**5.643**
NIQE↓	6.812	6.892	7.299	7.129	5.910	4.851	**4.764**

Table 3. Ablation study results of variant networks on LOL-Blur.

	(a) w/o PPM	(b) w/o CurveNLU	(c) Concat	(d) w/o $\mathcal{L}_{en}$	(e) Ours
PSNR↑	21.85	25.20	25.31	24.05	**25.74**
SSIM↑	0.781	0.823	0.826	0.784	**0.850**

5.3 Ablation Study

In this subsection, we present an ablation study to demonstrate the effectiveness of the key steps in data synthesis pipeline and the main modules in LEDNet.

Low-Light Simulation Using EC-Zero-DCE. To demonstrate the effectiveness of the proposed low-light simulation, we construct a new LOL-simulation dataset by applying our EC-Zero-DC to darken the normal-light images in LOL dataset [41], thus we obtain low-/normal-light paired images for training. We retrain the network KinD++ [52] using the LOL-simulation dataset for comparison with the official model that was trained on the original LOL dataset. Figure 8(a) shows that our simulated method enables the network to generate more natural results with less noise and color distortion (indicated by the yellow arrows).

Clipping Reverse (CR). Figure 3(b) shows that CR helps generate more realistic blurs in saturated regions. Figure 8(b) provides a visual comparison on real-world blurry image, it suggests that applying CR in training data generation helps the network to generalize better in blur removal around saturated regions.

| Night images | LOL-Original | LOL-Simulation (EC-Zero-DCE) | Night blurry images | w/o Clipping Reverse | w/ Clipping Reverse |

Fig. 8. Ablation study on data synthesis pipeline. (a) Results comparison on different training datasets: original LOL dataset (LOL-Original) and our simulated LOL dataset (LOL-Simulation). The network trained on LOL-Simulation generates more natural results with less noise and color distortion. (b) Results comparison on different data synthesis pipelines. Applying Clipping Reverse in training data generation enables the network to be robust to handle blur in saturated regions.

Effectiveness of PPM. The PPM layer provides crucial global prior for stable training and artifacts suppression in low-light enhancement. In Table 3(a), The variant LEDNet without Pyramid Pooling Module (w/o PPM) significantly degrades the network performance. Besides, the network removing PPM suffers from noticeable artifacts in the enhanced images, as shown in Fig. 9.

Effectiveness of CurveNLU. Figure 10 shows the feature enhancement rate F_{in}/F_{out} of input F_{in} and output F_{out} of CurveNLU. As observed, feature adjustment in CurveNLU is spatially adaptive to different regions in the image. The merit of CurveNLU is also validated in Table 3.

Effectiveness of FASC Connections. Comparing variant LEDNet (c) and (e) in Table 3, the one with FASC connection achieves better performance compared to simple connection based on concatenation. This is because the saturated and unsaturated areas in the night scenes follow different blur models. The task in this paper poses more requirements of spatially-varying operations.

Effectiveness of Enhancement Loss. The enhancement loss $\mathcal{L}_{en}$ is necessary in our method. Removing it from training harm the performance as shown in Table 3(d). It is because this intermediate loss helps decompose our joint task into low-light enhancement and deblurring, which makes it easier to optimize.

| Input | w/o PPM | w/ PPM | Input | Feature Enhancment Rate |

Fig. 9. Result comparison of variant networks: without PPM and with PPM.

Fig. 10. CurveNLU enhancement rate F_{out}/F_{in} of different channels.

6   Conclusion

We have presented a novel data synthesis pipeline to model realistic low-light blurring. Based on the pipeline, we built a large-scale and diverse paired dataset (LOL-Blur) for learning and benchmarking the new joint task of low-light enhancement and deblurring. We have also proposed a simple yet effective model, LEDNet, which performs illumination enhancement and blur removal in a single forward pass. We showed that PPM is beneficial and introduced CurveNLU to make the learned network more stable and robust. We further described FASC for better deblurring. Our dataset and network offer a foundation for further exploration for low-light enhancement and deblurring in the dark.

Acknowledgment. This study is supported under the RIE2020 Industry Alignment Fund - Industry Collaboration Projects (IAF-ICP) Funding Initiative, as well as cash and in-kind contribution from the industry partner(s).

References

1. Chan, K.C., Zhou, S., Xu, X., Loy, C.C.: Investigating tradeoffs in real-world video super-resolution. In: CVPR (2022)
2. Chen, C., Chen, Q., Do, M.N., Koltun, V.: Seeing motion in the dark. In: ICCV (2019)
3. Chen, C., Chen, Q., Xu, J., Koltun, V.: Learning to see in the dark. In: CVPR (2018)
4. Chen, L., Fang, F., Zhang, J., Liu, J., Zhang, G.: OID: outlier identifying and discarding in blind image deblurring. In: Vedaldi, A., Bischof, H., Brox, T., Frahm, J.-M. (eds.) ECCV 2020. LNCS, vol. 12370, pp. 598–613. Springer, Cham (2020). https://doi.org/10.1007/978-3-030-58595-2_36
5. Chen, L., Zhang, J., Lin, S., Fang, F., Ren, J.S.: Blind deblurring for saturated images. In: CVPR (2021)
6. Chen, L., Zhang, J., Pan, J., Lin, S., Fang, F., Ren, J.S.: Learning a non-blind deblurring network for night blurry images. In: CVPR (2021)
7. Cho, S.J., Ji, S.W., Hong, J.P., Jung, S.W., Ko, S.J.: Rethinking coarse-to-fine approach in single image deblurring. In: CVPR (2021)
8. Gong, D., et al.: From motion blur to motion flow: a deep learning solution for removing heterogeneous motion blur. In: CVPR (2017)
9. Guo, C., et al.: Zero-reference deep curve estimation for low-light image enhancement. In: CVPR (2020)
10. Hu, X., et al.: Pyramid architecture search for real-time image deblurring. In: ICCV (2021)
11. Hu, Z., Cho, S., Wang, J., Yang, M.H.: Deblurring low-light images with light streaks. In: CVPR (2014)
12. Jiang, H., Zheng, Y.: Learning to see moving objects in the dark. In: ICCV (2019)
13. Jiang, Y., et al.: EnlightenGAN: deep light enhancement without paired supervision. TIP **30**, 2340–2349 (2021)
14. Ke, J., Wang, Q., Wang, Y., Milanfar, P., Yang, F.: MUSIQ: multi-scale image quality transformer. In: ICCV (2021)

15. Kupyn, O., Budzan, V., Mykhailych, M., Mishkin, D., Matas, J.: DeblurGAN: blind motion deblurring using conditional adversarial networks. In: CVPR (2018)
16. Kupyn, O., Martyniuk, T., Wu, J., Wang, Z.: DeblurGAN-V2: deblurring (orders-of-magnitude) faster and better. In: CVPR (2019)
17. Li, C., et al.: Low-light image and video enhancement using deep learning: a survey. arXiv:2104.10729 (2021)
18. Li, C., Guo, C., Loy, C.C.: Learning to enhance low-light image via zero-reference deep curve estimation. IEEE Trans. Pattern Anal. Mach. Intell. **44**(8), 4225–4238 (2022)
19. Li, D., et al.: ARVo: learning all-range volumetric correspondence for video deblurring. In: CVPR (2021)
20. Li, X., Chen, C., Zhou, S., Lin, X., Zuo, W., Zhang, L.: Blind face restoration via deep multi-scale component dictionaries. In: Vedaldi, A., Bischof, H., Brox, T., Frahm, J.-M. (eds.) ECCV 2020. LNCS, vol. 12354, pp. 399–415. Springer, Cham (2020). https://doi.org/10.1007/978-3-030-58545-7_23
21. Liu, J., Xu, D., Yang, W., Fan, M., Huang, H.: Benchmarking low-light image enhancement and beyond. IJCV **129**(4), 1153–1184 (2021)
22. Liu, R., Ma, L., Zhang, J., Fan, X., Luo, Z.: Retinex-inspired unrolling with cooperative prior architecture search for low-light image enhancement. In: CVPR (2021)
23. Lore, K.G., Akintayo, A., Sarkar, S.: LLNet: a deep autoencoder approach to natural low-light image enhancement. Pattern Recogn. **61**, 650–662 (2017)
24. Loshchilov, I., Hutter, F.: SGDR: stochastic gradient descent with warm restarts. arXiv:1608.03983 (2016)
25. Lv, F., Lu, F., Wu, J., Lim, C.: MBLLEN: low-light image/video enhancement using CNNs. In: BMVC (2018)
26. Ma, C., Yang, C.Y., Yang, X., Yang, M.H.: Learning a no-reference quality metric for single-image super-resolution. CVIU **158**, 1–16 (2017)
27. Maggioni, M., Boracchi, G., Foi, A., Egiazarian, K.: Video denoising, deblocking, and enhancement through separable 4-D nonlocal spatiotemporal transforms. TIP **21**(9), 3952–3966 (2012)
28. Mittal, A., Soundararajan, R., Bovik, A.C.: Making a "completely blind" image quality analyzer. IEEE Signal Process. Lett. **20**(3), 209–212 (2012)
29. Nah, S., et al.: NTIRE 2019 challenge on video deblurring and super-resolution: Dataset and study. In: CVPRW (2019)
30. Nah, S., Hyun Kim, T., Mu Lee, K.: Deep multi-scale convolutional neural network for dynamic scene deblurring. In: CVPR (2017)
31. Niklaus, S., Mai, L., Liu, F.: Video frame interpolation via adaptive separable convolution. In: ICCV (2017)
32. Rim, J., Lee, H., Won, J., Cho, S.: Real-world blur dataset for learning and benchmarking deblurring algorithms. In: Vedaldi, A., Bischof, H., Brox, T., Frahm, J.-M. (eds.) ECCV 2020. LNCS, vol. 12370, pp. 184–201. Springer, Cham (2020). https://doi.org/10.1007/978-3-030-58595-2_12
33. Shen, Z., et al.: Human-aware motion deblurring. In: ICCV (2019)
34. Su, S., Delbracio, M., Wang, J., Sapiro, G., Heidrich, W., Wang, O.: Deep video deblurring for hand-held cameras. In: CVPR (2017)
35. Sun, J., Cao, W., Xu, Z., Ponce, J.: Learning a convolutional neural network for non-uniform motion blur removal. In: CVPR (2015)
36. Tao, X., Gao, H., Shen, X., Wang, J., Jia, J.: Scale-recurrent network for deep image deblurring. In: CVPR (2018)
37. Wang, R., Xu, X., Fu, C.W., Lu, J., Yu, B., Jia, J.: Seeing dynamic scene in the dark: a high-quality video dataset with mechatronic alignment. In: CVPR (2021)

38. Wang, R., Zhang, Q., Fu, C.W., Shen, X., Zheng, W.S., Jia, J.: Underexposed photo enhancement using deep illumination estimation. In: CVPR (2019)
39. Wang, X., Xie, L., Dong, C., Shan, Y.: Real-ESRGAN: training real-world blind super-resolution with pure synthetic data. In: ICCVW (2021)
40. Wang, X., et al.: ESRGAN: enhanced super-resolution generative adversarial networks. In: Leal-Taixé, L., Roth, S. (eds.) ECCV 2018. LNCS, vol. 11133, pp. 63–79. Springer, Cham (2019). https://doi.org/10.1007/978-3-030-11021-5_5
41. Wei, C., Wang, W., Yang, W., Liu, J.: Deep retinex decomposition for low-light enhancement. In: BMVC (2018)
42. Yang, W., Wang, S., Fang, Y., Wang, Y., Liu, J.: From fidelity to perceptual quality: a semi-supervised approach for low-light image enhancement. In: CVPR (2020)
43. Yang, W., Wang, W., Huang, H., Wang, S., Liu, J.: Sparse gradient regularized deep retinex network for robust low-light image enhancement. TIP **30**, 2072–2086 (2021)
44. Zamir, S.W., et al.: CycleISP: real image restoration via improved data synthesis. In: CVPR (2020)
45. Zamir, S.W., et al.: Learning enriched features for real image restoration and enhancement. In: Vedaldi, A., Bischof, H., Brox, T., Frahm, J.-M. (eds.) ECCV 2020. LNCS, vol. 12370, pp. 492–511. Springer, Cham (2020). https://doi.org/10.1007/978-3-030-58595-2_30
46. Zamir, S.W., et al.: Multi-stage progressive image restoration. In: CVPR (2021)
47. Zhang, H., Dai, Y., Li, H., Koniusz, P.: Deep stacked hierarchical multi-patch network for image deblurring. In: CVPR (2019)
48. Zhang, J., et al.: Dynamic scene deblurring using spatially variant recurrent neural networks. In: CVPR (2018)
49. Zhang, K., Liang, J., Van Gool, L., Timofte, R.: Designing a practical degradation model for deep blind image super-resolution. In: ICCV (2021)
50. Zhang, K., et al.: Deblurring by realistic blurring. In: CVPR (2020)
51. Zhang, R., Isola, P., Efros, A.A., Shechtman, E., Wang, O.: The unreasonable effectiveness of deep features as a perceptual metric. In: CVPR (2018)
52. Zhang, Y., Guo, X., Ma, J., Liu, W., Zhang, J.: Beyond brightening low-light images. IJCV **129**(4), 1013–1037 (2021)
53. Zhang, Y., Zhang, J., Guo, X.: Kindling the darkness: a practical low-light image enhancer. In: ACM MM (2019)
54. Zhao, H., Shi, J., Qi, X., Wang, X., Jia, J.: Pyramid scene parsing network. In: CVPR (2017)
55. Zheng, C., Shi, D., Shi, W.: Adaptive unfolding total variation network for low-light image enhancement. In: CVPR (2021)
56. Zhou, S., Zhang, J., Pan, J., Xie, H., Zuo, W., Ren, J.: Spatio-temporal filter adaptive network for video deblurring. In: ICCV (2019)
57. Zhou, S., Zhang, J., Zuo, W., Xie, H., Pan, J., Ren, J.S.: DAVANet: stereo deblurring with view aggregation. In: CVPR (2019)

MPIB: An MPI-Based Bokeh Rendering Framework for Realistic Partial Occlusion Effects

Juewen Peng[1], Jianming Zhang[2], Xianrui Luo[1], Hao Lu[1],
Ke Xian[1(✉)], and Zhiguo Cao[1]

[1] Key Laboratory of Image Processing and Intelligent Control, Ministry of Education,
School of AIA, Huazhong University of Science and Technology, Wuhan, China
{juewenpeng,xianruiluo,hlu,kexian,zgcao}@hust.edu.cn
[2] Adobe Research, San Jose, USA
jianmzha@adobe.com
https://github.com/JuewenPeng/MPIB

Abstract. Partial occlusion effects are a phenomenon that blurry objects near a camera are semi-transparent, resulting in partial appearance of occluded background. However, it is challenging for existing bokeh rendering methods to simulate realistic partial occlusion effects due to the missing information of the occluded area in an all-in-focus image. Inspired by the learnable 3D scene representation, Multiplane Image (MPI), we attempt to address the partial occlusion by introducing a novel MPI-based high-resolution bokeh rendering framework, termed MPIB. To this end, we first present an analysis on how to apply the MPI representation to bokeh rendering. Based on this analysis, we propose an MPI representation module combined with a background inpainting module to implement high-resolution scene representation. This representation can then be reused to render various bokeh effects according to the controlling parameters. To train and test our model, we also design a ray-tracing-based bokeh generator for data generation. Extensive experiments on synthesized and real-world images validate the effectiveness and flexibility of this framework.

Keywords: Bokeh rendering · Multiplane image · Partial occlusion

1 Introduction

Bokeh effect is commonly used in photography to create an appealing blur effect in out-of-focus areas and make the subject stand out from the picture. Various post-processing methods, which simulate the bokeh effect from an all-in-focus image, have been proposed so far. However, as shown in Fig. 1, neither the physically based ones (*e.g.*, SteReFo [3]) nor the deep learning-based ones (*e.g.*, DeepLens [39]) can well handle the issue of partial occlusion: the out-of-focus

Supplementary Information The online version contains supplementary material available at https://doi.org/10.1007/978-3-031-20068-7_34.

© The Author(s), under exclusive license to Springer Nature Switzerland AG 2022
S. Avidan et al. (Eds.): ECCV 2022, LNCS 13666, pp. 590–607, 2022.
https://doi.org/10.1007/978-3-031-20068-7_34

All-in-Focus   SteReFo [3]   DeepLens [39]   MPIB (Ours)

Fig. 1. MPIB renders more realistic partial occlusion effects than other methods at the boundary between foreground and background. Best viewed by zooming in.

object close to the camera becomes blurred and semi-transparent, revealing the occluded in-focus area.

In the field of computer graphics, Schedl and Wimmer [31] first attempt to solve this problem by decomposing the scene into different depth layers, and blurring each layer with a fixed-size filter before compositing them together. This strategy works well given the complete scene information, however, it is less effective for methods with a single image as input [3,48]. A recent idea relevant to this layering strategy is Multiplane Image (MPI) proposed for novel view synthesis [50]. MPI aims to learn a 3D scene representation with multiple RGBA planes from a single image, which can then be used to synthesize different novel views of the scene. Despite its desirable characteristics of explicitly modeling occluded areas for each plane, we observe that current MPI-based view synthesis methods [16,35,37,50] are still inadequate in restoring the occluded surface with complicated textures.

To apply MPI to bokeh rendering and address the above challenges, we first analyse the difference of MPI representation and layer compositing formulation between the view synthesis and bokeh rendering. Then, based on this analysis, we propose a novel MPI-based framework, termed MPIB, for synthetic bokeh effect. Specifically, we combine an MPI representation module with a background inpainting module to obtain a high-resolution 3D scene representation. The background inpainting module aims to synthesize convincing contents in the occluded areas and lighten the burden of the scene representation. Once the scene representation is obtained, it can be reused to render different bokeh effects with adjustable controlling parameters, such as blur amount and refocused disparity.

Due to the difficulty of capturing accurate pairs of all-in-focus image and bokeh image in the real world, we design a ray-tracing-based bokeh generator for training. We also use it to synthesize a test dataset for the initial validation. Since the judgement of the bokeh effect is really subjective, we further conduct a user study on images collected from websites and compare our results with the latest iPhone 13 Cinematic Mode. Experimental results show that MPIB renders realistic partial occlusion effects and yields substantial improvements over state-of-the-art methods.

In summary, our main contributions are as follows.

- We present an analysis on how to apply the MPI representation and the layer composting scheme to bokeh rendering.
- We propose an MPI-based framework for high-resolution bokeh rendering and realistic partial occlusion effects.
- We design a ray-tracing-based bokeh generator, which creates almost real bokeh effects and can be used to produce training and test data.

2   Related Work

Bokeh Rendering. Bokeh rendering techniques can be classified into physically based methods and neural rendering methods. In the early years, most physically based methods [1,14,31,40,46] entail 3D scene information and are time-consuming. Recent methods [2,3,7,26,32,33,38,41,44,48], which render bokeh effects from a single image and a corresponding depth map, are more efficient and practical. One classic idea is layered rendering [3,48], *i.e.*, decomposing the scene into multiple layers and independently blurring each layer before compositing them from back to front. However, they do not consider potential depth inaccuracy and object occlusion, resulting in unrealistic partial occlusion effects.

To solve these problems, many neural rendering methods have been proposed recently. Xiao *et al.* [42] specialize in using a perfect depth map to render realistic bokeh effects in low resolution. Considering the difficulty of obtaining perfect depth maps in the real world, Wang *et al.* [39] propose a robust rendering system consisting of the depth prediction, lens blur, and guided upsampling modules. To further simplify the rendering process, many end-to-end networks [5,9–11,28] are proposed. They simulate the bokeh effect of DSLR cameras from a single wide depth-of-field image without inputting the depth map or any other controlling parameters and show a compelling performance on the bokeh dataset EBB! [9]. However, the simplicity comes at a cost. These networks are lack of flexibility. They cannot adjust bokeh effects, such as different blur amounts and focal planes. In this work, we focus on controllable bokeh rendering with an all-in-focus image, a potentially imperfect disparity map and some controlling parameters as input.

MPI Representation. Since Zhou *et al.* [50] first propose MPI to reconstruct the camera frustum from stereo images and synthesize novel views, this representation has been widely used in novel view synthesis methods [16,20,35,37,51] due to the appealing property of differentiability and explicitly modeling occluded contents. Srinivasan *et al.* [35] provide a theoretical analysis of MPI limits, and use the appearance flow [51] to improve the realism in occluded areas. Tucker *et al.* [37] apply the MPI representation to the single-view inputting case which is more practical but more challenging. Li *et al.* [16] propose an encoder-decoder architecture which is a continuous depth generalization of MPI by introducing the idea of neural radiance fields (NeRF) [21]. Different from the above works, we embed an additional disparity map into the model aside from the all-in-focus image and apply a lightweight guided upsampling network. It aims to enhance the generalization of the model and obtain the high-resolution scene representation with accurate and sharp object boundaries. In addition, we supervise our model with bokeh images instead of synthesized images in different views.

Image Inpainting. The goal of inpainting is to fill in missing contents of an image. Compared with traditional patch-based [4] and nearest neighbor-based [8] methods, neural networks have much stronger ability to capture spatial context of images and generate plausible contents for unseen parts, espcially after the introduction of adversarial training [6]. Therefore, deep learning-based inpainting has attracted a lot of attention and many CNN-based methods have been proposed [12,25,43]. Recent works attempt to replace the regular convolutions with partial [18], gated [45] or fourier [36] convolutions, and design new architectures [19,22,52] to address irregular masks and high-resolution inpainting. In this work, we utilize the off-the-shelf inpainting model [36] to facilitate our MPI representation and create more convincing partial occlusion effects.

3   MPIB: An MPI-Based Bokeh Rendering Framework

As shown in Fig. 2, our framework consists of 3 modules: background inpainting, MPI representation, and bokeh rendering. In the following, we first analyse how to apply MPI in bokeh rendering and introduce our rendering formula (Sect. 3.1). Then, we describe the structures of our background inpainting module (Sect. 3.2) and MPI representation module (Sect. 3.3). Finally, we provide the training details, including the proposed ray-tracing-based bokeh generator (Sect. 3.4).

3.1   MPI Representation and Layer Compositing Formulation

The well-known multiplane image (MPI) representation, introduced by Zhou *et al.* [50], consists of a set of fronto-parallel planes. Each plane encodes an RGB color image c_i and an alpha map α_i, *i.e.*, $\{(c_i, \alpha_i) \,|\, i = 1, 2, ..., N\}$, where N is the number of MPI planes. When applying the MPI representation to bokeh rendering, we make minor modifications. As proven in [38,44], the blur radius r of each pixel is

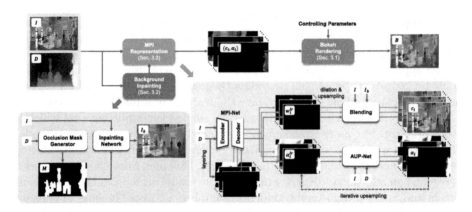

Fig. 2. Our framework MPIB takes an all-in-focus image and a potentially imperfect disparity map as input to obtain a 3D scene representation of multiple RGBA planes. This representation is generated by an MPI representation module and a background inpainting module. Then, the scene representation can be reused to produce multiple bokeh images according to different controlling parameters.

$$r = A \left| \frac{1}{z} - \frac{1}{z_f} \right| = A \left| d - d_f \right|, \tag{1}$$

where A reflects the overall blur amount of the image. z is the depth of the pixel and z_f is the refocused depth. We replace the depth z with the disparity (inverse depth) d to simplify the formula. One can see that r is the linear variation of d. For uniform sampling of the blur amount across different planes, we replace depth discretization in general MPI representation with disparity discretization.

In novel view synthesis, one can reconstruct the scene I by continuously using the "over" alpha compositing operation [15,27] to MPI planes with a back-to-front order:

$$I = \sum_{i=1}^{N} \left(c_i \alpha_i \prod_{j=i+1}^{N} (1 - \alpha_j) \right). \tag{2}$$

When applying Eq. 2 to the bokeh rendering, we blur each layer with a fixed-size kernel K_i, which is adaptive to the controlling parameters. The rendered bokeh image B can be formulated as

$$B = \sum_{i=1}^{N} \left((c_i \alpha_i * K_i) \prod_{j=i+1}^{N} (1 - \alpha_j * K_j) \right), \tag{3}$$

where $*$ is the convolution operation. To eliminate the artifacts caused by discretization, we add extra weight normalization to Eq. 3 as follows:

$$B = \frac{\sum_{i=1}^{N} \left((c_i \alpha_i * K_i) \prod_{j=i+1}^{N} (1 - \alpha_j * K_j) \right)}{\sum_{i=1}^{N} \left((\alpha_i * K_i) \prod_{j=i+1}^{N} (1 - \alpha_j * K_j) \right)}. \tag{4}$$

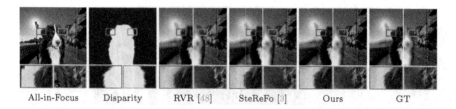

All-in-Focus   Disparity   RVR [48]   SteReFo [3]   Ours   GT

Fig. 3. Toy experiment. The scene is synthesized from two images with constant disparities. "GT" refers to the result of the ray-tracing-based bokeh generator proposed in Sect. 3.4. For each rendered bokeh image, the left half is refocused on the foreground while the right half is refocused on the background.

Typically, the transformation from scene irradiance to RGB values is nonlinear [44], so we conduct the gamma transformation to c_i and the inverse gamma transformation to B following common practice.

Previous layered rendering methods, such as RVR [48] and SteReFo [3], adopt a similar compositing strategy. However, they only consider visible parts of the image and calculate the alpha map of each plane manually. For clarity, we conduct a toy experiment in Fig. 3 where only two planes are used. We compare our approach with RVR, SteReFo, and the bokeh generator proposed in Sect. 3.4 (regarded as the ground truth). Note that the result of our approach is in an ideal situation with known background information. One can see that our result is most similar to the ground truth, and the occluded background is partly visible at the boundary of the blurred foreground, demonstrating the plausibility of our rendering formula and the importance of predicting occluded contents.

3.2 Background Inpainting Module

In background inpainting module, we combine an off-the-shelf inpainting model LaMa [36] with an occlusion mask generator to produce a background image. Since occlusion often occurs where the disparity of the scene changes significantly and the occluded area is on the side with a larger disparity, we design the occluded mask generator according to this principle.

At the beginning, we use the Sobel operator to calculate a 2-channel gradient map $G = \{G_x, G_y\}$ of the input disparity map D. By thresholding the gradient magnitude, we obtain a depth discontinuity mask and regard it as the initial occlusion mask M. Then, we remove short segments of M and G to reduce the impact of noise. Subsequently, we iteratively extend M in the direction of gradient increase. In each iteration, we first perform ℓ_2 normalization to G to obtain unit normal vectors G^n. Then, we forward warp G^n via the softmax splatting operation [23] using the same G^n as the optical flow to get the inner ring of G^n, and represent it with G^w. At last, we update G by

$$G = M \cdot G^n + (1 - M) \cdot G^w, \tag{5}$$

and update M to refer to the nonzero areas of G. In practice, as the input disparity map may not align well with the all-in-focus image at occluding boundaries,

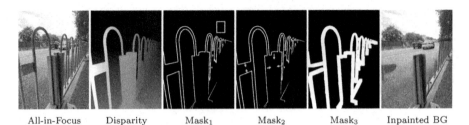

All-in-Focus   Disparity   Mask₁   Mask₂   Mask₃   Inpainted BG

Fig. 4. Generation of the occlusion mask and the inpainted background image. "$Mask_1$" is calculated by thresholding the gradient of the disparity map. "$Mask_2$" removes the short segments of "$Mask_1$". "$Mask_3$" extends the area of "$Mask_2$" in the direction of disparity increase. "Inpainted BG" is predicted by the inpainting method LaMa [36] using the all-in-focus image and the produced occlusion mask as input.

we finally dilate M by several pixels as processed in [34] to prevent the foreground color leakage and reduce inpainting artifacts. For ease of understanding, we visualize the process of producing an occlusion mask in Fig. 4.

Note that for complicated scenes, we can restrict the area of occlusion mask and predict more background images for MPI planes in different disparity levels. However, we show in Sect. 4.2 that one background image is sufficient for rendering real-world images in general.

3.3   High-Resolution MPI Representation Module

In MPI representation module, we first propose an encoder-decoder network MPI-Net to obtain an initial MPI representation as with [16]. For each image, the encoder runs only once, while the decoder runs multiple times to generate N planes. However, there are two main differences to be aware of. (i) We embed the disparity map D into the decoder instead of the discrete disparity values to pass more prior knowledge to the network, which will lead to the better layering and stronger generalization. Specifically, assume D is ranged from 0 to 1, we divide the range by $\{[\frac{i-1}{N}, \frac{i}{N}] \mid i = 1, 2, ..., N\}$, and calculate the coarse zone mask for each plane. Subsequently, we apply a single convolution layer to each zone mask to increase channels before feeding them into the decoder. (ii) To reduce the difficulty of training MPI-Net, we assume that the RGB image c_i of each plane is the per-pixel weighted average of the original all-in-focus image I and the inpainted background image I^b. Thus, for each plane, MPI-Net only predicts an alpha map α_i and a blend weight map w_i, and c_i can be produced by

$$c_i = w_i \cdot I^b + (1 - w_i) \cdot I. \tag{6}$$

To adapt our model to high-resolution input, we also propose a lightweight guided upsampling network AUP-Net to iteratively upsample the alpha map α_i by a factor of 2. Note that AUP-Net is guided by the high-resolution all-in-focus image I and its corresponding disparity map D. As for the blend weight

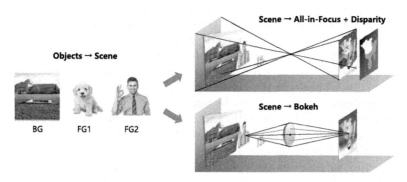

Fig. 5. Pipeline of ray-tracing-based bokeh generator. Given a background RGB image and two foreground RGBA images, we first construct a 3D scene through randomly setting the positions and disparities of different objects. Then, we can synthesize an all-in-focus image and a corresponding disparity map by compositing different object planes, and generate a bokeh image by backward tracing the path of light rays.

map w_i, we just perform slight dilation and bilinear upsampling. The reason for the dilation here is similar to the reason we dilated the occlusion mask earlier in Sect. 3.2. Although this operation may cause a small amount of visible information loss on c_i, it effectively prevents foreground colors from bleeding into background planes and reduces the risk of unpleasant boundary artifacts.

3.4   Model Training

Bokeh Generator and Training Data. To obtain ground-truth bokeh images, we design a ray-tracing-based bokeh generator (Fig. 5), which is capable of creating a bokeh image from a background RGB image and some foreground RGBA images with customized disparities and different controlling parameters. Specifically, for each image to be composited, we set its disparity map d as a plane equation of pixel coordinates (x, y):

$$d = \frac{1 - ax - by}{c}, \tag{7}$$

where a, b, c are three constants. We project all images to a 3D scene based on their disparities, and treat them as different objects. For each pixel (x, y) of the rendered result, we sample 2500 rays passing through the aperture, look for the intersection of each ray and the scene, and project the intersection to the sensor plane. The detailed calculation is in the supplementary material. Here, we directly provide the coordinates (x_n, y_n) of the projected intersection:

$$\begin{cases} x_n = x + \dfrac{1 - ax - by - cd_f}{aA\mu + bA\nu + c} A\mu, \\ y_n = y + \dfrac{1 - ax - by - cd_f}{aA\mu + bA\nu + c} A\nu, \end{cases} \tag{8}$$

where A is the blur parameter. d_f is the refocused disparity. (μ, ν) denotes the sampling point within the aperture, which meets $\mu^2 + \nu^2 \leq 1$. (x_n, y_n) is available if and only if it is inside the object. Specially, if (x_n, y_n) happens to be on the boundary, we suppose the ray with a proportion equal to the alpha value of (x_n, y_n) intersects the current plane, and the ray with the remaining proportion continues to propagate. In summary, we calculate the intersection of the ray and each plane from front to back, and the search process stops until the energy of the ray is exhausted. The final rendered result of (x, y) is the weighted average of the colors for all intersections.

In practice, we first randomly select 20k images from Places [49] as our background images. The foreground images originate from two sources. One is PhotoMatte85 [17] with 85 portrait RGBA images. The other is websites. We collect 300 images with pure background and extract their alpha maps by matting tools. During the training, each sample is synthesized online from 2 random foreground images and 1 background image with the resolution of 256×256. The disparity map is set within the range from 0 to 1. The ground-truth bokeh image is produced with the random blur parameter from 0 to 32, refocused disparity from 0 to 1, and gamma value from 1 to 4. To improve the generalization of the model, we augment the input disparity map with random noise, gaussian blur, dilation and erosion. We also use the intermediate synthesized results instead of the inpainted results as I^b to simplify and accelerate the training process.

Loss Functions. The training of MPI-Net and AUP-Net are independent. For MPI-Net, we use the following loss:

$$\mathcal{L}_{MPI} = \mathcal{L}_{bokeh} + 0.4\,\mathcal{L}_{disp} + 0.1\,\mathcal{L}_{alpha} + 0.1\,\mathcal{L}_{weight}, \tag{9}$$

where $\mathcal{L}_{bokeh}$ is a ℓ_1 loss, which encourages the rendered bokeh image B to match the ground truth B^* in both image space and gradient space. $\mathcal{L}_{disp}$ has the same form with $\mathcal{L}_{bokeh}$, which enforces the reconstructed disparity map D^{rc} to be consistent with the raw input disparity map D^* without augmentation. This term aims to assist MPI representation learning and improve the sensitivity of the model to object boundaries. As with [37], the reconstructed disparity is defined by

$$D^{rc} = \sum_{i=1}^{N} \left(d_i \alpha_i \prod_{j=i+1}^{N} (1 - \alpha_j) \right), \tag{10}$$

where $d_i = \frac{i-0.5}{N}$, which represents the average disparity of each plane. Next, $\mathcal{L}_{alpha}$ and $\mathcal{L}_{weight}$ are two ℓ_1 regularization losses, which constrain the predicted alpha maps and blend weight maps to be smooth, respectively.

For training AUP-Net, we use a similar loss:

$$\mathcal{L}_{AUP} = \mathcal{L}_{bokeh} + 0.4\,\mathcal{L}_{disp} + 0.1\,\mathcal{L}_{alpha} + 0.4\,\mathcal{L}_{self}. \tag{11}$$

$\mathcal{L}_{weight}$ is not used here because AUP-Net only processes alpha maps. Instead, we add a self-supervised loss $\mathcal{L}_{self}$ to accelerate the convergence and prevent the upsampled alpha map α_i and the input low-resolution alpha map α_i^{lr} from being too different.

$$\mathcal{L}_{self} = \mathcal{L}_{\ell_1}\left(\text{downsample}(\alpha_i), \alpha_i^{lr}\right). \tag{12}$$

Implementations. We implement our model by PyTorch [24]. The number of MPI planes is set to 32. In MPI-Net, we use ResNet-18 as the encoder, and use a decoder similar to [16]. AUP-Net is a lightweight network based on U-Net [30]. We show its detailed architecture in the supplementary material. When training AUP-Net, we forcely downsample the input by a factor of 2 before applying MPI-Net, and use AUP-Net to upsample the initial rendered result up to the original resolution. Both networks are trained for 40 epochs using the Adam optimizer [13] with a learning rate of 10^{-4}, and a batch size of 8. All experiments are conducted on four NVIDIA GeForce GTX 1080 Ti GPUs.

4   Experiments

4.1   Bokeh Rendering on Synthesized Dataset

Dataset. Current public bokeh datasets including EBB! [9], Aperture [48] and a Unity synthesized dataset [42] are unsuitable for evaluations of controllable bokeh rendering. The first two datasets are manually captured by a DSLR camera with unknown controlling parameters. There exist color inconsistency and scene misalignment between the wide and shallow DoF image pairs, and almost all images are focused on the front subject. For the last synthesized dataset, all scenes are built from randomized object geometries, so there is a huge gap between them and real-world images. In addition, the maximum blur size of this dataset is too small. As a result, we use our ray-tracing-based generator to synthesize a test dataset, which contains 100 new scenes (not the same with our training data) with the resolution of 1024×1024. Each scene is synthesized from 1 background image and 3 foreground images. Unlike [42], all images are derived from the real world. We provide two versions for disparity settings. In the first version, the disparity of each object is set to a constant value, while in the second version, it is set to a smoothly varying plane. Besides, for each all-in-focus image, we synthesize 16 bokeh images with 4 blur parameters from 20 to 80 and 4 refocused disparities, which correspond to the disparities of the 4 objects. The gamma values are set to 2.2 for all settings.

Metrics. To measure performance, we use LPIPS [47], PSNR and SSIM as metrics. Since the difficulty of bokeh rendering is mainly concentrated at occluding boundaries and the human eye is more sensitive to these areas, we additionally introduce two metrics $PSNR_{ob}$ and $SSIM_{ob}$, which only reflect the accuracy at occluding boundaries. More details are in the supplementary material.

Table 1. Quantitative results on the synthesized dataset. N_{bg} denotes the number of the inpainted images used in our background inpainting module. The best performance is in **boldface**, and the second best is <u>underlined</u>.

Method	Constant disparity for each object					Varying disparity for each object				
	LPIPS↓	PSNR↑	PSNR$_{ob}$↑	SSIM↑	SSIM$_{ob}$↑	LPIPS↓	PSNR↑	PSNR$_{ob}$↑	SSIM↑	SSIM$_{ob}$↑
Gather [38]	0.042	32.6	25.4	0.978	0.896	0.044	33.0	25.9	0.979	0.903
Scatter [38]	0.029	33.9	26.7	0.983	0.921	0.027	34.8	27.8	0.985	0.934
RVR [48]	0.103	28.8	21.9	0.951	0.783	0.113	28.9	22.0	0.951	0.787
SteReFo [3]	0.038	32.8	26.4	0.976	0.923	0.040	32.5	26.3	0.973	0.928
DeepLens [39]	0.068	29.5	24.9	0.945	0.897	0.055	29.8	24.9	0.957	0.911
DeepFocus [42]	0.083	33.4	<u>30.3</u>	0.938	0.923	0.063	35.2	<u>31.9</u>	0.968	0.952
Ours ($N_{bg}=1$)	<u>0.011</u>	<u>36.7</u>	30.0	<u>0.989</u>	<u>0.951</u>	<u>0.019</u>	<u>36.8</u>	30.5	<u>0.986</u>	<u>0.956</u>
Ours ($N_{bg}=3$)	**0.008**	**39.3**	**33.0**	**0.991**	**0.963**	**0.017**	**38.8**	**33.0**	**0.988**	**0.966**

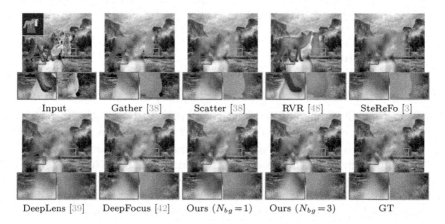

Input   Gather [38]   Scatter [38]   RVR [48]   SteReFo [3]

DeepLens [39]   DeepFocus [42]   Ours ($N_{bg}=1$)   Ours ($N_{bg}=3$)   GT

Fig. 6. Qualitative results on the synthetic dataset.

Compared Methods. We compare MPIB with 4 physically based rendering methods, including 2 pixel-wise rendering methods: Gather [38] and Scatter [38], and 2 layered rendering methods: RVR [48] and SteReFo [3]. We also test 2 neural rendering methods: DeepLens [39] and DeepFocus [42]. Note that as DeepFocus [42] cannot handle large blur sizes, directly applying it to high resolution will cause the collapse of the model. Thus, we downsample the input before feeding it into the network, and the rendered result is bilinearly upsampled without refining. More discussion about DeepFocus is in the supplementary material. To be fair, we discard the depth estimation modules in SteReFo [3] and DeepLens [39], and only preserve their rendering modules. Then, all methods can take the same all-in-focus image, disparity map and controlling parameters as input.

Comparison with State-of-the-Art. We show quantitative and qualitative results in Table 1 and Fig. 6. One can observe: (i) Among the physically based rendering methods, pixel-wise methods (Gather [38], Scatter [38]) perform well on the overall PSNR and SSIM due to the accurate bokeh rendering in depth-

Table 2. Pairwise comparison results of the user study. A number of more than 50% indicates that our approach gets more votes than the other method.

Method	Refocusing on the foreground				Refocusing on the background			
	Scatter [38]	SteReFo [3]	DeepLens [39]	DeepFocus [42]	Scatter [38]	SteReFo [3]	DeepLens [39]	DeepFocus [42]
Ours	89.4%	72.7%	83.4%	86.1%	82.9%	76.7%	77.2%	82.8%

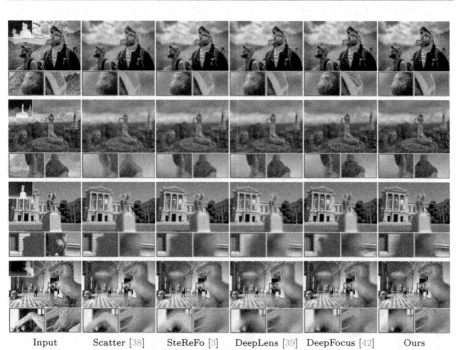

| Input | Scatter [38] | SteReFo [3] | DeepLens [39] | DeepFocus [42] | Ours |

Fig. 7. Qualitative results of the user study. The first 2 rows are refocused on the foreground. The last 2 rows are refocused on the background.

continuous areas, but cause serious color bleeding artifacts at occluding boundaries. For layered methods, SteReFo [3] is much better than RVR [48] as SteReFo uses the weight normalization during the rendering. Without this operation, halo artifacts will occur at occluding boundaries, just like RVR. (ii) Neural rendering methods render relatively smooth bokeh effects at boundaries. However, DeepLens [39] does not perform very well in metrics. The reason may be that its training data is synthesized by VDSLR [44], which applies manual color enhancement and is inconsistent with real rendering rules. DeepFocus [42] gets high $PSNR_{ob}$ and $SSIM_{ob}$, but it processes images in low resolution, which leads to poor LPIPS and unpleasant fuzziness and aliasing on refocused plane. (iii) All of the above methods cannot fill the occluded areas with convincing contents, and the rendered results look fake, particularly when the blur amount is large. (iv) Our approach outperforms other methods numerically and creates much more realistic partial occlusion effects. Besides, generating more background images can handle well the continuous occlusion, leading to better performance.

4.2   Bokeh Rendering on Real-World Images

In this section, all disparity inputs are predicted by DPT [29], and we use only one inpainted image in the background inpainting module.

User Study. Since numerical metrics cannot reflect the perceptual quality of the rendered result, we conduct a user study on real-world images. Specifically, we collect 50 all-in-focus images from websites, including both indoor and outdoor scenes. The average resolution of images is 1690×1354. For each image, we manually select 2 focal points, one on the foreground and the other on the background. Then, we use different methods to produce bokeh images under the same controlling parameters. During the test, we show each participant 4 images at a time, including an all-in-focus image, a darker all-in-focus image with the focal point labeled, and two bokeh images in random order produced by our approach and a method randomly selected from Scatter [38], SteReFo [3], DeepLens [39] and DeepFocus [42]. The participant is required to choose the method with more realistic bokeh effects or choose none if it is hard to judge. In addition, each participant needs to complete at least 10 tests before submitting results. Finally, 99 people participate in this survey, and there are 2097 valid pairwise comparisons. The data of the 2 focal points is counted separately. We show the comparison results in Table 2, where the number represents the preference of our approach over the other method. One can observe that whether the image is refocused on the foreground or the background, our approach is most favored. Some qualitative results are visualized in Fig. 7. See the supplementary material for more experimental details and visual results.

Input   iPhone 13   Ours   Ours^{large} Input   iPhone 13   Ours   Ours^{large}

Fig. 8. Comparison with iPhone 13 Cinematic Mode. Image resolution is 1080×1920. The superscript *large* denotes applying the larger blur amount in the rendering.

It is also worth noting that for other rendering methods, their rankings in this user study differ from the results on the synthetic dataset. For example, Scatter [38] gets high metrics on the synthetic dataset, but it is the least preferred in the user study due to the obvious boundary artifacts. This phenomenon demonstrates that the current metrics may fail to accurately measure the perceptual quality of rendered bokeh results.

Comparison with iPhone 13 Cinematic Mode. We further compare MPIB with the latest feature of iPhone 13 - Cinematic Mode, which can freely change the focus point after capturing. From Fig. 8, the upper limit of blur amount for iPhone 13 Cinematic Mode is small, and our approach creates more clear and natural bokeh effects in transition areas of the foreground and background.

4.3   Ablation Study

To investigate the impact of different components, we present ablation studies on the synthetic dataset. The results are shown in Table 3.

Table 3. Ablation study on the synthetic dataset. The best performance is in **boldface**. Our settings are underlined.

Experiment	Method	Constant disparity for each object					Varying disparity for each object				
		LPIPS↓	PSNR↑	PSNR$_{ob}$↑	SSIM↑	SSIM$_{ob}$↑	LPIPS↓	PSNR↑	PSNR$_{ob}$↑	SSIM↑	SSIM$_{ob}$↑
Inpainting model	EC [22]	0.012	**36.8**	**30.1**	**0.989**	0.949	0.019	36.8	30.6	0.986	0.955
	MADF [52]	0.012	36.7	30.0	**0.989**	0.949	0.020	36.7	30.4	0.986	0.955
	LaMa [36]	**0.011**	36.7	30.0	**0.989**	0.951	0.019	**36.8**	30.5	0.986	0.956
Number of MPI planes	8	0.027	34.1	28.5	0.977	0.930	0.090	31.6	27.5	0.932	0.902
	16	0.015	36.0	29.6	0.986	0.946	0.044	34.8	29.5	0.969	0.939
	32	0.011	36.7	30.0	0.989	0.951	0.019	36.8	30.5	0.986	0.956
	64	0.011	**36.8**	**30.1**	0.989	0.952	0.018	36.9	30.5	0.989	0.959
Weight normalization	w/o	0.012	36.2	29.7	0.989	0.950	0.019	36.2	30.1	0.986	0.956
	w/	0.011	36.7	30.0	0.989	0.951	0.019	36.8	30.5	0.986	0.956

Inpainting Model. As we use the off-the-shelf inpainting model to generate background image, we compare 3 inpainting methods: EC [22], MADF [52], and LaMa [36]. From Table 3, one can observe that their performance is similar, showing that our framework can adapt to different inpainting models.

Number of MPI Planes. Increasing the number of MPI planes improves the representation ability of scene geometry and reduces the discretization error, but it also brings more runtime consumption at the same time. We finally choose 32 planes to achieve a trade-off between the performance and the time consumption.

Weight Normalization. As discussed in Sect. 4.1, the weight normalization plays an important role in traditional layered rendering methods. However, the performance gain of this operation is not that significant in our layer composition. The reason is that the learned alpha maps cover the invisible background parts and overlap in areas where the disparity changes smoothly, which makes the denominator of Eq. 4 more inclined to be 1.

5   Conclusion

We have presented an analysis on how to apply the MPI representation and the layer compositing formulation to bokeh rendering, and proposed an MPI-based framework MPIB to render multiple high-resolution bokeh effects and handle realistic partial occlusion effects. Despite the fact that this framework works well in general, it still has some limitations, such as the fracture of the connected area due to the plane discretization, and the boundary artifacts caused by terrible inpainting results or the continuous occlusion, which are shown in the material. We will address these issues in our future work.

Acknowledgements. This work was funded by Adobe.

References

1. Abadie, G., McAuley, S., Golubev, E., Hill, S., Lagarde, S.: Advances in real-time rendering in games. In: ACM SIGGRAPH 2018 Courses (2018)
2. Barron, J.T., Adams, A., Shih, Y., Hernández, C.: Fast bilateral-space stereo for synthetic defocus. In: Proceedings of the IEEE Conference on Computer Vision and Pattern Recognition (CVPR), pp. 4466–4474 (2015)
3. Busam, B., Hog, M., McDonagh, S., Slabaugh, G.: SteReFo: efficient image refocusing with stereo vision. In: Proceedings of the IEEE International Conference on Computer Vision Workshops (ICCVW) (2019)
4. Criminisi, A., Perez, P., Toyama, K.: Object removal by exemplar-based inpainting. In: Proceedings of the IEEE Conference on Computer Vision and Pattern Recognition (CVPR), vol. 2, p. II. IEEE (2003)
5. Dutta, S., Das, S.D., Shah, N.A., Tiwari, A.K.: Stacked deep multi-scale hierarchical network for fast bokeh effect rendering from a single image. In: Proceedings of the IEEE Conference on Computer Vision and Pattern Recognition (CVPR), pp. 2398–2407 (2021)
6. Goodfellow, I., et al.: Generative adversarial nets. In: Advances in Neural Information Processing Systems (NIPS), vol. 27 (2014)
7. Hach, T., Steurer, J., Amruth, A., Pappenheim, A.: Cinematic bokeh rendering for real scenes. In: Proceedings of the European Conference on Visual Media Production (CVMP), pp. 1–10 (2015)
8. Hays, J., Efros, A.A.: Scene completion using millions of photographs. ACM Trans. Graph. (TOG) **26**(3), 4-es (2007)
9. Ignatov, A., Patel, J., Timofte, R.: Rendering natural camera bokeh effect with deep learning. In: Proceedings of the IEEE Conference on Computer Vision and Pattern Recognition Workshops (CVPRW), pp. 418–419 (2020)
10. Ignatov, A., et al.: Aim 2019 challenge on bokeh effect synthesis: methods and results. In: Proceedings of the IEEE International Conference on Computer Vision Workshops (ICCVW), pp. 3591–3598. IEEE (2019)
11. Ignatov, A., et al.: AIM 2020 challenge on rendering realistic bokeh. In: Bartoli, A., Fusiello, A. (eds.) ECCV 2020. LNCS, vol. 12537, pp. 213–228. Springer, Cham (2020). https://doi.org/10.1007/978-3-030-67070-2_13
12. Iizuka, S., Simo-Serra, E., Ishikawa, H.: Globally and locally consistent image completion. ACM Trans. Graph. (TOG) **36**(4), 1–14 (2017)
13. Kingma, D.P., Ba, J.: Adam: a method for stochastic optimization. In: Proceedings of the International Conference on Learning Representations (ICLR) (2014)
14. Lee, S., Eisemann, E., Seidel, H.P.: Real-time lens blur effects and focus control. ACM Trans. Graph. (TOG) **29**(4), 1–7 (2010)

15. Levoy, M.: Efficient ray tracing of volume data. ACM Trans. Graph. (TOG) **9**(3), 245–261 (1990)
16. Li, J., Feng, Z., She, Q., Ding, H., Wang, C., Lee, G.H.: MINE: towards continuous depth MPI with nerf for novel view synthesis. In: Proceedings of the IEEE International Conference on Computer Vision (ICCV), pp. 12578–12588 (2021)
17. Lin, S., Ryabtsev, A., Sengupta, S., Curless, B.L., Seitz, S.M., Kemelmacher-Shlizerman, I.: Real-time high-resolution background matting. In: Proceedings of the IEEE Conference on Computer Vision and Pattern Recognition (CVPR), pp. 8762–8771 (2021)
18. Liu, G., Reda, F.A., Shih, K.J., Wang, T.C., Tao, A., Catanzaro, B.: Image inpainting for irregular holes using partial convolutions. In: Proceedings of the European Conference on Computer Vision (ECCV), pp. 85–100 (2018)
19. Liu, H., Jiang, B., Song, Y., Huang, W., Yang, C.: Rethinking image inpainting via a mutual encoder-decoder with feature equalizations. In: Vedaldi, A., Bischof, H., Brox, T., Frahm, J.-M. (eds.) ECCV 2020. LNCS, vol. 12347, pp. 725–741. Springer, Cham (2020). https://doi.org/10.1007/978-3-030-58536-5_43
20. Mildenhall, B., et al.: Local light field fusion: practical view synthesis with prescriptive sampling guidelines. ACM Trans. Graph. (TOG) **38**(4), 1–14 (2019)
21. Mildenhall, B., Srinivasan, P.P., Tancik, M., Barron, J.T., Ramamoorthi, R., Ng, R.: NeRF: representing scenes as neural radiance fields for view synthesis. In: Vedaldi, A., Bischof, H., Brox, T., Frahm, J.-M. (eds.) ECCV 2020. LNCS, vol. 12346, pp. 405–421. Springer, Cham (2020). https://doi.org/10.1007/978-3-030-58452-8_24
22. Nazeri, K., Ng, E., Joseph, T., Qureshi, F., Ebrahimi, M.: EdgeConnect: structure guided image inpainting using edge prediction. In: Proceedings of the IEEE International Conference on Computer Vision Workshops (ICCVW) (2019)
23. Niklaus, S., Liu, F.: Softmax splatting for video frame interpolation. In: Proceedings of the IEEE Conference on Computer Vision and Pattern Recognition (CVPR), pp. 5437–5446 (2020)
24. Paszke, A., et al.: Automatic differentiation in PyTorch. In: Advances in Neural Information Processing Systems Workshops (NIPSW) (2017)
25. Pathak, D., Krahenbuhl, P., Donahue, J., Darrell, T., Efros, A.A.: Context encoders: feature learning by inpainting. In: Proceedings of the IEEE Conference on Computer Vision and Pattern Recognition (CVPR), pp. 2536–2544 (2016)
26. Peng, J., Luo, X., Xian, K., Cao, Z.: Interactive portrait bokeh rendering system. In: Proceedings of the IEEE International Conference on Image Processing (ICIP), pp. 2923–2927. IEEE (2021)
27. Porter, T., Duff, T.: Compositing digital images. ACM Trans. Graph. (TOG) 253–259 (1984)
28. Qian, M., et al.: BGGAN: bokeh-glass generative adversarial network for rendering realistic bokeh. In: Bartoli, A., Fusiello, A. (eds.) ECCV 2020. LNCS, vol. 12537, pp. 229–244. Springer, Cham (2020). https://doi.org/10.1007/978-3-030-67070-2_14
29. Ranftl, R., Bochkovskiy, A., Koltun, V.: Vision transformers for dense prediction. In: Proceedings of the IEEE International Conference on Computer Vision (ICCV), pp. 12179–12188 (2021)
30. Ronneberger, O., Fischer, P., Brox, T.: U-net: convolutional networks for biomedical image segmentation. In: Navab, N., Hornegger, J., Wells, W.M., Frangi, A.F. (eds.) MICCAI 2015. LNCS, vol. 9351, pp. 234–241. Springer, Cham (2015). https://doi.org/10.1007/978-3-319-24574-4_28

31. Schedl, D.C., Wimmer, M.: A layered depth-of-field method for solving partial occlusion. J. WSCG **20**(3), 239–246 (2012)
32. Shen, X., et al.: Automatic portrait segmentation for image stylization. Comput. Graph. Forum **35**(2), 93–102 (2016)
33. Shen, X., Tao, X., Gao, H., Zhou, C., Jia, J.: Deep automatic portrait matting. In: Leibe, B., Matas, J., Sebe, N., Welling, M. (eds.) ECCV 2016. LNCS, vol. 9905, pp. 92–107. Springer, Cham (2016). https://doi.org/10.1007/978-3-319-46448-0_6
34. Shih, M.L., Su, S.Y., Kopf, J., Huang, J.B.: 3D photography using context-aware layered depth inpainting. In: Proceedings of the IEEE Conference on Computer Vision and Pattern Recognition (CVPR), pp. 8028–8038 (2020)
35. Srinivasan, P.P., Tucker, R., Barron, J.T., Ramamoorthi, R., Ng, R., Snavely, N.: Pushing the boundaries of view extrapolation with multiplane images. In: Proceedings of the IEEE Conference on Computer Vision and Pattern Recognition (CVPR), pp. 175–184 (2019)
36. Suvorov, R., et al.: Resolution-robust large mask inpainting with Fourier convolutions. In: Proceedings of the IEEE Winter Conference on Applications of Computer Vision (WACV), pp. 2149–2159 (2022)
37. Tucker, R., Snavely, N.: Single-view view synthesis with multiplane images. In: Proceedings of the IEEE Conference on Computer Vision and Pattern Recognition (CVPR), pp. 551–560 (2020)
38. Wadhwa, N., et al.: Synthetic depth-of-field with a single-camera mobile phone. ACM Trans. Graph. (TOG) **37**(4), 1–13 (2018)
39. Wang, L., et al.: DeepLens: shallow depth of field from a single image. ACM Trans. Graph. (TOG) **37**(6), 1–11 (2018)
40. Wu, J., Zheng, C., Hu, X., Xu, F.: Rendering realistic spectral bokeh due to lens stops and aberrations. Vis. Comput. **29**(1), 41–52 (2013)
41. Xian, K., Peng, J., Zhang, C., Lu, H., Cao, Z.: Ranking-based salient object detection and depth prediction for shallow depth-of-field. Sensors **21**(5), 1815 (2021)
42. Xiao, L., Kaplanyan, A., Fix, A., Chapman, M., Lanman, D.: DeepFocus: learned image synthesis for computational displays. ACM Trans. Graph. (TOG) **37**(6), 1–13 (2018)
43. Yang, C., Lu, X., Lin, Z., Shechtman, E., Wang, O., Li, H.: High-resolution image inpainting using multi-scale neural patch synthesis. In: Proceedings of the IEEE Conference on Computer Vision and Pattern Recognition (CVPR), pp. 6721–6729 (2017)
44. Yang, Y., Lin, H., Yu, Z., Paris, S., Yu, J.: Virtual DSLR: high quality dynamic depth-of-field synthesis on mobile platforms. Electron. Imaging **2016**(18), 1–9 (2016)
45. Yu, J., Lin, Z., Yang, J., Shen, X., Lu, X., Huang, T.S.: Free-form image inpainting with gated convolution. In: Proceedings of the IEEE International Conference on Computer Vision (ICCV), pp. 4471–4480 (2019)
46. Yu, X., Wang, R., Yu, J.: Real-time depth of field rendering via dynamic light field generation and filtering. Comput. Graph. Forum **29**(7), 2099–2107 (2010)
47. Zhang, R., Isola, P., Efros, A.A., Shechtman, E., Wang, O.: The unreasonable effectiveness of deep features as a perceptual metric. In: Proceedings of the IEEE Conference on Computer Vision and Pattern Recognition (CVPR), pp. 586–595 (2018)
48. Zhang, X., Matzen, K., Nguyen, V., Yao, D., Zhang, Y., Ng, R.: Synthetic defocus and look-ahead autofocus for casual videography. ACM Trans. Graph. (TOG) **38**, 1–16 (2019)

49. Zhou, B., Lapedriza, A., Khosla, A., Oliva, A., Torralba, A.: Places: a 10 million image database for scene recognition. IEEE Trans. Pattern Anal. Mach. Intell. (TPAMI) **40**(6), 1452–1464 (2017)
50. Zhou, T., Tucker, R., Flynn, J., Fyffe, G., Snavely, N.: Stereo magnification: learning view synthesis using multiplane images. ACM Trans. Graph. (TOG) **37**(4), 1–12 (2018)
51. Zhou, T., Tulsiani, S., Sun, W., Malik, J., Efros, A.A.: View synthesis by appearance flow. In: Leibe, B., Matas, J., Sebe, N., Welling, M. (eds.) ECCV 2016. LNCS, vol. 9908, pp. 286–301. Springer, Cham (2016). https://doi.org/10.1007/978-3-319-46493-0_18
52. Zhu, M., et al.: Image inpainting by end-to-end cascaded refinement with mask awareness. IEEE Trans. Image Process. (TIP) **30**, 4855–4866 (2021)

Real-RawVSR: Real-World Raw Video Super-Resolution with a Benchmark Dataset

Huanjing Yue, Zhiming Zhang, and Jingyu Yang$^{(\boxtimes)}$

School of Electrical and Information Engineering, Tianjin University, Tianjin, China
{huanjing.yue,zmzhang,yjy}@tju.edu.cn

Abstract. In recent years, real image super-resolution (SR) has achieved promising results due to the development of SR datasets and corresponding real SR methods. In contrast, the field of real video SR is lagging behind, especially for real raw videos. Considering the superiority of raw image SR over sRGB image SR, we construct a real-world raw video SR (Real-RawVSR) dataset and propose a corresponding SR method. We utilize two DSLR cameras and a beam-splitter to simultaneously capture low-resolution (LR) and high-resolution (HR) raw videos with $2\times$, $3\times$, and $4\times$ magnifications. There are 450 video pairs in our dataset, with scenes varying from indoor to outdoor, and motions including camera and object movements. To our knowledge, this is the first real-world raw VSR dataset. Since the raw video is characterized by the Bayer pattern, we propose a two-branch network, which deals with both the packed RGGB sequence and the original Bayer pattern sequence, and the two branches are complementary to each other. After going through the proposed co-alignment, interaction, fusion, and reconstruction modules, we generate the corresponding HR sRGB sequence. Experimental results demonstrate that the proposed method outperforms benchmark real and synthetic video SR methods with either raw or sRGB inputs. *Our code and dataset are available at* https://github.com/zmzhang1998/Real-RawVSR.

Keywords: Real-RawVSR · Raw video · Co-alignment · Bayer pattern

1 Introduction

Capturing images (videos) with a short-focus lens can enlarge the view angles by sacrificing the resolutions while capturing with a long-focus lens can increase the resolutions by sacrificing the view angles. Image (video) super-resolution (SR) is an effective way to get both wide angle and high-resolution (HR) images

---

J. Yang—This work was supported in part by the National Natural Science Foundation of China under Grant 62072331 and 62231018.

Supplementary Information The online version contains supplementary material available at https://doi.org/10.1007/978-3-031-20068-7_35.

© The Author(s), under exclusive license to Springer Nature Switzerland AG 2022
S. Avidan et al. (Eds.): ECCV 2022, LNCS 13666, pp. 608–624, 2022.
https://doi.org/10.1007/978-3-031-20068-7_35

(videos). Video SR reconstructs an HR video from a low-resolution (LR) input by exploring the spatial and temporal correlations of the input sequence. In recent years, the development of video SR has shifted from traditional model-driven to deep learning based methods [9,31,32,36].

The performance of these deep learning based SR methods heavily depends on the training datasets. Considering that the synthetic LR-HR datasets, such as DIV2K [3] and REDS [28], cannot represent the degradation models between real captured LR images and HR images, many real SR datasets are constructed to boost the real-world SR performance. However, most of these datasets are for static LR-HR images, such as RealSR [8] and ImagePairs [18]. Recently, Yang et al. [37] proposed the first real-world video SR dataset via capturing with a multi-camera system of iPhone 11 Pro Max. However, the parallax between the LR and HR cameras increased the difficulty for alignment and there are only 2× LR-HR sequence pairs in this dataset due to the limited focal lengths of phone cameras.

On the other hand, there is a trend to utilize raw images for real-scene image (video) restoration, such as low light enhancement [13,14], denoising [1,2,5,23, 33,38], deblurring [22], and super-resolution [35,39]. The main reason is that raw images have wide bit depths (12 or 14 bits), *i.e.*, containing the most original information, and its intensity is linear to the illumination. However, there is still little work exploring raw video SR. Liu et al. [24] proposed a raw video SR dataset by synthesizing LR raw frames by downsampling from the captured HR raw frames. Even though, there is still a gap between the synthesized LR raw frames and real captured ones, which makes the SR models trained on synthesized data cannot generalize well to real scenes.

Based on the above observations, we propose to construct a real-world raw video SR dataset to facilitate the raw VSR research. Specifically, we build a two-camera system with a beam-splitter to make sure that there is no parallax between the two cameras. In addition, we perform alignment on the captured LR-HR pairs to make them aligned. On the other hand, the current VSR methods [9, 32] are mostly based on sRGB frame inputs and the network design for raw sequence inputs has not been well explored. Therefore, we propose a raw VSR network tailored for raw inputs. Specifically, the raw frames are fed into the network in two forms. One is in its original Bayer pattern and the other is in the packed sub-frame version, namely that RGGB pixels are packed into four channels. The features from the two branches are co-aligned, interacted, and fused together to reconstruct the HR sRGB frame. In brief, our contributions can be summarized as follows.

- We construct the first aligned raw VSR dataset for real scenes, which contains LR-HR pairs for 2×, 3×, and 4× magnification in both raw and sRGB domains. By utilizing a beam splitter in our capturing system, we obtain LR-HR pairs without parallax. There are totally 450 video pairs and each video contains about 150 frames.
- We propose a novel raw VSR network by utilizing the raw frames in terms of the original Bayer pattern and its corresponding packed sub-frame pattern.

Specifically, we propose co-alignment, interaction, and fusion modules to take advantage of the complementary information from the two branches.

- We introduce a simple but effective color correction method (*i.e.,* channel-based correction), which is beneficial for training with image pairs having color differences. Experimental results demonstrate that our method outperforms benchmark VSR methods in both sRGB and raw domains.

2   Related Work

2.1   Image and Video SR Datasets

Image SR Datasets. The early image SR datasets usually synthesize LR images from the captured HR ones via bicubic downsampling, such as DIV2K dataset [3]. Considering the domain gap between synthesized and real captured LR images, many real-world SR datasets are constructed. For example, the City100 [12] and RealSR [8] datasets, which are captured with different focal length cameras, contain LR-HR pairs in sRGB domain. Zhang *et al.* claimed that using sRGB images to train the SR model is inferior to that trained by raw data [39]. Therefore, they constructed the first SR-Raw dataset for real-world computational zoom. Meanwhile, Xu *et al.* constructed a synthesized raw image dataset for raw image SR [35]. Hereafter, the ImagePairs dataset [18] is constructed by introducing a beam splitter into the capturing system, which enables them to capture a much larger dataset with LR-HR pairs in both raw and sRGB domains. These datasets have greatly promoted the performance of real image SR and laid the foundation for the construction of VSR datasets for real scenes.

Video SR Datasets. Similar to the development of image SR dataset, the video dataset is also shifted from the synthesized ones (such as REDS [28] and Vimeo-90k [36]) to real captured ones (such as RealVSR [37] and BurstSR dataset[1] [4]), from sRGB domain [36,37] to raw domain [4,24]. The RealVSR [37] dataset is constructed by capturing with two different focal length cameras in iPhone 11 Pro Max and the DoubleTake App. Since the focal lengths are limited for phone cameras, there are only 2× LR-HR sequence pairs in this dataset. Recently, RealBasicVSR [11] built a VideoLQ dataset to assess the generalize ability of real-world VSR methods. Since there are no ground truths for these videos, this dataset cannot be used for supervised training.

Inspired by the success of raw image SR, Bhat *et al.* constructed a BurstSR dataset [4] in the raw domain by capturing the burst LR raw images with a phone camera and the HR sRGB images with a DSLR camera. Liu *et al.* constructed the RawVD dataset [24] for videos, which synthesized the LR raw sequences from the captured HR raw sequences via a degradation model. However, as demonstrated in [4], a network trained with synthetic data is expected to have

---

[1] Since burst image SR is similar to video SR, we present them here other than in the image SR.

suboptimal performance when applied to real images. Therefore, we propose to construct a Real-RawVSR dataset by capturing real raw sequences with both short and long focal length cameras for different scaling factors, thus providing a real benchmark for raw VSR model training and evaluation.

2.2 Image and Video SR Methods

SR Methods for Synthesized Data. In the literature, most SR methods are designed based on the synthesized LR-HR pairs. For image SR, most works explore efficient modules to explore spatial correlations, such as the residual channel attention block in RCAN [40], the holistic attention block in HAN [29]. For video SR, both spatial and temporal correlations are essential for SR performance. Therefore, many methods focus on the alignment strategy, such as the optical flow based [6,19,36] and the deformable convolution [15] based, e.g. TDAN [31], EDVR [32]. Recently, BasicVSR [9] and its enhanced versions, i.e., IconVSR [9] and BasicVSR++ [10] have achieved superior SR performance by combining forward and backward bidirectional propagation information and optical flow based feature alignment. Hereafter, Zhou et al. proposed an effective iterative alignment algorithm and an efficient adaptive reweighting strategy to better utilize the temporal correlations [41].

SR Methods for Real Captured Data. Different from synthesized LR-HR pairs, there are usually spatial misalignment, color mismatching, and intensity variance in the real captured LR-HR pairs. Therefore, the SR methods for real data focus on dealing with these misalignments. Zhang et al. introduced the contextual bilateral loss to deal with the spatial misalignment [39], and Cai et al. proposed a Laplacian pyramid based kernel prediction network since the real degradation kernels are naturally non-uniform [8]. Besides, the NTIRE challenge on real-world image SR further boosts the SR performance [7,26]. Compared with real image SR, there is a few research on real VSR. RealVSR [37] proposed a Laplacian pyramid based loss to deal with the misalignment and color differences between the LR-HR frames. Considering that in-the-wild degradations could be exaggerated during temporal propagation, RealBasicVSR [11] proposed a pre-cleaning module to reduce noise and artifacts prior to temporal propagation.

SR Methods for Raw Images and Videos. The above methods are generally designed for sRGB images. For raw input SR, the network needs to simultaneously deal with both ISP and SR tasks. The work in [39] directly maps the raw input to an sRGB output via a ResNet. Different from it, Xu et al. proposed a dual CNN, where one branch is used for structure reconstruction and the other branch is for color restoration with the LR sRGB image as guidance [35]. Following it, the RawVSR method [24] also utilizes two branches for both detail and color reconstruction. However, the raw LR frames are synthesized.

To our knowledge, there is still no work exploring real-world raw VSR methods and the network design for raw sequence input has not been well explored. In this work, we propose a two-branch interaction network tailored for raw sequence inputs and propose co-alignment, interaction, and fusion modules to explore the complementary information between the two branches.

3   Real-RawVSR Dataset Construction

Hardware Design. Capturing LR-HR image pairs with short-long focal lengths are common settings for real image SR. This can be easily realized for static scene by capturing with the same camera [39]. For dynamic LR-HR video capturing, we need to utilize two cameras with different focal lengths. However, this will inevitably bring parallax problems caused by different shooting positions. Inspired by [17,18], which utilizes a beam splitter to divide the incident light into two light beams with a brightness ratio of 1:1, we also utilize this strategy, as shown in Fig. 1(a). In order to capture LR-HR frame pairs with different ratios, we utilize the DSLR camera with an 18–135 mm zoom lens instead of the mobile phone cameras. Therefore, a large beam splitter is expected to cover the lens of DSLR cameras. To this end, we utilize a large and cheap beam splitter with reflectance coating and antireflection coating, instead of a small and expensive beam splitter cube. In order to avoid the influence of natural light from other directions, we design and print a 3D model box to hold the beam splitter. In this way, the two cameras can receive natural light from the same viewpoint. The size of the beam splitter is $150 \times 150 \times 1\,(\mathrm{mm}^3)$, which is enough to cover the camera lens. We put the camera and beam splitter box on an optical plate, which is installed on a tripod, to improve its stability.

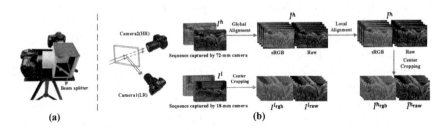

Fig. 1. The capturing hardware (a) and our coarse to fine alignment pipeline to generate aligned LR-HR pairs (b).

Data Collection. We use two Canon 60D cameras upgraded with a third-party software Magic Lantern[2] to capture raw videos in Magic Lantern Video (MLV) format. To keep the cameras in sync, we use an infrared remote control to signal both cameras to capture at the same time. During capturing, we keep the ISO of the two cameras ranging from 100 to 1600 to avoid noise, and the exposure time ranges from 1/400 s to 1/31 s to capture both slow and fast motions. All

---

[2] https://magiclantern.fm/.

the other settings are set to default values to simulate real capture scenarios. Then we use the MlRawViewer[3] software to process the MLV video to obtain the corresponding sRGB frames and raw frames in the DNG format. For each scene, we capture a short video with six seconds and the frame rate is 25 FPS, namely that each video contains approximately 150 frames in both raw and sRGB formats.

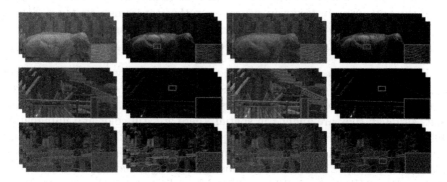

Fig. 2. Examples of videos in Real-RawVSR Dataset with the brightness and contrast of raw frames adjusted for better visualization. From left to right, each column lists LR frames ($I^{l_{rgb}}$, $I^{l_{raw}}$) and HR frames ($\tilde{I}^{h_{rgb}}$, $\tilde{I}^{h_{raw}}$) in both raw and sRGB domains.

Data Processing. As shown in Fig. 1(b), although there is no parallax between the LR-HR pair, the field of view (FoV) of the LR frame is much larger than that of the HR frame. In addition, due to the existence of lens distortion, there is still misalignment between the LR-HR pairs. Therefore, we utilize a coarse to fine alignment strategy to obtain aligned LR-HR pairs. In the following, we give details for sRGB frame and raw frame alignment, respectively.

1) **RGB frame alignment.** First, we estimate a homography matrix (H) between the upsampled LR ($\hat{I}^{l_{rgb}}$, the upsampling factor is estimated according to the ratio between the LR and HR focal lengths) and HR ($I^{h_{rgb}}$) frames using their matched SIFT [25] key points, which are selected by the RANSAC algorithm [16]. Note that, we perform alignment on $I^{h_{rgb}}$, to make the LR input of our network to be consistent with real captured LR frames, instead of performing alignment on $I^{l_{rgb}}$ as that in [37]. Then, the aligned HR frame is obtained by $\hat{I}^{h_{rgb}} = H I^{h_{rgb}}$. In this way, we can roughly crop the corresponding regions in the LR frame matched with the HR frame. Then, we utilize DeepFlow [34], which is a traditional flow estimation method, to perform pixel-wise alignment for the matching area. Finally, we crop the center area to eliminate the alignment artifacts around the border, generating the aligned LR-HR frames in RGB domain, denoted by ($I^{l_{rgb}}$, $\tilde{I}^{h_{rgb}}$).

---

[3] https://bitbucket.org/baldand/mlrawviewer/src/master/.

2) **Raw frame alignment.** The raw frames should go through the same pipeline as that of RGB frames to make $\tilde{I}_t^{h_{\text{raw}}}$ and $\tilde{I}_t^{h_{\text{rgb}}}$ be strictly aligned. However, directly applying the global and local alignment will destroy the Bayer pattern of raw inputs. Therefore, we first pack the Bayer pattern raw frame into RGGB sub-frames, whose size is half of that of RGB frames. Hence, we change the H matrix calculated from sRGB frames by rescaling the translation parameters with a ratio of 0.5. The deep flow vectors are also processed in the same way. In this way, we generate the raw frame pair $(I^{l_{\text{raw}}}, \tilde{I}^{h_{\text{raw}}})$. Note that, in this work, we utilize $(I^{l_{\text{raw}}}, \tilde{I}^{h_{\text{rgb}}})$ as training pairs. The provided raw pairs can enable future research on raw to raw SR.

We totally captured 600 groups of videos, and manually removed 150 videos with large alignment errors, with 450 videos remaining in our dataset. Figure 2 gives some examples of our aligned pairs in both raw and sRGB domains. Note that, although they are aligned in spatial, there are still color and illumination differences in each LR-HR pair. These phenomena also exist in other real captured LR-HR pairs [4,37,39]. Our captured scenes vary from indoor to outdoor, and the motion types include camera motions and object motions. The resolution of the original HR frame is 1728 × 972. After alignment and center cropping, the resolutions of the aligned HR and LR frames for 2× SR are 1440 × 640 and 720 × 320, respectively. For each magnification scale, there are 150 video pairs and each video contains about 150 frames. More detailed information about the dataset is presented in the supplementary file.

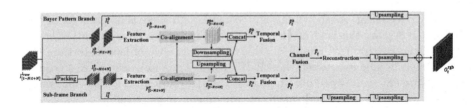

Fig. 3. The proposed Real-RawVSR network for 2× SR. The LR raw sequences $(I_{[t-N:t+N]}^{l_{\text{raw}}})$ are fed into the network in terms of both Bayer pattern and sub-frame forms. The final SR result O_t^{rgb} is obtained by feature interaction and fusion of the Bayer pattern and sub-frame branches.

4   The Proposed Method

We propose a Real-RawVSR network to reconstruct an HR sRGB frame O_t^{rgb} from $2N + 1$ consecutive LR raw frames $I_{[t-N:t+N]}^{l_{\text{raw}}}$. The existing raw image (video) SR methods [24,35] usually directly pack the Bayer pattern input into four (RGGB) different channels, where each channel contains the same color pixels. However, this will destroy the pixel order of the original raw frame. Inspired by [22], in this work, we propose to deal with raw frames in two branches, as shown in Fig. 3. The top branch deals with the original Bayer pattern input, and the bottom branch deals with the packed RGGB input. In this way, the top Bayer pattern branch benefits the spatial reconstruction while the bottom sub-frame branch can take advantage of longer neighboring pixels to generate details. To fully take advantage of the complementary information between the two branches, we propose co-alignment, interaction, and fusion modules. In the following, we give details of these modules.

4.1 Packing and Feature Extraction

As shown in Fig. 3, the input LR raw frames $I^{l_{raw}}_{[t-N:t+N]}$ are fed into the network in different forms for the two branches. The top Bayer pattern branch directly utilizes the raw frames themselves as input. The bottom sub-frame branch utilizes the packed version, namely that we extract the sub-frame with the same color from the Bayer pattern input and all the sub-frames form a new sequence. For simplicity, we denote the input of the Bayer pattern branch as $I^b_{[t-N:t+N]}$ and that of the sub-frame branch as $I^s_{[t-N:t+N]}$, whose channel number is four times of $I^b_{[t-N:t+N]}$. The Bayer pattern branch keeps the original order of raw pixels, which is good for spatial reconstruction. Although the sub-frame branch cannot keep the original pixel order, it can take advantage of far neighbor correlations to generate details. Therefore, they are complementary to each other, which helps to improve the SR results generated by one single branch. Then, the two inputs go through the feature extraction modules, respectively, where the feature extraction module is constructed by five residual blocks. Note that, the weights for the two feature extraction blocks are not shared since their inputs are in different forms. After the feature extraction module, we obtain $F^b_{[t-N:t+N]}$ with size $(2N + 1) \times C \times H \times W$ for the Bayer pattern branch and $F^s_{[t-N:t+N]}$ with size $(2N + 1) \times C \times H/2 \times W/2$ for the sub-frame branch, where $2N + 1$ is the frame number along the time dimension, C is the channel number, H is the height, and W is the width of features.

4.2 Co-alignment

Since there are temporal misalignments between neighboring frames, we need to warp neighboring frames to the center frame. Following [32], we utilize PCD alignment. Since we have two branches, a straightforward solution is performing the PCD alignment separately. We note that the two branches actually share the same offset. Therefore, we propose to calculate the alignment offsets from the sub-frame branch and then directly copy the calculated offsets to the Bayer pattern branch to perform the alignment operation. Namely that the two branches are co-aligned.

Given the features of two adjacent frames in the sub-frame branch F^s_t and F^s_{t+i}, we aim to align F^s_{t+i} with F^s_t. The aligned feature $\hat{F}^s_{t+i}$ at position $\mathbf{p}_0$ is

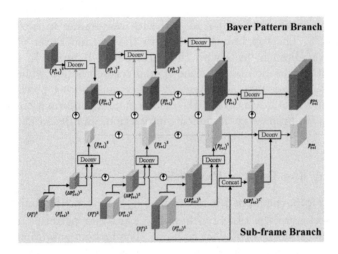

Fig. 4. The proposed co-alignment module. The top branch is for the Bayer pattern feature alignment and the bottom branch is for the sub-frame feature alignment. The two branches share the same offset with different sizes.

obtained via deformable convolution, which can be expressed by

$$\hat{F}^s_{t+i}(\mathbf{p}_0) = \sum_{k=0}^{K} w_k \cdot F^s_{t+i}(\mathbf{p}_0 + \mathbf{p}_k + \triangle \mathbf{p}_k) \cdot \triangle m_k, \tag{1}$$

where $\mathbf{w}_k$ and $\mathbf{p}_k$ represent the weight and predefined offset for the k-th location in the deformable convolution kernel. The learnable offset $\triangle \mathbf{p}_k$ and the modulation scalar $\triangle m_k$ are predicted from concatenated features of the neighboring and reference frames, denoted by

$$\triangle \mathbf{P}_{t+i} = f([F^s_{t+i}, F^s_t]), \tag{2}$$

where $\triangle \mathbf{P} = \{\triangle \mathbf{p}\}$ represents the set of offsets, and f represents a nonlinear mapping function realized by several convolution layers. For simplicity, we ignore the modulation scalar $\triangle m_k$ in the descriptions and figures. Following PCD alignment, we further utilize pyramidal processing and cascading refinement to deal with large motions, as shown in Fig. 4. The features $(F^s_{t+i})^l$ and $(F^s_t)^l$ are downsampled via strided convolution for $L-1$ times to form a pyramid with L levels. The pyramid features in the Bayer-pattern branch are constructed in the same way. The offsets in the lth level are calculated from the concatenated features in the lth level and the upsampled version of the offsets in the $(l+1)^{\text{th}}$ level. The upsampling is realized by bilinear interpolation and the offset values are magnified by two times. This process is denoted by

$$(\triangle \mathbf{P}^s_{t+i})^l = f([(F^s_{t+i})^l, (F^s_t)^l], 2((\triangle \mathbf{P}^s_{t+i})^{l+1})^{\uparrow 2}). \tag{3}$$

Since the input of the sub-frame branch is actually a down-sampling version of that in the Bayer pattern branch, the offset values for the Bayer pattern branch should be two times of that in the sub-frame branch. Therefore, the offsets for the Bayer pattern branch $(\triangle \mathbf{P}_{t+i}^b)^l$ in the lth level can be obtained via two times upsampling and two times magnification of the offsets $(\triangle \mathbf{P}_{t+i}^s)^l$ in the sub-frame branch. We denote this process as

$$(\triangle \mathbf{P}_{t+i}^b)^l = 2((\triangle \mathbf{P}_{t+i}^s)^l)^{\uparrow 2}. \tag{4}$$

Given the offsets, the aligned features for the two branches can be expressed by

$$(\hat{F}_{t+i}^s)^l = g(\text{Dconv}((F_{t+i}^s)^l, (\triangle \mathbf{P}_{t+i}^s)^l), ((\hat{F}_{t+i}^s)^{l+1})^{\uparrow 2}), \tag{5}$$

$$(\hat{F}_{t+i}^b)^l = g(\text{Dconv}((F_{t+i}^b)^l, (\triangle \mathbf{P}_{t+i}^b)^l), ((\hat{F}_{t+i}^b)^{l+1})^{\uparrow 2}), \tag{6}$$

where g represents the mapping function realized by seveal convolution layers and DConv represents deformable convolution expressed in Eq. 1. Note that, the two-branch DConv shares the same weights in the corresponding level. After alignment for L levels, we further use the offsets $(\triangle \mathbf{P}_{t+i}^s)^{1'}$ calculated between $(F_t^s)^1$ and $(\hat{F}_{t+i}^s)^1$ to refine $(\hat{F}_{t+i}^s)^1$ and $(\hat{F}_{t+i}^b)^1$, and generate the final alignment results $\hat{F}_{t+i}^{sa}$ and $\hat{F}_{t+i}^{ba}$ for the neighboring features in the two branches.

We would like to point out that using the proposed co-alignment strategy not only reduces computing complexity but also improves the final SR performance (see the ablation study). The main reason is that the offsets are optimized by both the Bayer pattern features and the sub-frame features, while the offsets calculated with separated alignment can only be optimized with their corresponding features. Therefore, the co-alignment strategy outperforms the sep-alignment.

4.3   Interaction

Since the features in the two branches are complementary, we further propose an interaction module to enrich the feature representations in the two branches. Specifically, the Bayer pattern branch features are downsampled via a 3×3 strided convolution (stride $= 2$) and Leaky Relu layer, and these downsampled features are concatenated with those in the sub-frame branch. Similarly, the sub-frame branch features are upsampled via pixel shuffle [30], which are then concatenated with the features in the Bayer pattern branch. In this way, we generate the interacted features $\hat{F}_c^b \in \mathbb{R}^{(4N+2) \times C \times H \times W}$ and $\hat{F}_c^s \in \mathbb{R}^{(4N+2) \times C \times H/2 \times W/2}$.

4.4   Temporal Fusion

Although we have aligned the neighboring frames to the reference frame, these frames still contribute differently to the reference frame SR. Therefore, we utilize attention based fusion to fuse the features together. First, we utilize a non-local temporal attention module [38] to aggregate long-range features to enhance the feature representations along the time dimension. Then, we utilize temporal spatial attention (TSA) [32] based fusion to fuse the features together. Finally, we obtain the temporal fused features $\tilde{F}_t^b$ with size $1 \times C \times H \times W$ and $\tilde{F}_t^s$ with size $1 \times C \times H/2 \times W/2$ for the two branches, respectively.

4.5   Channel Fusion

We utilize channel fusion to merge the features in the two branches together since the same channel of $\tilde{F}_t^b$ and $\tilde{F}_t^s$ may contribute differently to the final SR reconstruction. We adopt selective kernel convolution (SKF) [21] to fuse the two branches via channel-wise weighted average. We first upsample $\tilde{F}_t^s$ via pixel shuffle to make it have the same size as that of $\tilde{F}_t^b$. Then, the two features are added together, going through global average pooling along the channel dimension, generating a channel-wise weighting vector $z \in \mathbb{R}^{1 \times 1 \times C}$. Then, z goes through the squeeze and excitation layers, generating two weighting coefficients z^b and z^s. Hereafter, they are normalized via softmax, generating the final weighting coefficients $\hat{z}^b$ and $\hat{z}^s$. The final fused feature is obtained by $\tilde{F}_t = \hat{z}^b \tilde{F}_t^b + \hat{z}^s \tilde{F}_t^s$.

4.6   Reconstruction and Upsampling

The fused feature $\tilde{F}_t$ is fed into the reconstruction module, which is realized by 10 ResNet blocks, for the SR reconstruction. After reconstruction, we utilize the pixel shuffle layer to upsample it and then utilize a convolution layer to generate the three-channel output. We also utilize two long skip connections. One is for the LR Bayer input (I_t^b), which is first processed by a convolution layer and then upsampled by pixel shuffle to a three channel output. The other is for the LR sub-frame input (I_t^s), which is upsampled two times since its spatial size is half of the original input. The three outputs are added together to generate the final HR result O_t^{rgb}. For 4× magnification, similar to EBSR [27], we utilize a two-stage upsampling based long-skip connection.

4.7   Color Correction and Loss Function

As described in Sec. 3, the LR input $(I_t^{l_{\mathrm{rgb}}})$ and ground truth $(\tilde{I}_t^{h_{\mathrm{rgb}}})$ have differences in color and brightness. Directly utilizing pixel-wise loss between the output and the ground truth may lead the network to optimize color and brightness correction other than the essential task of SR, *i.e.*, detail generation. To solve this problem, inspired by [4], we utilize color correction before the loss calculation. Different from [4], we utilize channel-based color correction for RGB channels separately other than calculating a 3×3 color correction matrix to simultaneously correct them. This process can be denoted as

$$\hat{O}_t^c = \alpha^c O_t^c, \alpha^c = \phi(I_t^{l_c}, \tilde{I}_t^{h_c}), c \in \{r, g, b\}, \tag{7}$$

where α^c is the scaling factor for channel c, and it is calculated by minimizing the least square loss between the corresponding pixel pairs in $I_t^{l_c}$ and the downsampled version of $\tilde{I}_t^{h_c}$. Then, we can optimize the network with the Charbonnier loss [20] between the corrected output and the ground truth as

$$\mathcal{L} = \sqrt{\| \hat{O}_t^{\mathrm{rgb}} - \tilde{I}_t^{h_{\mathrm{rgb}}} \|_2^2 + \epsilon}, \text{ where } \epsilon = 1 \times 10^{-6}.$$

5   Experiments

5.1   Training Details

In our experiments, for each magnification factor, 130 videos are used for training and validation, and the other 20 videos are used for testing. To make the movements between neighboring frames more obvious, for each video, we extract frames from the original 150 frames with a step size of three, resulting in a 50-frame sequence. This strategy is also used in [28]. The raw data is pre-processed by black level subtraction and white level normalization. The frame number is 5, $i.e.$, $N = 2$. The channel number C of features is 64. All the convolution filter size is 3×3^4. During training, the Bayer pattern patch size is 128×128 and the batch size is 4. We train our model with Adam optimizer and the learning rate is set to 1e−4. The total iteration number is 300k. Our model is implemented in PyTorch and trained with an NVIDIA 3090 GPU.

Table 1. Quantitative comparison with state-of-the-art VSR methods. The best results are highlighted in bold and the second best results are underlined.

Scale		Bicubic	TOF [36]	TDAN [31]	EDVR [32]	BasicVSR [9]	RawEDVR	DBSR [4]	RawVSR [24]	Ours
2×	PSNR	35.32	35.62	36.14	<u>36.93</u>	36.72	36.74	36.16	36.55	**37.38**
	SSIM	0.9530	0.9555	0.9615	0.9674	0.9668	0.9670	0.9621	<u>0.9677</u>	**0.9705**
3×	PSNR	33.09	33.72	34.43	<u>35.25</u>	34.95	35.23	34.48	34.96	**35.62**
	SSIM	0.9169	0.9241	0.9352	0.9425	0.9408	<u>0.9442</u>	0.9370	0.9431	**0.9468**
4×	PSNR	31.19	32.17	32.84	<u>33.60</u>	33.27	33.55	32.86	33.46	**33.91**
	SSIM	0.8787	0.8928	0.9050	0.9139	0.9113	0.9153	0.9077	<u>0.9164</u>	**0.9182**
Params (M)		–	–	2.3	3.3	6.3	3.3	12.4	4.5	4.8
FLOPs (G)		–	–	360.3	463.3	370.0	464.7	254.7	622.9	494.9

5.2   Comparison with State-of-the-arts

We compare with six state-of-the-art VSR methods, including four methods in sRGB domain (TOFlow [36], EDVR [32], TDAN [31], and BasicVSR [9]) and two methods in raw domain (RawVSR [24] and DBSR [4]). In addition, we also revise EDVR by setting its input to the one channel Bayer pattern input and the original bilinear upsampling operation on the long skip connection is replaced by convolution and pixel shuffle operations. The revised version is denoted as RawEDVR. For a fair comparison, we retrain the above methods on our dataset and add the color correction strategy mentioned in Sect. 4.7 to all the compared methods to avoid the influence of color mis-matching. We use $(I_{[t-N:t+N]}^{l_{rgb}}, \tilde{I}_t^{h_{rgb}})$ as training pairs for sRGB domain methods and $(I_{[t-N:t+N]}^{l_{raw}}, \tilde{I}_t^{h_{rgb}})$ for raw domain methods. All the methods are trained with 5 consecutive frames as inputs.

---

[4] More details about the network structure are presented in the supplementary file.

The quantitative comparison results are shown in Table 1. Our method achieves the best results compared to all previous methods on all scaling factors. Specially, for 2× SR, our method outperforms EDVR and RawVSR by 0.45 dB and 0.83 dB, respectively. Note that, although the PSNR results of RawVSR and RawEDVR are worse than those of EDVR, the SSIM results of RawVSR and RawEDVR are generally better than those of EDVR. This demonstrates that the raw input is beneficial for the structure reconstruction, which is also verified by the visual comparison in Fig. 5. We also present the number of parameters and FLOPs (calculated for 4× SR with a 160 × 360 input) in Table 1. Our method has similar FLOPs as that of RawEDVR and is much lighter than RawVSR. This mainly benefits from the proposed co-alignment strategy, which saves about 100G FLOPs compared with separate alignment.

Figure 5 presents the visual comparison results for 2× and 4× SR. All the sRGB domain processing methods cannot deal with the false colors embedded in the LR input. RawVSR also cannot remove the false colors since it utilizes the LR sRGB input for guidance. It demonstrates that for real raw VSR, utilizing the LR sRGB input as guidance may be not a good choice. In addition, raw domain processing can generate better details compared with sRGB domain processing (see the second image). Our method can correct the false colors well and our generated details are much cleaner than those of other methods.

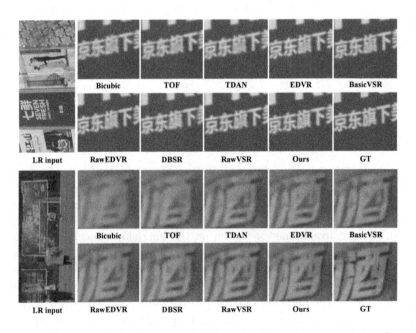

Fig. 5. Visual comparison for 2× and 4× VSR results. For each group, the top (bottom) row presents the results generated by sRGB (raw) domain processing methods.

5.3   Ablation Study

We evaluate the key modules in our network by replacing them with other straightforward solutions. 1) **Co-Alignment.** We evaluate the effectiveness of the co-alignment module by replacing it with a separate alignment, which performs alignment on the two branches separately. As shown in Table 2, co-alignment outperforms sep-alignment by 0.11 dB. The main reason is that the offsets calculated by co-alignment are more accurate than those calculated by sep-alignment. We also present the result by removing the alignment module, which is 0.19 dB less than our proposed method. 2) **Interaction.** If we remove the interaction module from our full model, the result will drop 0.15 dB. It verifies that interaction is beneficial for taking advantage of the complementary information in the two branches. 3) **Channel Fusion.** By replacing the selective kernel based fusion strategy with simple concatenation, the PSNR result will drop 0.06 dB. 4) **Color Correction.** If we do not utilize color correction, the result will be heavily degraded (30.65 dB) due to the color cast. In addition, our channel-based correction is better than the widely used matrix-based correction method by 0.1 dB. 5) **Single Branch.** We also present the results by training the Bayer pattern branch and sub-frame branch separately. We increase the parameters of the two variants by increasing their channel numbers to make their parameters almost the same as that of our full model. Our method outperforms the two variants by nearly 0.2 dB. It demonstrates that the gain of two branch processing is not from the large parameters but from our co-alignment and interaction modules.

Table 2. Ablation study ($4\times$) for the key modules in our network.

Alignment	Sep-alignment	✗	✓	✗
	Co-alignment	✗	✗	✓
	PSNR/SSIM	33.72/0.9173	33.80/0.9178	**33.91/0.9182**
Interaction	Interaction	✗	✓	
	PSNR/SSIM	33.76/0.9173	**33.91/0.9182**	
Channel Fusion	SKF	✗	✓	
	Concat	✓	✗	
	PSNR/SSIM	33.85/0.9180	**33.91/0.9182**	
Color Correction	Matrix-based	✗	✓	✗
	Channel-based	✗	✗	✓
	PSNR/SSIM	30.65/0.9102	33.81/0.9173	**33.91/0.9182**
Branch	Bayer branch	✓	✗	✓
	Sub-frame branch	✗	✓	✓
	PSNR/SSIM	33.73/0.9175	33.70/0.9167	**33.91/0.9182**

6   Conclusion and Discussion

We build the first real-world raw VSR dataset with three magnification ratios in both raw and sRGB domains, which provides a benchmark dataset for both training and evaluation of real raw VSR methods. Based on this dataset, we propose a Real-RawVSR method by dealing with the raw inputs in two branches. By utilizing the proposed co-alignment, interaction, and fusion modules, the complementary information of the two branches is well explored. Experiments demonstrate that the proposed method outperforms state-of-the-art raw and sRGB VSR methods.

Compared with VSR for synthetic LR inputs, dealing with real LR inputs is more difficult due to the color and brightness differences in the LR-HR pair. As reported in [37], the gap between different methods retrained on the same real dataset is much smaller than those trained on the synthetic dataset [32]. In this work, we focus on the network structure design for raw inputs and have achieved impressive gain over our baseline network EDVR. The proposed co-alignment and interaction strategy can be applied to other sRGB VSR methods to improve their performance in dealing with raw inputs. In the future, we would like to explore more effective losses to deal with the color and brightness differences.

References

1. Abdelhamed, A., Afifi, M., Timofte, R., Brown, M.S.: NTIRE 2020 challenge on real image denoising: dataset, methods and results. In: Proceedings of the IEEE/CVF Conference on Computer Vision and Pattern Recognition Workshops, pp. 496–497 (2020)
2. Abdelhamed, A., Timofte, R., Brown, M.S.: NTIRE 2019 challenge on real image denoising: methods and results. In: Proceedings of the IEEE/CVF Conference on Computer Vision and Pattern Recognition Workshops (2019)
3. Agustsson, E., Timofte, R.: NTIRE 2017 challenge on single image super-resolution: dataset and study. In: Proceedings of the IEEE conference on computer vision and pattern recognition workshops, pp. 126–135 (2017)
4. Bhat, G., Danelljan, M., Van Gool, L., Timofte, R.: Deep burst super-resolution. In: Proceedings of the IEEE/CVF Conference on Computer Vision and Pattern Recognition, pp. 9209–9218 (2021)
5. Brooks, T., Mildenhall, B., Xue, T., Chen, J., Sharlet, D., Barron, J.T.: Unprocessing images for learned raw denoising. In: Proceedings of the IEEE/CVF Conference on Computer Vision and Pattern Recognition, pp. 11036–11045 (2019)
6. Caballero, J., et al.: Real-time video super-resolution with spatio-temporal networks and motion compensation. In: Proceedings of the IEEE Conference on Computer Vision and Pattern Recognition, pp. 4778–4787 (2017)
7. Cai, J., Gu, S., Timofte, R., Zhang, L.: NTIRE 2019 challenge on real image super-resolution: methods and results. In: Proceedings of the IEEE/CVF Conference on Computer Vision and Pattern Recognition Workshops (2019)
8. Cai, J., Zeng, H., Yong, H., Cao, Z., Zhang, L.: Toward real-world single image super-resolution: a new benchmark and a new model. In: Proceedings of the IEEE/CVF International Conference on Computer Vision, pp. 3086–3095 (2019)

9. Chan, K.C., Wang, X., Yu, K., Dong, C., Loy, C.C.: BasicVSR: the search for essential components in video super-resolution and beyond. In: Proceedings of the IEEE/CVF Conference on Computer Vision and Pattern Recognition, pp. 4947–4956 (2021)

10. Chan, K.C., Zhou, S., Xu, X., Loy, C.C.: BasicVSR++: improving video super-resolution with enhanced propagation and alignment. arXiv preprint arXiv:2104.13371 (2021)

11. Chan, K.C., Zhou, S., Xu, X., Loy, C.C.: Investigating tradeoffs in real-world video super-resolution. arXiv preprint arXiv:2111.12704 (2021)

12. Chen, C., Xiong, Z., Tian, X., Zha, Z.J., Wu, F.: Camera lens super-resolution. In: Proceedings of the IEEE/CVF Conference on Computer Vision and Pattern Recognition, pp. 1652–1660 (2019)

13. Chen, C., Chen, Q., Do, M.N., Koltun, V.: Seeing motion in the dark. In: Proceedings of the IEEE/CVF International Conference on Computer Vision, pp. 3185–3194 (2019)

14. Chen, C., Chen, Q., Xu, J., Koltun, V.: Learning to see in the dark. In: Proceedings of the IEEE Conference on Computer Vision and Pattern Recognition, pp. 3291–3300 (2018)

15. Dai, J., Qi, H., Xiong, Y., Li, Y., Zhang, G., Hu, H., Wei, Y.: Deformable convolutional networks. In: Proceedings of the IEEE International Conference on Computer Vision, pp. 764–773 (2017)

16. Fischler, M.A., Bolles, R.C.: Random sample consensus: a paradigm for model fitting with applications to image analysis and automated cartography. Commun. ACM **24**(6), 381–395 (1981)

17. Jiang, H., Zheng, Y.: Learning to see moving objects in the dark. In: Proceedings of the IEEE/CVF International Conference on Computer Vision, pp. 7324–7333 (2019)

18. Joze, H.R.V., et al.: ImagePairs: Realistic super resolution dataset via beam splitter camera rig. In: Proceedings of the IEEE/CVF Conference on Computer Vision and Pattern Recognition Workshops, pp. 518–519 (2020)

19. Kappeler, A., Yoo, S., Dai, Q., Katsaggelos, A.K.: Video super-resolution with convolutional neural networks. IEEE Trans. Comput. Imaging **2**(2), 109–122 (2016)

20. Lai, W.S., Huang, J.B., Ahuja, N., Yang, M.H.: Deep laplacian pyramid networks for fast and accurate super-resolution. In: Proceedings of the IEEE Conference on Computer Vision and Pattern Recognition, pp. 624–632 (2017)

21. Li, X., Wang, W., Hu, X., Yang, J.: Selective kernel networks. In: Proceedings of the IEEE/CVF Conference on Computer Vision and Pattern Recognition, pp. 510–519 (2019)

22. Liang, C.H., Chen, Y.A., Liu, Y.C., Hsu, W.: Raw image deblurring. IEEE Trans. Multimed. **24**, 61–72 (2020)

23. Liu, J., et al.: Learning raw image denoising with bayer pattern unification and bayer preserving augmentation. In: Proceedings of the IEEE/CVF Conference on Computer Vision and Pattern Recognition Workshops (2019)

24. Liu, X., Shi, K., Wang, Z., Chen, J.: Exploit camera raw data for video super-resolution via hidden Markov model inference. IEEE Trans. Image Process. **30**, 2127–2140 (2021)

25. Lowe, D.G.: Object recognition from local scale-invariant features. In: Proceedings of the seventh IEEE International Conference on Computer Vision, vol. 2, pp. 1150–1157. IEEE (1999)

26. Lugmayr, A., Danelljan, M., Timofte, R.: NTIRE 2020 challenge on real-world image super-resolution: Methods and results. In: Proceedings of the IEEE/CVF Conference on Computer Vision and Pattern Recognition Workshops, pp. 494–495 (2020)
27. Luo, Z., et al.: EBSR: feature enhanced burst super-resolution with deformable alignment. In: Proceedings of the IEEE/CVF Conference on Computer Vision and Pattern Recognition, pp. 471–478 (2021)
28. Nah, S., et al.: NTIRE 2019 challenge on video deblurring and super-resolution: Dataset and study. In: Proceedings of the IEEE/CVF Conference on Computer Vision and Pattern Recognition Workshops (2019)
29. Niu, B., et al.: Single image super-resolution via a holistic attention network. In: Vedaldi, A., Bischof, H., Brox, T., Frahm, J.-M. (eds.) ECCV 2020. LNCS, vol. 12357, pp. 191–207. Springer, Cham (2020). https://doi.org/10.1007/978-3-030-58610-2_12
30. Shi, W., et al.: Real-time single image and video super-resolution using an efficient sub-pixel convolutional neural network. In: Proceedings of the IEEE Conference on Computer Vision and Pattern Recognition, pp. 1874–1883 (2016)
31. Tian, Y., Zhang, Y., Fu, Y., Xu, C.: TDAN: temporally-deformable alignment network for video super-resolution. In: Proceedings of the IEEE/CVF Conference on Computer Vision and Pattern Recognition, pp. 3360–3369 (2020)
32. Wang, X., Chan, K.C., Yu, K., Dong, C., Change Loy, C.: EDVR: video restoration with enhanced deformable convolutional networks. In: Proceedings of the IEEE/CVF Conference on Computer Vision and Pattern Recognition Workshops (2019)
33. Wang, Y., Huang, H., Xu, Q., Liu, J., Liu, Y., Wang, J.: Practical deep raw image denoising on mobile devices. In: Vedaldi, A., Bischof, H., Brox, T., Frahm, J.-M. (eds.) ECCV 2020. LNCS, vol. 12351, pp. 1–16. Springer, Cham (2020). https://doi.org/10.1007/978-3-030-58539-6_1
34. Weinzaepfel, P., Revaud, J., Harchaoui, Z., Schmid, C.: DeepFlow: large displacement optical flow with deep matching. In: Proceedings of the IEEE International Conference on Computer Vision, pp. 1385–1392 (2013)
35. Xu, X., Ma, Y., Sun, W.: Towards real scene super-resolution with raw images. In: Proceedings of the IEEE/CVF Conference on Computer Vision and Pattern Recognition, pp. 1723–1731 (2019)
36. Xue, T., Chen, B., Wu, J., Wei, D., Freeman, W.T.: Video enhancement with task-oriented flow. Int. J. Comput. Vision **127**(8), 1106–1125 (2019)
37. Yang, X., Xiang, W., Zeng, H., Zhang, L.: Real-world video super-resolution: A benchmark dataset and a decomposition based learning scheme. In: Proceedings of the IEEE/CVF International Conference on Computer Vision, pp. 4781–4790 (2021)
38. Yue, H., Cao, C., Liao, L., Chu, R., Yang, J.: Supervised raw video denoising with a benchmark dataset on dynamic scenes. In: Proceedings of the IEEE/CVF Conference on Computer Vision and Pattern Recognition, pp. 2301–2310 (2020)
39. Zhang, X., Chen, Q., Ng, R., Koltun, V.: Zoom to learn, learn to zoom. In: Proceedings of the IEEE/CVF Conference on Computer Vision and Pattern Recognition, pp. 3762–3770 (2019)
40. Zhang, Y., Li, K., Li, K., Wang, L., Zhong, B., Fu, Y.: Image super-resolution using very deep residual channel attention networks. In: Proceedings of the European conference on computer vision (ECCV), pp. 286–301 (2018)
41. Zhou, K., Li, W., Lu, L., Han, X., Lu, J.: Revisiting temporal alignment for video restoration. arXiv preprint arXiv:2111.15288 (2021)

Transform Your Smartphone into a DSLR Camera: Learning the ISP in the Wild

Ardhendu Shekhar Tripathi[1]([✉]), Martin Danelljan[1], Samarth Shukla[1],
Radu Timofte[1,2], and Luc Van Gool[1,3]

[1] ETH Zurich,Zürich, Switzerland
ardhenu-shekhar.tripathi@vision.ee.ethz.ch
[2] University of Wurzburg, Würzburg, Germany
[3] KU Leuven, Leuven, Belgium

Abstract. We propose a trainable Image Signal Processing (ISP) framework that produces DSLR quality images given RAW images captured by a smartphone. To address the color misalignments between training image pairs, we employ a color-conditional ISP network and optimize a novel parametric color mapping between each input RAW and reference DSLR image. During inference, we predict the target color image by designing a color prediction network with efficient Global Context Transformer modules. The latter effectively leverage global information to learn consistent color and tone mappings. We further propose a robust masked aligned loss to identify and discard regions with inaccurate motion estimation during training. Lastly, we introduce the ISP in the Wild (ISPW) dataset, consisting of weakly paired phone RAW and DSLR sRGB images. We extensively evaluate our method, setting a new state-of-the-art on two datasets. The code is available at https://github.com/4rdhendu/TransformPhone2DSLR.

Keywords: Color conditional ISP · Efficient global attention · Learning in the wild · Mate30Canon dataset

1 Introduction

An Image Signal Processing (ISP) pipeline is characterized by a sequence of low-level vision operations that are performed to convert RAW data from the camera sensor to sRGB images. Each camera has an inherent ISP that is implemented on the device through hand-designed operations. With the advent of mobile photography, smartphones have become the primary source of photo capture due to their portability. However, their strict size constraints enforces small sensor sizes and compact lenses, which inevitably leads to higher sensor noise compared to

Supplementary Information The online version contains supplementary material available at https://doi.org/10.1007/978-3-031-20068-7_36.

© The Author(s), under exclusive license to Springer Nature Switzerland AG 2022
S. Avidan et al. (Eds.): ECCV 2022, LNCS 13666, pp. 625–641, 2022.
https://doi.org/10.1007/978-3-031-20068-7_36

(a) Phone RAW   (b) LiteISP-Net [24].   (c) Ours   (d) DSLR sRGB

Fig. 1. Our learnable ISP generates a DSLR quality sRGB image from RAW data captured by a smartphone camera. Our approach recovers rich details and produces colors that are more consistent with the DSLR sRGB ground-truth, compared to LiteISPNet (best performing competing method). Shown are the full resolution results on our ISP in the Wild (ISPW) dataset. Best viewed with zoom.

DSLR cameras. In this work, we therefore strive towards mitigating the hardware constraints in mobile photography by designing a learnable alternative to the ISP pipeline, utilizing DSLR quality sRGB images as reference.

Compared to standard image enhancement/restoration tasks, learning the ISP mapping introduces new fundamental challenges, which require careful attention. In the paired learning setting, a primary issue is that the color mapping between the input RAW image and the DSLR sRGB image depends on partially unobserved factors, such as camera parameters and the environmental conditions. Further, the image pairs for training, each consisting of a smartphone RAW and a DSLR sRGB, inevitably contain substantial spatial misalignment that greatly complicate the learning. Despite recent efforts [4,8,24], these issues remain central in the strive towards a fully learning-based ISP solution.

In this work, we propose a learnable ISP framework that can be effectively trained *in the wild*, using only weakly paired DSLR reference images with unknown and varying color and spatial misalignments. Our approach is composed of an ISP network that maps the input phone RAW to a DSLR quality output. Contrary to much previous works, we further condition the network on a target color image. This allows our ISP network to fully focus on the denoising and demosaicing tasks, without having to guess the unknown color transformation. To allow the target color image to be used during training, we propose a flexible and efficient parametric color mapping. Our color mapping between the input RAW and output DSLR sRGB image is individually optimized for every training image pair. The resulting mapping is then applied to the input RAW image to generate the target color image for conditioning. Importantly, this approach effectively mitigates information leakage from the target ground truth into the network, while achieving a faithful color transformation.

In order to achieve the target color image during inference, we further propose a dedicated target DSLR color prediction network, which solely takes the RAW phone image as input. To predict an accurate target color image, exploiting both local and global cues in an image is essential. While local information capture high-frequency details, global information is important in order to achieve a globally consistent and realistic color mapping across the entire image. We achieve the latter by designing an efficient Global Context Transformer block, which aggregates global color information into a compact latent array through cross-attention operations. This both alleviates the quadratic complexity of standard transformer modules, and importantly enables a variable input size. Finally, we address the problem of misaligned ground-truth by introducing a robust masked aligned objective for training our ISP framework.

To aid in extensive benchmarking and evaluation of RAW-to-sRGB mapping approaches for weakly paired data, we introduce the ISP in the Wild (ISPW) dataset. This dataset comprises of pairs of RAW sensor data from a recent smartphone camera and sRGB images taken from a high-end DSLR camera. Our dataset consists of 197 captured 10+ MegaPixel image pairs, resulting in over 35,000 crops of size 320 × 320 for training, validation, and test. We perform extensive ablative and state-of-the-art experiments on the Zurich RAW-to-RGB (ZRR) dataset [8] and our ISPW dataset. Our approach outperforms all previous approaches by a significant margin, setting a new state-of-the-art on both datasets. Example visual results are provided in Fig. 1.**Contributions:** Our main contributions are summarized as: **(i)** We propose a color conditional trainable ISP in the wild. **(ii)** We propose a color prediction network that integrates a global-context transformer module for efficient and globally coherent prediction of the target colors. **(iii)** We condition on color information from the reference image during training by introducing a flexible parametric color mapping, which is efficiently optimized for a single RAW-sRGB training pair. **(iv)** We employ a loss masking strategy for robust learning under alignment errors. **(v)** We introduce the ISPW dataset for learning the camera ISP in the wild.

2   Related Work

Despite the successes of deep-learning for low-level vision tasks, its application to camera ISP in the wild has been much less explored. Among the existing methods, CycleISP [22] and Invertible-ISP [21] propose a full camera imaging pipeline in the forward and reverse directions. These methods learn the ISP in a well aligned setting, where the RAW-sRGB training pairs originate from the same device. For RAW-to-sRGB mapping in the wild, the goal of the AIM 2020 challenge [8] on learned image processing pipeline was to map the original low-quality RAW images captured by a phone to a DSLR sRGB image. In particular, the CNN approaches inspired by the Multi-level Wavelet CNNs (MWCNN) [13] obtained the best results. Among the MWCNN-based methods both, MW-ISPNet [8] and AWNet [4] employ different variations of a U-Net for generation of appealing sRGB images.

More recently, LiteISPNet [24] propose an aligned loss by explicitly calculating the optical flow between the predicted DSLR image and the ground truth.

The idea of the aligned loss using optical flow in case of misaligned data was first used in DeepBurstSR [2] for burst super-resolution. Prior to DeepBurstSR, other efforts to handle misaligned data include a contextual bilateral loss (CoBi) [23] or primarily relying on a deep perceptual loss function, as in MW-ISPNet [8] and AWNet [4].

Another bottleneck for the field has been the dearth of datasets for camera ISP learning and benchmarking. The datasets MIT5K [3], DND [16], SIDD [1] and Zoom-to-Learn [23] capture several images from the same device under different settings. Moreover, [1,3,16] collect images in very controlled settings, where accurate alignment is possible. They are therefore unfit for designing approaches for ISP in the wild. Further, DPED [7] provides RGB images from different devices but does not contain RAW images and thus cannot be used for our task of designing and training the full ISP pipeline. In contrast, we aim to learn the ISP from a constrained device, i.e. smartphone, using high-quality DSLR images. The BurstSR dataset [2] is designed for the burst super-resolution task. Most related is the ZRR dataset [8]. Our ISPW dataset contains RAW images collected via a more modern smartphone. Additionally, our ISPW dataset contains important meta information, such as the ISO and exposure settings, that can further be exploited by the community for controllable and conditional learning of the RAW-to-sRGB mapping for weakly paired data.

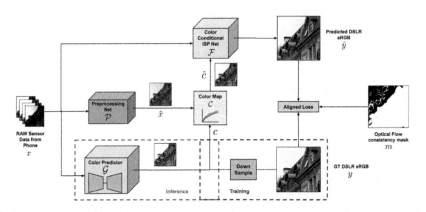

Fig. 2. An Overview of our learnable ISP framework: We learn a color conditional framework $\mathcal{F}(x, \hat{c})$ for RAW-to-sRGB mapping in the wild (Sect. 3.1). The estimated target color image $\hat{c}$ is achieved by our color mapping $\hat{c} = \mathcal{C}(x, c)$ (Sect. 3.3), which maps the raw input x to the color space of c. During training c is given by the downsampled ground truth. During inference, the DSLR-quality color content is predicted by the dedicated global attention based color prediction network $\mathcal{G}(x)$, using only the raw image x as input (Sect. 3.2). Finally, for robust learning of the ISP in the presence of even substantial misalignments (see Fig. 1), we propose a masked aligned loss (Sect. 3.4), which is robust to errors in the computed optical flow.

3   Method

In this work, we strive towards a fully deep learning based ISP module, which predicts a high-quality sRGB image $y \in \mathbb{R}^{3 \times H \times W}$ given the RAW image $x \in \mathbb{R}^{4 \times \frac{H}{2} \times \frac{W}{2}}$ captured by a mobile phone camera. Specifically, our aim is to learn such a module from a set of weakly paired training samples $\{(x^k, y^k)\}_k$. Our approach is illustrated in Fig. 2. It is comprised of a color conditional restoration network $\mathcal{F}(x, \hat{c})$ (Sect. 3.1). The color information $\hat{c}$ is provided by a dedicated color prediction network $\mathcal{G}(x)$ during inference (Sect. 3.2) and by the ground truth DSLR sRGB during training. To avoid the network from cheating during training, we propose a color mapping approach (Sect. 3.3) that maps the RAW sensor data to the target DSLR sRGB. During inference, our color mapping module works as a regularizer for our color predictor network in case of spurious inaccurate local colors predicted. Further, there also exists a spatial misalignment between the noisy mobile sensor data and the target DSLR sRGB image. To handle misalignment between the RAW-sRGB pairs, we propose a robust masked aligned loss (Sect. 3.4) that also takes into account the inaccuracies that are introduced during the alignment operation.

3.1   ISP Network

As motivated in Sect. 1, there exists an unknown color mapping between the input x^k and the target y^k, which further varies between each capture (x^k, y^k) due to changes in the parameters and environment. Modelling the ISP pipeline in the wild as a single feed-forward network $y = \mathcal{F}(x)$ can therefore prove detrimental to the learning of an accurate RAW-to-sRGB mapping as no fixed global color mapping exists. In order to learn effectively the RAW-to-sRGB mapping in these conditions, we propose a network $y = \mathcal{F}(x, \hat{c})$ that is conditioned on the desired output color information $\hat{c}$. During training, the color information is extracted from the RAW-sRGB pair using a flexible parametric formulation, which is detailed in Sect. 3.3. This allows us to capture a rich color mapping model from a single training pair (x^k, y^k), while preventing the network $\mathcal{F}$ to cheat. Additionally, our dedicated RAW pre-processing network discussed in Sect. 3.3 mitigates the ill-effects that noise in the RAW sensor data has on our color mapping estimation module. During inference, the color information $\hat{c}$ is predicted by a dedicated color predictor network $\mathcal{G}(x)$ (Sect. 3.2) and the color mapping module (Sect. 3.3). Compared to a handcrafted ISP pipeline, demosaicing, denoising, and detail enhancement is performed by our ISP net, while color correction, gamma, and tone is handled by the color prediction network (Sect. 3.2).

3.2   Color Prediction

In this section, we propose a low-resolution reference color prediction network $c = \mathcal{G}(x)$. This network aims to predict a low-resolution image c with the color content and dynamic range of the target DSLR camera. It is then the task of our

ISP network $\mathcal{F}$, to predict a detailed high-resolution image, conditioned on this color information. The measured colors and intensities depend on the camera parameters during capture, along with various other environmental factors, such as the properties of the illuminants in the scene. These conditions vary on a capture to capture basis. Hence, a simple feedforward network fails to capture the DSLR sRGB color accurately.

Color Prediction Network: To circumvent this drawback of feed-forward nets, we design an encoder-decoder based color prediction network (Fig. 3a).

$$c = \mathcal{G}(x) = D_{\text{DSLR}}\big(E_{\text{phone}}(x)\big). \tag{1}$$

Here, D_{DSLR} is the DSLR decoding network that predicts a low resolution target sRGB color. Predicting the target sRGB colors in low resolution makes the learning easier and leads to a faster convergence. We employ a U-Net inspired architecture (Fig. 3a) for our encoder-decoder. This is because U-Net [17] effectively expands the receptive field by integrating pooling operations and exploiting contextual information at different scales using skip connections. Further, a U-Net is relatively insensitive to small misalignments in the image due to the low-resolution of core features, achieved by successive pooling operations. Our U-Net encoder E_{phone} exploits local and global cues by integrating a successive convolutional layer and an efficient global context transformer.

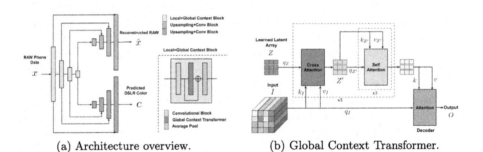

(a) Architecture overview.   (b) Global Context Transformer.

Fig. 3. Illustration of the full color prediction network (a) with its global context transformer module (b).

Global Context Transformer. For target color prediction, capturing a global context is pivotal since color in one patch of the image can be related to the color in a spatially distant patch of the same image. Hence, attending to different patches in the image may prove beneficial for predicting an accurate target color. Using standard transformers [19] for global attention is a viable option. However, its quadratic computational complexity w.r.t. the number of patches in the image/feature map makes it unsuitable for our color prediction network. Furthermore, our network needs to be able to process an image of arbitrary resolution, which brings further challenges to a standard transformer architecture.

We therefore design our Global Context Transformer block by taking inspiration from the Perceiver [9,10] architecture. Specifically, we perform cross attention operations between an auxiliary latent space $Z' \in \mathbb{R}^{K \times C}$ and the input feature map $I_l \in \mathbb{H}_l \times \mathbb{W}_l \times \mathbb{D}_l$, followed by self attention layers on Z'. Here, I_l is extracted from the U-Net encoder at level l. The latent space contains K tokens of dimension C, as is initialized by a learned constant array $Z \in \mathbb{R}^{K \times C}$. The majority of the computation thus happens on Z'. This reduces the complexity of the attention operations from quadratic to linear in the input size, and crucially enables a variable input image size.

Figure 3b details the architecture of our global context block. It comprises multiple cross and self-attention layers on the fixed-size auxiliary latent array Z'. Cross-attention has a complexity of $O(NK) = O(N)$ (here $N = \mathbb{H}_l \times \mathbb{W}_l$) since $K \ll N$ is a small constant. Moreover, self-attention is only performed on Z, leading to a complexity of $O(K^2) = O(1)$. Hence, decoupling the network depth from the input size. Through the global attention operations, the learned latent arrays Z' can encode color transformations. The final decoder module then maps information encapsulated in Z' to the output array O through cross attention with the input query q_I. We integrate our Global Context Transformer block in the contracting path of our color prediction module after each convolutional block (Fig. 3a). This aids in exploiting local cues as well as global cues while remaining computationally efficient.

Reconstruction Branch. In addition to the DSLR specific decoder, we also employ a decoder D_{phone} for reconstructing the RAW input x such that $\hat{x} = D_{\mathrm{phone}}(E_{\mathrm{phone}}(x))$ (Fig. 3a). Employing a RAW reconstruction decoder equips our color prediction framework to learn an optimal phone-specific embedding $E_{\mathrm{phone}}(x)$ that encodes various meta-information that was not provided with the RAW data for reconstructing the RAW input x. Hence, intuitively our DSLR-specific decoder learns a mapping from the phone ISP to the DSLR ISP.

3.3 Color Mapping Module

In this section we introduce our approach for estimating the color transformation between the RAW input x and a target color sRGB image c. For this, we design a module $\hat{c} = C(x, c)$ that estimates a color mapping between a single pair (x, c), and applies it to x. The result represents the RAW image x transformed according to the target color space in c. Our approach is particularly important during training, when c is derived from the ground-truth image y through downsampling and alignment. It supplies our ISP network, conditioned on $\hat{c}$, with the correct color transformation between the pair (x, y) while preventing information leakage from the ground-truth y. During inference, C works as a regularizer for our color predictor network (1) for spurious inaccurate local colors predicted.

Pre-processing Network: Real world training image pairs, apart from being weakly paired in terms of alignment, pose many other challenges. In particular, the RAW sensor data from the phone is prone to noise due to the limited sensor size, along with other interference from the environment. The noise may be signal-dependent or signal-independent. A noisy source image x inhibits the performance of the color mapping significantly. Hence, removing noise from the RAW data is pivotal. In this direction, we design a pre-processing module for removing noise from the RAW data, thereby aiding our color mapping module.

Our RAW pre-processing network $\mathcal{P}$ aims to retrieve the clean source image $\tilde{x}$ given a noisy RAW x,

$$\mathcal{P}(x) := \tilde{x} = x' - \eta(x'), \text{ where } x' = \Gamma(x). \tag{2}$$

Here, η is our noise estimation net and is implemented as a CNN with residual connections. For our framework, x' is a processed version of the mobile RAW sensor data x. We obtain x' by neglecting one of the green channels in x and normalizing the resulting 3-channel image between $[0, 1]$ uniformly. To further reduce the non-linearities in the color mapping, we apply a constant approximate gamma correction to obtain the final processed image x'. The processing operation $\Gamma(\cdot)$ is detailed in the supplementary.

Color Mapping: Formulating our color mapping scheme, we define a set of $\mathcal{B}$ equally spaced bins between the range of values in each channel of the source image $\tilde{x}$ (Eq. 2). The bth bin centroid for color channel j is denoted as k_b^j. The goal is to map the image $\tilde{x}$ to the target color image as,

$$\hat{c}_i^j = \sum_{b=1}^{\mathcal{B}} \hat{w}_{ib}^j (A_b^j \tilde{x}_i + B_b^j), \tag{3}$$

using a learned affine transformation $A_b^j \tilde{x}_i + B_b^j$ for each bin b. Here, $A_b^j \in \mathbb{R}^{1 \times 3}$ and $B_b^j \in \mathbb{R}$ are the parameters of the affine map, while $\tilde{x}_i \in \mathbb{R}^3$ (Eq. 2) denotes the color values at pixel i after the pre-processing network. The result $\hat{c}_i^j$ is the mapped intensity at channel j and location i. The soft bin assignment weights in (3) are calculated as $\hat{w}_{ib}^j = \text{SoftMax}_b(-\|\tilde{x}_i^j - k_b^j\|^2 / T)$, where, T is a temperature parameter. Hence, our color mapping (3) can be seen as an attention mechanism, with the source image attending to the learned values through the bin centroids. The motivation of learning an affine transformation instead of a fixed numeric value for each bin centroid is providing each bin more expressive power leading to better color mapping even with less number of bins.

In (3), the parameters (A_b^j, B_b^j) of the affine mapping are learned using only a single pair $(\tilde{x}, c)$. This is performed by minimizing the following squared error to the target color value c_i^j,

$$A_b^j, B_b^j = \underset{A,B}{\text{argmin}} \sum_i w_{ib}^j \|A\tilde{x}_i + B - c_i^j\|_2^2. \tag{4}$$

Here, the weights $w_{ib}^j = \text{SoftMax}_i(-\|\tilde{x}_i^j - k_b^j\|^2 / T)$. These set of weights signify how much each target intensity affects the affine transformation learned for each bin centroid. The objective (4) corresponds to a linear least squares problem, which can efficiently be solved in closed form as detailed in the supplementary.

3.4   Learning the Camera ISP

The RAW-sRGB pairs taken from two different devices are misaligned. The reasons are the different fields of view for both the cameras, parallax, and small motion of objects in the scene. Misalignment in the RAW-sRGB pair makes training the ISP pipeline difficult. Trying to learn in such a setting produces blurry results and significant color shift (Fig. 4). Hence, a robust loss applicable to the weakly paired setting is pivotal. In this section, we introduce an aligned masked loss for robust learning in a weakly paired setting. We then introduce the objectives for our main ISP network, pre-processing network, and the color prediction network. Lastly, we provide training strategies and details.

Alignment. We calculate aligned losses for learning our color conditional RAW-to-sRGB network in the wild. For alignment, we use the PWC-net [18] for computing optical flow. We denote by $c_{x'} = \mathcal{W}(c, f(c, x'))$ the color image c aligned with respect to the processed RAW x' (Sect. 3.3). Here, $f(c, x')$ is the optical flow from the color image c to the processed RAW x'. While we found PWC-Net to be robust to substantial color transformations between the input images, we use the processed RAW x' as input as it has a much smaller difference in color and intensity to the reference color image c. Further, the loss masking discussed next aids in a more robust loss calculation for inaccurately aligned regions.

Loss Masking. Although, employing an aligned L_1-loss partially handles the misalignment problem for ISP learning in the wild, the flow estimation itself can introduce errors. In particular, optical flow is often inaccurate in the presence of repeating patterns, occlusions, and homogeneous regions. This leads to an incorrect training signal which degrades the quality of the ISP network. We therefore propose a mask for our loss by identifying regions where the optical flow is inaccurate. Inspired by [15], we use the forward-backward consistency constraint to filter out regions with inaccurate flow. The optical-flow consistency mask m is set to 1 where the following condition holds true, and otherwise to 0:

$$\left| f(x', y^{\downarrow}) + f(x'_{y^{\downarrow}}, x') \right|^2 < \alpha_1 \left(\left| f(x', y^{\downarrow}) \right|^2 + \left| f(x'_{y^{\downarrow}}, x') \right|^2 \right) + \alpha_2. \tag{5}$$

Here, x' is the processed RAW sensor data (Sect. 3.3). And, $y^{\downarrow}$ is the target sRGB image bilinearly downsampled by a factor of 2. And, $x'_{y^{\downarrow}}$ is x' aligned with $y^{\downarrow}$. Thus, the mask m aids in masking out inaccurately aligned regions.

ISP Network Loss: The masked target sRGB prediction loss is given by:

$$\hat{y} = \mathcal{F}(x, \hat{c}), \text{ where } \hat{c} = \mathcal{C}(\tilde{x}, c_{\tilde{x}})$$
$$L_{\text{pred}}(\hat{y}, y) = \| m^{\uparrow} \odot \left(y_{\hat{y}} - \hat{y} \right) \|_1. \tag{6}$$

Here, $y_{\hat{y}}$ is the target DSLR sRGB aligned w.r.t. the final predicted sRGB $\hat{y}$. We did not see a significant difference in performance when we align the predicted sRGB $\hat{y}$ w.r.t. the target DSLR sRGB for our loss calculation (see supplementary). This choice further circumvents the need of differentiating through the warping process. During training, the color image $c = y^{\downarrow}$ is the 2× downsampled ground truth sRGB. Further, $c_{\tilde{x}}$ is the color image c aligned with $\tilde{x}$ (Eq. 2). Lastly, $m^{\uparrow}$ is the 2× upsampled mask m via nearest neighbour interpolation.

Pre-processing Network Loss: The pre-processing net (Sect. 3.3) aims at providing a source image that aids our learned parametric color mapping scheme (Sect. 3.3) and denoising the processed RAW x' (Sect. 3.3). Motivated by this, we design loss for our pre-processing net $\mathcal{P}$ as,

$$L_{\text{map}}(\mathcal{C}(\tilde{x}, c_{x'}), c_{x'}) = \|m \odot (\mathcal{C}(\tilde{x}, c_{x'}) - c_{x'})\|_1, \text{ and}$$
$$L_{\text{constraint}}(x', \tilde{x}) = \|b * x' - b * \tilde{x}\|_1. \tag{7}$$

Here, $\tilde{x}$ is the output of our Pre-processing Net (Eq. 2) and b is a predefined blurring kernel. The loss $L_{\text{constraint}}$ constrains $\mathcal{P}$ to keep the color of x'. The color image $c = y^\downarrow$ is the $2\times$ downsampled ground truth sRGB. And, $c_{x'}$ is the color image c aligned with x'. These losses aid the pre-processing network in not only denoising the RAW sensor data but also allows for the network to be flexible enough to learn a color space where the color mapping (Sect. 3.3) is optimal.

Color Prediction Network Loss: To train our target color prediction network (Sect. 3.2), we employ a color prediction loss on the predicted low resolution target color image $\hat{y}^{\text{clr}} = \mathcal{G}(x)$ and a reconstruction loss on the reconstructed RAW sensor data $\hat{x}$,

$$L_{\text{pred}}^{\text{clr}}(\hat{y}^{\text{clr}}, c_{x'}) = \left\|m \odot \left(\hat{y}^{\text{clr}} - c_{x'}\right)\right\|_1$$
$$L_{\text{reconstruct}}(\hat{x}, x) = \|x - \hat{x}\|_1 \tag{8}$$

Here, $c_{x'} = y_{x'}^\downarrow$ is the $2\times$ downsampled ground truth sRGB aligned with x'. Hence, $c_{x'}$ serves as the target color image for training our color prediction network in the loss $L_{\text{pred}}^{\text{clr}}$. The reconstruction loss $L_{\text{reconstruct}}$ further encourages the encoder $E_{\text{phone}}(x)$ to preserve important image details.

Training: Thanks to the independent objectives, we can train our color conditional ISP network $\mathcal{F}$ and the color prediction network $\mathcal{G}$ separately. This allows use of larger batch sizes and reduced training times significantly. A comparative study with the joint fine-tuning of both the networks is provided in the supplementary. The final training loss for $\mathcal{F}$ is given by (6) and (7). The loss for the color prediction net $\mathcal{G}$ is given by (8). Each batch for training both, $\mathcal{F}$ and $\mathcal{G}$ comprises 16 pairs of randomly sampled RAW phone images $x \in \mathbb{R}^{4\times80\times80}$ and DSLR sRGB images $y \in \mathbb{R}^{3\times160\times160}$. During training, we augment the data by applying random flips and 90 deg rotations. To increase the robustness of our color conditional ISP network $\mathcal{F}$, we employ color augmentations on the ground truth DSLR sRGB during training. Specifically, we randomly jitter the hue, saturation, brightness and contrast in a range $[-0.2, 0.2]$.

The blurring kernel b in (7) is a 9×9 Gaussian with the standard deviation in each of the dimension set to 2. The constants α_1 and α_2 for computing m are set to 0.01 and 0.5, respectively. The number of bins $\mathcal{B}$ in our color mapping 3.3 is set to 15 and the temperature parameter $T = (1/\mathcal{B})^2$. Finally, to handle vignetting (dark corners) that occurs in RAW sensor data, we append the RAW data with a pixel-wise function of 2D coordinate map for the inputs to our pre-processing net

$\mathcal{P}$ and the color prediction net $\mathcal{G}$. We use the ADAM algorithm [12] as optimizer with $\beta_1 = 0.9$ and $\beta_2 = 0.99$. The initial learning rate for training both our networks is set to $2e - 4$ which is halved at 50%, 75%, 90% and 95% of the total number of epochs respectively. The networks are trained separately for 100 epochs on a Nvidia V100 GPU. The training time for our $\mathcal{F}$ and $\mathcal{G}$ nets was 27 hours and 22 hours, respectively.

4 Dataset

We propose the ISP in the Wild (ISPW) dataset for learning the camera ISP in the wild. The ISPW dataset consists of a set of 197 high-resolution captures from a Canon 5D Mark IV DSLR camera (with a lens of focal length 24mm) and a Huawei Mate 30 Pro mobile phone. Each capture comprises of the RAW sensor data from the mobile phone ($4 \times 1368 \times 1824$) and 3 sRGB DSLR images ($3 \times 4480 \times 6720$) of the same scene taken at different exposure settings (EV values: -1, 0 and 1). All DSLR images were captured with an ISO of 100 for more detail and less noise. Further a small aperture of F18 was used for a large depth of field. The dataset was collected over several weeks in a variety of places and in various illumination and weather conditions to ensure diversity of samples. During the capture, both the devices were mounted on a tripod using a custom made rig to ensure no blur due to camera motion. Collection was focused on predominately static scenes in order to ease the alignment between the two cameras. However, small motion is inevitable in most settings, and thus need to be handled by our data processing and robust learning objectives. We split the ISPW dataset into 160, 17, and 20 high-resolution captures for training, validation, and test, respectively. We believe that it can serve as an important benchmarking and training set for RAW-to-sRGB mapping in the wild.

Data Processing: We describe the pre-processing pipeline for our ISPW data here. We consider the DSLR image taken at EV value 0 as the target DSLR sRGB in this work. We first crop out the matching field of view from the phone and the DSLR high-resolution captures using SIFT [14] and RANSAC [5]. Crops of size 320×320 are then extracted in a sliding manner (stride of 160) from both, the DSLR sRGB and the phone sRGB. Local alignment is performed by estimating the homography between two crops. The corresponding 4-channel RAW crop from the phone of size 160×160 is extracted using the coordinates of the 320×320 phone sRGB crop and paired with the DSLR sRGB crop. To filter out crops with extreme scene mismatch, we discard the pairs which have a normalized cross-correlation of less than 0.5 between them.

5 Experiments

Here, we perform extensive experiments to validate our approach. We evaluate our approach on the test sets of the ZRR dataset [8] and ISPW datasets (Sect. 4). The methods are compared in terms of the widely used PSNR and SSIM [20] metrics. For a fair comparison, we align the ground truth DSLR sRGB with the phone RAW for the computation of PSNR and SSIM metrics. See supplementary for more qualitative and quantitative results,

5.1   Ablative Analysis of the Color Mapping

Here, we study the effectiveness of our color mapping scheme (Sect. 3.3) compared to other alternatives. The results on the ZRR dataset are reported in Table 1.

NoColorPred: As a baseline for evaluating our color mapping scheme, we train $\mathcal{F}(x, \hat{c})$ with the color information $\hat{c}$ set to 0. This implies a simple feed-forward network setting. We do not include the color mapping module $\mathcal{C}$ in this version. NoColorPred achieves a PSNR of 21.27 dB and a SSIM of 0.844. This variation learns average and dull colors and is not able to account for various factors on which the color in an image depends. **ColorBlur:** Next, as in CycleISP [22], we train $\mathcal{F}(x, \hat{c})$ where the target color $\hat{c} = z * y_{x'}^{\downarrow}$ is achieved by blurring the 2x downsampled target DSLR sRGB (aligned with x') with a Gaussian kernel z during training. At inference, we apply the same blurring to our predicted target color $\hat{c} = z * \mathcal{G}(x)$. As in NoColorPred, we do not include the color mapping module $\mathcal{C}$ in this version. ColorBlur achieves a gain of 2.16 dB in PSNR over NoColorPred. Although being better than NoColorPred, ColorBlur fails to capture the sudden changes of color in the image contour.

We further evaluate different versions of the color mapping scheme $\mathcal{C}$. **LinearMap:** First, we consider learning a 3×3 global color correction matrix between the processed RAW x' and the color c for each training pair, as in [2]. LinearMap produces inaccurately colored images specially in terms of the contrast, since it cannot represent more complex color transformations and tone curves.

Table 1. Ablative study of our color mapping scheme (Sect. 3.3) on the ZRR dataset.

	NoColorPred	ColorBlur	LinearMap	ConstValMap	AffineMapIndep	AffineMapDep	+Preprocess
PSNR↑	21.27	23.43	21.89	22.65	23.78	24.41	25.24
SSIM↑	0.844	0.857	0.832	0.859	0.861	0.873	0.879

Table 2. Ablative study of our loss (Sect. 3.4) on the ZRR dataset.

	NoAlign	+AlignedLoss	+Mask
PSNR↑	20.56	24.62	25.24
SSIM↑	0.785	0.867	0.879

Table 3. Ablative study of our color prediction network (Sect. 3.2) on the ZRR dataset

	NoColorPred	+U-Net	+Reconstruct	+Global Context
PSNR ↑	21.27	24.09	24.43	25.24
SSIM ↑	0.844	0.865	0.871	0.879

ConstValMap: Here, we use a simplified version of our approach (Sect. 3.3) as $\mathcal{C}$ by using fixed values for each bin instead of the affine mapping learned in Sect. 3.3. Channel dependence is not exploited in this version for calculating the values. This achieves a substantial improvement of 0.76 dB in PSNR over LinearMap. Thus, proving the utility of using a more flexible color mapping formulation. **AffineMapIndep:** Setting $\mathcal{C}$ to our color mapping scheme (Sect. 3.3) but without any channel dependence boosts the PSNR by a further 1.13 dB over ConstValMap. Increasing the expressive power of each bin by predicting an affine transform instead of a constant is thus pivotal for better performance of our color conditional RAW-to-sRGB mapping. **AffineMapDep:** Here, $\mathcal{C}$ is set to our full formulation discussed in Sect. 3.3. Thus, exploiting channel dependence in $\mathcal{C}$ is beneficial as quantified by the PSNR increase of 0.63 dB w.r.t. AffineMapIndep. **+Preprocess:** Finally, we add our pre-processing network $\mathcal{P}$ (Sect. 3.3) to the AffineMapDep version. This gives an impressive boost of 0.83 dB in PSNR over AffineMapDep hence, validating the need to remove noise and pre-process the phone RAW before color mapping.

5.2 Ablative Study of the Training Loss

Here, we study the effect of our masked aligned loss (Sect. 3.4). The results on the ZRR dataset are reported in Table 2.

NoAlign: As a baseline for ablating our loss, we employ an unaligned L_1-loss for all our objectives (Eq. (6), (7) and (8)). The mask m is set to 1 at all locations. **+AlignedLoss** Further, employing alignment before the loss calculation leads to more crisp predictions, giving a large improvement of 4.06 dB in PSNR and a relative gain of 10.4% in SSIM. Although improving the results, the prediction lacks detail and is characterized by a noticeable color shift. This is due to the inaccuracies in optical flow computations that may occur due to occlusions and homogenous regions. **+Mask** Finally, our masking strategy using Eq. (5) leads to a significant gain of 0.62 dB in PSNR. (+Mask) produces a more detailed output with colors consistent with the target DSLR sRGB. This shows that accurate supervision using our masked loss during training is beneficial to our DSLR sRGB restoration network.

5.3 Ablative Study of the Color Prediction Network

Next, we study the effect of our color prediction module (Sect. 3.2). The results on the ZRR dataset are reported in Table 3.

NoColorPred: This is the same baseline as in Sect. 5.1, which employs no explicit color prediction or conditioning. **U-Net:** Integrating a low resolution U-Net based color predictor without the reconstruction branch or global context transformer leads to an impressive gain of 2.82 dB over NoColorPred. This demonstrates the effectiveness of conditioning $\mathcal{F}$ on the color image for robust ISP learning and prediction. **+Reconstruct:** Further, integrating a reconstruction branch in our color predictor helps $\mathcal{G}(x)$ in learning a more informative encoding $E_{\text{phone}}(x)$, leading to a 0.34 dB increase in PSNR. Thus, +Reconstruct facilitates our encoder in the color predictor module to encapsulate all the information into the encoding that is necessary for accurate color prediction. **+GlobalContext:** Finally, integrating the global context transformer (Sect. 3.2) in our U-Net color predictor $\mathcal{G}(x)$ provides our color conditional ISP net $\mathcal{F}(x, \hat{c})$ with a substantial gain of 0.81 dB. This clearly demonstrates the importance of exploiting global information in predicting coherent colors.

(a) MWISP- (b) AWNet (c) LiteISP- (d) Ours (e) OursFast (f) GT
Net   Net

Fig. 4. Visual results for state-of-the-art comparison on our ISPW dataset (first row) and the ZRR dataset (second row). Best viewed with zoom.

5.4 State-of-the-Art Comparison

In this section, we compare our color conditional ISP network with state-of-the-art methods for RAW-to-sRGB mapping, namely PyNet [6], MW-ISPNet [8], AWNet [4] and LiteISPNet [24]. We evaluate on the test splits of the ZRR dataset [8] and our ISPW dataset (Sect. 4). Among these methods, MW-ISPNet, AWNet and LiteISPNet employ discrete wavelet transforms for incorporating global context. To deal with misalignments, MW-ISPNet, AWNet and PyNet incorporate the VGG perceptual loss [11], while LiteISPNet employs an aligned loss using optical flow computation [18].

Table 4. State-of-the-art comparison on the ZRR [8] and our ISPW datasets.

	#Params(M)↓	ZRR dataset			ISPW dataset		
		PSNR↑	SSIM↑	Time(ms)↓	PSNR↑	SSIM↑	Time(ms)↓
PyNet [6]	47.6	22.73	0.845	62.7	–	–	–
MW-ISPNet [8]	29.2	23.13	0.849	111.3	22.43	0.746	99.4
AWNet [4]	52.2	23.52	0.855	63.4	23.10	0.787	50.8
LiteISPNet [24]	11.9	23.81	0.873	**23.3**	23.51	0.809	**17.2**
Ours	35.2	25.24	0.879	67.6	25.05	0.821	55.7
OursFast	**13.4**	**24.70**	**0.876**	18.2	**24.57**	**0.815**	13.8

Table 4 lists the quantitative results on the test split of the ZRR dataset that contains 1203 RAW-sRGB crop pairs of size 448 × 448. Our method outperforms all previous approaches by a significant margin, achieving a gain of 1.43 dB PSNR compared to the second best method: the very recent LiteISPNet. We then run the best performing methods on the test split of our ISPW dataset, that contains 3023 RAW-sRGB crop pairs of size 320 × 320. For a fair comparison, all the methods were retrained on our dataset using apt train settings. The performance gap between our color conditional ISP network and other methods is more stark for the ISPW dataset, with our approach achieving a PSNR 1.54 dB higher than the second best LiteISPNet. Efficiency is crucial for deploying the model on a smartphone. We therefore evaluate a *faster and lighter* version of our approach. In OursFast, we omit the color mapping regularization C after the color prediction network. We further reduce the number of parameters by $\sim 3\times$, by reducing the depth of all three networks and dimensionality of the Global Context Block. OursFast outperforms LiteISPNet by 1.06dB while being 20.2% faster on the ISPW dataset. Further details on the model complexity and execution times are given in the .

Figure 4 shows the visual results for our color conditional ISP compared to the top three performing methods. Compared to our approach, all the other three methods fail to capture the accurate color of the target DSLR sRGB. Moreover, the results for MW-ISPNet and AWNet are blurry due to their inability to handle misalignment well. On the other hand, although LiteISPNet employs an aligned loss, it fails to account for inconsistent flow computations hence leading to significant color shift and loss of detail. Conversely, our approach produces crisp DSLR-like sRGB predictions with accurate colors, thus proving the utility of our global attention based color predictor paired with our masked aligned loss. The blur and color shift effect is more intense for all other methods on our dataset that contains misaligned RAW-sRGB pairs. Finally, we calculate the average inference time per image for our method on both the datasets. We achieve an average per image inference times of 67.6 ms and 55.7 ms, respectively on the sRGB images of sizes 448×448 (ZRR dataset) and 320×320 (ISPW dataset).

6   Conclusion

We address the problem of mapping RAW sensor data from a phone to a high quality DSLR image by modelling it as a conditional ISP framework on the target color. To aid our color conditional ISP net during inference, we propose a novel encoder-decoder based color predictor that encapsulates an efficient global attention module. A flexible parametric color mapping scheme from RAW to the target color is integrated for a robust training and inference. Finally, we propose a masked aligned loss for filtering out regions with inconsistent optical flow during aligned loss calculations. We perform experiments on the ZRR dataset and our ISPW dataset, setting a new state-of-the-art on both the datasets.

Acknowledgement. This work was supported by the ETH Zürich Fund (OK), Huawei Technologies Oy (Finland) and Alexander von Humboldt Foundation.

References

1. Abdelhamed, A., Lin, S., Brown, M.S.: A high-quality denoising dataset for smartphone cameras. In: IEEE Conference on Computer Vision and Pattern Recognition (CVPR), June 2018

2. Bhat, G., Danelljan, M., Gool, L.V., Timofte, R.: Deep burst super-resolution. In: IEEE Conference on Computer Vision and Pattern Recognition, CVPR 2021, virtual, 19–25 June 2021. pp. 9209–9218. Computer Vision Foundation/IEEE (2021)

3. Bychkovsky, V., Paris, S., Chan, E., Durand, F.: Learning photographic global tonal adjustment with a database of input/output image pairs. In: The Twenty-Fourth IEEE Conference on Computer Vision and Pattern Recognition (2011)

4. Dai, L., Liu, X., Li, C., Chen, J.: AWNet: attentive wavelet network for image ISP. In: Bartoli, A., Fusiello, A. (eds.) ECCV 2020. LNCS, vol. 12537, pp. 185–201. Springer, Cham (2020). https://doi.org/10.1007/978-3-030-67070-2_11

5. Fischler, M.A., Bolles, R.C.: Random sample consensus: a paradigm for model fitting with applications to image analysis and automated cartography. Commun. ACM **24**(6), 381–395 (1981). https://doi.org/10.1145/358669.358692, http://doi.acm.org/10.1145/358669.358692

6. Ignatov, A., Gool, L.V., Timofte, R.: Replacing mobile camera ISP with a single deep learning model. In: 2020 IEEE/CVF Conference on Computer Vision and Pattern Recognition, CVPR Workshops 2020, Seattle, WA, USA, 14–19 June 2020, pp. 2275–2285. Computer Vision Foundation/IEEE (2020). https://doi.org/10.1109/CVPRW50498.2020.00276

7. Ignatov, A., Kobyshev, N., Timofte, R., Vanhoey, K., Van Gool, L.: Dslr-quality photos on mobile devices with deep convolutional networks. In: Proceedings of the IEEE International Conference on Computer Vision, pp. 3277–3285 (2017)

8. Ignatov, A., et al.: AIM 2020 challenge on learned image signal processing pipeline. In: Bartoli, A., Fusiello, A. (eds.) ECCV 2020. LNCS, vol. 12537, pp. 152–170. Springer, Cham (2020). https://doi.org/10.1007/978-3-030-67070-2_9

9. Jaegle, A., et al.: Perceiver IO: a general architecture for structured inputs & outputs. CoRR abs/2107.14795 (2021). http://arxiv.org/abs/2107.14795

10. Jaegle, A., Gimeno, F., Brock, A., Zisserman, A., Vinyals, O., Carreira, J.: Perceiver: general perception with iterative attention. CoRR abs/2103.03206 (2021). http://arxiv.org/abs/2103.03206

11. Johnson, J., Alahi, A., Fei-Fei, L.: Perceptual losses for real-time style transfer and super-resolution. In: Leibe, B., Matas, J., Sebe, N., Welling, M. (eds.) ECCV 2016. LNCS, vol. 9906, pp. 694–711. Springer, Cham (2016). https://doi.org/10.1007/978-3-319-46475-6_43

12. Kingma, D.P., Ba, J.: Adam: a method for stochastic optimization. In: Bengio, Y., LeCun, Y. (eds.) 3rd International Conference on Learning Representations, ICLR 2015, San Diego, CA, USA, 7–9 May 015, Conference Track Proceedings (2015). http://arxiv.org/abs/1412.6980

13. Liu, P., Zhang, H., Lian, W., Zuo, W.: Multi-level wavelet convolutional neural networks. IEEE Access **7**, 74973–74985 (2019)

14. Lowe, D.G.: Object recognition from local scale-invariant features. In: Proceedings of the International Conference on Computer Vision, Kerkyra, Corfu, Greece, September 20–25, 1999. pp. 1150–1157. IEEE Computer Society (1999). DOI: https://doi.org/10.1109/ICCV.1999.790410,http://doi.org/10.1109/ICCV.1999.790410

15. Meister, S., Hur, J., Roth, S.: Unflow: Unsupervised learning of optical flow with a bidirectional census loss. In: McIlraith, S.A., Weinberger, K.Q. (eds.) Proceedings of the Thirty-Second AAAI Conference on Artificial Intelligence, (AAAI-18), the 30th innovative Applications of Artificial Intelligence (IAAI-18), and the 8th AAAI Symposium on Educational Advances in Artificial Intelligence (EAAI-18), New Orleans, Louisiana, USA, February 2–7, 2018. pp. 7251–7259. AAAI Press (2018), www.aaai.org/ocs/index.php/AAAI/AAAI18/paper/view/16502

16. Plotz, T., Roth, S.: Benchmarking denoising algorithms with real photographs. In: Proceedings of the IEEE conference on computer vision and pattern recognition. pp. 1586–1595 (2017)

17. Ronneberger, O., Fischer, P., Brox, T.: U-net: Convolutional networks for biomedical image segmentation. In: Navab, N., Hornegger, J., III, W.M.W., Frangi, A.F. (eds.) Medical Image Computing and Computer-Assisted Intervention - MICCAI 2015–18th International Conference Munich, Germany, October 5–9, 2015, Proceedings, Part III. Lecture Notes in Computer Science, vol. 9351, pp. 234–241. Springer (2015). https://doi.org/10.1007/978-3-319-24574-4_28,http://doi.org/10.1007/978-3-319-24574-4_28

18. Sun, D., Yang, X., Liu, M., Kautz, J.: Pwc-net: Cnns for optical flow using pyramid, warping, and cost volume. CoRR abs/1709.02371 (2017), http://arxiv.org/abs/1709.02371

19. Vaswani, A., Shazeer, N., Parmar, N., Uszkoreit, J., Jones, L., Gomez, A.N., Kaiser, L., Polosukhin, I.: Attention is all you need. In: Guyon, I., von Luxburg, U., Bengio, S., Wallach, H.M., Fergus, R., Vishwanathan, S.V.N., Garnett, R. (eds.) Advances in Neural Information Processing Systems 30: Annual Conference on Neural Information Processing Systems 2017, December 4–9, 2017, Long Beach, CA, USA. pp. 5998–6008 (2017)

20. Wang, Z., Bovik, A.C., Sheikh, H.R., Simoncelli, E.P.: Image quality assessment: from error visibility to structural similarity. IEEE Trans. Image Process. **13**(4), 600–612 (2004), 10.1109/TIP.2003.819861, http://doi.org/10.1109/TIP.2003.819861

21. Xing, Y., Qian, Z., Chen, Q.: Invertible image signal processing. In: IEEE Conference on Computer Vision and Pattern Recognition, CVPR 2021, virtual, June 19–25, 2021. pp. 6287–6296. Computer Vision Foundation / IEEE (2021)

22. Zamir, S.W., Arora, A., Khan, S.H., Hayat, M., Khan, F.S., Yang, M., Shao, L.: Cycleisp: Real image restoration via improved data synthesis. In: 2020 IEEE/CVF Conference on Computer Vision and Pattern Recognition, CVPR 2020, Seattle, WA, USA, June 13–19, 2020. pp. 2693–2702. Computer Vision Foundation / IEEE (2020). DOI: 10.1109/CVPR42600.2020.00277

23. Zhang, X., Chen, Q., Ng, R., Koltun, V.: Zoom to learn, learn to zoom. In: IEEE Conference on Computer Vision and Pattern Recognition, CVPR 2019, Long Beach, CA, USA, June 16–20, 2019. pp. 3762–3770. Computer Vision Foundation / IEEE (2019). DOI: 10.1109/CVPR.2019.00388

24. Zhang, Z., Wang, H., Liu, M., Wang, R., Zhang, J., Zuo, W.: Learning raw-to-srgb mappings with inaccurately aligned supervision. CoRR abs/2108.08119 (2021), http://arxiv.org/abs/2108.08119

Learning Deep Non-blind Image Deconvolution Without Ground Truths

Yuhui Quan[1,2], Zhuojie Chen[1(✉)], Huan Zheng[2], and Hui Ji[2]

[1] School of Computer Science and Engineering, South China University of Technology, Guangzhou 510006, China
csyhquan@scut.edu.cn, zhuojie.chen.cs@foxmail.com
[2] Department of Mathematics, National University of Singapore, Singapore 119076, Singapore
huan_zheng@u.nus.edu, matjh@nus.edu.sg

Abstract. Non-blind image deconvolution (NBID) is about restoring a latent sharp image from a blurred one, given an associated blur kernel. Most existing deep neural networks for NBID are trained over many ground truth (GT) images, which limits their applicability in practical applications such as microscopic imaging and medical imaging. This paper proposes an unsupervised deep learning approach for NBID which avoids accessing GT images. The challenge raised from the absence of GT images is tackled by a self-supervised reconstruction loss that approximates its supervised counterpart well. The possible errors of blur kernels are addressed by a self-supervised prediction loss based on intermediate samples as well as an ensemble inference scheme based on kernel perturbation. The experiments show that the proposed approach provides very competitive performance to existing supervised learning-based methods, no matter under accurate kernels or erroneous kernels.

Keywords: Non-blind image deconvolution · Self-supervised learning · Unsupervised deep learning · Image deblurring

1 Introduction

Image deconvolution is a challenging problem often encountered in imaging systems and low-level vision. It is about estimating the latent image X from its degraded observation Y generated by

$$Y = K^* \otimes X + N, \tag{1}$$

Y. Quan—Is also with Pazhou Lab, Guangzhou 510335, China. He would like to thank the support in part by National Natural Science Foundation of China under Grant 61872151 and in part by Natural Science Foundation of Guangdong Province under Grant 2022A1515011755.
H. Ji—Would like thank the support in part by Singapore MOE AcRF under Grant R-146-000-315-114.

Supplementary Information The online version contains supplementary material available at https://doi.org/10.1007/978-3-031-20068-7_37.

© The Author(s), under exclusive license to Springer Nature Switzerland AG 2022
S. Avidan et al. (Eds.): ECCV 2022, LNCS 13666, pp. 642–659, 2022.
https://doi.org/10.1007/978-3-031-20068-7_37

where $\otimes$ denotes the convolution operation, $\boldsymbol{K}^*$ denotes a blur kernel, and $\boldsymbol{N}$ denotes image noise. When the kernel is given as a prior, the problem is called *Non-Blind Image Deconvolution* (NBID); otherwise, it is called blind image deconvolution (BID). The kernel often can be obtained by calibrating an imaging system and capturing the image of Dirac-like dots, or be captured using specific hardware. NBID also serves as a key module for BID, which is often called in the last stage of a BID method after the kernel estimation is finished. In this case, the estimated kernel used for NBID usually contains non-ignorable errors.

An image convolved by a blur kernel will have its high-frequency parts significantly attenuated or erased. Together with the unknown image noise and possible kernel errors, it makes NBID a challenging ill-posed inverse problem. In recent years, there have been extensive studies applying deep learning (DL) for NBID, which train a neural network (NN) to predict latent images from the pairs of degraded images and blur kernels; see *e.g.* [3,10–12,14,19,21,29,35,38,50,51]. While these methods differ in terms of architecture and training scheme, they are all based on supervised learning. That is, their NNs are trained over many pairs of blurred and ground truth (GT) images. Such a prerequisite on GT images limits their applications in certain domains, such as scientific imaging and medical imaging. In these domains, either GT images are very challenging to collect, or have restricted usage for privacy concerns. Such an issue cannot be effectively addressed by calling GT images from other domains, as it may result in poor generalization performance due to domain shifts and domain gaps.

1.1 Problem Setting and Main Idea

Motivated by the limitation of supervised DL-based NBID in the domains where the access to GT images is very limited, this paper proposes an unsupervised DL approach for NBID whose NN training does not involve any GT image. The unsupervised learning setting we study is as follows.

- **Training data:** Only a set of blurred image $\{Y_j\}_j$ and the associated kernels $\{K_j\}_j$ are provided for training; and the GT images $\{X_j\}_j$ are unavailable.
- **Error sources:** In the training data, there is noise N_j on each image Y_j and possible kernel error defined by $\Delta K_j = K_j - K_j^*$ with GT kernel K_j^*.

It is a challenging task to teach an NN to make accurate predictions in such a setting, as there is no GT image to define a loss that can measure the prediction accuracy. In addition, the possible kernel errors may confuse the learning process and lower the accuracy of the learned NBID process.

In the proposed approach, the challenge raised by the absence of GT images is tackled by generalizing the Recorrupted-to-Recorrupted (R2R) training [33] from denoising to NBID. It leads to a noise-resistant self-supervised reconstruction loss which approximates well a supervised loss defined over GT images in the range space induced by the blur kernel. Furthermore, by training with both kernel diversity and cross-image patch recurrence, the loss can also well approximate its supervised counterpart on the full image space.

In comparison to image noise, kernel errors are more challenging to handle. Without GT kernels for training, an NN is hardly aware of the existence of kernel errors, let alone learn to handle it. Our idea to handle kernel errors is viewing a deblurred image output by the NN as a "pseudo" GT and reblurring it with a different kernel to have a paired sample for "pseudo" supervised training. Such data augmentation is effective as long as the original kernel and the reblurring kernel are sufficiently different. In this case, the kernel for reblurring, even erroneous, is viewed as the GT kernel, and we apply a kernel error simulator to have its erroneous version. The rationale comes from that an imperfect blur kernel estimated by some existing method is also a physically valid blur kernel, or at least is very likely to approximate a valid blur kernel well. Based on the above data augmentation scheme, a self-supervised prediction loss is defined for enhancing to the kernel error robustness of the trained NN model.

In addition, an ensemble inference scheme is proposed to further improve the robustness to kernel errors. The scheme is based on the observation that, when restoring the latent image using many instances of the inaccurate kernel perturbed by random noise, the artifacts shown in the corresponding results have certain degrees of statistical independence. Then, the aggregation of these results is likely to attenuate the artifacts.

The proposed approach is applied with a popular off-the-shelf optimization-unrolling-based NN architecture composed of common building blocks. In the experiments on motion deblurring of natural images and microscopic deconvolution, we found that such an NN suffices to yield satisfactory performance, which competes against that of supervised learning-based NBID approaches.

1.2 Main Contributions

This work is one of the few attempts on unsupervised DL for NBID. Our main contributions lie in the design of loss functions and training/test schemes for NBID. See below for the summary of our main contributions.

- A self-supervised reconstruction loss function with good approximation to its supervised counterpart when being applied with kernel diversity and cross-image patch recurrence presented in training data;
- A self-supervised prediction loss function to improve the robustness of the trained model to kernel errors.
- An ensemble inference scheme based on kernel perturbations, which reduces the sensitivity of the NN to kernel errors in the test stage and works for both unsupervised models and supervised models.
- An unsupervised DL approach for NBID, which not only outperforms existing unsupervised methods, but also competes against the supervised ones.

2 Related Works

Non-DL-Based NBID. Conventional methods for NBID developed handcrafted image priors based on empirical image statistics to regularize the deconvolution process. There is abundant literature on it; see *e.g.* [13,20,36].

Supervised DL-Based NBID. Most supervised DL-based methods focus on NN architecture design. To have an NN working for different kernels, many recent methods unfold an iterative scheme of some regularization-based NBID approach; see *e.g.* [3,11,12,14,19,21,26,29,50,51]. These methods usually decompose each iteration into an inversion process using the image estimate from the previous iteration and a denoising process performed by a convolutional NN (CNN). There are also some studies directly neuralizing existing regularization-based methods via replacing the regularizer by a CNN; see *e.g.* [10,35].

In comparison to the robustness to image noise, the robustness to kernel errors receives less attention in existing NBID methods, even it is important for real applications. It is known that without a specific mechanism, a NBID method is sensitive to kernel errors; see *e.g.* [18,28,37,42]. There are only a few regularization-based methods considering kernel errors explicitly; see *e.g.* [18,37]. For DL-based methods, Vasu *et al.* [42] proposed an NN that fuses multiple estimates generated by a hyper-Laplacian regularized inverse with different regularization weights. By unfolding a total least squared estimator, Nan and Ji [28] proposed a dual-path NN with a kernel-error residual estimation module. Dong *et al.* [10] handles kernel errors by performing Wiener deconvolution in feature domain with a multi-scale refinement process.

Unsupervised DL for NBID. The study on unsupervised DL-based NBID is scant in the literature. Some studies (*e.g.* [44,53]) leverage the generative priors of untrained NNs to perform online internal learning on a test image. While avoiding using external training samples (including GTs), their performance is not satisfactory. Chen *et al.* [7] achieved a significant performance improvement by leveraging model uncertainty induced by dropout. However, all these methods need to train different models for different images, whose computational cost can be overwhelming. In contrast, the proposed approach trains a universal model for efficiently processing all test images in an offline manner. There are few works on offline unsupervised DL for NBID. One is Lim *et al.* [25] which uses unpaired blurred images and latent images to train an adversarial generative network with cycle consistency, which is not is GT-free.

There are also a number of unsupervised DL methods for solving linear inverse problems; see *e.g.* [5,17,32,43,46]. These methods are not specifically designed for NBID, and none of them concern the errors in measurement matrix, *i.e.*, kernel errors in our case.

3 Proposed Approach

Through the paper, the NN for NBID is denoted by $\mathcal{F}(\cdot, \cdot)$, which predicts the latent image from an input pair of degraded image $\boldsymbol{Y}$ and blur kernel $\boldsymbol{K}$.

3.1 Self-supervised Reconstruction Loss

To make the discussion more accessible, without loss of generality, we temporarily assume the input kernel is accurate in this subsection. Let $\mathcal{N}(\boldsymbol{0}, \sigma^2 \boldsymbol{I})$ denote the normal distribution with zero mean and diagonal variance matrix $\sigma^2 I$. Consider a training sample (Y, K^*), where K^* denotes the GT kernel. Suppose $N \sim \mathcal{N}(0, \sigma^2 I)$. We first introduce a self-supervised loss to address N:

$$\mathcal{L}^r := \mathbb{E}_{U \sim \mathcal{N}(0, \sigma^2 I)} \|Y - U - K^* \otimes \mathcal{F}(Y + U, K^*)\|_F^2. \tag{2}$$

This loss is motivated by the R2R unsupervised denoising loss [33]. It is resistant to the noise, as shown in Proposition 1.

Proposition 1. *Consider* $Y = K^* \otimes X + N$ *where* $N \sim \mathcal{N}(0, \sigma^2 I)$. *Then,*

$$\mathbb{E}_{N, U \sim \mathcal{N}(0, \sigma^2 I)} \|Y - U - K^* \otimes \mathcal{F}(Y + U, K^*)\|_F^2 \tag{3}$$
$$= \mathbb{E}_{N, U \sim \mathcal{N}(0, \sigma^2 I)} \|K^* \otimes [X - \mathcal{F}(Y + U, K^*)]\|_F^2 + \text{const.}$$

See supplementary materials for the proof. It can be seen that the noise in Y is effectively removed in the loss function even without accessing the GT X.

3.2 Approximate Supervision in Image Space with Kernel Diversity and Cross-Image Patch Recurrence

The loss $\mathcal{L}^r$ indeed provides a weak form of the supervised loss $\mathcal{L}^{gt}$ defined by

$$\mathcal{L}^{gt} := \|X - \mathcal{F}(Y, K^*)\|_F^2, \tag{4}$$

with training samples in the form of (Y, X, K^*). To see this, recall that for a kernel K^*, the space $\mathbb{R}^{M \times N}$ can be expressed as the direct sum of two orthogonal subspaces: null space $\text{Null}(K^*)$ and range space $\text{Range}(\widetilde{K^*})$, where $\widetilde{K^*}$ is the flipped version of K^* (see [15]), and

$$\text{Null}(K^*) = \{E \in \mathbb{R}^{M \times N} : K^* \otimes E = 0\}, \tag{5}$$
$$\text{Range}(\widetilde{K^*}) = \{\widetilde{K^*} \otimes X : X \in \mathbb{R}^{M \times N}\}. \tag{6}$$

It can be seen that $\mathcal{L}^r$ indeed measures the prediction error in $\text{Range}(\widetilde{K^*})$, not the full space $\mathbb{R}^{M \times N}$. In other words, $\mathcal{L}^r$ is equivalent to some norm defined in $\text{Range}(\widetilde{K^*})$: $\mathbb{E}_{U \sim \mathcal{N}_\sigma} \|X - \mathcal{F}(Y + U, K^*)\|_{\text{Range}(\widetilde{K^*})}^2$.

The remaining task is then how to measure the prediction error in $\text{Null}(K^*)$. While it is challenging with a single image, it is much easier when training the NN on a set of blurred images whose blur kernels have sufficient variations. Note that not every point in $\mathbb{R}^{M \times N}$ is an image. There are certain priors for images and one is patch recurrence [9]. The patch recurrence prior states that image patches are likely to repeat over the image [9] and across different images [47].

Suppose that the dataset we are processing have sufficient variations on blur kernels and have strong patch recurrence across images. Then, the loss function $\mathcal{L}^r$ indeed provides an approximate measure of the prediction accuracy over the full space. Recall that a deep NN can be viewed as processing image patches whose size is limited by its receptive field. Then, for each GT image patch P, suppose we have a set of its blurred correspondences $\{Q_j\}_j$ across many images with different kernels $\{K_j^*\}_j$. Then, with sufficient variations among $\{K_j^*\}_j$, we are likely to have $\cap_j \text{Null}(K_j^*) \approx \{0\}$, or equivalently $\cup_j \text{Range}(\widetilde{K_j^*}) = \mathbb{R}^{M \times N}$. As $\mathcal{L}^r$ measures the prediction error in each $\text{Range}(\widetilde{K^*})$, the summation of $\mathcal{L}^r$ over $\{Q_j\}_j$ provides the measure of prediction error on P. In other words, $\mathcal{L}^r$ provides an approximation to the supervised loss defined on GT images in this case. The assumption of kernel diversity in the training dataset is reasonable for many domains. For instance, in motion deblurring, when two motion blur kernels have different dominant orientations, the intersection of their null spaces are roughly close to a zero set; see e.g. [4,24,30].

3.3   Self-supervised Prediction Loss

For notational simplicity, kernel errors are omitted in the previous discussions. In the presence of kernel errors, the similar conclusion also holds. Suppose the input kernel, denoted by K, differs from the GT kernel K^*. Then, $\mathcal{L}^r$ will induce some errors related to $\Delta K = K - K^*$, and we have

$$\mathbb{E}_{N,U \sim \mathcal{N}_\sigma} \|Y - U - K \otimes \mathcal{F}(Y + U, K)\|_F^2 \tag{7}$$
$$= \mathbb{E}_{N,U \sim \mathcal{N}_\sigma} \|K \otimes X - \Delta K \otimes X + N - U - K \otimes \mathcal{F}(Y + U, K)\|_F^2$$
$$= \mathbb{E}_{N,U \sim \mathcal{N}_\sigma} \|K \otimes [X - \mathcal{F}(Y + U, K)]\|_F^2 + \delta(\Delta K \otimes X) + \text{const},$$

where $\delta(\Delta K \otimes X)$ denotes the error term induced by kernel errors, which distorts the measure on prediction error of the NN. In the next, we introduce an additional self-supervised prediction loss to handle such distortion.

The additional loss is defined over the intermediate estimates of the latent image during the training stage, as well as over the re-corrupted versions of the inaccurate kernels in training data. The intermediate estimates are used to simulate the GT images for training. The inaccurate kernels are used to mimic GT kernels which are applied to the simulated GT images to form blurred images as the input images for training. The re-corrupted kernels are used as the input erroneous kernels for training so as to improve the robustness to kernel errors.

Let $\mathbb{K}$ denote the set of kernels in training data. For a sample (Y, K) where K is erroneous, let Z_K denote the output from the NN in some intermediate training stage:

$$Z_K = \mathcal{F}(Y + U, K), \quad U \sim \mathcal{N}_\sigma, \tag{8}$$

which can be viewed as an approximation of the GT image corresponding to the pair $(Y + U, K)$, and the noise U comes from the definition of $\mathcal{L}^r$ in (2). Then, we synthesize a set of training samples with the triples: $\big($noisy blurred image $\overline{Z}_{\overline{K}}$, erroneous kernel $\mathcal{S}(\overline{K})$, latent Image $Z_K\big)$:

$$\overline{Z}_{\overline{K}} := \overline{K} \otimes Z_K + \overline{N}, \tag{9}$$

for $\overline{K} \sim \mathbb{K}/K$, where $\mathcal{S}$ is the error generator proposed in [28] for simulating the erroneous estimate of the GT kernel, and $\overline{N}$ denotes the white Gaussian

(WG) noise with variance randomly drawn from the range of noise variances of training samples. Such a set of triplets $\{(\overline{Z}_{\overline{K}}, \mathcal{S}(\overline{K}), Z_K)\}_{\overline{K} \sim \mathbb{K}/K}$ are used to supervise the training, using the self-supervised prediction loss defined by

$$\mathcal{L}^{\mathrm{p}} := \mathbb{E}_{\overline{N}, \overline{K} \sim \mathbb{K}/K, \mathcal{S} \sim \mathbb{S}} \| Z_K - \mathcal{F}(\overline{Z}_{\overline{K}}, \mathcal{S}(\overline{K})) \|_1. \tag{10}$$

When provided with accurate kernels, we fix $\mathcal{S}$ to an identity mapping. In this case, $\overline{Z}_{\overline{K}}$ varies with U, and thus $\mathcal{L}^{\mathrm{p}}$ still contributes.

An additional benefit from $\mathcal{L}^{\mathrm{p}}$ is that, it can further improve the accuracy of $\mathcal{L}^{\mathrm{r}}$ in measuring prediction errors. Recall that kernel variations are important for $\mathcal{L}^{\mathrm{r}}$ to measure the prediction error in the null space Null(K^*). The triplets $\{(\overline{Z}_{\overline{K}}, \mathcal{S}(\overline{K}), Z_K)\}_{\overline{K} \sim \mathbb{K}/K}$ increase kernel diversity due to the generator $\mathcal{S}$, and it also enforces cross-image patch recurrence, as for every $(\overline{Z}_{\overline{K}}, \mathcal{S}(\overline{K}))$, the output of $\mathcal{F}$ is expected to predict the same target.

To conclude, more pairs are generated during the intermediate training stage for NN training. The intermediate image estimates Z_K are used as pseudo GT images, and the inaccurate kernels K are used as pseudo GT kernels. The loss $\mathcal{L}^{\mathrm{p}}$ defined on these pairs can improve the robustness to kernel errors, as well as improve the effectiveness of $\mathcal{L}^{\mathrm{r}}$ in the kernel-induced null space.

3.4   Unsupervised Training and Ensemble Inference

Unsupervised Training. The NN is trained by minimizing the loss:

$$\mathcal{L} := \mathcal{L}^{\mathrm{r}} + \beta \mathcal{L}^{\mathrm{p}}, \tag{11}$$

with $\beta \in \mathbb{R}^+$. In training, β is first set to 0 so as to concentrate on minimizing Range($\widetilde{K}$) and then is increased to include $\mathcal{L}^{\mathrm{p}}$. For handling inaccurate kernels, after sufficient training in the first stage, we modify the loss $\mathcal{L}^{\mathrm{r}}$ to be

$$\mathbb{E}_{U \sim \mathcal{N}_\sigma, \mathcal{S} \sim \mathbb{S}} \| Y - U - \mathcal{S}(K) \otimes \mathcal{F}(Y + U, \mathcal{S}(K)) \|_{\mathrm{F}}^2, \tag{12}$$

where data augmentation on kernels is done the same as $\mathcal{L}^{\mathrm{p}}$.

Ensemble Inference via Kernel Perturbation. For further performance improvement in handling kernel errors of test data, we propose a simple yet effective ensemble inference scheme for a sample (Y, K) as follows:

$$X^{\mathrm{est}} = \mathbb{E}_{U \sim \mathcal{N}, V \sim \mathbb{V}_K} \mathcal{F}(Y + U, \frac{K + V}{\|K + V\|_1}), \tag{13}$$

with a perturbation set $\mathbb{V}_K$. We can see that the prediction is done by averaging over the estimates from both perturbed images and perturbed kernels. The motivation of kernel perturbation is that, when using randomly-perturbed kernels to restore the latent image, the artifacts in the recovered images caused by kernel errors tend to show certain degree of independence, which can be attenuated by averaging. The perturbation on input image is to ensure the consistency of noise characteristics between training and test.

The perturbation set $\mathbb{V}_K$ is constructed such that it does not cause any shift of the kernel, as the NBID results with different kernel shifts are not aligned and their average cannot cancel the artifacts well. To address this, we first generate a noise map with the same size as K, whose elements are sampled from $\mathcal{N}_{0.1\%}$. Then, the Fourier phase spectrum of the noise map is replaced by that of K, and the resulting noise map is used as V. This ensures the perturbation does not shift the kernel. It is worth mentioning that, experimentally while the ensemble inference with such perturbations brings noticeable improvement for inaccurate, it brings either negligible improvement or little degradation on the performance for accurate kernels.

3.5 NN Architecture

Following recent supervised DL methods for NBID (*e.g.* [21,50]), the NN used for the experiments is based on the unfolding of the half-quadratic splitting (HQS) scheme for solving a regularization model:

$$\min_{X} \|Y - K \otimes X\|_F^2 + \sum_p \psi(W_p \otimes X), \tag{14}$$

where $\psi(\cdot)$ is some prior-inducing regularization, $\{W_p\}_p$ is the set of 3×3 wavelet high-pass filters. The iteration scheme from HQS reads: for $t = 1, \cdots, T$,

$$X^{(t)} := \operatorname{argmin}_X \|Y - K \otimes X\|_F^2 + \sum_p \lambda_t \|A_p^{(t)} - W_p \otimes X\|_F^2,$$
$$A_p^{(t+1)} := \operatorname{argmin}_{A_p} \|A_p - W_p \otimes X^{(t)}\|_F^2 + \psi(A_p), \forall p, \tag{15}$$

where $\{\lambda_t\}_t$ are hyper-parameters simply set as: $\lambda_0 = 0.5\%$ and $\lambda_t = 10\%$ for $t > 0$. Accordingly, the NN is constructed by stacking two blocks alternatively; see Fig. 1 for an illustration of the detailed structure.

(a) *Inversion block* $\mathcal{G}^{(t)} : Y, \{A_p^{(t)}\}_p, K \rightarrow X^{(t)}$. It corresponds to the 1st step in the iteration, which is an unconstrained quadratic problem with an analytic solution. We adopt the FFT-based computation scheme with adaptive boundary padding [21] to calculate the analytic solution.

(b) *Denoising block* $\mathcal{H}^{(t)} : \{X^{(t)}\}_{t=0}^t \rightarrow \{A_p^{(t+1)}\}_p$. It corresponds to the 2nd step of the iteration, replaced by a U-Net to refine $W_p \otimes X^{(t)}$. The U-Net takes all previous estimates as the input for better performance. In the implementation, it first removes noise from $X^{(t)}$ and then applies W_p to obtain $A_p^{(t+1)}$.

We also enforce the loss in the intermediate outputs. Let $\mathcal{F}^{(t)} := \mathcal{G}^{(0)} \rightarrow \mathcal{H}^{(1)} \rightarrow \cdots \rightarrow \mathcal{H}^{(t)} \rightarrow \mathcal{G}^{(t)}$, for $t = 1, \cdots, T$. Indeed, $\mathcal{F}^{(t)}$ can be viewed as an NN with different depths. Then, the overall loss is defined on all $\mathcal{F}^{(t)}$s by

$$\mathcal{L}^{\text{total}} := \sum_{t=1}^{T-1} \mathcal{L}(\mathcal{F}^{(t)}) + \gamma \mathcal{L}(\mathcal{F}^{(T)}), \tag{16}$$

where γ is fixed to 1.25 in our implementation.

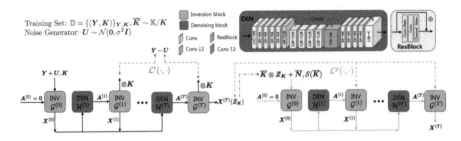

Fig. 1. Diagram of NN architecture used in the proposed approach

4   Performance Evaluation

4.1   Motion Deblurring with Erroneous Kernels

The proposed approach is evaluated on non-blind motion deblurring. To simulate practical scenarios, we follow [28] to prepare the training and test data. For training, random cropping is applied to the images of BSDS500 [2] to have 1500 sharp images of size 256×256, and the 192 motion kernels from [39] are used. The blurred images are generated by first randomly convolving each image with a blur kernel and then adding the WG noise of standard deviation 1%. Afterwards, we apply the BID method [31] to estimate a kernel from each blurred image. The blurred images and the estimated kernels are used as the training samples.

In our training data, each latent image only has one blurred correspondence. This differs from one popular setting in existing supervised NBID methods (*e.g.* [21,29,50]) where each image has multiple blurred correspondences with different kernels. Indeed, our setting is more realistic, especially for unsupervised learning. Data augmentation is applied to each pair of a blurred image and the corresponding kernel, using rotation by 90°, 180° or 270°, as well as flipping.

The test is conducted on three datasets: Levin *et al.*'s dataset [23], Sun *et al.*'s dataset, and a subset of Lai *et al.*'s dataset [22]. Several BID methods are called to estimate the kernels which are then used in the NBID process, including [31,41] for Levin *et al.*'s dataset, [8,27,48] for Sun *et al.*'s dataset, and [34,41,48,49] for Lai *et al.*'s dataset. The blurred images are corrupted by the WG noise with standard deviation 1%. In both training and test, the EdgeTapper is used for simulating realistic boundary conditions.

We fix $T = 5$ for our NN. In training, all the model weights are initialized by Kaiming [16] except that the biases are initialized by zeros. The Adam optimizer is used with 300 epochs. In the first 100 epochs, we zero β and set the learning rate to 10^{-4}. Afterwards, we set $\beta = 10^{-2}$ and the learning rate to 10^{-5}. We simply set the random noise U in both training and inference schemes to the WG noise with standard deviation estimated on the input image using [6]. When sampling $\overline{K}$ in $\mathcal{L}^{\mathrm{P}}$, we randomly pick up 10 instances and choose the one with the lowest correlation to K. In the test, we perform 10 inferences for averaging.

For experimental comparison, we include *(a)* supervised DL-based methods: IRCNN [51], FCNN [50], FDN [21], VEM [29], DWDN [10] and TLSNN [28]; *(b)* unsupervised DL-based methods: BPDIP [53], SURE [40] and EI EI [5]; and *(c)* non-DL-based method: DSPSI [45]. Among these methods, TLSNN, DWDN and DSPSI have specific mechanisms to handle kernel errors. The results of FDN, IRCNN, FCNN and TLSNN are quoted from [28]. The model of VEM is retrained on our data for better performance, while that of DWDN is not retrained as no performance gain is observed. The BPDIP is an online unsupervised DL method for NBID, while the SURE and EI are the offline ones for inverse problems but not applied to NBID before. Their loss functions are used to train our NN instead of their original ones for better performance and for a fair comparison.

See Table 1 for the quantitative comparison. The PSNR and SSIM are calculated using the shifting and boundary cut-off scheme of [28] for all the compared methods. For convenience, we name the proposed approach as UNID (Unsupervised Non-blind Image Deconvolution). In all cases, UNID outperformed other unsupervised DL-based methods. The BPDIP cannot leverage external training data and thus yielded much worse performance. Without an effective mechanism to deal with kernel errors, both SURE and EI showed inferior performance to UNID, and the performance of SURE is much worse. In most cases, UNID noticeably outperformed those supervised DL-based methods that do not treat kernel errors specifically. In comparison to the very recent supervised DL-based methods TLSNN and DWDN with specific treatments on kernel errors, UNID still provides comparable performance even it uses neither GT images nor accurate kernels for training. See Fig. 2 for a visual comparison, where UNID can deblur an image with comparable visual quality to that of the supervised NNs.

Table 1. PSNR(dB)/SSIM in motion deblurring with erroneous kernels (bold: highest values among all methods; underlined: highest values among GT-free methods)

	Dataset	Levin *et al.*'s		Sun *et al.*'s			Lai *et al.*'s			
	Kernels	[31]	[41]	[8]	[48]	[27]	[48]	[49]	[41]	[34]
Supervised	IRCNN	30.42/.86	29.56/.83	28.84/.81	29.54/.83	29.23/.82	19.99/.70	19.36/.67	19.46/.67	18.68/.68
	FCNN	31.12/.90	30.27/.88	29.79/.86	30.45/.86	29.84/.84	20.27/.74	19.52/.70	19.80/.70	19.12/.70
	FDN	31.19/.92	30.83/.90	29.69/.87	30.51/.88	29.82/.86	N/A	N/A	N/A	N/A
	VEM	31.83/.92	31.08/.91	30.32/.85	30.61/.86	29.82/.83	22.04/.70	21.95/.70	21.85/.68	21.04/.62
	DWDN	30.87/.91	30.66/.90	29.49/.87	30.29/.88	29.46/.85	**22.88/.77**	**22.70/.77**	**22.59/.75**	21.21/**.72**
	TLSNN	**31.97/.92**	**31.24/.91**	**30.44/.87**	**30.84**/.87	**30.27/.86**	22.53/.74	22.27/.73	22.31/.72	21.61/.70
w/o GT	DSPSI	29.55/.84	29.10/.82	28.57/.78	29.06/.79	28.74/.78	20.21/.72	19.87/.70	19.91/.69	19.35/.70
	SURE	28.59/.85	27.99/.81	26.91/.69	27.15/.71	27.17/.69	19.24/.65	18.91/.60	19.04/.60	18.39/.55
	BPDIP	28.71/.85	28.12/.84	26.99/.69	27.23/.70	27.14/.69	19.42/.66	19.05/.61	19.11/.60	18.50/.55
	EI	29.37/.85	29.58/.86	28.60/.80	29.05/.83	28.10/.79	20.77/.63	20.24/.63	20.45/.63	19.67/.61
	UNID	31.71/<u>.92</u>	30.66/.89	30.24/.86	30.82/.87	30.08/.85	22.43/.73	22.24/.73	22.04/.71	<u>21.65</u>/.70

4.2 Motion Deblurring with Accurate Kernels

A majority of existing studies on NBID (*e.g.* [3,12,14,19,29,35,50]) conducted experiments using accurate kernels in both training and test, which simulate the

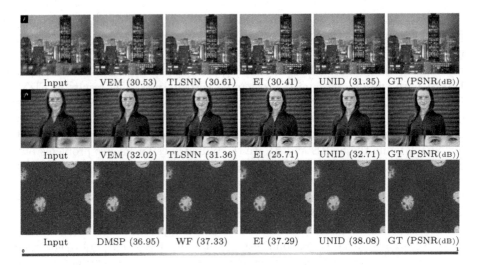

Fig. 2. NBID results of selected methods on motion deblurring with inaccurate kernels (top and middle) and on microscopic deconvolution (bottom)

scenarios where kernel errors are sufficiently small and thus negligible. Such a setting is also used to have a comprehensive evaluation. We follow [21, 29, 50] for the preparation of training and test data, similar to the previous experiment. The 1500 sharp images from random cropping of BSDS500 and the 192 motion kernels from [39] are used to generate the blurred images, with WG noise added whose standard deviation is randomly picked from $[1, 14]/255$. Also, each sharp image only is allowed to form one blurred image to be more realistic. The data augmentation is also applied to have sufficient training samples. An universal model is trained w.r.t. different noise levels. Since there is no kernel error, we lower the contribution of $\mathcal{L}^\mathrm{P}$ with $\beta = 10^{-3}$ in the second training stage.

Three datasets are used for test, including Levin *et al.*'s dataset [23], Sun *et al.*'s dataset [41] and Set12 [29]. The blurred images are generated by first convolving each sharp image with the eight motion kernels from [23] respectively and then adding the WG noise with standard deviations of 1%, 3%, 5% respectively. The blurred images and their associated kernels are used for test. The EdgeTapper for boundary simulation is also used in both training and test. Our UNID is compared to the previously-used IRCNN, FDN, VEM, BPDIP, SURE and EI. In addition, two supervised NNs, DMSP [3] and DPDNN [12], are included for comparison. The FDN, FCNN and VEM also use BSD500 for training, DPDNN is re-trained on BSD500, DMSP used with their pre-trained models as they have no training codes provided, and IRCNN is trained on its original noisy data instead of the blurred one. Existing works use different boundary cut-off strategies for evaluation. For a fair comparison, we cut the boundary with half kernel size when calculating the PSNR and SSIM for all methods.

Table 2. PSNR(dB)/SSIM in motion deblurring with accurate kernels (bold: highest values among all methods; underlined: highest values among GT-free methods)

	Dataset	Sun et al.'s			Levin et al.'s			Set12		
	STD	1%	3%	5%	1%	3%	5%	1%	3%	5%
Supervised	IRCNN	31.80/.88	28.93/.80	27.50/.74	31.11/.89	28.99/.85	27.58/.80	30.37/.87	27.95/.81	26.51/.76
	FDN	32.21/.89	28.88/.78	27.61/.73	31.95/.91	28.95/.84	27.45/.80	31.03/.88	27.92/.80	26.47/.76
	DMSP	32.00/.87	28.63/.77	27.48/.74	32.60/.90	29.30/.83	27.84/.81	31.20/.87	27.95/.79	26.43/.76
	DPDNN	31.24/.85	29.09/.80	27.90/.76	31.15/.89	28.95/.85	27.57/.81	30.11/.86	27.78/.81	26.53/.78
	VEM	32.20/.89	29.23/.80	**27.93**/.76	31.63/.91	29.33/.86	27.79/.81	30.97/.88	28.27/.82	26.79/.77
	DWDN	**32.37**/.89	29.19/.80	27.88/.75	**32.92**/.92	**29.85**/.87	28.23/.83	**31.37**/.89	**28.36**/.82	**26.89**/.78
w/o GT	SURE	27.32/.73	26.69/.71	25.65/.66	30.40/.88	27.41/.80	25.77/.71	28.69/.83	26.00/.74	24.58/.65
	BPDIP	27.50/.73	26.84/.71	25.71/.66	30.63/.88	27.53/.79	25.86/.72	28.86/.83	26.11/.73	24.65/.66
	EI	31.43/.86	28.80/.77	27.37/.72	31.32/.90	29.05/.85	27.49/.80	29.37/.86	27.50/.80	26.20/.74
	UNID	32.28/**.89**	**29.24**/.80	27.82/.74	32.12/**.92**	29.71/.86	28.16/.82	30.92/.88	28.23/**.82**	26.76/.77

See Table 2 for the quantitative results and comparison. Again, UNID outperformed other unsupervised models in all settings. Surprisingly, while UNID requires no GT images, it also outperformed the supervised models trained with GT images in many settings and it is very competitive to the top performers of the supervised models. All such results demonstrated the effectiveness of UNID.

4.3 Microscopic Deconvolution

Microscopic imaging in science is one domain where GT images are difficult to collect in practice. We follow the same evaluation scheme as [35]. The images of the fluorescence microscopy dataset [52] and the cell segmentation dataset [1] are first scaled to the range of $[0, 1]$ and cropped into patches of size 256×256, among which 975 (230) patches are used for training (test). There are kernels of size 7×7, 9×9, 11×11 or 13×13 provided, among which 25 (5) kernels are used for training (test); see [35] for the details on the kernels. For test, the GT images are first convoluted with one of the five test kernels respectively, and then corrupted by the WG noise with standard deviation $\sigma = 0.1\%, 0.5\%, 1\%, 5\%$ respectively. The training parameters are set the same as previous experiments. In addition, we also simulate erroneous kernels by approximating each GT kernel with a Gaussian kernel that minimizes their MSE. Our model trained by these erroneous kernels is denoted by UNID[†].

Similar to previous experiments, for practical scenario simulation, the blurred images for training are generated by convolving each GT image with only one randomly-selected kernel and adding the WG noise with σ randomly picked from $\{0.1\%, 0.5\%, 1\%, 5\%, 10\%\}$. This differs from the supervised learning setting in [35], and the same data augmentation as previous experiments is applied.

In addition to the aforementioned IRCNN, FDN, DMSP, SURE and EI, the WF-KPN-SA [35] (denoted by WF) is also included for comparison, whose results are quoted from [35]. See Table 3 for the quantitative comparison and Fig. 2 for a visual inspection. The boundary cutting scheme of [35] is used to calculate the PSNR and SSIM. The performance of UNID is noticeably better

Table 3. PSNR(dB)/SSIM results in microscopic NBID (bold: highest values among all methods; underlined: highest values among unsupervised methods)

STD	Supervised				Unsupervised				
	IRCNN	FDN	DMSP	WF	SURE	BPDIP	EI	UNID[†]	UNID
0.1%	33.33/.86	40.31/.94	**40.44/.94**	39.86/.94	37.65/.91	37.90/.92	39.41/.93	40.18/.94	40.30/<u>.94</u>
0.5%	36.88/.90	38.61/.92	39.16/.93	38.76/.93	37.21/.91	37.37/.91	38.24/.92	38.97/.93	**39.33/.93**
1%	36.80/.90	37.33/.91	37.73/.91	37.81/.92	36.60/.90	36.70/.90	36.87/.90	37.59/.90	**38.36/.92**
5%	32.44/.79	33.50/.84	34.31/.86	**34.58/.87**	31.67/.77	31.79/.77	32.27/.79	33.67/.83	34.32/.85

Table 4. PSNR(dB) results using different training loss functions

(a) PSNR(dB) results *w.r.t.* loss

Training Loss	Sun *et al.*'s Dataset			Levin *et al.*'s Dataset	
	[8]	[48]	[27]	[31]	[41]
Only $\mathcal{L}^{\mathrm{p}}$	28.04	28.11	27.83	28.03	27.60
Only $\mathcal{L}^{\mathrm{r}}$	29.92	30.50	29.72	30.96	30.11
Both	30.24	30.82	30.08	31.71	30.66
Fixed $\mathcal{L}^{\mathrm{r}}$	30.13	30.74	30.00	31.44	30.43
$\mathcal{L}^{\mathrm{gt}}$	30.27	30.87	30.13	31.91	30.87

(b) PSNR(dB) results *w.r.t.* kernel perturbations

Kernel Perturb.	Lai *et al.*'s Dataset				Sun *et al.*'s Dataset		
	[48]	[49]	[41]	[34]	[8]	[48]	[27]
Proposed	22.43	22.24	22.04	21.65	30.24	30.82	30.08
Disabled	21.54	20.96	21.13	20.37	29.31	29.49	28.80
Gaussian	22.30	22.15	22.02	20.98	29.48	30.05	29.60

than other unsupervised models and competitive to the supervised ones. Particularly, UNID outperformed all supervised models when $\sigma = 0.5\%, 1\%$. For other noise levels, UNID performed a bit worse than the top performers. The UNID[†] saw a certain performance decrease due to the kernel errors in training data, but its performance is still competitive among all methods and better than other unsupervised models.

4.4   Ablation Studies

Comparison of Different Loss Functions. To evaluate how the proposed self-supervised loss functions contribute to the performance, we use the following loss functions to retrain the NN with rigorous tuning-up: *(a)* $\mathcal{L}^{\mathrm{p}}$: only train with $\mathcal{L}^{\mathrm{p}}$; *(b)* $\mathcal{L}^{\mathrm{r}}$: only train with $\mathcal{L}^{\mathrm{r}}$; *(c)* Fixed $\mathcal{L}^{\mathrm{r}}$: do not change $\mathcal{L}^{\mathrm{r}}$ to (12) during training; and *(d)* $\mathcal{L}^{\mathrm{gt}}$: use (4) and the training data of [29] for supervised training.

See Table 4(a) for the results on two datasets, from which we have the following observations. First, the NN trained by UNID without GT images performs nearly as well as the one trained with GT images. Second, the loss $\mathcal{L}^{\mathrm{r}}$ is critical to the training, and the performance will have a significant decrease when training without it. This is because the restoration on $\mathrm{Range}(\widetilde{\boldsymbol{K}})$ corresponds to the major part of an image, and the $\mathcal{L}^{\mathrm{r}}$ relies on the success of restoration on $\mathrm{Range}(\widetilde{\boldsymbol{K}})$ as well. Third, the loss $\mathcal{L}^{\mathrm{p}}$ also has a noticeable contribution to the performance. Lastly, modifying $\mathcal{L}^{\mathrm{r}}$ to (12) brings slight improvement.

Performance Gain by Ensemble Inference. Two inference schemes are evaluated as baselines: one is the standard prediction scheme without kernel

w/o kernel perturbation Gaussian perturbation Proposed perturbation   GT

Fig. 3. Effects of kernel perturbations

Table 5. PSNR(dB) results of supervised models with ensemble inference

Dataset	Kernels	FDN	FDN*	VEM	VEM*	DWDN	DWDN*	UNID	UNID*
Sun *et al.*'s	[8]	29.40	30.28	29.69	30.30	29.49	29.98	29.31	30.24
	[48]	30.05	30.99	30.51	30.99	30.29	30.63	29.49	30.82
	[27]	29.12	30.21	29.82	30.07	29.46	29.85	28.80	30.08
Levin *et al.*'s	[31]	30.27	31.77	30.27	31.61	30.87	31.85	30.25	31.71
	[41]	30.11	30.80	30.11	30.76	30.66	31.00	29.80	30.66

perturbation (*i.e.* $\mathbb{V}_{\widetilde{K}} = \emptyset$) and the other uses WG noise with standard deviation 0.1% as the perturbation term. See Table 4(b) and Fig. 3 for the comparison. Our ensemble inference scheme outperformed the standard one, which shows that averaging predictions from perturbed kernels can improve the robustness to kernel errors. Furthermore, a trivial perturbation using WG noise also brings some improvement but not as significant as ours.

The proposed inference scheme with kernel perturbations is also applied to the supervised models including FDN [21], VEM [29], DWDN [10]. The resulting methods are marked by *. Table 5 lists the results. Note that the reported results of VEM differ from those in Sect. 4.1 as here we use the pre-trained model instead of the retrained one. It can seen that our ensemble inference scheme can bring noticeable performance gain: ranging from 0.25dB to 1.09dB on Sun *et al.*'s dataset and raning from 0.34dB to 1.5 dB on Levin *et al.*'s dataset. This demonstrates the applicability of ensemble inference to supervised models. Our UNID is also included for comparison. Even using the same inference scheme, it is still competitive to the supervised models.

5   Conclusion

While supervised DL has been the main driving force in the recent development of NBID methods, its applicability to real applications is limited by its requirement on GT images. In this paper, we developed a GT-free unsupervised DL approach to NBID, which provides a complement to existing supervised DL-based methods especially when GT images are of the limited amount or unavailable. Based on a self-supervised training scheme with rigorous mathematical treatment and an ensemble inference scheme based on kernel perturbation, the proposed approach can effectively handle kernels errors and image noise in both training and test data. Extensive experiments on uniform motion deblurring and microscopic deconvolution showed the effectiveness of the proposed approach.

References

1. Al-Kofahi, Y., Zaltsman, A., Graves, R., Marshall, W., Rusu, M.: A deep learning-based algorithm for 2-d cell segmentation in microscopy images. BMC Bioinf. **19**(1), 1–11 (2018)
2. Arbelaez, P., Maire, M., Fowlkes, C., Malik, J.: Contour detection and hierarchical image segmentation. IEEE Trans. Neural Netw. Learn. Syst. **33**(5), 898–916 (2010)
3. Bigdeli, S.A., Jin, M., Favaro, P., Zwicker, M.: Deep mean-shift priors for image restoration. In: Advances in Neural Information Processing Systems, pp. 763–772 (2017)
4. Cai, J.F., Ji, H., Liu, C., Shen, Z.: High-quality curvelet-based motion deblurring from an image pair. In: Proceedings of the IEEE Conference on Computer Vision and Pattern Recognition, 1566–1573 (2009)
5. Chen, D., Tachella, J., Davies, M.E.: Equivariant imaging: learning beyond the range space. In: Proceedings of the IEEE/CVF International Conference on Computer Vision (2021)
6. Chen, G., Zhu, F., Ann Heng, P.: An efficient statistical method for image noise level estimation. In: Proceedings of the IEEE International Conference on Computer Vision, pp. 477–485 (2015)
7. Chen, M., Quan, Y., Pang, T., Ji, H.: Nonblind image deconvolution via leveraging model uncertainty in an untrained deep neural network. Int. J. Comput. Vision **130**, 1770–789 (2022). https://doi.org/10.1007/s11263-022-01621-9
8. Cho, S., Lee, S.: Fast motion deblurring. In: Proceedings of the ACM SIGGRAPH Asia, pp. 1–8 (2009)
9. Dabov, K., Foi, A., Katkovnik, V., Egiazarian, K.: Image denoising by sparse 3-d transform-domain collaborative filtering. IEEE Trans. Image Process. **16**(8), 2080–2095 (2007)
10. Dong, J., Roth, S., Schiele, B.: Deep wiener deconvolution: wiener meets deep learning for image deblurring. In: Advances in Neural Information Processing Systems, vol. 33 (2020)
11. Dong, J., Roth, S., Schiele, B.: Learning spatially-variant map models for non-blind image deblurring. In: Proceedings of the IEEE/CVF Conference on Computer Vision and Pattern Recognition, pp. 4886–4895 (2021)
12. Dong, W., Wang, P., Yin, W., Shi, G.: Denoising prior driven deep neural ketwork for image restoration. IEEE Trans. Neural Netw. Learn. Syst. **41**(10), 2305–2318 (2019)
13. Dong, W., Zhang, L., Shi, G., Li, X.: Nonlocally centralized sparse representation for image restoration. IEEE Trans. Image Process. **22**(4), 1620–1630 (2012)
14. Eboli, T., Sun, J., Ponce, J.: End-to-end interpretable learning of non-blind image deblurring. In: Proceedings of the European Conference on Computer Vision (2020)
15. Folberth, J., Becker, S.: Efficient adjoint computation for wavelet and convolution operators [lecture notes]. IEEE Sig. Process. Mag. **33**(6), 135–147 (2016)
16. He, K., Zhang, X., Ren, S., Sun, J.: Delving deep into rectifiers: Surpassing human-level performance on ImageNet classification. In: Proceedings of the IEEE International Conference on Computer Vision, pp. 1026–1034 (2015)

17. Hendriksen, A.A., Pelt, D.M., Batenburg, K.J.: Noise2inverse: Self-supervised deep convolutional denoising for tomography. IEEE Trans. Comput. Imaging **6**, 1320–1335 (2020)
18. Ji, H., Wang, K.: Robust image deblurring with an inaccurate blur kernel. IEEE Trans. Image Process. **21**(4), 1624–1634 (2011)
19. Jin, M., Roth, S., Favaro, P.: Noise-blind image deblurring. In: Proceedings of the IEEE Conference on Computer Vision and Pattern Recognition, pp. 3834–3842 (2017)
20. Krishnan, D., Fergus, R.: Fast image deconvolution using hyper-laplacian priors. Adv. Neural Inf. Process. Syst. **22**, 1033–1041 (2009)
21. Kruse, J., Rother, C., Schmidt, U.: Learning to push the limits of efficient FFT-based image deconvolution. In: Proceedings of the IEEE International Conference on Computer Vision, pp. 4586–4594 (2017)
22. Lai, W.S., Huang, J.B., Hu, Z., Ahuja, N., Yang, M.H.: A comparative study for single image blind deblurring. In: Proceedings of the IEEE Conference on Computer Vision and Pattern Recognition, pp. 1701–1709 (2016)
23. Levin, A., Weiss, Y., Durand, F., Freeman, W.T.: Efficient marginal likelihood optimization in blind deconvolution. In: Proceedings of the IEEE Conference on Computer Vision and Pattern Recognition, pp. 2657–2664. IEEE (2011)
24. Li, W., Zhang, J., Dai, Q.: Exploring aligned complementary image pair for blind motion deblurring. In: Proceedings of the IEEE Conference on Computer Vision and Pattern Recognition, pp. 273–280 (2011)
25. Lim, S., Park, H., Lee, S.E., Chang, S., Sim, B., Ye, J.C.: Cyclegan with a blur kernel for deconvolution microscopy: optimal transport geometry. IEEE Trans. Comput. Imaging **6**, 1127–1138 (2020)
26. Meinhardt, T., Moller, M., Hazirbas, C., Cremers, D.: Learning proximal operators: using denoising networks for regularizing inverse imaging problems. In: Proceedings of the IEEE International Conference on Computer Vision, pp. 1781–1790 (2017)
27. Michaeli, T., Irani, M.: Blind deblurring using internal patch recurrence. In: Fleet, D., Pajdla, T., Schiele, B., Tuytelaars, T. (eds.) ECCV 2014. LNCS, vol. 8691, pp. 783–798. Springer, Cham (2014). https://doi.org/10.1007/978-3-319-10578-9_51
28. Nan, Y., Ji, H.: Deep learning for handling kernel/model uncertainty in image deconvolution. In: Proceedings of the IEEE/CVF Conference on Computer Vision and Pattern Recognition, pp. 2388–2397 (2020)
29. Nan, Y., Quan, Y., Ji, H.: Variational-EM-based deep learning for noise-blind image deblurring. In: Proceedings of the IEEE/CVF Conference on Computer Vision and Pattern Recognition, pp. 3626–3635 (2020)
30. Nayar, S.K., Ben-Ezra, M.: Motion-based motion deblurring. IEEE Trans. Pattern Anal. Mach. Intell. **26**(6), 689–698 (2004)
31. Pan, J., Sun, D., Pfister, H., Yang, M.H.: Blind image deblurring using dark channel prior. In: Proceedings of the IEEE Conference on Computer Vision and Pattern Recognition, pp. 1628–1636 (2016)
32. Pang, T., Quan, Y., Ji, H.: Self-supervised bayesian deep learning for image recovery with applications to compressive sensing. In: Vedaldi, A., Bischof, H., Brox, T., Frahm, J.-M. (eds.) ECCV 2020. LNCS, vol. 12356, pp. 475–491. Springer, Cham (2020). https://doi.org/10.1007/978-3-030-58621-8_28
33. Pang, T., Zheng, H., Quan, Y., Ji, H.: Recorrupted-to-recorrupted: unsupervised deep learning for image denoising. In: Proceedings of the IEEE/CVF Conference on Computer Vision and Pattern Recognition, pp. 2043–2052 (2021)

34. Perrone, D., Favaro, P.: Total variation blind deconvolution: the devil is in the details. In: Proceedings of the IEEE Conference on Computer Vision and Pattern Recognition, pp. 2909–2916 (2014)

35. Pronina, V., Kokkinos, F., Dylov, D.V., Lefkimmiatis, S.: Microscopy image restoration with deep wiener-kolmogorov filters. In: Proceedings of the European Conference on Computer Vision (2020)

36. Quan, Y., Ji, H., Shen, Z.: Data-driven multi-scale non-local wavelet frame construction and image recovery. J. Sci. Comput. **63**(2), 307–329 (2015)

37. Ren, D., Zuo, W., Zhang, D., Xu, J., Zhang, L.: Partial deconvolution with inaccurate blur kernel. IEEE Trans. Image Process. **27**(1), 511–524 (2017)

38. Ren, W., et al.: Deep non-blind deconvolution via generalized low-rank approximation. Adv. Neural Inf. Process. Syst. **31**, 297–307 (2018)

39. Schmidt, U., Jancsary, J., Nowozin, S., Roth, S., Rother, C.: Cascades of regression tree fields for image restoration. IEEE Trans. Neural Netw. Learn. Syst. **38**(4), 677–689 (2015)

40. Soltanayev, S., Chun, S.Y.: Training deep learning based denoisers without ground truth data. In: Advances in Neural Information Processing Systems (2018)

41. Sun, L., Cho, S., Wang, J., Hays, J.: Edge-based blur kernel estimation using patch priors. In: Proceedings of the IEEE International Conference on Computational Photography, pp. 1–8. IEEE (2013)

42. Vasu, S., Maligireddy, V.R., Rajagopalan, A.: Non-blind deblurring: handling kernel uncertainty with CNNs. In: Proceedings of the IEEE/CVF Conference on Computer Vision and Pattern Recognition, pp. 3272–3281 (2018)

43. Wang, W., Li, J., Ji, H.: Self-supervised deep image restoration via adaptive stochastic gradient langevin dynamics. In: Proceedings of the IEEE/CVF Conference on Computer Vision and Pattern Recognition, pp. 1989–1998 (2022)

44. Wang, Z., Wang, Z., Li, Q., Bilen, H.: Image deconvolution with deep image and kernel priors. In: Proceedings of the IEEE/CVF International Conference on Computer Vision Workshops (2019)

45. Whyte, O., Sivic, J., Zisserman, A.: Deblurring shaken and partially saturated images. Int. J. Comput. Vision **110**(2), 185–201 (2014). https://doi.org/10.1007/s11263-014-0727-3

46. Xia, Z., Chakrabarti, A.: Training image estimators without image ground-truth. In: Advances in Neural Information Processing Systems (2019)

47. Xu, J., Zhang, L., Zuo, W., Zhang, D., Feng, X.: Patch group based nonlocal self-similarity prior learning for image denoising. In: Proceedings of the IEEE international Conference on Computer Vision, pp. 244–252 (2015)

48. Xu, L., Jia, J.: Two-phase kernel estimation for robust motion deblurring. In: Daniilidis, K., Maragos, P., Paragios, N. (eds.) ECCV 2010. LNCS, vol. 6311, pp. 157–170. Springer, Heidelberg (2010). https://doi.org/10.1007/978-3-642-15549-9_12

49. Xu, L., Zheng, S., Jia, J.: Unnatural l0 sparse representation for natural image deblurring. In: Proceedings of the IEEE Conference on Computer Vision and Pattern Recognition, pp. 1107–1114 (2013)

50. Zhang, J., Pan, J., Lai, W.S., Lau, R., Yang, M.H.: Learning fully convolutional networks for iterative non-blind deconvolution. In: Proceedings of the IEEE Conference on Computer Vision and Pattern Recognition, pp. 6969–6977 (2017)

51. Zhang, K., Zuo, W., Gu, S., Zhang, L.: Learning deep CNN denoiser prior for image restoration. In: Proceedings of the IEEE Conference on Computer Vision and Pattern Recognition, vol. 2, pp. 2808–2817 (2017)

52. Zhang, Y., et al.: A poisson-gaussian denoising dataset with real fluorescence microscopy images. In: Proceedings of the IEEE/CVF Conference on Computer Vision and Pattern Recognition, pp. 11710–11718 (2019)
53. Zukerman, J., Tirer, T., Giryes, R.: BP-DIP: a backprojection based deep image prior. In: Proceedings of the European Signal Processing Conference (2020)

NEST: Neural Event Stack
for Event-Based Image Enhancement

Minggui Teng[1], Chu Zhou[2], Hanyue Lou[1], and Boxin Shi[1,3,4(✉)]

[1] NERCVT, School of Computer Science, Peking University, Beijing, China
shiboxin@pku.edu.cn
[2] KLMP (MOE), School of Artificial Intelligence, Peking University, Beijing, China
[3] Institute for Artificial Intelligence, Peking University, Beijing, China
[4] Beijing Academy of Artificial Intelligence, Beijing, China

Abstract. Event cameras demonstrate unique characteristics such as high temporal resolution, low latency, and high dynamic range to improve performance for various image enhancement tasks. However, event streams cannot be applied to neural networks directly due to their sparse nature. To integrate events into traditional computer vision algorithms, an appropriate event representation is desirable, while existing voxel grid and event stack representations are less effective in encoding motion and temporal information. This paper presents a novel event representation named Neural Event STack (**NEST**), which satisfies physical constraints and encodes comprehensive motion and temporal information sufficient for image enhancement. We apply our representation on multiple tasks, which achieves superior performance on image deblurring and image super-resolution than state-of-the-art methods on both synthetic and real datasets. And we further demonstrate the possibility to generate high frame rate videos with our novel event representation.

Keywords: Event camera · Image enhancement · Event representation

1 Introduction

Event cameras, such as Dynamic Vision Sensor (DVS) [16], can detect brightness changes and trigger events whenever the increase (decrease) of latent irradiance exceeds a preset threshold. They are widely used in image enhancement tasks since they possess clear advantages over traditional cameras in various aspects, such as high temporal resolution, low latency, and high dynamic range (HDR). However, event streams are represented as multiple four coordinates signals (x, y, t, p), and such continuous event signals cannot be processed by traditional computer vision algorithms directly, which brings a natural gap to leverage the advantages of events for image enhancement.

Project page: https://github.com/ChipsAhoyM/NEST.

Supplementary Information The online version contains supplementary material available at https://doi.org/10.1007/978-3-031-20068-7_38.

© The Author(s), under exclusive license to Springer Nature Switzerland AG 2022
S. Avidan et al. (Eds.): ECCV 2022, LNCS 13666, pp. 660–676, 2022.
https://doi.org/10.1007/978-3-031-20068-7_38

(a) Blurry image   (b) Event   (c) eSL-Net × 4   (d) Ours × 4

Fig. 1. An example result of NEST-guided image enhancement with 4× super-resolution. (a) Blurry image. (b) Corresponding events (color pair {blue, red} represents the event polarity {positive, negative} throughout this paper). (c) Result of eSL-Net [31]. (d) Our result. (Color figure online)

Finding a favored representation as input is important for event-based image enhancement tasks. Discretizing event signals in the time domain is an intuitive choice. This could be achieved by recording the timestamp of the last event in each pixel location [14], by inserting events into a voxel grid using a linearly weighted accumulation similar to bilinear interpolation [37], or by merging and stacking events within a time interval or a fixed number of events [32]. Despite their simplicity, when the number of channels divided from events increases, noisy events in such hand-crafted representations become hardly distinguishable from useful signals.

Neural representation has become a popular choice in event embedding procedures recently. Useful features could be extracted from event sequences with multi-layer perceptron (MLP) [6,25], spike neural network (SNN) [35], long short-term memory (LSTM) [3,20], and graph neural network (GNN) [1,15]. Despite their effectiveness in object recognition [1,3,6,15,20,35] and segmentation [25], these representations are not supposed to be optimized for image enhancement tasks, since they focus more on preserving semantic information well instead of caring about pixel-wise information, while the latter is crucial for image enhancement. The fact that hand-crafted event representations are prone to noise and neural representations sacrifice contextual information motivates us to propose a tailored representation for event-based image enhancement.

In this paper, we introduce Neural Event STack (**NEST**), which satisfies event physical constraints while faithfully encodes motion and temporal information with less noise involved. We first propose a NEST estimator to transform an event sequence into NESTs by a bidirectional convolutional long short-term memory (ConvLSTM) block [28] in a data-driven manner to fulfill event embedding. Tailored to the NEST, we then propose a NEST-guided Deblurring Net (D-Net) for image deblurring and a NEST-guided Super-resolution Net (S-Net) for image super-resolution, with simple architectures (a NEST-guided image enhancement example is shown in Fig. 1). By parallel processing multiple NESTs with D-Net and S-Net, high frame rate (HFR) videos can be restored with sharper edges and higher resolution.

Overall, this paper contributes in the following aspects:

Table 1. Comparison of LSTM-based event representations. H and W denote the image height and width, C denotes the number of channels, and T denotes the number of temporal bins.

Representation	Dimensions	Characteristics		
		Direction	Resolution	Hidden states
PhasedLSTM [20]	1D vector	Uni-direction	Fixed	Discarded
MatrixLSTM [3]	$C \times H \times W$			
NEST	$T \times C \times H \times W$	Bi-direction	Arbitrary	Preserved

- a neural representation (NEST) comprehensively encoding motion and temporal information from events in a noise-robust manner;
- event-based solutions for image deblurring and super-resolution taking benefit from the new representation;
- a unified framework for HFR video generation guided by NESTs.

We quantitatively and qualitatively evaluate our method on both synthetic and real datasets and demonstrate its superior performance over state-of-the-art methods.

2   Related Work

2.1   Event Representation

Event data possess many attractive advantages such as high speed and high dynamic range. However, it is difficult to apply computer vision algorithms designed for ordinary images to events, since event data are essentially different from image frames. Many algorithms try to find an event representation compatible with frame-based data, and they can be divided into two categories: hand-crafted representation and data-driven representation.

Hand-Crafted Representation. Lagorce et al. [14] proposed the time surface representation, obtained by keeping track of the timestamp of the last event that occurred in each location. Based on the time surface representation, Sironi et al. [30] proposed using histograms of averaged time surfaces (HATS), preserving more temporal information in histograms. To avoid the "motion overwriting" problem in the time surface representation, Zhu et al. [37] proposed the voxel grid representation, which inserts events into a voxel grid using a linearly weighted accumulation similar to bilinear interpolation. Wang et al. [32] proposed an event stack representation, which forms events as multiple frame event stacks by merging and stacking them within a time interval or a fixed number of events.

Data-Driven Representation. Recently data-driven models show higher robustness for event representation. Sekikawa et al. [25] proposed a recursive architecture and used MLP for computing a recursive formula. Gehrig et al. [6]

used MLP to encode time information of event sequences and summed up values from MLP to construct an event spike tensor. Inspired by biological mechanisms, Yao et al. [35] encoded events with attention SNN by processing events as asynchronous spikes. To better exploit the topological structure inside events sequences, Bi et al. [1] and Li et al. [15] used a graph to represent the event cloud with GNN and further conducted graph convolutions to obtain the event representation. Besides, to better exploit temporal information of events sequences, Neil et al. [20] proposed PhasedLSTM with a new time gate for processing asynchronous events. Cannici et al. [3] proposed the MatrixLSTM representation which integrates event sequences conditionally with LSTM cells. Although these representations show great potential in multiple computer vision tasks (e.g., object recognition, segmentation, and optical flow estimation), hand-crafted representations are still popular for image enhancement tasks, since data-driven representations for these tasks are not readily available. Particularly, LSTM-based methods show great potential in event representation. A comparison of LSTM-based event representations and their design choices are summarized in Table 1. The method in [3] emphasizes preserving sparsity when computing the MatrixLSTM, it is not suitable for image enhancement tasks due to the loss of connection around neighboring pixels. Thus, a proper event representation method tailored to image enhancement tasks is desired.

2.2 Event-Based Image Enhancement

Event-Based Image Deblurring. Pan et al. [21] proposed a simple and effective approach, the Event-based Double Integral (EDI) model, to reconstruct an HFR sharp video from a single blurry frame and corresponding event data. Jiang et al.[11] proposed a convolutional recurrent neural network and a differentiable directional event filtering module to recover sharp images. Lin et al. [17] proposed a deep CNN with a dynamic filtering layer to deblur and generate videos in a frame-aware manner. Wang et al. [31] proposed an event-enhanced sparse learning network named eSL-Net to address deblurring, denoising, and super-resolution simultaneously. Shang et al. [26] detected the nearest sharp frames with events, and then performed deblurring guided by the nearest sharp frames.

Event-Based Image Super-Resolution. Jing et al. [12] proposed an event-based video super-resolution framework, which reconstructs high-frequency low resolution (LR) frames interpolated with events and merges them to form a high resolution (HR) frame. Han et al. [7] proposed a two-stage network to fuse event temporal information with images and established event-based single image super-resolution as a multi-frame super-resolution problem.

For these event-based image enhancement methods, event stack is the most widely adopted choice [7,10–12,17,26,33] for representation due to simplicity, despite its poor robustness to noise. In the next section, we will first revisit the formulation of deblurring and super-resolution with events and analyze the demerits of applying the event stack representation method for image enhancement. We then propose the NEST representation to solve these problems.

3   NEST: Representation

In this section, we first derive the formulation of bidirectional event summations, which bridge the gap between low-quality images and high-quality images with events in Sect. 3.1. Based on bidirectional event summations, we briefly analyze the advantages and disadvantages of event stack representation. To avoid noisy events interference, we propose a neural representation to robustly implement bidirectional event summations in Sect. 3.2. Finally, we introduce the model design of our NEST estimator in Sect. 3.3.

3.1   Bidirectional Event Summation

An event e is a quadruple (x, y, t, p) triggered when the log intensity change exceeds a preset threshold c, $i.e.$,

$$| \log(\mathbf{I}_{x,y}^t) - \log(\mathbf{I}_{x,y}^{t-\Delta t})| \geq c, \tag{1}$$

in which $\mathbf{I}_{x,y}^t$ and $\mathbf{I}_{x,y}^{t-\Delta t}$ represent the instantaneous intensity at time t and $t - \Delta t$ respectively for pixel (x, y), and Δt denotes the time interval since the last event occurred at the same position. Polarity $p \in \{1, -1\}$ indicates the direction (increase or decrease) of intensity change. Eq. (1) applies to each pixel (x, y) independently, and pixel indices are omitted henceforth.

Given two instantaneous intensity frames $\mathbf{I}^{t_r}$ and $\mathbf{I}^{t_i}$, let's assume there are N_e events triggered between time t_r and t_i, denoted as $\{e_k\}_{k=1}^{N_e}$. According to the physical model of the event camera, if $t_r \leq t_i$, the event makes a connection between $\mathbf{I}^{t_r}$ and $\mathbf{I}^{t_i}$ as:

$$\mathbf{I}^{t_i} = \mathbf{I}^{t_r} \cdot \exp(\sum_{k=1}^{N_e} c_r \cdot e_k)$$

$$= \mathbf{I}^{t_r} \cdot \tilde{\mathbf{S}}_{r \to i}^{c_r} \quad (t_r \leq t_i), \tag{2}$$

where $\tilde{\mathbf{S}}_{r \to i}^{c_r}$ denotes event summation from time t_r to t_i in the exponential space with a time-varying threshold c_r. c_r approximately follows a normal distribution over time [22].

Deriving from Eq. (2), we can also obtain $\mathbf{I}^{t_r}$ from $\mathbf{I}^{t_i}$ by reversing the event summation $(t_r > t_i)$. Thus, we formulate the $bidirectional\ event\ summation$ $\mathbf{S}_{r \to i}^{c_r}$ to consider both cases, $i.e.$,

$$\mathbf{S}_{r \to i}^{c_r} = \begin{cases} \tilde{\mathbf{S}}_{r \to i}^{c_r} & (t_r \leq t_i), \\ 1/\tilde{\mathbf{S}}_{i \to r}^{c_i} & (t_r > t_i). \end{cases} \tag{3}$$

Combining Eq. (3), Eq. (2) can be further expanded to include both forward and reverse event summation:

$$\mathbf{I}^{t_i} = \mathbf{I}^{t_r} \cdot \mathbf{S}_{r \to i}^{c_r}. \tag{4}$$

Image Enhancement with Events. Ill-posedness is a common problem in image enhancement tasks, such as image deblurring and super-resolution. For image deblurring, a blurry image $\mathbf{B}$ can be modeled as the average over a sequence of latent sharp frames $\{\mathbf{I}^{t_i}\}_{i=1}^{N_f}$ [21]:

$$\mathbf{B} \approx \frac{1}{N_f} \sum_{i=1}^{N_f} \mathbf{I}^{t_i}, \tag{5}$$

in which N_f is the number of latent sharp frames. Obviously, there are multiple groups of latent frames satisfying Eq. (5), which brings difficulty to recover sharp frames from a single blurry image.

For image super-resolution, an HR frame can be reconstructed by a sequence of latent sharp frames $\{\mathbf{I}_{LR}^{t_i}\}_{i=1}^{N_f}$, i.e.,

$$\mathbf{I}_{SR}^{t_i} = \Uparrow \{\mathbf{I}_{LR}^{t_j}\}_{j=1}^{N_f}, \tag{6}$$

where $\Uparrow$ denotes the multi-frame super-resolution operator, combining information from multiple LR frames to recover details that are missing in individual frames. However, it is hard to record multiple latent sharp frames with traditional cameras, which means we need to generate an HR frame with a single LR frame leading to ill-posedness.

As Eq. (4) has shown the relationship of two latent frames by corresponding events, ill-posedness can be relieved by integrating image and events. By combining Eq. (4) and Eq. (5), we obtain:

$$\mathbf{B} \approx \mathbf{I}^{t_i} \cdot \left(\frac{1}{N_f} \sum_{j=1}^{N_f} \mathbf{S}_{i \to j}^{c_i}\right). \tag{7}$$

By substituting Eq. (4), we can rewrite Eq. (6) as follows:

$$\mathbf{I}_{SR}^{t_i} = \Uparrow \{\mathbf{I}_{LR}^{t_i} \cdot \mathbf{S}_{i \to j}^{c_i}\}_{j=1}^{N_f}. \tag{8}$$

Since the bidirectional event summations $\{\mathbf{S}_{i \to j}^{c_i}\}_{j=1}^{N_f}$ are independent of the latent frames, we can restore arbitrary sharp latent frames from a single blurry image or reconstruct arbitrary HR frames from a single LR frame with the corresponding events directly.

3.2   Neural Representation

According to Sect. 3.1, the bidirectional event summation establishes the relationship between low-quality (blurry, LR) images and high-quality (sharp, HR) images. As shown in Eq. (7) and Eq. (8), image deblurring needs the average value of the set, and image super-resolution depends on the magnitude difference of each element in the set for recovering details. Thus, the event signal can be discretized in the time domain to form bidirectional event summations $\{\mathbf{S}_{i \to j}^{c_i}\}_{j=1}^{N_f}$, which can guide image enhancement tasks.

Event stack forms events as multiple frames by merging and stacking them within a time interval or a fixed number of events [32]. Intuitively bidirectional event summations can be seen as a combination of event stacks with linear weights, which can be learned implicitly by a neural network, so that event stack works well in image enhancement tasks. However, event stack will be noise-sensitive when the time resolution increases since they become sparser with more channel numbers, which degrades the restored image quality. Thus, it is necessary to transform event stacks [32] into a more robust representation.

Inspired by data-driven representations in the deep learning field, to fully utilize such information to address these problems, we propose a robust neural representation, named $\underline{\text{N}}$eural $\underline{\text{E}}$vent $\underline{\text{ST}}$ack (**NEST**), to replace $\{\mathbf{S}_{i \to j}^{c_i}\}_{j=1}^{N_f}$ and guide image enhancement. NEST representation explicitly learns the combination parameters of event stack to achieve a robust representation. By substituting bidirectional event summations with NESTs, high-quality frames can be restored according to Eq. (7) and Eq. (8) as below:

$$\mathbf{I}^{t_i} = f_d\left(\mathbf{B}, \mathbf{E}^i\right), \tag{9}$$

$$\mathbf{I}_{SR}^{t_i} = f_s\left(\mathbf{I}_{LR}^{t_i}, \mathbf{E}^i\right), \tag{10}$$

where f_d and f_s are implicit functions derived from Eq. (7) and Eq. (8), and $\mathbf{E}^i$ denotes a NEST.

From Eq. (9) and Eq. (10), we could see that once the NEST $\mathbf{E}^i$ is properly estimated, image enhancement tasks such as deblurring and super-resolution can be solved in a more robust manner. Besides, since the NEST is implemented by deep neural networks in a data-driven manner, it naturally extracts semantic information in the event sequence, which can facilitate the reconstruction of high-quality images. Therefore, our goal turns into estimating NESTs first, and then using NESTs to guide image deblurring and super-resolution procedures. To achieve that goal, we propose three specific sub-networks for estimating NESTs and modeling the implicit functions f_d and f_s respectively, as introduced in the following sections.

3.3   NEST Estimator

To obtain robust event representation, we design a NEST estimator to transform event stacks [32] into NESTs. From Eq. (3), we can divide $\mathbf{E}^i$ into two parts. The preceding part $\{\mathbf{S}_{i \to j}^{c_i}\}_{j=1}^{i-1}$ is represented by $\mathbf{E}_p^i$, and the following part $\{\mathbf{S}_{i \to j}^{c_i}\}_{j=i}^{N_f}$ is represented by $\mathbf{E}_f^i$, which encodes the events before and after time t_i respectively. Therefore, we design the NEST estimator to encode preceding and following events separately as shown in Fig. 2. Such a network can be expressed as:

$$\{\mathbf{E}^i\}_{i=1}^{N_f} = \{(\mathbf{E}_p^i, \mathbf{E}_f^i)\}_{i=1}^{N_f} = f_n\left(\{\mathbf{e}_i^{i+1}\}_{i=1}^{N_f}\right), \tag{11}$$

where f_n denotes our NEST estimator and $\{\mathbf{e}\}_i^{i+1}$ represents the events triggered in t_i to t_{i+1}.

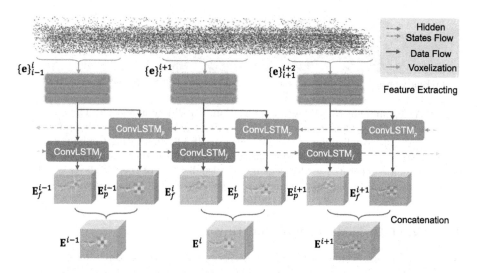

Fig. 2. The architecture of our NEST estimator, which consists of a parameter-shared feature extractor and a bidirectional ConvLSTM block. The input raw events $\{e\}_i^{i+1}$ (triggered in t_i to t_{i+1}) are first binned into an event stack (voxelization), and then transformed into a NEST $\mathbf{E}^i$. ConvLSTM$_p$ encodes the preceding part and ConvLSTM$_f$ for the following part of events.

We first use a feature extractor block, consisting of multiple dense convolution layers [9], to perform local event feature extraction. Recent work has shown that dense convolution can extract high-level features, and filter most noisy events [4]. Then a bidirectional ConvLSTM block [28] is used to construct NESTs, which can not only encode temporal information lying in events but also fuse spatial information and reconstruct gradient information by the convolution operation.

From the event formation model [5], the expectation of event noise is zero. Since NESTs are generated by bi-directional encoding, paired noisy events are combined with temporal-variant thresholds, effectively suppressing noisy events. Besides, thanks to the data-driven encoding operation, NESTs also contain contextual information of the scene, which cannot be encoded by hand-crafted representations like event stacks [32]. As the example shown in Fig. 3, NESTs contain the statistical event information such as event-triggered frequency (Fig. 3 (c)) to indicate the blurry region, and a rough segmentation (Fig. 3 (d)) of the captured frame to distinguish the less blurred background, which both serve as global priors for reconstructing the high-quality image.

4   NEST: Application

In this section, we conduct three experiments: image deblurring (Sect. 4.1), super resolution (Sect. 4.2), and HFR video generation (Sect. 4.3) guided by NESTs to validate the effectiveness of NEST.

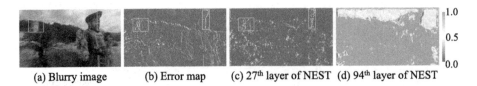

|(a) Blurry image | (b) Error map | (c) 27th layer of NEST | (d) 94th layer of NEST |

Fig. 3. An example of NEST layer visualization. (a) Blurry image. (b) The error map between blurry image and ground truth, indicating the blurry region with higher difference values. (c) Visualization of the 27th layer of NEST, illustrating the blurry region. As highlighted in orange boxes, the blurry region has a higher response value, since more events are generated in this region. (d) Visualization of the 94th layer of NEST, separating less blurry sky apart from the foreground with different response values.

4.1 NEST-Guided Image Deblurring

After embedding events as NESTs, we can use them to conduct image deblurring. Since NESTs contain not only motion information but also global semantic information (an example shown in Fig. 3 (c) and (d)), we propose the NEST-guided D-Net to perform image deblurring by making full use of motion and global semantic information. Guided by NESTs, the image deblurring can be viewed as multi-modality fusion tasks. Thus, we adopt a U-Net-like [23] network architecture to perform image deblurring. We also formulate it as the residual learning with global connection, by fusing motion and intensity information to calculate the residual between the blurry image and the sharp one.[1]

Experiment Result. Our experiment can be divided into 3 parts. The first part (I) compares NEST-guided image deblurring with a state-of-the-art learning-based video deblurring method ESTRNN [36] and three state-of-the-art event-based image deblurring methods: EDI [21], LEDVDI [17], and eSL-Net [31]. To validate the effectiveness of the NEST representation, the second part (II) compares with the event stack representation method and another two data-driven event representations combined with our D-Net (denoted EvST+D/S [32], EST+D/S [6] and MatrixLSTM+D/S [3]). Besides, the third part (III) replaces eSL-Net's event stack representation with NEST representation (named NEST+eSL) to better illustrate the robustness of NEST. For a fair comparison, we retrained ESTRNN [36] on our training dataset.[2]

The quantitative comparison results are shown in Table 2 (a) and qualitative comparisons are shown in Fig. 4. We can see that our method outperforms others on all metrics. Compared to the video deblurring method ESTRNN [36], our method recovers sharper details encoding inside NESTs. As for event-based methods and other event representation methods, our method restored sharp images with fewer artifacts, with NEST's robust event representation. Thanks to the motion and semantic information encoded inside the NESTs, our network can handle blurry images with complicated real scenarios. Besides, as compari-

---

[1] Detailed D-Net and S-Net configurations are in the supplementary material.

[2] ∗ denotes retraining on our training dataset.

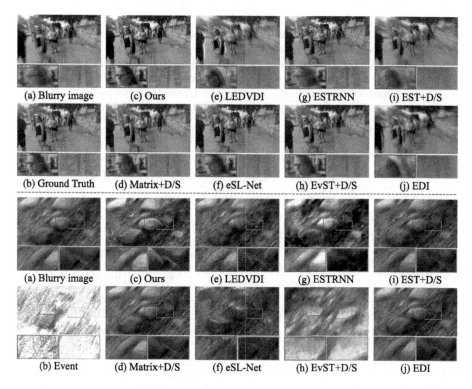

Fig. 4. Qualitative comparisons for deblurring application on synthetic data (upper) and real data (lower). (a) Blurry image. (b) Ground truth (synthetic data) / Event (real data). (c)~(j) Deblurring results of ours,Matrix+D/S [3], LEDVDI [17], eSL-Net [31], ESTRNN [36], EvST+D/S [32], EST+D/S [6], and EDI [21]. Close-up views are provided below each image.

son between eSL-Net [31] and NEST+eSL has shown Table 2, much lower LPIPS values demonstrate NEST representation can improve the performance.

4.2   NEST-Guided Image Super-Resolution

Event cameras show higher temporal resolution than traditional cameras, which demonstrates the possibility of performing single image super-resolution like multi-frame super-resolution with events to relieve the ill-posed issue. However, frame alignment is an unavoidable difficulty for multi-frame super-resolution. Fortunately, the high temporal resolution property of events only brings slight changes for consecutive latent frames. Besides, our NEST estimator adopts a bidirectional ConvLSTM block, which also aligns temporal information implicitly. To better exploit semantic information hidden in NESTs, we design the NEST-guided S-Net for image super-resolution.

In our S-Net, we use multiple Residual in Residual Dense Blocks (RRDBs) as proposed in ESRGAN [34] to extract different features from NESTs and images

Table 2. Quantitative comparisons for deblurring (a) and super-resolution (b) application on the synthetic testing dataset. ↑ (↓) indicates the higher (lower), the better. The best performances are highlighted in **bold**. Our experiment can be divided into 3 parts: The first part (I) is to compare with state-of-the-art image-based and event-based image enhancement methods; the second part (II) compares "X+D/S", where "X" is other event representation methods; and the third part (III) compares "NEST+X", where "X" is another state-of-the-art event-based image enhancement method;

Methods		Applications					
		(a) Deblurring			(b) Super-resolution		
		PNSR ↑	SSIM ↑	LPIPS ↓	PSNR ↑	SSIM ↑	LPIPS ↓
I	EDI [21]	20.96	0.5752	0.2537	–	–	–
	LEDVDI [17]	22.08	0.6222	0.1905	–	–	–
	ESTRNN* [36]	30.52	0.8901	0.1105	–	–	–
	SPSR* [18]	–	–	–	27.63	0.7471	0.2763
	RBPN* [8]	–	–	–	27.23	0.7738	0.2956
	EvIntSR [7]	–	–	–	27.52	0.7334	0.2893
II	EvST+D/S [32]	31.09	0.8977	0.0689	28.89	0.7992	0.3150
	EST+D/S [6]	24.10	0.6987	0.2253	13.14	0.6574	0.4765
	Matrix+D/S [3]	31.28	0.9022	0.0596	27.88	0.7966	0.2844
III	eSL-Net [31]	29.73	0.8697	0.1078	28.23	0.7783	0.3950
	NEST+eSL [31]	29.92	0.8935	0.0634	28.87	0.7961	0.3096
Ours		**32.56**	**0.9354**	**0.0422**	**29.43**	**0.8128**	**0.2745**

independently. Besides, we incorporate features extracted from NESTs to the image branch, fusing temporal and global semantic information hidden in the NESTs to guide image super-resolution. Finally, we add a pixel shuffle layer [27] to rearrange features and predict image residual between LR image and HR image. By employing it to the upsampled image with bilinear interpolation, the super-resolved image can be restored.

Experiment Results. Similar to deblurring application, the first part (I) compares NEST-guided image super-resolution with two state-of-the-art learning-based image super-resolution methods SPSR [18] (taking in a single frame) and RBPN [8] (taking in multiple frames from a video), and two state-of-the-art event-based image super-resolution methods: eSL-Net [31] and EvIntSR [7]. The second part (II) compares with event stack representation method and two data-driven event representations combined with our S-Net (denoted EvST+D/S [32], EST+D/S [6] and MatrixLSTM+D/S [3]). The third part (III) replaces eSL-Net's event stack representation with NEST (named NEST+eSL).

The quantitative comparison results are shown in Table 2 (b) and qualitative comparisons are shown in Fig. 5. As experiments on real data show in Fig. 5,

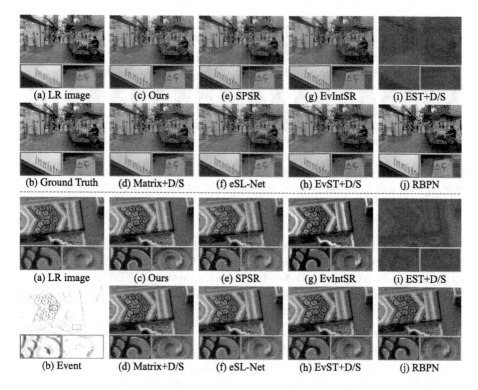

Fig. 5. Qualitative comparisons for super-resolution application on synthetic data (upper) and real data (lower). (a) LR image. (b) Ground truth (synthetic data) / Event (real data). (c)~(j) Super-resolved 4× results of ours, Matrix+D/S [3], SPSR [18], NEST+eSL [31], EvIntSR [7], EvST+D/S [32], EST+D/S [6], and RBPN [8]. Close-up views are provided below each image.

results obtained by compared methods are distorted by noise, since the quality of intensity frames captured by DAVIS346 cameras is lower than the outputs of traditional cameras. But our method is noise-resistant thanks to NEST's robust representation. Like the deblurring application, eSL-Net [31] can achieve better performance combined with NEST.[3]

4.3 NEST-Guided HFR Video Generation

As Eq. (11) shows, we can obtain multiple NESTs in one pass by ConvLSTM. As shown in Table 1, compared to other LSTM-based event representations such as MatrixLSTM [3] or PhasedLSTM [20], our method preserves the intermediate states of ConvLSTM cells. Therefore, it brings the possibility to extend our D-Net and S-Net to process multiple NESTs in parallel to produce HFR

---

[3] Qualitative comparison between eSL-Net and NEST+eSL on deblurring and SR applications can be found in the supplementary material.

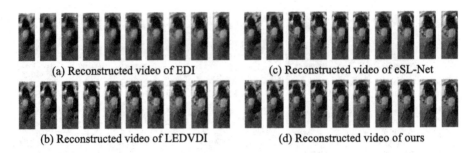

(a) Reconstructed video of EDI   (c) Reconstructed video of eSL-Net

(b) Reconstructed video of LEDVDI   (d) Reconstructed video of ours

Fig. 6. Qualitative comparisons for HFR video generation application on synthetic data. The crop of reconstructed video frames from (a) EDI [21], (b) LEDVDI [17], (c) eSL-Net [31], and (d) ours are shown.

videos without modifying the original architecture. To implement this, after event sequence was transformed into NESTs. We can then generate multiple sharp images in parallel by D-Net by combining multiple NESTs with a single blurry image. After that, S-Net can generate multiple deblurred HR frames from LR frames to form an HFR video.

Experiment Results. We conduct qualitative comparisons on synthetic data in Fig. 6 for generating HFR videos from a single blurry image, compared with three state-of-the-art event-based HFR video generation methods: EDI [21], LEDVDI [17], and eSL-Net [31]. The results demonstrate that our method can generate frames with sharper edges and better visual quality than other state-of-the-art methods.

4.4 Implementation Details

Loss Function. We use the same loss function for training D-Net and S-Net, which is defined as

$$\mathcal{L} = \alpha \cdot \mathcal{L}_2(\mathbf{I}_o, \mathbf{I}_{gt}) + \beta \cdot \mathcal{L}_{perc}(\mathbf{I}_o, \mathbf{I}_{gt}), \tag{12}$$

where $\mathbf{I}_o$ denotes output image, $\mathbf{I}_{gt}$ for ground truth, and α and β are set to 200 and 0.5 respectively. $\mathcal{L}_2$ denotes the loss on L_2 norm and $\mathcal{L}_{perc}$ for perceptual loss, which is defined as

$$\mathcal{L}_{perc}(\mathbf{I}_o, \mathbf{I}_{gt}) = \mathcal{L}_2(\phi_h(\mathbf{I}_o), \phi_h(\mathbf{I}_{gt})), \tag{13}$$

where ϕ_h denotes the feature map from h-th layer of VGG-19 network [29] pre-trained on ImageNet [24], and we use activations from $VGG_{3,3}$ and $VGG_{5,5}$ convolutional layer here.

Training Details. We implement our method using PyTorch on an NVIDIA 3090Ti GPU. D-Net and S-Net are both trained for 100 epochs and after the first 50 epochs, we linearly decay the learning rate to 0 over the next 50 epochs.

Table 3. Quantitative evaluation results of ablation study on the synthetic testing dataset.

Methods	Applications					
	(a) Deblurring			(b) Super-resolution		
	PSNR ↑	SSIM ↑	LPIPS ↓	PSNR ↑	SSIM ↑	LPIPS ↓
W/o global	30.74	0.8932	0.0569	28.66	0.7917	0.3075
W/o feature	31.68	0.9064	0.0520	29.20	0.8096	0.2768
Our complete model	**32.56**	**0.9354**	**0.0422**	**29.43**	**0.8128**	**0.2745**

The initial learning rate is set to 1×10^{-3} for D-Net and 1×10^{-4} for S-Net, respectively, and ADAM optimizer [13] is used in the training procedure.

Dataset. Our training and testing datasets are adopted from Wang *et al.* [31]. As their datasets only contain the gray-scale images, we regenerate RGB blurry images and LR images from the original REDS dataset [19] as Wang *et al.* [31] suggested. And our real data are captured by a DAVIS346 camera.

4.5 Ablation Study

We conduct a series of ablation studies. The quantitative comparison results of deblurring application are shown in Table 3 (a) and super-resolution application for Table 3 (b), to verify the validity of each model design choice. We first show the effectiveness of the feature extractor in the NEST estimator by removing it (W/o feature). Next, we show the effectiveness of learning the residual in D-Net and S-Net by removing the global connection (W/o global). As the results show, our complete model achieves the best performance.

5 Conclusion

We propose a novel event representation (NEST) and apply it to event-based image deblurring, super-resolution, and HFR video generation. Thanks to the advantage of NESTs, all these image enhancement methods demonstrate superior performance over state-of-the-art methods.

Discussion. Limited by the low quality of the intensity frame captured by a DAVIS346 camera, although this paper demonstrates convincing evidence of fusing event data to improve the quality of an intensity frame, the final quality still has a gap with sharp frames captured by a modern DLSR camera. In our future work, we hope to build an event-RGB hybrid camera to fuse with high-quality intensity frames. Although event cameras also demonstrate the high dynamic range property (130 dB for DAVIS240 [2]), due to the lack of HDR paired images in our training dataset, we do not optimize the results to handle the HDR issue from a single LDR image with corresponding events. Extending NEST with a well-designed HDR dataset and network is also left as our future work.

Acknowledgement. This work was supported by National Key R&D Program of China (2021ZD0109803) and National Natural Science Foundation of China under Grant No. 62136001, 62088102.

References

1. Bi, Y., Chadha, A., Abbas, A., Bourtsoulatze, E., Andreopoulos, Y.: Graph-based object classification for neuromorphic vision sensing. In: Proc. of International Conference on Computer Vision. pp. 491–501 (2019)
2. Brandli, C., Berner, R., Yang, M., Liu, S.C., Delbruck, T.: A 240 × 180 130 dB 3 μs latency global shutter spatiotemporal vision sensor. IEEE Journal of Solid-State Circuits **49**(10), 2333–2341 (2014)
3. Cannici, M., Ciccone, M., Romanoni, A., Matteucci, M.: A differentiable recurrent surface for asynchronous event-based data. In: Proc. of European Conference on Computer Vision. pp. 136–152 (2020)
4. Chen, H., Teng, M., Shi, B., Wang, Y., Huang, T.: Learning to deblur and generate high frame rate video with an event camera. arXiv preprint arXiv:2003.00847 (2020)
5. Duan, P., Wang, Z.W., Zhou, X., Ma, Y., Shi, B.: EventZoom: Learning to denoise and super resolve neuromorphic events. In: Proc. of Computer Vision and Pattern Recognition. pp. 12824–12833 (2021)
6. Gehrig, D., Loquercio, A., Derpanis, K.G., Scaramuzza, D.: End-to-end learning of representations for asynchronous event-based data. In: Proc. of International Conference on Computer Vision. pp. 5633–5643 (2019)
7. Han, J., Yang, Y., Zhou, C., Xu, C., Shi, B.: EvIntSR-Net: Event guided multiple latent frames reconstruction and super-resolution. In: Proc. of International Conference on Computer Vision. pp. 4882–4891 (2021)
8. Haris, M., Shakhnarovich, G., Ukita, N.: Recurrent back-projection network for video super-resolution. In: Proc. of Computer Vision and Pattern Recognition. pp. 3897–3906 (2019)
9. Huang, G., Liu, Z., Van Der Maaten, L., Weinberger, K.Q.: Densely connected convolutional networks. In: Proc. of Computer Vision and Pattern Recognition. pp. 4700–4708 (2017)
10. I., S.M.M., Choi, J., Yoon, K.: Learning to super resolve intensity images from events. In: Proc. of Computer Vision and Pattern Recognition. pp. 2765–2773 (2020)
11. Jiang, Z., Zhang, Y., Zou, D., Ren, J., Lv, J., Liu, Y.: Learning event-based motion deblurring. In: Proc. of Computer Vision and Pattern Recognition. pp. 3320–3329 (2020)
12. Jing, Y., Yang, Y., Wang, X., Song, M., Tao, D.: Turning frequency to resolution: Video super-resolution via event cameras. In: Proc. of Computer Vision and Pattern Recognition. pp. 7772–7781 (2021)
13. Kingma, D.P., Ba, J.: ADAM: A method for stochastic optimization. arXiv preprint arXiv:1412.6980 (2014)
14. Lagorce, X., Orchard, G., Galluppi, F., Shi, B.E., Benosman, R.B.: Hots: A hierarchy of event-based time-surfaces for pattern recognition. IEEE Transactions on Pattern Analysis and Machine Intelligence **39**(7), 1346–1359 (2016)
15. Li, Y., Zhou, H., Yang, B., Zhang, Y., Cui, Z., Bao, H., Zhang, G.: Graph-based asynchronous event processing for rapid object recognition. In: Proc. of International Conference on Computer Vision. pp. 934–943 (2021)

16. Lichtsteiner, P., Posch, C., Delbruck, T.: A 128 × 128 120 dB 15 μs latency asynchronous temporal contrast vision sensor. IEEE Journal of Solid-State Circuits **43**(2), 566–576 (2008)
17. Lin, S., Zhang, J., Pan, J., Jiang, Z., Zou, D., Wang, Y., Chen, J., Ren, J.: Learning event-driven video deblurring and interpolation. In: Proc. of European Conference on Computer Vision. pp. 695–710 (2020)
18. Ma, C., Rao, Y., Cheng, Y., Chen, C., Lu, J., Zhou, J.: Structure-preserving super resolution with gradient guidance. In: Proc. of Computer Vision and Pattern Recognition. pp. 7766–7775 (2020)
19. Nah, S., Baik, S., Hong, S., Moon, G., Son, S., Timofte, R., Mu Lee, K.: Ntire 2019 challenge on video deblurring and super-resolution: Dataset and study. In: Proc. of Computer Vision and Pattern Recognition Workshops. pp. 1996–2005 (2019)
20. Neil, D., Pfeiffer, M., Liu, S.C.: Phased LSTM: Accelerating recurrent network training for long or event-based sequences. In: Proc. of Neural Information Processing Systems. pp. 3882–3890 (2016)
21. Pan, L., Scheerlinck, C., Yu, X., Hartley, R., Liu, M., Dai, Y.: Bringing a blurry frame alive at high frame-rate with an event camera. In: Proc. of Computer Vision and Pattern Recognition. pp. 6820–6829 (2019)
22. Rebecq, H., Gehrig, D., Scaramuzza, D.: ESIM: an open event camera simulator. In: Conference on Robot Learning. pp. 969–982 (2018)
23. Ronneberger, O., Fischer, P., Brox, T.: U-Net: Convolutional networks for biomedical image segmentation. In: Proc. of International Conference on Medical Image Computing and Computer Assisted Intervention. pp. 234–241 (2015)
24. Russakovsky, O., Deng, J., Su, H., Krause, J., Satheesh, S., Ma, S., Huang, Z., Karpathy, A., Khosla, A., Bernstein, M., Berg, A.C., Fei-Fei, L.: ImageNet large scale visual recognition challenge. International Journal of Computer Vision **115**(3), 211–252 (2015)
25. Sekikawa, Y., Hara, K., Saito, H.: Eventnet: Asynchronous recursive event processing. In: Proc. of Computer Vision and Pattern Recognition. pp. 3887–3896 (2019)
26. Shang, W., Ren, D., Zou, D., Ren, J.S., Luo, P., Zuo, W.: Bringing events into video deblurring with non-consecutively blurry frames. In: Proc. of International Conference on Computer Vision. pp. 4531–4540 (2021)
27. Shi, W., Caballero, J., Huszár, F., Totz, J., Aitken, A.P., Bishop, R., Rueckert, D., Wang, Z.: Real-time single image and video super-resolution using an efficient sub-pixel convolutional neural network. In: Proc. of Computer Vision and Pattern Recognition. pp. 1874–1883 (2016)
28. Shi, X., Chen, Z., Wang, H., Yeung, D., Wong, W., Woo, W.: Convolutional LSTM network: A machine learning approach for precipitation nowcasting. In: Proc. of Neural Information Processing Systems. pp. 802–810 (2015)
29. Simonyan, K., Zisserman, A.: Very deep convolutional networks for large-scale image recognition. arXiv preprint arXiv:1409.1556 (2014)
30. Sironi, A., Brambilla, M., Bourdis, N., Lagorce, X., Benosman, R.: HATS: Histograms of averaged time surfaces for robust event-based object classification. In: Proc. of Computer Vision and Pattern Recognition. pp. 1731–1740 (2018)
31. Wang, B., He, J., Yu, L., Xia, G.S., Yang, W.: Event enhanced high-quality image recovery. In: Proc. of European Conference on Computer Vision (2020)
32. Wang, L., I., S.M.M., Ho, Y., Yoon, K.: Event-based high dynamic range image and very high frame rate video generation using conditional generative adversarial networks. In: Proc. of Computer Vision and Pattern Recognition. pp. 10081–10090 (2019)

33. Wang, L., Kim, T.K., Yoon, K.J.: EventSR: From asynchronous events to image reconstruction, restoration, and super-resolution via end-to-end adversarial learning. In: Proc. of Computer Vision and Pattern Recognition. pp. 8312–8322 (2020)

34. Wang, X., Yu, K., Wu, S., Gu, J., Liu, Y., Dong, C., Qiao, Y., Change Loy, C.: ESRGAN: Enhanced super-resolution generative adversarial networks. In: Proc. of European Conference on Computer Vision Workshops. pp. 63–79 (2018)

35. Yao, M., Gao, H., Zhao, G., Wang, D., Lin, Y., Yang, Z., Li, G.: Temporal-wise attention spiking neural networks for event streams classification. In: Proc. of International Conference on Computer Vision. pp. 10221–10230 (2021)

36. Zhong, Z., Gao, Y., Zheng, Y., Zheng, B.: Efficient spatio-temporal recurrent neural network for video deblurring. In: Proc. of European Conference on Computer Vision. pp. 191–207 (2020)

37. Zhu, A.Z., Yuan, L., Chaney, K., Daniilidis, K.: Unsupervised event-based learning of optical flow, depth, and egomotion. In: Proc. of Computer Vision and Pattern Recognition. pp. 989–997 (2019)

Editable Indoor Lighting Estimation

Henrique Weber[1]([⊠]) [iD], Mathieu Garon[2] [iD], and Jean-François Lalonde[1] [iD]

[1] Université Laval, Québec, Canada
henrique.weber.1@ulaval.ca
[2] Depix, Montréal, Canada
https://lvsn.github.io/EditableIndoorLight/

Abstract. We present a method for estimating lighting from a single perspective image of an indoor scene. Previous methods for predicting indoor illumination usually focus on either simple, parametric lighting that lack realism, or on richer representations that are difficult or even impossible to understand or modify after prediction. We propose a pipeline that estimates a parametric light that is easy to edit and allows renderings with strong shadows, alongside with a non-parametric texture with high-frequency information necessary for realistic rendering of specular objects. Once estimated, the predictions obtained with our model are interpretable and can easily be modified by an artist/user with a few mouse clicks. Quantitative and qualitative results show that our approach makes indoor lighting estimation easier to handle by a casual user, while still producing competitive results.

Keywords: Lighting estimation · Virtual object insertion · HDR

1 Introduction

Mixing virtual content realistically with real imagery is required in an increasing range of applications, from special effects to image editing and augmented reality (AR). This has created the need for capturing the lighting conditions of a scene with ever increasing accuracy and flexibility. In his seminal work, Debevec [6] suggested to capture the lighting conditions with a high dynamic range light probe. While it has been improved over the years, this technique, dubbed *image-based lighting*, is still at the heart of lighting capture for high end special effects in movies nowadays[1]. Since the democratization of virtual object insertion for consumer image editing and AR, capturing light conditions with light probes restricts non professional users to have access to the scene and to use specialized equipment. To circumvent those limitations, approaches for automatically estimating the lighting conditions directly from images have been proposed.

---

[1] See https://www.fxguide.com/fxfeatured/the-definitive-weta-digital-guide-to-ibl/.

Supplementary Information The online version contains supplementary material available at https://doi.org/10.1007/978-3-031-20068-7_39.

© The Author(s), under exclusive license to Springer Nature Switzerland AG 2022
S. Avidan et al. (Eds.): ECCV 2022, LNCS 13666, pp. 677–692, 2022.
https://doi.org/10.1007/978-3-031-20068-7_39

Input image   Lighting   Render   User edits lighting   Final render

Fig. 1. Our method produces an estimation of the indoor lighting from a single perspective image. Our lighting representation is composed of a 3D parametric light source, a texture map and a coarse 3D layout of the scene. With this information, it is possible to realistically insert 3D objects (like the golden armadillo and sphere) into the scene. Because our lighting representation is interpretable and intuitive, the user can experiment with possibilities by modifying, say, the position of the light source in order to achieve the desired look.

In this line of work, the trend has been to estimate more and more *complex* lighting representations. This is exemplified by works such as Lighthouse [25], which propose to learn a multi-scale volumetric representation from an input stereo pair. Similarly, Li et al. [19] learn a dense 2D grid of spherical gaussians over the image plane. Wang et al. [27] propose to learn a 3D volume of similar spherical gaussians. While these lighting representations have been shown to yield realistic and spatially-varying relighting results, they have the unfortunate downside of being hard to understand: they do not lend themselves to being easily editable by a user. This quickly becomes a source of limitation when erroneous automatic results need to be corrected for improved accuracy or when creative freedom is required.

In this work, we depart from this trend and propose a *simple, interpretable, and editable* lighting representation (Fig. 1). But what does it mean for a lighting representation to be editable? We argue that an editable lighting representation must: 1) *disentangle* various components of illumination; 2) allow an *intuitive control* over those components; and, of course, 3) enable *realistic relighting results*. Existing lighting representations in the literature do not possess all three properties. *Environment maps* [11,17,24] can be rotated but they compound light sources and environment textures together such that one cannot, say, easily increase the intensity of the light source without affecting everything else. Rotating the environment map inevitably rotates the entire scene, turning walls into ceilings, etc., when changing the elevation. *Dense and/or volumetric* representations [12,19,25,27] are composed of 2D (or 3D) grids containing hundreds of parameters, which would have to be modified in a consistent way to achieve the desired result, an unachievable task for most. *Parametric* representations [10] model individual light sources with a few intuitive parameters, which can be modified independently of the others, but cannot generate realistic reflections.

Our proposed representation is the first to offer all three desired properties and is composed of two parts: 1) a parametric light source for modeling shading in high dynamic range; and 2) a non-parametric texture to generate realistic reflections off of shiny objects. Our representation builds on the hypothesis (which we validate) that most indoor scenes can accurately be modeled by a *single*, dominant directional light source. We model this in high dynamic range with a parametric representation [10] that explicitly models the light source intensity, size, and 3D position. This representation is intuitive and can easily be edited by a user simply by moving the light source around in 3D.

This light source is complemented with a spatially-varying environment map texture, mapped onto a coarse 3D representation of the indoor scene. For this, we rely on a layout estimation network, which estimates a cuboid-like model of the scene from the input image. In addition, we also use a texture estimation network, whose output is conditioned on a combination of the input image, the scene layout and the parametric lighting representation. By explicitly tying the appearance of the environment texture with the position of the parametric light source, modifying the light source parameters (e.g. moving around the light) will automatically adjust the environment in a realistic fashion.

While our representation is significantly simplified, we find that it offers several advantages over the previous approaches. First, it renders both realistic shading (due to the high dynamic range of the estimated parametric light) and reflections (due to the estimated environment map texture). Second, it can efficiently be trained on real images, thereby alleviating any domain gap that typically arise when approaches need synthetic imagery for training [19,25,27]. Third—and perhaps most importantly—it is *interpretable and editable*. Since all automatic approaches are bound to make mistakes, it is of paramount importance in many scenarios that their output be adjustable by a user. By modifying the light parameters and/or the scene layout using simple user interfaces, our approach bridges the gap between realism and editability for lighting estimation.

2   Related Work

For succinctness, we focus on single-image indoor lighting estimation methods in the section below, and refer the reader to the recent survey on deep models for lighting estimation for a broader overview [8].

Lighting Estimation. Gardner et al. [11] proposed the first deep learning-based lighting estimation method for indoor scenes, and predicted an HDR environment map (equirectangular image) from a single image. This representation was also used in [17] for both indoors and outdoors, in [24] to take into account the object insertion position, in [23] which presented a real-time on-device approach, in [22] for scene decomposition, and in [3] which exploited the front and back cameras in current mobile devices. Finally, [28] propose to learn the space of indoor lighting using environment maps on single objects.

Other works explored alternative representations, such as spherical harmonics [12,20,34] that are useful for real-time rendering but are typically unsuitable for modeling high-frequency lighting (such as bright light sources) and are not ideal for non diffuse object rendering. [10] proposed to estimate a set of 3 parametric lights, which can easily be edited. However, that representation cannot generate realistic reflections. EMlight [33] propose a more expressive model by predicting gaussians on a spherical model. Similar to us, GMlight [31] back-projects the spherical gaussians to an estimated 3D model of the scene. This is further extended in [1] by the use of graph neural networks, and in [32] through the use of spherical wavelets dubbed "needlets".

Recently, methods have attempted to learn volumetric lighting representations from images. Of note, Lighthouse [25] learns multi-scale volumetric lighting from a stereo pair, [19] predicts a dense 2D grid of spherical gaussians which is further extended into a 3D volumetric representation by Wang et al. [27]. While these yield convincing spatially-varying results, these representations cannot easily be interacted by a user.

Scene Decomposition. Holistic scene decomposition [2] is deeply tied to lighting estimation as both are required to invert the image formation process. Li et al. [19] proposes to extract the scene geometry and the lighting simultaneously. Similarly, [7] extract only the geometry of the scene by estimating the normal and depth of the scene. These geometric representations are however non-parametric and thus difficult to edit or comprehend. [16] proposes a simplified parametric model where a room layout is recovered in the camera field of view. Similarly, [35] presents a method to estimate the layout given a panoramic image of an indoor scene. We use the method of [16] to estimate a panoramic layout given a perspective image, thus providing a simple cuboid representation that allows for spatially varying textured lighting representation.

3   Editable Indoor Lighting Representation

We begin by presenting our hybrid parametric/non-parametric lighting representation which aims at bridging the gap between realism and editability. We also show how that representation can be fitted to high dynamic range panoramas to obtain a training dataset, and conclude by presenting how it can be used for virtual object relighting.

3.1   Lighting Representation

Our proposed light representation, shown in Fig. 2, is composed of two main components: an HDR parametric light source $\mathbf{p}$; and an LDR textured cuboid $\mathcal{C}$.

Light Source. As in [10], the light source parameters $\mathbf{p}$ are defined as

$$\mathbf{p} = \{\mathbf{l}, d, s, \mathbf{c}, \mathbf{a}\}, \tag{1}$$

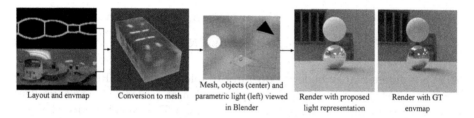

| Layout and envmap | Conversion to mesh | Mesh, objects (center) and parametric light (left) viewed in Blender | Render with proposed light representation | Render with GT envmap |

Fig. 2. To render a virtual object with our proposed lighting representation, the texture is first warped according to the layout (1st column), producing a textured mesh (2nd). This mesh is combined with an emitting sphere representing the parametric light (3rd) for rendering. The resulting rendering (4th) closely matches the ground truth rendering obtained with the HDR environment map (last).

where $\mathbf{l} \in \mathbb{R}^3$ is a unit vector specifying the light direction in XYZ coordinates, d is the distance in meters, s the radius (in meters), $\mathbf{c}, \mathbf{a} \in \mathbb{R}^3$ are the light source and ambient colors in RGB, respectively. Here, $\mathbf{l}$, d and s are defined with respect to the camera. In contrast with [10], we use a single light source.

Textured Cuboid. The cuboid $\mathcal{C} = \{\mathbf{T}, \mathbf{L}\}$ is represented by a texture $\mathbf{T} \in \mathbb{R}^{2H \times H \times 3}$, which is an RGB spherical image of resolution $2H \times H$ stored in equirectangular (latitude-longitude) format, and a scene layout $\mathbf{L} \in \mathbb{R}^{2H \times H}$. The layout is a binary image of the same resolution, also in equirectangular format, indicating the intersections of the main planar surfaces in the room (walls, floor, ceiling) as an edge map [9].

3.2 Ground Truth Dataset

The ground truth is derived from the Laval Indoor HDR Dataset [11], which contains 2,100 HDR panoramas (with approximate depth labels from [10]). We extract $\mathbf{p}$ and $\mathcal{C}$ from each panorama using the following procedure. First, the HDR panorama is clipped to LDR (we re-expose such that the 90th-percentile is 0.8 then clip to [0, 1]) and directly used as the texture $\mathbf{T}$. Then the intersection between the main surfaces are manually labelled to define the layout $\mathbf{L}$. Lastly, we extract a dominant parametric light source from the HDR panorama. In order to determine the main light source, the $N = 5$ brightest individual light sources are first detected using the region-growing procedure in [10]. A test scene (9 diffuse spheres arranged in a 3×3 grid on a diffuse ground plane, seen from top as in Fig. 4b) is rendered with each light source independently by masking out all other pixels—the brightest render determines the strongest light source.

An initial estimate of the light parameters $\mathbf{p}$ are obtained by the following. The distance d is approximated by using the average depth of the region, direction $\mathbf{l}$ as the region centroid, the angular size from the major and minor axes of an ellipse fitted to the same region. Finally, the light color $\mathbf{c}$ and ambient term $\mathbf{a}$ are initialized with a least-squares fit to a rendering of the test scene using the

HDR panorama. From the initial parameters, **p** is further refined:

$$\mathbf{p}^* = \arg\min_{\mathbf{p}} ||\mathcal{R}(\mathbf{p}) - \mathcal{R}(\tilde{\mathbf{P}})||_2 \,. \tag{2}$$

$\mathcal{R}(x)$ is a differentiable rendering operator (implemented with Redner [18]) that renders a test scene using **p**. The optimization is performed using gradient descent with Adam [15]. Finally, the texture map **T** is rescaled with the estimated ambient term $\mathbf{a}^*$ to ensure that the texture yields the same average RGB color.

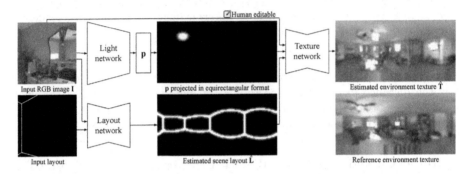

Fig. 3. Our method takes as input a perspective, RGB image and its scene layout representation, passes the RGB to a CNN to predict a parametric light, and passes the partial layout to another CNN to predict the full panorama layout. The parametric light is converted to a binary mask panorama, which is then sent together with the full layout prediction and the input RGB image to a third network which outputs an LDR texture with the light at the desired location.

3.3 Virtual Object Rendering

To render a virtual object using our lighting representation, we employ the Cycles rendering engine[2]. A scene, as shown in Fig. 2, is composed of a 3D emissive sphere for the parametric light **p** and the textured cuboid mesh $\mathcal{C}$. The cuboid mesh is derived by detecting the cuboid corners from the layout using high pass filters. We use the following geometric constraints to simplify the back-projection of the scene corners to 3D. First, the shape is limited to a cuboid, meaning that opposing faces are parallel. Second, the panorama layouts were trained using a camera elevation of $0°$ (pointing at the horizon) and height of 1.6 m above the ground. Using these constraints, the bottom corners can easily be projected on the ground plane, and the top corners can be used to compute the ceiling height (averaged from the 4 corners). A texture map can then be computed using every planar surfaces of the cuboid. Finally, the parametric light and the texture are rendered in two rendering passes. After rendering, the relit virtual object can be composited into the image using differential rendering [6].

---

[2] Available within Blender at https://www.blender.org.

4   Approach

Our approach, illustrated in Fig. 3, is composed of three main networks: light, layout, and texture which are combined together to estimate our light representation (c.f., Sect. 3) from an image. We assume that the layout of the input image is available, in practice this is obtained with an off-the-shelf solution [30].

Light Network. A "light" network is trained to learn the mapping from input image $\mathbf{I} \in \mathbb{R}^{128 \times 128 \times 3}$ to estimated lighting parameters $\mathbf{p}$ (Sect. 3) using a similar approach to [10]. Specifically, the light network is composed of a headless DenseNet-121 encoder [14] to produce a 2048-dimensional latent vector, followed by a fully-connected layer (512 units), and ultimately with an output layer producing the light source parameters $\mathbf{p}$.

The light network is trained on light parameters fitted on panoramas from the Laval Indoor HDR Dataset [11] using the procedure described in Sect. 3.2. To generate the input image from the panorama, we follow [11] and extract rectified crops from the HDR panoramas. The resulting images are converted to LDR by re-exposing to make the median intensity equal to 0.45, clipping to 1, and applying a $\gamma = 1/2.4$ tonemapping. The same exposure factor is subsequently applied to the color $\mathbf{c}$ and ambient a light parameters to ensure consistency. Note that the training process is significantly simplified compared to [11] as the network predicts only a single set of parameters.

We employ individual loss functions on each of the parameters independently: L2 for direction $\mathbf{l}$, depth d, size s, and ambient color a, and L1 for light color $\mathbf{c}$. In addition, we also employ an angular loss for both the ambient and light colors a and $\mathbf{c}$ to enforce color consistency. The weights for each term were obtained through a Bayesian optimization on the validation set (see supp. mat.).

Layout Network. The mapping from the input RGB image $\mathbf{I}$ and its layout (obtained with [30]) to the estimated scene layout $\hat{\mathbf{L}}$ (Sect. 3) is learned by the "layout" network whose architecture is that of pix2pixHD [26]. Both inputs are concatenated channel-wise. The layout network is trained on both the Laval and the Zillow Indoor Dataset [5], which contains 67,448 LDR indoor panoramas of 1575 unfurnished residences along with their scene layouts. To train the network, a combination of GAN, feature matching and perceptual losses are employed [26]. The same default weights as in [26] are used in training.

Texture Network. Finally, the estimated environment texture $\hat{\mathbf{T}}$ is predicted by a "texture" network whose architecture is also that of pix2pixHD [26]. It accepts as input a channel-wise concatenation of three images: the input RGB image $\mathbf{I}$, the estimated light parameters $\hat{\mathbf{p}}$ projected in an equirectangular format, and the estimated scene layout $\hat{\mathbf{L}}$. The equirectangular images are vertically concatenated to the input image. Note that the $\hat{\mathbf{p}}$ projection is performed using a subset of all parameters (direction $\mathbf{l}$ and size s only).

The texture network is also trained on both Laval and Zillow datasets. To obtain the required light source position from the Zillow dataset, we detect the largest connected component whose intensity is above the 98th percentile over the upper half of the panorama. To convert the Laval HDR panoramas to LDR, first a scale factor is found such as the crop taken from that panorama has its 90th percentile mapped to 0.8. This scale factor is then applied to the panorama such as its scale matches the one of the crop. The texture network is trained with the same combination of losses as the layout network.

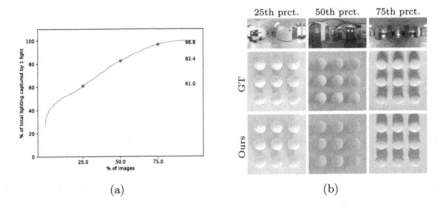

(a)   (b)

Fig. 4. Validation of our 1-light approximation. (a) Cumulative distribution of the contribution of the single strongest light with respect to the entire lighting environment of the scene. (b) Example images for different percentiles, where the rows correspond to the environment map (top), a synthetic scene (seen from the top) rendered with (middle) the ground truth environment map and (bottom) our 1-light representation. As expected, scenes where the strongest light does not contribute significantly have shadows that are less pronounced which may point to several light sources equally contributing to the overall energy (25th prct.). The strongest light source contributes to more than 80% of the total energy in at least 50% of the images in our test set, which confirms our assumption that most scenes can accurately be modeled with a single light source.

5   Experiments

5.1   Validation of Our 1-Light Approximation

We test our hypothesis that most indoor scenes are well-approximated by a single dominant light source with an ambient term. We render a scene with the ground truth environment map, and compare it with the renders obtained from the parametric lighting optimization procedure described in Sect. 3. Figure 4a shows the cumulative distribution of the contribution of the strongest light with respect to the entire lighting of the scene. Note that the strongest light source contributes to more than 60%/80%/95% of the total lighting for 25%/50%/75%

Table 1. Quantitative comparative metrics on (left) renderings of a diffuse scene, and (right) on the estimated environment maps directly. Each row is color-coded as best and second best . We also highlight the methods which produce lighting representations that can be interpreted and edited by a user ("Edit.").

	si-RMSE$_\downarrow$	RMSE$_\downarrow$	RGB ang.$_\downarrow$	PSNR$_\uparrow$	FID$_\downarrow$	Edit.
Ours	0.081	0.209	4.13°	12.79	89.58	yes
Gardner'19 (1) [10]	0.099	0.229	4.43°	12.25	356.8	yes
Gardner'19 (3) [10]	0.105	0.508	4.58°	10.87	335.6	yes
Gardner'17 [11]	0.123	0.628	8.29°	10.24	254.8	no
Garon'19 [12]	0.096	0.254	8.04°	9.70	314.9	no
Lighthouse [25]	0.120	0.253	14.53°	9.88	195.5	no
EMLight [33]	0.099	0.232	3.99°	10.38	121.09	no
EnvmapNet[a] [23]	0.097	0.286	7.67°	11.74	201.20	no

[a] Only their proposed ClusterID loss and tonemapping.

of the images in our test set. Figure 4b shows example images for each of these scenarios. We find that even if we expect indoor scenes to have multiple light sources, the vast majority can accurately be represented by a single *dominant* light.

5.2 Light Estimation Comparison

We now evaluate our method and compare it with recent state-of-the-art light estimation approaches. We first validate that our model performs better on quantitative metrics evaluated on physic-based renders of a scene using a test set provided by [11]. For each of the 224 panoramas in the test split, we extract 10 images using the same sampling distribution as in [11], for a total of 2,240 images for evaluation. We also show renders in various scenes to demonstrate how our solution is visually more appealing.

Quantitative Comparison. To evaluate the lighting estimates, we render a test scene composed of an array of spheres viewed from above (Sect. 3) and compute error metrics on the resulting rendering when compared to the ground truth obtained with the original HDR panorama. We report RMSE, si-RMSE [13], PSNR, and RGB angular error [17]. We also compute the FID[3] on the resulting environment maps to evaluate the realism of reflections (similar to [23]).

We evaluate against the following works. First, two versions of [10] are compared: the original (3) where 3 light sources are estimated, and a version (1) trained to predict a single parametric light. Second, we also compare to Lighthouse [25], which expects a stereo pair as input. As a substitute, we generate

---

[3] Implementation taken from https://pypi.org/project/pytorch-fid/.

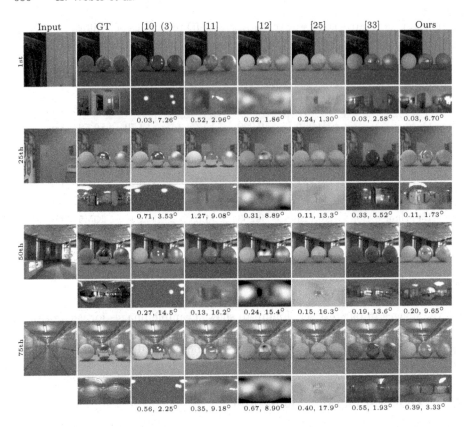

Fig. 5. Qualitative lighting estimation examples from our test set. To compare the estimated lighting, we render a simple scene composed of three spheres (diffuse, mirror, glossy) on a diffuse ground plane with different methods. From left to right: input image, ground truth lighting, Gardner'19 [10] (3 lights), Gardner'17 [11], Garon'19 [12], Lighthouse [25], EMLight [33], and ours. The second row shows the corresponding estimated lighting in equirectangular format (reprojected in the center of the image for the spatially-varying techniques such as [10,12,25] and ours). Finally, error metrics (RMSE and RGB angular) are also shown below each example for reference. Each group shows examples from different error percentiles for our method according to the RMSE metric. More examples can be found in the supplementary materials.

a second image with a small baseline using Synsin [29] (visual inspection confirmed this yields reasonable results). For [12], we select the coordinates of the image center for the object position. For [23], we implemented their proposed "Cluster ID loss" and tonemapping (Eq. 1 in [23]) but used pix2pixHD as backbone. Finally, we also compare against [33]. Results for each metrics are reported in Table 1, which shows that despite our model being simple, it achieves the best score in every metric. We argue that it is *because* of its simplicity that we can achieve competitive results. Our approach can be trained on real data (as opposed to [12,25] and does not require an elaborate 2-stage training process

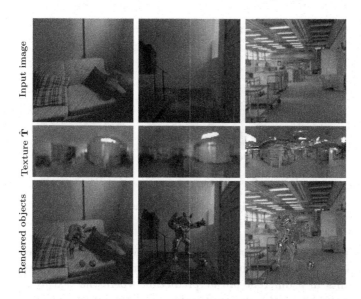

Fig. 6. Virtual object insertion in scenes with our estimated lighting. For simplicity, we assume the scene surrounding the objects is made of a flat ground plane, which catches shadows and is placed manually by an artist (the focus of our work being lighting estimation). For example, the figure shows a golden armadillo and sphere inserted into three different scenes. Note how the reflections on the objects and the shadows cast on the ground plans appear realistic.

(compared to [10]). We also demonstrate a significantly lower FID score than other methods thus bridging the gap between representation realism and HDR accuracy.

Qualitative Comparison. We also present qualitative results in Fig. 5 where predictions are rendered on 3 spheres with varying reflectance properties (diffuse, mirror, glossy). In addition, a tonemapped equirectangular view of the estimated light representation is provided under each render. We show an example from each error percentiles according to the RMSE metric. Our proposed method is perceptually better on the mirror spheres as other methods do not model high frequency details from the scene. We also notice accurate shadow and shading from all the spheres. We show objects realistically composited into photographs in Fig. 6. Note how the reflections of the virtual objects and their cast shadows on the ground plane perceptually match the input photograph. Finally, we also compare against [27] in Fig. 7.

5.3   Ablation Study on Input Layout

One may consider that requiring the image layout as input may make our method sensitive to its estimation. To show this is not the case, we perform an experiment

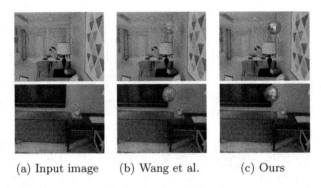

(a) Input image   (b) Wang et al.   (c) Ours

Fig. 7. Qualitative comparison against Wang et al. [27]

where we provide a black layout as input to the layout network (equivalent to no layout estimate). As can be seen in Fig. 8, providing a black layout as input simply results in a different layout prediction where the texture still remains coherent with the RGB input and estimated light direction. The FID of the generated panoramas with no input layout is 88.68 (compared to 89.58 from Table 1), showing that this essentially has no impact.

5.4   Ablation Study on the Texture Network

We also tested different configurations for the texture network in order to validate our design choices. More specifically, we trained the texture network providing as input: (1) only the RGB crop (FID of 167.39), (2) RGB crop and parametric light (FID of 97.13), and (3) RGB crop and layout (FID of 151.04). In contrast, our full approach obtained an FID of 89.57 (see Table 1).

6   Editing the Estimated Lighting

Because of its intuitive nature, it is simple and natural for a user to edit our estimated lighting representation, should the estimate not perfectly match the background image or simply for artistic purposes. Figure 9 shows that our approach simultaneously *disentangles* various components of illumination, allows an *intuitive control* over those components, and enables *realistic relighting results*. First, Fig. 9a shows that a user can rotate the light source about its azimuth angle. Note how the estimated texture (second row) is consistent with the desired light position (third row), while preserving the same overall structure. The renders (first row) exhibit realistic reflections and shadows that correspond to the desired lighting directions. A similar behaviour can be observed in Figs. 9b and 9c when the elevation angle and size are modified, respectively. In Fig. 9d, we show that it is also possible to edit the scene layout and obtain an estimated texture map $\hat{\mathbf{T}}$ that is consistent with the users request. We also show results of compositing virtual objects directly into a scene in Fig. 6. As shown in Fig. 1,

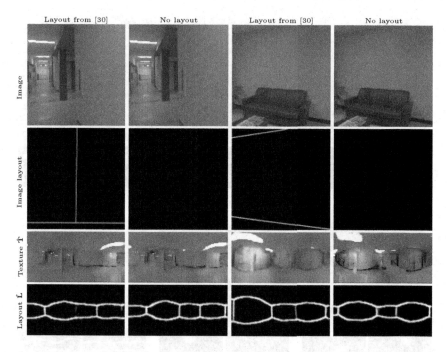

Fig. 8. Ablation on input image layout. We compare the output of our method (last two rows) as a function of whether or not it is given the estimated layout of the input image (with [30]). Our approach produces similar results in both cases.

realistic rendering results can intuitively be edited to achieve the desired look. To the best of our knowledge, the only other method which allows intuitive editing of indoor lighting estimate is that of Gardner et al. [10]. Unfortunately, realistic renders are limited to diffuse objects and cannot be extended to reflective objects as shown in Fig. 5.

7 Discussion

This paper proposes a lighting estimation approach which produces an intuitive, user-editable lighting representation given a single indoor input image. By explicitly representing the dominant light source using a parametric model, and the ambient environment map using a textured cuboid, our approach bridges the gap between generating realistic shading (produced by HDR light sources) and reflections (produced by textured environment maps) on rendered virtual objects. We demonstrate, through extensive experiments, that our approach provides competitive quantitative performance when compared to recent lighting estimation techniques. In particular, when compared to the only other approach which can be user-edited [10], our approach yields significant improved results.

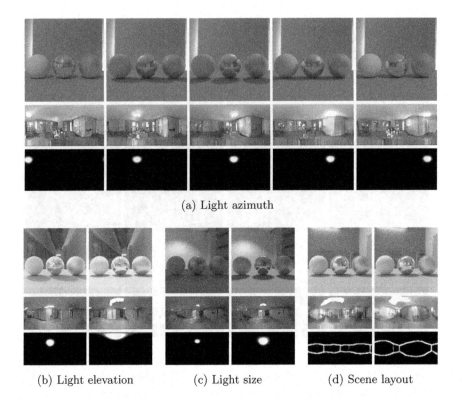

(a) Light azimuth

(b) Light elevation   (c) Light size   (d) Scene layout

Fig. 9. Using our representation, a user can easily edit the estimated light parameters and obtain relighting results consistent with their edits. For example, the user can change the (a) azimuth and (b) elevation angles of the light source; (c) the size of the light source; or (d) the layout of the scene. For all scenarios, we show rendered virtual objects in the first row, the estimated texture $\hat{\mathbf{T}}$ in the second, and the representation being edited in the last (light parameters $\hat{\mathbf{p}}$ for (a)–(c) and layout $\hat{\mathbf{L}}$ for (d)).

Limitations and Future Work. While our proposed approach estimates a 3D representation of the surrounding lighting environment, it does not reason about light occlusions in the scene as opposed to other techniques such as [12,19,27]. Incorporating these higher-order interactions while maintaining interpretability and editability of the output representation is an interesting direction for future research. In addition, the estimated environment textures were shown to produce realistic reflections on shiny objects, but a close inspection reveals that they are low resolution and contain some visual artifacts. It is likely that more recent image-to-image translation architectures [4,21] could be used to improve realism.

Acknowledgements. This research was supported by MITACS and the NSERC grant RGPIN-2020-04799. The authors thank Pascal Audet for his help.

References

1. Bai, J., et al.: Deep graph learning for spatially-varying indoor lighting prediction. arXiv preprint arXiv:2202.06300 (2022)
2. Barron, J.T., Malik, J.: Shape, illumination, and reflectance from shading. IEEE TPAMI **37**(8), 1670–1687 (2014)
3. Cheng, D., Shi, J., Chen, Y., Deng, X., Zhang, X.: Learning scene illumination by pairwise photos from rear and front mobile cameras. Comput. Graph. Forum **37**(7), 213–221 (2018)
4. Choi, Y., Uh, Y., Yoo, J., Ha, J.W.: Stargan v2: diverse image synthesis for multiple domains. In: CVPR (2020)
5. Cruz, S., Hutchcroft, W., Li, Y., Khosravan, N., Boyadzhiev, I., Kang, S.B.: Zillow indoor dataset: annotated floor plans with 360º panoramas and 3D room layouts. In: CVPR (2021)
6. Debevec, P.: Rendering synthetic objects into real scenes: bridging traditional and image-based graphics with global illumination and high dynamic range photography. In: Proceedings of the 25th Annual Conference on Computer Graphics and Interactive Techniques, pp. 189–198. SIGGRAPH (1998)
7. Eigen, D., Fergus, R.: Predicting depth, surface normals and semantic labels with a common multi-scale convolutional architecture. In: Proceedings of the IEEE International Conference on Computer Vision, pp. 2650–2658 (2015)
8. Einabadi, F., Guillemaut, J.Y., Hilton, A.: Deep neural models for illumination estimation and relighting: a survey. Comput. Graph. Forum **40**(6), 315–331 (2021)
9. Fernandez-Labrador, C., Facil, J.M., Perez-Yus, A., Demonceaux, C., Civera, J., Guerrero, J.J.: Corners for layout: End-to-end layout recovery from 360 images. IEEE Rob. Autom. Lett. **5**(2), 1255–1262 (2020)
10. Gardner, M.A., Hold-Geoffroy, Y., Sunkavalli, K., Gagne, C., Lalonde, J.F.: Deep parametric indoor lighting estimation. In: ICCV (2019)
11. Gardner, M.A., et al.: Learning to predict indoor illumination from a single image. ACM TOG **36**(6) (2017)
12. Garon, M., Sunkavalli, K., Hadap, S., Carr, N., Lalonde, J.F.: Fast spatially-varying indoor lighting estimation. In: CVPR (2019)
13. Grosse, R., Johnson, M.K., Adelson, E.H., Freeman, W.T.: Ground truth dataset and baseline evaluations for intrinsic image algorithms. In: 2009 IEEE 12th International Conference on Computer Vision, pp. 2335–2342. IEEE (2009)
14. Huang, G., Liu, Z., Van Der Maaten, L., Weinberger, K.Q.: Densely connected convolutional networks. In: CVPR (2017)
15. Kingma, D.P., Ba, J.: Adam: a method for stochastic optimization. arxiv preprint arxiv:1412.6980 (2014)
16. Lee, C.Y., Badrinarayanan, V., Malisiewicz, T., Rabinovich, A.: Roomnet: end-to-end room layout estimation. In: ICCV (2017)
17. LeGendre, C., et al.: Deeplight: learning illumination for unconstrained mobile mixed reality. In: CVPR (2019)
18. Li, T.M., Aittala, M., Durand, F., Lehtinen, J.: Differentiable monte carlo ray tracing through edge sampling. ACM TOG **37**(6), 1–11 (2018)
19. Li, Z., Shafiei, M., Ramamoorthi, R., Sunkavalli, K., Chandraker, M.: Inverse rendering for complex indoor scenes: shape, spatially-varying lighting and svbrdf from a single image. In: CVPR (2020)
20. Mandl, D., et al.: Learning lightprobes for mixed reality illumination. In: ISMAR (2017)

21. Park, T., Efros, A.A., Zhang, R., Zhu, J.-Y.: Contrastive learning for unpaired image-to-image translation. In: Vedaldi, A., Bischof, H., Brox, T., Frahm, J.-M. (eds.) ECCV 2020. LNCS, vol. 12354, pp. 319–345. Springer, Cham (2020). https://doi.org/10.1007/978-3-030-58545-7_19

22. Sengupta, S., Gu, J., Kim, K., Liu, G., Jacobs, D.W., Kautz, J.: Neural inverse rendering of an indoor scene from a single image. In: ICCV (2019)

23. Somanath, G., Kurz, D.: HDR environment map estimation for real-time augmented reality. In: CVPR (2021)

24. Song, S., Funkhouser, T.: Neural illumination: lighting prediction for indoor environments. In: CVPR (2019)

25. Srinivasan, P.P., Mildenhall, B., Tancik, M., Barron, J.T., Tucker, R., Snavely, N.: Lighthouse: predicting lighting volumes for spatially-coherent illumination. In: CVPR (2020)

26. Wang, T.C., Liu, M.Y., Zhu, J.Y., Tao, A., Kautz, J., Catanzaro, B.: High-resolution image synthesis and semantic manipulation with conditional gans. In: CVPR (2018)

27. Wang, Z., Philion, J., Fidler, S., Kautz, J.: Learning indoor inverse rendering with 3D spatially-varying lighting. In: ICCV (2021)

28. Weber, H., Prévost, D., Lalonde, J.F.: Learning to estimate indoor lighting from 3D objects. In: 3DV (2018)

29. Wiles, O., Gkioxari, G., Szeliski, R., Johnson, J.: Synsin: end-to-end view synthesis from a single image. In: CVPR (2020)

30. Yang, C., Zheng, J., Dai, X., Tang, R., Ma, Y., Yuan, X.: Learning to reconstruct 3D non-cuboid room layout from a single rgb image. In: Winter Conference on Applications of Computer Vision (2022)

31. Zhan, F., et al.: Gmlight: lighting estimation via geometric distribution approximation. IEEE TIP 31, 2268–2278 (2022)

32. Zhan, F., et al.: Sparse needlets for lighting estimation with spherical transport loss. In: ICCV (2021)

33. Zhan, F., et al.: Emlight: lighting estimation via spherical distribution approximation. In: AAAI (2021)

34. Zhao, Y., Guo, T.: POINTAR: efficient lighting estimation for mobile augmented reality. In: Vedaldi, A., Bischof, H., Brox, T., Frahm, J.-M. (eds.) ECCV 2020. LNCS, vol. 12368, pp. 678–693. Springer, Cham (2020). https://doi.org/10.1007/978-3-030-58592-1_40

35. Zou, C., Colburn, A., Shan, Q., Hoiem, D.: Layoutnet: reconstructing the 3D room layout from a single rgb image. In: CVPR (2018)

Fast Two-Step Blind Optical Aberration Correction

Thomas Eboli[✉], Jean-Michel Morel, and Gabriele Facciolo

Université Paris-Saclay, ENS Paris-Saclay, CNRS,
Centre Borelli, Gif-sur-Yvette, France
thomas.eboli@ens-paris-saclay.fr
https://github.com/teboli/fast_two_stage_psf_correction

Abstract. The optics of any camera degrades the sharpness of photographs, which is a key visual quality criterion. This degradation is characterized by the point-spread function (PSF), which depends on the wavelengths of light and is variable across the imaging field. In this paper, we propose a two-step scheme to correct optical aberrations in a single raw or JPEG image, *i.e.,* without any prior information on the camera or lens. First, we estimate local Gaussian blur kernels for overlapping patches and sharpen them with a non-blind deblurring technique. Based on the measurements of the PSFs of dozens of lenses, these blur kernels are modeled as RGB Gaussians defined by seven parameters. Second, we remove the remaining lateral chromatic aberrations (not contemplated in the first step) with a convolutional neural network, trained to minimize the red/green and blue/green residual images. Experiments on both synthetic and real images show that the combination of these two stages yields a fast state-of-the-art blind optical aberration compensation technique that competes with commercial non-blind algorithms.

Keywords: Point-spread function · Optical aberrations · Blind deblurring · Spatial Gaussian filter · Edge non-linear filtering

1 Introduction

Sharpness is a critical criterion for both photographers and scientific applications. In the absence of motion and with perfect focus, there will always be blur in the raw photographs, caused by the optics. The choice of the objective is thus important to take the best possible images and its quality is often characterized by its point spread function (or *PSF*), which is the combination of the optical aberrations transforming a white point in the ideal focal image into a colored spot. In real images, the PSF introduces optical aberrations degrading the global sharpness and introducing colored fringes next to the contrasted edges, see for instance in Fig. 1 for a mid-entry camera/lens pair.

Supplementary Information The online version contains supplementary material available at https://doi.org/10.1007/978-3-031-20068-7_40.

© The Author(s), under exclusive license to Springer Nature Switzerland AG 2022
S. Avidan et al. (Eds.): ECCV 2022, LNCS 13666, pp. 693–708, 2022.
https://doi.org/10.1007/978-3-031-20068-7_40

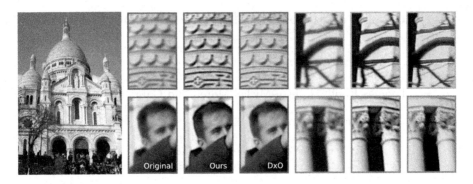

Fig. 1. We propose a blind method to correct the optical aberrations caused by the point-spread function of the lens, without any prior on the lens or the camera to restore the image. We sharpen and compensate the visible colored fringes in a 24 megapixels (4000 × 6000) photograph taken with a Sony α6000 camera and a Sony FE 35 mm $f/1.8$ lens at maximal aperture in 2 s on a NVIDIA 3090 GPU, achieving a visual result comparable to that of the non-blind algorithm of DxO PhotoLab (best seen on a computer screen). (Color figure online)

Since most cameras use glass or plastic lenses, the effects of the PSF cannot be avoided but only compensated by either switching to a better objective with a smaller colored spot, or post-processing the aberrated photographs. The first solution seems to be the most appealing since it solves the problem at its root but the top-of-the-line objectives are too expensive for most consumers. Furthermore, most pictures are taken nowadays with smartphone cameras that have low-quality and non-interchangeable lenses, hence the relevance of efficient algorithmic solutions. Optical aberration correction, along with denoising, demosaicking and distortion and vignetting correction, is among the earliest processing steps of any commercial editing software, *e.g.*, Adobe Lightroom or DxO PhotoLab. Figure 2 shows an example of such an image processing pipeline. However, these software rely on accurate calibration of camera/objective pairs, which are based on exhaustive measurements of all the possible camera settings.

In this paper, we propose a blind optical aberration compensation technique that can be applied to any raw or JPEG image *without* any prior knowledge of the camera or lens. Unlike the current state of the art that casts this problem correction as an instance of blind deblurring with RGB kernels [22,23,30], we follow [17] and decompose optical aberration compensation into a two-stage scheme that first removes lens blur and second compensates the remaining color fringes. We show a visual comparison with the non-blind commercial solution of DxO in Fig. 1. Our deblurring stage relies on the observation that the real RGB PSF measurements of [3] and the parametric kernels of [18] (which model local RGB kernels of real data), fit 2D Gaussian filters defined by just seven parameters. We confirm that these Gaussian filters verify the "mild blur" condition needed to apply the fast blind deblurring algorithm proposed in [8]. We thus adapt this approach to our problem to increase the sharpness of overlapping patches, assuming the blur is uniform on their supports. We correct the remaining effects due to the color-dependent warp by independently processing the red and blue channels using a small convolutional neural network (CNN) trained to minimize the red/green and blue/green image residuals. This is motivated by the analysis of color fringes in [7] showing that the profile of this image transformation is directly related to the intensity of the colored fringes. Thanks to the above decomposition, a shallow 160K-parameter CNN is enough to achieve state-of-the-art results. We finally gather the patches processed by the CNN.

Our approach presents several advantages over concurrent academic works and commercial solutions. First, the blind deblurring stage is very fast and memory-efficient since it leverages the Gaussian model of [18] and the approximated deconvolution scheme from [8]. Moreover, since our 2D Gaussian lens blur approximation only has a seven parameters, it is easy to compute. Yet, the method yields satisfactory visual results. Second, our approach does not suppose any parametric warp model to represent the displacements of the edges in the red and blue channels, which results in a more accurate prediction and in a method that may run either on crops or the full image. Furthermore, since the colored fringes are relatively thin, a small, fast and memory-efficient CNN architecture yields satisfactory results. Third, since the method is blind to the camera and lens settings, we restore any photograph without prior calibration with a target.

The contributions of this paper are summarized as follows:

- We decompose the optical aberration into blur and warp components and in particular, characterize the blur with local 2D Gaussian kernels with seven parameters. We validate this model with the PSFs measurements of [3];
- we sequentially compensate the blur and the warp. We apply the blind deblurring algorithm of [8] to sharpen the image, showcasing its effectiveness for optical aberration correction, and then remove the remaining color fringes with a novel 2-channel CNN trained to minimize the image residual between the red/blue and green channels;
- quantitative experiments on both synthetic and real images show that our method accurately compensates both the blur and the colored edges misalignments caused by the PSF. In particular it is 20 times faster and has 100 times less parameters than the current state of the art; and
- we show that our blind approach generalizes to real images even competing with commercial image editing software running in a non-blind setting. Our method processes a 12 megapixels image in 1 s on a GPU with a non-optimized code.

2   Related Work

Knowing the PSF associated to an image or a lens may be useful for two tasks: accurately evaluating the lens quality and removing the lens blur with a non-blind deblurring algorithm. The PSF may be estimated from a single photograph of a calibration target or from natural images. Trimeche *et al.* [29] and Joshi

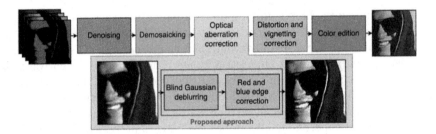

Fig. 2. Main stages of an editing software, processing a raw photograph into a JPEG image. We focus on the optical aberration correction module, usually just after denoising and demosaicking and before further color and geometry corrections. We decompose this block into two stages: (i) we improve sharpness with a blind deblurring algorithm, and (ii) we align the contrasted red and blue edges to remove the colored fringes at the vicinity of contrasted edges. (Color figure online)

et al. [16] take raw photographs of targets with contrasted edges, *e.g.,* a checkerboard, and solve an optimization problem to predict a grayscale local filter. The same idea is proposed by Brauers *et al.* [5], Delbracio *et al.* [9] and Heide *et al.* [14] who use carefully designed noise patterns to facilitate the optimization and achieve sub-pixel grayscale filters estimation. Instead of using edge and noise patterns, Schuler *et al.* [23] and Bauer *et al.* [3] take photographs of LED panels, which allow them to directly observe the local PSFs without any optimization, simply by recording how the white LED dots become colored spots in the images.

All these techniques may predict accurate estimates of the PSF but are only valid for specific lens settings and for a sparse set of locations in the image, making them unsuitable at non-measured pixel locations or lens settings. A few approaches intend to fill this void: Kee *et al.* [18] and Shih *et al.* [25] interpolate the PSF for various focal length/aperture aperture pairs by fitting a spatial Gaussian model and Hirsch and Schölkopf [15] predict RGB filters at unknown locations on the field of view with a kernel method.

However, if the goal is enhancing the image sharpness, blind kernel estimates designed to achieve the best deblurring, *i.e.,* without being faithful representations of the true local blurs, may suffice. For instance Joshi *et al.* [16] propose a variant of their target-based approach by assuming the latent sharp image has ideal step edges. Schuler *et al.* [24] predict a set of RGB linear filters covering the image, hypothesizing symmetries of the PSF, which is most of the time an inaccurate oversimplification for real lenses [10], and Yue *et al.* [30] and Sun *et al.* [26] additionally posit sharpness of the green channel, which is also an aggressive approximation when looking at real lens measurements [3]. Heide *et al.* [14] adopt instead a prior on the color and the location of edges across the color channels. After PSF estimation, correction boils down to non-blind deblurring by solving an inverse problem [19], or learned with a CNN [22]. In this paper, we adopt a 2D Gaussian model to approximate the local blur caused by the PSF,

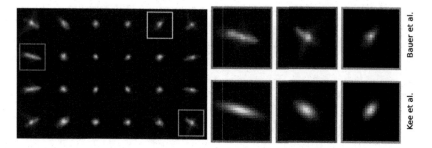

Fig. 3. A 4 × 6 subset of the Canon EF 16–35 mm f/2.8L II USM PS lens PSF measurement of Bauer *et al.* [3] at maximal aperture and shortest focal length, a panel of three zoomed local kernels and the Gaussian approximations of Kee *et al.* [18]. The spots, despite being non-parametric functions of the field of view, may be reasonably approximated with spatial Gaussian filters. (Color figure online)

which is validated by observations of [18] and that can be efficiently estimated from a single image [8]. Furthermore, [8] shows that no prior is needed to achieve satisfactory deblurring results with these simple kernels.

Blur is only one facet of a PSF, which also warps the color planes of a photograph, resulting in color fringes next to the edges. Boult and Wolberg [4] and Kang [17] align the red and blue channels with the green one by means of a radial warp model. Chang *et al.* [7] do not suppose any model on the warp and instead remove the fringes with a linear filter applied in the neighborhood if the most salient edges, in the red/green and blur/green image residuals. These image residuals contain all the information to characterize these colored artifacts and are used in the present work to train a CNN, a non-linear variant of [7].

3   Local PSF Parametric Model

3.1   Optical Aberrations Model

In the absence of diffraction, which is a realistic assumption for usual aperture sizes, typically below $f/11$, the PSF is the combination of the optical aberrations. The Seidel theory [27] decomposes them into five monochromatic aberrations: spherical, coma, astigmatism, field curvature and geometric distortion, and two chromatic aberrations: lateral and longitudinal.

The combination of the first four monochromatic and the longitudinal aberrations boils down to converting a point in the ideally focused image into a spot whose size depends on the wavelength and its position on the focal plane [17]. Geometric distortion bends parallel lines and necessitates two or more images to calibrate the camera [31], and is thus not addressed in this presentation. However, lateral aberrations are also geometric transformations, but which warp differently each color component of an edge, leading to visible colored fringes [7]. Figure 3 illustrates a PSF measurement of a real lens obtained by Bauer *et al.* [3].

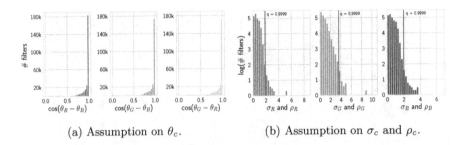

(a) Assumption on θ_c.   (b) Assumption on σ_c and ρ_c.

Fig. 4. Experimental validation of the assumptions on the parameter triplets $(\theta_c, \sigma_c, \rho_c)$. Left: We measure the similarity θ_R, θ_G and θ_B and show the strong correlation across the color channel directions. Right: We compute the histogram of σ_c and ρ_c ($c = R, G, B$) and its 0.9999-th quantile, and show that almost all standard deviation values are under 4. (Color figure online)

Kang [17] already proposed a forward model for optical aberrations with simultaneous blur and color warp. Chang et al. [7] set an order, that we follow in this paper, by running a sharpening stage prior to edge correction. From the above analysis, and considering also degradation caused by the sensor, (mosaicking, noise and saturation), we derive the following raw image formation model for a single color channel $c = (R, G, B)$:

$$r_c = s \circ m_c \left(g_c \circ w_c(u_c) + \varepsilon \right) \quad \text{with} \quad \varepsilon \sim \mathcal{N}(0, \alpha g_c \circ w_c(u_c) + \beta), \qquad (1)$$

where u_c and r_c are the sharp and raw color planes, w_c is the inter-color warp caused by lateral chromatic aberrations (recall that we neglect geometric distortion in this presentation), g_c is the spatially-varying blur caused by the remaining aberrations, $\circ$ is the composition operator, m_c is the decimation caused by the mosaicking filter, s is the sensor saturation and ε is the image noise modeled with the heteroscedastic normal model of [12], parameterized with shot and read noise weights α and β. We call v the denoised and demosaicked version of the raw image r, which should therefore be close to the RGB aberrated image *before* mosaicking and degradation with noise.

3.2   Blur Parametric Approximation

An image of the local blur may be obtained with photographs of a known reference like a target [9,16,29]. It gives an accurate estimate of the blur but only in a controlled environment with special gear. We instead follow Kee et al. [18] and approximate the local blur g_c in a color channel ($c = R, G, B$) with a zero-mean 2D Gaussian filter. Blur estimation thus boils down to a direct blind estimation of few parameters from any photograph.

Parametric Monochromatic Aberrations. A zero-mean 2D Gaussian is fully characterized by three parameters: the angle of the principal direction θ and the standard deviation values σ in θ and ρ in the direction $\theta + \pi/2$:

$$k(x) = [2\pi \det(\Sigma)]^{-\frac{1}{2}} \exp\left(-\frac{1}{2}x^\top \Sigma^{-1} x\right), \tag{2}$$

for the locations x in the support of k and with a covariance matrix Σ:

$$\Sigma = R(\theta)^\top \begin{bmatrix} \sigma^2 & 0 \\ 0 & \rho^2 \end{bmatrix} R(\theta), \tag{3}$$

where $R(\theta)$ is the 2D rotation matrix of angle θ.

Parametric Longitudinal Chromatic Aberrations. Incorporating the contribution of longitudinal chromatic aberrations yields a kernel k_c, or equivalently a triplet $(\theta_c, \sigma_c, \rho_c)$, for each color $c = (R, G, B)$. Thus, our RGB parametric local blur model has nine parameters.

Bounding the Parameters with Real Data. We use the real PSF measurements by Bauer *et al.* [3] and the non-blind Gaussian approximation technique of Kee *et al.* [18], both shown in Fig. 3, to reduce the set of parameters. Bauer *et al.* took photographs with 70 lens settings of a 52×78-point LED array, which yields about 280,000 local RGB PSF measurements (g_R, g_G, g_B). Since the aperture is kept between $f/1.4$ and $f/5.6$, the contribution of diffraction to the local spot is negligible.

Following Kee *et al.*, we compute the covariance matrices of the kernels k_c that best fit the measurements g_c $(c = R, G, B)$, and whose eigendecomposition return the triplets $(\theta_c, \sigma_c, \rho_c)$. From this large corpus of triplets, we draw two conclusions: (i) the direction θ_c is roughly the same for each color c, and (ii) the standard deviation values σ_c and ρ_c are contained in the segment $[0.2, 4]$. The first observation limits the actual number of parameters to be estimated to only seven, the information on the principal direction being contained in a single scalar θ, whereas the second observation ensures that we can use the fast blind deblurring technique of [8] to predict k_c.

We experimentally validate these claims by first computing the cosine similarity of the pairs of eigenvectors directed by θ_c of the approximate filters k_c $(c = R, G, B)$. We show in Fig. 4 (a) that these vectors are always aligned, confirming our first observation. Second, we plot in Fig. 4 (b) the cumulative distribution function of the standard deviation values σ_c and ρ_c and show that only a negligible amount of candidates are above 4. We also see that a realistic floor value is at 0.2, thus suggesting the standard deviations for modeling realistic parametric lens blurs are within a segment $[0.2, 4]$, validating our second claim. In conclusion, we can reasonably adapt the blind deblurring technique of Delbracio *et al.* [8] to estimate a local PSF blur with only seven blur parameters.

4   Proposed Method

We decompose the image into patches, *e.g.*, with 25% or 50% overlap, in which we assume that the blur is uniform, and we remove the local PSF in two steps.

Algorithm 1: Proposed PSF removal method

Data: Aberrated v, coefficients (C, σ_b), estimator ϕ_ν
Result: Aberration-free $\hat{u}$

1 Compute blur direction θ from v_G with Eq. (4);
2 Compute blur standard deviations σ_c and ρ_c ($c = R, G, B$) with Eq. (5);
3 Compute approximate filter k_c ($c = R, G, B$) with Eqs. (2) and (3);
4 Compute approximate inverse filter $p(k_c) = -3(k_c * k_c) - k_c + 3\delta$ ($c = R, G, B$);
5 Compute deblurred image z_c ($c = R, G, B$) with Eq. (6);
6 Compute aligned channel $\hat{u}_c$ ($c = R, B$) with Eq. (7);
7 Build $\hat{u} = [\hat{u}_R, z_G, \hat{u}_B]$;

We first remove the local uniform blur with the blind Gaussian deblurring technique of [8]. Second, we eliminate the colored artifacts caused by the warp next the salient deblurred edges using a CNN, which is inspired on the method [7]. The selected deblurring and colored artifact correction methods strike a good compromise between speed and accuracy. Other combinations of methods were also considered leading to worse results or much slower methods, *e.g.*, classical registration techniques for lateral aberration removal [17], or much slower methods, for instance recent CNNs for deblurring [22].

Algorithm 1 summarizes our approach for restoring a single patch. After all the patches are deblurred and processed by the CNN, we put them back to their initial locations in the image using a Hamming window to limit fusion artifacts.

4.1 Blind Gaussian Deblurring

As explained above, the combination of the monochromatic and longitudinal aberrations is a spatially-varying blur. We split the image into overlapping patches where the local blur is supposed uniform, and predict a zero-mean Gaussian kernel for which we approximate a deconvolution filter, adapting the procedure of [8]. In brief, this technique quickly estimates the parameters (ρ, σ, θ) from a blurry grayscale image, and run an approximate inverse filter for the corresponding 2D Gaussian kernel. It is particularly effective for "mild" blurs that may be captured by Gaussian kernels with standard deviation under 4.

This blind deblurring technique is valid in our context since PSFs are mostly small blurs according to the previous section and previous art [3,18,23]. The authors of [8] thus demonstrate that their approach achieves similar result to that of CNNs, but for a fraction of the speed and memory. We show in this work it is well suited for lens blur removal. Since, according to our analysis, the blur orientation is the same for all color channels we find θ by arbitrarily computing the infinite norm of the directional derivative of the green channel and picking the direction with the smallest value, *i.e.*, where the blur is the strongest:

$$\theta = \underset{\varphi}{\operatorname{argmin}} \|\nabla_\varphi n(v_G)\|_\infty, \tag{4}$$

where $\nabla_\varphi v = \cos(\varphi)\nabla_x v + \sin(\varphi)\nabla_y v$, ∇_x and ∇_y are the horizontal and vertical derivative operators, and n is a normalization function detailed in [8] and in the supplemental material. For the range of standard deviation values we are interested with, Delbracio et al. [8] empirically show that there exists an affine relationship between the variance of a Gaussian blur and the infinite norm of the image gradients in its principal directions θ and $\theta + \pi/2$. Let C be the slope and σ_b be the intercept of this model. The empirical affine model reads

$$\sigma_c = \sqrt{\frac{C^2}{\|\nabla_\theta n(v_c)\|_\infty^2} - \sigma_b^2} \quad \text{and} \quad \rho_c = \sqrt{\frac{C^2}{\|\nabla_{\theta+\frac{\pi}{2}} n(v_c)\|_\infty^2} - \sigma_b^2}, \qquad (5)$$

where $c \in \{R, G, B\}$ and θ is the direction previously computed. The hyperparameters are tuned with the protocol of [8]. Minimizing with the linear programming algorithm the sum of ℓ_1 differences between the norm of the gradient and the variance for 600 synthetic blurry images and known corresponding Gaussian filters yields $C = 0.415$ and $\sigma_b = 0.358$ for demosaicked images before gamma correction, and $C = 0.371$ and $\sigma_b = 0.453$ for JPEG images.

The resulting triplet $(\theta, \sigma_c, \rho_c)$ is used to build the covariance matrix defined in Eq. (3) and thus the 2D Gaussian kernel k_c ($c = R, G, B$). As in [8], we carry out non-blind deblurring by computing the approximate inverse filter $p(k) = -3(k*k) - 4k + 3\delta$ (δ denotes the Dirac filter), and deconvolve each color channel c ($c = R, G, B$) with:

$$z_c = p(k_c) * v_c. \qquad (6)$$

We have also tried an inverse filter obtained with Fourier transform, e.g., [11], but noticed that the filter $p(k_c)$ ($c = R, G, B$) achieves better results in our experiments. Each $h \times w$ image z_c is a sharp version of v_c, however due to lateral chromatic aberration, the red and blue channels still have shifted edges compared to their counterparts in the aberration-free image u, which results in artifacts in the vicinity of contrasted and sharp edges.

4.2 Red and Blue Edge Correction

Lateral chromatic aberrations introduce a shift between the color channels. Usual techniques for removing these colored artifacts use parametric red-to-green and blue-to-green warp models, for instance taking the form of a global radial transformation [4,17] or local translations [24,30]. In this context registration is hard since different color channels may have different edge profiles and in these contrasted areas demosaicking may produce incorrect color predictions, preventing perfect edge alignment and resulting in residual edge artifacts. Modeling the warp thus seems to be a harder problem than the original one. Conversely, we follow Chang et al. [7] remkarking that lateral aberrations result in color fringes next to the most salient edges; Filtering the edges, without any explicit model on the warp or information on the edge location, is enough for effective correction. In this work we propose a residual CNN, that takes as input z_G and z_R or z_B

and returns an image $\widehat{u}_R$ or $\widehat{u}_B$ whose edges should be aligned with those of z_G. If we call this CNN ϕ with parameter ν, our approach reads for $c = R, B$:

$$\widehat{u}_c = z_c - \phi_\nu(z_c, z_G). \tag{7}$$

We then combine $\widehat{u}_R$, z_G and $\widehat{u}_B$ into a single restored image. The network ϕ_ν is a UNet with four convolutional layers of respectively 16, 32, 64 and 64 feature maps in the encoder part and a mirrored structure in the decoder, each followed by batch normalization and ReLU activation.

Training of ϕ. For estimating the network parameters ν, we use synthetic supervisory data. We follow Brooks $et\ al.$ [6] to convert 128×128 JPEG patches into linear RGB ones, just after demosaicking, but without noise or aberrations. We then apply the forward model (1) to generate their aberrated and mosaicked raw counterparts. We sample orientations in $[0, \pi)$, and standard deviations in $[0.2, 4]$ to build an RGB Gaussian kernel to blur a given "unprocessed" training image u from the DIV2K dataset. Then translate the red and blue channels with subpixel shifts sampled in $[-4, 4]^2$ to model the local lateral chromatic aberration, add Poissonian-Gaussian noise, mosaick with the Bayer filter and clip its pixel values between 0 and 1, ultimately resulting in a raw image r. The translation value range is empirically set after having observed photographs taken with a couple of different lenses. Nonetheless, this arbitrary value leads to satisfactory restoration results in real images. To simulate the modules preceding the optical aberration brick in any image processing pipeline (see Fig. 1), we denoise and demosaick r respectively with the bilateral filter [28] and demosaicnet [13] to predict an aberrated RGB image v. We deblur v by removing the blur with Eqs. (4) to (6) to predict a sharp version z with aberrated edges.

As demonstrated by Chang $et\ al.$ [7], the chroma images $z_R - z_G$ and $z_B - z_G$ isolate the lateral chromatic aberrations and are sufficient to remove the colored artifacts. Thus, instead of training our model to minimize a loss of the sort $\|\widehat{u} - u\|_1$ as usual, we force ϕ to minimize these quantities for N synthetic image pairs $(u^{(i)}, v^{(i)})$ with the training loss

$$\sum_{i=1}^{N} \sum_{c \in \{R,B\}} \left\| \left(u_c^{(i)} - u_G^{(i)}\right) - \left(z_c^{(i)} - \phi_\nu(z_c^{(i)}, z_G^{(i)}) - z_G^{(i)}\right) \right\|_1, \tag{8}$$

where $z_c^{(i)} = p(k_c) * v_c^{(i)}$ $(c = R, G, B)$. Since the roles of the red and blue channels are symmetric, we have $2N$ supervisions from N pairs $(u^{(i)}, v^{(i)})$ $(i = 1, \ldots, N)$. We minimize Eq. (8) with the Adam optimizer whose initial learning rate is set to 3×10^{-4} and is multiplied by 0.5 when the validation loss plateaus for 10 epochs and with batch size set to 40.

5   Experiments

5.1   Blind Grayscale PSF Removal

We first measure the ability of the parametric estimation technique to help deblurring a real-world non-parametric PSF for a single color channel (the

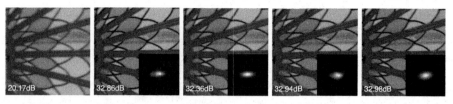

(a) Blurry.   (b) GT's kernel. (c) [18]'s kernel. (d) [1]'s kernel. (e) Our's kernel.

Fig. 5. Qualitative result for blind deblurring with different kernel estimators. From left to right: The synthetic blurry image, the version deblurred with the ground truth kernel from [3], the oracle Gaussian approximation [18], the parametric kernel from [1] and our estimate. We use the polynomial p previously defined to achieve non-blind deblurring. All the techniques, except that of Kee *et al.* [18] achieve similar results but ours is blind and fast.

impact of lateral chromatic aberrations is kept for later in this presentation). We compute blur estimates with a panel of blur estimation techniques including ours, and quantitatively evaluate their impact on deblurring.

We convolve grayscale images u with the green components g_G of the local PSFs of Bauer *et al.* [3] to generate blurry images v, from which we predict a blur kernel $\widehat{g_G}$ with various kernel estimation techniques. We then compute a deconvolution filter $p(\widehat{g_G})$ and estimate a deblurred version $p(g_G) * v$ for each kernel estimation method in our panel composed of the non-blind parametric model of Kee *et al.* [18] and the blind non-parametric algorithm of Anger *et al.* [1]. We quantitatively compare the performance of the blur estimators with the SSIM ratio of Kee *et al.* comparing the relative quality of the image deblurred with the ground-truth kernel g_G over that restored with $\widehat{g_G}$:

$$R(\widehat{g_G}, g_G) = \frac{\text{SSIM}[p(g_G) * v, u] + 2}{\text{SSIM}[p(\widehat{g_G}) * v, u] + 2}. \tag{9}$$

Since the kernels of Bauer *et al.* may not be centered in zero, we adopt the ground-truth shifting strategy of Levin *et al.* [21] and crop the 15 pixel on the borders to compute $\text{SSIM}[p(g_G) * v, u]$. Figure 6 (a) shows the plots of the ratios R for the different kernel estimators on 870 synthetic images of size 400×400. The non-blind parametric technique of Kee *et al.* is an upper-bound to ours and logically achieves the best result, nonetheless we are just under it with a marginal gap, and in a blind fashion. We also exceed the performance of the non-parametric algorithm of Anger *et al.*, validating our blind Gaussian model for PSF removal. Figure 5 shows a deblurring example for different kernel estimates.

5.2 Lateral Chromatic Aberration Compensation

We now validate the CNN ϕ to correct the lateral chromatic aberrations. However, to our knowledge, there is no benchmark or quantitative metric for this specific task. As a result, we have found that computing the norm of the image

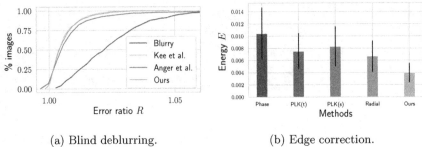

(a) Blind deblurring.   (b) Edge correction.

Fig. 6. Quantitative analysis of the blind deblurring and the edge corrections modules with the metrics R and E of Eqs (9) and (10). Left: Comparison of the SSIM ratios R in Eq. (9) for kernels estimated as by Kee *et al.* [18], Anger *et al.* [1] and with our approach (the more on the left, the better). Our blind method competes with the non-blind technique of Kee *et al.*. Right: Comparison of the energy E in Eq. (10) from Heide *et al.* [14] for edge corrections estimated by phase correlation [20], the pyramid Lucas-Kanade (PLK) algorithm of [2] predicting translations and similarities (PLK(t) and PLK(s)), the radial model of [17] and our CNN. Our approach achieves the best quantitative result. (Color figure online)

prior of Heide *et al.* [14] favoring aberration-free solutions, was the most relevant existing metric for this evaluation. Given an image z, we predict the red and blur corrected planes $\widehat{u}_R$ and $\widehat{u}_B$, compute their horizontal and vertical gradients with ∇_x and ∇_y, and evaluate the following energy:

$$E(\widehat{u}_R, \widehat{u}_B, z_G) = \sum_{c=R,B} \sum_{j=x,y} \|(\nabla_j z_G)/z_G - (\nabla_j \widehat{u}_c)/\widehat{u}_c\|_1, \qquad (10)$$

where the division is pixelwise. It may be seen as normalized variants of the color residuals of Chang *et al.* [7]. Note that this quantitative score does not necessitate a clean ground-truth, and thus can be used on real images. We thus take ten 24 megapixels photographs, of various environments (shown in the supplemental material), that are denoised and demosaicked with DxO PhotoLab 5, deblurred with our blind technique, and decomposed into 400×400 non-overlapping patches, resulting in 1,500 test images.

Figure 6 (b) compares the performance of our method with a classical radial model [17], and local parametric warps modeled with translations predicted with the phase correlation [20] or the pyramid Lucas-Kanade (PLK) [2] algorithms, or similarities also predicted with PLK. Our model achieves the best performance of the panel since it is trained to compensate the colored residuals. Note that phase correlation performs the worst among the considered methods, probably because the real blurs can affect differently the phase of different bands. The underconstrained PLK (similarity) method produces slightly worse results than the radial and PLK (translation) methods. A visual inspection of the restored images (reported in the supplementary material) confirms this quantitative analysis.

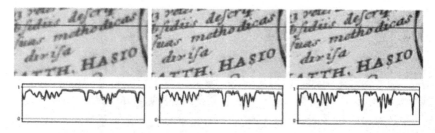

Fig. 7. Comparison of lateral chromatic aberration removal from a real raw image. From left to right: The blurry image, the version predicted by ϕ trained with the typical loss $\|\widehat{u}-u\|_1$ and the estimate from the one trained with the loss $\|(\widehat{u}-\widehat{u}_G)-(u-u_G)\|_1$. The model trained with the usual regression loss retains purplish edges whereas the variant gets rid of most of the aberrations. (Color figure online)

5.3 Real-World Examples

We test our method on real raw images and some datasets for existing images comparing our results with those of DxO PhotoLab 5. Figure 1 shows a real 24 megapixels photograph taken with a Sony $\alpha6000$ camera and a Sony FE 35mm $f/1.8$ lens set at maximal aperture to maximize the chromatic aberration. The raw image is denoised and demosaicked with DxO PhotoLab prior to optical aberration compensation. We show in the supplemental material additional qualitative results for different lenses.

Computational Efficiency. We evaluate the speed of the state-of-the-art CNN from [22] and our technique to process a 24 megapixel (6000×4000) photograph on a NVIDIA 3090 GPU. Our technique takes in average 1.7 s whereas that of [22] takes about 30 s on the same device. This is explained by the fact that our network only has 160K parameters for 33.1 gigaflops, whereas its counterpart counts 17 million parameters for 27.3 teraflops.

Impact of the Training Loss. We train ϕ_ν with a loss minimizing the red-green and blue-green residuals in the target u and prediction $\widehat{u}$ of the form $\|(\widehat{u}-\widehat{u}_G)-(u-u_G)\|_1$, which differs from the typical regression loss $\|\widehat{u}-u\|_1$. We show in Fig. 7 the advantage of the loss (8) leveraging the observations of Chang *et al.* on chromatic aberrations. The model trained with the typical regression loss leads to purplish edges next to the contrasted edges, *i.e.*, the edges across the three color channels have been aligned but the intensities of the red and blue ones do not match that of the green channel, whereas the one trained with Eq. (8) predicts an image without any color artifact.

Restoring JPEG Images. We have assumed so far that the raw image is available. However, we show that our blind method may also be applied to JPEG images when only this one is available. Figure 8 shows a restoration example from two images of [14,18] with the techniques of [22,30] and ours with the blur estimation coefficients (C, σ_b) calibrated for JPEG images (see Sect. 4.1). Our method, despite being blind, achieves the best visual result, predicting correct

(a) Blurry.   (b) Yue *et al.* [30].   (c) Li *et al.* [22].   (d) Ours.

Fig. 8. Comparison of aberration removal from a real JPEG images from [14, 18]. We eliminate the aberrations whereas the competitors retain colored edges and cannot restore finer details. (Color figure online)

colors and compensating the colored edges. Since the CNN is trained on linear images, prior to restoration we apply an inverse 2.2 gamma curve.

Limitation of the Gaussian Model. We showed good performance for eight mid-level camera/lens pairs in our experiments. This guarantees generalization of the Gaussian blur model to that category of photography gear, as claimed by previous art [3, 18, 23]. Yet, this model may be too restrictive in practice, especially for the first-entry lenses for which the lens blur may not be captured by a Gaussian kernel. We show failing examples in the material.

6   Conclusion

We have proposed a two-stage blind method for removing the lens blur, *i.e.*, its PSF, from a JPEG or raw image. The first module is a blind deblurring technique based on fast 2D Gaussian filter estimation on overlapping patches. We have shown that simple parametric kernels are good approximations of the combination of the monochromatic and longitudinal chromatic aberrations. The second module aligns the red and blue salient edges with the green ones and thus corrects the lateral chromatic aberration. Experiments have shown that the method generalizes to real-world images, even in the presence of the challenging purple fringes. Our approach is also fast, processing a 12 megapixels image in less than 1 s on a GPU, making it suitable for embedding in an ISP pipeline.

Acknowledgements. This work was partly financed by the DGA Astrid Maturation project "SURECAVI" no ANR-21-ASM3-0002, Office of Naval research grant N00014-17-1-2552. This work was performed using HPC resources from GENCI-IDRIS (grant 2022-AD011012453R1).

References

1. Anger, J., Facciolo, G., Delbracio, M.: Blind image deblurring using the ℓ_0 gradient prior. Image Process. Online (IPOL) **9**, 124–142 (2019)
2. Baker, S., Matthews, I.A.: Lucas-Kanade 20 years on: a unifying framework. Int. J. Comput. Vision (IJCV) **56**(3), 221–255 (2004)
3. Bauer, M., Volchkov, V., Hirsch, M., Schölkopf, B.: Automatic estimation of modulation transfer functions. In: Proceedings of the International Conference on Computational Photography (ICCP), pp. 1–12 (2018)
4. Boult, T.E., Wolberg, G.: Correcting chromatic aberrations using image warping. In: Proceedings of the conference on Computer Vision and Pattern Recognition (CVPR), pp. 684–687. IEEE (1992)
5. Brauers, J., Seiler, C., Aach, T.: Direct PSF estimation using a random noise target. In: Digital Photography. In: SPIE Proceedings, vol. 7537, p. 75370. SPIE (2010)
6. Brooks, T., Mildenhall, B., Xue, T., Chen, J., Sharlet, D., Barron, J.T.: Unprocessing images for learned raw denoising. In: Proceedings of the conference on Computer Vision and Pattern Recognition (CVPR), pp. 11036–11045 (2019)
7. Chang, J., Kang, H., Kang, M.G.: Correction of axial and lateral chromatic aberration with false color filtering. IEEE Trans. Image Process. (TIP) **22**(3), 1186–1198 (2013)
8. Delbracio, M., Garcia-Dorado, I., Choi, S., Kelly, D., Milanfar, P.: Polyblur: removing mild blur by polynomial reblurring. IEEE Trans. Comput. Imaging (TCI) **7**, 837–848 (2021)
9. Delbracio, M., Musé, P., Almansa, A., Morel, J.: The non-parametric sub-pixel local point spread function estimation is a well posed problem. Int. J. Comput. Vision (IJCV) **96**(2), 175–194 (2012)
10. Dube, B., Cicala, R., Closz, A., Rolland, J.: How good is your lens? Assessing performance with MTF full-field displays. Appl. Opt. **56**(20), 5661–5667 (2017)
11. Eboli, T., Sun, J., Ponce, J.: End-to-end interpretable learning of non-blind image deblurring. In: Proceedings of the European Conference on Computer Vision (ECCV), pp. 314–331 (2020)
12. Foi, A., Trimeche, M., Katkovnik, V., Egiazarian, K.O.: Practical Poissonian-Gaussian noise modeling and fitting for single-image raw-data. IEEE Trans. Image Process. (TIP) **17**(10), 1737–1754 (2008)
13. Gharbi, M., Chaurasia, G., Paris, S., Durand, F.: Deep joint demosaicking and denoising. ACM Trans. Graph. (ToG) **35**(6), 191:1–191:12 (2016)
14. Heide, F., Rouf, M., Hullin, M.B., Labitzke, B., Heidrich, W., Kolb, A.: High-quality computational imaging through simple lenses. ACM Trans. Graphics (ToG) **32**(5), 149:1–149:14 (2013)
15. Hirsch, M., Schölkopf, B.: Self-calibration of optical lenses. In: Proceedings of the International Conference on Computer Vision (ICCV), pp. 612–620 (2015)
16. Joshi, N., Szeliski, R., Kriegman, D.J.: PSF estimation using sharp edge prediction. In: Proceedings of the conference on Computer Vision and Patter Recognition (CVPR) (2008)
17. Kang, S.B.: Automatic removal of chromatic aberration from a single image. In: Proceedings of the Conference on Computer Vision and Pattern Recognition (CVPR) (2007)
18. Kee, E., Paris, S., Chen, S., Wang, J.: Modeling and removing spatially-varying optical blur. In: Proceedings of the International Conference on Computational Photography (ICCP), pp. 1–8. IEEE Computer Society (2011)

19. Krishnan, D., Fergus, R.: Fast image deconvolution using hyper-Laplacian priors. In: Advances in Neural Information Processing Systems (NeurIPS), pp. 1033–1041 (2009)

20. Leprince, S., Barbot, S., Ayoub, F., Avouac, J.: Automatic and precise orthorectification, coregistration, and subpixel correlation of satellite images, application to ground deformation measurements. IEEE Trans. Geosci. Remote Sens. **45**(6), 1529–1558 (2007)

21. Levin, A., Weiss, Y., Durand, F., Freeman, W.T.: Understanding and evaluating blind deconvolution algorithms. In: Proceedings of the conference on Computer Vision and Pattern Recognition (CVPR), pp. 1964–1971. IEEE Computer Society (2009)

22. Li, X., Suo, J., Zhang, W., Yuan, X., Dai, Q.: Universal and flexible optical aberration correction using deep-prior based deconvolution. In: Proceedings of the International Conference on Computer Vision (ICCV), pp. 2593–2601 (2021)

23. Schuler, C.J., Hirsch, M., Harmeling, S., Schölkopf, B.: Non-stationary correction of optical aberrations. In: Proceedings of the International Conference on Computer Vision (ICCV), pp. 659–666 (2011)

24. Schuler, C.J., Hirsch, M., Harmeling, S., Schölkopf, B.: Blind correction of optical aberrations. In: Proceedings of the European Conference on Computer Vision (ECCV), pp. 187–200 (2012)

25. Shih, Y., Guenter, B., Joshi, N.: Image enhancement using calibrated lens simulations. In: Proceedings of the European Conference on Computer Vision (ECCV), pp. 42–56 (2012)

26. Sun, T., Peng, Y., Heidrich, W.: Revisiting cross-channel information transfer for chromatic aberration correction. In: Proceedings of the International Conference on Computer Vision (ICCV), pp. 3268–3276 (2017)

27. Tang, H., Kutulakos, K.N.: What does an aberrated photo tell us about the lens and the scene? In: Proceedings of the International Conference on Computational Photography (ICCP), pp. 1–10 (2013)

28. Tomasi, C., Manduchi, R.: Bilateral filtering for gray and color images. In: Proceedings of the International Conference on Computer Vision (ICCV), pp. 839–846 (1998)

29. Trimeche, M., Paliy, D., Vehvilainen, M., Katkovnik, V.: Multichannel image deblurring of raw color components. In: Computational Imaging, vol. 5674, pp. 169–178. SPIE (2005)

30. Yue, T., Suo, J., Wang, J., Cao, X., Dai, Q.: Blind optical aberration correction by exploring geometric and visual priors. In: Proceedings of the conference on Computer Vision and Pattern Recognition (CVPR), pp. 1684–1692 (2015)

31. Zhang, Z.: A flexible new technique for camera calibration. IEEE Trans. Pattern Anal. Mach. Intell. (TPAMI) **22**(11), 1330–1334 (2000)

Seeing Far in the Dark with Patterned Flash

Zhanghao Sun[1]([✉]), Jian Wang[2], Yicheng Wu[2], and Shree Nayar[2]

[1] Stanford University, 350 Serra Mall, Stanford, CA 94305, USA
zhsun@stanford.edu
[2] Snap Inc., 229 W 43rd Street, New York, NY 10036, USA

Abstract. Flash illumination is widely used in imaging under low-light environments. However, illumination intensity falls off with propagation distance quadratically, which poses significant challenges for flash imaging at a long distance. We propose a new flash technique, named "patterned flash", for flash imaging at a long distance. Patterned flash concentrates optical power into a dot array. Compared with the conventional uniform flash where the signal is overwhelmed by the noise everywhere, patterned flash provides stronger signals at sparsely distributed points across the field of view to ensure the signals at those points stand out from the sensor noise. This enables post-processing to resolve important objects and details. Additionally, the patterned flash projects texture onto the scene, which can be treated as a structured light system for depth perception. Given the novel system, we develop a joint image reconstruction and depth estimation algorithm with a convolutional neural network. We build a hardware prototype and test the proposed flash technique on various scenes. The experimental results demonstrate that our patterned flash has significantly better performance at long distances in low-light environments. Our code and data are publicly available. (https://github.com/zhsun0357/Seeing-Far-in-the-Dark-with-Patterned-Flash).

Keywords: Computational photography · Flash imaging · Light fall off · Low-light imaging · Structured light

1 Introduction

Low-light imaging is critical in consumer photography, surveillance, robotics, and vision-based autonomous driving. Both hardware designs [18,28,33,37,43,49,58,

---

Z. Sun and J. Wang—These Authors Contributed Equally.
Z. Sun—This work was done during an internship at Snap Research.

Supplementary Information The online version contains supplementary material available at https://doi.org/10.1007/978-3-031-20068-7_41.

© The Author(s), under exclusive license to Springer Nature Switzerland AG 2022
S. Avidan et al. (Eds.): ECCV 2022, LNCS 13666, pp. 709–727, 2022.
https://doi.org/10.1007/978-3-031-20068-7_41

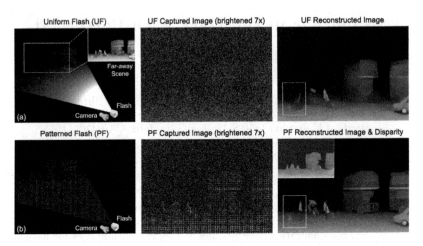

Fig. 1. (Better viewed on full screen to avoid visual artifacts) Conventional, uniform flash (UF) vs. the proposed patterned flash (PF). (a) In UF system, due to inverse square law of light, only close-by scenes are lit up, while the far-away scene is overwhelmed by sensor noise. The ground truth scene is in the inset of the left column. (b) In PF system, illumination power is concentrated into a dot array to enable long distance imaging in low-light environments. The reconstructed image contains important objects and details that are missing in UF reconstructed image (e.g., the pedestrian and the traffic cone in the white box). PF also supports depth estimation with the textured illumination pattern, as shown in the inset of the right column. (Color figure online)

71] and computational imaging algorithms [10,12,14,24,42] have been developed for this challenging task. Among these approaches, flash illumination is widely adopted given its outstanding performance and robustness. A flash can easily boost the illumination intensity hence the image signal level by $100 \sim 1000\times$ [6,18]. With high enough illumination level, it is sufficient to use short exposure time, casual capturing mode, and simple image processing while still getting high-quality images. However, flash has a fundamental drawback; its strength attenuates quadratically with distance. With a limited power budget (which is the practical constraint for most mobile devices like phones, drones, and wearable devices), the conventional flash illumination system is ineffective at a long distance. This raises robustness and safety issues in surveillance and navigation (e.g., missing important objects at night time). It also leads to irreversible content degradation in photography.

In this paper, we propose patterned flash (PF) technique for low-light imaging at a long distance. Instead of distributing the flash light uniformly across the camera's field of view (FOV), we concentrate it into a dot array pattern. Considering the same power budget, in a conventional uniform flash (UF) system, flash signals from far-away objects are overwhelmed by the sensor noise or fall below the sensitivity threshold of the sensor, leading to severe information loss (as shown in Fig. 1(a)). Contrarily, in the PF system (Fig. 1(b)), the perceived dot array contains higher signals from far-away objects, despite being sparse. By leveraging the redundancies in natural images and capabilities of modern neural networks, we can reconstruct far-away scenes with higher quality. As shown in the third column of Fig. 1, PF's reconstruction of red buses is better; more importantly, the pedestrian and the traffic cone (indicated by the white box) are completely missed in UF's result while still visible in PF's. Downstream tasks, including object detection [15,72] and semantic segmentation [11], can also benefit from this higher quality reconstruction. Note that concentrating optical power has also been proposed to improve the sensing distance of active 3D sensors [5,22,50,62], but in that context, photon noise from strong ambient light sources (e.g., sunlight), instead of sensor noise, dominates.

Apart from higher image quality at a long distance, PF introduces another advantage over UF. With a textured illumination pattern and a small baseline between the light source and the imaging device, the captured image contains depth information, as in the case of structured light (SL) 3D imaging techniques [20]. The slight differences to traditional SL are that our SL's pattern is weak in brightness, and ours has a comparatively micro baseline because of the long imaging distance. Since color and depth information highly correlate in the captured image, existing SL methods cannot be readily applied. The proposed algorithm solves this problem and can estimate sub-pixel disparity accurately.

In summary, our contributions are in three folds:

- We propose patterned flash (PF) for low-light imaging. It relieves flash's fundamental drawback, short distance.
- We develop a deep-learning-based joint image reconstruction and disparity estimation algorithm to reconstruct scene image and depth from the single captured patterned flash image.
- We evaluate our approach with simulations and real-world data captured by a hardware prototype. The results verify that the proposed system has significant improvement over the conventional uniform flash.

2   Related Work

2.1   Flash Imaging

The flash has long been used to enhance image signals in dim environments. It was also applied in many other computational imaging tasks, such as reflection removal [38], BRDF acquisition [31], white balance [29], illumination separation [30], image matting [59], edge detection [52] and geometric estimation [40]. In the context of using a flash to assist low-light imaging, there are three well-known problems, and some solutions have been proposed. (1) Flash images look harsh or unnatural. Flash changes the color tone of the scene, adds highlights to the human face, and makes the nearby objects much brighter than far away. Since the seminal work [16,51], flash/no-flash techniques have been intensively discussed in literature [21,39,67,70] which denoise the no-flash image with guidance from the flash image. True-tone flash has been widely used in smartphones which uses two

LEDs of different colors to mimic the color tone of the scene. (2) Flash is intrusive to human eyes. To make the flash more user-friendly and social friendly, previous research focused on using flashes that operate at wavelengths less sensitive to human eyes, e.g., dark flash (NUV and NIR) [37,64], deep-red flash [69], or using weak flash [27]. (3) Flash has a short effective range. Current methods either increase the power or shrink the FOV, and there has been little effort to solve this problem from a computational imaging perspective. High power (10 ~ 100 W) LEDs have been used to lighten large scenes at night (e.g., football field), but such systems cannot be applied to consumer devices and introduce heavy light pollution. Another approach is to concentrate light into a smaller FOV. Matrix headlight has been adopted in high-end vehicle models [3]; when necessary, it concentrates flash power into a smaller angular range to reach a longer distance. However, sacrificing FOV is a non-optimal solution.

More broadly, flash illumination or active illumination is also often used in other imaging modalities, where the environmental light level is low, including active hyper-spectral, short-wave infrared [57], middle-wave infrared [36], long-wave infrared [35], and near-ultraviolet imaging. These techniques also face the challenge of light fall off, and they may face more challenges than active, visible-light imaging in that the sensor qualities [54] and light emitters' optical efficiencies [61] are lower, or the power is constrained by safety concerns.

2.2   Low-Light Imaging Without Flash

Apart from flash imaging, there are other popular low-light imaging methods, which can be categorized into single image-based and burst-based methods. Usually, they require more ambient light than the flash-based methods. Efforts have been made to denoise a single image from early years of image processing to date [10,12,14,65]. Chen et al. [12] first introduced a modern neural network model on RAW data for low-light imaging. Wei et al. [65] demonstrated that carefully modeling sensor noise in the training data plays an important role in improving the denoising performance. Though progress has been made, it is fundamentally difficult to recover the scene details without hallucination in single-image-based methods. Burst-based imaging has achieved more impressive results recently [24,42,47,68]. By fusing a sequence of images taken with a short exposure time, SNR is greatly boosted. The major difficulty for this approach is aligning the burst frames; some algorithms are based on explicit optical flow estimation [24,42] while others utilize implicit kernel prediction networks [47,68]; for both approaches, the extremely low-light condition makes the image registrations unreliable, and then the reconstruction quality reduces significantly [47]. Burst-based methods also require the camera to be still and the scene to be static, which may not hold in some circumstances.

2.3   Structured Light (SL) 3D Imaging

SL is one of the most widely used techniques in 3D imaging [20]. Although there are advances which can speed up dot scanning [63], line scanning [8], and time-multiplexing gray code [60], the random dot pattern is usually adopted in consumer devices, like Microsoft Kinect [44] and Apple Face ID [45], because it supports single-shot depth estimation. Existing algorithms, like block matching or HyperDepth [17], assume the scene of interest is close, the baseline is sufficiently large, and the dots are saturated in the image. Depth can be accurately estimated by the number of pixel shifts of pattern dots. However, these algorithms can not be directly applied in our small-baseline system, since the sub-pixel disparities mainly lead to subtle color and intensity changes. Thus, the depth and image estimations are highly correlated. Saragadam et al. [56] proposed micro-baseline SL to estimate sub-pixel disparities, but it requires a triangular wave pattern profile. Riegler et al. [53] proposed a self-supervised learning approach by modeling the joint distribution of scene albedo and depth, but it requires sufficient ambient illumination to separate scene albedo and depth. Low-light environments make this separation impractical. The proposed PF is a novel SL system where color and depth information are naturally mixed. Estimating either attribute requires knowledge about the other one, and the baseline is very small. We propose a new algorithm that can estimate both accurately.

3   Image Formation Model

In the proposed PF system, we capture one RAW image $\mathbf{I} \in \mathbb{R}^{H \times W \times C}$, with the PF as the dominant illumination light source[1] (with H, W being spacial dimensions and C being the number of color channels). A reference pattern $\mathbf{P_r} \in \mathbb{R}^{H \times W \times C}$ is captured in the calibration stage, and the image/reference pair $\{\mathbf{I}, \mathbf{P_r}\}$ is used as the input into the reconstruction algorithm. Both $\mathbf{I}$ and $\mathbf{P_r}$ are $\in [0, 1]$. The image formation model for $\mathbf{I}$ can be expressed as:

$$\mathbf{I} = \frac{\mathcal{W}_\mathbf{d}[\mathbf{P_r}]}{\mathbf{d}^2} \odot \mathbf{A} + \mathcal{N} \tag{1}$$

In Eq. 1, $\mathcal{W}_\mathbf{d}$ is the depth-dependent warping operation. $\mathcal{W}_\mathbf{d}[\mathbf{P_r}]$ is the warped flash pattern. $\mathbf{d}$ is the scene depth, and $\mathbf{A}$ is the scene image. Here we include scene surface normal and material properties in $\mathbf{A}$. $\odot$ is the pixel-wise product. $\mathcal{N}$ includes photon noise, read noise, quantization noise, and other noise sources [65]. We leverage this image formation model in synthetic data generation, for network training and evaluation. We also implement a photometric loss based on this model for better supervision.

3.1   Signal-to-Noise Ratio Analysis

Here we theoretically analyze the advantage of PF over UF and elucidate the assumptions used in the comparison. In the UF system (Fig. 2(b)), each pixel receives signal s, the signal-noise-ratio at each pixel can be expressed as:

$$SNR_{UF} = s/\sqrt{s + \sigma_r^2} \tag{2}$$

---

[1] Our method can be extended to the scenarios with stronger ambient illumination. Please refer to supplementary material for details.

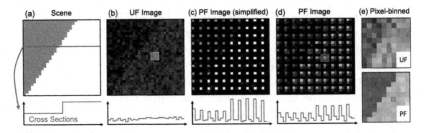

Fig. 2. Signal-noise-ratio comparisons and "pixel-binned" images. (a) Scene. (b-d) Comparisons between UF and PF captured images with cross-sections. (e) Comparisons between "pixel-binned" UF and PF images, as discussed in Sect. 3.1. The yellow and red pixels in upper and lower parts of (e) correspond to the $M \times M$ patches ($M = 3$ in this case) in (b) and (d), respectively. (Color figure online)

where σ_r is the standard deviation of signal-independent sensor noise (e.g., read noise), and photon shot noise of signal s has variance s.

In the PF system, however, suppose the entire signal in an $M \times M$ patch is concentrated in one camera pixel (Fig. 2(c), $M = 3$). The "in-pattern" pixel receives signal M^2s, and the SNR for this pixel can be expressed by SNR_{PF} in Eq. 3. However, this SNR enhancement is at the expense of lower spatial resolution. For a fair comparison, we average the entire signal in the UF image patch to get the SNR at the same spatial resolution (SNR_{UFavg} in Eq. 3). We notice that when σ_r dominates, SNR_{PF} can be around M times higher than SNR_{UFavg}. Generally, this holds in low-light conditions [19,23].

$$\begin{cases} SNR_{PF} = M^2s/\sqrt{M^2s + \sigma_r^2} \approx M^2s/\sigma_r \\ SNR_{UFavg} = M^2s/\sqrt{M^2s + M^2\sigma_r^2} \approx Ms/\sigma_r \end{cases} \tag{3}$$

For real-world patterns, $\mathbf{P_r}$ may not be exactly "1 in $M \times M$" (Fig. 2(d)). Each pattern dot is blurred, and the overall pattern contrast is lower. We can define a similar input signal SNR comparison. For a PF image, we set a threshold to define whether an image pixel falls within a pattern dot. Then we only extract "in pattern" image pixels from each $M \times M$ pixels patch (red rectangle in Fig. 2 (d)) and combine them into a low-resolution image (as shown in Fig. 2(e), lower part). For a UF image, we average the captured image to the same spatial resolution (as shown in Fig. 2(e), upper part). In the following, we use this "pixel-binning" method to visualize the quality of image signal before processing.

We also define the "average occupancy" of $\mathbf{P_r}$ as its mean value. A pattern with average occupancy $1/\Omega$ can be regarded as an equivalence of the simplified "1 in $\sqrt{\Omega} \times \sqrt{\Omega}$" pattern, and therefore has theoretical upper bound of input SNR gain $\sqrt{\Omega} \times$ (when signal $\rightarrow 0$ and contrast $\rightarrow \infty$). With smaller average occupancy, the pattern is sparser, and the SNR gain is larger. However, recovering the image content between pattern dots becomes more difficult. Empirically, we found average occupancy $= 1/16$ achieves good balance in this trade-off. Note that higher photon shot noise and lower flash pattern contrast would reduce

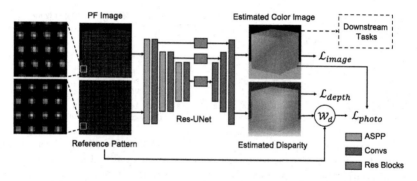

Fig. 3. Joint scene image and depth estimation. We use captured PF image and a reference pattern as input. The neural network predicts a scene image and a disparity map. We use three loss functions to supervise the network training: image loss $\mathcal{L}_{image}$, depth loss $\mathcal{L}_{depth}$, and photometric loss $\mathcal{L}_{photo}$. The reconstruction results can be further employed in downstream tasks (e.g., object detection).

the SNR gain from its theoretical limit. However, we demonstrate that, in both simulations and real-world experiments, PF improves image quality significantly.

4 Patterned Flash Processing

4.1 Network Architecture

The network architecture is shown in Fig. 3. The goal of our reconstruction algorithm is to jointly estimate a scene image $\widehat{\mathbf{A}}$ and the scene depth $\widehat{\mathbf{d}}$ from PF image $\mathbf{I}$. We use a U-Net [55] as backbone, with multiple residual blocks [26] as skip connections. Since information is distributed sparsely in $\mathbf{I}$, a big receptive field is required for feature extraction. We use an Atrous Spatial Pyramid Pooling (ASPP) module [13] to balance the receptive field and computational cost. For details of the network architecture, please refer to supplementary material.

4.2 Loss Functions

We train the network in a supervised manner, with ground truth color image $\mathbf{A}$ and depth $\mathbf{d}$. We use three types of loss functions; supervision on image reconstruction $\mathcal{L}_{image}$, supervision on depth estimation $\mathcal{L}_{depth}$, and photometric loss [53,73] $\mathcal{L}_{photo}$. The total loss is a weighted combination.

$$\mathcal{L} = \mathcal{L}_{image} + \lambda_1 \mathcal{L}_{depth} + \lambda_2 \mathcal{L}_{photo} \tag{4}$$

The image reconstruction loss consists of three parts, an L2 loss, a perceptual loss [32] (with VGG16 as feature extractor), and an L1 gradient loss.

$$\mathcal{L}_{image} = |\widehat{\mathbf{A}} - \mathbf{A}|^2 + \beta_1 |\text{VGG}(\widehat{\mathbf{A}}) - \text{VGG}(\mathbf{A})|^2$$
$$+ \beta_2(|\nabla_x \widehat{\mathbf{A}} - \nabla_x \mathbf{A}| + |\nabla_y \widehat{\mathbf{A}} - \nabla_y \mathbf{A}|) \tag{5}$$

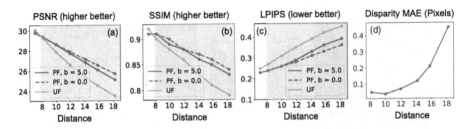

Fig. 4. Quantitative comparisons between PF and UF on synthetic data (distance unit defined in Sect. 6.1). (a, b) Image reconstruction quality from the PF system consistently outperforms that in the UF system at a long distance (green region). Also, increasing the baseline only slightly influences the image reconstruction performance. (c) Mean absolute error (MAE) of disparity estimation. (Color figure online)

For depth estimation supervision, we use an L2 loss.

$$\mathcal{L}_{depth} = |\widehat{\mathbf{d}} - \mathbf{d}|^2 \tag{6}$$

The photometric loss utilizes the image formation model to enforce a consistent depth and image prediction.

$$\mathcal{L}_{photo} = |\mathcal{W}_{\widehat{\mathbf{d}}}[\mathbf{P_r}] \odot \widehat{\mathbf{A}} - \mathcal{W}_{\mathbf{d}}[\mathbf{P_r}] \odot \mathbf{A}|^2 \tag{7}$$

5   Implementations

We train the network on data synthesized from FlyingThings3D dataset [46], with ground truth image and depth. We use experimentally captured reference patterns for both network training and evaluations. For each scene, we set a distance $\in [8, 16]$. Compared with imaging an object at distance $= 1$, this corresponds to an attenuation of the color image (normalized to $[0, 1]$) by $64\times \sim 256\times$. Note that we use a uniform attenuation factor across one scene in training data synthesis instead of a depth-dependent attenuation $1/\mathbf{d}^2$. This is to not weigh the farther objects less in loss function $\mathcal{L}_{image}$. We assume a heteroscedastic Gaussian noise model to account for both read and shot sensor noise. For an attenuated image $\mathbf{I_0}$, the noise variance is defined as $\sigma_r^2 + \sigma_s^2 \mathbf{I_0}$. For each scene, we randomly select $\sigma_r \in [0.002, 0.005]$ and $\sigma_s \in [0.015, 0.04]$. We also add a small "row noise", with $\sigma_{row} = 0.0005$, to be consistent with our CMOS sensor used in real-world experiments [65]. For each scene, we randomly choose the sign of disparities and randomly select a baseline between $0.5 \sim 5.0$, consistent with the unambiguous range defined by the reference pattern.

We train our model using the Adam optimizer [34], with learning rate 2×10^{-4}, for a total of roughly 200k iterations. The training process takes around 1.5 d on a single Nvidia Tesla-V100 GPU.

6   Simulation Results

6.1   Joint Image and Depth Estimation

We first evaluate the image reconstruction quality at discrete distances. We use an experimentally captured pattern with average occupancy $\sim 1/16$ (as discussed in Sect. 3.1), which is a real-world equivalence of "1 in 4×4" pattern. We fix the noise settings with $\sigma_r = 0.004$ and $\sigma_s = 0.02$. We set the distance values at $\{8, 10, 12, 14, 16, 18\}$ (the distances are defined such that no image attenuation at distance $= 1$), and assume the reference pattern is at distance $= 8$ in calibration. We use a baseline $= 5.0$, which leads to disparities $= \{0, 1.0, 1.7, 2.1, 2.5, 2.8\}$ pixels at the evaluation distances.[2] The evaluation is conducted on a test set with 128 scenes. The quantitative comparisons between these two approaches are shown in Fig. 4 (a, b, c). It can be seen that PF consistently outperforms UF at long distances (green region). When flash power is more attenuated (with a farther imaging distance), the difference between the two approaches is larger. Note that at closer range (e.g., < 8), PF has lower reconstruction quality compared with the UF. We attribute it to the fact that the PF system discards part of the high-frequency information. This is the major limitation of PF technique. For more discussions, please refer to Sect. 8.

We further evaluate the influence of the baseline. We evaluate PF image reconstruction with a zero baseline (disparity is always zero). As shown by the blue solid lines and dashed lines in Fig. 4 (a, b, c), the discrepancies in image reconstruction with and without baseline are generally small. When distance increases, performance of the system with baseline drops slightly faster due to more inaccurate depth estimation with lower signal levels. We also evaluate the mean absolute error (MAE) of disparity estimation (Fig. 4 (d)). The proposed system achieves sub-pixel disparity estimations in the distance range of interest, which provides a rough depth estimation.

As discussed in Sect. 3.1, we can directly compare the *captured* image quality through a "pixel-binning" method. The theoretical upper bound of input SNR gain, with the specific pattern being used, is $4\times$ (12dB). With the existence of photon shot noise and lower pattern contrast, we get $\sim$ 6dB input SNR gain across the distance range. A qualitative comparison of the "pixel-binned" input images is shown in the second column of Fig. 5. PF images contain most edges and textures in the scene, while some of these details are invisible in UF images, even after averaging. In this way, PF enables much more detailed reconstructions for far-away scenes (as shown in the third column of Fig. 5). We also show the disparity estimation results from PF images (thr fourth column of Fig. 5). Note that the algorithm is unable to predict a decent depth map from UF images.

6.2   Illumination Pattern Design

Designing optimal patterns in structured light has long been investigated [48, 66]. Since for natural scenes, important details appear with uniform probabilities

---

[2] The disparity estimation is not influenced by the reference's distance as long as the disparity is within reasonable range.

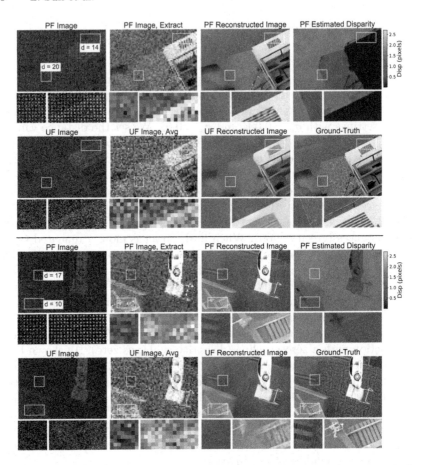

Fig. 5. Qualitative comparisons between patterned flash (PF) and uniform flash (UF) on synthetic data. PF preserves more details in the captured image (first and second columns), and supports higher quality reconstruction (third column). PF also provides disparity estimation, which is non-trivial with UF.

across the FOV, we also consider patterns with uniformly distributed sampling dots. Current structured light systems utilize random patterns due to less ambiguity in stereo matching. We compare a "regular" pattern with multiple "pseudo-random" patterns generated from jittering each dot in the regular pattern by $\{-1, 0, 1\}$ pixels. Two examples of the pseudo-random pattern are shown in Fig. 6(a, b). We empirically found that using pseudo-random pattern results in a slightly worse image reconstruction quality (Fig. 6(c)). This might be due to unavoidable "gap" regions in pseudo-random patterns, where information is missing and difficult to be completed (marked by red boxes in Fig. 6(a, b)). Also, in the proposed system and applications, the baseline is much smaller than the scene distance, and disparities are smaller than the unambiguous range in regular patterns. As an example, a 90° FOV camera, with 2000 × 2000 pixels, and

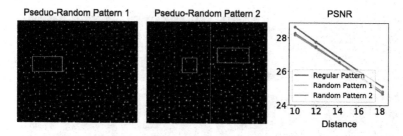

Fig. 6. Pattern design:"pseudo-random" pattern vs. "regular" pattern. (a, b) Part of example pseudo-random patterns generated from the regular pattern. Red boxes show big "gaps" in the patterns. (c) Quantitative comparison on image reconstruction quality between regular pattern and pseudo-random patterns. (Color figure online)

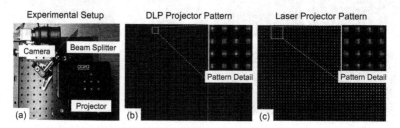

Fig. 7. (a) Photo of the hardware prototype, with a camera, a beam splitter (to enable tunable baseline between camera and projector from 0 ∼ 2 cm), and a projector. (b) DLP projector pattern (with zoomed in details). (c) Laser projector pattern (with zoomed in details).

a baseline = 3 cm between camera and flash light source, would perceive 2.25 pixels pattern dot shift when imaging an object at 20 m distance (suppose reference pattern is calibrated at 8 m). Therefore, we choose the regular pattern in our setup. More advanced pattern designs (e.g. Poisson disk sampling [9]) or even an end-to-end optimization on the illumination pattern [7,66] could be left for a future research work.

7 Experimental Results

We implement a patterned flash hardware prototype to evaluate our approach in a real-world environment, as shown in Fig. 7. The system consists of a machine-vision camera (Basler acA2040-120uc), a projector as the PF light source, and a beam splitter. The beamsplitter is used to remove the physical constraints from the bulky camera lens and the projector case, and enable tuning the baseline between the camera and the projector from 0 to 2 cm. We tested our system with two projectors: a DLP projector (Aaxa P300 Pico Projector) and a laser projector (AnyBeam Laser Projector). The DLP projector has a limited depth of focus but with a sharper projected pattern and higher power. The laser projector has a large depth of focus, but has less contrast and lower power. We set the

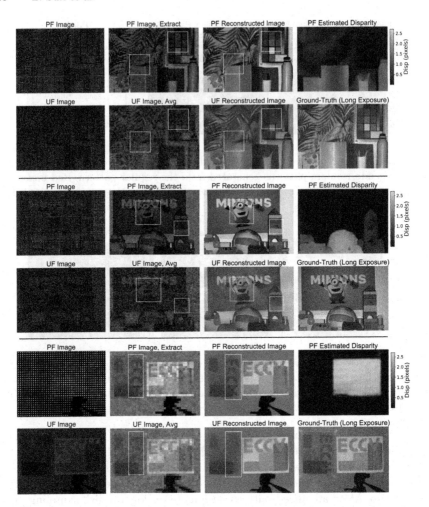

Fig. 8. Experimental results of PF vs. UF on real-world data with a DLP projector (first two rows) and a laser projector (third row). Notice that PF resolves more details, especially in the regions indicated by the white boxes.

projector display content as a regular pattern for PF, and as a uniform pattern for the UF. The two patterns are both projected onto a white wall for calibration. We adjust the projector brightness to make the two calibration patterns have the same per-channel average intensities for a fair comparison. We compare both the captured image and the reconstruction qualities in Fig. 8. In the first setup (Fig. 8 first two rows), the DLP projector projects a pattern with 57×80 dots, and the scene is set to be ~ 3 m away (limited by lab space), with a depth range ~ 50 cm (limited by projector depth of focus). In the second setup (Fig. 8(b)), the laser projector projects a pattern with 28×46 dots. The scene is set to be ~ 3 m aways, with depth range ~ 1.5 m.

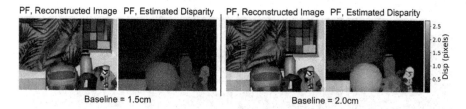

Fig. 9. Experimental image reconstruction and disparity estimation with different base-lines, with the same camera and DLP projector illumination settings as that in Fig. 8.

In Fig. 8, it can be seen that for both setups, PF out-performs UF, with higher visibility of objects under low flash illumination power, as highlighted by the white boxes. This can be observed in both "pixel-binned" images and reconstruction results. Specifically, UF fails to distinguish the outlines of objects (e.g., curtain textures in the first row and toy building blocks in the second row) while PF can faithfully reconstruct the fine textures. In the third row, we placed two boards at different distances. At close range, both PF and UF recovers the board content well enough, due to sufficiently high signal level. At a long distance, UF signals are overwhelmed by the sensor noise, and the reconstructed object is heavily blurred out. The PF system suffers from aliasing artifacts. However, this is a minor effect compared with the artifacts in reconstructed images from the UF. We also demonstrate depth estimation with the experimental setup. As shown in Fig. 8, we are able to estimate disparities in both regions with rich textures (e.g., curtain, stripes on the baseball) and non-textured regions (e.g., white wall, white notebook). Also, as shown in Fig. 9, we tune the baseline between the camera and DLP projector to generate different disparities for the same scene. When the baseline changes in a reasonable range, image reconstruction quality is not influenced.

Object Detection. We further demonstrate the advantage of PF, by applying face detection on the real-world reconstruction images. We use Google MediaPipe [1] as the detector. As shown in Fig. 10, the detector is able to both detect the face and the key points from the PF reconstructed image while it fails with the UF reconstructed image, especially for the mannequin with darker skin color. For more discussions and examples of applying PF reconstructed images in downstream tasks, please refer to the supplementary material.

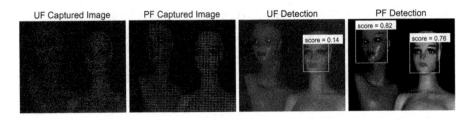

Fig. 10. Real-world face detection with UF and PF. The detector fails on UF reconstructed image but succeeds in PF reconstructed image, especially for the mannequin with darker skin color.

8   Discussions and Conclusions

In this paper, we propose patterned flash for low-light imaging at a long distance. From a noisy patterned flash image, we jointly reconstruct a color image and estimate depth. We build a hardware prototype and demonstrate compelling performance under low-light conditions compared to traditional uniform flash. The proposed technique has the potential to be implemented as an energy-efficient low-light imaging module, which improves visual quality and robustness in applications across disciplines, including photography, navigation, and surveillance.

Limitations and Envisioning. (1) In reality, the proposed system can be implemented with more stable and more compact devices. Diffractive optical element (DOE) [4], Vertical-cavity surface-emitting laser (VCSEL) arrays [2] or Microelectromechanical systems (MEMS) mirror can be used. (2) As mentioned in Sect. 6, at close range, patterned flash has lower image reconstruction quality compared with the uniform flash. This originates from the sparse nature of captured patterned flash signals. We envision two variants of the patterned flash system to solve this problem: (i) a combination of uniform and patterned flashes. Power can be distributed between the two light sources according to the required imaging distance and the relative importance of close or far-away objects. (ii) a lens-based system with a large aperture that focuses at infinity (or the maximum imaging distance of interest), to create patterned flash far away and uniform flash (blurred) nearby. (3) The sparse patterned flash signal might also lead to aliasing in the reconstructed image. However, this is a secondary effect when imaging at long distance, where the uniform flash fails to reconstruct even big structures. Also, when there is certain amount of ambient light or the flash has some uniform flash component, this problem can be relieved. Besides, image inpainting and super-resolution algorithms [25], [41] can be applied.

Acknowledgment. We would like to thank Jinhui Xiong and Yifan Peng for helpful discussions.

References

1. Google mediapipe face detector. https://google.github.io/mediapipe/ (2020). Accessed 1 Mar 2022
2. Vcsel array applications. https://vixarinc.com/wp-content/uploads/2020/07/ (2020). Accessed 1 Mar 2022
3. Audi led matrix headlights. https://media.audiusa.com/en-us/releases/444 (2021). Accessed 1 Mar 2022
4. Nil technology introduces flat, multifunctional optics platform for 3d sensing and lidar applications. https://www.nilt.com/nilt-introduces-flat-optics-for-3d-sensing-and-lidar/ (2021). Accessed 1 Mar 2022
5. Achar, S., Bartels, J.R., Whittaker, W.L.R., Kutulakos, K.N., Narasimhan, S.G.: Epipolar time-of-flight imaging. ACM Trans. Graph. (TOG) **36**(4), 6383–6392 (2017)
6. Altenburg, M.: Understanding flash photography: how to shoot great photographs using electronic flash. PSA J. **78**(7), 8–9 (2012)
7. Baek, S.H., Heide, F.: Polka lines: learning structured illumination and reconstruction for active stereo. In: Proceedings of the IEEE Conference on Computer Vision and Pattern Recognition (CVPR), pp. 5757–5767 (2021)
8. Bartels, J.R., Wang, J., Whittaker, W., Narasimhan, S.G., et al.: Agile depth sensing using triangulation light curtains. In: Proceedings of the IEEE/CVF International Conference on Computer Vision (ICCV), pp. 7900–7908 (2019)
9. Bridson, R.: Fast poisson disk sampling in arbitrary dimensions. SIGGRAPH Sketches **10**(1), 1 (2007)
10. Brooks, T., Mildenhall, B., Xue, T., Chen, J., Sharlet, D., Barron, J.T.: Unprocessing images for learned raw denoising. In: Proceedings of the IEEE Conference on Computer Vision and Pattern Recognition (CVPR), pp. 11036–11045 (2019)
11. Buchholz, T.-O., Prakash, M., Schmidt, D., Krull, A., Jug, F.: DENOISEG: joint denoising and segmentation. In: Bartoli, A., Fusiello, A. (eds.) ECCV 2020. LNCS, vol. 12535, pp. 324–337. Springer, Cham (2020). https://doi.org/10.1007/978-3-030-66415-2_21
12. Chen, C., Chen, Q., Xu, J., Koltun, V.: Learning to see in the dark. In: Proceedings of the IEEE Conference on Computer Vision and Pattern Recognition (CVPR), pp. 3291–3300 (2018)
13. Chen, L.C., Papandreou, G., Kokkinos, I., Murphy, K., Yuille, A.L.: DeepLab: semantic image segmentation with deep convolutional nets, atrous convolution, and fully connected CRFs. IEEE Trans. Pattern Anal. Mach. Intell. (PAMI) **40**(4), 834–848 (2017)
14. Dabov, K., Foi, A., Katkovnik, V., Egiazarian, K.: Image denoising by sparse 3-d transform-domain collaborative filtering. IEEE Trans. Image Process. (TIP) **16**(8), 2080–2095 (2007)
15. Duan, K., Bai, S., Xie, L., Qi, H., Huang, Q., Tian, Q.: Centernet: keypoint triplets for object detection. In: Proceedings of the IEEE/CVF International Conference on Computer Vision (ICCV), pp. 6569–6578 (2019)
16. Eisemann, E., Durand, F.: Flash photography enhancement via intrinsic relighting. ACM Trans. Graph. (TOG) **23**(3), 673–678 (2004)
17. Fanello, S.R., et al.: HyperDepth: learning depth from structured light without matching. In: Proceedings of the IEEE Conference on Computer Vision and Pattern Recognition (CVPR), pp. 5441–5450 (2016)

18. Flint, K.: Flash!: Photography, Writing, and Surprising Illumination. Oxford University Press, Oxford (2017)
19. Foi, A., Trimeche, M., Katkovnik, V., Egiazarian, K.: Practical poissonian-gaussian noise modeling and fitting for single-image raw-data. IEEE Trans. Image Process. (TIP) **17**(10), 1737–1754 (2008)
20. Geng, J.: Structured-light 3d surface imaging: a tutorial. Adv. Opt. Photonics **3**(2), 128–160 (2011)
21. Guo, X., Li, Y., Ma, J., Ling, H.: Mutually guided image filtering. IEEE Trans. Pattern Anal. Mach. Intell. (PAMI) **42**(3), 694–707 (2018)
22. Gupta, M., Yin, Q., Nayar, S.K.: Structured light in sunlight. In: Proceedings of the IEEE International Conference on Computer Vision (ICCV), pp. 545–552 (2013)
23. Hasinoff, S.W.: Photon, poisson noise (2014)
24. Hasinoff, S.W., et al.: Burst photography for high dynamic range and low-light imaging on mobile cameras. ACM Trans. Graph. (TOG) **35**(6), 1–12 (2016)
25. He, K., Chen, X., Xie, S., Li, Y., Dollár, P., Girshick, R.: Masked autoencoders are scalable vision learners. arXiv preprint arXiv:2111.06377 (2021)
26. He, K., Zhang, X., Ren, S., Sun, J.: Deep residual learning for image recognition. In: Proceedings of the IEEE Conference on Computer Vision and Pattern Recognition (CVPR), pp. 770–778 (2016)
27. Huawei: Huawei x2391–20-t 20t 9mp low-light its AI bullet camera. https://www.tepuhui.com/huawei-x2391-20-t-en (2022). Accessed 1 March 2022
28. Hubel, P.M., Liu, J., Guttosch, R.J.: Spatial frequency response of color image sensors: bayer color filters and foveon x3. In: Sensors and Camera Systems for Scientific, Industrial, and Digital Photography Applications V. vol. 5301, pp. 402–407. SPIE (2004)
29. Hui, Z., Sankaranarayanan, A.C., Sunkavalli, K., Hadap, S.: White balance under mixed illumination using flash photography. In: 2016 IEEE International Conference on Computational Photography (ICCP), pp. 1–10. IEEE (2016)
30. Hui, Z., Sunkavalli, K., Hadap, S., Sankaranarayanan, A.C.: Illuminant spectra-based source separation using flash photography. In: Proceedings of the IEEE Conference on Computer Vision and Pattern Recognition (CVPR), pp. 6209–6218 (2018)
31. Hui, Z., Sunkavalli, K., Lee, J.Y., Hadap, S., Wang, J., Sankaranarayanan, A.C.: Reflectance capture using univariate sampling of BRDFs. In: Proceedings of the IEEE International Conference on Computer Vision (ICCV), pp. 5362–5370 (2017)
32. Johnson, J., Alahi, A., Fei-Fei, L.: Perceptual losses for real-time style transfer and super-resolution. In: Leibe, B., Matas, J., Sebe, N., Welling, M. (eds.) ECCV 2016. LNCS, vol. 9906, pp. 694–711. Springer, Cham (2016). https://doi.org/10.1007/978-3-319-46475-6_43
33. Jung, Y.J.: Enhancement of low light level images using color-plus-mono dual camera. Opt. Express **25**(10), 12029–12051 (2017)
34. Kingma, D.P., Ba, J.: Adam: a method for stochastic optimization. arXiv preprint arXiv:1412.6980 (2014)
35. Koerperick, E.J., Norton, D.T., Olesberg, J.T., Olson, B.V., Prineas, J.P., Boggess, T.F.: Cascaded superlattice InAs/GaSb light-emitting diodes for operation in the long-wave infrared. IEEE J. Quant. Electron. **47**(1), 50–54 (2010)
36. Koerperick, E.J., Olesberg, J.T., Hicks, J.L., Prineas, J.P., Boggess, T.F.: High-power MWIR cascaded InAs-GaSb superlattice LEDs. IEEE journal of quantum electronics **45**(7), 849–853 (2009)
37. Krishnan, D., Fergus, R.: Dark flash photography. ACM Trans. Graph. (TOG) **28**(3), 96 (2009)

38. Lei, C., Chen, Q.: Robust reflection removal with reflection-free flash-only cues. In: Proceedings of the IEEE Conference on Computer Vision and Pattern Recognition (CVPR), pp. 14811–14820 (2021)
39. Li, Y., Huang, J.-B., Ahuja, N., Yang, M.-H.: Deep joint image filtering. In: Leibe, B., Matas, J., Sebe, N., Welling, M. (eds.) ECCV 2016. LNCS, vol. 9908, pp. 154–169. Springer, Cham (2016). https://doi.org/10.1007/978-3-319-46493-0_10
40. Li, Z., Xu, Z., Ramamoorthi, R., Sunkavalli, K., Chandraker, M.: Learning to reconstruct shape and spatially-varying reflectance from a single image. ACM Trans. Graph. (TOG) **37**(6), 1–11 (2018)
41. Liang, J., Cao, J., Sun, G., Zhang, K., Van Gool, L., Timofte, R.: SwinIR: Image restoration using swin transformer. In: Proceedings of the IEEE International Conference on Computer Vision (CVPR), pp. 1833–1844 (2021)
42. Liba, O., et al.: Handheld mobile photography in very low light. ACM Trans. Graph. (TOG) **38**(6), 1–16 (2019)
43. Ma, S., Gupta, S., Ulku, A.C., Bruschini, C., Charbon, E., Gupta, M.: Quanta burst photography. ACM Trans. Graph. (TOG) **39**(4), 1–79 (2020)
44. MacCormick, J.: How does the kinect work. Presentert ved Dickinson College **6** (2011)
45. Mainenti, D.: User perceptions of apple's face id. Information Science, Human Computer Interaction (DIS805) (2017)
46. Mayer, N., Ilg, E., Hausser, P., Fischer, P., Cremers, D., Dosovitskiy, A., Brox, T.: A large dataset to train convolutional networks for disparity, optical flow, and scene flow estimation. In: Proceedings of the IEEE Conference on Computer Vision and Pattern Recognition (CVPR), pp. 4040–4048 (2016)
47. Mildenhall, B., Barron, J.T., Chen, J., Sharlet, D., Ng, R., Carroll, R.: Burst denoising with kernel prediction networks. In: Proceedings of the IEEE Conference on Computer Vision and Pattern Recognition (CVPR), pp. 2502–2510 (2018)
48. Mirdehghan, P., Chen, W., Kutulakos, K.N.: Optimal structured light a la carte. In: Proceedings of the IEEE Conference on Computer Vision and Pattern Recognition (CVPR), pp. 6248–6257 (2018)
49. O'Connor, M.: Tested: Huawei p30 pro. Aust. Photogr. 66–68 (2019)
50. O'Toole, M., Achar, S., Narasimhan, S.G., Kutulakos, K.N.: Homogeneous codes for energy-efficient illumination and imaging. ACM Trans. Graph. (TOG) **34**(4), 1–13 (2015)
51. Petschnigg, G., Szeliski, R., Agrawala, M., Cohen, M., Hoppe, H., Toyama, K.: Digital photography with flash and no-flash image pairs. ACM Trans. Graph. (TOG) **23**(3), 664–672 (2004)
52. Raskar, R., Tan, K.H., Feris, R., Yu, J., Turk, M.: Non-photorealistic camera: depth edge detection and stylized rendering using multi-flash imaging. ACM Trans. Graph. (TOG) **23**(3), 679–688 (2004)
53. Riegler, G., Liao, Y., Donne, S., Koltun, V., Geiger, A.: Connecting the dots: Learning representations for active monocular depth estimation. In: Proceedings of the IEEE Conference on Computer Vision and Pattern Recognition (CVPR), pp. 7624–7633 (2019)
54. Rogalski, A.: Infrared and Terahertz Detectors. CRC Press, Boca Raton (2019)
55. Ronneberger, O., Fischer, P., Brox, T.: U-net: convolutional networks for biomedical image segmentation. In: Navab, N., Hornegger, J., Wells, W.M., Frangi, A.F. (eds.) MICCAI 2015. LNCS, vol. 9351, pp. 234–241. Springer, Cham (2015). https://doi.org/10.1007/978-3-319-24574-4_28

56. Saragadam, V., Wang, J., Gupta, M., Nayar, S.: Micro-baseline structured light. In: Proceedings of the IEEE International Conference on Computer Vision (ICCV), pp. 4049–4058 (2019)

57. Steiner, H., Sporrer, S., Kolb, A., Jung, N.: Design of an active multispectral SWIR camera system for skin detection and face verification. J. Sens. (2016)

58. Sukegawa, S., et al.: A 1/4-inch 8mpixel back-illuminated stacked CMOS image sensor. In: 2013 IEEE International Solid-State Circuits Conference Digest of Technical Papers (ISSCC), pp. 484–485. IEEE (2013)

59. Sun, J., Li, Y., Kang, S.B., Shum, H.Y.: Flash matting. In: ACM Transactions on Graphics (TOG), pp. 772–778 (2006)

60. Sun, Z., Zhang, Y., Wu, Y., Huo, D., Qian, Y., Wang, J.: Structured light with redundancy codes. arXiv preprint arXiv:2206.09243 (2022)

61. Tan, M.C., Connolly, J., Riman, R.E.: Optical efficiency of short wave infrared emitting phosphors. J. Phys. Chem. C 115(36), 17952–17957 (2011)

62. Wang, J., Bartels, J., Whittaker, W., Sankaranarayanan, A.C., Narasimhan, S.G.: Programmable triangulation light curtains. In: Proceedings of the European Conference on Computer Vision (ECCV), pp. 19–34 (2018)

63. Wang, J., Sankaranarayanan, A.C., Gupta, M., Narasimhan, S.G.: Dual structured light 3d using a 1d sensor. In: Leibe, B., Matas, J., Sebe, N., Welling, M. (eds.) ECCV 2016. LNCS, vol. 9910, pp. 383–398. Springer, Cham (2016). https://doi.org/10.1007/978-3-319-46466-4_23

64. Wang, J., Xue, T., Barron, J.T., Chen, J.: Stereoscopic dark flash for low-light photography. In: 2019 IEEE International Conference on Computational Photography (ICCP), pp. 1–10. IEEE (2019)

65. Wei, K., Fu, Y., Zheng, Y., Yang, J.: Physics-based noise modeling for extreme low-light photography. IEEE Trans. Pattern Anal. Mach. Intell. (PAMI) 44(11), 8520–8537 (2021)

66. Wu, Y., et al.: FreeCam3D: snapshot structured light 3d with freely-moving cameras. In: Vedaldi, A., Bischof, H., Brox, T., Frahm, J.-M. (eds.) ECCV 2020. LNCS, vol. 12372, pp. 309–325. Springer, Cham (2020). https://doi.org/10.1007/978-3-030-58583-9_19

67. Xia, Z., Gharbi, M., Perazzi, F., Sunkavalli, K., Chakrabarti, A.: Deep denoising of flash and no-flash pairs for photography in low-light environments. In: Proceedings of the IEEE Conference on Computer Vision and Pattern Recognition (CVPR), pp. 2063–2072 (2021)

68. Xia, Z., Perazzi, F., Gharbi, M., Sunkavalli, K., Chakrabarti, A.: Basis prediction networks for effective burst denoising with large kernels. In: Proceedings of the IEEE Conference on Computer Vision and Pattern Recognition (CVPR), pp. 11844–11853 (2020)

69. Xiong, J., Wang, J., Heidrich, W., Nayar, S.: Seeing in extra darkness using a deep-red flash. In: Proceedings of the IEEE Conference on Computer Vision and Pattern Recognition (CVPR), pp. 10000–10009 (2021)

70. Yan, Q., et al.: Cross-field joint image restoration via scale map. In: Proceedings of the IEEE International Conference on Computer Vision (ICCV), pp. 1537–1544 (2013)

71. Yang, H., Chao, C.K., Wei, M.K., Lin, C.P.: High fill-factor microlens array mold insert fabrication using a thermal reflow process. J. Micromech. Microeng. **14**(8), 1197 (2004)
72. Yu, K., Li, Z., Peng, Y., Loy, C.C., Gu, J.: ReconfigISP: reconfigurable camera image processing pipeline. In: Proceedings of the IEEE/CVF International Conference on Computer Vision (ICCV), pp. 4248–4257 (2021)
73. Zhang, Y., et al.: ActiveStereoNet: end-to-end self-supervised learning for active stereo systems. In: Proceedings of the European Conference on Computer Vision (ECCV), pp. 784–801 (2018)

PseudoClick: Interactive Image Segmentation with Click Imitation

Qin Liu[1,2] ⓘ, Meng Zheng[2] ⓘ, Benjamin Planche[2] ⓘ, Srikrishna Karanam[2] ⓘ, Terrence Chen[2], Marc Niethammer[1], and Ziyan Wu[2(✉)] ⓘ

[1] University of North Carolina at Chapel Hill, Chapel Hill, NC, USA
qin.liu19@cs.unc.edu, marc.niethammer@uii-ai.com
[2] United Imaging Intelligence, Cambridge, MA, USA
{meng.zheng,benjamin.planche,srikrishna.karanam,terrence.chen,
ziyan.wu}@uii-ai.com

Abstract. The goal of click-based interactive image segmentation is to obtain precise object segmentation masks with limited user interaction, *i.e.*, by a minimal number of user clicks. Existing methods require users to provide all the clicks: by first inspecting the segmentation mask and then providing points on mislabeled regions, iteratively. We ask the question: can our model directly predict where to click, so as to further reduce the user interaction cost? To this end, we propose `PseudoClick`, a generic framework that enables existing segmentation networks to propose candidate next clicks. These automatically generated clicks, termed pseudo clicks in this work, serve as an imitation of human clicks to refine the segmentation mask. We build `PseudoClick` on existing segmentation backbones and show how the click prediction mechanism leads to improved performance. We evaluate `PseudoClick` on 10 public datasets from different domains and modalities, showing that our model not only outperforms existing approaches but also demonstrates strong generalization capability in cross-domain evaluation. We obtain new state-of-the-art results on several popular benchmarks, *e.g.*, on the Pascal dataset, our model significantly outperforms existing state-of-the-art by reducing 12.4% number of clicks to achieve 85% IoU.

Keywords: Click imitation · Interactive image segmentation · Pseudo click

1 Introduction

Recent years have seen tremendous progresses in segmentation methods for various applications, *e.g.*, semantic object/instance segmentation [1,2], video understanding [3,4], autonomous driving [5–7], and medical image analysis [8,9]. The

Supplementary Information The online version contains supplementary material available at https://doi.org/10.1007/978-3-031-20068-7_42.

ⓒ The Author(s), under exclusive license to Springer Nature Switzerland AG 2022
S. Avidan et al. (Eds.): ECCV 2022, LNCS 13666, pp. 728–745, 2022.
https://doi.org/10.1007/978-3-031-20068-7_42

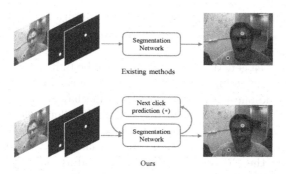

Fig. 1. The key difference between existing methods and our method is the ability for click prediction. (a) Illustration of existing methods. All clicks are provided by users. (b) Illustration of our method, which predicts the next click based on the current segmentation mask. This predicted pseudo click is used to refine the segmentation mask. Note the manual segmentation is not required at test time for the pseudo-click prediction.

success of these applications heavily relies on the availability of large-scale pixel-level annotation masks, which are very laborious and costly to obtain. Interactive image segmentation, which aims at extracting the object-of-interest using limited human interactions, is an efficient way to obtain these annotations.

While different interaction types have been investigated, including clicks [10,11], bounding boxes [12–14], and scribbles [15,16], we only focus on click-based interactive segmentation because it has the simplest interaction, and well-established training and evaluation protocols [10,11]. Compared with scribble-based methods [15,16], click-based interactive segmentation requires no heuristics or complex procedures to simulate user input. Recent work on click-based interactive segmentation has resulted in state-of-the-art segmentation performance using various inference-time optimization schemes [17], which are computationally expensive due to multiple backward passes during inference. More recently, Sofiiuk *et al.* proposed RITM [11], a simple feedforward approach requiring no inference-time optimization for click-based interactive segmentation that shows performance superior to all existing models when trained on the combined COCO [18] and LVIS [19] datasets with diverse and high-quality annotations.

While existing methods in this area have shown improved performance, *e.g.*, using inference-time optimization schemes [17] or iterative mask-guided training schemes [11], these methods still require users to provide all the clicks. Hence, users need to interactively inspect the resulting segmentation masks and then provide points for mislabeled regions. We ask the question: can the segmentation model directly predict where to click so as to further reduce the number of human clicks? To this end, we propose `PseudoClick`, a novel framework for interactive segmentation that equips existing segmentation backbones with the ability to predict user clicks automatically. As shown in Fig. 1, the key difference between existing methods and our proposed one is the ability to generate additional, beneficial, and "free" pseudo clicks as the prediction of human clicks for refining the segmentation mask.

PseudoClick is a generic framework that can be built upon existing segmentation backbones, including both CNNs and transformers. We equip an existing segmentation backbone with clicks prediction mechanism in the following procedures: we first introduce an error decoder, in parallel with the segmentation decoder of the backbone, that produces the false-positive (FP) and false-negative (FN) error maps for the current segmentation mask. We then extract a pseudo click from either the FP or the FN map, depending on which map contains the largest error. Specifically, a positive click should be generated from the FN map, while a negative click should be generated from the FP map. After that, the generated pseudo click (we generate one pseudo click each time) will be updated in the network input to refine the segmentation mask for the next forward pass. Note that the entire process is an imitation of the core human activity in interactive segmentation: visually estimating the segmentation errors, *i.e.*, over-segmentation (FP) or under-segmentation (FN), before determining what and where the next click should be.

We evaluate our method extensively on **10** public datasets (see Sect. 4.1). Evaluation results show that our model not only outperforms existing approaches but also demonstrates strong generalization capabilitity in cross-domain evaluation on medical images. On the Pascal dataset, our model significantly outperforms existing state-of-the-art by reducing 12.4% and 11.4% number of clicks to achieve 85% and 90% IoU, respectively. For the cross-domain evaluation on BraTS [20] and ssTEM [21], our method significantly outperforms existing approaches to a large margin. Our main contributions are:

1) We propose PseudoClick, a novel interactive segmentation framework that directly imitates human clicks through the segmentation network and refines the segmentation mask with these imitated pseudo clicks. Our proposed framework differs from existing interactive segmentation methods in that it provides additional, beneficial, and "free" clicks during the annotation process for a human-in-the-loop.

2) We show that PseudoClick is an efficient and generic framework that can be built upon different types of segmentation backbones, including both CNNs and transformers, with little effort in tuning the hyper-parameters and modifying the network architectures.

3) We evaluate PseudoClick thoroughly on benchmarks from multiple domains and modalities with extensive comparison and cross-domain evaluation experiments. The results show that PseudoClick not only outperforms existing state-of-the-art approaches on in-domain benchmarks but also demonstrates strong generalization capability on cross-domain evaluation.

2   Related Work

Click-based Interactive Image Segmentation. Click-based interactive segmentation has the simplest interaction and well-established training and evaluation protocols [10,11]. Xu *et al.* [10] first apply CNNs for interactive segmentation and propose a click simulation strategy for training that has inspired many future works [11,22,23]. Compared with previous click-based approaches [11,23,24], PseudoClick is unique because it is the first work that imitates human clicks and refines the segmentation with automatically generated pseudo clicks.

Other Types of Interactive Feedback. Other than clicks, different types of user interaction have been explored in this field, including bounding boxes [13], scribbles [25], and interactions from multiple modalities [26]. The main drawback of bounding box-based approaches is the lack of a specific object reference inside the selected region, as well as a clear approach to correct the predicted mask. Inside outside guidance (IOG) [13] addresses this issue by combining clicks with bounding points of the target object and by allowing corrections of the predicted mask. Our method differs from all these in that we only use clicks as the interaction. Instead of exploring more complicated interactions, we try to imitate user clicks and to decrease their number required to acquire predefined accuracy.

Imitation Learning and Beyond. Imitation learning aims at mimicking human behavior for a given task [27]. While this field has recently gained attention due to computing and sensing advances as well as the rising demand for intelligent applications [28,29], it has never been explored in the interactive segmentation tasks. We claim that our method is highly related to imitation learning in that it imitates the core user activity in the interactive annotation process: visually estimating the segmentation errors before determining what and where the next point should be. SeedNet [24] first proposes a reinforcement learning approach for automatically generating automatic click. However, their method is not an imitation of human clicks because it automatically generates a sequence of clicks for achieving an implicit long-term reward without human intervention given the initial two clicks. Therefore, it is more like a post-processing approach. In contrast, our method is an imitation of human clicks because it explicitly quantifies the FP&FN errors and then generates the next click based on the estimated errors (just like a human annotator would do). Our method imitates this process by introducing a pseudo click generation mechanism on existing segmentation backbones, as discussed in Sect. 3. Our idea of predicting FP&FN errors for segmentation is also related to the idea of "prediction loss" proposed in [30], but the two ideas are investigated in significantly different problem settings.

3   Method

As shown in Fig. 2, PseudoClick is a generic framework that builds upon existing segmentation framework with two additional modules: a segmentation error

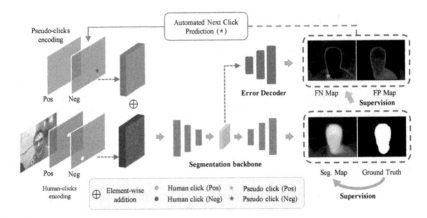

Fig. 2. PseudoClick overview. Given the image and clicks, the network outputs the segmentation map, along with two error maps that predict the false-positives and false-negatives of the segmentation mask, respectively. Then, a pseudo click will be generated from either the FP map or the FN map (see Sect. 3.2). After that, the network refines the segmentation mask in the second forward pass by adding the new pseudo click to the click encoding.

decoder module and a clicks-encoding module that consists of encoding masks for both human clicks and pseudo clicks. In Sect. 3.1, we first describe the segmentation error decoder that outputs two error maps from which pseudo clicks are generated. In Sect. 3.2, we further describe the pseudo clicks generation process. In Sect. 3.3, we then introduce the encoding mechanism that transforms pseudo clicks into spatial signal for feeding into the segmentation backbone. In Sect. 3.4, we introduce the loss function for training our models. In Sect. 3.5, we conclude the whole section by providing additional implementation details about the proposed method.

3.1 Segmentation Error Decoder

The segmentation error decoder is introduced in parallel with the segmentation decoder of the backbone. It generates two error maps that estimate the false positive (FP) and false negative (FN) errors of the segmentation mask. Both error maps are probability maps[1] that can be trained as two binary segmentation tasks. The FP and FN maps generated by the error decoder are supervised by the ground-truth FP map $\mathbf{M}_{fp}$ and ground-truth FN map $\mathbf{M}_{fn}$ that can be obtained from the ground truth mask $\mathbf{M}$ and the segmentation probability map $\mathbf{P}$ in the following way: $\mathbf{M}_{fp} = \neg\mathbf{M} \wedge (\mathbf{P} \geq \tau)$; $\mathbf{M}_{fn} = \mathbf{M} \wedge (\mathbf{P} < \tau)$, where τ is a probability threshold (which is set to 0.5 by default). Since training the

---

[1] Note that we call these *probability maps*, but in general they will likely be miscalibrated. If desired, calibration can be improved, for example, using the approach in [31].

segmentation error decoder is formulated as two binary segmentation tasks, the error decoders and the segmentation decoder can be trained end-to-end in a multi-task learning manner (See Sect. 3.4).

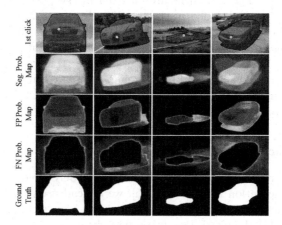

Fig. 3. Illustration of the output error maps of `PseudoClick`. Given the first click (dots in the first row), the network outputs a segmentation map (second row), along with estimated FP and FN error maps (third and fourth rows). Each column represents a test case. All test images are from the Cars dataset [32]. (Color figure online)

To help readers better understand the function of the proposed error decoder, we show in Fig. 3 the error maps generated by the error decoder. We observe that the error maps provide a meaningful estimation of the true errors, as one can easily estimate by comparing the segmentation mask (red masks in first row) with the ground truth (white masks in the last row). The accuracy of these error maps is essential for reliable pseudo clicks generation, introduced next.

3.2   Pseudo Clicks Generation

Given the predicted FP and FN error maps for the current segmentation mask, our method generates one pseudo click from either the FP or the FN map, depending on which map contains the largest error region. First, we transform the two error maps to two binary masks through a predefined threshold (*i.e.* 0.5), followed by extracting a positive/negative click from one of the two binary masks that contains the largest connected error region—the extracted pseudo click locates at the center of this region. If the largest error region is from the FP mask, then the extracted pseudo click is negative (*i.e.*, indicating that this region should not be segmented); if the largest error region is from the FN mask, then the extracted pseudo click is positive (*i.e.*, indicating that this region should be segmented). Finally, we encode the new pseudo click as a disk on the encoding maps designed exclusively for pseudo clicks, introduced next.

3.3   Pseudo Clicks Encoding

As shown in Fig. 2, human clicks and pseudo clicks are encoded separately as small binary disks in the corresponding encoding maps, resulting in two 2-channel disk maps. Positive clicks are encoded in the positive disk map while the negative clicks are encoded in the negative disk map. Note that our choice of using disk maps instead of Gaussian maps for clicks encoding is inspired by RITM [11], which shows that disk maps are more efficient and effective than Gaussian maps. We perform element-wise addition to merge the feature maps extracted from pseudo clicks and feature maps extracted from the combination of image and human clicks. The merged feature maps will be fed into the segmentation backbone for end-to-end training.

3.4   Loss Function

Although binary cross entropy (BCE) loss is widely used to supervise the interactive segmentation tasks [13,33–36], we instead use normalized focal loss (NFL) [37], which allows for faster convergence and better accuracy than BCE, as discussed in [11]. The NFL loss L can be written as:

$$L(\mathbf{P}(i,j)) = -\frac{1}{\sum_{i,j} \mathbf{P}(i,j)}(1 - \mathbf{P}(i,j))^{\gamma} \log \mathbf{P}(i,j) \tag{1}$$

where $\mathbf{P}(i,j)$ denotes the prediction $\mathbf{P}$ at point (i,j) and $\gamma > 0$ is a tunable focusing parameter (as in the focal loss [38]). Since the error branch can be supervised as two binary segmentation tasks (see Sect. 3.1), we also use the NFL loss for them during training. Therefore, the overall loss is a combination of three NFL loss functions:

$$L = \sum_{i,j}(\lambda_1 L_{seg}(i,j) + \lambda_2 L_{fp}(i,j) + \lambda_3 L_{fn}(i,j)) \tag{2}$$

where $\lambda_1, \lambda_2, \lambda_3 > 0$ represent the weights for each component; $L_{seg}(i,j)$, $L_{fp}(i,j)$, and $L_{fn}(i,j)$ denote $L(\mathbf{P}(i,j))$, $L(\mathbf{E}_{fp}(i,j))$, and $L(\mathbf{E}_{fn}(i,j))$, respectively.

3.5   Implementation Details

Click Simulation for Training and Evaluation. We automatically simulate human clicks based on the ground truth and current segmentation for fast training and evaluation. For training, we use a combination of random and iterative click simulation strategies, similar to [11]. The random click simulation strategy generates a set of positive and negative clicks without considering the order between them [10,17,39]. In contrast, the iterative simulation strategy generates clicks sequentially—a new click is generated based on the erroneous region of a prediction produced by a model using the set of previous clicks [36,40,41]. Once the model is trained, there are two modes to evaluate it: automatic evaluation and human evaluation. For automatic evaluation, we adopt the iterative click simulation strategy. Note that the automatically simulated clicks may be different from clicks generated by human evaluation. We present in the supplementary materials some qualitative results obtained via human evaluation.

Previous Segmentation as an Additional Input Channel. It is natural to incorporate the output segmentation mask from previous interaction as an input for the next correction, providing additional prior information that can help improve the segmentation quality. The previous segmentation mask is added as an additional channel to the RGB image, resulting in a 4-channel image as the input. This 4-channel image will be concatenated with the human clicks encoding maps, which have two channels (positive and negative clicks are encoded in separate channels). Note that the additional mask input is not shown in Fig. 2 for brevity. For the first interaction, we feed an empty mask to our model.

Post-processing Using Error Maps. Pseudo clicks are extracted from the error maps. Actually, the error maps can be directly used to refine the segmentation mask (*e.g.* via simple post-processing introduced in Sect. 4.4). We argue that post-processing based on FP&FN maps can be regarded as a by-product of our core contribution—PseudoClick—which takes a step further towards the general idea of click imitation.

4 Experiments

4.1 Evaluation Details

Datasets. We evaluate PseudoClick on **10** public datasets: GrabCut [16], Berkeley [42], DAVIS [43], Pascal [44], Semantic Boundaries Dataset (SBD) [45], Brain Tumor Segmentation challenge (BraTS) [20], ssTEM [21], Cars [32], COCO [18], and LVIS [19]. Since COCO and LVIS datasets share the same set of images and are complementary to each other in terms of annotation quality and object categories, they can be combined as an ideal training set for the interactive image segmentation task [11]. Therefore, we use the combined COCO+LVIS for training and the remaining 8 datasets for evaluation. Specifically, we use the training set of the COCO+LVIS dataset for training and its validation set for model selection. The Cars [32] dataset is only used for qualitative evaluation. We test the trained PseudoClick models on the test set of the remaining 7 datasets; no finetuning is conducted on these datasets. For the DAVIS and BraTS datasets, we do not use the original videos or volumes. Instead, we extract 345 and 369 2D slices from the two 3D datasets, respectively. We extracted from each volume in the BraTS the slice that contains the largest tumor area. The two medical image datasets, BraTS [20] and ssTEM [21], are used for cross-domain evaluation (see Sect. 4.3) because our models are trained with natural images, which are significantly different from images from medical domain. We refer the readers to the supplementary material for more details.

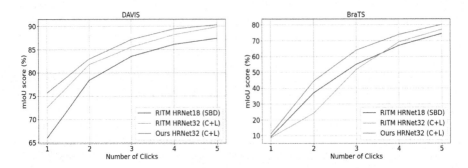

Fig. 4. Comparison of mIoU for the first five clicks on DAVIS and BraTS datasets.

Segmentation Backbone. We choose HRNet-18 and HRNet-32 [46] as backbones for our `PseudoClick` model. To show that `PseudoClick` is a generic framework that can be built upon most of existing segmentation backbones, we also implement `PseudoClick` on two recently proposed segmentation transformers: SegFormer-B5 [47] and HRFormer-base [48]. While the two transformers have shown promising preliminary results in our experiments, HRNet still outperforms them to a large margin under the same experimental settings.

Evaluation Modes and Metrics. We evaluate the trained models with two modes: automatic evaluation and human evaluation. For automatic evaluation, we simulate human clicks based on the ground truth and current segmentation mask (see Sect. 3.5); for human evaluation, a human-in-the-loop will provide clicks based on his/her subjective evaluation. We use the standard Number of Clicks (NoC) metric that measures the number of clicks required to achieve predefined Intersection over Union (IoU). Specifically, we use NoC@85 and NoC@90 as two main metrics to measure the number of clicks required to obtain 85% and 90% IoU, respectively.

More Implementation Details. We adopt the same data augmentation techniques as in RITM [11] for fair comparison. Pseudo-clicks were not counted in the NoC@85% or NoC@90% metrics as they are "free" in terms of human labor. We implement our models in Python, using PyTorch [49]. We train the models for 200 epochs on COCO+LVIS dataset with an initial learning rate 5×10^{-4}, which will decrease to 5×10^{-5} after the epoch 50. During training, we crop images with a fixed size of 320×480 and set the batch size to 32. We optimize using Adam with $\beta_1 = 0.9$, $\beta_2 = 0.999$. All models are trained and tested on a single NVIDIA RTX A6000 GPU.

4.2   Comparison with State-of-the-Art

We compare our results with existing state-of-the-art methods, including f-BRS [17], IA+SA [40], FCA [54], and RITM [11]. Table 1 shows the quantitative

Table 1. Evaluation results on GrabCut, Berkeley, DAVIS, SBD, and Pascal datasets. Our models are trained on either SBD or COCO+LVIS (denoted as C+L above) datasets. The best results are set in bold; the second best results are shown underlined. "H18" and "H32" represent "HRNet-18" and "HRNet-32", respectively. "PC" means the model is implemented with pseudo clicks. The metrics are NoC@85% and NoC@90%, representing the number of clicks required to achieve 85% and 90% IoU, respectively.

Method	GrabCut	Berkeley	SBD	DAVIS		Pascal	
	NoC@90	NoC@90	NoC@90	NoC@85	NoC@90	NoC@85	NoC@90
GC [15] ICCV01	10.00	14.22	15.96	15.13	17.41	–	–
RW [50] PAMI06	13.77	14.02	15.04	16.71	18.31	–	–
GM [51] IJCV09	14.57	15.96	17.60	18.59	19.50	–	–
GSC [52] CVPR10	9.12	12.57	15.31	15.35	17.52	–	–
ESC [52] CVPR10	9.20	12.11	14.86	15.41	17.70	–	–
DIOS [10] CVPR16	6.04	8.65	–	–	12.58	6.88	–
LD [53] CVPR18	4.79	–	10.78	5.05	9.57	–	–
BRS [33] CVPR19	3.60	5.08	9.78	5.58	8.24	–	–
f-BRS [17] CVPR20	2.72	4.57	7.73	5.04	7.41	–	–
IA+SA [40] ECCV20	3.07	4.94	–	5.16	–	3.18	–
FCA [54] CVPR20	2.08	3.92	–	–	7.57	2.69	–
SBD RITM-H18	2.04	3.22	<u>5.43</u>	4.94	6.71	2.51	3.03
C+L RITM-H32	1.56	<u>2.10</u>	5.71	4.11	5.34	2.19	2.57
SBD H18 w/ PC	2.04	3.23	**5.40**	4.81	6.57	2.34	2.74
SBD H32 w/ PC	1.84	2.98	5.61	4.74	6.16	2.37	2.78
C+L H32 w/o PC	<u>1.55</u>	2.11	5.68	<u>4.09</u>	<u>5.27</u>	<u>2.14</u>	<u>2.52</u>
C+L H32 w/ PC	**1.50**	**2.08**	5.54	**3.79**	**5.11**	1.94	**2.25**

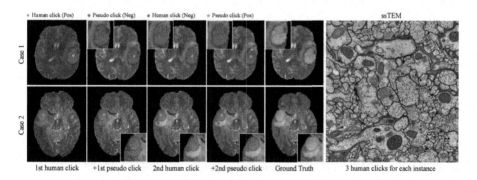

Fig. 5. Cross-domain evaluation on two medical image datasets: BraTS [20] (left) and ssTEM [21] (right). The evaluation is performed by a human annotator through our internally developed interactive segmentation GUI. For the BraTS dataset, we use two clicks for each image. For the ssTEM dataset, we strictly use three clicks for each instance. Note that our model is trained on natural images, but shows very robust results on the two medical datasets. (Color figure online)

results. Our proposed `PseudoClick` approach outperforms all the methods across the five benchmark datasets. For example, compared with RITM on the Pascal dataset, our model uses 12.4% and 11.4% fewer number of clicks for achieving

85% and 90% IoU, respectively. Figure 4 shows plots for mean IoU with respect to the first several clicks for the DAVIS and BraTS datasets. Our approach shows continuous improvement in terms of accuracy and stability. We also visualize the evaluation process of the proposed method on some images in Fig. 6. From the qualitative results, we can see that the pseudo clicks automatically generated from our model can accurately focus on false positive and false negative regions. Hence, they are able to refine the predicted segmentation masks and thereby alleviate human annotation effort. Computational analysis is shown in Fig. 7.

4.3 Cross-Domain Evaluation

To evaluate the generalization cability of the proposed method, we conduct cross-domain evaluation on two medical image datasets: BraTS [20] and ssTEM [21]. Specifically, we directly apply our `PseudoClick` models trained on SBD or COCO+LVIS datasets to the medical images without finetuning (medical images in grayscale are replicated 3 times channel-wise to be of the same channel dimension with RGB images). We report cross-domain evaluation results in Table 2 and Table 3. We observe that our models generalize very well to medical images without fine-tuning. Note that these results are evaluated by a human annotator. Some qualitative results on the two medical datasets are shown in Fig. 5.

Table 2. Cross-domain evaluation on the BraTS dataset. The evaluation measure is mean IoU (%) given 3 or 5 human clicks.

Method	Train	Finetune	Backbone	mIoU@3	mIoU@5
RITM [11]	SBD	N/A	HRNet18	54.9	74.4
RITM [11]	C+L	N/A	HRNet32	51.7	77.1
Ours	SBD	N/A	HRNet18	54.5	74.6
Ours	C+L	N/A	HRNet32	**64.0**	**80.1**

Table 3. Cross-domain evaluation on the ssTEM [21] dataset. The evaluation measure is mean IoU (%) given 2 or 3 human clicks. The results for IOG and Curve-GCN methods are copied from the corresponding papers.

Method	Train	Finetune	Backbone	#Clicks	mIoU
Curve-GCN [55]	CityScapes	N/A	ResNet-50	2	60.9
IOG [13]	Pascal	N/A	ResNet-101	3	83.7
RITM [11]	SBD	N/A	HRNet18	3	77.3
RITM [11]	C+L	N/A	HRNet32	3	86.4
Ours	SBD	N/A	HRNet18	3	80.9
Ours	C+L	N/A	HRNet32	3	**87.2**

Fig. 6. Qualitative evaluation of `PseudoClick` model on natural images. Top: segmentation results with one pseudo click. The first row shows the results of the first human click; the second row shows the improvement of the segmentation mask with the help of the first pseudo click. Bottom: segmentation results with IoU greater than 90% given several clicks. The first row shows the segmentation using only human clicks. The second row shows the segmentation with both human and pseudo clicks. The color and shape of a click follow the same rule shown in Fig. 5. (Color figure online)

4.4   Comparison Study

Segmentation Backbone Comparison. We have demonstrated in Table 1 that our method outperforms existing state-of-the-art when using HRNet-32 as its backbone. In this study, we implement other backbones including two recently proposed vision transformers, SegFormer [47] and HRFormer [48], that show encouraging results when compared with CNNs. Table 4 shows the comparison results. All models are pre-trained on ImageNet [56] and finetuned on COCO+LVIS dataset with NFL loss function. We use SegFormer-B5 [47] and HRFormer-Base [48] for the transformers. Models are trained and evaluated using pseudo clicks. The evaluation measure is NoC@85%. While the transformers achieve decent results, we actually spend little time in tuning the hyperparameters and modifying the architecture when transferring from CNNs to transformers. This demonstrates the flexibility and generalization capability of our framework.

Loss Functions Comparison. In this study, we train `PseudoClick` models using four different loss functions: binary cross entropy (BCE) loss, focal loss (FL) [38], Soft IoU loss [57], and normalized focal loss (NFL) [37]. Each experiment uses the HRNet32 model. All the four models are trained on the COCO+LVIS dataset. Results in Table 5 show that training with NFL leads to the best accuracy.

Table 4. Comparison study for different segmentation backbones.

Backbone	Berkeley	SBD	DAVIS	Pascal
ResNet51	1.94	3.49	4.87	2.18
ResNet101	1.85	3.44	4.14	2.02
SegFormer	2.54	4.10	4.11	2.26
HRFormer	1.84	4.53	4.80	2.62

Table 5. Comparison study for different loss functions.

Loss	Berkeley	SBD	DAVIS	Pascal
BCE	1.44	3.53	3.97	1.98
FL	1.43	3.54	3.79	2.01
Soft IoU	1.44	3.63	3.96	2.10
NFL	1.40	3.46	3.79	1.94

Table 6. Comparison study for different training datasets.

Train	Berkeley	SBD	DAVIS	Pascal
Pascal	2.33	5.87	5.67	2.66
SBD	1.67	3.51	4.74	2.37
LVIS	2.63	5.40	6.97	3.14
C+L	1.40	3.46	3.79	1.94

Table 7. Computational analysis. Speed is measured as second per click (including a pseudo click for ours) with a NVIDIA A6000 GPU.

Model	Param/M	FLOPs/G	Speed/s
RITM-H32	30.95	16.57	0.137
Ours-H32-PC	36.79	18.43	0.185

Training Datasets Comparison. In this study, we train PseudoClick models on four different training datasets: Pascal, SBD, LVIS, and COCO+LVIS. We test on four datasets: Pascal, SBD, Berkeley, and DAVIS. For each experiment, our model is based on HRNet32 and is trained with NFL loss function. We report results in Table 6. We observe that the model trained on COCO+LVIS shows the best performance, highlighting the benefit of combining COCO and LVIS for training interactive segmentation models. We also notice that on the Pascal dataset, model trained on COCO+LVIS dataset is even better than the model trained on Pascal dataset. This, again, highlights the strengths of COCO+LVIS dataset: 1) large dataset size. The number of annotated instances in COCO+LVIS dataset is 50× and 170× times larger than SBD and Pascal, respectively; 2) diverse and high annotation quality.

Post-processing vs. Pseudo Clicks. In this study, we directly use the two error maps for refining the segmentation mask. The two error maps serve as a regularization for the segmentation branch during training. As shown in Fig. 3, they quantize the segmentation mask reasonably well, and thus can be used for refining the segmentation mask. To achieve this goal, we simply subtract the two error maps from the segmentation map (all three maps are probability maps). We compare the post-processing with adding one pseudo click. The comparison results are shown in Table 8. We emphasize that the post-processing based on FP&FN maps can also be regarded as a contribution of our work as it is a by-product of our core contribution. Given two human clicks on the BraTS dataset, the relative mIoU obtained by adding one pseudo-click is 5.2% higher than the mIoU by post-processing, which is substantial considering the strong performance of post-processing.

Table 8. Adding one pseudo-click vs. post-processing. Comparison of post-processing and pseudo clicks for mask refinement given a fixed number of human clicks. The Baseline model above is our best `PseudoClick` model (C+L HRNet32) on the BraTS dataset.

mIoU@Human-clks	BraTS			DAVIS		
	2	3	5	2	3	5
Baseline (BL)	23.2	51.2	77.3	80.2	85.6	89.3
BL+post-processing	42.6	63.5	79.7	81.3	86.2	90.1
BL+1 pseudo-click	**44.8**	**64.0**	**80.1**	**83.7**	**87.4**	**90.8**

5   Limitations

The major limitation of the proposed method is that pseudo clicks may not be as accurate as human clicks, and therefore may cause the segmentation accuracy to drop. This may lead to extra work for users to withdraw the poorly placed pseudo clicks or to correct the error by putting more points. Fortunately, this issue has be greatly alleviated by separating the encoding maps for the two types of clicks. By separating the two encoding maps, the inaccurate pseudo clicks are tolerated during the training and less likely to cause accuracy to drop during evaluation. In the early stage of this project, we discovered this issue. After separating the two types of encoding maps, as implemented in our current architecture, this issue has been significantly eliminated.

6   Conclusion

We proposed `PseudoClick`, a novel interactive segmentation framework that automatically imitates human clicks and efficiently segments objects with the imitated pseudo clicks. `PseudoClick` is a general framework that can be built upon different types of segmentation backbones, including both CNNs and transformers, with little effort in tuning the hyper-parameters and modifying the network architectures. We evaluated `PseudoClick` thoroughly on benchmarks from multiple domains and modalities with extensive comparison and cross-domain evaluation experiments that demonstrated the effectiveness as well as the generalization capability of the proposed method.

Acknowledgments. Research reported in this publication was supported by the National Institutes of Health (NIH) under award number NIH 1R01AR072013. The content is solely the responsibility of the authors and does not necessarily represent the official views of the NIH.

References

1. Garcia-Garcia, A., Orts-Escolano, S., Oprea, S., Villena-Martinez, V., Garcia-Rodriguez, J.: A review on deep learning techniques applied to semantic segmentation, arXiv preprint arXiv:1704.06857 (2017)
2. Minaee, S., et al.: Image segmentation using deep learning: a survey. IEEE Trans. Pattern Anal. Mach. Intell. **44**(7), 3523–3542 (2021)
3. Yang, L., Fan, Y., Xu, N.: Video instance segmentation. In: Proceedings of the IEEE/CVF International Conference on Computer Vision, pp. 5188–5197 (2019)
4. Xu, N., et al.: YouTube-VOS: a large-scale video object segmentation benchmark, arXiv preprint arXiv:1809.03327 (2018)
5. Cordts, M., et al.: The cityscapes dataset for semantic urban scene understanding. In: Proceedings of the IEEE Conference on Computer Vision and Pattern Recognition, pp. 3213–3223 (2016)
6. Geiger, A., Lenz, P., Urtasun, R.: Are we ready for autonomous driving? the KITTI vision benchmark suite. In: 2012 IEEE Conference on Computer Vision and Pattern Recognition, pp. 3354–3361. IEEE (2012)
7. Neuhold, G., Ollmann, T., Rota Bulo, S., Kontschieder, P.: The mapillary vistas dataset for semantic understanding of street scenes. In: Proceedings of the IEEE International Conference on Computer Vision, pp. 4990–4999 (2017)
8. Shen, D., Wu, G., Suk, H.-I.: Deep learning in medical image analysis. Ann. Rev. Biomed. Eng. **19**, 221–248 (2017)
9. Litjens, G.: A survey on deep learning in medical image analysis. Med. Image Anal. **42**, 60–88 (2017)
10. Xu, N., Price, B., Cohen, S., Yang, J., Huang, T.S.: Deep interactive object selection. In: Proceedings of the IEEE Conference on Computer Vision and Pattern Recognition, pp. 373–381 (2016)
11. Sofiiuk, K., Petrov, I.A., Konushin, A.: Reviving iterative training with mask guidance for interactive segmentation, arXiv preprint arXiv:2102.06583 (2021)
12. Xu, N., Price, B., Cohen, S., Yang, J., Huang, T.: Deep grabcut for object selection, arXiv preprint arXiv:1707.00243 (2017)
13. Zhang, S., Liew, J.H., Wei, Y., Wei, S., Zhao, Y.: Interactive object segmentation with inside-outside guidance. In: Proceedings of the IEEE/CVF Conference on Computer Vision and Pattern Recognition, pp. 12234–12244 (2020)
14. Wu, J., Zhao, Y., Zhu, J.-Y., Luo, S., Tu, Z.: Milcut: a sweeping line multiple instance learning paradigm for interactive image segmentation. In: Proceedings of the IEEE Conference on Computer Vision and Pattern Recognition, pp. 256–263 (2014)
15. Boykov, Y.Y., Jolly, M.-P.: Interactive graph cuts for optimal boundary & region segmentation of objects in ND images. In: Proceedings Eighth IEEE International Conference on Computer Vision, ICCV 2001, vol. 1, pp. 105–112. IEEE (2001)
16. Rother, C., Kolmogorov, V., Blake, A.: GrabCut: interactive foreground extraction using iterated graph cuts. ACM Trans. Graph. (TOG) **23**(3), 309–314 (2004)

17. Sofiiuk, K., Petrov, I., Barinova, O., Konushin, A.: F-BRS: rethinking backpropagating refinement for interactive segmentation. In: Proceedings of the IEEE/CVF Conference on Computer Vision and Pattern Recognition, pp. 8623–8632 (2020)
18. Lin, T.-Y., et al.: Microsoft COCO: common objects in context. In: Fleet, D., Pajdla, T., Schiele, B., Tuytelaars, T. (eds.) ECCV 2014. LNCS, vol. 8693, pp. 740–755. Springer, Cham (2014). https://doi.org/10.1007/978-3-319-10602-1_48
19. Gupta, A., Dollar, P., Girshick, R.: Lvis: a dataset for large vocabulary instance segmentation. In: Proceedings of the IEEE/CVF Conference on Computer Vision and Pattern Recognition, pp. 5356–5364 (2019)
20. Baid, U., et al: The RSNA-ASNR-MICCAI BRATS 2021 benchmark on brain tumor segmentation and radiogenomic classification, arXiv preprint arXiv:2107.02314 (2021)
21. Gerhard, S., Funke, J., Martel, J., Cardona, A., Fetter, R.: Segmented anisotropic ssTEM dataset of neural tissue. figshare (2013)
22. Liu, Q., Xu, Z., Jiao, Y., Niethammer, M.: iSegFormer: interactive image segmentation with transformers, arXiv preprint arXiv:2112.11325 (2021)
23. Chen, X., Zhao, Z., Zhang, Y., Duan, M., Qi, D., Zhao, H.: FocalClick: towards practical interactive image segmentation. In: Proceedings of the IEEE/CVF Conference on Computer Vision and Pattern Recognition, pp. 1300–1309 (2022)
24. Song, G.: Seednet. In: CVPR (2018)
25. Cheng, H. K., Tai, Y.-W., Tang, C.-K.: Modular interactive video object segmentation: interaction-to-mask, propagation and difference-aware fusion. In: Proceedings of the IEEE/CVF Conference on Computer Vision and Pattern Recognition, pp. 5559–5568 (2021)
26. Ding, H., Cohen, S., Price, B., Jiang, X.: PhraseClick: toward achieving flexible interactive segmentation by phrase and click. In: Vedaldi, A., Bischof, H., Brox, T., Frahm, J.-M. (eds.) ECCV 2020. LNCS, vol. 12348, pp. 417–435. Springer, Cham (2020). https://doi.org/10.1007/978-3-030-58580-8_25
27. Hussein, A., Gaber, M.M., Elyan, E., Jayne, C.: Imitation learning: a survey of learning methods. ACM Comput. Surv. (CSUR) **50**(2), 1–35 (2017)
28. Osa, T., Pajarinen, J., Neumann, G., Bagnell, J.A., Abbeel, P., Peters, J.: An algorithmic perspective on imitation learning, arXiv preprint arXiv:1811.06711 (2018)
29. Zhang, T., et al.: Deep imitation learning for complex manipulation tasks from virtual reality teleoperation. In: 2018 IEEE International Conference on Robotics and Automation (ICRA), pp. 5628–5635. IEEE (2018)
30. Yoo, D., Kweon, I. S.: Learning loss for active learning. In: Proceedings of the IEEE/CVF Conference on Computer Vision and Pattern Recognition, pp. 93–102 (2019)
31. Ding, Z., Han, X., Liu, P., Niethammer, M.: Local temperature scaling for probability calibration. In: Proceedings of the IEEE/CVF International Conference on Computer Vision, pp. 6889–6899 (2021)
32. Krause, J., Stark, M., Deng, J., Fei-Fei, L.: 3d object representations for fine-grained categorization. In: 4th International IEEE Workshop on 3D Representation and Recognition (3dRR-13), Australia, Sydney (2013)
33. Jang, W.-D., Kim, C.-S.: Interactive image segmentation via backpropagating refinement scheme. In: Proceedings of the IEEE/CVF Conference on Computer Vision and Pattern Recognition, pp. 5297–5306 (2019)
34. Maninis, K.-K., Caelles, S., Pont-Tuset, J., Van Gool, L.: Deep extreme cut: from extreme points to object segmentation. In: Proceedings of the IEEE Conference on Computer Vision and Pattern Recognition, pp. 616–625 (2018)

35. Liew, J.H., Cohen, S., Price, B., Mai, L., Ong, S.H., Feng, J.: MultiSeg: semantically meaningful, scale-diverse segmentations from minimal user input. In: Proceedings of the IEEE/CVF International Conference on Computer Vision, pp. 662–670 (2019)

36. Majumder, S., Yao, A.: Content-aware multi-level guidance for interactive instance segmentation. In: Proceedings of the IEEE/CVF Conference on Computer Vision and Pattern Recognition, pp. 11602–11611 (2019)

37. Sofiiuk, K., Barinova, O., Konushin, A.: AdaptIS: adaptive instance selection network. In: Proceedings of the IEEE/CVF International Conference on Computer Vision, pp. 7355–7363 (2019)

38. Lin, T.-Y., Goyal, P., Girshick, R., He, K., Dollár, P.: Focal loss for dense object detection. In: Proceedings of the IEEE international conference on computer vision, pp. 2980–2988 (2017)

39. Benenson, R., Popov, S., Ferrari, V.: Large-scale interactive object segmentation with human annotators. In: Proceedings of the IEEE/CVF Conference on Computer Vision and Pattern Recognition, pp. 11700–11709 (2019)

40. Kontogianni, T., Gygli, M., Uijlings, J., Ferrari, V.: Continuous adaptation for interactive object segmentation by learning from corrections. In: Vedaldi, A., Bischof, H., Brox, T., Frahm, J.-M. (eds.) ECCV 2020. LNCS, vol. 12361, pp. 579–596. Springer, Cham (2020). https://doi.org/10.1007/978-3-030-58517-4_34

41. Mahadevan, S., Voigtlaender, P., Leibe, B.: Iteratively trained interactive segmentation, arXiv preprint arXiv:1805.04398 (2018)

42. Martin, D., Fowlkes, C., Tal, D., Malik, J.: A database of human segmented natural images and its application to evaluating segmentation algorithms and measuring ecological statistics. In: Proceedings Eighth IEEE International Conference on Computer Vision, ICCV 2001, vol. 2, pp. 416–423. IEEE (2001)

43. Perazzi, F., Pont-Tuset, J., McWilliams, B., Van Gool, L., Gross, M., Sorkine-Hornung, A.: A benchmark dataset and evaluation methodology for video object segmentation. In: Proceedings of the IEEE Conference on Computer Vision and Pattern Recognition, pp. 724–732 (2016)

44. Everingham, M., Van Gool, L., Williams, C.K., Winn, J., Zisserman, A.: The PASCAL visual object classes (VOC) challenge. Int. J. Comput. Vision **88**(2), 303–338 (2010)

45. Hariharan, B., Arbeláez, P., Bourdev, L., Maji, S., Malik, J.: Semantic contours from inverse detectors. In: 2011 International Conference on Computer Vision, pp. 991–998. IEEE (2011)

46. Wang, J., et al.: Deep high-resolution representation learning for visual recognition. IEEE Trans. Pattern Anal. Mach. Intell. **43**(10), 3349–3364 (2020)

47. Xie, E., Wang, W., Yu, Z., Anandkumar, A., Alvarez, J.M., Luo, P.: SegFormer: simple and efficient design for semantic segmentation with transformers, arXiv preprint arXiv:2105.15203 (2021)

48. Yuan, Y., et al.: HRFormer: high-resolution transformer for dense prediction, arXiv preprint arXiv:2110.09408 (2021)

49. Paszke, A., et al.: PyTorch: an imperative style, high-performance deep learning library. Adv. Neural Inf. Process. Syst. **32**, 8026–8037 (2019)

50. Grady, L.: Random walks for image segmentation. IEEE Trans. Pattern Anal. Mach. Intell. **28**(11), 1768–1783 (2006)

51. Bai, X., Sapiro, G.: A geodesic framework for fast interactive image and video segmentation and matting. In: 2007 IEEE 11th International Conference on Computer Vision, pp. 1–8. IEEE (2007)

52. Gulshan, V., Rother, C., Criminisi, A., Blake, A., Zisserman, A.: Geodesic star convexity for interactive image segmentation. In: 2010 IEEE Computer Society Conference on Computer Vision and Pattern Recognition, pp. 3129–3136. IEEE (2010)

53. Li, Z., Chen, Q., Koltun, V.: Interactive image segmentation with latent diversity. In: Proceedings of the IEEE Conference on Computer Vision and Pattern Recognition, pp. 577–585 (2018)

54. Lin, Z., Zhang, Z., Chen, L.-Z., Cheng, M.-M., Lu, S.-P.: Interactive image segmentation with first click attention. In: Proceedings of the IEEE/CVF Conference on Computer Vision and Pattern Recognition, pp. 13339–13348 (2020)

55. Ling, H., Gao, J., Kar, A., Chen, W., Fidler, S.: Fast interactive object annotation with curve-GCN. In: Proceedings of the IEEE/CVF Conference on Computer Vision and Pattern Recognition, pp. 5257–5266 (2019)

56. Deng, J., Dong, W., Socher, R., Li, L.-J., Li, K., Fei-Fei, L.: ImageNet: a large-scale hierarchical image database. In: 2009 IEEE conference on computer vision and pattern recognition, pp. 248–255. IEEE (2009)

57. Rahman, M.A., Wang, Y.: Optimizing intersection-over-union in deep neural networks for image segmentation. In: Bebis, G., et al. (eds.) ISVC 2016. LNCS, vol. 10072, pp. 234–244. Springer, Cham (2016). https://doi.org/10.1007/978-3-319-50835-1_22

Author Index

Printed in the United States
by Baker & Taylor Publisher Services